Third Canadian Edition

FINANCIAL INSTITUTIONS
MANAGEMENT

A RISK MANAGEMENT APPROACH

Anthony Saunders

Stern School of Business
New York University

Marcia Millon Cornett

Southern Illinois University

Patricia A. McGraw

Ryerson University

 **McGraw-Hill**
Ryerson

Toronto Montréal Boston Burr Ridge, IL Dubuque, IA Madison, WI New York
San Francisco St. Louis Bangkok Bogotá Caracas Kuala Lumpur Lisbon London
Madrid Mexico City Milan New Delhi Santiago Seoul Singapore Sydney Taipei

McGraw-Hill
Ryerson Limited
A Subsidiary of The **McGraw·Hill** Companies

Financial Institutions Management: A Risk Management Approach
Third Canadian Edition

Statistics Canada information is used with the permission of the Minister of Industry, as Minister responsible for Statistics Canada. Information on the availability of the wide range of data from Statistics Canada can be obtained from Statistics Canada's Regional Offices, its World Wide Web site at http://www.statcan.ca, and its toll free access number 1-800-263-1136.

ISBN: 0-07-091435-4

1 2 3 4 5 6 7 8 9 10   QPD   0 9 8 7 6

Printed and bound in the United States of America.

Care has been taken to trace ownership of copyright material contained in this text; however, the publisher will welcome any information that enables it to rectify any reference or credit for subsequent editions.

Editorial Director: Joanna Cotton
Publisher: Lynn Fisher
Marketing Manager: Joy Armitage-Taylor
Developmental Editor: Jennifer Matyczak
Associate Developmental Editor: Marcia Luke
Editorial Associate: Stephanie Hess
Manager, Editorial Services: Kelly Dickson
Supervising Editor: Joanne Limebeer
Copy Editor: Santo D'Agostino
Senior Production Coordinator: Paula Brown
Cover Design: Erin Smith/ArtPlus Limited
Cover Photos: Buildings: Masterfile, Globe: Workbook, Flag: Firstlight
Page Layout: Heather Brunton, Tom Lyons, Ruth Nicholson, Sue Kimball/ArtPlus Limited
Printer: Quebecor Printing Dubuque

Library and Archives Canada Cataloguing in Publication Data

Saunders, Anthony
  Financial institutions management : a risk management approach / Anthony
Saunders, Marcia Millon Cornett, Patricia A. McGraw. — 3rd Canadian ed.

Includes bibliographical references and index.
ISBN 0-07-091435-4

  1. Financial institutions—Canada—Management—Textbooks.   2. Risk
management—Canada—Textbooks.   I. Cornett, Marcia Millon   II. McGraw, Patricia
Anne, 1951-   III. Title.

HG185.C2S29 2006 fol.   332.1'068   C2005-906302-5

This book is dedicated to Pat, Nicholas, and Emily and to my mother, Evelyn.

Anthony Saunders

To the Millons and the Cornetts, especially Galen.

Marcia Millon Cornett

This book is dedicated to Gary, Bryan, Andrea, Tyler, Lavon, and Doreen.

Patricia A. McGraw

About the Authors

Anthony Saunders

Anthony Saunders is the John M. Schiff Professor of Finance and Chair of the Department of Finance at the Stern School of Business at New York University. Professor Saunders received his PhD from the London School of Economics and has taught both undergraduate- and graduate-level courses at NYU since 1978. Throughout his academic career, his teaching and research have specialized in financial institutions and international banking. He has served as a visiting professor all over the world, including INSEAD, the Stockholm School of Economics, and the University of Melbourne. He is currently on the Executive Committee of the Salomon Center for the Study of Financial Institutions, NYU.

Professor Saunders holds positions on the Board of Academic Consultants of the Federal Reserve Board of Governors as well as the Council of Research Advisors for the Federal National Mortgage Association. In addition, Dr. Saunders has acted as a visiting scholar at the Comptroller of the Currency and at the Federal Reserve Bank of Philadelphia. He also held a visiting position in the research department of the International Monetary Fund. He is an editor of the *Journal of Banking and Finance* and the *Journal of Financial Markets, Instruments and Institutions*, as well as the associate editor of eight other journals, including *Financial Management* and the *Journal of Money, Credit and Banking*. His research has been published in all the major money and banking and finance journals and in several books. In addition, he has authored or coauthored several professional books, the most recent of which is *Credit Risk Measurement: New Approaches to Value at Risk and Other Paradigms*, 2nd edition, John Wiley and Sons, New York, 2002.

Marcia Millon Cornett

Marcia Millon Cornett is the Rehn Professor of Business at Southern Illinois University at Carbondale. She received her BS degree in Economics from Knox College in Galesburg, Illinois, and her MBA and PhD degrees in Finance from Indiana University in Bloomington, Indiana. Dr. Cornett has written and published several articles in the areas of bank performance, bank regulation, and corporate finance. Articles authored by Dr. Cornett have appeared in such academic journals as the *Journal of Finance,* the *Journal of Money, Credit and Banking,* the *Journal of Financial Economics, Financial Management,* and the *Journal of Banking and Finance.* She served as an Associate Editor of *Financial Management* and is currently an Associate Editor for the *Journal of Banking and Finance, Journal of Financial Services Research, FMA Online,* the *Multinational Finance Journal* and the *Review of Financial Economics.* Dr. Cornett is currently a member of the Board of Directors, the Executive Committee, and the Finance Committee of the SIU Credit Union. Dr. Cornett has also taught at the University of Colorado, Boston College, and Southern Methodist University. She is a member of the Financial Management Association, the American Finance Association, and the Western Finance Association.

Patricia A. McGraw

Patricia A. McGraw is Associate Professor, Finance, at the School of Business Management, Ryerson University. Dr. McGraw holds a BSc degree in Geology and Chemistry from McGill University, an MSc in Geology from Dalhousie University, an MBA in Finance and Accounting from the University of Toronto, and a PhD in Interdisciplinary Studies from Dalhousie University. She has taught undergraduate and graduate finance courses at Dalhousie University and Ryerson University in Canada, at Lincoln University in Christchurch, New Zealand, and at Universiti Tenaga Nasional in Kuala Lumpur, Malaysia.

Professor McGraw has worked as an exploration geologist and as a corporate banker specializing in lending to resource companies. She has also consulted to the offshore natural gas industry. Her research and publications focus on lender environmental liability, capital market evolution, and capital structure and cost of capital in emerging markets.

Brief Contents

Contents

Preface to the Third Canadian Edition

"For us of course, things can change so abruptly, so violently, so profoundly, that futures like our grandparents' have insufficient 'now' to stand on. We have no future because our present is too volatile… . We have only risk management. The spinning of the given moment's scenarios. Pattern recognition."

William Gibson, *Pattern Recognition*, New York: Berkley Books, p. 57

Financial intermediaries (FIs) have always been in the business of risk management. However, the contracts that they create to manage and to transfer risk have changed significantly in the last 20 years in Canada, the United States, and globally. This has resulted in the development of different methods of "pattern recognition," that is, new risk management techniques that an FI can use to protect its customers and its shareholders and, as well, to satisfy regulators in protecting the financial system. Thus, the purpose of this textbook is to identify patterns, to develop scenarios, and to provide information about the risk management techniques used by financial institutions in Canada.

However, while the focus in the popular press is on "made in Canada" issues such as bank-bank mergers and bank-insurance mergers, the scope of Canadian FIs is much broader. Whether it is Sun Life Financial in India, Manulife Financial in Malaysia, Bank of Nova Scotia in Mexico, or Bank of Montreal in the United States, the global scope of Canada's FIs and the global nature of today's financial markets mean that the pattern recognition must extend beyond the Canadian border.

My purpose in adapting this textbook is to present a view of the Canadian financial services industry that situates it clearly within the North American market and to provide a sense of the global patterns that are shaping the future of this industry. It is my hope that the readers of this textbook will obtain an understanding of the issues that make these risk management companies so fascinating, and will be able to make use of the risk management techniques whether as an employee of an FI or as a consumer, business or personal, of the products of FIs.

Financial Institutions Management: A Risk Management Approach is aimed at upper level undergraduate and MBA audiences. The more technical sections are marked with a footnote. *These sections may be included or dropped from the chapter reading, depending on the rigour of the course, without harming the continuity of the chapters.*

Additional topics covered in the chapter appendices can be found at a central location, either at the back of the book (page 684) or at the Online Learning Centre **(www.mcgrawhill.ca/college/saunders)**.

What's New in the Third Canadian Edition

As well as having a new Canadian author, the Third Canadian Edition has been reorganized and changed substantially from the Second Canadian Edition in order to incorporate changes to the Canadian industry since 2000. This reflects a refocusing as the financial services industry has continued to evolve. The three-part structure (Part I: Introduction, Part II: Measuring Risk, Part III: Managing Risk) of the text is retained, but the chapters are expanded from 24 to 27 and rearranged to cover additional material. The new features and improvements are as follows:

- Part I: The Introduction now begins with Chapter 1 "Why Are Financial Intermediaries Special?" to focus attention on the functions of FIs and to set the stage for an in-depth discussion of each type of FI and its role in Canada's financial system.

- Chapters 2–6 provide up-to-date information on the structure of the industry, balance sheets, industry performance, and regulation for deposit-taking institutions, insurance companies, securities firms, investment banks, the funds industry, and finance companies. Tables and figures throughout have been updated and the discussion of mutual funds and pension funds has been expanded to acknowledge the special nature of funds and to include hedge funds.

- Part II has been reorganized to begin with two chapters on interest rate risk and end with a chapter on liquidity risk, emphasizing that the risks are interconnected. As well, information on technology risk has been added to the discussion of operational risk in Chapter 14. This chapter also discusses concerns of the Bank for International Settlements about outsourcing for FIs. A separate chapter on Sovereign Risk has also been added.

- Part III includes updated information on liability and liquidity management. The latest information on the new capital adequacy rules (Basel II) that are scheduled to run in parallel with Basel I starting in 2006, and to be fully implemented by November 1, 2007, is included in Chapter 20.

- There are now two chapters on diversification. Chapter 21 discusses product diversification from the viewpoint of cross-pillar mergers in Canada (bank-insurance) and within pillar (bank-bank) mergers to create large universal banks. Chapter 22 focuses on geographic diversification, particularly cross-border mergers with other North American and global FIs. This includes a discussion of the lifting of restrictions on U.S. interbranch banking that has set off mergers and acquisitions activities that are relevant to the current debate in Canada about large FI mergers.

- In line with the increase in globalization, the text focuses on Canadian FIs, but adopts a North American perspective, and discusses cross-border issues such as the effects of the U.S. Patriot Act and the Sarbanes-Oxley Act on the regulation and management of Canadian FIs.

- Internet problems are included in the end-of-chapter problems that guide students through Web sites as they collect and evaluate the requested data.

- Ethical Dilemmas boxes which highlight specific news stories relating to controversies involving financial institutions, Canadian, U.S. and global, have been added to many chapters.

Organization

Since the focus is on return and risk and the sources of that return and risk, this book relates ways in which the managers of modern FIs can expand return with a managed level of risk to achieve the best, or most favourable, return-risk outcome for FI owners.

Part I: Introduction

Chapter 1 introduces the special functions of FIs and takes an analytical look at how financial intermediation benefits the Canadian and the global economy. Chapters 2 to 6 provide an overview describing the key balance sheet and regulatory features of the major sectors of the Canadian financial services industry. Deposit-taking institutions are discussed in Chapter 2, insurance companies in Chapter 3, securities firms and investment banks in Chapter 4, mutual funds, pension funds, and hedge funds in Chapter 5, and finance companies in Chapter 6. Chapter 7 previews the risk measurement and management sections with an overview of the risks facing a modern FI.

Part II: Risk Measurement

Chapters 8 and 9 start the risk-measurement section by investigating the net interest margin as a source of profitability and risk, with a focus on the effects of interest rate volatility and the mismatching of asset and liability durations on FI risk exposure. Chapter 10 analyzes market risk, a risk that results when FIs actively trade bonds, equities, and foreign currencies.

Chapter 11 looks at the measurement of credit risk of individual loans and bonds and how this risk adversely affects an FI's profits through losses and provisions against the loan and debt security portfolio. Chapter 12 looks at the risk of loan (asset) portfolios and the effects of loan concentrations on risk exposure. Modern FIs do more than generate returns and bear risk through traditional maturity mismatching and credit extensions. They also are increasingly engaging in off-balance-sheet activities to generate fee income (Chapter 13), making technological investments to reduce costs (Chapter 14), pursuing foreign exchange activities and overseas financial investments (Chapter 15), and engaging in sovereign lending and securities activities (Chapter 16). Each of these has implications for the size and variability of an FI's profits and/or revenues. In addition, as a by-product of the provision of their interest rate and credit intermediation services, FIs face liquidity risk. The special nature of this risk is analyzed in Chapter 17.

Part III: Risk Management

Chapter 18 begins the risk-management section by looking at ways in which FIs can insulate themselves from liquidity risk. Chapter 19 looks at the key role deposit insurance and other guarantee schemes play in reducing liquidity risk. At the core of FI risk insulation is the size and adequacy of the owners' capital or equity investment in the FI, which is the focus of Chapter 20. Chapters 21 and 22 analyze how and why product diversification and geographic diversification—both domestic and international—can improve an FI's return-risk performance and the effect of regulation on the diversification opportunity set. Chapters 23 through 27 review various new markets and instruments that have been innovated or engineered to allow FIs to better manage three important types of risk: interest rate risk, credit risk, and foreign exchange risk. These markets and instruments and their strategic use by FIs include futures and forwards (Chapter 23); options, caps, floors, and collars (Chapter 24); swaps (Chapter 25); loan sales (Chapter 26); and securitization (Chapter 27).

Main Features

Throughout the text, special features have been integrated to encourage students' interaction with the text and to aid them in absorbing the material. Some of these features include:

In-chapter examples, which provide numerical demonstrations of the analytics described in various chapters.

EXAMPLE 8–3 Fixed Income Securities and the Maturity Model	Consider the value of a bond held by an FI that has one year to maturity, a face value of 100 (F) to be paid on maturity, one single annual coupon at a rate of 10 percent of the face value (C) and a current yield to maturity (R) (reflecting current interest rates) of 10 percent. The fair market price of the one-year bond, P_1^g, is equal to the present value of the cash flows on the bond:

$$P_1^g = \frac{F + C}{(1 + R)} = \frac{100 + 10}{1.1} = 100$$

Suppose the Bank of Canada tightens monetary policy so that the required yield on the bond rises instantaneously to 11 percent. The market value of the bond falls to:

$$P_1^g = \frac{100 + 10}{1.11} = 99.10$$

Thus, the market value of the bond is now only $99.10 per $100 of face value, whereas its original book value was $100. The FI has suffered a capital loss (ΔP_1) of $0.90 per $100 of face value in holding this bond, or:

$$\Delta P_1 = 99.10 - 100 = -\$0.90$$

Also, the percent change in the price is:

$$\Delta P_1 = \frac{99.10 - 100}{100} = -0.90\%$$

Bold key terms and marginal glossary, which emphasize the main terms and concepts throughout the chapter and aid in studying.

Ethical Dilemmas, Industry Perspectives, and Technology in the News boxes, which demonstrate the application of chapter material to real current events. See page xxiv for a complete listing.

Industry Perspectives

TRY DRIVING A CAR WITHOUT BRAKES......
Difficult to define

To understand why Canada and countries other than the US have moved faster on handling risk is to get a grasp of what exactly enterprise risk management is.

"It is really difficult to define," admits Suzanne Labarge, who, as former vice-chairman and chief risk officer (CRO) at the Royal Bank of Canada, knows a great deal about risk management. About seven years ago, when she was appointed CRO, she was not just the bank's first CRO, she was one of the first in Canada. Labarge, who recently retired from RBC Financial Group in Toronto, says, "At that point there were almost no CROs anywhere."

Entire seminars have been held to try to define, in a layman's term, what ERM means. Thousands of trees have died in pursuit of a definitive definition for ERM. Painfully complex computer models have been developed in pursuit of more effective risk management.

The US Society of Actuaries has also come up with one candidate. "Enterprise risk management is the discipline by which an entity in any industry assesses, controls, measures, exploits finances and monitors risk from all sources for the purpose of increasing the entity's short- and long-term value to its stakeholders."

Still, a simple explanation eludes the industry.

"If I'm at a cocktail party and someone asks me what enterprise risk management is, all I can think to say is 'Know thy risk,'" says Prakash Shimpi, practice leader with global responsibility for ERM for Towers Perrin in New York. "And if they want to know more, I would say the second step is: 'How much does that risk weigh?'"

At a meeting of CROs in New York last summer, co-hosted by the US Society of Actuaries, Standard & Poor's and the Casualty Actuary Society, the best definition they could come up with was that because it is in a state of flux, it is part art, part science and a work in progress.

But perhaps the most visual description comes from the vice-president internal audit and CRO of Hydro One Inc. "Put it this way," says John Fraser, "if a company doesn't have risk management, imagine what it would be like driving a car without brakes."

Source: Peter Morton, "Risky Business," *CA Magazine*, May 2005, Vol. 138, Iss. 4, pp. 24–29. Reproduced with permission from *CA Magazine*, published by the Canadian Institute of Chartered Accountants, Toronto, Canada.

Concept questions, which allow students to test themselves on the main concepts within each major chapter section and aid in studying.

International material highlights, which call out material relating to North American and global issues.

Consider the following simple example in Table 10–6, where an FI is trading two currencies: the Japanese yen and the Swiss franc. At the close of trade on December 1, 2006, it has a long position in Japanese yen of 500,000,000 and a long position in Swiss francs of 20,000,000. It wants to assess its VAR. That is, if tomorrow is that 1 bad day in 20 (the 5 percent worst case), how much does it stand to lose on its total foreign currency position? As shown in Table 10–6, six steps are required to calculate the VAR of its currency portfolio. It should be noted that the same methodological approach would be followed to calculate the VAR of any asset, liability, or derivative (bonds, options, etc.) as long as market prices were available on those assets over a sufficiently long historic time period.

Internet exercises and references, which guide the student to access the most recent data on the Web.

Internet Exercise

25. Canadian FIs are permitted by OSFI to use their own internal models in evaluating market risk. Go to CIBC's Web site (www.cibc.com) and download the latest Annual Report. Find the Risk Management section. What methods is CIBC now using to calculate market risk? What was CIBC's maximum daily value-at-risk on its trading activities? What was its minimum? What components are measured to give the total VAR? How has it changed since the 2004 data provided in Table 10–6? Does the Annual Report give you a good understanding of the market risk of this particular FI?

Comprehensive Teaching and Learning Package

We have developed a number of supplements for both teaching and learning to accompany this text:

For Instructors

Instructor's Online Learning Centre

(www.mcgrawhill.ca/college/saunders)

The Online Learning Centre includes a password-protected Web site for instructors. The site offers downloadable supplements, and PageOut, the McGraw-Hill Ryerson course Web site development centre.

Instructor's Resource CD-ROM

The Instructor's Resource CD-ROM contains all the necessary Instructor Supplements, including an **Instructors Manual** and **Test Bank** that feature detailed chapter contents, additional examples for use in the classroom, complete solutions to end-of-chapter questions and problem material, and additional problems for test material. Also included is a **PowerPoint** package, prepared by Lois Tullo, York University, which includes lecture outlines that you can customize for your own classes.

For Students

Student Online Learning Centre

(www.mcgrawhill.ca/college/saunders)

The Student Online Learning Centre, prepared by Larbi Hammami, McGill University, offers a wealth of learning materials, including online quizzes, appendices, Web links, Standard & Poor's questions, and much more. There is also a link to *Finance Around the World*, a tremendous resource that takes students to important and popular finance Web sites from around the globe.

Superior Service

Service takes on a whole new meaning with McGraw-Hill Ryerson and *Financial Institutions Management*. More than just bringing you the textbook, we have consistently raised the bar in terms of innovation and educational research—both in finance and in education in general. These investments in learning and the education community have helped us to understand the needs of students and educators across the country, and allowed us to foster the growth of truly innovative, integrated learning.

Integrated Learning

Your Integrated Learning Sales Specialist is a McGraw-Hill Ryerson representative who has the experience, product knowledge, training, and support to help you assess and integrate any of our products, technology, and services into your course for optimum teaching and learning performance. Whether it's helping your students improve their grades, or putting your entire course online, your *i*Learning Sales Specialist is there to help you do it. Contact your *i*Learning Sales Specialist today to learn how to maximize all of McGraw-Hill Ryerson's resources!

iLearning Services

McGraw-Hill Ryerson offers a unique *i*Services package designed for Canadian faculty. Our mission is to equip providers of higher education with superior tools and resources required for excellence in teaching. For additional information, visit www.mcgrawhill.ca/highereducation/iservices.

Course Management

McGraw-Hill Ryerson's course management system, PageOut, is the easiest way to create a Web site for your Financial Institutions Management course. There is no need for HTML coding, graphic design, or a thick how-to book. Just fill in a series of boxes in plain English and click on one of our professional designs. In no time, your course is online!

For the integrated instructor, we offer *Financial Institutions Management* content for complete online courses. Whatever your needs, you can customize the *Financial Institutions Management* Online Learning Centre content and author your own online course materials. It is entirely up to you. You can offer online discussion and message boards that will complement your office hours, and reduce the lines outside your door. Content cartridges are also available for course management systems, such as WebCT and Blackboard. Ask your *i*Learning Sales Specialist for details.

Teaching, Technology & Learning Conference Series

The educational environment has changed tremendously in recent years, and McGraw-Hill Ryerson continues to be committed to helping you acquire the skills you need to succeed in this new milieu. Our innovative Teaching, Technology & Learning Conference Series brings faculty together from across Canada with 3M Teaching Excellence award winners to share teaching and learning best practices in a collaborative and stimulating environment. Pre-conference workshops on general topics, such as teaching large classed and technology integration, will also be offered. We will also work with you at your own institution to customize workshops that best suit the needs of your faculty.

Acknowledgements

When considering the efforts of contributors, I am indebted and offer special thanks to the following reviewers, whose constructive suggestions have been incorporated as much as possible into the development of the Third Canadian Edition:

- Larbi Hammami, McGill University
- Yun Liu, University of Alberta
- Dev Gandhi, University of Ottawa
- Lois Tullo, York University
- Susan Christoffersen, McGill University
- Greg Hebb, St. Mary's University
- Charles Schell, University of Northern British Columbia
- Nancy Ursel, University of Windsor
- Karen Chiykowski, York University
- Ken Hartviksen, Lakehead University

I would also like to acknowledge Hugh Thomas from the Chinese University of Hong Kong, who, as the author of the first and second Canadian editions, has captured a dedicated user base for this text over the years. In addition, I thank McGraw-Hill Higher Education and McGraw-Hill Ryerson for their professional contributions, including Lynn Fisher, Publisher; Jennifer Matyczak, Developmental Editor; Joanne Limebeer, Supervising Editor; Santo D'Agostino, Copy Editor; and many others.

Finally, I look forward to teachers' comments, suggestions, and questions. It is my hope that this textbook will make a positive difference in your students' education.

Patricia A. McGraw
Ryerson University

Feature Boxes

Industry Perspectives

Technology in the News

Ethical Dilemmas

Introduction

Why Are Financial Intermediaries Special?

In this chapter, we look at the specialness of financial institutions (FIs) and discuss:

▸ the special functions that FIs provide

▸ how these special functions benefit the economy

▸ what makes some FIs more special than others

▸ how unique and long-lived the special functions of FIs are

INTRODUCTION

Bank Act
Federal legislation in Canada governing deposit-taking financial institutions.

four pillars
A term used to describe the separation of financial intermediation into four functions: banking, trust (fiduciary), insurance, and investment banking (securities).

universal bank
An FI that is permitted by regulators to offer a full range of financial services.

Prior to the revision of the **Bank Act** in 1992, financial institutions (FIs) in Canada were divided by function into **four pillars**: chartered banks, trust companies, insurance companies, and investment dealers. These FIs were prevented from providing services "cross-pillar." For example, prior to 1954, Canadian banks could not offer residential mortgages. In the 1970s and 1980s, new, relatively unregulated financial service industries sprang up (mutual funds, brokerage funds, etc.) that separated financial services functions even further. However, in the 21st century, regulatory barriers, technology, and financial innovations are changing so that, eventually, a full set of financial services may be offered by a single firm or **universal bank**. Not only have the boundaries between traditional industry sectors weakened, but competition has become global in nature as well. As the competitive environment changes, attention to profit and, more than ever, risk, becomes increasingly important. The major themes of this book are the measurement and management of the risks of financial institutions. Financial institutions (e.g., banks, credit unions, insurance companies, and mutual funds) perform the essential function of channeling funds from those with surplus funds (suppliers of funds) to those with shortages of funds (users of funds). At the beginning of 2005, the assets of just the banks in Canada were greater than $1.9 trillion. By comparison, the market capitalization of the 219 mining companies listed on the Toronto Stock Exchange (TSX) was $163 billion.

Although we might categorize or group FIs as life insurance companies, banks, finance companies, and so on, they face many common risks. Specifically, all FIs described in this chapter and Chapters 2 through 6 (1) hold some assets that are potentially subject to default or credit risk and (2) tend to mismatch the maturities of their balance sheet assets and liabilities to a greater or lesser extent and are thus exposed to interest rate risk. Moreover, all FIs are exposed to some degree of liability withdrawal or liquidity risk, depending on the type of claims they have sold to liability holders. In addition, most FIs are exposed to some type of underwriting risk, whether through the sale of securities or the issue of various types of credit guarantees on or off the balance sheet. Finally, all FIs are exposed to operating cost risks because the production of financial services requires the use of real resources and back-office support systems (labour and technology combined to provide services).

TABLE 1–1   **Areas of Financial Intermediaries' Specialness in the Provision of Services**

Information costs   The aggregation of funds in an FI provides greater incentive to collect information about customers (such as corporations) and to monitor their actions. The relatively large size of the FI allows this collection of information to be accomplished at a lower average cost (so-called economies of scale) than would be the case for individuals.

Liquidity and price risk   FIs provide financial claims to household savers with superior liquidity attributes and with lower price risk.

Transaction cost services   Similar to economies of scale in information production costs, an FI's size can result in economies of scale in transaction costs.

Maturity intermediation   FIs can better bear the risk of mismatching the maturities of their assets and liabilities.

Transmission of monetary supply   Deposit-taking institutions are the conduit through which monetary policy actions by the country's central bank (such as the Bank of Canada) affect the rest of the financial system and the economy.

Credit allocation   FIs are often viewed as the major, and sometimes only, source of financing for a particular sector of the economy, such as farming, small business, and residential real estate.

Intergenerational wealth transfers   FIs, especially life insurance companies and pension funds, provide savers with the ability to transfer wealth from one generation to the next.

Payment services   The efficiency with which deposit-taking institutions provide payment services such as cheque clearing directly benefits the economy.

Denomination intermediation   FIs, such as mutual funds, allow small investors to overcome constraints to buying assets imposed by large minimum denomination size.

Because of these risks and the special role that FIs play in the financial system, FIs are singled out for special regulatory attention.[1] In this chapter, we examine questions related to this specialness. In particular, what are the special functions that FIs—both deposit-taking institutions (banks, caisses populaires, and credit unions) and non-deposit-taking institutions (insurance companies, securities firms, investment banks, finance companies, and mutual funds)—provide? These special functions are summarized in Table 1–1.

FINANCIAL INTERMEDIARIES' SPECIALNESS

To understand the important economic function of FIs, imagine a simple world in which FIs do not exist. In such a world, households generating excess savings by consuming less than they earn would have the basic choice: They could hold cash as an asset or invest in the securities issued by corporations. In general, corporations issue securities to finance their investments in real assets and cover the gap between their investment plans and their internally generated savings such as retained earnings.

As shown in Figure 1–1, in such a world, savings would flow from households to corporations; in return, financial claims (equity and debt securities) would flow from corporations to household savers.

In an economy without FIs, the level of fund flows between household savers and the corporate sector is likely to be quite low. There are several reasons for this. Once they have lent money to a firm by buying its financial claims, households need to monitor, or check, the actions of that firm. They must be sure that the firm's management neither absconds with nor wastes the funds on any projects

---

[1] Some public utility suppliers, such as gas, electric, telephone, and water companies, are also singled out for regulation because of the special nature of their services and the costs imposed on society if they fail.

FIGURE 1–1

Flow of Funds in a World without FIs

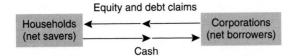

Equity and debt claims

Households (net savers) ← Corporations (net borrowers)

Cash

liquidity

The ease of converting an asset into cash.

price risk

The risk that the sale price of an asset will be lower than the purchase price of that asset.

financial intermediating

The provision of brokerage or asset transformation services by financial institutions to households and firms.

with low or negative net present values. Such monitoring actions are extremely costly for any given household because they require considerable time and expense to collect sufficiently high-quality information relative to the size of the average household saver's investments. Given this, it is likely that each household would prefer to leave the monitoring to others; in the end, little or no monitoring would be done. The resulting lack of monitoring would reduce the attractiveness and increase the risk of investing in corporate debt and equity.

The relatively long-term nature of corporate equity and debt, and the lack of a secondary market in which households can sell these securities, creates a second disincentive for household investors to hold the direct financial claims issued by corporations. Specifically, given the choice between holding cash and holding long-term securities, households may well choose to hold cash for **liquidity** reasons, especially if they plan to use savings to finance consumption expenditures in the near future.

Finally, even if financial markets existed (without FIs to operate them) to provide liquidity services by allowing households to trade corporate debt and equity securities among themselves, investors also face a **price risk** on sale of securities, and the secondary market trading of securities involves various transaction costs. That is, the price at which household investors can sell securities on secondary markets such as the Toronto Stock Exchange may well differ from the price they initially paid for the securities.

Because of (1) monitoring costs, (2) liquidity costs, and (3) price risk, the average household saver may view direct investment in corporate securities as an unattractive proposition and prefer either not to save or to save in the form of cash.

However, the economy has developed an alternative and indirect way to channel household savings to the corporate sector. This is to channel savings via FIs. Because of costs of monitoring, liquidity, and price risk, as well as for some other reasons, explained later, savers often prefer to hold the financial claims issued by FIs rather than those issued by corporations.

Consider Figure 1–2, which is a closer representation than Figure 1–1 of the world in which we live and the way funds flow in our economy. Notice how financial intermediaries or institutions are standing, or **intermediating**, between the household and corporate sectors.

These intermediaries fulfill two functions; any given FI might specialize in one or the other or might do both simultaneously. The first function is the brokerage function. When acting as a pure broker, an FI acts as an agent for the saver by providing information and transaction services. For example, full-service securities firms (e.g., RBC Dominion Securities) carry out investment research and make

FIGURE 1–2

Flow of Funds in a World with FIs

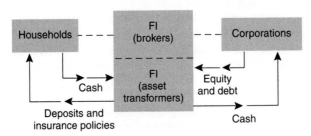

Households - - - FI (brokers) - - - Corporations

FI (asset transformers)

Cash — Equity and debt

Deposits and insurance policies — Cash

investment recommendations for their retail (or household) clients as well as conduct the purchase or sale of securities for commission or fees. Discount brokers (e.g., E*Trade) carry out the purchase or sale of securities at better prices and with greater efficiency than household savers could achieve by trading on their own. This efficiency results in reduced costs of trading, or **economies of scale** (see Chapter 21 for a detailed discussion). Independent insurance brokers identify the best types of insurance policies household savers can buy to fit their savings and retirement plans. In fulfilling a brokerage function, the FI plays an extremely important role by reducing transaction and information costs or imperfections between households and corporations. Thus, the FI encourages a higher rate of savings than would otherwise exist.[2]

The second function is the asset-transformation function. In acting as an **asset transformer,** the FI issues financial claims that are far more attractive to household savers than the claims directly issued by corporations. That is, for many households, the financial claims issued by FIs dominate those issued directly by corporations as a result of lower monitoring costs, lower liquidity costs, and lower price risk. In acting as asset transformers, FIs purchase the financial claims issued by corporations—equities, bonds, and other debt claims called **primary securities**—and finance these purchases by selling financial claims to household investors and other sectors in the form of deposits, insurance policies, and so on. The financial claims of FIs may be considered **secondary securities** because these assets are backed by the primary securities issued by commercial corporations that in turn invest in real assets. Specifically, FIs are independent market parties that create financial products whose value added to their clients is the transformation of financial risk.

Simplified balance sheets of a commercial firm and an FI are shown in Table 1–2. Note that in the real world, FIs hold a small proportion of their assets in the form of real assets such as bank branch buildings. These simplified balance sheets reflect a reasonably accurate characterization of the operational differences between commercial firms and FIs.

How can FIs purchase the direct or primary securities issued by corporations and profitably transform them into secondary securities more attractive to household savers? This question strikes at the very heart of what makes FIs special and important to the economy. The answer lies in the ability of FIs to better resolve the three costs facing a saver who chooses to invest directly in corporate securities.

economies of scale
The concept that the cost reduction in trading and other transaction services results from increased efficiency when FIs perform these services.

asset transformer
An FI issues financial claims that are more attractive to household savers than the claims directly issued by corporations.

primary securities
Securities issued by corporations and backed by the real assets of those corporations.

secondary securities
Securities issued by FIs and backed by primary securities.

TABLE 1–2
Simplified Balance Sheets for a Commercial Firm and an FI

Commercial Firm		Financial Intermediary	
Assets	**Liabilities**	**Assets**	**Liabilities**
Real assets (plant, machinery)	Primary securities (debt, equity)	Primary securities (debt, equity)	Secondary securities (deposits and insurance policies)

[2] Most recently, with the introduction of new derivative securities markets for financial futures, options, and swaps, financial institutions that participate in the markets reduce transaction and information costs for firms and consumers wanting to hedge their risks. Thus, FIs encourage better risk management than otherwise would exist. See F. Allen and A. M. Santomero, "The Theory of Financial Intermediation," *Journal of Banking and Finance* 21 (1998), pp. 1461–85; B. Scholtens and D. van Wensveen," A Critique of the Theory of Financial Intermediation," *Journal of Banking and Finance* 24 (2000), pp. 1243–51; F. Allen, "Do Financial Institutions Matter?" *Journal of Finance* 56 (2001), pp. 1165–75; and F. Allen and A. M. Santomero, "What Do Financial Intermediaries Do?" *Journal of Banking and Finance* 25 (2001), pp. 271–94.

Information Costs

One problem faced by an average saver directly investing in a commercial firm's financial claims is the high cost of information collection. Household savers must monitor the actions of firms in a timely and complete fashion after purchasing securities. Failure to monitor exposes investors to **agency costs,** that is, the risk that the firm's owners or managers will take actions with the saver's money contrary to the promises contained in the covenants of its securities contracts. Monitoring costs are part of overall agency costs. That is, agency costs arise whenever economic agents enter into contracts in a world of incomplete information and thus costly information collection. The more difficult and costly it is to collect information, the more likely it is that contracts will be broken. In this case the saver (the principal) could be harmed by the actions taken by the borrowing firm (the agent). One solution to this problem is for a large number of small savers to place their funds with a single FI. This FI groups these funds together and invests in the direct or primary financial claims issued by firms. This agglomeration of funds resolves a number of problems. First, the large FI now has a much greater incentive to collect information and monitor actions of the firm because it has far more at stake than does any small individual household. In a sense, small savers have appointed the FI as a **delegated monitor** to act on their behalf.[3] Not only does the FI have a greater incentive to collect information, the average cost of collecting information is lower. For example, the cost to a small investor of buying a $100 broker's report may seem inordinately high for a $10,000 investment. For an FI with $10 million under management, however, the cost seems trivial. Such economies of scale of information production and collection tend to increase the advantages to savers of using FIs rather than directly investing themselves.

Second, associated with the greater incentive to monitor and the costs involved in failing to monitor appropriately, FIs may develop new secondary securities that enable them to monitor more effectively. Thus, a richer menu of contracts may improve the monitoring abilities of FIs. Perhaps the classic example of this is the bank loan. Bank loans are generally shorter-term debt contracts than bond contracts. This short-term nature allows the FI to exercise more monitoring power and control over the borrower. In particular, the information the FI generates regarding the firm is frequently updated as its loan renewal decisions are made. When bank loan contracts are sufficiently short term, the banker becomes almost like an insider to the firm regarding informational familiarity with its operations and financial conditions. This more frequent monitoring often replaces the need for the relatively inflexible and hard-to-enforce covenants found in bond contracts.[4] Thus, by acting as a delegated monitor and producing better and more timely information, FIs reduce the degree of information imperfection and asymmetry between the ultimate suppliers and users of funds in the economy.

agency costs
Costs relating to the risk that the owners and managers of firms that receive savers' funds will take actions with those funds contrary to the best interests of the savers.

delegated monitor
An economic agent appointed to act on behalf of smaller agents in collecting information and/or investing funds on their behalf.

---

[3] For a theoretical modeling of the delegated monitor function, see D. W. Diamond, "Financial Intermediaries and Delegated Monitoring," *Review of Economic Studies* 51 (1984), pp. 393–414; and A. Winton, "Competition among Financial Intermediaries When Diversification Matters," *Journal of Financial Intermediation* 6 (1997), pp. 307–46.

[4] For a further description and discussion of the special or unique nature of bank loans, see E. Fama, "What's Different about Banks?" *Journal of Monetary Economics* 15 (1985), pp. 29–39; C. James, "Some Evidence on the Uniqueness of Bank Loans," *Journal of Financial Economics* 19 (1987), pp. 217–35; M. T. Billett, M. J. Flannery, and J. A. Garfinkel, "The Effect of Lender Identity on a Borrowing Firm's Equity Return," *Journal of Finance* 50 (1995), pp. 699–718; W. A. Kracaw and M. Zenner, "The Wealth Effects of Bank Financing Announcements in Highly Leveraged Transactions," *Journal of Finance* 57 (1996), pp. 1931–46; and S. Dahiya, M. Puri, and A. Saunders, "Bank Borrowers and Loan Sales: New Evidence on the Uniqueness of Bank Loans," *Journal of Business* 76 (2003), pp. 563–82.

Liquidity and Price Risk

In addition to improving t
financial or secondary clai
claims have superior liquidi
rities such as corporate e
deposit-taking institutions
with a fixed principal value
withdrawn immediately o
mutual funds issue shares t
almost fixed principal (dep
higher than those on bank c
cyholders to borrow against
notice. The real puzzle is h
highly liquid and low price
balance sheets while investi
rities issued by corporatio
confident enough to guara
investors and savers when they themselves invest in risky asset portfolios.
And why should savers and investors believe FIs' promises regarding the liquidity of their investments?

diversify

Reducing risk by holding a number of securities in a portfolio.

The answers to these questions lie in the ability of FIs to **diversify** away some but not all of their portfolio risks. The concept of diversification is familiar to all students of finance: Basically, as long as the returns on different investments are not perfectly *positively* correlated, by exploiting the benefits of size, FIs diversify away significant amounts of portfolio risk—especially the risk specific to the individual firm issuing any given security. Indeed, experiments have shown that equal investments in as few as 15 securities can bring significant diversification benefits to FIs and portfolio managers.[6] Further, as the number of securities in an FI's asset portfolio increases beyond 15 securities, portfolio risk falls, albeit at a diminishing rate. What is really going on here is that FIs exploit the law of large numbers in their investments, achieving a significant amount of diversification, whereas because of their small size, many household savers are constrained to holding relatively undiversified portfolios. This risk diversification allows an FI to predict more accurately its expected return on its asset portfolio. A domestically and globally diversified FI may be able to generate an almost risk-free return on its assets. As a result, it can credibly fulfill its promise to households to supply highly liquid claims with little price or capital value risk. A good example of this is the ability of a bank to offer highly liquid demand deposits—with a fixed principal value—as liabilities, while at the same time investing in risky loans as assets. As long as an FI is sufficiently large to gain from diversification and monitoring, its financial claims are likely to be viewed as liquid and attractive to small savers compared with direct investments in the capital market.

---

[5] Also, the largest commercial banks in the world make markets for swaps, allowing businesses to hedge various risks (such as interest rate risk and foreign exchange risk) on their balance sheets.

[6] For a review of such studies, see E. J. Elton, M. J. Gruber, S.J. Brown and W.N. Goetzmann, *Modern Portfolio Theory and Investment Analysis*, 6th ed. (New York: John Wiley & Sons, 2003), Chapter 2. For a Canadian perspective, see S. Cleary and D. Copp, "Diversification with Canadian Stocks: how much is enough?" Canadian Investment Review 12, Fall, 1999, pp. 21–25.

l Services

...ng discussion has concentrated on three general or special services ...by FIs: reducing household savers' monitoring costs, increasing their liq-...and reducing their price-risk exposure. Next, we discuss two other special ...ces provided by FIs: reduced transaction costs and maturity intermediation.

Reduced Transaction Costs

Just as FIs provide potential economies of scale in information collection, they also provide potential economies of scale in transaction costs. For example, small retail buyers face higher commission charges or transaction costs than do large wholesale buyers. By grouping their assets in FIs that purchase assets in bulk—such as in mutual funds and pension funds—household savers can reduce the transaction costs of their asset purchases. In addition, bid-ask (buy-sell) spreads are normally lower for assets bought and sold in large quantities.

Maturity Intermediation

An additional dimension of FIs' ability to reduce risk by diversification is that they can better bear the risk of mismatching the maturities of their assets and liabilities than can small household savers. Thus, FIs offer maturity intermediation services to the rest of the economy. Specifically, through maturity mismatching, FIs can produce new types of contracts, such as long-term mortgage loans to households, while still raising funds with short-term liability contracts. Further, while such mismatches can subject an FI to interest rate risk (see Chapters 8 and 9), a large FI is better able to manage this risk through its superior access to markets and instruments for hedging such as loan sales and securitization (Chapters 26 and 27); futures (Chapter 23); swaps (Chapter 25); and options, caps, floors, and collars (Chapter 24).

Concept Questions

1. What are the three major risks to household savers from direct security purchases?
2. What are two major differences between brokers (such as security brokers) and deposit-taking institutions (such as banks)?
3. What are primary securities and secondary securities?
4. What is the link between asset diversification and the liquidity of deposit contracts?

OTHER ASPECTS OF SPECIALNESS

The theory of the flow of funds points to three principal reasons for believing that FIs are special, along with two other associated reasons. In reality, academics, policymakers, and regulators identify other areas of specialness relating to certain specific functions of FIs or groups of FIs. We discuss these next.

The Transmission of Monetary Policy

The highly liquid nature of bank and other FI deposits has resulted in their acceptance by the public as the most widely used medium of exchange in the economy. Indeed, at the core of the three most commonly used definitions of the money supply—M1, M2, and M3[7]—lie deposit-taking institutions' deposit contracts. Because

---

[7] The Bank of Canada defines the money supply as M1: ($170.1 billion outstanding in March 2005) the currency in circulation (bank notes and coins) outside of banks plus personal chequing accounts and current accounts at banks; M2: ($636.0 billion outstanding in March 2005) equal to M1 plus personal savings accounts, other chequing accounts, term deposits, and non-personal notice deposits; and M3: ($918.9 billion in March 2005) equal to M1 plus M2 plus bank non-personal deposits plus foreign currency deposits of residents of Canada.

the liabilities of deposit-taking institutions are a significant component of the money supply that influences the rate of inflation, they play a key role in the *transmission of monetary policy* from the central bank to the rest of the economy. That is, chartered banks and other DTIs are the conduit through which monetary policy actions affect the rest of the financial sector and the economy in general. The aim of monetary policy in Canada is to protect the value of the dollar by controlling the level of inflation. The Bank of Canada carries out monetary policy primarily through setting the target overnight rate (the rate at which financial institutions lend money to each other for one day in the overnight inter-bank market). The target overnight rate in turn influences the loan rates and deposit rates offered by the deposit-taking institutions.

Credit Allocation

A further reason FIs are often viewed as special is that they are the major and sometimes the only source of finance for a particular sector of the economy pre-identified as being in special need of finance. Policymakers in Canada, the United States, and a number of other countries, such as the United Kingdom, have identified *residential real estate* as needing special subsidies. For example, Canada Mortgage and Housing Corporation (CMHC) insures residential mortgage loans where the downpayment is less than 25 percent. This has enhanced the specialness of FIs that most commonly service the needs of that sector. In a similar fashion, farming is an especially important area of the economy in terms of the overall social welfare of the population. Farm Credit Canada (FCC) provides loans to farmers unable to get credit elsewhere.

www.cmhc.ca

www.fcc-fac.ca

Intergenerational Wealth Transfers or Time Intermediation

The ability of savers to transfer wealth between youth and old age and across generations is also of great importance to the social well-being of a country. Because of this, life insurance (see Chapter 3) and pension funds (see Chapter 5) are often especially encouraged, via special taxation relief and other subsidy mechanisms, to service and accommodate those needs.

Payment Services

Deposit-taking institutions such as banks, credit unions, and caisses populaires (see Chapter 2) are special in that the efficiency with which they provide payment services directly benefits the economy. Important payment services are cheque-clearing, debit and credit transactions, and wire transfer services. For example, on any given day, billions of dollars worth of payments are effected through the large value transfer system (LVTs) operated by the Canadian Payments Association (see Chapter 14). Any breakdowns in this system probably would produce gridlock in the payment system with resulting harmful effects to the economy.

Denomination Intermediation

Both money market and debt-equity mutual funds are special because they provide services relating to denomination intermediation (see Chapter 5). Because they are sold in very large denominations, many assets are either out of reach of individual savers or would result in savers' holding highly undiversified asset portfolios. For example, the minimum size of a negotiable CD is $100,000 and commercial paper (short-term corporate debt) is often sold in minimum packages of $250,000 or more. Individually, a saver may be unable to purchase such instruments. However, by buying shares in a money market mutual fund along with other small investors, household savers overcome the constraints to buying assets imposed by large minimum denomination sizes. Such indirect access to these markets may allow small savers to generate higher returns on their portfolios as well.

SPECIALNESS AND REGULATION

In the preceding section, FIs were shown to be special because of the various services they provide to sectors of the economy. The general areas of FI specialness include:

- information services
- liquidity services
- price-risk reduction services
- transaction cost services
- maturity intermediation services

Areas of institution-specific specialness are as follows:

- money supply transmission (banks)
- credit allocation (credit unions, caisses populaires)
- intergenerational transfers (pension funds, life insurance companies)
- payment services (banks)
- denomination intermediation (mutual funds, pension funds, trust companies)

negative externalities
Action by an economic agent imposing costs on other economic agents.

Failure to provide these services or a breakdown in their efficient provision can be costly to both the ultimate sources (households) and users (firms) of savings. The **negative externalities**[8] affecting firms and households when something goes wrong in the FI sector of the economy make a case for regulation. That is, FIs are regulated to protect against a disruption in the provision of the services discussed above and the costs this would impose on the economy and society at large. For example, bank failures may destroy household savings and at the same time restrict a firm's access to credit. Insurance company failures may leave households totally exposed in old age to catastrophic illnesses and sudden drops in income on retirement. Further, individual FI failures may create doubts in savers' minds regarding the stability and solvency of FIs in general and cause panics and even runs on sound institutions. In addition, racial, sexual, age, or other discrimination—such as mortgage **redlining**—may unfairly exclude some potential financial service consumers from the marketplace. This type of market failure needs to be corrected by regulation. Although regulation may be socially beneficial, it also imposes private costs, or a regulatory burden, on individual FI owners and managers. For example, regulations prohibit banks from making loans to individual borrowers that exceed more than 25 percent of their total capital even though the loans may have a positive net present value to the bank. Consequently, regulation is an attempt to improve the social welfare benefits and mitigate the social costs of the provision of FI services. The private costs of regu-

redlining
The procedure by which a banker refuses to make loans to residents living inside given geographic boundaries.

---

[8] A good example of a negative externality is the costs faced by small businesses in a one-bank town if the local bank fails. These businesses could find it difficult to get financing elsewhere, and their customers could be similarly disadvantaged. As a result, the failure of the bank may have a negative or contagious effect on the economic prospects of the whole community, resulting in lower sales, production, and employment.

net regulatory burden
The difference between the private costs of regulations and the private benefits for the producers of financial services.

lation relative to its private benefits, for the producers of financial services, is called the **net regulatory burden.**[9]

Six types of regulation seek to increase the net social welfare benefits of financial intermediaries' services: (1) safety and soundness regulation, (2) monetary policy regulation, (3) credit allocation regulation, (4) consumer protection regulation, (5) investor protection regulation, and (6) entry and chartering regulation. Regulations are imposed differentially on the various types of FIs. For example, deposit-taking institutions are the most heavily regulated of the FIs. Regulation can also be imposed at the federal or the provincial level and occasionally at the international level, as in the case of bank capital requirements (see Chapter 20).

Finally, some of these regulations are functional in nature, covering all FIs that carry out certain functions, such as payment services, while others are institution specific.

Safety and Soundness Regulation

To protect depositors and borrowers against the risk of FI failure due, for example, to a lack of diversification in asset portfolios, regulators have developed layers of protective mechanisms. These mechanisms are intended to ensure the safety and soundness of the FI and thus to maintain the credibility of the FI in the eyes of its borrowers and lenders. In the first layer of protection are requirements encouraging FIs to diversify their assets. Thus, banks are required not to make loans exceeding 25 percent of their total equity capital funds to any one company or borrower (see Chapter 11).

The second layer of protection concerns the minimum level of capital or equity funds that the owners of an FI need to contribute to the funding of its operations (see Chapter 20). For example, FI regulation is concerned with the minimum ratio of capital to (risk) assets. The higher the proportion of capital contributed by owners, the greater the protection against insolvency risk to outside liability claimholders such as depositors and insurance policyholders. This is because losses on the asset portfolio due, for example, to the lack of diversification are legally borne by the equity holders first, and only after equity is totally wiped out by outside liability holders.[10] Consequently, by varying the required degree of equity capital, FI regulators can directly affect the degree of risk exposure faced by nonequity claimholders in FIs. (See Chapter 20 for more discussion on the role of capital in FIs.)

www.cdic.ca

The third layer of protection is the provision of guaranty funds such as the Canada Deposit Insurance Corporation (CDIC) to meet insolvency losses to small claimholders (see Chapter 19). By protecting FI claimholders, when an FI collapses and owners' equity or net worth is wiped out, these funds create a demand for regulation of the insured institutions to protect the funds' resources (see Chapter 19 for more discussion).

The fourth layer of regulation is monitoring and surveillance itself. Regulators subject all FIs, whether banks, securities firms, or insurance companies, to varying degrees of monitoring and surveillance. This involves on-site examination as well as an FI's production of accounting statements and reports on a timely basis for off-site evaluation. Just as savers appoint FIs as delegated monitors to evaluate the behaviour and actions of ultimate borrowers, society appoints regulators to monitor the behaviour and performance of FIs.

---

[9] Other regulated firms, such as gas and electric utilities, also face a complex set of regulations imposing a net regulatory burden on their operations.

[10] Thus, equity holders are junior claimants and debt holders are senior claimants to an FI's assets.

Finally, note that regulation is not without costs for those regulated. For example, society's regulators may require FIs to have more equity capital than private owners believe is in their own best interests. Similarly, producing the information requested by regulators is costly for FIs because it involves the time of managers, lawyers, and accountants. Again, the socially optimal amount of information may differ from an FI's privately optimal amount.[11]

As noted earlier, the differences between the private benefits to an FI from being regulated—such as insurance fund guarantees—and the private costs it faces from adhering to regulation—such as examinations—is called the *net regulatory burden*. The higher the net regulatory burden on FIs, the more inefficiently they produce any given set of financial services from a private (FI) owner's perspective.

Monetary Policy Regulation

www.bankofcanada.ca

outside money
The part of the money supply directly produced by the government or central bank, such as notes and coin.

inside money
The part of the money supply produced by the private banking system.

Another motivation for regulation concerns the special role banks play in the transmission of monetary policy from the Bank of Canada (the central bank) to the rest of the economy. The problem is that the central bank directly controls only the quantity of notes and coin in the economy—called **outside money**—whereas the bulk of the money supply consists of deposits—called **inside money.** In theory, a central bank can vary the quantity of cash or outside money and directly affect a bank's reserve position as well as the amount of loans and deposits a bank can create without formally regulating the bank's portfolio. In practice, regulators have chosen to impose formal controls.[12] Banks in Canada are not subject to reserve requirements but in many countries, including the United States, regulators commonly impose a minimum level of required cash reserves to be held against deposits (see Chapter 17). Some argue that imposing such reserve requirements makes the control of the money supply and its transmission more predictable. Such reserves also add to an FI's net regulatory burden if they are more than the institution believes are necessary for its own liquidity purposes. In general, whether banks or insurance companies, all FIs would choose to hold some cash reserves—even non-interest-bearing—to meet the liquidity and transaction needs of their customers directly. For well-managed FIs, however, this optimal level is normally low, especially if the central bank (or other regulatory body) does not pay interest on required reserves. As a result, FIs often view required reserves as similar to a tax and as a positive cost of undertaking intermediation.[13]

Credit Allocation Regulation

Credit allocation regulation supports the FI's lending to socially important sectors such as housing and farming. Canada does not have this type of regulation, but in the U.S. these regulations may require an FI to hold a minimum amount of assets

---

[11] Also, a social cost rather than social benefit from regulation is the potential risk-increasing behaviour (often called moral hazard) that results if deposit insurance and other guaranty funds provide coverage to FIs and their liability holders at less than the actuarially fair price (see Chapter 19 for further discussion).

[12] In classic central banking theory, the quantity of bank deposits *(D)* is determined as the product of 1 over the banking system's required (or desired) ratio of cash reserves to deposits *(r)* times the quantity of bank reserves *(R)* outstanding, where R comprises notes and coin plus bank deposits held on reserve at the central bank. $D = (1/r) \times R$. Thus, by varying R, given a relatively stable reserve ratio *(r)*, the central bank can directly affect D, the quantity of deposits or inside money that, as just noted, is a large component of the money supply. Even if not required to do so by regulation, banks would still tend to hold some cash reserves as a liquidity precaution against the sudden withdrawal of deposits or the sudden arrival of new loan demand.

[13] In the United States, bank reserves held with the central bank (the Federal Reserve, or the Fed) are non-interest-bearing. In some other countries, interest is paid on bank reserves, thereby lowering the "regulatory tax" effect. Canada eliminated bank reserves in 1994.

in one particular sector of the economy or to set maximum interest rates, prices, or fees to subsidize certain sectors. Examples of asset restrictions include insurance regulations that set maximums on the amount of foreign or international assets in which insurance companies can invest. Examples of interest rate restrictions are the usury laws on the maximum rates that can be charged on loans. The Canadian Criminal Code defines a criminal rate as an effective annual rate greater than 60 percent.

Such price and quantity restrictions may have justification on social welfare grounds—especially if society has a preference for strong (and subsidized) housing and farming sectors. However, they can also be harmful to FIs that have to bear the private costs of meeting many of these regulations. To the extent that the net private costs of such restrictions are positive, they add to the costs and reduce the efficiency with which FIs undertake intermediation.

Consumer Protection Regulation

www.fcac-acfc.gc.ca

In 2001, Bill C-8 was passed by the federal government to reform the financial services industry in Canada. The Financial Consumer Agency of Canada (www.fcac-acfc.gc.ca) was created to protect consumers of financial services by ensuring that FIs adhered to the consumer protection regulation in Canada. For example, the FCAC provides information for consumers on such services as bank accounts and investment products. The FCAC also examines and imposes fines on FIs who violate the consumer protection laws.

In addition, on July 21, 2003, eight Canadian FIs renewed a public commitment to provide low-cost banking services to Canadians. Thus, it can be argued that consumer protection laws impose a considerable net regulatory burden on FIs, but the offsetting benefit is the provision of equal access to mortgage and lending markets. As deregulation proceeds toward consolidation and universal banking (see Chapter 2) it is likely that such laws will be extended beyond banks to other financial services providers such as insurance companies.

Investor Protection Regulation

A considerable number of laws protect investors who use investment banks directly to purchase securities and/or indirectly to access securities markets through investing in mutual or pension funds. Various laws protect investors against abuses such as insider trading, lack of disclosure, outright malfeasance, and breach of fiduciary responsibilities (see Chapter 4). As with consumer protection legislation, compliance with these acts can impose a net regulatory burden on FIs.[14]

Entry Regulation

The entry and activities of FIs are also regulated (e.g., new bank chartering regulations). Increasing or decreasing the cost of entry into a financial sector affects the profitability of firms already competing in that industry. Thus, the industries heavily protected against new entrants by high direct costs (e.g., through required equity or capital contributions) and high indirect costs (e.g., by restricting individuals who can establish FIs) of entry produce bigger profits for existing firms than those in which entry is relatively easy (see Chapters 21 and 22). In addition, regulations

---

[14] There have been a number of moves to extend these regulations to hedge funds, which have traditionally been outside regulations and the securities acts as long as they have fewer than 100 "sophisticated" investors. It has been believed until recently that large sophisticated investors do not need such protections. However, recent scandals and failures relating to hedge funds and their investments—such as the failure of Long Term Capital Management in 1998 and its subsequent bailout—appear to be changing lawmakers' and regulators' perceptions.

(such as the Bank Act) define the scope of permitted activities under a given charter (see Chapter 21). The broader the set of financial service activities permitted under a given charter, the more valuable that charter is likely to be. Thus, barriers to entry and regulations pertaining to the scope of permitted activities affect the *charter value* of an FI and the size of its net regulatory burden.[15]

Concept Questions

1. Why should more regulation be imposed on FIs than on other types of private corporations?
2. Define the concept of net regulatory burden.
3. What six major types of regulation do FIs face?

THE CHANGING DYNAMICS OF SPECIALNESS

At any moment in time, each FI supplies a set of financial services (brokerage related, asset transformation related, or both) and is subject to a given net regulatory burden. As the demands for the special features of financial services change as a result of changing preferences and technology, one or more areas of the financial services industry become less profitable.[16] Similarly, changing regulations can increase or decrease the net regulatory burden faced in supplying financial services in any given area. These demand, cost, and regulatory pressures are reflected in changing market shares in different financial service areas as some contract and others expand. Clearly, an FI seeking to survive and prosper must be flexible enough to move to growing financial service areas and away from those that are contracting. If regulatory activity restrictions inhibit or reduce the flexibility with which FIs can alter their product mix, this will reduce their competitive ability and the efficiency with which financial services are delivered. That is, activity barriers within the financial services industry may reduce the ability to diversify and potentially add to the net regulatory burden faced by FIs.

Trends in Canada

Figure 1-3 shows the percentage distribution of the financial sector assets held in Canada in 2003 by banks, mutual fund companies, property and casualty insurance companies, life and health insurers, and credit unions/caisses populaires. The banks are highest at 56 percent, followed by mutual fund companies at 19 percent. The effect of mutual fund companies is understated in Figure 1-3 as the data for the banks, insurance companies, and credit unions/caisses populaires include the assets of their mutual fund subsidiaries. Mutual fund assets have increased from $42.2 billion in 1990 to $497.3 billion in 2004, almost a 12-fold increase over the 15-year period. The major banks took over the largest independent securities firms (Dominion Securities, McLeod Young Weir, Wood Gundy, among others) in the 1980s. The 1990s saw more consolidation in the financial services sector subsequent to the implementation of the revised Bank Act in 1992 that permitted banks to own trusts. Toronto-Dominion Bank took over Central Guaranty Trust in 1992 and Canada Trust in 2000, which resulted in the virtual

---

[15] Indeed, the higher an FI's charter value, the lower the incentive it has to take risk. See, for example, A. Saunders and B. Wilson, "An Analysis of the Charter Value and Its Risk Constraining Incentives," *Journal of Financial Services Research* 19 (April/June 2001), pp. 185–96.

[16] See, for example, F. S. Mishkin and P. E. Strahan, "What Will Technology Do to Financial Structure?" NBER Working Paper, no. 6842, January 1999.

FIGURE 1–3

Financial Services Assets in Canada by Sector, 2003

Source: Department of Finance, Canada, www.fin.gc.ca

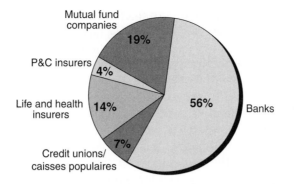

FIGURE 1–4

Financial Services Revenue in Canada by Sector, 2003

Source: Department of Finance, Canada, www.fin.gc.ca

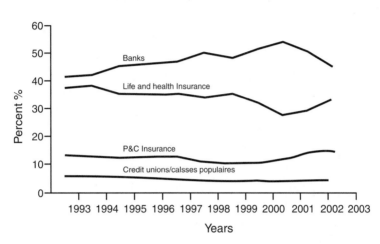

Source: Bank of Canada, Canadian Life and Health Insurance Association, Conference Board of Canada, Insurance Bureau of Canada

elimination of the trust industry as one of the four pillars. The asset allocation by sector has changed very little since 2000.[17]

Figure 1-4 shows the changing shares of revenue on a consolidated basis in the financial services sector for banks, life and health insurers, property and casualty insurers, and credit unions/caisses populaires from 1993–2003. Of note is the increase in the share of revenue of the banks up until 2000, reflecting their dominance and diversification into insurance, trust, and securities activities.

Traditional services provided by deposit-taking institutions (payment services, transaction cost services, information costs) have become relatively less significant as a portion of all services provided by FIs. In particular, FIs engaged in securities functions such as the sale of mutual funds and other investment products, differ from banks and insurance companies in that they give savers cheaper access to the direct securities markets. They do so by exploiting the comparative advantages of size and diversification, with the transformation of financial claims, such as maturity transformation, a lesser concern. Thus, mutual funds buy stocks, bonds, commercial paper, and Treasury bills directly in financial markets and

---

[17] The Bank Act determines who may operate as a bank in Canada and specifies which activities are allowed. For a detailed history of the Bank Act and its influence on Canadian financial markets, see P. L. Siklos, *Money, Banking, and Financial Institutions: Canada in the Global Environment*, 4th ed., 2004, Toronto: McGraw-Hill Ryerson, Chapter 19, pp. 355–363. See also M. Babad and C. Mulroney's book, *Pillars: The Coming Crisis in Canada's Financial Industry*, 1993, Toronto: Stoddart Publishing, for an early popular history and predictions of the impact of consolidation on Canada's financial services sector.

issue savers shares whose value is linked in a direct pro rata fashion to the value of the mutual fund's asset portfolio. To the extent that these funds efficiently diversify, they also offer price-risk protection and liquidity services.

The maturity and return characteristics of the financial claims issued by mutual funds closely reflect the maturities of the direct equity and debt securities portfolios in which they invest. In contrast, banks, credit unions, and insurance companies have lower correlations between their asset portfolio maturities and the promised maturity of their liabilities. Thus, banks may partially fund a 10-year commercial loan with demand deposits; a credit union may fund 25-year conventional mortgages with three-month time deposits.

To the extent that the financial services market is efficient and these trends reflect the forces of demand and supply, they indicate a current trend: Savers increasingly prefer the denomination intermediation and information services provided by mutual funds. These FIs provide investments that closely mimic diversified investments in the *direct* securities markets over the transformed financial claims offered by traditional FIs. This trend may also indicate that the net regulatory burden on traditional FIs—such as banks and insurance companies—is higher than that on investment companies. As a result, traditional FIs are unable to produce their services as cost efficiently as they could previously. It is increasingly important that FI managers deal with changing trends and reconsider how best to exploit any remaining competitive advantages to keep the net benefit of regulation positive for their FIs.

In addition to a decline in the use of traditional services provided by deposit-taking institutions and insurance companies and an increase in the services provided by investment banks and mutual funds, the early 2000s saw an overall weakening of public trust and confidence in the ethics followed by financial institutions. Specifically, tremendous publicity was generated concerning conflicts of interest in a number of financial institutions between analysts' research recommendations on stocks to buy or not buy and whether these firms played a role in underwriting the securities of the firms the analysts were recommending. As a result, several highly publicized securities violations resulted in criminal cases brought against securities law violators in the U.S. In particular, the New York State attorney general forced Merrill Lynch to pay a US $100 million penalty because of allegations that Merrill Lynch brokers gave investors overly optimistic reports about the stock of its investment banking clients. Such allegations of securities law violations can reach across the U.S.-Canada border and lead to a loss in public trust and confidence in many sectors of the FI industry (see the Ethical Dilemmas Box).

Future Trends

The growth of mutual funds coupled with the weakening of public trust and confidence (amid a multitude of regulatory investigations into the practices of investment advisors, brokers, and banks), and with investors' recent focus on direct investments in primary securities, may together signal the beginning of a trend away from intermediation as the most efficient mechanism for savers to channel funds to borrowers. While this trend may reflect changed investors' preferences toward risk and return, it may also reflect a decline in the relative costs of direct securities investment versus investment via FIs. This decline in costs has led to many FI products being "commoditized" and sold directly in financial markets; for example, many options initially offered over the counter by FIs eventually migrate to the public option markets as trading volume grows and trading terms become standardized.

Ethical Dilemmas

ENRON DEALINGS COST CIBC $80M; PENALTY SETTLES CHARGES BY N.Y. STOCK MARKET WATCHDOG, FORCED BY REGULATORS TO STOP DOING CERTAIN TRANSACTIONS

CIBC's dealings with disgraced Enron Corp. came home to roost yesterday as the bank was hit with an $80 million (U.S.) penalty.

The payment settles allegations by the U.S. stock market watchdog that the bank helped the energy company mislead investors.

As well, financial regulators in Canada and the United States required Canadian Imperial Bank of Commerce to stop doing the types of financing transactions it handled for Enron, and to submit to more scrutiny.

"They have put CIBC on a short leash," said Per Mokkelbost, a corporate finance professor at the University of Toronto's Rotman School of Management. In addition, the U.S. Department of Justice alleged yesterday that "CIBC and its personnel have violated federal criminal law" and "aided and abetted" Enron in questionable transactions.

But the bank is not being prosecuted because it has agreed to stop doing Enron-style financings for three years and has appointed a monitor to oversee this, said a letter from the justice department's Enron task force chief, Leslie Caldwell.

Two former CIBC executives have also agreed to pay a total of $623,000 (U.S.) in penalties to the U.S. Securities and Exchange Commission. A third former executive, Ian Schottlaender of CIBC's New York operation, is fighting allegations of wrongdoing.

The hardest hit executive is Daniel Ferguson of Toronto, an executive vice-president who left the bank earlier this month. He has agreed to pay $563,000 in penalties. Mark Wolf, formerly of CIBC's Houston office, agreed to pay $60,000.

None could be reached for comment.

CIBC is the first Canadian bank hit in the SEC's wide-ranging investigation of the December, 2001 Enron collapse, one of several corporate failures that shook investor confidence and sent stock markets plummeting. "It is a bit of a black eye for the financial system in Canada," said Mokkelbost.

Royal Bank and Toronto-Dominion Bank have also been named by U.S. court-appointed examiners for "aiding and abetting" the Enron debacle, in which financings were set up to look like sales of assets to hide the company's heavy borrowing. Enron went bankrupt two years ago this month because of its debt, inflated profits and accounting hocus-pocus.

TD and Royal have denied any knowledge of Enron's accounting fraud and said they did nothing wrong. CIBC reached its settlement without admitting or denying the SEC's allegations.

Officials at the SEC would not comment when asked if any other Canadian banks are under investigation. Spokespersons for Royal and TD said they were unaware of any probes.

CIBC chief executive John Hunkin said yesterday he is pleased the settlement agreement is "closing an unpleasant and painful chapter in our company's history."

The bank has already put into place some of the changes required by Canada's Office of the Superintendent of Financial Institutions and the U.S. Federal Reserve to make sure Enron-style structured financing transactions don't happen again, Hunkin added in a conference call with reporters and analysts.

"We have moved well beyond the events of three years ago... . CIBC is now on the path it needs to be."

After the bank suffered heavily from corporate loan losses in 2002, Hunkin reduced corporate lending in favour of earning more profits from branch banking operations, which provide a more stable earnings stream.

The Enron-style structured finance transactions will be wound down over the coming months and lost revenues will cost the bank about 10 cents per share in earnings, said chief financial officer Tom Woods. The bank had earnings per share of $5.21 in its most recent fiscal year.

Earlier this year, CIBC set up a reserve fund of $109 million (Cdn.) to handle any Enron liabilities — an amount that is equal to the $80 million (U.S.) payment wired by the bank to the SEC yesterday.

No further reserves will be set aside, despite the class-action lawsuits CIBC is facing from disgruntled investors, because the bank has insurance to cover any awards.

"These suits are without merit," Hunkin said.

The $80 million penalty includes $37.5 million in profits CIBC made from Enron, a penalty of the same amount and $5 million in interest.

While the fine pales in comparison to CIBC's profits of slightly more than $2 billion in the fiscal year ended Oct. 31, "you cannot look at the money only," said Mokkelbost.

"It is their reputation."

The penalties paid by CIBC and its executives will go into an interest-bearing fund for benefits of the Enron fraud, which cost investors $25 billion as the share price collapsed — including the life savings of many ordinary Enron employees.

The fund has now raised $400 million, including payouts of $80 million from Merrill Lynch, $101 million

➤

17

from Citibank Corp. and $135 million from JP Morgan Chase, said Linda Chatman Thomsen, deputy director of enforcement for the SEC.

That makes the CIBC tied for third-largest penalty issued by the American stock market watchdog.

The SEC alleged that the CIBC helped Enron "mislead its investors through a series of complex structured finance transactions over a period of several years preceding Enron's bankruptcy."

Between June, 1998, and October 2001, the CIBC and Enron set up 34 financings as asset sales for the purposes of accounting and financial reporting, "allowing Enron to hide from investors and rating agencies the true extent of its borrowings," the SEC said.

Enron used these "disguised loans" to increase earnings by $1 billion and avoid disclosing more than $2.6 billion in debt.

"Today's action demonstrates that neither financial institutions nor their executives can hide behind the technical complexities of structured transactions to avoid responsibility for contributing to fraudulent accounting and manipulated financial results," said Steve Cutler, director of enforcement for the SEC.

Source: By Rob Ferguson, *Toronto Star*, Dec 23, 2003, p. A1. Reprinted with permission, TorStar Syndication Services.

As Merton has noted, financial markets "tend to be efficient institutional alternatives to intermediaries when the products have standardized terms, can serve a large number of customers and are well-enough understood for transactors to be comfortable in assessing their prices . . . intermediaries are better suited for low volume products."[18]

A dominant issue for Canadian FIs in recent years is the merger of firms within the financial sector (see Chapter 22). Revisions to the Bank Act in the 1980s and 1990s allowed banks to own brokerage firms as well as trust companies and insurance subsidiaries (banks are still not allowed to sell insurance in their branches). This moved Canada's financial sector closer to universal banking and the creation of larger banks as well as larger insurance firms (Manulife Financial, Sun Life Financial). Some of this growth has come from expansion overseas (Bank of Nova Scotia's purchase of Mexico's Banco Inverlat) and in the U.S. (Manulife Financial's merger with John Hancock of Boston). However, the issue of bank-bank mergers as well as cross-pillar mergers of banks and insurance companies within Canada has yet to be resolved. The 1998 MacKay Report recognized that the safety and soundness of the financial system, fair and ethical competitive markets, and consumer protection were necessary aims for the regulation of the financial sector. The disallowance in 1998 by the Minister of Finance of two proposed mergers (Canadian Imperial Bank of Commerce with Toronto-Dominion Bank, and Royal Bank of Canada with Bank of Montreal) came with a promise of a ruling with respect to mergers that was still awaited in 2005.[19]

Direct financial markets are evolving fast. Because of technological advances, the costs of direct access to financial markets by savers are falling and the relative benefits to individual savers of investing through FIs are narrowing. The ability to reduce transactions costs by **e-trading** on the Internet rather than using a traditional stockbroker and paying brokerage fees has reduced the need for FIs to perform these services. In addition, large FIs such as the Royal Bank of Canada are adapting technology to serve their existing customers across banking and invest-

e-trading
Buying and selling shares on the Internet.

---

[18] R. Merton, "A Functional Perspective of Financial Intermediation," *Financial Management,* Summer 1995, p. 26.

[19] The MacKay Task Force, appointed by the Minister of Finance in 1996, submitted its report in 1998. See *Report of the Task Force on the Future of the Canadian Financial Services Sector*, September 1998, available at http://finservtaskforce.fin.gc.ca. In 2005, the Canadian and international media were still speculating on when the government would announce its merger policy. See P. C. Newman, "Big Five, Small Players," *Maclean's*, Toronto, January 10 2005, Vol. 118, Issue 2, pp. 38–39 and "Top Canadians fall behind," *The Banker*, London, February 2005, Vol. 155, Issue. 948, p. 96.

ment services (Chapter 14) as well as to meet the demands placed on FIs for information regarding money laundering and terrorism as a result of the terrorist attacks on the World Trade Center and the Pentagon in September 2001.

GLOBAL ISSUES

Numerous highly publicized actions involving conflicts of interest and loans to companies like Enron, the second largest bankruptcy in U.S. history, have forced Canadian as well as other globally-active FIs to comply with U.S. regulations as well as international regulations regarding capital adequacy such as Basel II (Chapter 20). Table 1–3 lists the 10 largest banks in the world, measured by total assets (U.S. dollars) at the beginning of 2004. Note that the Royal Bank of Canada was the highest ranked Canadian bank at number 50. Asset size relative to their global competitors is the yardstick used to measure Canadian FIs, a statistic that figures prominently in any discussion of FI mergers in Canada (Chapter 22).

Cross-border issues are important in determining the rules for foreign FIs operating in Canada (Chapter 2) as well as the expansion of FIs into new banking territory such as the newly-opened markets in China (Chapter 22).

The world's six most active banks, based on the percent of their assets held outside their home countries, are listed in Table 1–4. These include the two big Swiss banks as well as one U.S. financial institution (American Express Bank). Interestingly, although in 2003 Japanese banks occupied 3 of the top 10 places of banks in the world in terms of asset size (see Table 1–3), they are absent from the list of banks with the most active international operations. Indeed, domestic problems, including a record number of bad loans (especially in real estate), and a recession, have induced

TABLE 1–3
The 10 largest Banks in the World, (in millions of U.S. dollars)

Source: © The Banker. Financial Times Business Limited 2005. All Rights Reserved.

1. Mizuho Financial Group (Japan)	1,285,471
2. Citigroup (USA)	1,264,032
3. UBS (Switzerland)	1,120,543
4. Crédit Agricole Groupe (France)	1,105,378
5. HSBC Holdings (UK)	1,034,216
6. Deutsche Bank (Germany)	1,014,845
7. BNP Paribas (France)	988,982
8. Mitsubishi Tokyo Financial Group (Japan)	974,950
9. Sumitomo Mitsui Financial Group (Japan)	950,448
10. Royal Bank of Scotland (UK)	806,207

Note: Canadian FIs that were in the top 150 banks worldwide in 2003 were Royal Bank of Canada (50th), Scotiabank, Canadian Imperial Bank of Commerce, and Toronto-Dominion Bank (61–63, respectively), Bank of Montreal (66), Desjardins Group (123), and National Bank of Canada (142).

TABLE 1–4
Top Global Banks

Source: *The Banker,* "Top 50 Global Banks," February 2003. *www.thebanker.com*

Banks	Home Country	Percentage of Overseas Business*
1. American Express Bank	United States	86.17
2. UBS	Switzerland	84.41
3. Arab Banking Corporation	Bahrain	82.33
4. Credit Suisse Group	Switzerland	79.62
5. Standard Chartered	United Kingdom	69.64
6. Deutsche Bank	Germany	66.44

*Overseas business refers to the percentage of assets banks hold outside their home country.

Japanese banks to contract their foreign assets and international activities, as well as to merge. For example, the three-way merger between Industrial Bank of Japan, Fuji Bank, and Dai-Ichi Kangyo Bank in 2000 created the world's largest banking group, Mizuho Financial Group, with assets of over US $1,394 billion.[20]

Concept Questions

1. Is the share of bank assets growing as a proportion of total FI assets in Canada?
2. Describe the global challenges facing FIs in the early 2000s.

INTERNET EXERCISE

Go to the Web site of the Office of the Superintendent of Financial Institutions (OSFI) at www.osfi-bsif.ca and compare the total assets of the different types of FIs that OSFI regulates.

Go to www.osfi-bsif.ca. Click on "Banks." Scroll down and click on "Financial Data–Banks." Click on "Submit" to download the latest balance sheet for Domestic banks. Repeat the process for Life Insurance Companies, and Property and Casualty Insurance Companies.

Summary

This chapter described the various factors and forces impacting financial intermediaries and the specialness of the services they provide. These forces suggest that in the future, FIs that have historically relied on making profits by performing traditional special functions, such as asset transformation and the provision of liquidity services, will need to expand into selling financial services that interface with direct security market transactions, such as asset management, insurance, and underwriting services. This is not to say that specialized or niche FIs cannot survive but rather that only the most efficient FIs will prosper as the competitive value of a specialized FI charter declines.

The major theme of this book is the measurement and management of FI risks. In particular, although we might categorize or group FIs and label them life insurance companies, banks, finance companies, and so on, in fact, they face risks that are more common than different. Specifically, all the FIs described in this and the next five chapters (1) hold some assets that are potentially subject to default or credit risk and (2) tend to mismatch the maturities of their balance sheets to a greater or lesser extent and are thus exposed to interest rate risk. Moreover, all are exposed to some degree of saver withdrawal or liquidity risk depending on the type of claims sold to liability holders. And most are exposed to some type of underwriting risk, whether through the sale of securities or by issuing various types of credit guarantees on or off the balance sheet. Finally, all are exposed to operating cost risks because the production of financial services requires the use of real resources and back-office support systems.

In Chapters 7 through 27 of this textbook, we investigate the ways managers of FIs are measuring and managing this inventory of risks to produce the best return-risk trade-off for shareholders in an increasingly competitive and contestable market environment.

Questions and Problems

1. What are five risks common to financial institutions?
2. Explain how economic transactions between household savers of funds and corporate users of funds would occur in a world without financial intermediaries.

3. Identify and explain three economic disincentives that probably would dampen the flow of funds between household savers of funds and corporate users of funds in an economic world without financial intermediaries.

---

[20] It might also be noted that regulation is becoming more international as well—especially in Europe. See, for example, X. Vives, "Restructuring Regulation in the European Monetary Union," *Journal of Financial Services Research* 19 (February 2001), pp. 57–82.

4. Identify and explain the two functions in which FIs may specialize that would enable the smooth flow of funds from household savers to corporate users.

5. In what sense are the financial claims of FIs considered *secondary securities,* while the financial claims of commercial corporations are considered *primary securities?* How does the transformation process, or intermediation, reduce the risk, or economic disincentives, to savers?

6. Explain how financial institutions act as delegated monitors. What secondary benefits often accrue to the entire financial system because of this monitoring process?

7. What are five general areas of FI specialness that are caused by providing various services to sectors of the economy?

8. How do FIs solve the information and related *agency costs* when household savers invest directly in securities issued by corporations? What are agency costs?

9. What often is the benefit to the lenders, borrowers, and financial markets in general of the solution to the information problem provided by large financial institutions?

10. How do FIs alleviate the problem of liquidity risk faced by investors who wish to invest in the securities of corporations?

11. How do financial institutions help individual savers diversify their portfolio risks? Which type of financial institution is best able to achieve this goal?

12. How can financial institutions invest in high-risk assets with funding provided by low-risk liabilities from savers?

13. How can individual savers use financial institutions to reduce the transaction costs of investing in financial assets?

14. What is *maturity intermediation?* What are some of the ways the risks of maturity intermediation are managed by financial intermediaries?

15. What are five areas of institution-specific FI specialness, and which types of institutions are most likely to be the service providers?

16. How do deposit-taking institutions such as commercial banks assist in the implementation and transmission of monetary policy?

17. What is meant by credit allocation regulation? What social benefit is this type of regulation intended to provide?

18. Which intermediaries best fulfill the intergenerational wealth transfer function? What is this wealth transfer process?

19. What are two of the most important payment services provided by financial institutions? To what extent do these services efficiently provide benefits to the economy?

20. What is denomination intermediation? How do FIs assist in this process?

21. What is *negative externality?* In what ways do the existence of negative externalities justify the extra regulatory attention received by financial institutions?

22. If financial markets operated perfectly and costlessly, would there be a need for financial intermediaries?

23. What is mortgage redlining?

24. Why are FIs among the most regulated sectors in the world? When is the net regulatory burden positive?

25. What forms of protection and regulation do the regulators of FIs impose to ensure their safety and soundness?

26. What legislation has been passed specifically to protect investors who purchase securities? Give some examples of the types of abuses for which protection is provided.

27. How do regulations regarding barriers to entry and the scope of permitted activities affect the *charter value* of financial institutions?

28. What reasons have been given for the growth of mutual funds and investment companies at the expense of "traditional" banks and insurance companies?

29. What are some of the methods banking organizations have employed to reduce the net regulatory burden? What has been the effect on profitability?

30. What characteristics of financial products are necessary for financial markets to become efficient alternatives to financial intermediaries? Can you give some examples of the commoditization of products which were previously the sole property of financial institutions?

Web Questions

31. Go to the Bank of Canada's Web site at www.bankofcanada.ca. Find the latest figures for M1, M2, and M3 using the following steps. Click on "Rates and Statistics." Click on "Weekly Financial Statistics." Click on "available as a pdf file." Scroll down to BFS Table E1 on page 11. By what percentage have these measures of the money supply grown over the past year?

The Financial Services Industry: Deposit-Taking Institutions

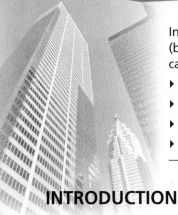

In this chapter we discuss federally-regulated deposit-taking financial institutions (banks, trusts, and loan companies) and other deposit-taking FIs (credit unions and caisses populaires) in terms of

▸ size, structure and composition of the industry group

▸ balance sheets and recent trends

▸ regulation

▸ industry performance

INTRODUCTION

The theme of this book is that the products sold and the risks faced by modern financial institutions are becoming increasingly similar, as are the techniques used to measure and manage those risks. To illustrate this, Tables 2–1A and 2–1B contrast the products sold by the financial services industry before the Bank Act revisions of the 1980s with those sold in 2005. In this chapter we begin by describing the major FI groups — banks, trusts and loans, credit unions, and caisses populaires — which are also called deposit-taking institutions (DTIs) because significant amounts of their funds come from customer deposits. In Chapters 3 through 6 other (non-deposit-taking) FIs will be described. We focus on four major characteristics of each group: (1) size, structure and composition of the industry group, (2) balance sheets and recent trends, (3) regulation, and (4) industry performance. Figure 2–1 presents a very simplified product-based balance sheet for deposit-taking institutions. Notice that deposit-taking institutions offer products to their customers on both sides of their balance sheets (loans on the asset side and deposits on the liability side). This joint-product nature of the deposit-taking institution business creates special challenges for management as they deal with the many risks facing these institutions. These risks will be discussed in Chapters 8 through 27.

Table 2–2 lists the largest Canadian deposit-taking institutions at the beginning of 2005 ranked by asset size. All but two of the ten FIs in Table 2–2 are banks (Desjardins Group, a caisse populaire, and Vancouver City Savings, a credit union), demonstrating the concentration of deposit-taking services in Canada and the dominance of the **Big Six** banks (Bank of Montreal, Bank of Nova Scotia, Canadian Imperial Bank of Commerce, National Bank of Canada, Royal Bank of Canada, and TD Canada Trust). There are nine financial services powerhouses in Canada, that is, what may be called "full-service" FIs. These include the six major banks and the three largest insurance companies, (Manulife Financial, Great-West Life Company, and Sun Life Financial), whose operations will be discussed in greater detail in Chapter 3.

The Big Six
The six largest banks in Canada (Bank of Montreal, Bank of Nova Scotia, Canadian Imperial Bank of Commerce, National Bank of Canada, Royal Bank of Canada, and TD Canada Trust)

TABLE 2–1A Products Sold by the Financial Services Industry, pre-1985

Institution	Payment Services	Savings Products	Fiduciary Services	Lending Business	Lending Consumer	Underwriting Issuance of Equity	Underwriting Issuance of Debt	Insurance and Risk Management Products
Deposit-taking institutions	X	X	X	X	X			
Insurance companies		X		*				X
Finance companies				*	X			
Securities firms		X	X			X	X	
Pension funds		X						
Mutual funds		X						

*Minor involvement.

TABLE 2–1B Products Sold by the Financial Services Industry, 2005

Institution	Payment Services	Savings Products	Fiduciary Services	Lending Business	Lending Consumer	Underwriting Issuance of Equity	Underwriting Issuance of Debt	Insurance and Risk Management Products
Deposit-taking institutions	X	X	X	X	X	X	X	X
Insurance companies	X	X	X	X	X	X	X	X
Finance companies	X	X	X	X	X	†	†	X
Securities firms	X	X	X	X	X	X	X	X
Pension funds		X	X	X				X
Mutual funds	X	X	X					X

†Selective involvement via affiliates

TABLE 2–2
The Largest Canadian Deposit-taking Institutions By Asset Size, Year End 2004 (billions of dollars)

Source: 2004 Company Annual Reports

Company	Assets
Royal Bank of Canada	$447.7
Toronto-Dominion Bank	311.0
Bank of Montreal	295.2
Bank of Nova Scotia	279.9
Canadian Imperial Bank of Commerce	278.8
Desjardins Group Inc.*	103.6
National Bank of Canada	88.8
HSBC Bank Canada*	43.3
Laurentian Bank Canada	16.6
Vancouver City Savings*	10.5

*As of December 31, 2004; all others as of October 31, 2004

FIGURE 2–1
A Simple Deposit-taking Institution Balance Sheet

Deposit-taking Institutions

Assets	Liabilities and Equity
Loans	Deposits
Other assets	Other liabilities and equity

BANKS

bank
A federally-regulated deposit-taking financial institution governed by the Bank Act and requiring a charter or letter of patent to operate.

Office of the Superintendent of Financial Institutions (OSFI)
The main regulator of federally-chartered FIs in Canada.

schedule I bank
A domestic Canadian FI, widely-held, chartered to conduct business under the Bank Act.

schedule II bank
A subsidiary, usually closely-held, of a foreign bank that is authorized to conduct business in Canada under the Bank Act.

schedule III Bank
A foreign bank branch that is authorized under the Bank Act to accept deposits only in amounts over $150,000.

contagion
Asset withdrawals from FIs because of financial system uncertainty and destabilization resulting from the failure of another FI.

Size, Structure, and Composition of the Industry

FIs that are allowed to operate as **banks** in Canada are governed by the Bank Act and regulated at the federal level by the **Office of the Superintendent of Financial Services (OSFI)**. OSFI provides a list of all of the banks that are currently allowed to operate in Canada on its Web site at www.osfi-bsif.gc.ca. Banks are divided into domestic chartered banks (**Schedule I banks**, 19 companies in 2005), and foreign banks whose activities are restricted as follows: (i) subsidiaries of foreign banks (**Schedule II banks**, 27 companies), (ii) foreign bank full service branches (**Schedule III banks**, 17 companies) that may only accept deposits over $150,000 (wholesale deposits), and (iii) foreign bank lending branches (5 companies) that are only allowed to provide lending services in Canada. In addition, there are 31 foreign bank representative offices that are not allowed to accept deposits and that are primarily focused on facilitating banking business for their clients from their home country. Canadian Schedule I banks must be widely-held, which means that no one person may hold more than 20 percent of the voting shares. A comparison of the assets of Canadian (Schedule I) and foreign banks (Schedule II) is presented in Table 2–3 where it can be seen that while the balance sheets have similar weights in each category, the Canadian domestic banks represented almost 95 percent of the $1.9 trillion total assets reported at October 31, 2004. The intent of regulators has been to maintain Canadian control of the financial services sector and to provide a safe and sound banking system. This has meant that the largest Canadian banks, the Big Six, have dominated the industry.

Compared to the U.S. and other countries, the concentration of assets, the payments system, and the coast-to-coast branch banking system have meant that the Canadian banking industry has been remarkably stable. The 1980s saw the first bank failures since the failure of the Home Bank in 1923. The Canadian Commercial Bank and the Northland Bank of Canada who both operated in Western Canada and who had major exposure to real estate and oil and gas loans, failed in 1985. However, their assets were only 0.75 percent of the total assets of the banking system at the time.[1] When these two banks got into trouble early in 1985, the Big Six banks worked together with the Bank of Canada and the Inspector General of Banks, the regulator at the time, to provide a rescue package, but the Canadian Commercial and Northland banks ultimately failed and "**contagion**" effects resulted in two other smaller banks, the Bank of British Columbia and the Continental Bank of Canada merging their operations with other banks. This stability contrasts with the reorganization and failures in the U.S. banking system which had a turbulent history with the Savings and Loan (S&L) crisis of the mid-1980s that saw the failure of almost 400 commercial banks in 1984 alone.

At the time of the FI failures in the 1980s, the Canadian and U.S. financial systems were still based on the concept of the "four pillars" (banking, trust or fiduciary functions, investment banking activities, and insurance). Each financial institution was prohibited from offering services outside of its own pillar. In Canada, this changed with the revision of the Bank Act in the 1980s. The shift towards universal banking started with the purchase of almost all of the independent investment dealers by the Big Six by the early 1990s. This was followed by the movement of banks into trust functions when the 1991 Bank Act revisions permitted them to own

---

[1] See J. F. Dingle, "Planning and Evolution: The Story of the Canadian Payments Association 1980–2002," The Bank of Canada and the Canadian Payments Association, May, 2003, Chapter 5, pp. 25–30, available at www.bankofcanada.ca for an account of the bank failures with respect to the stability of the payment system in Canada.

TABLE 2–3
Assets of Canadian and Foreign Banks, October 31, 2004 (billions of dollars)

Source: OSFI, *www.osfi-bsif.ca*

Asset Categories	Canadian Banks		Foreign Banks		Canadian & Foreign Banks	
	Amount	%	Amount	%	Total	%
Cash & deposits	$ 86.7	4.8	$ 8.5	8.6	$ 95.2	5.0
Securities	460.3	25.3	19.2	19.7	479.6	25.0
Non-mortgage loans	585.4	32.2	33.7	34.5	619.1	32.3
Mortgages	400.9	22.1	26.5	27.1	427.3	22.3
Insurance-related assets	2.4	0.1	0.0	0.0	2.4	0.1
Other Assets	281.2	15.5	10.0	10.2	291.1	15.2
Total Assets	1,816.8	100.0	97.8	100.0	1,914.6	100.0
Canadian Banks as percentage of total 94.9%						

trust companies. As a result, the trust pillar was virtually eliminated as a stand-alone function by the end of the 1990s. Banks have been permitted to own insurance subsidiaries since 1991, but they are still not permitted to sell insurance products (property and casualty and life insurance policies) side by side with banking services (e.g. mortgages and chequing accounts) and investment services (e.g. mutual funds) in their branches. However, this remnant of the four pillars may eventually be eliminated, by regulation or otherwise.[2]

The history of the North American financial services industry in Canada since the 1980s and the U.S. since the mid-1990s can thus be viewed as a move to universal banking. In Canada, this has resulted in the creation of the ten financial power-houses that are listed in Table 2–2. The consolidation of the financial services industry as a whole continues with issues related to banks' selling insurance products in their branches, and the perennial question of whether the Canadian banks should be allowed to merge with each other to create a larger concentration of banking assets in Canada and result in stronger FIs that are better able to operate in the global market place. See the Industry Perspectives box for a discussion by the Governor of the Bank of Canada, David Dodge, on the question of bank mergers, a political issue as much as an economic one in Canada that is discussed in more detail in Chapter 22.

spread
The difference between lending and deposit rates.

LIBOR
London inter-bank offer rate.

cost of funds
The market cost of all sources of capital used as the base rate in pricing loans.

Canadian banks fund themselves in the national markets and in the international interbank markets and they lend to larger corporations. This means that their **spreads** (i.e., the difference between lending and deposit rates) are subject to both North American market and global market conditions. To the extent that their lending is based on **LIBOR**, the interest rate charged to larger customers represents a market-based **cost of funds**. This has an effect on the return on equity (ROE) and the return on assets (ROAs) as reported along with the average interest rate spread in Table 2–4 for the big six banks from 1998–2004. The ROA averages 0.66 percent over the period and is less than 1 percent in every year. However, the ROE is positive in every year and is less than 10 percent only in 2002. This compares with a return on the S&P TSX Composite Index that was negative in 1998, 2000, and 2002. As of July, 2004, *The Banker* reported that, of the top 10 banks in the world ranked by asset size, only Citigroup (ROA of 2.08), HSBC Holdings (ROA of 1.24) and Royal Bank of Scotland (ROA of 1.36) had an average pre-tax return on assets greater than 1 percent. The average interest rate spread for the six Canadian banks

---

[2] The Royal Bank is setting up insurance "stores" with separate entrances next to its branches in order to comply with the rules that prohibit banks from providing insurance policies and loans in the same location. See S. B. Pasternak, "RBC to dodge federal rules by opening insurance stores next to Royal Bank branches," *Ottawa Citizen*, May 24, 2005, p. D1.

Industry Perspectives

DODGE SEEMS TO SUPPORT BANK MERGERS, ALBEIT IN DODGEAN WORDS; TOUTS SUCCESS OF INSURANCE COMBINES

OTTAWA — Bank of Canada Governor David Dodge waded into the politically sensitive bank merger debate yesterday, making arguments to a key Parliamentary committee that appeared to support consolidation in the sector.

Asked by MPs for his position on bank mergers, Mr. Dodge carefully avoided a direct answer to a question that the minority Liberal government is still wrestling with.

He did however hold up amalgamation in Canada's life insurance industry as a success story and played down the risks to small town Canada of a decline in financial services offerings that might result from bank mergers.

Mr. Dodge declined to talk to reporters after his comments to the House of Commons finance committee, but his statements were the strongest in recent memory on the subject.

The central bank governor suggested that mergers in the life insurance industry have helped that industry thrive.

"We have in the life insurance sector a sector which worldwide is recognized . . . [and] where consolidation has taken place and those institutions [are] making very considerable strides offshore to gain market" share, he told MPs. "And what that means is really good jobs at the head offices here in Canada and a real contribution to Canadian [gross domestic product]."

Mr. Dodge also said he thinks other financial institutions, such as credit unions, would fill any service gap left by merger-related branch closings in small-town Canada. "The worry about small communities is a very real one. But what is very interesting, and I think extraordinarily important, is that we have out there other institutions, in particular the credit unions, which in fact serve small communities very well," he told MPs.

"While there's a period undoubtedly where there will be branch closures . . . there is also here opportunities for other institutions to move in, and certainly what we have seen is a willingness — let me put me it more strongly — a desire of these institutions to come in and capitalize on what they perceive as the inefficiency of the large banks in dealing with these communities."

Source: By Steven Chase, *The Globe and Mail*, April 20, 2005, p. B8. Reprinted with permission from *The Globe and Mail*.

TABLE 2–4   ROA and ROE of Canadian Banks, 1998–2004

For the fiscal year ended Oct. 31	Return on Average Assets (%)	Return on Common Shareholders' Equity (%)	Return on Total Shareholders' Equity (%)	AVERAGE INTEREST RATE SPREAD (Percentages, all currencies)		
				Earned On Loans	Paid On Deposits	Average Spread
1998	0.57	14.71	13.41	7.14	4.50	2.64
1999	0.71	17.50	15.76	7.03	4.29	2.75
2000	0.72	16.81	15.27	7.64	4.77	2.86
2001	0.66	15.14	13.91	7.13	4.15	2.98
2002	0.44	9.90	9.38	5.36	2.37	2.99
2003	0.69	15.88	14.70	5.24	2.15	3.09
2004	0.81	18.31	17.03	4.87	1.89	2.97

Source: Canadian Bankers Association, *www.cba.ca*

has increased over time from 2.64 percent in 1998 to 2.97 percent in 2004, averaging 2.90 percent. Appendix 2A shows how a bank's ROE can be decomposed to examine the different underlying sources of profitability. This decomposition is often referred to as DuPont analysis. However, the use of balance sheet items for FI analysis has become less valuable as FIs, particularly banks, have moved more of their assets off of the balance sheet. The current trend by both FIs and their regulators has thus been to a risk-based analysis.

Balance Sheet and Recent Trends

Assets

Figure 2–2 shows the broad trends over the 1996–2004 period in the four principal earning asset areas of banks: Canadian securities, business loans, mortgages, and personal loans. Over the time period, mortgages have remained relatively steady at 47 percent of the total of these assets, while personal loans have increased only slightly. Canadian securities have increased as an asset source from 9 percent to 15 percent of the total, while business loans have declined from 24 percent to 16 percent over the 8 years. One important long-term influence has been the growth of the commercial paper market, which has become an alternative funding source for major corporations. This is an example of **disintermediation** whereby companies who have their own credit ratings are able to bypass a financial intermediary and go directly to the market to raise funds. Another has been the **securitization** of mortgages—the pooling and packaging of mortgage loans for sale in the form of bonds (see Chapter 27).

Look at the detailed balance sheet for all Canadian banks as of October 31, 2004 (Table 2–5) as reported to OSFI on a monthly basis. As noted previously, loans, personal and business, as well as mortgages make up a major portion of the assets. Hard assets (i.e., land, building and equipment) make up less than 1 percent of total assets. The securities are composed of those issued or guaranteed by the Canadian federal government, province, or municipality, as well as $199.5 billion in other debt securities and $142.6 billion of shares. Foreign assets make up 33.2 percent of the total assets, an indication of the international nature of the operations. It is notable that insurance-related assets, included with other assets, make up only 0.14 percent of the total, an indication that this cross-pillar diversification so far is small for these FIs.

A major inference that we can draw from this asset structure is that, with loans and mortgages at over 50 percent of the assets, credit or default risk exposure is a major risk faced by bank managers (see Chapters 11 and 12). Because banks are highly leveraged and therefore hold little equity (see below) compared with total assets, even a relatively small number of loan defaults could decrease the equity of a bank, moving it towards insolvency.[3]

disintermediation
The process by which firms go directly to the financial markets to raise funds without using an FI.

securitization
The removal of assets from the balance sheet by creating a contract that is sold in the financial market place.

FIGURE 2–2
Canadian Chartered Banks' Financial Assets 1996-2004

Source: Bank of Canada, *www.bankofcanada.ca*

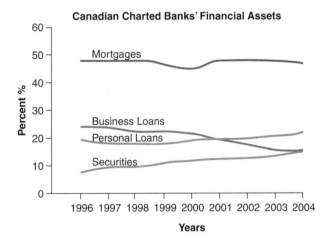

[3] Losses such as those due to defaults are charged off against the equity (stockholders' stake) in a bank. Loans are carried on the balance sheet net of an allowance for impairment, which is calculated according to criteria set by OSFI. The intent is to cause the bank to recognize potential loan losses on a timely basis and so not overstate the balance sheet position.

TABLE 2–5

Balance Sheet of Canadian Chartered Banks as of October 31, 2004 (millions of dollars)

Source: OSFI, *www.osfi-bsif.gc.ca*

ASSETS		
Cash assets	$ 86,138.6	4.74%
Securities:		
Government of Canada	64,704.5	3.56%
Other	395,627.0	21.78%
Loans, net of allowance for impairment:		
Non-mortgage	622,734.8	34.28%
Mortgage loans	400,869.3	22.06%
Land, building & equipment, net of depreciation	9,784.1	0.54%
Other assets	236,937.4	13.04%
Total assets	$1,816,795.8	100.00%

LIABILITIES		
Deposits:		
Demand	$ 195,601.1	10.77%
Notice	258,162.9	14.21%
Fixed term	749,200.0	41.24%
Subordinated debt	26,794.1	1.47%
Other liabilities	500,196.4	27.53%
Shareholders' equity:		
Preferred shares	7,350.9	0.40%
Common shares	26,657.0	1.47%
Contributed surplus and retained earnings	52,833.4	2.91%
Total liabilities and shareholders' equity	$1,816,795.8	100.00%

demand deposits
Deposits held at an FI that can be withdrawn by the depositor without notice.

fixed term deposits
Deposits held at an FI that cannot be withdrawn by the depositor prior to the maturity date. Often these deposits may be withdrawn prior to maturity with a penalty being paid by the depositor.

notice deposits
Deposits held at an FI that require notification to the FI before withdrawal. If the notice period is not met, the depositor could be denied access to the funds.

Canada Deposit Insurance Corporation (CDIC)
The corporation that insures eligible deposits of federally-regulated deposit-taking FIs in Canada, www.cdic.ca.

interbank borrowings
Short-term loans (deposits), usually overnight, received from other FIs.

Liabilities

Banks have two major sources of funds other than the equity provided by owners: deposits and borrowed or other liability funds. A major difference between banks and other firms is the banks' high leverage. For example, banks had an average ratio of total shareholders' equity to assets of 4.8 percent in 2004; this implies that 95.2 percent of their assets were funded by debt, either deposits or borrowed funds.

Note in Table 2–5 that deposits amounted to $1,203 billion or 66.2 percent of total liabilities and equity. Subordinated debt and other liabilities represented just 29.0 percent. Note also that **demand deposits** represented only 10.77 percent of liabilities and equity, **notice deposits** 14.21 percent and **fixed term deposits** represented over 41.24 percent. A good portion of these will be accounts insured by **Canada Deposit Insurance Corporation (CDIC)**, the deposit insurance company for deposit-taking institutions. Deposit insurance is discussed in greater detail in Chapter 19. Insurance liabilities are negligible at less than 1 percent (0.59 percent) of the total.

Overall, the liability structure of bank balance sheets tends to reflect a shorter maturity structure than does the asset portfolio with relatively more liquid instruments such as deposits and **interbank borrowings** used to fund less liquid assets such as loans. Thus, maturity mismatch or interest rate risk and liquidity risk are key exposure concerns for bank managers (see Chapters 8, 9, 17, and 18).

Equity

Bank equity capital (4.78 percent of total liabilities and shareholders' equity at October 31, 2004), consists mainly of preferred and common shares and retained earnings. Contributed surplus is a minor amount, representing the difference between a share's stated par value and what the original shareholders paid when they bought the newly-issued stock. OSFI requires banks to hold a minimum level of equity capital to act as a buffer against losses from their on- and off-balance-sheet activities (see Chapter 20). Because of the relatively low cost of deposit funding, banks may tend to hold equity close to the minimum levels set by regulators. As we discuss in subsequent chapters, this impacts banks' exposures to risk and their ability to grow—both on and off the balance sheet—over time.

INTERNET EXERCISE

Go to the Office of the Superintendent of Financial Institutions' Web site (www.osfi-bsif.gc.ca) and find the latest balance sheet information available for Canadian banks.

Go to www.osfi-bsif.gc.ca and click on "Banks." Scroll down and click on "Financial Data — Banks." Click on "Submit" to view the latest monthly balance sheet for the Canadian banks.

Off-Balance-Sheet Activities

The balance sheet itself does not reflect the total scope of bank activities. Banks conduct many fee-related activities off the balance sheet. Off-balance-sheet (OBS) activities are becoming increasingly important, in terms of their dollar value and the income they generate for banks—especially as the ability of banks to attract high-quality loan applicants and deposits becomes ever more difficult. OBS activities include issuing various types of guarantees (such as letters of credit), which often have a strong insurance underwriting element, and making future commitments to lend. Both services generate additional fee income for banks. Off-balance-sheet activities also involve engaging in derivative transactions—futures, forwards, options, and swaps.

off-balance-sheet asset
An item that moves onto the asset side of the balance sheet when a contingent event occurs.

Under current accounting standards, such activities are not shown on the current balance sheet. Rather, an item or activity is an **off-balance-sheet asset** if, when a contingent event occurs, the item or activity moves onto the asset side of the balance sheet or an income item is realized on the income statement. Conversely, an item or activity is an **off-balance-sheet liability** if, when a contingent event occurs, the item or activity moves onto the liability side of the balance sheet or an expense item is realized on the income statement.

off-balance-sheet liability
An item that moves onto the liability side of the balance sheet when a contingent event occurs.

By moving activities off the balance sheet, banks hope to earn additional fee income to complement the margins or spreads on their traditional lending business. At the same time, they can avoid regulatory costs or "taxes" since deposit insurance premiums are not levied on off-balance-sheet activities (see Chapter 13). As well, the **capital adequacy requirements** for on-balance-sheet loans differ from those for off-balance sheet items and in some cases, may make the off-balance-sheet activity more profitable (see Chapter 20). Thus the banks have both earnings and regulatory "tax-avoidance" incentives to undertake activities off their balance sheets.

capital adequacy requirements
Levels of equity capital that an FI is required by regulators to maintain in order to be allowed to continue in operation.

Off-balance-sheet activities, however, can involve risks that add to the overall insolvency exposure of an FI. In 2001, Allied Irish Bank incurred a US$750 million loss from foreign exchange derivative trades by a rogue trader, and in 2004 unauthorized trading of foreign currency options at National Australian Bank resulted in a loss of US$450 million. However, off-balance-sheet activities and instruments have both risk-reducing as well as risk-increasing attributes, and, when used appropriately, they can reduce or hedge an FI's interest rate, credit, and foreign exchange risks.

We show the notional, or face value of Canadian OBS activities, reported quarterly to OSFI, at December 31 2004 in Table 2–6. At the end of 2004, the OBS notional

TABLE 2–6   Aggregate Notional Amount of Off-Balance-Sheet Commitments by Canadian Banks at December 31, 2004 (in thousands of dollars)

	Contracts held for trading purposes	Notional Amount			
		Remaining term to maturity			
		Total Contracts	One year and less	Over 1 year to 5 years	Over 5 years
Derivatives					
Interest Rate Contracts					
OTC contracts	$4,766,860,661	$5,319,225,226	$2,163,482,589	$2,220,724,718	$935,017,918
Exchange-traded contracts	968,060,051	994,667,155	842,355,441	151,558,899	752,814
Foreign Exchange & Gold Contracts					
OTC contracts	2,136,889,646	2,339,781,725	1,767,772,025	407,338,559	164,671,140
Exchange-traded contracts	7,475,218	7,475,218	6,733,116	742,102	0
Other					
OTC contracts	500,938,267	514,450,647	250,774,107	217,500,644	46,175,898
Exchange-traded contracts	79,301,399	80,723,726	72,281,153	8,287,825	154,747
Total Derivative Contracts	8,459,525,241	9,256,323,697	5,103,398,432	3,006,152,749	1,146,772,514
Other Off-Balance Sheet Items		$ 561,098,458			

Source: OSFI, www.osfi-bsif.gc.ca

amount of derivative contracts was $9.26 trillion. Other off-balance-sheet items were a further $561 billion, for a total of $9.82 trillion, an amount that is over 5 times the total on balance sheet assets of $1.9 trillion reported for the same period. It should be noted that the notional, or face value of OBS activities does not accurately reflect the risk to the bank undertaking such activities. The potential for the bank to gain or lose is based on the possible change in the market value over the life of the contract rather than the notional, or face value of the contract, normally less than 3 percent of the notional value of an OBS contract. For example, the market value of a swap today is the difference between the present value of the cash flows expected to be received minus the present value of the cash flows expected to be paid.

The growth in the use of derivative securities activities by banks has been a direct response to the increased interest rate risk, credit risk, and foreign exchange risk exposures they have faced, both domestically and internationally. In particular, these contracts offer banks a way to hedge these risks without having to make extensive changes on the balance sheet. However, as shown in Table 2–6, of the total notional amount of derivatives contracts of $9.3 trillion reported, $8.5 trillion or 91.4 percent were held for trading purposes, indicating that this is a profitable source of income for the banks. The exposure is limited since, as shown, 55 percent of the contracts have a maturity of less than one year, but $7.4 trillion of the contracts are over the counter rather than exchange-traded, an indication of the market-making function of the banks as well as a market risk.

Although the simple notional dollar amount of OBS items overestimates their risk exposure amounts, the increase in these activities in the 1990s has been phenomenal and has pushed regulators into imposing capital requirements on such activities and into explicitly recognizing an FI's solvency risk exposure from pursuing such activities as we describe in Chapter 20.

Other Activities

Banks engage in other fee-generating activities that cannot easily be identified from analyzing their on- and off-balance-sheet accounts.

Trust Services

Up until the 1960s, banks were not permitted to offer National Housing Act (NHA) approved mortgages as were the trusts companies. This meant that trust company assets were concentrated in mortgage loans. However, the revision of the Bank Act in 1991 allowed banks to own trust companies and set off a series of takeovers by the banks. Federally-regulated trusts are governed by OSFI under the Trust and Loans Companies Act (44 firms were listed in 2005). There are also some provincially-regulated trusts. Trusts offer similar services to banks (i.e., deposit-taking, loans), as well as fiduciary activities such administering estates, trusts, and pension plans. Since banks are prohibited from providing these fiduciary services directly, the banks offer these types of services through their subsidiaries. For example, TD Waterhouse, the securities arm of TD Canada Trust, the result of a merger of Toronto-Dominion Bank with Canada Trust, offers estate planning, tax planning and other trust services. TD's banking customers can access TD Waterhouse directly from its web site, an advantage of a full-service FI. The largest trust companies are owned by the banks (for example, The Bank of Nova Scotia Trust Company, CIBC Trust Company, and The Canada Trust Company). The total assets of federally-regulated trusts were $63.7 billion at December 31, 2004. In many cases, the deposits of trust companies are covered by deposit insurance from CDIC. The advantage for banks of offering deposit services, investment services, and trust services is the **cross-selling** of services to customers, providing banks with additional revenue. As well, with internet banking and on-line access to accounts, a bank client is less likely to move to another institution because of the difficulty of establishing on-line accounts with another FI.

cross-selling
The marketing of other services such as mutual funds or insurance to a customer along with traditional banking.

Loan Companies

In addition to operating trust subsidiaries, the banks also participate in loan companies, of which there were 22 listed by OSFI in 2005. A loan company may be federally (falling under the Trust and Loan Companies Act) or provincially regulated, may offer deposit-taking services that are covered by CDIC's deposit insurance, and conduct other activities similar to a bank. The total assets of the loan companies regulated by OSFI were $150.8 billion at December 31, 2004. The 22 loan companies supervised by OSFI primarily represent the mortgage arms of the chartered banks (e.g. Bank of Montreal Mortgage Corporation, TD Mortgage Corporation).

Correspondent Banking

Correspondent banking is the provision of banking services to other banks that do not have the staff resources to perform the service themselves. These services include cheque-clearing and collection, foreign exchange trading, hedging services, and participation in large loan and security issuances. The nature of the Canadian economy means that firms rely heavily on both exporting and importing which implies a risk of non-payment and also foreign exchange risk. In addition to supplying over the counter foreign exchange contracts (forwards), the banks also provide letters of credit that allow a seller to be guaranteed that they will be paid in an exporting agreement with an unknown party (Chapter 15).

letters of credit
Letters from a bank to an exporter (importer) stating that it will pay the amount of the contract to on the completion of certain conditions.

Regulation

The current regulatory system for banks in Canada dates back to July, 1987, when the government enacted the Financial Institutions and Deposit Insurance Amendment Act and the Office of the Superintendent of Financial Institutions Act. The Department of Insurance and the Office of the Inspector General of Banks joined to form one national regulator, OSFI, to supervise federally-regulated deposit-taking institutions. OSFI's role has, since then, been to ensure the safety and soundness of the financial system in Canada under the Bank Act. As a member of global committees that determine capital requirements for international banks (set by the Bank for International Settlements, BIS, and discussed in detail in Chapter 20), OSFI enforces those rules through its reporting requirements and inspection of the FIs under its jurisdiction. As well, OSFI sets rules relating to the safety and soundness of the national and international payments systems (discussed in Chapter 17).

The Bank of Canada is responsible for ensuring the integrity of the financial markets system in Canada, primarily through its monetary policy. As such, the Bank of Canada participates indirectly in regulation of banks, primarily by producing research on capital markets and identifying global and national trends that may affect different aspects of the financial services industry.

www.fcac-acfg.gc.ca

Depositors are protected by the Canada Deposit Insurance Company (CDIC), which insures specified deposits of both federal and provincial deposit-taking institutions. Canadian consumers of banking products are also protected by the **Financial Consumer Agency of Canada (FCAC)**, which was established in 2001 to enforce consumer protection laws related to FIs in Canada. One of the initiatives related to consumers was the commitment of eight Canadian financial institutions to provide low-cost accounts for consumers.[4]

Regulations

www.cdnpay.ca
www.ida.ca
www.mfda.ca
www.cdic.ca
www.fintrac.gc.ca
www.assuris.ca
www.pacicc.com

Banks are among the most regulated firms in the global economy. Because of the inherent special nature of banking and banking contracts, as discussed in Chapter 1, regulators impose numerous restrictions on their product and geographic activities. In Canada, the division of powers between the provinces and the federal government under the British North America (BNA) Act meant that there are additional national and provincial regulatory agencies that come into play when an FI operates across provincial borders. The creation of one federal regulator (OSFI) was intended to simplify the regulatory framework and reduce the regulatory burden for FIs, as well as to firmly establish responsibility for the implementation of the BIS capital adequacy regulations (Basel I). In addition, the move cross-pillar to include insurance and securities functions means that, though banks are primarily governed by the Bank Act administered by OSFI at the federal level, provincial regulators also are involved for each province, as shown in Table 2–7. Although there is discussion of a move to one federal regulator for securities firms, the issue has not as yet been resolved.

---

[4] See the Department of Finance Web site at www.fin.gc.ca for additional details and news related to Canada's financial services sector. See also the FCAC's Web site at www.fcac-acfc.gc.ca for the list of acts and regulations that the FCAC is responsible for enforcing.

prudential regulator
The government agency responsible for ensuring compliance with good management practices within an FI to ensure the safety and soundness of the financial system.

market conduct regulator
The government agency responsible for enforcing adherence to regulations regarding FIs behaviour towards consumers of financial services.

self-regulating organizations (SROs)
FI industry groups who regulate the conduct and business practices of their members.

Table 2–7 shows the list of federal and provincial regulators of the bank financial groups in Canada and their responsibilities. At the federal level, OSFI is the **prudential regulator**, responsible for monitoring the solvency and risk management of an FI. FCAC is the **market conduct regulator** charged with ensuring that consumers of financial services are treated ethically and fairly. In addition, there are many **self-regulating organizations (SROs)** such as the Canadian Payments Association (CPA), the Investment Dealers Association of Canada (IDA), and the Mutual Fund Dealers Association of Canada (MFDA) which are industry associations which police their members. Other regulators at the federal level are CDIC which establishes deposit insurance coverage and the Financial Transactions and Reports Analysis Centre of Canada (FINTRAC) which oversees the reporting of terrorist activities as well as money laundering.[5] In addition to the reporting of insurance activities as required by OSFI and provincial insurance regulators, bank insurance subsidiaries who are members may have their policies covered by Assuris, which protects life insurance policy holders in the event of the failure of a life insurance company, and the Property and Casualty Insurance Compensation Corporation (PACICC), which protects property and casualty (P&C) policyholders.

The major source of compliance for banks comes from the monthly and quarterly reporting requirements to OSFI, which include such things as allowance for impairments, average assets and liabilities, capital adequacy and market risk, as well as an income statement, interest rate risk, and details of mortgage loans. OSFI maintains a table of guidelines for all of the FIs that they supervise (banks, foreign bank branches, trust and loan companies, co-operative credit and retail associations, life insurance, and property and casualty insurance) at their Web site, which covers capital adequacy requirements, prudential limits, and accounting guidelines.

Industry Performance

provision for loan losses
Bank management's recognition of expected bad loans for the period.

net interest income
Total interest income less total interest expense before provision for credit losses.

Table 2–8 presents selected performance ratios for eight members of the Canadian Bankers Association, which represent more than 90 percent of the assets of banks in Canada. The return on assets was below 1 percent in every year, a low amount compared to U.S. banks, which achieved a return on assets higher than 1 percent (ranging from 1.31 in 1999 to 1.40 in 2003). The return on total shareholder's equity exceeded 10 percent in every year except 2002, a year associated with the highest loan loss provision to average total assets which was equal to 0.56 percent. However, the loan loss provision to average total assets was equal to 0.22 and 0.06 percent in 2003 and 2004, likely reflecting the low interest rate climate. When interest rates start to climb, then the **provision for loan losses** should also be expected to increase as borrowers feel the financial stress and become less able to meet their interest obligations. **Net interest income** as a percent of average total assets has held relatively steady over the period, but non-interest expense has climbed from 2.30 percent in 1998 to 2.68 percent in 2004. Other income as a percentage of total assets has increased from 1.62 percent to 2.05 percent between 1998 and 2004, likely an indication of the increasing expansion of fee-generating activities of the banks. The low

---

[5] Money laundering and terrorism have become significant global issues for FIs since the terrorist attacks on the World Trade Centre in New York on September 11, 2001. It is estimated by the International Monetary Fund (IMF) that money laundering could range between US$600 billion and US$1.5 trillion per year. OSFI provides a list of known terrorist organizations on its Web site and is developing the approach that will be applied to Canadian FIs. FINTRAC is charged with ensuring compliance with the Proceeds of Crime (Money Laundering)m and Terrorist Financing Act. See N. W. R. Burbidge, "International Anti-Money Laundering and Anti-Terrorist Financing: The Work of the Office of the Superintendent of Financial Institutions in Canada," *Journal of Money Laundering Control*, Vol. 7, No. 4, 2004, pp. 320–332 and "A Matter of Compliance," *CGA Magazine*, March/April 2005, Vol. 39, Issue 2, p. 12.

TABLE 2–7   Who Regulates Bank Financial Groups In Canada?

JURISDICTION	PRUDENTIAL REGULATOR	MARKET CONDUCT REGULATOR	
FEDERAL	OSFI	FCAC	
NATIONAL			
Alberta	Alberta Finance, Financial Institutions	Alberta Ministry of Government Services, Consumer Services Division	
British Columbia	Financial Institutions Commission (British Columbia)	British Columbia Ministry of the Attorney General, Community Justice Branch, Consumer services Division	
Manitoba	Manitoba Consumer and Corporate Affairs	Manitoba Consumer and Corporate Affairs, Consumer Bureau	
New Brunswick	New Brunswick Department of Justice	New Brunswick Department of Justice, Consumer Affairs Branch	
Newfoundland	Newfoundland Department of Government Services and Lands, Commercial and Corporate Affairs Branch	Newfoundland Department of Government Services and Lands, Consumer and Commercial Affairs	
Nova Scotia	Nova Scotia Department of Environment and Labour, Financial Institutions Section	Nova Scotia Department of Business and Consumer Services	
Ontario	Financial Services Commission of Ontario	Ontario Ministry of Consumer and Business Services, General Enquiries Unit	
Prince Edward Island	Prince Edward Island Ministry of the Attorney General, Consumer, Corporate and Insurance Division	(same as prudential regulator)	
Québec	Autorité des marchés financières	(same as prudential regulator)	
Saskatchewan	Saskatchewan Financial Services Commission	(same as prudential regulator)	
Northwest Territories	Northwest Territories Department of Finance	Northwest Territories, Municipal and Community Affairs, Community Operations Programs, Consumer Services	
Nunavut	Nunavut Department of Justice	Nunavut, Department of Community Government and Transportation	
Yukon	Yukon Department of Justice, Corporate Affairs and Registrar of Securities	Yukon Department of Justice, Consumer Services Branch	

Source: Canadian Bankers Association, 2004

SECURITIES REGULATOR	INSURANCE REGULATOR	SROs	OTHER
		CPA	**Fintrac, CDIC**
		IDA, MFDA	**Assuris, PACICC**
Alberta Securities Commission	(see SROs)	Alberta Insurance Council	
British Columbia Securities Commission	(SEE SROs)	Insurance Council of British Columbia	
Manitoba Securities Commission	(see SROs)	Insurance Council of Manitoba	
Department of Justice Securities Administration	Superintendent of Insurance (Department of Justice, Insurance Branch)		
(same as prudential regulator)	(same as prudential regulator)		
Nova Scotia Securities Commission	Superintendent of Insurance, Department of Environment and Labour		
Ontario Securities Commission	(same as prudential regulator)		
(same as prudential regulator)	(same as prudential regulator)		
(same as prudential regulator)	• Chambre de l'assurance de dommages • Chambre de la sécurité financière		
(same as prudential regulator)	(see SROs)	Insurance Council of Saskatchewan	
Registrar of Securities, Northwest Territories	Superintendent of Insurance		
Registrar of Securities, Nunavut	Superintendent of Insurance, Department of Finance/ Fiscal Policy and Taxation		
(same as prudential regulator)	Superintendent of Insurance, Department of Justice		

TABLE 2–8   Selected Indicators for Canadian banks, 1998–2004

	1998	1999	2000	2001	2002	2003	2004
Return on average assets (ROA) (%)	0.57	0.71	0.71	0.66	0.44	0.69	0.81
Return on total shareholders' equity (ROE) (%)	13.39	15.89	15.25	13.89	9.34	14.65	16.88
Net interest income/average total assets (%)	1.84	1.83	1.83	1.93	2.01	1.88	1.83
Other income/average total assets (%)	1.62	1.95	2.27	2.11	1.81	1.94	2.05
Loan loss provision/average total assets (%)	0.2	0.23	0.27	0.39	0.56	0.22	0.06
Non-interest expenses/average total assets	2.3	2.45	2.64	2.71	2.62	2.64	2.68
Average interest rate spread (%)	2.63	2.74	2.85	2.98	2.98	3.08	2.99

Source: Canadian Bankers Association, 2005 Includes data for 8 banks (BMO Financial Group, Canadian Western Bank, CIBC, Laurentian Bank of Canada, National Bank of Canada, RBC Financial Group, Scotiabank, and TD Bank Financial Group)

interest rate climate has been good for these banks as the average interest rate spread has increased from 2.63 percent in 1998 to average 3.01 percent in the last four years.

Several explanations have been offered for the strong performance of banks during the early 2000s. First, lower interest rates made debt cheaper to service and kept many households and small firms borrowing. Second, lower interest rates made home purchasing more affordable. Thus, the housing market boomed throughout the period. Third, the development of new financial instruments, such as credit derivatives and mortgage-backed securities helped banks shift credit risk from their balance sheets to financial markets and other FIs such as insurance companies. Finally, improved information technology has helped banks manage their risk better.

However, as mentioned in Chapter 1, the early 2000s saw a weakening in the public trust and confidence in the ethics followed by financial institutions. A number of banks continue to deal with ethics-related issues. For example, in 2003, J. P. Morgan Chase, Citigroup, and CIBC settled with the New York District Attorney over allegations that the banks wrongly helped Enron hide its debt prior to the energy company's filing for bankruptcy in 2001. Also, ethical issues related to the trading of mutual funds in the U.S. caused the Ontario Securities Commission to review the trading practices of 105 Ontario mutual fund managers from November 2003 to December 2004. The Commission's report discussed **late trading** and **market timing** issues and resulted in fines of $205.6 million levied against 5 fund managers.[6] Related to the ethical issues are conflicts of interest that can arise between the market-oriented trading culture of the securities subsidiaries of the banks and the gatekeeper role of the traditional banker. These issues are illustrated by the court case of CIBC against its former employees related to Genuity Capital Markets, an investment banking firm set up in direct competition with CIBC World Markets (see the Ethical Dilemmas Box).

late trading
Illegally buying or selling mutual fund securities after the close of trading at the current price rather than at the next day's price as required by law.

market timing
Frequent short-term trading of mutual fund securities by a fund manager to take advantage of changes in price, but that are not in the best interests of the funds' investors.

Also certain to affect the future performance of banks as well as credit unions and caisses populaires is the extent to which banks adopt the newest technology (Chapter 14), including the extent to which industry participants embrace the internet and online banking. Early entrants into internet banking have introduced new technology in markets with demographic and economic characteristics that help ensure customer acceptance. In addition, keeping up to date with advances in technology helps FIs to provide better customer service, both for retail customers and for business customers, which ultimately helps FIs to retain customers.[7]

---

[6] See Ontario Securities Commission, *Report on Mutual Fund Trading Practices Probe*, March 2005, available at www.osc.gov.on.ca.

[7] The approach of the Royal Bank of Canada to its technology for its retail and wholesale is discussed in "RBC treads the integration path in its client-first strategy," *The Banker*, June 6, 2006, p. 118.

Going into the holiday season, the mighty Canadian Imperial Bank of Commerce was prepared to shrug off the creation of an upstart investment dealer, staffed by its former stars.

Even after a dozen of its deal makers defected in a single morning, 2,000-employee-strong brokerage house CIBC World Markets was determined to simply soldier on. The plan was to reload on talent, promote the young and keen, and match wits with newly created Genuity Capital Markets, along with far fiercer rivals — the other Canadian bank-owned firms and the major U.S. and European houses.

Right up to the bank's chief executive officer, John Hunkin, everyone understood that proven financiers would gravitate to the buzz, the excitement, and the potential payoff that could come with owning a small, high-end boutique such as Genuity, run by former CIBC World Markets head David Kassie. Nothing the bank did was going to stop their flight.

But as the traders, the takeover specialists, the mining financiers cleaned their desks on Dec. 17 and said their goodbyes, what started as whispers on trading desks and in hallways became a roar. CIBC World Markets staff who were staying behind began to openly complain that their former colleagues had been hard at work building Genuity, while still on the CIBC World Markets payroll. They claimed the defectors had been busy for months at work, e-mailing one another, setting meetings, lining up their new jobs.

So a decision was made to crack open the bank's e-mail records, a move that bank sources say was okayed, reluctantly, by Mr. Hunkin himself. Over the Christmas break, IT staff found message after message between the departed employees.

It all added up to what CIBC now claims in a lawsuit was a "secretive, well-orchestrated and calculated scheme" to steal away both top performers and corporate clients. Two Genuity founders who are now being sued, merger and acquisitions specialist Philip Evershed and tech stock whiz Daniel Daviau, each got more than $3-million in salary and severance packages from the bank last spring, on the condition that they not solicit CIBC World Markets employees for 21 months.

Another major shareholder in Genuity, Earl Rotman, was on the dealer's payroll as a vice-chairman until the end of December, and received $3.3-million. Thumbed messages from this fall, all contained in the 655-page lawsuit, link all three to now-departed staff.

With e-mails in hand, CIBC started down the road to what has now blossomed into a nasty, public court battle with its progeny. What's at issue, from the bank's perspective, is not Genuity. No, this lawsuit is about concepts such as duty, integrity, honour and trust.

CIBC is suing because its CEO and board see the courts as their only recourse, the only way to signal to every remaining employee, and every client, that the bank's corporate culture stands for honesty and fair dealing, and these aren't just words. The bank is asking the Ontario Superior Court to hold its former employees accountable to an ethical standard that should be expected from an organization that paid them extremely well for their services, that made them very rich.

The fight is not over the establishment of a small rival. It's about the slippery way it seems to have been done.

Genuity is already girding for battle. The best litigators have been lined up, and they'll argue Genuity's founders broke no rules in hiring those who had already decided to leave. And, by the way, the lawyers will say, big-brother bank has no right peeking into people's private BlackBerry messages.

While the outcome is impossible to predict, there seems no middle ground for a settlement. The bank needs a victory in court to make its moral point. It's got the resources to go 15 rounds. Genuity must command the trust of clients, and will be hard-pressed to win their patronage with its integrity impugned.

The striking thing about this lawsuit is that CIBC can't look forward to any sort of tangible win, no matter what the court decides. Why, the $10-million in damages demanded in this suit isn't even a rounding error on a rounding error at the bank. And CIBC, which one Bay Street analyst describes as the bank "most likely to walk into a sharp object," can only look forward to endless negative press, stories that hammer away at the departure of its best and brightest, and that glorify Genuity.

Maybe CIBC brass were naive. Senior executives at other dealers say, with the benefit of hindsight, that CIBC World Markets executives should have met with Mr. Kassie and his friends last summer, and fired some kind of warning shot. But hindsight's not worth much.

Right up to the board of directors, CIBC brass take the view that they must act, that they must go to court, and that they must win. Otherwise, the code of ethics set for bank employees, the standard of conduct expected of those who have been so richly rewarded, will have been shown to stand for nothing.

Source: By Andrew Willis, *The Globe and Mail*, Page B2, January 8, 2005. Reprinted with permission from *The Globe and Mail*.

In addition to the development of internet banking as a complement to the traditional services offered by banks, a new segment of the industry has arisen that consists of internet-only banks such as such as ING Bank. So far, internet-only banks have failed to capture more than a small fraction of the banking market.

Concept Questions

1. What are the major assets held by banks?
2. What are the major sources of funding for banks?
3. Describe the responsibilities of the regulatory agencies responsible for banks in Canada.
4. What has the trend in ROA and ROE been in the banking industry?

CREDIT UNIONS AND CAISSES POPULAIRES

credit unions (CUs)
Co-operative deposit-taking financial institutions that are owned by their members.

caisses populaires (CPs)
Co-operative deposit-taking financial institutions similar to credit unions that are owned by their members and operate primarily in Quebec.

co-operative financial institutions
Generic term used for FIs owned by their members.

mutual organizations
Savings banks in which the depositors are also the legal owners of the bank.

Credit unions (CUs) and **caisses populaires (CPs)** (which primarily operate in Quebec) are **co-operative financial institutions** who are owned by their members (depositors). The shares are covered by share and deposit insurance and the owner of the shares may receive dividends from the credit union. These co-operatives are also called **mutual organizations**. The cooperative credit movement has been important globally as it is based on the principle that a local community can provide banking services. [8] In this respect, cooperatives in Canada have been an alternative to the major banks, which were seen as unfriendly to retail customers and small borrowers by providing low deposit rates paired with high interest rates on loans. Thus universities, labour unions, cultural organizations and even towns formed credit cooperatives to pool the resources of the community. This was particularly important in Quebec and British Columbia where two of these independent FIs (Desjardins Group Inc. and Vancouver City Savings) now rank in the top 10 of the deposit-taking FIs in Canada based on asset size (see Table 2–2). Credit unions, both large and small, will have a role to play in the issue of bank mergers (see Chapter 22) as they are an integral part of small towns and remote communities in Canada and will continue to provide banking services even if bank mergers result in branch closings. The role of credit unions has been noted by David Dodge, the Governor of the Bank of Canada (See the Industry Perspectives box).

The primary objective of credit unions is to satisfy the deposit-taking and lending needs of their members. CU member deposits (shares) are used to provide loans to other members in need of funds. Any earnings from these loans are used to pay higher rates on member deposits, charge lower rates on member loans, or attract new members to the CU. Because credit unions do not issue common stock, the members are legally the owners of a CU.

Size, Structure, and Composition of the Industry and Recent Trends

Credit unions and caisses populaires are the most numerous of the deposit-taking FIs in Canada. However, like other FIs, they have declined in number from over

---

[8] Whereas in developed countries like Canada and the United States credit cooperatives account for a relatively small proportion of the financial services industry, in many less developed countries they play an important role in mobilizing savings at the rural level. One very important credit union-type FI, first developed in Bangladesh and extended to other developing countries has been the Grameen Bank. See, for example, H. K. Hassan and L. Reneria-Guerrero, "The Experience of the Grameen Bank of Bangladesh in Community Development," *International Journal of Social Economics* 24, No. 12 (1997), pp. 1488–1523. Credit cooperatives still provide deposit functions and lending to rural areas of China. These small FIs are part of the regulatory challenge facing China as it modernizes its financial architecture. See A. Yeh, "Beijing orders eight credit co-ops to close: Panic among depositors: Rumours one lender near default fuel run on savings," *National Post*, July 6, 2005, p. FP13.

TABLE 2–9 Statistics for Credit Unions and Caisses Populaires, Fourth Quarter 2004

AFFILIATED CREDIT UNIONS & CAISSES POPULAIRES					
($millions) Province	Total Loans	Total Assets	Total Credit Unions	Total Locations	Total Members
Credit Union Central Class					
British Columbia	$25,973	$32,342	56	347	1,489,582
Alberta	8,141	9,843	60	205	590,000
Saskatchewan	6,700	9,024	110	332	536,114
Manitoba	7,465	9,120	57	175	502,184
Ontario(1)	11,877	14,252	180	519	1,088,645
New Brunswick	712	929	23	44	123,219
Nova Scotia	970	1,318	37	84	168,891
Prince Edward Island	453	591	10	15	62,724
Newfoundland	401	490	14	41	42,495
Subtotal	$62,752	$77,909	547	1,762	4,603,854
Federation Class					
L'Alliance	594	769	13	26	71,028
TOTAL	$63,346	$78,678	560	1,788	4,674,882
NON-AFFILIATED CREDIT UNIONS & CAISSES POPULAIRES					
Caisses Populaires					
Ontario-La Fed(1)	$1,952	$2,43	24	59	165,895
Manitoba	485	584	7	28	30,804
New Brunswick	1,618	2,025	33	85	198,314
TOTAL CPs (excl QB)	$4,055	$5,045	64	172	395,013
Quebec	$64,630	$78,809	548	1,418	5,187,263
TOTAL (All)	$68,685	$83,854	612	1,590	5,582,276
Credit Unions					
Ontario (1)	$2,409	$4,832	24	91	335,187
TOTAL	$71,094	$88,686	636	1,681	5,917,463
CANADIAN CREDIT UNION & CAISSE POPULAIRE SYSTEM					
TOTAL	$134,440	$167,364	1,196	3,469	10,592,345

(1) Ontario—Results are provisional.

Source: Credit Union Central of Canada, *www.cucentral.ca*

www.cucentral.ca

2,000 in 1999 to 1,196 in 2004. CUs and CPs are mostly regulated at the provincial level, but Credit Union Central of Canada (CUCC), as well as six provincial organizations are federally-regulated and report to OSFI. Table 2–9 presents statistics on the CUs and CPs in Canada for the fourth quarter of 2004. As can be seen from Table 2–9, the total membership of credit unions and caisses populaires in Canada in 2004 was 10,592,345, roughly 30 percent of the Canadian population. British Columbia and Ontario had the largest number of CU members, but over 50 percent of the members (5,187,263) live in Quebec, a demonstration of the strength of the co-operative movement in Quebec and the source of the success of Desjardins Group Inc. presented in Table 2–2 previously as one of the largest deposit-taking FIs in Canada. In addition, the total assets of $167.4 billion are made up of $134.4 billion in loans (80.3 percent). Total members' deposits of $142.7 billion funded 85.3 percent of assets.

To attract and keep customers, CUs and CPs have expanded their services to compete with banks. For example, CUs and CPs offer products and services ranging from mortgages and auto loans to credit lines and automated teller machines. In addition, CUCC lists other co-operatives operating in Canada such as Agrifinance, which provides agricultural loans, Co-operative Trust Company of Canada, providing fiduciary and trust services, The Co-operators Group Limited, a property & casualty insurance company, as well as Credential Financial Inc, which provides wealth management services and Ethical Funds, a mutual fund company.

Balance Sheets

Table 2–10 shows the balance sheet of the 7 co-operatives that report to OSFI (Credit Union Central of British Columbia, Credit Union Central of Ontario Limited, Credit Union Central of Nova Scotia, Credit Union Central of Alberta Limited, Credit Union Central of Canada, Co-operative Credit Society of Manitoba Limited, and Credit Union Central of Saskatchewan) for year-end 2003. Of the $12.5 billion assets reported, 56.55 percent represent securities of federal and provincial governments, municipalities and school corporations. The remaining assets are composed of loans ($5.25 billion, 42 percent) and land, building and equipment and other assets ($241.7 million, 2 percent). The greatest dollar amount of loans is for residential mortgages, both insured and uninsured ($1.54 billion, 12.3 percent). The concentration in loans and mortgages increases the credit risk of these FIs. Also, the funding of these longer-term loans with deposits creates a maturity mis-match and therefore an interest rate risk.

On the liability side, deposits make up $10.1 billion, or 80.7 percent of total liabilities and equity. Members' equity funded 6.3 percent of total assets. Each depositor receives one vote to elect the Board of Directors and so participates in lending and investment issues. Thus, since the deposits and equity are owned by the members, corporate governance is different for these FIs than for the banks where the shareholders' funds are different from the depositors and the shares are by law are widely-held.

Regulation

With the exception of the 7 co-operatives who chose to be regulated federally by OSFI, the regulation of credit unions and caisses populaires is primarily at the provincial level. The provincial regulators are charged with ensuring that the CUs and CPs follow sound financial practices and in most provinces, require that external auditors prepare their annual financial statements. In addition, each firm is inspected by the provincial regulator on an annual basis.

Depositors' funds are protected at varying levels by provincial organizations. These may take the form of deposit insurance, deposit guarantee corporations, stabilization funds or a central credit union.

Industry Performance

Given the mutual-ownership status of this industry, growth in ROA (or profits) is not necessarily the primary goal of CUs and CPs. Rather, as long as capital or equity levels are sufficient to protect a CU or CP against unexpected losses on its credit portfolio as well as other financial and operational risks, this not-for-profit industry has a primary goal of serving the deposit and lending needs of its members. This contrasts with the emphasis placed on profitability by stockholder-owned banks.

TABLE 2–10   Assets and Liabilities of Federally-Regulated Cooperative Credit Associations, December 2003 (in thousands of dollars)

ASSETS

	Credit Union Central of British Columbia	Credit Union Central of Ontario Ltd.	Credit Union Central of Nova Scotia	Credit Union Central of Alberta Limited	Credit Union Central of Canada	Co-operative Credit Society of Manitoba Limited	Credit Union Central of Saskatchewan	Total 2003
Cash resources		$ 31,807	$ 14	$ 40,214	$ 6,655	$ 1,437	$ 204	$ 80,331
Deposits with regulated financial institutions	$1,159,869	40,500	165,695	12,315	138,081		124,897	1,631,357
Securities issued or guaranteed by federal and/or provincial governments	392,040	312,543	107,564	77,680		65,457	497,811	1,453,095
Securities issued or guaranteed by Canadian municipalities and/or school corporations	186,090					15,532	20,904	222,526
Other Securities								0
Debt	1,610,920	889,015	38,177	802,832	19,648	1,075,733	872,869	5,309,194
Shares	31,978	13,528	3,851	3,738	4,331	10,171	22,838	90,433
Loans								
To Credit Unions	411,481	114,192	6,332	103,691	58,194	64,887	98,240	857,017
To regulated financial institutions	2,000		2,158				508	4,668
To Canadian federal governments, provinces, municipal or school corporations		2,380	24,167				26,547	
To Member Co-operative Associations	10,274		2,827				8,610	21,711
Lease receivables					151		56,302	56,453
To individuals for non-business purposes	711		9,522		25,702		153,484	189,399
Reverse repurchase agreements		185,794						185,794
To individuals and others for business purposes	4,186	20,401			49,448	139	167,939	242,113
Mortgage Loans								
Residential								
Insured	8,822	2,965	200,589	2,793		146	590,928	806,243
Uninsured	56,495	7,040	133,014	7,285		761	528,275	732,870
Non-residential	27,039	91,418	72,508	44,773			123,571	359,309
Land, Building and Equipment, less accumulated depreciation	11,029	1,756	2,784	10,439	624	4,384	29,169	60,185
Other Assets	13,432	14,867	7,617	30,311	2,050	29,702	63,512	181,491
Total Assets	$3,926,366	$1,725,824	$745,032	$1,160,238	$304,884	$1,268,349	$3,360,041	$12,510,734

Source: OSFI, www.osfi-bsif.gc.ca

TABLE 2–10   Assets and Liabilities of Federally-Reguiated Cooperative Credit Associations, December 2003 (in thousands of dollars) (continued)

LIABILITIES AND MEMBERS' EQUITY								
	Credit Union Central of British Columbia	Credit Union Central of Ontario Ltd.	Credit Union Central of Nova Scotia	Credit Union Central of Alberta Limited	Credit Union Central of Canada	Co-operative Credit Society of Manitoba Limited	Credit Union Central of Saskatchewan	Total 2003
Deposits								
Credit Unions	$3,021,793	$1,298,740	$297,797	$912,638	$42,924	$1,160,797	$1,477,870	$8,212,559
Others	116,456	17,242	376,548			16,593	1,351,696	1,878,535
Cheques and other items in transit (net)	27,823	−2,248						25,575
Advances from Credit Union Central of Canada or Bank of Canada	100,000				159,048			259,048
Liabilities of consolidated subsidiaries, other than deposits					71,615		212,894	284,509
Other liabilities	442,715	306,20	14,423	84,800	4,461	22,505	98,025	973,849
Non-controlling interests in subsidiaries			13,804				32,989	46,793
Subordinated debt			4,484				39,500	43,984
Members' equity								
Common/members shares	105,485	85,942	26,665	137,171	27,733	65,453	81,948	530,397
Preferred shares								0
Contributed surplus								0
Other								0
Retained earnings	112,094	19,228	11,311	25,629	-897	3,001	85,119	255,485
Total Liabilities and Members' Equity	$3,926,366	$1,725,824	$745,032	$1,160,238	$304,884	$1,268,349	$3,380,041	$12,510,734

Concept Questions

1. How do credit unions and caisses populaires differ from banks?
2. Why have credit unions and caisses populaires prospered in recent years?
3. What is the major asset held by credit unions and caisses populaires?

GLOBAL ISSUES: JAPAN, CHINA, AND GERMANY

While Canadian deposit-taking institutions prospered and U.S. depository institution performance deteriorated only slightly in the early 2000s, not all countries fared as well. In April 2001, the Japanese government announced plans for a government-backed purchase of ¥11,000 billion (US $90 billion) of shares of Japanese banks as part of an increasingly frantic drive to avert a banking crisis, recover from a 16-year low in the levels of Japanese stock markets, and stem the country's economic decline. This was the third major attempt to bail out the banking system since 1998. Previous attempts had been unsuccessful. For example, in March 2001, Fitch Investors Service (a major international rating agency) put 19 of the biggest Japanese banks on its credit watch list. The purchase of bank shares was intended to offset losses from writing off bad loans (estimated to be as high as ¥32,000 billion (US $260 billion) in bank portfolios. Foreign financial institutions were also solicited in attempts to prevent a complete financial collapse in Japan. For instance, in October 2003, Goldman Sachs set up an investment fund to buy as much as ¥1 trillion (US $9.1 billion) in nonperforming loans from the Sumi-tomo Mitsui Banking Corporation. Earlier, in January 2003, Goldman agreed to buy ¥150.3 billion (US $1.4 billion) of preferred shares from Sumitomo. Merrill Lynch and Deutsche Bank also bought troubled assets from Japanese banks. These efforts, along with a strengthening Japanese economy, appear to have averted a disaster. By the end of 2003, Japanese banks posted their largest earnings in years. Specifically, as of September 2003, Japan's eight biggest banking groups all reported positive six-month net profits.[9]

In China, however, the banking industry deteriorated in the early 2000s. China's four state-run banks had about US $120 billion in nonperforming loans, accounting for about 21 percent of total loans. Private economists put the percentage of nonperforming loans closer to 50 percent of total loans. Looking to clean up its troubled banking sector, the China Banking Regulatory Commission unveiled a comprehensive plan to overhaul the country's banking system, one that included a shift by China from restricting overseas competition to allowing it. The plan gives foreign banks greater scope to operate. Measures include raising the ceiling on foreign ownership in Chinese financial institutions from 15 percent to 20 percent for a single investor, expanding the number of cities where foreign branches can do some local currency business, and easing capital requirements for branches.

Also experiencing trouble in the early 2000s were Germany's largest banks, which were experiencing their worst downturn since World War II. German banks' problems were due to mounting bad loans (the result of low growth and high unemployment in Germany for nearly a decade) which resulted in plummeting profits and share prices. Further, smaller local banks increasingly competed for loan business, contributing to a crisis for the country's biggest banks. Backed by government guarantees on their own borrowing, small banks enjoyed high credit ratings and low cost of funds. This resulted in a tradition of low lending rates that left these banks with 67 percent of the small business loan market and 39 percent of all chequing accounts. Without a robust stream of loan income, the large German banks were heavily reliant on trading and fee income from securities business. But that income dried up with the fall in the stock market.

Islamic banking
Banking services based on the Qu'ranic principles banning interest and usury.

An additional issue globally has been **Islamic banking**, which, while not a large feature of the North American banking scene, is prominent in other countries, particularly Pakistan and Malaysia, where traditional banks and Islamic banks co-exist. In some respects Islamic banks share the features of cooperative credit institutions in their community-based approach. However, the growth of Islamic finance has been hindered by the development of regulations to ensure their safety and soundness with respect to the global financial system. For Islamic banks, this means the development of appropriate risk management techniques and capital adequacy measures.[10]

Figure 2–4 shows where Canadian banks and insurance companies rank globally by market capitalization as of June 30 2004. The highest ranking Canadian FI is Manulife Financial in 31st place, followed by Royal Bank of Canada ranked at 36.

---

[9] See "Respite for Japanese Banks," *The Wall Street Journal*, November 26, 2003. p. C12; and "Japan's Banks Post Profits," *The Wall Street Journal*, May 25, 2004, p. C14.

[10] See F. Bokhari, "Pakistan The Outlook for Islamic Banking," *The Banker*, May 1, 2005, Z. Awad, "Islamic banking has global reach: The problem is that there are not industry-wide regulations and practices to govern it," *Investment Executive*, July 2005, p. 39, and S. Emling, "Islamic banking grows more popular, even in U.S.," Cox News Service, April 21, 2005.

FIGURE 2–4   Global Ranking of Banks and Insurance Companies by Market Capitalization, June 30 2004.

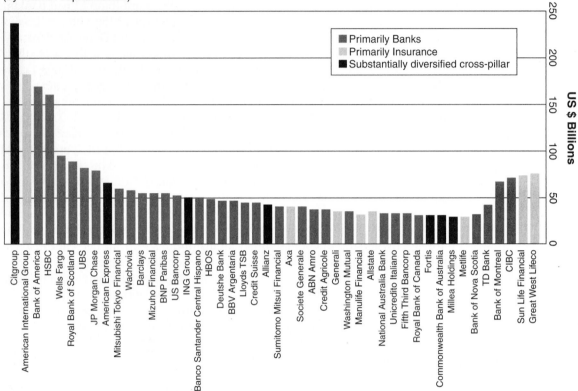

**Where Canada's Banks and Insurance Companies
Rank in the World (June 30, 2004)**
(by market capitalization)*

* Size of business based on total value of outstanding stock.
Source: Canadian Bankers Association, *www.cba.ca*

Of interest is the indication of the degree diversification shown in the figure, with the large, global financial conglomerate Citigroup ranked as number one. Only seven of the companies shown (Citigroup, American Express, U.S.; ING Group The Netherlands; Allianz, Fortis, Belgium; Commonwealth Bank of Australia, and Millea Holdings, Australia) are classified as substantially diversified across pillars.

Summary

This chapter provided an overview of the major activities of the deposit-taking institutions in Canada which rely heavily on deposits to fund their activities, although borrowed funds are becoming increasingly important for the largest institutions. Historically, the four-pillar approach in Canada meant that banks concentrated on business lending and on investing in securities, whereas trusts, credit unions and caisses populaires concentrated on mortgage and consumer lending. These differences have been eroded as a result of competitive forces, regulation, and changing financial and business technology, both within Canada and globally. The creation of large financial service firms operating cross-pillar has meant that the issue of competition is an important one in Canada that will figure prominently in the debate about mergers of large FIs.

Questions and Problems

1. What are the differences between Schedule I, Schedule II, and Schedule III banks?
2. What factors have caused the decrease in loan volume relative to other assets on the balance sheets of banks? How has each of these factors been related to the change and development of the financial services industry during the 1990s and early 2000s? What strategic changes have banks implemented to deal with changes in the financial services environment?
3. What are the major uses of funds for banks in Canada? What are the primary risks to a bank caused by each use of funds? Which of the risks is most critical to the continuing operation of a bank?
4. What are the major sources of funds for banks in Canada? How is the landscape for these funds changing and why?
5. How does the liability maturity structure of a bank's balance sheet compare with the maturity structure of the asset portfolio? What risks are created or intensified by these differences?

6. What types of activities are normally classified as off-balance-sheet (OBS) activities?
   a. How does an OBS activity move onto the balance sheet as an asset or liability?
   b. What are the benefits of OBS activities to a bank?
   c. What are the risks of OBS activities to a bank?
7. What factors normally are given credit for the revitalization of the banking industry during the 1990s? How is Internet banking expected to provide benefits in the future?
8. What factors are given credit for the strong performance of commercial banks in the early 2000s?
9. How does the asset structure of credit unions compare with the asset structure of banks?
10. Compare and contrast the performance of the Canadian deposit-taking institution industry with those of Japan, China, and Germany.

Web Questions

11. Go to OSFI's Web site at **www.osfi-bsif.gc.ca** and find the most recent monthly balance sheet for Canadian Chartered Banks using the following steps. Click on "Banks." Scroll down and click on "Financial Data—Banks." Click on "Submit" to retrieve the latest balance sheet. Repeat the process for Foreign Banks by selecting "Foreign Bank Subsidiaries" and select the most recent balance sheet. Compare the balance sheet of the domestic banks with the foreign banks. How have the assets of both changed since December 2004? Are foreign subsidiaries increasing or decreasing their share of assets in Canada?
12. Go to Credit Union Central of Canada's Web site at **www.cucentral.ca** and download the most recent information on number, assets, and membership in credit unions and caisses populaires using the following steps. Click on "Financial Data" and then click on the latest quarterly report. This will provide a summary of the required data.

Appendix 2A   Financial Statement Analysis Using a Return on Equity (ROE) Framework

View Appendix 2A on page 684 of this book.

Appendix 2B   Technology in Commercial Banking

View Appendix 2B on page 685 of this book.

CHAPTER 3

The Financial Services Industry: Insurance Companies

In this chapter we discuss the main features of (1) life insurance companies and (2) property and casualty insurance companies by concentrating on:

▸ the size, structure and composition of the industry in which they operate

▸ balance sheets and recent trends

▸ regulation, and

▸ global competition and trends in the industry

INTRODUCTION

The primary function of insurance companies is to protect individuals and corporations (policyholders) from adverse events. By accepting premiums, insurance companies promise policyholders compensation if certain specified events occur. These policies represent financial liabilities to the insurance company. With the premiums collected, insurance companies invest in financial securities such as corporate bonds and stocks. The industry is classified into two major groups: life, and property and casualty (P&C). Life insurance provides protection against the possibility of untimely death, illnesses, and retirement. Property insurance protects against personal injury and liability such as accidents, theft, and fire. However, as will become clear, insurance companies also sell a variety of investment products in a similar fashion to other financial service firms, such as mutual funds (Chapter 5) and deposit-taking institutions (Chapter 2).

LIFE INSURANCE COMPANIES

Size, Structure, and Composition of the Industry

demutualization

Conversion from a mutual insurance company owned by policyholders to a stockholder-controlled insurance firm.

As competition in the insurance industry increased in the late 1990s, many of the largest global insurance firms converted from being mutual companies owned by their policyholders to stockholder-controlled companies, a process called **demutualization**. Figure 3–1 illustrates the difference between a mutual insurer and a stock insurance company. Demutualization allows an insurance firm to gain access to the equity markets in order to raise additional capital for future business expansions and compete with the much larger banking industry. The ability to raise capital is also important from a regulatory standpoint since a mutual company cannot readily raise capital to offset a decline in asset values. Because a mutual company is owned by its policy holders, the existing capital and reserves (equal to accumulated past profits) have to be distributed to the insurer's policyholders.

FIGURE 3–1
Mutual versus
Stock Insurance
Companies

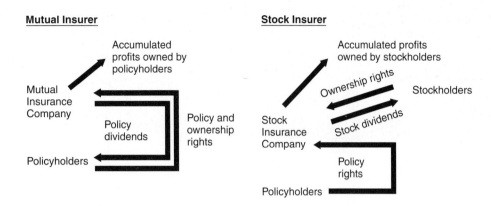

In 1957, the Canadian and British Insurance Companies Act was amended to allow insurance companies to mutualize in order to prevent U.S. takeovers of Canadian companies. As a result, in the 1960s, Mutual of Canada (a mutual since 1870) and North American Life Insurance (which mutualized in 1931) were joined by Canada Life, Sun Life, Equitable Life, Confederation Life, and Manufacturers Life as federally-regulated mutual companies. The reversal of demutualization in Canada (e.g., Manulife and Sun Life), the United States (e.g. Metropolitan Life and Prudential) as well as in other countries (e.g., Australia and the United Kingdom) has set the stage for further global consolidation as well as bank-insurance company mergers that are currently prohibited in Canada.[1]

In Canada, the number of firms declined from 163 firms in 1990 to 120 companies in 2000. In 2005, 95 firms were regulated by the Office of the Superintendent of Financial Services (OSFI), comprised of 42 Canadian and 53 foreign life insurance companies. The consolidation has taken the form of Canadian insurers acquiring the assets of other Canadian companies, such as Great-West Life's acquisition of London Life and Canada Life, and Sun Life's acquisition of Clarica Life Insurance in 2002. In addition, Canadian companies have been expanding their operations abroad. The most notable was the US$11 billion merger of Manulife Financial with the U.S. company, John Hancock, that was concluded in April, 2004. Maritime Life, based in Halifax as a wholly-owned subsidiary of John Hancock, became part of Manulife, and ceased reporting separately to OSFI in December, 2004. Table 3–1 shows the top ten Canadian companies ranked by revenue at December 31, 2004. Total assets are also shown as well as the return on common equity for the three top firms.

www.gwl.ca
www.sunlife.ca

www.manulife.ca

Life insurance allows individuals and their beneficiaries to protect against losses in income through premature death or retirement. By pooling risks, life insurance transfers income-related uncertainties from the insured individual to a group. While life insurance may be the core activity area, modern life insurance companies also sell annuity contracts, manage pension plans, and provide accident and health insurance (Figure 3–2 shows the distribution of premiums written for the various lines of insurance in 2003). We discuss these different activity lines in the following sections.

---

[1] For a legislative history of the Insurance Companies Act, see G. Goldstein, "Bill C-59: An Act to amend the Insurance Companies Act—the Issues (Notes)," December 2, 1998 at www.parl.gc.ca. For background to the insurance industry in Canada see L. B. Mussio, *Sun Ascendant: A History of Sun Life of Canada*, McGill Queen's University Press, 2005. L. Kryzanowski and G. Roberts, "Capital Forbearance: Depressions-era Experience of Life Insurance Companies," *Canadian Journal of Administrative Sciences*, March 1998, 15, 1, pp. 1–16 provides further history of Sun Life and Canadian regulators in the 1930s.

TABLE 3–1
Biggest Canadian Life Insurance Companies by Revenue, December 2004 ($ billions)

Source: *Globe and Mail Report on Business One Thousand 2005, OSFI, and company annual reports*

Company	Revenue	Assets	Return on Common Equity
Manulife Financial Corporation	$27.3	$184.2	15.93%
The Great-West Life Assurance Company	21.9	71.1	20.52%
Sun Life Financial Inc.	21.8	107.8	11.84%
Industrial Alliance Pacific Life Insurance	3.7	1.96	
Desjardins Financial Security Life	2.8	5.2	
Medavie Blue Cross	1.5	0.17	
SSQ Financial Group	1.0	2.5	
RBC Life Insurance Company	0.9	3.9	
Transamerica Life Canada	0.8	4.1	
Empire Life Insurance	0.7	2.82	

FIGURE 3–2
Distribution of Premiums Written on Various Life Insurance Lines, 2003

Source: Canadian Life and Health Insurance Association, *www.clhia.ca*

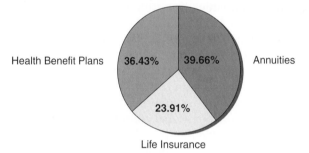

One problem that naturally faces life insurance companies (as well as property & casualty insurers) is the so-called adverse selection problem. Adverse selection is a problem in that customers who apply for insurance policies are more likely to be those most in need of insurance (i.e., someone with chronic health problems is more likely to purchase a life insurance policy than someone in perfect health). Thus, in calculating the probability of having to pay out on an insurance contract and, in turn, determining the insurance premium to charge, insurance companies' use of health (and other) statistics representing the overall population may not be appropriate (since the insurance company's pool of customers is more prone to health problems than the overall population). Insurance companies deal with the adverse selection problem by establishing different pools of the population based on health and related characteristics (such as income). By altering the pool used to determine the probability of losses to a particular customer's health characteristics, the insurance company can more accurately determine the probability of having to pay out on a policy and can adjust the insurance premium accordingly.

As the various types of insurance policies and services offered are described below, notice that some policies (such as universal life policies and annuities) provide not only insurance features but also savings components. For example, universal life policy payouts are a function of the interest earned on the investment of the policyholder's premiums.

Life Insurance

The four basic classes or lines of life insurance are distinguished by the manner in which they are sold or marketed to purchasers. These classes are (1) individual life, (2) group life, (3) industrial life, and (4) credit life.

Individual Life   Individual life insurance involves policies marketed on an individual basis, usually in units of $1,000, on which policyholders make periodic premium payments. Despite the enormous variety of contractual forms, there are essentially five basic contractual types. The first three are traditional forms of life insurance, and the last two are newer contracts that originated in the 1970s and 1980s as a result of increased competition for savings from other segments of the financial services industry. The three traditional contractual forms are term life, whole life, and endowment life. The two newer forms are variable life and universal life. The key features of each of these contractual forms are as follows:

- *Term life.* A term life policy is the closest to pure life insurance, with no savings element attached. Essentially, the individual receives a payout contingent on death during the coverage period. The term of coverage can vary from as little as 1 year to 40 years or more.

- *Whole life.* A whole life policy protects the individual over an entire lifetime. In return for periodic or level premiums, the individual's beneficiaries receive the face value of the life insurance contract on death. Thus, there is certainty that if the policyholder continues to make premium payments, the insurance company will make a payment—unlike term insurance. As a result, whole life has a savings element as well as a pure insurance element.

- *Endowment life.* An endowment life policy combines a pure (term) insurance element with a savings element. It guarantees a payout to the beneficiaries of the policy if death occurs during some endowment period (e.g., prior to reaching retirement age). An insured person who lives to the endowment date receives the face amount of the policy.

- *Variable life.* Unlike traditional policies that promise to pay the insured the fixed or face amount of a policy if a contingency arises, variable life insurance invests fixed premium payments in mutual funds of stocks, bonds, and money market instruments. Usually, policyholders can choose mutual fund investments to reflect their risk preferences. Thus, variable life provides an alternative way to build savings compared with the more traditional policies such as whole life because the value of the policy increases or decreases with the asset returns of the mutual fund in which the premiums are invested.

- *Universal life and variable universal life.* Universal life allows both the premium amounts and the maturity of the life contract to be changed by the insured, unlike traditional policies that maintain premiums at a given level over a fixed contract period. In addition, for some contracts, insurers invest premiums in money, equity, or bond mutual funds—as in variable life insurance—so that the savings or investment component of the contract reflects market returns. In this case, the policy is called variable universal life.

Group Life Insurance   Group life insurance covers a large number of insured persons under a single policy. Usually issued to corporate employers, these policies may be either contributory (where both the employer and employee cover a share of the employee's cost of the insurance) or noncontributory (where the employee does not contribute to the cost of the insurance) for the employees. Cost economies represent the principal advantage of group life over ordinary life policies. Cost economies result from mass administration of plans, lower costs for evaluating individuals through medical screening and other rating systems, and reduced selling and commission costs.

Industrial Life   Industrial life insurance currently represents a very small area of coverage. Industrial life usually involves weekly payments directly collected by representatives of the companies. To a large extent, the growth of group life insurance has led to the demise of industrial life as a major activity class.

Credit Life   Credit life insurance is sold to protect lenders against a borrower's death prior to the repayment of a debt contract such as a mortgage or car loan. Usually, the face amount of the insurance policy reflects the outstanding principal and interest on the loan. Credit life insurance can also be sold by deposit-taking institutions in their branches in Canada.

Other Life Insurer Activities

The other major activities of life insurance companies involve the sale of investment and retirement products (annuities, pension plans, RRSPs, RRIFs) and accident and health insurance.

Investment   Annuities represent the reverse of life insurance activities. Whereas life insurance involves different contractual methods of *building up* a fund, annuities involve different methods of *liquidating* a fund, such as paying out a fund's proceeds. As with life insurance contracts, many different types of annuity contracts have been developed. Specifically, they can be sold to an individual or a group and on a fixed or a variable basis by being linked to the return on some underlying investment portfolio. Individuals can purchase annuities with a single payment or with payments spread over a number of years. The annuity builds up a fund whose returns are tax deferred; that is, they are not subject to capital gains taxes on their investments. Payments may be structured to start immediately, or they can be deferred (at which time taxes are paid based on the income tax rate of the annuity receiver). These payments may cease on death or continue to be paid to beneficiaries for a number of years after death. Payments received by individuals from annuity contracts are declared as income that may or may not be taxable as determined by the Income Tax Act available from the Canada Revenue Agency (CRA), at www.cra-grc.gc.ca. Annuity sales provided premiums of $20.9 billion in 2004, representing 39.66% of the total premium income as shown in Figure 3–2. Although annuities were the largest source of premium income, primarily from the growth in retirement products such as pension plans and **registered retirement savings plans (RRSPs)**, premium income from annuities has declined from 53 percent of total premium income in 2000.[2] Life insurance has held steady at around 24 percent (versus 25 percent in 2000), whereas health insurance premium income has increased from 22 percent in 2000 to 36 percent in 2003.

Annuity premiums include group retirement plans such as private pension plans known as registered pension plans in Canada (Pension plans are covered in more detail in Chapter 5, Appendix B). According to the Canadian Life and Health Insurance Association (CLHIA), individual annuities amounted to $9.6 billion in 2003 whereas group annuities were $11.3 billion. Individual premiums come from demand for assets placed in an RRSP, and from **registered retirement income funds (RRIFs)**. Individuals in Canada are able to shelter income from tax during their earning years via RRSPs, but must transfer the funds to a RRIF after retirement and pay the tax on withdrawal. Individual and group RRSPs provided 37 percent of the life insurance industry's total 2003 annuity premiums.

Registered Retirement Savings Plan (RRSP)
Retirement savings fund that allows Canadians to shield a portion of their income from tax, but must be liquidated by age 69. RRSPs are usually converted to RRIFs.

Registered Retirement Income Fund (RRIF)
A fund that is designed to provide a regular income to an individual and allow the individual to defer payment and tax on money withdrawn from an RRSP.

---

[2] As discussed in Chapter 21, life insurers are facing increasingly intense competition from banks in the annuity product market.

Accident and Health Insurance   Though life insurance protects against mortality risk, accident and health insurance protect against morbidity, or ill health, risk. Canada's public health system provides coverage for many medical services but health insurance provides additional coverage, often through extended health care plans provided by employers as benefits to their employees. These include dental plans, travel insurance, disability insurance, and accidental death and dismemberment insurance. At year-end 2003, 26.5 million people in Canada were insured for extended health care, and total health insurance premiums were $19.2 billion, 36 percent of total premium income. Life insurers provide over 90 percent of the health insurance in Canada, and the remainder is provided by property and casualty insurance. In many respects, the loss exposures faced by insurers in health insurance are more similar to those faced under property-casualty insurance than to those faced under traditional life insurance, as discussed below.

Balance Sheet and Recent Trends

Assets

Because of the long-term nature of their liabilities (as a result of the long-term nature of life insurance policyholders' claims) and the need to generate competitive returns on the savings elements of life insurance products, life insurance companies concentrate their asset investments at the longer end of the maturity spectrum (e.g., bonds, equities, and government securities). Look at Table 3–2, where we show the distribution of life insurance companies' assets.

As you can see, in 2004, for the firms reporting to OSFI, 56.2 percent of life insurance assets were invested in bonds and debentures, 15.2 percent in mortgage loans, 5.6 percent in preferred and common shares, and 5.0 percent in short-term investments, with other assets, including cash, accrued investment income, accounts receivable, **policy loans** (loans made to policyholders using their policies as collateral), real estate, other loans and invested assets, deferred income taxes, and goodwill making up the remainder. The decline in mortgage loans from 23.4 percent of assets in 1996 to 15.2 percent in 2004 can be attributed to a decline in commercial real estate values. Similarly, the decline in preferred and common shares

policy loans
Loans made by an insurance company to its policyholders using their policies as collateral.

TABLE 3–2   Distribution of Assets of Canadian Life Insurance Companies

	1996	1997	1998	1999	2000	2001	2002	2003	2004
Cash	0.8%	1.1%	1.0%	1.7%	1.4%	1.0%	0.9%	1.2%	1.2%
Short Term Investments	4.3%	3.5%	3.3%	3.8%	5.0%	4.7%	4.9%	4.5%	5.0%
Accrued Investment Income	1.2%	1.2%	1.2%	1.1%	1.1%	1.1%	1.1%	1.0%	1.0%
Accounts Receivable	1.5%	1.6%	1.7%	2.0%	2.2%	1.5%	1.7%	1.6%	1.3%
Policy Loans	4.4%	4.7%	4.9%	4.6%	3.5%	3.7%	3.8%	3.5%	3.2%
Bonds and Debentures	48.6%	52.0%	53.0%	52.4%	51.4%	55.5%	57.7%	56.7%	56.2%
Mortgage Loans	23.4%	21.8%	20.5%	18.8%	18.7%	15.4%	13.8%	14.4%	15.2%
Preferred and Common Shares	5.1%	5.5%	5.5%	6.0%	6.8%	7.0%	5.7%	5.4%	5.6%
Real Estate	4.4%	3.9%	3.6%	3.6%	3.7%	3.2%	3.1%	3.1%	3.2%
Other Loans and Invested Assets	0.6%	0.8%	0.9%	1.2%	1.2%	1.3%	1.6%	1.7%	1.7%
Deferred Income Taxes	0.7%	0.9%	0.8%	0.8%	0.6%	0.7%	0.4%	0.5%	0.4%
Goodwill and Other Assets	4.8%	3.0%	3.6%	4.1%	4.5%	4.9%	5.3%	6.4%	6.1%
Total Assets	100.0%	100.0%	100.0%	100.0%	100.0%	100.0%	100.0%	100.0%	100.0%
Total Assets in Segregated Funds	36.3%	48.4%	58.4%	69.6%	74.0%	63.7%	57.7%	68.7%	75.5%
Total Assets ($ billions)	225.98	232.90	251.84	257.51	244.47	289.87	266.74	287.09	305.57

Source: Office of Superintendent of Financial Institutions, *www.osfi-bsif.gc.ca*

can be related to the downturn in the stock market starting with the collapse of the stock market in late 2001, with the resulting increase in investments in bonds and debentures. The CLHIA reported that, for 2003, life and health insurance companies had Canadian investments totalling $27.2 billion in provincial, municipal and federal bonds, $119.8 billion in corporate securities, and $45.3 billion in mutual funds, a significant participation in Canadian capital markets. While banks are the major issuers of new mortgages (sometimes keeping the mortgages on their books and sometimes selling them to secondary market investors), insurance companies hold mortgages as investment securities. That is, they purchase many mortgages in the secondary markets (see Chapters 26 and 27). The major trends have been a long-term increase in the proportion of bonds[3] and a decline in the proportion of mortgages in the balance sheet (see below). Thus, insurance company managers must be able to measure and manage the credit risk, interest rate risk, and other risks associated with these securities.

segregated funds
Investment funds held and managed separately by life and health insurance companies in Canada.

In Canada, life and health insurance companies offer shares in investment funds called **segregated funds** that are similar to the mutual funds offered by other FIs, and that are similarly invested in equities, bonds and money market instruments. These funds have been popular since the early 2000s when many investors saw their retirement savings in stocks and mutual funds reduced by the downturn in the market. Segregated funds must return a minimum percentage (usually 75 percent or more) of the capital invested to the investor at the maturity, reducing the risk of capital loss. Also, segregated funds are a means of **creditor proofing** assets, a feature of interest to small business owners. Segregated funds must be managed separately from the other assets of the firm, and insurance companies report the amount of their assets held as segregated funds to OSFI separately. It can be seen that segregated funds have increased from 36.3 percent of total assets in 1996 to 75.5 percent of total assets in 2004, reflecting the growth of individual and group pension plans.

creditor proofing
The placing of assets in a vehicle that cannot be claimed by creditors in the event of the owners' bankruptcy.

Liabilities

actuarial liabilities
A liability item for insurers that reflects their expected payment commitment on existing policy contracts.

The aggregate balance sheet for the life insurance industry at the end of 2004 is shown in Table 3–3. Looking at the liability side, we see that 68.1 percent represent **actuarial liabilities** under insurance policies and annuity contracts. These are based on actuarial assumptions regarding the insurers' expected future liability commitments to pay out on present contracts, including death benefits, matured endowments (lump sum or otherwise), and the cash **surrender values of policies** (the cash value paid to the policyholder if the policy is surrendered before it matures). Even though the actuarial assumptions underlying policy reserves are normally very conservative, unexpected fluctuations in future required payouts can occur; thus, underwriting life insurance is risky. For example, mortality rates—and life insurance payouts—might unexpectedly increase above those defined by historically based mortality tables as a result of a catastrophic epidemic illness such as AIDS. To meet unexpected future losses, the life insurer holds a capital and surplus reserve fund with which to meet such losses (and reduce insolvency risk). The total of policyholders' and shareholders' equity at year-end 2004 was $37.5 billion, 12 percent of the total liabilities and equity. The ratio of total liabilities to equity is thus 7.11. The equity accounts provide a surplus to meet unexpected underwriting losses as do the insurer's investment income from its asset portfolio plus any new premium income flows.

surrender value of a policy
The cash value of a policy received from the insurer if a policyholder surrenders the policy before maturity. The cash surrender value is normally only a portion of the contract's face value.

---

[3] The bull market of the 1980s and 1990s probably constitutes a major reason for the large percentage of assets invested in equities.

TABLE 3–3
Canadian Life
Insurance Industry
Balance sheet,
2004 (in thousands
of dollars)

Source: OSFI, *www.osfi-bsif.gc.ca*

	2004	
Cash	$ 3,679,191	1.2%
Short Term Investments	15,162,048	5.0%
Accrued Investment Income	3,015,112	1.0%
Accounts Receivable	3,882,550	1.3%
Policy Loans	9,862,839	3.2%
Bonds and Debentures	171,591,400	56.2%
Mortgage Loans	46,579,218	15.2%
Preferred and Common Shares	17,035,560	5.6%
Real Estate	9,873,180	3.2%
Other Loans and Invested Assets	5,207,091	1.7%
Deferred Income Taxes	1,163,506	0.4%
Goodwill and Other Assets	18,519,790	6.1%
Total Assets	**$305,571,485**	**100.0%**
Liabilities		
Net Actuarial Liabilities Under Insurance Policies and Annuity Contracts	$207,234,130	68.1%
Other Insurance Policy and Contract Liabilities	13,809,179	4.5%
Trust and Banking Deposits	4,217,270	1.4%
Accounts Payable	6,369,973	2.1%
Mortgage Loans and Other Real Estate Encumbrances	288,634	0.1%
Other Liabilities	12,871,703	4.2%
Net Deferred Gains (Losses) on Disposal of Portfolio Investments	11,201,245	3.7%
Non Controlling Interests	3,885,281	1.3%
Future Income Taxes	1,588,279	0.5%
Subordinated Debt	4,898,224	1.6%
Other Debt	548,338	0.2%
Total Liabilities	**$266,912,256**	**87.7%**
Policyholders' Equity		
Participating Account	$ 2,095,666	0.7%
Non-Participating Account (Mutual Companies Only)	158,631	0.1%
Currency Translation Account	−22,096	0.0%
Shareholders' Equity		0.0%
Capital Stock	15,077,887	5.0%
Contributed Surplus	646,071	0.2%
Retained Earnings	21,779,487	7.2%
Currency Translation Account	−2,195,858	−0.7%
Total Policyholders' and Shareholders' Equity	**37,539,788**	**12.3%**
Total Liabilities and Equity	**$304,452,044**	**100.0%**

Regulation

At the federal level, Canadian health and life insurers (42 firms in 2005) and branches of foreign-owned life insurance companies (53 firms) are regulated by OSFI under the Insurance Companies Act. These companies hold more than 90 percent of the industry's assets. Total assets of foreign life insurance companies in Canada were only $8.3 billion compared to the $305.6 billion of the Canadian life insurers. However, on a global basis, the foreign insurance companies operating in Canada represent some of the largest life insurers in the world, including the AXA

Group of France, Metropolitan Life of the United States, and Prudential Assurance of the United Kingdom. OSFI's regulatory approach is primarily prudential, meaning that its focus is on the safety and soundness of the health and life insurers so that these FIs do not pose a risk to the Canadian financial system. To, this end, OSFI provides guidelines that pertain specifically to health and life insurers at its Web site. These guidelines include minimum capital and surplus requirements (which will be discussed in detail in Chapter 20) as well as guidelines for innovative instruments, large exposure limits, securities lending, asset securitization, derivatives best practices, money laundering, and outsourcing. As well, accounting guidelines and reporting requirements are specified. Effective February 1998, OSFI issued guidelines with standards for sound business and financial practices specifically for life insurance companies that address capital management, credit risk management, foreign exchange risk management, interest rate risk management and liquidity management, among others, all of the risks that will be addressed for FIs in subsequent chapters.

Health and life insurers are also regulated at the provincial level. In each province in which they do business, the insurer must abide by the market conduct regulation and licencing requirements.

www.assuris.ca

The Canadian Life and Health Insurance Compensation Corporation (Assuris) is a private, non-profit corporation that is financed by the life and health insurance companies. Assuris provides a guarantee, subject to limits, of existing life insurance policies, accident and sickness policies, and annuity contracts in the event of the bankruptcy of an insurance company. Assuris insures up to $200,000 on claims in case of bankruptcy of an insurer, and up to $60,000 in cash policy coverage. In addition, the

www.clhio.ca

Canadian Life and Health Insurance OmbudService (CLHIO) provides support for consumers who have concerns about life and health insurance companies.

Concept Questions

1. What is the difference between a life insurance contract and an annuity contract?
2. Describe the different forms of life insurance.
3. Why do life insurance companies invest in long-term assets?
4. What is the major source of life insurance underwriting risk?
5. Who are the main regulators of the life insurance industry?

PROPERTY & CASUALTY INSURANCE

Size, Structure, and Composition of the Industry

The property and casualty (P&C) insurance industry performs the important function of spreading risk of personal or business loss over many policyholders. The industry is much less concentrated than the life and health insurance industry, and, because it does not have a savings function, it is much smaller in size. However, estimates of the Insurance Bureau of Canada (IBC) place the industry employment at over 100,000 people spread across Canada and divided between primary insurers and reinsurers, brokers, independent adjusters, and appraisers. **Primary insurers** are the originators of a policy, whereas **reinsurance** provides "insurance for insurers" by spreading the risk across many insurers. The major reinsurers are large international companies so that a major catastrophe such as the terrorist attacks in New York in 2001 and in London in 2005, which may result in large insurance claims, could increase property insurance premiums in Canada and globally.

primary insurers
Originators of insurance policies.

reinsurance
The payment of a premium to transfer the risk of a part of a claim to another insurer, called a reinsurer.

Like the life and health insurance industry, the P&C industry is regulated jointly by provincial bodies with respect to marketing and licencing issues, and by OSFI with respect to solvency issues. At December, 2004, OSFI listed 187 companies authorized to operate in Canada, 90 Canadian firms and 97 foreign firms. Many of the Canadian firms are subsidiaries of large, global firms such as Allianz, Allstate, ING, Munich Reinsurance, and Swiss RE. Assets of the Canadian firms totaled $59.3 billion at December, 2004. This represented just 3.1% of the $1.98 trillion on balance sheet assets of the Canadian banks and 19.4% of the $305.6 billion assets of the Canadian life insurance companies that OSFI supervises. At the present time, some Canadian banks have insurance subsidiaries who report to OSFI, but they are not allowed to sell insurance through their branch networks, a regulation that has been challenged by the banks but that has so far limited their expansion into this field. This issue will be discussed under product diversification in Chapter 21.

Property & Casualty Insurance

Property insurance covers the loss of real and personal property. Casualty—or, perhaps more accurately, liability—insurance concerns protection against legal liability exposures. However, the distinctions between the two broad areas of property and liability insurance are increasingly becoming blurred. Some insurance lines are marketed to both individuals and commercial firms (e.g. automobile insurance) and other lines are marketed to one specific group (e.g., boiler and machinery insurance). To understand the importance of each line in terms of premium income and losses incurred, look at Table 3–4, which shows the **net premiums written** (NPW) (the entire amount of premiums on insurance contracts written) for major P&C lines as well as the **claims ratio**. Major insurance lines include the following:

- *Property insurance.* Protects personal and commercial property against fire, lightning, and other damage (27.5 percent of net premiums written in 2004; 31.1 percent in 1996).
- *Automobile insurance.* Provides protection against (1) losses resulting from legal liability due to the ownership or use of a vehicle (auto liability) and (2) theft of or damage to vehicles (auto physical damage). Auto insurance represents the largest category of premiums of all types of insurance (55.5 percent of net premiums written in 2004 versus 54.0 percent in 1996).
- *Liability insurance (other than auto).* Provides either individuals or commercial firms with protection against non-automobile-related legal liability. For commercial firms, this includes protection against liabilities relating to their business operations (other than personal injury to employees covered by workers' compensation insurance) and product liability hazards (9.5 percent in 2004 versus 9.2 percent in 1996).

The claims ratio for automobile insurance is highest at 67.09, reflecting higher payouts and less surplus from premiums to cover claims and provide a buffer against loss of capital. Figure 3–3 shows net premiums written and claims incurred from 1986 to 2003 for the Canadian P&C industry. Like the spread on a loan, the difference between net premiums written and claims incurred affects the profitability of the industry. Premiums are estimates and if they do not cover claims (e.g., environmental cleanup costs that exceed the original expected loss) then the insurer's capital is affected. However, profitable years always bring calls for government inquiries and controls on high insurance premiums.[4]

net premiums written (NPW)
The entire amount of premiums on insurance contracts written.

claims ratio
Ratio of premiums written to claims paid out.

---

[4] Escalating automobile insurance premiums in the early 2000s across the country, but particularly in Ontario, led some consumers of automobile insurance to pay accident costs themselves rather than make a claim and see their insurance premiums escalate or perhaps be denied insurance and be unable to drive their cars. Some provincial governments (e.g. Nova Scotia) froze insurance premiums. The high insurance profits of 2004 brought calls for lowering of premiums. See "Insurer profit raises questions by consumer advocates," *Canada NewsWire*, Ottawa, February 18 2005, p. 1; "Ontario auto rates drop more than 10% in 2004," *Canadian Underwriter*, February 2005 Vol. 72(2), p. 6; R. Cornejo, "Balance Tilts to Profit in Canada's Auto Market," *Best's Review*, May 2005, Vol. 106(1), p. 10; and S. van Zyl, "Auto Insurance: WILL IT BITE BACK?" *Canadian Underwriter*, May 2005, Vol. 72(5), pp. 8–12.

TABLE 3–4   Property and Casualty Insurance Industry Underwriting by Lines, Canadian and Foreign
P&C Companies, 2004 (thousands of dollars)

	Canadian Net Written	Net Incurred	Claims Ratio	Foreign Net Written	Net Incurred	Claims Ratio
Property:						
Personal	$ 3,437,580	$ 2,005,155	62.59	$ 425,459	$ 185,785	42.48
Commercial	2,295,357	1,050,129	47.11	1,461,468	498,994	35.6
Total	$ 5,732,938	$ 3,055,284	56.24	$1,886,927	$ 684,779	37.24
Aircraft	−3,571	1,072	40.98	154,088	18,407	12.51
Automobile:						
Liability	5,451,460	3,940,437	74.6	667,518	620,539	87.98
Personal Accident	2303128	1627260	71.97	404,789	313,475	0.69
Other	3,859,192	2,006,899	53.56	461,362	277,450	54.26
Total	$11,612,780	$ 7,574,596	67.09	$1,533,669	$1,211,464	72.63
Boiler and Machinery	178,503	80,906	43.7	75,289	26,800	35.2
Credit	3,187	3,032	97.65	21,732	14,027	64.01
Credit Protection	7,460	647	8.67	0	0	0
Fidelity	73,206	32,220	46.09	49,767	13,542	26.64
Hail	7,213	4.043	56.05	2,566	3,422	145.31
Legal Expense	1,859	197	15.03	204	74	36.27
Liability	1,984,004	1,375,299	72.56	1,622,767	1,306,283	82.43
Mortgage	496,105	24,781	11.35	0	0	0
Other Approved Products	0	0	11.35	0	0	0
Surely	196,036	55,408	30.2	10,464	−1,648	−15.15
Title	1,555	237	15.24	145,896	48,748	0
Marine	109,351	48,623	46.01	113,428	48,836	40.23
Accident and Sickness	593,088	304,649	53.61	135,673	49,844	36.87
Total	$20,993,713	$12,560,993	62.89	$5,752,470	$3,424,578	59.01

Source: OSFI, *www.osfi-bsif.gc.ca*

FIGURE 3–3
Net premiums and
claims of the P&C
industry in Canada,
1986–2003

Source: The Insurance
Bureau of Canada Fact
Book, 2004, *www.ibc.ca*

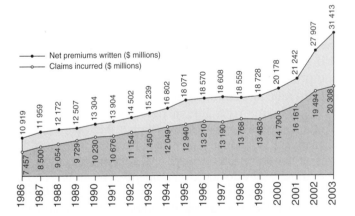

Balance Sheet and Recent Trends

The Balance Sheet and Underwriting Risk

The balance sheet of the Canadian P&C firms reporting to OSFI at the end of 2004
is shown in Table 3–5. Similar to life insurance companies, P&C insurers invest the
majority of their assets in long-term securities, thus subjecting them to credit and

interest rate risks. Bonds and debentures ($25.9 billion), preferred shares ($2.5 billion), and common shares ($4.4 billion) constituted 55.3 percent of total assets in 2004. P&C insurers, unlike life insurers, have more uncertain payouts on their insurance contracts (i.e., they incur greater levels of liquidity risk). Thus, their asset structure includes many assets with relatively fixed returns that can be liquidated easily and at low cost. Looking at their liabilities, we can see that major components are the unpaid claims and adjustment expenses ($26.95 billion) item, which relates to expected administrative and related costs of adjusting (settling) these claims. This item constitutes 45.4 percent of total liabilities and equity. **Unearned premiums** (a reserve set-aside that contains the portion of a premium that has been paid before insurance coverage has been provided) are also a major liability, representing 23.0 percent of total liabilities and capital.

unearned premiums
Reserve set-aside that contains the portion of a premium that has been paid before insurance coverage has been provided.

To understand how and why a loss reserve on the liability side of the balance sheet is established, we need to understand the risks of underwriting P&C insurance. In particular, P&C underwriting risk results when the premiums generated on a given insurance line are insufficient to cover (1) the claims (losses) incurred insuring against the peril and (2) the administrative expenses of providing that

TABLE 3–5
Balance Sheet for the Canadian Property & Casualty Industry, 2004 (thousands of dollars)

Assets		Percent of Total Assets
Cash	$ 1,816,190	3.1%
Investment Income Due and Accrued	305,304	0.5%
Investments:		
Term Deposits	1,380,992	2.3%
Bonds and Debentures	25,899,203	43.7%
Mortgage Loans	467,848	0.8%
Preferred Shares	2,536,927	4.3%
Common Shares	4,379,892	7.4%
Real Estate	122,044	0.2%
Other Investments	796,596	1.3%
Total Investments	**$35,583,502**	60.0%
Receivables:		
Agents and Brokers	1,156,410	1.9%
Policyholders	344,645	0.6%
Instalment Premiums	3,865,323	6.5%
Other Insurers	679,725	1.1%
Facility Association and the "P.R.R."	1,231,393	2.1%
Subsidiaries, Affiliates and Partnerships	302,689	0.5%
Income Taxes	23,172	0.0%
Other Receivables	139,018	0.2%
Recoverable from Reinsurers:		
Unearned Premiums	2,051,375	3.5%
Unpaid Claims and Adjustment Expenses	6,510,337	11.0%
Other Recoverables on Unpaid Claims	275,782	0.5%
Investment in Subsidiaries, Affiliates and Partnerships	1,406,940	2.4%
Real Estate for Insurer's Own Use	144,124	0.2%
Deferred Policy Acquisition Expenses	2,179,265	3.7%
Future Income Taxes	614,769	1.0%
Other Assets	696,994	1.2%
Total Assets	**$59,326,957**	100.0%

TABLE 3–5
(continued)

Source: OSFI, www.osfi-bsif.gc.ca

Liabilities		Percent of Total
Overdrafts	$ 92,963	0.2%
Borrowed Money and Accrued Interest	3,230	0.0%
Payables:		0.0%
Agents and Brokers	363,978	0.6%
Policyholders	53,888	0.1%
Other Insurers	387,577	0.7%
Subsidiaries, Affiliates and Partnerships	397,739	0.7%
Expenses Due and Accrued	784,789	1.3%
Income Taxes Due and Accrued	595,244	1.0%
Other Taxes Due and Accrued	254,705	0.4%
Policyholder Dividends and Rating Adjustments	14,653	0.0%
Encumbrances on Real Estate	30,968	0.1%
Unearned Premiums	13,630,140	23.0%
Unpaid Claims and Adjustment Expenses	26,952,582	45.4%
Unearned Commissions	406,951	0.7%
Premium Deficiency	0	0.0%
Future Income Taxes	69,725	0.1%
Other Liabilities	933,267	1.6%
Total Liabilities	**$44,972,398**	**75.8%**
Equity		
Share Capital Issued and Paid	5,470,486	9.2%
Contributed Surplus	750,150	1.3%
Other	−51,952	−0.1%
Retained Earnings	8,053,805	13.6%
Reserves	132,070	0.2%
Total Equity	**$14,354,559**	**24.2%**
Total Liabilities and Equity	**$59,326,957**	**100.0%**

insurance (legal expenses, commissions, taxes, etc.) after taking into account (3) the investment income generated between the time premiums are received and the time claims are paid. Thus, underwriting risk may result from (1) unexpected increases in loss rates, (2) unexpected increases in expenses, and/or (3) unexpected decreases in investment yields or returns. Next, we look more carefully at each of these three areas of P&C underwriting risk.

Loss Risk   The key feature of claims loss exposure is the actuarial *predictability* of losses relative to premiums earned. This predictability depends on a number of characteristics or features of the perils insured, specifically:

- *Property versus liability.* In general, the maximum levels of losses are more predictable for property lines than for liability lines. For example, the monetary value of the loss of, or damage to, an auto is relatively easy to calculate, while the upper limit to the losses an insurer might be exposed to in a product liability line—for example, asbestos damage to workers' health under other liability insurance—may be difficult, if not impossible, to estimate.

- *Severity versus frequency.* In general, loss rates are more predictable on low-severity, high-frequency lines than they are on high-severity, low-frequency lines. For example, losses in fire, auto, and homeowners peril lines tend to involve events expected to occur with a high frequency and to be independently distributed across any pool of the insured. Furthermore, the dollar loss on each event in the insured pool tends to be relatively small. Applying the law of large numbers, insurers can estimate the expected loss potential of such lines—the **frequency of loss** times the size of the loss (**severity of loss**)—within quite small probability bounds. Other lines, such as earthquake, hail, and financial guaranty insurance, tend to insure very low-probability (frequency) events. Here the probabilities are not always stationary, the individual risks in the insured pool are not independent, and the severity of the loss could be enormous. This means that estimating expected loss rates (frequency times severity) is extremely difficult in these coverage areas. For example, in the U.S., since the September 11 terrorist attacks, coverage for high-profile buildings in big cities, as well as other properties considered potential targets, remains expensive. This higher uncertainty of losses forces P&C firms to invest in more short-term assets and hold a larger percentage of capital and reserves than life insurance firms hold.[5]

- *Long tail versus short tail.* Some liability lines suffer from a long-tail risk exposure phenomenon that makes the estimation of expected losses difficult. This **long-tail loss** arises in policies in which the insured event occurs during a coverage period but a claim is not filed or reported until many years later. The delay in filing of a claim is in accordance with the terms of the insurance contract and often occurs because the detrimental consequences of the event are not known for a period of time after the event actually occurs. Losses incurred but not reported have caused insurers significant problems in lines such as medical malpractice and other liability insurance where product damage suits (e.g., the Dalkon shield case and asbestos cases) have mushroomed many years after the event occurred and the coverage period expired.[6] For example, in 2002 Halliburton, a major U.S. corporation, agreed to pay US $4 billion in cash and stock, and to seek bankruptcy protection for a subsidiary to settle more than 300,000 asbestos claims. Questions still remain about how much insurance companies will be required to reimburse Halliburton for the cost of asbestos case settlements and when. The company had only US $1.6 billion of expected insurance on its books for asbestos claims.

- *Product inflation versus social inflation.* Loss rates on all P&C property policies are adversely affected by unexpected increases in inflation. Such increases were triggered, for example, by the oil price shocks of 1973, 1978, and potentially, 2004–2005. However, in addition to a systematic unexpected inflation risk in each line, there may be line-specific inflation risks. The inflation risk of property lines is likely to reflect the approximate underlying inflation risk of the economy.

frequency of loss
The probability that a loss will occur.

severity of loss
The size of the loss.

long-tail loss
A claim that is made some time after a policy was written.

---

[5] An alternative to managing risk on a P&C insurer's balance sheet is to purchase reinsurance from a reinsurance company. Reinsurance is essentially insurance for insurance companies. It is a way for primary insurance companies to protect against unforeseen or extraordinary losses. Depending on the contract, reinsurance can enable the insurer to improve its capital position, expand its business, limit losses, and stabilize cash flows, among other things. In addition, the reinsurer, drawing information from many primary insurers, will usually have a far larger pool of data for assessing risks. Reinsurance takes a variety of forms. It may represent a layer of risk, such as losses within certain limits, say, $5 million to $10 million, that will be paid by the reinsurer to the primary insurance company for which a premium is paid, or a sharing of both losses and profits for certain types of business. Insurers and reinsurers also typically issue catastrophe bonds. The bonds pay high interest rates and diversify an investor's portfolio because natural disasters occur randomly and are not associated with (independent of) economic factors. Depending on how the bond is structured, if losses reach the threshold specified in the bond-offering, the investor may lose all or part of the principal or interest. For example, a deep-discount or zero-coupon catastrophe bond would pay $100(1 - \alpha)$ on maturity, where α is the loss rate due to the catastrophe. Thus, Munich Re issued a U.S. $250 million catastrophe bond in 2001 where α (the loss rate) reflected losses incurred on all reinsurer policies over a 24-hour period should an event (such as a flood or hurricane) occur and losses exceed a certain threshold. The required yield on these bonds reflected the risk-free rate plus a premium reflecting investors' expectations regarding the probability of the event's occurring.

[6] In some product liability cases, such as those involving asbestos, the nature of the risk being covered was not fully understood at the time many of the policies were written.

Liability lines may be subject to social inflation, as reflected in the courts' willingness to award punitive and other liability damages at rates far above the underlying rate of inflation. Such social inflation has been particularly prevalent in commercial liability and medical malpractice insurance in the U.S.

loss (claims) ratio
Ratio that measures pure losses incurred to premiums earned.

The **loss ratio** (also called the claims ratio) measures the actual losses incurred on a line. It measures the ratio of losses incurred to **premiums earned** (premiums received and earned on insurance contracts because time has passed with no claim being filed). Thus, a loss ratio less than 100 means that premiums earned were sufficient to cover losses incurred on that line. Aggregate loss ratios for the period 1993–2003 are shown in Table 3–6. Notice that the earned loss ratio generally increased over the time period, reaching a high of 80.0 percent in 2001, and a low of 69.6 percent in 2003. This ratio includes loss adjustment expenses (LAE)—see below—as well as (pure) losses. However, the earned loss ratio does not tell the whole story as the expense of providing insurance coverage must also be considered.

premiums earned
Premiums received and earned on insurance contracts because time has passed with no claim being filed.

Expense Risk   The two major sources of expense risk to P&C insurers are (1) loss adjustment expenses (LAE) and (2) commissions and other expenses. Loss adjustment expenses relate to the costs surrounding the loss settlement process; for example, many P&C insurers employ adjusters who determine the liability of the insurer and the size of the adjustment or settlement to be made. The other major area of expense occurs in the commission costs paid to insurance brokers and sales agents and other expenses related to the acquisition of business. As mentioned above, the loss ratio reported in Table 3–6 includes LAE. The expense ratio reported in Table 3–6 reflects commissions and other (non-LAE) expenses for P&C insurers over the 1993–2003 period. In contrast to the increasing trend in the loss ratio, the expense ratio generally decreased over the period shown. Expense can account for significant portions of the overall costs of operations. In 2003, for example, expenses—other than LAE—amounted to 28.6 percent of premiums written. Clearly, sharp rises in insurance broker commissions and other operating costs can rapidly render an insurance line unprofitable.

combined ratio
Ratio that measures the overall underwriting profitability of a line; it is equal to the loss ratio plus the ratios of loss adjustment expenses to premiums earned and commission and other acquisition costs to premiums written as a proportion of premiums earned.

A common measure of the overall underwriting profitability of a line, which includes both loss and expense experience, is the **combined ratio.** Technically, the combined ratio is equal to the loss ratio plus the ratios of LAE to premiums earned,

TABLE 3–6   **P&C Industry Financial Results and Underwriting Ratios**

Financial results ($000,000)	1993	1994	1995	1996	1997	1998	1999	2000	2001	2002	2003
Net premiums written	15,239	16,482	18,071	18,570	18,608	18,559	18,728	20,178	21,242	27,507	31,413
Net premiums earned[1] (x)	14,906	15,904	17,510	18,182	18,464	18,382	18,561	19,480	20,192	25,334	29,175
Net claims incurred (y)	11,490	12,043	12,840	13,210	13,190	13,768	13,483	14,790	16,161	19,494	20,388
Total claims and expenses (z)	16,379	17,013	18,234	18,794	18,938	19,824	19,647	21,167	22,414	26,810	28,718
Underwriting profit (loss)	(1,351)	(1,027)	(631)	(517)	(421)	(1,366)	(1.027)	(1,614)	(2,155)	(1,390)	559
Net investment income	2,671	2,061	2,508	3,111	3,324	2,864	2.543	3,251	2,762	2,248	3,020
Net profit	1,077	809	1,462	1,876	2,000	1,101	1,094	1,094	465	340	2,531
Ratios											
Return on equity (ROE)[2]	9.5%	6.8%	11.7%	13.6%	13.1%	6.8%	6.5%	6.3%	2.6%	1.7%	11.6%
Earned loss ratio (y÷x)	77.1%	75.7%	73.3%	72.7%	71.4%	74.9%	72.6%	75.9%	80.0%	76.9%	69.9%
Operating expense ratio [(z-y)/x]	32.8%	31.3%	30.8%	30.7%	31.1%	33.0%	33.2%	32.8%	31.0%	28.9%	28.6%
Combined ratio [z/x]	109.9%	107.0%	104.1%	103.4%	102.6%	107.8%	105.9%	108.7%	111.0%	105.8%	98.4%

[1] Excludes premiums collected in advance.
[2] Equity is calculated as the average of the equity figure for the fourth quarter of the current year and the equity figure for the fourth quarter of the previous year.

Source: Insurance Bureau of Canada, Fact Book of the General Insurance Industry in Canada, 2004, page 16, *www.ibc.ca*. Used with permission.

commissions and other acquisition costs and general expense costs to premiums written. If the combined ratio is less than 100, premiums alone are sufficient to cover both losses and expenses related to the line.

If premiums are insufficient and the combined ratio exceeds 100, the P&C insurer must rely on investment income earned on premiums for overall profitability. For example, in 2001 the combined ratio before dividend payments was 111.0 percent, indicating that premiums alone were insufficient to cover the costs of both losses and expenses related to writing P&C insurance. Table 3–6 presents the combined ratio and its components for the P&C industry for the years 1993–2003, as well as the return on equity. We see that with the exception of 2003, when the combined ratio was 98.4 percent, the level of premiums was not sufficient to cover the losses and expenses. However, the return on equity was positive in every year, reaching a minimum of 1.7 percent in 2002.

Investment Yield/Return Risk   As discussed above, when the combined ratio is more than 100, overall profitability can be ensured only by a sufficient investment return on premiums earned. That is, P&C firms invest premiums in assets between the time they are received and the time they are paid out to meet claims. For example, in 2002 net investment income to premiums earned (or the P&C insurers' investment yield) was 8.9 percent ($2,248 \div \$25,334$). As a result, the overall average profitability (or **operating ratio**) of P&C insurers was 96.9. It was equal to the combined ratio after dividends (105.8) minus the investment yield (8.9). Since the operating ratio was less than 100, P&C insurers were profitable in 2002. However, lower net returns on investments (e.g., 5 percent rather than 8.9 percent) would have meant that underwriting P&C insurance was marginally unprofitable (i.e., the operating ratio of insurers in this case would have been 100.8). Thus, the effect of interest rates and default rates on P&C insurers' investments is crucial to P&C insurers' overall profitability. That is, measuring and managing credit and interest rate risk are key concerns of P&C managers.

> **operating ratio**
> A measure of the overall profitability of a P&C insurer; it equals the combined ratio minus the investment yield.

Consider the following example. Suppose an insurance company's projected loss ratio is 79.8 percent and its expense ratio is 27.9 percent. The combined ratio for this insurance company is equal to:

$$\text{Loss ratio} + \text{Expense ratio} = \text{Combined ratio}$$
$$79.8 \quad + \quad 27.9 \quad = \quad 107.7$$

Thus, expected losses on all P&C lines and expenses exceeded premiums earned by 7.7 percent.

If the company's investment portfolio, however, yielded 12 percent, the operating ratio and overall profitability of the P&C insurer would be:

$$\text{Operating ratio} = \text{Combined ratio after dividends} - \text{Investment yield}$$
$$= \quad\quad 107.7 \quad\quad - \quad 12.0$$
$$= \quad\quad 95.7 \text{ percent}$$

and

$$\text{Overall profitability} = 100 - \text{Operating ratio}$$
$$= 100 - 95.7$$
$$= 4.3 \text{ percent}$$

As can be seen, the high investment returns (12 percent) make the P&C insurer profitable overall.

Given the importance of investment returns to P&C insurers' profitability, we can see from the balance sheet in Table 3–5 that bonds—both government and corporate—dominated the asset portfolios. Bonds constituted 43.7 percent of total assets and 72.8 percent of total investments in 2004.

Finally, if losses, expenses, and other costs are higher and investment yields are lower than expected so that operating losses are incurred, P&C insurers carry reserves (0.2 percent of total assets in 2004) to reduce the risk of insolvency.

Recent Trends

Table 3–7 lists the claims and payments for natural disasters for property and automobile insurance in Canada from 1987–2004. The major source for insurance company losses came from storms (hail, flooding, winds, and tornados) across Canada. The ice storm of 1998, which affected Southern Quebec (730,169 claims, $1.48 billion) and Eastern Ontario (165,562 claims, $165.56 million), was the only incident in Canada where total payouts have exceeded one billion dollars. By way of contrast, insurance incidents in the United States regularly exceed US$1 billion. Reinsurance means that large payouts affect global insurance rates and therefore rates in Canada. For example, Hurricane Katrina in 2005 cost insurers over US$35 billion. Manulife's reinsurance losses related to Hurricane Katrina were estimated to be $135 million.

Although catastrophes may be random, the period 1987–2004 was characterized by a number of catastrophes of historically high severity. A succession of catastrophes meant that, in the terminology of insurers, the global industry was in the trough of an underwriting cycle, or underwriting conditions were hard. These cycles are characterized by periods of rising premiums leading to increased profitability, such as has been seen for the automobile insurance industry in Canada from 2000–2004 (Figure 3–3). Following a period of solid but not spectacular rates of returns, the industry enters a down phase in which premiums soften as the supply of insurance products increases. Most analysts agree that a cycle that affects all lines simultaneously is unlikely. As an example of how bad things can be in this industry, Lloyd's of London, one of the world's most well-known and respected insurers, posted a £510 million loss in 1991, a result of four years or unprecedented accident claims.

The year 2001 saw yet another blow to the insurance industry and the world with the terrorist attacks on the World Trade Center and the Pentagon. Because of the tremendous impact these attacks had on the health of the U.S. insurance industry, the Bush administration proposed that the U.S. government pay the majority of the losses of the insurance industry due to the attacks. The proposal capped insurers' 2002 liabilities at US$12 billion, 2003 liabilities at US$23 billion, and 2004 liabilities at US$36 billion. Despite this bailout of the industry, many insurers did not survive and those that did were forced to increase premiums significantly.[7]

The traditional reaction to losses or poor profit results has been the exit from the industry—through failure or acquisition—of less profitable firms and a rapid increase in premiums among the remaining firms. As shown in Table 3–6, the combined ratio for Canadian P&C insurers finally declined below 100 in 2003. The decline in the earned loss ratio and the operating expense ratio, as well as the higher ROE, is starting to draw new entrants such as Arch Capital Group which is Bermuda-based and has operations in the U.S. and Europe. Arch intends to focus on **Directors and Officers (D&O) insurance**.[8]

Directors and Officers (D&O) insurance
Insurance that protects corporate directors and senior managers from legal claims.

---

[7] See "The Risk That Nobody Wants," *The Economist*, November 17, 2001, pp. 66–68.

[8] See R. Marquez, "New P&C insurer on Canadian scene," *The Insurance Journal*, June/July 2005.

TABLE 3–7
Canadian Natural Disaster Property and Automobile Insurance Payments, 1987–2004

Source: Insurance Bureau of Canada, *Fact Book of the General Insurance Industry in Canada, 2004*, pp. 18–19; *The System is Working*, February, 2005, *www.ibc.ca*.

Date and Place	Event	Total # of Claims	Total Loss ($000)
1987 Edmonton, Alberta	Tornado	58,506	148,337
1991 Calgary, Alberta	Hail	116,311	342,745
1993 Winnipeg, Manitoba	Flooding	n.a.	184,837
1996 Winnipeg, Calgary	Flooding, hail	93,841	351,138
1996 Saguenay, Quebec	Flooding	6,461	207,159
1998 Southern Quebec, Eastern Ontario	Ice storm	792,514	1,641,608
2003 British Columbia	Fires	n.a.	250,000*
2003 Nova Scotia, Prince Edward Island	Hurricane Juan	n.a.	115,000*
2004 Edmonton	Hail, flooding	n.a.	170,000*
2004 Peterborough, Ontario	Flooding	n.a.	90,000*

*Estimate

In summary, major issues for the P&C industry in Canada are its image with consumers, particularly with respect to automobile insurance and the perceived "gouging" of consumers with high insurance rates. Consumer access to insurance affects the industry's relationship with the federal and provincial governments and regulators, particularly with the financial sector reform that may see the sale of insurance in the branches of the major banks.

Regulation

Similar to life insurance companies, regulation of the property and casualty insurance industry is shared by the provincial and federal governments. Property and casualty insurers may be incorporated federally or provincially. OSFI, the federal regulator, is responsible for over 75 percent of the companies. OSFI provides a Table of Guidelines that are specific to property and casualty insurers, including investment concentration limits, securities lending, asset securitization, derivatives best practices, earthquake exposure, outsourcing, impaired loans, and accounting guidelines. Provincial regulators govern the marketing and licensing of property and casualty insurers.

www.pacicc.ca

Canadian property and casualty policyholders are protected from the insolvency of their insurers, up to certain limits, by the Property and Casualty Insurance Compensation Corporation (PACICC), which is industry-run. All Canadian provinces require PACICC coverage prior to licensing. In addition, foreign insurers are required to vest assets in Canada so that their policy holders are protected.

The deterioration of P&C insurers, particularly the decline in capital levels, prompted the Secretary of State for International Financial Institutions to request a report on the P&C insurance industry in Canada. In its report released in 2003, OSFI concluded that the investment portfolios were prudent and returns from these investment portfolios were able to carry the industry despite higher claims and declining premiums.[9]

Concept Questions

1. Why do P&C insurers hold more capital and reserves than do life insurers?
2. Why are life insurers' assets, on average, longer in maturity than those of P&C insurers?
3. Describe the main lines of insurance offered by P&C insurers.
4. What are the components of the combined ratio?
5. How does the operating ratio differ from the combined ratio?
6. Why does the combined ratio tend to behave cyclically?

[9] See N. Le Pan, Report on the Property and Casualty (P&C) Insurance Industry in Canada, September 19, 2003, at www.osfic-bcif.gc.ca for a detailed analysis of the industry to 2002.

GLOBAL ISSUES

Like the other sectors of the financial institutions industry, the insurance sector is becoming increasingly global. Table 3–8 lists the top 10 countries in terms of total premiums written in 2003 (in U.S. dollars) and their percentage share of the world market. Panel A lists the data for life insurers, while panel B lists the data for P&C insurers. Table 3–9 lists the top 10 insurance companies worldwide by total revenues. While North America, Japan, and Western Europe dominate the global market, all regions are engaged in the insurance business and many insurers are engaged internationally.

Globalization has certainly affected the U.S. insurance market. In the early 2000s, insurers headquartered outside the United States accounted for over 10 percent of all premiums written in the United States. Because of lax regulations, such as lower capital regulations, many insurance companies have set up offices in the Cayman Islands and the Bahamas. Indeed, it has been estimated that 44 percent of the insurance companies selling life insurance in the Caribbean are from outside the region. The pressure of the global economy, the inability of local insurers to serve all domestic customers, and the domestic demand for better economic performance have caused governments around the world to introduce and accelerate insurance market reform. This includes improving insurance and insurance supervision by formulating common principles and practices across nations. One consequence of these changes is that there have been a number of mergers of insurance companies across country borders, such as the Dutch ING Group's 2000 acquisition of the U.S. Aetna for US $7.75 billion.

TABLE 3–8
The World's Top Countries in Terms of Insurance Premiums Written

Source: Swiss Re, sigma No 3/2004.

Rank	Country	Premiums Written (in billions of US$)	Share of World Market
Panel A: Life Insurers			
1	United States	480.9	28.8%
2	Japan	381.3	22.8
3	United Kingdom	154.8	9.3
4	France	105.4	6.3
5	Germany	76.7	4.6
6	Italy	71.7	4.3
7	South Korea	42.0	2.5
8	China	32.4	1.9
9	Netherlands	25.4	1.5
10	Switzerland	24.7	1.5
Panel B: Property–Casualty Insurers			
1	United States	574.6	45.3%
2	Japan	97.5	7.7
3	Germany	94.1	7.4
4	United Kingdom	91.9	7.2
5	France	58.2	4.6
6	Italy	40.1	3.2
7	Canada	36.3	2.9
8	Spain	27.0	2.1
9	Netherlands	24.9	2.0
10	Australia	18.0	1.4

TABLE 3–9
World's Largest Insurance Companies by Total Revenues

Source: Insurance Information Institute Web site, 2004. *www.iii.org*

Rank	Company	Revenues (in millions of US$)	Home Country
Panel A: Life Insurers			
1	ING Group	88,102	Netherlands
2	AXA Group	62,051	France
3	Nippon Life Insurance	61,175	Japan
4	Assicurazioni Generali	55,105	Italy
5	Aviva	53,723	United Kingdom
6	Dai-Ichi Mutual Life	46,445	Japan
7	Sumitomo Life Insurance	42,220	Japan
8	Prudential	39,410	United Kingdom
9	MetLife	33,967	United States
10	Aegon	26,803	Netherlands
Panel B: Property–Casualty Insurers			
1	Allianz	74,178	Germany
2	American International Group	44,637	United States
3	Munich Re Group	41,974	Germany
4	State Farm Insurance	40,656	United States
5	Berkshire Hathaway	39,962	United States
6	Zurich Financial Services	38,400	Switzerland
7	Allstate	26,959	United States
8	Millea Holdings	26,018	Japan
9	Swiss Reinsurance	24,028	Switzerland
10	Royal and Sun Alliance	20,953	United Kingdom

As with commercial banks, Japanese non-life insurance companies suffered severe losses in the early 2000s. Six of the nine major non-life insurance groups that announced earnings (for the April through December 2003 period) saw their net premiums drop relative to the prior year. The main factor in the decline was the sluggish performance of automobile insurance, which accounts for roughly half the revenue for these firms. The total net premiums of the nine groups declined 0.5 percent on the year to ¥4.9 trillion (US$46.4 billion). Life insurers did not fare much better. In 2004, many Japanese life insurers took steps to boost reserves and repair their capital bases after two very difficult years. The sector is expected to continue facing problems due to asset deflation, low interest rates, and a shrinking market for life insurance products.

The property and casualty insurance industry has agreed, at the urging of the Ontario government, to disclose commission compensation to the public in the wake of a controversy over hidden payments to brokers.

Ontario Finance Minister Greg Sorbara announced the deal with the insurers and brokers in the Legislature yesterday. Both Mr. Sorbara and the head of a national regulatory body said they expected the measure to be adopted across the country.

Mr. Sorbara said the government asked property and casualty insurance companies to tell consumers just how much of their home and auto insurance premiums are pocketed by brokers in the form of sales commissions.

"The principle behind all that we're doing is that greater transparency is one of the important keys to a stronger and more competitive market and a more informed consumer," Mr. Sorbara said in an interview.

The announcement was welcomed by Jim Hall, chairman of the Canadian Council of Insurance Regulators, an umbrella group that represents regulators from each province and the federal government.

"I think it's a great first step," said Mr. Hall, who is Saskatchewan's Superintendent of Insurance.

Mr. Sorbara added that the industry, "which is a pan-Canadian industry, will simply use the same practices, whether asked to or not, in other jurisdictions."

The government's move comes amid a controversy over lucrative incentives that insurance companies pay brokers on top of their normal fees.

Brokers typically receive two types of payments: base commissions of 12.5 per cent for auto insurance and 20 per cent for home insurance, which are deducted from premiums paid by consumers; and so-called contingent commissions, ranging from 1 to 2 per cent of net premiums, paid by the insurer based on the profitability of the business steered to the company by the broker.

While the practice of paying contingent commissions has been common in the industry for decades, it has been hidden from consumers because insurance companies and brokers are not required to publicly disclose these payments.

Property and casualty insurers paid out contingent commissions totalling $290-million last year, according to figures obtained by Report on Business.

While these payouts accounted for only a small slice of a broker's overall compensation, they had a huge impact on the insurance companies' overall profitability. For example, ING Insurance Co. of Canada paid out $45.7-million in contingent commissions last year, and posted a profit of $123.6-million. Dominion of Canada General Insurance Co. paid $26.7-million in contingent commissions, a figure that exceeded its profit of $20.3-million.

Mr. Sorbara said in the Ontario Legislature that the industry has voluntarily agreed to bring in a new system of disclosure for both base and contingent commissions.

He said the details of precisely how such disclosure will be made to consumers will be determined by provincial insurance regulators, in consultation with the industry.

Stan Griffin, president of the Insurance Bureau of Canada, said his organization will work with the industry on a new disclosure policy. He said the new system could involve information brochures to clients listing commissions, or postings on websites.

"We have no opposition to the concept of disclosure. It's a question of how we are going to achieve it most effectively," he said.

Bruce Cran, president of the Consumers Association of Canada, was unimpressed with the announcement, which he described as a "Band-Aid" solution because the disclosure will not be mandatory. "I've been dealing with consumer issues for 40 years and I have never seen a single voluntary structure that's been put forward in any industry function properly. I'm disappointed if that's the best they can do."

Both provincial Opposition members and the Ontario Trial Lawyers Association called on the government yesterday to set up an independent public inquiry into the industry.

"These payments have been challenged in the U.S. Now, these practices appear to be affecting citizens of Ontario and must be investigated immediately," Robert Munroe, president of the association, said in a statement.

"Brokers are expected to advise their customers about insurance products best suited for their needs and not to simply steer business to a company in return for a commission that is hidden from the customer," he said.

Many of Canada's big insurers, including ING Canada, Manulife Financial Corp. and Sun Life Financial Inc., are reviewing their commission practices, while some of the big multinational brokers that operate here have stopped taking contingent commissions.

Mr. Sorbara said in the Legislature that there is no evidence here of the kind of allegations that have been levelled in the United States against Marsh & McLennan Cos. Inc.

Notwithstanding that, he said, Ontario has asked the Financial Services Commission of Ontario, which is responsible for regulating market conduct of insurance companies in the province, to review a range of industry practices.

Marsh was accused of bid rigging in a civil suit launched by New York Attorney-General Eliot Spitzer this month. The lawsuit has sparked regulatory probes across the United States and opened up contingent commissions to scrutiny. In Canada, insurance regulators say they reviewing these payments.

Source: By Karen Howlett and Paul Waldie, *The Globe and Mail*, Page B1, October 28, 2004. Reprinted with permission from *The Globe and Mail*.

Summary

This chapter examined the activities and regulation of insurance companies. The first part of the chapter described the various classes of life insurance and recent trends. The second part covered property and casualty companies. The various lines that make up property and casualty insurance are becoming increasingly blurred as multiple activity line coverages are offered. Both life and property and casualty are coming under threat from other financial service firms that offer similar or competitive products.

Questions and Problems

1. What is the primary function of an insurance company? How does this function compare with the primary function of a deposit-taking institution?
2. What is the adverse selection problem? How does adverse selection affect the profitable management of an insurance company?
3. What are the similarities and differences among the four basic lines of life insurance products?
4. Explain how annuity activities represent the reverse of life insurance activities.
5. Explain how life insurance and annuity products can be used to create a steady stream of cash disbursements and payments to avoid paying or receiving a single lump-sum cash amount.
6. a. Calculate the annual cash flows of a $1 million, 20-year fixed-payment annuity earning a guaranteed 10 percent per annum if payments are to begin at the end of the current year.
   b. Calculate the annual cash flows of a $1 million, 20-year fixed-payment annuity earning a guaranteed 10 percent per annum if payments are to begin at the end of year 5.
   c. What is the amount of the annuity purchase required if you wish to receive a fixed payment of $200,000 for 20 years? Assume that the annuity will earn 10 percent per annum.
7. You deposit $10,000 annually into a life insurance fund for the next 10 years, after which time you plan to retire.
   a. If the deposits are made at the beginning of the year and earn an interest rate of 8 percent, what will be the amount of retirement funds at the end of year 10?
   b. Instead of a lump sum, you wish to receive annuities for the next 20 years (years 11 through 30). What is the constant annual payment you expect to receive at the beginning of each year if you assume an interest rate of 8 percent during the distribution period?
   c. Repeat parts (a) and (b) above assuming earning rates of 7 percent and 9 percent during the deposit period and earning rates of 7 percent and 9 percent during the distribution period. During which period does the change in the earning rate have the greatest impact?

8. a. Suppose a 65-year-old person wants to purchase an annuity from an insurance company that would pay $20,000 per year until the end of that person's life. The insurance company expects this person to live for 15 more years and would be willing to pay 6 percent on the annuity. How much should the insurance company ask this person to pay for the annuity?
   b. A second 65-year-old person wants the same $20,000 annuity, but this person is much healthier and is expected to live for 20 years. If the same 6 percent interest rate applies, how much should this healthier person be charged for the annuity?
   c. In each case, what is the difference in the purchase price of the annuity if the distribution payments are made at the beginning of the year?
9. Contrast the balance sheet of a life insurance company with the balance sheet of a bank. Explain the balance sheet differences in terms of the differences in the primary functions of the two organizations.
10. Using the data in Table 3–2, how has the composition of assets of Canadian life insurance companies changed over time?
11. How do life insurance companies earn a profit?
12. How would the balance sheet of a life insurance company change if it offered to run a private pension fund for another company?
13. How does the regulation of insurance companies differ from the regulation of deposit-taking institutions?
14. How do guarantee funds for life insurance companies compare with deposit insurance for banks?
15. What are the two major activity lines of property and casualty insurance firms?
16. How have the product lines of property and casualty insurance companies changed over time?
17. Contrast the balance sheet of a property and casualty insurance company with the balance sheet of a bank. Explain the balance sheet differences in terms of the differences in the primary functions of the two organizations.

18. What are the three sources of underwriting risk in the property and casualty insurance industry?

19. How do unexpected increases in inflation affect property and casualty insurers?

20. Identify the four characteristics or features of the perils insured against by property and casualty insurance. Rank the features in terms of actuarial predictability and total loss potential.

21. Insurance companies will charge a higher premium for which of the insurance lines listed below? Why?

    a. Low-severity, high-frequency lines versus high-severity, low-frequency lines.

    b. Long-tail lines versus short-tail lines.

22. What does the loss ratio measure? What has been the long-term trend of the loss ratio? Why?

23. What does the expense ratio measure? Identify and explain the two major sources of expense risk to a property and casualty insurer. Why has the long-term trend in this ratio been decreasing?

24. How is the combined ratio defined? What does it measure?

25. What is the investment yield on premiums earned? Why has this ratio become so important to property and casualty insurers?

26. Use the data in Table 3–6. Since 1993, what has been the necessary investment yield for the industry to enable the operating ratio to be less than 100 in each year? How is this requirement related to the interest rate risk and credit risk faced by a property and casualty insurer?

27. An insurance company's projected loss ratio is 77.5 percent, and its loss adjustment expense ratio is 12.9 percent. The company estimates that commission payments will be 16 percent. What must be the minimum yield on investments to achieve a positive operating ratio?

28. a. What is the combined ratio for a property insurer who has a simple loss ratio of 73 percent, a loss adjustment expense of 12.5 percent, and a ratio of commissions and other acquisition expenses of 18 percent?

    b. What is the combined ratio adjusted for investment yield if the company earns an investment yield of 8 percent?

29. An insurance company collected $3.6 million in premiums and disbursed $1.96 million in losses. Loss adjustment expenses amounted to 6.6 percent. The total income generated from the company's investments was $170,000 after all expenses were paid. What is the net profitability in dollars?

Web Questions

30. Go to OSFI's Web site at **www.osfi-bsif.gc.ca**. Download the latest balance sheet for the life insurance industry as follows. Click on "Life Insurance Companies & Fraternals." Click on "Financial Data – Life Insurance Companies." Click on "Submit" to see the latest Total Assets for Canadian Life Insurers. How has the asset composition changed from Table 3–2? How many life insurance companies are regulated by OSFI? Submit a request for the Assets of Manulife, Sunlife, and Great-West Life. How have their total assets changed from Table 3–1?

31. Go to the Insurance Bureau of Canada's Web site at **www.ibc.ca** and download the latest version of the Fact Book of the General Insurance Industry in Canada. How has the return on equity, earned loss ratio, operating expense ratio and combined ratio changed since 2003? Have Canadian property and casualty insurers maintained their combined ratio below 100 percent? Have Canadian property and casualty insurers shown an underwriting loss or gain annually since 2003? Calculate the return on investment (net investment income/net premiums earned). Has the return on investment helped the industry?

The Financial Services Industry: Securities Firms and Investment Banks

In this chapter we present an overview of securities firms and investment banks in terms of:

▸ the size, structure and composition of the industry

▸ balance sheets and recent trends

▸ regulation of the industry

▸ global competition and trends in the industry

INTRODUCTION

broker-dealers
Securities firms that assist in the trading of existing securities.

investment banks
Firms that specialize in originating, underwriting, and distributing issues of new securities.

The securities industry in Canada performs two functions: (1) the raising of debt and equity securities, including the origination, underwriting, and placement of securities in money and capital markets for corporate or government issuers and (2) assistance in the trading of securities in the secondary markets including brokerage services and/or market making. Firms in the securities industry that specialize in the purchase, sale, and brokerage of existing securities (the retail side of the business) are called **broker-dealers**, whereas firms that specialize in originating, underwriting, and distributing issues of new securities are called **investment banks**.

Investment banking also includes corporate finance activities such as advising on mergers and acquisitions (M&As), as well as advising on the restructuring of existing corporations. Figure 4–1 reports merger activity for Canada for 1994–2004. Merger and acquisition activity on a year-to-year dollar basis increased from less than $50 billion in 1994 to over $200 billion in 2000. Merger activity fell between 2001 and 2003, but the industry picked up again in 2004 led by two large cross-border deals, the acquisition of Banknorth Group Inc. by Toronto-Dominion Bank, the largest deal at $4.97 billion, and the merger of Molson Inc. with Adolph Coors Company, a $4.53 billion deal. Merger activity in Canada parallels that of the United States as shown in Figure 4–2, which has the same peak in merger and acquisition activity in 2000 but with much larger deals totalling over US$1,800 billion at its peak. Canadian investment banks are in direct competition domestically with the major Wall Street investment firms (Merrill Lynch, JP Morgan, Goldman Sachs, Citigroup, Credit Suisse First Boston), which lead the world in terms of size, experience, research capability, and relationships. In fact, the history of the investment industry since the 1980s can be viewed as one of consolidation within Canada and increasing competition with globally dominant firms.[1]

---

[1] See Department of Finance, Canada, "Canada's Securities Industry," January 2005 (or the latest version) for a history and summary of the securities industry. See also the most recent "Capital Markets Report" produced by the Financial Markets Division of the Financial Sector Policy Branch available at www.fin.gc.ca. The Investment Dealer's Association of Canada publishes the *Chartbook: Securities Industry & Capital Markets Developments* annually that is available at their Web site at www.ida.ca.

FIGURE 4–1   Merger and Acquisitions in Canada, 1994–2004

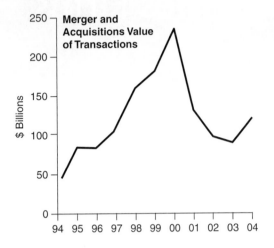

Source: Investment Dealers Association Chartbook, June 2005, page 7

FIGURE 4–2   U.S. Mergers and acquistions 1990–2003

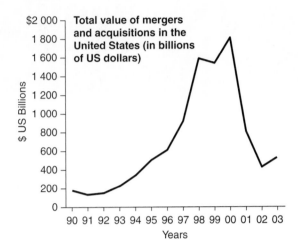

Source: Thomson Financial Securities Data, 2004. *www.tfibcm.com*

SIZE, STRUCTURE, AND COMPOSITION OF THE INDUSTRY

integrated firm
A securities firm offering a full range investment services to retail, institutional, and corporate customers.

underwriting
Assisting in the issue of new securities.

regulatory capital
Capital and margin requirements, including shareholders' equity and subordinated debt, as defined by the Investment Dealer's Association of Canada for its members.

Investment Dealer's Association of Canada (IDA)
The self-regulating organization (SRO) responsible for the regulation of its members in Canada.

The current structure of the securities industry dates back to the mid-to-late 1980s when the federal and provincial governments changed the Bank Act to allow banks, trust companies, and foreign firms to operate in the industry. This resulted in many securities firms, previously wholly-owned and operated as partnerships, being taken over by the major banks, creating the six largest integrated bank-owned firms (BMO Nesbitt Burns, CIBC World Markets, National Bank Financial, RBC Dominion Securities Limited, Scotia Capital, and TD Securities). The global stock market crash of 1987 accelerated the consolidation by making investment dealers cheap to acquire). Table 4–2 shows the investment firms acquired and the year of acquisition for the largest investment dealers in Canada ranked by their revenue in 2004.

As shown in Table 4–2, the Canadian securities industry can be divided into integrated, institutional, and retail firms based on their activities as follows:

(1) **integrated firms:** The integrated firms service retail customers (especially in acting as broker-dealers, assisting in the trading of existing securities) and corporate customers (such as **underwriting**, assisting in the issue of new securities), as well as institutional customers (servicing other FIs such as insurance companies, mutual funds, banks, trust companies, and pension funds). The 12 integrated firms generated 70.4 percent of the total operating revenue of the securities industry in 2004 and, as well, represented 53.1 percent of the total shareholders' equity of $8.372 billion and 61.1 percent of the **regulatory capital** (shareholders' equity and subordinated debt as defined by Regulation 100 of the **Investment Dealer's Association of Canada (IDA)**, for its members) of $15.1 billion as shown in Table 4–2. They derived 38 percent of their revenue from mutual fund and other commissions, followed by investment banking (new equity issues, 17.7 percent, new debt issues, 5.1 percent, and corporate advisory fees, 3.2 percent). Other fee income represented 11.9 percent of their operating revenue in 2004. The integrated firms had the highest return at 24 percent.

TABLE 4–1
Canadian Bank
Investment Firm
Acquisitions,
1987–1996

Source: Company Web sites
and Annual Reports, *The
Globe and Mail* Report on
Business One Thousand
2005, p. 87.

Firm	2004 Revenue ($ millions)	Company Acquired, Year of Acquisition
1. RBC Dominion Securities	3,751.0	Dominion Securities, 1988 Pemberton Willoughby Investment Co. 1989 McNeil Mantha, 1991 Richardson Greenshields, 1996
2. CIBC World Markets	3,521.0	Wood Gundy Inc., 1988
3. TD Securities	2,215.0	Marathon Brokerage, 1993
4. Scotia Capital	2,210.0	McLeod, Young, Weir, 1987
5. National Bank Financial	990.2	Lévesque Beaubien Geoffrion, 1988 First Marathon Securities, 1993
6. BMO Nesbitt Burns	n.a.*	Nesbitt Thomson, 1987 Burns Fry, 1994

*Note: BMO Nesbitt Burns had revenue for 2003 of $1,148.9 million, the last date for which information was available which
would have ranked the company fifth in 2004.

Institutional firm
A securities firm
offering services only
to other financial
institutions such as
insurance companies,
mutual funds, banks,
trust companies, and
pension funds.

retail firm
A securities firm
offering investment
services only to retail
investors, either at
full-service or on a
discount basis.

full service retail
A securities firm
which provides all
services to clients,
including back-office
functions.

retail introducer
A securities firm which
contracts with a full
service firm to carry
out specified trading
functions on its behalf.

discount brokers
Stockbrokers that con-
duct trades for cus-
tomers but do not offer
investment advice.

(2) **Institutional firms:** They offer investment services primarily to other FIs. These firms may be domestic (e.g. Maison Placements Canada Inc.) or subsidiaries of U.S. or European firms (e.g. Deutsche Bank Securities). As shown in Table 4–2, there are 48 domestic and 16 foreign institutional firms who generated 12.9 percent of the total operating revenue for the industry, but whose combined annual return in 2004 was much lower than the integrated firms at 10 percent. The major source of income for these firms in 2004 came from investment banking activities, particu- larly new equity issues. Commission fees are also important.

(3) **Retail firms:** They act primarily as investment advisors and brokers for retail customers. Retail firms can be divided into **full service retail** and **retail intro- ducer** firms. They also include specialized **discount brokers** who carry out trades for customers online or offline without offering investment advice or tips and usu- ally charge lower commissions than do full-service retail firms. As shown in Table 4–2, the revenue of retail firms comes from commissions on mutual funds as well as other securities. Retail firms provided 16.6 percent of the revenue of the industry in 2004, ranking behind the integrated firms.

In addition, there are specialized electronic trading securities firms (such as E*trade Canada, at www.canada.etrade.com) that provide a platform for cus- tomers to trade without the use of a broker. These trades are enacted on a com- puter via the internet. Also, venture capital firms pool money from individual investors and other FIs (e.g., hedge funds, pension funds, and insurance compa- nies) to fund relatively small new businesses (e.g., in biotechnology).[2]

Securities firms engage in as many as seven key activity areas.[3] Note that while each activity is available to a firm's customers independently, many of these activi- ties can be and are conducted simultaneously, such as mergers and acquisitions financed by new issues of debt and equity underwritten by the M&A advising firm.[4]

---

[2] Venture capital firms generally play an active management role in the firms in which they invest, often including a seat on the board of directors, and hold significant equity stakes. This differentiates them from traditional banking and securities firms.

[3] See Ernest Bloch, *Inside Investment Banking*, 2nd Ed. (Chicago: Irwin), for a similar list.

[4] See, for example, L. Allen, J. Jagtiani, S. Peristiani, and A. Saunders, "The Role of Bank Advisors in Mergers and Acquisitions," *Journal of Money, Credit and Banking* 3, no. 2 (April 2004), pp. 197–224.

TABLE 4–2   Structure and Statistics of the Securities Industry in Canada, 2004 (millions of dollars)

	Industry Total	Integrated Firms	Institutional	Retail Full Service	Retail Introducer
Number of firms	205	12	64	35	94
Number of employees	37,739	24,494	2,200	6,142	4,903
Shareholders' Equity	8,372	4,443	3,006	618	304
Regulatory Capital	15,108	9,228	4,497	887	497
Client Cash Holdings	22,109	18,918	591	2,043	557
Client Margin Debt Outstanding	9,478				
Annual Return (net profit/shareholders' equity)	20%	24%	10%	7%	6%
Revenue:					
Commission:					
Mutual Funds	1,413	12.0%	0.0%	20.8%	16.2%
Other	3,372	25.5%	30.0%	37.7%	32.1%
Investment Banking:					
New equity issues	2,172	17.7%	27.5%	11.1%	11.6%
New debt issues	502	5.1%	2.8%	1.7%	0.6%
Corporate advisory fees	446	3.2%	10.3%	0.7%	0.6%
Fixed Income Trading	595	6.3%	0.6%	2.2%	2.7%
Equity Trading	644	5.8%	5.1%	2.5%	4.5%
Net Interest	1,042	9.7%	5.7%	6.5%	5.8%
Fees	1,401	11.9%	3.2%	13.9%	20.4%
Other	793	2.9%	20.3%	2.8%	5.5%
Total revenue	12,380	100.0%	100.0%	100.0%	100.0%
Total Revenue	12,151	8,558	1,568	1,209	817
Percentage of industry total revenue	100.0%	70.4%	12.9%	9.9%	6.7%

Source: Investment Dealer's Association of Canada, *Securities Industry Performance First Quarter 2005*, www.ida.ca

1. Investing

www.tse.com

Investing involves managing not only pools of assets such as closed- and open-end mutual funds but also pension funds in competition with life insurance companies. Securities firms can manage such funds either as agents for other investors or as principals for themselves. The objective in funds management is to choose asset allocations to beat some return-risk performance benchmark such as the S&P TSX Composite Index or the S&P 500 index.[5] Since this business generates fees that are based on the size of the pool of assets managed, it tends to produce a more stable flow of income than does either investment banking or trading (discussed next).

2. Investment Banking

IPO

An initial, or first-time, public offering of debt or equity by a corporation.

Investment banking refers to activities related to underwriting and distributing new issues of debt and equity. New issues can be either primary, the first-time issues of companies (sometimes called **IPOs** [initial public offerings]), or secondary issues (the new issues of seasoned firms whose debt or equity is already trading). In recent years public confidence in the integrity of the IPO process has eroded significantly. Investigations have revealed that certain underwriters of IPOs have engaged in conduct contrary to the best interests of investors and the markets. Among the most harmful practices that have given rise to public concerns are spinning (in which cer-

---

[5] Or the "securities market line" given the fund's "beta."

FIGURE 4–3
Common Equity
Financings in
Canada, 2000
to Q1 2005

Source: Investment Dealer's
Association of Canada,
*Securities Industry Performance
First Quarter 2005, www.ida.ca*

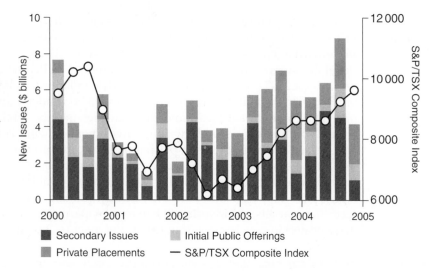

FIGURE 4–4
Securities Industry
Operating Profit,
1994–2004

Source: Investment Dealers
Association of Canada
Chartbook, June 2005

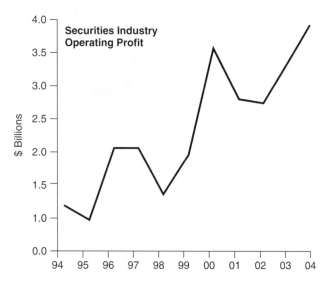

tain underwriters allocate "hot" IPO issues to directors and/or executives of potential investment banking clients in exchange for investment banking business) and
biased recommendations by research analysts (due to their compensation being tied
to the success of their firms' investment banking business). We discuss these issues
and some of the legal proceedings resulting from these practices below.[6]

Figure 4–3 shows the dollar value of common equity issues (secondary issues,
IPOs, private placements) from 2000 to Q1-2005. Higher levels of the S&P/TSX composite index result in higher levels of equity financing and higher levels of operating
profit for the industry as shown in Figure 4–4 with a record profit of $3.7 billion in
2004 following the downturn in 2001, 2002, and 2003.

---

[6] R. Aggarwal, N. R. Prabhala, and M. Puri, in "Institutional Allocation in Initial Public Offerings: Empirical Evidence," *The Journal of Finance*, June 2002, pp. 1421–42, document a positive relationship between institutional allocation and day-one IPO returns. The result is partly explained by the practice of giving institutions more shares in IPOs with strong premarket demand.

private placement
A securities issue placed with one or a few large institutional investors.

Securities underwritings can be undertaken through either public offerings or private offerings. In a private offering, the investment banker acts as a **private placement** agent for a fee, placing the securities with one or a few large institutional investors such as life insurance companies. The IDA's Directory of member services for 2005 lists 9 firms involved in private placements, including BMO Nesbitt Burns. In a public offering, the securities may be underwritten on a best-efforts or a firm commitment basis, and the securities may be offered to the public at large. With best-efforts underwriting, investment bankers act as *agents* on a fee basis related to their success in placing the issue. In firm commitment underwriting, the investment banker acts as a *principal,* purchasing the securities from the issuer at one price and seeking to place them with public investors at a slightly higher price. Finally, in addition to investment banking operations in the corporate securities markets, the investment banker may participate as an underwriter (primary dealer) in government, municipal, and asset-backed securities.

INTERNET EXERCISE

Go to the Thomson Financial Investment Banking/Capital Markets group Web site (**www.tfibcm.com**) and find the latest information available for top global underwriters of various securities.

Go to the Thomson Financial Investment Banking/Capital Markets group Web site at **www.tfibcm.com**. Click on "View the latest League Table Online." Click on "Debt & Equity." Under Press Releases, click on "Global Capital Markets Press Releases." This will download a file to your computer that will contain the most recent information on top underwriters for various securities.

3. *Market Making*

Market making involves creating a secondary market in an asset by a securities firm or investment bank. Thus, in addition to being primary dealers in government securities and underwriters of corporate bonds and equities, investment bankers make a secondary market in these instruments. Market making can involve either agency or principal transactions. *Agency* transactions are two-way transactions on behalf of *customers,* for example, acting as a *stockbroker* or dealer for a fee or commission. On the TSX, a market maker in a stock may, upon the placement of orders by its customers, buy the stock at $78 from one customer and immediately resell it at $79 to another customer. The $1 difference between the buy and sell price is usually called the bid–ask spread and represents a large portion of the market maker's profit. Many securities firms offer online trading services to their customers as well as direct access to a client representative (stockbroker). Thus, customers may now conduct trading activities from their homes and offices through their accounts at securities firms at a lower cost in terms of fees and commissions. Purely electronic securities trading firms offer investors (day traders) high-speed access to the stock markets. Accordingly, technology risk is an increasingly important issue for these FIs (see Chapter 14).

In *principal* transactions, the market maker seeks to profit on the price movements of securities and takes either long or short inventory positions for its own account. (Or an inventory position may be taken to stabilize the market in the securities.) In the example above, the market maker would buy the stock at $78 and hold it in its own portfolio in expectation of a price increase later on. Normally, market making can be a fairly profitable business; however, in periods of market stress or high volatility, these profits can rapidly disappear. For example, on the NYSE, market makers, in return for having monopoly power in market making for individual stocks (e.g., IBM), have an affirmative obligation to buy stocks from sellers even when the market is crashing. This caused a number of actual and near bankruptcies for NYSE market makers at the time of the October 1987 market crash. On NASDAQ, which has a system of competing market makers, liquidity was significantly impaired at the time of the crash and a number of firms had to withdraw from market making.[7] Finally, the recent moves toward decimalization of equities markets in the United States (i.e., expressing quotes in integers of 1 cent [e.g., $50.32] rather than rounding to eighths [e.g., 50 $^3/_8$]) has cut into traders' profits, as has competition from Internet-based or electronic-based exchanges such at The Island ECN and GlobeNet ECN.[8]

4. Trading

Trading is closely related to the market-making activities just described, where a trader takes an active net position in an underlying instrument or asset. There are at least four types of trading activities:

1. *Position trading* involves purchasing large blocks of securities on the expectation of a favourable price move. Such positions also facilitate the smooth functioning of the secondary markets in such securities.

2. *Pure arbitrage* entails buying an asset in one market at one price and selling it immediately in another market at a higher price.

3. *Risk arbitrage* involves buying blocks of securities in anticipation of some information release, such as a merger or takeover announcement or an interest rate announcement.[9]

4. *Program trading* is defined is the simultaneous buying and selling of a large portfolio of different stocks using computer programs to initiate such trades. Program trading is often associated with seeking a risk arbitrage between a cash market price and the *futures* market price of that instrument.

As with many activities of securities firms, such trading can be conducted on behalf of a customer as an agent (or broker), or on behalf of the firm as a principal.

5. Cash Management and Banking Services

Retail investment firms offer their customers the ability to invest in shares through a cash account, or to borrow on margin. As shown in Table 4–2, client cash holdings in the industry equalled $22.1 billion and margin debt outstanding, a credit risk for the securities firms, equalled $9.5 billion. The integrated firms owned by the major banks are able to offer their retail, business, and corporate clients on-line access to banking and investment accounts in addition to services such as investment advice, **private banking** (domestic and global), trust services, investment management, and financial planning.

private banking
The provision of wealth management services for high net worth clients.

---

[7] See, for example, W. A. Christie and P. H. Schultz, "Dealer Markets under Stress: The Performance of NASDAQ Market Makers during the November 15, 1991, Market Break," *Journal of Financial Services Research* 13 (June 1998), pp. 205–30.

[8] See, for example, R. Bloomfield, M. O'Hara, and G. Saar, "The Make or Take Decision in an Electronic Market: Evidence on the Evolution of Liquidity," *Journal of Financial Economics*, 75 (2005), pp. 165–199 and M.D. Griffiths, B.F. Smith, D.A.S. Turnbull, and R.W. White, "The Role of Tick Size in Upstairs Trading and Downstairs Trading," *Journal of Financial Intermediation* 7, pp. 393–417 (1998).

[9] It is termed *risk arbitrage* because if the event does not actually occur—for example, if a merger does not take place or the Bank of Canada does not change interest rates—the trader stands to lose money.

6. *Mergers and Acquisitions*

Investment banks are frequently involved in providing advice or assisting in mergers and acquisitions. For example, they will assist in finding merger partners, underwriting new securities to be issued by the merged firms, assessing the value of target firms, recommending terms of the merger agreement, and even helping target firms prevent a merger (for example, seeing that poison-pill provisions are written into a potential target firm's securities contracts). As noted in the introduction to this chapter, merger and acquisition activity stood at $525 billion in 2003. Table 4–3 lists the top ten financial advisors for Canadian completed mergers and acquisitions in 2004, ranked by market share based on value of transactions (in US dollars for easy comparison with the global rankings presented in Table 4–4) of the deals in which they participated. The total market for M&As in Canada in 2004 was $86.5 billion and 649 deals, a significant improvement over the period from 2001–2003. Only 19 of these deals were greater than $1 billion, with the majority (339) between $1 million and $100 million. While foreign firms including the U.S. heavyweights Merrill Lynch, JP Morgan, Goldman Sachs and Citigroup, rank in the top 10, the five large Canadian bank-owned integrated firms also have a presence in M&A advising, particularly for cross-border deals.[10] However, ranking and market share each year depend on the size and the number of deals in which investment advisors are able to participate. As shown in Table 4–4, Canadian deals are small compared to the worldwide completed mergers and acquisitions of US$1.516 trillion in 2004. The bank-owned integrated firms (e.g. CIBC World Markets) are active participants on Wall Street, providing expertise in resource financing, particularly oil and gas and mining.[11] Worldwide in 2004, the Americas ranked first in mergers and acquisitions with 54.6 percent of the total, followed by Europe at 28.1 percent, Asia-Pacific at 9.1 percent, Japan at 4.5 percent, and Africa/Middle East at 0.76 percent.

7. *Back-Office and Other Service Functions*

These functions include custody and escrow services, clearance and settlement services, and research and other advisory services—for example, giving advice on divestitures and asset sales. In performing these functions, a securities firm normally acts as an agent for a fee. As mentioned above, fees charged are often based on the total bundle of services performed for the client by the firm. The portion of the fee or commission allocated to research and advisory services is called soft dollars. When one area in the firm, such as an investment advisor, uses client commissions to buy research from another area in the firm, it receives a benefit because it is relieved from the need to produce and pay for the research itself. Thus, the advisor using soft dollars faces a conflict of interest between the need to obtain research and the client's interest in paying the lowest commission rate available.

income trust
A publicly-traded security created when, rather than issue shares, a firm places specific assets into a trust vehicle and distributes the income to investors, usually on a tax-free basis.

[10] The Canadian market is expected to be fueled by **income trusts**, a relatively new investment vehicle unique to the Canadian market, as trusts are added to the TSX index in 2006. See Investment Dealers Association of Canada, "Canada's M&A Activity: Headin' South, Eh?" January 2005 at www.ida.ca for a discussion of M&As in Canada. See also T. Ebden, "Paving the way for a fair exchange: Adding income trusts to the S&P/TSX composite index next spring is designed to help it better reflect Canada's economy," The *Globe and Mail*, June 29, 2005, p. E1.

[11] Often, in addition to providing M&A advisory services, an investment banker will be involved in underwriting new securities that help finance an M&A. See L. Allen, J. Jagtiani, S. Peristiani and A. Saunders, "The Role of Financial Advisors in Mergers and Acquisitions," *Journal of Money, Credit, and Banking* 36, no. 2 (April 2004), pp. 197–224. A. Saunders and A. Srinivasan, in "Investment Banking Relationships and Merger Fees," 2002, Working Paper, New York University, investigate the effect of prior investment banking relationships on merger advisory fees paid by acquiring firms. Their findings indicate that acquiring firms perceive benefits of retaining merger advisors with whom they have had a prior relationship (even at a cost of higher fees) and/or they face some other (higher) costs of switching to new bank advisors. Finally, V. Ivashina, V. Nair, A. Saunders, N. Massoud, and R. Stover, in "The Role of Banks in Takeovers," 2004, Working Paper, New York University, show that banks use the information generated in lending to increase the probability of takeovers.

TABLE 4–3
The Top Canadian
Advisors in 2004

Source: IDA, Capital Markets:
Notes and Commentaries,
January 2005, p. 5

Advisor	Market Share	Value (US$ billions)	Transactions
Merrill Lynch	19.3%	15.4	12
TD Securities	14.1%	11.2	18
Deutsche Bank	13.7%	10.9	9
CIBC World Markets Inc.	13.7%	10.9	41
BMO Nesbitt Burns Inc.	12.1%	9.6	21
JP Morgan	11.8%	9.4	13
Goldman Sachs	11.2%	8.9	13
Citigroup	8.2	6.5	6
RBC Capital Markets	6.5%	5.2	29
Scotia Capital Inc.	6.2%	4.9	14

Source: Bloomberg

TABLE 4–4   The Twenty-five Largest Financial Advisors Worldwide for Completed Mergers & Acquisitions, 2003 and 2004

Advisor	1/1/2004–12/31/2004				1/1/2003–12/31/2003	
	Number of Deals	Rank	Market Share	Rank Value $US mil	Number of Deals	Rank
KPMG Corporate Finance	361	1	1.7	18,898.7	385	1
JP Morgan	324	2	1.6	321,895.0	266	5
Citigroup	308	3	1.5	282,848.5	291	2
Goldman Sachs & Co	290	4	1.4	500,244.3	284	3
Morgan Stanley	277	5	1.3	355,163.5	248	6
UBS	247	6	1.2	203,958.8	240	7
Credit Suisse First Boston	242	7	1.2	166,783.1	272	4
Rothschild	226	8	1.1	145,353.6	190	10
Merrill Lynch & Co Inc.	200	9	1.0	317,034.8	166	12
Ernst & Young LLP	192	10	0.9	17,246.7	116	17
PricewaterhouseCoopers	189	11	0.9	24,369.1	205	8
Lazard	184	12	0.9	187,885.4	178	11
Deutsche Bank AG	167	13*	0.8	128,915.1	193	9
Lehman Brothers	167	13*	0.8	239,154.9	159	13
ABN AMRO	136	15	0.7	66,390.9	127	14
Houlihan Lokey Howard & Zukin	125	16	0.6	28,422.5	108	20
Nomura	114	17	0.6	26,477.0	122	15
Mizuho Financial Group	112	18	0.5	9,171.3	110	19
BNP Paribas SA	88	19	0.4	113,386.7	67	27
Banc of America Securities LLC	82	20*	0.4	122,780.0	88	21
Deloitte & Tuche LLP	82	20*	0.4	6,377.0	117	16
Daiwa Securities SMBC	81	22	0.4	18,082.8	57	29*
Jefferies & Co Inc	72	23	0.4	8,026.6	72	25
Mitsubishi Tokyo Fin'l Group	70	24	0.3	7,078.7	43	37
M&A International (France)	66	25	0.3	1,906.4	49	35
Subtotal with Financial Advisor	5,328	–	25.7	1,346,785.9	5,079	–
Subtotal without Financial Advisor	15,395	–	74.3	169,293.9	15,120	–
Industry Total	20,723	–	100.0	1,516,079.8	20,199	–

Source: Thomson Financial Securities Data Company 2005, www.tfibcm.com

FIGURE 4–5
Commission Income as a Percentage of Total Revenues

Source: Investment Dealers Association of Canada, *www.ida.ca*

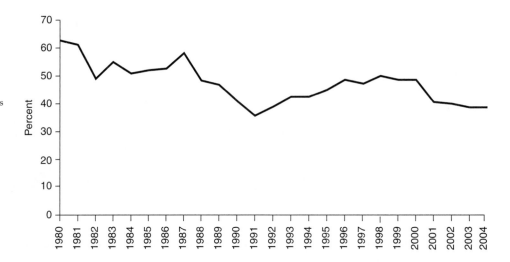

TABLE 4–5   Securities Industry Total Revenue by Source, 1987–2004

Revenue Source:	2004	2003	2002	2001	2000	1995	1990	1988	1987
Commissions	38%	38%	40%	41%	48%	45%	41%	47%	58%
Investment banking	25%	25%	22%	21%	17%	19%	18%	20%	20%
Fixed Income Trading	5%	7%	9%	10%	5%	14%	20%	11%	6%
Equity Trading	5%	6%	3%	4%	9%	5%	-2%	6%	6%
Net Interest	8%	10%	10%	11%	10%	10%	15%	9%	6%
Other	18%	13%	16%	13%	10%	8%	7%	6%	5%
Total	100%	100%	100%	100%	100%	100%	100%	100%	100%
Mutual Fund Commissions (as a percentage of total)	11%	10%	12%	12%	12%	9%	3%	2%	2%

Source: Investment Dealers Association of Canada, www.ida.ca

Concept Questions

1. Describe the difference between brokerage services and underwriting services.
2. What are the key areas of activities for securities firms?
3. Describe the difference between a best-efforts offering and a firm commitment offering.
4. What are the trading activities performed by securities firms?

BALANCE SHEET AND RECENT TRENDS

Recent Trends

In this section, we look at the balance sheet and trends in the securities firm and investment banking industry. Trends in this industry depend heavily on the state of the stock market. For example, a major effect of the 1987 stock market crash was a sharp decline in stock market trading volume and thus in commissions earned by securities firms over the 1987–91 period. Commission income began to recover only after 1992, with record equity trading volumes being achieved in 1995–2000 when stock market indexes hit new highs. As stock market values declined in 2001 and 2002, so did commission income. The overall level of commissions has declined from 63 percent of total revenues in 1980 to 38 percent in 2004. This reflects the

FIGURE 4–6
Securities Industry Net Profits, 1990–2004

Source: Investment Investment Dealers Association of Canada, *www.ida.ca*

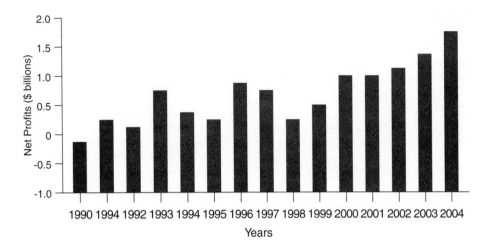

greater competition in the industry for customers, particularly after the banks formed the large integrated firms, whose effect was felt from the early 1990s, as well as the introduction of discount brokers.

Between 1991 and 2001, however, the securities industry generally showed a growth in profitability. For example, investment banking revenue grew from $424 million in 1990 to $3.12 billion in 2004 and after-tax return on equity rose from −20 percent in 1990 to 13 and 21 percent in 1995 and 2000, respectively. The principal reasons for this were improved trading profits and increased growth in new issue underwritings. Corporate debt issues became highly attractive to corporate treasurers because of relatively low long-term interest rates. Another sign of the resurgence in this industry during the 1990s appears in employment figures. Annual employment in the securities industry increased by 97 percent from 19,986 jobs in 1992 to 39,433 employees in 2000.

On the whole, as can be seen in Figure 4–6, with the exception of the slight decline in after-tax profits in 2001, the Canadian securities industry has seen increasing net after-tax profits in the period from 2000–2004. Table 4–6 provides a summary of statistics for the industry from 1992 to 2004.

Balance Sheet

A fourth quarter balance sheet for investment services firms, the retail brokers discussed previously, (including stock brokers and investment managers, North American Industry Classification System (NAICS) 2002–523) is shown in Table 4–7. Investments and accounts with affiliates as well as portfolio investments make up 67.4 percent of total assets. **Reverse repurchase agreements (reverse repos)**, securities purchased under agreement to resell (i.e., the broker gives a short-term loan to the repurchase agreement reseller) are included in the total assets. Because of the extent to which this industry's balance sheet consists of financial market securities, the industry is subjected to particularly high levels of market risk (see Chapter 10) and interest rate risk (see Chapters 8 and 9). Further, to the extent that many of these securities are foreign-issued securities, FI managers must also be concerned with foreign exchange risk (see Chapter 15) and sovereign risk (see Chapter 16).

With respect to liabilities, loans and accounts with affiliates accounted for 29.4 percent of total liabilities. Other borrowings accounted for 15.5 percent of total liabilities. Equity capital (share capital, contributed surplus, and retained earnings) exceeded

reverse repurchase agreements (reverse repos)
Securities purchased under agreement to resell.

TABLE 4–6   Securities Industry Statistics, 1992–2004

	2004	2003	2002	2001	2000	1999	1998	1997	1996	1995	1994	1993	1992
Highlights													
Number of Employees	37,739	37,262	37,949	37,121	39,433	36,175	34,445	32,990	29,636	25,901	24,284	22,553	19,986
Number of Firms	205	207	206	198	191	188	186	187	182	172	158	144	131
Firms with Profits	152	154	127	119	124	142	120	141	139	124	106	128	102
Firms with Losses	53	53	79	79	67	46	66	46	43	48	52	16	29
Operating Revenue	12,469	10,613	9,807	10,133	12,260	8,812	7,725	8,478	7,472	5,139	5,135	5,486	3,406
Operating Expenses	5,187	4,477	4,666	4,683	4,723	3,990	3,753	3,456	2,815	2,484	2,285	1,935	1,637
Operating Profit	3,934	3,321	2,735	2,793	3,565	1,946	1,345	2,070	2,061	961	1,200	1,734	676
Net Profit (Loss)	1,773	1,484	1,257	1,011	1,183	582	395	769	850	343	421	726	253
Shareholders Equity	8,372	7,076	6,995	5,681	5,526	4,850	3,745	3,526	3,344	2,562	2,000	1,957	1,394
Regulatory Capital	15,108	13,962	12,968	12,454	10,557	8,667	7,458	8,143	7,158	5,603	4,791	4,208	3,171
Client Cash Holdings	22,109	20,615	18,750	21,102	18,501	14,941	14,283	11,500	10,799	8,109	5,702	6,445	3,539
Client Margin Debt Outstanding	9,478	7,615	7.019	7,833	10,696	na	na	na	na	na	na	na	na
Productivity (000's) (Annual Revenue per Employee)	330	285	258	273	311	244	224	257	252	206	211	243	170
Annual Return (net profit shareholders equity)	21%	21%	18%	18%	21%	12%	11%	22%	25%	13%	21%	37%	18%

Source: Investment Dealers Association of Canada, www.ida.ca

total liabilities and represented 50.5 percent of total assets. The level of capital maintained by securities firms is governed by the rules of the securities regulators and by the IDA for its member firms, as noted previously. Capital adequacy will be discussed in Chapter 20.

Concept Questions

1. Describe the trend in profitability in the securities industry over the last 10 years.
2. What are the major assets held by broker–dealers?

REGULATION

www.csa-acvm.ca

The regulation of the securities industry in Canada is a provincial and territorial responsibility which is carried out by thirteen regulators who co-operate through the Canadian Securities Administrators (CSA). The securities industry has grown and trading has globalized. Cross-border trading and the issues that arise as a result of company inter-listing on Canadian and U.S. exchanges (222 firms, $533 billion trading value in 2004) has meant that the securities industry in Canada needs to have consistent regulation across the country. With this in mind, the Minister of Finance created the Wise Persons' Committee in 2003 whose report recommended that a single regulator be established to replace the provincial bodies.[12]

---

[12] See Committee to Review the Structure of Securities Regulation in Canada, "It's Time," December 2003, available at www.wpc-averties.ca. Additional documents, including the submissions received by the Committee are also available. However, the move towards a single securities regulator in Canada is seen as an intrusion by the federal government on a provincial matter. Quebec's Minister of Finance, Michel Audet, rejects the federal government's involvement in securities regulation as Quebec and other provinces would prefer to see a "passport system" which would allow securities firms access to all provincial markets while being regulated in their home province. See B. Marotte, "Audet snubs securities unification effort," The *Globe and Mail*, July 15, 2005, p. B3. In a speech given at the IDA's Annual Meeting, Joseph J. Oliver, President of the IDA, stated that while provincial squabbles hold back regulatory reform, market efficiency in Canada suffers. See J. J. Oliver, "Regulatory Reform: Waiting for Godot, Getting on With Life," June 27, 2005 at www.ida.ca.

TABLE 4–7
Balance Sheet for
Stock Brokers and
Investment Dealers,
2004 (in millions
of dollars)

Source: Statistics Canada,
www.statcan.ca

	2004
Assets	**180,364**
Cash and deposits	9,153
Accounts receivable and accrued revenue	19,768
Investments and accounts with affiliates	67,230
Portfolio investments	54,318
Loans	7,194
Mortgage	4,291
Non-mortgage	2,903
Allowance for losses on investments and loans	−222
Net capital assets	7,415
Other assets	15,507
Liabilities	**89,246**
Accounts payable and accrued liabilities	22,725
Loans and accounts with affiliates	26,273
Borrowings	13,844
Loans and overdrafts	6,163
From banks	2,663
From others	3,500
Bankers' acceptances and paper	1,585
Bonds and debentures	5,014
Mortgages	1,081
Deferred income tax	4,455
Other liabilities	21,950
Equity	**91,118**
Share capital	49,143
Contributed surplus	9,841
Retained earnings	32,134

**self-regulatory
organization (SRO)**
Industry-owned orga-
nization designated
by a provincial securi-
ties regulator to regu-
late its members.

www.rs.ca
www.cipf.ca
www.cfson-crcsf.ca

Currently, the provincial and territorial regulators establish legislation in their own jurisdictions, but they allow **self-regulatory organizations (SROs)** to carry out certain aspects of regulation. For example, the stock exchanges are SROs, as is the IDA and the Market Regulation Services Inc. (RS), owned jointly by the TSX Group and the IDA. Each SRO has a particular role in the regulation of securities firms. The IDA regulates its member firms for capital adequacy as well as code of conduct and provides details of the current regulations at its Web site, www.ida.ca. Also, since mutual funds have become such a large source of revenue for securities firms, having grown from 2 percent ($43 million) of commission income in 1988 to 11 percent in 2004 ($1.4 billion), securities dealers are also members of the Mutual Fund Dealers Association of Canada (MFDA) which is an SRO recognized in several provinces.

The Canadian Investor Protection Fund (CIPF), a trust fund set up by the TSX Group, the IDA and the Montreal Exchange (ME) provides investor protection of up to $1 million if a dealer were to become insolvent. Also, the Centre for Financial Services Ombudsnetwork (CFSON) provides dispute resolution for consumers free of charge. The complexity of the relationship of securities firms to their clients and the potential for a conflict of interest is shown in the Ethical Dilemmas Box. Many investment advisors, including Berkshire Group, referred investors to Portus Asset Management Inc., whose co-founder has been charged with moving US$35 million of clients' money into an account in Switzerland. Dealers have been asked to return the fees charged to clients.[13]

---

[13] See "Portus co-founder caught with hand in cookie jar, court is told," Canadian Press NewsWire, June 24, 2005 and A. Hoffman, "Dealers ask agents to return Portus fees: Move comes ahead of regulatory probe," The *Globe and Mail*, June 29, 2005, p. B1.

Disciplinary hearings being conducted by the Mutual Fund Dealers Association of Canada (MFDA) indicate many advisors are engaging in outside business activity without the knowledge of their employers, and much of this activity would not be approved if the firms did know about it. A recent notice sent out by the MFDA to members says some of this "inappropriate" outside business activity has resulted in "significant client harm." Activities primarily involve selling securities on the side, such as principal protected notes, private placements, flow-through shares and limited partnerships. There have also been problems with referral of securities-related business outside the firm. "Clients come to advisors for advice about their investment needs, and they have no idea what business is done inside the firm or what's done outside," says Karen McGuiness, vice-president of compliance for the MFDA. "Clients don't realize they may be buying a product that's not approved, and the risk that entails." The rules require that all securities-related business be conducted through the firm with the exception of deposit instruments sold by banks. Activities such as off-book trading and "selling away" are not allowed. Referral business involving other registrants, which is what happened when firms referred clients to Portus Asset Management Inc., must be done through the firm according to the rules regarding referral arrangements. These rules allow for two levels of oversight regarding the appropriateness of securities sold to clients, Ms. McGuiness says. Firstly, the securities sold must be approved by the firm, and secondly, they must be sold to clients for whom they are suitable based on the clients' goals, risk tolerance and investment knowledge. It is up to the advisor to make the suitability decision, based on knowledge of the individual client and written information given by the client in the Know Your Client form.

Source: Jade Hemeon, *National Post*, Page FP16, June 6, 2005.

While Canadian regulators are still wrestling with the establishment of a national securities regulator, the primary regulator of the securities industry in the United States is the Securities and Exchange Commission (SEC), established in 1934. Spurred on by the corporate governance scandals of Enron, Global Crossings, Tyco, Worldcom, and others, the SEC has already moved to limit state regulators' ability to control securities firms, and has enacted the Sarbanes-Oxley Act for corporate disclosure, which, along with the USA Patriot Act, has potential cross-border effects on Canadian companies, particularly for the integrated firms who also operate in the U.S. markets. The SEC has instituted rules requiring Wall Street analysts to vouch that their stock picks are not influenced by investment banking colleagues and that analysts disclose details of their compensation that would flag investors to any possible conflicts. If evidence surfaces that the analysts have falsely attested to the independence of their work, it could be used to bring enforcement actions. Violators could face a wide array of sanctions, including fines and other penalties, such as a suspension or banning from the securities industry. In addition, the SEC proposed that top officials from all public companies sign off on financial statements.

In the spring of 2003, an agreement between U.S. regulators and 10 of the largest securities firms required the firms to pay a record US$1.4 billion in penalties to settle charges involving investor abuse. The settlement centred on civil charges that securities firms routinely issued overly optimistic stock research to investors in order to gain favour with corporate clients and win their investment banking business. The agreement also settled charges that at least two big firms, Citigroup and Credit Suisse First Boston, improperly allocated shares to corporate executives to win banking business from their firms. The Wall Street firms agreed to the settlement without admitting or denying any wrongdoing. The agreement forced brokerage companies to make structural changes in the way they handle research—preventing analysts, for example, from attending certain investment banking meetings with bankers. The agreement also required securities firms to have separate reporting and supervisory structures for their research and banking operations. Additionally, it required that analysts' pay be tied to the quality and accuracy of their research rather than the amount of the investment banking business they generate.

Despite the fact that Bernard Ebbers, a Canadian and former Chief Executive Officer of Worldcom, was convicted of fraud in the U.S. and sentenced to 25 years in prison in 2005 for filing false financial reports in the US$11 billion conspiracy that brought down Worldcom, there have yet to be securities frauds in Canada on the scale of those in the U.S. However, in addition to the involvement of Canadian dealers in U.S. scandals (CIBC World Markets and Enron, as noted in Chapter 2), there have been some made-in-Canada scandals. For example, in May 2005 four traders at RBC Dominion Securities were accused of **wash trading**, a form of share price manipulation, by buying and selling more that $33 million worth of shares. The distortion in prices is alleged to have cost bystanders $232,000.[14]

wash trading
Manipulating share prices by related investors buying and selling the same security to give the appearance of a legitimate trade even though there has been no real change in ownership.

Securities firms and banks have historically been strongly supportive of efforts to combat money laundering, and the industry has been subject to laws that impose extensive reporting and record-keeping requirements. However, the USA Patriot Act, passed in response to the September 11 terrorist attacks, included additional provisions that financial services firms operating in the United States must implement. The new rules, which took effect on October 1, 2003, imposed three requirements. First, firms must verify the identity of any person seeking to open an account. Second, firms must maintain records of the information used to verify the person's identity. Third, firms must determine whether a person opening an account appears on any list of known or suspected terrorists or terrorist organizations. The new rules are intended to deter money laundering without imposing undue burdens that would constrain the ability of firms to serve their customers.

Canadian securities firms have been required to identify money laundering since 1993 and, in response to global concerns following September 11 2001, amendments to the Proceeds of Crime (Money Laundering) and Terrorist Financing Act 2001 require firms to report suspicious transactions, report large cash transactions, and obtain clear identification of their clients. The IDA maintains a section for its members on money laundering on its web site similar to that maintained by OSFI for federally-regulated banks and insurance companies.

Concept Questions

1. How does the regulation of the securities industry differ between Canada and the United States?
2. How and why does the regulatory framework differ for deposit-taking institutions, insurance companies, and securities firms?

GLOBAL ISSUES

Securities firms have followed other financial institutions in expanding their global operations. This can be seen in Table 4–8, which shows the top ten underwriters of global debt and equity in 2003 and 2004. The international nature of this group, despite the dominance of U.S. firms as top-ranked advisors for global securities issues (Table 4–9), means that the regulation of participants in the global markets will continue to be an issue in order to ensure financial market stability.

---

[14] See CBC News, "RBC traders face 'wash trading' allegations, Monday, May 30, 2005.

TABLE 4–8   Top Underwriters of Global Debt and Equity (US dollars)

| Bookrunners | Jan 1, 2004–Dec 31, 2004 | | | Jan 1, 2203–Dec 31, 2003 | |
	Proceeds ($millions)	Mkt Share	# of Issues	Rank	Mkt Share
Citigroup	534,486.2	9.4	1892	1	10.3
Morgan Stanley	413,554.2	6.8	1492	3	7.5
JP Morgan	385,797.5	6.8	1492	3	7.5
merrill Lynch & Co Inc	374,288.7	6.6	1564	4	7.2
Lehman Brothers	369,628.3	6.5	1292	5	6.7
Credit Suisse First Boston	362,441.5	6.4	1359	6	6.4
Deutsche Bank AG	334,834.7	5.9	1299	7	6.0
UBS	299,592.0	5.3	1175	9	5.5
Goldman Sachs & Co	285,859.4	5.0	855	8	5.6
Bank of America Securities LLC	203,734.6	3.6	780	10	3.9
Top 10 Totals	**3,564,217.1**	**62.8**	**13,042**	**3,571,618.6**	**66.7**
Industry Total	**5,693,011.6**	**100.0**	**20,066**	**5,361,518.8**	**100.0**

Source: Reprinted with permission of Thomson Financial Securities Data, 2005, www.tfibcm.com

TABLE 4–9   Who is Number 1 in Each Market?

| Type | Full Year 2004 | | Full Year 2003 | |
	Amount In US$ billions	Top-Ranked Manager	Amount In US$ billions	Top-Ranked Manager
Straight debt	5,187.0	Citigroup	4,972.7	Citigroup
Convertible debt	98.4	Morgan Stanley	164.8	J. P. Morgan Chase
US Investment-grade debt	688.6	Citigroup	665.0	Citigroup
US Mortgage-backed securities	729.3	Bear Stearns & Co Inc	915.9	UBS
US Asset-backed securities	856.7	Citigroup	604.5	J. P. Morgan
Common stock	508.1	Morgan Stanley	388.8	Goldman Sachs & Co.
IPOs (US issuers)	44.9	Morgan Stanley	14.1	Goldman Sachs & Co.
Global Loans	2,640.0	J. P. Morgan	1,965.7	J. P. Morgan
US Syndicated loans	1.339.0	J. P. Morgan	983.9	J. P. Morgan

Source: Thomson Financial Securities Data, 2005, *www.tfibcm.com*

Although firms in smaller capital markets such as Canada, Australia, and New Zealand, for example, have traditionally listed securities on U.S. exchanges and raised debt overseas when their markets were unable to accommodate their need for capital,[15] the phenomenon of U.S. firms going outside of their country to raise funds has been a relatively new trend, representing a 533 percent increase in all offerings by U.S. issuers between 1995 and 2003 as shown in Table 4–10. In fact, international offerings by U.S. issuers represented 39 percent of total offerings of US$2,999.0 billion in 2003, as shown in the upper panel of Table 4–10. At the same time, concerns about U.S. accounting practices as a result of the recent scandals, the burdensome nature of reporting accounting figures using U.S. accounting standards as well as local accounting standards (Sarbanes-Oxley, as

---

[15] For discussions of U.S. listing for Canadian and Mexican firms, see S. R. Foerster and A. G. Karolyi, "International Listings of stocks: The case of Canada and the U.S.," *Journal of International Business Studies*, 1993, Vol. 24, Iss. 4, pp. 763–785 and P. Y. Davis-Friday, T. J. Frecka, and J. M. Rivera, "The financial performance, capital constraints and information environment of cross-listed firms: Evidence from Mexico," *The International Journal of Accounting*, 2005, Vol. 40, Iss. 1, p. 1.

TABLE 4–10
Value of
International
Security Offerings
(U.S. in billions
of dollars)

Source: *Quarterly Review:
International Banking and
Financial Market Developments,*
Bank for International Settle-
ments, various issues.
www.bis.org

	1995	2001	2002	2003	Percent Change 1995–2003
Total international offerings					
Floating-rate debt	103.0	642.7	603.3	512.2	397.6
Straight debt	394.8	1,590.3	1,454.6	2,283.6	478.4
Convertible debt	18.1	72.2	42.7	88.0	386.2
Equity	54.6	149.4	102.3	115.2	111.0
Total offerings	570.5	2,454.6	2,202.9	2,999.0	427.5
International offerings by U.S. issuers					
Floating-rate debt	50.9	262.3	214.4	220.9	334.0
Straight debt	115.3	836.1	755.0	913.9	692.6
Convertible debt	8.5	32.9	16.5	32.2	278.8
Equity	10.0	24.8	1.2	1.9	−81.0
Total offerings	184.7	1,156.1	987.1	1,168.9	532.9

discussed above),[16] the decline in the U.S. stock market, and the fall in the value of the U.S. dollar against the euro and yen were all working to weaken the attractiveness of U.S. markets to foreign investors and issuers in the early 2000s. However, Canadian FIs are seasoned participants in the international capital markets and Canadian firms and their investment advisors continued to benefit from improved U.S.-Canadian dollar exchange rates and engaged in cross-border merger and acquisition activity in 2004. Five of the ten largest deals announced in Canada in 2004 (including, for example, the merger of breweries Molson Inc. and Adolph Coors Company, Jean Coutu Group's acquisition of Eckerd Drugstores, and the Toronto-Dominion Bank's acquisition of Banknorth Group Inc.) were cross-border deals.[17] Because of the importance of a strong global financial market to both developed and developing nations, the harmonization of regulations governing securities firms can be expected to continue.

**Concept
Questions**

1. What have been the trends in international securities offerings in the late 1990s and early 2000s?

---

[16] The Royal Bank of Canada announced that it is discontinuing the publication of its annual statements following U.S. accounting principles. In addition, it was announced recently that Canadian accounting standards will be aligned with International Accounting Standards. See J. Partridge, "RBC rekindles romance with Canadian accounting rules," *Globe and Mail Report on Business*, April 19, 2005.

[17] See Investment Dealer's Association of Canada, "Canada's M&A Activity: Headin' South, Eh? An Overview of Canada's M&A Trends in 2004 and its Impact on the Canadian Securities Industry," Capital Markets: Notes and Commentaries, January, 2005 at www.ida.ca.

Summary

This chapter presented an overview of the securities industry in Canada. Firms in this industry assist in getting new issues of debt and equity to the markets, often related to corporate mergers and restructurings, earning fees as financial advisors as well as from the underwriting function. Additionally, this industry facilitates trading and market making of securities after they are issued. We looked at the structure of the industry and changes over the last decade. We analyzed balance sheet information that highlighted the major assets and liabilities of firms in the industry and discussed the regulation of the industry and the implications of changes both within Canada and globally.

Questions and Problems

1. What are the different types of firms in the securities industry, and how does each type differ from the others?
2. What are the key activity areas for securities firms? How does each activity area assist in the generation of profits, and what are the major risks for each area?
3. What is the difference between an IPO and a secondary issue?
4. What is the difference between a private placement and a public offering?
5. What are the risk implications to an investment banker from underwriting on a best-efforts basis versus a firm commitment basis? If you operated a company issuing stock for the first time, which type of underwriting would you prefer? Why? What factors might cause you to choose the alternative?
6. How do agency transactions differ from principal transactions for market makers?
7. An investment banker agrees to underwrite a $500,000,000, 10-year, 8 percent semiannual bond issue for KDO Corporation on a firm commitment basis. The investment banker pays KDO on Thursday and plans to begin a public sale on Friday. What type of interest rate movement does the investment bank fear while holding these securities? If interest rates rise 0.05 percent, or 5 basis points, overnight, what will be the impact on the profits of the investment banker? What if the market interest rate falls 5 basis points?
8. An investment banker pays $23.50 per share for 4,000,000 shares of JCN Company. It then sells those shares to the public for $25 per share. How much money does JCN receive? What is the profit to the investment banker? What is the stock price of JCN?
9. XYZ, Inc., has issued 10,000,000 new shares. An investment banker agrees to underwrite these shares on a best-efforts basis. The investment banker is able to sell 8,400,000 shares for $27 per share, and it charges XYZ $0.675 per share sold. How much money does XYZ receive? What is the profit to the investment banker? What is the stock price of XYZ?
10. One of the major activity areas of securities firms is trading.
    a. What is the difference between pure arbitrage and risk arbitrage?
    b. What is the difference between position trading and program trading?
11. If an investor observes that the price of a stock trading in one exchange is different from the price in another exchange, what form of arbitrage is applicable, and how can the investor participate in that arbitrage?
12. An investor notices that an ounce of gold is priced at US $318 in London and US $325 in New York.
    a. What action could the investor take to try to profit from the price discrepancy?
    b. Under which of the four trading activities would this action be classified?
    c. If the investor is correct in identifying the discrepancy, what pattern should the two prices take in the short-term future?
    d. What may be some impediments to the success of this transaction?
13. What factors are given credit for the steady decline in brokerage commissions as a percentage of total revenues over the period beginning in 1987 and ending in 1991?
14. What factors are given credit for the resurgence of profitability in the securities industry beginning in 1991? Are firms that trade in fixed-income securities more or less likely to have volatile profits? Why?
15. How do the operating activities, and thus the balance sheet structures, of securities firms differ from the operating activities of deposit-taking institutions such as banks and insurance firms? How are the balance sheet structures of securities firms similar to those of other financial intermediaries?
16. Based on the data in Table 4–8, what were the second-largest single asset and the largest single liability of securities firms in 2004? Are these asset and liability categories related? Exactly how does a repurchase agreement work?
17. Identify the major regulatory organizations that are involved in the daily operations of the securities industry, and explain their role in providing smoothly operating markets.

Web Questions

18. Go to the Thomson Financial Securities Data Web site at **www.tfibcm.com** and find the most recent data on merger and acquisition volume and number of deals using the following steps. Click on "View the latest league Table Online." Click on "Mergers & Acquisitions." Under Press Releases, click on "Worldwide and US Financial Advisory Press Release." This will download a file onto your computer that will contain the most recent information on top underwriters for various securities. How has the dollar volume and number of deals changed since 2003, as reported in Figure 4–2?

The Financial Services Industry: Mutual Funds, Hedge Funds, and Pension Funds

In this chapter we provide an overview of (1) mutual funds, (2) hedge funds, and (3) pension funds, and highlight their rapid growth over the last decade. We look at:

▸ the size, structure and composition of each industry, highlighting historical trends, the different types, objectives, returns, and costs

▸ the balance sheets and recent trends

▸ the regulations and regulators, and

▸ global issues

INTRODUCTION

fund
A financial intermediary whose primary purpose is to acquire and manage financial assets for its owners.

mutual fund
An FI that pools the financial resources of individuals and companies and invests in diversified portfolios of assets, targeting a specific level of risk.

hedge fund
An FI that pools the financial resources of sophisticated investors and invests in a diversified pool of assets, usually high risk.

pension fund
A financial intermediary that pools the retirement savings of individuals, invests in a diversified portfolio of assets, and pays an income to its owners after retirement.

When the term "fund" is mentioned, most people automatically add the term "mutual" as an adjective. However, a **fund** can be defined more generally as a financial intermediary whose primary purpose is to acquire and manage financial assets (e.g., bonds, shares, money market securities) for its owners. The types of funds that will be discussed in this chapter are **mutual funds**, **hedge funds**, and **pension funds**. By pooling the financial resources of individuals and companies and investing in diversified portfolios of assets, funds provide opportunities for small savers to invest in financial securities and to diversify risk. Funds may also be able to generate greater economies of scale by incurring lower transactions costs and commissions than are incurred when individual investors buy securities directly. In this respect, funds are similar to deposit-taking FIs in converting savings into income-earning assets. However, while the 1990s saw savings transferred from banks and other deposit-taking institutions into funds, these funds differ for investors in the increased risk of a loss of capital, a market risk not present with government-insured deposits. Many investors saw their retirement savings devastated by the market downturn of 2001.

The growth in savings, as a result of an employment benefit (a pension fund, firm-operated or government-operated) or through individual efforts (often within a legal shelter such as a **Registered Retirement Savings Plan (RRSP)** or a **Registered Education Savings Plan (RESP)**) created FIs whose liability side is essentially all owners' equity. The fiduciary nature of pension funds was recognized early and regulations were established to govern them. Mutual funds were left to self-regulating organizations (SROs) for their control, and hedge funds, a product offered to knowledgeable investors, were left unregulated. The history of the last decade is thus one of growth in size and in regulation for these three types of FIs that developed into an industry whose primary service is **wealth management**, the provision of professional asset management to individual investors and companies.

By providing wealth management services, mutual funds, hedge funds, and pension funds are subject to interest rate risk, market risk, foreign exchange risk, and possibly off-balance sheet risks on the asset side of their balance sheet. With the exception of capital adequacy rules, the risk management of funds parallels that of other FIs.

MUTUAL FUNDS

Registered retirement savings plan (RRSP)
A retirement savings plan that allows Canadians to defer tax until retirement.

An open-ended mutual fund (the major type of mutual fund) continuously stands ready to sell new shares to investors and to redeem outstanding shares on demand at their fair market value. As a result of the tremendous increase in the market value of financial assets, such as equities, in the 1990s (for example, the S&P TSX Composite Index saw a return of over 25 percent in 1993, 1996, and 1999) and the relatively low-cost opportunity mutual funds provide to investors (particularly small investors) who want to hold such assets (through either direct mutual fund purchases or contributions to their registered retirement savings plans), the mutual fund industry boomed in size and customers in the 1990s.[1] In 2001, the market correction and a slowdown in the economy brought an end to such a rapid pace of growth. Further, allegations of trading abuses and excessive management fees resulted in a loss of confidence in mutual funds as an investment vehicle. Despite these issues, at the end of 2004 more than 1900 different mutual companies held total assets of $497.3 billion.[2]

SIZE, STRUCTURE, AND COMPOSITION OF THE INDUSTRY

Historical Trends

Registered Education Savings Plan (RESP)
A savings plan that allows Canadians to earn income for their children that is not taxed if used for educational purposes when withdrawn.

wealth management
The provision of professional portfolio management, tax planning, and retirement planning services to individuals and companies.

Table 5–1 presents information about the total assets, the number of funds, and the number of accounts collected by the Investment Funds Institute of Canada whose members represented 75–85% of the assets under management in Canada prior to September 1991 and 97% since that time. Table 5–1 shows that total assets have grown from $2.4 billion in 1970 to $497.5 billion at year-end 2004. Over the same time period, the number of funds has increased from 50 to 1,915, and the number of accounts has ballooned from 771.1 thousand to over 50 million. Since 1980, total assets decreased only in 2002. More recently, the increase between 2003 and year-end 2004 was 13.3%.

Table 5–2 shows the dollar value of Net New Sales of Canadian Common Share Funds and U.S. Common Share Funds and the annual returns on the S&P TSX Composite Index and the U.S. S&P 500 Composite Index from 1994 to 2004. The highest level of net new sales of Canadian Common Stock funds occurred in 1996 and 1997 when the return on the TSX was 25.7 percent and 13.0 percent, respectively. Higher levels of net sales of U.S. Common Stock Funds occurred between 1996 and 1998 when returns on the S&P 500 (Large Cap) Index exceeded 20 percent. However, these statistics may be misleading, as the limit for foreign content in registered retirement savings plans (RRSPs), a major source of investors in mutual funds in Canada, was increased from 10 per cent in 1990 to 30 percent in 2001, and

---

[1] Shareholder services offered by mutual funds include free exchanges of investments between a mutual fund company's funds, automatic investing, automatic reinvestment of dividends, and automatic withdrawals.

[2] See The Investment Funds Institute of Canada, www.ific.ca.

TABLE 5–1
Growth in the Mutual Fund Industry in Canada, 1970 to 2004

Source: Investment Funds Institute of Canada, *www.ific.ca*. Prior to 1991, funds reported averaged 75–80% of total assets under management in Canada and 97% of assets under management from September, 1991 to December, 2004.

YEAR	TOTAL ASSETS ($ billions)	# OF FUNDS	# OF ACCOUNTS (thousands)
1970	2.4	50	771.1
1980	3.6	87	479.6
1985	10.2	156	952.4
1990	24.9	422	2,587.9
1991	49.9	505	4,533.7
1992	67.3	543	5,514.2
1993	114.6	633	8,928.6
1994	127.3	813	13,486.3
1995	146.2	916	15,295.1
1996	211.8	954	22,297.8
1997	283.2	1,023	32,826.0
1998	326.6	1,030	40,948.7
1999	389.7	1,328	45,752.4
2000	418.9	1,605	53,645.5
2001	426.4	1,831	50,302.0
2002	391.3	1,956	53,188.9
2003	438.9	1,887	51,141.6
2004	497.3	1,915	50,871.8

TABLE 5–2
Net New Sales in the Canadian Mutual Funds Industry versus Annual Returns on the S&P TSX Composite Index and the S&P 500 Large Cap. Index.

Source: Investment Funds Institute of Canada, *www.ific.ca*, and Econstats, *www.econstats.com*

YEAR	Canadian Common Net New Sales ($ millions)	Return on S&P TSX Composite Index (%)	U.S. Common Net New Sales ($ millions)	Return on S&P 500 (Large Cap) (%)
1994	4,943.2	−2.50	−5.1	−1.54
1995	3,117.7	11.86	118.2	34.11
1996	11,415.5	25.75	1,073.5	20.26
1997	17,252.7	13.03	2,937.3	31.01
1998	8,091.7	−3.19	3,485.8	26.67
1999	−1,332.4	29.72	2,938.6	19.53
2000	3,593.4	6.18	3,952.3	−10.14
2001	1,622.8	−13.94	2,518.8	−13.04
2002	67.8	−13.97	1,866.7	−23.37
2003	−2,351.5	24.29	270.7	26.38
2004	−1,566.3	12.48	−18.9	8.99

Note: The TSX Composite Index replaced the TSE 300 Index in 2002.

clone fund
A mutual fund that is RRSP-eligible and that creates returns equivalent to a foreign stock portfolio using derivatives.

eliminated completely by the passing of Bill C-43 in June, 2005. With their purpose gone, foreign **clone funds**, (e.g. AGF RSP Japan), created to increase the foreign content of a mutual fund by using derivatives (e.g., forward contracts) to emulate the returns of a foreign stock portfolio, will be terminated and access to foreign content should be easier and cheaper for investors.

Industry participants consist of those who manufacture mutual funds, those who distribute funds, and those who do both such as banks and credit unions. Figure 5–1 shows the distribution of mutual fund assets by type of manager in 2005. Brokers and dealers dominate with 49 percent of the assets and banks and trusts are in second place at 35 percent.

FIGURE 5–1
Mutual Fund Assets
by Manager Type,
June 30, 2005

Source: Investment Funds
Institute of Canada,
www.ific.ca

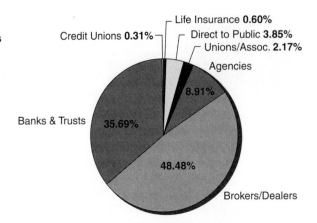

FIGURE 5–2
Ownership
Structure of Power
Corporation of
Canada, 2005

Source: K. Damsell, "A
Canadian conglomerate just
keeps on compounding."
The *Globe and Mail*,
March 15, 2005, p. B19.

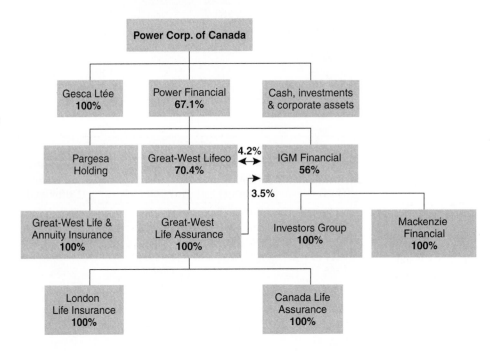

Mutual funds represent an investment security and are therefore regulated at the provincial level in Canada. A provincial regulator's goal is the protection of the investor by ensuring disclosure of information and market transparency. In order to sell mutual funds, an individual must meet the licencing requirements of their home province which includes training in the products sold. As well, training in the evaluation of the clients' investment goals, their risk tolerance, and their investment knowledge is included in order to ensure that the funds recommended are appropriate. Each dealer must be a member of a self-regulating organization such as the Investment Dealers Association of Canada (IDA). However, in addition to specific securities laws, the sale of funds by deposit-taking institutions and others regulated by the Office of the Superintendent of Financial Services (OSFI) means that the Bank Act, The Insurance Companies Act, the Trust and Loan Companies Act, and other federal and provincial statutes may also apply. The majority of Canadian mutual funds are regulated by the Ontario Securities Commission

www.ida.ca

www.osfi-bsif.ca

TABLE 5–3   The Top Ten Mutual Funds in Canada by Asset Size, December, 2004

Fund	Parent Company	December 2004 Assets
1 IGM Financial Inc.	Power Corp. of Canada	82,751,101
2 RBC Asset Management Inc.	Royal Bank	47,018,011
3 C.I. Mutual Funds Inc.	Independent	43,109,847
4 AIM Trimark Investments	AMVESCAP PLC, U.K.	42,119,569
5 CIBC Asset Management	CIBC	41,776,678
6 TD Asset Management Inc.	TD Canada Trust	36,253,372
7 Fidelity Investments Canada Limited	Fidelity Investments, U.S.	31,294,710
8 AGF Management Limited	Independent	23,279,731
9 Franklin Templeton Investments	Franklin Templeton Investments, U.S.	20,077,614
10 BMO Investments Inc.	Bank of Montreal	19,695,773
Total Assets		387,376,406
Note: IGM Financial's assets are made up of the following:		
Investors Group		44,509,827
Mackenzie Financial Corporation		37,132,645
Counsel Wealth Management		1,108,629

Source: Investment Funds Institute of Canada, *www.ific.ca*

(OSC), which is involved with other provincial securities regulators in harmonizing the regulations through the Canadian Securities Association (CSA).[3]

The number of mutual fund participants in Canada is concentrated and is declining as the industry becomes more consolidated, a trend noted by the IFIC to have continued in 2004.[4] The top ten companies at year-end 2004 are shown in Table 5–3. These top ten funds represent 77.9% of the $497.3 trillion mutual fund assets reported by IFIC at December 2004. IGM Financial Inc., owned by Power Group, became the largest fund manager and distributor in Canada during 2004. With assets of over $82 billion, IGM dwarfs even its closest rival, RBC Asset Management, which has assets of $47.0 billion and was the top ranking fund by asset size in 2003. Through its Web site, IGM Financial Inc. sells mortgages, insurance, and other banking products. Four of the top ten funds are owned by the big five banks, as is the eleventh in size, Scotia Securities Inc. and the sixteenth in size, National Bank Mutual Funds. Together, subsidiaries of the Big Six banks have total mutual fund assets of $165.2 billion, representing one-third of the total mutual fund assets reported in 2004. Although banks are still prohibited from selling insurance products through their branch networks, they are able to distribute mutual funds through their branches provided their sales people have been certified by the appropriate provincial regulator. In addition, the banks' clients are able to buy and sell mutual funds online from the same website where they can conduct their other banking. This gives the banks an advantage in extending their sales of funds. Both C.I. Mutual Funds and AGF Management are independent Canadian-owned funds, and three of the funds in Table 5–3 (AIM Trimark Investments, Fidelity Investments Canada Limited, and Franklin Templeton Investments) are owned by large foreign-based companies.

Power Corporation of Canada is a financial conglomerate whose controlling shareholder is the Desmarais family of Quebec. As shown in Figure 5–2, Power

---

[3] See Canadian Securities Association, "Striking a New Balance: A Framework for Regulating Mutual Funds and Their Managers", Concept Proposal 81–402, March 1, 2002 at www.osc.gov.on.ca.

[4] See E. Go, "Year 2004 in Review: IFIC's Review of the Annual Mutual Fund Industry's Statistics" at www.ific.ca.

Corporation has expanded into two areas of financial intermediation: its assets include life insurance (Great-West Life, London Life, Canada Life), as well as mutual funds (IGM Financial, Investors Group, Mackenzie Financial). Power Financial Corporation, owned 67.1 percent by Power Corporation, reported total assets of $104.2 billion in 2004.[5]

Different Types of Mutual Funds

bond funds
Funds that contain fixed-income capital market debt securities.

equity funds
Funds that contain primarily common stock securities.

balanced funds
Funds that contain bond and stock securities.

RRSP-eligible
A mutual fund or other security that meets the criteria of Canada Customs and Revenue Agency (CCRA) for inclusion in a Registered Retirement Savings Plan.

The mutual fund industry can be divided into two sectors: long-term funds and short-term funds. These are reported on an aggregate basis by the Bank of Canada as money market mutual funds and non-money market mutual funds as part of the money supply. Long-term funds include **bond funds** (comprised of fixed income securities with a maturity over one year), **equity funds** (comprised of primarily common stock securities), and **balanced funds** (comprised of common and preferred shares and bonds). Short-term funds include money market mutual funds which are invested in short-term paper, usually with maturities of less than six months. Since the goal of most mutual funds is to be **RRSP-eligible**, and since, as noted previously, there have been restrictions on the level of foreign content in RRSPs, mutual funds are further classified as to whether they contain foreign or U.S. common shares, foreign bonds, or foreign money market securities. There are also mortgage and real estate funds. Figure 5–4 shows the breakdown of the different fund types in Canada in 1994, 1999, and 2004. As can be seen from Figure 5–4, the composition of mutual fund assets changes over time, but the long-term funds dominate, with the short-term money market funds making up only 10 percent of total assets 2004. Foreign content has increased over time as government restrictions for maintaining the tax-deferred status of RRSPs have eased. In 2004, Canadian common shares represented 26 percent of the Canadian dollar value of the long-term funds, with U.S. common shares at 20 percent and foreign common shares at 7.5 percent. Money market funds are primarily invested in Canadian securities, with foreign content representing just 3.8 percent of the total. Since there are no limits on foreign content starting in 2005, foreign investment may be expected to climb, depending on the potential for diversification and the individual investor's appetite for international risk. However, international funds are seen as higher risk and, to the extent that Canadian markets provide sufficient diversification and returns, and investors are more risk-averse with where they place their retirement savings, there may not be a significant climb in the market for foreign funds. In addition, the increasing integration of North American financial markets (and global markets for commodities such as energy, for example) may make international diversification less attractive.[6]

INTERNET EXERCISE

Go to the Investment Funds Institute of Canada's Web site at www.ific.ca. Find the latest figures for the month-end dollar value of mutual fund assets by using the following steps:
Click on "Industry Statistics." Click on "Monthly Statistics." Click on "Overview Report." This will open an Excel spreadsheet that can be downloaded to your computer.

---

[5] For a snapshot of the extent of Power Corporation's reach in the Canadian mutual fund and insurance markets, see K. Damsell, "A Canadian conglomerate just keeps on compounding," the *Globe and Mail*, March 15, 2005, p. B19.

[6] See R. Rendon, "RRSPs go global," *Marketing*, March 21–March 28, 2005, Vol. 110, Iss. 11, p. 6.

FIGURE 5–3
Types of Mutual Fund Assets, 1994, 1999, 2004

Source: Investment Funds Institute of Canada, *www.ific.ca*

1994 Total Assets Month End

Total Money Market 12.3%
Real Estate 0.1%
Mortgage 10.1%
Dividend & Income 3.1%
Foreign Bond & Income 3.9%
Bond & Income 9.4%
US Common Shares 3.1%

Balanced 13.9%
Canadian Common Shares 22.4%
Foreign Common Shares 21.7%

Total (Excl. Not for Sale) 100%

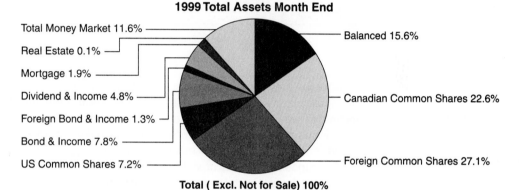

1999 Total Assets Month End

Total Money Market 11.6%
Real Estate 0.1%
Mortgage 1.9%
Dividend & Income 4.8%
Foreign Bond & Income 1.3%
Bond & Income 7.8%
US Common Shares 7.2%

Balanced 15.6%
Canadian Common Shares 22.6%
Foreign Common Shares 27.1%

Total (Excl. Not for Sale) 100%

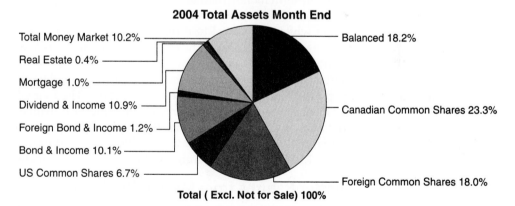

2004 Total Assets Month End

Total Money Market 10.2%
Real Estate 0.4%
Mortgage 1.0%
Dividend & Income 10.9%
Foreign Bond & Income 1.2%
Bond & Income 10.1%
US Common Shares 6.7%

Balanced 18.2%
Canadian Common Shares 23.3%
Foreign Common Shares 18.0%

Total (Excl. Not for Sale) 100%

Mutual Fund Objectives

Mutual funds are legally required to provide investors with a prospectus that outlines the fund's investment strategy and its costs. In addition, each fund produces an annual report that provides details of its activities, and also maintains a Web site to provide monthly and quarterly information, and, in some cases, a copy of the fund's prospectus. The goal is to fully inform existing and potential investors of its activities so that they can evaluate the risks and returns. Investment advisors and sellers of mutual funds must meet provincial requirements, which include a duty to ensure that the investor is informed and that the fund is appropriate for a particular client.

TABLE 5–4
Canadian Mutual
Fund Assets by
Fund Type,
December 31, 2004

Source: Investment Funds
Institute of Canada,
www.ific.ca

Fund Type	Total Assets Month End	Percent of Total
Balanced	90,333,725	18.2%
Canadian Common Shares	116,070,055	23.3%
Foreign Common Shares	89,451,986	18.0%
U.S. Common Shares	33,432,563	6.7%
Bond & Income	50,466,349	10.1%
Foreign Bond & Income	5,822,886	1.2%
Dividend & Income	54,246,567	10.9%
Mortgage	5,181,775	1.0%
Real Estate	1,827,013	0.4%
Total Non-Money Market	446,834,919	89.8%
Money Market	48,560,967	9.8%
Foreign Money Market	1,917,424	0.4%
Total Money Market	50,478,391	10.2%
Total	497,313,310	100.0%

Table 5–4 presents the December 31, 2004 data for mutual funds in Canada. As noted previously, the requirements of Canada Customs and Revenue Corporation (CCRA) mean that separate funds are produced for foreign assets. Within equity funds, Canadian, Foreign, and U.S. Common Share Funds make up a total of 48 percent, with balanced funds, which contain a mix of income and equity, adding a further 18 percent. Income funds (Bond & Income, Foreign Bond & Income, Dividend & Income), whose focus is on generating current income, make up another 22.2 percent, while the low-risk, short-term money market funds are only 10.2 percent of the assets reported.

The choice of the investor is to meet his or her investment objectives (e.g. diversification while satisfying RRSP requirements in order to keep the funds tax-sheltered), and also to minimize the fees paid, as discussed below. Table 5–5 lists the top 20 mutual funds by asset size as of February 28, 2005. The end of February marks the deadline for Canadians to contribute to their RRSPs and be able to claim the amount against their income taxes for the previous year. The four Global Equity funds are classified as 'Foreign' (Templeton Growth Fund Ltd., Trimark Select Growth, AGF International Value, and MD Growth), requiring that they meet the restrictions for foreign content if they are added to an RRSP. The rest of the top 20 funds by asset size are RRSP-eligible, reflecting the emphasis on retirement savings in Canada.

marked-to-market
Adjusting asset and balance sheet values to reflect current market prices.

Investor Returns from Mutual Fund Ownership

The return an investor gets from investing in mutual fund shares reflects three aspects of the underlying portfolio of mutual fund assets. First, income and dividends are earned on those assets; second, capital gains occur when assets are sold by a mutual fund at prices higher than the purchase price; third, capital appreciation in the underlying values of the assets held in a fund's portfolio add to the value of mutual fund shares. With respect to capital appreciation, mutual fund assets are normally **marked-to-market** daily. This means that the managers of the fund calculate the current value of each mutual fund share by computing the daily market value of the fund's total asset portfolio and then dividing this amount by the number of mutual fund shares outstanding. The resulting value is called the **net asset value (NAV)** or **net asset value per share (NAVPS)** of the fund. This is the price the investor gets when selling shares back to the fund that day or buying any new shares in the fund on that day.

**net asset value
(NAV)** *or* **net asset
value per share
(NAVPS)**
The net asset value of a mutual fund is equal to the market value of the assets in the mutual fund portfolio divided by the number of shares outstanding.

TABLE 5–5 The Largest Mutual Funds Ranked by Assets Held, February 28 2005

Fund Name	Asset Class	Assets ($ millions)	NAVPS ($) (April 7/05)	Return (%) 1 Year	3 Year	Load Type	MER (%)
Investors Dividend-A	Canadian Dividend	9,094.0	20.497	7.98	n.a.	BE	2.78
RBC Balanced	Canadian Balanced	7,138.1	11.690	6.95	5.94	NL	2.35
iUnits S&P/TSX 60 Index	Canadian Equity (Pure)	6,641.4	53.611	10.34	8.78	NL	0.17
Templeton Growth Fund Ltd.	Global Equity	6,063.4	10.390	2.81	1.22	OPT	2.40
Trimark Select Growth	Global Equity	5,514.7	17.337	−0.14	1.02	OPT	2.35
Mackenzie Ivy Canadian	Canadian Equity	5,406.8	28.497	9.28	4.79	OPT	2.46
RBC Monthly Income	Canadian Balanced	5,276.4	12.565	11.94	10.81	NL	1.19
TD Canadian Money Market	Canadian Money Market	5,261.3	10.000	1.45	1.79	NL	0.95
TD Canadian Bond	Canadian Bond	5,108.9	12.980	5.23	7.92	NL	1.07
Fidelity Canadian Asset Alloc.-A	Canadian Tactical Asset Allocation	4,960,2	23.140	9.29	6.96	OPT	2.48
RBC Dividend	Canadian Dividend	4,668.0	36.420	11.92	11.74	NL	1.77
RBC Premium Money Market	Canadian Money Market	4,241.7	10.000	2.03	2.36	NL	0.34
AGF International Value	Global Equity	4,144.6	37.760	−2.24	−3.08	OPT	2.80
Mackenzie Ivy Growth & Income	Canadian Balanced	4,104,4	22.412	7.53	5.24	OPT	2.20
TD Premium Money Market	Canadian Money Market	3,872.3	10.000	2.09	2.41	NL	0.32
MD Growth	Global Equity	3,854,1	10.550	2.46	2.32	NL	1.46
RBC Canadian Equity	Canadian Equity	3,793.3	20.177	10.85	9.32	NL	2.04
Trimark Select Canadian	Canadian Equity	3,788.8	12.059	9.73	8.44	OPT	2.34
RBC Canadian Money Market	Canadian Money Market	3,437.3	10.000	1.41	1.74	NL	0.96
CIBC Monthly Income	Canadian Balanced	3,350.8	13.410	12.37	11.38	NL	1.40

Note: BE = back end load, NL = no load, OPT = option to choose front end or back end load

Source: The *Globe and Mail* at *www.globefund.com*

EXAMPLE 5–1

Effect of Capital Appreciation on NAV

Suppose a mutual fund contains 1,000 shares of Canadian Tire currently trading at $37.75, 2,000 shares of Encana currently trading at $43.70, and 1,500 shares of CIBC currently trading at $46.67. The mutual fund currently has 15,000 shares outstanding held by investors. Thus, today, the NAV of the fund is calculated as

$$NAV = ((1,000 \times \$37.75) + (2,000 \times \$43.70) + (1,500 \times \$46.67)) \div 15,000 = \$13.01$$

If next month Canadian Tire shares increase to $45, Encana shares increase to $48, and CIBC shares increase to $50, the NAV (assuming the same number of shares outstanding) would increase to

$$NAV = ((1,000 \times \$45) + (2,000 \times \$48) + (1,500 \times \$50)) \div 15,000 = \$14.40$$

open-end mutual fund

The supply of shares in the fund is not fixed but can increase or decrease daily with purchases and redemptions of shares.

Most mutual funds are **open-end** in that the number of shares outstanding fluctuates up and down daily with the amount of share redemptions and new purchases. With open-end mutual funds, investors buy and sell shares from and to the mutual fund company. Thus, the demand for shares determines the number outstanding and the NAV of shares is determined solely by the market value of the underlying securities held in the mutual fund divided by the number of shareholders outstanding.

EXAMPLE 5–2

Effect of Investment Size on NAV

Consider the mutual fund in Example 5–1, but suppose that today 1,000 additional investors buy into the mutual fund at the current NAV of $13.01. This means that the fund manager now has $13,010 in additional funds to invest. Suppose the fund manager decides to use these additional funds to buy additional shares in Canadian Tire. At today's market price he or she can buy $13,010 ÷ $37.75 = 344 additional shares of Canadian Tire. Thus, the mutual fund's new portfolio of shares would be 1,344 in Canadian Tire, 2,000 in Encana, and 1,500 in CIBC. At the end of the month the NAV of the portfolio would be

$$\text{NAV} = ((1,344 \times \$45) + (2,000 \times \$48) + (1,500 \times \$50)) \div 16,000 = \$14.47$$

given the appreciation in value of all three stocks over the month.

Note that the fund's value changed over the month due to both capital appreciation and investment size. A comparison of the NAV in Example 5–1 with the one in this example indicates that the additional shares alone enabled the fund to gain a slightly higher NAV than had the number of shares remained static ($14.47 versus $14.40).

closed-end investment companies
Specialized investment companies that invest in securities and assets of other firms but have a fixed supply of shares outstanding themselves.

real estate investment trust (REIT)
A closed-end investment company that specializes in investing in mortgages, property, or real estate company shares.

Open-end mutual funds can be compared to most regular corporations traded on stock exchanges and to **closed-end investment companies,** both of which have a fixed number of shares outstanding at any given time. For example, **real estate investment trusts (REITs)** are closed-end investment companies that specialize in investment in real estate company shares and/or in buying mortgages. With closed-end funds, investors must buy and sell the investment company's shares on a stock exchange similar to the trading of corporate stock. Since the number of shares available for purchase at any moment in time is fixed, the NAV of the fund's shares is determined not only by the value of the underlying shares but also by the demand for the investment company's shares themselves. When demand is high, the shares can trade at more than the NAV of the securities held in the fund. In this case, the fund is said to be *trading at a premium,* that is, at more than the fair market value of the securities held. When the value of the closed-end fund's shares are less than the NAV of its assets, its shares are said to be *trading at a discount,* that is, at less than the fair market value of the securities held.

EXAMPLE 5–3

Market Value of Closed-End Mutual Fund Shares

Because of high demand for a closed-end investment company's shares, the 50 shares (N_S) are trading at $20 per share ($P_S$). The market value of the equity-type securities in the fund's asset portfolio, however, is $800, or $16 ($800 ÷ 50) per share. The market value balance sheet of the fund is shown below:

Assets		Liabilities and Equity	
Market value of asset portfolio	$800	Market value of closed-end fund shares ($P_S \times N_S$)	$1,000
Premium	$200		

The fund's shares are trading at a premium of $4 (200 ÷ 50) per share.

Because of low demand for a *second* closed-end fund, the 100 shares outstanding are trading at $25 per share. The market value of the securities in this fund's portfolio is $3,000, or each share has a NAV of $30 per share. The market value balance sheet of this fund is:

Assets		Liabilities and Equity	
Market value of asset portfolio	$3,000	Market value of closed-end fund shares (100 × $25)	$2,500
Discount	−$500		

Mutual fund investors can get information on the performance of mutual funds from several places. For example, for a comprehensive analysis of mutual funds, the *Globe and Mail* and Morningstar, Inc., offer information on over 10,000 open-end and closed-end funds. Neither the *Globe and Mail* nor Morningstar own, operate, or hold an interest in any mutual fund. Thus, they are recognized as leading providers of unbiased data and performance analysis (e.g., of returns) for the industry.

www.morningstar.ca

Mutual Fund Costs

Mutual funds charge shareholders a price or fee for the services they provide (i.e., management of a diversified portfolio of financial securities). Two types of fees are incurred by investors: sales loads and fund operating expenses. We discuss these next. The total cost to the shareholder of investing in a mutual fund is the sum of the annualized sales load and other fees charged.

Load versus No-Load Funds

An investor who buys a mutual fund share may be subject to a sales charge, sometimes as high as 8.5 percent. In this case, the fund is called a **load fund**.[7] Other funds that directly market shares to investors do not use sales agents working for commissions and have no up-front commission charges; these are called **no-load funds.**

The argument in favor of load funds is that their managers provide investors with more personal attention and advice than managers of no-load funds. However, the cost of this increased attention may not be worthwhile. It can be seen from Table 5–5 that, with the exception of the largest fund, Investors Dividend-A, which carries a back end load, and the U.S.-based funds which give the investor the option to choose to pay either a front-end or a back-end fee, the top funds in Canada are no load funds.

Fund Operating Expenses

In contrast to one-time up-front load charges on the initial investment in a mutual fund, annual fees are charged to cover all fund level expenses experienced as a percent of the fund assets. One type of fee (called a management fee) is charged to meet operating costs (such as administration and shareholder services). In addition, mutual funds generally require a small percentage (or fee) of investable funds to meet fund level marketing and distribution costs.

The amount the investor pays to the fund for investment management and administrative costs (excluding brokerage fees) is reported as a **management fee**. As shown in Table 5–5, the level of management fees is expressed as the **management expense ratio (MER)** which is the ratio of all the costs to operate a fund as a percentage of the average total assets in the fund. The quoted returns are net of the MER. The high MERs of the top foreign funds in Table 5–5, along with the appreciation of the Canadian currency, are reflected in the negative one-year returns reported for Trimark Select Growth (return = −0.14 percent, MER = 2.3 percent) and AGF International Value (return = −2.24 percent, MER = 2.80 percent). The focus on returns and the MER has meant that Canadian mutual funds are aware of their expenses, and can use a low MER as a marketing advantage.

The MER is often increased by the inclusion of a **trailer fee** (also called a trailer commission), which is an amount paid monthly or quarterly to the **investment advisor**

load fund
A mutual fund with an up-front sales or commission charge that has to be paid by the investor.

no-load fund
A mutual fund that does not charge up-front fees or commission charges on the sale of mutual fund shares to investors.

management fee
The amount paid to an investment manager for operating a mutual fund.

management expense ratio (MER)
A mutual fund's operating costs expressed as a percentage of its total average assets.

trailer fee
A commission paid monthly or quarterly to the investment advisor who sells a fund. It is payable as a percentage of the assets for as long as the investor owns the fund.

investment advisor
A person licenced to sell investment products to the public.

---

[7] Another kind of load, called a *back-end load*, is sometimes charged when mutual fund shares are sold by investors. Back-end loads, also referred to as deferred sales charges, are an alternative way to compensate the fund managers, or sales force for their services.

(i.e., the person who sells the fund to the investor) as long as the investor owns the fund. These fees are controversial as they may amount to 50 basis points or 0.5 percent per year of the amount of assets owned by the investor and, since they are essentially a sales commission, do not relate to the actual management of the funds year to year. The payment of trailer fees is included in the fund's prospectus, but many investors rely on their advisor's recommendations. The advisor has a conflict of interest and could recommend those funds for which he/she would receive a trailer fee.[8]

INTERNET EXERCISE

Go to the *Globe and Mail's* Globefund Web site and obtain data for the top mutual funds by asset size. Go to www.globefund.com. Click on "Fund Filter." Under "Total Assets" set the drop down menus to "Greater than or equal to" on the left and "$5,000 M" on the right. Click on "Go." The report listed will show you the top funds. You can change the information displayed by clicking on the "Report Type" tabs above the chart and selecting "Key Facts." This will show the funds by asset size. Have the rankings of the funds changed since February 28, 2005 as reported in Table 5–5? How have total assets changed?

EXAMPLE 5–4

Calculation of Mutual Fund Costs

The cost of mutual fund investing to the shareholder includes both the one-time sales load and any annual fees charged. Because the sales load is a one-time charge, it must be converted to an annualized payment incurred by the shareholder over the life of his or her investment. With this conversion, the total shareholder cost of investing in a fund is the sum of the annualized sales load plus any annual fees.

For example, suppose an investor purchases fund shares with a 4 percent front-end load and expects to hold the shares for 10 years. The annualized sales load[9] incurred by the investor is

$$4 \text{ percent}/10 \text{ years} = .4 \text{ percent per year}$$

Further, suppose the fund has a management expense ratio of 1 percent per year. The annual total shareholder cost for this fund is calculated as

$$.4 \text{ percent} + 1 \text{ percent} = 1.4 \text{ percent per year}$$

Concept Questions

1. Describe the difference between short-term and long-term mutual funds.
2. What have been the trends in the number of mutual funds since 1970?
3. What are the three biggest mutual fund companies? How have their funds performed in recent years?
4. Describe the difference between open-end and closed-end mutual funds.

---

[8] For a controversial discussion of mutual fund management fees, see M. Warywoda, "What Canadians Pay for Fund Management," June 10, 2003, at Morningstar.ca which found that MERs rose by approximately 60 basis points (0.6 percent) between 1995 and 2003. The industry disputed his methodology and his results. The question of MERs is still topical. See R. Carrick, "You're footing the bill for fund trailer fees," the *Globe and Mail*, July 10, 2003 and R. Carrick, "Who are the low-cost leaders?" the *Globe and Mail*, November 27, 2004. Since the mutual fund pricing is done on funds whose values and number of units outstanding may change on a daily basis, calculating the returns can be a difficult exercise, and the results subject to interpretation. See K. Ruckman, 'Expense ratios of North American mutual funds," *The Canadian Journal of Economics*, February 2003, Vol. 36, Iss. 1, p.192; A. Mawani, M. Milevsky, and K. Panyagometh, "The impact of personal income tax on returns and rankings of Canadian equity mutual funds," *Canadian Tax Journal*, 2003, Vol. 51, Iss. 2, p. 863; and R. Deaves, "The Comparative Performance of Load and No-Load Mutual Funds in Canada," *Canadian Journal of Administrative Sciences*, December 2004, 21(4), pp. 326–333.

[9] Convention in the industry is to annualize the sales load without adjusting for the time value of money.

REGULATION

www.mfda.ca

Mutual Fund Dealers Association of Canada (MFDA)
An SRO governing issues related to mutual funds in Canada.

The mutual fund industry is regulated by the provincial and territorial securities commissions (e.g., The Ontario Securities Commission, OSC) and thus is subject to the rules regarding securities sales and distribution. In addition, each mutual fund is a member of a self-regulating organization (SRO) such as the Investment Dealer's Association of Canada and the **Mutual Fund Dealers Association of Canada (MFDA)**. However, Canadian FIs and investors are globally oriented and integration of the Canadian and the U.S. financial markets means that cross-border issues are important for both Canadian FIs and Canadian regulators. The actions of the Securities and Exchange Commission (SEC), including the Sarbanes-Oxley Act of 2002, and the prosecution of brokers for insider trading and market timing have implications for Canadian markets and have focused global attention on corporate governance and stable and efficient capital markets.

In the early 2000s, the U.S. Securities and Exchange Commission (SEC) investigated securities violations by the mutual fund industry. The market for mutual funds was rocked by charges of **market timing**, **late trading** (also called **backward pricing**), and **directed brokerage fees**.

market timing
Excessive buying and selling of securities to take advantage of arbitrage opportunities between different markets.

Market timing involves short-term trading of mutual funds that seeks to take advantage of short-term discrepancies between the price of a mutual fund's shares and out-of-date values on the securities in the fund's portfolio. It is especially common in international funds as traders can exploit differences in time zones. Typically, market timers hold a fund for only a few days. For example, when Asian markets close with losses, but are expected to rebound the following day, market timers can buy a mutual fund, investing in Asian securities after the loss on that day and then sell the shares for a profit the next day. This single-day investment dilutes the profits of the fund's long-term investors, while market timers profit without much risk.

late trading (backward pricing)
Illegally buying or selling securities submitted after the closing time at that day's price.

The U.S. late trading allegations involved cases in which some investors were able to buy or sell mutual fund shares long after the price had been set at 4:00 PM Eastern time each day (i.e., after the close of the exchange). Under existing rules, investors have to place an order with their broker or another FI by 4:00 PM. If the mutual fund company has not have received the order until much later, legally must be **forward priced**, that is, processed at the next trading day's price. However, because of this time delay, some large U.S. investors had been able to illegally call their broker back after the market closed and alter or cancel their order. The Canadian system differs in that most orders are processed through the banks or through a clearing agency, FundSERV Inc. who automatically time-stamp the order and place it in the queue for next day pricing. This makes late trading difficult in Canada.

directed brokerage fees
Fees paid to brokerage firms for promoting a stock or mutual fund.

Directed brokerage involves arrangements between mutual fund companies and brokerage houses and whether those agreements improperly influenced which funds brokers recommended to investors. The U.S. investigation examined whether some mutual fund companies agreed to direct orders for stock and bond purchases and sales to brokerage houses that agreed to promote sales of the mutual fund company's products.

forward pricing
Execution of a security trade received after market hours at the following day's price.

Table 5–6 summarizes the U.S. investigations that resulted in some of the largest names in the U.S. securities industry (Bank of America, Charles Schwab, Citigroup, Merrill Lynch) being disciplined, destroying investor confidence in the fairness of the markets. In 2003, in response to the U.S. situation, an investigation into practices

TABLE 5–6   U.S. Mutual Fund Investigations in the Early 2000s

Company	Charge	Results
Alliance Capital	Market timing	$250 million settlement; 2 employees fired
Bank of America	Market timing/ late trading	$515 million settlement; 3 employees fired; several more employees resigned
Bank One	Market timing	2 managers resigned
Bear Stearns	Market timing	6 employees fired
Canary Capital	Market timing/ late trading	$40 million settlement
Charles Schwab	Late trading	2 employees fired
Citigroup	Market timing/ late trading	5 employees fired
Federated Investors	Market timing	Actions pending
Fred Alger & Co.	Market timing/ late trading	Vice chairman convicted of felony and fined $400,000; 2 employees fired
Janus Capital	Market timing	$226 million settlement; CEO and others resign; fee reductions of $125 million
Merrill Lynch	Market timing	3 employees fired
MFS Investment Management	Market timing	$225 million settlement; fee reductions of $125 million
Millennium Partners	Late trading	Fund trader pleads guilty and sentenced to up to 4 years in prison
Morgan Stanley	Directed brokerage; improper fees	$50 million settlement
PBHG Funds	Market timing	Co-founders resign
Pilgrim, Baxter & Associates	Market timing	2 founders resign
Prudential Securities	Market timing	12 employees fired; 7 employees facing charges
Putnam Investments	Market timing; improper fees	$110 million settlement; CEO resigns; 6 fund managers resign
Security Trust	Market timing	Company closed; CEO, president, and head of trading operations charged with grand larceny and fraud
Strong Capital Management	Market timing	$140 million settlement; chairman of mutual fund unit resigns; fee reductions of $35 million

Source: Author's research.

in Canada was set up with the provincial securities regulators, the IDA, and the MFDA. From late 2003–2004, Canadian mutual funds were questioned about market timing (which is not illegal in Canada but is not in the interests of all investors in the funds) and late trading. The report was released in March 2005, and agreements were made with 5 mutual fund dealers (CI Mutual Funds, $49.3 million, AGF Funds, $29.2 million, IG Investment Management, $19.2 million, and AIC, $58.8 million) to repay $156.5 million to investors harmed by the trading practices.

The result of both the Canadian and the U.S. investigations is the increased and ongoing scrutiny of the industry by investors and the movement towards more regulation in order to ensure a transparent system that is fair for investors and promotes efficient markets. The major proposals include independent committees to review issues of conflicts of interest but there is a tradeoff between industry independence and investor protection.[10]

Concept Questions

1. Who regulates mutual funds in Canada?

HEDGE FUNDS

History, Size, Structure, and Composition of the Industry

Hedge funds are a type of investment pool that solicits funds from wealthy individuals (also called high net worth individuals whose financial assets exceed $1 million) and other investors (e.g. banks, insurance companies) and invests these funds on their behalf. Hedge funds, however, are not technically mutual funds in that, in many cases, they are subject to virtually no regulatory oversight in Canada, the U.S., or globally. The absence of hedge fund regulations is due to the small number of investors permitted in each fund as well as the fact that investors are viewed as being sufficiently sophisticated so as not to need protection. Therefore, hedge funds are usually sold without a prospectus and generally are not required to publish financial statements on the System for Electronic Document Analysis and Retrieval (SEDAR).

Hedge funds grew in popularity in the 1990s as investors saw returns of over 40 percent after management fees (often more than 25 percent of the fund's profits).[11] They came to the forefront in the news in the late 1990s when one large hedge fund, Long-Term Capital Management (LTCM), nearly collapsed. The LTCM's troubles not only hurt its investors, but arguably came close to damaging the world's financial system through the credit risk exposure of other FIs. LTCM had lines of credit from financial institutions such as banks and brokerages that were used to increase the size of its investment pool and to take advantages of arbitrage opportunities. At its peak, LTCM only had approximately US$5 billion in capital supporting US$120 billion in investments, a debt to equity ratio of 24 times. To prevent LTCM's collapse, the U.S. Federal Reserve intervened by brokering a US$3.6 billion bailout by a consortium of some of the world's largest financial institutions.

Using traditional risk-adjusted measures of performance (such as Sharpe ratios), the performance of hedge funds has been very strong compared to traditional financial investments such as stocks and bonds.[12] Many hedge funds posted strong returns during the early 2000s even as stock returns were plummeting.

---

[10] The full report, Ontario Securities Commission Report on Mutual Fund Trading Practices Probe, March 2005, available online at www.osc.gov.on.ca, discusses the nature of the investigation as well as proposed policy and regulatory changes. A comparison of the U.S. and Canadian regulation of mutual funds is given in S. G. Kelman, "The Canadian Way," *CA magazine*, November 2004, 137 (9), pp. 36–38. See E. Church, "Watchdogs to put more bite in mutual fund conflict rules," *The Globe and Mail*, May 27, 2005, page B1 for a summary of the consultation process which is leading towards better governance in the industry and the restoration of investors' confidence in the markets.

[11] Although S. J. Brown, in "Hedge Funds: Omniscient or Just Plain Wrong," *Pacific Basin Finance Journal* 9 (2001) pp. 301–11, found that over the period 1989–1995, hedge funds earned, on average, 3 percent less than the S&P 500 index over the same period. Further, hedge fund risk was below that of the S&P 500 index.

[12] However, as pointed out by F. R. Edwards and S. Gaon in "Hedge Funds: What Do We Know?" *Journal of Applied Corporate Finance*, Fall 2003, pp. 58–71, data deficiencies in the reporting and collection of hedge fund returns somewhat reduce confidence in all measures of hedge fund performance. Further, the inability to explain returns of individual hedge funds with standard multifactor models leaves open the possibility that it is not possible to properly measure the risk associated with at least some hedge fund strategies. If so, risk-adjusted returns earned by hedge funds may be overstated.

TABLE 5–7
Canadian Hedge
Funds by Fund
Size ($ billions)

Source: Investor Economics
— Hedge Funds Report,
Winter 2005 Edition.

	No. of Funds	Total Assets ($ billions)	Share
Assets < $25 million	107	0.9	6.7%
Assets $25 to $100 million	60	3.5	24.5%
Assets > $100 million	24	9.6	68.4%
Total	191	14.1	100.0%

Though no hard data exists, industry sources estimate that there are over 7500 hedge funds in the U.S. in 2005, and global assets may be in excess of US$1 trillion. A report on the hedge fund industry by the IDA, using statistics estimated by Investor Economics, a consulting firm in Toronto, reported 191 Canadian hedge funds with assets of $26.6 billion in 2004. Of this, $14.1 billion represented Canadian-sponsored assets (Table 5–7). Initially, hedge fund managers found mainly wealthy individual investors to invest in their funds, but in the late 1990s, corporate pension plan sponsors, insurance companies, and university endowment funds became important investors such that $10.9 billion hedge fund assets were pension plan assets at June 2004.[13]

Some hedge funds take positions (using sophisticated computer models) speculating that some prices will rise faster than others. For example, a hedge fund may buy (take a long position in) a bond expecting that its price will rise. At the same time the fund will borrow (taking a short position) in another bond and sell it, promising to return the borrowed bond in the future. Generally, bond prices tend to move up and down together. Thus, if prices go up as expected, the hedge fund will gain on the bond it purchased while losing money on the bond it borrowed. The hedge fund will make a profit if the gain on the bond it purchased is larger than the loss on the bond it borrowed. If, contrary to expectations, bond prices fall, the hedge fund will make a profit if the gains on the bond it borrowed are greater than the losses on the bond it bought. Thus, regardless of the change in prices, the simultaneous long and short positions in bonds will minimize the risk of overall losses for the hedge fund. The IDA's report classifies this strategy as **non-directional** since the direction of market-movement is irrelevant and so the market risk exposure for the hedge fund is low.

Despite their name, hedge funds do not always "hedge" their investments to protect the fund and its investors against market price declines and other risks. The IDA's report points out that some strategies may be **event-driven** (e.g. potential mergers) and others are **opportunistic**, designed to take advantage of discrepancies in global macroeconomic conditions or markets. For example, though bond prices generally move in the same direction, the risk in hedge funds is that bond prices may unexpectedly move faster in some markets than others. In 1997 and 1998 computer models used by LTCM detected a price discrepancy between U.S. Treasury markets and other bonds (including high-yield corporate bonds, mortgage-backed securities, and European government bonds). LTCM consequently shorted U.S. Treasury securities (betting that their prices would fall) and took long positions in other types of bonds (betting their prices would rise). However, unexpectedly, in 1998 large drops in many foreign stock markets caused money to pour into the U.S. Treasury markets,

non-directional strategy
An arbitrage position that allows a hedge fund to benefit whether market prices go up or down.

event-driven strategy
A hedge designed to take advantage of a potential occurrence in the market such as purchase of shares of a merger target, or an investment in distressed debt.

opportunistic strategy
A hedge designed to take advantage of temporary pricing discrepancies in markets.

---

[13] See Hedge Fund Working Group, "Regulatory Analysis of Hedge Funds", May 18, 2005, Investment Dealers Association of Canada, www.ida.ca. The data for the IDA's analysis was provided by Investor Economics, "Hedge Fund Report," Volume 2, Winter 2005.

driving Treasury security prices up and yields down. This drop in U.S. Treasury yields drove rates on mortgages down, which pushed down the prices of many mortgage-backed securities. Further, the flight to U.S. Treasury security markets meant a drop in funds flowing into European bond markets and high-yield corporate bond markets. With all of their positions going wrong, LTCM experienced huge losses.[14]

REGULATION

In recent years, hedge funds have played an even bigger role in terms of global capital flows. During the early 2000s, riskier securities around the globe became popular investments for hedge funds eagerly searching for higher returns in a low-interest-rate environment. In early 2004, emerging market bond yields started to rise far more rapidly than those on U.S. Treasury bonds, increasing the gap in yields between the two as investors moved out of the riskier emerging country bond market. As a result, as rising interest rates negatively impacted emerging market hedge fund investments, many hedge funds saw decreases in returns. Consequently, there are fears that hedge funds may see a repeat of 1998. However, no one fund is likely to pose a systemic risk since, after LTCM, the amount of borrowing that banks extend to any one hedge fund client is far more carefully monitored by bank regulators. But, given the copycat nature of hedge fund management, there is concern that similar fund strategies by many hedge funds are combining to create potential systematic LTCM-type problems. Along with the use of similar investment strategies, many hedge funds are using the same risk models. These models are often historically based and are subject to similar errors in predicting the future.

The International Organization of Securities Commissions (IOSCO, www.iosco.org), whose members represent securities regulators in 181 countries, including Canada and the U.S., and over 90 percent of the world's securities markets, issued a report in 1999 following LTCM's near-collapse. The report recommended that regulators require FIs with a "material exposure" to highly leveraged institutions (HLIs) to (1) disclose their relationships to hedge funds and (2) to enhance their risk management, particularly the credit risk that arises from lending to hedge funds.[15] In Canada, as hedge funds expand from targeting the sophisticated large investor to the smaller "retail" customer, securities regulators are starting to be concerned, hence the IDA's 2005 report, Regulatory Analysis of Hedge Funds. Unlike mutual funds, hedge funds are not required to report their holdings and they are usually organized as limited partnerships and are structured so as to be exempt from securities laws that govern their marketing practices, conflicts of interest, and disclosure of financials. The IDA's report recommended that these guidelines be reviewed. Discussions about regulating hedge funds have been spurred on by the scandal surrounding Portus Alternative Asset Management Inc., a hedge fund that has caused losses for investors and other FIs who referred investors such as Manulife Securities International Ltd., a unit of Manulife

---

[14] As pointed out in W. Fung and F. S. Hsieh, "The Risk in Hedge Fund Strategies: Theory and Evidence from Fixed Income Traders," working paper, Duke University, 2001, a major reason for LTCM's large loss was that it was so highly leveraged compared to other funds. LTCM was two to four times more leveraged than the typical fund. As expressed in W. H. Brittain, "Hedge Funds and the Institutional Investor," *Journal of International Financial Management and Accounting*, 12:2, 2001, pp. 225–34. The effort to understand risks experienced in hedge funds often lacks the overall logical framework that is broadly accepted in the traditional investment world.

[15] See Technical Committee of the International Organization of Securities Commissions, "Hedge Funds and Other Highly Leveraged Institutions," November, 1999, at www.iosco.com.

The blue-chip board of directors at Manulife Financial Corp. snapped to attention on Valentine's Day.

Manulife's audit and risk-management committee, famous within the financial industry for its depth, gathered to discuss the evolving scandal involving Portus Alternative Asset Management Inc., and Manulife's exposure to the hedge fund firm. There were worried looks around the room. The seven committee members were stunned to learn that Manulife's chief accountant, the firm's controller and auditors, knew next to nothing about Portus, let alone how Manulife Securities International Ltd. (MSIL), a relatively unknown Waterloo, Ont.-based mutual fund unit of the giant insurer, became embroiled with the controversial investment firm.

"It was a splash in the face of the board and senior management. They were utterly seized by it," said a source familiar with the events that unfolded inside Manulife.

For days, senior executive vice-presidents at Manulife met for hours at a time, scrambling to figure out the insurer's exposure. After all, Manulife had steered about $235-million worth of business to Portus, which accounted for almost 35% of the $730-million worth of assets Portus had under management when the Ontario Securities Commission temporarily froze its operations in mid February. The OSC, along with seven other provincial securities regulators, is investigating Portus's sales and compliance practices. Worse for Manulife, none of the big bank-owned dealers had jumped on the Portus bandwagon the way the giant insurer had, for which it collected about $11-million in referral and syndication fees.

By the time Manulife's 14-member board met on Feb. 16, Jean-Paul Bisnaire, senior executive vice-president and general counsel, had been enlisted to launch an exhaustive internal review.

Sources told the Financial Post that during the hour-long meeting, Manulife chief executive Dominic D'Alessandro and Michael Wilson, former federal finance minister and chairman of UBS Global Asset Management, expressed concern that Manulife had more questions than it had answers. "They both threw a fit," said a source. More worrisome is that a handful of directors were remotely acquainted with MSIL, a wholly-owned subsidiary that seemed to have operated below the radar screen. Inevitably, they began peppering Mr. Bisnaire with questions about the quality of the due diligence performed by Manulife before its agents referred the Portus investments to its clients.

"The board was shell-shocked," said a source familiar with Manulife's internal probe into the matter. "I don't think there was a director who knew we had a company that didn't do due diligence before referring Manulife clients to other products that it didn't manufacture."

The company's top legal gun was given his orders: Figure out how Manulife got dragged into Portus's orbit, find out whether the investments were backed by Societe Generale Canada—and why most of Manulife's competitors took a pass on Portus. Until they

Financial that sells mutual funds. (See Ethical Dilemmas Box) The global growth of hedge funds means that disclosure and regulation of their activities can be expected to increase in the future.

PENSION FUNDS

Size, Structure, and Composition of the Industry

Growth of mutual funds and hedge funds may be driven by retirement savings as previously discussed, but pension funds are directly driven by government regulations regarding retirement savings in Canada, and represent the biggest funds in Canada. Retirement savings in Canada come from:

1. Government-funded or sponsored plans, e.g. the Canada Pension Plan and Quebec Pension Plan
2. Employer-sponsored pension plans, e.g. **trusteed pension funds**, profit sharing plans, group RRSPs, and
3. Individual savings, e.g. RRSPs.

trusteed pension funds (employer pension plans)
Registered pension plans (RPPs) usually sponsored by employers for the benefit of their employees and governed by a trust agreement.

had those answers, a cone of silence descended on the country's largest insurance company.

"We're not in the business of having our agents screw things around," said the source familiar with Manulife. "Dominic stands for integrity. There's nothing higher on the company's agenda than this."

In the meantime, Portus shut down its operations and terminated almost all of its 60 employees after the OSC banned it from trading and returning funds to its 26,000 clients. Even so, the once high-flying hedge fund firm, which markets funds of hedge funds, continued to insist client money is "safe." (Late yesterday, Portus was put into receivership.)

On Feb. 21, five days after Manulife's board met, Messrs. D'Alessandro and Bisnaire met with OSC chairman David Brown to inform the head of the country's largest securities regulator that Manulife was conducting an internal investigation.

Sources say the Manulife executives told Mr. Brown of their intention to protect the investments made by clients referred to Portus by Manulife with a guarantee. They also offered the company's assistance and co-operation to OSC staff.

Messrs. D'Alessandro and Bisnaire then met with Michael Watson, director of enforcement at the OSC, and members of his staff. Bev Margolian, executive vice-president and chief risk officer and Manulife's lawyers from Fasken Martineau DuMoulin LLP also attended.

During the meeting, the Post has learned Manulife was told the "OSC is fairly comfortable that it has ring-fenced" the notes from Societe Generale, which are held in an account at Royal Bank of Canada. Manulife is said to have informed OSC staff that MSIL clients accounted for approximately 33% of Portus' total client list of 26,000, and their investments totalled $235 million, or 34.5% of the hedge fund firm's total assets of $730-million.

According to confidential documents, Manulife says it believes the "OSC is able to get its hands on all but 15% or 18% of the $730 million."

Manulife began referring clients to Portus in September, 2003, at the time the firm was called Paradigm Alternative Asset Management Inc. Sources say Andrew Cairns, a 36-year-old vice-president and senior sales executive at Portus, was responsible for snaring the lucrative referral relationship with Manulife's mutual fund unit. Mr. Cairns is a former employee of Manulife, who left the company in 2002.

According to sources, Manulife told the OSC its referral agreement required that its sales representatives at MSIL would refer their clients to Portus to act as a portfolio manager of bank note trust accounts. The product was offered via an offering memorandum, which outlined how investors could purchase units that would invest in a series of bank notes from a Canadian chartered bank — Societe Generale Canada — that would at maturity pay the principal.

Source: Theresa Tedesco, *National Post*, Page FP1, March 5, 2005. Material reprinted with the express permission of National Post Company, a CanWest Partnership.

The top 100 pension funds in Canada had total assets of $584.6 billion in 2004, as shown in Table 5–8. The dollar value of pension assets are the next largest source of FI assets after the Big Six banks, but, in 2004, that was equal to only 35.4 percent of the reported $1.65 trillion assets of the six large Canadian banks. While the focus of hedge funds and mutual funds is the market and returns in order to attract investors, pension funds are focused on return and risk in order to meet their liabilities to their beneficiaries at retirement. With the exception of **vested assets**, which may be withdrawn by an employee and placed into a restricted RRSP, the assets of pension funds are only withdrawn to meet payments to beneficiaries. The risk for pension funds is that their asset growth, which comes from both investment returns and new contributions, will not meet their liabilities to their beneficiaries.

As shown in Table 5–8, the ten largest pension funds in Canada are employer-sponsored by provincial governments for civil servants (e.g., teachers, hospital workers) who usually negotiate a pension plan and its benefits as part of a union contract. Plans may be employer-sponsored, union-sponsored, or jointly sponsored. Pensions can be a significant portion of the benefit package of an employee,

vested assets
Contributions to a pension plan which are legally owned by the employee and may be withdrawn prior to retirement and transferred to another registered plan in which the assets are locked in until retirement.

TABLE 5–8   Top 25 Pension Funds in Canada by Asset Size, 2004

Rank	Organization	2004 ($ millions)	2003 ($ millions)	$Diff ($ million)	In-house (%)	Balanced (%)	Specialist (%)
1	Ontario Teacher's Pension	81,719.0	74,431.0	7,288.0	78.8	0	21.2
2	Quebec Government and Public Employees' Retirement Plan (RREGOP)[1]	60,100.0	54,900.0	5,200.0	100	0	0
3	Ontario Municipal Employees Retirement System (OMERS)	36,195.2	32,726.0	3,469.2	79	0	21
4	Hospitals of Ontario Pension Plan	21,077.0	18,657.0	2,420.0	85.9	0	14.1
5	B.C. Municipal Pension Fund	18,205.9	16,504.0	1,701.9	66	0	34
6	B.C. Public Service Pension Fund	13,846.5	12,747.4	1,099.1	65.1	0	34.9
7	Ontario Pension Board	13,053.0	12,275.0	7788.0	35.3	62.3	2.4
8	Public Service Pension Plan[2]	12,947.0	5,800.0	7,147.0	14	0	86
9	B.C. Teachers' Pension Plan	12,501.2	11,448.0	1,053.2	64.2	0	35.8
10	Quebec Teachers' Superannuation Plan (RRE)[3]	12,500.0	12,800.0	−300.0		0	0
11	Canadian National Railways	12,287.4	11,596.5	690.9	95.6	4.4	0
12	Alberta—Local Authorities Pension Plan	10,807.4	9,642.7	1,164.7	54.7	00	45.3
13	Bell Canada Pension Plan[4]	10,620,9	10,321.1	299.8	100	0	0
14	OPSEU Pension Trust	19,457.0	9,625.0	832.0	19.3	0	80.7
15	Régime de retraite du personnel d'encadrement (RRPE, Québec)[5]	10,400,0	9,400.0	1,000.0	0	100	0
16	Canada Pension Plan	10,214.0	8,797.0	1,417.0	11.3	0	88.7
17	Hydro-Quebec	9,999.7	9,239.0	760.7	47.3	0	52.7
18	Air Canada Pension Master Trust Fund	9,009.0	8,391.0	618.0	0	3.5	96.5
19	Quebec Construction Industry**	8,526.0	8,237.9	288.1			
20	General Motors of Canada Ltd.	7,400.0	6,600.0	800.0	6	0	94
21	Ontario Power Generation	7,056.0	6,440.0	616.0	0	0	100
22	Nova Scotia Public Service	7,043.0	6.652.0	3910	32	0	68
23	Canadian Pacific Railway	6,109.0	5,665.3	443.7	0	0	100
24	Quebec Civil Service Superannuation Plan (RRF)[6]	4,900.0	5,000.0	−100.0		0	0
25	Alberta—Public Service Pension Plan	4,466.1	4,056.1	410.0	63.1	0	36.9

Source: Benefits Canada, "Pensions Without Borders", May 2005, p. 24, *www.benefitscanada.com*, 2005.

defined contribution plan
A pension plan that sets up a separate account for each employee. A certain percentage is contributed each year and is made available to the employee on retirement.

and may be classified as a **defined contribution plan**, by which an employer contributes a certain percentage each year (e.g. a percentage of profits) for the benefit of the employee whose payments on retirement depend on the amount in the plan, or a **defined benefit plan**, whose payments to employees on retirement are known and employer contributions are determined by actuarial calculations based on factors such as mortality rates and investment returns. A plan's assets are held in trust for the benefit of employees, but **vesting**, which gives the employee the legal right to the funds, may occur after a specified period.

BALANCE SHEET AND RECENT TRENDS

defined benefit plan
A pension plan that pays benefits to retirees based on a formula.

The importance of pension funds as FIs in Canada comes from their ability to hold significant ownership of both corporate debt and corporate equity. This differs from the banks, which are precluded from having significant equity holdings in any one

FIGURE 5–4
Evolving Assets of the Top 100 Pension Funds in Canada, 2000–2004

Source: Benefits Canada, "Pensions Without Borders," May 2005, p. 21, *www.benefits canada.com*, 2005

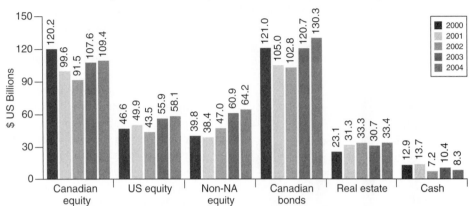

Evolving Assets of the Top 100 Pension Funds in Canada, 2000–2004

vesting
Granting of a legal right to an employee to receive funds in a pension plan regardless of whether they leave the company or the pension plan is dissolved.

company. Thus pension funds can be significant lenders (through investment in corporate bonds as well as through private placements) to and owners of domestic and foreign corporations. The growth of pension funds and their significant contribution to the capital of corporations, both in Canada and the United States, has led to the growth of shareholder activism and the push for pension funds to have representation on companies' boards of directors. In addition, pension funds have been limited to 30 percent foreign assets until 2005 whereas banks have had no limit on their foreign assets, which were 35 percent of total assets reported in 2004.

Figure 5–4 shows how the assets of the top pension funds in Canada have changed from 2000 to 2004. Unlike the mutual funds and the hedge funds, the liabilities of the pension funds are easier to forecast, particularly for those provinces (e.g. Ontario) that still have mandatory retirement. However, liquidity must be balanced with returns to meet their liabilities. The investment in assets also exposes the funds to interest rate risk, market risk, and foreign exchange risk. A major issue for the pension funds is the lifting of the 30 percent foreign content ceiling in 2005. Although many of the funds are at the 30 percent limit in 2005, many others have used clone funds and derivatives to increase their foreign content, as have the mutual funds.[16] As well, changes to the S&P/TSX Index to include income trusts in 2006 will have an impact on investment portfolios in Canada that use the return on the index as a benchmark. As long as the market performance in Canada remains strong, fund managers may not increase their foreign holdings, but the acquisition of foreign holdings should be cheaper for those funds who have used derivatives and who may now purchase foreign assets directly. If pension funds do decide to increase their foreign content, specialists in U.S., European, or Australasian equities may have an opportunity to increase their asset management in Canada.

privatization
The sale of government-owned assets to the private sector, often by IPO.

---

[16] See L.D. Johnson and W. W. Yu, "An analysis of the use of derivatives by the Canadian mutual fund industry," *Journal of International Money and Finance*, October 2004, Vol. 23, Iss. 6. pp. 947–970. Johnson and Yu found that derivative usage by mutual funds was low and had mixed results for risk and returns. The management of risk while limited to Canadian assets can be difficult given the level of concentration in the Canadian market. This issue is addressed in a report produced by William M. Mercer for the Pension Investment Association of Canada (PIAC), "Managing Risk in a Concentrated Market: Canadian Equity Benchmark Alternatives," 2000, available at www.piacweb.org, which covers the period when Nortel made up more than 15 percent of the TSE300 Index. The issue of concentrated markets also arises in other jurisdictions with small or developing capital markets such as New Zealand. See P. McGraw, "Privatization and the Corporate Cost of Capital in New Zealand: An Application of Fama and French (1999)," Review of Applied Economics April 2005, Vol. 1(1), pp. 1–20, which discusses the impact of a global market trend, **privatization**, on a small open economy.

FIGURE 5–5   **Active versus passive management of pension funds in Canada, 2004**

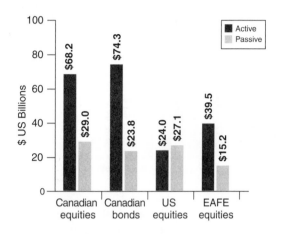

Source: Benefits Canada, "Pensions Without Borders," May 2005, p. 28

The search for returns along with the growth in size of pension fund assets has fuelled professional fund management in Canada. As shown in the three right-hand columns of Table 5–8, the management styles of pension funds vary from in-house (e.g., Bell Canada) to balanced (e.g., National Bank of Canada) to specialist (e.g., York University). In-house managers accounted for $279.0 billion of the assets, balanced managers for $33.5 billion, and specialist managers for $211.4 billion of the assets of the top 100 pension funds in Canada in 2004. In addition, the assets may be actively or passively managed. As shown in Figure 5–5, Canadian equities and bonds were more likely to be actively managed than investments in U.S. equities or European, Australasian, and Far East (EAFE) equities. Benefits Canada's list of the top 40 money managers in Canada in 2004 is shown in Table 5–9. From the last column, it can be seen that while some managers specialize in pension funds so that their pension assets equal their total assets, most funds manage pensions as well as other funds, earning a return on their investment in employees and their expertise. The largest manager of pension funds is the Caisse de dépôt et placement du Québec that manages the pensions of government employees in Quebec ($123.2 billion pension assets, 74.5 percent of the $165.36 billion assets under its management). Other asset managers are a mix of international (e.g., Barclays Global Investors Canada Limited) and Canadian (e.g., TD Asset Management Group).

Table 5–10 shows the revenue and expenditures of trusteed pension funds in Canada for 2001. Investment income represents 37 percent of the total revenue of the funds, a significant source of the long-term growth in assets of the funds. Contributions from employers and employees provided 22.3 percent of revenues. The major expenditures come from cash withdrawals, vested funds transferred to a locked-in fund controlled by the employee, at 39.6 percent of revenue and disbursements to pensioners at 39.6 percent. Disbursement to pensioners can be expected to increase over the coming years as the baby boom retires and starts drawing benefits. This demographic shift is of global significance, as it represents a switch from savings to consumption for global capital markets. The funding of the retirement of citizens in developed and developing countries was addressed by the World Bank in 2005, which produced a report recommending a move away from "pay as you go" plans (where current workers pay for the benefits of pensioners) to compulsory contributions of fully funded plans (where workers save part of their earnings). This represents a shift in thinking and the World Bank recently recommended that, as a significant public policy, countries adopt a five-pillar model of (1) public unfunded savings (2) private mandatory savings (3) voluntary savings (4) a tax-financed safety net and (5) other supports, primarily non-financial to ensure that their populations are supported in their retirement.[17]

---

[17] See *The Economist*, "Second thoughts on the third age," February 19, 2005, pp. 67–68. See also, Robert Holzman and Richard Hinz, "Old-Age Income Support in the 21st Century: The World Bank's Perspective on Pension Systems and Reform," The World Bank, June 2005.

TABLE 5–9   Top 40 Money Managers, 2004

Top 40 Money Managers					As of Dec. 31, 2004 ($ millions)	
			Total Pension Assets			
2004	**2003**	**Company**	**2004**	**2003**	**% Variance**	**Total Assets**
1	1	Calsse de depot et placement du Québec	123,202.0	97,190.0	26.8%	165,360.0
2	2	Barclays Global Investors Canada Limited	37,786.6	30,210.1	25.1%	51,003.5
3	4	TD Asset Management Group[1]	30,326.0	26,383.0	14.9%	106,630.0
4	3	Phillips, Hager & North Investments Management Ltd.	30,212.6	27,436.5	10.1%	50,378.8
5	5	Jarislowsky, Fraser Limited	26,258.0	23,536.0	11.6%	44,114.0
6	6	McLean Budden Ltd.	23,289.0	21,363.0	9.0%	33,480.0
7	7	State Street Global Advisors Ltd.	21,410.6	19,210.4	11.5%	28,981.6
8	12	Connor, Clark & Lunn Financial Group	15,434.5	10,233.6	50.8%	24,751.4
9	8	Greystone Managed Investments Inc.	15,335.9	13,398.9	14.5%	21,919.7
10	13	Addenda Capital Inc.	14,264.0	9,860.0	44.7%	21,404.0
11	10	Bimcor Inc.	12,816.4	12,518.0	2.4%	12,816.4
12	9	UBS Global Asset Management (Canada)	12,134.0	13,144.1	−7.7%	25,366.0
13	11	TAL Global Asset Management Inc.	10,533.9	12,165.0	−3.4%	54,115.8
14	17	Beutel Goodman & Company Ltd.	10,358.0	8,581.0	20.7%	11,750.0
15	15	AllanceBernstein Institutional Investment Mgmt.	10,166.0	9,510.0	6.9%	17,452.0
16	16	Legg Mason Canada Inc.	9,668.0	9,508.0	1.7%	12,745.0
17	14	Capital Guardian Trust Co.	9,613.3	9,732.3	−12%	10,932.0
18	21	Franklin Templeton Institutional	8,716.8	7,466.0	16.8%	15,928.0
19	18	Guardian Capital LP	8,212.0	7,522.0	9.2%	15,336.0
20	22	Natcan Investment Management	8,165.0	7,441.0	9.7%	28,533.0
21	20	JPMorgan Fleming Asset Management	8,143.6	7,474.5	9.0%	9,523.2
22	19	Northwater Capital Management Inc.	8,042.0	7,494.0	7.3%	8,344.0
23	24	GWL Investment Management Ltd.	7,342.8	6,760.6	8.6%	14,410.9
24	28	Letko, Brosseau & Associates Inc.	6,985.0	5,429.5	28.6%	10,957.0
25	25	New Brunswick Investment Management Corp.	6,917.9	6,233.0	11.0%	6,917.9
26	23	Standard Life Investments Inc.[2]	6,821.5	7,179.8	−5.0%	20,503.6
27	26	Bentall Capital	6,771.0	5,800.0	16.7%	10,089.0
28	27	Sprucegrove Investment Management Ltd.	6,650.5	5,482.5	21.3%	8,537.2
29		Wellington Management Company, LLP[3]	6,028.0	5,104.2	18.1%	7,998.0
30	32	Brandes Investment Partners, LLC	5,050.0	4,421.0	14.2%	12,949.0
31	33	AMI Partners Inc.	4,781.0	4,327.0	10.5%	5,076.0
32	34	YMG Capital Management Inc.	4,737.9	4,244.4	11.6%	15,057.1
33	30	MFC Global Investment Management	4,323.4	4,881.7	−11.4%	87,208.8
34	36	SEAMARK Asset Management Ltd.	4,124.3	3,903.5	5.7%	10,861.4
35	31	Sceptre Investment Counsel Limited	4,107.1	4,851.2	−15.3%	6,365.3
36	29	GE Asset Management[4]	4,020.7	4,966.4	−19.0%	4,544.0
37		AIM Trimark Investments	4,004.0	2,958.0	35.4%	43,022.0
38		Lelth Wheeler Investment Council Ltd.	3,896.0	2,700.0	44.3%	5,206.0
39		Foyston, Gordon & Payne Inc.	3,584.0	2,75.0	30.6%	7,178.0
40		lincluden Management Limited	3,538.0	3,170.1	11.6%	3,730.0
		Top 40 Total	547,771.3			
		2003 Top 70 Total	477,382.3			
		% Difference	14.7%			

Notes:
1. TD Assets Management Inc. and its affiliates
2. The total pension asset figure excludes $3,323.7 million and total asset figure excludes $5,177.9 million of U.K. assets managed by SLI North America.
3. Total pension asset figure for 2009 has been revised.
4. Total pension asset figure for 2009 has been revised.

Source: Benefits Canada, 2005, "A budget bonanza", April 2005, p. 44, *www.benefitscanada.com*
Note: EAFE denotes equities of Europe, Australasia, and the Far East

TABLE 5–10
Revenue and
Expenditures of
Trusteed Pension
Funds over $10
million in Canada,
2001 ($billions)

Source: Statistics Canada,
www.statcan.ca

	2001	Percentage of Revenue
Revenue:		
Employee contributions	5.2	8.8%
Employer contributions	8.0	13.5%
Total contributions	13.2	22.3%
Investment Income	22.0	37.1%
Net profit on sale of securities	7.7	13.0%
Miscellaneous	16.4	27.7%
Total non-contributions	24.1	40.7%
Total Revenue	59.3	100.0%
Expenditures:		
Pension payments out of funds	23.5	39.6%
Cost of pension purchased	0.4	0.6%
Cash withdrawals	16.3	27.6%
Administration Costs	1.7	2.8%
Net loss on sale of securities	7.8	13.2%
Other	1.0	1.6%
Total expenditures	50.7	85.4%

Regulation

Regulation of pension funds is entirely focused on the best interests of the owners or beneficiaries of the pensions' assets and the regulation, therefore, has not been left to SROs as for mutual funds. Some private pension plans (over 1000 in 2005) are regulated by and report to OSFI (e.g. Air Canada Pension Plan) and are subject to the Pension Benefits Standards Act of 1985. Others report to provincial bodies (i.e. Ontario Pension Board). Regulators are concerned with protecting the retirement savings of funds that may be in danger in the event of insolvency or bankruptcy proceedings, such as the reorganization of Air Canada in the early 2000s. OSFI may inspect the funds under its jurisdiction and, as well, provides guidelines for recommended industry practice that focuses on proper governance and accountability, as well as appropriate risk management practices.

Concept Questions

1. Why are mutual funds and hedge funds primarily self-regulated, whereas pension funds are regulated federally and provincially?
2. Compare the investment practices of mutual funds, hedge funds, and pension funds. Why might they differ?

GLOBAL ISSUES

As discussed above, because of their growth over the last decade, mutual funds, hedge funds, and pension funds have caught the attention of global regulators and market watchers. At issue is the stability of global financial markets and the concern about a repeat of the problems of the hedge fund LTCM.

The global magnitude of these funds is shown by the worldwide investment in mutual funds in Table 5–11. Mutual fund investment worldwide has increased over 300 percent from US$1.626 trillion in 1992 to US$6.543 trillion in 2003. This compares to growth of over 350 percent in U.S. funds. The relatively large return on U.S. stocks is the most likely reason for this growth in U.S. funds relative to other countries.

TABLE 5–11 Worldwide Assets of Open-End Investment Companies[1] (in millions of US dollars)

Non-U.S. countries	1999	2000	2001	2002	2003
Argentina	6,990	7,425	3,751	1,021	1,916
Australia	N/A	341,955	334,016	356,304	518,411
Austria	56,254	56,549	55,211	66,877	87,982
Belgium	65,461	70,313	68,661	74,983	98,724
Brazil	117,758	148,538	148,189	96,729	171,596
Canada	269,825	279,511	267,863	248,979	338,369
Chile	4,091	4,597	5,090	6,705	8,552
Czech Republic	1,473	1,990	1,778	3,297	4,083
Denmark[2]	27,558	32,485	33,831	40,153	49,533
Finland	10,318	12,698	12,933	16,516	29,967
France	656,132	721,973	713,378	845,147	1,148,446
Germany	237,312	238,029	213,662	209,168	276,319
Greece	36,397	29,154	23,888	26,621	38,394
Hong Kong	182,265	195,924	170,073	164,322	255,811
Hungary	1,725	1,953	2,260	3,992	3,936
India	13,065	13,507	15,284	20,364	29,800
Ireland	95,174	137,024	191,840	250,116	360,425
Italy	475,661	424,014	359,879	378,259	478,734
Japan	502,752	431,996	343,907	303,191	349,148
Korea	167,177	110,613	119,439	149,544	121,488
Liechtenstein	N/A	N/A	N/A	3,847	8,936
Luxembourg	661,084	747,117	758,720	803,869	1,104,112
Mexico	19,468	18,488	31,723	30,759	31,953
Netherlands	94,539	93,580	79,165	84,211	N/A
New Zealand	8,502	7,802	6,564	7,505	9,641
Norway	15,107	16,228	14,752	15,471	21,994
Philippines	117	108	211	474	792
Poland	762	1,546	2,970	5,468	8,576
Portugal	19,704	16,588	16,618	19,969	26,985
Romania	N/A	8	10	27	36
Russia	177	177	297	372	851
South Africa	18,235	16,921	14,561	20,983	34,460
Spain	207,603	172,438	159,899	179,133	255,344
Sweden	83,250	78,085	65,538	57,992	87,746
Switzerland	82,512	83,059	75,973	82,622	90,772
Taiwan	31,153	32,074	49,742	62,153	76,205
Turkey	N/A	N/A	N/A	6,002	14,164
United Kingdom	375,199	361,008	316,702	288,887	396,523
Total non-U.S.	**4,544,799**	**4,906,394**	**4,679,953**	**4,933,771**	**6,543,480**
Total U.S.	**6,846,339**	**6,964,667**	**6,974,951**	**6,390,360**	**7,414,084**
Total world	**11,391,138**	**11,871,061**	**11,654,904**	**11,324,131**	**13,957,564**

[1] Funds of funds are not included. Data include home-domiciled funds, except for Hong Kong, Korea, and New Zealand.
[2] Before 2003, data include special funds reserved for institutional investors.

Note: Components may not add to total because of rounding.
Source: Investment Company Institute, *2004 and 2004 Mutual Fund Fact Book* (Washington, D.C.: Investment Company Institute, May2004).Reprinted by permission of the Investment Company Institute. *www.ici.org*

In contrast, as this industry developed in countries throughout the world, the number of mutual funds worldwide (other than in the United States) increased over 150 percent from 18,183 in 1992 to 45,889 in 2003. The number of U.S. mutual funds increased 112 percent over this period.

As may be expected, the worldwide market for investment funds is most active in those countries with the most sophisticated securities markets (e.g. United States, Japan, France, Australia, and the United Kingdom). However, in the late 1990s and early 2000s, the Japanese economy resulted and the assets invested in mutual funds fell from US$502.7 billion in 1999 to US$432.0 (a drop of 14.1 percent) and the number of mutual funds fell from 3,444 to 2,884 (16.3 percent). Some FIs saw this decline in the Japanese market as an opportunity, and the U.S. Paine Webber Group teamed up with Yasuda Life Insurance Company and Merrill Lynch and bought the assets of the failed Japanese brokerage firm Yamaichi Securities in the late 1990s. Approximately 60 percent of Japan's savings was in low-yielding bank deposits or government-run institutions at the time.[18] The worldwide economic downturn in 2001–2002 also affected the global fund industry. Assets invested in non-U.S. mutual funds fell from US$4.91 trillion in 1999 to US$4.68 trillion in 2001. As the worldwide economic situation improved in 2003, so did assets invested in mutual funds, rising to US$6.54 trillion by year-end 2003.

A trend in the global markets in the 1990s has been the privatization of state-owned assets such as telephone companies and electric utilities. FIs have benefited from this process in generating fees for global advisors since privatization has been accomplished via IPOs and has resulted in the development of capital markets over the decade, providing a supply of assets for investment.[19]

Concept Questions

1. What have been the trends in the assets invested worldwide in mutual funds during the 1990s and early 2000s?

---

[18] It might be noted that as many European countries move away from state-sponsored pension plans to privately funded pension plans and retirement vehicles the rate of growth in mutual funds in these countries is likely to accelerate rapidly.

[19] See W. L. Megginson, R. C. Nash, J. M. Netter, and A. L. Schwartz, "The Long-Run Return to Investors in Share Issue Privatization", 2000, *Financial Management* 29(1), 67–77 and W. L. Megginson, J. M. Netter, "From State to market: A Survey of Empirical Studies on Privatization," 2001, *Journal of Economic Literature* 39, pp. 321–389. See also L. Booth, V. Aivazian, A. Demirguc-Kunt, and V. Maksimovic, "Capital Structures in Developing Countries," *The Journal of Finance*, Vol. LVI, No. 1, February, 2001, pp. 87–130 which discusses the impact of financial markets on capital structure.

Summary

This chapter provided an overview of mutual funds, hedge funds, and pension funds in Canada. Given the growth of savings, particularly retirement savings, in Canada, the amount of assets under administration, and the wealth management provided by FIs to diversify these funds for investors, Canadian and global regulators have focused attention on the activities of these funds and their potential to disrupt global market stability.

Questions and Problems

1. What is a mutual fund? In what sense is it a financial intermediary?

2. What are money market mutual funds? In what assets do these funds typically invest?

3. What are long-term mutual funds? In what assets do these funds usually invest?

4. Using the data in Figure 5–3, discuss the growth and ownership holding of long-term funds versus short-term funds.

5. How did the proportion of equities in long-term funds change between 1994 and 2004? How might an investor's preference for a mutual fund's objective change over time?

6. How does the risk of short-term funds differ from the risk of long-term funds?

7. What are the economic reasons for the existence of mutual funds; that is, what benefits do mutual funds provide for investors? Why do individuals rather than corporations hold most mutual funds shares?

8. What are the three possible components reflected in the return an investor receives from a mutual fund?

9. An investor purchases a mutual fund for $60. The fund pays dividends of $1.75, distributes a capital gain of $3, and charges a fee of $3 when the fund is sold one year later for $67.50. What is the net rate of return from this investment?

10. How is the net asset value (NAV) of a mutual fund determined? What is meant by the term *marked-to-market daily?*

11. A mutual fund owns 400 shares of Fiat, Inc., currently trading at $7, and 400 shares of Microsoft, Inc., currently trading at $70. The fund has 100 shares outstanding.
    a. What is the net asset value (NAV) of the fund?
    b. If investors expect the price of Fiat shares to increase to $9 and the price of Microsoft shares to decrease to $55 by the end of the year, what is the expected NAV at the end of the year?
    c. Assume that the expected price of the Fiat shares is realized at $9. What is the maximum price decrease that can occur to the Microsoft shares to realize an end-of-year NAV equal to the NAV estimated in (a)?

12. What is the difference between open-end and closed-end mutual funds? Which type of fund tends to be more specialized in asset selection? How does a closed-end fund provide another source of return from which an investor may either gain or lose?

13. Open-end Fund A owns 100 shares of Bell valued at $100 each and 50 shares of Toro valued at $50 each. Closed-end Fund B owns 75 shares of Bell and 100 shares of Toro. Each fund has 100 shares of stock outstanding.
    a. What are the NAVs of both funds using these prices?
    b. Assume that in one month the price of Bell stock has increased to $105 and the price of Toro stock has decreased to $45. How do these changes impact the NAV of both funds? If the funds were purchased at the NAV prices in (a) and sold at month end, what would be the realized returns on the investments?
    c. Assume that another 100 shares of Bell are added to Fund A. What is the effect on Fund A's NAV if the stock prices remain unchanged from the original prices?

14. What is the difference between a load fund and a no-load fund?

15. Suppose an individual invests $10,000 in a load mutual fund for two years. The load fee entails an up-front commission charge of 4 percent of the amount invested and is deducted from the original funds invested. In addition, annual fund operating expenses are 0.85 percent. The annual fees are charged on the average net asset value invested in the fund and are recorded at the end of each year. Investments in the fund return 5 percent each year paid on the last day of the year. If the investor reinvests the annual returns paid on the investment, calculate the annual return on the mutual fund over the two-year investment period.

16. Who are the primary regulators of the fund industry in Canada? How do their regulatory goals differ from those of other types of financial institutions?

17. How and why does the regulation of mutual funds, hedge funds, and pension funds differ?

18. Hedge funds are riskier than mutual funds. Discuss.

The Financial Services Industry: Finance Companies

In this chapter we provide an overview of finance companies, both private and crown corporations, in terms of:

▸ their size, structure and composition

▸ the services the industry provides

▸ the industry's competitive position

▸ the regulation of the industry, and

▸ global issues for the industry, including the role of the World Bank

INTRODUCTION

Our discussions so far have moved from highly-regulated FIs such as deposit-taking institutions (Chapter 2) to the relatively unregulated hedge funds covered in the last chapter. We now move to finance companies, an industry that, with the exception of the leasing arms of major banks, is unregulated. In addition, since many of the major players are private companies, it is difficult to measure the scope of the industry and its effect on the Canadian and North American economies. However, their role is important for small and medium-sized businesses and in supporting troubled companies. For example, GE Capital provided loans to keep Air Canada flying during its restructuring between 2003 and 2004 and $1.8 billion in refinancing as it came out of bankruptcy.

The primary function of finance companies is to make loans to both individuals and corporations. The services provided by finance companies include consumer lending, business lending, and mortgage financing. Some of their loans are similar to bank loans, such as consumer and car loans, but others are more specialized. The assets of finance companies are subject to credit risk, but this risk is mitigated because their loans are backed by collateral. Finance companies differ from banks in that they are not permitted to accept deposits but instead rely on short- and long-term debt (e.g. commercial paper) as a source of funds, often raising these funds in international markets. Their ability to offer loans is thus affected by their own ability to borrow. The downgrading of the debt of General Motors Corporation (GMC) and Ford Motor Credit Co. (Ford) to below investment grade in 2005 will have an effect on the operations of their financing subsidiaries. Finance companies are not subject to withdrawal risk as are banks, and, with the right credit conditions, are able to more closely match the maturities of their assets with those of their liabilities, controlling for liquidity risk. Additionally, finance companies often lend to customers that banks find too risky. However, since most of their assets are loans for capital expenditures, they are dependent on expansion in the economy for asset growth.

SIZE, STRUCTURE, AND COMPOSITION OF THE INDUSTRY

asset-based financing (ABF)/ asset-based lending (ABL)
A loan extended to a borrower based on the assets held as collateral.

structured finance
A unique loan and/or equity financing tailored to meet the specific needs of the borrower.

crown corporation
A firm owned by the federal or a provincial government, directly or indirectly.

www.gmacfs.com
www.fordcredit.com
www.citgroup.com
www.gecapital
canada.com

Finance companies offer lending services similar to banks, such as mortgages (residential and commercial), loans (e.g. **asset-based financing (ABF)** or **asset-based lending (ABL)**, **structured finance**, consumer loans), equipment leasing (e.g. automobile, aircraft), and credit cards. Finance companies in Canada are dominated by the unregulated institutions that are wholly-owned subsidiaries (and therefore private companies) of U.S.-based firms. General Motors Acceptance Corporation of Canada Limited (GMAC Canada) and Ford Motor Credit are the financing arms of the automobile manufacturers who provide most of the new car loans in Canada. In addition, there are **crown corporations** that also offer financing. Both these types of companies are shown in Table 6–1. In addition, while the major Canadian banks offer some asset-based financing through their commercial lending operations, Canadian Imperial Bank of Commerce (CIBC) formed CIT Business Credit Canada, a joint venture with CIT Group Inc., a large U.S.-based asset-backed lender, in order to compete for the larger deals. There has also been consolidation in the industry. Household Financial, in operation in Canada since 1928, whose assets were in excess of $2 billion (real estate mortgages, private-label credit cards, and personal loans) was taken over by HSBC Financial. These FIs are much less transparent in their activities, but they are performing more traditional, asset-based lending and providing competition for the large Canadian FIs who were discussed in Chapter 2.

The history of finance companies in North America has been the provision of loans to a clientele who are unable to get credit elsewhere. The first major finance company originated during the Depression in the United States when General Electric Corp. created General Electric Capital Corp. (GECC) as a means of financing appliance sales to cash-constrained customers who were unable to get installment credit from banks. Installment credit is a loan that is paid back to the lender with periodic payments (installments) consisting of varying amounts of interest and principal (e.g. car loans and home mortgages). A look at GECC's loan and lease portfolio today shows leases for almost 10,000 locomotive rail cars, 25,000 aircraft, and over US$1 billion in leveraged buyout financing.[1]

Because of the attractive rates they offer on some loans (such as the 0 percent financing offered on new car loans), their willingness to lend to riskier borrowers than banks, their often direct affiliation with manufacturing firms, and the relatively limited amount of regulation imposed on these firms, finance companies have been among the fastest growing FI groups in North America in recent years. Data collected by the U.S. Federal Reserve show the assets of U.S. finance companies equaled US$1,467.6 billion in 2003 as shown in Table 6–2 and US$104.3 billion in 1977 as shown in Table 6–3, a growth in assets of almost 1,307 percent in the last 26 years. GMAC Commercial Mortgage Corp. (GMACCM), a subsidiary of General Motors Acceptance Corp. (GMAC) is the largest commercial mortgage lender in the United States with a mortgage portfolio of over US$160 billion in place. The company announced in the late 1990s that it had

---

[1] See GECC's web at www.ge.com. In addition to its loans to Air Canada, GE Commercial Aviation Services has loaned over US$8 billion to global airlines. See D. Brady, B. Grow and L. Woellert, "Why GE is Keeping Loser Airlines Aloft," *Business Week*, February 2, 2005, Iss. 319, p. 35. For a perspective on GE in Canada, see J. Kirby, "Mr. Moneybags," *Canadian Business*, March 15–28, 2004, Vol. 77, Iss. 6, pp. 33–36. See A. Holloway, "Nice Assets, Here's the Cash," *Canadian Business*, March 15–28, 2004, Vol. 77, Iss. 6, pp. 39–40 and Y. Barcelo, "ABLS: Sharks or saviours?" *CA Magazine*, October 2004, Vol. 137, Iss. 8, pp. 22–28 for discussions of asset-based lending in Canada.

TABLE 6–1
Private and Crown-owned Finance Companies in Canada, 2004

Source: Company annual reports and Web sites

Company	Revenue ($ billions)	Assets ($ billions)
Privately-owned:		
CIT Group (Dec 04)*	n.a	US$2.4834
Ford Credit Canada (Dec 03)	1.9868	13.8365
GE Capital Canada**	n.a.	n.a.
GMAC of Canada, Ltd (Dec 04)	2.4109	n.a.

*Includes the assets of Newcourt Credit Group Inc.
**North American assets represent 8 percent of global assets of US$750.3 billion reported in 2004

Bank-owned asset backed lenders:
ABN-AMRO a division of ABN-AMRO Bank N.V. based in New York
CIT Business Credit Canada, a joint venture of CIBC and CIT Group
Congress Financial Corporation, owned by Wachovia Corporation, the fifth largest bank holding company in the U.S.
HSBC Financial Corporation Limited (formerly Household Financial Corporation), owned by U.K.-based HSBC Bank

Crown Corporations:		
The Business Development Bank of Canada (Mar 03)	$0.5660	$7.7914
Canada Mortgage and Housing Corp. (Dec 03)	$4.4300	$24.9680
Export Development Canada (Dec 03)	$1.5240	$21.1150
Farm Credit Canada (Mar 03)	$0.5721	$8.9911

TABLE 6–2
Assets and Liabilities of U.S. Finance Companies, 2003

Source: *Federal Reserve Bulletin,* June 2003, p. A30. *www.federalreserve.gov*

	Billions of US Dollars	Percent of Total Assets
Assets		
Accounts receivable gross	934.9	63.7%
Consumer	307.0	21.0
Business	453.9	30.9
Real estate	174.0	11.9
Less reserves for unearned income	(54.2)	(3.7)
Less reserves for losses	(24.0)	(1.6)
Accounts receivable net	856.7	58.4%
All other	610.9	41.6
Total assets	1,467.6	100.0%
Liabilities and Capital		
Bank loans	47.3	3.2%
Commercial paper	127.3	8.7
Debt due to parent	87.7	6.0
Debt not elsewhere classified	639.1	43.5
All other liabilities	344.4	23.5
Capital, surplus, and undivided profits	221.8	15.1
Total liabilities and capital	1,467.6	100.0%

mortgage broker
A firm which, for a fee, shops around to other FIs to find the most suitable mortgage at the best rates.

plans to expand its product mix to create one of the world's leading "one-stop" commercial finance companies and, in 2002, in line with this global strategy, Mortgage Intelligence, the largest independent **mortgage broker** in Canada, was purchased by GMAC Residential Funding of Canada, a wholly-owned subsidiary

TABLE 6–3
Assets and Liabilities of U.S. Finance Companies on December 31, 1977

Source: *Federal Reserve Bulletin*, June 1978, p. A39. *www.federalreserve.gov*

	Billions of US Dollars	Percent of Total Assets
Assets		
Accounts receivable gross	99.2	95.1%
Consumer	44.0	42.2
Business	55.2	52.9
Less reserves for unearned income and losses	(12.7)	(12.2)
Accounts receivable net	86.5	82.9%
Cash and bank deposit	2.6	2.5
Securities	0.9	0.9
All others	14.3	13.7
Total assets	104.3	100.0%
Liabilities and Capital		
Bank loans	5.9	5.7%
Commercial paper	29.6	28.4
Debt		
Short-term	6.2	5.9
Long-term	36.0	34.5
Other	11.5	11.0
Capital, surplus, and undivided profits	15.1	14.5
Total liabilities and capital	104.3	100.0%

sales finance institutions
Institutions that specialize in making loans to the customers of a particular retailer or manufacturer.

personal credit institutions
Institutions that specialize in making installment and other loans to consumers.

business credit institutions
Institutions that specialize in making business loans.

factoring
The process of purchasing accounts receivable from corporations (often at a discount), usually with no recourse to the seller if the receivables go bad.

of GMAC. Nevertheless, GECC's assets in North America represented just 8 percent (US$60 billion) of its total worldwide assets.

The three major types of finance companies are (1) sales finance institutions, (2) personal credit institutions, and (3) business credit institutions. **Sales finance institutions** (e.g., Ford Motor Credit) specialize in making loans to the customers of a particular retailer or manufacturer. Because sales finance institutions can frequently process loans faster and more conveniently (generally at the location of purchase) than deposit-taking institutions, this sector of the industry competes directly with deposit-taking institutions for consumer loans. **Personal credit institutions** (e.g., Household International Corp.) specialize in making installment and other loans to consumers. Personal credit institutions will make loans to customers that deposit-taking institutions find too risky to lend to (due to low income or a bad credit history). These institutions compensate for the additional risk by charging higher interest rates than deposit-taking institutions and/or accepting collateral (e.g., used cars) that deposit-taking institutions do not find acceptable. **Business credit institutions** (e.g., CIT Group) are companies that provide financing to corporations, especially through equipment leasing and **factoring,** in which the finance company purchases accounts receivable from corporate customers. These accounts are purchased at a discount from their face value, and the finance company specializes in and assumes the responsibility for collecting the accounts receivable. As a result, the corporate customer no longer has the worry of whether the accounts receivable may or may not be delayed and thus receives cash for sales faster than the time it takes customers to pay their bills. Many finance companies perform more than one of these three services (e.g., GMAC).

The industry is quite concentrated, with the largest 20 firms accounting for more than 75 percent of its assets. In addition, many of the largest finance companies, such as GMAC, tend to be wholly owned or captive subsidiaries of major

TABLE 6–4
The Largest U.S.
Finance Companies

Source: Insurance Information
Institute. 2003

Company Name	Total Receivables (in US$ millions)
General Electric Capital Services	233,086
Ford Motor Credit Company	202,528
Citigroup	130,400
Household International, Inc.	107,496
MBNA Corp.	107,258
SLM Corp.	79,557
First USA	74,000
American Express	73,800
Capital One Financial	59,746
Discover Bank	51,565

**captive finance
company**
A finance company
that is wholly
owned by a parent
corporation.

manufacturing companies. A major role of a **captive finance company** is to provide financing for the purchase of products manufactured by the parent, as GMAC does for cars. In turn, the parent company is often a major source of debt finance for the captive finance company.

Table 6–4 lists the top ten North American Finance Companies (in terms of total receivables) as of 2003. GECC is the largest with receivables totaling US $233.1 billion. In late 2000, Associates First Capital, then the fourth largest finance company and the largest consumer finance company, was acquired by Citigroup for US $31.1 billion. The acquisition resulted in Citigroup becoming the industry's third largest receivables financer with receivables of US $130.4 billion in 2003 (behind Ford Motor Credit Company with US $202.5 billion). A similar bank-finance company consolidation occurred in Canada in 2003 when Household Financial (which provides consumer loans, credit cards, car finance, and credit insurance) was purchased by the parent of HSBC Bank Canada, HSBC Holdings, a large international bank based in the United Kingdom. As of December 2004, Household Financial changed its name to HSBC Finance Corporation.

**Concept
Questions**

1. What are the three major types of finance companies? What types of customers does each serve?
2. What is a captive finance company?

BALANCE SHEET AND RECENT TRENDS

Assets

As mentioned above, finance companies provide three basic lending services: customer lending, consumer lending, and business lending. In Table 6–2 we show the balance sheet of U.S. finance companies in 2003. As you can see, business and consumer loans (called accounts receivable) are the major assets held by finance companies, accounting for 51.9 percent of total assets. Comparing the figures in Table 6–2 to those in Table 6–3 for 1977, we see that 95.1 percent of total assets were consumer and business loans in 1977. Over the last 26 years, finance companies have replaced consumer and business loans with increasing amounts of real estate loans and other assets, although these loans have not become dominant, as is the case with deposit-taking institutions. However, like banks, these activities create credit risk, interest rate risk, and liquidity risk that finance company managers must evaluate and manage.

TABLE 6–5
U.S. Finance
Company Loans
Outstanding from
1995 through 2003[1]
(in billions
of U.S. dollars)

Source: Federal Reserve
Board, "Flow of Fund
Accounts," various issues.
www.federalreserve.gov

	1995	2000	2003	Percent of Total, 2003
Consumer	285.8	475.9	538.3	40.4%
Motor vehicle loans	81.1	141.6	197.0	14.8
Motor vehicle leases	80.8	108.2	70.0	5.2
Revolving[2]	28.5	37.6	37.6	2.8
Other[3]	42.6	41.3	51.6	3.9
Securitized assets				
Motor vehicle loans	34.8	97.1	132.8	10.0
Motor vehicle leases	3.5	6.6	5.5	0.4
Revolving	n.a.	27.5	31.6	2.4
Other	14.7	16.0	12.2	0.9
Real estate	72.4	198.9	239.6	18.0
One- to four-family	n.a.	130.6	152.2	11.4
Other	n.a.	41.7	46.7	3.5
Securitized real estate assets[4]				
One- to four-family	n.a.	24.7	36.9	2.8
Other	n.a.	1.9	3.8	0.3
Business	331.2	525.0	553.2	41.6
Motor vehicles	66.5	75.5	74.9	5.6
Retail loans	21.8	18.3	18.2	1.4
Wholesale loans[5]	36.6	39.7	40.4	3.0
Leases	8.0	17.6	16.3	1.2
Equipment	188.0	283.5	277.6	20.9
Loans	58.6	70.2	74.6	5.6
Leases	129.4	213.3	203.0	15.3
Other business receivables[6]	47.2	99.4	105.0	7.9
Securitized assets[4]				
Motor vehicles	20.6	37.8	48.5	3.6
Retail loans	1.8	3.2	2.2	0.2
Wholesale loans	18.8	32.5	44.2	3.3
Leases	n.a.	2.2	2.1	0.1
Equipment	8.1	23.1	22.1	1.7
Loans	5.3	15.5	12.5	1.0
Leases	2.8	7.6	9.6	0.7
Other business receivables[6]	0.8	5.6	25.1	1.9
Total	689.5	1,199.8	1,331.1	100.0%

[1]Owned receivables are those carried on the balance sheet of the institution. Managed receivables are outstanding balances of pools upon which securities have been issued; these balances are no longer carried on the balance sheets of the loan originator.
[2]Excludes revolving credit reported as held by depository institutions that are subsidiaries of finance companies.
[3]Includes personal cash loans, mobile home loans, and loans to purchase other types of consumer goods, such as appliances, apparel, boats, and recreation vehicles.
[4]Outstanding balances of pools on which securities have been issued; these balances are no longer carried on the balance sheets of the loan originator.
[5]Credit arising from transactions between manufacturers and dealers, that is, floor plan financing.
[6]Includes loans on commercial accounts receivable, factored commercial accounts, and receivable dealer capital; small loans used primarily for business or farm purposes; and wholesale and lease paper for mobile homes, campers, and travel trailers.

Table 6–5 shows the breakdown of the industry's loans in the United States from 1995 through 2003 for consumer, real estate, and business lending. In recent years, the fastest growing areas of asset business have been in the nonconsumer finance areas, especially leasing and business lending. In December 2003 consumer loans constituted 40.4 percent of all finance company loans, mortgages represented 18.0 percent, and business loans comprised the largest category of loans at 41.6 percent.

Consumer Loans

Consumer loans consist of motor vehicle loans and leases, other consumer loans, and securitized loans from each category. Motor vehicle loans and leases are typically the major type of consumer loan. Finance companies generally charge higher rates for automobile loans than do banks. Nevertheless, sometime these rates get lowered dramatically. For example, because new car sale in the late 1990s were lower than normal, the auto finance companies owned by the major U.S. auto manufacturers slashed interest rates on new car loans, some to 0.0 percent.

subprime lender
A finance company that lends to high-risk customers.

The higher rates finance companies charge for consumer loans are mostly due to the fact that finance companies attract riskier customers than banks. In fact, customers who seek individual (or business) loans from finance companies are often those judged too risky to obtain loans from banks.[2] It is, in fact, possible for individuals to get a loan from a **subprime lender** finance company (a finance company that lends to high-risk customers) even with a bankruptcy on their records. For example, in 1997 Jayhawk Acceptance Corp., one of a group of U.S. finance companies that lent money to used-car buyers with poor or no credit, began marketing loans for tummy tucks, hair transplants, and other procedures. Jayhawk entered into contracts with doctors to lend money to their patients who were seeking cosmetic surgery or some types of dental procedures. Borrowers who paid the loans within a year paid an annual rate of 9.9 percent, but those who repaid within the maximum of two years paid 13.9 percent per year. Left unanswered, however, was what Jayhawk could repossess if a borrower defaulted on a loan. Banks would rarely do this. Most finance companies that offer these types of loans charge rates commensurate with the higher risk, and there are a few **loan shark** companies that prey on desperate consumers, charging exorbitant rates. This has meant that in the past, the industry has had to fight against a reputation for engaging in loan sharking and charging usurious rates, a criminal offence in Canada. A class action suit brought against Easyhome Ltd., which sells appliances and furniture on credit, alleged that it charged its customers a **criminal rate** in excess of 60 percent.[3]

loan sharks
Subprime lenders that charge unfairly exorbitant rates to desperate subprime borrowers.

criminal rate
An effective annual rate of interest greater than 60 percent.

www.cacfsc.com

Other consumer loans are **payday loans**, which are short-term, small sum, unsecured loans to people who would not qualify for a bank loan or a bank line of credit. The Canadian Association of Community Financial Service Providers (CACFSP) has a code of ethics and lists close to 50 companies (e.g. The Cash Store) providing loans in Canada in 2004. Their members do not offer internet services.

payday loans
Short-term, small sum, unsecured consumer loans.

Mortgages

Residential and commercial mortgages have become an important component in finance company portfolios. However, since finance companies are not subject to as extensive regulations as are banks, they are often willing to issue mortgages to riskier borrowers than banks, and they compensate for this additional risk by charging higher interest rates and fees. For example, in 2002, Home Loans Canada (HLC), a subsidiary of CIBC Mortgages Inc. and Household Financial Corporation

---

[2] We look at the analysis of borrower (credit) risk in Chapter 11.

[3] See the "Notice of the Proposed National Settlement of the easyhome class action" at www.easyhome.ca. Under section 347of the Criminal Code of Canada, it is unlawful to charge a **criminal rate**, defined as an effective annual rate of interest that is greater than 60 percent of the amount advanced and including fees, charges, and other expenses. However, recent Canadian court interpretations are modifying this law. See R. Pratt, R. Borins, and D. Salter, "'Unintentionally Usurious' Loans: Canada's Supreme Court Finds a New Way to Put Them Right," March 18, 2004, Osler, Hoskin & Harcourt LLP, available at www.osler.com.

(now HSBC Financial Corporation Ltd.) provided mortgages for self-employed entrepreneurs, both first and second mortgages for up to 85 to 90 percent of the value of the home. Because they have an irregular source of income, entrepreneurs have trouble qualifying for a regular or high ratio mortgage from a deposit-taking institution. Canada Mortgage and Housing Corporation (CMHC), a Crown corporation, provides mortgage insurance for **high ratio residential mortgages**, as well as information for Canadian consumers about real estate prices, mortgages, and other housing-related issues. FIs (such as banks, credit unions, caisses populaires) who are on the list of CMHC's approved lenders are able to provide mortgages to homebuyers that are insured by CMHC, reducing the default risk for the lender.

Mortgages include all loans secured by **liens** on any type of real estate. Mortgages can be made directly or as securitized mortgage assets. Securitization in mortgages involves the pooling of a group of mortgages with similar characteristics, the removal of these mortgages from the balance sheet, and the subsequent sale of interest in the pool to secondary market investors. Securitization of mortgages results in the creation of mortgage-backed securities (e.g. collateralized mortgage obligations) that can be traded in secondary mortgage markets, as we discuss in more detail in Chapter 27.[4]

Mortgages in the loan portfolio of a finance company can be first mortgages or second mortgages in the form of home equity loans. **Home equity loans** allow customers to borrow on a line of credit secured with a second mortgage on their home.

Business Loans

Business loans represent the largest portion of the loan portfolio of finance companies. Finance companies have several advantages over banks in offering services to small business customers.[5] First, as mentioned earlier, they are not subject to regulations that restrict the types of products and services they can offer. Second, because finance companies do not accept deposits, they have no bank-type regulators looking directly over their shoulders.[6] Third, being in many cases subsidiaries of corporate-sector holding companies, finance companies often have substantial industry and product expertise. Fourth, as mentioned in regard to consumer loans, finance companies are more willing to accept risky customers than are banks. Fifth, finance companies generally have lower overheads than banks have; for example, they do not need tellers or branches for taking deposits.

The major subcategories of business loans are retail and wholesale motor vehicle loans and leases, equipment loans, other business loans, and securitized business assets. Motor vehicle loans consist of retail loans that assist in transactions between the retail seller of the product and the ultimate consumer (i.e., passenger car fleets and commercial land vehicles for which licenses are required). Wholesale loans are loan agreements between parties other than the companies' consumers. For example, GMAC provides wholesale financing to GM dealers for inventory floor plans in which GMAC pays for GM dealers' auto inventory received from GM. GMAC puts a lien on each car on the showroom floor. Although the dealer pays periodic interest

---

high ratio residential mortgage
A mortgage loan in which the down payment is less than 10 percent.

liens
A legal charge on real property to secure a loan such as a mortgage loan.

home equity loans
Loans that let customers borrow on a line of credit secured with a second mortgage on their home.

---

[4] Mortgage servicing is a fee-related business whereby, after mortgages are securitized, the flow of mortgage repayments (interest and principal) has to be collected and passed on (by the mortgage servicer) to investors in either whole mortgage loan packages or securitization vehicles such as pass-through securities (see Chapter 28). In undertaking this intermediation activity, the servicer charges a fee.

[5] See M. Carey et al., "Does Corporate Lending by Banks and Finance Companies Differ? Evidence on Specialization in Private Debt Contracting," *Journal of Finance* 53 (June 1998), pp. 845–78.

[6] Finance companies do, of course, have market participants looking over their shoulders and monitoring their activities.

on the floor plan loan, it is not until the car is sold that the dealer pays for the car. These activities extend to retail and wholesale leasing of motor vehicles as well.

Business-lending activities of finance companies also include equipment loans, with the finance company either owning or leasing the equipment directly to its industrial customer or providing the financial backing for a leveraged lease, a working capital loan, or a loan to purchase or remodel the customer's facility. Finance companies often prefer to lease equipment rather than sell and finance the purchase of equipment. One reason for this is that repossession of the equipment in the event of default is less complicated when the finance company retains its title (by leasing). Further, a lease agreement generally requires no down payment, making a lease more attractive to the business customer. Finally, when the finance company retains ownership of the equipment (by leasing), it receives a tax deduction in the form of depreciation expense on the equipment.

www.cfla-acfl.ca

The Canadian Finance and Leasing Association (CFLA) estimated that in 2003, the assets of the asset-based financing industry totaled $116.7 billion. This means that the industry's assets have more than doubled from $50.0 billion in 1996.[7]

revolver
A credit facility which can be drawn down and repaid over the term of the loan.

Other business loans include loans to finance accounts receivable, factored commercial accounts, small farm loans, and wholesale and lease paper for mobile homes, campers, and trailers. GMAC Commercial Finance's web site also lists credits such as **revolvers** and **term loans**, constructions loans, secured and unsecured credits, and equipment financing. For example, in 2004, GE Commercial Finance, Bank of America, CIT Business Credit Canada Inc., and HSBC Bank Canada arranged a $650 million revolving asset-based facility for Hudson's Bay Company that is secured by the company's merchandise inventory. As well, asset-backed lending and leasing provide a way to extend credit to companies who are in a troubled industry or engaged in bankruptcy proceedings. For example, Stelco, the steelmaker based in Hamilton Ontario who entered protection from its creditors under the **Companies' Creditors Arrangement Act (CCCA)** in 2004, was given a $500 million secured loan by Deutsche Bank and CIT Business Credit Canada as part of its restructuring in 2005.

term loan
A credit facility that, once it is drawn down, must be repaid according to a schedule set out in the loan agreement.

Liabilities and Equity

Companies' Creditors Arrangement Act (CCCA)
Legislation that allows a company who owes its creditors more than $5 million to operate while protected from its creditors while it undergoes restructuring.

To finance asset growth, finance companies have relied primarily on short-term commercial paper and other debt (longer-term notes and bonds). Thus, management of liquidity risk is quite different from that in banks that mostly rely on deposits (see Chapter 2). As reported in Table 6–2, in 2003 commercial paper amounted to US $127.3 billion (8.7 percent of total assets), while other debt (debt due to parents and debt not elsewhere classified) totaled US $726.8 billion (49.5 percent) and bank loans totaled US $47.3 billion (3.2 percent). Comparing these figures with those for 1977 (in Table 6–3), commercial paper was used more in 1977 (28.4 percent of total liabilities and capital), while other debt (short- and long-term) was less significant as a source of financing (40.4 percent). Finance companies also now rely less heavily on bank loans for financing. In 1977, bank loans accounted for 5.7 percent of total financing. Much of the change in funding sources is due to the strong economy and low interest rates in the U.S. long-term debt markets in the early 2000s. Finally, in 2003 finance companies' capital-to-assets ratio was 15.1 percent, higher than the 14.5 percent in 1977.[8]

---

[7] See The Task Force on the Future of the Canadian Financial Services Sector, "Change Challenge Opportunity", September, 1998, p. 43. This report is also known as "The MacKay Report" after the Chairman of the Task Force.

[8] For more on the relative capital adequacy of finance companies versus banks, see M. L. Kwast and S. W. Passmore, "The Subsidy Provided by the Federal Safety Net: Theory, Measurement and Containment," Federal Reserve Board of Governors Working Paper 1997–58.

To finance assets, finance companies rely heavily on short-term commercial paper, with many having direct sale programs in which commercial paper is sold directly to mutual funds and other institutional investors on a continuous day-by-day basis. For example, in its 2004 Annual Report, CIT Group Inc. notes that it finances its operations with asset-backed commercial paper in Canada and the U.S. As well, they also had bank lines of credit as a back up to the commercial paper borrowings.[9]

Industry Performance

In the early 2000s, the outlook for the industry in North America as a whole is bright. Interest rates are at historical lows. Mortgage refinancing has grown and loan demand among lower- and middle-income consumers is strong. Because many of their potential borrowers have very low savings, no major slowdown in the demand for finance company services is expected. The most successful North American finance companies are becoming takeover targets for other financial service companies as well as industrial firms. For example, the acquisition of Household International by the British bank HSBC Holdings for US$14.9 billion was one of the largest M&As of any kind the U.S. in 2003.

Both Ford Credit and GMAC's debt were downgraded to non-investment grade (junk status) by Fitch Ratings and Standard and Poor's in 2005. This could increase the cost of financing Ford Credit's and GMAC's assets, affecting their ability to compete with other finance companies in pricing loans. A further prospect is for GM to sell GMAC, which earned US$2.9 billion in 2004, 80 percent of GM's net income and had an approximate market value of US$18 billion.[10]

Concept Questions

1. How do the consumer loan customers of finance companies differ from consumer loan customers at banks?
2. What advantages do finance companies offer over banks to small business customers?

REGULATION

The fortunes of GMAC and Ford raise issues from a regulatory standpoint. If we define a finance company as a firm (other than a deposit-taking institution) whose primary assets are loans to individuals and businesses (the definition used by the U.S. Federal Reserve), then finance companies, like deposit-taking institutions, are financial intermediaries that borrow funds for re-lending, making a profit on the difference between the interest rate on borrowed funds and the rate charged on the loans. Also like deposit-taking institutions, finance companies are subject to usury ceilings on the maximum loan rate assigned to any individual customer and are regulated by bankruptcy legislation as to the extent to which they can collect on delinquent loans. However, because finance companies do not accept deposits, they are not subject to extensive oversight by any specific regulator as are banks even though they offer services that compete directly with those of deposit-taking institutions (e.g. consumer installment loans and mortgages). Like any corporation, they are subject to securities regulations with respect to disclosure.

---

[9] Lines of credit as a backup for commercial paper became common in Canada in the 1980s when the commercial paper market developed and corporate customers became able to access the capital markets directly. A standby fee is usually charged by the banks to make this facility available to their customers.

[10] See "US high grade debt market springs back vigorously after Fitch junks GM," *Euroweek*, May 27, 2005, p. 1 and L. H. Hawkins, Jr., "Should GMAC Go on the Block?" Wall Street Journal, May 25, 2005, p. C1.

Further, since finance companies are heavy borrowers in the capital markets and do not enjoy the same regulatory "safety net" as banks, they need to signal their solvency and safety to investors.[11] Signals of solvency and safety are usually sent by holding higher equity or capital-asset ratios—and therefore lower leverage ratios—than banks hold. For example, in 2003 the aggregate balance sheet (Table 6–2) for U.S. finance companies shows a capital-asset ratio of 15.1 percent. This can be compared to the average capital-asset ratio for U.S. commercial banks of 9.10 percent (4.8 percent for the Big Six Canadian banks). Larger, captive finance companies also use default protection guarantees from their parent companies and/or guarantees such as letter of credit or lines of credit purchased for a fee from high-quality banks as additional protection against insolvency risk and as a device to increase their ability to raise additional funds in the capital and money markets. Thus, this group will tend to operate with lower capital-to-asset ratios than smaller finance companies. Given that there is little regulatory oversight of this industry, having sufficient capital and access to financial guarantees are critical to their continued ability to raise funds. Thus, finance companies operate more like non-financial, non-regulated companies than other types of financial institutions examined in this text. However, even though the borrowers would be able to find other financing, the impact of a failure of a large finance company in Canada or the U.S. brings back memories of the near-collapse of the unregulated hedge fund, LTCM in 1998 and raises the issue of regulation in the future.

Concept Questions

1. Since finance companies seem to compete in the same lending markets as banks, why aren't they subject to the same regulations as banks? Should they be?
2. How do finance companies signal solvency and safety to investors?

GOVERNMENT FINANCING ENTITIES

Crown Corporations in Canada

Crown corporation
A corporation owned by the federal government or by a provincial or territorial government.

Additional financing and export-related services to business are provided by the **Crown corporations** listed in Table 6–1, government entities who are in competition with other FIs in Canada. Each has a different mandate as follows:

The Business Development Bank of Canada (BDC) supports small and medium sized business in Canada by providing consulting services, financing, and **venture capital**.

venture capital
Business development financing provided in exchange for an equity position and some level of management control.

Canada Mortgage and Housing Corporation's (CMHC) mandate is the promotion of housing in Canada. They perform a major role in providing mortgage insurance for high ratio mortgages extended by approved lenders under the National Housing Act. In addition, CMHC provides a guarantee for mortgage-backed securities, as discussed in Chapter 27.

Export Development Canada (EDC) supports companies that are exporting and importing by providing services such as insurance, financing, and bonding, as well as advice on doing business outside of Canada.

www.bdc.ca
www.cmhc-schl.gc.ca
www.edc.ca
www.fcc-fac.ca

Farm Credit Canada (FCC) reports to the Minister of Agriculture and provides services such as loans, insurance, and venture capital to farmers in Canada.

---

[11] That is, they have no access to the deposit insurance fund nor may they borrow from the central bank. On the other hand, they do not have to pay deposit insurance premiums or meet regulatory imposed minimum capital standards.

None of these firms is large, but they do provide services to small and medium businesses, farmers, and home buyers, who may not be served by the other FIs previously discussed, either because they are too small or because they are too risky.

GLOBAL ISSUES

Because regulations in most foreign countries are not as restrictive as those in the United States, finance companies in foreign countries are generally subsidiaries of commercial banks or industrial firms. For those finance companies owned by commercial banks, as the bank goes, so does the finance company. For example, the economic recession in Japan in the late 1990s and early 2000s and the resulting huge volume of nonperforming property loans in Japanese commercial banks depleted the banks' capital and restricted their ability to lend to finance company subsidiaries. The result has been some attractive opportunities for others. For example, in January 1999 GE Capital Corporation (GECC) agreed to buy (for US $7 billion) Japan Leasing Corporation (JLC), the Japanese lending unit of Long-Term Credit Bank of Japan, in the biggest acquisition ever involving a Japanese company. GECC bought only the healthy assets of JLC shortly after its parent, Long-Term Credit Bank, was declared insolvent and nationalized because of its huge problems with nonperforming property loans. Historically, assets of companies such as JLC would never have been acquired by a foreign investor like GECC, but the extreme size of nonperforming property loans at Japan's biggest banks restricted their ability to undertake any rescue missions like that of JLC.

An issue related to financial services and global FIs is the development of a sound global financial system which means sound financial infrastructure, particularly in developing countries. Monetary and technical support for this development is provided by the **World Bank Group**, an international organization owned by its member companies. The World Bank provides loans, technical assistance, and advice through The International Bank for Reconstruction and Development (IBRD), The International Development Association (IDA), The International Finance Corporation (IFC), The Multilateral Investment Guarantee Group (MIGA), and The International Centre for Settlement of Investment Disputes (ICSID).

www.cdproject.net

FIs have also recognized that global warming has a potential impact on the value of their financial assets. Institutional investors, including the large global banks and insurance companies, have formed the Carbon Disclosure Project (CDP) which annually requests the FT500 largest companies in the world to respond to a survey regarding their greenhouse gas emissions. Three surveys have been completed (2003, 2004, 2005) and the results made public at the CDP's Web site, www.cdproject.net.

Summary

This chapter provided an overview of the finance company industry. This industry competes directly with deposit-taking institutions for its high-quality (prime) loan customers by specializing in consumer loans, real estate loans, and business loans. The industry also services subprime (high-risk) borrowers deemed too risky for most deposit-taking institutions. However, because firms in this industry do not accept deposits, they are not regulated to the same extent as are deposit-taking institutions. Because they do not have access to deposits for their funding, finance companies rely heavily on short- and long-term debt, especially commercial paper. Currently, the industry is generally growing and profitable although there are concerns about market stability related to the downgrading of GMAC's and Ford Credit's debt.

Questions and Problems

1. What is the primary function of finance companies? How do finance companies differ from commercial banks?

2. What are the three major types of finance companies? To which market segments do each of these types of companies provide service?

3. What have been the major changes in the accounts receivable balances of finance companies over the 26-year period 1977–2003?

4. What are the major types of consumer loans? Why are the rates charged by consumer finance companies typically higher than those charged by commercial banks?

5. Why have home equity loans become popular? What are securitized mortgage assets?

6. What advantages do finance companies have over commercial banks in offering services to small business customers? What are the major subcategories of business loans? Which category is the largest?

7. What have been the primary sources of financing for finance companies?

8. How do finance companies make money? What risks does this process entail? How do these risks differ for a finance company versus a commercial bank?

9. How does the amount of equity as a percentage of total assets compare for finance companies and banks? What accounts for this difference?

10. Why do finance companies face less regulation than do banks? How does this advantage translate into performance advantages? What is the major performance disadvantage?

Web Questions

11. Go to the Federal Reserve's Web site at **www.federalreserve.gov** and get the latest information on finance company consumer, real estate, and business lending using the following steps. Click on "Economic Research and Data." Click on "Statistics: Releases and Historical Data." Click on "Finance Companies: Releases." Click on the most recent date. This downloads a file onto your computer that contains the relevant data. How have these numbers changed since 2003, reported in Table 6–5?

CHAPTER 7

Risks of Financial Intermediation

In this chapter we introduce the various risks facing FIs that provide the framework for our discussions about the measurement and management of risk in the remaining chapters of the book:

▸ interest rate risk

▸ market risk

▸ credit risk

▸ off-balance sheet risk

▸ technology and operational risk

▸ foreign exchange risk

▸ country or sovereign risk

▸ liquidity risk, and

▸ insolvency risk

INTRODUCTION

"For us of course, things can change so abruptly, so violently, so profoundly, that futures like our grandparents' have insufficient 'now' to stand on. We have no future because our present is too volatile… . We have only risk management. The spinning of the given moment's scenarios. Pattern recognition."

William Gibson, Pattern Recognition[1]

Financial intermediaries have evolved into organizations whose quest is to find models that will achieve the best risk management, or "pattern recognition," in order to control their future. The pattern recognition takes the form of risk identification and measurement involving the entire organization (e.g. Bank of Montreal has "enterprise-wide risk management") and allowing them to understand how risks interact. Table 7–1 shows the risks discussed in the financial reports of selected Canadian FIs. The list includes most of those risks identified in the chapter objectives above, as well as additional areas of concern (e.g. environmental risk, reputational risk, regulatory risk). Even though they may not be specifically mentioned, other risks such as off-balance sheet risk and sovereign risk, are considered part of interest rate, liquidity, and foreign exchange risk.

The global issues that we have discussed in the first six chapters contribute to the volatile environment for FIs, making it difficult to achieve a major objective of FI management, that is, increasing the returns for the owners. Increased returns often come, however, at the cost of increased risk. By the end of this chapter, you will have a basic understanding of the variety and complexity of risks facing managers of modern FIs. As will become clear throughout the rest of the text-

---

[1] From *Pattern Recognition*, Copyright © 2004 by William Gibson. Used by permission.

TABLE 7-1   Risks Identified by Canadian FIs

	Interest Rate	Market	Credit	Opera-tional	Foreign Exchange	Liquidity	Other
Deposit-taking Institutions:							
Bank of Montreal	X	X	X	X	X	X	business, environmental, reputational
Bank of Nova Scotia	X	X	X	X	X	X	environmental
CIBC	X	X	X	X	X	X	equity, commodity
Desjardins Group		X	X	X	X	X	insurance
HSBC	X	X	X	X	X	X	structural, fiduciary
National Bank	X	X	X	X	X	X	regulatory
Royal Bank of Canada	X	X	X	X	X	X	insurance
TD Bank	X	X	X	X	X	X	strategic, regulatory, reputational
Insurance Companies:							
Manulife Financial	X	X	X	X	X	X	strategic, product
Sun Life Financial	X	X	X	X	X		insurance, mortality & morbidity

Source: Company 2004 Annual Reports

book, the effective management of these risks is central to an FI's performance and, it can be argued, the main business of FIs is to manage, not eliminate, risk for themselves and for their customers.[2]

INTEREST RATE RISK

interest rate risk
The risk incurred by an FI when the maturities of its assets and liabilities are mismatched.

Chapter 1 discussed asset transformation as a key special function of FIs. Asset transformation involves an FI's buying primary securities or assets and issuing secondary securities or liabilities to fund asset purchases. The primary securities purchased by FIs often have maturity and liquidity characteristics different from those of the secondary securities FIs sell. In mismatching the maturities of assets and liabilities as part of their asset-transformation function, FIs potentially expose themselves to **interest rate risk.**

EXAMPLE 7-1

Effect of an Interest Rate Increase on an FI's Profits When the Maturity of Its Assets Exceeds the Maturity of Its Liabilities

Consider an FI that issues $100 million of liabilities of one-year maturity to finance the purchase of $100 million of assets with a two-year maturity. We show this situation in the following time lines:

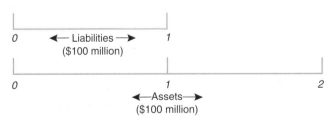

---

[2] These risks are not necessarily unique to financial institutions. Every global, non-financial corporation faces these risks as well, and managers of these firms must deal with them just as do managers of FIs. The book's Web site contains an overview of the evaluation of FI performance and risk exposure (Deposit-taking Institutions' Financial Statements and Analysis). Included are several accounting ratio-based measures of risk.

In these time lines the FI can be viewed as being "short-funded." That is, the maturity of its liabilities is less than the maturity of its assets.

Suppose the cost of funds (liabilities) for an FI is 9 percent per annum and the interest return on an asset is 10 percent per annum. Over the first year the FI can lock in a profit spread of 1 percent (10 percent − 9 percent) times $100 million by borrowing short term (for one year) and lending long term (for two years). Thus, its profit is $1 million (.01 × $100 m).

However, its profits for the second year are uncertain. If the level of interest rates does not change, the FI can *refinance* its liabilities at 9 percent and lock in a 1 percent, or $1 million, profit for the second year as well. There is always a risk, however, that interest rates will change between years 1 and 2. If interest rates were to rise and the FI can borrow new one-year liabilities only at 11 percent in the second year, its profit spread in the second year would actually be negative; that is, 10 percent − 11 percent = −1 percent, or the FI's loss is $1 million (−.01 × $100 m). The positive spread earned in the first year by the FI from holding assets with a longer maturity than its liabilities would be offset by a negative spread in the second year. Note that if interest rates were to rise by more than 1 percent in the second year, the FI would stand to take losses over the two-year period as a whole. As a result, when an FI holds longer-term assets relative to liabilities, it potentially exposes itself to **refinancing risk.** This is the risk that the cost of rolling over or reborrowing funds could be more than the return earned on asset investments. The classic example of this type of mismatch was demonstrated by U.S. savings institutions during the 1980s.

refinancing risk
The risk that the cost of rolling over or reborrowing funds will rise above the returns being earned on asset investments.

↳ *ie when short-funded*

EXAMPLE 7–2

Effect of an Interest Rate Decrease When the Maturity of an FI's Liabilities Exceeds the Maturity of Its Assets

An alternative balance sheet structure would have the FI borrowing $100 million for a longer term than the $100 million of assets in which it invests. In the time lines below the FI is "long-funded." The maturity of its liabilities is longer than the maturity of its assets. Using a similar example, suppose the FI borrowed funds at 9 percent per annum for two years and invested the funds in an asset that yields 10 percent for one year. This situation is shown as follows:

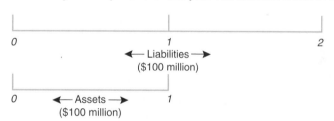

In this case, the FI is also exposed to an interest rate risk; by holding shorter-term assets relative to liabilities, it faces uncertainty about the interest rate at which it can reinvest funds in the second period. As before, the FI locks in a one-year profit spread of 1 percent, or $1 million. At the end of the first year, the asset matures and the funds that have been borrowed for two years have to be reinvested. Suppose interest rates fall between the first and second years so that in the second year the return on $100 million invested in new one-year assets is 8 percent. The FI would face a loss, or negative spread, in the second year of 1 percent (that is, 8 percent asset return minus 9 percent cost of funds), or the FI loses $1 million (−.01 × $100 m). The positive spread earned in the first year by the FI from holding assets with a shorter maturity than its liabilities is offset by a negative spread in the second year. Thus, the FI is exposed to **reinvestment risk;** by holding shorter-term assets relative to liabilities, it faced uncertainty about the interest rate at which it could reinvest funds borrowed for a longer period. In recent years, good examples of this exposure have been provided by banks that have borrowed fixed-rate deposits while investing in floating-rate loans, that is, loans whose interest rates are changed or adjusted frequently.

reinvestment risk
The risk that the returns on funds to be reinvested will fall below the cost of funds.

↳ *ie when long-funded*

↑ Int rates → ↑ discount rate → ↓ MV Asset/Liab

If: Asset Maturity > Liab Maturity then when Int rates ↑ ↓ MV Asset > ↓ MV Liab

In addition to a potential refinancing or reinvestment risk that occurs when interest rates change, an FI faces *market value* risk as well. Remember that the market (or fair) value of an asset or liability is conceptually equal to the present value of current and future cash flows from that asset or liability. Therefore, rising interest rates increase the discount rate on those cash flows and reduce the market value of that asset or liability. Conversely, falling interest rates increase the market values of assets and liabilities. Moreover, mismatching maturities by holding longer-term assets than liabilities means that when interest rates rise, the market value of the FI's assets falls by a greater amount than its liabilities. This exposes the FI to the risk of economic loss and, potentially, the risk of insolvency.

If holding assets and liabilities with mismatched maturities exposes FIs to reinvestment (or refinancing) and market value risks, FIs can seek to hedge, or protect against, interest rate risk by matching the maturity of their assets and liabilities.[3] This has resulted in the general philosophy that matching maturities is somehow the best policy to hedge interest rate risk for FIs that are averse to risk. Note, however, that matching maturities is not necessarily consistent with an active asset-transformation function for FIs. That is, FIs cannot be asset transformers (e.g., transforming short-term deposits into long-term loans) and direct balance sheet matchers or hedgers at the same time. While reducing exposure to interest rate risk, matching maturities may also reduce the FI's profitability because returns from acting as specialized risk-bearing asset transformers are reduced. As a result, some FIs emphasize asset-liability maturity mismatching more than others. For example, banks traditionally hold longer-term assets than liabilities, whereas life insurance companies tend to match the long-term nature of their liabilities with long-term assets. Finally, matching maturities hedges interest rate risk only in a very approximate rather than complete fashion. The reasons for this are technical, relating to the difference between the average life (or duration) and maturity of an asset or liability and whether the FI partly funds its assets with equity capital as well as debt liabilities. In the preceding simple examples, the FI financed its assets completely with borrowed funds. In the real world, FIs use a mix of debt liabilities and stockholders' equity to finance asset purchases. When assets and debt liabilities are not equal, hedging risk (i.e., insulating FI's stockholder's equity values) may be achieved by not exactly matching the maturities (or average lives) of assets and liabilities. We discuss the causes of interest rate risk and methods used to measure interest rate risk in detail in Chapters 8 and 9. We discuss the methods and instruments used to hedge interest rate risk in Chapters 23 through 25.[4]

---

[3] This assumes that FIs can directly "control" the maturities of their assets and liabilities. As interest rates fall, many mortgage borrowers seek to "prepay" their existing loans and refinance at a lower rate. This prepayment risk—which is directly related to interest rate movements—can be viewed as a further interest rate–related risk. Prepayment risk is discussed in detail in Chapter 27.

[4] We assumed in our examples that interest payments are paid only at the end of each year and could be changed only then. In reality, many loan and deposit rates adjust frequently or float as market rates change. For example, suppose a bank makes a one-year loan whose interest rate and interest rate payments are adjusted each quarter while fully funding the loan with a one-year CD that pays principal and interest at the end of the year. Even though the maturities of the loan and CD are equal to a year, the FI would not be fully hedged in a cash flow sense against interest rate risk since changes in interest rates over the year affect the cash flows (interest payments) on the loan but not those on deposits. In particular, if interest rates were to fall, the FI might lose on the loan in terms of net interest income (interest revenue minus interest expense). The reason for this loss is that the average life of the loan in a cash flow sense is less than that of the deposit because cash flows on the loan are received, on average, earlier than are those paid on the deposit.

Concept Questions	1. What is refinancing risk? What type of FI best illustrated this concept in the 1980s?
	2. Why does a rise in the level of interest rates adversely affect the market value of both assets and liabilities?
	3. Explain the concept of maturity matching.
	4. Is perfect hedging possible with maturity matching? To what extent is it desirable in view of the asset transforming function of FIs?

MARKET RISK

market risk
The risk incurred in the trading of assets and liabilities due to changes in interest rates, exchange rates, and other asset prices.

Market risk arises when FIs actively trade assets and liabilities (and derivatives) rather than holding them for longer-term investment, funding, or hedging purposes. Market risk is closely related to interest rate, equity return, and foreign exchange risk in that as these risks increase or decrease, the overall risk of the FI is affected. However, market risk adds another dimension resulting from its trading activity. Market risk is the incremental risk incurred by an FI when interest rate, foreign exchange, and equity return risks are combined with an active trading strategy, especially one that involves short trading horizons such as a day. Conceptually, an FI's trading portfolio can be differentiated from its investment portfolio on the basis of time horizon and secondary market liquidity. The trading portfolio contains assets, liabilities, and derivative contracts that can be quickly bought or sold on organized financial markets. The investment portfolio (banking book) contains assets and liabilities that are relatively illiquid and held for longer holding periods. Table 7–2 shows a hypothetical breakdown between banking book and trading book assets and liabilities. As can be seen, the banking book contains the majority of loans and deposits plus other illiquid assets. The trading book contains long and short positions in instruments such as bonds, commodities, foreign exchange (FX), equities, and derivatives.

With the increasing securitization of bank loans (e.g., mortgages), more and more assets have become liquid and tradable. Of course, with time, every asset and liability can be sold. While bank regulators have normally viewed tradable assets as those being held for horizons of less than one year, private FIs take an even shorter-term view. In particular, FIs are concerned about the fluctuation in value—or value at risk (VAR)—of their trading account assets and liabilities for periods as short as one day—so-called daily earnings at risk (DEAR)—especially if such fluctuations pose a threat to their solvency.

To see the type of risk involved in active trading, consider the case of Barings, the 200-year-old British merchant bank that failed as a result of trading losses in February 1995. In this case, the bank (or, more specifically, one trader, Nick Leeson)

TABLE 7–2
The Investment (Banking) Book and Trading Book of a Bank

	Assets	**Liabilities**
Banking book	Loans	Capital
	Other illiquid assets	Deposits
Trading book	Bonds (long)	Bonds (short)
	Commodities (long)	Commodities (short)
	FX (long)	FX (short)
	Equities (long)	Equities (short)
	Derivatives* (long)	Derivatives* (short)

*Derivatives are off-balance-sheet items (as discussed in Chapter 13).

was betting that the Japanese Nikkei Stock Market Index would rise by buying futures on that index (some US $8 billion worth). However, for a number of reasons—including the Kobe earthquake—the index actually fell. As a result, over a period of one month, the bank lost over US $1.2 billion on its trading positions, rendering the bank insolvent.[5] That is, the losses on its futures positions exceeded the bank's own equity capital resources. Of course, if the Nikkei Index had actually risen, the bank would have made very large profits and might still be in business.

As the above example illustrates, market, or trading, risk is present whenever an FI takes an open or unhedged long (buy) or sell (short) position in bonds, equities, and foreign exchange (as well as in commodities and derivative products), and prices change in a direction opposite to that expected. As a result, the more volatile are asset prices in the markets in which these instruments trade, the greater are the market risks faced by FIs that adopt open trading positions. This requires FI management (and regulators) to establish controls to limit positions taken by traders as well as to develop models to measure the market risk exposure of an FI on a day-to-day basis. These market risk measurement models are discussed in Chapter 10.

Concept Questions

1. What is market, or trading, risk?
2. What modern conditions have led to an increase in this particular type of risk for FIs?

CREDIT RISK

credit risk
The risk that the promised cash flows from loans and securities held by FIs may not be paid in full.

Credit risk arises because of the possibility that promised cash flows on financial claims held by FIs, such as loans or bonds, will not be paid in full. Virtually all types of FIs face this risk. However, in general, FIs that make loans or buy bonds with long maturities are more exposed than are FIs that make loans or buy bonds with short maturities. This means, for example, that banks and life insurance companies are more exposed to credit risk than are money market mutual funds and property & casualty insurance companies. If the principal on all financial claims held by FIs was paid in full on maturity and interest payments were made on the promised dates, FIs would always receive back the original principal lent plus an interest return. That is, they would face no credit risk. If a borrower defaults, however, both the principal loaned and the interest payments expected to be received are at risk. As a result, many financial claims issued by corporations and held by FIs promise a limited or fixed upside return (principal and interest payments to the lender) with a high probability and a large downside risk (loss of loan principal and promised interest) with a much smaller probability. Good examples of financial claims issued with these return-risk trade-offs are fixed-income coupon bonds issued by corporations and bank loans. In both cases, an FI holding these claims as assets earns the coupon on the bond or the interest promised on the loan if no borrower default occurs. In the event of default, however, the FI earns zero interest on the asset and may lose all or part of the principal lent, depending on its ability to lay claim to some of the borrower's assets through legal bankruptcy and insolvency proceedings. Accordingly, a key role of FIs involves screening and monitoring loan applicants to ensure that FI managers fund the most creditworthy loans (see Chapter 11).

---

[5] In 1995 Barings was acquired as a subsidiary of ING, a Dutch bank, and was fully integrated into ING in 2000.

FIGURE 7–1
The Probability
Distribution of
Dollar Returns
on Risky Debt
(Loans/Bonds)

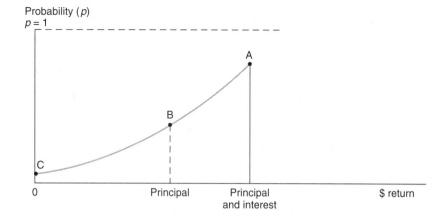

Figure 7–1 presents the probability distribution of dollar returns for an FI investing in risky loans or bonds. The distribution indicates a high probability (but less than 1) of repayment of principal and promised interest in full (point A). Problems with a borrower's cash flows can result in varying degrees of default risk. These range from partial or complete default on interest payments—the range between point A and point B in Figure 7–1—and partial or complete default on the principal lent, the range between point B and point C. Notice, too, that the probability of a complete default on principal and interest (point C) is often small. Nevertheless, because the probability of partial or complete default on bond and loan interest and principal exists, an FI must estimate expected default risk on these assets and demand risk premiums commensurate with the perceived risk exposure.

The potential loss an FI can experience from lending suggests that FIs need to monitor and collect information about borrowers whose assets are in their portfolios and to monitor those borrowers over time. Thus, managerial monitoring efficiency and credit risk management strategies directly affect the return and risks of the loan portfolio. Moreover, the credit risk distribution in Figure 7–1 is for an investment in a single asset exposed to default risk. One of the advantages FIs have over individual household investors is the ability to diversify some credit risk away by exploiting the law of large numbers in their asset investment portfolios (see Chapter 1). In the framework of Figure 7–1, diversification across assets, such as loans exposed to credit risk, reduces the overall credit risk in the asset portfolio and thus increases the probability of partial or full repayment of principal and/or interest. That is, the long-tailed downside risk of the return distribution is moderated.

FIs earn the maximum dollar return when all bonds and loans pay off interest and principal in full. In reality, some loans or bonds default on interest payments, principal payments, or both. Thus, the mean return on the asset portfolio would be less than the maximum possible in a risk-free, no-default case. The effect of risk diversification is to truncate or limit the probabilities of the bad outcomes in the portfolio. In effect, diversification reduces individual **firm-specific credit risk,** such as the risk specific to holding the bonds or loans of General Motors, while leaving the FI still exposed to **systematic credit risk,** such as factors that simultaneously increase the default risk of all firms in the economy (e.g., an economic recession). We describe methods to measure the default risk of individual corporate claims such as bonds and loans in Chapter 11. In Chapter 12, we investigate methods of measuring the risk in portfolios of such claims. Chapter 26 discusses various methods—for exam-

firm-specific credit risk
The risk of default of the borrowing firm associated with the specific types of project risk taken by that firm.

systematic credit risk
The risk of default associated with general economywide or macroconditions affecting all borrowers.

ple, loan sales, reschedulings, and a good bank–bad bank structure—to manage and control credit risk exposures better, while Chapters 23 to 25 discuss the role of the recently innovated credit derivative markets in hedging credit risk.

Concept Questions

1. Why does credit risk exist for FIs?
2. How does diversification affect an FI's credit risk exposure?

OFF-BALANCE-SHEET RISK

off-balance-sheet risk
The risk incurred by an FI due to activities related to contingent assets and liabilities.

One of the most striking trends for many modern FIs has been the growth in their off-balance-sheet activities and thus their **off-balance-sheet risk.** While all FIs to some extent engage in off-balance-sheet activities, most attention has been drawn to the activities of banks, especially large banks. By contrast, off-balance-sheet activities have been less of a concern to smaller deposit-taking institutions and many insurance companies. An off-balance-sheet activity, by definition, does not appear on an FI's current balance sheet since it does not involve holding a *current primary* claim (asset) or the issuance of a *current secondary* claim (liability). Instead, off-balance-sheet activities affect the *future* shape of an FI's balance sheet in that they involve the creation of contingent assets and liabilities that give rise to their potential (future) placement on the balance sheet. Thus, accountants place them "below the bottom line" of an FI's asset and liability balance sheet. A good example of an off-balance-sheet activity is the issuance of a **standby letter of credit (LC or L/C)** by a bank to support the import activities of one of its customers. For example, the foreign seller of goods to a Canadian importing company may require the importer to provide a standby letter of credit by which the bank guarantees that it will pay for the goods only in the event that its customer defaults. A **commercial letter of credit**, also called a documentary letter of credit, requires the bank to pay the foreign seller on presentation of the appropriate documents as specified in the letter of credit. In either case, the bank charges a fee which it includes in its income statement, but does not record the transaction on the balance sheet. Canadian banks show the dollar value of letters of credit in notes to their annual financial statements. The bank will conduct a credit analysis of its customer before issuing the letter of credit but, if the bank pays the commercial letter of credit when the seller of the goods presents the documents and its customer does not pay, the bank may experience a credit loss on the transaction.

standby letter of credit (LC or L/C)
An irrevocable credit guarantee that the issuing FI will pay a third party should its customer default on its obligation.

commercial letter of credit
A written undertaking that the issuing FI will pay a third party on the presentation of specified documents evidencing the shipment of goods.

The ability to earn fee income while not loading up or expanding the balance sheet has become an important motivation for FIs to pursue off-balance-sheet business. Unfortunately, this activity is not risk free. Significant losses in off-balance-sheet activities can cause an FI to fail, just as major losses due to balance sheet default and interest rate risks can cause an FI to fail.

Letters of credit are just one example of off-balance-sheet activities. Others include loan commitments and positions in forwards, futures, swaps, and other derivative securities. While some of these activities are structured to reduce an FI's exposure to credit, interest rate, or foreign exchange risks, mismanagement or speculative use of these instruments can result in major losses to FIs. We detail the specific nature of the risks of off-balance-sheet activities more fully in Chapter 13.

Concept Questions

1. Why are letters of credit an off-balance-sheet item?
2. Why are FIs motivated to pursue off-balance-sheet business? What are the risks?

TECHNOLOGY AND OPERATIONAL RISKS

www.bis.org

Technology and operational risks are closely related and in recent years have caused great concern to FI managers and regulators alike. The Bank for International Settlements (BIS), the principal organization of central banks in the major economies of the world, defines operational risk (inclusive of technological risk) as "the risk of loss resulting from inadequate or failed internal processes, people, and systems or from external events."[6] A number of FIs add reputational risk and strategic risk (e.g., due to a failed merger) as part of a broader definition of operational risk.

Technological innovation has been a major growth area of FIs in recent years. In the 1980s and 1990s, banks, insurance companies, and investment companies all sought to improve operational efficiency with major investments in internal and external communications, computers, and an expanded technological infrastructure. For example, most Canadian FIs provide depositors with the capability to check account balances, transfer funds between accounts, manage finances, pay bills, and perform other functions from their home personal computers. The clearing of both electronic funds and paper-based transactions is conducted through the national clearing and settlement system that is operated by the Canadian Payments Associations (CPA). The Automated Clearing Settlement System (ACSS) clears cheques, wire transfers, direct deposits, pre-authorized debits, bill payments, and point-of-sale transactions, while the Large Value Transfer System (LVTS), the first of its kind in the world, provides real-time transfer of irrevocable payments across Canada.

The major objectives of technological expansion are to lower operating costs, increase profits, and capture new markets for the FI. In current terminology, the objective is to allow the FI to exploit, to the fullest extent possible, better potential economies of scale and economies of scope in selling its products. **Economies of scale** refer to an FI's ability to lower its average costs of operations by expanding its output of financial services. **Economies of scope** refer to an FI's ability to generate cost synergies by producing more than one output with the same inputs. For example, an FI could use the same information on the quality of customers stored in its computers to expand the sale of both loan products and insurance products. That is, the same information (e.g., age, job, size of family, income) can identify both potential loan and life insurance customers. The attempt to better exploit such economies of scope lies behind megamergers such as that of Manulife Financial with John Hancock. In addition to enhancing global competitiveness by increasing their size, economies of scale and economies of scope are given as consideration when potential mergers of financial institutions, particularly among the Big Six banks and also between banks and insurance companies, are discussed in Canada.

economies of scale
The degree to which an FI's average unit costs of producing financial services fall as its outputs of services increase.

economies of scope
The degree to which an FI can generate cost synergies by producing multiple financial service products.

technology risk
The risk incurred by an FI when technological investments do not produce the cost savings anticipated.

Technology risk occurs when technological investments do not produce the anticipated cost savings in the form of either economies of scale or scope. Diseconomies of scale, for example, arise because of excess capacity, redundant technology, and/or organizational and bureaucratic inefficiencies (red tape) that become worse as an FI grows in size. Diseconomies of scope arise when an FI fails to generate perceived synergies or cost savings through major new technology investments. We describe the measurement and evidence of economies of scale and scope in FIs in Chapter 14. Technological risk can result in major losses in the

---

[6] See Basel Committee on Bank Supervision, "Sound Practices for the Management and Supervision of Operational Risk," July 2002, p. 2, Basel, Switzerland.

competitive efficiency of an FI and, ultimately, in its long-term failure. Similarly, gains from technological investments can produce performance superior to an FI's rivals as well as allow it to develop new and innovative products, enhancing its long-term survival chances.

operational risk
The risk that existing technology or support systems may malfunction or break down.

Operational risk is partly related to technology risk and can arise whenever existing technology malfunctions or back-office support systems break down.

For example, the summer of 2004 saw a string of computer glitches that affected customer accounts and transactions at three major banks. In June, a programming error at the Royal Bank of Canada held up millions of customer transactions from coast to coast for a week. A claims adjuster was hired to sort out the problem. In July, a computer malfunction created duplicate debits and over 60,000 customers at Canadian Imperial Bank of Commerce overdrew their accounts. At TD Bank, a computer problem made automated teller machines and online banking unavailable to customers for three hours. Even though such computer breakdowns are rare, their occurrence can cause major dislocations in the FIs involved and potentially disrupt the financial system in general.

Operational risk is not exclusively the result of technological failure. For example, employee fraud and errors constitute a type of operational risk that often negatively affects the reputation of an FI (see Chapter 14). For example, human error at Canadian Imperial Bank of Commerce in 2004 resulted in the much-publicized scandal of confidential customer information being faxed to a scrap yard dealer in the United States. This incident led to an investigation by the Privacy Commissioner. Fraudulent activities and human errors by employees result in an overall loss of reputation and, in turn, loss of business.

Concept Questions

1. What is the difference between economies of scale and economies of scope?
2. How is operational risk related to technology risk?
3. How does technological expansion help an FI better exploit economies of scale and economies of scope? When might technology risk interfere with these goals?

FOREIGN EXCHANGE RISK

Increasingly, FIs have recognized that both direct foreign investment and foreign portfolio investments can extend the operational and financial benefits available from purely domestic investments. For example, Bank of Nova Scotia invested over $1 billion in Grupo Financiero Inverlat, a Mexican bank, between 1996 and 2004, creating Scotiabank Inverlat. To the extent that the returns on domestic and foreign investments are imperfectly correlated, there are potential gains for an FI that expands its asset holdings and liability funding beyond the domestic frontier.

The returns on domestic and foreign direct investing and portfolio investments are not perfectly correlated for two reasons. The first is that the underlying technologies of various economies differ, as do the firms in those economies. For example, one economy may be based on agriculture while another is industry based. Given different economic infrastructures, one economy could be expanding while another is contracting. The second reason is that exchange rate changes are not perfectly correlated across countries. This means the dollar–euro exchange rate may be appreciating while the dollar–yen exchange rate may be falling.

One potential benefit from an FI's becoming increasingly global in its outlook is an ability to expand abroad directly through branching or acquisitions or by developing a financial asset portfolio that includes foreign securities as well as domestic securities. For example, the removal of the limits on foreign assets in pension funds in 2005 is expected to change the composition of their portfolios and to eliminate clone funds and the use of derivatives to circumvent the restriction. Even so, foreign investment exposes an FI to **foreign exchange risk.** Foreign exchange risk is the risk that exchange rate changes can adversely affect the value of an FI's assets and liabilities denominated in foreign currencies.

foreign exchange risk
The risk that exchange rate changes can affect the value of an FI's assets and liabilities located abroad.

To understand how foreign exchange risk arises, suppose that an FI makes a loan to a British company in pounds sterling (£). Should the British pound depreciate in value relative to the dollar, the principal and interest payments received by investors would be devalued in dollar terms. Indeed, were the British pound to fall far enough over the investment period, when cash flows are converted back into dollars, the overall return could be negative. That is, on the conversion of principal and interest payments from sterling into dollars, foreign exchange losses can offset the promised value of local currency interest payments at the original exchange rate at which the investment occurred.

In general, an FI can hold assets denominated in a foreign currency and/or issue foreign liabilities. Consider an FI that holds £100 million British pound loans as assets and funds £80 million of them with British pound certificates of deposit. The difference between the £100 million in pound loans and £80 million in pound CDs is funded by dollar CDs (i.e., £20 million pounds' worth of dollar CDs). See Figure 7–2. In this case, the FI is *net long* £20 million in British assets; that is, it holds more foreign assets than liabilities. The FI suffers losses if the exchange rate for pounds falls or depreciates against the dollar over this period. In dollar terms, the value of the British pound loan assets falls or decreases in value by more than the British pound CD liabilities do. That is, the FI is exposed to the risk that its net foreign assets may have to be liquidated at an exchange rate lower than the one that existed when the FI entered into the foreign asset–liability position.

Instead, the FI could have £20 million more foreign liabilities than assets; in this case, it would be holding a *net short* position in foreign assets, as shown in Figure 7–3. Under this circumstance, the FI is exposed to foreign exchange risk if the pound appreciates against the dollar over the investment period. This occurs because the value of its British pound liabilities in dollar terms rose faster than the return on its pound assets. Consequently, to be approximately hedged, the FI must match its assets and liabilities in each foreign currency.

FIGURE 7–2
The Foreign Asset and Liability Position: Net Long Asset Position in Pounds

FIGURE 7–3
The Foreign Asset and Liability Position: Net Short Asset Position in Pounds

Note that the FI is fully hedged only if we assume that it holds foreign assets and liabilities of exactly the same maturity.[7] Consider what happens if the FI matches the size of its foreign currency book (British pound assets = British pound liabilities = £100 million in that currency) but mismatches the maturities so that the pound sterling assets are of six-month maturity and the liabilities are of three-month maturity. The FI would then be exposed to foreign interest rate risk—the risk that British interest rates would rise when it has to roll over its £100 million British CD liabilities at the end of the third month. Consequently, an FI that matches both the size and maturities of its exposure in assets and liabilities of a given currency is hedged, or immunized, against foreign currency and foreign interest rate risk. To the extent that FIs mismatch their portfolio and maturity exposures in different currency assets and liabilities, they face both foreign currency and foreign interest rate risks. As already noted, if foreign exchange rate and interest rate changes are not perfectly correlated across countries, an FI can diversify away part, if not all, of its foreign currency risk. We discuss the measurement and evaluation of an FI's foreign currency risk exposure in depth in Chapter 15.

Concept Questions

1. Explain why the returns on domestic and foreign portfolio investments are not, in general, perfectly correlated.
2. A bank is net long in European assets. If the euro appreciates against the dollar, will the bank gain or lose?
3. A bank is net short in European assets. If the euro appreciates against the dollar, will the bank gain or lose?

COUNTRY OR SOVEREIGN RISK

As we noted in the previous section, a globally oriented FI that mismatches the size and maturities of its foreign assets and liabilities is exposed to foreign currency and foreign interest rate risks. Even beyond these risks, and even when investing in dollars, holding assets in a foreign country can expose an FI to an additional type of foreign investment risk called **country or sovereign risk.** Country or sovereign risk is a different type of credit risk that is faced by an FI that purchases assets such as the bonds and loans of foreign corporations. For example, when a domestic corporation is unable or unwilling to repay a loan, an FI usually has recourse to the domestic bankruptcy courts and eventually may recoup at least a portion of its original investment when the assets of the defaulted firm are liquidated or restructured. By comparison, a foreign corporation may be unable to repay the principal or interest on a loan even if it would like to. Most commonly, the government of the country in which the corporation is headquartered may prohibit or limit debt payments because of foreign currency shortages and adverse political reasons.

For example, in 1982, the Mexican and Brazilian governments announced a debt moratorium (i.e., a delay in their debt repayments) to Western creditors. The large global banks had made substantial loans to these countries and their government-owned corporations (such as Pemex, the Mexican state-run oil company). As a result, banks such as RBC and BNS eventually had to make additions to their loan loss reserves to meet expected losses on these loans. More recently, Canadian, U.S., European, and Japanese banks had enhanced sovereign risk expo-

country or sovereign risk
The risk that repayments from foreign borrowers may be interrupted because of interference from foreign governments.

[7] Technically speaking, hedging requires matching the durations (average lives of assets and liabilities) rather than simple maturities (see Chapter 9).

sures to countries such as Argentina, Russia, Thailand, South Korea, Malaysia, and Indonesia. Financial support given to these countries by the International Monetary Fund (IMF), the World Bank, and the U.S., Japanese, and European governments enabled the banks to avoid the full extent of the losses that were possible. Nevertheless, Indonesia had to declare a moratorium on some of its debt repayments, and Russia defaulted on payments on its short-term government bonds. In 1999, some banks agreed to settle their claims with the Russian government, receiving less than five cents for every dollar owed them. Finally, in 2001, the government of Argentina, which had pegged its peso to the dollar on a one-to-one basis since the early 1990s, had to default on its government debt largely because of an overvalued peso and the adverse effect this had on its exports and foreign currency earnings. In December 2001, Argentina ended up defaulting on US $130 billion in government-issued debt and, in 2002, passed legislation that led to defaults on US $30 billion of corporate debt owed to foreign creditors. Argentina's economic problems continued into 2003; in September 2003 it defaulted on a $3 billion loan repayment to the IMF.

In the event of such restrictions, reschedulings, or outright prohibitions on the payment of debt obligations by sovereign governments, the FI claimholder has little, if any, recourse to the local bankruptcy courts or an international civil claims court. The major leverage available to an FI to ensure or increase repayment probabilities and amounts is its control over the future supply of loans or funds to the country concerned. However, such leverage may be very weak in the face of a country's collapsing currency and government. Chapter 16 discusses how country or sovereign risk is measured and considers possible financial market solutions to the country risk exposure problems of a globally oriented FI.

Concept Questions

1. Can a bank be subject to sovereign risk if it lends only to AAA or the highest-quality foreign corporations?
2. What is one major way an FI can discipline a country that threatens not to repay its loans?

LIQUIDITY RISK

liquidity risk
The risk that a sudden surge in liability withdrawals may leave an FI in a position of having to liquidate assets in a very short period of time and at low prices.

Liquidity risk arises when an FI's liability holders, such as depositors or insurance policyholders, demand immediate cash for the financial claims they hold with an FI or when holders of off-balance-sheet loan commitments (or credit lines) suddenly exercise their right to borrow (draw down their loan commitments). When liability holders demand cash immediacy—that is, "put" their financial claims back to the FI—the FI must either borrow additional funds or sell assets to meet the demand for the withdrawal of funds. The most liquid asset of all is cash, which FIs can use to directly meet liability holders' demands to withdraw funds. Although FIs limit their cash asset holdings because cash earns no interest, low cash holdings are usually not a problem. Day-to-day withdrawals by liability holders are generally predictable, and FIs can normally expect to borrow additional funds to meet any sudden shortfalls of cash on the money and financial markets.

However, there are times when an FI can face a liquidity crisis. Because of a lack of confidence by liability holders in the FI or some unexpected need for cash, liability holders may demand *larger* withdrawals than normal. When all, or many, FIs face abnormally large cash demands, the cost of additional purchased or borrowed funds rises and the supply of such funds becomes restricted. As a consequence, FIs may have to sell some of their less liquid assets to meet the withdrawal demands of liability holders. This results in a more serious liquidity risk, especially as some assets with "thin" markets generate lower prices when the asset sale is immediate than when the FI has more time to negotiate the sale of an asset. As a result, the liquidation of some assets at low or fire-sale prices (the price an FI receives if an asset must be liquidated immediately at less than its fair market value) could threaten an FI's profitability and solvency. Good examples of such illiquid assets are bank loans to small firms. Such serious liquidity problems may eventually result in a run in which all liability claim-holders seek to withdraw their funds simultaneously from the FI because they fear that it will be unable to meet their demands for cash in the near future. This turns the FI's liquidity problem into a solvency problem and can cause it to fail.[8]

We examine the nature of normal, abnormal, and run-type liquidity risks and their impact on banks, insurance companies, and other FIs in more detail in Chapter 17. In addition, we look at ways an FI can better manage liquidity and liability risk exposures in Chapter 18. Chapter 19 discusses the roles of deposit insurance and other liability guarantee schemes in deterring deposit (liability) runs.

Concept Questions

1. Why might an FI face a sudden liquidity crisis?
2. What circumstances might lead an FI to liquidate assets at fire-sale prices?

INSOLVENCY RISK

Insolvency risk
The risk that an FI may not have enough capital to offset a sudden decline in the value of its assets relative to its liabilities.

Insolvency risk is a consequence or outcome of one or more of the risks described above: interest rate, market, credit, off-balance-sheet, technology, foreign exchange, sovereign, and liquidity risks. Technically, insolvency occurs when the capital or equity resources of an FI's owners are driven to, or near to, zero because of losses incurred as the result of one or more of the risks described above. Consider the failures of the Canadian Commercial Bank (CCB) and the Northland Bank of Canada (NBC) in 1985. Both concentrated their operations in Western Canada, investing in oil and gas, and real estate loans. A decline in the Canadian dollar and increases in interest rates caused the loan portfolios of both banks to deteriorate and led to difficulties in rolling over deposits (liquidity risk). Despite interim support from the other chartered banks and borrowings from the Bank of Canada, the capital of both banks deteriorated (solvency risk) and they eventually were allowed to fail. Similarly, in 1984, the U. S. bank, Continental Illinois National Bank and Trust Company, experienced defaults of its loans to the oil and gas sector, became unable to obtain funding, and U.S. federal regulators assumed control.[9]

---

[8] The situation of several Ohio savings institutions in 1985 is an extreme example of liquidity risk. A group of 70 Ohio savings institutions was insured by a private fund, the Ohio Deposit Guarantee Fund (ODGF). One of these savings banks, Home State Savings Bank (HSSB), had invested heavily in a Florida-based government securities dealer, EMS Government Securities, Inc., which eventually defaulted on its debts to HSSB (note the interaction between credit risk and liquidity risk). This in turn made it difficult for HSSB to meet deposit withdrawals of its customers. HSSB's losses from the ESM default were, in fact, so large that the ODGF could not cover them. Not only was HSSB unable to cover the deposit withdrawals, but other Ohio savings institutions insured by ODGF were inundated with deposit withdrawals to the extent that they could not cover them as well. As a result, ODGF-insured institutions were temporarily closed and the Ohio state legislature had to step in to cover depositors' claims.

[9] See J. F. Dingle, Planning an Evolution: The Story of the Canadian Payments Association, 1980–2002, May 2003, The Bank of Canada and The Canadian Payments Association, Chapter 5, and I. Swary, "The Stock Market Reaction to Regulatory Action in the Continental Illinois Crisis," *Journal of Business*, No. 3, 1986, pp. 451–474.

In general, the more equity capital to borrowed funds an FI has—that is, the lower its leverage—the better able it is to withstand losses, whether due to adverse interest rate changes, unexpected credit losses, or other reasons. Thus, both management and regulators of FIs focus on an FI's capital (and adequacy) as a key measure of its ability to remain solvent and grow in the face of a multitude of risk exposures. The issue of what is an adequate level of capital to manage an FI's overall risk exposure is discussed in Chapter 20.

Concept Questions

1. When does insolvency risk occur?
2. How is insolvency risk related to the other risks discussed in this chapter?

OTHER RISKS AND THE INTERACTION OF RISKS

In this chapter we have concentrated on nine major risks continuously impacting an FI manager's decision-making process and risk management strategies. These risks were interest rate risk, market risk, credit risk, off-balance-sheet risk, technology and operational risk, foreign exchange risk, country or sovereign risk, liquidity risk, and insolvency risk. Even though the discussion generally described each independently, in reality, these risks are often interdependent. For example, when interest rates rise, corporations and consumers find maintaining promised payments on their debt more difficult.[10] Thus, over some range of interest rate movements, credit, interest rate, and off-balance-sheet risks are positively correlated. Furthermore, the FI may have been counting on the funds from promised payments on its loans for liquidity management purposes. Thus, liquidity risk is also correlated with interest rate and credit risks. The inability of a customer to make promised payments also affects the FI's income and profits and, consequently, its equity or capital position. Thus, each risk and its interaction with other risks ultimately affects solvency risk. Similarly, foreign exchange rate changes and interest rate changes are also highly correlated. When the Bank of Canada changes a key interest rate through its monetary policy actions, exchange rates are also likely to change.

Various other risks, often of a more discrete or event type, also impact an FI's profitability and risk exposure, although, as noted earlier, many view discrete or event risks as part of operational risks. Discrete risks might include events external to the FI, such as a sudden change in taxation. Such changes can affect the attractiveness of some types of assets over others, as well as the liquidity of an FI's balance sheet.

Changes in regulatory policy constitute another type of external, discrete, or event risk. These include lifting the regulatory barriers to lending or to entry or on products offered (see Chapter 21). Other discrete or event risks involve sudden and unexpected changes in financial market conditions due to war, revolution, or sudden market collapse, such as the 1929 and 1987 stock market crashes or the September 2001 terrorist attacks in the United States. These can have a major impact on an FI's risk exposure. Other event risks include fraud, theft, earthquakes, storms, malfeasance, and breach of fiduciary trust; all of these can ultimately cause an FI to fail or be severely harmed. Yet each is difficult to model and predict.

Finally, more general macroeconomic or systematic risks, such as increased inflation, inflation volatility, and unemployment, can directly and indirectly impact an FI's level of interest rate, credit, and liquidity risk exposure. For example, infla-

---

[10] Rising interest rates may also negatively impact derivative contract holders, who may then be inclined to default. This credit risk on derivatives is often called counter-party risk.

tion was very volatile in the 1979–82 period in Canada and the United States. Interest rates reflected this volatility. During periods in which FIs face high and volatile inflation and interest rates, interest rate risk exposure from mismatching balance sheet maturities tends to rise. Credit risk exposure also rises because borrowing firms with fixed-price product contracts often find it difficult to keep up their loan payments when inflation and interest rates rise abruptly.

Concept Questions

1. What is meant by the term *event risk*?
2. What are some examples of event and general macroeconomic risks that impact FIs?

Summary

This chapter provided an introductory view of nine major risks faced by modern FIs. They face *interest rate risk* when their assets and liabilities maturities are mismatched. They incur *market risk* on their trading assets and liabilities if there are adverse movements in interest rates, exchange rates, or other asset prices. They face *credit risk* or default risk if their clients default on their loans and other obligations. Modern-day FIs also engage in a significant number of off-balance-sheet activities that expose them to *off-balance-sheet risks:* contingent asset and liability risks. The advent of sophisticated technology and automation exposes FIs to both *technological risk* and *operational risk.* If FIs conduct foreign business, they are subject to additional risks, namely *foreign exchange* and *sovereign risks. Liquidity risk* is a result of a serious run on an FI because of excessive withdrawals or problems in refinancing. Finally, *insolvency risk* occurs when an FI's capital is insufficient to withstand a decline in the value of assets relative to liabilities. However, even though we treat these risks at times as stand-alone, risk management for financial institutions involves focusing on enterprise-wide risk management. The effective management of risks determines the future success or failure of a modern FI. The chapters that follow analyze each of these risks in greater detail.

Questions and Problems

1. What is the process of *asset transformation* performed by a financial institution? Why does this process often lead to the creation of *interest rate risk?* What is interest rate risk?

2. What is *refinancing risk?* How is refinancing risk part of interest rate risk? If an FI funds long-term assets with short-term liabilities, what will be the impact on earnings of an increase in the rate of interest? A decrease in the rate of interest?

3. What is *reinvestment risk?* How is reinvestment risk part of interest rate risk? If an FI funds short-term assets with long-term liabilities, what will be the impact on earnings of a decrease in the rate of interest? An increase in the rate of interest?

4. The sales literature of a mutual fund claims that the fund has no risk exposure since it invests exclusively in federal government securities which are free of default risk. Is this claim true? Explain why or why not.

5. What is *economic or market value risk?* In what manner is this risk adversely realized in the economic performance of an FI?

6. A financial institution has the following balance sheet structure:

Assets	
Cash	$ 1,000
Bond	10,000
Total assets	**$11,000**

Liabilities and Equity	
Certificate of deposit	$10,000
Equity	1,000
Total liabilities and equity	**$11,000**

The bond has a 10-year maturity and a fixed-rate coupon of 10 percent. The certificate of deposit has a 1-year maturity and a 6 percent fixed rate of interest. The FI expects no additional asset growth.

a. What will be the net interest income at the end of the first year? *Note:* Net interest income equals interest income minus interest expense.

b. If at the end of year 1, market interest rates have increased 100 basis points (1 percent), what will be the net interest income for the second year? Is this result caused by reinvestment risk or refinancing risk?

c. Assuming that market interest rates increase 1 percent, the bond will have a value of $9,446 at the end of year 1. What will be the market value of equity for the FI?

d. If market interest rates had decreased 100 basis points by the end of year 1, would the market value of equity be higher or lower than $1,000? Why?

e. What factors have caused the changes in operating performance and market value for this firm?

7. How does the policy of matching the maturities of assets and liabilities work (a) to minimize interest rate risk and (b) against the asset-transformation function of FIs?

8. Corporate bonds usually pay interest semiannually. If a company decided to change from semiannual to annual interest payments, how would this affect the bond's interest rate risk?

9. Two 10-year bonds are being considered for an investment that may have to be liquidated before the maturity of the bonds. The first bond is a 10-year premium bond with a coupon rate higher than its required rate of return, and the second bond is a zero-coupon bond that pays only a lump-sum payment after 10 years with no interest over its life. Which bond would have more interest rate risk? That is, which bond's price would change by a larger amount for a given change in interest rates? Explain your answer.

10. Consider again the two bonds in problem 9. If the investment goal is to leave the assets untouched until maturity, such as for a child's education or for one's retirement, which of the two bonds has more interest rate risk? What is the source of this risk?

11. A mutual fund bought $1,000,000 of two-year government notes six months ago. During this time, the value of the securities has increased, but for tax reasons the mutual fund wants to postpone any sale for two more months. What type of risk does the mutual fund face for the next two months?

12. A bank invested $50 million in a two-year asset paying 10 percent interest per annum and simultaneously issued a $50 million, one-year liability paying 8 percent interest per annum. What will be the impact on the bank's net interest income if at the end of the first year all interest rates have increased by 1 percent (100 basis points)?

13. What is *market risk?* How do the results of this risk surface in the operating performance of financial institutions? What actions can be taken by an FI's management to minimize the effects of this risk?

14. What is *credit risk?* Which types of FIs are more susceptible to this type of risk? Why?

15. What is the difference between *firm-specific credit risk* and *systematic credit risk?* How can an FI alleviate firm-specific credit risk?

16. Many banks and savings institutions that failed in the 1980s in the United States had made loans to oil companies in Louisiana, Texas, and Oklahoma. When oil prices fell, these companies, the regional economy, and the banks and savings institutions all experienced financial problems. What types of risk were inherent in the loans that were made by these banks and savings institutions?

17. What is the nature of an off-balance-sheet activity? How does an FI benefit from such activities? Identify the various risks that these activities generate for an FI, and explain how these risks can create varying degrees of financial stress for the FI at a later time.

18. What is *technology risk?* What is the difference between *economies of scale* and *economies of scope?* How can these economies create benefits for an FI? How can these economies prove harmful to an FI?

19. What is the difference between technology risk and *operational risk?* How does internationalizing the payments system among banks increase operational risk?

20. What two factors provide potential benefits to FIs that expand their asset holdings and liability funding sources beyond their domestic economies?

21. What is *foreign exchange risk?* What does it mean for an FI to be *net long* in foreign assets? What does it mean for an FI to be *net short* in foreign assets? In each case, what must happen to the foreign exchange rate to cause the FI to suffer losses?

22. If the euro is expected to depreciate in the near future, would a Canadian-based FI in Paris prefer to be net long or net short in the euro in its asset positions? Discuss.

23. If international capital markets are well integrated and operate efficiently, will FIs be exposed to foreign exchange risk? What are the sources of foreign exchange risk for FIs?

24. If an FI has the same amount of foreign assets and foreign liabilities in the same currency, has that FI necessarily reduced to zero the risk involved in these international transactions? Explain.

25. An insurance company invests $1,000,000 in a private placement of British bonds. Each bond pays £300 in interest per year for 20 years. If the current exchange rate is £1.7612/$, what is the nature of the insurance company's exchange rate risk? Specifically, what type of exchange rate movement concerns this insurance company?

26. Assume that a bank has assets located in London that are worth £150 million on which it earns an average of 8 percent per year. The bank has £100 million in liabilities on which it pays an average of 6 percent per year. The current spot rate is £1.50/$.

    a. If the exchange rate at the end of the year is £2.00/$, will the dollar have appreciated or depreciated against the pound?

    b. Given the change in the exchange rate, what is the effect in dollars on the net interest income from the foreign assets and liabilities? *Note:* The net interest income is interest income minus interest expense.

    c. What is the effect of the exchange rate change on the value of assets and liabilities in dollars?

27. Six months ago, Qualitybank, LTD., issued a US $100 million, one-year maturity CD denominated in euros. On the same date, US $60 million was invested in a € denominated loan and US $40 million was invested in a U.S. Treasury bill. The exchange rate on this date was €1.7382/US $. Assume no repayment of principal and an exchange rate today of €1.3905/US $.

    a. What is the current value of the CD principal (in US dollars and euros)?

    b. What is the current value of the euro-denominated loan principal (in dollars and euros)?

    c. What is the current value of the U.S. Treasury bill (in US dollars and euros)?

    d. What is Qualitybank's profit/loss from this transaction (in US dollars and euros)?

28. Suppose you purchase a 10-year, AAA-rated Swiss bond for par that is paying an annual coupon of 8 percent. The bond has a face value of 1,000 Swiss francs (SF). The spot rate at the time of purchase is SF1.50/$. At the end of the year, the bond is downgraded to AA and the yield increases to 10 percent. In addition, the SF appreciates to SF1.35/$.

    a. What is the loss or gain to a Swiss investor who holds this bond for a year? What portion of this loss or gain is due to foreign exchange risk? What portion is due to interest rate risk?

    b. What is the loss or gain to a Canadian investor who holds this bond for a year? What portion of this loss or gain is due to foreign exchange risk? What portion is due to interest rate risk?

29. What is *country or sovereign risk?* What remedy does an FI realistically have in the event of a collapsing country or currency?

30. Characterize the risk exposure(s) of the following FI transactions by choosing one or more of the risk types listed below:

    a. Interest rate risk

    b. Credit risk

    c. Off-balance-sheet risk

    d. Technology risk

    e. Foreign exchange risk

    f. Country or sovereign risk

    (1) A bank finances a $10 million, six-year fixed-rate corporate loan by selling one-year certificates of deposit.

    (2) An insurance company invests its policy premiums in a long-term government bond portfolio.

    (3) A French bank sells two-year fixed-rate notes to finance a two-year fixed-rate loan to a British entrepreneur.

    (4) A Japanese bank acquires an Austrian bank to facilitate clearing operations.

    (5) A mutual fund completely hedges its interest rate risk exposure by using forward contingent contracts.

    (6) A bond dealer uses his own equity to buy Mexican debt on the less-developed country (LDC) bond market.

    (7) A securities firm sells a package of mortgage loans as mortgage-backed securities.

31. Consider these four types of risks: credit, foreign exchange, market, and sovereign. These risks can be separated into two pairs of risk types in which each pair consists of two related risk types, with one being a subset of the other. How would you pair off the risk types, and which risk type could be considered a subset of the other type in the pair?

32. What is *liquidity risk?* What routine operating factors allow FIs to deal with this risk in times of normal economic activity? What market reality can create severe financial difficulty for an FI in times of extreme liquidity crises?

33. Why can *insolvency risk* be classified as a consequence or outcome of any or all of the other types of risks?

34. Discuss the interrelationships among the different sources of bank risk exposure. Why would the construction of a bank risk-management model to measure and manage only one type of risk be incomplete?

Measuring **Risk**

Interest Rate Risk I

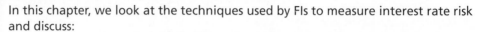

In this chapter, we look at the techniques used by FIs to measure interest rate risk and discuss:

▸ monetary policy, a key determinant of interest rate risk

▸ the repricing model for measuring interest rate risk

▸ the maturity model for measuring interest rate risk

▸ the term structure of interest rates and the shape of the yield curve (Appendix A, on page 688 of this book), and bond pricing and price volatility (Appendix B, available on the book's Web site, www.mcgrawhill.ca/college/saunders)

INTRODUCTION

net worth
The value of an FI to its owners; this is equal to the difference between the market value of assets and that of liabilities.

net interest income (NII)
The difference between an FI's interest income and interest expense.

www.bmo.com

www.osfi-bsif.gc.ca

www.bis.org

In Chapter 7 we established that while performing their asset-transformation functions, FIs often mismatch the maturities of their assets and liabilities. In so doing, they expose themselves to interest rate risk. For example, in the 1980s a large number of U.S. savings and loan companies became economically insolvent (i.e. the **net worth** or equity of their owners was eradicated) when interest rates unexpectedly increased. All FIs tend to mismatch their balance sheet maturities to some degree, but excessive interest rate risk can have an impact on the income statement as well as on the balance sheet by squeezing **net interest income (NII)**, the difference between an FI's interest income and interest expense. However, measuring interest rate risk exposure by looking only at the size of the maturity mismatch can be misleading.

This chapter analyzes two of the simpler methods used to measure an FI's interest rate risk. The repricing or funding gap model concentrates on the effect of interest rate changes on an FI's net interest income. Because of its simplicity, smaller deposit-taking institutions (DTIs) still use this model as their primary measure of interest rate risk. However, though all of the big FIs in Canada report their interest rate gap in their annual reports, most large FIs are adopting more sophisticated value-at-risk (VaR) models, which we will discuss in Chapter 10. For example, Bank of Montreal uses market value exposure (MVE), earnings volatility (EV), value at risk (VaR), simulations, sensitivity analysis, stress testing, and gap analysis to understand and manage its interest rate risk.[1] The Office of the Superintendent of Financial Institutions (OSFI) requires gap analysis to be reported quarterly for federally-regulated DTIs, but has recently issued a guideline that supports the Bank for International Settlements (BIS, the organization of the world's major Central Banks) whose final report issued in 2004 recommends market value accounting and the duration model to be applied by internationally active banks and their regulators to their banking book.[2] Canadian regulators played an important role in

---

[1] See Bank of Montreal's Annual Report 2004, p. 64, available at www.bmo.com.

[2] In this case, a longer horizon (e.g. one year) would be taken compared with that used to measure interest rate risk in the trading book (e.g. one day).

developing the principles, and Nicholas Le Pan, the Superintendent of OSFI, served as the Deputy Chairman of the Basel Committee.[3]

www.bankofcanada.ca

Before introducing the models, we turn to a discussion of the Bank of Canada's monetary policy, a key determinant of interest rate risk. Appendix A to this chapter reviews background information on the term structure of interest rates and discusses the shape of the yield curve. Appendix B to the chapter, located at the book's Web site, reviews bond pricing and price volatility.

THE BANK OF CANADA AND INTEREST RATE RISK

overnight rate

The rate that major financial institutions charge on one-day funds borrowed and lent to each other. It is at the middle of the operating band.

bank rate

The rate charged by the Bank of Canada on overnight loans to financial institutions.

operating band

The range (0.5 percent wide) of the overnight rates charged by the Bank of Canada. The bottom of the band is the rate the Bank of Canada will pay on deposits. The top of the band is the rate charged by the Bank of Canada on loans (the bank rate).

federal funds rate

The rate charged by the U.S. Federal Reserve on overnight loans to FIs.

www.federalreserve. gov

Since 1998, Canada's central bank, the Bank of Canada, has followed the practice of setting a target rate of inflation (2 per cent in 2005) and then adjusting the target for the **overnight rate**, the rate that FIs charge each other for one-day funds, to achieve its inflation target. The **bank rate**, the rate the Bank of Canada charges for one-day loans it makes to FIs, is always the upper limit of the **operating band**, and the overnight rate is at the middle of the band. The lower limit of the operating band is the rate the Bank of Canada will pay on funds deposited with the Bank.

The target overnight rate is the main instrument used by the Bank of Canada to carry out monetary policy. If the Bank of Canada forecasts that production is below capacity and so it expects that inflation will be below its target rate, it may lower the target overnight rate so that money is cheaper. Companies and consumers will respond by increasing their borrowing and production, and spending in Canada will rise. If the opposite is true and inflation is expected to rise above the target rate, then the bank rate will be set higher, putting pressure on companies and consumers to decrease their spending and bringing inflation levels back into line. The Bank of Canada recognizes that rate changes will not have immediate effects and therefore the Bank forecasts 18 to 24 months into the future. The Bank schedules eight fixed days every year on which it will set the bank rate. In addition, the Bank publishes quarterly monetary policy reports in January, April, July, and October that update its view of the economy and give an indication of where the Bank expects rates to be.

Global financial integration requires the Bank of Canada to pay attention to the actions of other central banks, particularly the central bank in the United States, the Federal Reserve (the Fed). Since 1993, the Federal Reserve has used interest rates—the **federal funds rate**—as its main target variable to guide monetary policy. Under this regime the Fed simply announces after each monthly meeting whether the federal funds rate target has been increased, decreased, or left unchanged. It also should be noted that although Federal Reserve actions are targeted mostly at short-term rates (especially the federal funds rate), changes in short-term rates usually feed through to the whole term structure of interest rates. The linkages between short-term rates and long-term rates and the theories of the term structure of interest rates are discussed in Appendix A, available at the book's Web site.

Figure 8–1 shows a comparison of the bank rate with the U.S. federal funds rate for the period from 1965–2005. The rates in both countries vary over time, declining to their lowest levels between 2003 and 2005. In addition, the bank rate is generally higher than the fed funds rate. This reflects the Bank of Canada's focus on the U.S.-Canadian dollar exchange rate and the flow of funds between the two countries as

---

[3] See Basel Committee on Banking Supervision, "Principles for the Management and Supervision of Interest Rate Risk," Bank for International Settlements, Basel, Switzerland, July, 2004 and Office of the Superintendent of Financial Institutions, "Guideline B-12: Interest Rate Risk Management," February 2005.

FIGURE 8–1   **Comparison of the Bank Rate and the Federal Funds Rate, 1965–2005**

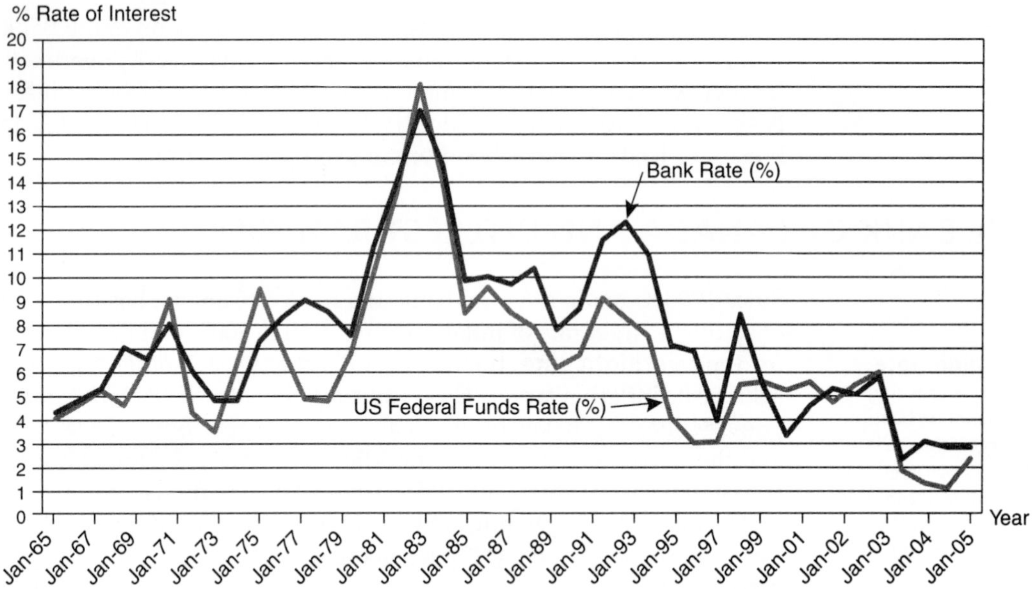

Source: Bank of Canada, "Comparison of the Bank Rate and the Federal Funds Rate 1965–2005." www.bankofcanada.ca

a result of interest rate differentials. In recent years, the Canadian government has eliminated its deficit while the U.S. deficit has widened. This has caused the Canadian dollar, along with the Euro and other currencies, to rise in value relative to the U.S. dollar, which is used as a global bench mark for commodities such as metals and oil and gas. As well, global developments, such as the Chinese government's decision to allow the yuan to float relative to the U.S. dollar, come into play. The complex interactions between exchange rates and monetary policy in Canada are discussed in more detail in Chapter 15 when we discuss foreign exchange risk.

Financial market integration increases the speed with which interest rate changes and associated volatility are transmitted among countries. The increased globalization of financial market flows in recent years has made the measurement and management of interest rate risk a prominent concern facing many modern FI managers. For example, investors across the world carefully evaluate the statements made by the Chairman of the U.S. Federal Reserve Board of Governors. Even hints of increased U.S. interest rates may have a major effect on world interest rates, as well as foreign exchange rates and stock prices. This emphasizes that, although we isolate risks in our discussions here, complex FIs engage in enterprise-wide risk management that takes into account interactions between risks.

We analyze the different ways an FI might measure the exposure it faces in running a mismatched maturity book (or gap) between its assets and its liabilities in a world of interest rate volatility by looking at the simplest models still in use, the repricing (or funding gap) model and the maturity model before moving on to the duration model in Chapter 9.

Concept Questions

1. How is the Bank of Canada's monetary policy linked to the degree of interest rate uncertainty faced by FIs?

INTERNET EXERCISE

The Bank of Canada publishes a Monetary Policy Update quarterly. Go to the Bank of Canada's Web site at www.bankofcanada.ca. Look for the latest Monetary Policy Update. Download it to your computer and then answer the following questions. What is the current inflation target? Does the Bank of Canada expect interest rates to increase or decrease in the next quarter? What are the highlights of the report? What are the major influences that the Bank sees in determining rates in the next 3 to 6 months? Are there any issues that would concern an FI that is managing its interest rate risk?

THE REPRICING MODEL

repricing gap
The difference between assets whose interest rates will be repriced or changed over some future period (rate-sensitive assets) and liabilities whose interest rates will be repriced or changed over some future period (rate-sensitive liabilities).

The repricing, or funding gap, model is essentially a book value accounting cash flow analysis of the **repricing gap** between the interest revenue earned on an FI's assets and the interest paid on its liabilities (or its net interest income) over a particular period of time. The assets or liabilities are **rate sensitive**, that is, the interest rate charged or earned will change (i.e., be repriced) over that period. Consider a bank that has divided its assets and liabilities into the following **maturity buckets**:[4]

1. One day.
2. More than one day to three months.
3. More than three months to six months.
4. More than 6 months to 12 months.
5. More than one year to five years.
6. More than five years.

rate-sensitive asset or liability
An asset or liability that is repriced at or near current market interest rates within a maturity bucket.

Under the repricing gap approach, a bank reports the gaps in each maturity bucket by calculating the rate sensitivity of each asset (RSA) and each liability (RSL) on its balance sheet. **Rate sensitivity** here means that the asset or liability is repriced at or near current market interest rates within a certain time horizon (or maturity bucket). More simply, it means how long the FI manager must wait to change the posted interest rates on any asset or liability. In many cases this occurs on a date prior to maturity.

maturity bucket
The sum of an FI's rate sensitive assets or liabilities that are repriced over a particular time period.

Table 8–1 shows the asset and liability repricing gaps of an FI, categorized into each of the six previously defined maturity buckets. Although the cumulative repricing gap over the whole balance sheet must, by definition, be zero [see Table 8–1, column (4)], the advantage of the repricing model lies in its information value and its simplicity in pointing to an FI's *net interest income exposure* (or profit exposure) to interest rate changes in different maturity buckets.[5]

refinancing risk
The risk that the cost of rolling over or reborrowing funds will rise above the returns being earned on asset investments.

For example, suppose that an FI has a negative $10 million difference between its assets and liabilities being repriced in one day (one-day bucket). Assets and liabilities that are repriced each day are likely to be interbank borrowings or repurchase agreements (see Chapter 2). Thus, a negative gap (RSA < RSL) exposes the FI to **refinancing risk,** in that a rise in these short-term rates would lower the FI's *net interest income* since the FI has more rate-sensitive liabilities than assets in this bucket. In other words, assuming equal changes in interest rates on RSAs and

---

[4] As of November 1997, OSFI's Reporting Manual requires FIs to report quarterly and to use 10 maturity buckets for their floating rate assets and liabilities: 1 day to one month, one month to 3 months, 3 months to 6 months, 1 year to 2 years, 2 years to 3 years, 3 years to 4 years, 4 years to 5 years, 5 years to 7 years, and greater than 7 years. For illustration purposes, we consider only 6 periods.

[5] If we include equity capital as a long-term (over five years) liability.

TABLE 8–1
Repricing Gap
(in millions
of dollars)

	1 Assets	2 Liabilities	3 Gaps	4 Cumulative Gap
1. One day	20	30	−10	−10
2. More than one day–three months	30	40	−10	−20
3. More than three months–six months	70	85	−15	−35
4. More than 6 months–12 months	90	70	+20	−15
5. More than one year–five years	40	30	+10	−5
6. Over five years	10	5	+5	0
	260	260		

RSLs, interest expense will increase by more than interest revenue. Conversely, if the FI has a positive $20 million difference between its assets and liabilities being repriced in 6 months to 12 months, it has a positive gap (RSA > RSL) for this period and is exposed to **reinvestment risk,** in that a drop in rates over this period would lower the FI's net interest income; that is, interest income will decrease by more than interest expense. Specifically, let:

reinvestment risk
The risk that the returns on funds to be reinvested will fall below the cost of the funds.

ΔNII_i = Change in net interest income in the ith bucket

GAP_i = Dollar size of the gap between the book value of rate-sensitive assets and rate-sensitive liabilities in maturity bucket i

ΔR_i = Change in the level of interest rates impacting assets and liabilities in the ith bucket

Then:

$$\Delta NII_i = (GAP_i)\,\Delta R_i = (RSA_i - RSL_i)\,\Delta R_i$$

In this first bucket, if the gap is negative $10 million and short-term interest rates rise 1 percent, the annualized change in the FI's future net interest income is:[6]

$$\Delta NII_i = (-\$10 \text{ million}) \times .01 = -\$100,000$$

(handwritten margin note:) Repricing model doesn't take chg in mkt value of assets/liab due to Δ in rates - only measures impact on current NII

This approach is very simple and intuitive. Remember, however, from Chapter 7 and our overview of interest rate risk that capital or market value losses also occur when rates rise. The capital loss effect that is measured by both the maturity and duration models developed later in this chapter and in Chapter 9 is not accounted for in the repricing model. The reason is that in the book value accounting world of the repricing model, assets and liability values are reported at their *historic* values or costs. Thus, interest rate changes affect only current interest income or interest expense—that is, net interest income on the FI's income statement—rather than the market value of assets and liabilities on the balance sheet.[7]

The FI manager can also estimate cumulative gaps (CGAP) over various repricing categories or buckets. A common cumulative gap of interest is the one-year repricing gap estimated from Table 8–1 as:

$$CGAP = (-\$10) + (-\$10) + (-\$15) + \$20 = -\$15 \text{ million}$$

---

[6] One can also calculate an "average" gap. If it is assumed that assets and liabilities reprice on *average* halfway through the period, the one-year gap measure calculated above will be divided by 2.

[7] For example, a 30-year bond purchased 10 years ago when rates were 13 percent would be reported as having the same book (accounting) value as when rates are 7 percent. Using market value, gains and losses to asset and liability values would be reflected in the balance sheet as rates changed.

TABLE 8–2
Simple FI Balance Sheet (in millions of dollars)

Assets		Liabilities	
1. Short-term consumer loans (one-year maturity)	50	1. Equity capital (fixed)	20
2. Long-term consumer loans (two-year maturity)	25	2. Demand deposits	40
3. Three-month Treasury bills	30	3. Savings deposits	30
4. Six-month Treasury bills	35	4. Three-month GICs	40
5. Three-year Government of Canada bonds	70	5. Three-month bankers acceptances	20
6. 10-year, fixed-rate mortgages	20	6. Six-month commercial paper	60
7. 25-year, floating-rate mortgages (rate adjusted every six months)	40	7. One-year term deposits	20
		8. Two-year term deposits	40
	270		270

If ΔR_i is the average interest rate change affecting assets and liabilities that can be repriced within a year, the cumulative effect on the bank's net interest income is:[8]

$$\Delta NII_i = (CGAP)\,\Delta R_i$$
$$= (-\$15 \text{ million})(.01) = -\$150,000$$

We can now look at how an FI manager would calculate the cumulative one-year gap from a balance sheet. Remember that the manager asks: Will or can this asset or liability have its interest rate changed within the next year? If the answer is yes, it is a rate-sensitive asset or liability; if the answer is no, it is not rate sensitive.

Consider the simplified balance sheet facing the FI manager in Table 8–2. Instead of the original maturities, the maturities are those remaining on different assets and liabilities at the time the repricing gap is estimated.

Rate-Sensitive Assets

Looking down the asset side of the balance sheet in Table 8–2, we see the following one-year rate-sensitive assets (RSAs):

1. *Short-term consumer loans: $50 million.* These are repriced at end of the year and just make the one-year cutoff.

2. *Three-month T-bills: $30 million.* These are repriced on maturity (rollover) every three months.

3. *Six-month T-bills: $35 million.* These are repriced on maturity (rollover) every six months.

4. *25-year floating-rate mortgages: $40 million.* These are repriced (i.e., the mortgage rate is reset) every six months. Thus, these long-term assets are rate-sensitive assets in the context of the repricing model with a one-year repricing horizon.

Summing these four items produces total one-year rate-sensitive assets (RSAs) of $155 million. The remaining $115 million of assets are not rate sensitive over the one-year repricing horizon—that is, a change in the level of interest rates will not affect the size of the interest revenue generated by these assets over the next year.[9]

---

[8] Note that a change in the dollar value and mix of rate-sensitive assets and liabilities (or a change in CGAP) also affects the FI's net income.

[9] We are assuming that the assets are noncallable over the year and that there will be no prepayments (runoffs, see below) on the mortgages within a year.

Although the $115 million in long-term consumer loans, 3-year Government of Canada bonds, and 10-year, fixed-rate mortgages generate interest revenue, the size of revenue generated will not change over the next year, since the interest rates on these assets are not expected to change (i.e., they are fixed over the next year).

Rate-Sensitive Liabilities

Looking down the liability side of the balance sheet in Table 8–2, we see the following liability items clearly fit the one-year rate or repricing sensitivity test:

1. *Three-month GICs $40 million.* These mature in three months and are repriced on rollover.

2. *Three-month bankers acceptances: $20 million.* These also mature in three months and are repriced on rollover.

3. *Six-month commercial paper: $60 million.* These mature and are repriced every six months.

4. *One-year term deposits: $20 million.* These get repriced right at the end of the one-year gap horizon.

Summing these four items produces one-year rate-sensitive liabilities (RSLs) of $140 million. The remaining $130 million is not rate sensitive over the one-year period. The $20 million in equity capital and $40 million in demand deposits (see the following discussion) do not pay interest and are therefore classified as non-interest-paying. The $30 million in savings deposits (see the following discussion) and $40 million in two-year term deposits generate interest expense over the next year, but the level of the interest expense generated will not change if the general level of interest rates changes. Thus, we classify these items as rate-insensitive liabilities.

Note that demand deposits (or transaction accounts in general) were not included as RSLs. We can make strong arguments for and against their inclusion as rate-sensitive liabilities.

Against Inclusion

Although explicit interest is paid on transaction accounts such as chequing/savings accounts, the rates paid by FIs do not fluctuate directly with changes in the general level of interest rates (particularly when the general level of rates is rising). Moreover, many demand deposits act as **core deposits** for FIs, meaning they are a long-term source of funds.

core deposits
Those deposits that act as an FI's long-term source of funds.

For Inclusion

If interest rates rise, individuals draw down (or run off) their demand deposits, forcing the bank to replace them with higher-yielding, interest-bearing, rate-sensitive funds. This is most likely to occur when the interest rates on alternative instruments are high. In such an environment, the opportunity cost of holding funds in demand deposit accounts is likely to be larger than it is in a low–interest rate environment.

Similar arguments for and against inclusion of retail savings accounts can be made. Banks adjust these rates infrequently. However, savers tend to withdraw funds from these accounts when rates rise, forcing banks into more expensive fund substitutions.

The four repriced liabilities ($40 + $20 + $60 + $20) sum to $140 million, and the four repriced assets ($50 + $30 + $35 + $40) sum to $155 million. Given this, the cumulative one-year repricing gap (CGAP) for the bank is:

$$CGAP = \text{One-year rate-sensitive assets} - \text{one-year rate-sensitive liabilities}$$
$$= \text{RSA} - \text{RSL}$$
$$= \$155 - \$140 = \$15 \text{ million}$$

TABLE 8–3

Effect of CGAP on the Relation between Changes in Interest Rates and Changes in Net Interest Income, Assuming Rate Changes for RSAs Equal Rate Changes for RSLs

Row	CGAP	Change in Interest Rates	Change in Interest Revenue		Change in Interest Expense	Change in NII
1	>0	⇑	⇑	>	⇑	⇑
2	>0	⇓	⇓	>	⇓	⇓
3	<0	⇑	⇑	<	⇑	⇓
4	<0	⇓	⇓	<	⇓	⇑

Interest rate sensitivity can also be expressed as a percentage of assets (*A*) (typically called the *gap ratio*):

$$\frac{CGAP}{A} = \frac{\$15 \text{ million}}{\$270 \text{ million}} = .056 = 5.6\%$$

Expressing the repricing gap in this way is useful since it tells us (1) the direction of the interest rate exposure (positive or negative CGAP) and (2) the scale of that exposure as indicated by dividing the gap by the asset size of the institution. In our example the bank has 5.6 percent more RSAs than RSLs in one-year-and-less buckets as a percentage of total assets.

Equal Changes in Rates on RSAs and RSLs

The CGAP provides a measure of an FI's interest rate sensitivity. Table 8–3 highlights the relation between CGAP and changes in NII when interest rate changes for RSAs are equal to interest rate changes for RSLs. For example, when CGAP (or the gap ratio) is positive (or the FI has more RSAs than RSLs), NII will rise when interest rates rise (row 1, Table 8–3), since interest revenue increases more than interest expense does.

EXAMPLE 8–1

Effect of Rate Changes on Net Interest Income When CGAP Is Positive

Suppose that interest rates rise by 1 percent on both RSAs and RSLs. The CGAP would project the expected annual change in net interest income (Δ*NII*) of the bank as approximately:

$$\Delta NII = CGAP \times \Delta R$$
$$= (\$15 \text{ million}) \times .01$$
$$= \$150,000$$

Similarly, if interest rates fall equally for RSAs and RSLs (row 2, Table 8–3), NII will fall when CGAP is positive. As rates fall, interest revenue falls by more than interest expense. Thus, NII falls. Suppose that for our FI, rates fall by 1 percent. The CGAP predicts that NII will fall by approximately:

$$\Delta NII = CGAP \times \Delta R$$
$$= (\$15 \text{ million}) \times -.01$$
$$= -\$150,000$$

It is evident from this equation that the larger the absolute value of CGAP, the larger the expected change in NII (i.e., the larger the increase or decrease in the FI's interest revenue relative to interest expense). In general, when CGAP is positive, the change in NII is positively related to the change in interest rates. Conversely, when CGAP (or the gap ratio) is negative, if interest rates rise by equal amounts for RSAs and RSLs (row 3, Table 8–3), NII will fall (since the FI has more RSLs than

FIGURE 8–2
Three-Month CD Rates versus Prime Rates for 1990–2004

Bank of Canada, "Three-Month CD Rates versus Prime Rates for 1990–2004." www.bankofcanada.ca

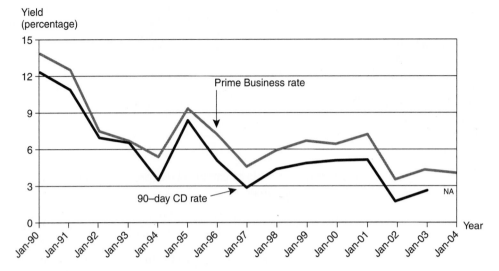

RSAs). Thus, an FI would want its CGAP to be positive when interest rates are expected to rise. Similarly, if interest rates fall equally for RSAs and RSLs (row 4, Table 8–3), NII will increase when CGAP is negative. As rates fall, interest expense decreases by more than interest revenue. In general then, when CGAP is negative, the change in NII is negatively related to the change in interest rates. Thus, an FI would want its CGAP to be negative when interest rates are expected to fall. We refer to these relationships as **CGAP effects.**

CGAP effects
The relations between changes in interest rates and changes in net interest income.

Unequal Changes in Rates on RSAs and RSLs

The previous section considered changes in net interest income as interest rates changed, assuming that the change in rates on RSAs was exactly equal to the change in rates on RSLs (in other words, assuming the interest rate spread between rates on RSAs and RSLs remained unchanged). This is not often the case; rather, rate changes on RSAs generally differ from those on RSLs (i.e., the spread between interest rates on assets and liabilities changes along with the levels of these rates). See Figure 8–2, which plots quarterly CD rates (liabilities) and prime lending rates (assets) for the period 1990–2004. Notice that although the rates generally move in the same direction, they are not perfectly correlated. In this case, as we consider the effect of rate changes on NII, we have a spread effect in addition to the CGAP effects.[10]

EXAMPLE 8–2

Influence of Spread Effect on Net Interest Income

To understand spread effect, assume for a moment that RSAs equal RSLs equals $155 million. Suppose that rates rise by 1.2 percent on RSAs and by 1 percent on RSLs (i.e., the spread between the rates on RSAs and RSLs increases by 1.2 percent − 1 percent = 0.2 percent). The resulting change in NII is calculated as:

$$\Delta NII = (RSA \times \Delta R_{RSA}) - (RSL \times \Delta R_{RSL})$$
$$= \Delta\text{Interest revenue} - \Delta\text{Interest expense}$$
$$= (\$155 \text{ million} \times 1.2\%) - (\$155 \text{ million} \times 1.0\%)$$
$$= \$155 \text{ million} (1.2\% - 1.0\%)$$
$$= \$310,000$$

---

[10] The spread effect therefore presents a type of basis risk for the FI. The FI's net interest income varies as the difference (basis) between interest rates on RSAs and interest rates on RSLs varies. We discuss basis risk in detail in Chapter 24.

TABLE 8–4
Effect of CGAP
on the Relation
between Changes
in Interest Rates
and Changes in
Net Interest Income,
Allowing for
Different Rate
Changes for RSAs
and RSLs

Row	CGAP	Change in Interest Rates	Change in Spread	NII
1	>0	⇑	⇑	⇑
2	>0	⇑	⇓	⇑⇓
3	>0	⇓	⇑	⇑⇓
4	>0	⇓	⇓	⇓
5	<0	⇑	⇑	⇑⇓
6	<0	⇑	⇓	⇓
7	<0	⇓	⇑	⇑
8	<0	⇓	⇓	⇑⇓

spread effect
The effect that a change
in the spread between
rates on RSAs and
RSLs has on net
interest income as
interest rates change.

If the spread between the rate on RSAs and RSLs increases, when interest rates rise (fall), interest revenue increases (decreases) by more (less) than interest expense. The result is an increase in NII. Conversely, if the spread between the rates on RSAs and RSLs decreases, when interest rates rise (fall), interest revenue increases (decreases) less (more) than interest expense, and NII decreases. In general, the **spread effect** is such that, regardless of the direction of the change in interest rates, a positive relation occurs between changes in the spread (between rates on RSAs and RSLs) and changes in NII. Whenever the spread increases (decreases), NII increases (decreases).

See Table 8–4 for various combinations of CGAP and spread changes and their effects on NII. The first four rows in Table 8–4 consider an FI with a positive CGAP; the last four rows consider an FI with a negative CGAP. Notice in Table 8–4 that both the CGAP and spread effects can have the same effect on NII. In these cases, FI managers can accurately predict the direction of the change in NII as interest rates change. When the two work in opposite directions, however, the change in NII cannot be predicted without knowing the size of the CGAP and expected change in the spread.

www.scotiabank.com

The interest rate exposure of an FI depends on its size and its view of rates. For example, in its 2003 Annual Report, the Bank of Nova Scotia (BNS) reported a moderate cumulative negative interest rate gap on its Canadian and foreign assets (including off-balance sheet instruments and prepayments on consumer and mortgage loans) of −$2.5 billion at October 31, 2003. It increased this gap to a positive one-year cumulative gap of $3.1 billion at October 31, 2004 as it expected rates to increase. BNS estimated that a 100 basis point increase in rates would increase its net income after-tax by $65 million over 12 months.[11]

The repricing gap is the measure of interest rate risk historically used by FIs, and it is still the main measure of interest rate risk used by small FIs. In contrast to the market value-based models of interest rate risk discussed below and in Chapter 9, the repricing gap model is conceptually easy to understand and can easily be used to forecast changes in profitability for a given change in interest rates. The repricing gap can be used to allow an FI to structure its assets and liabilities or to go off the balance sheet to take advantage of a projected interest rate change. However, the repricing gap model has some major weaknesses that have resulted in regulators' calling for the use of more comprehensive models (e.g., the duration gap model) to measure interest rate risk. We next discuss some of the major weaknesses of the repricing model.[12]

[11] See 2004 Scotiabank Annual Report, p. 58, available at www.scotiabank.com.

[12] See E. Brewer, "Bank Gap Management and the Use of Financial Futures," Federal Reserve Bank of Chicago, *Economic Perspectives,* March–April 1985, for an excellent analysis of the repricing model and its strengths and weaknesses.

<table>
<tr><td>

**Concept
Questions**

</td><td>

1. Why is it useful to express the repricing gap in terms of a percentage of assets? What specific information does this provide?

2. How can banks change the size and the direction of their repricing gap?

</td></tr>
</table>

WEAKNESSES OF THE REPRICING MODEL

The repricing model has four major shortcomings: (1) It ignores market value effects of interest rate changes, (2) it is overaggregative, (3) it fails to deal with the problem of rate-insensitive asset and liability runoffs and prepayments, and (4) it ignores cash flows from off-balance-sheet activities. In this section we discuss each of these weaknesses in more detail.

Market Value Effects

As was discussed in the overview of FI risks (Chapter 7), interest rate changes have a market value effect in addition to an income effect on asset and liability values. That is, the present value of the cash flows on assets and liabilities changes, in addition to the immediate interest received or paid on them, as interest rates change. In fact, the present values (and where relevant, the market prices) of virtually all assets and liabilities on an FI's balance sheet change as interest rates change. The repricing model ignores the market value effect—implicitly assuming a book value accounting approach. As such, the repricing gap is only a *partial* measure of the true interest rate exposure of an FI. As we discuss the market value-based measures of interest rate risk (below and in Chapter 9), we will highlight the result of ignoring the market value effect on the ability to accurately measure the overall interest rate risk of an FI.

Overaggregation

The problem of defining buckets over a range of maturities ignores information regarding the distribution of assets and liabilities within those buckets. For example, the dollar values of RSAs and RSLs within any maturity bucket range may be equal; however, on average, liabilities may be repriced toward the end of the bucket's range, while assets may be repriced toward the beginning, in which case a change in interest rates will have an effect on asset and liability cash flows that will not be accurately measured by the repricing gap approach.

Look at the simple example for the three-month to six-month bucket in Figure 8–3. Note that $50 million more RSAs than RSLs are repriced between months 3 and 4, while $50 million more RSLs than RSAs are repriced between months 5 and 6. The bank in its call report would show a zero repricing gap for the three-month to six-month bucket $(+50 + (-50) = 0)$. But as you can easily see, the bank's assets and liabilities are *mismatched* within the bucket. Clearly, the shorter the range over which bucket gaps are calculated, the smaller this problem is. If an FI manager calculated one-day bucket gaps out into the future, this would give a more accurate picture of the net interest income exposure to rate changes. Reportedly, many large banks have internal systems that indicate their repricing gaps on any given day in the future (252 days' time, 1,329 days' time, etc.). This suggests that although regulators require the report-

FIGURE 8–3
The Over-aggregation Problem: The Three-Month to Six-Month Bucket

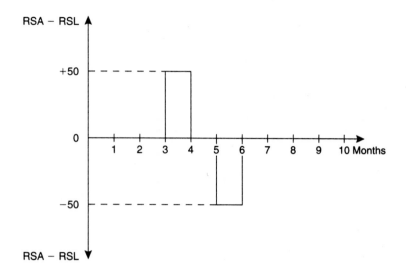

ing of repricing gaps over only relatively wide maturity bucket ranges, FI managers could set in place internal information systems to report the daily future patterns of such gaps.[13]

The Problem of Runoffs

In the simple repricing model discussed above, we assumed that all consumer loans matured in 1 year or that all conventional mortgages matured in 30 years. In reality, the FI continuously originates and retires consumer and mortgage loans as it creates and retires deposits. For example, today, some 30-year original maturity mortgages may have only 1 year left before they mature; that is, they are in their 29th year. In addition, these loans may be listed as 30-year mortgages (and included as not rate sensitive), yet they will sometimes be prepaid early as mortgage holders refinance their mortgages and/or sell their houses. Thus, the resulting proceeds will be reinvested at current market rates within the year. In addition, even if an asset or liability is rate insensitive, virtually all assets and liabilities (e.g., long-term mortgages) pay some principal and/or interest back to the FI in any given year. As a result, the FI receives a **runoff** cash flow from its rate-insensitive portfolio that can be reinvested at current market rates; that is, this runoff cash flow component of a rate-insensitive asset or liability is itself rate sensitive. The FI manager can deal easily with this in the repricing model by identifying for each asset and liability item the estimated dollar cash flow that will run off within the next year and adding these amounts to the value of rate-sensitive assets and liabilities.

Consider Table 8–5. Notice in this table that while the original maturity of an asset or liability may be long term, these assets and liabilities still generate some

runoff
Periodic cash flow of interest and principal amortization payments on long-term assets, such as conventional mortgages, that can be reinvested at market rates.

---

[13] Another way to deal with the overaggregation problem is by adjusting the buckets for the time to interest rate repricing within the bucket. Let RSA and RSL be rate-sensitive assets and liabilities in a bucket, let R denote initial interest rates on an asset or liability, and let K denote new interest rates after repricing. Let t be the proportion of the bucket period for which the asset's (liability's) old interest rate (R) is in effect, and thus, $1 - t$ is the proportion of the bucket period in which the new interest rate (K) is in operation:

$$\Delta NII = RSA[\{(1 + R_A)^{tA} \times (1 + K_A)^{1-tA}\} - (1 + R_A)] - RSL[\{(1 + R_L)^{tL} \times (1 + K_L)^{1-tL}\} - (1 + R_L)]$$

See Brewer, "Bank Gap Management," for more details.

TABLE 8–5   Runoffs of Different Assets and Liabilities (in millions of dollars)

Assets			Liabilities		
Item	**Amount Runoff in Less Than One Year**	**Amount Runoff in More Than One Year**	**Item**	**Amount Runoff in Less Than One Year**	**Amount Runoff in More Than One Year**
1. Short-term consumer loans	50	—	1. Equity	—	20
2. Long-term consumer loans	5	20	2. Demand deposits	30	10
3. Three-month T-bills	30	—	3. Savings deposits	15	15
4. Six-month T-bills	35	—	4. Three-month GICs	40	—
5. Three-year notes	10	60	5. Three-month bankers acceptances	20	—
6. 10-year mortgages	2	18	6. Six-month commercial paper	60	—
7. 30-year floating-rate mortgages	40	—	7. One-year time deposits	20	—
			8. Two-year time deposits	20	20
	172	98		205	65

cash flows that can be reinvested at market rates. Table 8–5 is a more sophisticated measure of the one-year repricing gap that takes into account the cash flows received on each asset and liability item during that year. Adjusted for runoffs, the repricing gap (in millions) is:

$$GAP = \$172 - \$205 = -\$33$$

As implied above, the runoffs themselves are not independent of interest rate changes. Specifically, when interest rates rise, many people may delay repaying their mortgages (and the principal on those mortgages), causing the runoff amount of $2 million on 10-year mortgages in Table 8–5 to be overly optimistic. Similarly, when interest rates fall, people may prepay their fixed-rate mortgages to refinance at a lower interest rate. Then runoffs could balloon to a number much greater than $2 million. This sensitivity of runoffs to interest rate changes is a further weakness of the repricing model.[14]

Cash Flows from Off-Balance-Sheet Activities

The RSAs and RSLs used in the repricing model generally include only the assets and liabilities listed on the balance sheet. Changes in interest rates will affect the cash flows on many off-balance-sheet instruments as well. For example, an FI might have hedged its interest rate risk with an interest rate futures contract (see Chapter 23). As interest rates change, these futures contracts—as part of the marking-to-market process—produce a daily cash flow (either positive or negative) for the FI that may offset any on-balance-sheet gap exposure. These offsetting cash flows from futures contracts are ignored by the simple repricing model and should (and could) be included in the model.

Concept Questions

1. What are four major weaknesses of the repricing model?
2. What does runoff mean?

---

[14] In the case of fixed-rate mortgage loans, the FI manager would need to estimate potential prepayments of principal during the year based on interest rate forecasts and mortgage holders' sensitivity to the forecasted change in rates (see Chapter 27 on prepayment models).

THE MATURITY MODEL

book value accounting
Accounting method in which the assets and liabilities of the FI are recorded at historic values.

market value accounting
Accounting method in which the assets and liabilities of the FI are revalued according to the current level of interest rates.

marking to market
Valuing securities at their current market price.

As mentioned above, a weakness of the repricing model is its reliance on book values rather than market values of assets and liabilities. Indeed, in most countries, FIs report their balance sheets by using **book value accounting.** This method records the historic values of securities purchased, loans made, and liabilities sold. Investment assets (i.e., those expected to be held to maturity) may be recorded at book values, while those assets expected to be used for trading (trading securities or available-for-sale securities) may be reported according to market value. The recording of market values means that assets and liabilities are revalued to reflect current market conditions. Thus, if a fixed-coupon bond had been purchased at $100 per $100 of face value in a low-interest rate environment, a rise in current market rates reduces the present value of the cash flows from the bond to the investor. Such a rise also reduces the price—say, to $97—at which the bond could be sold in the secondary market today. That is, the **market value accounting** approach reflects economic reality, or the true values of assets and liabilities if the FI's portfolio were to be liquidated at today's securities prices rather than at the prices when the assets and liabilities were originally purchased or sold. This practice of valuing securities at their market value is referred to as **marking to market.** We discuss book value versus market value accounting and the effect that the use of the alternative methods has in measuring the value of an FI in more detail in Chapter 20. In the maturity and duration model, developed below and in Chapter 9, the effects of interest rate changes on the market values of assets and liabilities are explicitly taken into account. This contrasts with the repricing model, discussed above, in which such effects are ignored.

EXAMPLE 8–3

Fixed Income Securities and the Maturity Model

Consider the value of a bond held by an FI that has one year to maturity, a face value of 100 (*F*) to be paid on maturity, one single annual coupon at a rate of 10 percent of the face value (*C*) and a current yield to maturity (*R*) (reflecting current interest rates) of 10 percent. The fair market price of the one-year bond, P_1^B, is equal to the present value of the cash flows on the bond:

$$P_1^B = \frac{F + C}{(1 + R)} = \frac{100 + 10}{1.1} = 100$$

Suppose the Bank of Canada tightens monetary policy so that the required yield on the bond rises instantaneously to 11 percent. The market value of the bond falls to:

$$P_1^B = \frac{100 + 10}{1.11} = 99.10$$

Thus, the market value of the bond is now only $99.10 per $100 of face value, whereas its original book value was $100. The FI has suffered a capital loss (ΔP_1) of $0.90 per $100 of face value in holding this bond, or:

$$\Delta P_1 = 99.10 - 100 = -\$0.90$$

Also, the percent change in the price is:

$$\Delta P_1 = \frac{99.10 - 100}{100} = -0.90\%$$

This example simply demonstrates the fact that:

$$\frac{\Delta P}{\Delta R} < 0$$

A rise in the required yield to maturity reduces the price of fixed-income securities held in FI portfolios. Note that if the bond under consideration were issued as a liability by the FI (e.g., a fixed-interest deposit such as a CD) rather than being held as an asset, the effect would be the same—the market value of the FI's deposits would fall. However, the economic interpretation is different. Although rising interest rates that reduce the market value of assets are bad news, the reduction in the market value of liabilities is good news for the FI. The economic intuition is straightforward. Suppose the FI issued a one-year deposit with a promised interest rate of 10 percent and principal or face value of $100.[15] When the current level of interest rates is 10 percent, the market value of the liability is 100:

$$P_1^D = \frac{100 + 10}{(1.1)} = 100$$

Should interest rates on new one-year deposits rise instantaneously to 11 percent, the FI has gained by locking in a promised interest payment to depositors of only 10 percent. The market value of the FI's liability to its depositors would fall to $99.10; alternatively, this would be the price the FI would need to pay the depositor if it repurchased the deposit in the secondary market:

$$P_1^D = \frac{100 + 10}{(1.11)} = 99.10$$

That is, the FI gained from paying only 10 percent on its deposits rather than 11 percent if they were newly issued after the rise in interest rates.

As a result, in a market value accounting framework, rising interest rates generally lower the market values of both assets and liabilities on an FI's balance sheet. Clearly, falling interest rates have the reverse effect: They increase the market values of both assets and liabilities.

EXAMPLE 8–4 *Effect of Maturity on Change in Bond Value*	In the preceding example, both the bond and the deposit were of one-year maturity. We can easily show that if the bond or deposit had a two-year maturity with the same annual coupon rate, the same increase in market interest rates from 10 to 11 percent would have had a more *negative* effect on the market value of the bond's (and deposit's) price. That is, before the rise in required yield:

$$P_2^B = \frac{10}{(1.1)} + \frac{10 + 100}{(1.1)^2} = 100$$

After the rise in market yields from 10 to 11 percent:

$$P_2^B = \frac{10}{(1.11)} + \frac{10 + 100}{(1.11)^2} = 98.29$$

and

$$\Delta P_2^B = 98.29 - 100 = -1.71$$

The resulting percentage change in the bond's value is:

$$\%\Delta P_2^B = (98.29 - 100)/100 = -1.71\%$$

---

[15] In this example we assume for simplicity that the promised interest rate on the deposit is 10 percent. In reality, for returns to intermediation to prevail, the promised rate on deposits would be less than the promised rate (coupon) on assets.

If we extend the analysis one more year, the market value of a bond with three years to maturity, a face value of $100, and a coupon rate of 10 percent is:

$$P_3^B = \frac{10}{(1.1)} + \frac{10}{(1.1)^2} + \frac{10 + 100}{(1.1)^3} = 100$$

After the rise in market rates from 10 to 11 percent, market value of the bond is:

$$P_3^B = \frac{10}{(1.11)} + \frac{10}{(1.11)^2} + \frac{10 + 100}{(1.11)^3} = 97.56$$

This is a change in the market value of:

$$\Delta P_3^B = 97.56 - 100 = -2.44$$

or

$$\%\Delta P_3^B = \frac{97.56 - 100}{100} = -2.44\%$$

This example demonstrates another general rule of portfolio management for FIs: The *longer* the maturity of a fixed income asset or liability, the larger its fall in price and market value for any given increase in the level of market interest rates. That is:

$$\frac{\Delta P_1}{\Delta R} < \frac{\Delta P_2}{\Delta R} < \cdots < \frac{\Delta P_{30}}{\Delta R}$$

Note that although the two-year bond's fall in price is larger than the fall of the one-year bond's, the difference between the two price falls, $\%\Delta P_2 - \%\Delta P_1$, is -1.71% − $(-0.9\%) = -0.81\%$. The fall in the three-year, 10 percent coupon bond's price when yield increases to 11 percent is -2.44 percent. Thus, $\%\Delta P_3 - \%\Delta P_2 = -2.44\%$ − $(-1.71\%) = -0.73\%$. This establishes an important result: Although P_3 falls more than P_2 and P_2 falls more than P_1, the size of the capital loss increases at a diminishing rate as we move into the higher maturity ranges. This effect is graphed in Figure 8–4.

So far, we have shown that for an FI's fixed-income assets and liabilities:

1. A rise (fall) in interest rates generally leads to a fall (rise) in the market value of an asset or liability.

2. The longer the maturity of a fixed-income asset or liability, the larger the fall (rise) in market value for any given interest rate increase (decrease).

3. The fall in the value of longer-term securities increases at a diminishing rate for any given increase in interest rates.

FIGURE 8–4
The Relationship between ΔR, Maturity, and ΔP (Capital Loss)

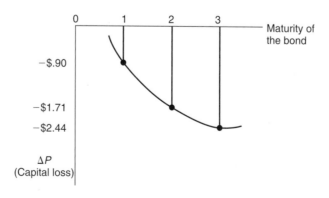

The Maturity Model with a Portfolio of Assets and Liabilities

The preceding general rules can be extended beyond an FI holding an individual asset or liability to a portfolio of assets and liabilities. Let M_A be the weighted-average maturity of an FI's assets and M_L the weighted-average maturity of an FI's liabilities such that:

$$M_i = W_{i1}M_{i1} + W_{i2}M_{i2} + \cdots + W_{in}M_{in}$$

where

M_i = Weighted-average maturity of an FI's assets (liabilities), $i = A$ or L

W_{ij} = Importance of each asset (liability) in the asset (liability) portfolio as measured by the market value of that asset (liability) position relative to the market value of all the assets (liabilities)

M_{ij} = Maturity of the jth asset (or liability), $j = 1 \ldots n$

This equation shows that the maturity of a portfolio of assets or liabilities is a weighted average of the maturities of the assets or liabilities that constitute that portfolio. In a portfolio context, the same three principles prevail as for an individual security:

1. A rise in interest rates generally reduces the market values of an FI's asset and liability portfolios.

2. The longer the maturity of the asset or liability portfolio, the larger the fall in value for any given interest rate increase.

3. The fall in value of the asset or liability portfolio increases with its maturity at a diminishing rate.

Given the preceding, the net effect of rising or falling interest rates on an FI's balance sheet depends on the extent and direction in which the FI mismatches the maturities of its asset and liability portfolios. That is, the effect depends on whether its **maturity gap,** $M_A - M_L$, is greater than, equal to, or less than zero.

maturity gap
Difference between the weighted-average maturity of the FI's assets and liabilities.

Consider the case in which $M_A - M_L > 0$; that is, the maturity of assets is longer than the maturity of liabilities. This is the case for most banks. These FIs tend to hold large amounts of relatively longer-term fixed-income assets such as conventional mortgages, consumer loans, commercial loans, and bonds, while issuing shorter-term liabilities, such as fixed interest payments promised to the depositors.[16]

Consider the simplified portfolio in Table 8–6 and notice that all assets and liabilities are marked to market; that is, we are using a market value accounting framework. Note that in the real world, reported balance sheets differ from Table 8–6 because historic or book value accounting rules are used. In Table 8–6 the difference between the market value of the FI's assets (A) and the market value of its liabilities such as deposits (L) is the net worth or true equity value (E) of the FI. This is the economic value of the FI owners' stake in the FI. In other words, it is the money the owners would get if they could liquidate the FI's assets and liabilities at today's prices in the financial markets by selling off loans and bonds and repurchasing deposits at the best prices. This is also clear from the balance sheet identity:

$$E = A - L$$

---

[16] These assets generate periodic interest payments such as coupons that are fixed over the asset's life. In Chapter 9 we discuss interest payments fluctuating with market interest rates, such as on an adjustable rate mortgage.

TABLE 8–6
The Market Value Balance Sheet of an FI

Assets	Liabilities
Long-term assets (*A*)	Short-term liabilities (*L*)
	Net worth (*E*)

TABLE 8–7
Initial Market Values of an FI's Assets and Liabilities (in millions of dollars)

Assets	Liabilities
$A = 100$ ($M_A = 3$ years)	$90 = L$ ($M_L = 1$ year)
	$10 = E$
100	100

TABLE 8–8
An FI's Market Value Balance Sheet after a Rise in Interest Rates of 1 Percent with Longer-Term Assets (in millions of dollars)

Assets	Liabilities
$A = 97.56$	$L = 89.19$
	$E = 8.37$
97.56	97.56

$$\text{or} \quad \begin{array}{ccccc} \Delta E & = & \Delta A & - & \Delta L \\ -1.63 & = & (-2.44) & - & (-0.81) \end{array}$$

As was demonstrated earlier, when interest rates rise, the market values of both assets and liabilities fall. However, in this example, because the maturity on the asset portfolio is longer than the maturity on the liability portfolio, for any given change in interest rates, the market value of the asset portfolio (*A*) falls by more than the market value of the liability portfolio (*L*). For the balance sheet identity to hold, the difference between the changes in the market value of its assets and liabilities must be made up by the change in the market value of the FI's equity or net worth:

$$\begin{array}{ccc} \Delta E & = \quad \Delta A & - \quad \Delta L \\ \text{(change in FI} & \text{(change in market} & \text{(change in market} \\ \text{net worth)} & \text{value of assets)} & \text{value of liabilities)} \end{array}$$

To see the effect on FI net worth of having longer-term assets than liabilities, suppose that initially the FI's balance sheet looks like the one in Table 8–7. The $100 million of assets is invested in three-year, 10 percent coupon bonds, and the liabilities consist of $90 million raised with one-year deposits paying a promised interest rate of 10 percent. We showed earlier that if market interest rates rise 1 percent, from 10 to 11 percent, the value of three-year bonds falls 2.44 percent while the value of one-year deposits falls 0.9 percent.[17] Table 8–8 depicts this fall in asset and liability market values and the associated effects on FI net worth.

---

[17] The market value of deposits (in millions of dollars) is initially:

$$P_1^D = \frac{9 + 90}{1.1} = 90$$

When rates increase to 11 percent, the market value decreases:

$$P_1^D = \frac{9 + 90}{1.11} = 89.19$$

The resulting change is:

$$\Delta P_1^D = \frac{89.19 - 90}{90} = -90\%$$

TABLE 8–9
An FI Becomes Insolvent after a 7 Percent Rate Increase (figures in millions of dollars)

Assets	Liabilities
$A = 84.53$	$L = 84.62$
	$E = -0.09$
84.53	84.53

or
$$\Delta E = \Delta A - \Delta L$$
$$-10.09 = -15.47 - (-5.38)$$

Because the FI's assets have a three-year maturity compared with its one-year liabilities, the value of its assets has fallen by more than the value of its liabilities. The FI's net worth declines from $10 million to $8.37 million, a loss of $1.63 million, or 16.3 percent! Thus, it is clear that with a *maturity gap* of two years:

$$M_A - M_L = 2 \text{ years}$$
$$(3) - (1)$$

a 1 percentage point rise in interest rates can cause the FI's owners or stockholders to take a big hit to their net worth. Indeed, if a 1 percent rise in interest rates leads to a fall of 16.3 percent in the FI's net worth, what increase in interest rates would make E fall by $10 million so that all the owners' net worth would be eliminated? For the answer to this question, look at Table 8–9. If interest rates were to rise a full 7 percent, from 10 to 17 percent, the FI's equity (E) would fall by just over $10 million, rendering the FI economically insolvent.[18]

EXAMPLE 8–5

Extreme Maturity Mismatch

Suppose the FI had adopted an even more extreme maturity gap by investing all its assets in 30-year fixed-rate bonds paying 10 percent coupons while continuing to raise funds by issuing one-year deposits with promised interest payments of 10 percent, as shown in Table 8–10. Assuming annual compounding and a current level of interest rates of 10 percent, the market price of the bonds (in millions of dollars) is initially:

$$P^B_{30} = \frac{10}{(1.1)} + \frac{10}{(1.1)^2} + \dots + \frac{10}{(1.1)^{29}} + \frac{10 + 100}{(1.1)^{30}} = 100$$

If interest rates were to rise by 1.5 percent to 11.5 percent, the price (in millions of dollars) of the 30-year bonds would fall to:

$$P^B_{30} = \frac{10}{(1.115)} + \frac{10}{(1.115)^2} + \dots + \frac{10}{(1.115)^{29}} + \frac{10 + 100}{(1.115)^{30}} = 87.45,$$

a drop of $12.55, or as a percentage change, $\%\Delta P^B_{30} = (87.45 - 100)/100 = -12.55\%$. The market value of the FI's one-year deposits would fall to:

$$P^D_1 = \frac{9 + 90}{(1.115)} = 88.79$$

a drop of $1.21 or $(88.79 - 90)/90 = -1.34\%$.

---

[18] Here we are talking about economic insolvency. The legal and regulatory definition may vary, depending on what type of accounting rules are used.

TABLE 8–10
An FI with an Extreme Maturity Mismatch (millions of dollars)

Assets	Liabilities
$A = 100$ ($M_A = 30$ years)	$L = 90$ ($M_L = 1$ year)
	$E = 10$
100	100

TABLE 8–11
The Effect of a 1.5 Percent Rise in Interest Rates on the Net Worth of an FI with an Extreme Asset and Liability Mismatch (figures in millions of dollars)

Assets	Liabilities
$A = 87.45$	$L = 88.79$
	$E = -1.34$
87.45	87.45

or

$$\Delta E = \Delta A - \Delta L$$
$$-11.34 = (-12.55) - (-1.21)$$

Look at Table 8–11 to see the effect on the market value balance sheet and the FI's net worth after a rise of 1 percent in interest rates. It is clear from Table 8–11 that when the mismatch in the maturity of the FI's assets and liabilities is extreme (29 years), a mere 1 percent increase in interest rates completely eliminates the FI's $10 million in net worth and renders it completely and massively insolvent (net worth is –$1.34 million after the rise in rates). In contrast, a smaller maturity gap (such as the two years from above) requires a much larger change in interest rates (i.e., 7 percent) to wipe out the FI's equity. Thus, interest rate risk increases as the absolute value of the maturity gap increases.

immunize
Fully protect an FI's equity against interest rate risk.

From the preceding examples, you might infer that the best way for an FI to **immunize,** or protect, itself from interest rate risk is for its managers to match the maturities of its assets and liabilities, that is, to construct its balance sheet so that its maturity gap, the difference between the weighted-average maturity of its assets and liabilities, is zero ($M_A - M_L = 0$). However, as we discuss next, maturity matching does not always protect an FI against interest rate risk.

Concept Questions

1. How does book value accounting differ from market value accounting?
2. In a market value accounting framework, what impact do rising interest rates have on the market values of an FI's assets and liabilities?
3. Using the example in Table 8–10, what would be the effect on this FI's net worth if it held one-year discount bonds (with a yield of 10 percent) as assets? Explain your findings.

WEAKNESSES OF THE MATURITY MODEL

The maturity model has two major shortcomings: (1) It does not account for the degree of leverage in the FI's balance sheet, and (2) it ignores the timing of the cash flows from the FI's assets and liabilities. As a result of these shortcomings, a strategy of matching asset and liability maturities moves the FI in the direction of hedging itself against interest rate risk, but it is easy to show that this strategy does not always eliminate all interest rate risk for an FI.

To show the effect of leverage on the ability of the FI to eliminate interest rate risk using the maturity model, assume that the FI is initially set up as shown in Table 8–12. The $100 million in assets is invested in one-year, 10 percent coupon bonds, and the

TABLE 8–12
Initial Market Values of an FI's Assets and Liabilities with a Maturity GAP of Zero (in millions of dollars)

Assets	Liabilities
$A = 100 \ (M_A = 1 \text{ year})$	$L = \quad 90 \ (M_L = 1 \text{ year})$
	$E = \quad 10$
$\overline{\quad\quad 100 \quad\quad}$	$\overline{\quad\quad 100 \quad\quad}$

TABLE 8–13
FI's Market Value Balance Sheet after a 1 Percent Rise in Interest Rates (in millions of dollars)

Assets	Liabilities
$A = 99.09$	$L = 89.19$
	$E = \quad 9.90$
$\overline{\quad\quad 99.09 \quad\quad}$	$\overline{\quad\quad 99.09 \quad\quad}$

or
$$\Delta E = \Delta A - \Delta L$$
$$-0.10 = -0.91 - (-0.81)$$

$90 million in liabilities are in one-year deposits paying 10 percent. The maturity gap $(M_A - M_L)$ is now zero. A 1 percent increase in interest rates results in the balance sheet in Table 8–13. In Table 8–13, even though the maturity gap is zero, the FI's equity value falls by $0.10 million. The drop in equity value is due to the fact that not all the assets (bonds) were financed with deposits; rather, equity was used to finance a portion of the FI's assets. As interest rates increased, only $90 million in deposits were directly affected, and $100 million in assets were directly affected.

An FI choosing to directly match the maturities and values of its assets and liabilities (so that $M_A = M_L$ and $A = L) does not necessarily achieve perfect immunization, or protection, against interest rate risk. Consider the example of an FI that issues a one-year CD to a depositor. This CD has a face value of $100 and an interest rate promised to depositors of 15 percent. Thus, on maturity at the end of the year, the FI has to repay the borrower $100 plus $15 interest, or $115, as shown in Figure 8–5.

Suppose the FI lends $100 for one year to a corporate borrower at a 15 percent annual interest rate (thus, $A = L). However, the FI requires half of the loan ($50) to be repaid after six months and the last half to be repaid at the end of the year. Note that although the maturity of the loan equals the maturity of the deposit of 1 year and the loan is fully funded by deposit liabilities, the cash flow earned on the loan may be greater or less than the $115 required to pay off depositors, depending on what happens to interest rates over the one-year period. You can see this in Figure 8–6.

At the end of the first six months, the FI receives a $50 repayment in loan principal plus $7.50 in interest ($100 \times 1/2$ year $\times$ 15 percent), for a total midyear cash flow of $57.50. At the end of the year, the FI receives $50 as the final repayment of loan principal plus $3.75 interest ($50 \times 1/2$ year $\times$ 15 percent) plus the reinvestment income earned from relending the $57.50 received six months earlier. If interest rates do not change over the period, the FI's extra return from its ability to reinvest part of the cash flow for the last six months will be ($57.50 \times 1/2 \times 15$ percent) = 4.3125. We summarize the total cash flow on the FI's one-year loan in Table 8–14.

As you can see, by the end of the year, the cash paid in on the loan exceeded the cash paid out on the deposit by $0.5625. The reason for this is the FI's ability to reinvest part of the principal and interest over the second half of the year at 15 percent. Suppose that interest rates, instead of staying unchanged at 15 percent throughout the whole one-year period, had fallen to 12 percent over the last six months in the

FIGURE 8–5
One-Year CD
Cash Flows

```
0                                    1 year
|────────────────────────────────────|
▲                                    ▲
FI borrows                           FI pays principal
$100                                 plus interest to
                                     depositor = $115
```

FIGURE 8–6
One-Year Loan
Cash Flows

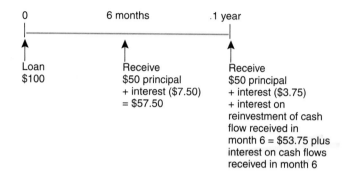

```
0                6 months          1 year
|────────────────────|────────────────|
▲                    ▲                ▲
Loan                 Receive          Receive
$100                 $50 principal    $50 principal
                     + interest ($7.50)   + interest ($3.75)
                     = $57.50         + interest on
                                      reinvestment of cash
                                      flow received in
                                      month 6 = $53.75 plus
                                      interest on cash flows
                                      received in month 6
```

TABLE 8–14 Cash Flow on a Loan with a 15 Percent Interest Rate

Cash Flow at 1/2 Year	
Principal	$ 50.00
Interest	7.50
Cash Flow at 1 Year	
Principal	$ 50.00
Interest	3.75
Reinvestment income	4.3125
	$115.5625

TABLE 8–15 Cash Flow on the Loan When the Beginning Rate of 15 Percent Falls to 12 Percent

Cash Flow at 1/2 Year	
Principal	$ 50.00
Interest	7.50
Cash Flow at 1 Year	
Principal	$ 50.00
Interest	3.75
Reinvestment income	3.45
	$114.70

year. This fall in rates would affect neither the promised deposit rate of 15 percent nor the promised loan rate of 15 percent because they are set at time 0 when the deposit and loan were originated and do not change throughout the year. What is affected is the FI's *reinvestment income* on the $57.50 cash flow received on the loan at the end of six months. It can be relent for the final six months of the year only at the new, lower interest rate of 12 percent (see Table 8–15).

The only change to the asset cash flows for the bank comes from the reinvestment of the $57.50 received at the end of six months at the lower interest rate of 12 percent. This produces the smaller reinvestment income of $3.45 ($57.50 × 1/2 × 12 percent) rather than $4.3125 when rates stayed at 15 percent throughout the year. Rather than making a profit of $0.5625 from intermediation, the FI loses $0.3. Note that this loss occurs as a result of interest rates changing, even when the FI had matched the maturity of its assets and liabilities ($M_A = M_L = 1$ year), as well as the dollar amount of loans (assets) and deposits (liabilities) (i.e., $A = L).

Despite the matching of maturities, the FI is still exposed to interest rate risk because the *timing* of the *cash flows* on the deposit and loan are not perfectly matched.

In a sense, the cash flows on the loan are received, on average, earlier than cash flows are paid out on the deposit, where all cash flows occur at the end of the year. The next chapter shows that only by matching the average lives of assets and liabilities—that is, by considering the precise timing of arrival (or payment) of cash flows—can an FI immunize itself against interest rate risk.

Concept Questions

1. Can an FI achieve perfect immunization against interest rate risk by matching the maturities of its assets and liabilities? Explain your answer.
2. Suppose the average maturity of an FI's assets is equal to its liabilities. If interest rates fall, why could an FI's net worth still decline? Explain your answer.

Summary

This chapter introduced two methods of measuring an FI's interest rate risk exposure: the repricing model and the maturity model. The repricing model looks at the difference, or gap, between an FI's rate-sensitive assets and rate-sensitive liabilities to measure interest rate risk, whereas the maturity model uses the difference between the average maturity of an FI's assets and that of its liabilities to measure interest rate risk. The chapter showed that both the repricing model and the maturity model have difficulty in accurately measuring the interest rate risk of an FI. In particular, the repricing model ignores the market value effects of interest rate changes, and the maturity model ignores the timing of the arrival of cash flows on assets and liabilities. More complete and accurate measures of an FI's exposure are duration and the duration gap, which are explained in the next chapter.

Questions and Problems

1. How has the increased level of financial market integration affected interest rates?

2. What is the repricing gap? In using this model to evaluate interest rate risk, what is meant by rate sensitivity? On what financial performance variable does the repricing model focus? Explain.

3. What is a maturity bucket in the repricing model? Why is the length of time selected for repricing assets and liabilities important in using the repricing model?

4. Download the most recent Annual Report of two different Canadian banks. Search the documents for the gap analysis. Which of these two banks has the largest positive or negative gap? Why do they hold this position?

5. Calculate the repricing gap and the impact on net interest income of a 1 percent increase in interest rates for each of the following positions:
   - Rate-sensitive assets = $200 million
     Rate-sensitive liabilities = $100 million
   - Rate-sensitive assets = $100 million
     Rate-sensitive liabilities = $150 million
   - Rate-sensitive assets = $150 million
     Rate-sensitive liabilities = $140 million

   a. Calculate the impact on net interest income of each of the above situations, assuming a 1 percent decrease in interest rates.

   b. What conclusion can you draw about the repricing model from these results?

6. What are the reasons for not including demand deposits as rate-sensitive liabilities in the repricing analysis for a commercial bank? What is the subtle but potentially strong reason for including demand deposits in the total of rate-sensitive liabilities? Can the same argument be made for passbook savings accounts?

7. What is the gap ratio? What is the value of this ratio to interest rate risk managers and regulators?

8. Which of the following assets or liabilities fit the one-year rate or repricing sensitivity test?
   91-day Treasury bills
   1-year Treasury bills
   20-year Government of Canada bonds
   20-year floating-rate corporate bonds with annual repricing
   25-year floating-rate mortgages with repricing every two years
   25-year floating-rate mortgages with repricing every six months

Overnight funds borrowed from the Bank of Canada
9-month fixed-rate CDs
1-year fixed-rate CDs
5-year floating-rate CDs with annual repricing
Common stock

9. Consider the following balance sheet for WatchoverU Bank, Inc. (in millions of dollars):

Assets	
Floating-rate mortgages	
(currently 10% annually)	50
25-year fixed-rate loans	
(currently 7% annually)	50
Total assets	100

Liabilities and Equity	
Demand deposits (currently 6% annually)	70
Time deposits (currently 6% annually)	20
Equity	10
Total liabilities and equity	100

a. What is WatchoverU's expected net interest income at year-end?
b. What will be the net interest income at year-end if interest rates rise 2 percent?
c. Using the cumulative repricing gap model, what is the expected net interest income for a 2 percent increase in interest rates?

10. What are some of the weaknesses of the repricing model? How have large banks solved the problem of choosing the optimal time period for repricing? What is runoff cash flow, and how does this amount affect the repricing model's analysis?

11. Use the following information about a hypothetical government security dealer named Merrill Burns Canada. Market yields are in parentheses, and amounts are in millions.

Assets	
Cash	10
1-Month T-bills (7.05%)	75
3-Month T-bills (7.25%)	75
2-Year Canada bonds (7.50%)	50
8-Year Canada bonds (8.96%)	100
5-Year provincial government debt	
(floating rate) (8.20% reset every 6 months)	25
Total assets	335

Liabilities and Equity	
Overnight repos	170
Subordinated debt	150
7-year fixed rate (8.55%)	
Equity	15
Total liabilities and equity	335

a. What is the funding or repricing gap if the planning period is 30 days? 91 days? 2 years? Recall that cash is a non-interest-earning asset.
b. What is the impact over the next 30 days on net interest income if all interest rates rise 50 basis points? Decrease 75 basis points?
c. The following one-year runoffs are expected: $10 million for two-year Canada bonds and $20 million for eight-year Canada bonds. What is the one-year repricing gap?
d. If runoffs are considered, what is the effect on net interest income at year- end if interest rates rise 50 basis points? Decrease 75 basis points?

12. What is the difference between book value accounting and market value accounting? How do interest rate changes affect the value of bank assets and liabilities under the two methods? What is marking to market?

13. Why is it important to use market values as opposed to book values in evaluating the net worth of an FI? What are some of the advantages of using book values as opposed to market values?

14. Consider a $1,000 bond with a fixed-rate, 10 percent annual coupon (Cpn %) and a maturity (N) of 10 years. The bond currently is trading to a market yield to maturity (YTM) of 10 percent. Complete the following table:

N	Cpn %	YTM %	Price	From Par, $ Change in Price	From Par, % Change in Price
8	10	9			
9	10	9			
10	10	9			
10	10	10	$1,000.00		
10	10	11			
11	10	11			
12	10	11			

Use this information to verify the principles of interest rate–price relationships for fixed-rate financial assets.

15. Consider a 12-year, 12 percent annual coupon bond with a required return of 10 percent. The bond has a face value of $1,000.

a. What is the price of the bond?
b. If interest rates rise to 11 percent, what is the price of the bond?
c. What has been the percentage change in price?
d. Repeat parts (a), (b), and (c) for a 16-year bond.
e. What do the respective changes in bond prices indicate?

16. Consider a five-year, 15 percent annual coupon bond with a face value of $1,000. The bond is trading at a market yield to maturity of 12 percent.
    a. What is the price of the bond?
    b. If the market yield to maturity increases 1 percent, what will be the bond's new price?
    c. Use your answers to parts (a) and (b) to find the percentage change in the bond's price as a result of the 1 percent increase in interest rates.
    d. Repeat parts (b) and (c) assuming a 1 percent decrease in interest rates.
    e. What do the differences in your answers indicate about the rate–price relationships of fixed-rate assets?

17. What is a maturity gap? How can the maturity model be used to immunize an FI's portfolio? What is the critical requirement that allows maturity matching to have some success in immunizing the balance sheet of an FI?

18. Nearby Bank has the following balance sheet (in millions of dollars):

Assets	
Cash	60
5-year Canada bonds	60
25-year mortgages	200
Total assets	320

Liabilities and Equity	
Demand deposits	140
1-year certificates of deposit	160
Equity	20
Total liabilities and equity	320

What is the maturity gap for Nearby Bank? Is Nearby Bank more exposed to an increase or a decrease in interest rates? Explain why.

19. County Bank has the following market value balance sheet (in millions of dollars, all interest at annual rates):

Assets	
Cash	20
15-year commercial loan at 10% interest, balloon payment	160
25-year mortgages at 8% interest, monthly amortizing	300
Total assets	480

Liabilities and Equity	
Demand deposits	100
5-year CDs at 6% interest, balloon payment	210
20-year debentures at 7% interest	120
Equity	50
Total liabilities and equity	480

a. What is the maturity gap for County Bank?
b. What will be the maturity gap if the interest rates on all assets and liabilities increase 1 percent?
c. What will happen to the market value of the equity?
d. If interest rates increase 2 percent, would the bank be solvent?

20. Given that bank balance sheets typically are accounted in book value terms, why should regulators or anyone else be concerned about how interest rates affect the market values of assets and liabilities?

21. If a bank manager is certain that interest rates are going to increase within the next six months, how should the bank manager adjust the bank's maturity gap to take advantage of this anticipated increase? What if the manager believed rates would fall? Would your suggested adjustments be difficult or easy to achieve?

22. Consumer Bank has $20 million in cash and a $180 million loan portfolio. The assets are funded with demand deposits of $18 million, a $162 million CD, and $20 million in equity. The loan portfolio has a maturity of two years, earns interest at an annual rate of 7 percent, and is amortized monthly. The bank pays 7 percent annual interest on the CD, but the interest will not be paid until the CD matures at the end of two years.
    a. What is the maturity gap for Consumer Bank?
    b. Is Consumer Bank immunized, or protected, against changes in interest rates? Why or why not?
    c. Does Consumer Bank face interest rate risk? That is, if market interest rates increase or decrease 1 percent, what happens to the value of the equity?
    d. How can a decrease in interest rates create interest rate risk?

23. FI International holds seven-year Acme International bonds and two-year Beta Corporation bonds. The Acme bonds are yielding 12 percent and the Beta bonds are yielding 14 percent under current market conditions.
    a. What is the weighted-average maturity of FI's bond portfolio if 40 percent is in Acme bonds and 60 percent is in Beta bonds?
    b. What proportion of Acme and Beta bonds should be held to have a weighted-average yield of 13.5 percent?
    c. What will be the weighted-average maturity of the bond portfolio if the weighted-average yield is realized?

24. An insurance company has invested in the following fixed-income securities: (a) $10,000,000 of five-year Government of Canada bonds paying 5 percent interest and selling at par value, (b) $5,800,000 of

10-year bonds paying 7 percent interest with a par value of $6,000,000, and (c) $6,200,000 of 20-year subordinated debentures paying 9 percent interest with a par value of $6,000,000.

a. What is the weighted-average maturity of this portfolio of assets?

b. If interest rates change so that the yields on all the securities decrease 1 percent, how does the weighted-average maturity of the portfolio change?

c. Explain the changes in the maturity values if the yields increase 1 percent.

d. Assume that the insurance company has no other assets. What will be the effect on the market value of the company's equity if the interest rate changes in (b) and (c) occur?

25. The following is a simplified FI balance sheet:

Assets	
Loans	$1,000
Total assets	$1,000

Liabilities and Equity	
Deposits	$ 850
Equity	150
Total liabilities and equity	$1,000

The average maturity of loans is four years, and the average maturity of deposits is two years. Assume that loan and deposit balances are reported as book value, zero-coupon items.

a. Assume that the interest rate on both loans and deposits is 9 percent. What is the market value of equity?

b. What must be the interest rate on deposits to force the market value of equity to be zero? What economic market conditions must exist to make this situation possible?

c. Assume that the interest rate on both loans and deposits is 9 percent. What must be the average maturity of deposits for the market value of equity to be zero?

26. Gunnison Insurance has reported the following balance sheet (in thousands):

Assets	
2-year Government of Canada bonds	$175
15-year municipal bonds	165
Total assets	$340

Liabilities and Equity	
1-year commercial paper	$135
5-year note	160
Equity	45
Total liabilities and equity	$340

All securities are selling at par equal to book value. The two-year Canadas are yielding 5 percent, and the 15-year municipal bonds are yielding 9 percent. The one-year commercial paper pays 4.5 percent, and the five-year notes pay 8 percent. All instruments pay interest annually.

a. What is the weighted-average maturity of the assets for Gunnison?

b. What is the weighted-average maturity of the liabilities for Gunnison?

c. What is the maturity gap for Gunnison?

d. What does your answer to part (c) imply about the interest rate exposure of Gunnison Insurance?

e. Calculate the values of all four securities of Gunnison Insurance's balance sheet assuming that all interest rates increase 2 percent. What is the dollar change in the total asset and total liability values? What is the percentage change in these values?

f. What is the dollar impact on the market value of equity for Gunnison? What is the percentage change in the value of the equity?

g. What would be the impact on Gunnison's market value of equity if the liabilities paid interest semiannually instead of annually?

27. Scandia Bank has issued a one-year, $1 million CD paying 5.75 percent to fund a one-year loan paying an interest rate of 6 percent. The principal of the loan will be paid in two installments: $500,000 in six months and the balance at the end of the year.

a. What is the maturity gap of Scandia Bank? According to the maturity model, what does this maturity gap imply about the interest rate risk exposure faced by Scandia Bank?

b. What is the expected net interest income at the end of the year?

c. What would be the effect on annual net interest income of a 2 percent interest rate increase that occurred immediately after the loan was made? What would be the effect of a 2 percent decrease in rates?

d. What do these results indicate about the ability of the maturity model to immunize portfolios against interest rate exposure?

28. EDF Bank has a very simple balance sheet. Assets consist of a two-year, $1 million loan that pays an interest rate of LIBOR plus 4 percent annually. The loan is funded with a two-year deposit on which the bank pays LIBOR plus 3.5 percent interest annually. LIBOR currently is 4 percent, and both the loan and the deposit principal will be paid at maturity.

  a. What is the maturity gap of this balance sheet?

  b. What is the expected net interest income in year 1 and year 2?

  c. Immediately prior to the beginning of year 2, LIBOR rates increase to 6 percent. What is the expected net interest income in year 2? What would be the effect on net interest income of a 2 percent decrease in LIBOR?

  d. How would your results be affected if the interest payments on the loan were received semiannually?

  e. What implications do these results have for the effectiveness of the maturity model as an immunization strategy?

29. What are the weaknesses of the maturity model?

Appendix 8A   Term Structure of Interest Rates

View Appendix 8A on page 688 of this book.

Appendix 8B   The Basics of Bond Valuation

View Appendix 8B at the Web site for this textbook (**www.mcgrawhill.ca/college/saunders**).

Interest Rate Risk II

In this chapter, we present the duration model and duration gap as measures of an FI's interest rate risk. We show:

▸ the basic arithmetic needed to calculate the duration of an asset or liability

▸ the economic meaning of duration

▸ how duration can be used to immunize an FI's portfolio against interest rate risk

▸ some of the problems in applying the duration measure to real-world FIs' balance sheets, and

▸ advanced issues relating to duration (see Appendix 9A on page 692 of this book)

INTRODUCTION

This second chapter on interest rate risk presents a value-based model for managing interest rate risk: the duration model. Duration, which measures the average life of an asset or liability, also has economic meaning as the interest sensitivity (or interest elasticity) of that asset or liability's value. Thus, duration and the duration gap are more accurate measures of an FI's interest rate risk exposure than is the simple maturity model described in Chapter 8. Unlike the repricing model, duration gap considers market values and the maturity distributions of an FI's assets and liabilities, and, unlike the maturity model, duration gap considers the degree of leverage on an FI's balance sheet as well as the timing of the payment or arrival of cash flows of assets and liabilities. Thus, duration gap is a more comprehensive measure of an FI's interest rate risk. As a result, although insurance companies have traditionally used duration analysis to model the effect of interest rate risk on their future claim payouts, other FIs and their regulators are increasingly focusing on this model, in conjunction with scenario analysis and enterprise risk management, to determine an appropriate level of capital reserves to mitigate exposure to interest rate risk (Chapter 20).

DURATION

Duration is a more complete measure of an asset or liability's interest rate sensitivity than is maturity because duration takes into account the time of arrival (or payment) of all cash flows as well as the asset's (or liability's) maturity. Consider the example of the one-year loan at the end of Chapter 8. This loan had a 15 percent interest rate and required repayment of half the $100 in principal at the end of six months and the other half at the end of the year. The promised cash flows *(CF)* received by the FI from the borrower at the end of one-half year and at the end of the year appear in Figure 9–1.

$CF_{1/2}$ is the $50 promised repayment of principal plus the $7.50 promised interest payment ($100 \times \frac{1}{2} \times 15\%$) received after six months. CF_1 is the promised cash flow at the end of the year and is equal to the second $50 promised principal repayment plus $3.75 promised interest ($50 \times \frac{1}{2} \times 15\%$). To compare the relative

FIGURE 9–1
Promised Cash
Flows on the
One-Year Loan

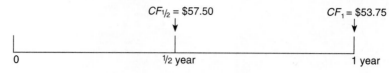

FIGURE 9–2
PV of the Cash
Flows from the Loan

sizes of these two cash flows, we should put them in the same dimensions. This is the case because $1 of principal or interest received at the end of a year is worth less to the FI in terms of the time value of money than $1 of principal or interest received at the end of six months. Assuming that the current required interest rates are 15 percent per annum, we calculate the present values (PV) of the two cash flows (CF) shown in Figure 9–2 as:

$$CF_{1/2} = \$57.5 \qquad PV_{1/2} = \$57.5/(1.075) = \$53.49$$
$$CF_1 = \$53.75 \qquad PV_1 = \$53.75/(1.075)^2 = \$46.51$$
$$CF_{1/2} + CF_1 = \$111.25 \qquad PV_{1/2} + PV_1 = \$100.00$$

Note that since $CF_{1/2}$, the cash flows received at the end of one-half year, are received earlier, they are discounted at $(1 + \frac{1}{2} R)$, where R is the current annual interest rate on the loan. This is smaller than the discount rate on the cash flow received at the end of the year $(1 + \frac{1}{2} R)^2$.[1] Figure 9–2 summarizes the PVs of the cash flows from the loan.

duration
The weighted-average time to maturity on an investment.

(using PV of CF to weight)

bie. when the invstmt is recovered using PV

Technically speaking, **duration** is the *weighted-average* time to maturity on the loan using the relative present values of the cash flows as weights. On a time value of money basis, duration measures the period of time required to recover the initial investment on the loan. Any cash flows received prior to the loan's duration reflect recovery of the initial investment, while cash flows received after the period of the loan's duration and before its maturity are the profits, or return, earned by the FI. As Figure 9–2 shows, the FI receives some cash flows at one-half year and some at one year. Duration analysis weights the time at which cash flows are received by the relative importance in present value terms of the cash flows arriving at each point in time. In present value terms, the relative importance of the cash flows arriving at time $t = \frac{1}{2}$ year and time $t = 1$ year are as follows:

Time (t)	Weight (x)				
1/2 year	$X_{1/2} =$	$\dfrac{PV_{1/2}}{PV_{1/2} + PV_1}$	$= \dfrac{53.49}{100.00}$	$= .5349$	$= 53.49\%$
1 year	$X_1 =$	$\dfrac{PV_1}{PV_{1/2} + PV_1}$	$= \dfrac{46.51}{100.00}$	$= .4651$	$= 46.51\%$
				1.0	100%

---

[1] We use here the formula for calculating the present values of cash flows on a security that pays cash flows semiannually. This approach is more accurate, since it reflects the semiannual payment and compounding of interest on the loan. See the Department of Finance's Web site (www.fin.gc.ca) for a guide to calculating prices on Government of Canada securities.

www.fin.gc.ca

FIGURE 9–3
PV of the Cash Flows of the Deposit

That is, in present value terms, the FI receives 53.49 percent of cash flows on the loan with the first payment at the end of six months ($t = \frac{1}{2}$) and 46.51 percent with the second payment at the end of the year ($t = 1$). By definition, the sum of the (present value) cash flow weights must equal 1:

$$X_{1/2} + X_1 = 1$$

$$.5349 + .4651 = 1$$

We can now calculate the duration (D), or the weighted-average time to maturity, of the loan using the present value of its cash flows as weights:

$$D_1 = X_{1/2}(\tfrac{1}{2}) + X_1(1)$$

$$= .5349(\tfrac{1}{2}) + .4651(1) = .7326 \text{ years}$$

Thus, while the maturity of the loan is one year, its duration, or average life in a cash flow sense, is only .7326 years. On a time value of money basis, the initial investment in the loan is recovered (albeit not realized) after .7326 years. After that time the FI earns a profit, or return, on the loan. The duration is less than the maturity of the loan because in present value terms 53.49 percent of the cash flows are received at the end of one-half year. Note that duration is measured in years since we weight the time (t) at which cash flows are received by the relative present value importance of cash flows ($X_{1/2}$, X_1, etc.).

To learn why the FI was still exposed to interest rate risk while matching maturities under the maturity model in the example at the end of Chapter 8, we next calculate the duration of the one-year, $100, 15 percent interest certificate of deposit. The FI promises to make only one cash payment to depositors at the end of the year; that is, $CF_1 = \$115$, which is the promised principal ($100) and interest repayment ($15) to the depositor. Since weights are calculated in present value terms:[2]

$$CF_1 = \$115, PV_1 = \$115/1.15 = \$100$$

We show this in Figure 9–3. Because all cash flows are received in one payment at the end of the year, $X_1 = PV_1/PV_1 = 1$, the duration of the deposit is:

$$D_D = X_1 \times (1)$$

$$D_D = 1 \times (1) = 1 \text{ year}$$

Thus, only when all cash flows are limited to one payment at the end of the period with no intervening cash flows does duration equal maturity. This example also illustrates that although the maturity gap between the loan and the deposit is zero, the duration gap is negative:

$$M_L - M_D = 1 - 1 = 0$$

$$D_L - D_D = .7326 - 1 = -.2674 \text{ years}$$

As will become clearer, to measure and to hedge interest rate risk, the FI needs to manage its duration gap rather than its maturity gap.

---

[2] Since the CD is like an annual coupon bond, the annual discount rate is $1/(1 + R) = 1/1.15$.

Concept Questions

1. Why is duration considered a more complete measure of an asset or liability's interest rate sensitivity than maturity?
2. When is the duration of an asset equal to its maturity?

Weighted Avg Time to Maturity
(weighted based on PV)

A GENERAL FORMULA FOR DURATION

You can calculate the duration for any fixed-income security that pays interest annually using the following general formula:[3]

$$D = \frac{\sum_{t=1}^{N} CF_t \times DF_1 \times t}{\sum_{t=1}^{N} CF_t \times DF_t} = \frac{\sum_{t=1}^{N} PV_t \times t}{\sum_{t=1}^{N} PV_t}$$

where

D = Duration measured in years

CF_t = Cash flow received on the security at end of period t

N = Last period in which the cash flow is received

DF_t = Discount factor = $1/(1 + R)^t$, where R is the annual yield or current level of interest rates in the market

$\sum_{t=1}^{N}$ = Summation sign for addition of all terms from $t = 1$ to $t = N$

PV_t = Present value of the cash flow at the end of the period t, which equals $CF_t \times DF_t$

For bonds that pay interest semiannually, the duration equation becomes:[4]

$$D = \frac{\sum_{t=1/2}^{N} \dfrac{CF_t \times t}{(1 + R/2)^{2t}}}{\sum_{t=1/2}^{N} \dfrac{CF_t}{(1 + R/2)^{2t}}} \approx \frac{PV \times t}{PV}$$

to receive CF

where $t = \frac{1}{2}, 1, 1\frac{1}{2}, \ldots, N$

Notice that the denominator of the duration equation is the present value of the cash flows on the security (which in an efficient market will be equal to the current market price). The numerator is the present value of each cash flow received on the security multiplied or weighted by the length of time required to receive the cash flow. To help you fully understand this formula, we next look at some examples.

---

[3] In the following material a number of useful examples and formulas were suggested by G. Hawawini of INSEAD. For more discussion of the duration model and a number of those examples, see G. Hawawini, "Controlling the Interest Rate Risk of Bonds: An Introduction to Duration Analysis and Immunization Strategies," *Financial Markets and Portfolio Management* 1 (1986–87), pp. 8–18.

[4] In general, the duration equation is written as:

$$D = \frac{\sum_{t=1/m}^{N} \dfrac{CF_t \times t}{(1 + R/m)^{mt}}}{\sum_{t=1/m}^{N} \dfrac{CF_t}{(1 + R/m)^{mt}}}$$

where m = number of times per year interest is paid.

TABLE 9–1
The Duration of a Six-Year Eurobond with 8 Percent Coupon and Yield

t	CF_t	DF_t	$CF_t \times DF_t$	$CF_t \times DF_t \times t$
1	80	0.9259	74.07	74.07
2	80	0.8573	68.59	137.18
3	80	0.7938	63.51	190.53
4	80	0.7350	58.80	235.20
5	80	0.6806	54.45	272.25
6	1,080	0.6302	680.58	4,083.48
			1,000.00	4,992.71

$$D = \frac{4,992.71}{1,000} = 4.993 \text{ years}$$

TABLE 9–2
The Duration of a Two-Year Government of Canada Bond with 8 Percent Coupon and 12 Percent Yield

t	CF_t	DF_t	$CF_t \times DF_t$	$CF_t \times DF_t \times t$
$1/2$	40	.9434	37.74	18.87
1	40	.8900	35.60	35.60
$1 1/2$	40	.8396	33.58	50.37
2	1,040	.7921	823.78	1,647.56
			930.70	1,752.40

$$D = \frac{1,752.40}{930.70} = 1.883 \text{ years}$$

The Duration of Interest-Bearing Bonds

EXAMPLE 9–1

The Duration of a Six-Year Eurobond

Eurobonds pay coupons *annually.* Suppose the annual coupon is 8 percent, the face value of the bond is $1,000, and the current yield to maturity (R) is also 8 percent. We show the calculation of its duration in Table 9–1.

As the calculation indicates, the duration or weighted-average time to maturity on this bond is 4.993 years. In other words, on a time value of money basis, the initial investment of $1,000 is recovered after 4.993 years. Between 4.993 years and maturity (6 years), the bond produces a profit or return to the investor.

EXAMPLE 9–2

The Duration of a Two-Year Government of Canada Bond

Government of Canada bonds and U.S. Treasury bonds pay coupon interest semiannually. Suppose the annual coupon rate is 8 percent, the face value is $1,000, and the annual yield to maturity (R) is 12 percent. See Table 9–2 for the calculation of the duration of this bond.[5] As the calculation indicates, the duration, or weighted-average time to maturity, on this bond is 1.883 years. Table 9–3 shows that if the annual coupon rate is lowered to 6 percent, duration rises to 1.909 years. Since 6 percent coupon payments are lower than 8 percent, it takes longer to recover the initial investment in the bond. In Table 9–4 duration is calculated for the original 8 percent bond, assuming that the yield to maturity increases to 16 percent. Now duration falls from 1.883 years (in Table 9–2) to 1.878 years. The higher the yield to maturity on the bond, the more the investor earns on reinvested coupons and the shorter the time needed to recover the initial investment. Finally, when the maturity on a bond decreases to 1 year (see Table 9–5), its duration falls to 0.980 years. Thus, the shorter the maturity on the bond, the more quickly the initial investment is recovered.

[5] Here we use the formula for discounting bonds with semiannual coupons: $(1 + R/2)^x$ where x is the number of semiannual coupon payments. Thus, at $t = 1/2$, the discount rate is (1.06), at $t = 1$ the discount rate is $(1.06)^2$, and so on.

TABLE 9–3
Duration of a Two-Year Government of Canada Bond with 6 Percent Coupon and 12 Percent Yield

t	CF_t	DF_t	$CF_t \times DF_t$	$CF_t \times DF_t \times t$
$1/2$	30	0.9434	28.30	14.15
1	30	0.8900	26.70	26.70
$1 1/2$	30	0.8396	25.19	37.78
2	1,030	0.7921	815.86	1,631.71
			896.05	1,710.34

$$D = \frac{1,710.34}{896.05} = 1.909 \text{ years}$$

TABLE 9–4
Duration of a Two-Year Government of Canada Bond with 8 Percent Coupon and 16 Percent Yield

t	CF_t	DF_t	$CF_t \times DF_t$	$CF_t \times DF_t \times t$
$1/2$	40	0.9259	37.04	18.52
1	40	0.8573	34.29	34.29
$1 1/2$	40	0.7938	31.75	47.63
2	1,040	0.7350	764.43	1,528.86
			867.51	1,629.30

$$D = \frac{1,629.30}{867.51} = 1.878 \text{ years}$$

TABLE 9–5
Duration of a One-Year Government of Canada Bond with 8 Percent Coupon and 12 Percent Yield

t	CF_t	DF_t	$CF_t \times DF_t$	$CF_t \times DF_t \times t$
$1/2$	40	0.9434	37.74	18.87
1	1,040	0.8900	925.60	925.60
			963.34	944.47

$$D = \frac{944.47}{963.34} = 0.980 \text{ years}$$

Next, we look at two other types of bonds that are useful in understanding duration.

The Duration of a Zero-Coupon Bond

The Government of Canada and the U.S. Treasury have created zero-coupon bonds that allow securities firms and other investors to strip individual coupons and the principal from regular bonds and sell them to investors as separate securities. Elsewhere, such as in the Eurobond markets, corporations have issued discount or zero-coupon bonds denominated in both Canadian and U.S dollars directly. Canadian and U.S. T-bills and commercial paper usually are issued on a discount basis and are additional examples of discount bonds. These bonds sell at a discount from face value on issue, pay the face value (e.g., $1,000) on maturity, and have no intervening cash flows, such as coupon payments, between issue and maturity. The current price an investor is willing to pay for such a bond is equal to the present value of the single, fixed (face value) payment on the bond that is received on maturity (here, $1,000), or:

$$P = \frac{1,000}{(1 + R)^N} \approx PV \ @ \ maturity \ of \ single \ pymt$$

where R is the required annually compounded yield to maturity, N is the number of years to maturity, and P is the price. Because there are no intervening cash flows such as coupons between issue and maturity, the following must be true:

$$D_B = M_B$$

That is, the duration of a zero-coupon bond equals its maturity. Note that only for zero-coupon bonds are duration and maturity equal. Indeed, for any bond that pays some cash flows prior to maturity, its duration will always be less than its maturity.

The Duration of a Consol Bond (Perpetuities)

consol bond
A bond that pays a fixed coupon each year forever.

Although consol bonds have yet to be issued in Canada, they are of theoretical interest in exploring the differences between maturity and duration. A **consol bond** pays a fixed coupon each year. The novel feature of this bond is that it *never* matures; that is, it is a perpetuity:

$$M_c = \infty$$

In fact, consol bonds that were issued by the British government in the 1890s to finance the Boer Wars in South Africa are still outstanding. However, while its maturity is theoretically infinity, the formula for the duration of a consol bond is:[6]

$$D_c = 1 + \frac{1}{R}$$

where R is the required yield to maturity. Suppose that the yield curve implies $R = 5$ percent annually; then the duration of the consol bond would be:

$$D_c = 1 + \frac{1}{.05} = 21 \text{ years}$$

Thus, while maturity is infinite, duration is finite. Specifically, on the basis of the time value of money, recovery of the initial investment on this perpetual bond takes 21 years. After 21 years, the bond produces profit for the bondholder. Moreover, as interest rates rise, the duration of the consol bond falls. Consider the 1979–82 period, when some yields rose to around 20 percent on long-term government bonds. Then:

$$D_c = 1 + \frac{1}{.2} = 6 \text{ years}$$

Concept Questions

1. What does the denominator of the duration equation measure?
2. What does the numerator of the duration equation measure?
3. Calculate the duration of a one-year, 8 percent coupon, 10 percent yield bond that pays coupons quarterly.
4. What is the duration of a zero-coupon bond?
5. What feature is unique about a consol bond compared with other bonds?

---

[6] For reasons of space, we do not provide a formal proof here. Interested readers might refer to G. Hawawini, "Controlling the Interest Rate Risk of Bonds: An Introduction to Duration Analysis and Immunization Strategies," *Financial Markets and Portfolio Management* 1 (1986–87), pp. 8–18.

FEATURES OF DURATION

From the preceding examples, we derive three important features of duration relating to the maturity, yield, and coupon interest of the security being analyzed.

Duration and Maturity

A comparison of Tables 9–5, 9–2, and 9–6 indicates that duration *increases* with the maturity of a fixed-income asset or liability, but at a *decreasing* rate:

$$\frac{\partial D}{\partial M} > 0 \qquad \frac{\partial^2 D}{\partial M^2} < 0$$

To see this, look at Figure 9–4, where we plot duration against maturity for a three-year, a two-year, and a one-year bond using the *same yield of 12 percent* for all three and assuming an annual coupon of 8 percent (with semiannual payments of 4 percent) on each bond. As the maturity of the bond increases from one year to two years (Tables 9–5 and 9–2), duration increases by 0.903 years, from 0.980 years to 1.883 years. Increasing maturity an additional year, from two years to three years (Tables 9–2 and 9–6), increases duration by 0.826, from 1.883 years to 2.709 years.

Duration and Yield

A comparison of Tables 9–2 and 9–4 indicates that duration decreases as yield increases:

$$\frac{\partial D}{\partial R} < 0$$

TABLE 9–6
Duration of a Three-Year Government of Canada Bond with 8 Percent Coupon and 12 Percent Yield (coupon interest paid semiannually)

t	CF_t	DF_t	$CF_t \times DF_t$	$CF_t \times DF_t \times t$
$\frac{1}{2}$	40	0.9434	37.74	18.87
1	40	0.8900	35.60	35.60
$1\frac{1}{2}$	40	0.8396	33.58	50.37
2	40	0.7921	31.68	63.36
$2\frac{1}{2}$	40	0.7473	29.89	74.72
3	1,040	0.7050	733.16	2,199.48
			901.65	2,442.40

$$D = \frac{2,442.40}{901.65} = 2.709 \text{ years}$$

FIGURE 9–4
Duration versus Maturity

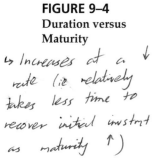

↳ *Increases at a rate (ie relatively takes less time to recover initial invstmt as maturity ↑)*

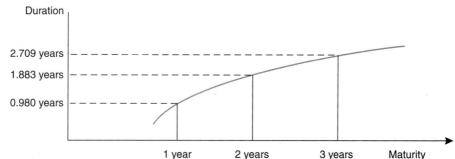

Duration & Yield
is As yield ↑ you
recover initial
invstmt faster (ie
duration ↓)

As the yield on the bond increased from 12 percent to 16 percent (Tables 9–2 and 9–4), the duration on the bond decreased from 1.883 years to 1.878 years. This makes sense intuitively because higher yields discount later cash flows more heavily and the relative importance, or weights, of those later cash flows decline when compared with earlier cash flows on an asset or liability.

Duration and Coupon Interest

A comparison of Tables 9–3 and 9–2 indicates that the higher the coupon or promised interest payment on the security, the lower its duration:

$$\frac{\partial D}{\partial C} < 0$$

As the coupon rate on the Government of Canada bond increased from 6 percent to 8 percent in Tables 9–3 and 9–2, the duration on the bond decreased from 1.909 years to 1.883 years. This is due to the fact that the larger the coupons or promised interest payments, the more quickly cash flows are received by investors and the higher are the present value weights of those cash flows in the duration calculation. On a time value of money basis, the investor recoups the initial investment faster when coupon payments are larger.

Concept Questions

1. Which has the longest duration, a 30-year, 8 percent, zero-coupon or discount bond or an 8 percent infinite maturity consol bond?
2. What is the relationship between duration and yield to maturity on a financial security?
3. Do high-coupon bonds have high or low durations?

THE ECONOMIC MEANING OF DURATION

So far we have calculated duration for a number of different fixed-income assets and liabilities. Now we are ready to make the direct link between the number measured in years we call duration and the interest rate sensitivity of an asset or liability or of an FI's entire portfolio.

In addition to being a measure of the average life, in a cash flow sense, of an asset or liability, duration is also a *direct* measure of the interest rate sensitivity, or elasticity, of an asset or liability. In other words, the larger the numerical value of *D*, the more sensitive the price of that asset or liability is to changes or shocks in interest rates.

Consider the following equation showing that the current price of a bond is equal to the present value of the coupons and principal payment on the bond:

$$P = \frac{C}{(1 + R)} + \frac{C}{(1 + R)^2} + \cdots + \frac{C + F}{(1 + R)^N} \qquad \textbf{(9.1)}$$

where

P = Price on the bond
C = Coupon (annual)
R = Yield to maturity
N = Number of periods to maturity
F = Face value of the bond

We want to find out how the price of the bond (P) changes when yields (R) rise. We know that bond prices fall, but we want to derive a direct measure of the size of this fall (i.e., its degree of price sensitivity).

Taking the derivative of the bond's price (P) with respect to the yield to maturity (R), we can show that:[7]

$$\frac{dP}{dR} = -\frac{1}{1 + R}[P \times D]$$ **(9.2)**

By cross multiplying:

$$\frac{dP}{dR} \times \frac{1 + R}{P} = -D$$ **(9.3)**

or, alternatively:

$$\frac{\dfrac{dP}{P}}{\dfrac{dR}{(1 + R)}} = -D$$ **(9.4)**

interest elasticity
The percentage change in the price of a bond for any given change in interest rates.

The economic interpretation of equation (2) is that the number D is the **interest elasticity,** or sensitivity, of the security's price to small interest rate changes. That is, D describes the percentage price fall of the bond (dP/P) for any given (present value) increase in required interest rates or yields ($dR/(1 + R)$).

---

[7] The first derivative of the bond's price in equation (1) with respect to the yield to maturity (R) is:

$$\frac{dP}{dR} = \frac{-C}{(1 + R)^2} + \frac{-2C}{(1 + R)^3} + \ldots + \frac{-N(C + F)}{(1 + R)^{N+1}}$$ **(9A)**

By rearranging, we get:

$$\frac{dP}{dR} = -\frac{1}{1 + R}\left[\frac{C}{(1 + R)} + \frac{2C}{(1 + R)^2} + \ldots + \frac{N(C + F)}{(1 + R)^N}\right]$$ **(9B)**

We have shown that duration (D) is the weighted-average time to maturity using the present value of cash flows as weights; that is, by definition:

$$D = \frac{1 \times \dfrac{C}{(1 + R)} + 2 \times \dfrac{C}{(1 + R)^2} + \ldots + N \times \dfrac{(C + F)}{(1 + R)^N}}{\dfrac{C}{(1 + R)} + \dfrac{C}{(1 + R)^2} + \ldots + \dfrac{(C + F)}{(1 + R)^N}}$$ **(9C)**

Since the denominator of the duration equation is simply the price (P) of the bond that is equal to the present value of the cash flows on the bond, then:

$$D = \frac{1 \times \dfrac{C}{(1 + R)} + 2 \times \dfrac{C}{(1 + R)^2} + \ldots + N \times \dfrac{(C + F)}{(1 + R)^N}}{P}$$ **(9D)**

Multiplying both sides of this equation by P, we get:

$$P \times D = 1 \times \frac{C}{(1 + R)} + 2 \times \frac{C}{(1 + R)^2} + \ldots + N \times \frac{C + F}{(1 + R)^N}$$ **(9E)**

The term on the right side of equation (E) is the same term as that in square brackets in equation (B). Substituting equation (E) into equation (B), we get:

$$\frac{dP}{dR} = -\frac{1}{1 + R}[P \times D]$$

FIGURE 9–5
Proportional
Relationship
between Price
Changes and Yield
Changes on a Bond
Implied by the
Duration Model

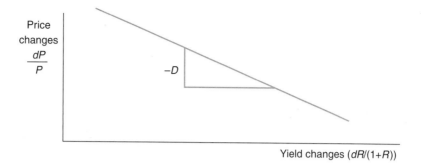

Equation (4) can be rearranged in another useful way for interpretation regarding interest sensitivity:

$$\frac{dP}{P} = -D \left[\frac{dR}{1 + R} \right] \qquad (9.5)$$

Equation (5) and Figure 9–5, its graphic representation, show that for small changes in interest rates, bond prices move *in an inversely proportional* fashion according to the size of D. Clearly, for any given change in interest rates, long-duration securities suffer a larger capital loss (or receive a higher capital gain) should interest rates rise (fall) than do short-duration securities. By implication, gains and losses under the duration model are *symmetric*. That is, if we repeated the above examples but allowed interest rates to *decrease* by one basis point annually (or 1/2 basis point semiannually), the percentage increase in the price of the bond (dP/P) would be proportionate with D. Further, the capital gains would be a mirror image of the capital losses for an equal (small) increase in interest rates.

modified duration
Duration divided by
1 plus the interest rate.

The duration equation can be rearranged, combining D and (1 + R) into a single variable D/(1 + R), to produce what practitioners call **modified duration** (MD). For annual compounding of interest:

$$\frac{dP}{P} = -MD \, dR$$

where

$$MD = \frac{D}{1 + R}$$

This form is more intuitive because we multiply MD by the simple change in interest rates rather than the discounted change in interest rates as in the general duration equation. Next, we use duration to measure the interest sensitivity of an asset or liability.

EXAMPLE 9–3

*The Six-Year
Eurobond*

Consider Example 9–1 for the six-year Eurobond with an 8 percent coupon and 8 percent yield. We determined in Table 9–1 that its duration was approximately D = 4.993 years. Suppose that yields were to rise by one basis point (1/100th of 1 percent) from 8 to 8.01 percent. Then

$$\frac{dP}{P} = -(4.993) \left[\frac{.0001}{1.08} \right]$$

$$= -.000462$$

$$\text{or} \ -0.0462\%$$

The bond price had been $1,000, which was the present value of a six-year bond with 8 percent coupons and 8 percent yield. However, the duration model predicts that the price of the bond would fall to $999.538 after the increase in yield by one basis point. That is, the price would fall by .0462 percent, or by $0.462.[8]

EXAMPLE 9–4

*The Consol
Bond*

Consider a consol bond with an 8 percent coupon paid annually, an 8 percent yield, and a calculated duration of 13.5 years ($D_c = 1 + 1/.08 = 13.5$). Thus, for a one basis point change in the yield (from 8 percent to 8.01 percent):

$$\frac{dP}{P} = -(13.5)\left[\frac{.0001}{1.08}\right]$$

$$= -.00125$$

$$\text{or } -0.125\%$$

As you can see, for any given change in yields, long-duration securities suffer a greater capital loss or receive a greater capital gain than do short-duration securities.

Semiannual Coupon Bonds

For fixed-income assets or liabilities whose interest payments are received semiannually or more frequently than annually, the formula in equation (5) has to be modified slightly. For semiannual payments:

$$\frac{dP}{P} = -D\left[\frac{dR}{1 + \frac{1}{2}R}\right] \tag{9.6}$$

The only difference between equation (6) and equation (5) is the introduction of a $\frac{1}{2}$ in the discount rate term $1 + \frac{1}{2}R$ to take into account the semiannual payments of interest.

EXAMPLE 9–5

*Semiannual
Coupon, Two-
Year Maturity
Treasury Bonds*

Recall from Example 9–2 the two-year bond with semiannual coupons whose duration we derived in Table 9–2 as 1.883 years when annual yields were 12 percent. A one-basis-point rise in interest rates would have the following predicted effect on its price:

$$\frac{dP}{P} = -1.883\left[\frac{.0001}{1.06}\right]$$

$$= -.000178$$

or the price of the bond would fall by 0.0178 percent from $930.70 to $930.53. That is, a price fall of 0.0178 percent in this case translates into a dollar fall of $0.17.[9]

---

[8] To calculate the dollar change in value, we can rewrite the equation as $dP = (P)(-D)(dR/(1 + R)) = (\$1,000)(-4.993)(.0001/1.08) = -\$0.462$.

[9] To calculate the dollar change in value, we can rewrite the equation as $dP = (P)(-D)(dR/(1 + R/2)) = (\$930.70)(-1.883)(.0001/1.06) = -\$0.17$.

Concept Questions

1. What is the relation between the duration of a bond and the interest elasticity of a bond?
2. How would the formula in equation (6) have to be modified to take into account quarterly coupon payments and monthly coupon payments?

DURATION AND IMMUNIZATION

So far, you have learned how to calculate duration and you understand that the duration measure has economic meaning because it indicates the interest sensitivity, or elasticity, of an asset or liability's value. For FIs, the major relevance of duration is as a measure for managing interest rate risk exposure. Also important is the role of duration in allowing the FI to immunize its balance sheet or some subset of that balance sheet against interest rate risk. In the following sections we consider two examples of how FIs can use the duration measure for immunization purposes. The first is its use by insurance company and pension fund managers to help meet promised cash flow payments to policyholders or beneficiaries at a particular time in the future. The second is its use to immunize or insulate the whole balance sheet of an FI against interest rate risk.

Duration and Immunizing Future Payments

Frequently, pension fund and life insurance company managers face the problem of structuring their asset investments so they can pay out a given cash amount to policyholders in some future period. The classic example of this is an insurance policy that pays the holder some lump sum on reaching retirement age. The risk to the life insurance company manager is that interest rates on the funds generated from investing the holder's premiums could fall. Thus, the accumulated returns on the premiums invested could not meet the target or promised amount. In effect, the insurance company would be forced to draw down its reserves and net worth to meet its payout commitments. (See Chapter 3 for a discussion of this risk.)

Suppose that we are in 2007 and the insurer has to make a guaranteed payment to a policyholder in five years, 2012. For simplicity, we assume that this target guaranteed payment is $1,469, a lump-sum policy payout on retirement, equivalent to investing $1,000 at an annually compounded rate of 8 percent over five years. Of course, realistically, this payment would be much larger, but the underlying principles of the example do not change by scaling the payout amount (up or down).

To immunize, or protect, itself against interest rate risk, the insurer needs to determine which investments would produce a cash flow of exactly $1,469 in five years regardless of what happens to interest rates in the immediate future. The FI investing either in a five-year maturity and duration zero-coupon bond or in a coupon bond with a five-year duration would produce a $1,469 cash flow in five years no matter what happened to interest rates in the immediate future. Next, we consider the two strategies: buying five-year maturity (and duration) deep-discount bonds and buying five-year duration coupon bonds.

Buy Five-Year Maturity Discount Bonds

Given a $1,000 face value and an 8 percent yield and assuming annual compounding, the current price per five-year discount bond would be $680.58 per bond:

$$P = 680.58 = \frac{1,000}{(1.08)^5}$$

If the insurer bought 1.469 of these bonds at a total cost of $1,000 in 2007, these investments would produce exactly $1,469 on maturity in five years ($1,000 $\times$ (1.08)^5 = $1,469). The reason is that the duration of this bond portfolio exactly matches the target horizon for the insurer's future liability to its policyholder. Intuitively, since no intervening cash flows or coupons are paid by the issuer of the zero-coupon discount bonds, future changes in interest rates have no reinvestment income effect. Thus, the return would be unaffected by intervening interest rate changes.

Suppose no five-year discount bonds exist. Then the portfolio manager may seek to invest in appropriate duration coupon bonds to hedge interest rate risk. In this example the appropriate investment would be in five-year duration coupon-bearing bonds.

Buy a Five-Year Duration Coupon Bond

We demonstrated earlier in Table 9–1 that a six-year maturity Eurobond paying 8 percent coupons with an 8 percent yield to maturity had a duration of 4.993 years, or approximately five years. If we buy this six-year maturity, five-year duration bond in 2007 and hold it for five years, until 2012, the term exactly matches the target horizon of the insurer. The cash flows generated at the end of five years will be $1,469 whether interest rates stay at 8 percent or instantaneously (immediately) rise to 9 percent or fall to 7 percent. Thus, buying a coupon bond whose duration exactly matches the time horizon of the insurer also immunizes the insurer against interest rate changes.

EXAMPLE 9–6 *Interest Rates Remain at 8 Percent*	The cash flows received by the insurer on the bond if interest rates stay at 8 percent throughout the five years would be 1. Coupons, 5 × $80 $ 400 2. Reinvestment income 69 3. Proceeds from sale of bond at end of fifth year 1,000 $1,469

We calculate each of the three components of the insurer's income from the bond investment as follows:

1. *Coupons.* The $400 from coupons is simply the annual coupon of $80 received in each of the five years.
2. *Reinvestment income.* Because the coupons are received annually, they can be reinvested at 8 percent as they are received, generating an additional cash flow of $69.[10]

---

[10] Receiving annual coupons of $80 is equivalent to receiving an annuity of $80. There are tables and formulas that help us calculate the value of $1 received each year over a given number of years that can be reinvested at a given interest rate. The appropriate terminal value of receiving $1 a year for five years and reinvesting at 8 percent can be determined from the Future Value of an Annuity Factor (FVAF) Tables, whose general formula is:

$$FVAF_{n,R} = \left[\frac{(1 + R)^n - 1}{R} \right]$$

In our example:

$$FVAF_{5, 8\%} = \left[\frac{(1 + .08)^5 - 1}{.08} \right] = 5.867$$

Thus, the reinvestment income for $80 of coupons per year is:

Reinvestment income = (80 × 5.867) − 400 = 469 − 400 = 69

Note that we take away $400 since we have already counted the simple coupon income (5 × $80).

3. *Bond sale proceeds.* The proceeds from the sale are calculated by recognizing that the six-year bond has just one year left to maturity when it is sold by the insurance company at the end of the fifth year. That is:

↓ *Sell*	*$1,080*
Year 5	*Year 6*
(2012)	*(2013)*

What fair market price can the insurer expect to get when selling the bond at the end of the fifth year with one year left to maturity? A buyer would be willing to pay the present value of the $1,080—final coupon plus face value—to be received at the end of the one remaining year (i.e., in 2013), or:

$$P_5 = \frac{1{,}080}{1.08} = \$1{,}000$$

Thus, the insurer would be able to sell the one remaining cash flow of $1,080, to be received in the bond's final year, for $1,000.

Next, we show that since this bond has a duration of five years, matching the insurer's target period, even if interest rates were to instantaneously fall to 7 percent or rise to 9 percent, the expected cash flows from the bond would still exactly sum to $1,469. That is, the coupons + reinvestment income + principal at the end of the fifth year would be immunized. In other words, the cash flows on the bond are protected against interest rate changes.

EXAMPLE 9–7

Interest Rates Fall to 7 Percent

In this example with falling interest rates, the cash flows over the five years would be:

1. Coupons, 5 × $80	$ 400
2. Reinvestment income	60
3. Bond sale proceeds	1,009
	$1,469

The total proceeds over the five years are unchanged from what they were when interest rates were 8 percent. To see why this occurs, consider what happens to the three parts of the cash flow when rates fall to 7 percent:

1. *Coupons.* Are unchanged since the insurer still gets five annual coupons of $80 = $400.
2. *Reinvestment income.* The coupons can now only be reinvested at the lower rate of 7 percent. Reinvestment income is only $60.[11]
3. *Bond sale proceeds.* When the six-year maturity bond is sold at the end of the fifth year with one cash flow of $1,080 remaining, investors are now willing to pay more:

$$P_5 = \frac{1{,}080}{1.07} = 1{,}009$$

---

[11] This reinvestment income is calculated as follows.

$$FVAF_{5,\,7\%} = \left[\frac{(1 + .07)5 - 1}{.07} \right] = 5.751$$

Reinvestment income = (5.751 × 80) − 400 = 60, which is $9 less than it was when rates were 8 percent.

That is, the bond can be sold for $9 more than it could have when rates were 8 percent. The reason for this is that investors can get only 7 percent on newly issued bonds, while this older bond was issued with a higher coupon of 8 percent.

A comparison of reinvestment income with bond sale proceeds indicates that the fall in rates has produced a *gain* on the bond sale proceeds of $9. This exactly offsets the loss of reinvestment income of $9 due to reinvesting at a lower interest rate. Thus, total cash flows remain unchanged at $1,469.

EXAMPLE 9–8

Interest Rates Rise to 9 Percent

In this example with rising interest rates, the proceeds from the bond investment are:

1. Coupons, 5 × $80 $ 400
2. Reinvestment income [(5.985 × 80) − 400]   78
3. Bond sale proceeds (1,080/1.09)   991
                                                      $1,469

Notice that the rise in interest rates from 8 percent to 9 percent leaves the final terminal cash flow unaffected at $1,469. The rise in rates has generated $9 extra reinvestment income ($78 − $69), but the price at which the bond can be sold at the end of the fifth year has declined from $1,000 to $991, equal to a capital loss of $9. Thus, the gain in reinvestment income is exactly offset by the capital loss on the sale of the bond.

These examples demonstrate that matching the duration of a coupon bond—or any other fixed–interest rate instrument, such as a loan or mortgage—to the FI's target or investment horizon *immunizes* the FI against instantaneous shocks to interest rates. The gains or losses on reinvestment income that result from an interest rate change are exactly offset by losses or gains from the bond proceeds on sale.

Immunizing the Whole Balance Sheet of an FI

So far we have looked at the durations of individual instruments and ways to select individual fixed-income securities to protect FIs such as life insurance companies and pensions funds with precommitted liabilities such as future pension plan payouts. The duration model can also evaluate the overall interest rate exposure for an FI, that is, measure the **duration gap** on its balance sheet.

duration gap
A measure of overall interest rate risk exposure for an FI.

The Duration Gap for a Financial Institution

To estimate the overall duration gap of an FI, we determine first the duration of an FI's asset portfolio (A) and the duration of its liability portfolio (L). These can be calculated as:

$$D_A = X_{1A}D_1^A + X_{2A}D_2^A + \cdots + X_{nA}D_n^A$$

and

$$D_L = X_{1L}D_1^L + X_{2L}D_2^L + \cdots + X_{nL}D_n^L$$

where

$$X_{1j} + X_{2j} + \cdots + X_{nj} = 1 \quad \text{and} \quad j = A, L$$

The X_{ij}'s in the equation are the market value proportions of each asset or liability held in the respective asset and liability portfolios. Thus, if new 30-year Government of Canada bonds were 1 percent of a life insurer's portfolio and D_1^A (the duration of those bonds) was equal to 9.25 years, then $X_{1A}D_1^A = .01(9.25) = 0.0925$. More simply, the duration of a portfolio of assets or liabilities is a market value weighted average of the individual durations of the assets or liabilities on the FI's balance sheet.[12]

Consider an FI's simplified market value balance sheet:

Assets ($)	Liabilities ($)
$A = 100$	$L = 90$
	$E = 10$
$\overline{100}$	$\overline{100}$

From the balance sheet:

$$A = L + E$$

and

$$\Delta A = \Delta L + \Delta E$$

or

$$\Delta E = \Delta A - \Delta L$$

That is, when interest rates change, the change in the FI's equity or net worth (E) is equal to the difference between the change in the market values of assets and liabilities on each side of the balance sheet. This should be familiar from our discussion of the maturity model in Chapter 8. The difference here is that we want to relate the sensitivity of an FI's net worth (ΔE) to its duration mismatch rather than to its maturity mismatch. As we have already shown, duration is a more accurate measure of the interest rate sensitivity of an asset or liability than is maturity.

Since $\Delta E = \Delta A - \Delta L$, we need to determine how ΔA and ΔL—the changes in the market values of assets and liabilities on the balance sheet—are related to duration.[13]

From the duration model (assuming annual compounding of interest):

$$\frac{\Delta A}{A} = -D_A \frac{\Delta R}{(1 + R)} \qquad \textbf{(9.7)}$$

$$\frac{\Delta L}{L} = -D_L \frac{\Delta R}{(1 + R)} \qquad \textbf{(9.8)}$$

Here we have simply substituted $\Delta A/A$ or $\Delta L/L$, the percentage change in the market values of assets or liabilities, for $\Delta P/P$, the percentage change in any single bond's price and D_A or D_L, the duration of the FI's asset or liability portfolio, for D_i, the duration on any given bond, deposit, or loan. The term $\Delta R/(1 + R)$ reflects the shock to interest rates as before.[14] To show dollar changes, these equations can be rewritten as:

$$\Delta A = -D_A \times A \times \frac{\Delta R}{(1 + R)} \qquad \textbf{(9.9)}$$

---

[12] This derivation of an FI's duration gap closely follows G. Kaufman, "Measuring and Managing Interest Rate Risk: A Primer," Federal Reserve Bank of Chicago, *Economic Perspectives,* 1984, pp. 16–29.

[13] In what follows, we use the Δ (change) notation instead of d (derivative notation) to recognize that interest rate changes tend to be discrete rather than infinitesimally small. For example, in real-world financial markets, the smallest observed rate change is usually one basis point, or 1/100th of 1 percent.

and

$$\Delta L = -D_L \times L \times \frac{\Delta R}{(1 + R)} \qquad \textbf{(9.10)}$$

We can substitute these two expressions into the equation $\Delta E = \Delta A - \Delta L$. Rearranging and combining this equation[15] results in a measure of the change in the market value of equity:

$$\Delta E = -[D_A - D_L k] \times A \times \frac{\Delta R}{1 + R}$$

where $k = L/A$ is a measure of the FI's leverage, that is, the amount of borrowed funds or liabilities rather than owners' equity used to fund its asset portfolio. The effect of interest rate changes on the market value of an FI's equity or net worth (ΔE) breaks down into three effects:

1. *The leverage adjusted duration gap* $= [D_A - D_L k]$. This gap is measured in years and reflects the degree of duration mismatch in an FI's balance sheet. Specifically, the larger this gap is *in absolute terms*, the more exposed the FI is to interest rate shocks.

2. *The size of the FI.* The term A measures the size of the FI's assets. The larger the scale of the FI, the larger the dollar size of the potential net worth exposure from any given interest rate shock.

3. *The size of the interest rate shock* $= \Delta R/(1 + R)$. The larger the shock, the greater the FI's exposure.

Given this, we express the exposure of the net worth of the FI as:

$$\Delta E = -[\text{Leverage adjusted duration gap}] \times \text{Asset size} \times \text{Interest rate shock}$$

---

[14] We assume that the level of rates and the expected shock to interest rates are the same for both assets and liabilities, which means that the FI's spread (the difference between the rate on earning assets and interest-bearing liabilities) is zero. However, as long as the FI has more earning assets than interest-bearing liabilities, it will have a positive level for net interest income. This assumption is standard in Macauley duration analysis. While restrictive, this assumption can be relaxed. However, if this is done, the duration measure changes, as is discussed later in Appendix A to this chapter.

[15] We do this as follows:

$$\Delta E = \left[-D_A \times A \times \frac{\Delta R}{(1 + R)} \right] - \left[-D_L \times L \times \frac{\Delta R}{(1 + R)} \right]$$

Assuming that the level of rates and the expected shock to interest rates are the same for both assets and liabilities:

$$\Delta E = [-D_A A + D_L L] \frac{\Delta R}{(1 + R)}$$

or

$$\Delta E = -[D_A A - D_L L] \frac{\Delta R}{(1 + R)}$$

To rearrange the equation in a slightly more intuitive fashion, we multiply and divide both $D_A A$ and $D_L L$ by A (assets):

$$\Delta E = -\left[D_A \frac{A}{A} - D_L \frac{L}{A} \right] \times A \times \frac{\Delta R}{(1 + R)}$$

or $\quad \Delta E = -[D_A - D_L k] \times A \times \dfrac{\Delta R}{(1 + R)}$

Interest rate shocks are largely external to the FI and often result from changes in the Bank of Canada's monetary policy (as discussed in the first section of Chapter 8). The size of the duration gap and the size of the FI, however, are under the control of management. The Industry Perspectives box highlights how a sharp drop in mortgage rates left Fannie Mae (a key U.S. mortgage provider) with its highest-ever reported duration gap.

Using an example, the next section explains how a manager can use information on an FI's duration gap to restructure the balance sheet to immunize stockholders' net worth against interest rate risk (i.e., to set the balance sheet up *before* a change in interest rates, so that ΔE is nonnegative for an expected change in interest rates).

EXAMPLE 9–9

Interest Rates Rise to 9 Percent

Suppose the FI manager calculates that:

$$D_A = 5 \text{ years}$$
$$D_L = 3 \text{ years}$$

Then the manager learns from an economic forecasting unit that rates are expected to rise from 10 to 11 percent in the immediate future; that is:

$$\Delta R = 1\% = .01$$
$$1 + R = 1.10$$

The FI's initial balance sheet is assumed to be:

Assets ($ millions)	Liabilities ($ millions)
$A = 100$	$L = 90$
	$E = 10$
100	100

The FI's manager calculates the potential loss to equity holders' net worth (E) if the forecast of rising rates proves true as follows:

$$\Delta E = -(D_A - kD_L) \times A \times \frac{\Delta R}{(1 + R)}$$

$$= -(5 - (.9)(3)) \times \$100 \text{ million} \times \frac{.01}{1.1} = -\$2.09 \text{ million}$$

The FI could lose $2.09 million in net worth if rates rise 1 percent. Since the FI started with $10 million in equity, the loss of $2.09 million is almost 21 percent of its initial net worth. The market value balance sheet after the rise in rates by 1 percent would look like this:[16]

Assets ($ millions)	Liabilities ($ millions)
$A = 95.45$	$L = 87.54$
	$E = 7.91$
95.45	95.45

---

[16] These values are calculated as follows:

$$\Delta A/A = -5(.01/1.1) = -.04545 = -4.545\%$$
$$100 + (-.04545)100 = 95.45$$

and

$$\Delta L/L = -3(.01/1.1) = -.02727 = -2.727\%$$
$$90 + (-.02727)90 = 87.54$$

Industry Perspectives

MORTGAGE MISMATCH: HOME REFINANCINGS WIDEN FANNIE'S RISK

A key measure of interest rate risk at Fannie Mae widened sharply last month, boosting part of the bond market but raising new questions about the effects of the home-refinancing boom on Fannie's own finances. In its monthly release of financial data, the giant government-sponsored mortgage company acknowledged that what is known as the "duration gap" between its mortgage assets and debt liabilities ended August at the highest level the company has ever reported publicly, "reflecting the recent sharp drop in mortgage rates." But the company said it can handle the added risk, and its profit projections remain the same.

Nevertheless, the disclosure somewhat rattled Fannie investors. As of 4 PM in the New York Stock Exchange composite trading, Fannie Mae shares fell $1.72 to $70.98 each. The disclosure creates "a general level of concern when you see a huge financial institution reporting what seems to be a mis-hedging of their assets and liabilities," says Robert Young, a mortgage analyst at Salomon Smith Barney. "It looks like a pretty sizable gap."

Fannie Mae's current predicament is related to the recent refinancing boom. With mortgage rates at their lowest levels in a generation, more borrowers are paying off their mortgages early and taking out new ones with lower rates. When that happens, Fannie replaces those mortgages with new loans that could have lower interest rates—creating a possible mismatch between the mortgages it now owns and the debt on its books. The duration gap is one way the company measures its success in matching its mortgage assets and its liabilities. The gap swung from negative nine months in July to negative 14 months in August. That doesn't mean that the company is in trouble. But it does mean Fannie Mae's huge $747 billion loan portfolio has greater exposure to a sudden shift in interest rates. Fannie Mae likes to have the duration of [its] assets and liabilities more closely matched; its stated target is to maintain a duration gap of within plus or minus six months.

Bond market investors care about the disclosure because it suggests Fannie Mae will have to take steps to get its assets and liabilities back in line, with possible implications for the rest of the bond market. Treasury prices rose yesterday, in part on expectations that Fannie Mae might soon become a big buyer of longer-dated Treasury debt in a move to better hedge its portfolio. . . .

Source: *The Wall Street Journal*, September 17, 2002, p. C1, by Patrick Barta. Reprinted by permission of *The Wall Street Journal*. © 2002 Dow Jones & Company, Inc. All Rights Reserved Worldwide. www.wsj.com

Even though the rise in interest rates would not push the FI into economic insolvency, it reduces the FI's net worth-to-assets ratio from 10 (10/100) to 8.29 percent (7.91/95.45). To counter this effect, the manager might reduce the FI's adjusted duration gap. In an extreme case, the gap might be reduced to zero:

$$\Delta E = -[0] \times A \times \Delta R/(1 + R) = 0$$

To do this, the FI should not directly set $D_A = D_L$, which ignores the fact that the FI's assets (A) do not equal its borrowed liabilities (L) and that k (which reflects the ratio L/A) is not equal to 1. To see the importance of factoring in leverage, suppose the manager increased the duration of the FI's liabilities to five years, the same as D_A. Then:

$$\Delta E = -[5 - (.9)(5)] \times \$100 \text{ million} \times (.01/1.1) = -\$0.45 \text{ million}$$

The FI is still exposed to a loss of $0.45 million if rates rise by 1 percent. An appropriate strategy would involve changing D_L until:

$$D_A = kD_L = 5 \text{ years}$$

For example,

$$\Delta E = -[5 - (.9)5.55] \times \$100 \text{ million} \times (.01/1.1) = 0$$

In this case the FI manager sets D_L = 5.55 years, or slightly longer than D_A = 5 years, to compensate for the fact that only 90 percent of assets are funded by borrowed liabilities, with the other 10 percent funded by equity. Note that the FI manager has at least three other ways to reduce the adjusted duration gap to zero:

1. *Reduce D_A*. Reduce D_A from 5 years to 2.7 years (equal to kD_L or (.9)3) such that:

$$[D_A - kD_L] = [2.7 - (.9)(3)] = 0$$

2. *Reduce D_A* and *increase D_L*. Shorten the duration of assets and lengthen the duration of liabilities at the same time. One possibility would be to *reduce D_A* to 4 years and to *increase D_L* to 4.44 years such that:

$$[D_A - kD_L] = [4 - (.9)(4.44)] = 0$$

3. *Change k and D_L*. Increase k (leverage) from .9 to .95 and increase D_L from 3 years to 5.26 years such that:

$$[D_A - kD_L] = [5 - (.95)(5.26)] = 0$$

Concept Questions

1. Refer to the example of the insurer in Examples 9–6 through 9–8. Suppose rates fell to 6 percent. Would the FI's portfolio still be immunized? What if rates rose to 10 percent?
2. How is the overall duration gap for an FI calculated?
3. How can a manager use information on an FI's duration gap to restructure, and thereby immunize, the balance sheet against interest rate risk?
4. Suppose D_A = 3 years, D_L = 6 years, k = .8, and A = $100 million. What is the effect on owners' net worth if $\Delta R/(1 + R)$ rises 1 percent? (ΔE = $1,800,000)

IMMUNIZATION AND REGULATORY CONSIDERATIONS

In the above section we assumed that the FI manager wants to structure the duration of assets and liabilities to immunize the equity or net worth stake (E) of the FI's equity owners from interest rate shocks. However, regulators periodically monitor the solvency or capital position of FIs. As we discuss in greater detail in Chapter 20 on capital adequacy, regulators set minimum target ratios for an FI's capital (or net worth) to assets. The simplest is the ratio of FI capital to its assets, or:

$$\frac{E}{A} = \text{Capital (net worth) ratio}$$

Given the regulations imposed on the minimum level of the capital ratio, if an FI's asset levels change significantly through time, FI managers may be most interested in immunizing against changes in the capital ratio ($\Delta(E/A)$) due to interest rate risk rather than changes in the level of capital (ΔE). For example, suppose the FI manager is close to the minimum regulatory required E/A (or capital) ratio and wants to immunize the FI against any fall in this ratio if interest rates rise.[17] That is, the immunization target is no longer ΔE = 0 when rates change but $\Delta(E/A)$ = 0.

Obviously, immunizing ΔE against interest rate risk cannot result in the same management strategy as immunizing $\Delta(E/A)$. A portfolio constructed to immunize

---

[17] In actuality, federally regulated deposit-taking institutions (DTIs) in Canada are subject to a risk-based capital adequacy framework that is covered in detail in Chapter 20.

ΔE would have a different duration match from that required to immunize $\Delta(E/A)$. Or, more simply, the manager could satisfy either the FI's stockholders or the regulators *but not both* simultaneously.

More specifically, when the objective is to immunize equity capital against interest rate risk, that is, to set $\Delta E = 0$, the FI manager should structure the balance sheet so that the leverage adjusted duration gap is zero:

$$\Delta E = 0 = D_A - kD_L$$

or set

$$D_A = kD_L$$

By comparison, to immunize the capital ratio, that is, to set $\Delta(E/A) = 0$ the manager needs to set:[18]

$$D_A = D_L$$

In this scenario, the leverage adjustment effect (k) drops out. If $D_A = 5$, then immunizing the capital ratio would require setting $D_L = 5$.

Concept Questions

1. Is immunizing a bank's net worth the same as immunizing its net worth–assets ratio? If not, why not?

In the next section, we analyze weaknesses of the duration model. Specifically, there are several practical problems in estimating duration and duration gaps for real-world FIs.

DIFFICULTIES IN APPLYING THE DURATION MODEL

www.bis.org

Critics of the duration model have often claimed that it is difficult to apply in real-world situations. However, duration measures and immunization strategies are useful in most real-world situations. In fact, the model proposed by the Bank for International Settlements to monitor bank interest rate risk taking is based heavily on the duration model. In this section, we look at the various criticisms of the duration model and discuss ways a modern FI manager would deal with them in practice. In the Appendix to the chapter, we present some of the more advanced issues associated with these weaknesses.

Duration Matching Can Be Costly

Critics charge that although in principle an FI manager can change D_A and D_L to immunize the FI against interest rate risk, restructuring the balance sheet of a large and complex FI can be both time-consuming and costly. Although this argument may have been true historically, the growth of purchased funds, asset securitization, and loan sales markets has considerably eased the speed and lowered the transaction costs of major balance sheet restructurings. (See Chapters 26 and 27 for a discussion of these strategies.) Moreover, an FI manager could still manage risk exposure using the duration model by employing techniques other than direct portfolio rebalancing to immunize against interest rate risk. Managers can get many of the same results of direct duration matching by taking

---

[18] See Kaufman, "Measuring and Managing Interest Rate Risk: A Primer," for a proof.

hedging positions in the markets for derivative securities, such as futures and forwards (Chapter 23); options, caps, floors, and collars (Chapter 24); and swaps (Chapter 25).[19]

Immunization Is a Dynamic Problem

Immunization is an aspect of the duration model that is not well understood. Let's go back to the earlier immunization example in which an insurer sought to buy bonds to provide an accumulated cash flow of $1,469 in five years no matter what happened to interest rates. We showed that buying a six-year maturity, 8 percent coupon bond with a five-year duration immunizes the insurer against an instantaneous change in interest rates. The word *instantaneous* is very important here; it means a change in interest rates immediately after purchasing the bond. However, interest rates can change at any time over the holding period. Further, the duration of a bond changes as time passes, that is, as it approaches maturity or the target horizon date. In addition, duration changes at a different rate than does real or calendar time.

To understand this time effect, consider the initially hedged position in which the insurer bought the five-year duration (six-year maturity), 8 percent coupon bond in 2007 to match its cash flow target of $1,469 in 2012. Suppose the FI manager puts the bond in the bottom drawer of a desk and does not think about it for a year, believing that the insurance company's position is fully hedged. After one year has passed (in 2008), suppose interest rates (yields) have fallen from 8 percent to 7 percent and the manager opens the drawer of the desk and finds the bond. Knowing the target date is now only four years away, the manager recalculates the duration of the bond. Imagine the manager's shock on finding that the same 8 percent coupon bond with a 7 percent yield and only five years left to maturity has a duration of 4.33 years. This means the insurance company is no longer hedged; the 4.33-year duration of this bond portfolio *exceeds* the investment horizon of four years. As a result, the manager has to restructure the bond portfolio to remain immunized. One way to do this is to sell some of the five-year bonds (4.33-year duration) and buy some bonds of shorter duration so that the overall duration of the investment portfolio is four years.

For example, suppose the insurer sold 50 percent of the five-year bonds with a 4.33-year duration and invested the proceeds in 3.67-year duration and maturity zero-coupon bonds. Because duration and maturity are the same for discount bonds, the duration of the asset portfolio is:

$$D_A = [4.33 \times .5] + [3.67 \times .5] = 4 \text{ years}$$

This simple example demonstrates that immunization based on duration is a dynamic strategy. In theory, the strategy requires the portfolio manager to rebalance the portfolio continuously to ensure that the duration of the investment portfolio exactly matches the investment horizon (i.e., the duration of liabilities). Because continuous rebalancing may not be easy to do and involves costly transaction fees, most portfolio managers seek to be only approximately dynamically immunized against interest rate changes by rebalancing at discrete intervals, such as quarterly. That is, there is a trade-off between being perfectly immunized and the transaction costs of maintaining an immunized balance sheet dynamically.

---

[19] In particular, instead of direct immunization of a positive duration gap ($D_A > D_L$), an FI manager could sell futures (forwards), take the fixed-rate side of an interest rate swap, buy put options on bonds, and/or buy an interest rate cap.

FIGURE 9–6
Duration versus
True Relationship

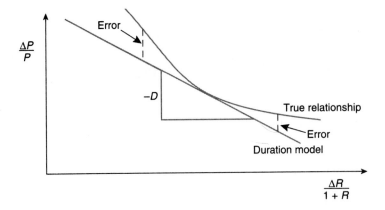

Large Interest Rate Changes and Convexity

Duration accurately measures the price sensitivity of fixed-income securities for small changes in interest rates of the order of one basis point. But suppose interest rate shocks are much larger, of the order of 2 percent, or 200 basis points. Then duration becomes a less accurate predictor of how much the prices of securities will change and therefore a less accurate measure of interest rate sensitivity. Looking at Figure 9–6, you can see the reason for this. Note first the change in a bond's price due to yield changes according to the duration model and second, the true relationship, as calculated directly, using the exact present value calculation for bond valuation.

The duration model predicts that the relationship between interest rate shocks and bond price changes will be proportional to D (duration). However, by precisely calculating the true change in bond prices, we would find that for large interest rate increases, duration overpredicts the *fall* in bond prices, while for large interest rate decreases, it underpredicts the *increase* in bond prices. That is, the duration model predicts symmetric effects for rate increases and decreases on bond prices. As Figure 9–6 shows, in actuality, for rate increases, the *capital loss effect* tends to be smaller than the *capital gain effect* is for rate decreases. This is the result of the bond price-yield relationship exhibiting a property called *convexity* rather than *linearity*, as assumed by the basic duration model.

convexity
The degree of curvature of the price-yield curve around some interest rate level.

Note that **convexity** is a desirable feature for an FI manager to capture in a portfolio of assets. Buying a bond or a portfolio of assets that exhibits a lot of convexity, or curvature, in the price-yield curve relationship is similar to buying partial interest rate risk insurance. Specifically, high convexity means that for equally large changes of interest rates up and down (e.g., plus or minus 2 percent), the capital gain effect of a rate decrease more than offsets the capital loss effect of a rate increase. As we show in the Appendix to the chapter, all fixed-income assets or liabilities exhibit some convexity in their price-yield relationships.[20]

To see the importance of accounting for the effects of convexity in assessing the impact of large rate changes on an FI's portfolio, consider the six-year Eurobond with an 8 percent coupon and yield. According to Table 9–1 (on page 220), its duration is 4.993 years and its current price P_0 is $1,000 at a yield of 8 percent:

---

[20] To be more precise, fixed-income securities without special option features such as callable bonds and mortgage-backed securities exhibit convexity. A callable bond tends to exhibit negative convexity (or concavity), as do some mortgage-backed securities.

FIGURE 9–7

The Price–Yield
Curve for the Six-
Year Eurobond

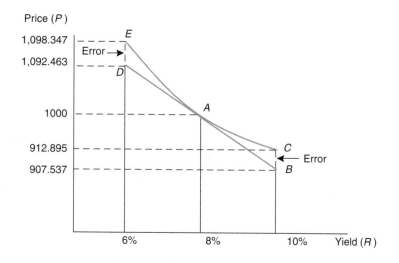

$$P_0 = \frac{80}{(1.08)} + \frac{80}{(1.08)^2} + \frac{80}{(1.08)^3}$$

$$+ \frac{80}{(1.08)^4} + \frac{80}{(1.08)^5} + \frac{1,080}{(1.08)^6} = 1,000$$

This is point *A* on the price-yield curve in Figure 9–7.

If rates rise from 8 to 10 percent, the duration model predicts that the bond price will fall by 9.2463 percent; that is:

$$\frac{\Delta P}{P} = -4.993 \left[\frac{.02}{1.08} \right] = -9.2463\%$$

or, from a price of $1,000 to $907.537 (see point *B* in Figure 9–7). However, calculating the exact change in the bond's price after a rise in yield to 10 percent, we find that its true value is:

$$P_0 = \frac{80}{(1.1)} + \frac{80}{(1.1)^2} + \frac{80}{(1.1)^3}$$

$$+ \frac{80}{(1.1)^4} + \frac{80}{(1.1)^5} + \frac{1,080}{(1.1)^6} = 912.895$$

This is point *C* in Figure 9–7. As you can see, the true or actual fall in price is less than the predicted fall by $5.358. This means that there is over a 0.5 percent error using the duration model. The reason for this is the natural convexity to the price-yield curve as yields rise.

Reversing the experiment reveals that the duration model would predict the bond's price to rise by 9.2463 percent if yields fell from 8 to 6 percent, resulting in a predicted price of $1,092.463 (see point *D* in Figure 9–7). By comparison, the true or actual change in price can be computed as $1,098.347 by estimating the present value of the bond's coupons and its face value with a 6 percent yield (see point *E* in Figure 9–7). The duration model has underpredicted the bond price increase by $5.884, or by over 0.5 percent of the true price increase.

An important question for the FI manager is whether a 0.5 percent error is big enough to be concerned about. This depends on the size of the interest rate change and the size of the portfolio under management. Clearly, 0.5 percent of a large number will still be a large number!

Summary

This chapter analyzed the duration model approach to measuring interest rate risk. The duration model is superior to the simple maturity model in that it incorporates the timing of cash flows as well as maturity effects into a simple measure of interest rate risk. The duration measure could be used to immunize a particular liability as well as the whole FI balance sheet. However, as the concluding section of the chapter indicates, a number of potential problems exist in applying the duration model in real-world scenarios. Despite these weaknesses, the duration model is fairly robust and can deal with a large number of real-world complexities, such as credit risk, convexity, floating interest rates, and uncertain maturities.

Questions and Problems

1. What are the two different general interpretations of the concept of duration, and what is the technical definition of this term? How does duration differ from maturity?

2. Two bonds are available for purchase in the financial markets. The first bond is a two-year, $1,000 bond that pays an annual coupon of 10 percent. The second bond is a two-year, $1,000 zero-coupon bond.

   a. What is the duration of the coupon bond if the current yield to maturity (YTM) is 8 percent? 10 percent? 12 percent? (*Hint:* You may wish to create a spreadsheet program to assist in the calculations.)

   b. How does the change in the current YTM affect the duration of this coupon bond?

   c. Calculate the duration of the zero-coupon bond with a YTM of 8 percent, 10 percent, and 12 percent.

   d. How does the change in the current YTM affect the duration of the zero-coupon bond?

   e. Why does the change in the YTM affect the coupon bond differently than it affects the zero-coupon bond?

3. A one-year, $100,000 loan carries a market interest rate of 12 percent. The loan requires payment of accrued interest and one-half of the principal at the end of six months. The remaining principal and the accrued interest are due at the end of the year.

   a. What is the duration of this loan?

   b. What will be the cash flows at the end of six months and at the end of the year?

   c. What is the present value of each cash flow discounted at the market rate? What is the total present value?

   d. What proportion of the total present value of cash flows occurs at the end of six months? What proportion occurs at the end of the year?

   e. What is the weighted-average life of the cash flows on the loan?

   f. How does this weighted-average life compare with the duration calculated in part (a) above?

4. What is the duration of a five-year, $1,000 Government of Canada bond with a 10 percent semiannual coupon selling at par? Selling with a YTM of 12 percent? 14 percent? What can you conclude about the relationship between duration and yield to maturity? Plot the relationship. Why does this relationship exist?

5. Consider three bonds each of which has a 10 percent semiannual coupon and trades at par.

   a. Calculate the duration for a bond that has a maturity of four years, three years, and two years.

   b. What conclusions can you reach about the relationship between duration and the time to maturity? Plot the relationship.

6. A six-year, $10,000 CD pays 6 percent interest annually. What is the duration of the CD? What would be the duration if interest were paid semiannually? What is the relationship of duration to the relative frequency of interest payments?

7. What is a consol bond? What is the duration of a consol bond that sells at a YTM of 8 percent? 10 percent? 12 percent? Would a consol trading at a YTM of 10 percent have a greater duration than a 20-year zero-coupon bond trading at the same YTM? Why?

8. Maximum Pension Fund is attempting to balance one of the bond portfolios under its management. The fund has identified three bonds that have five-year maturities and trade at a YTM of 9 percent. The bonds differ only in that the coupons are 7 percent, 9 percent, and 11 percent.

   a. What is the duration for each bond?

   b. What is the relationship between duration and the amount of coupon interest that is paid? Plot the relationship.

9. An insurance company is analyzing three bonds and is using duration as the measure of interest rate risk. All three bonds trade at a YTM of 10 percent and have $10,000 par values. The bonds differ only in the amount of annual coupon interest they pay: 8, 10, and 12 percent.

a. What is the duration for each five-year bond?

b. What is the relationship between duration and the amount of coupon interest that is paid?

10. You can obtain a loan for $100,000 at a rate of 10 percent for two years. You have a choice of paying the principal at the end of the second year or amortizing the loan, that is, paying interest and principal in equal payments each year. The loan is priced at par.

a. What is the duration of the loan under both methods of payment?

b. Explain the difference in the two results.

11. How is duration related to the interest elasticity of a fixed-income security? What is the relationship between duration and the price of the fixed-income security?

12. You have discovered that the price of a bond rose from $975 to $995 when the YTM fell from 9.75 percent to 9.25 percent. What is the duration of the bond?

13. Calculate the duration of a two-year, $1,000 bond that pays an annual coupon of 10 percent and trades at a yield of 14 percent. What is the expected change in the price of the bond if interest rates decline by 0.50 percent (50 basis points)?

14. The duration of an 11-year, $1,000 Government of Canada bond paying a 10 percent semiannual coupon and selling at par has been estimated at 6.9 years.

a. What is the modified duration of the bond (modified duration $= D/(1 + R)$)?

b. What will be the estimated price change of the bond if market interest rates increase 0.10 percent (10 basis points)? If rates decrease 0.20 percent (20 basis points)?

c. What would the actual price of the bond be under each rate change situation in part (b) using the traditional present value bond pricing techniques? What is the amount of error in each case?

15. Suppose you purchase a five-year, 13.76 percent bond that is priced to yield 10 percent.

a. Show that the duration of this annual payment bond is equal to four years.

b. Show that if interest rates rise to 11 percent within the next year and your investment horizon is four years from today, you will still earn a 10 percent yield on your investment.

c. Show that a 10 percent yield also will be earned if interest rates fall next year to 9 percent.

16. Consider the case in which an investor holds a bond for a period of time longer than the duration of the bond, that is, longer than the original investment horizon.

a. If market interest rates rise, will the return that is earned exceed or fall short of the original required rate of return? Explain.

b. What will happen to the realized return if market interest rates decrease? Explain.

c. Recalculate parts (b) and (c) of problem 15 above, assuming that the bond is held for all five years, to verify your answers to parts (a) and (b) of this problem.

d. If either calculation in part (c) is greater than the original required rate of return, why would an investor ever try to match the duration of an asset with his or her investment horizon?

17. Two banks are being examined by the regulators to determine the interest rate sensitivity of their balance sheets. Bank A has assets composed solely of a 10-year, 12 percent $1 million loan. The loan is financed with a 10-year, 10 percent $1 million CD. Bank B has assets composed solely of a 7-year, 12 percent zero-coupon bond with a current (market) value of $894,006.20 and a maturity (principal) value of $1,976,362.88. The bond is financed with a 10-year, 8.275 percent coupon $1,000,000 face value CD with a YTM of 10 percent. The loan and the CDs pay interest annually, with principal due at maturity.

a. If market interest rates increase 1 percent (100 basis points), how do the market values of the assets and liabilities of each bank change? That is, what will be the net effect on the market value of the equity for each bank?

b. What accounts for the differences in the changes in the market value of equity between the two banks?

c. Verify your results above by calculating the duration for the assets and liabilities of each bank, and estimate the changes in value for the expected change in interest rates. Summarize your results.

18. If you use only duration to immunize your portfolio, what three factors affect changes in the net worth of a financial institution when interest rates change?

19. Financial Institution XY has assets of $1 million invested in a 30-year, 10 percent semiannual coupon Government of Canada bond selling at par. The duration of this bond has been estimated at 9.94 years. The assets are financed with equity and a $900,000, two-year, 7.25 percent semiannual coupon capital note selling at par.

a. What is the leverage adjusted duration gap of Financial Institution XY?

b. What is the impact on equity value if the relative change in all market interest rates is a decrease of 20 basis points? *Note:* The relative change in interest rates is $\Delta R/(1 + R/2) = -0.0020$.

c. Using the information you calculated in parts (a) and (b), infer a general statement about the desired duration gap for a financial institution if interest rates are expected to increase or decrease.

d. Verify your inference by calculating the change in market value of equity assuming that the relative change in all market interest rates is an increase of 30 basis points.

e. What would the duration of the assets need to be to immunize the equity from changes in market interest rates?

20. The balance sheet for Gotbucks Bank, Inc. (GBI) is presented below ($ millions).

Assets	
Cash	30
Loans (floating)	125
Loans (fixed)	65
Total assets	220

Liabilities and Equity	
Core deposits	20
Euro CDs	180
Equity	20
Total liabilities and equity	220

Notes to the balance sheet: The floating loan rate is LIBOR + 4 percent, and currently LIBOR is 11 percent. Fixed-rate loans have five-year maturities, are priced at par, and pay 12 percent annual interest. Core deposits are fixed rate for two years at 8 percent paid annually. Euros currently yield 9 percent.

a. What is the duration of the fixed-rate loan portfolio of Gotbucks Bank?

b. If the duration of the floating-rate loans is 0.36 years, what is the duration of GBI's assets?

c. What is the duration of the core deposits if they are priced at par?

d. If the duration of the Euro CDs is 0.401 years, what is the duration of GBI's liabilities?

e. What is GBI's duration gap? What is its interest rate risk exposure?

f. What is the impact on the market value of equity if the relative change in all market interest rates is an increase of 1 percent (100 basis points)? Note that the relative change in interest rates is $\Delta R > (1 + R) = 0.01$.

g. What is the impact on the market value of equity if the relative change in all market interest rates is a decrease of 0.5 percent (-50 basis points)?

h. What variables are available to GBI to immunize the bank? How much would each variable need to change to get DGAP to equal zero?

21. Hands Insurance Company issued a $90 million, one-year zero-coupon note at 8 percent add-on annual interest (paying one coupon at the end of the year). The proceeds were used to fund a $100 million, two-year corporate loan at 10 percent annual interest. Immediately after these transactions were simultaneously closed, all market interest rates increased 1.5 percent (150 basis points).

a. What is the true market value of the loan investment and the liability after the change in interest rates?

b. What impact did these changes in market value have on the market value of the FI's equity?

c. What was the duration of the loan investment and the liability at the time of issuance?

d. Use these duration values to calculate the expected change in the value of the loan and the liability for the predicted increase of 1.5 percent in interest rates.

e. What was the duration gap of Hands Insurance Company after the issuance of the asset and note?

f. What was the change in equity value forecasted by this duration gap for the predicted increase in interest rates of 1.5 percent?

g. If the interest rate prediction had been available during the time period in which the loan and the liability were being negotiated, what suggestions would you have offered to reduce the possible effect on the equity of the company? What are the difficulties in implementing your ideas?

22. The following balance sheet information is available (amounts in thousands of dollars and duration in years) for a financial institution:

	Amount	Duration
T-bills	90	0.50
T-notes	55	0.90
Government bonds	176	
Loans	2,724	7.00
Deposits	2,092	1.00
Bank of Canada funds	238	0.01
Equity	715	

The Government of Canada bonds are five-year maturities paying 6 percent semiannually and selling at par.

a. What is the duration of the bond portfolio?

b. What is the average duration of all the assets?

c. What is the average duration of all the liabilities?

d. What is the leverage adjusted duration gap? What is the interest rate risk exposure?

e. What is the forecasted impact on the market value of equity caused by a relative upward shift in the entire yield curve of 0.5 percent [i.e., $\Delta R/(1 + R) = 0.0050$]?

f. If the yield curve shifts downward 0.25 percent [i.e., $\Delta R/(1 + R) = -0.0025$, what is the forecasted impact on the market value of equity?

g. What variables are available to the financial institution to immunize the balance sheet? How much would each variable need to change to get DGAP to equal 0?

23. Assume that a goal of a regulatory agency of a financial institution is to immunize the ratio of equity to total assets, that is, $D(E/A) = 0$. Explain how this goal changes the desired duration gap for the institution. Why does this differ from the duration gap necessary to immunize the total equity? How would your answers to part (h) in problem 20 and part (g) in problem 22 change if immunizing equity to total assets was the goal?

24. Identify and discuss three criticisms of using the duration model to immunize the portfolio of a financial institution.

25. In general, what changes have occurred in the financial markets that would allow financial institutions to restructure their balance sheets more rapidly and efficiently to meet desired goals? Why is it critical for an investment manager who has a portfolio immunized to match a desired investment horizon to rebalance the portfolio periodically? What is convexity? Why is convexity a desirable feature to capture in a portfolio of assets?

26. A financial institution has an investment horizon of two years, 9.5 months. The institution has converted all assets into a portfolio of 8 percent, $1,000 three-year bonds that are trading at a YTM of 10 percent. The bonds pay interest annually. The portfolio manager believes that the assets are immunized against interest rate changes.

a. Is the portfolio immunized at the time of the bond purchase? What is the duration of the bonds?

b. Will the portfolio be immunized one year later?

c. Assume that one-year, 8 percent zero-coupon bonds are available in one year. What proportion of the original portfolio should be placed in zeros to rebalance the portfolio?

27. MLK Bank has an asset portfolio that consists of $100 million of 30-year, 8 percent coupon $1,000 bonds that sell at par.

a. What will be the bonds' new prices if market yields change immediately by ±0.10 percent? What will be the new prices if market yields change immediately by ±2.00 percent?

b. The duration of these bonds is 12.1608 years. What are the predicted bond prices in each of the four cases using the duration rule? What is the amount of error between the duration prediction and the actual market values?

c. Given that convexity is 212.4, what are the bond price predictions in each of the four cases using the duration plus convexity relationship? What is the amount of error in these predictions?

d. Diagram and label clearly the results in parts (a), (b), and (c).

The following questions and problems are based on material in Appendix 9A to the chapter.

28. Estimate the convexity for each of the following three bonds, all of which trade at YTM of 8 percent and have face values of $1,000.

A 7-year, zero-coupon bond

A 7-year, 10 percent annual coupon bond

A 10-year, 10 percent annual coupon bond that has a duration value of 6.994 years (i.e., approximately 7 years)

Rank the bonds in terms of convexity, and express the convexity relationship between zeros and coupon bonds in terms of maturity and duration equivalencies.

29. A 10-year, 10 percent annual coupon $1,000 bond trades at a YTM of 8 percent. The bond has a duration of 6.994 years. What is the modified duration of this bond? What is the practical value of calculating modified duration? Does modified duration change the result of using the duration relationship to estimate price sensitivity?

Appendix 9A   Incorporating Convexity into the Duration Model

View Appendix 9A on page 692 of this book.

In this chapter, we define market risk and discuss:

- the three major approaches that are being used to measure market risk:
  (1) RiskMetrics,
  (2) historic or back simulation, and
  (3) Monte Carlo simulation
- the link between market risk and required capital levels

INTRODUCTION

In recent years, the trading activities of FIs have raised considerable concern among regulators and FI analysts. Some of these trading losses have been spectacular. For example, in 1995, after Barings, the U.K. merchant bank, was forced into insolvency as a result of losses on its trading in Japanese stock index futures in February, a similar incident took place at the New York branch of a leading Japanese FI, Daiwa Bank, in September. The largest trading loss in recent history involving a "rogue trader" occurred in June 1996 when Sumitomo Corp. (a Japanese bank) lost US$2.6 billion in commodity futures trading. The currency market volatility in Eastern Europe and Asia in 1997 continued in 1998 with additional losses on Russian bonds as the ruble fell in value and bond prices collapsed. Major U.S. banks (e.g., Bank of America) were forced to write off hundreds of millions of dollars in losses on their holdings of Russian government securities, and CIBC reported a one-day loss ("negative net trading revenue") of $93 million on August 27 1998, six days where trading losses were higher than $20 million, and trading losses on 69 percent of the days in the fourth quarter of 1998.

As markets have become more complex, Canadian regulators such as Nicholas Le Pan, Superintendent of OSFI, have worked to create the Basel II capital rules to protect the global financial system. As well, Canadian FIs have been at the cutting edge in developing risk management models, and simulations and scenario testing have evolved from the stand-alone, simplistic models (e.g. gap analysis) discussed in Chapters 8 and 9, to an enterprise-wide focus on risk identification and control. As shown in the Industry Perspectives Box, Royal Bank of Canada appointed Suzanne Labarge as one of the first Chief Risk Officers (CROs) in Canada in 1998. She was a Deputy Superintendent with OSFI prior to her appointment at RBC. Labarge, along with Douglas Brooks, CRO at Sun Life Financial, have helped to bring Canadian FIs to the forefront of enterprise risk management for both insurance and banking.[1]

www.osfi-bsif.gc.ca
www.royalbank.com
www.sunlife.ca

principles-based regulation
Regulation of FIs based on generally accepted management principles that must be met.

rules-based regulation
Regulation based on rules applicable to all FIs.

---

[1] Canadian companies are leaders of enterprise risk management (ERM), along with the U.K and Australia (Australian Standard AS-NZ 4360:2004, is called the "Bible of risk management"), because of Canada's small size, OSFI's principles-based approach rather than the U.S. regulators' rules-based regulation, and the global nature of the risks that face Canadian FIs. Basel II is an example of **principles-based regulation** in that it allows FIs to use their own internally-generated models to report their risk management. The U.S. Sarbanes-Oxley Act is **rules-based regulation** that allows for little individual variation from compliance. See P. Morton, "Risky business," *CA Magazine*, May 2005, Vol. 138, Iss. 4, pp. 24–29.

Industry Perspectives

TRY DRIVING A CAR WITHOUT BRAKES......
Difficult to define

To understand why Canada and countries other than the US have moved faster on handling risk is to get a grasp of what exactly enterprise risk management is.

"It is really difficult to define," admits Suzanne Labarge, who, as former vice-chairman and chief risk officer (CRO) at the Royal Bank of Canada, knows a great deal about risk management. About seven years ago, when she was appointed CRO, she was not just the bank's first CRO, she was one of the first in Canada. Labarge, who recently retired from RBC Financial Group in Toronto, says, "At that point there were almost no CROs anywhere."

Entire seminars have been held to try to define, in a layman's term, what ERM means. Thousands of trees have died in pursuit of a definitive definition for ERM. Painfully complex computer models have been developed in pursuit of more effective risk management.

The US Society of Actuaries has also come up with one candidate. "Enterprise risk management is the discipline by which an entity in any industry assesses, controls, measures, exploits finances and monitors risk from all sources for the purpose of increasing the entity's short- and long-term value to its stakeholders."'

Still, a simple explanation eludes the industry.

"If I'm at a cocktail party and someone asks me what enterprise risk management is, all I can think to say is 'Know thy risk,'" says Prakash Shimpi, practice leader with global responsibility for ERM for Towers Perrin in New York. "And if they want to know more, I would say the second step is: 'How much does that risk weigh?'"

At a meeting of CROs in New York last summer, co-hosted by the US Society of Actuaries, Standard & Poor's and the Casualty Actuary Society, the best definition they could come up with was that because it is in a state of flux, it is part art, part science and a work in progress.

But perhaps the most visual description comes from the vice-president internal audit and CRO of Hydro One Inc. "Put it this way," says John Fraser, "if a company doesn't have risk management, imagine what it would be like driving a car without brakes."

Source: Peter Morton, "Risky Business," *CA Magazine*, May 2005, Vol. 138, Iss. 4, pp. 24–29. Reproduced with permission from *CA Magazine*, published by the Canadian Institute of Chartered Accountants, Toronto, Canada.

As we move through the text, we are developing a framework for understanding the risk exposures of FIs. We now move on from our discussions of interest rate risk in Chapters 8 and 9 to add another layer of complexity, market risk.

MARKET RISK DEFINED

Conceptually, an FI's trading portfolio can be differentiated from its investment portfolio on the basis of time horizon and liquidity. The trading portfolio contains assets, liabilities, and derivative contracts that can be quickly bought or sold on organized financial markets (such as long and short positions in bonds, commodities, foreign exchange, equity securities, interest rate swaps, and options). The investment portfolio (or, in the case of banks, the banking book) contains assets and liabilities that are relatively illiquid and held for longer holding periods (such as consumer and business loans, retail deposits, and branches). Table 10–1 shows a breakdown between banking book and trading book assets and liabilities. Note that capital produces a cushion against losses on either the banking or trading books (see Chapter 20).

With the increasing securitization of bank loans (e.g., mortgages), more and more assets have become liquid and tradable (e.g. mortgage-backed securities). Of course, with time, every asset and liability can be sold. Bank regulators have normally viewed tradable assets as those being held for horizons of less than one year, and FIs take an even shorter-term view. In particular, FIs are concerned about the fluctuation in value—or value at risk (VAR or VaR)—of their trading account assets and liabilities for periods as short as one day (called Daily VAR)—especially if such fluctuations pose a threat to their solvency.

TABLE 10–1
The Investment
Book and Trading
Book of a Bank

	Assets	Liabilities
Banking Book	Loans	Capital
	Other illiquid assets	Deposits
Trading Book	Bonds (long)	Bonds (short)
	Commodities (long)	Commodities (short)
	FX (long)	FX (short)
	Equities (long)	Equities (short)
	Derivatives* (long)	Derivatives* (short)

*Derivatives are off balance sheet (as discussed in Chapter 7).

market risk
Risk related to the
uncertainty of an
FI's earnings on its
trading portfolio
caused by changes
in market conditions.

Market risk (or value at risk) can be defined as the risk related to the uncertainty of an FI's earnings on its trading portfolio caused by changes in market conditions such as the price of an asset, interest rates, market volatility, and market liquidity.[2, 3] Thus, risks such as interest rate risk (discussed in the last two chapters) and foreign exchange risk (discussed in Chapter 15) affect market risk. However, market risk emphasizes the risks to FIs that actively trade assets and liabilities (and derivatives) rather than hold them for longer-term investment, funding, or hedging purposes. Income from trading activities is increasingly replacing income from traditional FI activities of deposit taking and lending. The resulting earnings uncertainty can be measured over periods as short as a day or as long as a year. Moreover, market risk can be defined in absolute terms as a *dollar* exposure amount or as a relative amount against some benchmark. The sections that follow concentrate on absolute dollar measures of market risk. We look at three major approaches that are being used to measure market risk: RiskMetrics, historic or back simulation, and Monte Carlo simulation.

So important is market risk in determining the viability of an FI that since 1999, OSFI has included market risk in determining the required level of capital a federally regulated FI must hold.[4] The link between market risk and required capital levels is also discussed in the chapter.

MARKET RISK MEASUREMENT

There are at least five reasons market risk measurement (MRM) is important:

1. *Management information.* MRM provides senior management with information on the risk exposure taken by FI traders. Management can then compare this risk exposure to the FI's capital resources.

---

[2] J. P. Morgan, *Introduction to RiskMetrics* (New York: J. P. Morgan, October 1994), p. 2. There is an ongoing debate about whether spread risk is a part of market risk or credit risk. J. P. Morgan, includes spread risk as credit risk (and includes it in the CreditMetrics measure [see Chapter 11]) rather than as part of market risk. OSFI defines market risk for capital adequacy purposes as "the risk of losses in on- and off-balance sheet positions arising from movements in market prices, including interest rates, exchange rates, and equity values." (OSFI, Capital Adequacy Requirements A-Part I, January 2001).

[3] Market risk used by FI managers and regulators is not synonymous with systematic market risk analyzed by investors in securities markets. Systematic (market) risk reflects the comovement of a security with the market portfolio (reflected by the security's beta), although beta is used to measure the market risk of equities, as noted below.

[4] This requirement was introduced in 1996 in the EU and in 1998 in the U.S. OSFI applies the market risk framework to deposit-taking institutions whose trading book assets or trading book liabilities (market value) represent 10% of total assets, or are greater than $1 billion.

2. *Setting limits.* MRM considers the market risk of traders' portfolios, which will lead to the establishment of economically logical position limits per trader in each area of trading.

3. *Resource allocation.* MRM involves the comparison of returns to market risks in different areas of trading, which may allow the identification of areas with the greatest potential return per unit of risk into which more capital and resources can be directed.

4. *Performance evaluation.* MRM, relatedly, considers the return-risk ratio of traders, which may allow a more rational bonus (compensation) system to be put in place. That is, those traders with the highest returns may simply be the ones who have taken the largest risks. It is not clear that they should receive higher compensation than traders with lower returns and lower risk exposures.

www.bis.org
www.osfi-bsif.gc.ca

5. *Regulation.* The Bank for International Settlements (BIS) and OSFI currently regulate market risk through capital requirements (discussed later in this chapter). OSFI allows Canadian federally-regulated FIs to use internally-developed models to calculate their capital requirements. All of the Big Six banks therefore have their own models to evaluate market risks. The banks will run parallel Basel I and Basel II systems from November 1, 2005 and switch over to Basel II on November 1, 2007.[5]

Concept Questions

1. What is market risk?
2. Why is market risk measurement important for FIs?

CALCULATING MARKET RISK EXPOSURE

Large banks, insurance companies, and mutual funds have all developed market risk models. In the development of these internal models three major approaches have been followed:

- RiskMetrics (or the variance/covariance approach).
- Historic or back simulation.
- Monte Carlo simulation.

We consider RiskMetrics[6] first and then compare it with other internal model approaches, such as historic or back simulation.

THE RISKMETRICS MODEL

The ultimate objective of market risk measurement models can best be seen from the following quote by Dennis Weatherstone, former chairman of J. P. Morgan (JPM), now J. P. Morgan Chase: "At close of business each day tell me what the market risks are across all businesses and locations." In a nutshell, the chairman of J. P. Morgan wants a single *dollar* number at 4:15 PM New York time that tells him J. P. Morgan's market risk exposure the next day—especially if that day turns out to be a "bad" day.

---

[5] Since regulators are concerned with the social costs of a failure or insolvency, including contagion effects and other externalities, regulatory models will normally tend to be more conservative than private sector models that are concerned only with the private costs of failure.

[6] J. P. Morgan (JPM) first developed RiskMetrics in 1994. In 1998 the development group formed a separate company, partly owned by JPM. The material presented in this chapter is an overview of the RiskMetrics model. The details, additional discussion, and examples are found in "Return to RiskMetrics: The Evolution of a Standard," April 2001, available at the J. P. Morgan Chase Web site, **www.jpmorganchase.com** or **www.riskmetrics.com**.

TABLE 10–2　JPM's Trading Business

	Fixed Income	Foreign Exchange STIRI*	Commodities	Derivatives	Equities	Emergency Markets	Proprietary	Total
Number of active locations	14	12	5	11	8	7	11	14
Number of independent risk-taking units	30	21	8	16	14	11	19	120
Thousands of transactions per day	>5	>5	<1	<1	>5	<1	<1	>20
Billions of dollars in daily trading volume	>10	>30	1	1	<1	1	8	>50

*Short-term interest rate instruments.

Source: J. P. Morgan, *Introduction to RiskMetrics* (New York: J. P. Morgan, October 1994). www.jpmorganchase.com

This is nontrivial, given the extent of JPM's trading business. As shown in Table 10–2, when JPM developed its RiskMetrics Model in 1994 it had 14 active trading locations with 120 independent units trading fixed-income securities, foreign exchange, commodities, derivatives, emerging-market securities, and proprietary assets, with a total daily volume exceeding US $50 billion. This scale and variety of activities is typical of the major banks, large overseas banks (e.g., Deutsche Bank and Barclays), and major insurance companies.

Here, we will concentrate on measuring the market risk exposure of a major FI on a daily basis using the RiskMetrics approach. As will be discussed later, measuring the risk exposure for periods longer than a day (e.g., five days) is under certain assumptions a simple transformation of the daily risk exposure number.

Essentially, the FI is concerned with how much it can potentially lose if market conditions move adversely tomorrow; that is:

Market risk = Estimated potential loss under adverse circumstances

daily value at risk (daily VAR)
Market risk exposure over the next 24 hours.

More specifically, the market risk is measured in terms of the FI's **daily value at risk (daily VAR)**[7] and has three components:

$$\text{Daily value at risk} = \begin{pmatrix} \text{Dollar market} \\ \text{value of} \\ \text{the position} \end{pmatrix} \times \begin{pmatrix} \text{Price} \\ \text{sensitivity of} \\ \text{the position} \end{pmatrix} \times \begin{pmatrix} \text{Potential} \\ \text{adverse move} \\ \text{in yield} \end{pmatrix} \quad \textbf{(10.1)}$$

Since price sensitivity multiplied by adverse yield move measures the degree of price volatility of an asset, we can also write equation (1) as equation (2):

$$\text{Daily value at risk} = \begin{pmatrix} \text{Dollar market} \\ \text{value of} \\ \text{the position} \end{pmatrix} \times \begin{pmatrix} \text{Price} \\ \text{volatility} \end{pmatrix} \quad \textbf{(10.2)}$$

---

[7] Although Risk Metrics calls market risk exposure daily earnings at risk (DEAR), we adopt the more common usage, daily value at risk, also called daily VAR, daily VaR, or often shortened to VAR or VaR.

How price sensitivity and an adverse yield move will be measured depends on the FI and its choice of a price-sensitivity model as well as its view of what exactly is a potentially adverse price (yield) move.

We concentrate on how the RiskMetrics model calculates daily earnings at risk in three trading areas—fixed income, foreign exchange (FX), and equities—and then on how it estimates the aggregate risk of the entire trading portfolio to meet Dennis Weatherstone's objective of a single aggregate dollar exposure measure across the whole bank at 4:15 PM each day.[8]

The Market Risk of Fixed-Income Securities

Suppose an FI has a $1 million market value position in zero-coupon bonds of seven years to maturity with a face value of $1,631,483.[9] Today's yield on these bonds is 7.243 percent per annum. These bonds are held as part of the trading portfolio. Thus,

$$\text{Dollar market value of position} = \$1 \text{ million}$$

The FI manager wants to know the potential exposure the FI faces should interest rates move against the FI as the result of an adverse or reasonably bad market move the next day. How much the FI will lose depends on the bond's price volatility. From the duration model in Chapter 9 we know that:

$$\text{Daily price volatility} = (\text{Price sensitivity to a small change in yield})$$
$$\times (\text{Adverse daily yield move})$$

$$= (MD) \times (\text{Adverse daily yield move}) \qquad \textbf{(10.3)}$$

The modified duration (MD) of this bond is:[10]

$$MD = \frac{D}{1 + R} = \frac{7}{(1.07243)} = 6.527$$

given that the yield on the bond is $R = 7.243$ percent. To estimate price volatility, multiply the bond's MD by the expected adverse daily yield move.

EXAMPLE 10–1

Daily Value at Risk on Fixed-Income Securities

Suppose we define bad yield changes such that there is only a 5 percent chance that the yield changes will exceed this amount in either direction—or, since we are concerned only with bad outcomes, and we are long in bonds, that there is 1 chance in 20 (or a 5 percent chance) that the next day's yield increase (or shock) will exceed this given adverse move.

---

[8] It is clear from the above discussion that interest rate risk (see Chapters 8 and 9) is part of market risk. However, in market risk models, we are concerned with the interest rate sensitivity of the fixed-income securities held as part of an FI's active trading portfolio. Many fixed-income securities are held as part of an FI's investment portfolio. While the latter are subject to interest rate risk, they will not be included in a market risk calculation.

[9] The face value of the bonds is $1,631,483—that is, $1,631,483/(1.07243)^7 = \$1,000,000$ market value. In the original model, prices were determined using a discrete rate of return, R_j. In the 2001 document "Return to RiskMetrics: The Evolution of a Standard," April 2001, prices are determined using a continuously compounded return, e^{-rt}. The change was implemented because continuous compounding has properties that facilitate mathematical treatment. For example, the logarithmic return on a zero-coupon bond equals the difference of interest rates multiplied by the maturity of the bond. That is:

$$\log \left(\frac{e^{-\bar{r}t}}{e^{-rt}} \right) = (\bar{r} - r)t$$

where $\bar{r}$ is the expected return.

[10] Assuming annual compounding for simplicity.

If we assume that yield changes are normally distributed,[11] we can fit a normal distribution to the histogram of recent past changes in seven-year zero-coupon interest rates (yields) to get an estimate of the size of this adverse rate move. From statistics, we know that (the middle) 90 percent of the area under the normal distribution is to be found within ± 1.65 standard deviations (σ) from the mean—that is, 1.65σ—and 10 percent of the area under the normal distribution is found beyond $\pm 1.65\sigma$ (5 percent under each tail, -1.65σ and $+1.65\sigma$, respectively). Suppose that during the last year the mean change in daily yields on seven-year zero-coupon bonds was 0 percent[12] the standard deviation was 10 basis points (or 0.001). Thus, 1.65σ is 16.5 basis points (bp).[13] In other words, over the last year, daily yields on seven-year, zero-coupon bonds have fluctuated (either positively or negatively) by more than 16.5 bp 10 percent of the time. Adverse moves in yields are those that decrease the value of the security (i.e., the yield increases). These occurred 5 percent of the time, or 1 in 20 days. This is shown in Figure 10–1.

We can now calculate the potential daily price volatility on seven-year discount bonds using equation (3) as:

$$\text{Price volatility} = (MD) \times (\text{Potential adverse move in yield})$$
$$= (6.527) \times (.00165)$$
$$= .01077 \text{ or } 1.077\%$$

Given this price volatility and the initial market value of the seven-year bond portfolio, then equation (2) can be used to calculate the daily earnings at risk as:[14]

$$\text{Daily value at risk} = (\text{Dollar market value of position}) \times (\text{Price volatility})$$
$$= (\$1,000,000) \times (.01077)$$
$$= \$10,770$$

That is, the potential daily loss on the $1 million position is $10,770 if the 1 bad day in 20 occurs tomorrow.

We can extend this analysis to calculate the potential loss over 2, 3, . . ., N days. If we assume that yield shocks are independent and daily volatility is approximately constant,[15] and that the FI is locked in to holding this asset for N number of days, then the N-day market value at risk (VAR) is related to daily value at risk (daily VAR) by:

$$VAR = \text{daily } VAR \times \sqrt{N}$$

---

[11] In reality, many asset return distributions—such as exchange rates and interest rates—have "fat tails." Thus, the normal distribution will tend to underestimate extreme outcomes. This is a major criticism of the RiskMetrics modeling approach. (See later footnote and references.)

[12] If the mean were nonzero (e.g., −1 basis point), this could be added to the 16.5 bp (i.e., 15.5 bp) to project the yield shock

[13] RiskMetrics weights more recent observations more highly than past observations (this is called *exponential weighting*). This allows more recent news to be more heavily reflected in the calculation of σ. Regular σ calculations put an equal weight on all past observations.

[14] Since we are calculating loss, we drop the minus sign here.

[15] The assumptions that daily volatility is constant and that there is no autocorrelation in yield shocks are strong assumptions. Much recent literature suggests that shocks are autocorrelated in many asset markets over relatively long horizons. To understand why we take the square root of N, consider a five-day holding period. The σ_5^2, or five-day variance of asset returns, will equal the current one-day variance σ_1^2 times 5 under the assumptions of constant daily variance and no autocorrelation in shocks, or:

$$\sigma_5^2 = \sigma_1^2 \times 5$$

The standard deviation of this equation is:

$$\sigma_5 = \sigma_1 \times \sqrt{5}$$

or since daily VAR is measured in the same dimensions as a standard deviation (σ), in the terminology of RiskMetrics, the five-day value at risk (VAR_5) is:

$$VAR_5 = \text{daily } VAR \times \sqrt{5}$$

FIGURE 10–1
Adverse Rate Move,
Seven-Year Rates

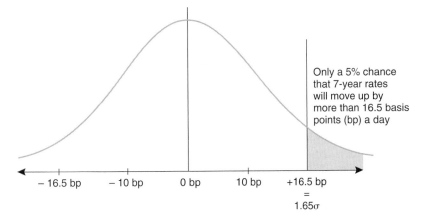

Only a 5% chance that 7-year rates will move up by more than 16.5 basis points (bp) a day

−16.5 bp   −10 bp   0 bp   10 bp   +16.5 bp
= 1.65σ

That is, the earnings the FI has at risk, should interest rate yields move against the FI, are a function of the value or earnings at risk for one day (daily VAR) and the (square root of the) number of days that the FI is forced to hold the securities because of an illiquid market. Specifically, daily VAR assumes that the FI can sell all the bonds tomorrow, even at the new lower price. In reality, it may take many days for the FI to unload its position. This relative illiquidity of a market exposes the FI to magnified losses (measured by the square root of N).[16] If N is five days, then:

$$VAR = \$10,770 \times \sqrt{5} = \$24,082$$

If N is 10 days, then:[17]

$$VAR = \$10,770 \times \sqrt{10} = \$34,057$$

In the above calculations, we estimated price sensitivity using modified duration. However, the RiskMetrics model generally prefers using the present value of cash flow changes as the price-sensitivity weights over modified durations. Essentially, each cash flow is discounted by the appropriate zero-coupon rate to generate the daily earnings at risk measure. If we used the direct cash flow calculation in this case, the loss would be $10,771.2.[18] The estimates in this case are very close.

Foreign Exchange

Large FIs actively trade in foreign exchange (FX). Remember that:

$$\text{daily } VAR = (\text{Dollar value of position}) \times (\text{Price volatility})$$

EXAMPLE 10–2

Daily Value at Risk of Foreign Exchange Contracts

Suppose the FI had a €1.6 million trading position in spot euros at the close of business on a particular day. The FI wants to calculate the daily value at risk from this position (i.e., the risk exposure on this position should the next day be a bad day in the FX markets with respect to the value of the euro against the dollar).

---

[16] In practice, a number of FIs calculate N internally by dividing the position held in a security by the median daily volume of trading of that security over recent days. Thus, if trading volume is low because of a "one-way market," in that most people are seeking to sell rather than buy, then N can rise substantially; that is, $N = (\$ \text{ position in security/median daily } \$ \text{ volume of trading})$.

[17] Under the BIS 1998 market risk capital requirements, a 10-day holding period ($N = 10$) is assumed to measure exposure.

[18] The initial market value of the seven-year zero was $1,000,000, or $1,631,483/(1.07243)^7. The (loss) effect on each $1 (market value) invested in the bond of a rise in rates by 1 bp from 7.243 percent to 7.253 percent is .0006528. However, the adverse rate move is 16.5 bp. Thus:

daily $VAR = (\$1 \text{ million}) \times (.0006528) \times (16.5) = \$10,771.2$

The first step is to calculate the dollar value of the position:

Dollar equivalent value of position = (FX position) × (€/$ spot exchange rate)

= (€1.6 million) × ($ per unit of foreign currency)

If the exchange rate is €1.60/$1 or $0.625/€ at the daily close, then

Dollar value of position = (€ 1.6 million) × ($0.625/€)

= $1 million

Suppose that, looking back at the daily changes in the €/$ exchange rate over the past year, we find that the volatility, or standard deviation (σ), of daily changes in the spot exchange rate was 56.5 bp. However, suppose that the FI is interested in adverse moves—that is, bad moves that will not occur more than 5 percent of the time, or 1 day in every 20. Statistically speaking, if changes in exchange rates are historically "normally" distributed, the exchange rate must change in the adverse direction by 1.65σ (1.65 × 56.5 bp) for this change to be viewed as likely to occur only 1 day in every 20 days:[19]

FX volatility = 1.65 × 56.5 bp = 93.2 bp or 0.932%

In other words, during the last year, the euro declined in value against the dollar by 93.2 bp 5 percent of the time. As a result:

daily *VAR* = (Dollar value of position) × (FX volatility)

= ($1 million) × (.00932)

= $9,320

This is the potential daily earnings exposure to adverse euro to dollar exchange rate changes for the FI from the €1.6 million spot currency holdings.

Equities

Many large FIs also take positions in equities. As is well known from the Capital Asset Pricing Model (CAPM), there are two types of risk to an equity position in an individual stock i:[20]

$$\text{Total risk} = \text{Systematic risk} + \text{Unsystematic risk}$$
$$(\sigma_{it}^2) = (\beta_i^2 \sigma_{mt}^2) + (\sigma_{eit}^2)$$

beta
Systematic (undiversifiable) risk reflecting the comovement of the returns on a specific stock with returns on the market portfolio.

Systematic risk reflects the comovement of that stock with the market portfolio reflected by the stock's **beta** (β_i) and the volatility of the market portfolio (σ_{mt}), whereas unsystematic risk is specific to the firm itself (σ_{eit}).

In a very well diversified portfolio, unsystematic risk (σ_{eit}^2) can be largely diversified away (i.e., will equal zero), leaving behind systematic (undiversifiable) market risk ($\beta_i^2\sigma_{mt}^2$). If the FI's trading portfolio follows (replicates) the returns on the stock market index, the β of that portfolio will be 1, since the movement of returns on the FI's portfolio will be one to one with the market,[21] and the standard deviation of the portfolio, σ_{it}, will be equal to the standard deviation of the stock market index, σ_{mt}.

---

[19] Technically, 90 percent of the area under a normal distribution lies between ±1.65σ from the mean. This means that 5 percent of the time, daily exchange rate changes will increase by more than 1.65σ, and 5 percent of the time, will decrease by 1.65σ. This case concerns only adverse moves in the exchange rate of euros to dollars (i.e., a depreciation of 1.65σ).

[20] This assumes that systematic and unsystematic risks are independent of each other.

[21] If $\beta \neq 1$, as in the case of most individual stocks, daily VAR = dollar value of position × β_i × 1.65σ_m, where β_i is the systematic risk of the ith stock.

EXAMPLE 10–3

Daily Value at Risk on Equities

Suppose the FI holds a $1 million trading position in stocks that reflect a stock market index (e.g., the S&P TSX Composite Index). Then β = 1 and the daily VAR for equities is:

daily VAR = (Dollar market value of position) × (Stock market return volatility)
= ($1,000,000) × (1.65 σ_m)

If, over the last year, the σ_m of the daily returns on the stock market index was 2 percent, then 1.65 σ_m = 3.3 percent (i.e., the adverse change or decline in the daily return on the stock market exceeded 3.3 percent only 5 percent of the time). In this case:

daily VAR = ($1,000,000) × (0.033)
= $33,000

That is, the FI stands to lose at least $33,000 in earnings if adverse stock market returns materialize tomorrow.[22]

In less well diversified portfolios or portfolios of individual stocks, the effect of unsystematic risk σ_{eit} on the value of the trading position would need to be added. Moreover, if the CAPM does not offer a good explanation of asset pricing compared with, say, multi-index arbitrage pricing theory (APT), a degree of error will be built into the daily VAR calculation.[23]

Portfolio Aggregation

The preceding sections analyzed the daily earnings at risk of individual trading positions. The examples considered a seven-year, zero-coupon, fixed-income security ($1 million market value); a position in spot euros ($1 million market value); and a position in the stock market index ($1 million market value). The individual daily VARs were:

1. Seven-year zero-coupon bonds = $10,770
2. Euro spot = $9,320
3. Equities = $33,000

However, senior management wants to know the aggregate risk of the entire trading position. To calculate this, we *cannot* simply sum the three VARs—$10,770 + $9,320 + $33,000 = $53,090—because that ignores any degree of offsetting covariance or correlation among the fixed-income, FX, and equity trading positions. In particular, some of these asset shocks (adverse moves) may be negatively correlated. As is well known from modern portfolio theory, negative correlations among asset shocks will reduce the degree of portfolio risk.

---

[22] If we consider a single equity security with a beta (β) = 1.25 (i.e., one that is more sensitive than the market, such that as market returns increase [decrease] by 1 percent, the security's return increases [decreases] by 1.25 percent), then with a $1 million investment and the same (assumed) volatility (σ) of 2 percent (such that 1.65 × .02 = 0.033, or 3.3 percent), the FI would stand to lose at least $41,250 in daily earnings if adverse stock returns materializes (i.e., daily VAR = $1,000,000 × 1.25 × 0.033 = $41,250).

[23] As noted in the introduction, derivatives are also used for trading purposes. In the calculation of its daily VAR, a derivative has to be converted into a position in the underlying asset (e.g., bond, FX, or equity).

TABLE 10–3
Correlations (ρ_{ij}) among Assets

	Seven-Year Zero	€/$1	Stock Index
Seven-year zero	—	−.2	.4
€/$1		—	.1
Stock index			—

EXAMPLE 10–4

Calculation of the daily VAR of a Portfolio

Table 10–3 shows a hypothetical correlation matrix between daily seven-year zero-coupon bond yield changes, €/$ spot exchange rate changes, and changes in daily returns on a stock market index. From Table 10–3, the correlation between the seven-year zero-coupon bonds and €/$ exchange rates, $\rho_{z,\epsilon}$, is negative (−.2), while the seven-year zero-coupon yield changes with stock returns, $\rho_{z,m}$, (.4) and €/$ shocks, $\rho_{m,\epsilon}$, (.1) are positively correlated.

Using this correlation matrix along with the individual asset DEARs, we can calculate the risk or standard deviation of the whole (three-asset) trading portfolio as:[24]

$$\text{daily VAR portfolio} = \begin{bmatrix} [\text{VAR}_z]^2 + (\text{VAR}_\epsilon)^2 + (\text{VAR}_m)^2 \\ + (2 \times \rho_{z\epsilon} \times \text{VAR}_z \times \text{VAR}_\epsilon) \\ + (2 \times \rho_{z,m} \times \text{VAR}_z \times \text{VAR}_m) \\ + (2 \times \rho_{m,\epsilon} \times \text{VAR}_m \times \text{VAR}_\epsilon)] \end{bmatrix}^{1/2} \quad (10.4)$$

This is a direct application of modern portfolio theory (MPT) since VARs are directly similar to standard deviations. Substituting into this equation the calculated individual VARs (in thousands of dollars), we get:

$$\text{daily VAR portfolio} = \begin{bmatrix} [(10.77)^2 + (9.32)^2 + (33)^2 + 2(-.2)(10.77)(9.32) \\ + 2(.4)(10.77)(33) + 2(.1)(9.32)(33)] \end{bmatrix}^{1/2}$$

$$= \$39,969$$

The equation indicates that considering the risk of each trading position as well as the correlation structure among those positions' returns results in a lower measure of portfolio trading risk ($39,969) than when risks of the underlying trading positions (the sum of which was $53,090) are added. A quick check will reveal that had we assumed that all three assets were perfectly positively correlated (i.e., $\rho_{ij} = 1$), daily VAR for the portfolio would have been $53,090 (i.e., equal to the sum of the three VARs). Clearly, even in abnormal market conditions, assuming that asset returns are perfectly correlated will exaggerate the degree of actual trading risk exposure.

Table 10–4 shows the type of spreadsheet used by U.S. FIs to calculate VAR. As you can see, in this example, positions can be taken in 13 different country (currency) bonds in eight different maturity buckets.[25] There is also a column for FX risk (and, if necessary, equity risk) in these different country markets, although in this example, the FI has no FX risk exposure (all the cells are empty).

---

[24] This is a standard relationship from modern portfolio theory in which the standard deviation or risk of a portfolio of three assets is equal to the square root of the sum of the variances of returns on each of the three assets individually plus two times the covariances among each pair of these assets. With three assets there are three covariances. Here we use the fact that a correlation coefficient times the standard deviations on each pair of assets equals the covariance between each pair of assets. Note that DEAR is measured in dollars and has the same dimensions as a standard deviation. We discuss Modern Portfolio Theory in more detail in Chapter 12.

[25] Bonds held with different maturity dates (e.g., six years) are split into two and allocated to the nearest two of the eight maturity buckets (here, five years and seven years) using three criteria: (1) The sum of the current market *value* of the two resulting cash flows must be identical to the market value of the original cash flow; (2) the market *risk* of the portfolio of two cash flows must be identical to the overall market risk of the original cash flow; and (3) the two cash flows have the same *sign* as the original cash flow. See J. P. Morgan, "RiskMetrics—Technical Document," November 1994, and "Return to RiskMetrics: The Evolution of a Standard," April 2001. **www.jpmorganchase.com** or **www.riskmetrics.com**.

TABLE 10–4   Portfolio Daily VAR Spreadsheet

	Interest Rate Risk Notional Amounts (U.S. $ millions equivalents)									FX Risk		Total	
	1 Month	1 Year	2 Years	3 Years	4 Years	5 Years	7 Years	10 Years	Interest VAR	Spot FX	FX VAR	Portfolio Effect	Total VAR
Australia										AUD			
Brazil										BRL			
Canada										CAD			
Denmark	19			−30				11	48	DKK			48
European Union	−19			30				−11	27	EUR			27
Hong Kong										HKD			
Japan										YEN			
Mexico										MXN			
Singapore										SGD			
Sweden										SEK			
Switzerland										CHF			
United Kingdom										GBP			
United States						10		10	76	USD			76
Total						10		10	151				151
							Portfolio effect		(62)				(62)
							Total VAR ($000s)		89				89

Source: J. P. Morgan, *RiskMetrics* (New York: J. P. Morgan, 1994). www.jpmorgan.com, www.riskmetrics.com

In the example in Table 10–4, while the FI is holding offsetting long and short positions in both Danish and Euro bonds, it is still exposed to trading risks of $48,000 and $27,000, respectively (see the column Interest VAR). This happens because the European Union yield curve is more volatile than the Danish and shocks at different maturity buckets are not equal. The VAR figure for a U.S. bond position of long $20 million is $76,000. Adding these three positions yields a VAR of $151,000. However, this ignores the fact that Danish, European Union, and U.S. yield shocks are not perfectly correlated. Allowing for diversification effects (the portfolio effect) results in a total VAR of only $89,000. This would be the number reported to the FI's senior management. Most financial institutions establish limits for value at risk, daily earnings at risk, position limits, and dollar trading loss limits for their trading portfolios. Actual activity compared with these limits is then monitored daily. Should a risk exposure level exceed approved limit levels, management must provide a strategy for bringing risk levels within approved limits. Table 10–5 reports the average, minimum, and maximum daily value at risk reported by five large Canadian banks in 2004 for their trading portfolios. Table 10–6 shows the makeup of the $7.3 million average VAR reported by CIBC for 2004 for its trading portfolio. As can be seen by the table, CIBC calculates

www.bmo.com
www.cibc.com
www.nbc.ca
www.scotiabank.com

TABLE 10–5
Total Daily VAR
for the trading
portfolios of
Canadian Banks,
2004* (in millions
of dollars)

Source: 2004 Annual Reports

Name	Average VAR for the year 2004	Minimum VAR during 2004	Maximum VAR during 2004
Bank of Montreal	18.9	14.1	28.4
CIBC	7.3	5.4	10.5
National Bank	5.0	2.7	7.6
Royal Bank	13	8	25
Scotiabank	8.8	4.2	19.0

* The figures are based on the banks' internal models and may be based on methodologies that differ from RiskMetrics.

TABLE 10–6   VAR by Risk Type for the trading and non-trading portfolios of CIBC, 2004

$ million as at or for the year ended October 31	2004							2003
	Year-end	Average	High	Low	Year-end	Average	High	Low
Interest rate risk	6.0	4.4	8.8	2.1	2.5	3.7	8.1	1.9
Credit spread risk	2.9	2.7	5.0	2.2	2.6	4.3	7.0	2.3
Equity risk	4.7	5.2	7.4	4.3	5.4	6.3	9.7	4.1
Foreign exchange risk	0.2	0.7	2.1	0.2	1.0	0.6	1.7	0.2
Commodity risk	2.0	1.5	3.2	0.8	0.8	1.3	2.7	0.7
Diversification effect[1]	(7.0)	(7.2)	NM[2]	NM[2]	(6.1)	(7.0)	NM	NM
Total risk	8.8	7.3	10.5	5.4	6.2	9.2	16.4	5.3

(1) Aggregate VAR is less than the sum of the VAR of the different market risk, types due to risk offsets resulting from portfolio diverstration.
(2) Not meaningful. It is not meaningful to complete a diverstication effect because the high and low may occur on different days for different risk types.

Source: CIBC 2004 Annual Report, p. 82, *www.cibc.com*

interest rate risk and credit spread risk related to trading in Canadian, U.S. and global government and corporate debt and derivatives markets. The equity risk arises from trading primarily U.S., Canadian, and European stocks. Foreign exchange risk represents exposure to the U.S. dollar, the Euro, the British pound and the Japanese yen. Commodity risk arises from North American natural gas and oil product indices. Since the risks are correlated, the total is adjusted for the effects of diversification, a reduction from the average VAR of $7.3 million in 2004. The average VAR has also decreased slightly from 2003.[26]

As an indication of the complexity of the calculations for a large FI, the number of markets covered by J. P. Morgan Chase's traders and the number of correlations among those markets require the daily production and updating of over 450 volatility estimates (σ) and correlations (ρ). The data are updated daily, requiring a significant investment in computer technology and time.

Concept Questions

1. What is the ultimate objective of market risk measurement models?
2. Refer to Example 10–1. What is the VAR for this bond if σ is 15 bp?
3. Refer to Example 10–4. What is the VAR of the portfolio if the returns on the three assets are independent of each other?

[26] See CIBC's 2004 Annual Report, pp. 82–85 at www.cibc.com.

HISTORIC (BACK SIMULATION) APPROACH

A major criticism of VAR models is the need to assume a symmetric (normal) distribution for all asset returns.[27] Clearly, for some assets, such as options and short-term securities (bonds), this is highly questionable. For example, the most an investor can lose if he or she buys a call option on an equity is the call premium; however, the investor's potential upside returns are unlimited. In a statistical sense, the returns on call options are nonnormal since they exhibit a positive skew.[28]

Because of these and other considerations discussed below, the large majority of FIs (e.g. RBC, CIBC, BNS, BMO, and National Bank) that have developed market risk models have employed a historic or back simulation approach. The advantages of this approach are that (1) it is simple, (2) it does not require that asset returns be normally distributed, and (3) it does not require that the correlations or standard deviations of asset returns be calculated.

The essential idea is to take the current market portfolio of assets (FX, bonds, equities, etc.) and revalue them on the basis of the actual prices (returns) that existed on those assets yesterday, the day before that, and so on. Frequently, the FI will calculate the market or value risk of its current portfolio on the basis of prices (returns) that existed for those assets on each of the last 500 days. It will then calculate the 5 percent worst case—the portfolio value that has the 25th lowest value out of 500. That is, on only 25 days out of 500, or 5 percent of the time, would the value of the portfolio fall below this number based on recent historic experience of exchange rate changes, equity price changes, interest rate changes, and so on.

Consider the following simple example in Table 10–6, where an FI is trading two currencies: the Japanese yen and the Swiss franc. At the close of trade on December 1, 2006, it has a long position in Japanese yen of 500,000,000 and a long position in Swiss francs of 20,000,000. It wants to assess its VAR. That is, if tomorrow is that 1 bad day in 20 (the 5 percent worst case), how much does it stand to lose on its total foreign currency position? As shown in Table 10–6, six steps are required to calculate the VAR of its currency portfolio. It should be noted that the same methodological approach would be followed to calculate the VAR of any asset, liability, or derivative (bonds, options, etc.) as long as market prices were available on those assets over a sufficiently long historic time period.

---

[27] Another criticism is that VAR models like RiskMetrics ignore the (risk in the) payments of accrued interest on an FI's debt securities. Thus, VAR models will underestimate the true probability of default and the appropriate level of capital to be held against this risk (see P. Kupiec, "Risk Capital and VAR," *The Journal of Derivatives*, Winter 1999, pp. 41–52). Also, Johansson, Seiles, and Tjarnberg find that because of the distributional assumptions, while RiskMetrics produces reasonable estimates of downside risk for FIs with highly diversified portfolios, FIs with small, undiversified portfolios will significantly underestimate their true risk exposure using RiskMetrics (see, F. Johansson, M. J. Seiles, and M. Tjarnberg, "Measuring Downside Portfolio Risks," *The Journal of Portfolio Management*, Fall 1999, pp. 96–107). Further, a number of authors have argued that many asset distributions have "fat tails" and that RiskMetrics, by assuming the normal distribution, underestimates the risk of extreme losses. See, for example, Salih F. Neftci, "Value at Risk Calculations, Extreme Events and Tail Estimations," *Journal of Derivatives*, Spring 2000, pp. 23–37. One alternative approach to dealing with the "fat-tail" problem is extreme value theory. Simply put, one can view an asset distribution as being explained by two distributions. For example, a normal distribution may explain returns up to the 95 percent threshold, but for losses beyond that threshold another distribution, such as the generalized Pareto distribution, may provide a better explanation of loss outcomes such as the 99 percent level and beyond. In short, the normal distribution is likely to underestimate the importance and size of observations in the tail of the distribution, which is, after all, what value at risk models are meant to be measuring (see also Alexander J. McNeil, "Extreme Value Theory for Risk Managers," Working Paper, Department of Mathematics, ETH Zentrom, Ch-8092, Zurich, Switzerland, May 17, 1999). Finally, VAR models by definition concern themselves with risk rather than return. It should be noted that minimizing risk may be highly costly in terms of the return the FI gives up. Indeed, there may be many more return–risk combinations preferable to that achieved at the minimum risk point in the trading portfolio. Recent upgrades to RiskMetrics (see the RiskMetrics Web site at **www.riskmetrics.com**) allow management to incorporate a return dimension to VAR analysis so that management can evaluate how trading portfolio returns differ as VAR changes.

[28] For a normal distribution, its skew (which is the third moment of a distribution) is zero.

TABLE 10–7   Hypothetical Example of the Historic, or Back Simulation, Approach Using Two Currencies, as of December 1, 2006

	Yen	Swiss Franc
Step 1. Measure Exposures		
1. Closing position on December 1, 2006	500,000,000	20,000,000
2. Exchange rate on December 1, 2006	¥130/$1	SF 1.4/$1
3. U.S. $ equivalent position on December 1, 2006	3,846,154	14,285,714
Step 2. Measure Sensitivity		
4. 1.01 × current exchange rate	¥131.3	SF 1.414
5. Revalued position in $	3,808,073	14,144,272
6. Delta of position ($) (measure of sensitivity to a 1% adverse change in exchange rate, or row 5 minus row 3)	−38,081	−141,442

Step 3. Measure risk of December 1, 2006, closing position using exchange rates that existed on each of the last 500 days

November 30, 2006	Yen	Swiss Franc
7. Change in exchange rate (%) on November 30, 2006	0.5%	0.2%
8. Risk (delta × change in exchange rate)	−19,040.5	−28,288.4
9. Sum of risks = −$47,328.9		

Step 4. Repeat Step 3 for each of the remaining 499 days

November 29, 2006
    ⋮

April 15, 2005
    ⋮

November 30, 2004
    ⋮

Step 5. Rank days by risk from worst to best

Date	Risk ($)
1. May 6, 2005	−105,669
2. Jan 27, 2006	−103,276
3. Dec 1, 2004	−90,939
⋮	⋮
25. Nov 30, 2006	−47,328.9
⋮	⋮
499. April 8, 2006	+98,833
500. July 28, 2005	+108,376

Step 6. VAR (25th worst day out of last 500)

VAR = −47,328.9 (November 30, 2006)

- *Step 1: Measure exposures.* Convert today's foreign currency positions into dollar equivalents using today's exchange rates. Thus, an evaluation of the FX position of the FI on December 1, 2006, indicates that it has a long position of $3,846,154 in yen and $14,285,714 in Swiss francs.

- *Step 2: Measure sensitivity.* Measure the sensitivity of each FX position by calculating its delta, where delta measures the change in the dollar value of each FX position if the yen or the Swiss franc depreciates (declines in value) by 1 percent against the dollar.[29] As can be seen from Table 10–6, line 6, the delta for the Japanese yen position is −$38,081, and for the Swiss franc position, it is − $141,442.

- *Step 3: Measure risk.* Look at the actual percentage changes in exchange rates, yen/$ and SF/$, on each of the past 500 days. Thus, on November 30, 2006, the yen declined in value against the dollar over the day by 0.5 percent while the Swiss franc declined in value against the dollar by 0.2 percent. (It might be noted that if the currencies were to appreciate in value against the dollar, the sign against the number in row 7 of Table 10–6 would be negative; that is, it takes fewer units of foreign currency to buy a dollar than it did the day before). As can be seen in row 8, combining the delta and the actual percentage change in each FX rate means a total loss of $47,328.9 if the FI had held the current ¥500,000,000 and SF 20,000,000 positions on that day (November 30, 2006).

- *Step 4: Repeat Step 3.* Step 4 repeats the same exercise for the yen and Swiss franc positions but uses actual exchange rate changes on November 29, 2006; November 28, 2006; and so on. That is, we calculate the FX losses and/or gains on each of the past 500 trading days, excluding weekends and holidays, when the FX market is closed. This amounts to going back in time over two years. For each of these days the actual change in exchange rates is calculated (row 7) and multiplied by the deltas of each position (the numbers in row 6 of Table 10–6). These two numbers are summed to attain total risk measures for each of the past 500 days.

- *Step 5: Rank days by risk from worst to best.* These risk measures can then be ranked from worst to best. Clearly the worst-case loss would have occurred on this position on May 6, 2005, with a total loss of $105,669. Although this worst-case scenario is of interest to FI managers, we are interested in the 5 percent worst case, that is, a loss that does not occur more than 25 days out of the 500 days (25 ÷ 500 equals 5 percent). As can be seen, in our example, the 25th worst loss out of 500 occurred on November 30, 2006. This loss amounted to $47,328.9.

- *Step 6: VAR.* If it is assumed that the recent past distribution of exchange rates is an accurate reflection of the likely distribution of FX rate changes in the future—that exchange rate changes have a stationary distribution—then the $47,328.9 can be viewed as the FX value at risk (VAR) exposure of the FI on December 1, 2006. That is, if tomorrow (in our case, December 2, 2006) is a bad day in the FX markets, and given the FI's position of long yen 500 million and long Swiss francs 20 million, the FI can expect to lose $47,328.9 (or more) with a 5 percent probability. This VAR measure can then be updated every day as the FX position changes and the delta changes. For example, given the nature of FX trading, the positions held on December 5, 2006, could be very different from those held on December 1, 2006.[30]

---

[29] That is, in the case of FX, delta measures the dollar change in FX holdings for a 1 percent change in the foreign exchange rate. In the case of equities, it would measure the change in the value of those securities for a 1 percent change in price, while for bonds, it measures the change in value for a 1 percent change in the price of the bond (note that delta measures sensitivity of a bond's value to a change in yield, not price).

[30] As in RiskMetrics, an adjustment can be made for illiquidity of the market, in this case, by assuming the FI is locked into longer holding periods. For example, if it is estimated that it will take five days for the FI to sell its FX position, then the FI will be interested in the weekly (i.e., five trading days) changes in FX rates in the past. One immediate problem is that with 500 past trading days, only 100 weekly periods would be available, which reduces the statistical power of the VAR estimate (see below).

The Historic (Back Simulation) Model versus RiskMetrics

One obvious benefit of the historic, or back simulation, approach is that we do not need to calculate standard deviations and correlations (or assume normal distributions for asset returns) to calculate the portfolio risk figures in row 9 of Table 10–6.[31] A second advantage is that it directly provides a worst-case scenario number, in our example, a loss of $105,669—see step 5. RiskMetrics, since it assumes asset returns are normally distributed—that returns can go to plus and minus infinity—provides no such worst-case scenario number.[32]

The disadvantage of the back simulation approach is the degree of confidence we have in the 5 percent VAR number based on 500 observations. Statistically speaking, 500 observations are not very many, so there will be a very wide confidence band (or standard error) around the estimated number ($47,328.9 in our example). One possible solution to the problem is to go back in time more than 500 days and estimate the 5 percent VAR based on 1,000 past daily observations (the 50th worst case) or even 10,000 past observations (the 500th worst case). The problem is that as one goes back farther in time, past observations may become decreasingly relevant in predicting VAR in the future. For example, 10,000 observations may require the FI to analyze FX data going back 40 years. Over this period we have moved through many very different FX regimes: from relatively fixed exchange rates in the 1950–70 period, to relatively floating exchange rates in the 1970s, to more managed floating rates in the 1980s and 1990s, to the abolition of exchange rates and the introduction of the euro in January 2002. Clearly, exchange rate behaviour and risk in a fixed-exchange rate regime will have little relevance to an FX trader or market risk manager operating and analyzing risk in a floating-exchange rate regime.

This seems to confront the market risk manager with a difficult modeling problem. There are, however, at least two approaches to this problem. The first is to weight past observations in the back simulation unequally, giving a higher weight to the more recent past observations.[33] The second is to use a Monte Carlo simulation approach, which generates additional observations that are consistent with recent historic experience. The latter approach, in effect, amounts to simulating or creating artificial trading days and FX rate changes.

The Monte Carlo Simulation Approach[34]

To overcome the problems imposed by a limited number of actual observations, we can generate additional observations (in our example, FX changes). Normally, the simulation or generation of these additional observations is structured using a Monte Carlo simulation approach so that returns or rates generated reflect the probability with which they have occurred in recent historic time periods. The first step is to calculate the historic variance-covariance matrix (Σ) of FX changes.

---

[31] The reason is that the historic, or back simulation, approach uses actual exchange rates on each day that explicitly include correlations or comovements with other exchange rates and asset returns on that day.

[32] The 5 percent number in RiskMetrics tells us that we will lose more than this amount on 5 days out of every 100; it does not tell us the maximum amount we can lose. As noted in the text, theoretically, with a normal distribution, this could be an infinite amount. See P. Christoffersen, "Meaningful Risk Measures", *Canadian Investment Review*, Winter 2003, Vol. 16, Iss. 4, pp. R15 for a discussion of this issue.

[33] See L. Allen, J. Boudoukh, and A. Saunders, *Understanding Market, Credit and Operational Risk: The Value at Risk Approach* (New York: Blackwell, 2004), Chapters 1–3.

[34] This section, which contains more technical details, may be included in or dropped from the chapter reading depending on the rigor of the course.

This matrix is then decomposed into two symmetric matrices, A and A'.[35] This allows the FI to generate scenarios for the FX position by multiplying the A' matrix, which reflects the historic volatilities and correlations among FX rates, by a random number vector z:[36] 10,000 random values of z are drawn for each FX exchange rate.[37] This simulation approach results in realistic FX scenarios being generated as historic volatilities and correlations among FX rates are multiplied by the randomly drawn values of z. The VAR of the current position is then calculated as in Table 10–7, except that in the Monte Carlo approach, the VAR is the 500th worst simulated loss out of 10,000.[38]

Concept Questions

1. What are the advantages of the historic, or bank simulation, approach over RiskMetrics to measure market risk?
2. What are the steps involved with the historic, or back simulation, approach to measuring market risk?
3. What is the Monte Carlo simulation approach to measuring market risk?

REGULATORY MODELS: THE BIS STANDARDIZED FRAMEWORK

The development of internal market risk models was partly in response to proposals by the Bank for International Settlement (BIS) in 1993 to measure and regulate the market risk exposures of banks by imposing capital requirements on their trading portfolios.[39] As noted in Chapter 7, the BIS is a organization encompassing the largest central banks in the world. After refining these proposals over a number of years, the BIS decided on a final approach to measuring market risk and the capital reserves necessary for an FI to hold to withstand and survive market risk losses. These required levels of capital held to protect against market risk exposure are in addition to the minimum level of capital banks are required to hold for credit risk purposes (see Chapter 20). Since January 1998[40] banks in the countries that are members of the BIS can calculate their market risk exposures in one of two ways. The first is to use a simple standardized framework (to be discussed below). The second, with regulatory approval, is to use their own internal models, which are similar to the models described above. However, if an internal model is approved for use in calculating capital requirements for the FI, it is subject to regulatory audit and certain constraints. Before looking at these constraints, we examine the BIS standardized framework for fixed-income securities, foreign exchange, and equities. Additional details of this model can be found at the BIS Web site, **www.bis.org**.[41]

www.bis.org

---

[35] The only difference between A and A' is that the numbers in the rows of A become the numbers in the columns of A'. The technical term for this procedure is the Cholesky decomposition, where $\Sigma = AA'$.

[36] Where z is assumed to be normally distributed with a mean of zero and a standard deviation of 1 or $z \sim N(0, 1)$.

[37] Technically, let y be an FX scenario; then $y = A'z$. For each FX rate, 10,000 values of z are randomly generated to produce 10,000 values of y. The y values are then used to revalue the FX position and calculate gains and losses.

[38] See, for example, J. P. Morgan, *RiskMetrics,* Technical Document, 4th ed., 1997.

[39] BIS, Basel Committee on Banking Supervision, "The Supervisory Treatment of Market Risks," Basel, Switzerland, April 1993; "Proposal to Issue a Supplement to the Basel Accord to Cover Market Risks," Basel, Switzerland, April 1995; and "The New Basel Capital Accord: Third Consultive Paper," Basel, Switzerland, April 2003.

[40] The requirements were introduced earlier in 1996 in the European Union.

[41] BIS, The Basel Committee on Banking Supervision, "Amendment to the Capital accord to Incorporate Market Risks," Basel, Switzerland, January 1996.

TABLE 10–8   **BIS Market Risk Calculation (Debt Securities, Sample Market Risk Calculation)**

Panel A: FI Holdings and Risk Charges

(1) Time Band	(2) Issuer	(3) Position ($)	Specific Risk		General Market Risk	
			(4) Weight (%)	(5) Charge	(6) Weight (%)	(7) Charge
0–1 month	Government	5,000	0.00	0.00	0.00	0.00
1–3 months	Government	5,000	0.00	0.00	0.20	10.00
3–6 months	Qual Corp	4,000	0.25	10.00	0.40	16.00
6–12 months	Qual Corp	(7,500)	1.00	75.00	0.70	(52.50)
1–2 years	Government	(2,500)	0.00	0.00	1.25	(31.25)
2–3 years	Government	2,500	0.00	0.00	1.75	43.75
3–4 years	Government	2,500	0.00	0.00	2.25	56.25
3–4 years	Qual Corp	(2,000)	1.60	32.00	2.25	(45.00)
4–5 years	Government	1,500	0.00	0.00	2.75	41.25
5–7 years	Qual Corp	(1,000)	1.60	16.00	3.25	(32.50)
7–10 years	Government	(1,500)	0.00	0.00	3.75	(56.25)
10–15 years	Government	(1,500)	0.00	0.00	4.50	(67.50)
10–15 years	Non Qual	1,000	8.00	80.00	4.50	45.00
15–20 years	Government	1,500	0.00	0.00	5.25	78.75
> 20 years	Qual Corp	1,000	1.60	16.00	6.00	60.00
Specific risk				229.00		
Residual general market risk						66.00

Panel B: Calculation of Capital Charge

(1)	(2)	(3)	(4)	(5)	(6)	(7) Charge
1. Specific Risk						229.00

2. Vertical Offsets within Same Time Bands

Time Band	Longs	Shorts	Residual*	Offset	Disallowance	Charge
3–4 years	56.25	(45.00)	11.25	45.00	10.00%	4.50
10–15 years	45.00	(67.50)	(22.50)	45.00	10.00	4.50

3. Horizontal Offsets within Same Time Zones

Zone 1						
0–1 month	0.00					
1–3 months	10.00					
3–6 months	16.00					
6–12 months		(52.50)				
Total zone 1	26.00	(52.50)	(26.50)	26.00	40.00%	10.40
Zone 2						
1–2 years		(31.25)				
2–3 years	43.75					
3–4 years	11.25					
Total zone 2	55.00	(31.25)	23.75	31.25	30.00%	9.38
Zone 3						
4–5 years	41.25					
5–7 years		(31.50)				
7–10 years		(56.25)				
10–15 years		(22.50)				
15–20 years	78.75					
>20 years	60.00					
Total zone 3	180.00	(111.25)	68.75	111.25	30.00%	33.38

(continued)

TABLE 10–8 (*concluded*)

Time Band	Longs	Shorts	Residual*	Offset	Disallowance	Charge
4. Horizontal Offsets between Time Zones						
Zones 1 and 2	23.75	(26.50)	(2.75)	23.75	40.00%	9.50
Zones 1 and 3	68.75	(2.75)	66.00	2.75	150.00%	4.12
5. Total Capital Charge						
Specific risk						229.00
Vertical disallowances						9.00
Horizontal disallowances						
Offsets within same time zones						53.16
Offsets between time zones						13.62
Residual general market risk after all offsets						66.00
Total						370.78

*Residual amount carried forward for additional offsetting as appropriate.
Note: Qual Corp is an investment grade debt issue (e.g., rated BBB and above). Non Qual is a below investment grade debt issue (e.g., rated BB and below), that is, a junk bond.

Fixed Income

We can examine the BIS standardized framework for measuring the market risk on the fixed-income (or debt security) trading portfolio by using the example for a typical FI provided by the BIS (see Table 10–8). Panel A in Table 10–8 lists the security holdings of an FI in its trading account. The FI holds long and short positions in [column (3)] various quality debt issues [column (2)] with maturities ranging from one month to over 20 years [column (1)]. Long positions have positive values; short positions have negative values. To measure the risk of this trading portfolio, the BIS uses two capital charges: (1) a specific risk charge [columns (4) and (5)] and (2) a general market risk charge [columns (6) and (7)].

Specific Risk Charge

specific risk charge
A charge reflecting the risk of a decline in the liquidity or credit risk quality of the trading portfolio.

The **specific risk charge** is meant to measure the risk of a decline in the liquidity or credit risk quality of the trading portfolio over the FI's holding period. As column (4) in panel A of Table 10–8 indicates, Treasuries have a zero risk weight, while junk bonds (e.g., 10- to 15-year nonqualifying "Non Qual" corporate debt) have a risk weight of 8 percent. As shown in Table 10–8, multiplying the absolute dollar values of all the long and short positions in these instruments [column (3)] by the specific risk weights [column (4)] produces a specific risk capital or requirement charge for each position [column (5)]. Summing the individual charges for specific risk gives the total specific risk charge of $229.[42]

General Market Risk Charge

general market risk charges
Charges reflecting the modified duration and interest rate shocks for each maturity.

The **general market risk charges** or weights—column (6)—reflect the product of the modified durations and interest rate shocks expected for each maturity.[43] The weights in Table 10–7 range from zero for the 0 to 1-month Treasuries to 6 percent for the long-term (longer than 20 years to maturity) quality corporate debt securities. The positive or negative dollar values of the positions in each instrument [column (3)] are multi-

---

[42] Note that the risk weights for specific risks are not based on obvious theory, empirical research, or past experience. Rather, the weights are based on regulators' perceptions of what was appropriate when the model was established.

plied by the general market risk weights [column (6)] to determine the general market risk charges for the individual holdings [column (7)]. Summing these gives the total general market risk charge of $66 for the whole fixed-income portfolio.

Vertical Offsets

vertical offsets
Additional capital charges assigned because long and short positions in the same maturity bucket but in different instruments cannot perfectly offset each other.

The BIS model assumes that long and short positions, in the same maturity bucket but in different instruments, cannot perfectly offset each other. Thus, the $66 general market risk charge tends to underestimate interest rate or price risk exposure. For example, the FI is short $1,500 in 10- to 15-year government securities producing a market risk charge of $67.50 and is long $1,000 in 10- to 15-year junk bonds (with a risk charge of $45). However, because of basis risk—that is, the fact that the rates on Treasuries and junk bonds do not fluctuate exactly together—we cannot assume that a $45 short position in junk bonds is hedging an equivalent ($45) risk value of government securities of the same maturity. Similarly, the FI is long $2,500 in three- to four-year government securities (with a general market risk charge of $56.25) and short $2,000 in three- to four-year quality corporate bonds (with a risk charge of $45). To account for this, the BIS requires additional capital charges for basis risk, called **vertical offsets** or disallowance factors. We show these calculations in part 2 of panel B in Table 10–8.

In panel B, column 1 lists the time bands for which the bank has both a long and short position. Columns (2) and (3) list the general market risk charges—from column (7) of panel A—resulting from the positions, and column (4) lists the difference (or residual) between the charges. Column (5) reports the smallest value of the risk charges for each time band (or offset). As listed in column (6), the BIS disallows 10 percent[44] of the $45 position in corporate bonds in hedging $45 of the government bond position. This results in an additional capital charge of $4.50 ($45 × 10 percent).[45] The total charge for all vertical offsets is $9.

Horizontal Offsets within Time Zones

horizontal offsets
Additional capital charges required because long and short positions of different maturities do not perfectly hedge each other.

In addition, the debt trading portfolio is divided into three maturity zones: zone 1 (1 month to 12 months), zone 2 (more than 1 year to 4 years), and zone 3 (more than 4 years to 20 years plus). Again because of basis risk (i.e., the imperfect correlation of interest rates on securities of different maturities), short and long positions of different maturities in these zones will not perfectly hedge each other. This results in additional (horizontal) disallowance factors of 40 percent (zone 1), 30 percent (zone 2), and 30 percent (zone 3).[46] Part 3 of the bottom panel in Table 10–8 shows these calculations. The **horizontal offsets** are calculated using the sum of the general market risk charges from the long and short positions in each time zone—columns (2) and (3). As with the vertical offsets, the smallest of these totals is the offset value

---

[43] For example, for 15- to 20-year government securities in Table 10–8, the modified duration is assumed to be 8.75 years, and the expected interest rate shock is 0.60 percent. Thus, 8.75 × 0.6 = 5.25, which is the general market risk weight for these securities shown in Table 10–8. Multiplying 5.25 by the $1,500 long position in these securities results in a general market risk charge of $78.75. Note that the shocks assumed for short-term securities, such as three-month T-bills, are larger (at 1 percent) than those assumed for longer-maturity securities. This reflects the fact that short-term rates are more impacted by monetary policy. Finally, note that the standardized model combines unequal rate shocks with estimated modified durations to calculate market risk weights. Technically, this violates the underlying assumptions of the duration model, which assumes parallel yield shifts (see Chapter 9) at each maturity.

[44] Note again that the disallowance factors were set subjectively by regulators.

[45] Intuitively, this implies that long-term government bond rates and long-term junk bond rates are approximately 90 percent correlated. However, in the final plan, it was decided to cut vertical disallowance factors in half. Thus, a 10 percent disallowance factor becomes a 5 percent disallowance factor, and so on.

[46] The zones were also set subjectively by regulators.

against which the disallowance is applied. For example, the total zone 1 charges for long positions equal $26.00 and for short positions ($52.50). A disallowance of 40 percent of the offset value (the smaller of these two values), $26.00, is charged, that is, $10.40 ($26 × 40 percent). Repeating this process for each of the three zones produces additional (horizontal offset) charges totaling $53.16.

Horizontal Offsets between Time Zones

Finally, because interest rates on short maturity debt and long maturity debt do not fluctuate exactly together, a residual long or short position in each zone can only partly hedge an offsetting position in another zone. This leads to a final set of offsets, or disallowance factors, between time zones, part 4 of panel B of Table 10–8. Here the BIS model compares the residual charges from zones 1 ($26.50) and 2 ($23.75). The difference, $2.75, is then compared with the residual from zone 3 ($68.75). The smaller of each zone comparison is again used as the offset value against which a disallowance of 40 percent for adjacent zones[47] and 150 percent[48] for nonadjacent zones, respectively, is applied. The additional charges here total $13.62.

Summing the specific risk charges ($229), the general market risk charge ($66), and the basis risk or disallowance charges ($9.00 + $53.16 + $13.62) produces a total capital charge of $370.78 for this fixed-income trading portfolio.[49]

Foreign Exchange

The standardized model or framework requires the FI to calculate its net exposure in each foreign currency—yen, euros, and so on—and then convert this into dollars at the current spot exchange rate. As shown in Table 10–9, the FI is net long (million-dollar equivalent) $50 yen, $100 euros, and $150 pounds while being short $20 Australian dollars and $180 Swiss francs. Its total currency long position is $300, and its total short position is $200. The BIS standardized framework imposes a capital requirement equal to 8 percent times the maximum absolute value of the aggregate long or short positions. In this example, 8 percent times $300 million = $24 million. This method of calculating FX exposure assumes some partial, but not complete, offsetting of currency risk by holding opposing long or short positions in different currencies.

Equities

As discussed in the context of the RiskMetrics market value model, the two sources of risk in holding equities are (1) a firm-specific, or unsystematic, risk element and (2) a market, or systematic, risk element. The BIS charges for unsystematic risk by adding the long and short positions in any given stock and applying a 4 percent charge against the gross position in the stock (called the x-factor). Suppose stock number 2, in Table 10–10, is Microsoft. The FI has a long $100 million and short $25 million position in that stock. Its gross position that is exposed to unsystematic (firm-specific) risk is $125, which is multiplied by 4 percent to give a capital charge of $5 million.

---

[47] For example, zones 1 and 2 are adjacent to each other in terms of maturity. By comparison, zones 1 and 3 are not adjacent to each other.

[48] This adjustment of 150 percent was later reduced to 100 percent.

[49] This number can also be recalculated in risk-adjusted asset terms to compare with risk-adjusted assets on the banking book. Thus, if capital is meant to be a minimum of 8 percent of risk-adjusted assets, then $370.78 × (1/1.08), or $370.78 × 12.5 = $4,634.75 is the equivalent amount of trading book risk-adjusted assets supported by this capital requirement.

TABLE 10–9
Example of the BIS Standardized Framework Measure of Foreign Exchange Risk (in millions of dollars)

Source: BIS, 1993.
www.bis.org

Once a bank has calculated its net position in each foreign currency, it converts each position into its reporting currency and calculates the risk (capital) measure as in the following example, in which the position in the reporting currency (dollars) has been excluded:

Yen*	Euros	GB£	A$	SF
+50	+100	+150	−20	−180
	+300		−200	

The capital charge would be 8 percent of the higher of the longs and shorts (i.e., 300).

*All currencies in $ equivalents.

TABLE 10–10   BIS Capital Requirement for Equities (Illustration of x plus y Methodology)

Under the proposed two-part calculation, there would be separate requirements for the position in each individual equity (i.e., the gross position) and for the net position in the market as a whole. Here we show how the system would work for a range of hypothetical portfolios, assuming a capital charge of 4 percent for the gross positions and 8 percent for the net positions.

Stock	Sum of Long Positions	Sum of Short Positions	*x*-Factor Gross Position (sum of cols. 2 and 3)	4 Percent of Gross	*y*-Factor Net Position (difference between cols. 2 and 3)	8 Percent of Net	Capital Required (gross + net)
1	100	0	100	4	100	8	12
2	100	25	125	5	75	6	11
3	100	50	150	6	50	4	10
4	100	75	175	7	25	2	9
5	100	100	200	8	0	0	8
6	75	100	175	7	25	2	9
7	50	100	150	6	50	4	10
8	25	100	125	5	75	6	11
9	0	100	100	4	100	8	12

Source: BIS, 1993. www.bis.org

Market, or systematic, risk is reflected in the net long or short position (the so-called y-factor). In the case of Microsoft, this risk is $75 million ($100 long minus $25 short). The capital charge would be 8 percent against the $75 million, or $6 million. The total capital charge (x-factor + y-factor) is $11 million for this stock.

This approach is very crude, basically assuming the same systematic risk factor (β) for every stock. It also does not fully consider the benefits from portfolio diversification (i.e., that unsystematic risk can be diversified away).

Concept Questions

1. What is the difference between the BIS specific risk and general market risk in measuring trading portfolio risk?
2. What methods did the BIS model propose for calculating FX trading exposure?
3. How are unsystematic and systematic risks in equity holdings by FIs reflected in charges assessed under the BIS model?

THE BIS REGULATIONS AND LARGE BANK INTERNAL MODELS

As discussed above, the BIS capital requirement for market risk exposure introduced in January 1998 allows large banks (subject to regulatory permission) to use their own internal models to calculate market risk instead of the standardized framework. (We examine the initiatives taken by the BIS and the major central banks, in controlling bank risk exposure through capital requirements in greater detail in Chapter 20.) However, the required capital calculation has to be relatively conservative compared with that produced internally. A comparison of the BIS requirement for large banks using their internal models with RiskMetrics indicates the following, in particular:

1. In calculating daily VAR, the FI must define an adverse change in rates as being in the 99th percentile rather than in the 95th percentile (multiply σ by 2.33 rather than by 1.65 as under RiskMetrics).
2. The FI must assume the minimum holding period to be 10 days (this means that RiskMetrics' daily VAR would have to be multiplied by $\sqrt{10}$).[50]

The FI must consider its proposed capital charge or requirement as the *higher* of:

1. The previous day's VAR (value at risk $\times \sqrt{10}$).
2. The average daily VAR over the previous 60 days times a multiplication factor with a minimum value of 3, i.e., capital charge = (VAR) $\times (\sqrt{10}) \times (3)$. In general, the multiplication factor makes required capital significantly higher than VAR produced from private models.

However, to reduce the burden of capital needs, an additional type of capital can be raised by FIs to meet the capital charge (or requirement). Suppose the portfolio VAR was $10 million using the 1 percent worst case (or 99th percentile).[51] The minimum capital charge would be:[52]

$$\text{Capital charge} = (\$10 \text{ million}) \times (\sqrt{10}) \times (3) = \$94.86 \text{ million}$$

As explained in Chapters 7 and 20, capital provides an internal insurance fund to protect an FI, its depositors and other liability holders, and the insurance fund (e.g., CDIC) against losses. The BIS permits three types of capital to be held to meet this capital requirement: Tier 1, Tier 2, and Tier 3. Tier 1 capital is essentially retained earnings and common stock, Tier 2 is essentially long-term subordinated debt (over five years), and Tier 3 is short-term subordinated debt with an original maturity of at least two years. Thus, the $94.86 million in the example above can be raised by any of the three capital types subject to the two following limitations: (1) Tier 3 capital is limited to 250 percent of Tier 1 capital, and (2) Tier 2 capital can be substituted for Tier 3 capital up to the same 250 percent limit. For example, sup-

---

[50] It is proposed that this will be changed to a minimum holding period of five days under Basel II (at the end of 2006). See "The New Basel Capital Accord: Third Consultive Paper," Basel, Switzerland, April 2003. Note that this will reduce market risk capital requirements.

[51] Using 2.33σ rather than 1.65σ.

[52] The idea of a minimum multiplication factor of 3 is to create a scheme that is "incentive compatible." Specifically, if FIs using internal models constantly underestimate the amount of capital they need to meet their market risk exposures, regulators can punish those FIs by raising the multiplication factor to as high as 4. Such a response may effectively put the FI out of the trading business. The degree to which the multiplication factor is raised above 3 depends on the number of days an FI's model underestimates its market risk over the preceding year. For example, an underestimation error that occurs on more than 10 days out of the past 250 days will result in the multiplication factor's being raised to 4.

pose Tier 1 capital was $27.10 million and the FI issued short-term Tier 3 debt of $67.76 million. Then the 250 percent limit would mean that no more Tier 3 (or Tier 2) debt could be issued to meet a target above $94.86 ($27.1 × 2.5 = $67.76) without additional Tier 1 capital being added. This capital charge for market risk would be added to the capital charge for credit risk and operational risk to get the FI's total capital requirement. The different types of capital and capital requirements are discussed in more detail in Chapter 20.

Since 1998, Canadian banks have needed OSFI's approval to use their internal models for market risk. For example, in 1998, CIBC received OSFI's approval to use its proprietary model in Canada and from the Bank of England to apply the model to its U.K. subsidiary, CIBC World Markets plc. Bank of Montreal's approval from OSFI came in 1999, while TD Bank's approval was received in 2004.

www.td.com

Concept Questions

1. What is the BIS standardized framework for measuring market risk?
2. What is the effect of using the 99th percentile (1 percent worst case) rather than the 95th percentile (5 percent worst case) on the measured size of an FI's market risk exposures?

Summary

In this chapter we analyzed the importance of measuring an FI's market risk exposure. This risk is likely to continue to grow in importance as more and more loans and previously illiquid assets become marketable and as the traditional franchises of commercial banks, insurance companies, and investment banks shrink. Given the risks involved, both private FI management and regulators are investing increasing resources in models to measure and track market risk exposures. We analyzed in detail three approaches FIs have used to measure market risk: RiskMetrics, the historic (or back simulation) approach, and the Monte Carlo simulation approach. The three approaches were also compared in terms of simplicity and accuracy. Market risk is also of concern to regulators. Beginning in November, 1999, banks in Canada have had to hold a capital requirement against the risk of their trading positions. The novel feature of the regulation of market risk is that given large FIs have the option to calculate capital requirements based on their own internal models rather than the regulatory model.

Questions and Problems

www.mcgrawhill.ca/college/saunders

1. What is meant by *market risk*?
2. Why is the measurement of market risk important to the manager of a financial institution?
3. What is meant by value at risk (VAR)? What are the three measurable components? What is the price volatility component?
4. Follow Bank has a $1 million position in a five-year, zero-coupon bond with a face value of $1,402,552. The bond is trading at a yield to maturity of 7.00 percent. The historical mean change in daily yields is 0.0 percent, and the standard deviation is 12 basis points.
   a. What is the modified duration of the bond?
   b. What is the maximum adverse daily yield move given that we desire no more than a 5 percent chance that yield changes will be greater than this maximum?
   c. What is the price volatility of this bond?
   d. What is the daily value at risk for this bond?
5. What is What would be the VAR for the bond in problem 4 for a 10-day period? With what statistical assumption is our analysis taking liberties? Could this treatment be critical?
6. The daily VAR for a bank is $8,500. What is the VAR for a 10-day period? A 20-day period? Why is the VAR for a 20-day period not twice as much as that for a 10-day period?
7. The mean change in the daily yields of a 15-year, zero-coupon bond has been five basis points (bp) over the past year with a standard deviation of 15 bp. Use these data and assume that the yield changes are normally distributed.

a. What is the highest yield change expected if a 90 percent confidence limit is required; that is, adverse moves will not occur more than 1 day in 20?

b. What is the highest yield change expected if a 95 percent confidence limit is required?

8. In what sense is duration a measure of market risk?

9. Bank Alpha has an inventory of AAA-rated, 15-year zero-coupon bonds with a face value of $400 million. The bonds currently are yielding 9.5 percent in the over-the-counter market.

a. What is the modified duration of these bonds?

b. What is the price volatility if the potential adverse move in yields is 25 basis points?

c. What is the daily VAR?

d. If the price volatility is based on a 90 percent confidence limit and a mean historical change in daily yields of 0.0 percent, what is the implied standard deviation of daily yield changes?

10. Bank Two has a portfolio of bonds with a market value of $200 million. The bonds have an estimated price volatility of 0.95 percent. What are the daily VAR and the 10-day VAR for these bonds?

11. Bank Three has determined that its inventory of 20 million euros (€) and 25 million British pounds (£) is subject to market risk. The spot exchange rates are $0.40/€ and $1.28/£, respectively. The σ's of the spot exchange rates of the € and £, based on the daily changes of spot rates over the past six months, are 65 bp and 45 bp, respectively. Determine the bank's 10-day VAR for both currencies. Use adverse rate changes in the 95th percentile.

12. Bank of Four's stock portfolio has a market value of $10,000,000. The beta of the portfolio approximates the market portfolio, whose standard deviation (σ_m) has been estimated at 1.5 percent. What is the five-day VAR of this portfolio using adverse rate changes in the 99th percentile?

13. Jeff Resnick, vice president of operations of Choice Bank, is estimating the aggregate daily VAR of the bank's portfolio of assets consisting of loans (L), foreign currencies (FX), and common stock (EQ). The individual daily VARs are $300,700; $274,000; and $126,700, respectively. If the correlation coefficients (ρ_{ij}) between L and FX, L and EQ, and FX and EQ are 0.3, 0.7, and 0.0, respectively, what is the daily VAR of the aggregate portfolio?

14. Calculate the daily VAR for the following portfolio with and without the correlation coefficients.

Assets	Estimated daily VAR	$(\rho_{S, FX})$	$(\rho_{S, B})$	$(\rho_{FX, B})$
Stocks (S)	$300,000	−0.10	0.75	0.20
Foreign Exchange (FX)	200,000			
Bonds (B)	250,000			

What is the amount of risk reduction resulting from the lack of perfect positive correlation between the various asset groups?

15. What are the advantages of using the back simulation approach to estimate market risk? Explain how this approach would be implemented.

16. Export Bank has a trading position in Japanese yen and Swiss francs. At the close of business on February 4, the bank had ¥300,000,000 and SF 10,000,000. The exchange rates for the most recent six days are given below.

Exchange Rates per Dollar at the Close of Business

	2/4	2/3	2/2	2/1	1/29	1/28
Japanese yen	112.13	112.84	112.14	115.05	116.35	116.32
Swiss francs	1.4140	1.4175	1.4133	1.4217	1.4157	1.4123

a. What is the foreign exchange (FX) position in dollar equivalents using the FX rates on February 4?

b. What is the definition of delta as it relates to the FX position?

c. What is the sensitivity of each FX position; that is, what is the value of delta for each currency on February 4?

d. What is the daily percentage change in exchange rates for each currency over the five-day period?

e. What is the total risk faced by the bank on each day? What is the worst-case day? What is the best-case day?

f. Assume that you have data for the 500 trading days preceding February 4. Explain how you would identify the worst-case scenario with a 95 percent degree of confidence.

g. Explain how the 5 percent value at risk (VAR) position would be interpreted for business on February 5.

h. How would the simulation change at the end of the day on February 5? What variables and/or processes in the analysis may change? What variables and/or processes will not change?

17. What is the primary disadvantage of the back simulation approach in measuring market risk? What effect does the inclusion of more observation days have as a remedy for this disadvantage? What other remedies can be used to deal with the disadvantage?

18. How is Monte Carlo simulation useful in addressing the disadvantages of back simulation? What is the primary statistical assumption underlying its use?

19. In the BIS standardized framework for regulating risk exposure for the fixed-income portfolios of banks, what do the terms *specific risk* and *general market risk* mean? Why does the capital charge for general market risk tend to underestimate the true interest rate or price risk exposure? What additional offsets, or disallowance factors, are included in the analysis?

20. An FI has the following bonds in its portfolio: long 1-year government bills, short 3-year governmet bonds, long 3-year AAA-rated corporate bonds, and long 12-year B-rated (nonqualifying) bonds worth $40, $10, $25, and $10 million, respectively (market values). Using Table 10–8, determine the following:

    a. Charges for specific risk.

    b. Charges for general market risk.

    c. Charges for basis risk: vertical offsets within same time bands only (i.e., ignoring horizon effects).

    d. The total capital charge, using the information from parts (a) through (c).

21. Explain how the capital charge for foreign exchange risk is calculated in the BIS standardized model. If an FI has an $80 million long position in euros, a $40 million short position in British pounds, and a $20 million long position in Swiss francs, what will be the capital charge required against FX market risk?

22. Explain the BIS capital charge calculation for unsystematic and systematic risk for an FI that holds various amounts of equities in its portfolio. What would be the total capital charge required for an FI that holds the following portfolio of stocks? What criticisms can be levied against this treatment of measuring the risk in the equity portfolio?

Company	Long	Short
Encana	$45 million	$25 million
RIM	$55 million	$12 million
CIBC	$20 million	
Air Canada		$15 million

23. What conditions were introduced by BIS in 1998 to allow large banks to use internally generated models for the measurement of market risk? What types of capital can be held to meet the capital charge requirements?

24. Dark Star Bank has estimated its average VAR for the previous 60 days to be $35.5 million. DEAR for the previous day was $30.2 million.

    a. Under the latest BIS standards, what is the amount of capital required to be held for market risk?

    b. Dark Star has $15 million of Tier 1 capital, $37.5 million of Tier 2 capital, and $55 million of Tier 3 capital. Is this amount of capital sufficient? If not, what minimum amount of new capital should be raised? Of what type?

Internet Exercise

25. Canadian FIs are permitted by OSFI to use their own internal models in evaluating market risk. Go to CIBC's Web site (www.cibc.com) and download the latest Annual Report. Find the Risk Management section. What methods is CIBC now using to calculate market risk? What was CIBC's maximum daily value-at-risk on its trading activities? What was its minimum? What components are measured to give the total VAR? How has it changed since the 2004 data provided in Table 10–6? Does the Annual Report give you a good understanding of the market risk of this particular FI?

In this chapter, we discuss credit or default risk and look at:

▸ the types of loans (business, real estate, individual, consumer, and others) and their characteristics

▸ how interest and fees are incorporated to calculate the return on a loan

▸ how the return on a loan versus the quantity of credit made available for lending is used by FIs to make decisions on business credit versus consumer and residential mortgage lending

▸ the various models used to measure credit risk, including qualitative models, credit scoring models, and newer models of credit risk measurement

▸ two privately developed credit risk measurement models; CreditMetrics and Credit Risk+ (see Appendixes A and B on pages 702 and 705 of this book), and

▸ the cash flow and financial ratio analysis widely used in the credit analysis process for mortgage, consumer and business loans (see Appendix C on page 707 of this book)

INTRODUCTION

As discussed in Chapter 1, financial intermediaries (FIs) are special because of their ability to efficiently transform financial claims of household savers into claims issued to corporations, individuals, and governments. An FI's ability to evaluate information and to control and monitor borrowers allows it to transform these claims at the lowest possible cost to all parties. One of the specific types of financial claim transformation discussed in Chapter 1 is credit allocation. That is, FIs transform claims of household savers (in the form of deposits) into loans issued to corporations, individuals, and governments. The FI accepts the credit risk on these loans in exchange for a fair return sufficient to cover the cost of funding (e.g., covering the costs of borrowing, or issuing deposits) to household savers and the credit risk involved in lending.

In this chapter, the first of two chapters on credit risk, we discuss various approaches to analyzing and measuring the credit or default risk on individual loans (and bonds). In the next chapter, we consider methods for evaluating the risk of loan portfolios, or loan concentration risk. Methods for hedging and managing an FI's credit risk are left to Chapters 23 to 27. Measurement of the credit risk on individual loans or bonds is crucial if an FI manager is to (1) price a loan or value a bond correctly and (2) set appropriate limits on the amount of credit extended to any one borrower or the loss exposure it accepts from any particular counterparty. The Ethical Dilemmas box highlights how the default of one major borrower can have a significant impact on the value and reputation of many FIs. Thus, managers need to manage the FI's loan portfolio to protect the FI from the failure of a single borrower. Management of the overall loan portfolio is equally important. In recent years Japanese FIs have suffered losses from an overconcentration of loans in real estate and in Asia. Indeed, in the early 2000s bad loans of the top eight Japanese

Royal Bank of Canada continued its cleanup of past problems in the U.S. yesterday with the announcement of $49 million (U.S.) in payments to both settle a lawsuit by collapsed energy trader Enron Corp. and to boost the bank's chances of collecting money from the bankrupt firm. Canada's largest bank will pay $25 million to resolve claims it aided Enron's accounting fraud, the bank said in a statement. It did not admit any wrongdoing. It will pay another $24 million to Enron in exchange for the company dropping its objection to RBC collecting on $114 million in loans the bank made to the company.

When a company goes bankrupt, banks are typically at the front of the line to collect any money eventually paid to creditors. But when Enron sued the banks, the banks moved to the back of the line, RBC spokesman David Moorcroft said. The $24 million payment moves RBC back to the front of the line. "We are very pleased with the agreement," Moorcroft told the Star. "We expect to recover more than $24 million" from Enron.

Enron spokeswoman Jennifer Lowney warned, however, "The average recovery of claims, and it varies, is about 20 cents on the dollar."

Other financial institutions facing similar Enron suits are Canadian Imperial Bank of Commerce, Toronto-Dominion Bank, Barclays PLC, Citigroup Inc., Credit Suisse First Boston Inc., Deutsche Bank AG, JPMorgan Chase & Co. and Merrill Lynch & Co., according to U.S. Bankruptcy Court filings.

Both CIBC and TD have set aside money in the past to cover their costs in the suit, but Royal had not, leading to some apprehension about how much the bank might eventually have to pay. But CIBC World Markets analyst Quentin Broad said the settlement was smaller than analysts had expected.

"Everybody knew that Royal, number 1, had exposure and, number 2, had not put up any sort of reserve or anticipated payment, as has the TD Bank and CIBC," he said.

"So people were certainly left out there pondering how much it might be. And I would say that $25 million plus the $24 million, taken together even, was well within expectations."

The cost of the settlement will be recorded as a charge against earnings in the bank's fiscal third quarter, which ends July 31. The bank reports its quarterly earnings on Aug. 26.

Enron is suing the banks in a so-called "MegaClaims" lawsuit as it tries to raise money to pay creditors owed a total of $74 billion.

"This settlement reflects our assessment that RBC played the smallest role of any of the financial institutions involved in this case," Enron interim chief executive Stephen Cooper said. "This is the second settlement in the MegaClaims litigation in recent weeks and we are pleased that we were once again able to achieve a meaningful cash recovery for the estate." Royal Bank of Scotland last month agreed to pay Enron $41.8 million.

Enron won approval last year for a plan to exit bankruptcy, and exists solely to sell assets and resolve creditors' claims.

"They are trying to make as much money as they can for the estate so they can pay out the claims of its creditors—of which we are one," Moorcroft said.

The agreement must still be approved by the U.S. bankruptcy court for the southern district of New York. If approved, it would mark a step in RBC's attempts to turn around past missteps in the U.S. as it tries to rebuild its troubled American franchise.

The bank sold its ailing Houston-based RBC Mortgage for about $109 million (U.S.) in May, and plans to refine the operations of its other American subsidiaries—Centura retail bank and Dain Rauscher brokerage.

Centura will focus on businesses, business owners and professionals, the bank has said, while Dain Rauscher will concentrate on providing a broader array of products. In December 2003, CIBC paid an $80 million penalty to settle allegations by U.S. regulators that it helped the energy company mislead investors. The following month it spent $50 million to set up an investor hotline and to train staff to prevent future problems.

Source: Stuart Laidlaw, *Toronto Star*, July 29, 2005, page F1. Reprinted with permission—TorStar Syndication Services.

banks exceeded US$43 billion, and a majority of Japanese banks reported losses as a result of having to write off these loans. In addition, Japanese life insurers were heavily exposed through their over 14 trillion yen (US$129 billion) loan exposure to Japanese banks.

CREDIT QUALITY PROBLEMS

Over the past two decades the credit quality of many FIs' lending and investment decisions has attracted a great deal of attention. In the 1980s there were tremendous problems with bank loans to less developed countries (LDCs). In the early 1990s attention switched to the problems of commercial real estate loans (to which banks and insurance companies were all exposed) as well as **junk bonds** (rated as speculative or less than investment grade securities by bond-rating agencies such as Dominion Bond Rating Service (DBRS), Moody's or Standard & Poors). In the late 1990s concerns shifted to the rapid growth in low-quality auto loans and credit cards as well as the declining quality in commercial lending standards as loan delinquencies started to increase. In the late 1990s and early 2000s, attention has focused on problems with telecommunication companies, new technology companies, and a variety of sovereign countries including at various times Argentina, Brazil, Russia, and South Korea.

junk bond
A bond rated as speculative or less than investment grade by bond-rating agencies such as Moody's.

www.dbrs.com
www.moodys.com
www.standardand-poors.com

The credit quality of the loans of all major Canadian banks has varied over the last two decades. As shown in Figure 11–1, gross impaired loans as a percentage of total loans peaked around 6 per cent in 1988 and again in 1992, settling below 2 percent from 1996 to 2004. However, since statistics became available in 1994, non-mortgage business loans have shown much higher impaired rates ranging from above 10 per cent in 1994 to around 4 per cent in 2004. These figures reflect the higher credit risk of business loans, but also show that Canadian banks are subject to global conditions such as the high rate of global corporate debt default which peaked in 2002–2003 related to the Enron bankruptcy, among others. For example, in 2002, Toronto-Dominion Bank reported a net loss of $76 million related to its exposure to telecoms and utilities, and increased its gross impaired loans to $2.5 billion, 2 per cent of its loans.

www.td.com

INTERNET EXERCISE

Find the latest information for impaired assets for Canadian banks published by the Office of the Superintendent of Financial Institutions using the following steps. Go to OSFI's Web site at www.osfi-bsif.gc.ca. Under the heading "Deposit-taking Institutions," click on "Banks." Then click on "Financial Data – Banks." Click on "Quarterly" and from the drop down menu, click on "Impaired Assets (excluding the memo items)." Click on "Submit" and the table of the most recent Quarter's results for all banks reporting to OSFI will appear. Data for individual banks is also available via the drop down menu.

---

[1] Nonperforming loans are loans that are 90 days or more past due or are not accruing interest.

[2] Losses drain capital through the income statement item "provision for loan losses." The provision for loan losses is a noncash, tax-deductible expense representing the FI management's prediction of loans at risk of default for the current period. As credit quality problems arise, the FI recognizes its expected bad loans by recording this expense, which reduces net income and, in turn, the FI's capital. The provision for loan losses is then allocated to the allowance for loan losses listed on the balance sheet. The allowance for loan and lease losses is a cumulative estimate by the FI's management of the percentage of the gross loans (and leases) that will not be repaid to the FI. Although the maximum amount of the provision of loan losses and the reserve for loan losses is influenced by tax laws, the FI's management actually sets the level based on loan growth and recent loan loss experience. The allowance for loan losses is an accumulated reserve that is adjusted each period as management recognizes the possibility of additional bad loans and makes appropriate provisions for such losses. Actual losses are then deducted from, and recoveries are added to (referred to as net write-offs), their accumulated loans and lease loss reserve balance. See Appendix 2C, "Financial Statements and Analysis" (located at the book's Web site, **www.mcgrawhill.ca/college/saunders**) for a more detailed discussion of these items.

FIGURE 11–1   **Gross Impaired Loans to Total Loans**

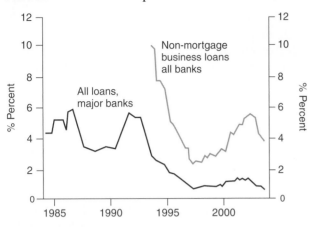

Source: Bank of Canada, "Gross Impaired Loans to Total Loans." www.bankofcanada.ca

Credit quality problems, in the worst case, can cause an FI to become insolvent or can result in such a significant drain on capital[2] and net worth that they adversely affect its growth prospects and ability to compete with other domestic and international FIs.[3]

However, credit risk does not apply only to traditional areas of lending and bond investing. As banks and other FIs have expanded into credit guarantees and other off-balance-sheet activities (see Chapter 13), new types of credit risk exposure have arisen, causing concern among managers and regulators. Thus, credit risk analysis is now important for a whole variety of contractual agreements between FIs and counterparties.[4]

Concept Questions

1. What are some of the credit quality problems faced by FIs over the last two decades?
2. What are some of the newer, nontraditional activities that create credit risk for today's FIs?

TYPES OF LOANS

Although most FIs make loans, the types of loans made and the characteristics of those loans differ considerably. This section analyzes the major types of loans made by Canadian banks. Remember from Chapters 2 through 6, however, that other FIs, such as trust and mortgage loan companies, life insurance companies, credit unions, and caisses populaires also engage in lending, especially in the real estate area. We also discuss important aspects of other FIs' loan portfolios.

Table 11–1 shows a recent breakdown of the aggregate loan portfolio of Canadian banks into four broad classes: business, mortgages, individual, and all others. We look briefly at each of these loan classes in turn.

Business Loans

The figures in Table 11–1 disguise a great deal of heterogeneity in the business loan portfolio. Business loans can be made for periods as short as a few weeks to as long as eight years or more. Traditionally, short-term business loans (those with an original maturity of one year or less) are used to finance firms' working capital needs and other short-term funding needs, while long-term commercial loans are used to finance credit needs that extend beyond one year, such as the purchase of real assets (machinery), new venture start-up costs, and permanent increases in working capital. They can be made in quite small amounts, such as $100,000, to small businesses or in packages as large as $10 million or more to major corporations. Large loans are often syndicated. A **syndicated loan** is provided by a group

syndicated loan
A loan provided by a group of FIs as opposed to a single lender.

---

[3] Not only is the book value of the FI's capital affected by credit quality problems in its loan portfolio, but studies have found that returns on banks' common stocks decrease significantly on the announcement of bankruptcy and default by borrowers of their bank. See S. Dahiya, A. Saunders, and A. Srinivasan, "Financial Distress and Bank Lending Relationships," *Journal of Finance,* February 2003, pp. 375–401 and S.V. Jayanti and G. Booth, "The impact of Latin American debt moratoria on Canadian bank stocks, *Canadian Journal of Administrative Sciences,* September 1993, Vol. 10, Iss. 3, pp. 201–212.

[4] This is one of the reasons for bank regulators' setting capital requirements against credit risk (see Chapter 20).

TABLE 11–1

Loans of All Banks, October 31, 2004 (in billions of dollars)

Source: Office of Superintendent of Financial Institutions Canada, www.osif.gc.ca

	Amount	Percent
Total loans*	849,874.4	100.0
Business loans	205,912.0	24.2
Mortgages	400,869.3	47.2
Personal loans	210,302.6	24.7
Other**	33,790.5	3.9

*Excludes interbank loans and reverse purchase agreements.
**Includes call loans to investment dealers, lease receivables, and loans to domestic and foreign governments.

secured loan
A loan that is backed by a first claim on certain assets (collateral) of the borrower if default occurs.

unsecured loan
A loan that has only a general claim to the assets of the borrower if default occurs.

spot loan
The loan amount is withdrawn by the borrower immediately.

loan commitment
A credit facility with a maximum size and a maximum period of time over which the borrower can withdraw funds; a line of credit.

of FIs as opposed to a single lender. A syndicated loan is structured by the lead FI (or agent) and the borrower. Once the terms (rates, fees, and covenants) are set, pieces of the loan are sold to other FIs. In addition, business loans can be secured or unsecured. A **secured loan** (or asset-backed loan) is backed by specific assets of the borrower; if the borrower defaults, the lender has a first lien or claim on those assets. In the terminology of finance, secured debt is senior to an **unsecured loan** (or junior debt) that has only a general claim on the assets of the borrower if default occurs. As we explain later in this chapter, there is normally a trade-off between the security or collateral backing of a loan and the loan interest rate or risk premium charged by the lender on a loan.[5]

In addition, loans can be made at either fixed or floating rates of interest. A fixed-rate loan has the rate of interest set at the beginning of the contract period. This rate remains in force over the loan contract period no matter what happens to market rates. Suppose, for example, IBM borrowed $10 million at 10 percent for one year, but the FI's cost of funds rose over the course of the year. Because this is a fixed-rate loan, the FI bears all the interest rate risk. This is why many loans have floating-rate contractual terms. The loan rate can be periodically adjusted according to a formula so that the interest rate risk is transferred in large part from the FI to the borrower. As might be expected, longer-term loans are more likely to be made under floating-rate contracts than are relatively short-term loans.[6]

Finally, loans can be made either spot or under commitment. A **spot loan** is made by the FI, and the borrower uses or takes down the entire loan amount immediately. With a **loan commitment**, or line of credit, by contrast, the lender makes an amount of credit available, such as $10 million; the borrower has the option to draw down any amount up to the $10 million at any time over the commitment period. In a fixed-rate loan commitment, the interest rate to be paid on any drawdown is established when the loan commitment contract originates. In a floating-rate commitment, the borrower pays the loan rate in force when the loan is actually drawn down. For example, suppose the $10 million IBM loan was made under a one-year

[5] The major Canadian banks are active participants in the international syndicated loans market. Details of the North American market are provided in J. Armstrong, "The Syndicated Loan Market: Developments in the North American Context," *Bank of Canada Financial System Review*, (June 2003), pp.69–73. N. T Khoury, K. V. Smith, and P. I MacKay, "Comparing Working Capital Practices in Canada, the United States, and Australia: A Note," *Canadian Journal of Administrative Sciences*, March 1999, Vol. 16, Iss. 1, pp. 53–57 survey of small firms (sales between $500,000 and $5 million), showed that 60.4 percent were always required to provide collateral as part of their bank borrowing. The trade-off between collateral and loan interest rates has been confirmed by A. Berger and G. Udell, "Lines of Credit, Collateral and Relationship Lending in small Firm Finance," *Journal of Business* 68 (July 1995), pp. 351–82.

[6] However, floating-rate loans are more credit risky than fixed-rate loans, holding all other contractual features the same. This is because floating-rate loans pass the risk of all interest rate changes onto borrowers. Thus, in rising interest rate environments, floating-rate borrowers may find themselves unable to pay the interest on their loans and may be forced to default. The benefit of floating-rate loans to lenders is that they better enable FIs to hedge the cost of rising interest rates on liabilities (such as deposits). This suggests that controlling interest rate risk may be at the expense of enhanced credit risk.

loan commitment. When the loan commitment was originated (say, January 2007), IBM borrows nothing. Instead, it waits until six months have passed (say, July 2007) before it draws down the entire $10 million. IBM pays the loan rate in force as of July 2007. We discuss the special features of loan commitments more fully in Chapter 13.

Finally, as we noted in Chapter 2, business loans are declining in importance in bank loan portfolios. The major reason for this has been the rise in nonbank loan substitutes, especially commercial paper. **Commercial paper** is an unsecured short-term debt instrument issued by corporations either directly or via an underwriter to purchasers in the financial markets. By using commercial paper, a corporation can sidestep banks and the loan market to raise funds often at rates below those banks charge. The market for commercial paper in Canada, particularly asset-backed commercial paper (ABCP) has grown phenomenally since the 1980s.[7] As of October 2004 the Bank of Canada reported $111.4 billion commercial paper outstanding with $14.4 billion to non-financial corporations. Of that total, $62.8 billion was securitized and provided cheap short-term credit for corporations. Also, $8.363 billion was issued in U.S. dollars, a feature of the Canadian debt market whereby both Canadian non-financial corporations and FIs are able to access the deeper, more liquid U.S. capital markets.[8]

commercial paper
Unsecured short-term debt instrument issued by corporations.

Mortgage Loans

Real estate loans at Canadian FIs are primarily mortgage loans and some revolving home equity loans.[9] Table 11–2 shows the residential (insured and uninsured) and non-residential mortgages for banks, trusts, and loan companies reporting to OSFI. Residential mortgage loans are the largest component of the mortgage portfolio. The characteristics of these loans, including size of the loans, the ratio of the loan to the property's price (the loan price or loan value ratio), the maturity of the mortgage, and the mortgage interest rate differ widely. The mortgage rate differs according to whether the mortgage has a fixed rate or a floating rate, also called a variable or adjustable rate. **Variable rate mortgages (VRMs)** have their contractual rates periodically adjusted to some underlying index, usually the FIs prime lending rate. The proportion of fixed-rate mortgages to VRMs in FI portfolios varies with the interest rate cycle. In low-interest rate periods, borrowers prefer fixed-rate mortgages. As a result, the proportion of VRM to fixed-rate mortgages can vary considerably over the rate cycle.

variable rate mortgage (VRM)
A mortgage whose interest rate adjusts with movements in an underlying market index interest rate.

Residential mortgages are long-term loans, usually based on an amortization period of 25 years. House prices can fall below the amount of the loan outstanding—that is, the loan-to-value ratio rises—and the residential mortgage portfolio can also be susceptible to default risk. For example, from 1979–82, a period of volatility in the economy, Canadian 5-year mortgage rates varied from 11.05 percent to 21.46 percent, housing prices declined, and mortgage defaults increased as did mortgage foreclosures.[10]

---

[7] A discussion of the commercial paper market in Canada is provided by P. Toovey and J. Kiff, "Developments and Issues in the Canadian market for Asset-Backed Commercial Paper," *Bank of Canada Financial System Review*, June 2003, pp. 43–49.

[8] A discussion of the Canadian corporate credit market and statistics is provided by S. Anderson, R. Parker, and A. Spence, "Development of the Canadian Corporate Debt Market: Some Stylized Facts and Issues," *Bank of Canada Financial System Review*, December 2003, pp. 35–41.

[9] Under home equity loans, borrowers use their homes as collateral backing for loans.

[10] See R. O Weagley, "Mortgage Default: A Demand Choice Unknown at Purchase," *The Service Industries Journal*, July 1987, Vol. 7, Iss. 3, pp. 319–339.

TABLE 11–2
Residential and non-residential mortgages held by Chartered Banks, Trusts, and Loan Companies in Canada, October 31, 2004 (millions of dollars)

Source: OSFI

www.osfi-bsif.gc.ca

	Banks	Trust Cos.	Loan Cos.	Total	Percent
Residential:					
Insured	168,636.1	9,422.4	59,851.7	237,910.2	44.5
Uninsured	210,751.7	9,515.0	52,180.7	272,447.3	50.9
Non-residential:	21,481.6	2,720.0	671.7	24,873.3	4.6
Total	400,869.4	21,657.3	112,704.1	535,230.7	100.0
Percent	74.9	4.0	21.1	100.0	

Individual (Consumer) Loans

Another major type of loan is the individual, or consumer, loan, such as personal and auto loans. Commercial banks, finance companies, retailers, savings institutions, credit unions, and oil companies also provide consumer loan financing through credit cards, such as Visa, MasterCard, and proprietary credit cards issued by, for example, Sears and Canadian Tire. A typical credit card transaction is illustrated in Figure 11–2. The largest credit card issuer in Canada is VISA which had 25.2 million cards issued and $135 billion of purchases in 2004. VISA has 38 percent of the Canadian market followed by MasterCard at 17 percent.[11]

Table 11–3 shows the major types of personal, non-mortgage loans at Canadian Chartered banks reported for October, 2004. **Personal lines of credit**, revolving loans that allow consumers to borrow and repay up to the approved amount or credit limit, are the major source of consumer credit, followed by **personal loan plans** that are generally fixed rate, fixed-term loans and then credit cards. Credit cards and lines of credit are revolving loans. With a **revolving loan** the borrower has a credit line on which to draw as well as to repay up to a maximum over the life of the credit contract.

The delinquency rate (over 90 days) on VISA and MasterCard year end outstanding amounts reported by the Canadian Bankers Association (CBA) has declined from 0.9% to 0.8% from 1999 to 2003. The CBA also reports that the percentage of total mortgages in arrears (three or more months) has declined from 0.53% in 1999 to 0.26% in 2004. However, consumer credit, excluding mortgages, from chartered banks, trust and mortgage loan companies, life insurance companies, credit unions and caisses populaires has grown by 37 percent from 2000 to 2004 as shown in Figure 11–3. The growth in consumer credit and the low default rates demonstrates the importance of risk evaluation for FIs prior to the credit decision for these types of loans.

Table 11–4 shows indicative interest rates on car, personal, and credit card loans as of February 2005. These rates differ depending on features such as collateral backing, maturity, default rate experience, and non-interest rate fees. In addition, competitive conditions in each market as well as usury ceilings (60 percent effective annual rate in Canada) all affect the rate structure for consumer loans.

Other Loans

The "other" loans category includes secured call and other short-term loans to investment dealers and brokers,[12] loans to the federal and provincial governments, loans to municipal and school corporations, and loans to foreign (sovereign) governments. Sovereign loans are discussed in Chapter 16.

personal line of credit
A revolving loan that allows a consumer to borrow and pay back an amount up to the approved credit limit.

www.cba.ca

personal loan plans
Consumer loans that have a fixed rate, a fixed term, and amortized payments.

revolving loan
A credit line on which a borrower can both draw and repay many times over the life of the loan contract.

---

[11] American Express had 5 percent, and Diner's Club less than 1 percent, of the Canadian market in 2004. However, 40% of consumer purchases are via debit cards. See D. Flavelle, "Passion for plastic persists," the *Toronto Star*, February 9, 2005.

[12] A call loan is a loan contract enabling the lender (e.g., the bank) to request repayment of a loan at any time in the contract period. A noncallable loan leaves the timing of the repayment in the hands of the borrower subject to the limit of the maturity of the loan. For example, most broker loans to investment banks are callable within the day and have to be repaid immediately at the bank lender's request.

FIGURE 11–2   Payment Flows in a Typical Credit Card Transaction

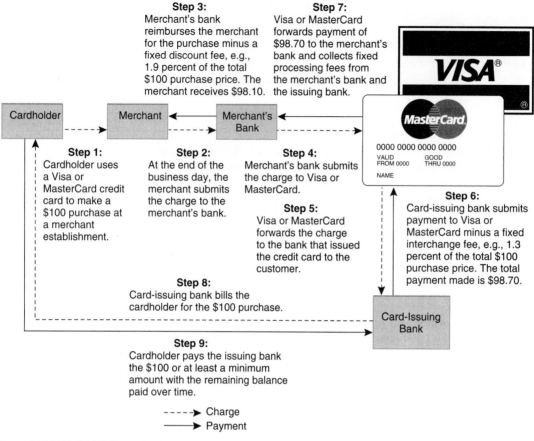

Source: GAO (1994) (GAO/GGD-94-23), p. 57.

TABLE 11–3   Loans of All Banks, October 31, 2004 (in millions of dollars)

Personal loan plans	40,064	21.9%
Credit cards	35,836	19.4%
Personal lines of credit	89,349	48.9%
Other	17,570	9.6%
Total	182,819	100.0%

Source: Bank of Canada, "Personal, non-mortgage loans at Canadian Chartered Banks, October 2004." www.bankofcanada.ca

TABLE 11–4   Average Interest Rates on Personal Loans, February 2005

48-month Car Loan	8.45%
3-year unsecured, fixed, personal loan	11.89%
Unsecured line of credit	7.95%
Secured line of credit	5.68%
Bank credit card	16.50%

Source: AOL Personal Finance at www.bankrate.com/can/rate

Concept Questions

1. What are the major types of loans made by Canadian banks? What are the basic distinguishing characteristics of each type of loan?
2. Will more VRMs be originated in high- or low-interest-rate environments? Explain your answer.
3. In Table 11–4, explain why credit card loan rates are much higher than car loan rates.

FIGURE 11–3
Consumer credit, excluding mortgages, at Canadian FIs

Source: Adapted from Statistics Canada, CANSIM database, http://cansim2. statcan.ca/cgi-win/ CNSMCGI.EXE, Table 176-0027, October 15, 2005.

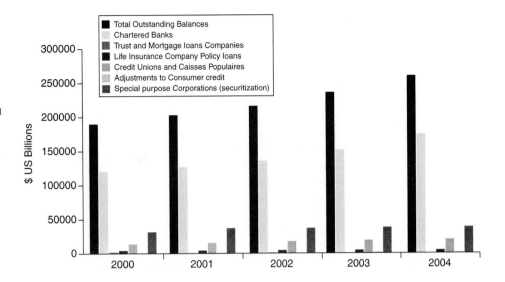

CALCULATING THE RETURN ON A LOAN

An important element in the credit management process, once the decision to make a loan has been made, is its pricing. This includes adjustments for the perceived credit risk or default risk of the borrower as well as any fees and collateral backing the loan.[13] This section demonstrates one method used to calculate the return on a loan: the traditional *return on assets approach.* Although we demonstrate the return calculations using examples of business loans, the techniques can be used to calculate the return on other loans (such as credit card or mortgage loans) as well.

The Contractually Promised Return on a Loan

The previous description of loans makes it clear that a number of factors impact the promised return an FI achieves on any given dollar loan (asset) amount. These factors include the following:

1. The interest rate on the loan.
2. Any fees relating to the loan.
3. The credit risk premium on the loan.
4. The collateral backing of the loan.
5. Other nonprice terms (especially compensating balances and reserve requirements).

First, let us consider an example of how to calculate the promised return on a loan. Suppose that an FI makes a spot one-year, $1 million loan. The loan rate is set as follows:

$$\text{Base lending rate } (BR) = 12\%$$
$$+ \text{ Credit risk premium or margin } (m) = \underline{\ 2\%}$$
$$BR + m = 14\%$$

---

[13] FIs have recently developed relationship pricing programs, which offer discounts on interest rates for customers based on the total amount of fee-based services used and investments held at the FI. Relationship pricing is in contrast to (the more traditional) transaction pricing, in which customers pay a stated rate for a service regardless of the total amount of other (nonloan) business conducted with the FI.

LIBOR
The London Interbank Offered Rate, which is the rate for interbank dollar loans of a given maturity in the offshore or Eurodollar market.

prime lending rate
The base lending rate periodically set by banks.

compensating balance
A percentage of a loan that a borrower is required to hold on deposit at the lending institution.

The base lending rate (*BR*) could reflect the FI's weighted-average cost of capital or its marginal cost of funds, such as the commercial paper rate, or **LIBOR**—the London Interbank Offered Rate, which is the rate for interbank dollar loans of a given maturity in the Eurodollar market. The center of the Eurodollar market is London. Alternatively, it could reflect the **prime lending rate.** The prime rate is most commonly used in pricing longer-term loans, whereas the LIBOR rate is more commonly used in pricing short-term loans. Traditionally, the prime rate has been the rate charged to the FI's lowest-risk customers. Now, it is more of a base rate to which positive or negative risk premiums can be added. In other words, the best and largest borrowers now commonly pay below prime rate to be competitive with the commercial paper market.[14]

Direct and indirect fees and charges relating to a loan generally fall into three categories:

1. A loan origination fee (*of*) charged to the borrower for processing the application.
2. A compensating balance requirement (*b*) to be held as non-interest-bearing demand deposits. **Compensating balances** are a percentage of a loan that a borrower cannot actively use for expenditures. Instead, these balances must be kept on deposit at the FI. For example, a borrower facing a 10 percent compensating balance requirement on a $100 loan would have to place $10 on deposit (traditionally on demand deposit) with the FI and could use only $90 of the $100 borrowed. This requirement raises the effective cost of loans for the borrower since less than the full loan amount ($90 in this case) can actually be used by the borrower and the deposit rate earned on compensating balances is less than the borrowing rate. Thus, compensating balance requirements act as an additional source of return on lending for an FI.[15]
3. A reserve requirement (*RR*) imposed by the Central Bank on the FI's demand deposits, including any compensating balances. Currently, the Bank of Canada does not impose reserve requirements on Canadian deposit-taking institutions, but the U.S. Federal Reserve still imposes reserve requirements on banks operating in the U.S.

While credit risk may be the most important factor ultimately affecting the return on a loan, these other factors should not be ignored by FI managers in evaluating loan profitability and risk. FIs can compensate for high credit risk in a number of ways other than charging a higher explicit interest rate or risk premium on a loan or restricting the amount of credit available. In particular, higher fees, high compensating balances, and increased collateral backing all offer implicit and indirect methods of compensating an FI for lending risk.

The contractually promised gross return on the loan, *k*, per dollar lent—or ROA per dollar lent—equals:[16]

$$1 + k = 1 + \frac{of + (BR + m)}{1 - [b(1 - RR)]}$$

---

[14] For more information on the prime rate, see P. Nabar, S. Park, and A. Saunders, "Prime Rate Changes: Is There an Advantage in Being First?" *Journal of Business* 66 (1993), pp. 69–92; and L. Mester and A. Saunders, "When Does the Prime Rate Change?" *Journal of Banking and Finance* 19 (1995), pp. 743–64, and P. McGraw, K. Panyagometh, and G. Roberts, "The Evolution of Corporate Borrowers: Prime versus LIBOR," (July 27, 2004), http://ssrn.com/abstract:60414.

[15] They also create a more stable supply of deposits and thus mitigate liquidity problems.

[16] This formula ignores present value aspects that could easily be incorporated. For example, fees are earned in up-front undiscounted dollars while interest payments and risk premiums are normally paid on loan maturity and thus should be discounted by the FI's cost of funds.

This formula may need some explanation. The numerator is the promised gross cash inflow to the FI per dollar, reflecting direct fees (*of*) plus the loan interest rate (*BR* + *m*). In the denominator, for every $1 in loans the FI lends, it retains *b* as non-interest-bearing compensating balances. Thus, 1 − *b* is the net proceeds of each $1 of loans received by the borrower from the FI, ignoring reserve requirements. However, since *b* (compensating balances) are held by the borrower at the FI as demand deposits, the Central Bank may require deposit-taking institutions to hold non-interest-bearing reserves at the rate *RR* against these compensating balances. Thus, the FI's net benefit from requiring compensating balances must consider the cost of holding additional non-interest-bearing reserve requirements. The net outflow by the FI per $1 of loans is 1− [*b*(1 − *RR*)] or, 1 minus the reserve adjusted compensating balance requirement. With *RR* = 0 in Canada, the denominator reduces to 1 − *b*. Canada eliminated reserve requirements in 1992.

EXAMPLE 11–1 *Calculation of ROA on a Loan*	Suppose a bank does the following: 1. Sets the loan rate on a prospective loan at 14 percent (where *BR* = 12% and *m* = 2%). 2. Charges a 1/8 percent (or 0.125 percent) loan origination fee to the borrower. 3. Imposes a 10 percent compensating balance requirement to be held as non-interest-bearing demand deposits. 4. Sets aside reserves, at a rate of 10 percent of deposits.

Plugging the numbers from our example into the return formula, we have:[17]

$$1 + k = 1 + \frac{.00125 + (.12 + .02)}{1 - [(.10)(.9)]}$$

$$1 + k = 1 + \frac{.14125}{.91}$$

$$1 + k = 1.1552 \text{ or } k = 15.52\%$$

This is, of course, greater than the simple promised interest return on the loan, *BR* + *m* = 14%.

In the special case where fees (*of*) are zero and the compensating balance (*b*) is zero:

$$of = 0$$

$$b = 0$$

the contractually promised return formula reduces to:

$$1 + k = 1 + (BR + m)$$

That is, the credit risk premium or margin (*m*) is the fundamental factor driving the promised return on a loan once the base rate on the loan is set.

Note that as commercial and corporate lending markets have become more competitive, both origination fees (*of*) and compensating balances (*b*) are becoming less important. For example, where compensating balances are still charged, the bank may now allow them to be held as time deposits, and they earn interest.

---

[17] If we take into account the present value effects on the fees and the interest payments and assume that the bank's discount rate (*d*) was $12\frac{1}{2}$ percent, then the *BR* + *m* term needs to be discounted by 1 + *d* = 1.125 while fees (as up-front payments) are undiscounted. In this case, *k* is 13.81 percent.

As a result, borrowers' opportunity losses from compensating balances have been reduced to the difference between the loan rate and the compensating balance time-deposit rate. Further, compensating balance requirements are very rare on international loans such as Eurodollar loans.[18] Finally, note that for a given promised gross return on a loan, k, FI managers can use the pricing formula to find various combinations of fees, compensating balances, and risk premiums they may offer their customers that generate the same returns.

The Expected Return on a Loan

The promised return on the loan $(1 + k)$ that the borrower and lender contractually agree on includes both the loan interest rate and non-interest rate features such as fees. The promised return on the loan, however, may well differ from the expected and, indeed, actual return on a loan because of default risk. **Default risk** is the risk that the borrower is unable or unwilling to fulfill the terms promised under the loan contract. Default risk is usually present to some degree in all loans. Thus, at the time the loan is made, the expected return $[E(r)]$ per dollar lent is related to the promised return as follows:

default risk
The risk that the borrower is unable or unwilling to fulfill the terms promised under the loan contract.

$$E(r) = p(1 + k) - 1$$

where p is the probability of repayment of the loan. To the extent that p is less than 1, default risk is present. This means the FI manager must (1) set the risk premium (m) sufficiently high to compensate for this risk and (2) recognize that setting high risk premiums as well as high fees and base rates may actually reduce the probability of repayment (p). That is, k and p are not independent. Indeed, over some range, as fees and loan rates increase, the probability that the borrower pays the promised return may decrease (i.e., k and p may be negatively related). As a result, FIs usually have to control for credit risk along two dimensions: the price or promised return dimension $(1 + k)$ and the quantity or credit availability dimension. Further, even after adjusting the loan rate (by increasing the risk premium on the loan) for the default risk of the borrower, there is no guarantee that the FI will actually receive the promised payments. The measurement and pricing approaches discussed in the chapter consider credit risk based on probabilities of receiving promised payments on the loan. The actual payment or default on a loan once it is issued may vary from the probability expected.

In general, compared with business loans, the quantity dimension controls credit risk differences on retail (e.g., consumer) loans more than the price dimension does. We discuss the reasons for this in the next section. That is followed by a section that evaluates various ways FI managers can assess the appropriate size of m, the risk premium on a loan. This is the key to pricing loan risk exposures correctly.

Concept Questions

1. Calculate the promised return (k) on a loan if the base rate is 13 percent, the risk premium is 2 percent, the compensating balance requirement is 5 percent, fees are $1/2$ percent, and reserve requirements are 10 percent. (16.23%)
2. What is the expected return on this loan if the probability of default is 5 percent. (10.42%)

---

[18] For a number of interesting examples using similar formulas, see J. R. Brick, *Commercial Banking: Text and Readings* (Haslett, Mich.: Systems Publications Inc., 1984), chap. 4. If compensating balances held as deposits paid interest at 8 percent ($r_d = 8\%$), then the numerator (cash flow) of the bank in the example would be reduced by $b \times r_d$, where $r_d = .08$ and $b = .1$. In this case, the $k = 14.64$ percent. This assumes that the reserve requirement on compensating balances held as time deposits (RR) is 10 percent. However, while currently reserve requirements on demand deposits in the U.S. are 10 percent, the reserve requirement on time deposits is 0 percent (zero). Recalculating but assuming $RR = 0$ and interest of 8 percent on compensating balances, we find $k = 14.81$ percent. In the Canadian context, reserve requirements are always equal to zero.

CONSUMER VERSUS BUSINESS CREDIT DECISIONS

Consumer

Because of the small dollar size of the loans in the context of an FI's overall investment portfolio and the higher costs of collecting information on household borrowers (consumer loans), most loan decisions made at this level tend to be accept or reject decisions. Borrowers who are accepted are often charged the same rate of interest and by implication the same credit risk premium. In the terminology of finance, retail customers (consumer loans) are more likely to be sorted or rationed by loan quantity restrictions than by price or interest rate differences.[19] That is, at the consumer level an FI controls its credit risks by **credit rationing** rather than by using a range of interest rates or prices. Thus, the FI may offer the wealthy individual a loan of up to $60,000, while the same FI may offer the less wealthy individual a loan of up to $10,000, both at the same interest rate. Residential mortgage loans provide another good example. While two borrowers may be accepted for mortgage loans, an FI discriminates between them according to the loan-to-value ratio—the amount the FI is willing to lend relative to the market value of the house being acquired—rather than by setting different mortgage rates.[20]

credit rationing
Restricting the quantity of loans made available to individual borrowers.

Business

In contrast to the retail level, at the business level FIs use both interest rates and credit quantity to control credit risk. Thus, when FIs quote a prime lending rate (*BR*) to business borrowers, lower-risk borrowers may be charged a lending rate below the prime lending rate. Higher-risk borrowers are charged a markup on the prime rate, or a credit (default) risk premium (*m*), to compensate the FI for the additional credit risk involved.

As long as they are compensated with sufficiently high interest rates (or credit risk premiums), over some range of credit demand, FIs may be willing to lend funds to high-risk borrowers. However, as discussed earlier, increasing loan interest rates (*k*) may decrease the probability (*p*) that a borrower will pay the promised return. For example, a borrower who is charged 15 percent for a loan—a prime rate of 10 percent plus a credit risk premium of 5 percent—may be able to make the promised payments on the loan only by using the funds to invest in high-risk investments with some small chance of a big payoff. However, by definition, high-risk projects have relatively high probabilities that they will *fail* to realize the big payoff. If the big payoff does not materialize, the borrower may have to default on the loan. In an extreme case, the FI receives neither the promised interest and fees on the loan nor the original principal lent. This suggests that very high contractual interest rate charges on loans may actually reduce an FI's expected return on loans because high interest rates induce the borrower to invest in risky projects.[21] Alternatively, only borrowers that

---

[19] This does not mean that rates cannot vary across FIs. For example, finance companies associated with car manufacturers (e.g., GMAC) offered 0.0 percent financing on car loans for much of the early 2000s. Unrecognized by many car buyers, the lenders' costs of funds were incorporated into an increased price for the car. Deposit-taking institutions, not able to recover their costs of funds in this manner, offered varying rates in an attempt to compete with finance companies. However, for a given FI, the rate offered on car loans would be the same for all borrowers.

[20] However, as the cost of information falls and comprehensive databases on individual households' credit-worthiness are developed, the size of a loan for which a single interest rate becomes optimal will shrink.

[21] In the context of the previous section, a high *k* on the loan reflecting a high base rate (*BR*) and risk premium (*m*) can lead to a lower probability of repayment (*p*) and thus a lower *E(r)* on the loan, where $E(r) = p(1 + k) - 1$. Indeed, for very high *k*, the expected return on the loan can become negative.

FIGURE 11–4
Relationship between the Promised Loan Rate and the Expected Return on the Loan

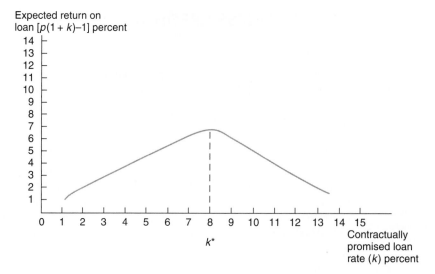

intend to use the borrowed funds to invest in high-risk projects (high-risk borrowers) may be interested in borrowing from FIs at high interest rates. Low-risk borrowers drop out of the potential borrowing pool at high-rate levels. This lowers the average quality of the pool of potential borrowers. We show these effects in Figure 11–4.[22]

At very low contractually promised interest rates (k), borrowers do not need to take high risks in their use of funds and those with relatively safe investment projects use FI financing. As interest rates increase, borrowers with fairly low-risk, low-return projects no longer think it is profitable to borrow from FIs and drop out of the pool of potential borrowers. Alternatively, borrowers may switch their use of the borrowed funds to high-risk investment projects to have a (small) chance of being able to pay off the loan. In terms of Figure 11–4, when interest rates rise above k^* (8 percent), the additional expected return earned by the FI through higher contractually promised interest rates (k) is increasingly offset by a lower probability of repayment on the loan (p). In other words, because of the potential increase in the probability of default when contractually promised loan rates are high, an FI charging wholesale borrowers loan rates in the 9 to 14 percent region can earn a *lower* expected return than will an FI charging 8 percent.

This relationship between contractually promised interest rates and the expected returns on loans suggests that beyond some interest rate level, it may be best for the FI to *credit ration* its loans, that is, to not make loans or to make fewer loans. Rather than seeking to ration by price (by charging higher and higher risk premiums to borrowers), the FI can establish an upper ceiling on the amounts it is willing to lend to maximize its expected returns on lending.[23] In the context of Figure 11–4, borrowers may be charged interest rates up to 8 percent, with the most risky borrowers also facing more restrictive limits or ceilings on the amounts they can borrow at any given interest rate.

---

[22] See also J. Stiglitz and A. Weiss, "Credit Rationing in Markets with Imperfect Information," *American Economic Review* 71 (1981), pp. 393–410.

[23] Indeed, it has been found that the availability of bank credit depends not just on interest rates, but on the borrower's credit quality as well. Specifically, banks sometimes tighten their credit standards (forgoing riskier loans even when higher interest rates can be charged) to maximize their expected return on lending. See C. S. Lown, D. P. Morgan, and S. Rohatgin, "Listening to Loan Officers: The Impact of Commercial Credit Standards on Lending and Output," *FRBNY Economic Policy Review*, July 2000, pp. 1–16. In addition, the degree of competition in the loan market, and hence the price elasticity of demand for loans, will affect the availability of bank credit. That is, as competition for loans increases, the point (interest rate) at which banks switch from risk-based pricing to credit rationing may increase as well, and vice versa.

Concept Questions

1. Can an FI's return on its loan portfolio increase if it cuts its loan rates?
2. What might happen to the expected return on a wholesale loan if an FI eliminates its fees and compensating balances in a low–interest rate environment?

MEASUREMENT OF CREDIT RISK

To calibrate the default risk exposure of credit and investment decisions as well as to assess the credit risk exposure in off-balance-sheet contractual arrangements such as loan commitments, an FI manager needs to measure the probability of borrower default. The ability to do this depends largely on the amount of information the FI has about the borrower. At the consumer level, much of the information needs to be collected internally or purchased from external credit agencies. At the business level, these information sources are bolstered by publicly available information, such as certified accounting statements, stock and bond prices, and analysts' reports. Thus, for a publicly traded company, more information is produced and is available to an FI than is available for a small, single-proprietor corner store. The availability of more information, along with the lower average cost of collecting such information, allows FIs to use more sophisticated and usually more quantitative methods in assessing default probabilities for large borrowers compared with small borrowers. However, advances in technology and information collection are making quantitative assessments of even smaller borrowers increasingly feasible and less costly.[24] The simpler details (such as cash flow and ratio analysis) associated with the measurement of credit risk for consumer and business loans are discussed in Appendix 11C to the chapter, located at the book's Web site (**www.mcgrawhill.ca/college/saunders**).

In principle, FIs can use very similar methods and models to assess the probabilities of default on both bonds and loans. Even though loans tend to involve fewer lenders to any single borrower as opposed to multiple bondholders, in essence, both loans and bonds are contracts that promise fixed (or indexed) payments at regular intervals in the future. Loans and bonds stand ahead of the borrowing firm's equity holders in terms of the priority of their claims if things go wrong. Also, bonds, like loans, include **covenants** restricting or encouraging various actions to enhance the probability of repayment. Covenants can include limits on the type and amount of new debt, investments, and asset sales the borrower may undertake while the loan or bonds are outstanding. Financial covenants are also often imposed restricting changes in the borrower's financial ratios such as its leverage ratio or current ratio. For example, a common restrictive covenant included in many bond and loan contracts limits the amount of dividends a firm can pay to its equity holders. Clearly, for any given cash flow, a high dividend payout to stockholders means that less is available for repayments to bondholders and lenders. Moreover, bond yields, like wholesale loan rates, usually reflect risk premiums that vary with the perceived credit quality of the borrower and the collateral or security backing of the debt. Given this, FIs can use many of the following models that analyze default risk probabilities either in making lending decisions or when considering investing in corporate bonds offered either publicly or privately.[25]

covenants
Restrictions written into bond and loan contracts either limiting or encouraging the borrower's actions that affect the probability of repayment.

---

[24] These advances include database services and software for automating credit assessment provided by companies such as Dun & Bradstreet.

[25] For more discussion of the similarities between bank loans and privately placed debt, see M. Berlin and L. Mester, "Debt Covenants and Renegotiation," *Journal of Financial Intermediation* 2 (1992), pp. 95–133; M. Carey et al., "The Economics of Private Placement: A New Look," *Financial Markets, Institutions and Instruments* 2, no. 3 (1993); and M. Carey et al., "Does Corporate Lending by Banks and Finance Companies Differ? Evidence on Specialization in Private Debt Contracting," *Journal of Finance* 53 (June 1998), pp. 845–78.

Concept Questions

1. Is it more costly for an FI manager to assess the default risk exposure of a publicly traded company or a small, single-proprietor firm? Explain your answer.
2. How do loan covenants help protect an FI against default risk?

DEFAULT RISK MODELS

Economists, analysts, and FI managers have employed many different models to assess the default risk on loans and bonds. These vary from relatively qualitative to the highly quantitative models. Further, these models are not mutually exclusive; an FI manager may use more than one model to reach a credit pricing or loan quantity rationing decision. As will be discussed below in more detail, a great deal of time and effort has recently been expended by FIs in building highly technical credit risk evaluation models. Many of these models use ideas and techniques similar to the market risk models discussed in Chapter 10. We analyze a number of models in three broad groups: qualitative models, credit scoring models, and newer models.

Qualitative Models

In the absence of publicly available information on the quality of borrowers, the FI manager has to assemble information from private sources—such as credit and deposit files—and/or purchase such information from external sources—such as credit rating agencies. This information helps a manager make an informed judgment on the probability of default of the borrower and price the loan or debt correctly.

In general, the amount of information assembled varies with the size of the potential debt exposure and the costs of collection. However, a number of key factors enter into the credit decision. These include (1) *borrower-specific* factors which are idiosyncratic to the individual borrower, and (2) *market-specific* factors, which have an impact on all borrowers at the time of the credit decision. The FI manager then weights these factors subjectively to come to an overall credit decision. Because of their reliance on the subjective judgment of the FI manager, these models are often called expert systems. Commonly used borrower-specific and market-specific factors are discussed next.

Borrower-Specific Factors

Reputation   The borrower's reputation involves the borrowing-lending history of the credit applicant. If, over time, the borrower has established a reputation for prompt and timely repayment, this enhances the applicant's attractiveness to the FI. A long-term customer relationship between a borrower and lender forms an **implicit contract** regarding borrowing and repayment that extends beyond the formal explicit legal contract on which borrower-lender relationships are based. The importance of reputation, which can be established only over time through repayment and observed behavior, works to the disadvantage of small, newer borrowers. This is one of the reasons initial public offerings of debt securities by small firms often require higher yields than do offerings of older, more seasoned firms.[26]

Leverage   A borrower's **leverage** or capital structure—the ratio of debt to equity—affects the probability of its default because large amounts of debt, such as bonds and loans, increase the borrower's interest charges and pose a significant claim on its cash flows. As shown in Figure 11–5, relatively low debt-equity ratios may not

implicit contract
Long-term customer relationship between a borrower and lender based on reputation.

leverage
The ratio of a borrower's debt to equity.

---

[26] For the link between bank finance and the cost of initial public offerings of securities, see C. James and P. Weir, "Borrowing Relationships, Intermediation, and the Costs of Issuing Public Securities," *Journal of Financial Economics* 28 (1992), pp. 149–71.

FIGURE 11–5   **Relationship between the Cost of Debt, the Probability of Default, and Leverage**

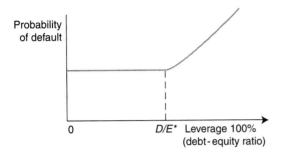

significantly impact the probability of debt repayment. Yet beyond some point, the risk of bankruptcy increases, as does the probability of some loss of interest or principal for the lender. Thus, highly leveraged firms, such as firms recently engaged in leveraged buyouts (LBOs) financed in part by FIs' provision of junk bonds or below-investment-grade debt, may find it necessary to pay higher risk premiums on their borrowings if they are not rationed in the first place.[27]

Volatility of Earnings   As with leverage, a highly volatile earnings stream increases the probability that the borrower cannot meet fixed interest and principal charges for any given capital structure. Consequently, newer firms or firms in high-tech industries with a high earnings variance over time are less attractive credit risks than are those with long and more stable earnings histories.

Collateral   As discussed earlier, a key feature in any lending and loan-pricing decision is the degree of collateral, or assets backing the security of the loan. Many loans and bonds are backed by specific assets should a borrower default on repayment obligations. Mortgage bonds give the bondholder first claim to some specific piece of property of the borrower, normally machinery or buildings; debentures give a bondholder a more general and more risky claim to the borrower's assets. Subordinated debentures are even riskier because their claims to the assets of a defaulting borrower are junior to those of both mortgage bondholders and debenture bondholders. Similarly, loans can be either secured (collateralized) or unsecured (uncollateralized).[28]

Market-Specific Factors

The Business Cycle   The position of the economy in the business cycle phase is enormously important to an FI in assessing the probability of borrower default. For example, during recessions, firms in the consumer durable goods sector that produce autos, refrigerators, or houses do badly compared with those in the nondurable goods sector producing tobacco and foods. People cut back on luxuries during a recession but are less likely to cut back on necessities such as food. Thus, corporate borrowers in the consumer durable goods sector of the economy are especially prone to default risk. Because of cyclical concerns, FIs are more likely to increase the relative degree of credit rationing in recessionary phases. This has especially adverse consequences for smaller borrowers with limited or no access to alternative credit markets such as the commercial paper market.[29]

---

[27] However, S. J. Grossman and O. D. Hart argue that high debt (leverage) may be a signal of managerial efficiency and may in fact lower bankruptcy risk. Similar arguments have been made about the efficiency incentives for managers in junk bond–financed LBOs. That is, firms with a lot of debt have to be "lean and mean" to meet their repayment commitments. See "Corporate Financial Structure and Managerial Incentives," in *The Economics of Information and Uncertainty*, ed. J. McCall (Chicago: Chicago University Press, 1982).

[28] However, collateralized loans are still subject to some default risk unless these loans are significantly overcollateralized; that is, assets are pledged with market values exceeding the face value of the debt instrument. There is also some controversy as to whether posting collateral signifies a high- or low-risk borrower. Arguably, the best borrowers do not need to post collateral since they are good credit risks, whereas only more risky borrowers need to post collateral. That is, posting collateral may be a signal of more rather than less credit risk. See, for example, A. Berger and G. Udell, "Lines of Credit, Collateral and Relationship Lending in Small Firm Finance," *Journal of Business,* 1995, pp. 351–381.

[29] For a good discussion of the sensitivity of different U.S. industries' default rates to the business cycle, see J. D. Taylor, "Cross-Industry Differences in Business Failure Rates: Implications for Portfolio Management," *Commercial Lending Review,* 1998, pp. 36–46. The Bank of Canada provides a good discussion of the impact of economic conditions on impaired loans and lending in Canada in its semi-yearly publication, *Financial System Review.* See in particular, the *Financial System Review* issues for December 2002, 2003, and 2004 downloadable at www.bankofcanada.ca.

The Level of Interest Rates High interest rates indicate restrictive monetary policy actions by the Bank of Canada. FIs not only find funds to finance their lending decisions scarcer and more expensive but also must recognize that high interest rates are correlated with higher credit risk in general. As discussed earlier, high interest rate levels may encourage borrowers to take excessive risks and/or encourage only the most risky customers to borrow.

So far, we have delineated just a few of the qualitative borrower- and economy-specific factors an FI manager may take into account in deciding on the probability of default on any loan or bond.[30] Rather than letting such factors enter into the decision process in a purely subjective fashion, the FI manager may weight these factors in a more objective or quantitative manner. We discuss quantitative credit scoring models used to measure credit risk next.

Concept Questions

1. Make a list of 10 key borrower characteristics you would assess before making a mortgage loan.
2. How should the risk premium on a loan be affected if there is a reduction in a borrower's leverage?

Credit Scoring Models

credit scoring models
Mathematical models that use observed loan applicant's characteristics either to calculate a score representing the applicant's probability of default or to sort borrowers into different default risk classes.

Credit scoring models are quantitative models that use observed borrower characteristics either to calculate a score representing the applicant's probability of default or to sort borrowers into different default risk classes. By selecting and combining different economic and financial borrower characteristics, an FI manager may be able to:

1. Numerically establish which factors are important in explaining default risk.
2. Evaluate the relative degree or importance of these factors.
3. Improve the pricing of default risk.
4. Be better able to screen out bad loan applicants.
5. Be in a better position to calculate any reserves needed to meet expected future loan losses.

The primary benefit from credit scoring is that credit lenders can more accurately predict a borrower's performance without having to use more resources. With commercial loan credit scoring models taking into account all necessary regulatory parameters and posting an 85 percent accuracy rate on average, according to credit scoring experts,[31] using these models means fewer defaults and write-offs for business loan lenders.

To use credit scoring models, the manager must identify objective economic and financial measures of risk for any particular class of borrower. For consumer debt, the objective characteristics in a credit scoring model might include income, assets, age, occupation, and location. For commercial debt, cash flow information and financial ratios such as the debt-equity ratio are usually key factors.[32] After data are identified, a statistical technique quantifies, or scores, the default risk probability or default risk classification.

---

[30] More generally, J. F. Sinkey identifies five Cs of credit that should be included in any subjective (qualitative) credit analysis: character (willingness to pay), capacity (cash flow), capital (wealth), collateral (security), and conditions (economic conditions). See *Commercial Bank Financial Management—In the Financial Services Industry,* 5th ed. (New York: Macmillan, 1998).

[31] See "Credit Scoring Heats Up," *Collections and Credit Risk,* September 2003, p. 34.

[32] A. N. Berger, W. S. Frame, and N. H. Miller, in "Credit Scoring and the Availability, Price, and Risk of Small Business Credit," 2002, Working Paper, Federal Reserve Board, find that small business credit scoring is associated with expanded credit supply, higher average interest rates, and greater risk levels for small business loans. Their findings are consistent with a net increase in lending to small businesses that would otherwise not receive credit without the use of credit scoring.

Credit scoring models include these three broad types: (1) linear probability models, (2) logit models, and (3) linear discriminant analysis. Appendix: 11C to the chapter (located at the book's Web site, **www.mcgrawhill.ca/college/saunders**) looks at credit scoring models used to evaluate mortgages and consumer loans. In this section we look at credit scoring models used to evaluate commercial and corporate loans.

Linear Probability Model and Logit Model

The linear probability model uses past data, such as financial ratios, as inputs into a model to explain repayment experience on old loans. The relative importance of the factors used in explaining past repayment performance then forecasts repayment probabilities on new loans. That is, factors explaining past repayment performance can be used for assessing p, the probability of repayment discussed earlier in this chapter (a key input in setting the credit premium on a loan or determining the amount to be lent) and the probability of default (PD).

Briefly, we divide old loans (i) into two observational groups: those that defaulted ($PD_i = 1$) and those that did not default ($PD_i = 0$). Then we relate these observations by linear regression to a set of j causal variables (X_{ij}) that reflect quantitative information about the ith borrower, such as leverage or earnings. We estimate the model by linear regression of this form:

$$PD_i = \sum_{j=1}^{n} \beta_j X_{ij} + \text{error}$$

where β_j is the estimated importance of the jth variable (leverage) in explaining past repayment experience.

If we then take these estimated β_js and multiply them by the observed X_{ij} for a prospective borrower, we can derive an expected value of PD_i for the prospective borrower. That value can be interpreted as the probability of default for the borrower: $E(PD_i) = (1 - p_i) = $ expected probability of default, where p_i is the probability of repayment on the loan.

EXAMPLE 11–2 *Estimating the Probability of Repayment on a Loan Using Linear Probability Credit Scoring Models*	Suppose there were two factors influencing the past default behaviour of borrowers: the leverage or debt-equity ratio (*D/E*) and the sales-asset ratio (*S/A*). Based on past default (repayment) experience, the linear probability model is estimated as: $$PD_i = .5(D/E_i) + .1(S/A_i)$$ Assume a prospective borrower has a *D/E* = .3 and an *S/A* = 2.0. Its expected probability of default (PD$_i$) can then be estimated as: $$PD_i = .5(.3) + .1(2.0) = .35$$

Although this technique is straightforward as long as current information on the X_{ij} is available for the borrower, its major weakness is that the estimated probabilities of default can often lie outside the interval 0 to 1. The logit model overcomes this weakness by restricting the estimated range of default probabilities from the linear regression model to lie between 0 and 1.[33]

---

[33] Essentially this is done by plugging the estimated value of PD_i from the linear probability model (in our example, $PD_i = .35$) into the following formula:

$$F(PD_i) = \frac{1}{1 + e^{-PD_i}}$$

where e is exponential (equal to 2.718) and $F(PD_i)$ is the logistically transformed value of PD_i.

Linear Discriminant Models

Whereas linear probability and logit models project a value for the expected probability of default if a loan is made, discriminant models divide borrowers into high or low default risk classes contingent on their observed characteristics (X_j).

Consider the discriminant analysis model developed by E. I. Altman for publicly traded manufacturing firms in the United States that has been adopted and used by FIs around the world. The indicator variable Z is an overall measure of the default risk classification of a commercial borrower.[34] This in turn depends on the values of various financial ratios of the borrower (X_j) and the weighted importance of these ratios based on the past observed experience of defaulting versus nondefaulting borrowers derived from a discriminant analysis model.[35]

Altman's discriminant function (credit-classification model) takes the form:

$$Z = 1.2X_1 + 1.4X_2 + 3.3X_3 + 0.6X_4 + 1.0X_5$$

where

X_1 = Working capital/total assets ratio
X_2 = Retained earnings/total assets ratio
X_3 = Earnings before interest and taxes/total assets ratio
X_4 = Market value of equity/book value of long-term debt ratio
X_5 = Sales/total assets ratio

The higher the value of Z, the lower the default risk classification of the borrower.[36] Thus, low or negative values of Z may be evidence of the borrower being a member of a relatively high default risk class.

EXAMPLE 11–3

Calculation of Altman's Z Score

Suppose that the financial ratios of a potential borrowing firm took the following values:

$X_1 = .2$
$X_2 = 0$
$X_3 = -.20$
$X_4 = .10$
$X_5 = 2.0$

The ratio X_2 is zero and X_3 is negative, indicating that the firm has had negative earnings or losses in recent periods. Also, X_4 indicates that the borrower is highly leveraged. However, the working capital ratio (X_1) and the sales/assets ratio (X_5) indicate that the firm is reasonably liquid and is maintaining its sales volume. The Z score provides an overall score or indicator of the borrower's credit risk since it combines and weights these five factors according to their past importance in explaining borrower default. For the borrower in question:

$$Z = 1.2 (.2) + 1.4(0) + 3.3(-.20) + 0.6(.10) + 1.0 (2.0)$$
$$= 0.24 + 0 - .66 + 0.06 + 2.0$$
$$= 1.64$$

According to Altman's credit scoring model, any firm with a Z score less than 1.81 should be placed in the high default risk region.[37] Thus, the FI should not make a loan to this borrower until it improves its earnings.

---

[34] The Z score is a default indicator and is not a direct probability of default (*PD*) measure.

[35] E. I. Altman, "Managing the Commercial Lending Process," in *Handbook of Banking Strategy*, eds. R. C. Aspinwall and R. A. Eisenbeis (New York: John Wiley & Sons, 1985), pp. 473–510.

[36] Working capital is current assets minus current liabilities.

[37] Discriminant analysis models produce such a switching point, $Z = 1.81$. This is the mean difference between the average Z scores of the defaulting firms and the nondefaulting firms. For example, suppose the average Z for nondefaulting firms was 2.01 and for defaulting firms it was 1.61. The mean of these two scores is 1.81. See G. Turvey, "Credit Scoring for Agricultural Loans: A Review with Applications," *Agricultural Finance Review* 51 (1991), pp. 43–54, for more details.

There are a number of problems in using the discriminant analysis model to make credit risk evaluations.[38] The first problem is that these models usually discriminate only between two extreme cases of borrower behaviour: no default and default. As discussed in Chapter 7, in the real world various gradations of default exist, from nonpayment or delay of interest payments (nonperforming assets) to outright default on all promised interest and principal payments. This problem suggests that a more accurate or finely calibrated sorting among borrowers may require defining more classes in the discriminant analysis model.

The second problem is that there is no obvious economic reason to expect that the weights in the discriminant function—or, more generally, the weights in any credit scoring model—will be constant over any but very short periods. The same concern also applies to the variables (X_j). Specifically, because of changing real and financial market conditions, other borrower-specific financial ratios may come to be increasingly relevant in explaining default risk probabilities. Moreover, the linear discriminant model assumes that the X_j variables are independent of one another.[39]

The third problem is that these models ignore important, hard-to-quantify factors that may play a crucial role in the default or no default decision. For example, reputation of the borrower and the nature of long-term borrower-lender relationships could be important borrower-specific characteristics, as could macrofactors such as the phase of the business cycle. These variables are often ignored in credit scoring models. Moreover, traditional credit scoring models rarely use publicly available information, such as the prices of outstanding public debt and equity of the borrower.[40]

A fourth problem relates to default records kept by FIs. Currently, no centralized database on defaulted business loans for proprietary and other reasons exists. Some task forces set up by consortiums of commercial banks, insurance companies, and consulting firms are currently seeking to construct such databases largely in response to proposed reforms to bank capital requirements (see Chapter 20). However, it may well be many years before they are developed.[41] This constrains the ability of many FIs to use traditional credit scoring models (and quantitative models in general) for larger business loans—although their use for smaller consumer loans, such as credit card loans, where much better centralized databases exist, is well established.

The newer credit risk models use *financial theory* and more widely available *financial market* data to make inferences about default probabilities on debt and loan instruments. Consequently, these models are most relevant in evaluating loans to larger borrowers in the corporate sector. This is the area in which a great deal of current research is taking place by FIs, as noted in Appendixes 11A and 11B (located on pages 702 and 705 of this book). Below we consider a number of these newer approaches or models of credit risk, including:

---

[38] Most of these criticisms also apply to the linear probability and logit models.

[39] Recent work in nonlinear discriminant analysis has sought to relax this assumption. Moreover, work with neural networks, which are complex computer algorithms seeking links or correlations between the X_j variables to improve on Z classifications, shows some promise. See P. K. Coats and L. F. Fant, "Recognizing Financial Distress Patterns: Using a Neural Network Tool," *Financial Management,* Summer 1993, pp. 142–55; and "New Tools for Routine Jobs," *The Financial Times,* September 24, 1994.

[40] For example, S. C. Gilson, K. John, and L. Lang show that three years of low or negative stock returns can usefully predict bankruptcy probabilities. In fact, this market-based approach is supplementary to the market-based information models discussed in later sections of this chapter. See "An Empirical Study of Private Reorganization of Firms in Default," *Journal of Financial Economics,* 1990, pp. 315–53.

[41] A recent, successful example of such a database is "1986–1992 Credit-Loss Experience Study: Private Placement Bonds," *Society of Actuaries,* Schaumburg, IL, 1996. For an analysis of these data, see M. Carey, "Credit Risk in Private Debt Portfolios," *Journal of Finance,* June 1998, pp. 1363–87.

1. Term structure of credit risk approach.
2. Mortality rate approach.
3. Risk-Adjusted Return on Capital (RAROC) models.
4. Option models (including the KMV credit monitor model).
5. CreditMetrics (see Appendix 11A on page 702 of this book).
6. Credit Risk+ (see Appendix 11B on page 705 of this book).

While some of these models focus on different aspects of credit risk, they are all linked by a strong reliance on modern financial theory and financial market data.[42]

Concept Questions

1. Suppose the estimated linear probability model looked as follows: $Z = 0.3X_1 + 0.1X_2 +$ error, where

    X_1 = Debt-equity ratio; and X_2 = Total assets − Working capital ratio

    Suppose, for a prospective borrower, $X_1 = 1.5$ and $X_2 = 3.0$. What is the projected probability of default for the borrower? (75%)

2. Suppose $X_3 = .5$ in Example 11–3. Show how this would change the default risk classification of the borrower. ($Z = 3.95$)

3. What are two problems in using discriminant analysis to evaluate credit risk?

NEWER MODELS OF CREDIT RISK MEASUREMENT AND PRICING

Term Structure Derivation of Credit Risk

One market-based method of assessing credit risk exposure and default probabilities is to analyze the risk premiums inherent in the current structure of yields on corporate debt or loans to similar risk-rated borrowers. Rating agencies such as Standard & Poor's (S&P) categorize corporate bond issuers into at least seven major classes according to perceived credit quality. The first four quality ratings—AAA, AA, A, and BBB—indicate investment-quality borrowers. Non-investment-grade securities with ratings such as BB, B, and CCC, are known as high-yield or junk bonds. Different quality ratings are reflected in the degree to which corporate bond yields exceed those implied by the Treasury (credit risk-free) yield curve.

www.standardand-poors.com

Look at the spreads shown in Figure 11–6 for zero-coupon corporate (grade B) bonds over similar maturity zero-coupon Government debt (called Treasury strips). Because **Treasury strips** and **zero-coupon corporate bonds** are single-payment discount bonds, it is possible to extract required credit risk premiums and implied probabilities of default from actual market data on interest rates. That is, the spreads between risk-free discount bonds issued by the Government of Canada and discount bonds issued by corporate borrowers of differing quality reflect perceived credit risk exposures of corporate borrowers for single payments at different times in the future. FIs can use these credit risk probabilities on existing debt to decide whether or not to issue additional debt to a particular credit risk borrower.

Treasury strips, zero-coupon corporate bonds
Bonds that are created or issued bearing no coupons and only a face value to be paid on maturity. As such, they are issued at a large discount from face value. (Also called deep-discount bonds.)

Next, we look at the simplest case of extracting an implied probability of default for an FI considering buying one-year bonds from or making one-year loans to a risky borrower. Then, we consider multiyear loans and bonds. In each case, we show that we can extract a market view of the credit risk—the expected probability of default—of an individual borrower.[43]

---

[42] For further details on these newer models, see A. Saunders and L. Allen, *Credit Risk Measurement: New Approaches to Value at Risk and Other Paradigms*, 2nd ed. (John Wiley and Sons: New York, 2002).

[43] Technically, these credit risk models are often called intensity-based models or reduced form models. For a full review, see A. Saunders and L. Allen, *Credit Risk Measurement: New Approaches to Value at Risk and Other Paradigms*, 2nd ed. (John Wiley and Sons: New York, 2002), Chapter 5.

FIGURE 11–6
Corporate and
Government
Discount Bond
Yield Curves

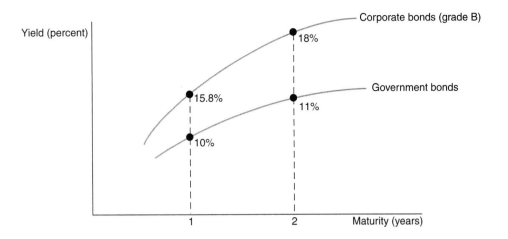

Probability of Default on a One-Period Debt Instrument

Assume that the FI requires an expected return on a one-year (zero-coupon) corporate debt security equal to at least the risk-free return on one-year (zero-coupon) Treasury bonds. Let p be the probability that the corporate debt, both principal and interest, will be repaid in full; therefore, $1 - p$ is the probability of default. If the borrower defaults, the FI is (for now) assumed to get nothing (i.e., the recovery rate is zero or the loss given default is 100 percent).[44] By denoting the contractually promised return on the one-year corporate debt security as $1 + k$ and on the credit risk–free one-year Treasury security as $1 + i$, the FI manager would just be indifferent between corporate and Treasury securities when[45]

$$p(1 + k) = 1 + i$$

or, the expected return on corporate securities is equal to the risk-free rate.

EXAMPLE 11–4	Suppose, as shown in Figure 11–7, the interest rates in the market for one-year zero-coupon government bonds and for one-year zero-coupon grade B corporate bonds are, respectively:

EXAMPLE 11–4

Calculating the Probability of Default on a One-Year Bond (Loan) Using Term Structure Derivation of Credit Risk

Suppose, as shown in Figure 11–7, the interest rates in the market for one-year zero-coupon government bonds and for one-year zero-coupon grade B corporate bonds are, respectively:

$$i = 10\%$$

and

$$k = 15.8\%$$

This implies that the probability of repayment on the security as perceived by the market is:

$$p = \frac{1 + i}{1 + k} = \frac{1.100}{1.158} = .95$$

[44] This is a key assumption. If the recovery rate is nonzero (which in reality is true, since in recent years banks have recovered on average up to 40 percent of a defaulted loan and 50 percent of a senior secured bond), then the spread between the corporate bond return and the Treasury bond return will reflect both the probability of default as well as the loss given default (the latter is equal to 1 minus the recovery rate). To disentangle the probability of default from the loss given default, we need to make assumptions about the size of the loss given default (LGD) or the statistical process that either the PD and/or the LGD follow, such as the Poisson process. One simple case assuming LGD is known is discussed later in this chapter.

[45] This assumes that the FI manager is not risk averse; that is, this is a risk-neutral valuation method and the probabilities so derived are called risk-neutral probabilities. In general these will differ from probabilities estimated from historic data on defaults. See Saunders and Allen, *Credit Risk Management,* Chapter 5.

If the probability of repayment is .95, this implies a probability of default $(1 - p)$ equal to .05. Thus, in this simple one-period framework, a probability of default of 5 percent on the corporate bond (loan) requires the FI to set a risk premium (ϕ) of 5.8 percent.[46]

$$\phi = k - i = 5.8\%$$

Clearly, as the probability of repayment (p) falls and the probability of default $(1 - p)$ increases, the required spread ϕ between k and i increases.

This analysis can easily be extended to the more realistic case in which the FI does not expect to lose all interest and all principal if the corporate borrower defaults.[47] Realistically, the FI lender can expect to receive some partial repayment even if the borrower goes into bankruptcy. For example, Altman and Bana estimated that when firms defaulted on their bonds in 2002, the investor lost on average 74.7 cents on the dollar (i.e., recovered around 25.3 cents on the dollar).[48] Table 11–5 gives recovery rates on defaulted debt by seniority from 1978–2002. As discussed earlier in this chapter, many loans and bonds are secured or collateralized by first liens on various pieces of property or real assets should a borrower default. Let γ be the proportion of the loan's principal and interest that is collectible on default, where in general γ is positive.

The FI manager would set the expected return on the loan to equal the risk-free rate in the following manner:

$$[(1 - p)\,\gamma\,(1 + k)] + [p\,(1 + k)] = 1 + i$$

The new term here is $(1 - p)\,\gamma\,(1 + k)$; this is the payoff the FI expects to get if the borrower defaults.

As might be expected, if the loan has collateral backing such that $\gamma > 0$, the required risk premium on the loan will be less for any given default risk probability $(1 - p)$. Collateral requirements are a method of controlling default risk; they act as a direct substitute for risk premiums in setting required loan rates. To see this, solve for the risk premium ϕ between k (the required yield on risky corporate debt) and i (the risk-free rate of interest):

$$k - i = \phi = \frac{(1 + i)}{(\gamma + p - p\gamma)} - (1 + i)$$

If $i = 10$ percent and $p = .95$ as before but the FI can expect to collect 90 percent of the promised proceeds if default occurs ($\gamma = .9$), then the required risk premium $\phi = 0.6$ percent.[49]

Interestingly, in this simple framework, γ and p are perfect substitutes for each other. That is, a bond or loan with collateral backing of $\gamma = .7$ and $p = .8$ would have

---

[46] In the real world a bank could partially capture this required spread in higher fees and compensating balances rather than only in the risk premium. In this simple example, we are assuming away compensating balances and fees. However, they could easily be built into the model. For additional information on this model, see A. Ginzburg, K. J. Maloney, and R. Wilner, "Risk Rating Migration and the Valuation of Floating Rate Debt," Citicorp Working Paper, March 1994; and R. Litterman and T. Iben, "Corporate Bond Valuation and the Term Structure of Credit Spreads," *Journal of Portfolio Management*, 1989, pp. 52–64.

[47] See J. B. Yawitz, "Risk Premia on Municipal Bonds," *Journal of Financial and Quantitative Analysis* 13 (1977), pp. 475–85; and J. B. Yawitz, "An Analytical Model of Interest Rate Differentials and Different Default Recoveries," *Journal of Financial and Quantitative Analysis* 13 (1977), pp. 481–90.

[48] E. I. Altman and G. Bana, "Defaults and Returns on High-Yield Bonds: The Year 2002 in Review and the Market Outlook," Working Paper, New York University Salomon Center, February 2003.

[49] For example, from Table 11–5 the average recovery rate on bonds that were senior secured in 1987 was 90.68 percent (although these bonds recover on average 52.86 percent), recovery rates are usually calculated in one of two ways: first, by looking at the prices of loans or bonds in the secondary market postdefault or, second (if they are not actively traded), by calculating the net present value of the expected cash flows that are projected to be recovered postdefault.

TABLE 11–5   Recovery Rates (RR) on Defaulted Debt by Seniority, 1978–2002

Year	Senior Secured		Senior Unsecured		Senior Subordinated		Subordinated		Discount and Zero Coupon		All Securities	
	Number	RR%	Number	RR%	Number	RR%	Number	RR%	Number	RR%	Number	RR%
2002	37	52.81	254	21.82	21	32.79	—	—	28	26.47	340	25.32
2001	9	40.95	187	28.84	48	18.37	—	—	37	15.05	281	25.48
2000	13	39.58	47	25.40	61	25.96	26	26.62	17	23.61	164	25.83
1999	14	26.90	60	42.54	40	23.56	2	13.88	11	17.30	127	31.14
1998	6	70.38	21	39.57	6	17.54	—	—	1	17.00	34	37.27
1997	4	74.90	12	70.94	6	31.89	1	60.66	2	19.00	25	53.89
1996	4	59.08	4	50.11	9	48.99	4	44.23	3	11.99	24	51.91
1995	5	44.64	9	50.50	17	39.01	1	20.00	1	17.50	33	41.77
1994	5	48.66	8	51.14	5	19.81	3	37.04	1	5.00	22	39.44
1993	2	55.75	7	33.38	10	51.50	9	28.38	4	31.75	32	38.83
1992	15	59.85	8	35.61	17	58.20	22	49.13	5	19.82	67	50.03
1991	4	44.12	69	55.84	37	31.91	38	24.30	9	27.89	157	40.67
1990	12	32.18	31	29.02	38	25.01	24	18.83	11	15.63	116	24.66
1989	9	82.69	16	53.70	21	19.60	30	23.95	—	—	76	35.97
1988	13	67.96	19	41.99	10	30.70	20	35.27	—	—	62	43.45
1987	4	90.68	17	72.02	6	56.24	4	35.25	—	—	31	66.63
1986	8	48.32	11	37.72	7	35.20	30	33.39	—	—	56	36.60
1985	2	74.25	3	34.81	7	36.18	15	41.45	—	—	27	41.78
1984	4	53.42	1	50.50	2	65.88	7	44.68	—	—	14	50.62
1983	1	71.00	3	67.72	—	—	4	41.79	—	—	8	55.17
1982	—	—	16	39.31	—	—	4	32.91	—	—	20	38.03
1981	1	72.00	—	—	—	—	—	—	—	—	1	72.00
1980	—	—	2	26.71	—	—	2	16.63	—	—	4	21.67
1979	—	—	—	—	—	—	1	31.00	—	—	1	31.00
1978	—	—	1	60.00	—	—	—	—	—	—	1	60.00
Total/ Average	172	52.86	806	33.62	368	29.67	247	31.03	130	20.40	1723	32.93

Source: E. I. Altman and G. Bana, "Defaults and Returns on High-Yield Bonds: The Year 2002 in Review and the Market Outlook," Working Paper, New York University Salomon Center, February 2003. www.stern.nyu.edu/-ealtman

the same required risk premium as one with $\gamma = .8$ and $p = .7$. An increase in collateral γ is a direct substitute for an increase in default risk (i.e., a decline in p).

Probability of Default on a Multiperiod Debt Instrument

We can extend this type of analysis to derive the credit risk or default probabilities occurring in the market for longer-term loans or bonds (i.e., two-year bonds). To do this, the manager must estimate the probability that the bond will default in the second year conditional on the probability that it does not default in the first year. The probability that a bond will default in any given year is clearly conditional on the fact that the default has not occurred earlier. The probability that a bond will default in any given year, t, is the **marginal default probability** for that year, $1 - p_t$. However, for, say, a two-year loan, the marginal probability of default in the second year $(1 - p_2)$ can differ from the marginal probability of default in the first year $(1 - p_1)$. If we use these marginal default probabilities, the **cumulative default probability** at some time between now and the end of year 2 is:

$$Cp = 1 - [(p_1)(p_2)]$$

marginal default probability
The probability that a borrower will default in any given year.

cumulative default probability
The probability that a borrower will default over a specified multiyear period.

EXAMPLE 11–5

Calculating the Probability of Default on a Multiperiod Bond

Suppose the FI manager wanted to find out the probability of default on a two-year bond. For the one-year loan, $1 - p_1 = .05$ is the marginal and total or cumulative probability (Cp) of default in year 1. Later in this chapter we discuss ways in which p_2 can be estimated by the FI manager, but for the moment suppose that $1 - p_2 = .07$. Then:

$$1 - p_1 = .05 = \text{marginal probability of default in year 1}$$
$$1 - p_2 = .07 = \text{marginal probability of default in year 2}$$

The probability of the borrower surviving—not defaulting at any time between now (time 0) and the end of period 2—is $p_1 \times p_2 = (.95)(.93) = .8835$.

$$Cp = 1 - [(.95)(.93)] = .1165$$

There is an 11.65 percent probability of default over this period.

We have seen how to derive the one-year probability of default from yield spreads on one-year bonds. We now want to derive the probability of default in year 2, year 3, and so on. Look at Figure 11–6; as you can see, yield curves are rising for both government issues and corporate bond issues. We want to extract from these yield curves the *market's expectation* of the multiperiod default rates for corporate borrowers classified in the grade B rating class.[50]

Look first at the government yield curve. The condition of efficient markets and thus **no arbitrage** profits by investors requires that the return on buying and holding the two-year government discount bond to maturity just equals the expected return from investing in the current one-year discount government bond and reinvesting the principal and interest in a new one-year discount government bond at the end of the first year at the expected one-year **forward rate**. That is:

$$(1 + i_2)^2 = (1 + i_1)(1 + f_1) \tag{11.1}$$

The term on the left side is the return from holding the two-year discount bond to maturity. The term on the right side results from investing in two successive one-year bonds, where i_1 is the current one-year bond rate and f_1 is the expected one-year bond rate or forward rate next year. Since we can observe directly from the government bond yield curve the current required yields on one- and two-year government bonds, we can directly infer the market's expectation of the one-year government bond rate next period or the one-year forward rate, f_1:

$$1 + f_1 = \frac{(1 + i_2)^2}{(1 + i_1)} \tag{11.2}$$

We can use the same type of analysis with the corporate bond yield curve to infer the one-year forward rate on corporate bonds (grade B in this example). The one-year rate expected on corporate securities (c_1) one year into the future reflects the market's default risk expectations for this class of borrower as well as the more general time value factors also affecting f_1:

$$1 + c_1 = \frac{(1 + k_2)^2}{(1 + k_1)} \tag{11.3}$$

no arbitrage
The inability to make a profit without taking risk.

forward rate
A one-period rate of interest expected on a bond issued at some date in the future.

---

[50] To use this model, one has to place borrowers in a rating class. One way to do this for unrated firms would be to use the Z score model to calculate a Z ratio for this firm. E. I. Altman has shown that there is a high correlation between Z scores and Standard & Poor's and Moody's bond ratings. Once a firm is placed in a bond rating group (e.g., B) by the Z score model, the term structure model can be used to infer the expected (implied) probabilities of default for the borrower at different times in the future. See "Valuation, Loss Reserves, and Pricing of Commercial Loans," *Journal of Commercial Bank Lending,* August 1993, pp. 9–25.

The expected rates on one-year bonds can generate an estimate of the expected probability of repayment on one-year corporate bonds in one year's time, or what we have called p_2. Since:

$$p_2 (1 + c_1) = 1 + f_1$$

then:

$$p_2 = \left[\frac{1 + f_1}{1 + c_1} \right] \qquad \textbf{(11.4)}$$

Thus, the expected probability of default in year 2 is:

$$1 - p_2 \qquad \textbf{(11.5)}$$

In a similar fashion, the one-year rates expected in two years' time can be derived from the Treasury and corporate term structures so as to derive p_3, and so on.

EXAMPLE 11–6

Calculating the Probability of Default on a Multiperiod Bond Using Term Structure Derivation of Credit Risk

From the government bond yield curve in Figure 11–6, the current required yields on one- and two-year Treasuries are $i_1 = 10$ percent and $i_2 = 11$ percent, respectively. If we use equation (2), the one-year forward rate, f_1, is:

$$1 + f_1 = \frac{(1.11)^2}{(1.10)} = 1.12$$

or

$$f_1 = 12\%$$

The expected rise in one-year rates from 10 percent (i_1) this year to 12 percent (f_1) next year reflects investors' perceptions regarding inflation and other factors that directly affect the time value of money.

Further, the current yield curve, in Figure 11–6, indicates that appropriate one-year discount bonds are yielding $k_1 = 15.8$ percent and two-year bonds are yielding $k_2 = 18$ percent. Thus, if we use equation (3), the one-year rate expected on corporate securities, c_1, is:

$$1 + c_1 = \frac{(1.18)^2}{(1.158)} = 1.202$$

or

$$c_1 = 20.2\%$$

We summarize these calculations in Table 11–6. As you can see, the expected spread between one-year corporate bonds and government bonds in one year's time is higher than the spread for current one-year bonds. Thus, the default risk premium increases with the maturity on the corporate (risky) bond.

From these expected rates on one-year bonds, if we use equations (4) and (5), the expected probability of repayment on one-year corporate bonds in one year's time, p_2, is:

$$p_2 = \frac{[1.12]}{[1.202]} = .9318$$

and the expected probability of default in year 2 is:

$$1 - p_2 = 1 - .9318 = .0682$$

or

$$6.82\%$$

The probabilities we have estimated are marginal probabilities conditional on default not occurring in a prior period. We also discussed the concept of the *cumulative probability* of default that would tell the FI the probability of a loan or bond investment defaulting over a particular time period. In the example developed earlier, the cumulative probability that corporate grade-B bonds would default over the next two years is:

$$Cp = 1 - [(p_1)(p_2)]$$

$$Cp = 1 - [(.95)(.9318)] = 11.479\%$$

As with the credit scoring approach, this model creates some potential problems. Its principal advantages are that it is clearly forward-looking and based on market expectations. Moreover, if there are liquid markets for government and corporate discount bonds—such as Treasury strips and corporate zero-coupon bonds—then we can easily estimate expected future default rates and use them to value and price loans. However, the market for corporate discount bonds is quite small. Although a discount yield curve for corporate bonds could be extracted mathematically from the corporate bond coupon yield curve (see Chapter 26), these bonds often are not very actively traded and prices are not very transparent. Given this, the FI manager might have to consider an alternative way to use bond or loan data to extract default rate probabilities for all but the very largest corporate borrowers. We consider a possible alternative next.[51]

Concept Questions

1. What is the difference between the marginal default probability and the cumulative default probability?
2. How should the posting of collateral by a borrower affect the risk premium on a loan?

Mortality Rate Derivation of Credit Risk

Rather than extracting *expected* default rates from the current term structure of interest rates, the FI manager may analyze the *historic* or past default risk experience, the **mortality rates,** of bonds and loans of a similar quality. Consider calculating p_1 and p_2 using the mortality rate model.[52] Here p_1 is the probability of a grade B bond or loan surviving the first year of its issue; thus $1 - p_1$ is the **marginal mortality rate,** or the probability of the bond or loan defaulting in the first year of issue. While p_2 is the probability of the loan surviving in the second year given that default has not occurred during the first year, $1 - p_2$ is the marginal mortality rate for the second year. Thus, for each grade of corporate borrower quality, a marginal mortality rate (MMR) curve can show the historical default rate experience of bonds in any specific quality class in each year after issue on the bond or loan.

Note in Figure 11–7 that as grade B bonds age, their probability of dying increases in each successive year. Of course, in reality, any shape to the mortality curve is possible. It is possible that MMRs can be flat, decline over time, or show a more complex functional form. These marginal mortality rates can be estimated from actual data on bond and loan defaults. Specifically, for grade B quality bonds (loans):

$$MMR_1 = \frac{\text{Total value of grade B bonds defaulting in year 1 of issue}}{\text{Total value of grade B bonds outstanding in year 1 of issue}}$$

mortality rate
Historic default rate experience of a bond or loan.

marginal mortality rate
The probability of a bond or loan defaulting in any given year after issue.

---

[51] For a discussion of and empirical evidence on the lack of price transparency in the U.S. corporate bond markets, see A. Saunders, A. Srinivasan, and I. Walter, "Price Formation in the OTC Corporate Bond Markets: A Field Study of the Inter-Dealer Market," *Journal of Economics and Business,* January–February 2002, pp. 95–113.

[52] For further reading, see E. I. Altman, "Measuring Corporate Bond Mortality," *Journal of Finance,* September1989, pp. 909–22; Altman and Bana, "Defaults and Returns on High-Yield Bonds"; and Saunders and Allen, *Credit Risk Measurement,* Chapter 8.

TABLE 11–6 Government and Corporate
Rates and Rate Spreads

	Current One-Year Rate	Expected One-Year Rate
Government	10.0%	12.0%
Corporate (B)	15.8	20.2
Spread	5.8	8.2

FIGURE 11–7 Hypothetical Marginal Mortality Rate
Curve for Grade B Corporate Bonds

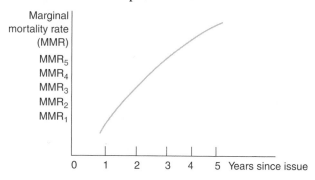

Source: Excerpted, with permission, from *Default Risk, Mortality Rates, and the Performance of Corporate Bonds*, 1989. Copyright 1989. Association for Investment Management and Research, Charlottesville, VA. All rights reserved.

$$MMR_2 = \frac{\text{Total value of grade B bonds defaulting in year 2 of issue}}{\begin{array}{c}\text{Total value of grade B bonds outstanding in year 2 of issue}\\ \text{adjusted for defaults, calls, sinking fund redemptions, and}\\ \text{maturities in the prior year}\end{array}}$$

Table 11–7 shows the estimated mortality and cumulative default rates for samples of 1,513 rated corporate bonds over the 1971–2002 period. From Table 11–7 it can be seen that mortality rates are higher the lower the rating of the bond.

The mortality rate approach has a number of conceptual and applicability problems. Probably the most important of these is that, like the credit scoring model, it produces historic, or backward-looking, measures. Also, the estimates of default rates and therefore implied future default probabilities tend to be highly sensitive to the period over which the FI manager calculates the MMRs. For example, WorldCom had an S&P rating of BBB just prior to its defaulting on its debt in 2002. Note in Table 11–7 the second year's marginal mortality rate for BBB bonds (3.42%) is much higher than those of years 3 and 4 and is even higher than that of the second year mortality rate for BB bonds. This is primarily due to the default of World-Com in 2002. In addition, the estimates tend to be sensitive to the number of issues and the relative size of issues in each investment grade.[53]

Concept Questions

1. In Table 11–7, the CMR over 3 years for CCC rated corporate bonds is 33.17 percent. Check this calculation using the individual year MMRs.
2. Why would any FI manager buy loans that have a CMR of 33.17 percent? Explain your answer.

RAROC Models

RAROC
Risk-adjusted return on capital.

A popular model used to evaluate (and price) credit risk based on market data is the RAROC model. The **RAROC** (risk-adjusted return on capital) was pioneered by Bankers Trust (acquired by Deutsche Bank in 1998) and has now been adopted by virtually all the large banks in the United States and Europe, although with some significant proprietary differences between them.

---

[53] For example, even though the estimates in Table 11–7 are based on 1,513 observations of bonds, these estimates still have quite wide confidence bands. See P. H. McAllister and J. J. Mingo, "Commercial Loan Risk Management, Credit Scoring and Pricing: The Need for a New Shared Data Base," *Journal of Commercial Lending*, May 1994, pp. 6–20; and Saunders and Allen, *Credit Risk Measurement*, Chapter 8.

TABLE 11–7   **Mortality Rates by Original Rating—All Rated* Corporate Bonds, 1971–2002**

		Years after Issuance									
		1	2	3	4	5	6	7	8	9	10
AAA	Marginal	0.00%	0.00%	0.00%	0.00%	0.03%	0.00%	0.00%	0.00%	0.00%	0.00%
	Cumulative	0.00	0.00	0.00	0.00	0.03	0.03	0.03	0.03	0.03	0.03
AA	Marginal	0.00	0.00	0.33	0.17	0.00	0.00	0.00	0.00	0.03	0.02
	Cumulative	0.00	0.00	0.33	0.50	0.50	0.50	0.50	0.50	0.53	0.55
A	Marginal	0.01	0.10	0.02	0.09	0.04	0.10	0.05	0.20	0.11	0.06
	Cumulative	0.01	0.11	0.13	0.22	0.26	0.36	0.41	0.61	0.72	0.78
BBB	Marginal	0.25	3.42	1.52	1.44	0.92	0.57	0.80	0.26	0.17	0.35
	Cumulative	0.25	3.66	5.13	6.49	7.35	7.88	8.62	8.85	9.01	9.33
BB	Marginal	1.23	2.62	4.53	2.15	2.49	1.14	1.67	0.67	1.76	3.78
	Cumulative	1.23	3.82	8.17	10.15	12.39	13.39	14.83	15.40	16.89	20.03
B	Marginal	3.19	7.14	7.85	8.74	6.22	4.28	3.88	2.39	2.07	0.87
	Cumulative	3.19	10.10	17.16	24.40	29.10	32.14	34.77	36.33	37.65	38.19
CCC	Marginal	6.70	14.57	16.16	11.28	3.36	10.26	5.35	3.25	0.00	4.18
	Cumulative	6.70	20.29	33.17	40.71	42.70	48.58	51.33	52.92	52.92	54.88

*Rated by S&P at issuance.

Source: E. I. Altman and G. Bana, "Defaults and Returns on High-Yield Bonds: The Year 2002 in Review and the Market Outlook," Working Paper, New York University Salomon Center, February 2003.

The essential idea behind RAROC is that rather than evaluating the actual or contractually promised annual ROA on a loan, as on p. 299 (that is, net interest and fees divided by the amount lent), the lending officer balances expected interest and fee income less the cost of funds against the loan's expected risk. Thus, the numerator of the RAROC equation is net income (accounting for the cost of funding the loan) on the loan. Further, rather than dividing annual loan income by assets lent, it is divided by some measure of asset (loan) risk or what is often called capital at risk, since (unexpected) loan losses have to be written off against an FI's capital:[54]

$$RAROC = \frac{\text{One year net income on a loan}}{\text{Change in loan's market value}}$$

A loan is approved only if RAROC is sufficiently high relative to a benchmark return on capital (ROE) for the FI, where ROE measures the return stockholders require on their equity investment in the FI. The idea here is that a loan should be made only if the risk-adjusted return on the loan adds to the FI's equity value as measured by the ROE required by the FI's stockholders. Thus, for example, if an FI's ROE is 15 percent, a loan should be made only if the estimated RAROC is higher than the 15 percent required by the FI's stockholders as a reward for their investment in the FI. Alternatively, if the RAROC on an existing loan falls below an FI's RAROC benchmark, the lending officer should seek to adjust the loan's terms to make it "profitable" again. Therefore, RAROC serves as both a credit risk measure and a loan pricing tool for the FI manager.

One problem in estimating RAROC is the measurement of loan risk or change in the loan's market value (the denominator in the RAROC equation). Chapter 9 on duration showed that the percentage change in the market value of an asset such as

---

[54] Traditionally, expected loan losses are covered by a bank's loss reserve (or provisions), while unexpected or extreme loan losses are being met by a bank's capital reserves.

a loan ($\Delta LN/LN$) is related to the duration of the loan and the size of the interest rate shock ($\Delta R/(1 + R)$), where R is the base rate, BR, plus the credit risk premium, m:

$$\frac{\Delta LN}{LN} = -D_{LN}\frac{\Delta R}{1 + R}$$

The same concept is applied here, except that (assuming that the base rate remains constant) interest rate shocks are the consequence of credit quality (or credit risk premium) shocks (i.e., shocks to m). We can thus rewrite the duration equation with the following interpretation to estimate the loan risk or capital at risk on the loan:

$$\Delta LN \quad = \quad -D_{LN} \quad \times \quad LN \quad \times \quad (\Delta R/(1 + R))$$

| (change in loan's market value) | (duration of the loan) | (risk amount or size of loan) | (expected maximum change in the loan rate due to a change in the credit premium (m) or risk factor on the loan) |

While the loan's duration (say, 2.7 years) and the loan amount (say, $1 million) are easily estimated, it is more difficult to estimate the maximum change in the credit risk premium on the loan over the next year. Since publicly available data on loan risk premiums are scarce, we turn to publicly available corporate bond market data to estimate premiums. First, an S&P credit rating (AAA, AA, A, and so on) is assigned to a borrower. Thereafter, the available risk premium changes of all the bonds traded in that particular rating class over the last year are analyzed. The ΔR in the RAROC equation equals:

$$\Delta R = \text{Max} [\Delta(R_i - R_G) > 0]$$

where $\Delta(R_i - R_G)$ is the change in the yield spread between corporate bonds of credit rating class i (R_i) and matched duration treasury bonds (R_G) over the last year. In order to consider only the worst-case scenario, a maximum change in yield spread is chosen, as opposed to the average change. In general, it is common to pick the 1 percent worst case or 99th percentile of credit risk changes.

EXAMPLE 11–7

Calculation of RAROC on a Loan

Suppose we want to evaluate the credit risk of a loan to a AAA borrower. Assume there are currently 400 publicly traded bonds in that class (i.e., bonds issued by firms of a rating type similar to that of the borrower). The first step is to evaluate the actual changes in the credit risk premiums ($R_i - R_G$) on each of these bonds for the past year (in this example, the year 2006). These (hypothetical) changes are plotted in the frequency curve of Figure 11–6. They range from a fall in the risk premiums of negative 2 percent to an increase of 3.5 percent. Since the largest increase may be a very extreme (unrepresentative) number, the 99 percent worst-case scenario is chosen (i.e., only 4 bonds out of 400 had risk premium increases exceeding the 99 percent worst case). For the example shown in Figure 11–6 this is equal to 1.1 percent.

The estimate of loan (or capital) risk, assuming that the current average level of rates (R) on AAA bonds is 10 percent, is:

$$\Delta LN = -D_{LN} \times LN \times \frac{\Delta R}{1 + R}$$

$$= -(2.7)(\$1 \text{ million})\left(\frac{.011}{1.1}\right)$$

$$= -\$27,000.$$

FIGURE 11–8
Hypothetical
Frequency
Distribution of
Yield Spread
Changes for All
AAA Bonds in 2006

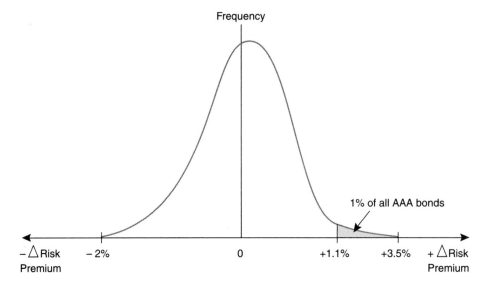

Thus, while the face value of the loan amount is $1 million, the risk amount, or change in the loan's market value due to a decline in its credit quality, is $27,000.

To determine whether the loan is worth making, the estimated loan risk is compared with the loan's income (spread over the FI's cost of funds plus fees on the loan). Suppose the projected (one-year) spread plus fees is as follows:

$$\text{Spread} = 0.2\% \times \$1 \text{ million} = \$2,000$$
$$\text{Fees} = 0.1\% \times \$1 \text{ million} = \underline{\$1,000}$$
$$\$3,000$$

The loan's RAROC is:

$$RAROC = \frac{\text{One-year net income on loan}}{\text{Loan risk (or capital risk)}(\Delta LN)} = \frac{\$3,000}{\$27,000} = 11.1\%$$

Note that RAROC can be either forward looking, comparing the projected income over the next year on the loan with ΔLN, or backward looking, comparing the actual income generated on the loan over the past year with ΔLN.

If the 11.1 percent exceeds the FI's internal RAROC benchmark (based on its cost of capital, or ROE), the loan will be approved. If it is less, the loan will be rejected outright or the borrower will be asked to pay higher fees and/or a higher spread to increase the RAROC to acceptable levels.

Other FIs have adopted different ways of calculating ΔLN in their versions of RAROC. Some FIs, usually the largest ones with very good loan default databases, divide one-year income by the product of an unexpected loss rate and the proportion of the loan lost on default, also called the loss given default. Thus:

$$RAROC =$$

$$\frac{\text{One-year net income per dollar loaned}}{\text{Unexpected default rate} \times \text{Proportion of loan lost on default (loss given default)}}$$

Suppose expected income per dollar lent is 0.3 cents, or .003. The 99th percentile historic (extreme case) default rate for borrowers of this type is 4 percent, and the dollar proportion of loans of this type that cannot be recaptured is 80 percent. Then:[55]

$$RAROC = \frac{.003}{(.04)(.8)} = \frac{.003}{(.032)} = 9.375\%$$

Concept Questions

1. Describe the basic concept behind RAROC models.

Option Models of Default Risk[56]

Theoretical Framework

In recent years, following the pioneering work of Nobel prize winners Merton, Black, and Scholes, we now recognize that when a firm raises funds by issuing bonds or increasing its bank loans, it holds a very valuable default or repayment option.[57] That is, if a borrower's investment projects fail so that it cannot repay the bondholder or the bank, it has the option of defaulting on its debt repayment and turning any remaining assets over to the debtholder. Because of limited liability for equity holders, the borrower's loss is limited on the downside by the amount of equity invested in the firm.[58] On the other hand, if things go well, the borrower can keep most of the upside returns on asset investments after the promised principal and interest on the debt have been paid. Moody's KMV Corporation (which was purchased by Moody's in 2002) turned this relatively simple idea into a credit monitoring model. Many of the largest U.S. FIs are now using this model to determine the expected default risk frequency (EDF) of large corporations.[59] Before we look at the KMV credit monitor model, we will take a closer look at the theory underlying the option approach to default risk estimation.

www.moodyskmv. com

The Borrower's Payoff from Loans

Look at the payoff function for the borrower in Figure 11–9, where S is the size of the initial equity investment in the firm, B is the value of outstanding bonds or loans (assumed for simplicity to be issued on a discount basis), and A is the market value of the assets of the firm.

---

[55] Calculating the unexpected default rate commonly involves calculating the standard derivation (σ) of annual default rates on loans of this type and then multiplying σ by a factor such that 99 percent (or higher) of defaults are covered by capital. For example, if the loss distribution was normally distributed, then the σ of default rates would be multiplied by 2.33 to get the extreme 99 percent default rate. For many FIs, default rates are skewed to the right and have fat tails suggesting a multiplier much larger than 2.33. For example, to get coverage of 99.97 percent of defaults, Bank of America has historically used a multiplier of 6. Finally, the denominator can also be adjusted for the degree of correlation of the loan with the rest of the FI's portfolio. See, for example, Edward Zaik et al., "RAROC at Bank of America: From Theory to Practice," *Journal of Applied Corporate Finance*, Summer 1996, pp. 83–93.

[56] This section, which contains more technical details, may be included in or dropped from the chapter reading depending on the rigor of the course. Students unfamiliar with the basics of options may want to review the section "Basic Features of Options" in Chapter 24 of the text.

[57] R. C. Merton, "On the Pricing of Corporate Debt: The Risk Structure of Interest Rates," *Journal of Finance* 29 (1974), pp. 449–70; and F. Black and M. Scholes, "The Pricing of Options and Corporate Liabilities," *Journal of Political Economy* 81 (1973), pp. 637–59.

[58] Given limits to losses in personal bankruptcy, a similar analysis can be applied to consumer loans.

[59] See KMV Corporation Credit Monitor, KMV Corporation, San Francisco, 1994; S. P. Choudhury, "Choosing the Right Box of Credit Tricks," *Risk Magazine*, November 1997 pp. 61–62; and Saunders and Allen, *Credit Risk Measurement*, Chapter 4.

FIGURE 11–9
**Payoff Function
to Corporate
Borrowers
(Stockholders)**

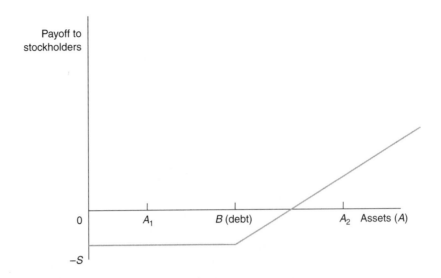

If the investments in Figure 11–9 turn out badly such that the firm's assets are valued at point A_1, the limited-liability stockholder–owners of the firm will default on the firm's debt, turn its assets (such as A_1) over to the debt holders, and lose only their initial stake in the firm (S). By contrast, if the firm does well and the assets of the firm are valued highly (A_2), the firm's stockholders will pay off the firm's debt and keep the difference ($A_2 - B$). Clearly, the higher A_2 is relative to B, the better off are the firm's stockholders. Given that borrowers face only a limited downside risk of loss of their equity investment but a very large potential upside return if things turn out well, equity is analogous to buying a call option on the assets of the firm (see also Chapter 24 on options).

The Debt Holder's Payoff from Loans

Consider the same loan or bond issue from the perspective of the FI or bondholder. The maximum amount the FI or bondholder can get back is B, the promised payment. However, the borrower who possesses the default or repayment option would rationally repay the loan only if $A > B$, that is, if the market value of assets exceeds the value of promised debt repayments. A borrower whose asset value falls below B would default and turn over any remaining assets to the debt holders. The payoff function to the debt holder is shown in Figure 11–10.

After investment of the borrowed funds has taken place, if the value of the firm's assets lies to the right of B, the face value of the debt—such as A_2—the debt holder or FI will be paid off in full and receive B. On the other hand, if asset values fall in the region to the left of B—such as A_1—the debt holder will receive back only those assets remaining as collateral, thereby losing $B - A_1$. Thus, the value of the loan from the perspective of the lender is always the minimum of B or A, or min $[B,A]$. That is, the payoff function to the debt holder is similar to writing a put option on the value of the borrower's assets with B, the face value of debt, as the *exercise price*. If $A > B$, the loan is repaid and the debt holder earns a small fixed return (similar to the premium on a put option), which is the interest rate implicit in the discount bond. If $A < B$, the borrower defaults and the debt holder stands to lose both interest and principal. In the limit, default for a firm with no assets left results in debt holders' losing all their principal and interest. In actuality, if there are also costs of bankruptcy, the debt holder can potentially lose even more than this.

FIGURE 11–10
Payoff Function
to the Debt Holder
(the FI) from a Loan

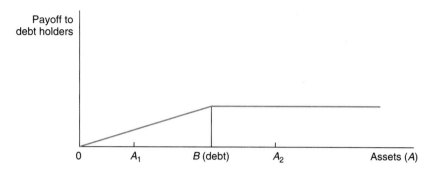

Applying the Option Valuation Model to the Calculation of Default Risk Premiums

Merton has shown that in the context of the preceding options framework, it is quite straightforward to express the market value of a risky loan made by a lender to a borrower as:[60]

$$F(\tau) = Be^{-i\tau}[(1/d)N(h_1) + N(h_2)] \qquad (11.6)$$

where

$\tau =$ Length of time remaining to loan maturity; that is, $\tau = T - t$, where T is the maturity date and time t is today.

$d =$ Borrower's leverage ratio measured as $Be^{-i\tau}/A$, where the market value of debt is valued at the rate i, the risk-free rate of interest.

$N(h) =$ Value computed from the standardized normal distribution statistical tables. This value reflects the probability that a deviation exceeding the calculated value of h will occur.

$$h_1 = -\left[\frac{1}{2}\sigma^2\tau - \ln(d)\right]/\sigma\sqrt{\tau}$$

$$h_2 = -\left[\frac{1}{2}\sigma^2\tau + \ln(d)\right]/\sigma\sqrt{\tau}$$

$\sigma^2 =$ Measures the asset risk of the borrower. Technically, it is the variance of the rate of change in the value of the underlying assets of the borrower.

More important, written in terms of a yield spread, this equation reflects an equilibrium default risk premium that the borrower should be charged:

$$k(\tau) - i = (-1/\tau)\ln[N(h_2) + (1/d)N(h_1)]$$

where

$k(\tau) =$ Required yield on risky debt (the contractually promised return from earlier)

$\ln =$ Natural logarithm

$i =$ Risk-free rate on debt of equivalent maturity (here, one period)

Thus, Merton has shown that the lender should adjust the required risk premium as d and σ^2 change, that is, as leverage and asset risk change.

---

[60] See Merton, "On the Pricing of Corporate Debt."

EXAMPLE 11–8

Calculating the Value of and Interest Rate on a Loan Using the Option Model[61]

Suppose that:

B = \$100,000
τ = 1 year
i = 5 percent
d = 90% or .9
σ = 12%

That is, suppose we can measure the market value of a firm's assets (and thus $d = Be^{-i\tau}/A$) as well as the volatility of those assets (σ). Then, substituting these values into the equations for h_1 and h_2 and solving for the areas under the standardized normal distribution, we find that:

$$N(h_1) = .174120$$
$$N(h_2) = .793323$$

where

$$h1 = \frac{-\left[\frac{1}{2}(.12)^2 - \ln(.9)\right]}{.12} = -.938$$

and

$$h2 = \frac{-\left[\frac{1}{2}(.12)^2 - \ln(.9)\right]}{.12} = +.818$$

The current market value of the loan is:

$$L(t) = Be^{-i\tau}[N(h_2) + (1/d)N(h_1)]$$

$$= \frac{\$100,000}{1.05127}[.793323 + (1.1111)(.17412)]$$

$$= \frac{\$100,000}{1.05127}[.986788]$$

$$= \$93,866.18$$

and the required risk spread or premium is:

$$k(\tau) - i = \left(\frac{-1}{\tau}\right)\ln[N(h_2) + (1/d)N(h_1)]$$

$$= (-1)\ln[.986788]$$

$$= 1.33\%$$

Thus, the risky loan rate $k(\tau)$ should be set at 6.33 percent when the risk-free rate (i) is 5 percent.

Theoretically, this model is an elegant tool for extracting premiums and default probabilities; it also has important conceptual implications regarding which variables to focus on in credit risk evaluation [e.g., the firm's market value of assets (A) and asset risk (σ^2)]. Even so, this model has a number of real-world implementation problems. Probably the most significant is the fact that neither the market value of a firm's assets (A) nor the volatility of the firm's assets (σ^2) is directly observed.

www.moodyskmv. com

The KMV model in fact recognizes this problem by using an option pricing model (OPM) approach to extract the implied market value of assets (A) and the asset volatility of a given firm's assets (σ^2).[62] The KMV model uses the value of equity in

---

[61] This numerical example is based on D. F. Babbel, "Insuring Banks against Systematic Credit Risk," *Journal of Futures Markets* 9 (1989), pp. 487–506.

[62] See S. Kealhofer, "Quantifying Credit Risk I: Default Prediction," *Financial Analysts Journal,* January/February 2003, pp. 30–44.

FIGURE 11–11
Expected Default Frequency Using the KMV Model

Source: KMV Corporation Credit Monitor. Reprinted by permission of KMV Corporation. www.moodyskmv.com

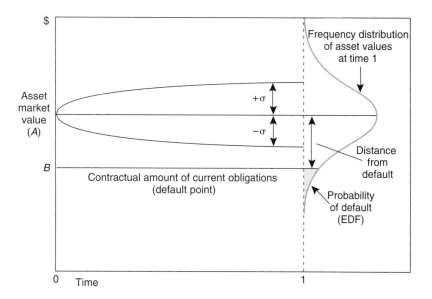

a firm (from a stockholder's perspective) as equivalent to holding a call option on the assets of the firm (with the amount of debt borrowed acting similarly to the exercise price of the call option). From this approach, and the link between the volatility of the market value of the firm's equity and that of its assets, it is possible to derive the asset volatility (risk) of any given firm (σ) and the market value of the firm's assets (A).[63] Using the implied value of σ for assets and A, the market value of assets, the likely distribution of possible asset values of the firm relative to its current debt obligations can be calculated over the next year.[64] As shown in Figure 11–11, the expected default frequency (EDF) that is calculated reflects the probability that the market value of the firm's assets (A) will fall below the promised repayments on its short-term debt liabilities (B) in one year. If the value of a firm's assets falls below its debt liabilities, it can be viewed as being economically insolvent. Simulations by KMV have shown that EDF models outperform both Z score-type models and S&P rating changes as predictors of corporate failure and distress.[65] An example for Enron Corp., which filed for Chapter 11 bankruptcy protection on June 25, 2001, is shown in Figure 11–12.

---

[63] More specifically, it does this by using the equity (stock market) value of the firm's shares (E) and the volatility of the value of the firm's shares (σ_E). Since equity can be viewed as a call option on the firm's assets and the volatility of a firm's equity value will reflect the leverage adjusted volatility of its underlying assets, we have in general form:

$$\bar{E} = f(A, \sigma, \bar{B}, \bar{r}, \bar{\tau})$$

and

$$\bar{\sigma}_E = g(\sigma)$$

where the bars denote values that are directly measurable. Since we have two equations and two unknowns (A, σ), we can directly solve for both A and σ and use these, along with the firm's outstanding short-term liabilities or current liabilities, to calculate the EDF (expected default frequency).

[64] Suppose the value of the firm's assets (A) at the time zero is $100 million and the value of its short-term debt is $80 million. Suppose that the implied volatility (σ) of asset values was estimated at $12.12 million, and it is assumed that asset-value changes are normally distributed. The firm becomes distressed only if the value of its assets falls to $80 million or below (falls by $20 million). Such a fall is equal to 1.65σ, i.e., $1.65 \times \$12.12$ million = $20 million. From statistics, we know that the area of the normal distribution (in each tail) lying $\pm 1.65\ \sigma$ from the mean is theoretically 5 percent. Thus, the KMV model would suggest a theoretical 5 percent probability of the firm's going into distress over the next year (by time 1). However, KMV calculates empirical EDFs, since we do not know the true distribution of asset values (A) over time. Essentially, it asks this question: In practice, how many firms that started the year with asset values 1.65 σ distance from default (see Figure 11–11) actually defaulted at the end of the year? This value may or may not equal 5 percent.

[65] Moody's KMV provides monthly EDFs for over 6,000 U.S. companies and 20,000 companies worldwide.

FIGURE 11–12
KMV and S&P
Ratings for
Enron Corp.

Source: KMV Corporation,
San Francisco, California.
www.moodyskmv.com

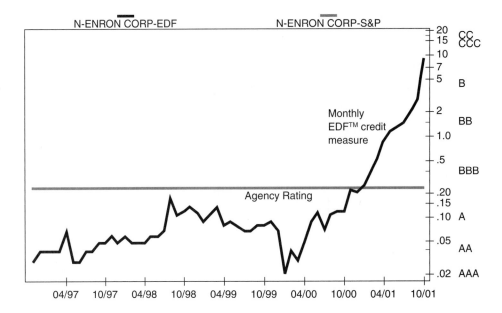

Note that the KMV score (expected default frequency) is rising faster than the rating agencies are downgrading the firm's debt. Indeed, the rating agency ratings are very slow to react to, if not totally insensitive to, the increase in Enron's risk. The KMV EDF score starts to rise over a year prior to Enron's bankruptcy. Thus, the KMV EDF score gives a better early warning of impending default.[66]

**Concept
Questions**

1. Which is the only credit risk model discussed in this section that is really forward looking?
2. How should the risk premium on a loan be affected if there is a reduction in a borrower's leverage and the underlying volatility of its earnings?
3. What is the link between the implied volatility of a firm's assets and its expected default frequency?

---

[66] One reason is that the KMV score is extracted from stock market data that is highly sensitive to new information about a firm's future prospects. Indeed, the acquisition of KMV by Moody's allowed the rating agency to move closer to including market-based information in its rating process. See "Implications of the Acquisition of KMV for Moody's Ratings," Moody's Investors Service, March 2002.

Summary

This chapter discussed different approaches to measuring credit or default risk on individual loans (bonds). The different types of loans made by FIs and some of their basic characteristics were first examined. The expected return on a loan was shown to depend on factors such as origination fees, compensating balances, interest rates, and maturity. The various models to assess default risk include both qualitative and quantitative models. The qualitative models usually contain both firm-specific factors, such as reputation and leverage, and market-specific factors, such as the business cycle and the level of interest rates. Quantitative models, such as the linear probability model, the logit model, and the linear discriminant model, were shown to provide credit scores that can rank or classify loans by expected default risk. The more rigorous of the quantitative models make use of both financial theory and financial data. These include the term structure and mortality rate models as well as the RAROC (risk-adjusted return on capital) and option-based models. (Two additional models, CreditMetrics and Credit Risk+, are discussed in Appendixes 11A and 11B on pages 702 and 705 of this book.) In the next chapter we look at methods to evaluate the risk of loan portfolios, or loan concentration risk.

Questions and Problems

1. Why is credit risk analysis an important component of FI risk management? What recent activities by FIs have made the task of credit risk assessment more difficult for both FI managers and regulators?

2. Differentiate between a secured loan and an unsecured loan. Who bears most of the risk in a fixed-rate loan? Why would FI managers prefer to charge floating rates, especially for longer-maturity loans?

3. How does a spot loan differ from a loan commitment? What are the advantages and disadvantages of borrowing through a loan commitment?

4. Why is commercial and corporate lending declining in importance in Canada and the United States? What effect does this decline have on overall business lending activities?

5. What are the primary characteristics of residential mortgage loans? Why does the ratio of variable rate mortgages to fixed-rate mortgages in the economy vary over the interest rate cycle? When would the ratio be highest?

6. What are the two major classes of consumer loans at Canadian banks? How do revolving loans differ from nonrevolving loans?

7. How does the credit card transaction process assist in the credit monitoring function of financial institutions? Which major parties receive a fee in a typical credit card transaction? Do the services provided warrant the payment of these associated fees?

8. What are compensating balances? What is the relationship between the amount of compensating balance requirement and the return on the loan to the FI?

9. Canada Bank offers one-year loans with a stated rate of 9 percent but requires a compensating balance of 10 percent. What is the true cost of this loan to the borrower? How does the cost change if the compensating balance is 15 percent? If the compensating balance is 20 percent?

10. West Coast Bank offers one-year loans with a 9 percent stated or base rate, charges a 0.25 percent loan origination fee and imposes a 10 percent compensating balance requirement, and must pay a 6 percent reserve requirement. The loans typically are repaid at maturity.
    a. If the risk premium for a given customer is 2.5 percent, what is the simple promised interest return on the loan?
    b. What is the contractually promised gross return on the loan per dollar lent?
    c. Which of the fee items has the greatest impact on the gross return?

11. Why are most consumer loans charged the same rate of interest, implying the same risk premium or class? What is credit rationing? How is it used to control credit risks with respect to loans?

12. Why could a lender's expected return be lower when the risk premium is increased on a loan? In addition to the risk premium, how can a lender increase the expected return on a commercial or corporate loan? A consumer loan?

13. What are covenants in a loan agreement? What are the objectives of covenants? How can these covenants be negative? Affirmative?

14. Identify and define the borrower-specific and market-specific factors that enter into the credit decision. What is the impact of each type of factor on the risk premium?
    a. Which of these factors is more likely to adversely affect small businesses rather than large businesses in the credit assessment process by lenders?
    b. How does the existence of a high debt ratio typically affect the risk of the borrower? Is it possible that high leverage may reduce the risk of bankruptcy (or the risk of financial distress)? Explain.
    c. Why is the volatility of the earnings stream of a borrower important to a lender?

15. Why is the degree of collateral as specified in the loan agreement of importance to the lender? If the book value of the collateral is greater than or equal to the amount of the loan, is the credit risk of the lender fully covered? Why or why not?

16. Why are FIs consistently interested in the expected level of economic activity in the markets in which they operate? Why is monetary policy of the Bank of Canada important to FIs?

17. What are the purposes of credit scoring models? How could these models possibly assist an FI manager in better administering credit?

18. Suppose the estimated linear probability model is $PD = .3X_1 + .2X_2 - 0.5X_3 + $ error, where $X_1 = 0.75$ is the borrower's debt/equity ratio, $X_2 = 0.25$ is the volatility of borrower earnings, and $X_3 = 0.10$ is the borrower's profit ratio.
    a. What is the projected probability of default for the borrower?
    b. What is the projected probability of repayment if the debt–equity ratio is 2.5?
    c. What is a major weakness of the linear probability model?

19. Describe how a linear discriminant analysis model works. Identify and discuss the criticisms which have been made regarding the use of this type of model to make credit risk evaluations.

20. MNO, Inc., a publicly traded manufacturing firm, has provided the following financial information in its application for a loan.

Assets	
Cash	$ 20
Accounts receivable	90
Inventory	90
Plant and equipment	500
Total assets	$700

Liabilities and Equity	
Accounts payable	$ 30
Notes payable	90
Accruals	30
Long-term debt	150
Equity	400
Total liabilities and equity	$700

Also assume sales = $500, cost of goods sold = $360, taxes = $56, interest payments = $40, and net income = $44; the dividend payout ratio is 50 percent, and the market value of equity is equal to the book value.

a. What is the Altman discriminant function value for MNO, Inc.? Recall that:

Net working capital = Current assets minus current liabilities.

Current assets = Cash + Accounts receivable + Inventories.

Current liabilities = Accounts payable + Accruals + Notes payable.

EBIT = Revenues − Cost of goods sold − Depreciation.

Taxes = (EBIT − Interest) (Tax rate).

Net income = EBIT − Interest − Taxes.

Retained earnings = Net income (1 − Dividend payout ratio).

b. Should you approve MNO, Inc.'s, application to your bank for a $500 capital expansion loan?

c. If sales for MNO were $300, the market value of equity was only half of book value, and the cost of goods sold and interest were unchanged, what would be the net income for MNO? Assume the tax credit can be used to offset other tax liabilities incurred by other divisions of the firm. Would your credit decision change?

d. Would the discriminant function change for firms in different industries? Would the function be different for retail lending in different geographic sections of the country? What are the implications for the use of these types of models by FIs?

21. Consider the coefficients of Altman's Z score. Can you tell by the size of the coefficients which ratio appears most important in assessing creditworthiness of a loan applicant? Explain.

22. If the rate on one-year T-bills currently is 6 percent, what is the repayment probability for each of the following two securities? Assume that if the loan is defaulted, no payments are expected. What is the market-determined risk premium for the corresponding probability of default for each security?

a. One-year AA-rated bond yielding 9.5 percent.
b. One-year BB-rated bond yielding 13.5 percent.

23. A bank has made a loan charging a base lending rate of 10 percent. It expects a probability of default of 5 percent. If the loan is defaulted, the bank expects to recover 50 percent of its money through the sale of its collateral. What is the expected return on this loan?

24. Assume that a one-year T-Bill is currently yielding 5.5 percent and a AAA-rated discount bond with similar maturity is yielding 8.5 percent.

a. If the expected recovery from collateral in the event of default is 50 percent of principal and interest, what is the probability of repayment of the AAA-rated bond? What is the probability of default?

b. What is the probability of repayment of the AAA-rated bond if the expected recovery from collateral in the case of default is 94.47 percent of principal and interest? What is the probability of default?

c. What is the relationship between the probability of default and the proportion of principal and interest that may be recovered in case of default on the loan?

25. What is meant by the phrase *marginal default probability*? How does this term differ from *cumulative default probability*? How are the two terms related?

26. Calculate the term structure of default probabilities over three years using the following spot rates from the Government of Canada and corporate bond (pure discount) yield curves. Be sure to calculate both the annual marginal and the cumulative default probabilities.

	Spot 1 year	Spot 2 year	Spot 3 year
Government bonds	5.0%	6.1%	7.0%
BBB-rated bonds	7.0	8.2	9.3

27. The bond equivalent yields for Government of Canada and A-rated corporate bonds with maturities of 93 and 175 days are given below:

	93 days	175 days
Government	8.07%	8.11%
A-rated corporate	8.42	8.66
Spread	0.35	0.55

a. What are the implied forward rates for both an 82-day Government of Canada and an 82-day A-rated bond beginning in 93 days? Use daily compounding on a 365-day year basis.

b. What is the implied probability of default on A-rated bonds over the next 93 days? Over 175 days?

c. What is the implied default probability on an 82-day A-rated bond to be issued in 93 days?

28. What is the mortality rate of a bond or loan? What are some of the problems with using a mortality rate approach to determine the probability of default of a given bond issue?

29. The following is a schedule of historical defaults (yearly and cumulative) experienced by an FI manager on a portfolio of commercial and mortgage loans.

a. Complete the blank spaces in the table.

b. What are the probabilities that each type of loan will not be in default after five years?

c. What is the measured difference between the cumulative default (mortality) rates for commercial and mortgage loans after four years?

30. The table below shows the dollar amounts of outstanding bonds and corresponding default amounts for every year over the past five years. Note that the default figures are in millions, while those outstanding are in billions. The outstanding figures reflect default amounts and bond redemptions.

What are the annual and cumulative default rates of the above bonds?

31. What is RAROC? How does this model use the concept of duration to measure the risk exposure of a loan? How is the expected change in the credit premium measured? What precisely is ΔLN in the RAROC equation?

32. A bank is planning to make a loan of $5,000,000 to a firm in the steel industry. It expects to charge a servicing fee of 50 basis points. The loan has a maturity of 8 years with a duration of 7.5 years. The cost of funds (the RAROC benchmark) for the bank is 10 percent. Assume the bank has estimated the maximum change in the risk premium on the steel manufacturing sector to be approximately 4.2 percent, based on two years of historical data. The current market interest rate for loans in this sector is 12 percent.

a. Using the RAROC model, determine whether the bank should make the loan.

b. What should be the duration in order for this loan to be approved?

c. Assuming that the duration cannot be changed, how much additional interest and fee income will be necessary to make the loan acceptable?

d. Given the proposed income stream and the negotiated duration, what adjustment in the loan rate would be necessary to make the loan acceptable?

33. A firm is issuing two-year debt in the amount of $200,000. The current market value of the assets is $300,000. The risk-free rate is 6 percent, and the standard deviation of the rate of change in the underlying assets of the borrower is 10 percent. Using an options framework, determine the following:

a. The current market value of the loan.

b. The risk premium to be charged on the loan.

34. A firm has assets of $200,000 and total debts of $175,000. With an option pricing model, the implied volatility of the firm's assets is estimated at $10,730. Under the KMV method, what is the expected default frequency (assuming a normal distribution for assets)?

			Years after Issuance		
Loan Type	1 Year	2 Years	3 Years	4 Years	5 Years
Commercial:					
Annual default	0.00%	_____	0.50%	_____	0.30%
Cumulative default	_____	0.10%	_____	0.80%	_____
Mortgage:					
Annual default	0.10%	0.25%	0.60%	_____	0.80%
Cumulative default	_____	_____	_____	1.64%	_____

			Years after Issuance		
Loan Type	1 Year	2 Years	3 Years	4 Years	5 Years
A-rated: Annual default ($millions)	0	0	0	1	2
Outstanding ($billions)	100	95	93	91	88
B-rated: Annual default ($millions)	0	1	2	3	4
Outstanding ($billions)	100	94	92	89	85
C-rated: Annual default ($millions)	1	3	5	5	6
Outstanding ($billions)	100	97	90	85	79

35. CC Bank (CCB) has outstanding a $5,000,000 face value, adjustable rate loan to a company that has a leverage ratio of 80 percent. The current risk-free rate is 6 percent, and the time to maturity on the loan is exactly 1/2 year. The asset risk of the borrower, as measured by the standard deviation of the rate of change in the value of the underlying assets, is 12 percent. The normal density function values are given below.

h	N(h)	h	N(h)
−2.55	0.0054	2.50	0.9938
−2.60	0.0047	2.55	0.9946
−2.65	0.0040	2.60	0.9953
−2.70	0.0035	2.65	0.9960
−2.75	0.0030	2.70	0.9965

a. Use the Merton option valuation model to determine the market value of the loan.
b. What should be the interest rate for the last six months of the loan?

The questions and problems that follow refer to Appendixes 11A and 11B on pages 702 and 705 of this book. Refer to the example information in Appendix 11A for problems 36 and 37.

36. From Table 11A–1, what is the probability of a loan upgrade? A loan downgrade?
a. What is the impact of a rating upgrade or downgrade?
b. How is the discount rate determined after a credit event has occurred?
c. Why does the probability distribution of possible loan values have a negative skew?
d. How do the capital requirements of the Credit-Metrics approach differ from those of the BIS and OSFI?

37. A five-year fixed-rate loan of $100 million carries a 7 percent annual interest rate. The borrower is rated BB. Based on hypothetical historical data, the probability distribution given below has been determined

for various ratings upgrades, downgrades, status quo, and default possibilities over the next year. Information also is presented reflecting the forward rates of the current Treasury yield curve and the annual credit spreads of the various maturities of BBB bonds over Treasuries.

a. What is the present value of the loan at the end of the one-year risk horizon for the case where the borrower has been upgraded from BB to BBB?
b. What is the mean (expected) value of the loan at the end of year 1?
c. What is the volatility of the loan value at the end of year 1?
d. Calculate the 5 percent and 1 percent VARs for this loan assuming a normal distribution of values.
e. Estimate the approximate 5 percent and 1 percent VARs using the actual distribution of loan values and probabilities.
f. How do the capital requirements of the 1 percent VARs calculated in parts (d) and (e) above compare with the capital requirements of the BIS and OSFI?

38. How does the Credit Risk+ model of Credit Suisse Financial Products differ from the CreditMetrics model?

39. An FI has a loan portfolio of 10,000 loans of $10,000 each. The loans have a historical average default rate of 4 percent, and the severity of loss is 40 cents per dollar.

a. Over the next year, what are the probabilities of having default rates of 2, 3, 4, 5, and 8 percent?
b. What would be the dollar loss on the portfolios with default rates of 4 and 8 percent?
c. How much capital would need to be reserved to meet the 1 percent worst-case loss scenario? What proportion of the portfolio's value would this capital reserve be?

Rating	Probability Distribution %	New Loan Value plus Coupon $	Forward Rate Spreads at Time t		
			t	r_t%	s_t%
AAA	0.01	114.82	1	3.00	0.72
AA	0.31	114.60	2	3.40	0.96
A	1.45	114.03	3	3.75	1.16
BBB	6.05		4	4.00	1.30
BB	85.48	108.55			
B	5.60	98.43			
CCC	0.90	86.82			
Default	0.20	54.12			

Web Questions

40. Go to the Bank of Canada's Web site at www.bankofcanada.ca and find the most recent statistics for Canadian Chartered Bank Loan assets using the following steps. Click on "Rates and Statistics." Click on "Weekly Financial Statistics." Download the most recent report.
    a. Open the file and find BFS Table C1. What percentage of the total loans is represented by personal loan plans? How much by credit cards? How has the amount of business loans changed over the past 24 months? What percentage of total mortgage loans was residential? What was the percentage change in the total dollar amount of mortgage loans over the last 24 months?
    b. From the same file, find BFS Table F1. How have conventional 1 year and 5 year mortgage rates changed since 2005 as reported in Table 11–4? Look at the other financial market statistics in BFS Table F1. How can you relate the change in mortgage rates to the economic climate in Canada (other interest rates, Bank of Canada monetary policy)?
41. Go to the Bank of Canada's Web site at www.bankofcanada.ca and download the Financial System Review for June, 2004. Go to the discussion on the Canadian housing market and look at Charts 12–15. How have residential mortgages changed as a percentage of total bank credit? What was the most popular mortgage term in Canada in June 2000? How has the use of variable-rate mortgages changed over time? What governs the provision of mortgage insurance in Canada? How has mortgage insurance affected the mortgage market?

Appendix **11A**   **CreditMetrics**

View Appendix 11A on page 702 of this book.

Appendix **11B**   **Credit Risk+**

View Appendix 11B on page 705 of this book.

Appendix **11C**   **Credit Analysis**

View Appendix 11C on page 707 of this book.

Credit Risk: Loan Portfolio and Concentration Risk

In this chapter, we examine credit risk in the context of a loan portfolio. We consider:

▸ the benefits of loan portfolio diversification

▸ the models used by FI managers to assess the risk of the overall loan portfolio

▸ the potential use of loan portfolio models in setting maximum concentration limits for business or borrowing sectors, and

▸ the regulatory approach of OSFI to the measurement and control of the default risk of a loan portfolio

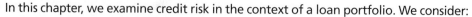

INTRODUCTION

The models discussed in the previous chapter describe alternative ways by which an FI manager can measure the default risks of *individual* debt instruments such as loans and bonds. Rather than looking at credit risk one loan at a time, this chapter concentrates on the ability of an FI manager to measure credit risk in a loan (asset) *portfolio context* and the benefit from loan (asset) diversification. The consequences of ignoring portfolio risk can be significant. For example, in 1986, a year after the failures of the Canadian Commercial Bank and Northland Bank of Canada caused by exposure to oil and gas and real estate loans in Western Canada, the Royal Bank's (RBC's) Senior Vice-President and Controller Dominic D'Alessandro, now CEO of the insurance conglomerate Manulife Financial, announced loan loss provisions for oil and gas loans of $275 million. The provision reduced RBC's earnings after-tax by $25 million to $30 million. RBC, known as Canada's energy bank, had 7.2 percent of its total assets of $97.53 billion in energy loans. A total of $240 million represented loans to Dome Petroleum, a Calgary oil company that was in trouble because of low prices for oil and gas. Dome's situation was causing concern for Toronto-Dominion Bank which had loaned $738 million to Dome as well.[1] Thus, while the risk-return characteristics of each loan in its portfolio are a concern for an FI, the risk-return of the overall loan portfolio affects an FI's overall credit exposure. FIs have internal models to analyze this risk and, since 1994, the Office of the Superintendent of Financial Institutions (OSFI) has allowed banks, foreign bank branches, and federal trust and loan companies to self-assess their credit risks and develop their own approaches. However, as long as FIs lend, there will be ups and downs and, in 2002, after trying to buy investment banking business through cheap corporate loans, Canadian banks became over-exposed to the U.S. telecommunications industry and re-evaluated their lending practices. (See the Industry Perspectives Box.)

www.manulife.ca
www.rbc.com
www.osfi-bsif.gc.ca
www.td.com

---

[1] See A. Freeman, "Big Canada Bank Sees Oil, Gas Loan Loss Provision," *Wall Street Journal*, June 4, 1986, p. 1. Different regulations influence an FI's income statement and capital. Canadian accounting rules at the time allowed loan losses to be averaged over a five-year period. A change in Canadian GAAP guidelines in 1996 required the discounting of the expected cash flows by the interest rate on the loan at the time of the impairment. See I. Hasan and L. D. Wall, "Determinants of the Loan Loss Allowance: Some Cross-Country Comparisons," *The Financial Review*, 2004, 38, pp. 129–152 for a study of loan loss practices in Canada, the United States, Japan, and 21 other countries.

Industry Perspectives

TIES THAT BIND: RISKY BUSINESS

Canadian banks improved their lending practices in the early 1990s after a series of bad corporate loans left them reeling. But last year banks saw the return of corporate loan losses ans we saw our bank stocks tumble. Now they're tinkering with lending practices again and asking us not to worry—after all, it's just temporary.

LOSSES DEVELOP Corporate loan defaults send bank profits plummeting in the early '90s. In 1992, Royal Bank alone has loan-loss provisions totaling $2.35 billion—including $800 million owed by developer Olympia & York. Banks are criticized for lending to businesses without sufficient collateral.

BEAUTIFUL LOANERS Banks vow to "deal agressively" with their loan problems. Royal reviews its lending practices and CIBC restructures its risk management operations. Small businesses "squeezed by banks that have been 'O&Yed,' find it harder to borrow, says Catherine Swift at the Canadian Federation of Independent Business.

BANK ON PROFITS By the mid-'90s, loan losses are out and record financial totals are in. In 1995, the $900 mil-

lion in profits for Canada's chartered banks matches the drop in loan-loss provisions from the previous year. In 1998, Scotiabank cites risk management as a major operational factor behind record profits.

CREDIT CRUNCH Massive loan defaults by firms such as Teleglobe Inc. and Enron Corp. raise concerns about banks' risk management practices. A two-week span in October 2001 sees four major banks issue credit warnings. Share prices drop and loan-loss provisions soar. "The credit markets are going to hell in a handbasket," comments Bob Hoye, editor of the Vancouver-based *Institutional Advisors* newsletter.

CREDIT WHERE DUE After announcing significant loan losses, CIBC pledges in May to cut its corporate loan book by one-third and introduce more severe lending polices. Royal Bank and Laurentian Bank also pledge to reduce their exposure to corporate lending. New federal regulations require banks to allocate provisions on specific sectors as well as their overall portfolios.

Source: Steve Brearton, "Ties that bind: Risky Business," *CA Magazine*, October 2002, Vol. 135, Iss. 8, p. 11. Reproduced with permission from *CA Magazine*, published by the Canadian Institute of Chartered Accountants, Toronto, Canada.

SIMPLE MODELS OF LOAN CONCENTRATION RISK

migration analysis
A method to measure loan concentration risk by tracking credit ratings of firms in particular sectors or ratings class for unusual declines.

www.standardand poors.com

www.moodys.com

loan migration matrix
A measure of the probability of a loan being upgraded, downgraded, or defaulting over some period.

FIs widely employ two simple models to measure credit risk concentration in the loan portfolio beyond the purely subjective model of "we have already lent too much to this borrower." The first is **migration analysis**, which tracks the movement (transition) of a loan portfolio from one credit rating to another, based on historical relative frequency. Lending officers track S&P, Moody's, or their own internal credit ratings of certain pools of loans or certain sectors, for example, oil and gas. If the credit ratings of a number of firms in a sector or rating class decline faster than has been historically experienced, FIs curtail lending to that sector or rating class.

A **loan migration matrix** (or transition matrix) shows the historic experience of a pool of loans in terms of their credit rating changes (migration) over time. Table 12–2 shows a hypothetical credit migration matrix in which loans are classified into one of three rating classes (most FIs use 10 to 13 classes) ranked in descending order from 1 to 3 with D* used for loans in default.[2] The rows in Table 12–2 list the rating at which the portfolio of loans began the year, and the columns list the rating at which the portfolio ended the year. The numbers in the table are called transition

[2] For 2004, the Bank of Montreal (BMO) reported using a sixteen-point scale over a one year time horizon to evaluate credit default risk. BMO assigned an internal rating based on Moody's and Standard and Poor's and tracked the migration of the counterparty between grades. See BMO's most recent annual report at www.bmo.com. A recent survey of credit portfolio management by FIs found the range of credit rating classes to be 5 to 22. See "2002 Survey of Credit Portfolio Management Practices," International Association of Credit Portfolio Managers, International Swaps and Derivatives Association, Risk Management Association, October 2002.

TABLE 12–1
A Hypothetical
Rating Migration,
or Transition,
Matrix

		Risk Rating at End of Year			
		1	2	3	D*
Risk rating at beginning of year	1	.85	.10	.04	.01
	2	.12	.83	.03	.02
	3	.03	.13	.80	.04

*D = default.

probabilities, reflecting the proportions of loans that began the year at, for example, rating 2, remaining at rating 2 at the end of the year, being upgraded to a 1, being downgraded to a 2, or defaulting (D).

For example, for loans that began the year at rating 2, historically (on average) 12 percent have been upgraded to 1; 83 percent have remained at 2; 3 percent have been downgraded to 3; and 2 percent have defaulted by the end of the year. Suppose that the FI is evaluating the credit risk of its current portfolio of loans of borrowers rated 2 and that over the last few years, a much higher percentage (say, 5 percent) of loans has been downgraded to 3 and a higher percentage (say, 3 percent) has defaulted than is implied by the historic transition matrix. The FI may then seek to restrict its supply of lower-quality loans (e.g., those rated 2 and 3), concentrating more of its portfolio on grade 1 loans.[3] At the very least, the FI should seek higher credit risk premiums on lower-quality (rated) loans. Not only is migration analysis used to evaluate commercial loan portfolios, it is widely used to analyze credit card portfolios and consumer loans as well although most Canadian FIs use credit scoring models for personal loans.[4]

concentration limits
External limits set on the maximum loan size that can be made to an individual borrower.

The second simple model requires management to set some firm external limit on the maximum amount of loans that will be made to an individual borrower or sector. The FI determines **concentration limits** on the proportion of the loan portfolio that can go to any single customer by assessing the borrower's current portfolio, its operating unit's business plans, its economists' economic projections, and its strategic plans. Typically, FIs set concentration limits to reduce exposures to certain industries and increase exposures to others. When two industry groups' performances are highly correlated, an FI may set an aggregate limit of less than the sum of the two individual industry limits. FIs also typically set geographic limits. They may set aggregate portfolio limits or combinations of industry and geographic limits.

EXAMPLE 12–1

Calculating Concentration Limits for a Loan Portfolio

Suppose management is unwilling to permit losses exceeding 10 percent of an FI's capital to a particular sector. If management estimates that the amount lost per dollar of defaulted loans in this sector is 40 cents, the maximum loans to a single sector as a percent of capital, defined as the concentration limit, is:

$$\text{Concentration limit} = \text{Maximum loss as a percent of capital} \times \frac{1}{\text{Loss rate}}$$

$$= 10\% \times [1/.4]$$

$$= 25\%$$

---

[3] The theory underlying the use of the average one-year transition matrix (based on historic data) as a benchmark is that actual transactions will fluctuate randomly around these average transitions. In the terminology of statistics, actual transitions follow a stable Markov (chain) process.

[4] See, for example, J. Z. Wei, "A multifactor, credit migration model for sovereign and corporate debts," *Journal of International Money and Finance*, October 2003, Vol. 22, Iss. 5, pp. 709–735.

FIGURE 12–1
Industry classifications used by Canadian Imperial Bank of Commerce, 2004

Source: 2004 Annual Report, page 78, www.cibc.com.

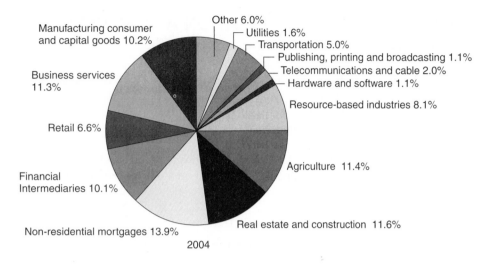

2004

In recent years, regulators have limited loan concentrations to *individual borrowers* to a certain percentage of the FI's capital, for example, 10%. In some countries, such as Chile, limits are mandated by sector or industry. OSFI applies a 'prudent person approach,' and requires each FI to have written investment and lending policies. Since 1994, OSFI has set **large exposure limits** on credit risk for Canadian banks, federally regulated trust and loan companies, and foreign bank branches. The exposure is limited to a maximum of 25 per cent of the FI's total capital as defined in calculating its risk-based capital adequacy ratio. The FI is expected to set lower internal limits and reach the maximum only on an exception basis. Canadian life insurance companies regulated by OSFI are also subject to a maximum exposure of 25 per cent of their capital. The aggregate book value of investments of a property and casualty insurance company to an entity or group cannot exceed 5 per cent of the company's assets.[5]

large exposure limits
Maximum amount of credit or investment exposure a federally-regulated FI may have to a single entity.

www.cibc.com

In 2004, Canadian Imperial Bank of Commerce (CIBC) set concentration limits for its business and government loan portfolio by geographic location (90.3 per cent of its business and government loan portfolio was in North America), by individual borrower or related borrower, by product or type of lending, and by industry sector, as shown in Figure 12–1. CIBC's largest exposure was to non-residential mortgages (13.9 percent), followed by real estate and construction (11.6 percent), and business services (11.3 percent). CIBC also controls exposure through loan sales, as discussed in Chapter 26.

Concept Questions

1. What would the concentration limit be if the loss rate on bad loans is 25 cents on the dollar?
2. What would the concentration limit be if the maximum loss (as a percent of capital) is 15 percent instead of 10 percent? 25 percent?

Next we look at the use of more sophisticated portfolio theory–based models to set concentration limits. Although these models have a great deal of potential, data availability and other implementation problems have, until recently, hindered their use. The basic idea is to select the portfolio of loans that maximizes the return on the loan portfolio for any given level of risk (or that minimizes the degree of portfolio risk for any given level of returns).

---

[5] See Guideline B-1 (Prudent Person Approach) and B-2 (Large Exposure Limits) for federally regulated FIs at www.osfi-bsif.gc.ca.

LOAN PORTFOLIO DIVERSIFICATION AND MODERN PORTFOLIO THEORY (MPT)

To the extent that an FI manager holds widely traded loans and bonds as assets or, alternatively, can calculate loan or bond returns, portfolio diversification models can be used to measure and control the FI's aggregate credit risk exposure. Suppose the manager can estimate the expected returns of each loan or bond ($\overline{R}_i$) in the FI's portfolio.

After calculating the individual security return series, the FI manager can compute the expected return ($\overline{R}_p$) on a portfolio of assets as:

$$\overline{R}_p = \sum_{i=1}^{N} X_i \overline{R}_i \qquad \textbf{(12.1)}$$

In addition, the variance of returns or risk of the portfolio (σ_i^2) can be calculated as:

$$\sigma_p^2 = \sum_{i=1}^{n} X_i^2 \sigma_i^2 + \sum_{i=1}^{n} \sum_{\substack{j=1 \\ i \neq j}}^{n} X_i X_j \sigma_{ij} \qquad \textbf{(12.2)}$$

or:

$$\sigma_p^2 = \sum_{i=1}^{n} X_i^2 \sigma_i^2 + \sum_{i=1}^{n} \sum_{\substack{j=1 \\ i \neq j}}^{n} X_i X_j \rho_{ij} \sigma_i \sigma_j \qquad \textbf{(12.3)}$$

where

$\overline{R}_p$ = Expected or mean return on the asset portfolio
Σ　= Summation sign
$\overline{R}_i$　= Mean return on the ith asset in the portfolio
X_i　= Proportion of the asset portfolio invested in the ith asset (the desired concentration amount)
σ_i^2 = Variance of returns on the ith asset
σ_{ij} = Covariance of returns between the ith and jth assets
ρ_{ij} = Correlation between the returns on the ith and jth assets[6]

The fundamental lesson of modern portfolio theory (MPT) is that by taking advantage of its size, an FI can diversify considerable amounts of credit risk as long as the returns on different assets are imperfectly correlated with respect to their default risk adjusted returns.[7]

Consider the σ_p^2 in equation (2). If many loans have negative covariances or correlations of returns (ρ_{ij} are negative)—that is, when one borrower's loans do

---

[6] The correlation coefficient reflects the joint movement of asset returns or default risks in the case of loans and lies between the values $-1 \leq \rho \leq +1$, where ρ is the correlation coefficient. As can be seen from equations (2) and (3), the covariance between any two assets (σ_{ij}) is related to the correlation coefficient (ρ_{ij}) by $\sigma_{ij} = \rho_{ij} \sigma_i \sigma_j$.

[7] One objection to using modern portfolio theory for loans is that the returns on individual loans are not normally or symmetrically distributed. In particular, most loans have limited upside returns and long-tail downside risks; see the discussion in Chapter 11, Appendix A, "CreditMetrics," and Chapter 9 in A. Saunders and L. Allen, *Credit Risk Measurements: New Approaches to Value at Risk and Other Paradigms*, 2nd ed. (New York: John Wiley & Sons, 2002). Also, concerns about maintaining relationships with traditional customers may limit the ability of an FI to diversify. The relationship limit on diversification has been called the "paradox of credit." That is, banks specialize in monitoring and generating information about their key customers (see Chapter 1), yet such monitoring specialization may lead to a highly concentrated loan portfolio. Relationship concerns may inhibit the loan portfolio's being managed in a fashion similar to a mutual fund's management of an equity portfolio.

FIGURE 12–2
FI Portfolio
Diversification

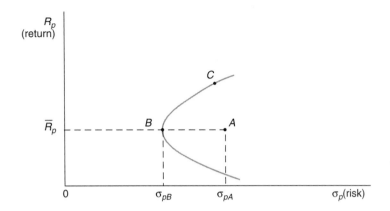

badly and another's do well—the sum of the individual credit risks of loans viewed independently overestimates the risk of the whole portfolio. This is what we meant in Chapter 5 when we stated that by pooling funds, FIs can reduce risk by taking advantage of the law of large numbers in their investment decisions.

EXAMPLE 12–2

Calculation of Return and Risk on a Two-Asset Portfolio

Suppose that an FI holds two loans with the following characteristics:[8]

Loan i	X_i	$\bar{R}_i$	σ_i	σ_i^2	
1	.40	10%	.0980	.0096	$\rho_{12} = -.84$
2	.60	12	.0857	.007344	$\sigma_{12} = .70548$

The return on the loan portfolio is:

$$R_p = .4\,(10\%) + .6\,(12\%) = 11.2\%$$

while the risk of the portfolio is:

$$\sigma_p^2 = (.4)^2\,(.0096) + (.6)^2\,(.007344) + 2\,(.4)(.6)(-.84)(.098)(.0857) = .0007935$$

thus, $\sigma_p = \sqrt{.0007935} = .0282 = 2.82\%$.

Notice that the risk (or standard deviation of returns) of the portfolio, σ_p (2.82 percent), is less than the risk of either individual asset (9.8 percent and 8.57 percent, respectively). The negative correlation between the returns of the two loans (−.84) results in an overall reduction of risk when they are put together in an FI's portfolio.

To see more generally the advantages of diversification, consider Figure 12–2. Note that A is an undiversified portfolio with heavy investment concentration in just a few loans or bonds. By fully exploiting diversification potential with bonds or loans whose returns are negatively correlated or that have a low positive correlation with those in the existing portfolio, the FI manager can lower the credit risk on the portfolio from σ_{pA} to σ_{pB} while earning the same expected return. That is, portfolio B is the efficient (lowest-risk) portfolio associated with portfolio return level $\bar{R}_p$. By varying the proportion of the asset portfolio invested in each asset (in other words, by varying the required portfolio return level $\bar{R}_p$ up and down), the manager can identify an entire frontier of efficient portfolio mixes (weights) of loans and bonds. Each portfolio mix is efficient in the sense that it offers the low-

---

[8] Note that variance (σ^2) is measured in percent squared; standard deviation (σ) is measured in percent.

est risk level to the FI manager at each possible level of portfolio returns. However, as you can see in Figure 12–2, of all possible efficient portfolios that can be generated, portfolio *B* produces the lowest possible risk level for the FI manager. That is, it maximizes the gains from diversifying across all available loans and bonds so that the manager cannot reduce the risk of the portfolio below σ_{pB}. For this reason, σ_{pB} is usually labeled the **minimum risk portfolio.**

minimum risk portfolio
Combination of assets that reduces the variance of portfolio returns to the lowest feasible level.

Even though *B* is clearly the minimum risk portfolio, it does not generate the highest returns. Consequently, portfolio *B* may be chosen only by the most risk-averse FI managers, whose sole objective is to minimize portfolio risk regardless of the portfolio's return. Most portfolio managers have some desired return-risk trade-off in mind; they are willing to accept more risk if they are compensated with higher expected returns.[9] One such possibility would be portfolio *C* in Figure 12–2. This is an efficient portfolio in that the FI manager has selected loan proportions (X_i) to produce a portfolio risk level that is a minimum for that higher expected return level. This portfolio dominates all other portfolios that can produce the same expected return level.[10]

Portfolio theory is a highly attractive tool. Still, over and above the intuitive concept that diversification is generally good, a question arises as to its applicability for banks, insurance companies, and thrifts. These FIs often hold significant amounts of regionally specific nontraded or infrequently traded loans and bonds.

Concept Questions

1. What is the main point in using MPT for loan portfolio risk?
2. Why would an FI not always choose to operate with a minimum risk portfolio?

KMV Portfolio Manager Model

www.moodyskmv.com

Despite the nontraded aspect of many loans, a great deal of recent research has gone into developing modern portfolio theory models for loans. Below we look at one approach developed by Moody's KMV Corporation called **Portfolio Manager.**[11]

KMV Portfolio Manager
A model that applies modern portfolio theory to the loan portfolio.

Any model that seeks to estimate an efficient frontier for loans, as in Figure 12–2, and thus the optimal or best proportions (X_i) in which to hold loans made to different borrowers, needs to determine and measure three things [see equations (1), (2),

---

[9] The point that is chosen depends on the risk aversion of managers and the degree of separation of ownership from control. If the FI is managed by agents who perform the task of maximizing the value of the firm, they act as risk-neutral agents. They would know that stockholders, who are well diversified, could, through homemade diversification, hold the shares of many firms to eliminate borrower-specific risk. Thus, managers would seek to maximize expected return subject to any regulatory constraints on risk-taking behavior (i.e., they probably would pick a point in region C in Figure 12–1). However, if managers are risk averse because of their human capital invested in the FI and make lending decisions based on their own risk preferences rather than those of the stockholders, they are likely to choose a relatively low-risk portfolio, something closer to the minimum risk portfolio. Other agency issues such as bonuses to lending officers based on asset growth may also influence lending decisions. Internal controls thus are important for FIs. For more on agency issue and bank risk taking, see A. Saunders, E. Strock, and N. G., Travlos, "Ownership Structure, Deregulation, and Bank Risk Taking," *Journal of Finance* 45 (1990), pp. 643–54. The trade-off between portfolio return and portfolio risk can now be solved using new methods of optimization called genetic algorithm-based techniques. See A. Mukherjee, R. Bisuras, K. Deb, and A. Mathur, "Multi-Objective Evolutionary Algorithms for the Risk-Return Trade-off in Bank Loan Management," KanGAL Report Number 200/005.

[10] Rather than selecting a point on the loan efficient frontier that reflects managerial risk aversion, as in Figure 12–1 point C (see footnote 9), the FI manager would pick a point that maximizes firm value. This would be the point where the return of the portfolio minus the risk-free rate divided by the standard deviation of portfolio returns is maximized, that is the maximum of $[(R_p - R_f)/\sigma_p)]$. In MPT this is often called the Sharpe ratio. Diagramatically, this is a point on the efficient frontier where a straight line drawn from the vertical axis, from a point equal to R_f, is just tangential to the efficient frontier. At this tangency point, it is impossible to improve upon the risk-return trade-off.

[11] Other portfolio models have been developed, including CreditMetrics, Credit Risk+, and Credit Portfolio View (McKinsey and Company). See Saunders and Allen, *Credit Risk Measurement*. A recent survey of credit portfolio management by FIs found that 69 percent of the financial institutions that used a credit portfolio model used Portfolio Manager. See "2002 Survey of Credit Portfolio Management Practices," International Association of Credit Portfolio Managers, International Swaps and Derivatives Association, and Risk Management Association, October 2002.

and (3)]: the expected return on a loan to borrower i (R_i), the risk of a loan to borrower i (σ_i), and the correlation of default risks between loans made to borrowers i and j (ρ_{ij}).

In its simplest model, KMV measures each of these as follows:

$$R_i = AIS_i - E(L_i) = AIS_i - [EDF_i \times LGD_i] \qquad \textbf{(12.4)}$$

$$\sigma_i = UL_i = \sigma_{Di} \times LGD_i = \sqrt{EDF_i(1 - EDF_i)} \times LGD_i \qquad \textbf{(12.5)}$$

ρ_{ij} = Correlation between the systematic return components
of the asset returns of borrower i and borrower j.

Each of these needs some explanation.

Return on the Loan (R_i)

The return on a loan is measured by the so-called annual all-in-spread (AIS), which measures annual fees earned on the loan by the FI plus the annual spread between the loan rate paid by the borrower and the FI's cost of funds. Deducted from this is the expected loss on the loan [$E(L_i)$]. This expected loss is equal to the product of the expected probability of the borrower defaulting over the next year, or its expected default frequency (EDF_i)—as discussed in Chapter 11—times the amount lost by the FI if the borrower defaults [the loss given default, or LGD_i]. Also, if desired, the return on the loan can be expressed in excess return form by deducting the risk-free rate on a security of equivalent maturity.

Risk of the Loan (σ_i)

The risk of the loan reflects the volatility of the loan's default rate (σ_{Di}) around its expected value times the amount lost given default (LGD_i). The product of the volatility of the default rate and the LGD is called the unexpected loss on the loan (UL_i) and is a measure of the loan's risk, or σ_i. To measure the volatility of the default rate, assume that loans can either default or repay (no default); then defaults are binomially distributed, and the standard deviation of the default rate for the ith borrower (σ_{Di}) is equal to the square root of the probability of default times 1 minus the probability of default ($\sqrt{(EDF)(1 - EDF)}$).

Correlation (ρ_{ij})

To measure the unobservable default risk correlation between any two borrowers, the KMV Portfolio Manager model uses the systematic asset return components of the two borrowers and calculates a correlation that is based on the historical comovement between those returns. According to KMV, default correlations tend to be low and lie between .002 and .15. This makes intuitive sense. For example, what is the probability that both IBM and General Motors will go bankrupt at the same time? For both firms, their asset values would have to fall below their debt values at the same time over the next year! The likelihood of this is small except in a very severe or extreme recession or extremely high growth in each firm's short-term debt obligations. The generally low (positive) correlations between the default risks of borrowers is also good news for FI managers in that it implies that by spreading loans across many borrowers, they can reduce portfolio risk significantly.[12]

---

[12] The Portfolio Manager model of KMV also can be used to assess the risk of extending more loans to any one borrower. If more loans are extended to one borrower, fewer loans can be made to others (assuming a fixed amount of loans). Technically, since the variance of the loan portfolio is:

$$UL_p^2 = \sum_{i=1}^{n} X_i^2 UL_i^2 + \sum_{i=1}^{n} \sum_{j=1}^{n} X_i X_j UL_i UL_j \rho_{ij}$$

| **EXAMPLE 12–3** | Suppose that an FI holds two loans with the following characteristics: | | | | | | |

Calculation of Return and Risk on a Two-Asset Portfolio Using KMV Portfolio Manager

Loan i	X_i	Annual Spread between Loan Rate and FI's Cost of Funds	Annual Fees	Loss to FI Given Default	Expected Default Frequency	
1	.60	5%	2%	25%	3%	$\rho_{12} = -.25$
2	.40	4.5	1.5	20	2	

The return and risk on loan 1 are:

$$R_1 = (.05 + .02) - [.03 \times .25] = 0.0625 \text{ or } 6.25\%$$

$$\sigma_1 = [\sqrt{.03(.97)}] \times .25 = .04265 \text{ or } 4.265\%$$

The return and risk on loan 2 are:

$$R_2 = (.045 + .015) - [.02 \times .20] = 0.056 \text{ or } 5.60\%$$

$$\sigma_2 = [\sqrt{.02(.98)}] \times .20 = .028 \text{ or } 2.80\%$$

The return and risk of the portfolio are then:

$$R_p = .6 (6.25\%) + .4 (5.60\%) = 5.99\%$$

$$\sigma_p^2 = (.6)^2 (.04265)^2 + (.4)^2 (.028)^2 + 2 (.6)(.4)(-.25)(.04265)(.028) = .0006369$$

thus, $\sigma_p = \sqrt{.0006369} = .0252 = 2.52\%$.

Reportedly, a number of large FIs are using the KMV model (and other similar models) to actively manage their loan portfolios.

Concept Questions

1. How does KMV measure the return on a loan?
2. If *EDF* = 0.1 percent and *LGD* = 50 percent, what is the unexpected loss (σ_i) on the loan?
3. How does KMV calculate loan default correlations?

Partial Applications of Portfolio Theory
Loan Volume-Based Models

As discussed above, direct application of modern portfolio theory is often difficult for FIs lacking information on market prices of assets because many of the assets— such as loans—are not bought and sold in established markets. However, sufficient

---

The marginal risk contribution of a small amount of additional loans to borrower *i* can be calculated as:

$$\text{Marginal risk contribution} = \frac{dUL_p}{dX_i}$$

where UL_p is the standard deviation (in dollars) of the loan portfolio. Clearly, the marginal risk contribution (dUL_p) of an additional amount of loans to borrower *i*, (dX_i), will depend not just on the risk of loan *i* on a stand-alone basis, but also on (i) the correlation of loan *i* with *j* other loans, (ii) the risk of the *j* other loans, and (iii) where the funds to increase loan *i* come from. In particular, if $dX_i > 0$, then the sum of the proportion of all remaining loans must decrease unless new funds are raised. Indeed, in the presence of a binding funding constraint $\sum_{j=1}^{n} dx_j$ where $j \neq i$, the key insight is that a loan to a BBB-rated borrower may well be more valuable to an FI (in an MPT sense) if it has a lower correlation with other loans than a loan to an A-rated borrower; that is, it is the loan's marginal risk contribution to total portfolio risk that is important, not its stand-alone risk.

loan volume data may be available to allow managers to construct a modified or partial application of MPT to analyze the overall concentration or credit risk exposure of the FI.[13] Such loan volume data include:

1. *Bank regulatory reports:* Federally-regulated deposit-taking institutions report monthly to the Bank of Canada and classify their loans as business, personal, residential and non-residential mortgages, as well as those to financial institutions and to domestic and foreign governments. They report geographically for inside and outside of Canada, as well as reporting their impaired assets to OSFI. The information is available on an aggregate basis and can be used to estimate the notional allocation of loans among categories or types.[14]

2. *Data on shared national credits.* A U.S. database on large commercial and industrial loans that categorizes loan volume by two-digit Standard Industrial Classification (SIC) codes. For example, loans made to SIC code 49 are loans to public utilities. Because this database provides a picture of the allocation of large loans across sectors, it is analogous to the market portfolio or basket of commercial and industrial loans and, given the interconnection between the Canadian and U.S. economies, could provide a surrogate database for Canadian lending.

3. *Commercial databases.* Data on 100,000-plus loans by bank and by borrower on the *Loan Pricing Corporation's Dealscan* database. The Dealscan database provides pricing and details for global corporate loans from 1988 onwards. Data on over 1800 Canadian companies is available.[15]

These data therefore provide *market benchmarks* against which an individual FI can compare its own internal allocations of loans across major lending sectors such as real estate and oil and gas.

By comparing its own allocation, or the proportions (X_{ij}), of loans in any specific area with the national allocations across borrowers (X_i, where i designates different loan groups), the jth FI can measure the extent to which its loan portfolio deviates from the market portfolio benchmark. This indicates the degree to which the FI has developed *loan concentrations* or relatively undiversified portfolios in various areas.

Consider Table 12–2. In this table we evaluate the first level of the loan asset allocation problem, which is the amount to be lent to each major loan sector or type. Here we show hypothetical numbers for four types of loans: real estate, commercial and industrial, individual, and others. Column (1) shows the loan allocation proportions at the national level for all banks; this is the market portfolio allocation. Column (2) lists the allocations assumed to be chosen by bank A, and column (3) shows the allocations chosen by bank B.

---

[13] This partial application of portfolio theory was first suggested by L. B. Morgan, "Managing a Loan Portfolio like an Equity Fund," *Bankers Magazine,* January–February 1989, pp. 228–35.

[14] Some countries, such as Italy, go further and break down a bank's loan portfolio into greater detail including industry and geographic concentrations. In Canada, data is published monthly by the Bank of Canada (www.bankofcanada.ca) on an aggregate basis and by OSFI (www.osfi-bsif.gc.ca) on an aggregate basis and for the individual deposit-taking institutions under its supervision.

[15] For details regarding the nature of the Canadian borrowers included in Dealscan see J. Chant, "Corporate Linkages and Bank Lending in Canada: Some First Results," Bank of Canada Conference Proceedings (The Evolving Financial System and Public Policy, December 2003), www.bankofcanada.ca. See also S. Aintablian and G. S. Roberts, "A note on market response to corporate loan announcements in Canada," *Journal of Banking & Finance,* Volume 24, Issue 3, March 2000, pp. 381–393 for an analysis of Canadian loan information in Dealscan. Dealscan also provides data on pricing of new loans. See the discussion in E. Altman, A. Gande, and A. Saunders, "Informational Efficiency of Loans versus Bonds: Evidence from Secondary Market Prices," Stern School of Business Working Paper, 2003; and S. Dahiya et al., "Financial Distress and Bank Lending Relationships," *Journal of Finance,* 2003, pp. 375–90. As these databases expand, tests of full MPT models for loans become easier.

TABLE 12–2
Allocation of the Loan Portfolio to Different Sectors (in percentages)

	(1) National	(2) Bank A	(3) Bank B
Real estate	45%	65%	10%
Business	30	20	25
Personal	15	10	55
Others	10	5	10
	100%	100%	100%

Note that bank A has concentrated loans more heavily in real estate lending than the national average, while bank B has concentrated loans more heavily in lending to individuals. To calculate the extent to which each bank deviates from the national benchmark, we use the standard deviation of bank A's and bank B's loan allocations from the national benchmark. Of course, the national benchmark may be inappropriate as the relevant market portfolio for a very small regional bank, insurance company, or thrift. In this case, the FI could construct a regional benchmark from the call report data of banks (or similar data collected by insurance company and thrift regulators) in a given regional area, such as the American Southwest, or, alternatively, a peer group benchmark of banks of a similar asset size and location.

We calculate the relative measure of loan allocation deviation as:[16]

$$\sigma_j = \sqrt{\frac{\sum_{i=1}^{N} (X_{ij} - X_i)^2}{N}} \qquad \textbf{(12.6)}$$

where

σ_j = Standard deviation of bank j's asset allocation proportions from the national benchmark

X_{ij} = Asset allocation proportions of the jth bank

X_i = National asset allocations

N = Number of observations or loan categories, $N = 4$

EXAMPLE 12–4

Calculating Loan Allocation Deviation

Refer again to Table 12–2. Applying equation (6) to bank A's loan portfolio, we get the deviation in its loan portfolio allocation as follows:

$$(X_{1A} - X_1)^2 = (.65 - .45)^2 = .0400$$
$$(X_{2A} - X_2)^2 = (.20 - .30)^2 = .0100$$
$$(X_{3A} - X_3)^2 = (.10 - .15)^2 = .0025$$
$$(X_{4A} - X_4)^2 = (.05 - .10)^2 = .0025$$

and

$$\sum_{i=1}^{4} = .0550$$

---

[16] For small samples such as this, it is really more appropriate for the divisor of equation (6) to be $N - 1$ rather than N.

Therefore, $\sigma_A = (.0550/4)^2 = 11.73\%$. Repeating this process for bank B's loan portfolio, we get:

$$(X_{1B} - X_1)^2 = (.10 - .45)^2 = .1225$$
$$(X_{2B} - X_2)^2 = (.25 - .30)^2 = .0025$$
$$(X_{3B} - X_3)^2 = (.55 - .15)^2 = .1600$$
$$(X_{4B} - X_4)^2 = (.10 - .10)^2 = \underline{.0000}$$

and

$$\sum_{i=1}^{4} = .2850$$

Therefore, $\sigma_B = (.2850/4)^2 = 26.69\%$. As you can see, bank B deviates more significantly from the national benchmark than bank A because of its heavy concentration on loans to individuals.

Deviation from the national benchmark is not necessarily bad; a bank may specialize in this area of lending because of its comparative advantage in information collection and monitoring of personal loans (perhaps due to its size or location). The standard deviation simply provides a manager with a measure of the degree to which an FI's loan portfolio composition deviates from the national average or benchmark. Nevertheless, to the extent that the national composition of a loan portfolio represents a more diversified market portfolio, because it aggregates across all banks, the asset proportions derived nationally (the X_i) are likely to be closer to the *most efficient portfolio composition* than the X_{ij} of the individual bank. This partial use of modern portfolio theory provides an FI manager with a sense of the relative degree of loan concentration carried in the asset portfolio. Finally, although the preceding analysis has referred to the loan portfolio of banks, any FI can use this portfolio theory for any asset group or, indeed, the whole asset portfolio, whether the asset is traded or not. The key data needed are the allocations of a peer group of regional or national financial institutions faced with similar investment decision choices.

Loan Loss Ratio-Based Models

systematic loan loss risk
A measure of the sensitivity of loan losses in a particular business sector relative to the losses in an FI's loan portfolio.

A second partial application of MPT is a model based on historic loan loss ratios.[17] This model involves estimating the **systematic loan loss risk** of a particular (SIC) sector or industry relative to the loan loss risk of an FI's total loan portfolio. This systematic loan loss can be estimated by running a time-series regression of quarterly losses of the ith sector's loss rate on the quarterly loss rate of an FI's total loans:

$$\left(\frac{\text{Sectoral losses in the } i\text{th sector}}{\text{Loans to the } i\text{th sector}}\right) = \alpha + \beta_i\left(\frac{\text{Total loan losses}}{\text{Total loans}}\right)$$

where α measures the loan loss rate for a sector that has no sensitivity to losses on the aggregate loan portfolio (i.e., its $\beta = 0$) and β_i measures the systematic loss sensitivity of the ith sector loans to total loan losses. For example, regression results showing that the consumer sector has a β of 0.2 and the real estate sector has a β of 1.4, suggest that loan losses in the real estate sector are systematically higher relative to the total loan losses of the FI (by definition, the loss rate β for the whole loan portfolio is 1). Similarly, loan losses in the consumer sector are systematically lower relative to the total loan losses of the FI. Consequently, it may be prudent for the FI to maintain lower concentration limits for the real estate sector as opposed to the con-

---

[17] See E. P. Davis, "Bank Credit Risk," Bank of England, Working Paper Series no. 8, April 1993.

sumer sector, especially as the economy moves toward a recession and total loan losses start to rise. The implication of this model is that sectors with lower βs could have higher concentration limits than high β sectors—since low β loan sector risks (loan losses) are less systematic, that is, are more diversifiable in a portfolio sense.[18]

EXAMPLE 12–5

Calculating Loan Loss Ratios

Using regression analysis on historical loan losses, a finance company has estimated the following:

$$X_{C\&I} = 0.003 + 0.75X_L \quad \text{and} \quad X_{con} = 0.005 + 1.25X_L$$

where $X_{C\&I}$ = the loss rate in the commercial and industrial loan sector, X_{con} = the loss rate in the consumer loan sector, and X_L = the loss rate for the finance company's loan portfolio. If the finance company's total loan loss rate increases by 15 percent, the expected loss rate increase in the commercial and industrial loan sector will be:

$$X_{C\&I} = 0.003 + 0.75\,(.15) = 11.55\%$$

and in the consumer loan sector will be:

$$X_{con} = 0.005 + 1.25\,(.15) = 19.25\%$$

To protect against this increase in losses, the finance company should consider reducing its concentration of consumer loans.

Regulatory Models

As noted in the introduction to this chapter, bank and insurance regulators around the world have also been investigating ways to measure concentration risk. After examining various quantitative approaches, the U.S. Federal Reserve in 1994 issued a final ruling on its proposed measure of credit concentration risk. The method adopted is largely subjective and is based on examiner discretion. The reasons given for rejecting the more technical models were that (1) at the time, the methods for identifying concentration risk were not sufficiently advanced to justify their use and (2) insufficient data were available to estimate more quantitative-type models, although the development of models like KMV (as well as CreditMetrics and Credit Risk+, discussed in the Appendixes in Chapter 11) may make bank regulators change their minds.

The board of directors of a Canadian FI has a legal obligation to develop and follow "investment and lending policies, standards and procedures that a reasonable and prudent person would apply in respect of a portfolio of investments and loans to avoid undue risk of loss and obtain a reasonable return."[19] OSFI's B-1 (1993) and B-2 (1994) Guidelines for Canadian deposit-taking institutions and federally regulated insurance companies set limits for concentrations as previously noted, allow the FIs to develop in-house models to measure credit risk, and also require them to ensure that the staff assigned to monitor the risks are appropriately trained. In Chapter 20, we look at the details of how credit risk is one component used to determine a deposit-taking institution's required level of capital.

www.osfi-bsif.gc.ca

---

[18] This type of approach suggests a possible extension to factor analysis (on the lines of multifactor models). Basically, it involves regressing SIC sector losses against various factors (market risk, interest rate risk, etc.) to see which sectors have the greatest (least) factor sensitivity. See also J. Neuberger, "Conditional Risk and Return in Bank Holding Company Stocks: A Factor-GARCH Approach," Federal Reserve Bank of San Francisco, Working Paper, May 1994.

[19] See "B-1 Prudent Person Approach" and "B-2 Guideline, Large Exposure Limits" for the various federally-regulated FIs at www.osfi-bsif.gc.ca.

Concept Questions

1. Suppose the returns on different loans were independent. Would there be any gains from loan portfolio diversification?
2. How would you find the minimum risk loan portfolio in a modern portfolio theory framework?
3. Should FI managers select the minimum risk loan portfolio? Why or why not?
4. Explain the reasoning behind the U.S. Federal Reserve's 1994 decision to rely more on a subjective rather than a quantitative approach to measuring credit concentration risk. Is that view valid today? How does the U.S. approach differ from OSFI's approach?

Summary

This chapter discussed the various approaches available to an FI manager to measure credit portfolio and concentration risk. It showed how portfolio diversification can reduce the loan risk exposure of an FI. Two simple models that allow an FI to monitor and manage its loan concentration risk were also discussed: migration analysis, which relies on rating changes to provide information on desirable and undesirable loan concentrations, and a model that sets concentration limits based on an FI's capital exposure to different lending sectors. The application of the fully fledged MPT model to the credit (loan) concentration issue was also analyzed as was the Moody's KMV Portfolio Manager model. In addition, a model that applies portfolio theory to loan loss ratios in different sectors to determine loan concentrations was discussed. Finally, the approaches of regulators to measuring loan concentrations were described.

Questions and Problems

1. How do loan portfolio risks differ from individual loan risks?

2. What is migration analysis? How do FIs use it to measure credit risk concentration? What are its shortcomings?

3. What does loan concentration risk mean?

4. A manager decides not to lend to any firm in sectors that generate losses in excess of 5 percent of equity.

   a. If the average historical losses in the automobile sector total 8 percent, what is the maximum loan a manager can lend to a firm in this sector as a percentage of total capital?

   b. If the average historical losses in the mining sector total 15 percent, what is the maximum loan a manager can make to a firm in this sector as a percentage of total capital?

5. An FI has set a maximum loss of 12 percent of total capital as a basis for setting concentration limits on loans to individual firms. If it has set a concentration limit of 25 percent to a firm, what is the expected loss rate for that firm?

6. Explain how modern portfolio theory can be applied to lower the credit risk of an FI's portfolio.

7. The Bank of Tinytown has two $20,000 loans with the following characteristics: Loan A has an expected return of 10 percent and a standard deviation of returns of 10 percent. The expected return and standard deviation of returns for loan B are 12 percent and 20 percent, respectively.

   a. If the covariance between A and B is .015 (1.5 percent), what are the expected return and the standard deviation of this portfolio?

   b. What is the standard deviation of the portfolio if the covariance is −.015 (−1.5 percent)?

   c. What role does the covariance, or correlation, play in the risk reduction attributes of modern portfolio theory?

8. Why is it difficult for FIs to measure credit risk using modern portfolio theory?

9. What is the minimum risk portfolio? Why is this portfolio usually not the portfolio chosen by FIs to optimize the return-risk trade-off?

10. The obvious benefit to holding a diversified portfolio of loans is to spread risk exposures so that a single event does not result in a great loss to the bank. Are there any benefits to not being diversified?

11. A bank vice president is attempting to rank, in terms of the risk-reward trade-off, the loan portfolios of three loan officers. Information on the portfolios is noted below. How would you rank the three portfolios?

Expected Portfolio	Standard Return	Deviation
A	10%	8%
B	12	9
C	11	10

12. An FI uses Moody's KMV Portfolio Manager model to evaluate the risk-return characteristics of the loans in its portfolio. A specific $10 million loan earns 2 percent per year in fees, and the loan is priced at a 4 percent spread over the cost of funds for the bank. Because of collateral considerations, the loss to the bank if the borrower defaults will be 20 percent of the loan's face value. The expected probability of default is 3 percent. What is the anticipated return on this loan? What is the risk of the loan?

13. What data is available on loan information at the national and regional levels? How can they be used to analyze credit concentration risk?

14. Information concerning the allocation of loan portfolios to different market sectors is given below.

Allocation of Loan Portfolios in Different Sectors (%)

Sectors	National	Bank A	Bank B
Corporate & Commercial	30%	50%	10%
Consumer	40	30	40
Real Estate	30	20	50

Bank A and bank B would like to estimate how much their portfolios deviate from the national average.

a. Which bank is further away from the national average?

b. Is a large standard deviation necessarily bad for a bank using this model?

15. Assume that the averages for FIs engaged in mortgage lending have their assets diversified in the following proportions: 20 percent residential, 30 percent commercial, 20 percent international, and 30 percent mortgage-backed securities. A bank has the following ratios: 30 percent residential, 40 percent commercial, and 30 percent international. How does this bank differ from the average?

16. Using regression analysis on historical loan losses, a bank has estimated the following:

$$X_C = 0.002 + 0.8X_L, \quad \text{and} \quad X_h = 0.003 + 1.8X_L$$

where X_C = loss rate in the commercial sector, X_h = loss rate in the consumer (household) sector, and X_L = loss rate for its total loan portfolio.

a. If the bank's total loan loss rates increase by 10 percent, what are the expected loss rate increases in the commercial and consumer sectors?

b. In which sector should the bank limit its loans and why?

17. What guidelines on credit concentrations has OSFI provided for federally-regulated FIs?

18. An FI is limited to holding no more than 8 percent of the securities of a single issuer. What is the minimum number of securities it should hold to meet this requirement? What if the requirements are 2 percent, 4 percent, and 7 percent?

Internet Exercise

Go to the Web site for a Canadian bank and download the pdf file containing the latest Annual Report. Search the document using 'credit' or 'credit risk' to find the management's discussion of credit risk. What models does this FI use for evaluating and controlling the risks of its corporate and commercial loans? What models does the FI use for evaluating its consumer loans? Does the FI use other techniques (e.g., loan sales) to reduce its concentration to credit risk?

Off-Balance-Sheet Risk

This chapter examines the various off-balance-sheet (OBS) activities of FIs. We discuss:

▸ the effect of OBS activities on an FI's risk exposure, return performance, and solvency

▸ the different types of OBS activities (credit substitutes, e.g. loan commitments, letters of credit, loans sold; derivative contracts; and other OBS exposure, e.g. when issued trading, settlement risk, and affiliate risk) and the risks associated with each, and

▸ the role of OBS activities in reducing the risk of an FI

INTRODUCTION

Off-balance-sheet (OBS) activities can involve risks that add to an FI's overall risk exposure. Though some part of OBS risk is related to interest rate risk, credit risk, and other risks, these items also introduce unique risks that must be managed by FIs. For example, the US$2.6 billion loss incurred by Sumitomo Corp. of Japan from commodity futures trading, and the US$1.5 billion in losses and eventual bankruptcy of Orange County in California have all been linked to FI off-balance sheet activities in derivatives. For example, in May 1998 Credit Suisse First Boston paid US$52 million to Orange County to settle a lawsuit alleging that it had been in part responsible for that county's investments in risky securities and derivatives transactions. Table 13–1 lists some of the other large losses for FIs. Many of the losses are related to trading in derivatives. Derivative securities (futures, forwards, options and swaps) are examined in detail in Chapters 23 through 25.

Prior to 2003, major losses by Canadian FIs were relatively minor. However, the U.S. Securities and Exchange Commission (SEC) investigated Canadian Imperial Bank of Canada's (CIBC's) structured finance transactions with Enron, the U.S. energy trader that failed in 2001. SEC charged that CIBC took a 3 percent equity holding in 34 structured financing deals (essentially loans carried off the balance sheet) that allowed Enron to treat them as transactions with independent entities, providing US$1 billion in revenues and hiding US$2.5 billion in debt. As a result, in 2003, CIBC paid the SEC a settlement of US$80 million without admitting any wrongdoing and agreed with the Federal Reserve Bank of New York and OSFI to adopt new policies. Subsequently, 10 large FIs (CIBC, Toronto-Dominion Bank, Royal Bank of Canada, Citigroup, JP Morgan, Barclays PLC, Royal Bank of Scotland, Credit Suisse First Boston, Deutsche Bank, and Merrill Lynch & Co.) were sued by Enron in the "MegaClaims lawsuit." In 2005, Royal Bank agreed to pay US$25 million to settle, and the other FIs were in the process of settling. However, in a separate class action lawsuit lead by the University of California, CIBC agreed to pay US$2.4 billion, the largest settlement so far and one with severe consequences for CIBC. As seen in the Ethical Dilemmas Box, the risks of CIBC's OBS deals with Enron affected the solvency of the FI, bringing its capital ratio to 7.5 percent, above the 7 percent required by OSFI. The total settlement by FIs related to the class action lawsuit was US$7.12 billion by August, 2005, with more to come.[1]

www.cibc.com
www.royalbank.com
www.td.com

---

[1] For Enron-related news accounts see B. Schecter, "Royal Bank pays $25 million to exit Enron lawsuit," *CanWest News*, July 29, 2005, p. 1 and R. Smith, "CIBC to Pay $2.4 billion Over Enron; Canadian Bank Is Settling Investors' Fraud Claims; Spotlight on Merrill, CSFB," *Wall Street Journal* (Eastern edition), August 3, 2005, p. A.3.

TABLE 13–1   Some Big Losses on OBS Activities

Date	Case	Settlement/Loss
1994	Bankers Trust payout to Gibson Greeting and Procter & Gamble over derivatives losses	US$0.212 billion
1995	Nicholas Leeson, a "rogue trader" in derivatives at Barings, Britain's oldest investment bank	US$1.38 billion
1996	Kyriacos Papouis, NatWest Bank, losses on mispricing of derivatives caused by two years of unauthorized trading	£77 million
1997	Chase Manhattan loses through trading complex derivative products related to emerging markets debt	US$200 million
1998	Long-term Capital Management, hedge fund losses in derivatives and other securities	US$3.65 equity infusion
2000	Rogue trader causes loss on speculative trading in foreign currency at Trans Canada Pipelines Limited, the largest pipeline company in North America based in Calgary	C$77 million
2001	Rogue trader, John Rusnak, causes losses on foreign exchange trades at Allied Irish Bank in Boston	US$750 million
2003	Trader Stephen Duthie accused by Ontario Securities Commission of improper trading in unhedged US Treasury notes causing losses and the collapse of Phoenix Hedge Fund LP in Canada in 1998	C$125 million
2005	The class action lawsuit brought by Enron's shareholders starts to work itself out as FIs (CIBC US$2.4 billion, JP Morgan Chase US$2.2 billion, Citigroup US$2 billion) settle for their role in hiding Enron's debt via off-balance sheet entities	US$7.12 billion

Source: Adapted from Dan Atkinson, "UBS Pledged Derivatives Explanation," *Manchester Guardian*, 1998. Copyright Guardian Newspapers Limited 1998.

It is important to keep in mind that, though they can increase an FI's risk, OBS activities can also reduce or hedge the interest rate, credit, and foreign exchange risks. That is, OBS activities have both risk-increasing and risk-reducing attributes. OBS activities have been one way for Canadian FIs to replace income lost to disintermediation (e.g., commercial paper replacing loans as a source of financing for large firms). Thus, OBS activities have become a profitable source of fee income because they have not required the regulatory capital (prior to 2006, 100 percent for corporate loans, regardless of default risk, as discussed in Chapter 20) and therefore earn a higher return for the FI.[2]

OFF-BALANCE-SHEET ACTIVITIES AND FI SOLVENCY

www.osfi-bsif.gc.ca

One of the most important choices facing an FI manager is the relative scale of an FI's on- and off-balance-sheet activities. The total notional OBS items reported to OSFI by domestic banks at Quarter 3, 2005 was $10.80 billion. Total on-balance-sheet assets were $2.03 billion. Most of us are aware of on-balance-sheet activities because they appear on an FI's published asset and liability balance sheets. For

---

[2] This fee income can have both direct (e.g., a fee from the sale of a letter of credit) and indirect (through improved customer relationships) effects that have a positive income impact in other product areas. In cases where customers feel aggrieved with respect to derivatives purchased from a dealer FI, off-balance-sheet activities can have important negative reputational effects that have an adverse impact on the future flow of fees and other income.

Though it did not admit wrongdoing, CIBC paid up to resolve a suit that alleged it helped Enron raise money, hide debt and inflate revenues. The tab, larger than expected on the Street, exceeds payments made by much larger Enron bankers Citigroup and J.P. Morgan Chase.

CIBC is swallowing a $2.8-billion (Canadian) pretax charge to cover this settlement and other Enron-related suits, a stunning figure for a bank that earned just $1.99-billion in profit for all of 2004. The bank had previously set aside just $300-million in legal reserves for its involvement with Enron.

Following the settlement, the bank is suspending its share buyback program until it can nurse its balance sheet back to health, and will likely freeze any dividend increases.

Industry observers are also expecting the bank to be downgraded by credit rating agencies.

Gerry McCaughey, who signed off on the agreement less than 24 hours after he replaced John Hunkin as chief executive officer of the bank, is already running out of options after his first day on the job.

CIBC has essentially abandoned its foreign growth plans in the past two years following some painful episodes south of the border, including the failure of its U.S. electronic banking subsidiary, Amicus.

That hasn't bothered investors, who have been drawn to CIBC for its income trust-like strategy: return most of your profit to shareholders, either by repurchasing stock or providing generous dividend increases. Without these tools, however, many are questioning how badly the stock will be punished, and suggest that Mr. McCaughey will have to sit tight and focus on rebuilding the balance sheet.

The bank said its important Tier 1 capital ratio will decline to 7.5 per cent, and cautioned it will not likely be able to reach its internal objective of 8.5 per cent before mid-2006.

"It completely evaporates their excess capital," said Robert Wessel, an analyst with National Bank Financial Inc. "Before, they had a choice whether or not to deploy capital [on acquisitions] or return it to shareholders. Now they don't have a need to deploy or return."

Stephen Forbes, a spokesman for the bank, said CIBC's goal was to put the lawsuit behind it and elim-inate the "uncertainties, burden and expense" of further litigation.

Under Mr. Hunkin, CIBC made an aggressive push into the U.S. investment banking scene in the late 1990s and had aspirations of being mentioned in the same breath as its larger, more powerful Wall Street rivals. But this was not what the bank's shareholders had in mind.

Earlier this summer, J.P. Morgan Chase & Co. paid $2.2-billion (U.S.) to end its involvement in the lawsuit, while Citigroup Inc. paid $2-billion. A host of other banks and brokerages, including Toronto-Dominion Bank and Royal Bank of Canada, have yet to reach an agreement.

Several analysts said the CIBC deal will cast a pall over Canadian banking stocks as the market speculates about how much TD and RBC may have to shell out for similar settlements with Enron investors.

For CIBC, the Enron settlement marks a costly and painful culmination of various regulatory problems that have afflicted the bank in recent years. In late 2003, the bank paid $80-million to U.S. regulators to settle allegations it aided and abetted the accounting fraud at Enron. Two weeks ago, just before Mr. Hunkin left his post, it struck a $125-million deal with the U.S. Securities and Exchange Commission and New York State Attorney-General Eliot Spitzer to settle its alleged role in a mutual fund trading scandal.

Then there have been the other distractions, such as the embarrassing faxing snafu last year in which private customer information was errantly sent to a Virginia junkyard.

The bank is still named in a separate suit filed by the company itself against several of its lenders and banking partners. RBC settled its part in this suit last week for $49-million. The bank will pay $25-million to Enron, and an additional $24-million to advance its bankruptcy claims against the company.

Included in CIBC's $2.8-billion (Canadian) in reserve charges is approximately $200-million to fund a possible settlement with Enron, an action that has been dubbed the "MegaClaims" litigation.

Source: Sinclair Stewart, *The Globe and Mail*, August 3, 2005, Page B1. Reprinted with permission from *The Globe and Mail*.

example, an FI's deposits and holdings of bonds and loans are on-balance-sheet activities. By comparison, off-balance-sheet activities are less obvious and often are invisible to all but the best-informed investor or regulator. In accounting terms, *off-balance-sheet items* usually appear "below the bottom line," frequently just as footnotes to financial statements. In economic terms, however, off-balance-sheet items

contingent assets and liabilities
Assets and liabilities off the balance sheet that potentially can produce positive or negative future cash flows for an FI.

are **contingent assets and liabilities** that affect the future, rather than the current, shape of an FI's balance sheet. As such, they have a direct impact on the FI's future profitability and solvency performance. Consequently, efficient management of these OBS items is central to controlling overall risk exposure in a modern FI.

From a valuation perspective, OBS assets and liabilities have the potential to produce positive or negative *future* cash flows. As a result, the true value of an FI's capital or net worth is not simply the difference between the market value of assets and liabilities on its balance sheet today but also reflects the difference between the current market value of its off-balance-sheet or contingent assets and liabilities.

off-balance-sheet asset
An item or activity that, when a contingent event occurs, moves onto the asset side of the balance sheet.

An item or activity is an **off-balance-sheet asset** if, when a contingent event occurs, the item or activity moves onto the asset side of the balance sheet. Conversely, an item or activity is an **OBS liability** if, when the contingent event occurs, the item or activity moves onto the liability side of the balance sheet. For example, as we discuss in more detail later, FIs sell various performance guarantees, especially guarantees that their customers will not default on their financial and other obligations. Examples of such guarantees include letters of credit and standby letters of credit. Should a customer default occur, the FI's contingent liability (its guaranty) becomes an actual liability and it moves onto the liability side of the balance sheet. Indeed, FI managers and regulators are just beginning to recognize and measure the risk of OBS activities and their impact on the FI's value.

off-balance-sheet liability
An item or activity that, when a contingent event occurs, moves onto the liability side of the balance sheet.

Since off-balance-sheet items are contingent assets and liabilities and move onto the balance sheet with a probability less than 1, their valuation is difficult and often highly complex. Because many off-balance-sheet items involve option features, the most common methodology has been to apply contingent claims/option pricing theory models of finance. For example, one relatively simple way to estimate the value of an OBS position in options is by calculating the **delta of an option**—the sensitivity of an option's value to a unit change in the price of the underlying security, which is then multiplied by the notional value of the option's position. (The delta of an option lies between 0 and 1.) Thus, suppose an FI has bought call options on bonds (i.e., it has an OBS asset) with a face or **notional value** of $100 million and the delta is calculated[3] at .25. Then the contingent asset value of this option position would be $25 million:

delta of an option
The change in the value of an option for a unit change in the price of the underlying security.

notional value
The face value of an OBS item.

$$d = \text{Delta of an option} = \frac{\text{Change in the option's price}}{\text{Change in price of underlying security}} = \frac{dO}{dS} = .25$$

$$F = \text{Notional or face value of options} = \$100 \text{ million}$$

The delta equivalent or contingent asset value = delta × face value of option = .25 × $100 million = $25 million. Of course, to figure the value of delta for the option, one needs an option pricing model such as Black-Scholes or a binomial model. In general, the delta of the option varies with the level of the price of the underlying security as it moves in and out of the money;[4] that

---

[3] A 1-cent change in the price of the bonds underlying the call option leads to a 0.25 cent (or quarter-cent) change in the price of the option.

[4] For example, for an in-the-money call option the price of the underlying security exceeds the option's exercise price. For an out-of-the money call option, the price of the underlying security is less than the option's exercise price. In general, the relationship between the value of an option and the underlying value of a security is nonlinear. Thus, using the delta method to derive the market value of an option is at best an approximation. To deal with the nonlinearity of payoffs on options, some analysts take into account the gamma as well as the delta of the option (gamma measures the change in delta as the underlying security price varies). For example, the standardized model of the BIS used to calculate the market risk of options incorporates an option's delta, its gamma, and its vega (a measure of volatility risk). See Bank for International Settlements, *Standardized Model for Market Risk* (Basel, Switzerland, BIS, 1996). See also J. P. Morgan, *RiskMetrics,* 4th ed., 1996.

is, $0 < d < 1$.[5] Note that if the FI sold options, they would be valued as a contingent liability.[6]

Loan commitments and letters of credit are also off-balance-sheet activities that have option features.[7] Specifically, the holder of a loan commitment or credit line who decides to draw on that credit line is exercising an *option to borrow*. When the buyer of a guaranty defaults, this buyer is exercising a *default* option. Similarly, when the counterparty to a derivatives transaction is unable or unwilling to meet its obligation to pay (e.g., in a swap), this is considered an exercise of a default option.

With respect to swaps, futures, and forwards, a common approach is to convert these positions into an equivalent value of the underlying assets. For example, a $20 million, 10-year, fixed-floating interest rate swap in which an FI receives 20 semiannual fixed interest rate payments of 8 percent per annum (i.e., 4 percent per half year) and pays floating rate payments every half year indexed to LIBOR, can be viewed as the equivalent, in terms of valuation, of an on-balance-sheet position in two $20 million bonds. That is, the FI can be viewed as being long $20 million (holding an asset) in a 10-year bond with an annual coupon of 8 percent per annum and short $20 million (holding a liability) in a floating-rate bond of 10 years' maturity whose rate is adjusted every six months.[8] The market value of the swap can be viewed as the present value of the difference between the cash flows on the fixed-rate bond and the expected cash flows on the floating-rate bond. This market value is usually a very small percent of the notional value of the swap. In our example of a $20 million swap, the market value is about 3 percent of this figure,[9] or $600,000.

Given these valuation models, we can calculate, in an approximate sense, the current or market value of each OBS asset and liability and its effect on an FI's solvency. Consider Tables 13–2 and 13–3. In Table 13–2 the value of the FI's net worth (E) is calculated in the traditional way as the difference between the market values of its on-balance-sheet assets (A) and liabilities (L). As we discussed in Chapter 8:

$$E = A - L$$
$$10 = 100 - 90$$

Under this calculation, the market value of the stockholders' equity stake in the FI is 10 and the ratio of the FI's capital to assets (or capital–assets ratio) is 10 percent. Regulators and FIs often use the latter ratio as a simple measure of solvency (see Chapter 20 for more details).

A truer picture of the FI's economic solvency should consider the market value of both its visible on-balance-sheet and OBS activities. Specifically, the FI manager

---

[5] In the context of the Black-Scholes model, the value of the delta on a call option is $d = N(d_1)$, where $N(.)$ is the cumulative normal distribution function and $d_1 = [\ln(S/X) + (r + \sigma^2/(2\tau)]/\sigma \sqrt{T}$.

[6] Note that a cap or a floor is a complex option—that is, a collection of individual options (see Chapter 24).

[7] See S. I. Greenbaum, H. Hong, and A. Thakor, "Bank Loan Commitments and Interest Rate Volatility," *Journal of Banking and Finance* 5 (1981), pp. 497–510; T. Ho and A. Saunders, "Fixed Rate Loan Commitments, Takedown Risk, and the Dynamics of Hedging with Futures," *Journal of Financial and Quantitative Analysis* 18 (1983), pp. 499–516; O. E. Ergungor, "Theories of Bank Loan Commitments: A Literature Review," Working Paper, Federal Reserve Bank of Cleveland, September 2000; and P. Andre, R. Mathieu, and P. Chang, "A note on: Capital adequacy and the information content of term loans and lines of credit", *Journal of Banking & Finance*, 25 (2001), pp. 431–444.

[8] An interest rate swap does not normally involve principal payments on maturity. In the case above, the two principal amounts on the fixed- and floating-rate bonds cancel each other out.

[9] This is based on calculations by J. Kambhu, F. Keane, and C. Benadon, "Price Risk Intermediation in the Over-the-Counter Derivatives Markets: Interpretation of a Global Survey," Federal Reserve Bank of New York, *Economic Policy Review*, April 1996, pp. 1–15.

TABLE 13–2
Traditional Valuation of an FI's Net Worth

Assets		Liabilities	
Market value of assets (*A*)	100	Market value of liabilities (*L*)	90
		Net worth (*E*)	10
	100		100

TABLE 13–3
Valuation of an FI's Net Worth with On- and Off-Balance-Sheet Activities Valued

Assets		Liabilities	
Market value of assets (*A*)	100	Market value of liabilities (*L*)	90
		Net worth (*E*)	5
Market value of contingent assets (*CA*)	50	Market value of contingent liabilities (*CL*)	55
	150		150

should value contingent or future assets and liability claims as well as current assets and liabilities. In our example, the current market value of the FI's contingent assets (*CA*) is 50, while the current market value of its contingent liabilities (*CL*) is 55. Since the market value of contingent liabilities exceeds the market value of contingent assets by 5, this difference is an additional obligation, or claim, on the net worth of the FI. That is, stockholders' true net worth (*E*) is really:

$$E = (A - L) + (CA - CL)$$
$$= (100 - 90) + (50 - 55)$$
$$= 5$$

rather than 10, as it was when we ignored off-balance-sheet activities. Thus, economically speaking, contingent assets and liabilities are contractual claims that directly impact the economic value of the FI. Indeed, from both the stockholders' and regulators' perspectives, large increases in the value of OBS liabilities can render an FI economically insolvent just as effectively as can losses due to mismatched interest rate gaps and default or credit losses from on-balance-sheet activities. For example, in 1998, J. P. Morgan had to recognize $587 million in currency swaps as nonperforming, of which $489 million were related to currency swaps with SK, a Korean investment company. Two of those swaps involved the exchange of Thai baht for Japanese yen in which SK would benefit if the Thai baht rose in value. As it turned out, soon after the contract was entered into, the baht collapsed and SK disputed the legality of the contract.[10] In 2002, Royal Bank of Canada (RBC) was sued by Cooperatieve Centrale Raiffeisen-Boerenleenbank B.A. (Rabobank) to nullify obligations under a total return swap. RBC is carrying the receivables due of US$517 million (Cdn.$805 million) on its books as "Other Assets," but discloses the amount in a note to the financial statements.[11]

Concept Questions

1. Define a contingent asset and a contingent liability.
2. Suppose an FI had a market value of assets of 95 and a market value of liabilities of 88. In addition, it had contingent assets valued at 10 and contingent liabilities valued at 7. What is the FI's true net worth position?

[10] See "J. P. Morgan in Korean Battle on Derivatives," *New York Times,* February 27, 1998, p. D1.
[11] See Royal Bank of Canada's 2004 Annual Report, Note 18, p. 92 at www.royalbank.com.

RETURNS AND RISKS OF OFF-BALANCE-SHEET ACTIVITIES

In the 1980s, rising losses on loans to less developed and Eastern European countries, increased interest rate volatility, and squeezed interest margins for on-balance-sheet lending due to nonbank competition induced many large commercial banks to seek profitable OBS activities. By moving activities off the balance sheet, banks hoped to earn more fee income to offset declining margins or spreads on their traditional lending business. At the same time, they could avoid regulatory costs or taxes, since reserve requirements, deposit insurance premiums, and capital adequacy requirements were not levied on off-balance-sheet activities. Thus, banks had both earnings and regulatory tax-avoidance incentives to move activities off their balance sheets.[12]

www.bis.org

notional amount
The face value of a financial contract.

The dramatic growth in OBS activities caused OSFI to introduce a reporting system in 1996 to satisfy the Bank for International Settlements (BIS) capital requirements, which we discuss in detail in Chapter 20. Table 13–4 shows the level of OBS activities of Canadian banks, reported quarterly to OSFI at their **notional amount**, which overestimates their current market, or contingent claims value. Even so, the notional amount of OBS contracts reported has increased by almost 90% between Q4 1996 and Q3 2005, a phenomenal growth rate. In 2005, most of the off-balance sheet exposure for Canadian banks came from over the counter (OTC) interest rate derivative contracts (50.5% of the total notional amount), followed by OTC foreign exchange and gold contracts (25.5%). At 5.1%, the other OBS items (guarantees and standby letters of credit, securities lending, documentary and commercial letters of credit, lease commitments, loan commitments, and loans sold) reported to OSFI comprise a relatively small amount of risk exposure for the domestic Canadian banks.

The picture for individual banks can be different, though. Table 13–5 shows on-balance-sheet and OBS assets for the Royal Bank of Canada reported at year-end 2004. The notional amounts of the OBS assets are 6.3 times the on-balance sheet assets, represented by credit related amounts at 6.7 percent ($181.86 billion) and derivative contracts at 93.3 percent ($2.52 billion). However, the notional amounts overstate RBC's risk. When converted to the credit equivalent amounts as required by OSFI (discussed in Chapter 20), the credit equivalent is only $92.45 billion.

Other large caisses populaires and insurance companies engage in many of these OBS activities as well.[13]

The Major Types of OBS Activities

From Tables 13–4 and 13–5, the major types of OBS activities for Canadian banks are:

- credit instruments: loan commitments, standby letters of credit and letters of credit
- derivatives contracts: futures, forwards, swaps, and options, and
- other OBS contracts: when issued securities, loans sold

The next section analyzes these OBS activities in more detail and pays particular attention to the types of risk exposure an FI faces when engaging in such activities. As we discussed earlier, precise market valuation of these contingent assets and liabilities can be extremely difficult because of their complex contingent claim features

---

[12] For a modeling of the incentives to go off balance sheet due to capital requirements, see G. G. Pennacchi, "Loan Sales and the Cost of Bank Capital," *Journal of Finance* 43 (1988), pp. 375–96. Also, Chapter 26 goes into further details on incentives relating to loan sales.

[13] See the 2004 Annual Report of Desjardins Group, Table 27, p. 100 and Manulife Financial, Note 21, pp. 106–107. See also S. Figlewski, "The Use of Futures and Options by Life Insurance Companies," *Best's Review*, 1989; and R. L. Shockley and A. V. Thakor, "Bank Loan Commitment Contracts: Data, Theory and Tests," *Journal of Money, Credit and Banking* 29 (November 1997) (part 1), pp. 517–34.

TABLE 13–4   **Off-balance-sheet Items of Canadian Banks**

(Notional Amounts, billions of Cdn. dollars)	1996 Q4	2000 Q4	2003 Q4	2005 Q3	%
Derivatives:					
Interest Rate Contracts					
OTC	2,717.0	4,067.4	5,400.1	5,747.8	50.5
Exchange-traded	338.1	699.6	990.2	1,314.0	11.5
Foreign Exchange & Gold Contracts:					
OTC	1,938.0	2,234.2	2,251.3	2,900.0	25.5
Exchange-traded	9.3	6.8	9.6	9.1	0.1
Other:					
OTC	37.2	267.7	371.8	593.6	5.2
Exchange-traded	6.0	90.6	72.9	235.7	2.1
Total Derivative Contracts	5,046.6	7,366.3	9,096.0	10,800.2	94.9
Other Off-Balance Sheet Items	487.2	732.5	575.1	586.0	5.1
Total OBS	5,533.8	8,098.8	9,761.1	11,386.3	100

Source: OSFI Quarterly Reports for all banks www.osfi-bsif.gc.ca

FIGURE 13–1
Structure of a Loan Commitment

Loan Commitments

loan commitment agreement
A contractual commitment to make a loan up to a stated amount at a given interest rate in the future.

These days, most commercial loans are made by firms that take down (or borrow against) prenegotiated lines of credit or loan commitments rather than borrow spot loans (see Chapter 11's discussion). A **loan commitment agreement** is a contractual commitment by an FI to lend to a firm a certain maximum amount (say, $10 million) at given interest rate terms (say, 12 percent). The loan commitment agreement also defines the length of time over which the borrower has the option to take down this loan. In return for making this loan commitment, the FI may charge an **up-front fee** (or facility fee) of, say, $\frac{1}{8}$ percent of the commitment size, or $12,500 in this example. In addition, the FI must stand ready to supply the full $10 million at any time over the commitment period—say, one year. Meanwhile, the borrower has a valuable option to take down any amount between $0 and $10 million. The FI also may charge the borrower a **back-end fee** (or commitment fee) on any unused balances in the commitment line at the end of the period.[14] In this example, if the borrower takes down only $8 million in funds over the year and the fee on *unused* commitments is $\frac{1}{4}$ percent, the FI will generate additional revenue of $\frac{1}{4}$ percent times $2 million, or $5,000. Figure 13–1 presents a summary of the structure of this loan commitment.

up-front fee
The fee charged for making funds available through a loan commitment.

back-end fee
The fee imposed on the unused balance of a loan commitment.

and option aspects. At a very minimum, FI managers should understand not only the general features of the risk exposure associated with each major OBS asset and liability but also how each one can impact the return and profitability of an FI.

---

[14] This can be viewed as an excess capacity charge; see A. V. Thakor and G. Udell, "An Economic Rationale for the Pricing Structure of Bank Loan Commitments," *Journal of Banking and Finance* 11 (1987), pp. 271–90.

TABLE 13–5 Balance sheet and Off-balance-sheet Assets of Royal Bank of Canada, October 31, 2004

($ millions, except percentage amounts)	Balance sheet amount
Balance sheet assets	
Cash and deposits with banks	$ 11,096
Securities	
Issued or guaranteed by Canadian or other OEDC governments	29,536
Other	99,410
Residential mortgages (3)	
Insured	36,321
Conventional	47,822
Other loans and acceptances (3)	
Issued or guaranteed by Canadian or other OECD governments	14,523
Other	128,923
Other assets	61,565
	$429,196

	Contract amount	Credit conversion factor	Credit equivalent amount
Off-balance sheet financial instruments			
Credit instruments			
Guarantees and standby letters of credit			
Financial	$ 15,097	100%	$15,097
Non-financial	3,523	50%	1,761
Documentary and commercial letters of credit	592	20%	118
Securities lending	27,055	100%	27,055
Commitments to extend credit			
Original term to maturity of 1 year or less	45,682	–	–
Original term to maturity of more than 1 year	28,912	50%	14,456
Uncommitted amounts	60,972	–	–
Note issuance/revolving underwriting facilities	23	50%	12
	$ 181,856		$58,499
Derivatives (4)	2,522,309		33,954
Total off-balance-sheet financial instruments	$2,704,165		$92,453

Source: RBC Annual Report, p. 64A, at www.royalbank.com

EXAMPLE 13–1

Calculation of the Promised Return on a Loan Commitment

It is quite easy to show how the unique features of loan commitments affect the promised return $(1 + k)$ on a loan. In Chapter 11 we developed a model for determining $(1 + k)$ on a spot loan. This can be extended by allowing for partial drawdown and the up-front and back-end fees commonly found in loan commitments. For a one-year loan commitment, let:

BR = Interest on the loan = 12%

m = Risk premium = 2%

f_1 = Up-front fee on the whole commitment = $\frac{1}{8}$%

f_2 = Back-end fee on the unused commitment = $\frac{1}{4}$%

td = Expected (average) drawdown rate $(0 < td < 1)$ on the loan commitment = 75%

Then the general formula for the promised return $(1 + k)$ of the loan commitment is:[15]

$$1 + k = 1 + \frac{f_1 + f_2(1 - td) + (BR + m)td}{td}$$

$$1 + k = 1 + \frac{.00125 + .0025(.25) + (.12 + .02).75}{.75}$$

$$1 + k = 1 + \frac{.106875}{0.75} = 1.1425 \text{ or } k = 14.25\%$$

Note that only when the borrower actually draws on the commitment do the loans made under the commitment appear on the balance sheet. Thus, only when the $8 million loan is taken down exactly halfway through the one-year commitment period (i.e., six months later), does the balance sheet show a new $8 million loan being created. When the $10 million commitment is made at time 0, nothing shows on the balance sheet. Nevertheless, the FI must stand ready to make the full $10 million in loans on any day within the one-year commitment period; that is, at time 0 a new contingent claim on the resources of the FI was created.

This raises the question: What contingent risks are created by the loan commitment provision? At least four types of risk are associated with the extension of loan commitments: interest rate risk, drawdown or takedown risk, credit risk, and aggregate funding risk.

Interest Rate Risk

Interest rate risk is a contingent risk emanating from the fact that the FI precommits to make loans available to a borrower over the commitment period at either (1) some fixed interest rate as a fixed-rate loan commitment or (2) some variable rate as a variable-rate loan commitment. Suppose the FI precommits to lend a maximum of $10 million at a fixed rate of 12 percent over the year and its cost of funds rises. The cost of funds may well rise to a level that makes the spread between the 12 percent commitment rate and the FI's cost of funds negative or very small. Moreover, 12 percent may be much less than the rate the customer would have to pay if forced to borrow on the spot loan market under current interest rate conditions. When rates do rise over the commitment period, the FI stands to lose on its portfolio of fixed-rate loan commitments as borrowers exercise to the full amount their very valuable options to borrow at below-market rates.[16]

One way the FI can control this risk is by making commitment rates float with spot loan rates, for example, by indexing loan commitments to the prime or LIBOR rate. If the prime rate rises during the commitment period, so does the cost of commitment loans to the borrower—the borrower pays the market rate in effect when the commitment is drawn on. Nevertheless, this fixed formula rate solution does not totally eradicate interest rate risk on loan commitments. For example, suppose that the prime rate rises 1 percent but the cost of funds rises 1.25 percent; the spread between the indexed commitment loan and the cost of funds narrows by .25 percent. This spread risk is often called **basis risk**.[17]

basis risk
The variable spread between a lending rate and a borrowing rate or between any two interest rates or prices.

---

[15] This formula closely follows that in John R. Brick, *Commercial Banking: Text and Readings* (Haslett, MI: Systems Publication, Inc., 1984), Chapter 4. Note that for simplicity we have used undiscounted cash flows. Taking into account the time value of money means that we would need to discount both f_2 and $BR + m$ since they are paid at the end of the period. If the discount factor (cost of funds) is $d = 10$ percent, then $k = 12.95$ percent. The calculation can be expanded for multi-year loan commitments by assuming appropriate discount rates and drawdowns.

[16] In an options sense, the loans are in the money to the borrower.

[17] Basis risk arises because loan rates and deposit rates are not perfectly correlated in their movements over time.

Drawdown or Takedown Risk

Another contingent risk is takedown risk. Specifically, in making the loan commitment, the FI must always stand ready to provide the maximum of the commitment line—$10 million in our example. The borrower has the flexible option to borrow anything between $0 and the $10 million ceiling on any business day in the commitment period usually with a short notice period of 3 days. This exposes the FI to a degree of future liquidity risk or uncertainty (see Chapter 17). The FI can never be absolutely sure when, during the commitment period, the borrower will demand the full $10 million or some proportion thereof in cash.[18] For example, in February 2002, Tyco International unexpectedly drew down US$14.4 billion in credit lines from banks shut out of the commercial paper market when investors began to doubt its accounting practices. Canadian banks were reported to have US$1 billion in loans to Tyco, $500 million at TD Bank alone. To some extent, at least, the back-end fee on unused amounts is designed to create incentives for the borrower to take down lines in full to avoid paying this fee. However, in actuality, many lines are only partially drawn upon.[19]

Credit Risk

FIs also face a degree of contingent credit risk in setting the interest or formula rate on a loan commitment. Specifically, the FI often adds a risk premium based on its current assessment of the creditworthiness of the borrower. For example, the borrower may be judged as a AA credit risk paying 1 percent above prime rate. However, suppose that over the one-year commitment period the borrowing firm gets into difficulty; its earnings decline so that its creditworthiness is downgraded to BBB. The FI's problem is that the credit risk premium on the commitment had been preset to the AA level for the one-year commitment period. To avoid being exposed to dramatic declines in borrower creditworthiness over the commitment period, most FIs include an *adverse material change in conditions clause* by which the FI can cancel or reprice a loan commitment. However, exercising such a clause is really a last resort tactic for an FI because it may put the borrower out of business and result in costly legal claims for breach of contract.[20]

Aggregate Funding Risk

www.bankofcanada.ca

Many large borrowing firms, such as GM, Ford, and IBM, take out multiple commitment or credit lines with many FIs as insurance against future credit crunches.[21] In a credit crunch, the supply of spot loans to borrowers is restricted, possibly as a result of restrictive monetary policy actions of the Bank of Canada. Another cause is an FI's increased aversion toward lending, that is, a shift to the left in the loan supply function at all interest rates. In such credit crunches, borrowers with long-standing loan

---

[18] Indeed, the borrower could come to the bank and borrow different amounts over the period ($1 million in month 1, $2 million in month 2, etc.). The only constraint is the $10 million ceiling. See Ho and Saunders, "Fixed Rate Loan Commitments," for a modeling approach to drawdown risk. We discuss this liquidity risk aspect of loan commitments further in Chapter 17.

[19] See A. Melnick and S. Plaut, "Loan Commitment Contracts, Terms of Lending, and Credit Allocations," *Journal of Finance* 41 (1986), pp. 425–36; R. L. Shockley and A. V. Thakor, "Bank Loan Commitment Contracts"; and E. Asarnow and J. Marker, "Historical Performance of the U.S. Corporate Loan Market 1988–1993," *Journal of Commercial Lending,* Spring 1995, pp. 13–22. Asarnow and Marker show that the average takedown rates vary widely by borrower credit rating, from a takedown rate of only 0.1 percent by a AAA borrower to 20 percent for BBB and 75 percent for CCC.

[20] Potential damage claims can be enormous if the borrower goes out of business and attributes this to the cancelation of loans under the commitment contract. There are also important reputational costs to take into account in canceling a commitment to lend.

[21] Recent research by Donald P. Morgan, "The Credit Effects of Monetary Policy: Evidence Using Loan Commitments," *Journal of Money, Credit, and Banking* 30 (February 1998), pp. 102–18, has found evidence of this type of insurance effect. Specifically, in credit crunches, spot loans may decline, but loans made under commitment do not.

commitments are unlikely to be as credit constrained as those without loan commitments. However, this also implies that borrowers' aggregate demand to take down loan commitments is likely to be greatest when the FI's borrowing and funding conditions are most costly and difficult. In difficult credit conditions, this aggregate commitment takedown effect can increase the cost of funds above normal levels while many FIs scramble for funds to meet their commitments to customers. This is similar to the *externality effect* common in many markets when all participants simultaneously act together and adversely affect the costs of each individual participant.

The four contingent risk effects just identified—interest rate risk, drawdown or takedown risk, credit risk, and aggregate funding risk—appear to imply that loan commitment activities increase the insolvency exposure of FIs that engage in such activities. However, an opposing view holds that loan commitment contracts may make an FI less risky than had it not engaged in them. This view maintains that to be able to charge fees and sell loan commitments or equivalent credit rationing insurance, the FI must convince borrowers that it will still be around to provide the credit needed in the *future*.[22] To convince borrowers that an FI will be around to meet its future commitments, managers may have to adopt *lower*-risk portfolios *today* than would otherwise be the case. By adopting lower-risk portfolios, managers increase the probability that the FI will be able to meet all its long-term on- and off-balance-sheet obligations. Interestingly, empirical studies have confirmed that banks making more loan commitments have lower on-balance-sheet portfolio risk characteristics than those with relatively low levels of commitments; that is, safer banks have a greater tendency to make loan commitments.[23]

Commercial Letters of Credit and Standby Letters of Credit

commercial letters of credit

Contingent guarantees sold by an FI to underwrite the trade or commercial performance of the buyer of the guaranty.

In selling **commercial letters of credit** (LCs) and **standby letters of credit** (SLCs) for fees, FIs add to their contingent future liabilities. Both LCs and SLCs are essentially *guarantees* sold by an FI to underwrite the *performance* of the buyer of the guaranty (such as a corporation). In economic terms, the FI that sells LCs and SLCs is selling insurance against the frequency or severity of some particular future occurrence. Further, similar to the different lines of insurance sold by property–casualty insurers, LC and SLC contracts differ as to the severity and frequency of their risk exposures. We look next at an FI's risk exposure from engaging in LC and SLC off-balance-sheet activities.

standby letters of credit

Guarantees issued to cover contingencies that are potentially more severe and less predictable than contingencies covered under trade-related or commercial letters of credit.

Commercial Letters of Credit

Commercial letters of credit are widely used in both domestic and international trade. For example, they ease the shipment of grain between a farmer in Saskatchewan and a purchaser in British Columbia or the shipment of goods between a Canadian importer and a foreign exporter. The FI's role is to provide a formal guaranty that payment for goods shipped or sold will be forthcoming regardless of whether the buyer of the goods defaults on payment. We show a very simple LC example in Figure 13–2 for an international transaction between a Canadian importer and a German exporter.

Suppose the importer sent an order for $10 million worth of machinery to a German exporter, as shown by arrow 1 in Figure 13–2. However, the German exporter may be reluctant to send the goods without some assurance or guaranty of being paid once the

---

[22] A. W. A. Boot and A. V. Thakor, "Off-Balance-Sheet Liabilities, Deposit Insurance, and Capital Regulation," *Journal of Banking and Finance* 15 (1991), pp. 825–46.

[23] See, for example, R. B. Avery and A. N. Berger, "Loan Commitments and Bank Risk Exposure," *Journal of Banking and Finance* 15 (1991), pp. 173–92.

FIGURE 13–2
Simple Letter of
Credit Transaction

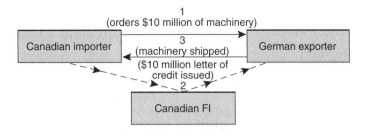

goods are shipped. The importer may promise to pay for the goods in 90 days, but the German exporter may feel insecure either because it knows little about the creditworthiness of the importer or because the importer has a low credit rating (say, B or BB). To persuade the German exporter to ship the goods, the importer may have to turn to a large Canadian FI with which it has developed a long-term customer relationship. In its role as a lender and monitor, the FI can better appraise the importer's creditworthiness. The FI can issue a contingent payment guaranty—that is, an LC to the German exporter on the importer's behalf—in return for an LC fee paid by the importer.[24] In our example, the FI would send to the German exporter an LC guaranteeing payment for the goods in 90 days regardless of whether the importer defaults on its obligation to the German exporter (see arrow 2 in Figure 13–2). Implicitly, the FI is replacing the importer's credit risk with its own credit risk guaranty. For this substitution to work effectively, in guaranteeing payment, the FI must have a higher credit standing or better credit quality reputation than the importer.[25] Once the FI issues the LC and sends it to the German exporter, the exporter ships the goods to the importer, as shown by arrow 3. The probability is very high that in 90 days' time, the importer will pay the German exporter for the goods sent and the FI keeps the LC fee as profit. The fee is, perhaps, 10 basis points of the face value of the letter of credit, or $10,000 in this example.

A small probability exists, however, that the importer will be unable to pay the $10 million in 90 days and will default. Then the FI would be obliged to make good on its guaranty. The cost of such a default could mean an FI must pay $10 million, although it would have a creditor's claim against the importer's assets to offset this loss. Clearly, the LC fee should exceed the expected default risk on the LC, which is equal to the probability of default times the expected net payout on the LC, after adjusting for the FI's ability to reclaim assets from the defaulting importer and any monitoring costs.[26] A more detailed version of an LC transaction is presented in Appendix 13A to the chapter, located at the book's Web site (**www.mcgrawhill.ca/college/saunders**).

---

[24] The FI subsequently notifies the German exporter that, upon meeting the delivery requirements, the exporter is entitled to draw a time draft against the letter of credit at the importer's FI (i.e., withdraw money) for the amount of the transaction. After the export order is shipped, the German exporter presents the time draft and the shipping papers to its own (foreign) FI, who forwards these to the importer's FI. The FI stamps the time draft as accepted and the draft becomes a banker's acceptance listed *on the balance sheet*. At this point, the FI either returns the stamped time draft (now a banker's acceptance) to the German exporter's FI and payment is made on the maturity date (e.g., in 90 days), or the FI immediately pays the foreign FI (and implicitly the exporter) the discounted value of the banker's acceptance. In either case, the foreign FI pays the German exporter for the goods. When the banker's acceptance matures, the importer must pay its FI for the purchases, and the FI sends the importer the shipping papers.

[25] In fact, research has found that, when the market becomes aware that a line of credit is granted, the FI customer experiences a significant increase in its stock price. See M. Mosebach, "Market Response to Banks Granting Lines of Credit," *Journal of Banking and Finance* 23 (1999), pp. 1701–23 and S. Aintablian and G.S. Roberts, "A note on market response to corporate loan announcements in Canada," *Journal of Banking & Finance*, Vol. 24, Iss. 3, March 2000, pp. 381–393.

[26] Hassan finds that stockholders view commercial letter of credit activities by banks as risk reducing. See M. K. Hassan, "The Market Perception of the Riskiness of Large U.S. Bank Commercial Letters of Credit," *Journal of Financial Services Research* 6 (1992), pp. 207–21.

Standby Letters of Credit

Standby letters of credit perform an insurance function similar to that of commercial and trade letters of credit. However, the structure and type of risks covered are different. FIs may issue SLCs to cover contingencies that are potentially more *severe,* less *predictable* or frequent, and not necessarily trade related.[27] These contingencies include performance bond guarantees whereby an FI may guarantee that a real estate development will be completed in some interval of time. Alternatively, the FI may offer default guarantees to back an issue of commercial paper (CP) to allow issuers to achieve a higher credit rating and a lower funding cost than would otherwise be the case. The $3.523 billion non-financial guarantees shown in Table 13–5 for RBC include loan default commitments or guarantees, also called credit enhancements.

Without credit enhancements, for example, many firms would be unable to borrow in the CP market or would have to borrow at a higher funding cost. P1 borrowers, who offer the highest-quality commercial paper, normally pay 40 basis points less than P2 borrowers, the next quality grade. By paying a fee of perhaps 25 basis points to an FI, the FI guarantees to pay CP purchasers' principal and interest on maturity should the issuing firm itself be unable to pay. The SLC backing of CP issues normally results in the paper's placement in the lowest default risk class (P1) and the issuer's savings of up to 15 basis points on issuing costs—40 basis points (the P2–P1 spread) minus the 25-basis-point SLC fee equals 15 basis points.

Note that in selling the SLCs, FIs are competing directly with another of their OBS products, loan commitments. Rather than buying an SLC from an FI to back a CP issue, the issuing firm might pay a fee to an FI to supply a loan commitment. This loan commitment would match the size and maturity of the CP issue, for example, a $100 million ceiling and 45 days maturity. If, on maturity, the CP issuer has insufficient funds to repay the CP holders, the issuer has the right to take down the $100 million loan commitment and to use those funds to meet CP repayments. Often, the up-front fees on such loan commitments are less than those on SLCs; therefore, many CP-issuing firms prefer to use loan commitments.

It needs to be stressed that banks are not the only issuers of SLCs. Not surprisingly, performance bonds and financial guarantees are an important business line of property & casualty insurers. The growth in these lines for property & casualty insurers has come at the expense of banks. Moreover, foreign banks increasingly are taking a share of the U.S. market in SLCs. The reason for the loss in this business line by U.S. banks is that to sell guarantees such as SLCs credibly, the seller must have a better credit rating than the customer. In recent years, few U.S. banks or their parent holding companies have had AA ratings. Other domestic U.S. FIs and Canadian and other foreign banks, on the other hand, have more often had AA ratings. High credit ratings not only make the guarantor more attractive from the buyer's perspective but also make the guarantor more competitive because its cost of funds is lower than that of less creditworthy FIs.

Derivative Contracts: Futures, Forwards, Swaps, and Options

FIs can be either users of derivative contracts for hedging (see Chapters 23 through 25) and other purposes or dealers that act as counterparties in trades with customers for a fee. Of the total notional derivatives amounts reported in Table 13–4 for Q3 2005, TD and RBC accounted for 26.5 and 24.8 percent of the total $10.8 bil-

---

[27] G. O. Koppenhaver uses a similar definition to distinguish between LCs and SLCs. See "Standby Letters of Credit," Federal Reserve Bank of Chicago, *Economic Perspectives,* 1987, pp. 28–38.

www.royalbank.com
www.td.com
www.bmo.com
www.cibc.com
www.scotiabank.ca
www.nbc.ca

lion, followed by Bank of Montreal (16.9 percent), CIBC (10.4 percent), Bank of Nova Scotia (8.1 percent) and National Bank of Canada (3.9 percent). OTC contracts are by far the greater portion of OBS exposure for the banks on a notional basis. By comparison, although approximately 530 U.S. banks were users of derivatives in 2003, the big three dealer banks (J. P. Morgan Chase, Bank of America, and Citigroup) accounted for 87 percent of the US$65.8 billion reported to the U.S. Office of the Comptroller of the Currency.

Contingent credit risk is likely to be present when FIs expand their positions in forwards, futures, swaps, and option contracts. This risk relates to the fact that the counterparty to one of these contracts may default on payment obligations, leaving the FI unhedged and having to replace the contract at today's interest rates, prices, or exchange rates.[28] Further, such defaults are most likely to occur when the counterparty is losing heavily on the contract and the FI is in the money on the contract. This type of default risk is much more serious for forward (and swap) contracts than for futures contracts. This is so because **forward contracts**[29] are nonstandard contracts entered into bilaterally by negotiating parties such as two FIs, and all cash flows are required to be paid at one time (on contract maturity). Thus, they are essentially over-the-counter (OTC) arrangements with no external guarantees should one or the other party default on the contract. For example, the contract seller might default on a forward foreign exchange contract that promises to deliver £10 million in three months' time at the exchange rate of $1.40 to £1 if the cost to purchase £1 for delivery is $1.60 when the forward contract matures. By contrast, **futures contracts** are standardized contracts guaranteed by organized exchanges such as Montréal Exchange or the New York Futures Exchange (NYFE), a part of the New York Board of Trade (NYBOT). Futures contracts, like forward contracts, make commitments to deliver foreign exchange (or some other asset) at some future date. If a counterparty defaults on a futures contract, however, the exchange assumes the defaulting party's position and the payment obligations. For example, when Barings, the British merchant bank, was unable to meet its margin calls on Nikkei Index futures traded on the Singapore futures exchange (SIMEX) in 1995, the exchange stood ready to assume Barings' US$8 billion position in futures contracts and ensure that no counterparty lost money. Thus, unless a systematic financial market collapse threatens the exchange itself, futures are essentially default risk free.[30] In addition, default risk is reduced by the daily marking to market of contracts. This prevents the accumulation of losses and gains that occurs with forward contracts. These differences are discussed in more detail in Chapter 23.

An option is a contract that gives the holder the right, but not the obligation, to buy (a call option) or sell (a put option) an underlying asset at a prespecified price for a specified time period. Option contracts can also be purchased or sold by an FI, trading either over the counter (OTC) or bought/sold on organized exchanges. If the options are standardized options traded on exchanges, such as bond options,

forward contracts
Nonstandard contracts between two parties to deliver and pay for an asset in the future.

futures contracts
Standardized contract guaranteed by organized exchanges to deliver and pay for an asset in the future.

www.nybot.com
www.m-x.ca

---

[28] In fact, J. F. Sinkey, Jr., and D. A. Carter, in "The Reaction of Bank Stock Prices to News of Derivative Losses by Corporate Clients," *Journal of Banking and Finance* 23 (1999), pp. 1725–43, find that when large nonfinancial firms announced losses from derivative deals, the FI serving as the derivatives dealer experiences significant stock price declines. Thus, FIs are exposed to OBS risk as a party to a derivatives contract as well as a derivative dealer (acting as a third party, but not a direct party, to the contract).

[29] Conceptually, a swap contract can be viewed as a succession of forward contracts.

[30] More specifically, there are at least four reasons why the default risk of a futures contract is less than that of a forward contract: (1) daily marking to market of futures, (2) margin requirements on futures that act as a security bond, (3) price limits that spread out over extreme price fluctuations, and (4) default guarantees by the futures exchange itself.

they are virtually default risk free.[31] If they are specialized options purchased OTC such as interest rate caps (see Chapter 24), some element of default risk exists.[32]

A swap is an agreement between two parties (called counterparties) to exchange specified periodic cash flows in the future based on some underlying instrument or price (e.g., a fixed or floating rate on a bond or note). Similar to options, swaps are OTC instruments normally susceptible to counterparty risk (see Chapter 25). If interest rates (or foreign exchange rates) move a lot, one party can be faced with considerable future loss exposure, creating incentives to default.

Credit derivatives (including forwards, options, and swaps) allow FIs to hedge their credit risk. They can be used to hedge the credit risk on individual loans or bonds or portfolios of loans and bonds. The emergence of these new derivatives is important since more FIs fail as a result of credit risk exposures than either interest rate or FX risk exposures. We discuss these derivatives in more detail in Chapters 23 through 25.

In general, default risk on OTC contracts increases with the time to maturity of the contract and the fluctuation of underlying prices, interest rates, or exchange rates.[33] Most empirical evidence suggests that derivative contracts have generally reduced FI risk or left it unaffected.[34]

Forward Purchases and Sales of When Issued Securities

when issued (WI) trading
Trading in securities prior to their actual issue.

www.bankofcanada.ca

Very often banks and other FIs—especially investment banks—enter into commitments to buy and sell securities before issue. This is called **when issued (WI) trading.** These OBS commitments can expose an FI to future or contingent interest rate risk. FIs often include these securities as a part of their holdings of forward contracts.

An example of a WI commitment is that taken on with new T-bills in the week prior to the announcement of T-bill auction results. The Bank of Canada releases a call for tenders for three-month, six-month, and one-year Government of Canada treasury bills on Thursday afternoon and the auction is held the following Thursday afternoon, as shown in Figure 13–3. Secondary trading (the "when-issued" market) for these bills occurs until the settlement date, which is the day following the auction of the bills. There are nine primary dealers who maintain a market in the securities and 22 government securities distributors who are investment dealers and banks. Normally, primary dealers sell the yet-to-be-issued T-bills for forward

---

[31] Note that the options can still be subject to interest rate risk; see our earlier discussion of the delta on a bond option.

[32] Under an interest rate cap, in return for a fee, the seller promises to compensate the buyer if interest rates rise above a certain level. If rates rise a lot more than expected, the cap seller may have an incentive to default to truncate the losses. Thus, selling a cap is similar to an FI selling interest rate risk insurance (see Chapter 24 for more details).

[33] Reputational considerations and the need for future access to markets for hedging deter the incentive to default (see Chapter 25 as well).

[34] See, for example, L. Angbazo, "Commercial Bank Net Interest Margins, Default Risks, Interest Rate Risk and Off-Balance-Sheet Banking," *Journal of Banking and Finance* 21 (January 1997), pp. 55–87, who finds no link between interest rate risk and FIs' use of derivatives; and G. Gorton and R. Rosen, "Banks and Derivatives," Working Paper, University of Pennsylvania, Wharton School, February 1995. Gorton and Rosen find that swap contracts have generally reduced the systemic risk of the U.S. banking system. J. T. Harper and J. R. Wingender, "An Empirical Test of Agency Cost Reduction Using Interest Rate Swaps," *Journal of Banking and Finance* 24 (2000), pp. 1419–31, find that the use of interest rate swaps is positively related to a reduction in a firm's agency costs. Nevertheless, B. Hirtle, "Derivatives, Portfolio Composition and Bank Holding Company Interest Rate Risk Exposure," *Journal of Financial Services Research,* 1997, pp. 243–66, finds that the use of interest rate derivatives corresponded to greater interest rate risk exposure during the 1991–94 period for U.S. bank holding companies. Finally, N. Y. Naik and P. K. Yadav, "Risk Management with Derivatives by Dealers and Market Quality in Government Bond Markets," *Journal of Finance* 58 (2003), pp. 1873–1904, find that intermediaries use futures contracts to offset or hedge changes in their spot positions. They find that larger intermediaries engage in greater amounts of market risk taking and hedge their spot exposure to a lesser extent than smaller intermediaries. They do not find that larger intermediaries earn more profit from their selective risk taking than smaller intermediaries.

FIGURE 13–3
T-Bill Auction
Time Line

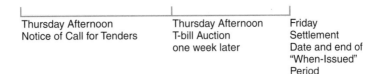

| Thursday Afternoon Notice of Call for Tenders | Thursday Afternoon T-bill Auction one week later | Friday Settlement Date and end of "When-Issued" Period |

delivery to customers in the secondary market at a small margin above the price they expect to pay at the primary auction. This can be profitable if the primary dealer gets all the bills needed at the auction at the appropriate price or interest rate to fulfill these forward WI contracts. A primary dealer that makes a mistake regarding the tenor of the auction (i.e., the level of interest rates) faces the risk that the commitments entered into to deliver T-bills in the WI market can be met only at a loss. For example, an overcommitted dealer may have to buy T-bills from other dealers at a loss right after the auction results are announced to meet the WI T-bill delivery commitments made to its customers.[35]

Loans Sold

We discuss in more detail in Chapter 26 the types of loans FIs sell, their incentives to sell, and the way they can be sold. Increasingly, banks and other FIs originate loans on their balance sheets, but rather than holding them to maturity, they quickly sell them to outside investors. These outside investors include other banks, insurance companies, mutual funds, and even corporations. In acting as loan originators and loan sellers, FIs are operating more in the fashion of loan brokers than as traditional asset transformers (see Chapter 1).

recourse
The ability to put an asset or loan back to the seller if the credit quality of that asset deteriorates.

When an outside party buys a loan with absolutely no **recourse** to the seller of the loan should the loan eventually go bad, loan sales have no OBS contingent liability implications for FIs. Specifically, *no recourse* means that if the loan the FI sells goes bad, the buyer of the loan must bear the full risk of loss (see arrow 1 in Figure 13–4). In particular, the buyer cannot put the bad loan back to the seller or originating bank. Suppose the loan is sold with recourse. Then, loan sales present a long-term contingent credit risk to the seller. Essentially, the buyer of the loan holds a long-term option to put the loan back to the seller (arrow 2), which the buyer can exercise should the credit quality of the purchased loan deteriorate. In reality, the recourse or nonrecourse nature of loan sales is often ambiguous. For example, some have argued that FIs generally are willing to repurchase bad no recourse loans to preserve their reputations with their customers.[36] Obviously, reputational concerns may extend the size of a selling FI's contingent liabilities for OBS activities.[37]

Concept
Questions

1. What are the four risks related to loan commitments?
2. What is the major difference between a commercial letter of credit and a standby letter of credit?
3. What is meant by counterparty risk in a forward contract?
4. Which is more risky for an FI, loan sales with recourse or loan sales without recourse?

---

[35] The Investment Dealers Association of Canada provides a compliance bulletin for when-issued trades of government debt at www.ida.ca as does the Bank of Canada at www.bankofcanada.ca.

[36] G. Gorton and G. Pennacchi, "Are Loan Sales Really Off Balance Sheet?" in *Off-Balance-Sheet Activities,* ed. J. Ronen, A. Saunders, and A. C. Sondhi (New York: Quorum Books, 1989), pp. 19–40. We discuss loan sales in more detail in Chapter 26.

[37] However, C. Pavel finds that there is little relationship between bank loan sales and bank risk. See C. Pavel, "Loan Sales Have Little Effect on Bank Risk," *Economic Perspectives,* Federal Reserve Bank of Chicago, May–June 1988, pp. 23–31.

FIGURE 13–4
Loans Sold with
and without
Recourse

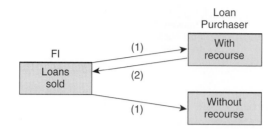

OTHER OFF-BALANCE-SHEET RISKS

So far we have looked at five different OBS activities of banks that report to OSFI each quarter. Remember that many other FIs engage in these activities as well. Thus, credit unions, insurance companies, and investment banks all engage in futures, forwards, swaps, and options transactions of varying forms. Life insurers are heavily engaged in making loan commitments in commercial mortgages, property & casualty companies underwrite large amounts of financial guarantees, and investment banks engage in when issued securities trading. Moreover, the five activities just discussed are not the only OBS activities that can create contingent liabilities or risks for an FI. Next, we briefly introduce two other activities that can create them; we discuss the activities at greater length in later chapters.

www.chips.org
www.cdnpay.ca

clearing
The exchange and reconcile of payments in order to transfer funds from one FI to another.

Settlement Risk

Canadian FIs send their domestic Canadian and U.S. dollar payments via the systems operated by the Canada Payments Association (CPA) of which 10 FIs and the Bank of Canada are Direct Clearers. The Automated Clearing Settlement System (ACSS) is involved in **clearing** ninety-nine per cent of the daily volume of transactions in Canada, but these represent only 15 per cent of the total value. The Large Value Transfer System (LVTS) clears 85 per cent of the total daily value (Cdn. $115 billion) and is used for irrevocable payments. The LVTS is the first of its kind in the world and gives real time **settlement**, eliminating settlement risk for these types of transactions within Canada.

settlement
The adjustment of financial positions of individual FIs at the Bank of Canada.

settlement risk
Intraday credit risk associated with wire transfer activities.

CHIPS is an international and private network owned by approximately 55 participating or member banks. Unlike the ACSS and the LVTS, funds or payment messages sent on the CHIPs network *within* the day are provisional messages that become final and are settled only at the end of the day, giving rise to an intraday, or within-day, **settlement risk** that does not appear on the FI's balance sheet. The balance sheet at best summarizes only the end-of-day-closing position or book of an FI and thus intraday settlement risk represents an additional form of OBS risk for FIs participating on private wholesale wire transfer system networks. The payments system in Canada is discussed in more detail in Chapter 14.

affiliate risk
The risk imposed on a parent company or holding company due to the potential failure of another unit in the group.

Affiliate Risk

Affiliate risk is the risk imposed on the parent company group or holding company group due to the potential failure of another unit in the group. A **holding company** is a corporation that owns the shares (normally more than 25 percent) of other corporations. Currently, in Canada, federally-regulated FIs are permitted to operate with a **parent-subsidiary company structure** where each member of the group is subject to the same regulatory oversight as the parent. However, Bill C-8, passed in June, 2001 would allow Canadian FIs to operate in a holding company

holding company
A corporation that owns the shares (normally more than 25 percent) of other corporations.

FIGURE 13–5
One-Bank and
Multibank Holding
Company
Structures

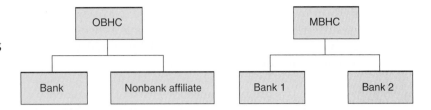

parent-subsidiary corporate structure
A corporate structure where the subsidiaries are owned and controlled by the parent and subject to the same level of regulatory oversight.

structure. The regulations have yet to be amended to allow this type of organizational structure. Most developed countries allow bank holding company structures. For example, Citigroup is a one-bank U.S. holding company (OBHC) that owns all the shares of Citibank. Citigroup engages in certain permitted nonbank activities such as data processing through separately capitalized affiliates or companies that it owns. Similarly, a number of other holding companies are multi-bank holding companies (MBHCs) that own shares in a number of different banks. J.P. Morgan Chase is an MBHC that holds shares in banks throughout the United States. The organizational structures of these two holding companies are presented in Figure 13–5.

Legally, in the context of OBHCs, the bank and the nonbank affiliate are separate companies, as are bank 1 and bank 2 in the context of MBHCs. Thus, in Figure 13–5, the failure of the nonbank affiliate and bank 2 should have no effect on the financial resources of the bank in the OBHC or on bank 1 in the MBHC. In reality, the failure of an affiliated firm or bank imposes affiliate risk on another bank in a holding company structure. Both creditors and regulators may look to the holding company, that is, the corporation that owns the shares of the affiliate for support for a failed affiliate, particularly if they have similar names such as Town Bank and Town Bank Credit Card Company.

Special Purpose Entity (SPE)
A separate company or trust created for the sale of specific assets.

At the present time, affiliate risk for FIs operating in Canada arises primarily from the use of **Special Purpose Entities** (SPEs, also called Variable Interest Entities or VIEs) that are created as vehicles for the securitization of assets. For example, the Royal Bank of Canada securitizes its credit card receivables and the TD Bank securitizes residential mortgage loans, credit card receivables, and commercial mortgage loans by selling them to an SPE. The risk arises when the assets have been removed from the bank's balance sheet but the bank retains an interest in the securitized assets. The mechanisms of securitization will be discussed in greater detail in Chapter 27.[38]

THE ROLE OF OBS ACTIVITIES IN REDUCING RISK

This chapter has emphasized that OBS activities may add to the riskiness of an FI's activities. Indeed, most contingent assets and liabilities have various characteristics that may accentuate an FI's default and/or interest rate risk exposures. Even so, FIs use some OBS instruments—especially forwards, futures, options, and swaps—to reduce or manage their interest rate risk, foreign exchange risk, and credit risk exposures in a manner superior to what would exist in their absence.[39] When used to hedge on-balance-sheet interest rate, foreign exchange, and credit risks, these instru-

outsourcing
The contracting out of services to an entity outside of the company.

[38] The Bank for International Settlements (BIS) has been concerned about securitization and **outsourcing** as sources of risk for globally active FIs. See A. Jobst, "The Basel Securitisation Framework Explained," forthcoming in *Journal of Financial Regulation and Compliance*, Vol. 13, No. 1 and The Basel Committee on Banking Supervision, The Joint Forum, "Outsourcing in Financial Services," February 2005, at www.bis.org.

[39] As we discuss in Chapter 24, there are strong tax disincentives to using derivatives for purposes other than direct hedging.

ments can actually work to reduce FIs' overall insolvency risk.[40] Although we do not fully describe the role of these instruments as hedging vehicles in reducing an FI's insolvency exposure until Chapters 23 through 26, you can now recognize the inherent danger in the overregulation of OBS activities and instruments. For example, the risk that a counterparty might default on a forward foreign exchange contract risk is very small. It is probably much lower than the insolvency risk an FI faces if it does not use forward contracts to hedge its foreign exchange assets against undesirable fluctuations in exchange rates. (See Chapters 15 and 23 for some examples of this.)

Despite the risk-reducing attributes of OBS derivative securities held by FIs, the expanded use of derivatives has caused many regulators to focus on the risk-increasing attributes of these securities and the possible detrimental effect the risk may have on global financial markets. The result has been an increase in the amount of regulation proposed for these activities. Despite these rules and regulations passed in the early 1990s, huge losses on derivative securities by FIs such as Bankers Trust (in 1994), Barings (in 1995), and Long Term Capital Management (in 1998) have resulted in the call for additional regulation. Partially as a result of these concerns, the regulatory costs of hedging have risen (e.g., through the imposition of special capital requirements or restrictions on the use of such instruments [see Chapter 20]). As a result, FIs may have a tendency to underhedge, thereby increasing, rather than decreasing, their insolvency risk.

Finally, fees from OBS activities provide a key source of noninterest income for many FIs, especially the largest and most creditworthy ones. The importance of noninterest incomes for large banks is shown in Table 14–1 in the next chapter. Thus, increased OBS earnings can potentially compensate for increased OBS risk exposure and actually reduce the probability of insolvency for some FIs.[41]

Concept Questions

1. While recognizing that OBS instruments may add to the riskiness of an FI's activities, explain how they also work to reduce the overall insolvency risk of FIs.
2. Other than hedging and speculation, what reasons do FIs have for engaging in OBS activities?

---

[40] For example, the London International Financial Futures and Options Exchange (LIFFE) introduced in 2001 a swapnote, which is a futures contract whose settlement price is based on swap market rates. Swapnotes provide an effective mechanism for FIs to hedge interest rate risk with minimal basis risk (see Chapter 25).

[41] In addition, by allowing risk-averse managers to hedge risk, derivatives may induce the managers to follow more value-maximizing investment strategies. That is, derivatives may allow manager–stockholder agency conflicts over the level of risk taking to be reduced. See, for example, D. R. Nance, C. W. Smith, Jr., and C. W. Smithson, "On the Determinants of Corporate Hedging," *Journal of Finance*, 1993, pp. 267–84.

Summary

This chapter showed that an FI's net worth or economic value is linked not only to the value of its traditional on-balance-sheet activities but also to the contingent asset and liability values of its off-balance-sheet activities. The risks and returns of several off-balance-sheet items were discussed in detail: loan commitments; commercial and standby letters of credit; derivative contracts such as futures, options, and swaps; forward purchases; and sales of when issued securities and loans sold. In all cases, it is clear that these instruments have a major impact on the future profitability and risk of an FI. Two other risks associated with off-balance-sheet activities—settlement risk and affiliate risk—were also discussed. The chapter concluded by pointing out that although off-balance-sheet activities can be risk increasing, they can also be used to hedge on-balance-sheet exposures, resulting in lower risks as well as generating fee income to the FI.

Questions and Problems

1. Classify the following items as (1) on-balance-sheet assets, (2) on-balance-sheet liabilities, (3) off-balance-sheet assets, (4) off-balance-sheet liabilities, or (5) capital account.
   a. Loan commitments.
   b. Loan loss reserves.
   c. Letter of credit.
   d. Bankers acceptance.
   e. Rediscounted bankers acceptance.
   f. Loan sales without recourse.
   g. Loan sales with recourse.
   h. Forward contracts to purchase.
   i. Forward contracts to sell.
   j. Swaps.
   k. Loan participations.
   l. Securities borrowed.
   m. Securities lent.
   n. Loss adjustment expense account (PC insurers).

2. How does one distinguish between an off-balance-sheet asset and an off-balance-sheet liability?

3. Contingent Bank has the following balance sheet in market value terms (in millions of dollars).

Assets		Liabilities	
Cash	20	Deposits	220
Mortgages	220	Equity	20
Total assets	240	Total liabilities and equity	240

In addition, the bank has contingent assets with $100 million market value and contingent liabilities with $80 million market value. What is the true stockholder net worth? What does the term *contingent* mean?

4. Why are contingent assets and liabilities like options? What is meant by the delta of an option? What is meant by the term *notional value?*

5. An FI has purchased options on bonds with a notional value of $500 million and has sold options on bonds with a notional value of $400 million. The purchased options have a delta of 0.25, and the sold options have a delta of 0.30. What is (a) the contingent asset value of this position, (b) the contingent liability value of this position, and (c) the contingent market value of net worth?

6. What factors explain the growth of off-balance-sheet activities in the 1980s through the early 2000s among FIs?

7. What are the characteristics of a loan commitment that an FI may make to a customer? In what manner and to whom is the commitment an option? What are the various possible pieces of the option premium? When does the option or commitment become an on-balance-sheet item for the FI and the borrower?

8. A FI makes a loan commitment of $2,500,000 with an up-front fee of 50 basis points and a back-end fee of 25 basis points on the unused portion of the loan. The takedown on the loan is 50 percent.
   a. What total fees does the FI earn when the loan commitment is negotiated?
   b. What are the total fees earned by the FI at the end of the year, that is, in future value terms? Assume the cost of capital for the FI is 6 percent.

9. A FI has issued a one-year loan commitment of $2,000,000 for an up-front fee of 25 basis points. The back-end fee on the unused portion of the commitment is 10 basis points. The FI's cost of funds is 6 percent, the interest rate on the loan is 10 percent. The customer is expected to draw down 80 percent of the commitment at the beginning of the year.
   a. What is the expected return on the loan without taking future values into consideration?
   b. What is the expected return using future values? That is, the net fee and interest income are evaluated at the end of the year when the loan is due.
   c. What is the expected return using future values but with the funding of demand deposits replaced by certificates of deposit that have an interest rate of 5.5 percent?

10. Suburb Bank has issued a one-year loan commitment of $10,000,000 for an up-front fee of 50 basis points. The back-end fee on the unused portion of the commitment is 20 basis points. The bank has a cost of funds of 7 percent and will charge an interest rate on the loan of 9 percent. The customer is expected to draw down 60 percent of the commitment.
   a. What is the expected return on this loan?
   b. What is the expected return per annum on the loan if the draw-down on the commitment does not occur until the end of six months?

11. How is an FI exposed to interest rate risk when it makes loan commitments? In what way can an FI control for this risk? How does basis risk affect the implementation of the control for interest rate risk?

12. How is an FI exposed to credit risk when it makes loan commitments? How is credit risk related to interest rate risk? What control measure is available to an FI for the purpose of protecting against credit risk? What is the realistic opportunity to implement this control feature?

13. How is an FI exposed to takedown risk and aggregate funding risk? How are these two contingent risks related?

14. Do the contingent risks of interest rate, takedown, credit, and aggregate funding tend to increase the insolvency risk of an FI? Why or why not?

15. What is a letter of credit? How is a letter of credit like an insurance contract?

16. A German bank issues a three-month letter of credit on behalf of its customer in Germany, who is planning to import $100,000 worth of goods from Canada. It charges an up-front fee of 100 basis points.
    a. What up-front fee does the bank earn?
    b. If the exporter decides to discount this letter of credit after it has been accepted by the German bank, how much will the exporter receive, assuming that the interest rate currently is 5 percent and that 90 days remain before maturity?
    c. What risk does the German bank incur by issuing this letter of credit?

17. How do standby letters of credit differ from commercial letters of credit? With what other types of FI products do SLCs compete? What types of FIs can issue SLCs?

18. A corporation is planning to issue $1,000,000 of 270-day commercial paper for an effective annual yield of 5 percent. The corporation expects to save 30 basis points on the interest rate by using either an SLC or a loan commitment as collateral for the issue.
    a. What are the net savings to the corporation if a bank agrees to provide a 270-day SLC for an up-front fee of 20 basis points (of the face value of the loan commitment) to back the commercial paper issue?
    b. What are the net savings to the corporation if a bank agrees to provide a 270-day loan commitment to back the issue? The bank will charge 10 basis points for an up-front fee and 10 basis points for a back-end fee for any unused portion of the loan. Assume the loan is not needed, and that the fees are on the face value of the loan commitment.
    c. Should the corporation be indifferent to the two alternative collateral methods at the time the commercial paper is issued?

19. Explain how the use of derivative contracts such as forwards, futures, swaps, and options creates contingent credit risk for an FI. Why do OTC contracts carry more contingent credit risk than do exchange-traded contracts? How is the default risk of OTC contracts related to the time to maturity and the price and rate volatilities of the underlying assets?

20. What is meant by when issued trading? Explain how forward purchases of when issued government T-bills can expose FIs to contingent interest rate risk.

21. Distinguish between loan sales with and without recourse. Why would banks want to sell loans with recourse? Explain how loan sales can leave banks exposed to contingent interest rate risks.

22. The manager of Shakey Bank sends a $2 million funds transfer payment message via CHIPS to the Trust Bank at 10 AM. Trust Bank sends a $2 million funds transfer message via CHIPS to Hope Bank later that same day. What type of risk is inherent in this transaction? How will the risk become reality?

23. Explain how settlement risk is incurred in the interbank payment mechanism and how it is another form of off-balance-sheet risk.

24. What is the difference between a parent-subsidiary structure and a holding company structure? How might Canadian FIs change when the Bank Act is amended to permit holding company structures? Do you expect that the risks will be different for the FIs? How might the failure of an affiliate affect the holding company even if the affiliate were structured separately?

25. Defend the statement that although off-balance-sheet activities expose FIs to several forms of risks, they also can alleviate the risks of FIs.

Web Questions

26. Go to OSFI's web site at www.osfi-bsif.gc.ca to update Table 13–6. Click on "Banks." Click on "Financial Data—Banks." Click on "Quarterly" and use the dropdown menu to choose "Summary Off-Balance-sheet Items (Summary of CAR4)." Submit your request and then answer the following questions from the spreadsheet that pops up. What is the dollar value increase in total OBS assets reported by the banks since Table 13–6 was prepared? Are OTC interest rate derivatives still the largest category? Use the dropdown menu at the top of the page to obtain the results for Royal Bank of Canada and TD Bank. Are RBC and TD still the two largest users of derivatives of the six major banks? Click on "Monthly" and find the latest Consolidated Balance Sheet for the banks. How does the growth in reported OBS assets compare with the growth in on-balance sheet assets for the banks over the same time period?

Appendix 13A   A Letter of Credit Transaction

View Appendix 13A at the Web site for this textbook (**www.mcgrawhill.ca/college/saunders**).

Technology and Other Operational Risks

This chapter focuses on operational risk and considers:

▸ the factors that influence operational returns and risks of FIs (with an emphasis on technology)

▸ the importance of optimal management control of labour, capital, and other input sources and their costs

▸ how well-managed FIs can use operational cost savings to increase profits and thus reduce the probability of insolvency

▸ how operational risk is addressed at Canadian FIs and

▸ how Basel II will change the way operational risk is addressed at Canadian FIs

INTRODUCTION

Chapters 7 through 13 concentrated on the financial risks that arise as FIs perform their asset-transformation and/or brokerage functions on or off the balance sheet. However, financial risk is only one part of a modern FI's risk profile. As with regular corporations, FIs have a real or production side to their operations that results in additional costs and revenues.

Central to FIs' decision-making processes is the cost of inputs, or factors used to produce services both on and off the balance sheet. Two important factors are labour (tellers, credit officers) and capital (buildings, machinery, furniture). Crucial to the efficient management and combination of these inputs (which result in financial outputs at the lowest cost) is technology. Technological innovation has been a major concern of FIs in recent years. Since the 1980s, banks, insurance companies, and investment companies have sought to improve operational efficiency with major investments in internal and external communications, computers, and an expanded technological infrastructure. Internet and wireless communications technologies are having a profound effect on financial services—they are a completely different way of providing financial services. A global financial service firm such as the U.S.-based bank, Citigroup, has operations in more than 100 countries connected in real time by a proprietary-owned satellite system. Operational risk is partly related to technology risk and can arise when existing technology malfunctions or back-office support systems break down. Further, back-office support systems combine labour and technology to provide clearance, settlement, and other services to back FIs' underlying on- and off-balance-sheet transactions.

According to Hitachi Data Systems, back-office system failures usually occur four times per year in the average firm. Recovery time from system failures average 12 hours. The terrorist attacks on the World Trade Center and the Pentagon in the U.S. created back-office system failures of an unforeseen magnitude. For example, over a week after the attacks, Bank of New York was still having trouble with some crucial communications links. The risks of technological malfunctions for FIs were highlighted in June, 2004, when the Royal Bank of Canada experienced a programming error that affected their main and backup computer systems. The

www.bis.org

reputational risk
The potential an FI's actions to cause a loss of trust of clients, the market, and regulators.

operational risk
The potential for losses from failed systems, personnel, or external events.

problem, which lasted for a week, resulted in customers overdrawing their accounts when their paycheques were not deposited on time. This operational risk cost the bank the trust of their clients (**reputational risk**) and increased their non-interest expense by $11 million in 2004.[1]

Technology and operational risks are closely related and have caused great concern to FI regulators. The Bank of International Settlements (BIS), the principal organization of the world's central banks, defines **operational risk** as "the risk of losses resulting from inadequate or failed internal processes, people, and systems or from external events." Operational risk, including risks from outsourcing, have become so significant that the BIS has proposed that, as of 2006, banks should be made to carry a capital cushion against losses from this risk.[2] We discuss the BIS proposal briefly in this chapter and in more detail in Chapter 20.

WHAT ARE THE SOURCES OF OPERATIONAL RISK?

These are at least five sources of operational risk:[3]

1. Technology (e.g., technological failure and deteriorating systems).
2. Employees (e.g., human error and internal fraud).
3. Customer relationships (e.g., contractual disputes).
4. Capital assets (e.g., destruction by fire or other catastrophes).
5. External (e.g., external fraud).

Increasingly important to the profitability and riskiness of modern FIs has been item 1: technology.

TECHNOLOGICAL INNOVATION AND PROFITABILITY

technology
Computers, audio and visual communication systems, and other information systems, which can be applied to an FI's production of services.

www.cba.ca

Broadly defined, **technology** includes computers, visual and audio communication systems, and other information technology (IT). The Canadian Banker's Association (CBA) reports that, between 1996 and 2003, the six largest Canadian banks spent $24.8 billion, an average of $3.5 billion per year, on technology such as computer hardware and software, capital leases related to computer equipment, data and voice communication equipment, and development expenses related to these items.[4] An efficient technological base for an FI can result in:

1. Lower costs, by combining labour and capital in a more efficient mix.
2. Increased revenues, by allowing a wider array of financial services to be produced or innovated and sold to customers.

---

[1] The Royal Bank's management of operational risk includes self-assessment and control of risk, compilation of a loss event database, and the identification of key risk indicators. See Royal Bank of Canada's 2004 Annual Report, p. 61A, as well as C. Conrath, "Anatomy of a royal snafu: a look inside RBC's recent battle with its technology demons," *ComputerWorld Canada*, June 25, 2004, Vol. 20, Iss. 13. Canadian Imperial Bank of Commerce (CIBC) and TD Canada Trust (TD) also experienced computer problems in the summer of 2004. See F. Sheikh, "Computer glitches paralyse CIBC, TD banking systems," *Computing Canada*, August 13, 2004, Vol. 30, Iss. 11, pp. 1–2.

[2] See Basel Committee on Bank Supervision, "Overview of the New Basel Capital Accord," Bank for International Settlements, April 2003, p. 120. Other BIS papers on operational risk are "Working Paper on the Regulatory Treatment of Operational Risk," September 2001, "Sound Practices for the Management and Supervision of Operational Risk," February 2003, and "Outsourcing in Financial Services," February 2005, available at www.bis.org.

[3] See, for example, D. Hoffman and M. Johnson, "Operating Procedures," Risk Magazine, October 1996, pp. 60–63.

[4] Canadian Bankers Association, "The Banking Industry in Canada: Taking a Closer Look," June 2004, page 26. See also The Strategic Counsel, "Technology and Banking: A Survey of Consumer Attitudes" (2004) which surveyed 1200 Canadians about the impact of technology on their banking habits. A summary of the survey's findings is available at the CBA's Web site, www.cba.ca.

TABLE 14–1
Earnings and Other Data for All Banks Reporting to OSFI (in millions of dollars)

Source: Office of Superintendent of Financial Services, www.osfi-bsif.gc.ca

Financial Data	1996	1999	2002	2004*
Interest income	63,383	76,293	69,592	48,592
Interest expense	−40,875	−51,788	−36,091	−23,261
Net interest income	22,508	24,506	33,501	25,331
Charge for impairment	−2,139	−3,177	−9,719	−1,195
Deposit service charges	2,090	2,455	3,402	2,676
Credit & debit card fees	1,432	1,641	2,212	1,758
Loan fees	1,056	1,654	1,775	1,132
Mutual fund & underwriting fees	3,858	7,599	9,790	8,324
Trading income	1,029	6,192	3,259	3,673
All other	3,836	7,397	10,842	8,346
Noninterest income	13,301	26,938	31,280	25,910
Salaries, pensions & benefits	−12,526	−18,362	−23,826	−18,645
Premises & equipment	−4,424	−6,366	−7,907	−5,844
All other	−5,874	−9,357	−12,693	−9,323
Noninterest expenses	−22,284	−34,085	−44,427	−33,811
Income taxes	−4,080	−4,542	−2,391	−4,580
Non-controlling interests in subsidiaries	124	−150	−508	−434
Extraordinary items	0	−9	8	0
Net income (%)	6,640	9,481	7,745	11,221
Total assets ($ billion)	1,014.6	1,367.2	1,688.5	1,816.8
Return on assets	0.65%	0.69%	0.46%	0.62%

*as of the third quarter; all other data for Q4 of the relevant year

The importance of an FI's operating costs and the efficient use of technology affecting these costs is clearly demonstrated by this simplified profit function:

Earnings or profit before taxes = (Interest income − interest expense) + (Other income − Noninterest expense) − (Provision for loan losses)

www.osfi-bsif.gc.ca

Table 14–1 breaks down the profit data for Canadian banks reporting to the Office of Superintendent of Financial Services (OSFI) over the 1996–2004 period into the different components impacting profits. For example, through the third quarter of 2004, interest income of $48,592 million and interest expense of $23,261 million produce net interest income of $25,331 million. However, the banks also had total noninterest income of $25,910 (including service charges on deposits of $2,676) and noninterest expenses of $33,811 million (including salaries, pensions, and employee benefits of $18,645 million and premises and equipment expenses of $5,844 million). Thus, banks' net noninterest income was −$7,901 million. After considering provisions for impaired loans of $1,195 million, non-controlling interest in subsidiaries ($434 million), extraordinary items ($0) and taxes ($4,580 million), after-tax net income was $11,221 million. Underscoring the importance of operating costs is the fact that noninterest expenses amounted to 145% of interest expenses and were 3 times net income in 2004.

INTERNET EXERCISE

Go to the Web site for the Office of Superintendent of Financial Services and find the latest information available for Canadian banks. Go to OSFI's Web site at www.osfi-bsif.gc.ca. Click on "Banks." Click on "Financial Data." Click on "Quarterly." Click on the dropdown menu and select "Summary Income Statement." Click "Submit" to view and print the latest quarterly information.

Technology is important because well-chosen technological investments have the potential to increase both the FI's net interest margin, or the difference between interest income and interest expense, and other net income. Therefore, technology can directly improve profitability, as the following examples show:

1. *Interest income* can increase if the FI sells a broader array of financial services as a result of technological developments. These may include cross selling financial products by having the computer identify customers and then having the FI telemarket financial service products directly and over the Internet.

2. *Interest expense* can be reduced if access to markets for liabilities is directly dependent on the FI's technological capability. For example, the wire transfer systems linking domestic and international interbank lending markets are based on interlocking computer network systems. Moreover, an FI's ability to originate and sell commercial paper is increasingly computer driven. Thus, failure to invest in the appropriate technology may lock an FI out of a lower-cost funding market.[5]

3. *Other income* increases when fees for FI services, especially those from off-balance-sheet activities, are linked to the quality of the FI's technology. For example, letters of credit are now commonly originated electronically by customers; swaps, caps, options, and other complex derivatives are usually traded, tracked, and valued using high-powered computers and algorithms. FIs could not offer innovative derivative products to customers without investments in suitable IT. Further, new technology has resulted in an evolution of the payment systems (see below), which has increased the amount of fee income (noninterest income) as a percent of total operating income (interest income plus noninterest income) for FIs. For example, referring again to Table 14–1, we see that noninterest income as a percent of total operating income was 17.35 percent in 1996 and increased to 34.78 percent by 2004.

4. *Noninterest expenses* can be reduced if the collection and storage of customer information as well as the processing and settlement of numerous financial products are computer based rather than paper based. This is particularly true of security-related back-office activities.

Concept Questions

1. What are some of the advantages of an efficient technological base for an FI? How can it be used to directly improve profitability?
2. Looking at Table 14–1, determine if noninterest expenses and noninterest income have been increasing or decreasing as a percent of total bank costs over the 1996–2004 period.

THE EFFECT OF TECHNOLOGY ON WHOLESALE AND RETAIL FINANCIAL SERVICE PRODUCTION

The previous discussion established that modern technology has the potential to directly affect a modern FI's profit-producing areas. The following discussion focuses on some specific technology-based products found in modern retail and wholesale operations of financial institutions.[6] Note that this is far from a complete list.

---

[5] Commercial paper is an important source of funding for Canadian FIs. In 2002, 90 per cent of outstanding asset-backed commercial paper (ABCP) was attributed to the major Canadian banks, who were also responsible for US$31.5 million of ABCP issuance in the United States as well as for European U.S. dollar issues totaling US$3.7 billion at September 30 2002. See P. Toovey and J. Kiff, "Developments and Issues in the Canadian Market for Asset-Backed Commercial Paper," *Bank of Canada Financial System Review*, June 2003, pp. 43–48.

[6] A. K. Pennathur, in "'Clicks and Bricks': e-Risk Management for Banks in the Age of the Internet," *Journal of Banking and Finance* 25 (2001), pp. 2103–23, outlines various risks associated with the provision of these services.

Wholesale Financial Services

Probably the most important area in which technology has had an impact on wholesale or corporate customer services is an FI's ability to provide cash management or working capital services. Cash management services include "services designed to collect, disburse and transfer funds—on a local, regional, national or international basis—and to provide information about the location and status of those funds."[7] Cash management service needs have largely resulted from (1) corporate recognition that excess cash balances result in a significant opportunity cost due to lost or forgone interest and (2) corporate need to know cash or working capital position on a real-time basis. Among the services modern FIs provide to improve the efficiency with which corporate clients manage their financial positions are the following:

1. *Controlled disbursement accounts.* An account feature that establishes in the morning almost all payments to be made by the customer in a given day. The FI informs the corporate client of the total funds it needs to meet disbursements, and the client wire transfers the amount needed. These chequing accounts are debited early each day so that corporations can obtain an early insight into their net cash positions.

2. *Account reconciliation.* A chequing feature that records which of the firm's cheques have been paid by the FI.

float

The interval between the deposit of a cheque and when funds become available for depositor use; that is, the time is takes a cheque to clear at a bank.

3. *Wholesale lockbox.* A centralized collection service for corporate payments to reduce the delay in cheque clearing, or the **float**. In a typical lockbox arrangement, a local FI sets up a lockbox at the post office for a corporate client located outside the area. Local customers mail payments to the lockbox rather than to the out-of-town corporate headquarters. The FI collects these cheques several times per day and deposits them directly into the customer's account. Details of the transaction are wired to the corporate client.

4. *Electronic lockbox.* Same type of service as item 3 but receives online payments for public utilities and similar corporate clients.

5. *Funds concentration.* Redirects funds from accounts in a large number of FIs or branches to a few centralized accounts at one FI.

6. *Electronic funds transfer.* Includes overnight payments, automated payment of payrolls or dividends, and automated transmission of payments messages by SWIFT, an international electronic message service owned and operated by global FIs that instructs FIs to make specific payments.

7. *Cheque deposit services.* Encoding, endorsing, microfilming, and handling customers' cheques.

8. *Electronic initiation of letters of credit.* Allows customers in a network to access FI computers to initiate letters of credit.

9. *Treasury management software.* Allows efficient management of multiple currency and security portfolios for trading and investment purposes.[8]

10. *Electronic data interchange.* A specialized application of electronic mail, allowing businesses to transfer and transact invoices, purchase orders, and shipping notices automatically, using FIs as clearinghouses.

11. *Facilitation of business-to-business e-commerce.* A few of the largest Canadian and U.S. banks have begun to offer firms the technology for electronic business-to-business

---

[7] Salomon Brothers, "Transaction Processing: Raising the Technological Hurdle," U.S. Equity Research (Commercial Banks), January 6, 1997, p. 5.

[8] Computerized pension fund management and advisory services could be added to this list.

commerce. The banks are essentially undertaking automation of the entire information flow associated with the procurement and distribution of goods and services among businesses.

12. *Electronic billing.* Provides the presentment and collection services for companies that send out substantial volumes of recurring bills. Banks combine the e-mail capability of the Internet to send out bills with their ability to process payments electronically through the interbank payment networks.[9]

13. *Verification of identities.* Using encryption technology, banks certify the identities of its own account holders and serve as the intermediary through which its business customers can verify the identities of account holders at other banks.

14. *Assistance to small businesses entering into e-commerce.* Help to smaller firms in setting up the infrastructure—interactive Web site and payment capabilities—for engaging in e-commerce.

Retail Financial Services

Retail customers have demanded efficiency and flexibility in their financial transactions. Using only cheques or holding cash is often more expensive and time-consuming than using retail-oriented electronic payments technology and, increasingly, the Internet. Further, securities trading is increasingly moving toward electronic platforms not tied to any specific location. Electronic trading networks have lowered the costs of trading and allowed for better price determination. For example, customers of a major bank can obtain information on their account balances, pay their bills online, and trade stocks in their brokerage. accounts and their RRSP accounts from one Web site. Some of the most important retail payment product innovations include:

1. *Automated teller machines (ATMs).* Allows customers 24-hour access to their deposit accounts. They can pay bills as well as withdraw cash from these machines. In addition, if the FI's ATMs are part of a bank network (such as CIRRUS), retail depositors can gain direct nationwide—and in many cases international—access to their deposit accounts by using the ATMs of other banks in the network to draw on their accounts.[10]

2. *Point-of-sale (POS) debit cards.* Allows customers who choose not to use cash, cheques, or credit cards for purchases to buy merchandise using debit card/point-of-sale (POS) terminals. The merchant avoids the cheque float and any delay in payment associated with credit card receivables since the FI offers the debit card/POS service immediately and transfers funds directly from the customer's deposit account to the merchant's deposit account at the time of card use. Unlike cheque or **credit card transactions**, **debit card transactions** result in an immediate transfer of funds from the customers' account to the merchant's account.[11] Moreover, the customer never runs up a debit to the card issuer as is common with a credit card.

credit card transaction
An extension of credit to a cardholder and a transfer of payment by the card issuer (e.g., bank, credit union) to the merchant.

debit card transaction
A withdrawal (debit) directly from a customer's account with an FI.

---

[9] Firms and households have been slow to embrace this technology because of the presence of coordination problems in the electronic payments sector. These systems involve significant up-front costs for billers and customers. If billers believe that most of their customers will not establish connections to the system, they will not purchase the equipment for fear that they will be unable to recover their fixed investment costs.

[10] Using another bank's ATM usually results in an access fee to the customer that averages $1 but can be as high as $5.

[11] In the case of bank-supplied credit cards, the merchant normally gets compensated very quickly but not instantaneously by the credit card issuer (usually one or two days). The bank then holds an account receivable against the card user. However, even a short delay can represent an opportunity cost for the merchant. In 2003, MasterCard and Visa agreed to settle an antitrust suit consenting to lower fees, modify card policies, and pay over U.S. $3 billion in damages to about 5 million merchants (including Wal-Mart and Sears). The merchants argued that these card associations illegally tied their debit cards to their credit cards, forcing retailers for pay higher fees. The debit transactions are processed on ATM/POS networks.

3. *Home banking.* Connects customers to their deposit and brokerage accounts and provides services such as electronic securities trading and bill paying via personal computers.

4. *Preauthorized debits/credits.* Includes direct deposits of payroll cheques into bank accounts as well as direct payments of mortgage and utility bills.

5. *Payment of bills via telephone.* Allows direct transfer of funds from the customer's FI account to outside parties either by voice command or by touch-tone telephone.

6. *E-mail billing.* Allows customers to receive and pay bills using the Internet, thus saving postage and paper.

7. *Online banking.* Allows customers to conduct retail banking and investment services offered via the Internet.[12] In some cases this involves building a new online Internet-only "bank," such as ING Direct, a virtual bank which has about one million customers and $14 billion in assets in Canada.

www.ingdirect.ca

8. *Smart cards (store-value cards).* Allows the customer to store and spend money for various transactions using a card that has a chip storage device, usually in the form of a strip. These have become increasingly popular at universities.[13, 14]

Concept Questions

1. Describe some of the wholesale financial services provided to corporate customers that have been improved by technology.
2. Describe some of the automated retail payment products available today. What advantages do these products offer the retail customer?

THE EFFECT OF TECHNOLOGY ON REVENUES AND COSTS

The previous section presented an extensive list of current products or services being offered by FIs that are built around a strong technological base and, increasingly, the Internet. Technological advances allow an FI to offer such products to its customers and potentially to earn higher profits. The investment of resources in many of these products is risky, however, because product innovations may fail to attract sufficient business relative to the initial cash outlay and the future costs related to these investments once they are in place. In the terminology of finance, a number of technologically based product innovations may turn out to be *negative* net present value projects because of uncertainties over revenues and costs and how quickly rivals will mimic or copy any innovation. Another factor is agency conflicts, in which managers undertake growth-oriented investments to increase an FI's size; such investments may be inconsistent with stockholders' value-maximizing objectives. As a

---

[12] In addition to cash management services, technology also enhances the ability of FIs to offer security services (e.g., local and global custody and transfer).

[13] Dexit is an example of FIs teaming up with communications companies to implement new technology. Dexit is a pre-paid service via radio frequency used for small cash purchases that is offered in downtown Toronto in conjunction with Bell Canada, TD Canada, National Bank of Canada, and TELUS Mobility. See www.dexit.com.

identity theft
The theft of electronic identification (debit or credit cards) to gain illegal access to customer accounts.

[14] Associated with the increased use of electronic transfers is **identity theft**, the use of credit or debit cards illegally to access FIs' customers' accounts. The Bank Act limits credit card users to a maximum liability of $50 if their cards are used illegally, but debit cards are not covered by the same limits on illegal fund withdrawals or transfers. See W. McLellan, "The legal limbo of debit cards," *The Ottawa Citizen*, June 26 2005, p. D1; and D. Flavelle and R. Ross, "Visa card with chip to fight fraud on way," *Toronto Star*, June 28, 2005, p. D01. In addition, Equifax Canada Inc., which provides credit checks on consumer bank loans and credit cards, had a security breach that allowed 605 consumer files to be accessed illegally. See S. Avery, "Criminals breach Equifax Canada security for second time," Canadian Press NewsWire, June 16, 2005.

result, losses on technological innovations and new technology could weaken an FI because scarce capital resources were invested in value-decreasing products.[15]

This leads one to consider whether direct or indirect evidence is available that indicates whether technology investments to update the operational structure of FIs have increased revenues or decreased costs. Most of the direct or indirect evidence has concerned the effects of size on financial firms' operating costs; indeed, it is the largest FIs that appear to be investing most in IT and other technological innovations.

We first discuss the evidence on the product revenue side and then discuss the evidence on the operating cost side. However, before looking at these revenue and cost aspects, we should stress that the success of technologically related innovation cannot be evaluated independently from regulation and regulatory changes. For example, while Canadians take their nationwide branch banking for granted, the introduction of full interstate banking in the U.S. in 1997, as well as the rapid consolidation in the U.S. financial services industry (e.g., as a result of mergers of large banks and the development of national branch systems) have created opportunities for Canadian FIs in the U.S. market. Product and geographic diversification, supported by technological advances, are discussed in more detail in Chapters 21 and 22.

Technology and Revenues

One potential benefit of technology is that it allows an FI to cross-market both new and existing products to customers. Such joint selling does not require the FI to produce all the services sold within the same branch or financial services outlet. For example, a commercial bank may link up with an insurance company to jointly market each other's loan, credit card, and insurance products. This arrangement has proved popular in Germany, where some of the largest banks have developed sophisticated cross-marketing arrangements with large insurance companies. In the United States, Citicorp's merger with Travelers to create Citigroup was explicitly designed to cross-market banking, insurance, and securities products in over 100 countries. However, Citigroup management admitted after the completion of the merger that it may take 10 or more years to integrate computer systems to a sufficient degree to achieve this objective.

Although there has been considerable cross-selling of retail banking and brokerage services, Canadian banks are not allowed to offer life insurance products through their branches. A merger of an insurance company and a bank requires the approval of the Minister of Finance. The bank-bank mergers and bank-insurance mergers are expected to be addressed by the review of the Bank Act, which is mandatory in 2006. This issue is discussed in more detail in Chapters 21 and 22.

The rate of adoption of technology by consumers determines the profitability of the investment. For example, despite large investments in technology globally by FIs, according to the Bank for International Settlements, debit card use in Canada was 76.4 transactions per inhabitant versus 54 transactions per inhabitant in the United

---

[15] Standard capital budgeting techniques can be applied to technological innovations and new FI products. Let:

I_0 = Initial capital outlay for developing an innovation or product at time 0

R_i = Expected net revenues or cash flows from product sales in future years i, $i = 1, \ldots, N$

d = FI's discount rate reflecting its risk-adjusted cost of capital

Thus, a negative net present value (NPV) project would result if:

$$I_0 > \frac{R_1}{(1 + d)} + \ldots + \frac{R_N}{(1 + d)^N}$$

Clearly, the profitability of any product innovation is negatively related to the size of the initial setup and development costs (I_0) and the FI's cost of capital (d), and positively related to the size of the stream of expected net cash flows (R_i) from selling the services.

TABLE 14–2   Delivery Channels for Canadian Bank Transactions, 1999–2003

| DELIVERY CHANNELS | Number of transactions (in millions) | | | | | |
	2003	2002	2001	2000	1999	% change 2002–2003
ABM	**1,131.8**	**1,206.6**	**1,209.0**	**1,239.4**	**1,156.5**	**−6.2%**
Deposits	258.9	249.2	249.9	244.5	214.9	3.9%
Withdrawals	765.0	848.6	846.2	875.1	838.8	−9.8%
Transfers	43.2	43.7	45.4	48.5	42.4	−1.1%
Bill Payments	64.7	65.1	67.5	71.3	60.3	−0.7%
DEBIT CARDS	**1854.7**	**1,749.6**	**1,590.6**	**1,289.8**	**N/A**	**6.0%**
POS Purchases	1854.7	1,749.6	1,590.6	1289.8	N/A	6.0%
PC/INTERNET BANKING	**192.1**	**147.0**	**100.9**	**47.2**	**26.6**	**30.7%**
Transfers	57.0	43.3	29.0	10.5	6.4	31.7%
Bill Payments	135.1	103.7	71.9	36.7	20.2	30.3%
TELEPHONE BANKING	**87.7**	**92.1**	**94.6**	**74.0**	**63.4**	**−4.8%**
Transfers	18.8	17.3	17.0	16.1	13.7	8.6%
Bill Payments	68.9	74.8	77.6	57.9	49.7	−7.9%

Source: Canadian Bankers Association, www.cba.ca

States in 2003. Table 14–2 shows the volume of transactions by delivery channel for six Canadian banks from 1999 to 2003. The number of transactions by personal computer (PC)/Internet banking for transfers and bill payments both increased by more than 30 percent between 2002 and 2003. The use of automated banking machines (ABMs) for transfers and bill payments decreased, as did cash withdrawals as retail customers increased their usage of debit cards for point of sale (POS) purchases.

Finally, we cannot ignore the issue of service quality and convenience. For example, while ATMs and Internet banking may potentially lower FI operating costs compared with employing full-service tellers, the inability of machines to address customers' concerns and questions flexibly may drive retail customers away and revenue losses may counteract any cost-savings effects. Customers still want to interact with a person for many transactions. However, a survey of 1200 consumers in May–June 2004, indicated that the primary means of bill payment in Canada was through the computer/online. Figure 14–1 summarizes the data of this survey of how Canadians pay their bills. Though 26 percent pay their bills by computer/online, 14 percent still pay at a branch.[16]

Technology and Costs

Traditionally, FIs have considered the major benefits of technological advances to be on the cost side rather than the revenue side. After a theoretical look at how technology favourably or unfavourably affects an FI's costs, we look at the direct and indirect evidence of technology-based cost savings for FIs. In general, technology may favourably affect an FI's cost structure by allowing it to exploit either economies of scale or economies of scope.

[16] The 2004 survey also found that 23 per cent of the survey respondents used online banking primarily, triple the number since the first survey in 2000. For further details see: Canadian Bankers Association, "Technology and Banking: A Survey of Consumer Attitudes" (2004) available at www.cba.ca.

FIGURE 14–1
How Canadians Pay Bills

Source: Canadian Bankers Association, The Banking Industry in Canada: Taking A Closer Look, May 2005, p. 29, www.cba.ca

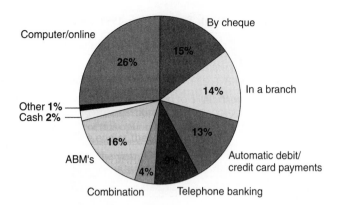

FIGURE 14–2
Economies of Scale in FIs

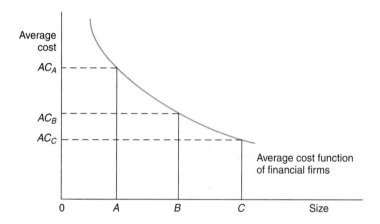

Economies of Scale

As financial firms become larger, the potential scale and array of the technology in which they can invest generally expands.[17] As noted above, the largest FIs make the largest expenditures on technology-related innovations. If improved technology lowers an FI's average costs of financial service production, larger FIs may have an **economy of scale** advantage over smaller financial firms. Economies of scale imply that the unit or average cost of producing FI services in aggregate (or some specific service such as deposits or loans) falls as the size of the FI expands.

Figure 14–2 shows economies of scale for three different-sized FIs. The average cost of producing an FI's output of financial services is measured as:

economy of scale
A drop in the average costs of production as the output of an FI increases.

$$AC_i = \frac{TC_i}{S_i}$$

where

AC_i = Average costs of the ith FI

TC_i = Total costs of the ith FI

S_i = Size of the FI measured by assets, deposits, or loans.[18]

---

[17] Economies of scale and scope can result from a variety of factors other than technology (e.g., geographic diversification or merger with another FI). In this section, however, we demonstrate these economies using a framework of technological investments.

[18] It is arguable that the size of a modern FI should be measured by including off-balance-sheet assets (contingent value) as well.

FIGURE 14–3 Effects of Technological Improvement

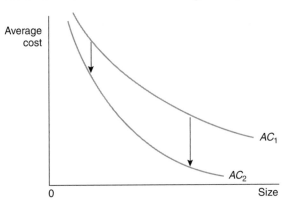

FIGURE 14–4 Diseconomies of Scale

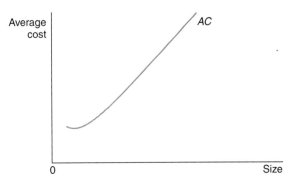

The largest FI in Figure 14–2 (size C) has a lower average cost of producing financial services than do smaller firms B and A. This means that at any given price for financial service firm products, firm C can make a bigger profit than either B or A. Alternatively, firm C can undercut B and A in price and potentially gain a larger market share. The long-run implication of economies of scale on the FI sector is that the larger and most cost-efficient FIs will drive out smaller FIs, leading to increased large-firm dominance and concentration in financial services production. Such an implication is reinforced if time-related operating or technological improvements increasingly benefit larger FIs more than smaller FIs. For example, satellite technology and supercomputers, in which enormous technological advances are being made, may be available to only the largest FIs. The effect of improving technology over time, which is biased toward larger projects, is to shift the AC curve downward over time but with a larger downward shift for large FIs (see Figure 14–3). In Figure 14–3, AC_1 is the hypothetical AC curve prior to cost-reducing technological innovations. AC_2 reflects the cost-lowering effects of technology on FIs of all sizes but with the greatest benefit accruing to those of the largest size.

As noted earlier, technological investments are risky; if their future revenues do not cover their costs of development, they reduce the value of the FI and its net worth to the FI's owners. On the cost side, large-scale investments may result in excess capacity problems and integration problems as well as cost overruns and cost control problems. Then small FIs with simple and easily managed computer systems and/or those leasing time on large FIs' computers (e.g. President's Choice Financial is operated by CIBC) without bearing the fixed costs of installation and maintenance may have an average cost advantage. In this case, technological investments of large-sized FIs result in higher average costs of financial service production, causing the industry to operate under conditions of **diseconomies of scale** (see Figure 14–4). Diseconomies of scale imply that small FIs are more cost efficient than large FIs and that in a freely competitive environment for financial services, small FIs prosper.

At least two other possible shapes for the AC function exist (see Figure 14–5). In panel (a) of Figure 14–5, the financial services industry reflects economies of scale at first and then diseconomies of scale as firms grow larger. This suggests that a best or most efficient size for an FI exists at point S^* and that too much technology investment can be as bad as too little. Panel (b) of Figure 14–5 represents constant returns to scale. Any potential cost-reducing effects of technology are spread evenly over FIs of all sizes. That is, technology investments are neutral rather than favoring one size of FI over another.

diseconomy of scale

Increase in the average costs of production as the output of an FI increases.

FIGURE 14–5
Other Average Cost Functions

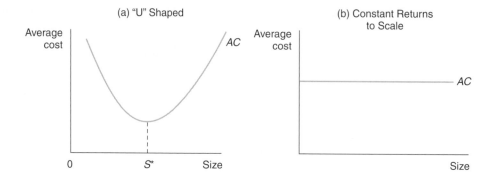

Economies of Scope

Although technological investments may have positive or negative effects on FIs in general and these effects may well differ across FIs of different size, technology tends to be applied more in some product areas than in others. That is, FIs are multiproduct firms producing services involving different technological needs. Moreover, technological improvements or investments in one financial service area (such as lending) may have incidental and synergistic benefits in lowering the costs of producing financial services in other areas (such as securities underwriting and brokerage). Specifically, computerization allows the storage and joint use of important information on customers and their needs. The simple *economy of scale* concept ignores these interrelationships among products and the "jointness" in the costs of producing financial products. In particular, FIs' abilities to generate synergistic cost savings through joint use of inputs in producing multiple products is called *economies of scope* as opposed to economies of scale.

economies of scope
The ability of FIs to generate synergistic cost savings through joint use of inputs in producing multiple products.

Technology may allow two FIs to jointly use their input resources, such as capital and labor, to produce a set of financial services at a lower cost than if financial service products were produced independently of one another. **Economies of scope** exist if these firms merge. That is, the cost of joint production via cost synergies is less than the separate and independent production of these services.

EXAMPLE 14–1

Calculation of Average Cost

Let TC_B be a bank's total cost of producing lending services to a corporate client. Suppose that the total operating costs of producing these services is $50,000 for a loan volume (L_B) of $10 million. Such costs include information collection and monitoring as well as account maintenance and processing. Thus, the average cost (AC_B) of loan production for the bank is:

$$AC_B = \frac{TC_B}{L_B} = \frac{\$50,000}{\$10,000,000} = .005 = .5\%$$

At the same time, a specialized investment bank is selling commercial paper for the same corporate customer. The investment bank's total cost (TC_S) of running the commercial paper operation is $10,000 for a $1 million issue ($P_S$). These costs include the cost of underwriting the issue as well as placing the issue with outside buyers. Thus:

$$AC_S = \frac{TC_S}{P_S} = \frac{\$10,000}{\$1,000,000} = .01 = 1\%$$

Consequently, the total average cost (TAC) of separately producing the loan services through the bank and the commercial paper issuance through the investment bank is:

$$TAC = \frac{\$60,000}{\$11,000,000} = 0.54\%$$

Suppose, instead, a single FI produces both $10 million of lending services and $1 million commercial paper issuance services for the same customer (i.e., $P_{FS} = \$11$ million). Loans and commercial paper are substitute sources of funds for corporate customers. For an FI to originate a loan and commercial paper requires very similar expertise both in funding that issue and in credit risk assessment and monitoring. Common technologies in the loan and commercial paper production functions suggest that a single FI simultaneously (or jointly) producing both loan and commercial paper services for the same client at a total cost TC_{FS} should be able to do this at a lower average cost than could the specialized FIs that separately produce these services. That is, the single FI should be able to produce the $11,000,000 ($P_{FS}$) of financial services at a lower cost (say $TC_{FS} = \$51,000$), than should two specialized FIs. Accordingly:

$$AC_{FS} = \frac{TC_{FS}}{P_{FS}} = \frac{\$51,000}{\$11,000,000} = 0.46\% < 0.54\%$$

Formally, if AC_{FS} is the total average cost of a nonspecialized financial services firm, then economies of scope imply that:

$$AC_{FS} < TAC$$

diseconomies of scope
The costs of joint production of FI services are higher than they would be if they were produced independently.

Nevertheless, **diseconomies of scope** may occur instead; FIs find costs actually higher from joint production of services than if they were produced independently. For example, suppose an FI purchases some very specialized information-based technology to ease the loan production and processing function. The FI could use any excess capacity this system has in other service areas. However, this process could be a relatively inefficient technology for other service areas and could add to the overall costs of production compared with using a specialized technology for each service or product area.

Concept Questions

1. What are two risk factors involved in an FI's investment of resources in innovative technological products?
2. Does the existence of economies of scale for FIs mean that in the long run small FIs cannot survive?
3. If there are diseconomies of scope, do specialized FIs have a relative cost advantage or disadvantage over product-diversified FIs?
4. Make a list of the potential economies of scope or cost synergies if two Canadian FIs were allowed to merge. How would the merger of two large Canadian banks differ from the merger of a bank and an insurance company?

TESTING FOR ECONOMIES OF SCALE AND ECONOMIES OF SCOPE

To test for economies of scale and economies of scope, FIs must clearly specify both the inputs to their production process and the cost of those inputs. Basically, the two approaches to analyzing the cost functions of FIs are the production and the intermediation approaches.

The Production Approach

The production approach views FIs' outputs of services as having two underlying inputs: labour and capital. If $w =$ wage costs of labour, $r =$ rental costs of capital, and $y =$ output of services, the total cost function (C) for the FI is:

$$C = f(y, w, r)$$

The Intermediation Approach

The intermediation approach views the output of financial services as being produced by labour and capital as well as funds the intermediary uses to produce intermediated services. Thus, deposit costs would be an input in the banking and trust industries, while premiums or reserves would be inputs in the insurance industry, and:

$$C = f(y, w, r, k)$$

where k reflects the cost of funds for the FI.

Concept Questions

1. Describe the basic concept behind the production approach to testing for economies of scale and economies of scope.
2. How does the intermediation approach differ from the production approach?

EMPIRICAL FINDINGS ON COST ECONOMIES OF SCALE AND SCOPE AND IMPLICATIONS FOR TECHNOLOGY EXPENDITURES

A large number of studies have examined economies of scale and scope in different financial service industry sectors.[19] With respect to banks, most of the early studies failed to find economies of scale for any but the smallest banks. More recently, better data sets and improved methodologies have suggested that economies of scale may exist for banks up to the $10 billion to $25 billion size range. With respect to economies of scope either among deposits, loans, and other traditional banking product areas or between on-balance-sheet products and off-balance-sheet products such as loan sales, the evidence that cost synergies exist is at best very weak. Similarly, the smaller number of studies involving nonbank financial service firms such as savings and loans, co-ops, insurance companies, and securities firms almost always report neither economies of scale nor economies of scope.[20]

Economies of Scale and Scope and X-Inefficiencies

A number of more recent studies which primarily use data for U.S. FIs have looked at the *dispersion* of costs in any given FI size class rather than the shape of the average cost functions. These efficiency studies find quite dramatic cost differences of 20 percent or more among banks, thrifts, and insurance companies in any given size class ($100 million asset size class, $200 million asset size class, etc.). Moreover, these studies find that only a small part of the cost differences among FIs in any size

---

[19] Good reviews are found in J. A. Clark, "Economies of Scale and Scope at Depository Financial Institutions: A Review of the Literature," Federal Reserve Bank of Kansas City, *Economic Review,* September–October 1988, pp. 16–33; L. Mester, "Efficient Production of Financial Services: Scale and Scope Economies," Federal Reserve Bank of Philadelphia, *Economic Review,* January–February 1987, pp. 15–25; A. Berger, W. C. Hunter, and S. B. Timme, "The Efficiency of Financial Institutions: A Review and Preview of Research Past, Present and Future," *Journal of Banking and Finance* 17 (1993), pp. 221–49; and R. DeYoung, "Learning-by-Doing, Scale Efficiencies, and Financial Performance at Internet-Only Banks," Federal Reserve Bank of Chicago Working Paper, June 2002. Three major production function forms have been tested: The Cobb-Douglas, the trans-log, and the Box-Cox flexible functional form.

[20] A. Berger, D. Humphrey, and L. B. Pulley, "Do Consumers Pay for One-Stop Banking? Evidence from an Alternative Revenue Function," *Journal of Banking and Finance* 20 (1996), pp. 1601–21, look at revenue economies of scope (rather than cost economies of scope) between loans and deposits over the 1978–90 period and find no evidence of revenue economies of scope. J. D. Cummins, S. Tennyson, and M. A. Weiss, "Consolidation and Efficiency in the U.S. Life Insurance Industry," *Journal of Banking and Finance* 23 (1999), pp. 325–57, find that mergers and acquisitions in the insurance industry do produce economies of scale, while efficiency gains are significantly smaller in non-M&A life insurers.

X-inefficiency
The production of less than efficient levels of output from a given level of input.

class can be attributed to economies of scale or scope.[21] This suggests that cost inefficiencies related to managerial performance and other hard-to-quantify factors (so-called **X-inefficiencies**) may better explain cost differences and operating cost efficiencies among financial firms than technology-related investments per se.[22]

There is little strong, direct evidence that larger multiproduct financial service firms enjoy cost advantages over smaller, more specialized financial firms. Nor do economies of scope and scale explain many of the cost differences among FIs of the same size. These empirical findings raise questions about the benefits of technology investments and technological innovation. While a majority of the studies tested for economies of scope and scale rather than the benefits of technology, these results are consistent with the relatively low payoff from technological innovation. To the extent that large FIs obtain benefits, they may well be on the revenue generation/new product innovation side rather than on the cost side. Indeed, recent studies looking at output and input efficiencies for banks and insurance companies derived from revenue and profit functions found that large FIs tend to be more efficient in revenue generation than smaller FIs and that such efficiencies may well offset scope and scale cost inefficiencies related to size.[23]

Finally, the real benefits of technological innovation may be long term and dynamic, related to the evolution of the Canadian and U.S. payments system away from cash and cheques and toward electronic means of payment.[24] Such benefits are difficult to obtain in traditional economy of scale and scope studies, which are largely static and ignore the more dynamic aspects of efficiency gains. This dynamic technological evolution not only has affected the fundamental role of FIs in the financial system but also has generated some new and subtle types of risks for FIs and their regulators. In the next section we take a closer look at the effects of technology on the payments system.

Concept Questions

1. What does the empirical evidence reveal about economies of scale and scope?
2. What conclusion is suggested by recent studies that have focused on the dispersion of costs across banks of a given asset size?

TECHNOLOGY AND THE EVOLUTION OF THE PAYMENTS SYSTEM

To better understand the changing nature of the payments system, look at Tables 14–3 to 14–5. Nonelectronic methods—mostly cheques—accounted for 23.0 percent of noncash transactions, but this represented only 11.8 percent of the dollar *value* of

---

[21] See A. N. Berger and L. J. Mester, "Inside the Black-Box: What Explains Differences in the Efficiencies of Financial Institutions," *Journal of Banking and Finance* 21 (1997), pp. 895–947, for an extensive review of these efficiency studies. See also K. Mukherjee, S. C. Ray, and S. M. Miller, "Productivity Growth in Large U.S. Commercial Banks: The Initial Post-Deregulation Experience," *Journal of Banking and Finance* 25 (2001), pp. 913–39; and A. Akhigbe and J. E. McNulty, "The Profit Efficiency of Small U.S. Commercial Banks," *Journal of Banking and Finance* 27 (2003), pp. 307–25.

[22] See, for example, T. T. Milbourn, A. W. A. Boot, and A. V. Thakor, "Megamergers and Expanded Scope: Theories of Bank Size and Activity Diversity," *Journal of Banking and Finance* 23 (1999), pp. 195–214.

[23] See Berger and Mester, "Inside the Black-Box"; J. Cummins, S. Tennyson, and M. A. Weiss, "Efficiency, Scale Economies and Consolidation in the U.S. Life Insurance Industry," *Journal of Banking and Finance,* February 1999, pp. 325–57; and R. DeYoung and K. P. Roland, "Product Mix and Earnings Volatility at Commercial Banks: Evidence from a Degree of Total Leverage Model," *Journal of Financial Intermediation* 10 (2001), pp. 54–84. In contrast to the majority of the research, a recent study of 201 large U.S. commercial banks in the postderegulation period (after 1984) finds overall productivity growth at a rate of about 4.5 percent per year on average. The growth in productivity reflected largely adjustments in technology. See Mukherjee et al., "Productivity Growth in Large U.S. Commercial Banks."

[24] For example, D. Hancock, D. B. Humphrey, and J. A. Wilcox, "Cost Reductions in Electronic Payments: The Roles of Consolidation, Economies of Scale, and Technical Change," *Journal of Banking and Finance* 23 (1999), pp. 391–421, find that when the Fed consolidated its Fedwire electronic funds transfer operations, reductions in production costs were partially attributable to technological advances.

TABLE 14–3
Canadian Cashless Payments: Volume, Value, and Average Transaction Amount, 2002

Source: Bank for International Settlements, Statistics on Payment Systems in Selected Countries, Basel, Switzerland, March 2004, www.bis.org

	Volume, (billions)	Percent	Value, ($ billions)	Percent	Transaction Average Value ($)
Cheque	1.5	23.0	4820.5	11.8	3,182
Debit card	2.4	36.4	105.0	0.3	44
Credit card	1.5	22.7	153.0	0.4	103
Credit transfers	0.7	10.0	35,502.1	86.8	53,987
Direct debits	0.5	7.9	308.0	0.7	592
	6.6		40,888.6		

TABLE 14–4
Percentage of Total Volume of Noncash Paper and Electronic Transactions, 2002

Source: Bank for International Settlements, Statistics on Payment Systems in Selected Countries, Basel, Switzerland, Table 13, March 2004, www.bis.org

	Paper (Cheque)	Debit and Credit Cards	Credit Transfers	Direct Debits	Electronic
Canada	23.0	59.1	10.0	7.9	77.0
United States	49.9	41.7	5.0	3.4	51.1
Germany	1.2	16.6	45.0	36.9	98.8*
United Kingdom	21.0	41.2	17.7	20.1	79.0

*Includes card-based e-money of 0.3%. Card-based e-money is not measurable for the U.S., Canada, and the U.K.

TABLE 14–5
Percentage of Total Value of Noncash Paper and Electronic Transactions, 2002

Source: Bank for International Settlements, Statistics on Payment Systems in Selected Countries, Basel, Switzerland, Table 14, March 2004, www.bis.org

	Paper (Cheque)	Debit and Credit Cards	Credit Transfers	Direct Debits	Electronic
Canada	11.8	0.6	86.8	0.8	88.2
United States	4.9	0.3	93.7	1.1	95.1
Germany	2.3	0.4	85.4	11.8	97.7
United Kingdom	2.2	0.2	96.9	0.7	97.8

noncash transactions. By comparison, while electronic methods of payment— credit cards, debit cards, and credit transfer systems and direct debits—accounted for only 77.0 percent in volume, they accounted for 95.1 percent in value. Wire transfer systems alone accounted for 88.2 percent of all dollar transactions measured in value.

As can be seen from Tables 14–4 and 14–5, the use of electronic methods of payment is far higher in other major developed countries than in the United States. For example, in Canada, Germany, and the United Kingdom electronic transactions account for over 77 percent of total transactions measured by number of transactions. To some extent, the United States is only now starting to catch up with these countries. Part of the reason for this involves culture and tradition in the United States. For example, cheques have been obsolete in Germany for some time, but in the United States people still prefer to write cheques. As a result, U.S. FIs have been slow in adopting and using online banking and electronic payment methods extensively. The speed with which this electronic payments gap will be closed will in large part depend on two factors: the speed with which the trend toward consolidation and automated banking continues and the degree and speed of technological innovation. Note that in terms of dollar values of transactions completed electronically (Table 14–5), the United States is comparable with the other reported countries; 95.1 percent in the United States compared with 88.2 percent, 97.7 percent, and 97.8 percent in Canada, Germany, and the United Kingdom, respectively.

Canada has two systems for the clearing of non-cash payments. As noted in Chapter 13, the **Large Value Transfer System (LVTS)** handles time-sensitive, large value transactions. The **Auto Clearing Settlement System (ACSS)** processes regular bill payments (e.g., debit card transactions, cheques, automatic bill payments). The LVTS thus operates essentially as a wholesale type of system while the ACSS is the system for smaller retail transactions.

The payments system has been viewed in Canada as a source of systemic risk to the financial system. For this reason, in 1996, the Payment Clearing and Settlement Act gave the Bank of Canada responsibility for the payment systems that could put the overall financial system at risk including, since 1999, the LVTS. The focus has been to develop a system that serves Canadians nationally with the best technology and with a view to competition and economies of scale and scope. The additional focus has also been on cross-border transactions within North America, particularly the United States, but with a view to the internationalization of capital flows. Two studies provide details of the current view of the payments system in Canada. The first is James Dingle's history of the Canadian Payments Association from 1980 to 2002. The second is a 2001 BIS study that outlines the future of payment systems from a global perspective.[25]

Another way to see the enormous growth in the use of electronic transfers in Canada is to consider the percentage of electronic versus items flowing through the Auto Clearing Settlement System (ACSS) between 1990 and 2004. According to the Canada Payments System, the volume of electronic transactions grew from 13.4 per cent in 1990 to 75.96 percent in 2004. On a dollar value basis, electronic transactions increased from 0.6 percent in 1990 to 30.33 percent of the value of the transactions through the ACSS in 2004. Although the value of paper transactions was still 69.7 percent in 2004, the volume of electronic transactions through the ACCS has exceeded the number of paper transactions since 1997. Canada Payments Association's systems cleared, on average, 18.8 million items each business day in 2003, an average daily value of $142 billion.

According to the data in Table 14–6, Canada is not the only country in which wholesale wire transfer systems have come to dominate the payment systems. The United States, the United Kingdom, Switzerland, and Japan also have very large wire transfer systems measured as a percentage of local gross domestic product (GDP). In 2001 as a result of the single currency (the euro) and the European Monetary Union, a single wholesale wire transfer system for Europe fully emerged, linking all countries that are members of the European Monetary Union. The transaction system is called TARGET (Trans-European Automated Real-Time Gross-Settlement Express Transfer).

Risks That Arise in an Electronic Transfer Payment System

At least six important risks have arisen along with the growth of wire transfer systems. We mentioned some of these while discussing off-balance-sheet activities in Chapter 13; here, we go into more detail.

Large Value Transfer System (LVTS)
The payment system operated by Canada Payments Association for time-sensitive, large value transactions that are irrevocable.

Auto Clearing Settlement System (ACSS)
The payment system for ordinary transactions operated by Canada Payments Association.

[25] See J. Dingle, *Planning an Evolution: The Story of the Canadian Payments Association, 1980–2002*, May 2003, The Bank of Canada and the Canadian Payments Association, available at www.cdnpay.ca. See also The Bank for International Settlements, Group of Ten, "Report on Consolidation in the Financial Sector, 2001," Basel, Switzerland, which discusses the payment system in Chapter 6 and is available at www.bis.org. The difference in customs, regulations, and culture between countries, even between close neighbours such as Canada and the United States, is an issue in the globalization of payments systems. See *American Banker*, "National Differences a Hurdle to Globalization," July 29, 1998, Vol. 163, Iss. 143, p. 6.

TABLE 14–6
Wholesale Wire Transfer Systems in Selected Countries 2002

Source: The Bank for International Settlements, *Statistics on Payment Systems in Selected Countries*, Basel, Switzerland, March 2004, Table 15. www.bis.org

	Number of Transactions (thousands)	Annual Value of Transactions (US$ billions)	Ratio of Transactions Value to GDP (at annual rate)
Japan			
FXYCS	9,238	$ 48,887	12.3%
BOJ-NET	4,788	143,989	36.2
Netherlands			
Interpay	2,812,350	1,582	3.8
Top	4,548	19,670	46.8
Sweden			
K-RIX	1,100	11,731	48.7
Bank Giro System	363,000	416	1.7
Switzerland			
SIC	177,000	28,767	107.2
DTA/LSV	103,300	229	0.9
United Kingdom			
CHAPS-Sterling	25,563	77,863	49.7
BACS	3,734,774	3,574	2.3
Check/credit	1,817,000	2,170	1.4
United States			
Fedwire	115,000	405,762	38.8
CHIPS	63,300	315,709	30.2
European Union			
TARGET	64,519	372,927	—
Euro 1	34,401	45,241	—
Canada			
LVTS	3,903	18,573	25.1

Settlement Risk

www.cdnpay.ca
www.cls-services.com

The Canada Payments Association (CPA) operates the payment systems in Canada. Members of the CPA include the Bank of Canada, all of the domestic banks, and authorized foreign banks. In addition, other deposit-taking institutions (credit unions, caisses populaires, savings and loans) as well as insurance companies, securities dealers and mutual funds are also eligible for membership. Clearing of accounts is done through the LVTS and the ACSS as mentioned previously, and the settlement of accounts occurs through adjustments to the accounts of approximately 12 financial institutions that have settlement accounts at the Bank of Canada. If an FI is unable to cover its LVTS or ACSS obligations, the Bank of Canada lends funds to the FI on an overnight basis at the upper band of the Bank Rate. As a participant in the clearing and settlement system, the Bank of Canada also settles obligations for the government of Canada.

Since 2002, the LVTS has been used for the settlement of Canadian dollar transfers in foreign exchange transactions through a process called **continuous linked settlement (CLS)**. This process occurs between 1 a.m. and 6 a.m., Monday through Friday, resulting in a 24-hour-a-day operation at the CPA, and has virtually eliminated settlement risk on foreign exchange transactions by providing real time and irrevocable settlement across international time zones.[26]

continuous linked settlement (CLS)
The method of settling global foreign exchange transactions used by CLS Bank to eliminate settlement risk.

---

[26] See J. Dingle, "The Elements of the Global Network for Large-Value Funds Transfers, Bank of Canada Working Paper No. 2—1–1 (2001) at pages 14–15 for a detailed description of the settlement of a foreign currency transaction involving U.S. dollars and Japanese yen through the international payments systems. See also the Web site for CLS Group at www.cls-services.com. CLS Bank eliminates the settlement risk of foreign exchange transactions by offsetting each party's account. The Bank of Canada acts as the banker for CLS Bank in Canada.

FIGURE 14–6 LVTS Daily Operating Schedule

12:30 a.m – 1 a.m	1 a.m – 7 a.m	7 a.m – 6 p.m	6 p.m – 6:30 p.m	6:30 p.m – 7:30 p.m
CLS participants pledge collateral to the Bank of Canada, set debit caps for Tranche 1 activity and lines of credit for Tranche 2 activity.	CLS transactions. Participants may adjust debit caps, lines of credit, collateral.	Payment transactions start. Non-CLS participants send debit caps, bilateral lines of credit, and collateral to the Bank of Canada between 7 a.m and 8 a.m. Participants can track their positions and adjust Tranche 1, Tranche 2, and collateral during the day.	LVTS closes. Transactions between participants occur to reduce the need for overnight borrowing from the Bank of Canada.	The Bank of Canada settles each participant's account irrevocably and releases unused collateral.

Source: Bank of Canada, "LVTS Operating Schedule." www.bankofcanada.ca

Figure 14–6 illustrates the operations of the LVTS system on a daily basis. The settlement risk is virtually eliminated by the requirement that each direct participant in the LVTS be a member of the CPA, use the SWIFT network for telecommunications, and keep a settlement account at the Bank of Canada. In addition, there are limits on the net amount that each participant is able to owe, and each participant pledges collateral at the Bank of Canada, which provides liquidity to the system if one of the participants defaults. The participants have a choice between Tranche 1 payments, which are covered by the collateral pledged to the Bank of Canada, and Tranche 2 payments, which are bilateral lines of credit granted by each participant to every other participant. These are set daily and can be monitored and adjusted during the day. If the collateral is insufficient to settle the accounts when a participant fails, then the surviving FIs will absorb the losses, and, in the event of more than one participant failing, the Bank of Canada guarantees settlement. Participants with overdrafts at the Bank of Canada at the end of the day, either through their LVTS operations or through the ACCS, borrow overnight at the upper band of the Bank Rate.

www.chips.org

In the United States, a large value transfer system is operated in New York called the Clearing House Interbank Payment System (CHIPS). On CHIPS, net payment flows often reflect a daily pattern similar to the LVTS except that, as a privately owned pure net settlement system, the beginning-of-day position must be zero for all banks. Big banks often run an overdraft during the day (called a daylight overdraft) then seek to borrow funds in the afternoon to cover net debit positions created earlier in the day. CHIPs does not charge banks explicit fees for running daylight overdrafts, but it treats a bank's failure to settle at the end of the day very differently than does the LVTS. On the LVTS, all payments are in good funds; that is, the transfers are irrevocable. By contrast, because CHIPS is a private network, all within-day transfers are provisional and become final only on settlement among CHIPS members at the end of the day. In this case, if a bank (bank Z) with a daylight overdraft were to fail, CHIPS might have to resolve this by unwinding all the failing bank's transactions over that day with the other $(N - 1)$ remaining banks. Banks Z's individual failure could result in a systemic crisis in the banking and financial system among the remaining $(N - 1)$ banks in the system. While no settlement failure has occurred recently on CHIPS, any such failure could be potentially disastrous, with financial ramifications far exceeding those of the October 1987 stock market crash[27] or the 1997 Asian financial market crisis.[28]

International Technology Transfer Risk

In recent years Canada and the United States have been at the forefront in making technology investments and financial service innovations in the payments system. For example, North American FIs have been pioneers of ATMs, yet such networks have grown relatively slowly in countries such as Sweden and Belgium, often because of prohibitive charges imposed for the use and leasing of domestic telephone lines (see Table 14–7).

This suggests that financial service firms have often been unable to transfer profitably their domestic technological innovations to international markets to gain competitive advantage, at least in the short term.[29] In contrast, foreign financial service firms entering the North American market gain direct access to, and knowledge of, technology–based products at a very low cost.

Crime and Fraud Risk

The increased replacement of cheques and cash by electronic transfers as methods of payment or exchange has resulted in an increase in the efficiency of the execution of transactions, but it has also resulted in new problems regarding theft, data snooping, and white-collar crime. Because huge sums are transferred across the networks each day and some bank employees have specialized knowledge of personal identification numbers (PINS) and other entry codes, the incentive for white-collar crime appears to have increased. For example, a manager at the Sri Lankan branch of the now defunct BCCI reportedly stole a computer chip from a telex machine in the bank's Oman branch and used it to transfer $10 million from three banks in the United States and Japan to his own account in Switzerland.[30]

Moreover, considerable security problems exist in trying to develop the Internet as a form of electronic payment system. Internet transactions can be intercepted by third parties. Financial institutions are accordingly concerned about open credit or debit card details on the Internet. Any version of electronic payment via the Internet must not only meet the requirements of recognition and acceptability associated with physical cash but also provide the same high level of security that

---

[27] Simulations by D. B. Humphrey of CHIPS unwinding following an assumed bank failure show that up to 50 banks might be unable to meet their payment obligations on CHIPS following any one bank's failure to settle, implying a massive systematic collapse of the payment system. See "Payments Finality and Risk Settlement Failure," in *Technology and the Regulation of Financial Markets: Securities, Futures, and Banking,* ed. A. Saunders and L. J. White (Lexington, MA: Lexington Books, 1986), pp. 97–120. Interestingly, in a paper conducting similar simulations for Italy (P. Angelini, G. Maresca, and D. Russo, "An Assessment of Systemic Risk in the Italian Clearing System," *Bank of Italy,* Discussion Paper No. 207, 1993), these systemic costs were much lower. This was largely due to the lower importance of wholesale wire transfers in Italy.

[28] To lower this settlement risk problem and to introduce an element of payment finality, CHIPS members have contributed more than $4 billion to a special escrow fund that became operational in October 1990. CHIPS members can use this fund to replace the message commitments of any failed bank, therefore preventing the potentially disastrous unwinding effects just described. However, it is estimated that this fund is sufficient to cover only the failure of its two largest financial institution members. At the end of the day, the central banks would have to mount a rescue to prevent an international failure contagion from spreading throughout the domestic and international financial system. Of course, this implies a subsidy from regulators and taxpayers to the private domestic and international banking system. See Computer Sciences Corp., *Sustaining Stable Financial Markets throughout the Millennium* (Waltham, MA: CSC, 1998).

[29] Long-term benefits may yet be realized as a result of telecommunications deregulation globally and through better customer recruitment and marketing of products in foreign environments. See S. Claessens, T. Glaessner, and D. Klingebiel, "E-finance in Emerging Markets: Is Leapfrogging Possible?" *Financial Markets Institutions & Instruments*, February 2002, pp. 1–124, for an update on e-banking in emerging markets.

[30] Office of Technology Assessment, *U.S. Banks and International Telecommunications,* October 1992, chap. 5, pp. 27–35.

TABLE 14–7
Cash Dispensers
and ATMs

Source: The Bank for International Settlements, *Statistics on Payment Systems in Selected Countries*, Basel, Switzerland, May 2003, Table 5. www.bis.org

	1991	1995	1999	2001
Number of Machines per 1,000,000 Inhabitants				
Belgium	105	360	606	669
Canada[†]	467	600	873	1,142
France	284	395	538	606
Germany	161	436	563	603
Italy	204	378	524	593
Japan	795	1,013	944	918
Netherlands	222	378	422	445
Singapore	—	—	470	435
Sweden	258	267	291	289
Switzerland	347	532	655	694
United Kingdom	309	358	460	612
United States	331	466	832	1,137
Number of Transactions per Inhabitant				
Belgium	8.1	14.3	17.4	21.5
Canada[†]	33.6	45.7	47.2	47.8
France	11.0	15.8	17.0	19.1
Germany	—	13.4	18.4	19.4
Italy	2.9	5.8	8.7	9.7
Japan	2.4	3.8	3.1	3.1
Netherlands	13.7	23.2	28.5	28.0
Singapore	—	—	2.6	2.1
Sweden	24.1	31.8	35.0	37.7
Switzerland	6.6	10.0	12.2	19.6
United Kingdom	18.5	25.2	33.1	36.6
United States	25.3	36.9	39.9	47.7
Average Value of Transactions (US$)*				
Belgium	117.4	138.1	111.3	92.8
Canada[†]	56.7	51.0	65.3	69.5
France	82.7	81.3	64.8	54.7
Germany	—	196.6	155.9	140.2
Italy	239.2	198.3	170.6	144.9
Japan	356.5	450.6	501.3	474.4
Netherlands	92.2	119.3	93.7	88.2
Singapore	—	—	140.0	124.7
Sweden	120.6	112.6	100.2	81.4
Switzerland	224.6	246.9	173.2	111.9
United Kingdom	81.0	77.3	88.8	84.0
United States	67.0	67.7	68.0	68.0

* Converted at yearly average exchange rates.
† Average value of a cash withdrawal only.

is demanded of cash payments but which the Internet itself cannot guarantee. After the terrorist attacks on September 11, 2001, the U.S. Congress passed the USA Patriot Act of 2001. The act contains a number of specific amendments to existing criminal laws designed to streamline early detection and investigation of suspected terrorist activity conducted through financial institutions. For example, in accordance with the Patriot Act, in April 2004 the FBI and federal regulators began a probe into large cash withdrawals from Riggs National Bank by Saudi Arabian citizens/customers and accused Riggs of failing to alert regulators of suspicious

Technology in the News

PATRIOT ACT ARRIVES FOR FUND COMPANIES

Nearly two years after passage of the USA Patriot Act, another piece of the law kicked in this month, requiring mutual funds to bring their customer identification programs into compliance with rules issued by the Treasury Department and the Securities and Exchange Commission. The USA Patriot Act, which amended the Bank Secrecy Act in establishing minimum standards for identifying customers who open accounts at financial institutions, became effective in June, but banks and financial institutions had until 1 October to comply.

In the mutual fund business, every fund provider's so-called customer identification program (CIP) must define its methods for profiling new individual and corporate customers who are opening accounts, as well as define its methods for maintaining data on them. Fund companies must obtain and verify the following pieces of data from each new customer: name; street address; date of birth (for individuals); and a Social Security number, tax identification number or, for non-US investors, a foreign government–issued ID card…

Patriot Act compliance will undoubtedly cost mutual fund companies millions, in compliance costs, which in turn will place ever-greater earnings pressure on an already beleaguered industry. Tower-Group, the Needham, Massachusetts–based financial consultancy, estimated in a recent report, for example, that U.S. funds will spend at least $288 million on Patriot Act compliance in the first year, and $140 million in each succeeding year for the foreseeable future. Such hefty costs will likely be absorbed by the major players, but smaller funds may have no choice but to pass them on to customers. The cost of compliance actually represents less than 0.2 percent of annual mutual fund fees, but in an environment of increasing regulatory scrutiny "it's one more straw on the camel's back," the TowerGroup report states.

Funds have little choice but to comply: The Patriot Act provides for both civil and criminal penalties for noncompliance. Fund company officials say they're concerned about those penalties, but are optimistic that they will avoid them…

Source: *Funds International,* Lafferty Publications Limited, October 29, 2003, p. 4.

transactions. The Office of the Comptroller of the Currency (OCC) also classified Riggs as a "troubled institution" for failing to adequately tighten its money laundering controls despite an order from the OCC to do so. Regulators also pursued a second line of inquiry into whether Riggs violated "know your customer" record keeping laws in its dealings with foreign customers. Treasury Department investigators were looking into the relationship between Riggs and high risk foreign customers. But as Technology in the News box 1 points out, compliance with the Patriot Act can be quite costly for FIs operating in the U.S.

The U.S. Patriot Act has had unforeseen consequences for Canadian FIs. OSFI keeps an up-to-date list of suspected terrorist organizations on its web site, and provides guidelines to deposit-taking institutions regarding the *Proceeds of Crime (Money Laundering) and Terrorism Financing Act* introduced in 2003. All federally regulated FIs except property and casualty insurance companies are required to implement programs to detect and prevent money-laundering in order to protect their reputations and the stability of the financial system. OSFI works with the **Financial Transactions and Reports Analysis Centre of Canada** (FINTRAC, www.fintrac.gc.ca) to counteract money laundering and terrorist activities, which come under the Criminal Code of Canada, and the Royal Canadian Mounted Police (RCMP) may subpoena customer account information to investigate a crime. However, U.S. authorities have much broader powers to search under the Patriot Act and, since both Royal Bank of Canada and CIBC outsource management of their credit card

Financial Transactions and Reports Analysis Centre of Canada (FINTRAC)
A government of Canada operation that tracks and analyzes money laundering, terrorist activity, and threats to Canadian security.

operations to Total Systems Services, a U.S. company, Canadian customer's transactions are open to scrutiny and the FIs are not permitted to let customers know if they are under investigation.[31]

Regulatory Risk

The improvement in FIs' computer and telecommunications networks also enhances the power of FIs' vis-à-vis regulators, effectively aiding regulatory avoidance. Thus, as implied earlier, regulation not only can affect the profitability of technological innovations, but also can spur or hinder the rate and types of innovation.[32, 33] As a result of regulation in Canada and in the United States, banking in the relatively unregulated Cayman Islands has experienced considerable growth. The 500 or more FIs located there do most of their business via public and private telecommunications networks.[34] The use of telecommunications networks and technological improvements has changed, perhaps irreversibly, the balance of power between large multinational FIs and governments—both local and national—in favor of the former. Such a shift in power may create incentives for countries to lower their regulations to attract entrants; that is, the shift may increase the incentives for competitive deregulation. This trend may be potentially destabilizing to the market in financial services, with the weakest regulators attracting the most entrants.[35]

Tax Avoidance

The development of international wire networks as well as international financial service firm networks has enabled FIs to shift funds and profits by using internal pricing mechanisms, thereby minimizing their overall domestic tax burden and maximizing their foreign tax credits. For example, prior to 1986, many large Canadian and U.S. banks paid almost no corporate income taxes, despite large reported profits, by rapidly moving profits and funds across different tax regimes. This raised considerable public policy concerns and was a major reason underlying the 1987 tax reforms in Canada. These reforms changed the rules for issuing preferred shares.[36]

Competition Risk

As financial services become more technologically based, they are increasingly competing with nontraditional financial service suppliers. Also, once established, nonfinancial firms can easily purchase financial services technology. For example, General Motors has established a credit card operation linked to the purchase of its

---

[31] See T. Hamilton, "Prospect of U.S. Patriot Act-snooping bothers Canadians. Who's trustworthy? Canadians, American disagree," *Toronto Star*, October 11, 2004, p. D01; and S. Laidlaw, "Banks up customer surveillance; U.S.A. Patriot Act's long arm reaching into Canadian bank, credit card accounts. Bankers can't tell customers they are under investigation," *Toronto Star*, December 29, 2004, p. E01.

[32] A further example of regulatory risk impacts on technology and operating costs in general is the cost of converting European banks' systems from local currencies into the euro. This may cost European banks $150 billion or more. See "A Year before the Millennium Bug, There's the Euro Problem," *New York Times*, March 9, 1998, p. 1.

[33] The importance of accounting for technological change in the design of regulatory policies has been emphasized by the Chairman of the Federal Reserve. See A. Greenspan, "Technological Change and the Design of Bank Supervising Policies," in *33rd Annual Conference on Bank Structure and Competition* (Federal Reserve Bank of Chicago, May 1997), pp. 1–8.

[34] A major reason for the growth in Cayman Islands banking was the desire of large U.S. banks to avoid or reduce the cost of the Federal Reserve's non-interest-bearing reserve requirements. Many attribute its current popularity to drug- or crime-related secret money transactions. See I. Walter, *Secret Money: The World of International Financial Secrecy* (London: Allen and Unwin, 1985).

[35] A closely associated risk for regulators is that increased use of international wire transfer systems weakens the power of central banks to control the domestic money supply.

[36] See I. Fooladi, P. McGraw, and G. Roberts, "Preferred share rules freeze out the individual investor," CA Magazine (April 1988), pp. 38–41.

TABLE 14–8
A Summary of Operational Risks Faced by FIs

Source: C. Marshall, *Measuring and Managing Operational Risks in Financial Institutions: Tools, Techniques and Other Resources* (Singapore: John Wiley and Sons, 2001).

Source of Risk	Specific Problem
Employee risk	Employee turnover
	Key personnel risk
	Fraud risk
	Error
	Rogue trading
	Money laundering
	Confidentiality breach
Technology risk	Programming error
	Model risk
	Mark-to-market error
	Management information
	IT systems outage
	Telecommunications failure
	Technology provider failure
	Contingency planning
Customer risk	Contractual disagreement
	Dissatisfaction
	Default
Capital asset risk	Safety
	Security
	Operating costs
	Fire/flood
External risk	External fraud
	Taxation risk
	Legal risk
	War
	Collapse of markets
	Reputation risk
	Relationship risk

vehicles at a discount. Thus, technology exposes existing FIs to the increased risk of erosion of their franchises as costs of entry fall and the competitive landscape changes.[37]

Concept Questions

1. Describe the six risks faced by FIs with the growth of wire transfer payment systems.
2. What steps has the Canada Payments System taken to lower settlement risk for the LVTS?

OTHER OPERATIONAL RISKS

While technology risk has become increasingly important to the profitability and riskiness of modern FIs, it is not the sole source of operational risk. Early in the chapter we listed four other sources of operational risk. These are employees, customer relationships, capital assets, and external risks. Table 14–8 lists a summary of the problems these sources of operational risk can create, including how the other sources of operational risk interact with technology risk. For example, employee risk includes employee turnover and fraud, as well as programming errors by employees. Similarly,

---

[37] For an excellent overview of the issues relating to the risks of payment systems, see D. Hancock and D. B. Humphrey, "Payment Transactions, Instruments and Systems: A Survey," *Journal of Banking and Finance* 21 (December 1997), pp. 1573–1624.

FIGURE 14–7
Optimal Risk
Management Effort

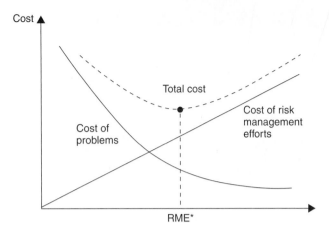

Extent of risk managment efforts

the failure of a third-party technology provider to perform as promised, resulting an FI's online banking services being interrupted, may cause the FI to lose customers.[38]

Like technology risk, these other sources of operational risk can result in direct costs (e.g., loss of income), indirect costs (e.g., client withdrawals and legal costs), and opportunity costs (e.g., forgone business opportunities) for an FI that reduce profitability and value. To offset these costs, FI managers spend considerable effort and resources to prevent, control, finance, and insulate the FI from losses due to operational risk. These efforts include (see Marshall, 2001):

1. *Loss prevention:* Training, development, and review of employees.
2. *Loss control:* Planning, organization, backup (e.g., computer systems).
3. *Loss financing:* External insurance (e.g., catastrophe insurance).
4. *Loss insulation:* FI capital.

Risk management efforts, of course, come at a cost to the FI. As illustrated in Figure 14–7, the greater the commitment of resources to risk management efforts, the lower the costs resulting from operational risks. However, the resources spent in preventing costs of operational risk may, at some point, be greater than the cost of the risk itself. In maximizing profits and value, FIs will invest in these risk management efforts until the costs of such efforts just offset operating losses from not undertaking such efforts (point RME* in Figure 14–7). See Marshall (2001), p. 317.

As discussed previously, the Royal Bank of Canada has a three-pronged approach to operational risk (self-assessment and control, a loss event database, and the identification of key risk indicators). Similarly, Bank of Montreal has an "Operational Risk Framework" that it uses to identify, quantify, and control the risks inherent in its operations, as well as to meet the requirements of OSFI and CDIC.[39]

www.cdic.ca

The Ethical Dilemmas Box presents a case study on German "loan factories" considered by the BIS that presents a regulator's view of the risks inherent in outsourcing for FIs. Thus, while an FI may wish to outsource credit granting activities for cost and efficiency reasons, all 5 of the risks listed in Table 14–8 could be relevant in this case.

---

[38] See "E Is for Risk," *Risk: Operational Risk Special Report,* November 1999, pp. 6–9. This section is based in part on Christopher Marshall, *Measuring and Managing Operational Risks in Financial Institutions: Tools, Techniques, and Other Resources* (Singapore: John Wiley and Sons, 2001).

[39] See BMO Financial Group Annual Report 2004, pp. 65–66.

In Germany, an increasing number of credit institutions outsource loan handling to specialised, unregulated service providers, called "loan factories". These service providers specialise in back-office-services concerning loans and mortgages and, in some cases, decide whether to grant a loan.

In 2003 a credit institution wanted to outsource not only the servicing of loans, but also the decision to grant a loan in standard retail-lending business and in the non-standard business up to €2.5 m. The result of the assessment by the supervisor was that in the non-standard-business the credit institution was unable to monitor and oversee the loans granted by the loan factory. Though the business is run by he credit institution, which bears the risk emerging from

it, the decision on granting the loans had been made by the service provider.

Issues that emerged as part of this scenario included:
- The outsourcing of decisions concerning the incurrence of new exposure is permissible only if it does not impair management's ability to manage risks adequately.
- This aforementioned would only be met if the regulated entity stringently committed the service provider to apply precise and verifiable evaluation and assessment criteria. With the systems currently used by the financial industry, this is only possible in the standardised retail lending business.

Source: Basel Committee on Banking Supervision, The Joint Forum, "Outsourcing in Financial Services," February 2005, p. 20. Original text available free of charge at www.bis.org.

Concept Questions

1. Using the German loan factory case presented in the Ethical Dilemmas box, identify how operational risk might arise from employee risk, technology risk, customer risk, capital asset risk, and external risk if an FI were to outsource its credit decisions.
2. What risk management efforts are involved in controlling operational risk?

REGULATORY ISSUES AND TECHNOLOGY AND OPERATIONAL RISKS

As stated earlier, operational risk is the risk of direct or indirect loss resulting from inadequate or failed internal processes, people, or systems, and from external events. Certainly, as FIs' use of technology increases, operational risk increases as well. However, little has been done to oversee or regulate these increasing risks. In this section, we look at two areas that have been directly affected by the increase in operational risk.

1. *Operational Risk and FI Insolvency.* Research by Operational Research Inc., an operational risk consultancy firm, estimates that since 1980, FIs have lost over US $200 billion due to operational risk.[40] Regulators have recognized the significance of operational risk for FIs. Specifically, in 1999 the Basel Committee (of the BIS) on Banking Supervision said that operational risks "are sufficiently important for banks to devote necessary resources to quantify the level of such risks and to incorporate them (along with market and credit risk) into their assessment of their overall capital adequacy."[41] In its follow-up consultative documents released in January 2001 and April 2003, the Basel Committee proposed three specific methods by which deposit-taking institutions (DTIs) could calculate the required capital (effective 2006) to protect themselves against operational risk. These methods are the Basic Indicator Approach, the Standardized Approach, and the Advanced Measurement Approach.[42] We discuss each of the methods in more detail in Chapter 20.

---

[40] See C. Smithson, "Measuring Operational Risk," *Risk,* March 2000, pp. 58–59.

[41] See "Basel Committee on Banking Supervision, 1999; A New Capital Adequacy Framework," Bank for International Settlements, Basel, Switzerland, June 1999, p. 50.

[42] See "Basel Committee on Banking Supervision, 2001; The New Basel Capital Accord," January 2001, and "Overview of The New Basel Capital Accord," April 2003, Bank for International Settlements, Basel, Switzerland, (www.bis.org). The Advanced Measurement Approach offers three alternative methodologies for capital reserve calculations for the most sophisticated and largest banks in the world.

Technology in the News

NO DETERRENCE FOR THOSE ENGAGING IN INTERNET FRAUD

Internet fraud has all the perks of growing marijuana, but has a better upside in a couple of critical areas.

Like cultivating B.C. bud, there's millions of dollars to be made stealing credit card numbers, selling them anonymously online, and racking up thousands of dollars in purchases in someone else's name.

But when it comes to violence or the fear of getting nabbed by the police, Internet fraud presents virtually no risk.

While Vancouver is the top source in North America for stolen credit card numbers, one case involving a Richmond young offender is a prime example of where the justice system is lagging far behind this type of criminal activity.

Last November, the local youth—who can't be identified under terms of the Youth Criminal Justice Act—and a relative from Surrey were arrested by the Vancouver Police following a year-long international undercover operation. The pair were among nearly two dozen suspects arrested around the world, accused of creating forged documents and manufacturing credit cards. Police claim some 1.7 million stolen credit cards and $4 million was netted by the group. It's been nearly nine months since the Richmond and Surrey arrests, and about six months since the Crown received the report from police investigators, and yet charges still haven't been laid. "The Crown is still reviewing the file and trying to decide on charges," Vancouver Police Const. Mark Fenton said.

This type of crime has been around for years, but police lack the resources and know-how to combat Internet fraud and only now are police agencies beginning to address the issue.

"We're the only ones who have been tackling this stuff," Fenton said of the Vancouver Police's two-man Computer Crime Unit.

With police forces traditionally concentrating on tackling crime within their own jurisdictions, the area of Internet fraud is nobody's responsibility since it knows no boundaries on the nebulous Internet.

"It's a global problem, not a local problem," Fenton said.

Recently, police arrested a 25-year-old Abbotsford man in a "full-blown counterfeit credit card and false identification factory."

Seized were 4,000 blank credit cards, card-manufacturing equipment, fake social insurance cards, birth certificates and driver licences. There was also enough credit card data to fill all of the blank cards, police said, which could have cost the banks $20 million.

This arrest was the fruit of work involving police departments in Vancouver, Calgary and Abbotsford, as well as the Secret Service and investigators from the Royal Bank of Canada.

Fenton said there really is no deterrence for people engaging in Internet fraud.

The courts haven't seen a prosecution in this area, and currently there are only four people (one in Edmonton, two in Calgary and now possibly one in Abbotsford) facing charges in Canada in connection with the Web site.

On the surface, it may appear the victims of 'Net fraud' are just the banking institutions, but Fenton said that's not true.

Individual victims often face a painstaking task that can take years to reclaim their good financial name.

And identity theft hasn't been dealt with by the courts as far as Fenton is aware.

"Only now are they starting to realize how much of a problem this is."

Source: *The Leader*, Surrey, B.C., August 3, 2005, page 14.

---

2. *Consumer Protection.* A KPMG Information Security Survey 2000 reported that business customers hesitate to put their personal and financial information on the Internet for two reasons. First, they are worried about who has access to this information and how it will be used. Second, they worry that credit card or bank account details will be stolen or used fraudulently.[43] As Technology in the News points out, these worries are well founded. The advent of electronic banking is making consumer protection an increasingly important responsibility for regulators of FIs. Global standards and

---

[43] See R. Coles, "Safety Net," *The Banker,* September 2000, pp. 7–8; and "E Is for Risk."

protocols that can be credibly enforced will become increasingly necessary to assure the customer's desired degree of privacy.

With respect to security risk, because Internet transactions involve open systems, they are susceptible to interception and fraud. Cryptographic techniques for ensuring transaction security are rapidly improving and are almost fully secure for consumer transactions. Further, technological developments are soon expected that will provide protection needed for large transactions as well. Availability of these technologies does not ensure that FIs will use them (especially if their costs are high). Consequently, regulators may need to oversee (or even mandate) the implementation of these technologies if FIs are slow to use them operationally.

Concept Questions

1. What are the three approaches proposed by the Basel Committee on Banking Supervision for measuring capital requirements associated with operational risk?
2. What steps have been or are being taken to ensure privacy and protection against fraud in the use of personal and financial consumer information placed on the Internet?

Summary

This chapter analyzed the operating cost side of FIs' activities, including the effects of the growth of technology-based innovations. The impact of technology was first examined separately for wholesale and retail services before an analysis was presented of its effects on cost and revenues. Technology-based investments can potentially result in new product innovations and lower costs, but the evidence for such cost savings is mixed. Moreover, new and different risks appear to have been created by modern technology. These include settlement risk, international technology transfer risk, crime or fraud risk, regulatory avoidance risk, taxation avoidance risk, and competition risk. Nevertheless, although the chapter focuses on the cost and benefits of technology to an FI, a more fundamental issue may not be technology's costs and benefits but the need to invest in technology to survive as a modern full-service FI.

Questions and Problems

1. Explain how technological improvements can increase an FI's interest and noninterest income and reduce interest and noninterest expenses. Use some specific examples.

2. Table 14–1 shows data on earnings, expenses, and assets for banks that report to OSFI. Calculate the annual growth rates in the various income, expense, earnings, and asset categories from 1996 to 2004. If part of the growth rates in assets, earnings, and expenses can be attributed to technological change, in what areas of operating performance has technological change appeared to have the greatest impact? What growth rates are more likely to be caused by economywide economic activity?

3. Compare the effects of technology on an FI's wholesale operations with the effects of technology on an FI's retail operations. Give some specific examples.

4. What are some of the risks inherent in being the first to introduce a financial innovation?

5. The operations department of a major FI is planning to reorganize several of its back-office functions. Its current operating expense is $1,500,000, of which $1,000,000 is for staff expenses. The FI uses a 12 percent cost of capital to evaluate cost-saving projects.

   a. One way of reorganizing is to outsource overseas a portion of its data entry functions. This will require an initial investment of approximately $500,000 after taxes. The FI expects to save $150,000 in annual operating expenses after tax for the next 7 years. Should it undertake this project, assuming that this change will lead to permanent savings?

   b. Another option is to automate the entire process by installing new state-of-the-art computers and software. The FI expects to realize more than $500,000 per year in after-tax savings, but the initial investment will be approximately $3,000,000. In addition, the life of this project is limited to seven years, at which time new computers and software will need to be installed. Using this seven-year planning horizon, should the FI invest in this project? What level of after-tax savings would be necessary to make this plan comparable in value creation to the plan in part (a)?

6. City Bank upgrades its computer equipment every five years to keep up with changes in technology. Its next upgrade is two years from today and is budgeted to cost $1,000,000. Management is considering moving up the date by two years to install some new computers with a breakthrough software that could generate significant cost savings. The cost for this new equipment also is $1,000,000. What should be the savings per year to justify moving up the planned upgrade by two years? Assume a cost of capital of 15 percent.

7. Identify and discuss three benefits of technology in generating revenue for FIs.

8. Distinguish between economies of scale and economies of scope.

9. What information on the operating costs of FIs does the measurement of economies of scale provide? If economies of scale exist, what implications do they have for regulators?

10. What are diseconomies of scale? What are the risks of large-scale technological investments, especially to large FIs? Why are small FIs willing to outsource production to large FIs against which they are competing? Why are large FIs willing to accept outsourced production from smaller FI competition?

11. What information on the operating costs of FIs is provided by the measurement of economies of scope? What implications do economies of scope have for regulators?

12. Buy Bank had $130 million in assets and $20 million in expenses before the acquisition of Sell Bank, which had assets of $50 million and expenses of $10 million. After the merger, the bank had $180 million in assets and $35 million in costs. Did this acquisition generate either economies of scale or economies of scope?

13. A bank with assets of $2 billion and costs of $200 million has acquired an investment banking firm subsidiary with assets of $40 million and expenses of $15 million. After the acquisition, the costs of the bank are $180 million and the costs of the subsidiary are $20 million. Does the resulting merger reflect economies of scale or economies of scope?

14. What are diseconomies of scope? How could diseconomies of scope occur?

15. A survey of a local market has provided the following average cost data: Mortgage Bank A (MBA) has assets of $3 million and an average cost of 20 percent. Life Insurance Company B (LICB) has assets of $4 million and an average cost of 30 percent. Corporate Pension Fund C (CPFC) has assets of $4 million and an average cost of 25 percent. For each firm, average costs are measured as a proportion of assets. MBA is planning to acquire LICB and CPFC with the expectation of reducing overall average costs by eliminating the duplication of services.

    a. What should be the average cost after acquisition for the bank to justify this merger?

    b. If MBA plans to reduce operating costs by $500,000 after the merger, what will be the average cost of the new firm?

16. What is the difference between the production approach and the intermediation approach to estimating cost functions of FIs?

17. What are some of the conclusions of empirical studies on economies of scale and scope? How important is the impact of cost reductions on total average costs? What are X-inefficiencies? What role do these factors play in explaining cost differences among FIs?

18. Why does the United States lag behind most other industrialized countries in the proportion of annual electronic noncash transactions per capita? What factors probably will be important in causing the gap to decrease?

19. What are the differences between the LVTS and CHIPS payment systems?

20. What provision has been taken by the members of the CPA to reduce the settlement risk problem in the LVTS?

21. Why do FIs in the United States face a higher degree of international technology risk than do the FIs in other countries, especially some European countries?

22. What has been the impact of rapid technological improvements in the electronic payment systems on crime and fraud risk?

23. What are usury ceilings? How does technology create regulatory risk?

24. How has technology altered the competition risk of FIs?

25. What actions has the BIS taken to protect deposit-taking institutions from insolvency due to operational risk?

Web Questions

26. Go to the BIS Web site at **www.bis.org** and find the most recent data on the volume and value of payment system transactions in Canada (Table 14–2) using the following steps. Click on "Publications and Statistics." Click on "Publications of the Committee on Payment and Settlement Systems." Click on the most recent release of "Statistics on Payment Systems in Selected Countries." Click on "Full Publication." Under Bookmarks, click on "Canada." This will bring the file onto your computer that contains the relevant data (in Tables 9 and 10). How have these numbers changed since 2002 as reported in Table 14–3?

27. Go to the BIS Web site at **www.bis.org** and find the most recent data on the volume and value of worldwide wire transfer systems (Table 14–6). Click on "Publications and Statistics." Click on "Publications of the Committee on Payment and Settlement Systems." Click on the most recent release of "Statistics on Payment Systems in Selected Countries." Click on "Comparative tables only." This will bring the file onto your computer that contains the relevant data (in Table 15). How have these numbers changed since 2002 as reported in Table 14–6?

This chapter looks at how FIs: (1) evaluate (2) measure, and (3) hedge their foreign exchange risk:

▸ when their assets and liabilities are denominated in foreign currencies, and

▸ when they take major positions as traders in the spot and forward foreign currency markets

INTRODUCTION

The globalization of the financial services industry has meant that FIs are increasingly exposed to foreign exchange (FX) risk. FX risk can occur as a result of trading in foreign currencies, making foreign currency loans (such as a loan in sterling to a corporation), buying foreign-issued securities (U.K. sterling-denominated gilt-edged bonds or German euro-government bonds), or issuing foreign currency-denominated debt (sterling certificates of deposit) as a source of funds. Canadian FIs and their business customers may be particularly exposed to exchange rate risk relative to the U.S. dollar both for trade and the pricing of commodities such as oil and gas, metals, and forest products. In particular, as shown in the Industry Perspectives box, exchange rate movements are related to the Bank of Canada's monetary policy and, therefore, interest rate risk (as discussed in Chapters 8 and 9). This has been particularly important between 2003 and 2005 as the U.S. dollar has declined relative to other world currencies and as pressures have grown for the Chinese government to re-value the yuan, which has been pegged to the U.S. dollar.

The greater the volatility of foreign exchange rates, the greater the fluctuations in value of an FI's foreign portfolio (see Chapter 10 where we discussed market risk). Extreme foreign exchange risk was evident in 1997 when a currency crisis occurred in Asia. The crisis began July 2 when the Thai baht fell nearly 50 percent in value relative to the U.S. dollar, which led to contagious drops in the value of other Asian currencies and eventually affected currencies other than those in Asia (e.g. the Brazilian real and the Russian ruble). On November 20, 1997, almost five months after the baht's drop in value, the value of the South Korean won dropped by 10 percent relative to the U.S. dollar. As a result of these currency shocks, the earnings of some FIs were adversely impacted. For example, Canadian Imperial Bank of Commerce (CIBC) suffered a trading loss of $70 million in its first quarter (November 1997 to January 1998) related to its Asian exposure and $427 million in the fourth quarter as world markets worried about Asia and Eastern Europe. CIBC's reported total trading revenue declined by $612 million between 1997 and 1998.

www.cibc.com

SOURCES OF FOREIGN EXCHANGE RISK EXPOSURE

Canada's largest banks are major players in foreign currency trading and dealing, taking significant positions in foreign currency assets and liabilities (see also Chapter 10 on market risk, where we looked at methods of calculating value at risk on foreign

Industry Perspectives

MONETARY POLICY AND EXCHANGE RATE MOVEMENTS

Over the past two years, the Canadian dollar has appreciated by about 25 per cent relative to the U.S. dollar, from an average of 65 cents U.S. in January 2003 to an average of 82 cents U.S. in January 2005.

Understanding the causes of exchange rate movements is important because the implications for the Canadian economy of a change in the exchange rate depend crucially on the cause of the change, and may therefore require a different monetary policy response. From the standpoint of monetary policy, these causes can be divided into two broad types: those that stem from changes in the demand for Canadian goods and services, and those that do not. Developments over the past two years provide a useful illustration of these two types of forces.

The first type relates to the strengthening global economic recovery, which led to a substantial increase in world commodity prices and to strong foreign demand for Canadian products, especially raw materials. This development represented a direct increase in Canadian aggregate demand. The associated appreciation of the Canadian dollar dampened the increase in aggregate demand and helped to facilitate the adjustment of the Canadian economy by encouraging a shift in activity towards Canada's commodity-exporting sector. To the extent that the dampening effect on aggregate demand exactly offsets the direct increase in demand, there would be no need for a policy response.

The second type, independent of the demand for Canadian goods and services, relates to the general weakening of the U.S. dollar against most major floating currencies. This reflects growing concerns about a shortage of savings in the United States, partly related to the expanding U.S. fiscal deficit, and a surplus of savings elsewhere, mainly in Asia. The associated appreciation of the Canadian dollar works to reduce foreign demand for Canadian products. All other things being equal, this would require monetary policy to be more stimulative than it otherwise would have been.

Over the past two years, an important challenge for Canadian monetary policy has been to determine the relative importance of these two main forces on the Canadian dollar and the net impact on Canadian aggregate demand. For the early part of this period, both forces were at play, although the stronger world demand and rising commodity prices appeared to be producing most of the dollar's momentum. In the past few months, however, the weakening U.S. dollar appears to have become the relatively more important factor, especially against a background of broadly stable commodity prices.

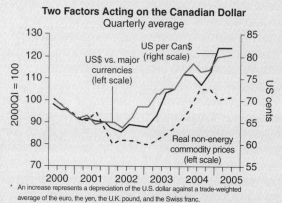

Two Factors Acting on the Canadian Dollar
Quarterly average

* An increase represents a depreciation of the U.S. dollar against a trade-weighted average of the euro, the yen, the U.K. pound, and the Swiss franc.

Note: The letter "a" denotes average of daily rates up to 24 January 2005.
The letter "e" denotes estimate based on available indicators.

Source: Bank of Canada, "Monetary Policy Report Update," January 2005, p. 3, www.bankofcanada.ca

www.royalbank.com   exchange contracts). The Royal Bank of Canada ranks 15th in global market share, trading approximately US$40 billion per day of the US$1.9 trillion traded on average in global markets in 2004.[1] Table 15–1 shows the annual outstanding dollar value of Canadian banks' on-balance-sheet foreign assets and liabilities for the period 1996 to 2004. The 2004 figure for foreign assets (claims) was $645.4 billion, with foreign liabilities of $665.4 billion. As you can see, Canadian banks reported negative net foreign assets each year. Foreign assets made up an average of 40 percent of the banks' total on balance sheet assets over the time period. Loans were

---

[1] See T. Grant, "The power of the money changers" and "Hedge funds throwing their weight around in global currency markets," *Globe and Mail,* August 5, 2005, p.B9.

TABLE 15–1 Foreign Currency Assets and Liabilities Reported by Canadian Banks, 1996–2004 (millions of dollars), as at December 31

	1996	1997	1998	1999	2000	2001	2002	2003	2004
Liabilities & S/H Equity	433,363	574,745	685,852	593,308	653,562	761,369	770,925	665,470	665,448
Deposits	75,112	92,237	81,463	75,945	74,324	78,769	75,074	73,152	67,720
Securities	75,853	104,734	142,800	154,937	168,775	213,760	214,440	237,799	248,143
Loans	206,535	264,284	304,986	260,077	279,236	305,523	278,203	215,156	206,000
Derivative-related	40,283	61,946	105,676	46,477	76,587	85,688	107,485	73,716	73,121
Other Assets	19,187	24,883	32,414	26,012	28,316	43,187	53,029	39,301	50,454
Total Foreign Assets	416,969	548,084	667,339	563,448	627,240	726,927	728,231	639,123	645,438
Net Foreign Assets	−16,393	−26,661	−18,513	−29,861	−26,322	−34,442	−42,694	−26,347	−20,010
Total Assets	1,107,388	1,322,127	1,433,613	1,399,432	1,551,461	1,711,437	1,761,953	1,769,611	1,898,703
Foreign Assets/ Total Assets	37.7%	41.5%	46.5%	40.3%	40.4%	42.5%	41.3%	36.1%	34.0%

Source: Office of Superintendent of Financial Institutions, www.osfi-bsif.gc.ca

TABLE 15–2 Foreign Exchange Turnover in Canada in April 2004 by Currency Pair (in millions of dollars)

	Directly against the U.S. dollar					All other currency pairs	Total
	Canadian dollar	Euro	Japanese yen	U.K. pound	Other		
Summary by instrument							
Total spot	169,480	79,596	43,536	27,763	35,206	30,098	385,679
(Currency share, per cent)	(44.0)	(20.6)	(11.3)	(7.2)	(9.1)	(7.8)	(100.0)
Total outright forwards and FX swaps	439,356	82,949	49,347	52,336	100,728	22,057	747,773
(Currency share, per cent)	(58.8)	(11.1)	(6.6)	(7.0)	(13.5)	(3.0)	(100.0)
Total turnover	608,836	162,545	92,883	80,099	135,934	52,155	1,132,452
(Currency share, per cent)	(53.7)	(14.4)	(8.2)	(7.1)	(12.0)	(4.6)	(100.0)

Source: Bank of Canada, "Triennial Central Bank Survey of Foreign Exchange and Over-the-Counter (OTC) Derivatives Markets," March 2005, Table 6, www.bankofcanada.ca

the highest dollar amount at $206.5 billion followed by $75.8 billion in securities in 1996. The amount of loans in 2004 was slightly down from 1996 at $206.0 billion, but foreign securities had increased to represent the largest category of foreign assets at $248.1 billion.

The Bank of Canada has conducted a survey of the foreign exchange and Over-the-Counter (OTC) derivatives markets triennially since 1983. Table 15–2 summarizes the foreign currency exchange turnover in Canada as reported by the April, 2004 survey. The results, by instrument, demonstrate that spot transactions and outright forwards and FX swaps in U.S. dollars against the Canadian dollar constituted the largest amount of foreign exchange transactions in Canada (53.7 percent), followed by the Euro (14.4 percent), other currencies (12.0 percent), the Japanese yen (8.2 percent) and the U.K. pound (7.1 percent) against the U.S. dollar. Foreign exchange transactions of all other currency pairs except the U.S. dollar

TABLE 15–3
Sample FI
Positions in
Foreign Currencies
and Foreign Assets
and Liabilities
(in currency of
denomination)

	(1) Assets	(2) Liabilities	(3) FX Bought*	(4) FX Sold*	(5) Net Position†
U.S. dollars (thousands)	126,812	130,875	367,077	369,335	−6,321
Japanese yen (millions)	43,969	43,869	183,081	187,711	−4,530
Swiss francs (thousands)	52,152	57,423	377,101	384,344	−12,514
British pounds (thousands)	225,987	223,079	519,818	528,657	−5,931
Euros (thousands)	1,113,381	1,072,384	1,848,576	1,867,959	21,614

* Includes spot, future, and forward contracts.
† Net position = (Assets − Liabilities) + (FX bought − FX sold).

represented only 4.6 percent of the total turnover of US$1.13 billion made by the Canadian FIs surveyed in April 2004. This is not surprising since the Bank for International Settlements reports that daily average global trading in the U.S. dollar was US$461.3 billion in April 2004, a 19.2 percent share of the total.[2]

Table 15–3 gives the categories of foreign currency positions (or investments) of a hypothetical FI in major currencies. Columns (1) and (2) refer to the assets and liabilities denominated in foreign currencies that are held in the portfolios. Columns (3) and (4) refer to foreign currency trading activities (the **spot foreign exchange** and **forward foreign exchange** contracts bought—a long position—and sold—a short position—in each major currency). Foreign currency trading dominates this FI's direct portfolio investments. Even though the aggregate trading positions appear very large—for example, 183,081 million yen—the overall or net exposure position can be relatively small (e.g., the net position in yen was −4,530 million yen).

An FIs' overall FX exposure in any given currency can be measured by the **net position exposure,** which is measured in column (5) of Table 15–3 as:

$$\text{Net exposure}_i = (\text{FX assets}_i - \text{FX liabilities}_i) + (\text{FX bought}_i - \text{FX sold}_i)$$
$$= \text{Net foreign assets}_i + \text{Net FX bought}_i$$

where

$$i = i\text{th currency}$$

Clearly, an FI could match its foreign currency assets to its liabilities in a given currency and match buys and sells in its trading book in that foreign currency to reduce its foreign exchange net exposure to zero and thus avoid FX risk. It could also offset an imbalance in its foreign asset-liability portfolio by an opposing imbalance in its trading book so that its net exposure position in that currency would be zero.

Notice in Table 15–3 that this FI had a positive net FX exposure in one of the five major currencies, euros. A *positive* net exposure position implies the FI is overall **net long in a currency** (i.e., the FI has bought more foreign currency than it has sold) and faces the risk that the foreign currency will fall in value against the dollar, the domestic currency. A *negative* net exposure position implies that the FI is **net short in a foreign currency** (i.e., the FI has sold more foreign currency than it has purchased) and faces the risk that the foreign currency could rise in value against the dollar. Thus, failure to maintain a fully balanced position in any given currency exposes an FI to fluctuations in the FX rate of that currency against the dollar.

spot foreign exchange
Foreign currency traded for immediate delivery.

forward foreign exchange
Foreign currency traded for future delivery.

net exposure
The degree to which an FI is net long (positive) or net short (negative) in a given currency.

net long (short) in a currency
Holding more (fewer) assets than liabilities in a given currency.

[2] Bank of Canada, "Triennial Central Bank Survey of Foreign Exchange and Over-the-Counter (OTC) Derivatives Markets," March 2005, Table 9, available at www.bankofcanada.ca and Bank for International Settlements, "Triennial Central Bank Survey," March 2004, at www.bis.org. See also E. Santor, "Banking Crises, Contagion, and Foreign-Asset Exposures of Canadian Banks," Bank of Canada Conference Proceedings, *The Evolving Financial System and Public Policy* (2004), available at www.bankofcanada.ca for a detailed analysis of the exposure of Canadian banks to foreign assets.

Table 15–1 shows the FX exposures only for Canadian banks, but most nonbank FIs also have some FX exposure either through asset-liability holdings or currency trading, for their own account or for their customers. The absolute sizes of these exposures are smaller for three reasons: smaller asset sizes, prudent person concerns[3], and regulations. In Canada, foreign investment was 22.5 percent of the market value of the total assets of trusteed pension funds in the first quarter of 2002. Prior to 1990 when limits on foreign investments were proposed, trusteed pension funds in Canada had less than 6 percent of their total assets invested abroad.[4]

While the levels of claims and positions in foreign currencies held by financial institutions have increased in recent years, the global volume of foreign currency trading declined between 1998 and 2001, and then increased dramatically between 2001 and 2004. The Bank for International Settlements reported that average daily turnover in the foreign exchange markets was US $1,490 trillion in 1996, declining to US$1,200 trillion in 2001, and increasing to $1,880 trillion in 2004. The increase between 2001 and 2004 was 57 percent at current exchange rates. A report by G. Galati and M. Melvin in the BIS Quarterly Review of December 2004 attributed the decline in trading between 1998 and 2001 to the impending introduction of the Euro in 2002, growth in electronic brokerages that reduced the number of trading operations, corporate mergers that eliminated the need for foreign exchange transactions, banking consolidations, and the financial events of 1998 that increased global risk aversion and led to lower global liquidity. Between 2001 and 2004, money managers were seeking higher yields and used foreign exchange contracts as an alternative to equity and fixed income assets. Higher volatility in the markets resulted in increased hedging, pushing up the volume of trading. Also, interest rate differentials played a part as **carry trades** were popular whereby a money manager would buy a higher interest rate currency such as the Australian or New Zealand dollar and fund the trade by borrowing a lower interest rate currency such as the U.S. dollar, the Japanese yen, or the Swiss franc, thus betting that the exchange rate would not change and wipe out the interest rate differential. Since the U.S. dollar depreciated by 30 percent against the Australian dollar and 15 percent against the Canadian dollar and the Japanese yen between April 2001 and early 2004, the carry trade strategy would have been highly profitable in many cases. In addition, traders also engaged in and profited from **momentum trading** by holding long positions in currencies that were experiencing long-run swings in exchange rates.[5]

With the introduction of the euro in January 2002, the cross-trading of member currencies has completely disappeared. For example, with the euro in place, cash flows from subsidiaries based in one European country can be put directly into the accounts of a parent company without complicated foreign exchange adjustments. As a result, with the European Monetary Unit (EMU) fully implemented, multinational companies are likely to continue to reduce the number of banking relationships and foreign exchange transactions that they need. Currency unions that have been discussed from time to time for other countries could also act to reduce global foreign

carry trades
The purchase by an investor of a currency in a country with high interest rates funded by borrowing in a currency with low interest rates.

momentum trading
Taking a large position in a currency (or other financial asset) in order to take advantage of long-term increases in exchange rates.

---

[3] Prudent person concerns are especially important for pension funds.

[4] For example, foreign assets held by Canadian trusteed pension funds were limited to 20 percent of total book value of assets in 1998. The limit was raised to 25 percent in 2000 and 30 percent in 2001. See Statistics Canada, Quarterly Estimates of Trusteed Pension Funds, First Quarter, 2002. The 2005 federal budget removed all limits on foreign assets in pension funds as discussed in Chapter 5.

[5] See BIS, Triennial Central Bank Survey, March 2004. Also, see G. Galati and M. Melvin, "Why has FX trading surged? Explaining the 2004 triennial survey," BIS Quarterly Review, December 2004, pp. 67–74, and G. Galati, "Why has global FX turnover declined? Explaining the 2001 triennial survey," BIS Quarterly Review, December 2001, pp. 39–47, for discussions of the global foreign exchange markets between 1998 and 2004.

exchange transactions in the future. For example, the use of a common dollar between Australia and New Zealand or Canada and the United States has been raised.[6]

Foreign Exchange Rate Volatility and FX Exposure

As Chapter 10 on market risk discussed, we can measure the potential size of an FI's FX exposure by analyzing the asset, liability, and currency trading mismatches on its balance sheet and the underlying volatility of exchange rate movements. Specifically, we can use the following equation:

$$\text{Dollar loss/gain in currency } i = [\text{Net exposure in foreign currency } i \text{ measured in dollars}] \times \text{Shock (volatility) to the } \$/\text{Foreign currency } i \text{ exchange rate}$$

The larger the FI's net exposure in a foreign currency and the larger the foreign currency's exchange rate volatility,[7] the larger is the potential dollar loss or gain to an FI's earnings (i.e., the greater its daily value at risk). The underlying causes of FX volatility reflect fluctuations in the demand for and supply of a country's currency. That is, conceptually, an FX rate is like the price of any good and will appreciate in value relative to other currencies when demand is high or supply is low and will depreciate in value when demand is low or supply is high. For example, in October 1998 the U.S. dollar fell (depreciated) in value on one day from 121 yen/$ to 112 yen/$, or by over 7 percent. The major reason for this was the purchase of yen by hedge funds and the sale of U.S. dollars to repay Japanese banks for the yen loans they had borrowed at low interest rates earlier in 1998. While not as rapid a decline, in the early 2000s the U.S. dollar fell in value by almost 20 percent relative to the yen (from 134.0 in early 2002 to 107.8 in October 2003), much of which was due to an improving Japanese economy and intervention by Japan's Central Bank. A final example is the devaluation of the Argentinian peso in 2002. The Bank of Nova Scotia took an after-tax charge to earnings of $540 million in 2002 and sold its subsidiary after 40 years of operating in Argentina. See Chapter 10 for more details on measuring FX exposure.

www.scotiabank.com

Concept Questions	1. How is the net foreign currency exposure of an FI measured?
	2. If a bank is long in British pounds (£), does it gain or lose if the dollar appreciates in value against the pound?
	3. A bank has £10 million in assets and £7 million in liabilities. It has also bought £52 million in foreign currency trading. What is its net exposure in pounds? (£55 million)

FOREIGN CURRENCY TRADING

The FX markets of the world have become one of the largest of all financial markets, with trading turnover averaging as high as US$1.8 trillion a day in recent years, 90 times the daily trading volume on the New York Stock Exchange.[8] London continues to be the largest market, followed by New York and Tokyo.[9] Foreign

---

[6] See P. Murray and James Powell, "Dollarization in Canada: The Buck Stops There," Bank of Canada Technical Report No. 90 (2002), as well as J. Powell, "A History of the Canadian Dollar," Bank of Canada (2003), at www.bankofcanada.ca.

[7] In the case of RiskMetrics the shock (or volatility) measure would equal 1.65 times the historic volatility (standard deviation) of the currency's exchange rate with the dollar. This shock, when multiplied by the net exposure in that currency (measured in dollars), provides an estimate of the loss exposure of the FI if tomorrow is that "1 bad day in 20" (see Chapter 10 for more details).

[8] The early 2000s saw a drop in FX trading, with daily volume falling to $1.2 trillion in 2003. Up to 95 percent of all currency trading is now conducted via electronic brokers (resulting in a reduction in the number of people working in the industry).

[9] On a global basis, approximately 31 percent of trading in FX occurs in London, 19 percent in New York, and 8 percent in Tokyo. Canada's share was 2.2 percent in 2004, tenth of the 52 countries participating in the BIS Triennial Central Bank Survey available at www.bis.org.

exchange trading has been called the fairest market in the world because of its immense volume and the fact that no single institution can control the market's direction. Although professionals refer to global foreign exchange trading as a market, it is not really one in the traditional sense of the word. There is no central location where foreign exchange trading takes place. Moreover, the FX market is essentially a 24-hour market, moving among Tokyo, London, and New York throughout the day. Therefore, fluctuations in exchange rates and thus FX trading risk exposure continues into the night even when other FI operations are closed. This clearly adds to the risk from holding mismatched FX positions. Most of the volume is traded among the top international banks, which process currency transactions for everyone from large corporations to governments around the world. Online foreign exchange trading is increasing, and the transnational nature of the electronic exchange of funds makes secure, Internet-based trading an ideal platform. Online trading portals—terminals where currency transactions are being executed—are a low-cost way of conducting spot and forward foreign exchange transactions. Reuters speculates that the number of global FIs using online trading systems will grow from 200 banks in 2003 to 700 banks by 2007.[10]

FX Trading Activities

An FI's position in the FX markets generally reflects four trading activities:

1. The purchase and sale of foreign currencies to allow customers to partake in and complete international commercial trade transactions.
2. The purchase and sale of foreign currencies to allow customers (or the FI itself) to take positions in foreign real and financial investments.
3. The purchase and sale of foreign currencies for hedging purposes to offset customer (or FI) exposure in any given currency.
4. The purchase and sale of foreign currencies for speculative purposes through forecasting or anticipating future movements in FX rates.

In the first two activities, the FI normally acts as an *agent of* its customers for a fee but does not assume the FX risk itself. Of the 11 Canadian FIs who participated in the BIS Triennial Central Bank Survey, four banks accounted for more than 75 percent of the US$54 million average daily foreign exchange market turnover in Canada reported for April 2004. Royal Bank of Canada's Annual Report showed a notional amount of foreign exchange contracts of $949 billion at October 31, 2004. Citigroup is the dominant supplier of FX to retail customers in the United States. As of 2003, the aggregate value of Citigroup's principal amount of foreign exchange contracts totaled US$1,435 billion. In the third activity, the FI acts defensively as a hedger to reduce FX exposure. For example, it may take a short (sell) position in the foreign exchange of a country to offset a long (buy) position in the foreign exchange of that same country. Thus, FX risk exposure essentially relates to **open positions** taken as a principal by the FI for speculative purposes, the fourth activity. An FI usually creates an open position by taking an unhedged position in a foreign currency in its FX trading with other FIs. FIs can make speculative trades directly with other FIs or arrange them through specialist FX brokers. Speculative trades can be instituted through a variety of FX instruments. Spot currency trades are the most common, with FIs seeking to make a profit on the difference between buy and sell prices (i.e., on movements in the bid-ask prices over time). However, FIs can also take speculative positions in foreign exchange forward contracts, futures, and options.

open position
An unhedged position in a particular currency.

---

[10] See "The Institutional Investor Guide to Foreign Exchange as an Asset Class," *Institutional Investor,* February 2003, p. 4.

TABLE 15–4   Foreign Exchange Trading Revenue of the Big Six Banks (millions of dollars, as reported for year end October 31)

	1996	1997	1998	1999	2000	2001	2002	2003	2004
Bank of Montreal	83	92	114	118	112	126	69	69	85
Bank of Nova Scotia	67	45	77	150	152	246	187	201	171
CIBC	38	78	50	154	199	179	152	171	169
National Bank	50	39	46	50	52	61	67	66	72
Royal Bank	n.a.	226	267	290	301	340	264	301	278
TD Bank	80	81	112	145	200	247	217	248	230

Source: Bank Annual Reports

The Profitability of Foreign Currency Trading

Remember from the previous section that most profits or losses on foreign trading come from taking an open position or speculating in currencies. Revenues from market making—the bid-ask spread—or from acting as agents for retail or wholesale customers generally provide only a secondary or supplementary revenue source.

Note the trading income from FX trading for the six large Canadian banks in Table 15–4. As can be seen, total trading revenue is variable, but generally grew for each FI between 1996 and 2001. The level of operations is not large compared to the rest of the banks' operations, and is small relative to the major U.S. banks. For example, Citigroup and J. P. Morgan Chase, the dominant FX trading banks in the U.S., reported foreign exchange trading income of US$2,277.0 million and US$1,225.0 million, respectively, at December 2004. The decline in the volatility of FX rates among major European countries as well as the increase in volatility in Asian currencies decreased banks' trading profits in the 1990s. As noted previously, the drop in foreign exchange trading revenue at CIBC between 1997 and 1998 was related to the currency crisis in Asia. The decline in European FX volatility is the result of two forces. The first is the reduction in inflation rates in these countries, and the second is the fixing of exchange rates among European countries as they moved toward full monetary union and the replacement of local currencies with the euro. Specifically, in May 1998, 11 countries in the European Union[11] fixed their exchange rates with each other and on January 1, 1999, all FIs and stock exchanges in these countries began using euros (electronically). On January 1, 2002, the euro went into physical circulation, and on July 1, 2002, local currencies were no longer accepted. While, as noted above, there has been increased FX volatility in many emerging-market countries, such as those of Thailand, Indonesia, and Malaysia,[12] the importance of these currencies in the FX trading activities of major FIs remains relatively small.

www.citigroup.com

www.jpmorganchase.com

Concept Questions

1. What are the four major FX trading activities?
2. In which trades do FIs normally act as agents, and in which trades as principals?
3. What is the source of most profits or losses on foreign exchange trading? What foreign currency activities provide a secondary source of revenue?

FOREIGN ASSET AND LIABILITY POSITIONS

The second dimension of an FI's FX exposure results from any mismatches between its foreign financial asset and foreign financial liability portfolios. As discussed earlier,

---

[11] These countries were Austria, Belgium, Finland, France, Germany, Ireland, Italy, Luxemburg, Netherlands, Portugal, and Spain.

[12] For example, in 1997 these currencies fell over 50 percent in value relative to the U.S. dollar. In the fall of 1998 Malaysia introduced capital controls and restrictions on trading in its currency.

an FI is long a foreign currency if its assets in that currency exceed its liabilities, while it is short a foreign currency if its liabilities in that currency exceed its assets. Foreign financial assets might include Swiss franc–denominated bonds, British pound–denominated gilt-edged securities, or peso-denominated Mexican bonds. Foreign financial liabilities might include issuing British pound CDs or a yen-denominated bond in the Euromarkets to raise yen funds. The globalization of financial markets has created an enormous range of possibilities for raising funds in currencies other than the home currency. This is important for FIs that wish to not only diversify their source and use of funds but also exploit imperfections in foreign banking markets that create opportunities for higher returns on assets or lower funding costs.

The Return and Risk of Foreign Investments

This section discusses the extra dimensions of return and risk from adding foreign currency assets and liabilities to an FI's portfolio. Like domestic assets and liabilities, profits (returns) result from the difference between contractual income from or costs paid on a security. With foreign assets and liabilities, however, profits (returns) are also affected by changes in foreign exchange rates.

EXAMPLE 15–1

Calculating the Return of Foreign Exchange Transaction

Suppose that an FI has the following assets and liabilities:

Assets	Liabilities
$100 million Loans (one-year) in dollars	$200 million CDs (one-year) in dollars
$100 million equivalent U.K. loans (one-year) (loans made in sterling)	

The FI is raising all of its $200 million liabilities in dollars (one-year CDs) but investing 50 percent in dollar assets (one-year maturity loans) and 50 percent in U.K. pound sterling assets (one-year maturity loans).[13] In this example, the FI has matched the duration of its assets and liabilities ($D_A = D_L = 1$ year) but has mismatched the currency composition of its asset and liability portfolios. Suppose the promised one-year CD rate is 8 percent, to be paid in dollars at the end of the year, and that one-year, credit risk-free loans in Canada are yielding only 9 percent. The FI would have a positive spread of 1 percent from investing domestically. Suppose, however, that credit risk-free one-year loans are yielding 15 percent in the United Kingdom.

To invest in the United Kingdom, the FI decides to take 50 percent of its $200 million in funds and make one-year maturity U.K. sterling loans while keeping 50 percent of its funds to make dollar loans. To invest $100 million (of the $200 million in CDs issued) in one-year loans in the United Kingdom, the FI engages in the following transactions (illustrated in panel (a) of Figure 15–1).

1. At the beginning of the year, sells $100 million for pounds on the spot currency markets. If the exchange rate is $1.60 to £1, this translates into $100 million/1.6 = £62.5 million.
2. Takes the £62.5 million and makes one-year U.K. loans at a 15 percent interest rate.
3. At the end of the year, sterling revenue from these loans will be £62.5(1.15) = £71.875 million.[14]
4. Repatriates these funds back to Canada at the end of the year. That is, the FI sells the £71.875 million in the foreign exchange market at the spot exchange rate that exists at that time, the end of the year spot rate.

---

[13] For simplicity, we ignore the leverage or net worth aspects of the FI's portfolio.

[14] No default risk is assumed.

FIGURE 15–1

Time Line for a Foreign Exchange Transaction

(a) Unhedged Foreign Exchange Transaction

FI lends $100 million for pounds

FI receives £62.5(1.15)

0   1 year

(b) Foreign Exchange Transaction Hedged On the Balance Sheet

FI lends $100 million for pounds

FI receives £62.5(1.15)

FI receives (from a CD) $100 million for

FI pays £62.5(1.11) with dollars at

0   1 year

(c) Foreign Exchange Transaction Hedged with Forwards

FI lends $100 million for pounds

FI sells a one-year pounds for dollars forward contract with a stated forward rate of $1.55/£1 and nominal value of £62.5 (1.15)

FI receives £62.5(1.15) from borrower and delivers funds to forward buyer receiving £62.5 × (1.15) × 1.55 guaranteed.

0   1 year

Suppose the spot foreign exchange rate has not changed over the year; it remains fixed at $1.60/£1. Then the dollar proceeds from the U.K. investment will be:

$$£71.875 \text{ million} \times \$1.60/£1 = \$115 \text{ million}$$

or, as a return,

$$\frac{\$115 \text{ million} - \$100 \text{ million}}{\$100 \text{ million}} = 15\%$$

Given this, the weighted return on the bank's portfolio of investments would be:

$$(.5)(.09) + (.5)(.15) = .12 \text{ or } 12\%$$

This exceeds the cost of the FI's CDs by 4 percent (12% − 8%).

Suppose, however, that at the end of the year the British pound had fallen in value relative to the dollar, or the dollar had appreciated in value relative to the pound. The returns on the U.K. loans could be far less than 15 percent even in the absence of interest rate or credit risk. For example, suppose the exchange rate had fallen from $1.60/£1 at the beginning of the year to $1.45/£1 at the end of the year when the FI needed to repatriate the principal and interest on the loan. At an exchange rate of $1.45/£1, the pound loan revenues at the end of the year translate into:

$$£71.875 \text{ million} \times \$1.45/£1 = \$104.22 \text{ million}$$

or as a return on the original dollar investment of:

$$\frac{\$104.22 - \$100}{\$100} = .0422 = 4.22\%$$

The weighted return on the FI's asset portfolio would be:

$$(.5)(.09) + (.5)(.0422) = .0661 = 6.61\%$$

In this case, the FI actually has a loss or has a negative interest margin (6.61% − 8% = −1.39%) on its balance sheet investments.

The reason for the loss is that the depreciation of the pound from $1.60 to $1.45 has offset the attractive high yield on British pound sterling loans relative to domestic loans. If the pound had instead appreciated (risen in value) against the dollar over the year—say, to $1.70/£1—then the U.S. FI would have generated a dollar return from its U.K. loans of:

$$£71.875 \times \$1.70 = \$122.188 \text{ million}$$

or a percentage return of 22.188 percent. Then the FI would receive a double benefit from investing in the United Kingdom: a high yield on the domestic British loans plus an appreciation in sterling over the one-year investment period.

Risk and Hedging

Since a manager cannot know in advance what the pound/dollar spot exchange rate will be at the end of the year, a portfolio imbalance or investment strategy in which the FI is *net long* $100 million in pounds (or £62.5 million) is risky. As we discussed, the British loans would generate a return of 22.188 percent if the pound appreciated from $1.60 to $1.70 but would produce a return of only 4.22 percent if the pound depreciated in value against the dollar to $1.45.

In principle, an FI manager can better control the scale of its FX exposure in two major ways: on-balance-sheet hedging and off-balance-sheet hedging. On-balance-sheet hedging involves making changes in the on-balance-sheet assets and liabilities to protect FI profits from FX risk. Off-balance-sheet hedging involves no on-balance-sheet changes but rather involves taking a position in forward or other derivative securities to hedge FX risk.

On-Balance-Sheet Hedging

The following example illustrates how an FI manager can control FX exposure by making changes on the balance sheet.

EXAMPLE 15–2

Hedging on the Balance Sheet

Suppose that instead of funding the $100 million investment in 15 percent British loans with dollar CDs, the FI manager funds the British loans with $100 million equivalent one-year pound sterling CDs at a rate of 11 percent (as illustrated in panel (b) of Figure 15–1). Now the balance sheet of the bank would look like this:

Assets	Liabilities
$100 million Cdn. loans (9%)	$100 million Cdn. CDs (8%)
$100 million U.K. loans (15%) (loans made in sterling)	$100 million U.K. CDs (11%) (deposits raised in sterling)

In this situation, the FI has both a matched maturity and currency foreign asset–liability book. We might now consider the FI's profitability or spreads between the return on assets and the cost of funds under two scenarios: first, when the pound depreciates in value against the dollar over the year from $1.60/£1 to $1.45/£ and second, when the pound appreciates in value over the year from $1.60/£1 to $1.70/£1.

The Depreciating Pound

When the pound falls in value to $1.45/£1, the return on the British loan portfolio is 4.22 percent. Consider now what happens to the cost of $100 million in pound liabilities in dollar terms:

1. At the beginning of the year, the FI borrows $100 million equivalent in sterling CDs for one year at a promised interest rate of 11 percent. At an exchange rate of $1.60£, this is a sterling equivalent amount of borrowing of $100 million/1.6 = £62.5 million.
2. At the end of the year, the bank has to pay back the sterling CD holders their principal and interest, £62.5 million (1.11) = £69.375 million.
3. If the pound had depreciated to $1.45/£ over the year, the repayment in dollar terms would be £69.375 million × $1.45/£1 = $100.59 million, or a dollar cost of funds of 0.59 percent.

Thus, at the end of the year the following occurs:

Average return on assets:

$$(0.5)(0.9) + (0.5)(0.422) = .0661 = 6.61\%$$

Canadian asset return + U.K. asset return = Overall return

Average cost of funds:

$$(0.5)(.08) + (0.5)(.0059) = .04295 = 4.295\%$$

Canadian cost of funds + U.K. cost of funds = Overall cost

Net return:

Average return on assets − Average cost of funds

$$6.61\% - 4.295\% = 2.315\%$$

The Appreciating Pound

When the pound appreciates over the year from $1.60/£1 to $1.70/£1, the return on British loans is equal to 22.188. Now consider the dollar cost of British one-year CDs at the end of the year when the FI has to pay the principal and interest to the CD holder:

$$£69.375 \text{ million} \times \$1.70/£1 = \$117.9375 \text{ million}$$

or a dollar cost of funds of 17.9375 percent. Thus, at the end of the year:

Average return on assets:

$$(0.5)(.09) + (0.5)(.22188) = .15594 \text{ or } 15.594\%$$

Average cost of funds:

$$(0.5)(.08) + (0.5)(.179375) = .12969 \text{ or } 12.969\%$$

Net return:

$$15.594 - 12.969 = 2.625\%$$

Thus, by directly matching its foreign asset and liability book, an FI can lock in a positive return or profit spread whichever direction exchange rates change over the investment period. For example, even if domestic U.S. banking is a relatively low-profit activity (i.e., there is a low spread between the return on assets and the cost of funds), the FI could be quite profitable overall. Specifically, it could lock in a large positive spread—if it exists—between deposit rates and loan rates in foreign markets. In our example, a 4 percent positive spread existed between British one-year loan rates and deposit rates compared with only a 1 percent spread domestically.

Note that for such imbalances in domestic spreads and foreign spreads to continue over long periods of time, financial service firms would have to face significant barriers to entry in foreign markets. Specifically, if real and financial capital is free to move, FIs would increasingly withdraw from the Canadian market and reorient their operations toward the United Kingdom. Reduced competition would widen loan deposit interest spreads in Canada, and increased competition would contract U.K. spreads, until the profit opportunities from foreign activities disappeared. We discuss FIs' abilities, and limits on their abilities, to engage in cross-border financial and real investments further in Chapter 22.[15]

Hedging with Forwards

Instead of matching its $100 million foreign asset position with $100 million of foreign liabilities, the FI might have chosen to remain unhedged on the balance sheet.[16] As a lower-cost alternative, it could hedge by taking a position in the forward market for foreign currencies—for example, the one-year forward market for selling sterling for dollars. We discuss the nature and use of forward contracts by FI managers more extensively in Chapter 23; however, here we introduce them to show how they can insulate the FX risk of the FI in our example. Any forward position taken would not appear on the balance sheet; it would appear as a contingent off-balance-sheet claim, which we described in Chapter 13 as an item below the bottom line. The role of the forward FX contract is to offset the uncertainty regarding the future spot rate on sterling at the end of the one-year investment horizon. Instead of waiting until the end of the year to transfer sterling back into dollars at an unknown spot rate, the FI can

forward exchange rate
The exchange rate agreed to today for future (forward) delivery of a currency.

enter into a contract to sell forward its *expected* principal and interest earnings on the loan, at today's known **forward exchange rate** for dollars/pounds, with delivery of sterling funds to the buyer of the forward contract taking place at the end of the year. Essentially, by selling the expected proceeds on the sterling loan forward, at a known (forward FX) exchange rate today, the FI removes the future spot exchange rate uncertainty and thus the uncertainty relating to investment returns on the British loan.

EXAMPLE 15–3	Consider the following transactional steps when the FI hedges its FX risk immediately by sell-ing its expected one-year sterling loan proceeds in the forward FX market (illustrated in panel (c) of Figure 15–1).
Hedging with Forwards	

1. The FI sells $100 million for pounds at the *spot* exchange rate *today* and receives $100 million/1.6 = £62.5 million.

2. The FI then immediately lends the £62.5 million to a British customer at 15 percent for one year.

---

[15] In the background of the previous example was the implicit assumption that the FI was also matching the durations of its foreign assets and liabilities. In our example, it was issuing one-year duration sterling CDs to fund one-year duration sterling loans. Suppose instead that it still had a matched book in size ($100 million) but funded the one-year 15 percent British loans with three-month 11 percent sterling CDs.

$$D_{£A} - D_{£L} = 1 - .25 = .75 \text{ years}$$

Thus, sterling assets have a longer duration than do sterling liabilities.

If British interest rates were to change over the year, the market value of sterling assets would change by more than the market value of sterling liabilities. This effect should be familiar from Chapter 9. More importantly, the FI would no longer be locking in a fixed return by matching in the size of its foreign currency book since it would have to take into account its potential exposure to capital gains and losses on its sterling assets and liabilities due to shocks to British inter-est rates. In essence, an FI is hedged against both foreign exchange rate risk and foreign interest rate risk only if it matches both the size and the durations of its foreign assets and liabilities in a specific currency. For a detailed discussion of this risk, see T. Grammatikos, A. Saunders, and I. Swary, "Returns and Risks of U.S. Bank Foreign Currency Activities," *Journal of Finance* 41 (1986), pp. 670–81; K. C. Mun and G. E. Morgan, "Should Interest and Foreign Exchange Risk Management Be Integrated in International Banking?" Working Paper, Virginia Polytechnic Institute, 1994; and J. J. Choi and E. Elyasiani, "Derivative Exposure and the Interest Rate and Exchange Rate Risks of U.S. Banks," *Journal of Financial Services Research* 12 (1997), pp. 267–86.

[16] An FI could also hedge its on-balance-sheet FX risk by taking off-balance-sheet positions in futures, swaps, and options on foreign currencies. Such strategies are discussed in detail in Chapters 23 through 25.

3. The FI also sells the expected principal and interest proceeds from the sterling loan forward for dollars at today's forward rate for one-year delivery. Let the current forward one-year exchange rate between dollars and pounds stand at $1.55/£1, or at a 5 cent discount to the spot pound; as a percentage discount:

$$(\$1.55 - \$1.60)/\$1.6 = -3.125\%$$

This means that the forward buyer of sterling promises to pay:

$$£62.5 \text{ million } (1.15) \times \$1.55/£ = £71.875 \text{ million} \times \$1.55/£1 = \$111.406 \text{ million}$$

to the FI (the forward seller) in one year when the FI delivers the £71.875 million proceeds of the loan to the forward buyer.

4. In one year, the British borrower repays the loan to the FI plus interest in sterling (£71.875 million).

5. The FI delivers the £71.875 million to the buyer of the one-year forward contract and receives the promised $111.406 million.

Barring the sterling borrower's default on the loan or the forward buyer's reneging on the forward contract, the FI knows from the very beginning of the investment period that it has locked in a guaranteed return on the British loan of:

$$\frac{\$111.406 - \$100}{\$100} = .11406 = 11.406\%$$

Specifically, this return is fully hedged against any dollar/pound exchange rate changes over the one-year holding period of the loan investment. Given this return on British loans, *the overall expected return* on the FI's asset portfolio is:

$$(.5)(.09) + (.5)(.11406) = .10203 \text{ or } 10.203\%$$

Since the cost of funds for the FI's $200 million CDs is an assumed 8 percent, it has been able to lock in a risk-free return spread over the year of 2.203 percent regardless of spot exchange rate fluctuations between the initial foreign (loan) investment and repatriation of the foreign loan proceeds one year later.

Can this profitability of hedging with forwards last? In the preceding example, it is profitable for the FI to increasingly drop domestic loans and invest in hedged foreign U.K. loans, since the hedged dollar return on foreign loans of 11.406 percent is so much higher than 9 percent domestic loans. As the FI seeks to invest more in British loans, it needs to buy more spot sterling. This drives up the spot price of sterling in dollar terms to more than $1.60/£1. In addition, the FI would need to sell more sterling forward (the proceeds of these sterling loans) for dollars, driving the forward rate to below $1.55/£1. The outcome would widen the dollar forward-spot exchange rate spread on sterling, making forward hedged sterling investments less attractive than before. This process would continue until the U.S. cost of FI funds just equals the forward hedged return on British loans. That is, the FI could make no further profits by borrowing in dollars and making forward contract-hedged investments in U.K. loans.

interest rate parity theorem
Relationship in which the discounted spread between domestic and foreign interest rates equals the percentage spread between forward and spot exchange rates.

Interest Rate Parity Theorem

We discussed above that foreign exchange spot market risk can be reduced by entering into forward foreign exchange contracts. In general, spot rates and forward rates for a given currency differ. The forward exchange rate is determined by the spot exchange rate and the interest rate differential between the two countries. The specific relationship that links spot exchange rates, interest rates, and forward exchange rates is described as the **interest rate parity theorem** (IRPT).

Intuitively, the IRPT implies that by hedging in the forward exchange rate market, an investor realizes the same returns whether investing domestically or in a foreign country. This is a so-called no-arbitrage relationship in the sense that the investor cannot make a risk-free return by taking offsetting positions in the domestic and foreign markets. That is, the hedged dollar return on foreign investments just equals the return on domestic investments. The eventual equality between the cost of domestic funds and the hedged return on foreign assets, or the IRPT, can be expressed as:

$$1 + r_t^D = \frac{1}{S_t} \times [1 + r_{ukt}^L] \times F_t$$

Rate on domestic investment = Hedged return on foreign (U.K.) investment where

$1 + r_t^D = 1$ plus the interest rate on CDs for the FI at time t

$S_t = \$/£$ spot exchange rate at time t

$1 + r_{ukt}^L = 1$ plus the interest rate on U.K. loans at time t

$F_t = \$/£$ forward exchange at time t

EXAMPLE 15–4

An Application of Interest Rate Parity Theorem

Suppose $r_t^D = 8$ percent and $r_{ukt}^L = 15$ percent, as in our preceding example. As the FI moves into more British loans, suppose the spot exchange rate for buying pounds rises from $1.60/£1 to $1.63/£1. In equilibrium, the forward exchange rate would have to fall to $1.5308/£1 to eliminate completely the attractiveness of British investments to the FI manager. That is:

$$(1.08) = \left(\frac{1}{1.63}\right)[1.15](1.5308)$$

This is a *no-arbitrage* relationship in the sense that the hedged dollar return on foreign investments just equals the FI's dollar cost of domestic CDs. Rearranging, the IRPT can be expressed as:

$$\frac{r_t^D - r_{ukt}^L}{1 + r_{ukt}^L} \simeq \frac{F_t - S_t}{S_t}$$

$$\frac{.08 - .15}{1.15} \simeq \frac{1.5308 - 1.63}{1.63}$$

$$-.0609 \simeq -.0609$$

That is, the discounted spread between domestic and foreign interest rates is, in equilibrium, equal to the percentage spread between forward and spot exchange rates.

Suppose that in the preceding example, the annual rate on domestic time deposits is 8.1 percent (rather than 8 percent). In this case, it would be profitable for the investor to put excess funds in domestic rather than the U.K. deposits. In fact, the arbitrage opportunity that exists results in a flow of funds out of U.K. time deposits into domestic time deposits. According to the IRPT, this flow of funds would quickly drive up the dollar–British pound exchange rate until the potential profit opportunities from domestic deposits are eliminated. The implication of IRPT is that in a competitive market for deposits, loans, and foreign exchange, the potential profit opportunities from overseas investment for the FI manager are likely to be small and fleeting.[17] Long-term violations of IRPT are likely to occur only if there are major imperfections in international deposit, loan, and other financial markets, including barriers to cross-border financial flows.

---

[17] Note that in a fully competitive market for loans and deposits (and free movement of exchange rates), not only would the domestic deposit rate equal the hedged return on U.K. loans (8 percent in our example), but the domestic loan rate (for risk-free loans) would also be driven into equality with the domestic CD rate, that is, would fall from 9 percent to 8 percent.

TABLE 15–5
Correlations
of Long-Term
Government Bond
Annual Returns in
Local Currencies,
January 1986–
December 1998

Source: A Saunders and
A. Schmeits, "The Determinants of Bank Lending
Rates: Evidence from the
Netherlands and Other
Countries," Working Paper.
Stern School of Business,
New York University,
June 2001.

	United States	United Kingdom	Germany	Netherlands
United States	1.00	.8692	.5882	.6000
United Kingdom	.8692	1.00	.7632	.7705
Germany	.5882	.7632	1.00	.9932
Netherlands	.6000	.7705	.9932	1.00

Multicurrency Foreign Asset-Liability Positions

So far, we have used a one-currency example of a matched or mismatched foreign asset-liability portfolio. Many FIs, including banks, mutual funds, and pension funds, hold multicurrency asset-liability positions. As for multicurrency trading portfolios, diversification across many asset and liability markets can potentially reduce the risk of portfolio returns and the cost of funds. To the extent that domestic and foreign interest rates or stock returns for equities do not move closely together over time, potential gains from asset-liability portfolio diversification can offset the risk of mismatching individual currency asset-liability positions.

Theoretically speaking, the one-period nominal interest rate (r_k) on fixed-income securities in any particular country has two major components. First, the **real interest rate** reflects underlying real sector demands and supplies for funds in that currency. Second, the *expected inflation rate* reflects an extra amount of interest lenders demand from borrowers to compensate the lenders for the erosion in the principal (or real) value of the funds they lend due to inflation in goods prices expected over the period of the loan. Formally:[18]

real interest rate
The difference between
a nominal interest
rate and the expected
rate of inflation.

$$r_k = rr_k + i_k^e$$

where

r_k = Nominal interest rate in country k

rr_k = Real interest rate in country k

i_k^e = Expected one-period inflation rate in country k

If real savings and investment demand and supply pressures, as well as inflationary expectations, are closely linked or integrated across countries, we expect to find that nominal interest rates are highly correlated across financial markets. For example, if, as the result of a strong demand for investment funds, German real interest rates rise, there may be a capital outflow from other countries toward Germany. This may lead to rising real and nominal interest rates in other countries as policymakers and borrowers try to mitigate the size of their capital outflows. On the other hand, if the world capital market is not very well integrated, quite significant nominal and real interest deviations may exist before equilibrating international flows of funds materialize. Foreign asset or liability returns are likely to be relatively weakly correlated, and significant diversification opportunities exist.

Table 15–5 lists the correlations among the returns on long-term government bonds in major bond markets for 1986–1998. Looking at correlations between foreign bond market monthly returns and U.S. bond market monthly returns, you can see that the correlations across bond markets vary from a high of .9932 between Germany and

---

[18] This equation is often called the Fisher equation after the economist who first publicized this hypothesized relationship among nominal rates, real rates, and expected inflation. As shown, we ignore the small cross-product term between the real rate and the expected inflation rate.

the Netherlands to a low of .5882 between the United States and Germany. Further, these correlations are all positive and they are generally quite high, similar to correlations computed for stock returns among the same countries.[19]

Concept Questions

1. The cost of one-year dollar CDs is 8 percent, one-year dollar loans yield 10 percent, and U.K. sterling loans yield 15 percent. The dollar/pound spot exchange is $1.50/£1, and the one-year forward exchange rate is $1.48/£1. Are one-year dollar loans more or less attractive than U.K. sterling loans?
2. What are two ways an FI manager can control FX exposure?
3. Suppose the one-year expected inflation rate in Canada is 8 percent and nominal one-year interest rates are 10 percent. What is the real rate of interest? (2%)

---

[19] From the Fisher relationship, high correlations may be due to high correlations of real interest rates over time and/or inflation expectations.

Summary

This chapter analyzed the sources of FX risk faced by modern FI managers. Such risks arise through mismatching foreign currency trading and/or foreign asset-liability positions in individual currencies. While such mismatches can be profitable if FX forecasts prove correct, unexpected outcomes and volatility can impose significant losses on an FI. They threaten its profitability and, ultimately, its solvency in a fashion similar to interest rate, off-balance-sheet, and technology risks. This chapter discussed possible ways to mitigate such risks, including direct hedging through matched foreign asset-liability books, hedging through forward contracts, and hedging through foreign asset and liability portfolio diversification.

Questions and Problems

1. What are the four FX risks faced by FIs?
2. What is the spot market for FX? What is the forward market for FX? What is the position of being net long in a currency?
3. X-IM Bank has ¥ 14 million in assets and ¥ 23 million in liabilities and has sold ¥ 8 million in foreign currency trading. What is the net exposure for X-IM? For what type of exchange rate movement does this exposure put the bank at risk?
4. What two factors directly affect the profitability of an FI's position in a foreign currency?
5. The following are the foreign currency positions of an FI, expressed in dollars.

Currency	Assets	Liabilities	FX Bought	FX Sold
Swiss francs (SF)	$125,000	$50,000	$10,000	$15,000
British pound (£)	50,000	22,000	15,000	20,000
Japanese yen (¥)	75,000	30,000	12,000	88,000

a. What is the FI's net exposure in Swiss francs?
b. What is the FI's net exposure in British pounds?
c. What is the FI's net exposure in Japanese yen?
d. What is the expected loss or gain if the SF exchange rate appreciates by 1 percent?
e. What is the expected loss or gain if the £ exchange rate appreciates by 1 percent?
f. What is the expected loss or gain if the ¥ exchange rate appreciates by 2 percent?

6. What are the four FX trading activities undertaken by FIs? How do FIs profit from these activities?

7. CB Bank issued $200 million of one-year CDs in Canada at a rate of 6.50 percent. It invested part of this money, $100 million, in the purchase of a one-year bond issued by a Canadian firm at an annual rate of 7 percent. The remaining $100 million was invested in a one-year Brazilian government bond paying an annual interest rate of 8 percent. The exchange rate at the time of the transactions was Brazilian real 1/$.

a. What will be the net return on this $200 million investment in bonds if the exchange rate between the Brazilian real and the Canadian dollar remains the same?

b. What will be the net return on this $200 million investment if the exchange rate changes to real 1.20/$?

c. What will the net return on this $200 million investment be if the exchange rate changes to real 0.80/$?

8. An FI has purchased a 16 million one-year swiss franc loan that pays 12 percent interest annually. The spot rate for swiss franc is SF1.60/$. Sun Bank has funded this loan by accepting a British pound (£)-denominated deposit for the equivalent amount and maturity at an annual rate of 10 percent. The current spot rate of the British pound is $1.60/£.

a. What is the net interest income earned in dollars on this one-year transaction if the spot rates at the end of the year are SF1.70/$ and $1.85/£?

b. What should be the £ to $ spot rate in order for the bank to earn a net interest margin of 4 percent?

c. Does your answer to part (b) imply that the dollar should appreciate or depreciate against the pound?

d. What is the total effect on net interest income and principal of this transaction given the end-of-year spot rates in part (a)?

9. An FI recently made a one-year $10 million loan that pays 10 percent interest annually. The loan was funded with a Swiss francs-denominated one-year deposit at an annual rate of 8 percent. The current spot rate is SF 1.60/$.

a. What will be the net interest income in dollars on the one-year loan if the spot rate at the end of the year is SF 1.58/$?

b. What will be the net interest return on assets?

c. How far can the SF appreciate before the transaction will result in a loss for the FI?

d. What is the total effect on net interest income and principal of this transaction given the end-of-year spot rates in part (a)?

10. What motivates FIs to hedge foreign currency exposures? What are the limitations to hedging foreign currency exposures?

11. What are the two primary methods of hedging FX risk for an FI? What two conditions are necessary to achieve a perfect hedge through on-balance-sheet hedging? What are the advantages and disadvantages of off-balance-sheet hedging in comparison to on-balance-sheet hedging?

12. North Bank has been borrowing in the U.S. markets and lending abroad, thus incurring foreign exchange risk. In a recent transaction, it issued a one-year US$2 million CD at 6 percent and funded a loan in euros at 8 percent. The spot rate for the euro was €1.45/US$ at the time of the transaction.

a. Information received immediately after the transaction closing indicated that the euro will depreciate to €1.47/US$ by year-end. If the information is correct, what will be the realized spread on the loan? What should have been the bank interest rate on the loan to maintain the 2 percent spread?

b. The bank had an opportunity to sell one-year forward euros at €1.46. What would have been the spread on the loan if the bank had hedged forward its foreign exchange exposure?

c. What would have been an appropriate change in loan rates to maintain the 2 percent spread if the bank intended to hedge its exposure using forward contracts?

13. A bank purchases a six-month US$1 million Eurodollar deposit at an annual interest rate of 6.5 percent. It invests the funds in a six-month Swedish krone bond paying 7.5 percent per year. The current spot rate is US$0.18/SK.

a. The six-month forward rate on the Swedish krone is being quoted at US$0.1810/SK. What is the net spread earned on this investment if the bank covers its foreign exchange exposure using the forward market?

b. What forward rate will cause the spread to be only 1 percent per year?

c. Explain how forward and spot rates will both change in response to the increased spread.

d. Why will a bank still be able to earn a spread of 1 percent knowing that interest rate parity usually eliminates arbitrage opportunities created by differential rates?

14. Explain the concept of interest rate parity. What does this concept imply about the long-run profit opportunities from investing in international markets? What market conditions must prevail for the concept to be valid?

15. Assume that annual interest rates are 8 percent in Canada and 4 percent in Japan. An FI can borrow (by issuing CDs) or lend (by purchasing CDs) at these rates. The spot rate is $0.60/¥.

a. If the forward rate is $0.64/¥, how could the FI arbitrage using a sum of $1 million? What is the expected spread?

b. What forward rate will prevent an arbitrage opportunity?

16. How does the lack of perfect correlation of economic returns between international financial markets affect the risk-return opportunities for FIs holding multi-currency assets and liabilities? Refer to Table 15–5. Which country pairings seem to have the highest correlation of returns on long-term government bonds?

17. What is the relationship between the real interest rate, the expected inflation rate, and the nominal interest rate on fixed-income securities in any particular country? Refer to Table 15–5. What factors may be the reasons for the relatively high correlation coefficients?

18. What is economic integration? What impact does the extent of economic integration of international markets have on the investment opportunities for FIs?

19. An FI has $100,000 of net positions outstanding in British pounds (£) and –$30,000 in Swiss francs (SF). The standard deviation of the net positions as a result of exchange rate changes is 1 percent for the SF and 1.3 percent for the £. The correlation coefficient between the changes in exchange rates of the £ and the SF is 0.80.

a. What is the risk exposure to the FI of fluctuations in the £/$ rate?

b. What is the risk exposure to the FI of fluctuations in the SF/$ rate?

c. What is the risk exposure if both the £ and the SF positions are combined?

20. A mutual fund manager is looking for some profitable investment opportunities and observes the following one-year interest rates on government securities and exchange rates: $r_{US} = 12\%$, $r_{UK} = 9\%$, S = US$1.50/£, f = US$1.6/£, where S is the spot exchange rate and f is the forward exchange rate. Which of the two types of government securities would constitute a better investment?

Web Questions

21. Go to the Royal Bank's Web site at **www.royalbank.com** and download RBC's latest annual report. Using the search function in Adobe Acrobat, search the document using the phrase "notional amount of derivatives" and find the table that lists RBC's holdings of derivatives for trading and other purposes. Which derivative had the highest notional amount? Which foreign exchange derivative had the highest notional amount? Search the document using the phrase "trading revenue." How has RBC's trading income from foreign exchange changed in the past year? How does RBC's trading income from foreign exchange compare with its trading income from other sources?

22. The Canadian Foreign Exchange Committee (CFEC) is an organization of the major participants in the foreign exchange market in Canada. Its membership includes the Bank of Canada and the Department of Finance. The CFEC publishes monthly statistics on foreign exchange trading in Canada. Go to the CFEC's Web site at **www.cfec.ca** and click on "FX Volumes and Rates." Download the latest report on FX volumes. How has the market volume in spot and forward contracts changed over the time period? How have the market volumes of foreign exchange swaps changed? Has the total Canadian dollar foreign exchange market volume increased or decreased over the time period?

23. Go to the FDIC Web site at **www.fdic.gov** and find the most recent values for foreign exchange trading revenue at J.P. Morgan Chase and Citigroup using the following steps. Click on "Analysts." Click on "Statistics on Depository Institutions (SDI)." Click on "Enter SDI." Click on "ID Home." Click on "Find Bank Holding Cos." At "*BHC Name:*," enter "Citigroup" then click on "find." Under "BHC ID," click on "*1951350.*" Under "ID Report Selections:" select "Income and Expenses," then click on "Generate Report." Click on "*Tradingaccount gains & fees.*" This will bring the file onto your computer that contains revenue from foreign exchange exposures. Repeat this process for J.P. Morgan Chase and BHC ID *1039502.* Compare the FX activities of RBC with J.P. Morgan Chase and Citigroup. How does FX exposure and management differ cross-border?

Sovereign Risk

In this chapter, we examine sovereign risk, also called country risk, and discuss:

▸ credit risk versus sovereign risk

▸ country risk evaluation models, and

▸ sovereign debt markets

INTRODUCTION

www.worldbank.org

www.imf.org

sovereign risk
The risk of a foreign government's limiting or preventing domestic borrowers in its jurisdiction from repaying amounts owed to external lenders.

In the 1970s, major international banks rapidly expanded their loans to Eastern European, Latin American, and other less developed countries (LDCs). This was largely to meet these countries' demand for funds beyond those provided by the World Bank and the International Monetary Fund (IMF), to aid their development, and to allow the international banks to recycle "petrodollar" funds from huge U.S. dollar holders such as Saudi Arabia, dollars that helped to create the LIBOR market. Making LDC loans resulted in **sovereign risk** for the banks, the risk of a foreign government's limiting or preventing domestic borrowers in its jurisdiction from repaying the principal and interest on debt owed to external lenders. In many cases, these loans appear to have been made with little judgment regarding the credit quality of the sovereign country in which the borrower resided or consideration as to whether that body was a government-sponsored organization (e.g., Pemex, the state-owned Mexican oil company) or a private corporation.

loan loss provision
An amount deducted from income and used to a write-off bad loans as the losses are realized.

www.osfi-bsif.gc.ca

www.cibc.com

The debt repayment problems of Poland and other Eastern European countries at the beginning of the 1980s and the debt moratoria announced by the Mexican and Brazilian governments in the fall of 1982 had a major and long-lasting impact on the banks' balance sheets and profits. In 1987, the newly-formed Office of the Superintendent of Financial Institutions (OSFI) required Canadian banks to increase their **loan loss provisions** to 30 to 40 percent of their loans outstanding to 34 countries, including Mexico, Argentina, and Brazil. The Canadian banks made combined provisions of $8.5 billion on loans of $20.5 billion. The net dollar exposure of $12 billion ($20.5 − $8.5 billion) represented 66 percent of the big six Canadian banks' common equity. In 1989, Canadian Imperial Bank of Commerce (CIBC), which held $1.17 billion in non-Mexican LDC debt, increased its loan-loss provisions by $525 million and took an after-tax charge to its 1989 earnings of $300 million. CIBC also restructured its Mexican debt which totaled $604 million at the time. By comparison, the U.S. banks' average exposure to LDC debt in 1989 was 120 percent of total equity. Citicorp (now Citigroup) alone set aside US$5 billion in loan loss reserves after Brazil declared a debt moratorium on its US$68 billion commercial bank debt.[1]

Notwithstanding their experience with LDC lending a decade earlier, international FIs began once again to invest considerable amounts in emerging market countries in

---

[1] See C. Melnbardis, "Big banks' red ink will be black again soon, analysts say," *The Gazette*, Montreal, August 24, 1987, p. B.5; S. Santedicola, "Bank profits up despite increase in debt reserves," *Financial Post*, Toronto, September 12, 1988, p.27; and "Canadian Bank Boosts Provisions for Losses on Its LDC Lending," *The Wall Street Journal*, October 16, 1989, p. 1.

the late 1980s to early 1990s. Rather than making loans, however, the FIs concentrated their investments in debt and equity claims.[2] However, with rising trade deficits and declining foreign exchange reserves, as the result of an overvalued peso, Mexico devalued the peso on December 29, 1994.[3] The Mexican devaluation—as with the Mexican loan moratorium 12 years earlier—had devastating short-term repercussions on the Mexican capital markets as well as on other emerging markets. The run on emerging market debt and equity markets was ameliorated only when U.S. President Clinton, along with the IMF, put together a US$50 billion international aid package, providing loan guarantees over three to five years to help restructure the debt. The IMF and the Bank for International Settlements (BIS) provided loans of US$17.8 billion and $10 billion, respectively. Mexican oil revenues were promised as collateral for the U.S. financial guarantees and, by January 1997, the Mexican economy had improved and the Mexican government paid back all of its loans in full to the U.S. government.[4]

Emerging markets in Asia faltered in 1997 when an economic and financial crisis in Thailand, a relatively small country in terms of financial markets, produced worldwide reactions. In early July, the devaluation of the Thai baht resulted in contagious devaluations of currencies throughout Southeast Asia (including those of Indonesia, Singapore, Malaysia, and South Korea) and the devaluations eventually spread to South America and Russia. Hong Kong, who pegged its currency to the U.S. dollar, was forced to take precautionary action by increasing interest rates and using China's foreign currency reserves to stabilize the Hong Kong dollar. In Russia, financial speculation was fueled in part by the belief that the Russian government would not default on its bonds or let any of its major companies default on theirs.[5]

Possibly as a reaction to the events (losses) experienced with the Latin American countries in the 1980s or to improved sovereign risk assessment techniques,[6] (see later discussion) North American FIs held their exposure in Asia in the mid- and late-1990s to approximately one-third of the investment made by Japanese and European banks. As can be seen in Figure 16–1, in December 1997, foreign banks had US$381 billion in loans and other debt outstanding to emerging market Asian countries with 10 percent (US$38.9 billion) to Canadian and U.S. banks. In 1999, North American banks wrote off hundreds of millions of dollars in losses as they accepted a payoff of less than five cents on the dollar for Russian securities.

As Asian currencies collapsed, financial institutions in countries such as Japan and Hong Kong failed or were forced to merge or restructure. Investment bank power-houses such as Yamaichi Securities, Japan's fourth-largest securities firm, and Peregrine Investment Holding, Ltd., one of Hong Kong's largest investment banks, failed as currency values fell. Commercial banks in Japan and Hong Kong that had lent heavily to other Southeast Asian countries failed in record numbers as well. Estimates of problem loans held by Japanese banks totaled US$577.5 billion in September 1997, compared with US$210 billion in early August 1997.[7] Financial support given to these

---

[2] The Basel I capital regulations came into effect for internationally active banks in the early 1990s, reducing the returns on commercial loans that required 100 percent capital. This is an example of how regulations can influence international financial markets. We discuss Basel I and II in more detail in Chapter 20.

[3] Mexico's foreign exchange reserves fell from US$25 billion at the end of 1993 to US$6 billion at the end of 1994.

[4] See "The Mexican Rescue Plan," *The New York Times*, February 1, 1995, p. 1 and "Mexico Will Close Out Its Debt to U.S.," *The Wall Street Journal*, January 16, 1997, p. A10.

[5] See T. L. O'Brien, "Risk Takers' Safety Net: From Rock 'n' Roll to Russia: Having a Likely Rescuer Fosters Moral Hazard," *The New York Times,* May 1, 1999, p. B11.

[6] See N. Kochan, "Controversial Calls: Credit Rating Agencies May Be Too Negative on Latin American Sovereign Risk Following Their Misjudgements in Asia and Russia," *LatinFinance,* November 1999, pp. 37–39.

[7] See "Japan Plans Crackdown on Bad Loans," *The Wall Street Journal,* December 26, 1997, p. A5.

FIGURE 16–1   Foreign Banks' Share of Asian Debt in December 1997, excluding Singapore and Hong Kong

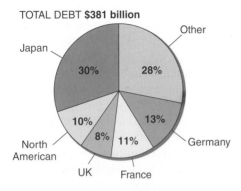

TOTAL DEBT **$381 billion**

Other 28%
Japan 30%
North American 10%
UK 8%
France 11%
Germany 13%

Source: Adapted from "Foreign Banks' Share of Asian Debt in June 1997," Basel Committee on Banking Supervision, IAIS and IOSCO's Joint Forum. Original text available free of charge at www.bis.org, www.iosco.org, and www.iaisweb.org

TABLE 16–1   Statistics on External Debt Outstanding, Argentina, June 2003

Type of Debt	Amount Outstanding (in millions of U.S. dollars)
Bank loans	25,052
Debt securities issued abroad	84,740
Brady bonds	6,846
Multilateral claims	30,798
Total	147,436

Source: World Bank, Joint BIS-IMF-OECD-World Bank Statistics on External Debt, November 2003. www.worldbank.org

www.scotiabank.com

MYRAs
Multiyear restructuring agreements, the official terminology for a sovereign loan rescheduling.

Brady bonds
Bonds issued by an LDC that are swapped for an outstanding loan to that LDC.

countries by the International Monetary Fund (IMF) and the U.S., Japanese, and European governments enabled the banks largely to avoid the full extent of the possible losses. Nevertheless, Indonesia had to declare a moratorium on some of its debt repayments, while Russia defaulted on payments on its short-term government bonds.

Most recently, in the early 2000s, concerns were raised about the ability of Argentina and Turkey to meet their debt obligations and the effects this would have on other emerging market countries.[8] For example, in December 2001, Argentina defaulted on US$130 billion in government-issued debt, and in 2002, passed legislation that led to defaults on US$30 billion of corporate debt owed to foreign creditors. The situation continued to deteriorate, and in November 2002 Argentina's government paid only US$79.5 million of an US$805 million repayment (that had become more than 30 days delinquent) due to the World Bank. Table 16–1 shows the total external debt outstanding for Argentina as of June 2003. In an attempt to resolve the country's problem and restructure its debt, in January 2004 Argentina's government set up a voluntary register for creditors holding the country's defaulted bonds. However, as Argentina pulled out of its crisis, it was offering debtholders only 25 cents on the dollar for their holdings.[9]

In 2002, the Bank of Nova Scotia (BNS) sold its subsidiary in Argentina and left a country where it had done business for 40 years, taking an after-tax charge against earnings of $540 million. Thus, while international lending by FIs provides the focus of this chapter, sovereign risk for FIs also comes from their operations in foreign countries that expose them to an investment risk that can be classified as an equity risk in a foreign subsidiary. We cover this type of geographic diversification in Chapter 22.

These recurring experiences confirm the importance of assessing the country or sovereign risk of a borrowing country before making lending or other investment decisions such as buying foreign bonds or equities. We next look at measures of sovereign risk that FI managers can use as screening devices before making loans or other investment decisions. Appendix A to this chapter (available on page 718 of this book) looks at the ways FIs have managed sovereign risk problems, including entering into **multiyear restructuring agreements (MYRAS)**, debt-equity swaps, loan sales, and **Brady bond** conversions.

---

[8] See "Gloom Over the River Plate," *The Economist,* July 14, 2001, pp. 11, 12; "How the Bug Can Spread," *The Economist,* July 21, 2001, pp. 20, 21; "Austerity or Bust," *The Economist,* July 21, 2001, pp. 29, 30; "Analysts Worry of Ripple Effect in Argentina's Latest Debt Plan," *The New York Times,* November 3, 2001, pp. C1; and "Experts See Record Default in Argentine Debt Revision," *The New York Times,* November 3, 2001, pp. A4.

[9] See "After Huge Default, Argentina Squeezes Small Bondholders," *The Wall Street Journal*, January 14, 2004, p. A1.

CREDIT RISK VERSUS SOVEREIGN RISK

rescheduling
Changing the contractual terms of a loan, such as its maturity and interest payments.

To understand the difference between the sovereign risk and the credit risk on a loan or a bond, consider what happens to a domestic firm that refuses to repay, or is unable to repay, its loans. The lender would probably seek to work out the loan with the borrower by **rescheduling** its promised interest and principal payments on the loan into the future. Ultimately, continued inability or unwillingness to pay would likely result in bankruptcy proceedings and eventual liquidation of the firm's assets. Consider next a dollar loan made by an FI to a private Indonesian corporation. Suppose that this first-class corporation always maintained its debt repayments in the past; however, the Indonesian economy and the Indonesian government's reserve position are in bad shape. As a result, the Indonesian government refuses to allow any further debt repayment to be made in dollars to outside creditors. This puts the Indonesian borrower automatically into default even though, when viewed on its own, the company is a good credit risk. The Indonesian government's decision is a *sovereign* or *country risk event* in large part independent of the credit standing of the individual loan to the borrower. Further, unlike the situation in Canada, where the lender might seek a legal remedy in the local bankruptcy courts, there is no international bankruptcy court to which the lender can take the Indonesian government. That is, the lender's legal remedies to offset a sovereign country's default or moratoria decisions are very limited.

This situation suggests that making a lending decision to a party residing in a foreign country is a *two-step* decision. First, lenders must assess the underlying *credit quality* of the borrower, as it would do for a normal domestic loan, including setting an appropriate credit risk premium or credit limits (see Chapter 11). Second, lenders must assess the *sovereign risk quality* of the country in which the borrower resides. Should the credit risk or quality of the borrower be assessed as good but the sovereign risk be assessed as bad, the lender should not make the loan. When making international lending or foreign bond investment decisions, an FI manager should consider sovereign risk above considerations of private credit risk.

Concept Questions

1. What is the difference between credit risk and sovereign risk?
2. In deciding to lend to a party residing in a foreign country, what two considerations must an FI weigh?

DEBT REPUDIATION VERSUS DEBT RESCHEDULING

A good deal of misunderstanding exists regarding the nature of a sovereign risk event. In general, a sovereign country's (negative) decisions on its debt obligations or the obligations of its public and private organizations may take two forms: repudiation and rescheduling.

repudiation
Outright cancelation of all current and future debt obligations by a borrower.

Debt repudiation. **Repudiation** is an outright cancelation of all a borrower's current and future foreign debt and equity obligations. Since World War II, only China (1949), Cuba (1961), and North Korea (1964) have followed this course.[10] The low level of repudiations partly reflects recent international policy toward the poorest countries in the world. Specifically, in the fall of 1996,

---

[10] With respect to equity, repudiation can include direct nationalization of private sector assets.

www.worldbank.org

www.imf.org

the World Bank, the International Monetary Fund, and major governments around the world agreed to forgive the external debt of the world's poorest, most heavily indebted poor countries (HIPCs). The HIPC initiative broke new ground by removing debt obligations from countries that pursue economic and social reform targeted at measurable poverty reduction. By 2003, 6 countries had received irrevocable debt relief under the HIPC initiative, and an additional 20 countries had begun to receive interim debt relief. Together, these countries had their outstanding debt reduced by US$40 billion. About 35 countries are expected to ultimately qualify for HIPC assistance. Repudiations on debt obligations were far more common before World War II, as we discuss later in this chapter.

Debt rescheduling. Rescheduling has been the most common form of sovereign risk event. Specifically, a country (or a group of creditors in that country) declares a moratorium or delay on its current and future debt obligations and then seeks to ease credit terms through a rescheduling of the contractual terms, such as debt maturity and/or interest rates. Such delays may relate to the principal and/or the interest on the debt (South Korea in January 1998 and Argentina in 2001[11] are recent examples of debt reschedulings).

One of the interesting questions in the provision of international financial services is why we have generally witnessed international debtor problems (of other than the poorest highly indebted countries) being met by reschedulings in the post-World War II period, whereas a large proportion of debt problems were met with repudiations before World War II. A fundamental reason given for this difference in behaviour is that until recently, most postwar international debt has been in *bank loans,* while before the war it was mostly in the form of *foreign bonds.*[12]

International loan rather than bond financing makes rescheduling more likely for reasons related to the inherent nature of international loan versus bond contracts. First, there are generally fewer FIs in any international lending syndicate compared with thousands of geographically dispersed bondholders. The relatively small number of lending parties makes renegotiation or rescheduling easier and less costly than when a borrower or a bond trustee has to get thousands of bondholders to agree to changes in the contractual terms on a bond.[13]

Second, many international loan syndicates comprise the same groups of FIs, which adds to FI cohesiveness in loan renegotiations and increases the probability of consensus being reached. For example, Citigroup was chosen the lead bank negotiator by other banks in five major loan reschedulings in the 1980s,[14] as well as in both the Mexican and South Korean reschedulings. J. P. Morgan Chase is the lead bank involved in the recent loan reschedulings of Argentina.

Third, many international loan contracts contain cross-default provisions that state that if a country were to default on just one of its loans, all the other loans it has outstanding would automatically be put into default as well. Cross-default clauses prevent a country from selecting a group of weak lenders for special default treatment and make the outcome of any individual loan default decision potentially very costly for the borrower.

---

[11] See "Argentina Plans Debt Swap in Billions, Delaying Payments," *The New York Times,* May 25, 2001, p. C4; and "Cavallo Pawns an Uncertain Future," *The Economist,* June 9, 2001, p. 64.

[12] See B. Eichengreen and R. Portes, "The Anatomy of Financial Crises," in *Threats to International Financial Stability,* ed. R. Portes and A. K. Swoboda (Cambridge: Cambridge University Press, 1987), pp. 10–15.

[13] In January 1998 the rescheduling of South Korean loans required the agreement of just over 100 banks.

[14] See T. Grammatikos and A. Saunders, "Additions to Bank Loan Loss Reserves," *Journal of Monetary Economics* 25 (1990), pp. 289–304.

A further set of reasons rescheduling is likely to occur on loans relates to the behaviour of governments and regulators in lending countries. One of the overwhelming public policy goals in recent years has been to prevent large FI failures in countries such as Canada, the United States, Japan, Germany, and the United Kingdom. Thus, government-organized rescue packages for LDCs arranged either directly or indirectly via World Bank/IMF guarantees or the Brady Plan are ways of subsidizing large FIs and/or reducing the incentives for LDCs to default on their loans. To the extent that banks are viewed as special (see Chapter 1), domestic governments may seek political and economic avenues to reduce the probability of foreign sovereign borrowers defaulting on or repudiating their debt contracts. Governments and regulators appear to view the social costs of default on international bonds as less worrisome than those on loans. The reason is that bond defaults are likely to be more geographically and numerically dispersed in their effects, and bondholders do not play a key role in the provision of liquidity services to the domestic and world economy. It should also be noted that the tendency of the IMF/governments to bail out countries and thus, indirectly, FI lenders such as the major North American, Japanese, and European FIs has not gone without criticism. Specifically, it has been argued that unless FIs and countries are ultimately punished, they will have no incentives to avoid similar risks in the future. This is one reason sovereign debt crises keep recurring.

Concept Questions

1. What is the difference between debt repudiation and debt rescheduling?
2. Provide four reasons we see sovereign loans being rescheduled rather than repudiated.

COUNTRY RISK EVALUATION

In evaluating sovereign risk, an FI can use alternative methods, varying from the highly quantitative to the very qualitative. Moreover, as in domestic credit analysis, an FI may rely on outside evaluation services or develop its own internal evaluation or sovereign risk models. Of course, to make a final assessment, an FI may use many models and sources together because different measures of country risk are not mutually exclusive.

We begin by looking at three country risk assessment services available to outside investors and FIs: the *Euromoney Index,* the *Economist Intelligence Unit,* and the *Institutional Investor Index.* We then look at ways an FI manager might make internal risk assessments regarding sovereign risk.

Outside Evaluation Models

The Euromoney Index

LIBOR
The London Interbank Offered Rate; the rate charged on prime interbank loans on the Euromarket.

When originally published in 1979, the *Euromoney Index* was based on the spread in the Euromarket of the required interest rate on that country's debt over the London Interbank Offered Rate (**LIBOR**), adjusted for the volume and maturity of the issue. More recently, this has been replaced by an index based on a large number of economic and political factors weighted subjectively according to their perceived relative importance in determining country risk problems.

The Economist Intelligence Unit

www.economist.com

A sister index to *The Economist,* The Economist Intelligence Unit (EIU) rates country risk by combined economic and political risk on a 100 (maximum) point scale.

FIGURE 16–2

The Economist
Intelligence Unit
Country Risk
Ratings

Source: EIU ViewsWire, New
York, June and July, 2005
www.eiu.com

The higher the number, the worse the sovereign risk rating of the country. The EIU country risk ratings reported in 2005 are presented in Figure 16–2.

The Institutional Investor Index

Normally published twice a year, this index is based on surveys of the loan officers of major multinational banks. These officers give subjective scores regarding the credit quality of given countries. Originally, the score was based on 10, but since 1980 it has been based on 100, with a score of 0 indicating certainty of default and 100 indicating no possibility of default. The *Institutional Investor* then weighs the scores received from the officers surveyed by the exposure of each bank to the country in question. For a sampling of the *Institutional Investor's* country credit ratings as of September 2003, see Table 16–2. For example, in September 2003, loan officers around the world assessed Switzerland as the country with the least chance of default, while they assessed Somalia as the country with the highest chance of default.

TABLE 16–2
Institutional Investor's 2003 Country Credit Ratings

Source: *Institutional Investor,* September 2003. www. institutionalinvestor.com

Rank			Institutional		
March 2003	September 2003	Country	Investor Credit Rating	Six-Month Change	One-Year Change
1	1	Switzerland	94.0	−1.3	−2.2
2	2	Luxembourg	93.3	−1.0	−1.4
5	3	Norway	92.9	0.1	−0.2
3	4	United States	92.8	−0.5	−0.3
5	5	United Kingdom	92.3	−0.5	−1.8
4	6	Netherlands	92.2	−1.0	−2.4
8	7	France	91.7	−0.5	−1.2
10	8	Denmark	91.0	0.7	0.5
12	9	Finland	90.6	0.7	−0.5
9	*10	Austria	90.3	−0.3	−0.4
11	*11	Canada	90.3	0.4	0.9
13	12	Sweden	89.3	0.2	0.0
15	13	Ireland	87.5	0.6	−1.0
14	14	Belgium	87.2	−1.1	−2.3
7	15	Germany	86.8	−5.5	−7.2
16	16	Spain	85.7	−0.4	−1.3
19	17	Australia	84.3	1.0	−0.2
17	18	Singapore	84.2	−1.4	−1.9
18	19	Italy	83.1	−1.2	−3.1
22	20	New Zealand	81.1	1.2	−0.1
21	21	Portugal	80.4	−1.2	−3.8
34	22	Kuwait	79.2	15.6	16.3
20	23	Japan	77.2	−4.8	−5.5
24	24	Taiwan	74.0	−0.3	−0.7
23	25	Greece	73.1	−1.5	−2.2
25	26	Iceland	72.4	−0.8	−1.2
30	27	Slovenia	69.2	2.8	0.8
27	28	South Korea	68.5	0.3	2.9
26	29	Hong Kong	67.8	−0.8	0.1
33	30	Czech Republic	65.6	1.9	1.6
122	*144	Serbia and Montenegro	16.1	−1.4	−0.4
137	*145	Ethiopia	16.1	1.4	0.1
129	*146	Haiti	15.8	−0.5	1.0
—	*147	Madagascar	15.8	—	—
121	148	Côte d'Ivoire	15.7	−2.0	−2.8
135	149	Zambia	15.3	−0.4	−0.5
131	150	Niger	14.7	−1.4	1.1
136	151	Chad	14.4	−0.8	−0.4
141	152	Tajikistan	14.3	1.2	1.6
—	153	Comoros	13.9	—	—
—	154	São Tomé and Principe	13.6	—	—
140	155	Myanmar	13.5	0.4	−0.3
—	156	East Timor	13.1	—	—
—	157	Central African Republic	12.8	—	—
146	158	Congo Republic	12.6	2.2	2.1
139	159	Cuba	12.3	−1.4	−3.4
—	160	Eritrea	12.0	—	—

(continued)

TABLE 16–2
(*continued*)

Rank		Country	Institutional Investor Credit Rating	Six-Month Change	One-Year Change
March 2003	September 2003				
144	161	Zimbabwe	11.0	0.2	−0.9
—	162	Guinea–Bissau	10.6	—	—
145	*163	Sudan	10.5	0.0	0.8
142	*164	Burundi	10.5	−0.8	−0.8
147	165	Sierra Leone	8.5	−0.7	−1.1
150	166	Iraq	8.4	0.4	−1.8
—	167	Rwanda	8.2	—	—
148	168	Afghanistan	7.6	−1.3	0.7
151	169	North Korea	7.5	0.8	0.2
149	170	Democratic Republic of the Congo	7.3	−1.0	−1.4
143	171	Liberia	6.6	−4.3	−3.0
—	172	Somalia	6.5	—	—
Global average rating			39.6	−2.5	−2.9

*Order determined by actual results before rounding.

Internal Evaluation Models

Statistical Models

By far, the most common approach to evaluating sovereign country risk among large FIs has been to develop sovereign country risk-scoring models based on key economic ratios for each country, similar to the domestic credit risk-scoring models discussed in Chapter 11.

An FI analyst begins by selecting a set of macro- and microeconomic variables and ratios that might be important in explaining a country's probability of rescheduling. Then the analyst uses past data on rescheduling and nonrescheduling countries to see which variables best discriminate between those countries that rescheduled their debt and those that did not. This helps the analyst identify a set of key variables that best explain rescheduling and a group of weights indicating the relative importance of these variables. For example, domestic credit risk analysis can employ discriminant analysis to calculate a Z score rating of the probability of corporate bankruptcy. Similarly, in sovereign risk analysis we can develop a Z score to measure the probability that a country will reschedule (see Chapter 11 for discussion of the Z score model).[15]

The first step in this country risk analysis (CRA) is to pick a set of variables that may be important in explaining rescheduling probabilities. In many cases analysts select more than 40 variables. Here we identify the variables most commonly included in sovereign risk probability models.[16]

---

[15] Alternatively, analysts could employ linear probability, logit, or probit models.

[16] See, for example, K. Saini and P. Bates, "Statistical Techniques for Determining Debt-Servicing Capacity for Developing Countries: Analytical Review of the Literature and Further Empirical Results," Federal Reserve Bank of New York Research Paper no. 7818, September 1978, for an early attempt in using statistical models to predict sovereign risk problems. More recent examples can be found in A. Saunders and L. Allen, *Credit Risk Measurement: New Approaches to Value at Risk and Other Paradigms,* 2nd ed. (New York: John, Wiley and Sons, 2002). See also C. W. Calomiris, "Lessons from the Tequila Crisis for Successful Financial Liberalization," *Journal of Banking and Finance* 23 (1999), pp. 1457–61; F. Drudi and R. Giordano, "Default Risk and Optimal Debt Management," *Journal of Banking and Finance* 24 (2000), pp. 861–91; F. Ferri, L. Liu, and F. Majnoni, "The Role of Rating Agency Assessments in Less Developed Countries: Impact of the Proposed Basel Guidelines," *Journal of Banking and Finance* 25 (2001), pp. 115–48; and R. Brooks, R. W. Faff, and D. Hillier, "The National Market Impact of Sovereign Rating Changes, "*Journal of Banking and Finance* 28 (2004), pp. 233–50.

TABLE 16–3
Debt Service Ratio
for Various
Countries, 2003

Source: *The Economist* Web
site, December 2003.
www.economist.com

Country	Debt Service Ratio %	Country	Debt Service Ratio %
Argentina	376	Malaysia	57
Brazil	531	Philippines	145
Chile	221	Poland	203
China	56	Russia	142
Colombia	347	Singapore	10
Costa Rica	100	South Korea	76
Hong Kong	30	Turkey	354
Indonesia	224		

The Debt Service Ratio (DSR)

$$DSR = \frac{\text{Interest plus amortization on debt}}{\text{Exports}}$$

An LDC's exports are its primary way of generating hard currencies. The larger the debt repayments in hard currencies are in relation to export revenues, the greater the probability that the country will have to reschedule its debt. Thus, there should be a *positive* relationship between the size of the **debt service ratio** and the probability of rescheduling. Table 16–3 shows the scheduled debt service ratios of various countries. Note that several countries are servicing debt obligations at several times the level of their exports (e.g., Argentina's debt service ratio is 376 percent, Brazil's debt service ratio is 531 percent).

debt service ratio
The ratio of a country's interest and amortization obligations to the value of its exports.

The Import Ratio (IR)

$$IR = \frac{\text{Total imports}}{\text{Total foreign exchange reserves}}$$

Many LDCs must import manufactured goods since their inadequate infrastructure limits their domestic production. In times of famine, even food becomes a vital import. To pay for imports, the LDC must run down its stock of hard currencies—its foreign exchange reserves. The greater its need for imports—especially vital imports—the quicker a country can be expected to deplete its foreign exchange reserves. For example, Chile's import ratio was 113 percent in 2003, implying that Chile imported more goods and services than it had foreign reserves to pay for. Since the first use of reserves is to buy vital imports, the larger the ratio of imports to foreign exchange reserves, the higher the probability that the LDC will have to reschedule its debt repayments. This is so because these countries generally view repaying foreign debtholders as being less important than supplying vital goods to the domestic population. Thus, the **import ratio** and the probability of rescheduling should be *positively* related.

import ratio
The ratio of a country's imports to its total foreign currency reserves.

Investment Ratio (INVR)

$$INVR = \frac{\text{Real investment}}{\text{GNP}}$$

The **investment ratio** measures the degree to which a country is allocating resources to real investment in factories, machines, and so on, rather than to consumption. The higher this ratio, the more productive the economy should be in the future and the lower the probability that the country would need to reschedule its debt: This implies a *negative* relationship between *INVR* and the probability of rescheduling.

investment ratio
The ratio of a country's real investment to its GNP.

An opposing view is that a higher investment ratio allows an LDC to build up its investment infrastructure. The higher ratio puts it in a stronger bargaining position with external creditors since the LDC would rely less on funds in the future and would be less concerned about future threats of credit rationing by FIs should it request a rescheduling. This view argues for a *positive* relationship between the investment ratio and the probability of rescheduling, especially if the LDC invests heavily in import competing industries.[17] Just before the collapse of their economies (in the mid-1990s) investment ratios in Thailand and Malaysia were 34 and 26 percent, respectively, while Brazil's investment ratio was close to zero. More recently, the investment ratio in the United Kingdom averaged 12 percent in the early 2000s.

Variance of Export Revenue (VAREX)

$$VAREX = \sigma_{ER}^2$$

An LDC's export revenues may be highly variable as a result of two risk factors. *Quantity risk* means that the production of the raw commodities the LDC sells abroad—for example, coffee or sugar—is subject to periodic gluts and shortages. *Price risk* means that the international dollar prices at which the LDC can sell its exportable commodities are subject to high volatility as world demand for and supply of a commodity, such as copper, vary. The more volatile an LDC's export earnings, the less certain creditors can be that at any time in the future it will be able to meet its repayment commitments. That is, there should be a *positive* relationship between σ_{ER}^2 and the probability of rescheduling.

Domestic Money Supply Growth (MG)

$$MG = \frac{\Delta M}{M}$$

The faster the domestic growth rate of an LDC's money supply [$\Delta M/M$, which measures the change in the money supply (ΔM) over its initial level (M)], the higher the domestic inflation rate and the weaker that country's currency becomes in domestic and international markets.[18] When a country's currency loses credibility as a medium of exchange, real output is often adversely impacted, and the country must increasingly rely on hard currencies for both domestic and international payments, the most recent case being Argentina in 2003. These inflation, output, and payment effects suggest a *positive* relationship between domestic money supply growth and the probability of rescheduling.

We can summarize the expected relationships among these five key economic variables and the probability of rescheduling (p) for any country as:

$$p = f(DSR, IR, INVR, VAREX, MG \dots)$$
$$+ \quad ++ \text{ or } - \quad + \quad +$$

After selecting the key variables, the FI manager normally places countries into two groups or populations:

P_1 = Bad (reschedulers)

P_2 = Good (nonreschedulers)

---

[17] See S. Acharya and I. Diwan, "Debt Conversion Schemes of Debtor Countries as a Signal of Creditworthiness: Theory and Evidence," *International Economic Review* 34 (1993), pp. 795–815.

[18] The purchasing power parity (PPP) theorem argues that high relative inflation rates lead to a country's currency depreciating in value against other currencies.

Then the manager uses a statistical methodology such as discriminant analysis (see Chapter 11) to identify which of these variables best discriminates between the population of rescheduling borrowers and that of nonrescheduling borrowers. Once the key variables and their relative importance or weights have been identified, the discriminant function can classify as good or bad current sovereign loans or sovereign loan applicants using currently observed values for the *DSR, IR*, and so on. Again, the methodology is very similar to the credit scoring models discussed in Chapter 11.

Problems with Statistical CRA Models

Even though this methodology has been one of the most common forms of CRA used by FIs, it is fraught with problems. This section discusses six major problems in using traditional CRA models and techniques. We do not imply in any way that these techniques should not be used but instead indicate that FI managers should be aware of the potential pitfalls in using such models.

Measurement of Key Variables Very often the FI manager's information on a country's DSR or IR is out of date because of delays in collection of data and errors in measurement. For example, the Bank for International Settlements (BIS) collects aggregate loan volume data for countries; frequently, this information is six months old or more before it is published. This example illustrates the problem: the Bank of Nova Scotia may know today the current amount of its outstanding loans to Indonesia, but it is unlikely to know with any great degree of accuracy Indonesia's total outstanding external loans and debt with every other lender in the world.

www.bis.org

Moreover, these measurement problems are compounded by forecast errors when managers use these statistical models to predict the probabilities of rescheduling with future or projected values of key variables such as *DSR* and *IR*.

Population Groups Usually, analysts seek to find variables that distinguish between only two possible outcomes: reschedulers and nonreschedulers. In actuality, a finer distinction may be necessary—for example, a distinction between those countries announcing a moratorium on only interest payments and those announcing a moratorium on both interest and principal payments. Thus, Peru, which in the early 1980s limited its total debt repayments to a small proportion of its export revenues, should be viewed as a higher-risk country than a country that delayed the interest payments on its debt for a few months because of short-term foreign exchange shortages.

Political Risk Factors Traditionally, CRA statistical credit-scoring models incorporate only economic variables. While there may be a strong correlation between an economic variable such as money supply growth and rescheduling, the model may not capture very well purely political risk events such as *strikes, elections, corruption,* and *revolutions.* For example, the election of a strongly nationalist politician may reduce the probability of repayment and increase the probability of rescheduling. Similarly, a considerable part of the debt repayment and banking crisis problems in Southeast Asia has been attributed to cronyism and corruption.

www.heritage.org

Since 1995, the Index of Economic Freedom (compiled by the Heritage Foundation) has provided a measure that summarizes the economic freedom of over 160 countries in the world. The Heritage Foundation defines economic freedom as "the absence of government coercion or constraint on the production, distribution, or consumption of goods and services beyond the extent necessary for citizens to protect and maintain liberty itself."[19] The index includes measures of trade policy, fiscal burden of govern-

---

[19] See *2004 Index of Economic Freedom* (Washington, DC: Heritage Foundation, 2004), Chapter 5, p. 50.

TABLE 16–4
Economic Freedom Index for Various Countries

Source: The Heritage Foundation Web site, January 2005. www.heritage.org

Country	Overall Economic Freedom Index
Hong Kong	1.35
Singapore	1.60
Luxembourg	1.63
Estonia	1.65
New Zealand	1.70
Ireland	1.70
United Kingdom	1.75
Australia	1.79
United States	1.85
Canada	1.91
Turkmenistan	4.00
Haiti	4.04
Venezuela	4.09
Uzbekistan	4.10
Cuba	4.29
Laos	4.33
Zimbabwe	4.36
Libya	4.40
Burma	4.60
North Korea	5.00

ment, government intervention in the economy, monetary policy, capital flows and foreign investment, banking and finance, wages and prices, prosperity rights, regulation, and black market activities. Each country is assigned a score ranging from 1 to 5 for each of the 10 individual factors as well as an overall score based on the average of these factors. A score of 1 signifies policies most conducive to economic freedom; a score of 5, policies least conducive to economic freedom. Table 16–4 lists the economic freedom index for the highest- and lowest-rated countries as of 2005.

An alternative quantitative measure of country risk is the Corruption Perceptions Index produced by Transparency International. Figure 16–3 shows the corruption index for 18 out of 133 countries covered for 2004. The least corrupt countries are assigned a score of 10, while the most corrupt countries are assigned a score of 0.[20]

Portfolio Aspects Traditional CRA considers each country separately. However, many large banks with LDC or sovereign risk exposures hold a portfolio of LDC loans. In a portfolio context, the risk of holding a well-diversified portfolio of LDC sovereign loans may be smaller than that of having a portfolio heavily concentrated in non-oil-producing LDC loans. In particular, the lender may distinguish between those key risk indicator variables having a *systematic* effect on the probability of repayment across a large number of sovereign countries and those variables having an *unsystematic* effect by impacting only one or a few countries.

---

[20] J. deHaan and W. J. Kooi, in "Does Central Bank Independence Really Matter? New Evidence for Developing Countries Using a New Indicator," *Journal of Banking and Finance* 24 (2000), pp. 643–64, find that the turnover rate of central bank governors is also an indicator of central bank independence, which in turn is found to affect the economic health (and, consequently, country risk) of the countries examined. C. Pantzalis, D. A. Stangeland, and H. J. Turtle, in "Political Elections and the Resolution of Uncertainty: The International Evidence," *Journal of Banking and Finance* 24 (2000), pp. 1575–1604, find that stock markets react positively in less-free countries when a political election is won by the opposition or lost by the incumbent government.

FIGURE 16–3
Corruption
Perceptions Index,
2004

Source: Transparency
International, October 2004.
www.transparency.org

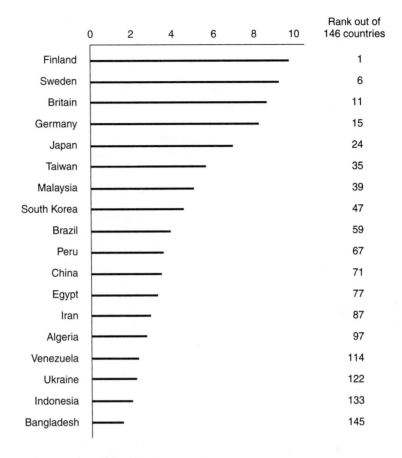

Rank out of 146 countries
1
6
11
15
24
35
39
47
59
67
71
77
87
97
114
122
133
145

Systematic and Unsystematic Risks

One way to address this problem is to employ a portfolio framework for sovereign risk analysis. Such an analysis would identify those indicator variables that have a *systematic* impact across all borrowers' probability of repayment and those that tend to be country specific (or *unsystematic*).[21] The indicator variables that the FI manager should really be concerned with are the *systematic* variables since they cannot be diversified away in a multisovereign loan portfolio. By comparison, unsystematic, or country-specific, risks can be diversified away. Consider the following model:

$$X_i = a_i + b_i \overline{X} + e_i$$

where

X_i = Key variable or country risk indicator for country i (e.g., the *DSR* for country i)

$\overline{X}$ = Weighted index of this key risk indicator across all countries to which the lender makes loans (e.g., the *DSR* for each country weighted by the shares of loans for each country in the FI's portfolio)

e_i = Other factors impacting X_i for any given country

Expressing this equation in variance terms, we get:

$$VAR(X_i) = b_i^2 VAR(\overline{X}) + VAR(e_i)$$

Total risk = Systematic risk + Unsystematic risk

---

[21] See L. S. Goodman, "Diversifiable Risks in LDC Lending: A 20/20 Hindsight View," *Studies in Banking and Finance* 3 (1986), pp. 249–62.

From this equation, you can see that the total risk or variability of any given risk indicator for a country, such as the *DSR* for Nigeria, can be divided into a nondiversifiable *systematic* risk element that measures the extent to which that country's *DSR* moves in line with the *DSR*s of all other debtor countries and an unsystematic risk element that impacts the *DSR* for Nigeria independently. The greater the size of the *unsystematic* element relative to the systematic risk element, the less important this variable is to the lender since it can be diversified away by holding a broad array of LDC loans.

L. S. Goodman found that for the 1970–83 period, the *DSR* had a high systematic element across countries, as did export revenue variance (*VAREX*).[22] This implies that when one LDC country was experiencing a growing debt burden relative to its exports, so were all others. Similarly, when commodity prices or world demand collapsed for one debtor country's commodity exports, the same occurred for other debtor countries as well. A possible reason for the high systematic risk of the *DSR* is the sensitivity of this ratio to rising nominal and real interest rates in the developed (or lending) countries. As we discussed in Chapter 15, international interest rates tend to be positively correlated over time. A possible reason for the high systematic risk of the export variance is the tendency of prices and world demands for commodities to reflect simultaneously economic conditions such as recessions and expansions in developed countries.

By comparison, money supply growth ($\Delta M/M$) and the import ratio appear to have low systematic elements.[23] This is not surprising since control over the money supply and the use of domestic reserves are relatively discretionary variables for LDC governments. Thus, while Argentina may choose a money supply growth rate of 50 percent per annum, the Chilean government may choose a target rate of 10 percent per annum. Similarly, the Argentinean and Chilean economies may have very different demands for imports, and the scale of vital imports may differ quite widely across LDCs. Using this type of analysis allows an FI manager to focus on relatively few variables such as the *DSR*s and export variances that affect the risk of the LDC sovereign loan portfolio.

In another study[24] of systematic risk versus nonsystematic risk, for 54 LDCs over the 1974–87 period, looking at *Institutional Investor* ratings of a country as the risk indicator variable, it was found that the systematic versus nonsystematic risk components varied from 97 percent versus 3 percent for Argentina to 41 percent versus 59 percent for Russia. This would suggest, all else being equal, that an FI should hold more Russian than Argentinean loans—although the experience of FIs in 2002 with Russian defaults and in 2003 with Argentinian defaults may call into question the appropriateness of the portfolio approach and especially, the ability of FIs to diversify away unsystematic sovereign risk in a contagious crisis. More recently, value at risk models have been applied to (Dutch) government bond portfolios.[25] Similar to the discussion in Chapter 12, this line of research examines total losses on portfolios of government debt in the worst-case (say, 1 percent) scenario.[26]

---

[22] Ibid.

[23] Ibid.

[24] See M. Palmer and T. B. Sanders, "A Model for Diversifying International Loan Portfolios," *Journal of Financial Services Research*, 1996, pp. 359–71.

[25] See P. J. G. Vlaar, "Value at Risk Models for Dutch Bond Portfolios," *Journal of Banking and Finance* 24 (2000), pp. 1131–54.

[26] VAR models might also be applied to a country's FX revenues—to evaluate its ability to withstand shocks or crises.

Incentive Aspects CRA statistical models often identify variables based on rather loose or often nonexistent analyses of the borrower or lender's incentives to reschedule. Rarely are the following questions asked: What are the *incentives* or *net benefits* to an LDC seeking a rescheduling? What are the incentives or net benefits to an FI that grants a rescheduling? That is, what determines the demand for rescheduling by LDCs and the supply of rescheduling by FIs? Presumably, only when the benefits outweigh the costs for both parties does rescheduling occur. Consider the following benefits and costs of rescheduling for borrowers on the one hand and FIs on the other.

Borrowers

Benefits

- By rescheduling its debt, the borrower lowers the present value of its future payments in hard currencies to outside lenders. This allows it to increase its consumption of foreign imports and/or increase the rate of its domestic investment.

Costs

- By rescheduling now, the borrower may close itself out of the market for loans in the future. As a result, even if the borrower encounters high-growth investment opportunities in the future, it may be difficult or impossible to finance them.
- Rescheduling may result in significant interference with the borrower's international trade since it would be difficult to gain access to instruments such as letters of credit, without which trade may be more costly.[27]

Lenders (FIs)

Benefits

- Once a loan has been made, a rescheduling is much better than a borrower default. With a rescheduling, the FI lender may anticipate some present value loss of principal and interest on the loan; with an outright default, the FI stands to lose all its principal and future interest repayments.
- The FI can renegotiate fees and various other collateral and option features into a rescheduled loan.
- There may be tax benefits to an FI's taking a recognized write-down or loss in value on a rescheduled LDC loan portfolio.[28]

Costs

- Through rescheduling, loans become similar to long-term bonds or even equity, and the FI often becomes locked into a particular loan portfolio structure.
- Those FIs with large amounts of rescheduled loans are subject to greater regulatory attention. For example, in the United States, such FIs may be placed on the regulators' problem list of FIs.[29]

All these relevant economic incentive considerations go into the demand for and the supply of rescheduling; however, it is far from clear how the simple statistical

---

[27] See Chapter 13 on letters of credit.

[28] For example, in 1998 Deutsche Bank took a loan loss provision of nearly $800 million against its Asian loan portfolio (see "Study Shows How World Banks Panicked Over Asian Troubles," *The New York Times,* January 30, 1998, p. D1).

[29] The problem list singles out banks for special regulatory attention. Normally, examiners rate a problem list bank as 4 or 5 on a rating scale of 1 to 5, where 1 is good and 5 is bad.

models just described incorporate this complex array of incentives. At a very minimum, statistical models should clearly reflect the underlying theory of rescheduling.[30]

Stability A final problem with simple statistical CRA models is that of stability. The fact that certain key variables may have explained rescheduling in the past does not mean that they will perform or predict well in the future. Over time, new variables and incentives affect rescheduling decisions, and the relative weights on the key variables change. This suggests that the FI manager must continuously update the CRA model to incorporate all currently available information and ensure the best predictive power possible. This is particularly true in today's new global environment of enhanced trade and competition with major changes in production technology taking place in countries such as China and India.

Using Market Data to Measure Risk: The Secondary Market for LDC Debt

Since the mid-1980s, a secondary market for trading LDC debt has developed among large commercial and investment banks in New York and London. The volume of trading grew dramatically from around U.S.$2 billion per year in 1984 to over U.S.$6 billion today, with trading often taking place in the high-yield (or junk bond) departments of the participating FIs.[31] Trading declined to U.S.$4.2 billion in 1998 after the Russian debt defaults and again in 1999 after Ecuador's failure to pay interest on its Brady bonds (see below). Trading has also been adversely affected by schemes of the more successful emerging market countries to get investors to swap Brady bonds for domestic government bonds (see below). The early 2000s were characterized by increasing trading activity and growing investor confidence in emerging markets, sparked in large part by Brazil's rapid economic recovery, Mexico's upgraded credit rating to investment grade, and Russia's successful debt restructuring.

These markets provide quoted prices for LDC loans and other debt instruments that an FI manager can use for CRA. Before we look at how this might be done, we describe the structure and development of the markets for LDC loans and related debt instruments, including the determinants of market demand and supply.

The Structure of the Market

This secondary market in LDC debt has considerably enhanced the liquidity of LDC loans on bank and other FI balance sheets.[32] The following are the market players that sell and buy LDC loans and debt instruments.

Sellers

- large FIs willing to accept write-downs of loans on their balance sheets
- small FIs wishing to disengage themselves from the LDC loan market

---

[30] See J. Bulow and K. Rogoff, "A Constant Recontracting Model of Sovereign Debt," *Journal of Political Economy* 97 (1989), pp. 155–78.

[31] See "Loads of Debt," *The Economist*, March 22, 1997, p. 5. The Loan Syndication Trading Association has reported that trading in domestic corporate loans plus sovereign loans exceeded US$110 billion in total in 2003. The market comprises over 100 traders/dealers.

[32] LDC loans change hands when one creditor assigns the rights to all future interest payments and principal payments to a buyer. In most early market transactions, the buyer had to get the permission of the sovereign debtor country before the loan could be assigned to a new party. The reason for this was that the country might have concerns as to whether the buyer was as committed to any new money deals as part of restructuring agreements as the original lender. Most recent restructuring agreements, however, have removed the right of assignment from the borrower (the sovereign country). This has increased liquidity in the LDC loan market.

- FIs willing to swap one country's LDC debt for another's to rearrange their portfolios of country risk exposures

Buyers

- wealthy investors, hedge funds (see Chapter 5, Appendix A), FIs, and corporations seeking to engage in debt-for-equity swaps or speculative investments
- FIs seeking to rearrange their LDC balance sheets by reorienting their LDC debt concentrations

The Early Market for Sovereign Debt

Consider the quote sheet from Salomon Brothers, in Table 16–5, for May 2, 1988—a relatively early stage of LDC loan market development. As indicated in Table 16–5, FIs such as investment banks and major commercial banks act as market makers, quoting two-way bid–ask prices for LDC debt.[33] Thus, an FI or an investor could have bought US$100 of Peruvian loans from Salomon for US$9 in May 1988, or at a 91 percent discount from face value. However, in selling the same loans to Salomon, the investor would have received only US$7 per US$100, or a 93 percent discount. The bid–ask spreads for certain countries were very large in this period; for example, Sudan's US$2 bid and US$10 ask exemplified a serious lack of market demand for the sovereign loans of many countries.

Today's Market for Sovereign Debt

In recent years there have been a large number of changes in the structure of the market. Now there are four market segments: Brady bonds, sovereign bonds, performing loans, and nonperforming loans.

Brady Bonds The first segment of the market (and the largest) is that for Brady bonds. These reflect programs under which the U.S. and other FIs exchanged their dollar loans for dollar bonds issued by the relevant less developed countries (LDCs). These bonds have a much longer maturity than that promised on the original loans and a lower promised original coupon (yield) than the interest rate on the original loan. However, the principal has usually been collateralized through the issuing country's purchasing U.S. treasury bonds and holding them in a special-purpose escrow account. Should that country default on its Brady bonds the buyers of the bonds could access the dollar bonds held as collateral. These loan-for-bond restructuring programs, also called debt-for-debt swaps, were developed under the auspices of the U.S. Treasury's 1989 Brady Plan and international organizations such as the IMF. Once loans were swapped for bonds by banks and other FIs, they could be sold on the secondary market. For example, in March 2002, the 30-year Brazilian discount Brady bonds had a bid price of US$90.75 per US$100 of face value. These bonds have their principal repayments collateralized by U.S. Treasury bonds. Table 16–6 lists the amount of Brady bonds outstanding for several countries.

Sovereign Bonds The second segment of the LDC debt market is that for sovereign bonds. Beginning in May 1996, as the debt position and economies of some LDCs improved,[34] a number started buy-back, or repurchase, programs for their Brady bonds. For example, in April 2003 Mexico sold US$2.5 billion of sovereign bonds to

---

[33] Major market makers include the Dutch ING bank, as well as Lehman, Citigroup, J. P. Morgan, Bankers Trust, and Merrill Lynch.

[34] In fact, Mexico has experienced such a turnaround. It is now embroiled in a lawsuit with Citigroup for prepaying on its Brady debt. See "Mexico's Debt Situation Takes a New Twist," *The New York Times*, June 27, 2000, p. 02.

TABLE 16–5   Indicative Prices for Less Developed Country Bank Loans (US$)

Country	Indicative Cash Prices		Swap Index		Trading Commentary
	Bid ($)	Offer ($)	Sell	Buy	
Algeria	91.00	93.00	5.22	6.71	Longer-dated paper resurfacing as cash substitute in swaps.
Argentina	29.00	30.00	0.66	0.67	Less volume this period; consolidation exercise slows note trades.
Bolivia	10.00	13.00	0.52	0.54	Minimal current activity.
Brazil	53.00	54.00	1.00	1.02	Rally topping out as supply catches up with auction interest.
Chile	60.50	61.50	1.19	1.22	Market firm and rising as deal calendar fills.
Colombia	67.00	68.00	1.42	1.47	Resurgence of interest as high-quality exit.
Costa Rica	13.00	16.00	0.54	0.56	Market building reserves of patience to deal with this name again.
Dominican Republic	17.00	20.00	0.57	0.59	Trading picks up at lower levels.
Ecuador	31.00	33.00	0.66	0.70	Occasional swaps surfacing.
Honduras	25.00	28.00	0.63	0.65	Viewed as expensive on a relative value basis.
Ivory Coast	30.00	33.00	0.67	0.70	Newly sighted by fee swappers.
Jamaica	33.00	36.00	0.70	0.73	Slow but serious inquiry continues.
Mexico	52.50	53.50	0.99	1.01	Prices continue upward drift on lower, lumpy flow.
Morocco	50.00	51.00	0.94	0.96	Fee swappers oblige sellers by jumping into the wider breach versus Latins.
Nicaragua	3.00	4.00	0.48	0.49	Avoided by the surviving court tasters.
Nigeria	28.50	30.50	0.66	0.68	Retail stonewalls dealer interest.
Panama	20.00	23.00	0.59	0.61	Recent bidding stirs the mud.
Peru	7.00	9.00	0.51	0.52	Debt-for-debt workouts and debt-for-goods deals continue.
Philippines	52.00	53.00	0.98	1.00	Prices drift higher with good interest in non-CB names.
Poland	43.25	44.50	0.83	0.85	Somewhat slower trading this period.
Romania	82.00	84.00	2.61	2.94	Bidding improves on expectations of 1988 principal payments.
Senegal	40.00	45.00	0.78	0.85	Trading talk more serious.
Sudan	2.00	10.00	0.48	0.52	Still on the mat.
Turkey	97.50	99.00	18.80	47.00	CTLDs remain well bid.
Uruguay	59.50	61.50	1.16	1.22	Remains a patience-trying market.
Venezuela	55.00	55.75	1.04	1.06	Trading stronger as uptick in Chile brings swaps back into range.
Yugoslavia	45.50	47.00	0.86	0.89	More frequent trading.
Zaire	19.00	23.00	0.58	0.61	New interest develops.

Source: Salomon Brothers Inc., May 2, 1988.

help finance the repurchase of the country's U.S. dollar–denominated Brady Bonds. The difference between a Brady bond and a sovereign bond is that a Brady bond's value partly reflects the value of the U.S. Treasury bond collateral underlying the principal and/or interest on the issue. By contrast, sovereign bonds are uncollateralized and their price or value reflects the credit risk rating of the country issuing the bonds. The benefit to the country is the "saving" from not having to

TABLE 16–6
Brady Bonds and Bank Loans Outstanding, June 2003 (in billions of US dollars)

Source: World Bank Web site, January 2004. www.worldbank.org

Country	Brady Bonds Outstanding	Bank Loans Outstanding
Argentina	6.85	25.05
Brazil	17.78	58.20
Bulgaria	2.44	0.82
Costa Rica	0.43	3.03
Côte d'Ivoire	2.23	2.22
Dominican Republic	0.46	2.70
Ecuador	0.00	1.83
Mexico	1.27	45.69
Nigeria	1.44	1.99
Peru	2.47	4.23
Philippines	1.16	12.26
Poland	2.79	16.81
Russia	0.00	35.32
Uruguay	0.46	2.08
Venezuela	7.67	11.16

pledge U.S. Treasury bonds as collateral. The cost is the higher interest spreads required on such bonds. Thus, the US$2.8 billion June 1997 issue by Brazil of 30-year dollar-denominated bonds (rated BB – grade by Standard & Poor's) was sold at a yield spread of nearly 4 percent over U.S. Treasuries at the time of issue.[35] In July 2001, Argentinian sovereign bonds were trading at spreads of over 15 percent above U.S. Treasury rates, with the J. P. Morgan Emerging Market Bond Index showing a spread of nearly 10 percent over U.S. Treasuries. This reflected the serious economic problems in Argentina and the contagious effects these were having on other sovereign bond markets.[36]

Performing Loans The third segment of the LDC debt market is that for performing LDC loans. Performing loans are original or restructured outstanding sovereign loans on which the sovereign country is currently maintaining promised payments to lenders or debt holders. Any discounts from 100 percent reflect expectations that these countries may face repayment problems in the future. Table 16–6 reports external bank loans outstanding for several countries as of June 2003.

Nonperforming Loans The fourth and final segment of the LDC market is that for nonperforming loans. Nonperforming loans reflect the secondary market prices for the sovereign loans of countries where there are no interest or principal payments currently being made. These are normally traded at very deep discounts from 100 percent.

---

[35] A. Gande and D. Parsley found that the credit rating on sovereign debt of one country can affect the credit rating and thus the yield spread in other countries' debt. For example, a one-category downgrade (e.g., from BB to B) is associated with a 12-basis point increase in spreads of sovereign bonds. However, positive rating events have no discernible impact on sovereign bond debt (see "News Spillovers in the Sovereign Debt Market," *Journal of Financial Economics,* forthcoming). Further, D. Duffie, L. H. Pedersen, and K. J. Singleton find that Russian yield spreads in the 1990s and 2000 varied significantly over time (responding to political events) and were negatively correlated with Russian foreign currency reserves and oil prices. Their model suggests that Russian sovereign bonds may have been overpriced in September 1997 (see "Modeling Sovereign Yield Spreads: A Case Study of Russian Debt," *Journal of Finance* 58 (February 2003), pp. 119–59).

[36] See "Gloom Over the River Plate," *The Economist,* June 14, 2001, pp. 11–12.

LDC Market Prices and Country Risk Analysis

By combining LDC debt prices with key variables, FI managers can potentially predict future repayment problems. For example, in the markets for which LDC debt is quite heavily traded, such as Mexico and Brazil, these prices reflect market consensus regarding the current and expected future cash flows on these loans and, implicitly, the probability of rescheduling or repudiation of these loans. Because market prices on LDC loans have been available monthly since 1985, the FI manager might construct a statistical CRA model to analyze which key economic and political variables or factors have driven changes in secondary market prices. Basically, this would involve regressing periodic changes in the prices of LDC debt in the secondary market on a set of key variables such as those described earlier in this section. Table 16–7 presents the results of a study by E. Boehmer and W. L. Megginson of the factors driving the secondary market prices of 10 LDC countries' loans over a 32-month period, July 1985–July 1988.

As you can see, the most significant variables affecting LDC loan sale prices (P) over this period were a country's debt service ratio (TDGNP and TDEX), its import ratio (NIRES), its accumulated debt in arrears (ARR), and the amount by which FIs had already made loan loss provisions against these LDC loans (USP). Also important were variables that reflect the debt moratoria for Peru and Brazil (PDUM and BDUM) and that indicate whether a debt-for-equity swap program was in place. Interestingly, debt-for-equity swap programs appear to depress prices. (We discuss these programs in more detail in Appendix A to the chapter).

Once managers have estimated a statistical model, they can use the estimate of parameters $\beta_1, \beta_2, \ldots, \beta_n$ along with forecasts for a given LDC's debt service ratio and other key variables to derive predicted changes in LDC asset prices. That is, this approach might allow the FI manager to come up with another set of forecasts regarding changes in sovereign risk exposure to a number of sovereign debtors.

This approach is subject to many of the same criticisms as the traditional statistical models of country risk prediction. Specifically, the parameters of the model may be unstable; managers can measure variables, such as the DSR and the import ratio, only with error; and the LDC loan market may not be price efficient.[37] In addition, the link between these key variables and the change in secondary market price is something of a black box in terms of links to the underlying theoretical incentives of borrowers and lenders to engage in future reschedulings or repudiations of their debt obligations.

Concept Questions

1. Are the credit ratings of countries in the *Institutional Investor* rating scheme forward looking or backward looking?
2. What variables are most commonly included in sovereign risk prediction models? What does each one measure?
3. What are the major problems involved with using traditional CRA models and techniques?
4. Which sovereign risk indicators are the most important for a large FI, those with a high or those with a low systematic element?
5. Why is the supply of Brady bonds in decline?

---

[37] However, in S. H. Lee, H. M. Sung, and J. L. Urrutia, "The Behavior of Secondary Market Prices of LDC Syndicated Loans," *Journal of Banking and Finance* 20 (1996), pp. 537–54, it is shown that returns on LDC loans traded in the secondary market conform to those expected to exist in an efficient market. In fact, recent research has found that, in general, international and, particularly, emerging markets are becoming increasingly efficient. See B. Eftekhari and S. E. Satchell, "International Investors' Exposure to Risk in Emerging Markets," *Journal of Financial Research*, Spring 1999, pp. 83–106. Additionally, J. J. Choi, S. Hauser, and K. J. Kopecky, in "Does the Stock Market Predict Real Activity? Time Series Evidence from the G-7 Countries," *Journal of Banking and Finance* 23 (1999), pp. 1771–92, found a significant relationship between lagged real stock returns and the growth rate in industrial production for the G-7 countries.

TABLE 16–7
Variables Affecting Secondary Market Prices

Source: E. Boehmer and W. L. Megginson, "Determinants of Secondary Market Prices for Developing Country Syndicated Loans," *Journal of Finance* 45 (1990), pp. 1517–40.

The following regression equation is estimated:

$$P_{it} = \beta_1 \times \text{Intercept} + \beta_2 \times \text{TDGNP}_{it} + \beta_3 \times \text{TDEX}_{it} + \beta_4 \times \text{NETDS}_{it} + \beta_5 \times \text{NIRES}_{it}$$
$$+ \beta_6 \times \text{INT}_{it} + \beta_7 \times \text{ARR}_{it} + \beta_8 \times \text{USP}_{it} + \beta_9 \times \text{BDUM}_{it} + \beta_{10} \times \text{PDUM}_{it}$$
$$+ \beta_{11} \times \text{CONVDUM}_{it} + U_{it}$$

where

P =	LDC secondary market loan prices
TDGNP =	Ratio of total long-term debt to GNP
TDEX =	Ratio of total long-term debt to exports
NETDS =	Ratio of net exports to debt service
NIRES =	Ratio of net imports to hard currency reserves
INT =	Monthly London Interbank Offered Rate (a short-term interest rate)
ARR =	Level of incurred payment arrears
USP =	Cumulative developing country specific loan provisioning by U.S. FIs
BDUM =	Unity for Brazil from January to December of 1987 and zero otherwise to capture the effects of the debt moratorium
PDUM =	Unity for Peru over the whole sampling period and zero otherwise to account for the unilateral limitation of debt service payments
CONVDUM =	Unity for all months in which a country maintained legislation for debt-to-equity conversions

Parameter	Estimate	*t*-Statistic
Intercept	88.51760	13.47
TDGNP	−18.11610	−4.75
TDEX	−0.10437	−3.57
NETDS	−0.30754	−0.50
NIRES	5.79548	1.28
INT	0.22825	0.30
ARR	−0.00574	−2.68
USP	−0.00100	−13.69
BDUM	−10.92820	−6.61
PDUM	−36.07240	−8.31
CONVDUM	−5.43157	−6.75

Degrees of freedom: 309
Adjusted R^2: 0.96

Summary

This chapter reviewed the problems FIs face from sovereign or country risk exposures. Sovereign risk is the risk of a foreign government's limiting or preventing domestic borrowers in its jurisdiction from repaying the principal and interest on debt owed to external lenders. In recent years this risk has caused enormous problems for banks lending to LDCs, and Latin American and Asian countries. We reviewed various models for country risk analysis (CRA), including those produced by external monitoring agencies such as Euromoney, The Economist Intelligence Unit, and the Institutional Investor and those that could be constructed by an FI manager for internal evaluation purposes. Such statistical CRA models have problems and pitfalls. An alternative approach using secondary market prices on LDC loans and bonds was also described. In Appendix A (on page 718 of this book), we analyze the advantages and disadvantages of using four alternative mechanisms for dealing with problem sovereign credits from the perspective of the lender: debt-equity swaps, MYRAs, loan sales, and bond-for-loan swaps.

Questions and Problems

1. What risks are incurred in making loans to borrowers based in foreign countries? Explain.

2. What is the difference between debt rescheduling and debt repudiation?

3. Identify and explain at least four reasons that rescheduling debt in the form of loans is easier than rescheduling debt in the form of bonds.

4. What three country risk assessment models are available to investors? How is each model compiled?

5. What types of variables normally are used in a CRA Z score model? Define the following ratios and explain how each is interpreted in assessing the probability of rescheduling.

   a. Debt service ratio.
   b. Import ratio.
   c. Investment ratio.
   d. Variance of export revenue.
   e. Domestic money supply growth.

6. An FI manager has calculated the following values and weights to assess the credit risk and likelihood of having to reschedule the loan. From the Z score calculated from these weights and values, is the manager likely to approve the loan? Validation tests of the Z score model indicated that scores below 0.500 were likely to be nonreschedulers, while scores above 0.700 indicated a likelihood of rescheduling. Scores between 0.500 and 0.700 do not predict well.

Variable	Country Value	Weight
DSR	1.25	0.05
IR	1.60	0.10
INVR	0.60	0.35
VAREX	0.15	0.35
MG	0.02	0.15

7. Countries A and B have exports of US$2 and US$6 billion, respectively. The total interest and amortization on foreign loans for both countries are US$1 and US$2 billion, respectively.

   a. What is the debt service ratio (DSR) for each country?

   b. Based only on this ratio, to which country should lenders charge a higher risk premium?

   c. What are the shortcomings of using only these ratios to determine your answer in (b)?

8. What shortcomings are introduced by using traditional CRA models and techniques? In each case, what adjustments are made in the estimation techniques to compensate for the problems?

9. How do price and quantity risks affect the variability of a country's export revenue?

10. The average σ_{ER}^2 (or VAREX = variance of export revenue) of a group of countries has been estimated at 20 percent. The individual VAREX of two countries in the group, Holland and Singapore, has been estimated at 15 percent and 28 percent, respectively. The regression of individual country VAREX on the average VAREX provides the following beta (coefficient) estimates:

$$\beta_H = \text{Beta of Holland} = 0.80$$
$$\beta_S = \text{Beta of Singapore} = 0.20$$

   a. Based only on the VAREX estimates, which country should be charged a higher risk premium? Explain.

   a. If FIs include unsystematic risk in their estimation of risk premiums, how would your conclusions to (a) be affected? Explain.

11. Explain the following relation:

$$p = f(IR, INVR)$$
$$+, + \text{ or } -$$

where

   p = Probability of rescheduling
   IR = Total imports/Total foreign exchange reserves
   $INVR$ = Real investment/GNP

12. What is systematic risk in terms of sovereign risk? Which of the variables often used in statistical models tend to have high systematic risk? Which variables tend to have low systematic risk?

13. What are the benefits and costs of rescheduling to the following?

   a. A borrower.
   b. A lender.

14. Who are the primary sellers of LDC debt? Who are the buyers? Why are FIs often both sellers and buyers of LDC debt in the secondary markets?

15. Identify and describe the four market segments of the secondary market for LDC debt.

The following questions and problems are based on material presented in Appendix 16A.

16. What are the risks to an investing company participating in a debt-for-equity swap?

17. Global Bank holds a US$200 million loan to Argentina. The loans are being traded at bid-offer prices of 91–93 per 100 in the London secondary market.

a. If Global has an opportunity to sell this loan to an investment bank at a 7 percent discount, what are the savings after taxes compared with the revenue selling the loan in the secondary market? Assume the tax rate is 40 percent.

b. The investment bank in turn sells the debt at a 6 percent discount to a real estate company planning to build apartment complexes in Argentina. What is the profit after taxes to the investment bank?

c. The real estate company converts this loan into pesos under a debt-for-equity swap organized by the Argentinean government. The official rate for dollar to peso conversion is P1.05/US$. The free market rate is P1.10/US$. How much did the real estate company save by investing in Argentina through the debt-for-equity swap program as opposed to directly investing US$200 million using the free market rates?

d. How much would Global benefit from doing a local currency debt-for-equity swap itself? Why doesn't the bank do this swap?

18. Zlick Company plans to invest US$20 million in Chile to expand its subsidiary's manufacturing output. Zlick has two options. It can convert the US$20 million at the current exchange rate of 410 pesos to a dollar (i.e., P410US$), or it can engage in a debt-for-equity swap with its bank, City Bank, by purchasing Chilean debt and then swapping that debt into Chilean equity investments.

a. If City Bank quotes bid-offer prices of 94–96 for Chilean loans, what is the bank expecting to receive from Zlick Corporation (ignore taxes)? Why would City Bank want to dispose of this loan?

b. If Zlick decides to purchase the debt from City Bank and convert it to equity, it will have to exchange it at the official rate of P400/US$. Is this option better than investing directly in Chile at the free market rate of P410/US$?

c. What official exchange rate will cause Zlick to be indifferent between the two options?

19. What is concessionality in the process of rescheduling a loan?

20. Which variables typically are negotiation points in an LDC multiyear restructuring agreement (MYRA)? How do changes in these variables provide benefits to the borrower and to the lender?

21. How would the restructuring, such as rescheduling, of sovereign bonds affect the interest rate risk of the bonds? Is it possible that such restructuring would cause the FI's cost of capital not to change? Explain.

22. A bank is in the process of renegotiating a loan. The principal outstanding is US$50 million and is to be paid back in two installments of US$25 million each, plus interest of 8 percent. The new terms will stretch the loan out to five years with only interest payments of 6 percent, no principal payments, for the first three years. The principal will be paid in the last two years in payments of US$25 million along with the interest. The cost of funds for the bank is 6 percent for both the old loan and the renegotiated loan. An up-front fee of 1 percent is to be included for the renegotiated loan.

a. What is the present value of the existing loan for the bank?

b. What is the present value of the rescheduled loan for the bank?

c. Is the concessionality positive or negative for the bank?

23. A bank is in the process of renegotiating a three-year nonamortizing loan. The principal outstanding is US$20 million, and the interest rate is 8 percent. The new terms will extend the loan to 10 years at a new interest rate of 6 percent. The cost of funds for the bank is 7 percent for both the old loan and the renegotiated loan. An up-front fee of 50 basis points is to be included for the renegotiated loan.

a. What is the present value of the existing loan for the bank?

b. What is the present value of the rescheduled loan for the bank?

c. What is the concessionality for the bank?

d. What should be the up-front fee to make the concessionality zero?

24. A US$20 million loan outstanding to the Nigerian government is currently in arrears with City Bank. After extensive negotiations, City Bank agrees to reduce the interest rate from 10 percent to 6 percent and to lengthen the maturity of the loan to 10 years from the present 5 years remaining to maturity. The principal of the loan is to be paid at maturity. There will be no grace period, and the first interest payment is expected at the end of the year.

a. If the cost of funds is 5 percent for the bank, what is the present value of the loan prior to the rescheduling?

b. What is the present value of the rescheduled loan to the bank?

c. What is the concessionality of the rescheduled loan if the cost of funds remains at 5 percent and an up-front fee of 5 percent is charged?

d. What up-front fee should the bank charge to make the concessionality equal zero?

25. A bank was expecting to receive US$100,000 from its customer based in Great Britain. Since the customer

has problems repaying the loan immediately, the bank extends the loan for another year at the same interest rate of 10 percent. However, in the rescheduling agreement, the bank reserves the right to exercise an option for receiving the payment in British pounds, equal to £81,500.

a. If the cost of funds to the bank is also assumed to be 10 percent, what is the value of this option built into the agreement if only two possible exchange rates are expected at the end of the year, £1.75/US$ or £1.55/US$, with equal probability?

b. How would your answer differ if the probability of the exchange rate being being £1.75/US$ is 70 percent and that of £1.55/US$ is 30 percent?

c. Does the currency option have more or less value as the volatility of the exchange rate increases?

26. What are the major benefits and costs of loan sales to an FI?

27. What are the major costs and benefits of converting debt to Brady bonds for an FI?

Web Questions

28. Go to the Heritage Foundation Web site at **www.heritage.org** and find the most recent Economic Freedom Index for Canada using the following steps. Click on "20XX Index of Economic Freedom." Click on "Countries." Click on "Canada." This will bring the file onto your computer that contains the relevant data. What factors led to this rating?

29. Go to the World Bank Web site at **www.worldbank.org** and find the amount of Brady bonds currently outstanding in Brazil using the following steps. Click on "Data and Statistics." Click on "Data by Country." Click on "BIS, IMF, OECD, and World Bank Joint Initiative on Debt Reporting." Click on "Joint Statistics on External Debt (Home)." Click on "25 countries are also available in HTML format." Under Brazil, click on "Joint BIS-IMF-OECD-World Bank Statistics on External Debt." This will bring the file onto your computer that contains the relevant data.

Appendix 16A   Mechanisms for Dealing with Sovereign Risk Exposure

View Appendix 16A on page 718 of this book.

Liquidity Risk

In this chapter, we consider liquidity risk and:

▸ identify the causes of liquidity risk on an FI's balance sheet, both on the asset and on the liability side

▸ discuss the methods used to measure an FI's liquidity risk exposure,

▸ discuss the consequences of extreme liquidity risk, including deposit liability drains and bank runs

▸ examine regulatory mechanisms put in place to ease liquidity problems and prevent runs on deposit-taking institutions, and

▸ examine the reasons for differences in liquidity risk among banks (high exposure), life insurance companies (moderate exposure), and mutual funds, pension funds, and property and casualty insurance companies (low exposure)

INTRODUCTION

liquidity risk
The risk that a sudden surge in liability withdrawals may require an FI to liquidate assets in a very short period of time and at low prices.

As defined in Chapter 7, **liquidity risk** is the risk that a sudden surge in liability withdrawals may require an FI to liquidate assets in a very short period of time and at low prices. For example, in 1998, the hedge fund, Long Term Capital Management (LTCM), as discussed in Chapter 5, was unable to meet the margin calls (liability withdrawals) on its highly leveraged short positions. When the Russian government defaulted on its debt, the financial markets made a "flight to liquidity" and caught LTCM in its downdraft, driving up the prices of U.S. Treasuries and driving down the values of the securities held by LTCM as it tried to liquidate assets to pay its debt. A US$3.625 billion bailout was organized by the U.S. Federal Reserve Bank of New York, and LTCM's losses on their investments were over US$4.6 billion.[1]

Chapters 8 through 16 examined how the major problems of interest rate risk, market risk, credit risk, off-balance-sheet risk, operational and technology risk, foreign exchange risk, and sovereign risk can threaten the solvency of an FI. This chapter looks at the problems created by liquidity risk. Unlike risks that threaten the very solvency of an FI, liquidity risk is a normal aspect of the everyday management of an FI. Only in extreme cases do liquidity risk problems develop into solvency risk problems.

CAUSES OF LIQUIDITY RISK

Liquidity risk arises for two reasons: a liability-side reason and an asset-side reason. The liability-side reason occurs when an FI's liability holders, such as depositors or insurance policyholders, seek to cash in their financial claims immediately.

---

[1] While LTCM's value at risk (VaR) models used to evaluate their strategies were generally correct, they failed to incorporate an adjustment for liquidity. See F. Portnoy, "The Domino Effect," in *Infectious greed: how deceit and risk corrupted the financial markets*, New York: Times Books, Chapter 8, pp. 262–266 for a general discussion of LTCM and its VaR models, as well as a perspective on the effect of unregulated FIs (hedge funds) on the financial system.

When liability holders demand cash by withdrawing deposits, the FI needs to borrow additional funds or sell assets to meet the withdrawal. The most liquid asset is cash; FIs use this asset to pay claim holders who seek to withdraw funds. However, FIs tend to minimize their holdings of cash reserves as assets because those reserves pay no interest. To generate interest revenues, most FIs invest in less liquid and/or longer-maturity assets. While most assets can be turned into cash eventually, for some assets this can be done only at a high cost when the asset must be liquidated immediately. The price the asset holder must accept for immediate sale may be far less than it would receive with a longer horizon over which to negotiate a sale. Thus, some assets may be liquidated only at low **fire-sale prices,** thus threatening the solvency of the FI. Alternatively, rather than liquidating assets, an FI may seek to purchase or borrow additional funds.

fire-sale price
The price received for an asset that has to be liquidated (sold) immediately.

The second cause of liquidity risk is asset-side liquidity risk: supplying off-balance-sheet loan commitments. As we described in Chapter 13, a loan commitment allows a customer to borrow (draw down) funds from an FI (over a commitment period) on demand. When a borrower draws on its loan commitment, the FI must fund the loan on the balance sheet immediately; this creates a demand for liquidity. As it can with liability withdrawals, an FI can meet such a liquidity need by running down its cash assets, selling off other liquid assets, or borrowing additional funds.

To analyze the differing degrees of importance of liquidity risk across FIs, we next consider liquidity risk problems faced by deposit-taking institutions, insurance companies, and mutual and pension funds.

Concept Questions

1. What are the sources of liquidity risk?
2. Why is cash more liquid than loans for an FI?

LIQUIDITY RISK AT DEPOSIT-TAKING INSTITUTIONS

Liability-Side Liquidity Risk

As discussed in Chapter 2, a deposit-taking institution's (DTI's) balance sheet typically has a large amount of short-term liabilities, such as demand deposits and other transaction accounts, which fund relatively long-term assets. Demand deposit accounts and other transaction accounts are contracts that give the holders the right to put their claims back to the DTI on any given day and demand immediate repayment of the face value of their deposit claims in cash.[2] Thus, an individual demand deposit account holder with a balance of $10,000 can demand cash to be repaid immediately, as can a corporation with $100 million in its demand deposit account.[3] In theory, at least, a DTI that has 20 percent of its liabilities in demand deposits and other transaction accounts must stand ready to pay out that amount by liquidating an equivalent amount of assets on any banking day. Table 17–1 shows the aggregate balance sheet of the assets and liabilities of Canadian

---

[2] Accounts with this type of put option include demand deposits, interest bearing chequing accounts with minimum balance requirements, and (chequing accounts with minimum balance and number-of-cheques-written restrictions). We describe these accounts in more detail in Chapter 18. Deposit-taking institutions typically liquidate deposit account contracts immediately upon request of the customer. Many savings account contracts, however, give a DTI some powers to delay withdrawals by requiring notification of withdrawal a certain number of days before withdrawal or by imposing penalty fees such as loss of interest.

[3] Technology is compounding the risk in these withdrawals. The Internet enables depositors to transfer money between FIs quickly to take advantage of higher rates.

TABLE 17–1
Assets and
Liabilities of
Canadian Banks,
October 31, 2004 (in
billions of dollars)

Source: Statistics Canada,
www.statscan.ca

Assets			Liabilities*		
Total cash assets	27.0	1.75%	Total deposits	1,056.9	73.39%
Total investments	360.0	23.38%	Borrowings	56.3	3.91%
Total loans	991.8	64.42%	Other liabilities	326.9	22.70%
Other assets	160.7	10.44%	Total liabilities	1,440.1	100.00%
Total assets	1,539.5	100.00%			

* Excluding bank equity capital.

banks. As seen in this table, total deposits are 73.39 percent of total liabilities. By comparison, cash assets are only 1.75 % percent of total assets. Also note that borrowed funds are 3.91% percent of total liabilities.

In reality, a deposit-taking institution knows that normally only a small proportion of its deposits will be withdrawn on any given day. Most demand deposits act as consumer **core deposits** on a day-by-day basis, providing a relatively stable or long-term source of savings and time deposit funds for the DTI. Moreover, deposit withdrawals may in part be offset by the inflow of new deposits (and income generated from the DTI's on- and off-balance-sheet activities). The DTI manager must monitor the resulting net deposit withdrawals or net deposit drains.[4] Specifically, over time, a DTI manager can normally predict—with a good degree of accuracy—the probability distribution of **net deposit drains** (the difference between deposit withdrawals and deposit additions) on any given normal banking day.[5]

Consider the two possible distributions shown in Figure 17–1. In panel (a) of Figure 17–1, the distribution is assumed to be strongly peaked at the 5 percent net deposit withdrawal level—this DTI expects approximately 5 percent of its net deposit funds to be withdrawn on any given day with the highest probability. In panel (a) a net deposit drain means that the DTI is receiving insufficient additional deposits (and other cash inflows) to offset deposit withdrawals.

The DTI in panel (a) has a mean, or expected, net positive drain on deposits, so its new deposit funds and other cash flows are expected to be insufficient to offset deposit withdrawals. The liability side of its balance sheet is contracting. Table 17–2 illustrates an actual 5 percent net drain of deposit accounts (or, in terms of dollars, a drain of $5 million).

For a DTI to be growing, it must have a mean or average deposit drain such that new deposit funds more than offset deposit withdrawals. Thus, the peak of the net deposit drain probability distribution would be at a point to the left of zero. See the −2 percent in panel (b) in Figure 17–1, where the distribution of net deposit drains is peaked at −2 percent, or the FI is receiving net cash inflows with the highest probability.

core deposits
Those deposits
that provide a DTI
with a long-term
funding source.

net deposit drains
The amount by which
cash withdrawals
exceed additions;
a net cash outflow.

---

[4] Also a part of liquidity risk (although not as likely to cause an FI to fail) is an unexpected inflow of funds. For example, in the early 2000s as stock prices fell, investors liquidated their mutual fund shares and deposited these funds in their banks and credit unions. With interest rates at historic lows, deposit-taking institutions faced a problem of finding sufficiently attractive (in a return sense) loans and securities in which to invest these funds.

[5] Apart from predictable daily seasonality to deposit flows, there are other seasonal variations, many of which are, to a greater or lesser degree, predictable. For example, many retail DTIs face above-average deposit outflows around the end of the year and in the summer (due to Christmas and the vacation season). Also, the rural branches of many DTIs face a deposit inflow–outflow cycle that closely matches the agricultural cycle of the local crop or crops. In the planting and growing season, deposits tend to fall, while in the harvest season, deposits tend to rise (as crops are sold). J. H. Gilkeson, J. A. List, and C.K. Ruff, in "Evidence of Early Withdrawal in Time Deposit Portfolios," *Journal of Financial Services Research* 15:2 (1999), pp. 103–22, find that early withdrawals of time deposits are also somewhat predictable in that, for all but the very short-term deposits, the size of early withdrawals is significantly related to changes in interest rates relative to the rate paid on existing time deposits. The size of the penalties for early withdrawals is also found to affect the size of these withdrawals.

FIGURE 17–1
Distribution of
Net Deposit Drains

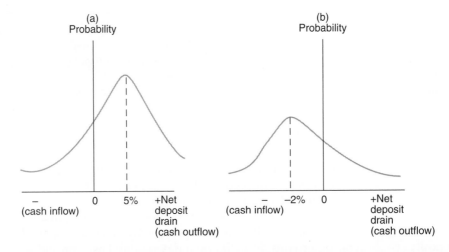

TABLE 17–2
Effect of Net
Deposit Drains
on the Balance
Sheet (in millions
of dollars)

Before the Drain				After the Drain			
Assets		**Liabilities**		**Assets**		**Liabilities**	
Assets	100	Deposits	70	Assets	100	Deposits	65
		Borrowed funds	10			Borrowed funds	10
		Other liabilities	20			Other liabilities	20
	100		100		100		95

A DTI can manage a drain on deposits in two major ways: (1) purchased liquidity management and/or (2) stored liquidity management. Traditionally, DTI managers have relied on stored liquidity management as the primary mechanism of liquidity management. Today, many DTIs—especially the largest banks with access to the money market and other nondeposit markets for funds—rely on purchased liquidity (or liability) management to deal with the risk of cash shortfalls.[6] A more extensive discussion of liability management techniques is left to Chapter 18. Here we briefly discuss the alternative methods of liquidity risk management.

Purchased Liquidity Management

A DTI manager who purchases liquidity may turn to the interbank markets for short-term funds. These could be the repurchase agreement markets[7] or via the Large Value Transfer System (LVTS) that allows the major Canadian FIs who are **LVTS participants** to borrow from the Bank of Canada at the Bank Rate or from other member FIs who have excess funds.[8]

Alternatively, the DTI manager could issue additional fixed-maturity wholesale certificates of deposit or even sell some notes and bonds.[7] In the example above, as long as the total amount of funds raised equals $5 million, the DTI in Table 17–2 could fully fund its net deposit drain. However, this can be expensive for the DTI

LVTS participant
A member of the
Canadian Payments
Association who
settles directly with
the Bank of Canada
and participates in
the LVTS.

---

[6] However, using the loan-to-deposit ratio as their main indicator of proper management strategy, J. P. Lajaunie, T. O. Stanley, and C. Roger argue that the vast majority of U.S. commercial banks should focus on nonpurchased liquidity management strategies. See "Liability Management and Commercial Banks: Fact or Fiction," *Journal of Financial and Economic Practice*, Spring 2003, pp. 53–66.

[7] Securities companies and institutional investors use the repurchase agreement market extensively for liquidity management purposes.

[8] The Bank of Canada plays a role in maintaining the liquidity of the financial system. See the section "Bank Runs, the Bank of Canada, and Deposit Insurance" in this chapter and Chapter 19 for more discussion.

TABLE 17–3
Adjusting to a
Deposit Drain
through Liability
Management (in
millions of dollars)

Assets		Liabilities	
Assets	100	Deposits	65
		Borrowed funds	15
		Other liabilities	20
	100		100

since it is paying *market rates* for funds in the wholesale money market to offset net drains on low-interest-bearing deposits.[9] Thus, the higher the cost of purchased funds relative to the rates earned on assets the less attractive this approach to liquidity management becomes. Further, since   )st of these funds are not covered by deposit insurance, their availability may be limited should the depository institution incur insolvency difficulties. Table 17–3 shows the DI's balance sheet if it responds to deposit drains by using purchased liquidity management techniques.

purchased liquidity management
An adjustment to a deposit drain that occurs on the liability side of the balance sheet.

Note that **purchased liquidity management** has allowed the DI to maintain its overall balance sheet size of $100 million without disturbing the size and composition of the asset side of its balance sheet—that is, the complete adjustment to the deposit drain occurs on the liability side of the balance sheet. In other words, purchased liquidity management can insulate the asset side of the balance sheet from normal drains on the liability side of the balance sheet. This is one of the reasons for the enormous growth in recent years of FI purchased liquidity management techniques and associated purchased fund markets such as borrowings from the Bank of Canada, repurchase agreements, and wholesale CDs. (We describe and discuss these instruments in more detail in Chapter 18.) Indeed, in the early 2000s regulators expressed concerns about the increased use of these (wholesale) funding sources by DTIs. Regulators noted that during the 1990s, as savers put more into investments (instead of DTI deposit accounts), DTIs were unable to increase deposits as fast as loans (and loan commitments) increased on the asset side of the balance sheet. In the event of a liquidity crunch (for example, because of an economic slowdown), additional (wholesale) funds could be hard to obtain.[10]

Stored Liquidity Management

stored liquidity management
An adjustment to a deposit drain that occurs on the asset side of the balance sheet.

Instead of meeting the net deposit drain by purchasing liquidity in the wholesale money markets, the DI could use **stored liquidity management.** That is, the FI could liquidate some of its assets, utilizing its stored liquidity. Traditionally, DTIs have held stored cash reserves at the Bank of Canada and in their vaults for this very purpose. Canada and the United Kingdom have no official central bank-designated cash reserve requirements while the U.S. Federal Reserve requires 3 percent on the first US$42.1 million and 10 percent on the rest of an FIs demand deposit and transaction account holdings.

www.bankofcanada.ca

Suppose, in our example, that on the asset side of the balance sheet the DTI normally holds $9 million of its assets in cash. We depict the situation before the net drain in liabilities in Table 17–4. As depositors withdraw $5 million in deposits, the DTI can meet this directly by using the excess cash stored in its vaults or held on deposit at other DTIs or at the Bank of Canada. If the reduction of $5 million in deposit liabilities is met by a $5 million reduction in cash assets held by the DTI, its balance sheet will be as shown in Table 17–5.

---

[9] While chequing accounts generally pay no explicit interest, other transaction accounts do. However, the rates paid are normally sticky, are slow to adjust to changes in market interest rates, and lie below purchased fund rates (see Chapter 18).

[10] See "Regulators Press for Safeguards," *Financial Times*, June 4, 2001, p. 24.

TABLE 17–4   Composition of the DTI's Balance Sheet (in millions of dollars)

Assets		Liabilities	
Cash	9	Deposits	70
Other assets	91	Borrowed funds	10
		Other liabilities	20
	100		100

TABLE 17–5   Stored Liquidity Adjustment to Deposit Drain (in millions of dollars)

Assets		Liabilities	
Cash	4	Deposits	65
Other assets	91	Borrowed funds	10
		Other liabilities	20
	95		95

When the DTI uses its cash as the liquidity adjustment mechanism, both sides of its balance sheet contract. In this example, the DTI's total assets and liabilities shrink from $100 to $95 million. The cost to the DTI from using stored liquidity, apart from decreased asset size,[11] is that it must hold excess non-interest-bearing assets in the form of cash on its balance sheet.[12] Thus, the cost of using cash to meet liquidity needs is the forgone return (or opportunity cost) of being unable to invest these funds in loans and other higher-income-earning assets.

Finally, note that while stored liquidity management and purchased liquidity management are alternative strategies for meeting deposit drains, a DTI can combine the two methods by using some purchased liquidity management and some stored liquidity management to meet liquidity needs.

Asset-Side Liquidity Risk

Just as deposit drains can cause a DTI liquidity problems, so can the exercise by borrowers of their loan commitments and other credit lines. Table 17–6 shows the effect of a $5 million exercise of a loan commitment by a borrower. As a result, the DTI must fund $5 million in additional loans on the balance sheet.[13] Consider panel (a) in Table 17–6 (the balance sheet before the commitment exercise) and panel (b) (the balance sheet after the exercise). In particular, the exercise of the loan commitment means that the DTI needs to provide $5 million in loans immediately to the borrower (other assets rise from $91 to $96 million). This can be done either by purchased liquidity management (borrowing an additional $5 million in the money market and lending these funds to the borrower) or by stored liquidity management (decreasing the DTI's excess cash assets from $9 million to $4 million). We present these two policies in Table 17–7.

Measuring a DTI's Liquidity Exposure

Sources and Uses of Liquidity

As discussed above, a DTI's liquidity risk can arise from a drain on deposits or from new loan demand, and the subsequent need to meet those demands through liquidating assets or borrowing funds. Therefore, a DTI manager must be able to measure its liquidity position on a daily basis, if possible. A useful tool is a net liquidity statement that lists sources and uses of liquidity and thus provides a measure of a DTI's net liquidity position.

---

[11] It should be noted that there is no empirical evidence showing a significant correlation between a DTI's asset size and profits.

[12] DTIs could hold highly liquid interest-bearing assets such as T-bills, but these are still less liquid than cash and immediate liquidation may result in some small capital value losses.

[13] Larger DTIs with more extensive commercial loan portfolios tend to be more susceptible to this type of risk than are smaller retail-oriented (or consumer-oriented) DTIs.

TABLE 17–6
Effects of a Loan
Commitment
Exercise (in
millions of dollars)

(a) Before				(b) After			
Cash	9	Deposits	70	Cash	9	Deposits	70
Other assets	91	Borrowed funds	10	Other assets	96	Borrowed funds	10
		Other liabilities	20			Other liabilities	20
	100		100		105		100

TABLE 17–7
Adjusting the
Balance Sheet to a
Loan Commitment
Exercise (in
millions of dollars)

(a) Purchased Liquidity Management				(b) Stored Liquidity Management			
Cash	9	Deposits	70	Cash	4	Deposits	70
Other assets	96	Borrowed funds	15	Other assets	96	Borrowed funds	10
		Other liabilities	20			Other liabilities	20
	105		105		100		100

The DTI can obtain liquid funds in two ways. First, it can sell its liquid assets such as T-bills immediately with little price risk and low transaction cost.[14] Second, it can borrow funds in the money/purchased funds market up to a maximum amount (this is an internal guideline based on the manager's assessment of the credit limits that the purchased or borrowed funds market is likely to impose on the DTI). As an FI manager deals with liquidity risk, historical sources and uses of liquidity statements can assist the manager in determining where future liquidity issues may arise.

Peer Group Ratio Comparison

Another way to measure a DTI's liquidity exposure is to compare certain key ratios and balance sheet features of the DTI such as its loans to assets, loans to deposits, loans and loan commitments to assets, loans and loan commitments to deposits, cash and securities to total assets, and core deposits to total deposits. Table 17–8 shows these ratios for the 6 large Canadian banks. A high ratio of loans to deposits (and loans and loan commitments to deposits) means that the DTI relies heavily on the short-term money market rather than on core deposits to fund loans. This could mean future liquidity problems if the DTI is at or near its borrowing limits in the purchased funds market. As noted previously, Canadian banks rely on the commercial paper market for funding. Similarly, a high ratio of loans and loan commitments to assets indicates the need for a high degree of liquidity to fund any unexpected drawdowns of these loans—high commitment DTIs (e.g., BMO, Scotia-bank, from Table 17–8) often face more liquidity risk exposure than do low-commitment FIs (e.g., TD Bank).

www.bmo.com
www.scotiabank.com
www.td.com

Financing Gap and the Financing Requirement

A fourth way to measure liquidity risk exposure is to determine the DTI's financing gap. As we discussed earlier, even though demand depositors can withdraw their funds immediately, they do not do so in normal circumstances. On average, most demand deposits stay at DTIs for quite long periods—often two years or more. Thus, a DTI manager often thinks of the average deposit base, including demand deposits, as a core source of funds that over time can fund a DTI's average amount of loans.

---

[14] In recent years, as the loan sales and securitization markets have grown, many banks have added to their sources statement loan assets that can be immediately sold or securitized. Chapters 26 and 27 describe the loan sales and securitization markets.

TABLE 17–8   Liquidity Ratios for Canadian Banks, 2004

	Loans/Assets	Loans and Loan Commitments/ Assets	Loans/ Deposits	Loans and Loan Commitments/ Deposits	Cash and Securities/ Total Assets	Core Deposits/ Total Deposits
BMO	56.9%	89.2%	86.2%	135.0%	25.8%	58.2%
CIBC	55.8%	74.8%	81.7%	109.5%	30.4%	n.a.
National Bank	51.8%	56.8%	86.1%	94.4%	43.1%	n.a.
RBC	51.6%	69.0%	81.7%	109.2%	32.6%	60.0%
Scotiabank*	61.2%	98.5%	87.5%	140.9%	24.6%	52.0%
TD Bank**	46.9%	60.1%	70.5%	90.4%	41.5%	63.0%
Average	54.2%	75.9%	81.7%	129.5%	31.6%	n.a.

*Core deposits include capital
**Core deposits as a percentage of total funding
Source: Canadian Banker's Association, Company 2004 Annual Reports and authors' calculations

financing gap
The difference between a DTI's average loans and average (core) deposits.

We define a **financing gap** as the difference between a DTI's average loans and average (core) deposits, or:

$$\text{Financing gap} = \text{Average loans} - \text{Average deposits}$$

If this financing gap is positive, the DTI must fund it by using its cash and liquid assets and/or borrowing funds in the money market. Thus:

$$\text{Financing gap} = - \text{Liquid assets} + \text{Borrowed funds}$$

We can write this relationship as:

$$\text{Financing gap} + \text{Liquid assets} = \text{Financing requirement (borrowed funds)}$$

financing requirement
The financing gap plus a DTI's liquid assets.

As expressed in this fashion, the liquidity and managerial implications of the **financing requirement** (the financing gap plus a DTI's liquid assets) are that the level of core deposits and loans as well as the amount of liquid assets determines the DTI's borrowing or purchased fund needs. In particular, the larger a DTI's financing gap and liquid asset holdings, the larger the amount of funds it needs to borrow in the money markets and the greater is its exposure to liquidity problems from such a reliance.

The balance sheet in Table 17–9 indicates the relationship between the financing gap, liquid assets, and the borrowed fund financing requirement. See also the following equation:

$$\text{Financing gap} + \text{Liquid assets} = \text{Financing requirement}$$
$$(\$5 \text{ million}) \qquad (\$5 \text{ million}) \qquad (\$10 \text{ million})$$

A widening financing gap can warn of future liquidity problems since it may indicate increased deposit withdrawals (core deposits falling below $20 million in Table 17–9) and increasing loans due to increased exercise of loan commitments (loans rising above $25 million). If the DTI does not reduce its liquid assets—they stay at $5 million—the manager must resort to more money market borrowings. As these borrowings rise, sophisticated lenders in the money market may be concerned about the DTI's creditworthiness. They may react by imposing higher risk premiums on borrowed funds or establishing stricter credit limits by not rolling over funds

TABLE 17–9
Financing
Requirement
of a DTI (in
millions of dollars)

Assets		Liabilities	
Loans	25	Core deposits	20
Liquid assets	5	Financing requirement (borrowed funds)	10
Total	30	Total	30
		Financing gap	5

lent to the DTI. If the DTI's financing requirements exceed such limits, it may become insolvent. A good example of an excessive financing requirement was Continental Bank of Canada. Following the failure of Canadian Commercial Bank and Northland Bank of Canada in 1985, financial markets in Canada were jittery and short-term funds moved out of the smaller FIs into larger, safer institutions. This loss of deposits forced Continental Bank, whose assets were of good quality, to seek a 6-month $1.4 billion loan from the Bank of Canada, and then to arrange a $1.5 billion 3-month standby line of credit with the other major banks that cost $750,000 in facility fees. Despite these efforts, Continental never regained the confidence of the market, and it ultimately merged with Lloyds Bank International, becoming a Schedule B Bank (the equivalent of today's Schedule II banks).[15]

BIS Approach: Maturity Ladder/Scenario Analysis

www.bis.org

In February 2000, recognizing that liquidity is crucial to the ongoing viability of a DTI, the Bank for International Settlements (BIS) outlined a Maturity Laddering method for measuring liquidity risk, and specifically, net funding (financing) requirements.[16] At a minimum, liquidity measurement involves assessing all cash inflows against its outflows, as outlined in Table 17–10. Once identified, a maturity ladder model allows a comparison of cash inflows and outflows on a day-to-day basis and/or over a series of specified time periods. Daily and cumulative net funding requirements can then be determined from the maturity ladder.

For the DTI in Table 17–10, for example, excess cash of $4 million is available over the one-day time horizon. However, a cumulative net cash shortfall of $46 million is expected to exist over the next month. The DTI will need to start planning immediately to obtain additional funding to fill this net funding requirement. Over the six-month period, the DTI has cumulative excess cash of $1,104 million. If these expectations hold true, the DTI will need to find a place to invest these excess funds until they are needed.

---

[15] See "Continental Bank's care package." *Financial Post*, November 9, 1985, p. 4, and "Continental Bank merges with Lloyds," *Toronto Star*, October 2, 1986, p. B.1. Other smaller FIs were affected as Morguard Bank of Canada was sold to Security Pacific Bank Canada, and Mercantile Bank of Canada merged with National Bank of Canada. Bank of B.C. and other FIs in Western Canada struggled with higher cost of funds that limited their ability to expand. See S. Horvitch, "Turmoil persists for smaller banks," *Financial Post*, February 1, 1986, p. 4, and A. Toulin, "Banks face an uphill battle in regaining lost confidence," *Toronto Star*, April 3, 1986, p. F.1. See also B. Smith and R. W. White, "The capital market impact of recent Canadian bank failures," *Canadian Journal of Administrative Sciences*, June 1990, Vol. 7, Iss. 2, p. 41, which demonstrates the "flight to quality" of deposits from regional to national banks. Around the same time, U.S. FIs experienced similar problems. The large money centre bank, Chicago-based Continental Illinois Bank, failed in 1984 when large money market lenders (such as Japanese banks) failed to roll over their borrowed funds. See L. Wall and D. R. Peterson, "The Effect of Continental Illinois' Failure on the Performance of Other Banks," *Journal of Monetary Economics*, 1990, pp. 77–79.

[16] See "Sound Practices for Managing Liquidity in Banking Organizations," Basel Committee on Banking Supervision, BIS, Basel, Switzerland, February 2000, available at www.bis.org.

TABLE 17–10
Net Funding
Requirement Using
the BIS Maturity
Laddering Model
(in millions of
dollars)

	1 Day	1 Month	6 Months
Cash Inflows			
Maturing assets	10	150	1,500
Salable nonmaturing assets	12	250	4,000
Access to deposit liabilities	15	200	2,000
Established credit lines	12	100	750
Ability to securitize	5	50	400
	54	750	8,650
Cash Outflows			
Liabilities falling due	30	490	4,500
Committed lines of credit that can be drawn on and other contingent liabilities	16	300	2,960
Cash outflows from unanticipated events	4	10	40
	50	800	7,500
Net funding requirement	4	(50)	1,150
Cumulative net funding requirement	4	(46)	1,104

The relevant time frame for active liquidity management is generally quite short, including intraday liquidity. However, the appropriate time frame will depend on the nature of a DTI's business. DTIs that rely on short-term funding concentrate primarily on managing their liquidity in the very short term (e.g., the BIS recommends a five-day horizon. DTIs that are less dependent on short-term funding might actively manage their net funding requirements over a slightly longer period. In addition, DTIs should analyze and monitor their liquidity positions over the longer term. Typically, a DTI may find substantial funding gaps in distant periods and thus need to plan ways to fill these gaps by influencing the maturity of transactions to offset the future funding gap.

While liquidity is typically managed under normal conditions, the BIS cautions that DTIs must also be prepared to manage liquidity under abnormal conditions. Analyzing liquidity thus entails generating and analyzing various what-if scenarios. Under each scenario, the DTI should try to account for any significant positive or negative liquidity swings that could occur. These scenarios should take into account factors both internal (bank specific) and external (market related). Under the BIS Scenario Analysis, a DTI needs to assign a timing of cash flows for each type of asset and liability by assessing the probability of the behavior of those cash flows under the scenario being examined. Accordingly, the timing of cash inflows and outflows on the maturity ladder can differ among scenarios, and the assumptions may differ quite sharply. For example, a DTI may believe, based on its historical experience, that its ability to control the level and timing of future cash flows from a stock of salable assets in a DTI-specific funding crisis would deteriorate little from normal conditions. However, in a market crisis, this capacity may fall off sharply if few institutions are willing or able to make cash purchases of less liquid assets.

The evolution of a DTI's liquidity profile under each scenario can be portrayed graphically, as in Figure 17–2. A stylized liquidity graph enables the evolution of the cumulative net excess or shortages of funds to be compared under the major scenarios (e.g., normal conditions, general market crisis conditions, DTI-specific crisis conditions). The DTI can use this profile to provide additional insights into

FIGURE 17–2
Cumulative Excess
or Shortages of
Funds for a High-
Quality DTI under
Various Market
Conditions

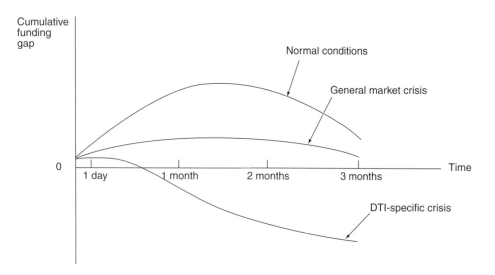

how consistent and realistic the assumptions are for its liquidity. For example, in Figure 17–2, a high-quality bank may look very liquid under normal circumstances and remain so in a general market crisis, but may suffer a liquidity crisis only in a DTI-specific crisis. In contrast, a lower-quality DTI might be equally illiquid in a general and a DTI-specific crisis. Because a DTI's future liquidity position can be affected by factors that cannot always be accurately predicted, it is critical that assumptions used to determine its funding requirements be reviewed and revised frequently.

Liquidity Planning

As implied by the BIS maturity ladder approach, liquidity planning is a key component in measuring (and being able to deal with) liquidity risk and its associated costs. Specifically, liquidity planning allows managers to make important borrowing priority decisions before liquidity problems arise. Such planning can lower the cost of funds (by determining an optimal funding mix) and can minimize the amount of excess reserves that a DTI needs to hold.

A liquidity plan has a number of components. The first component is the delineation of managerial details and responsibilities. Responsibilities are assigned to key management personnel should a liquidity crisis occur. The plan identifies those managers responsible for interacting with various government agencies such as the Bank of Canada, CDIC, and OSFI. It also specifies areas of managerial responsibility in disclosing information to the public—including depositors. The second component of a liquidity plan is a detailed list of fund providers who are most likely to withdraw, as well as the pattern of fund withdrawals. For example, in a crisis, financial institutions such as mutual funds and pension funds are more likely than correspondent banks and small business corporations to withdraw funds quickly from FIs. In turn, correspondent banks and small corporations are more likely than individual depositors to withdraw funds quickly. This makes liquidity exposure sensitive to the effects of future funding composition changes. Further, DTIs face particularly heavy seasonal withdrawals of deposits in the quarter before Christmas. The third component of liquidity planning is the identification of the size of potential deposit and fund withdrawals over various time horizons in the future (one week, one month, one quarter, etc.) as well as alternative private market funding sources to meet such

www.bankofcanada.ca
www.cdic.ca
www.osfi-bsif.gc.ca

TABLE 17–11
Deposit
Distributions
and Possible
Withdrawals
Involved in a DTI's
Liquidity Plan (in
millions of dollars)

Deposits from		250	
Mutual funds		60	
Pension funds		50	
Correspondent banks		15	
Small businesses		70	
Individuals		55	
Expected Withdrawals		**Average**	**Maximum**
One week		40	105
One month		55	140
Three months		75	200
Sequence of Deposit Withdrawal Funding	**One Week**	**One Month**	**Three Months**
New deposits	10	35	75
Investment portfolio asset liquidation	50	60	75
Borrowings from other FIs	30	35	45
Borrowings from the Bank of Canada	15	10	5

withdrawals (e.g., emergency loans from other FIs and the Bank of Canada). The fourth component of the plan sets internal limits on separate subsidiaries' and branches' borrowings as well as bounds for acceptable risk premiums to pay in each market. In addition, the plan details a sequencing of assets for disposal in anticipation of various degrees or intensities of deposit/fund withdrawals. Such a plan may evolve from a DTI's asset–liability management committee and may be relayed to various key departments of the DTI (e.g., the money desk and the treasury department), which play vital day-to-day roles in liability funding.

Consider, for example, Table 17–11. The data are for a DTI that holds $250 million in deposits from mutual funds, pension funds, correspondent banks, small businesses, and individuals. The table includes the average and maximum expected withdrawals over the next one-week, one-month, and one-quarter periods. The liquidity plan for the DTI outlines how to cover expected deposit withdrawals should they materialize. In this case, the DTI will seek to cover expected deposit withdrawals over the next three months, first with new deposits, then with the liquidation of marketable securities in its investment portfolio, then with borrowings from other FIs, and finally, if necessary, with borrowings from the Bank of Canada.

Liquidity Risk, Unexpected Deposit Drains, and Bank Runs

Under normal conditions and with appropriate management planning, neither net deposit withdrawals nor the exercise of loan commitments pose significant liquidity problems for DTIs because borrowed funds availability or excess cash reserves are adequate to meet anticipated needs. For example, even in December and the summer vacation season, when net deposit withdrawals are high, DTIs anticipate these *seasonal* effects by holding larger than normal excess cash reserves or borrowing more than normal on the wholesale money markets.

Major liquidity problems can arise, however, if deposit drains are abnormally *large* and unexpected. Abnormal deposit drains (shocks) may occur for a number of reasons, including:

1. Concerns about a DTI's solvency relative to those of other DTIs.

2. Failure of a related DTI leading to heightened depositor concerns about the solvency of other DTIs (the contagion effect).

3. Sudden changes in investor preferences regarding holding nonbank financial assets (such as T-bills or mutual fund shares) relative to deposits.

bank run
A sudden and unexpected increase in deposit withdrawals from a DTI.

www.scotiabank.com

In such cases, any sudden and unexpected surges in net deposit withdrawals risk triggering a **bank run** that could eventually force a bank into insolvency. Macroeconomic factors can also trigger a bank run, as shown in the Industry Perspectives box which describes the Bank of Nova Scotia's experience in Argentina. BNS's story has the added feature of sovereign risk. In Argentina, government actions appeared to exacerbate the situation, whereas in Canada, actions by the Bank of Canada and regulators have forestalled this type of bank run.[17]

Deposit Drains and Bank Run Liquidity Risk

At the core of bank run liquidity risk is the fundamental and unique nature of the *demand deposit contract*. Specifically, demand deposit contracts are first-come, first-served contracts in the sense that a depositor's place in line determines the amount he or she will be able to withdraw from a DTI. In particular, a depositor either gets paid in full or gets nothing.[18] Because demand deposit contracts pay in full only a certain proportion of depositors when a DTI's assets are valued at less than its deposits—and because depositors realize this—any line outside a DTI encourages other depositors to join the line immediately even if they do not need cash today for normal consumption purposes. Thus, even the DTI's core depositors rationally seek to withdraw their funds immediately when they observe a sudden increase in the lines at their DTI.

As a bank run develops, the demand for net deposit withdrawals grows. The DTI may initially meet this by decreasing its cash reserves, selling off liquid or readily marketable assets such as T-bills and T-bonds, and seeking to borrow in the money markets. As a bank run increases in intensity, more depositors join the withdrawal line, and a liquidity crisis develops. Specifically, the DTI finds it difficult, if not impossible, to borrow on the money markets at virtually any price. Also, it has sold all its liquid assets, cash, and bonds as well as any salable loans (see Chapter 26). The DTI is likely to have left only relatively illiquid loans on the asset side of the balance sheet to meet depositor claims for cash. However, these loans can be sold or liquidated only at very large discounts from face value. A DTI needing to liquidate long-term assets at fire-sale prices to meet continuing deposit

---

[17] For more analysis regarding the contagion effects, see A. Kanas, "Pure Contagion Effects in International Banking: The Case of BCCI's failure," *Journal of Applied Economics*, May 2005, Vol. 8, Iss. 1, pp. 101–124. The failure of Bank of Credit and Commerce International (BCCI) in the 1990s was one of the largest bank failures in the world whose story has all the elements of drama, including money laundering, corruption, and terrorist cells. Kanas looks at BCCI's failure in the U.K., the U.S., and Canada and finds no evidence of contagion effects in Canada or the U.S. S. J. Kamath and J. R. Tilley, "Canadian International Banking and the Debt Crisis," *Columbia Journal of World Business*, Winter 1987, Vol. 22, Iss. 4. pp. 75–87 examines effects from the 1980s LDC debt crisis, and S. V. Jayanti, A. M. Whyte, and A. Quang Do, "Bank Failures and contagion effects: Evidence from Britain and Canada," *Journal of Economics and Business*, May 1996, Vol. 48, Iss. 2, pp. 103–116 compares the 1985 Canadian bank failures with the U.K. experience. Jayanti et al conclude that the actions of regulators determine the market effects, as do L. Kryzanowski and G. S. Roberts, "Capital forbearance: Depression-era experience of life insurance companies," *Canadian Journal of Administrative Sciences*, March 1998, Vol. 15, Iss. 1, pp. 1–16.

[18] We are assuming no deposit insurance exists that guarantees payments of deposits and no borrowing from the Bank of Canada that alters consumers' incentives to engage in a bank run as we describe later in Chapter 19. Bankruptcies of Canadian FIs occurred between 1983–86 when 15 members of the Canada Deposit Insurance Corporation (CDIC) failed. Two of the failures were banks and the remaining FIs were trust companies. However, there have been no documented occurrences of contagion while deposit insurance has been in place. See G. Dionne, "The Foundations of Risk Regulation for Banks: A Review of the Literature," Bank of Canada Conference Proceedings, The Evolving Financial System and Public Policy, December, 2003, p.177–215, www.bankofcanada.ca.

Industry Perspectives

The Bank of Nova Scotia is seeking more than $600 million US in damages from the government of Argentina, claiming "discriminatory" actions cost the Canadian bank its investment in a former subsidiary.

Scotiabank alleges the government made unfair moves regarding Scotiabank Quilmes, whose licence was revoked in August 2002 amid an economic crisis in the South American country.

The bank eventually wrote off its holding in Quilmes, which at the time had 1,700 employees and 91 branches, with a $540-million-Cdn. after-tax charge.

"Scotiabank is seeking damages as compensation for the loss of its investment, the cost to it of winding up Scotiabank Quilmes, and harm to its reputation," the bank stated Thursday as it filed a notice of arbitration with the Argentine Attorney General.

The arbitration process could take two to three years, the bank said.

"This is the first time in the bank's 173-year history that it has made a claim of this nature, but a series of expropriatory and discriminatory actions taken by the Argentine government directly caused the loss of its investment and violated its treaty rights of fair treatment," Scotiabank stated.

"As a result, the bank and its shareholders experienced significant damages and as such it intends to vigorously pursue the right to compensation."

Argentina's economy crumbled into chaos in 2001, eventually leading to the largest government debt default in history.

There was a drastic run on bank deposits, as the population tried to grab its money while the currency crumbled. That caused the government to freeze withdrawals from retail bank accounts on Dec. 1, 2001, and restrict the transfer of funds abroad.

One month later medium-term Scotiabank Quilmes notes became due.

Scotiabank says the Argentine Central Bank would not grant permission for Quilmes to make payments on the notes, even though it had enough cash to do so, forcing Quilmes to default. Rating agencies downgraded the bank's debt and institutional investors withdrew deposits.

Quilmes' liquidity plummeted and "the Central Bank refused to provide adequate and timely liquidity support equal to that provided to other Argentine banks," Scotiabank said.

In February 2002, Argentina offered local banks bonds to compensate them for the decision to convert U.S.-dollar loans to pesos. Quilmes did not receive bonds.

Additionally, Scotiabank says Quilmes was forced to return deposits in excess of a government-mandated cap.

During this time, it says, the Argentine central bank was assisting other banks but refused to extend "sufficient" liquidity support to Quilmes.

In April 2002, the central bank froze Quilmes' operations because of its low liquidity, then "obstructed" to restructure, Scotiabank said.

In August 2002, the central bank revoked Quilmes' licence and the operation shut down. Its assets were transferred to a trust run by two Argentine banks.

Source: Tara Perkins, CNW Group, Toronto, April 7, 2005.

---

drains faces the strong possibility that the proceeds from such asset sales are insufficient to meet depositors' cash demands. The DTI's liquidity problem then turns into a solvency problem; that is, the DTI must close its doors.

The incentives for depositors to run first and ask questions later creates a fundamental instability in the banking system in that an otherwise sound DTI can be pushed into insolvency and failure by unexpectedly large depositor drains and liquidity demands. This is especially so in periods of contagious runs, or **bank panics,** when depositors lose faith in the banking system as a whole and engage in a run on all DTIs by not materially discriminating among them according to their asset qualities.[19]

bank panic
A systemic or contagious run on the deposits of the banking industry as a whole.

---

[19] See Kaufman, "Bank Contagion," for an excellent review of the nature and causes of bank runs and panics. There is strong evidence of contagious bank runs or panics in 1930–32 in the United States. See A. Saunders and B. Wilson, "Informed and Uninformed Depositor Runs and Panics: Evidence from the 1929–33 Period," *Journal of Financial Intermediation* 5 (1996), pp. 409–23.

Bank Runs, The Bank of Canada, and Deposit Insurance

Regulators have recognized the inherent instability of the banking system due to the all-or-nothing payoff features of the deposit contract. As a result, regulatory mechanisms are in place to ease DTIs' liquidity problems and to deter bank runs and panics. The two major liquidity risk insulation devices are *deposit insurance* and *borrowing from the Bank of Canada*. Because of the serious social welfare effects that a contagious run on DTIs could have, government regulators of deposit-taking institutions have established guarantee programs offering deposit holders varying degrees of insurance protection to deter runs. Specifically, if a deposit holder believes a claim is totally secure, even if the DTI is in trouble, the holder has no incentive to run. The deposit holder's place in line no longer affects his or her ability to obtain the funds. Deposit insurance deters runs as well as contagious runs and panics.

In addition to deposit insurance, central banks such as the Bank of Canada have traditionally provided overnight lending facilities to meet DTIs' short-term non-permanent liquidity needs. The Bank of Canada has three roles as **lender of last resort (LLR)** in providing liquidity to the financial system. As previously noted, through the LVTS, the Bank of Canada provides daily and overnight funds to cover temporary shortfalls of an FI. The Bank can also provide emergency lending assistance (ELA) to solvent deposit-taking financial institutions for a longer time period, as they did for Continental Bank of Canada. During extreme conditions, the Bank of Canada can also buy securities issued by financial and non-financial Canadian or foreign firms and government entities.[20]

lender of last resort (LLR)
The role of a central bank in providing funds to a country's FIs during a liquidity crisis.

Concept Questions

1. List two benefits and two costs of using (a) purchased liquidity management and (b) stored liquidity management to meet a deposit drain.
2. What are the three major sources of DTI liquidity? What are the two major uses?
3. What are the measures of liquidity risk used by FIs?

LIQUIDITY RISK AND LIFE INSURANCE COMPANIES

Deposit-taking institutions are not the only FIs exposed to liquidity risk or run problems. Like DTIs, life insurance companies hold cash reserves and other liquid assets to meet policy cancelations (surrenders) and other working capital needs that arise in the course of writing insurance. The early cancelation of an insurance policy results in the insurer's having to pay the insured the **surrender value** of that policy.[21] In the normal course of business, premium income and returns on an insurer's asset portfolio are sufficient to meet the cash outflows required when policyholders cash in or surrender their policies early. As with DTIs, the distribution or pattern of premium income minus policyholder liquidations is normally predictable. When premium income is insufficient to meet surrenders, however, a

surrender value
The amount received by an insurance policy-holder when cashing in a policy early.

---

[20] See The Bank of Canada, "Bank of Canada Lender-of-Last-Resort Policies," *Financial System Review*, December 2004, pp. 49–55.

[21] A surrender value is usually some proportion or percent less than 100 percent of the face value of the insurance contract. The surrender value continues to grow as funds invested in the policy earn interest (returns). Earnings to the policyholder are taxed if and when the policy is actually surrendered or cashed in before the policy matures. Some insurance companies have faced run problems resulting from their sale of guaranteed investment contracts (GICs). A GIC, similar to a long-term, fixed-rate bank deposit, is a contract between an investor and an insurance company. As market interest rates rose, many investors withdrew their funds early and reinvested elsewhere in higher-return investments. This created both liquidity and refinancing problems for life insurers that supplied such contracts and eventually led to restrictions on withdrawals.

life insurer can sell some of its relatively liquid assets, such as government bonds. In this case, bonds act as a buffer or reserve asset source of liquidity for the insurer.

Nevertheless, concerns about the solvency of an insurer can result in a run in which new premium income dries up and existing policyholders seek to cancel their policies by cashing them in early. To meet exceptional demands for cash, a life insurer could be forced to liquidate the other assets in its portfolio, such as commercial mortgage loans and other securities, potentially at fire-sale prices.[22]

Concept Questions

1. What is likely to be a life insurance company's first source of liquidity when premium income is insufficient?
2. Can a life insurance company be subjected to a run? If so, why?

LIQUIDITY RISK AND PROPERTY & CASUALTY INSURERS

As discussed in Chapter 3, property & casualty (P & C) insurers sell policies insuring against certain contingencies impacting either real property or individuals. Unlike those of life insurers, P & C contingencies (and policy coverages) are relatively short term, often one to three years. With the help of mortality tables, claims on life insurance policies are generally predictable. P & C claims (such as those associated with natural disasters such as the Quebec ice storm and the Winnipeg flood discussed in Chapter 3), however, are virtually impossible to predict. As a result, P & C insurers' assets tend to be shorter term and more liquid than those of life insurers. P & C insurers' contracts and premium-setting intervals are usually relatively short term as well, so problems caused by policy surrenders are less severe. P & C insurers' greatest liquidity exposure occurs when policyholders cancel or fail to renew policies with an insurer because of insolvency risk, pricing, or competitive reasons. This may cause an insurer's premium cash inflow, when added to its investment returns, to be insufficient to meet policyholders' claims. Alternatively, large unexpected claims may materialize and exceed the flow of premium income and income returns from assets causing severe liquidity crises and failures among smaller P & C insurers.[23]

Concept Questions

1. What is the greatest cause of liquidity exposure faced by property & casualty insurers?
2. Is the liquidity risk of property & casualty insurers in general greater or less than that of life insurers?

MUTUAL FUNDS, HEDGE FUNDS, AND PENSION FUNDS

open-end fund
An investment fund that sells an elastic or nonfixed number of shares in the fund to outside investors.

Mutual funds sell shares as liabilities to investors and invest the proceeds in assets such as bonds and equities. As discussed in Chapter 5, by far the majority of mutual funds are **open-end funds;** that is, they can issue an unlimited supply of shares to investors. Open-end funds must also stand ready to buy back previously issued shares from investors at the current market price for the fund's shares. Thus, at a given market price, P, the supply of open-end fund shares is perfectly elastic. The price at which an open-end mutual fund stands ready to sell

---

[22] Life insurers also provide a considerable amount of loan commitments, especially in the commercial property area. As a result, they face asset-side loan commitment liquidity risk in a fashion similar to that of DTIs.

[23] Also, claims may arise in long-tail lines where a contingency takes place during the policy period but a claim is not lodged until many years later. As mentioned in Chapter 3, one example is the claims regarding damage caused by asbestos contacts.

TABLE 17–12
Run Incentives of
DTI Depositors
versus Mutual
Fund Investors

Deposit-taking Institution		Mutual Fund	
Assets	**Liabilities**	**Assets**	**Liabilities**
Assets $90	$100 Deposits (100 depositors with $1 deposits)	Assets $90	$100 Shares (100 shareholders with $1 shares)

net asset value (NAV)
The price at which
mutual funds shares
are sold (or can be
redeemed). It equals
the total market value
of the assets of the
fund divided by the
number of shares in
the funds outstanding.

new shares or redeem existing shares is the **net asset value (NAV)** of the fund. NAV is the current or market value of the fund's assets less any accrued liabilities divided by the number of shares in the fund. A mutual fund's willingness to provide instant liquidity to shareholders while it invests funds in equities, bonds, and other long-term instruments could expose it to liquidity problems similar to those banks, and life insurance companies face when the number of withdrawals (or fund shares cashed in) rises to abnormally and unexpectedly high levels. Indeed, mutual funds can be subject to dramatic liquidity runs if investors become nervous about the NAV of the mutual funds' assets.[24] However, the fundamental difference in the way mutual fund contracts are valued compared with the valuation of DTI deposit and insurance policy contracts mitigates the incentives for mutual fund shareholders to engage in runs. Specifically, if a mutual fund were to be liquidated, its assets would be distributed to fund shareholders on a pro rata basis rather than the first-come, first-served basis employed under deposit and insurance contracts.

To illustrate this difference, we can directly compare the incentives for mutual fund (and hedge fund) investors to engage in a run with those of DTI depositors. Table 17–12 shows a simple balance sheet of an open-end mutual fund and a DTI. When they perceive that a DTI's assets are valued below its liabilities, depositors have an incentive to engage in a run on the DTI to be first in line to withdraw. In the example in Table 17–12, only the first 90 bank depositors would receive $1 back for each $1 deposited. The last 10 would receive nothing at all.

Now consider the mutual fund with 100 shareholders who invested $1 each for a total of $100, but whose assets are worth $90. If these shareholders tried to cash in their shares, *none* would receive $1. Instead, a mutual fund values its balance sheet liabilities on a market value basis; the price of any share liquidated by an investor is:

$$P = \frac{\text{Value of assets}}{\text{Shares outstanding}} = \text{NAV (net asset value)}$$

Thus, unlike deposit contracts that have fixed face values of $1, the value of a mutual fund's shares reflects the changing value of its assets divided by the number of shares outstanding.

In Table 17–12, the value of each shareholder's claim is:

$$P = \frac{\$90}{100} = \$.9$$

That is, each mutual fund shareholder participates in the fund's loss of asset value on a *pro rata*, or proportional, basis. Technically, whether first or last in line, each mutual fund shareholder who cashes in shares on any given day receives the same net asset value per share of the mutual fund. In this case, it is 90 cents, representing

---

[24] For example, this happened to the value of assets held by mutual funds specializing in equities of Asian countries such as Indonesia and Thailand as well as Russia during the emerging market crisis of 1997–98.

a loss of 10 cents per share. All mutual fund shareholders realize this and know that investors share asset losses on a pro rata basis; being the first in line to withdraw has no overall advantage as it has at DTIs.

This is not to say that mutual funds bear no liquidity risk, but that the incentives for mutual fund shareholders to engage in runs that produce the extreme form of liquidity problems faced by DTIs and life insurance companies are generally absent.[25]

Pension funds differ in that amounts paid out are controlled by the nature of the plan and therefore have been generally well-insulated from the meltdowns that affected LTCM and the banks. However, pension funds, as well as mutual funds and hedge funds are subject to the same economy-wide liquidity risks that affect their returns.[26]

Concept Questions

1. What would be the impact on their liquidity needs if DTIs offered deposit contracts of an open-end mutual fund type rather than the traditional all-or-nothing demand deposit contract?
2. How do the incentives of mutual fund investors to engage in runs compare with the incentives of DTI depositors?

---

[25] A sudden surge of mutual fund shareholder redemptions might require a mutual fund manager to sell some of its less marketable bonds and equities at fire-sale prices. Long-Term Capital Management, faced severe liquidity problems when trying to unwind large positions in many asset markets at the end of 1998. For example, some mortgage-backed securities markets (see Chapter 27) were insufficiently deep to be able to absorb the massive sale of hedge fund assets without major price dislocations.

[26] T. Anthony, "Avoiding a Run for Your Money," *Canadian Investment Review*, Fall 2004, Vol. 17, Iss. 3, pp. 29–34 discusses adjustments to portfolio management to recognize this type of risk for defined benefit pension plans, particularly with the aging of the Canadian population. Some of the principles can be extended to mutual funds and hedge funds as retirees increase their cash demands as their investment needs decrease.

Summary

Liquidity risk, as a result of heavier-than-anticipated liability withdrawals or loan commitment exercise, is a common problem faced by FI managers. Well-developed policies for holding liquid assets or having access to markets for purchased funds are normally adequate to meet liability withdrawals. However, very large withdrawals can cause asset liquidity problems that can be compounded by incentives for liability claim holders to engage in runs at the first sign of a liquidity problem. These incentives for depositors and life insurance policyholders to engage in runs can push normally sound FIs into insolvency. Mutual funds are able to avoid runs because liabilities are marked to market so that losses are shared equally among liability holders. Since such insolvencies have costs to society as well as to private shareholders, regulators have developed mechanisms such as deposit insurance and borrowing from the central bank to alleviate liquidity problems. We discuss these mechanisms in detail in Chapter 19.

Questions and Problems

1. How does the degree of liquidity risk differ for different types of financial institutions?

2. What are the two reasons liquidity risk arises? How does liquidity risk arising from the liability side of the balance sheet differ from liquidity risk arising from the asset side of the balance sheet? What is meant by fire-sale prices?

3. What are core deposits? What role do core deposits play in predicting the probability distribution of net deposit drains?

4. The probability distribution of the net deposit drain of a DTI has been estimated to have a mean of 2 percent and a standard deviation of 1 percent. Is this DTI increasing or decreasing in size? Explain.

5. How is a DTI's distribution pattern of net deposit drains affected by the following?
   a. The holiday season.
   b. Summer vacations.
   c. A severe economic recession.
   d. Double-digit inflation.

6. What are two ways a DTI can offset the liquidity effects of a net deposit drain of funds? How do the two methods differ? What are the operational benefits and costs of each method?

7. What are two ways a DTI can offset the effects of asset-side liquidity risk such as the drawing down of a loan commitment?

8. A DTI with the following balance sheet (in millions) expects a net deposit drain of $15 million.

Assets		Liabilities and Equity	
Cash	10	Deposits	68
Loans	50	Equity	7
Securities	15		
Total assets	75	Total liabilities and equity	75

Show the DTI's balance sheet if the following conditions occur:

a. The DTI purchases liabilities to offset this expected drain.

b. The stored liquidity management method is used to meet the expected drain.

9. AllStarBank has the following balance sheet (in millions):

Assets		Liabilities and Equity	
Cash	30	Deposits	110
Loans	90	Borrowed funds	40
Securities	50	Equity	20
Total assets	170	Total liabilities and equity	170

AllStarBank's largest customer decides to exercise a $15 million loan commitment. How will the new balance sheet appear if AllStar uses the following liquidity risk strategies?

a. Asset management.

b. Liability management.

10. A DTI has assets of $10 million consisting of $1 million in cash and $9 million in loans. The DTI has core deposits of $6 million, subordinated debt of $2 million, and equity of $2 million. Increases in interest rates are expected to cause a net drain of $2 million in core deposits over the year.

a. The average cost of deposits is 6 percent, and the average yield on loans is 8 percent. The DTI decides to reduce its loan portfolio to offset this expected decline in deposits. What will be the effect on net interest income and the size of the DTI after the implementation of this strategy?

b. If the interest cost of issuing new short-term debt is expected to be 7.5 percent, what would be the effect on net interest income of offsetting the expected deposit drain with an increase in interest-bearing liabilities?

c. What will be the size of the DTI after the drain if the DTI uses this strategy?

d. What dynamic aspects of DTI management would further support a strategy of replacing the deposit drain with interest-bearing liabilities?

11. Define each of the following four measures of liquidity risk. Explain how each measure would be implemented and utilized by a DTI.

a. Sources and uses of liquidity.

b. Peer group ratio comparisons.

c. Liquidity index.

d. Financing gap and financing requirement.

12. A DTI has $10 million in T-bills and a $5 million line of credit to borrow in the repo market. The DTI currently has borrowed $6 million in interbank funds and $2 million from the Bank of Canada to meet seasonal demands.

a. What is the DTI's total available (sources of) liquidity?

b. What is the DTI's current total uses of liquidity?

c. What is the net liquidity of the DTI?

d. What conclusions can you derive from the result?

13. Plainbank has $10 million in cash and equivalents, $30 million in loans, and $15 million in core deposits.

a. Calculate the financing gap.

b. What is the financing requirement?

c. How can the financing gap be used in the day-to-day liquidity management of the bank?

14. How can an FI's liquidity plan help reduce the effects of liquidity shortages? What are the components of a liquidity plan?

15. What is a bank run? What are some possible withdrawal shocks that could initiate a bank run? What feature of the demand deposit contract provides deposit withdrawal momentum that can result in a bank run?

16. The following is the balance sheet of a DTI (in millions):

Assets		Liabilities and Equity	
Cash	2	Demand deposits	50
Loans	50		
Plant and equipment	3	Equity	5
Total	55	Total	55

The asset-liability management committee has estimated that the loans, whose average interest rate is 6 percent and whose average life is three years, will have to be discounted at 10 percent if they are to be sold in less than two days. If they can be sold in four days, they will have to be discounted at 8 percent.

If they can be sold later than a week, the DTI will receive the full market value. Loans are not amortized; that is, the principal is paid at maturity.

a. What will be the price received by the DTI for the loans if they have to be sold in two days? In four days?

b. In a crisis, if depositors all demand payment on the first day, what amount will they receive? What will they receive if they demand to be paid within the week? Assume no deposit insurance.

17. What government safeguards are in place to reduce liquidity risk for DTIs?

18. What are the levels of defense against liquidity risk for a life insurance company? How does liquidity risk for a property & casualty insurer differ from that for a life insurance company?

19. How is the liquidity problem faced by mutual funds different from that faced by DTIs and insurance companies?

20. A mutual fund has the following assets in its portfolio: $40 million in fixed-income securities and $40 million in stocks at current market values. In the event of a liquidity crisis, the fund can sell the assets at 96 percent of market value if they are disposed of in two days. The fund will receive 98 percent if the assets are disposed of in four days. Two shareholders, A and B, own 5 percent and 7 percent of equity (shares), respectively.

a. Market uncertainty has caused shareholders to sell their shares back to the fund. What will the two shareholders receive if the mutual fund must sell all the assets in two days? In four days?

b. How does this situation differ from a bank run? How have bank regulators mitigated the problem of bank runs?

21. A mutual fund has $1 million in cash and $9 million invested in securities. It currently has 1 million shares outstanding.

a. What is the net asset value (NAV) of this fund?

b. Assume that some of the shareholders decide to cash in their shares of the fund. How many shares at its current NAV can the fund take back without resorting to a sale of assets?

c. As a result of anticipated heavy withdrawals, the fund sells 10,000 shares of stock currently valued at $40. Unfortunately, it receives only $35 per share. What is the net asset value after the sale? What are the cash assets of the fund after the sale?

d. Assume that after the sale of stock, 100,000 shares are sold back to the fund. What is the current NAV? Is there a need to sell more securities to meet this redemption?

Web Questions

22. Go to the Statistics Canada Web site at www.statcan.ca. In the Search Box, enter "Banking balance sheet." Click on the first item returned, "Banking Balance sheet and income statement." Use information in this table to update Table 17–1. How have the assets and liabilities of Canadian banks changed since October 2004?

Managing Risk

Liability and Liquidity Management

In this chapter, we consider how an FI can manage liquidity risk and discuss:

▸ the various liquid assets and liabilities an FI might use to manage liquidity risk

▸ the risk-return tradeoffs of using these assets and liabilities to manage liquidity risk, and

▸ the specific issues associated with liquidity risk management in deposit-taking institutions, insurance companies, and other FIs

INTRODUCTION

Deposit-taking institutions as well as life insurance companies are especially exposed to liquidity risk (see Chapter 17). The essential feature of this risk is that an FI's assets are relatively illiquid when liquid claims are suddenly withdrawn (or not renewed). The classic case is a bank run in which depositors demand cash as they withdraw their claims from a bank and the bank is unable to meet those demands because of the relatively illiquid nature of its assets. For example, the bank could have a large portfolio of nonmarketable small business or real estate loans.

To reduce the risk of a liquidity crisis, FIs can insulate their balance sheets from liquidity risk by efficiently managing their liquid asset positions or managing the liability structure of their portfolios. In reality, an FI manager can optimize over both liquid asset and liability structures to insulate the FI against liquidity risk. In addition to ensuring that FIs can meet expected and unexpected liability withdrawals, two additional motives exist for holding liquid assets: monetary policy implementation and taxation reasons.

LIQUID ASSET MANAGEMENT

A liquid asset can be turned into cash quickly and at a low transaction cost with little or no loss in principal value. Specifically, a liquid asset is traded in an active market so that even large transactions in that asset do not move the market price or move it very little. Good examples of liquid assets are newly issued T-bills, and other government debt. The ultimate liquid asset is, of course, cash. While it is obvious that an FI's liquidity risk can be reduced by holding large amounts of assets such as cash, T-bills, and Government of Canada bonds, FIs usually face a return or interest earnings penalty from doing this. Because of their high liquidity and low default risks, such assets often bear low returns that reflect their essentially risk-free nature. By contrast, nonliquid assets often must promise additional returns or liquidity risk premiums to compensate an FI for the relative lack of marketability and often greater default risk of the instrument.

Holding relatively small amounts of liquid assets exposes an FI to enhanced illiquidity and risk of a bank run. Excessive illiquidity can result in an FI's inability to meet required payments on liability claims and, at the extreme, in insolvency. It can even lead to contagious effects that negatively impact other FIs (see Chapter 17). Consequently, regulators have often imposed minimum liquid asset reserve requirements that differ in nature and scope for various FIs and according to country. The requirements depend on the liquidity risk exposure perceived for the FI's type and other regulatory objectives. For example, the Federal Reserve Bank of the United States strengthens its monetary policy by setting a minimum ratio of liquid reserve assets to deposits that limits the ability of deposit-taking institutions (DTIs) to expand lending. An increase in the reserve requirement results in a decrease in lending and subsequent decrease in the money supply. Conversely, a decrease in the reserve ratio means that DTIs are able to lend a greater percentage of their deposits, thus increasing credit availability in the economy.[1] As noted in Chapter 17, the Bank of Canada is one of several central banks (another example is the Reserve Bank of New Zealand) that carry out monetary policy to control inflation by setting a target for the overnight rate rather than by imposing reserve requirements. Thus the Bank of Canada has set the reserve requirements for banks at zero since 1994. However, it still stands as the lender of last resort in providing overnight liquidity and emergency lending assistance to deposit-taking institutions in Canada.

www.bankofcanada.ca

Concept Questions

1. Why do regulators set minimum liquid asset requirements for FIs?

THE COMPOSITION OF THE LIQUID ASSET PORTFOLIO

The composition of an FI's liquid asset portfolio, especially among cash and government securities, is determined partly by earnings considerations and partly by the type of minimum liquid asset reserve requirements the central bank imposes. In many countries, such as the United Kingdom, reserve ratios have historically been imposed to encompass both cash and liquid government securities such as T-bills.[2] Thus, a 20 percent **liquid assets ratio** requires a DTI to hold $1 of cash plus government securities for every $5 of deposits. Many states in the United States impose liquid asset ratios on life insurance companies that require minimum cash and government securities holdings in their balance sheets. By contrast, the minimum liquid asset requirements on DTIs in the United States have been cash based and have excluded government securities. As a result, government securities are less useful because they are not counted as part of reserves held by DTIs and at the same time yield lower promised returns than loans. Nevertheless, many DTIs view government securities holdings as performing a useful **secondary** or **buffer reserve** function. In times of a liquidity crisis, when significant drains on cash reserves occur, these securities can be turned into cash quickly and with very little loss of principal value because of the deep nature of the markets in which these assets are traded.

liquid assets ratio
A minimum ratio of liquid assets to total assets set by the central bank.

secondary or buffer reserves
Nonreserve assets that can be quickly turned into cash.

Concept Questions

1. In general, would it be better to hold three-month T-bills or 10-year government bonds as buffer assets? Explain.

---

[1] For example, in the United States the Federal Reserve system is divided into 12 districts that are the "operating arms" of the central banking system. Each of the 12 regional banks deals specifically with the liquidity issues in its section of the country.

[2] The United Kingdom no longer imposes minimum reserve requirements on banks.

RETURN-RISK TRADE-OFF FOR LIQUID ASSETS

In optimizing its holdings of liquid assets, an FI must trade the benefit of cash immediacy for lower returns. In a jurisdiction which, like Canada or the United Kingdom, does not impose reserve requirements, an FI is able to optimize its liquid asset holdings by matching its assets holdings with the liquidity needs of its short-term liabilities such as deposit withdrawals. A further consideration in the liquid asset mix for large Canadian FIs is the requirement for members of the Large Value Transfer System (LVTS) to provide collateral on a daily basis for the largest transaction that they expect to clear through the payment system. Since LVTS transactions are instantaneous and irrevocable, the collateral acts as a form of co-insurance to protect other LVTS participants and the Bank of Canada should a member experience liquidity difficulties during the day. If an LVTS participant were unable to make its payments, the Bank of Canada would sell the securities held as collateral to meet the FI's obligations. Thus, the collateral is highly liquid and is limited to securities issued or guaranteed by the Government of Canada or provincial governments, deposits held at the Bank of Canada, bankers' acceptances, commercial paper, short-term paper or bonds issued by municipalities, and corporate bonds.[3]

Liquidity Management as a Knife-Edge Management Problem

The management of a DTI's liquidity is something of a knife-edge situation because holding too many liquid assets penalizes an FI's earnings, and thus, its stockholders. An FI manager who holds excessive amounts of liquid assets is unlikely to survive long. Similarly, a manager who holds too little liquid assets faces increased risks of liquidity crises, which would result in regulatory intervention. Again, such a manager's tenure at the FI may be relatively short.

LIABILITY MANAGEMENT

Liquidity and liability management are closely related. One aspect of liquidity risk control is the buildup of a prudential level of liquid assets. Another aspect is the management of the DTI's liability structure to reduce the need for large amounts of liquid assets to meet liability withdrawals. However, excessive use of purchased funds in the liability structure can result in a liquidity crisis if investors lose confidence in the DTI and refuse to roll over such funds.

Funding Risk and Cost

Unfortunately, constructing a low-cost, low-withdrawal-risk liability portfolio is more difficult than it sounds. This is true because those liabilities, or sources of DTI funds, that are the most subject to withdrawal risk are often the least costly to the DTI. That is, a DTI must trade off the benefits of attracting liabilities at a low funding cost with a high chance of withdrawal against liabilities with a high funding cost and low liquidity. For example, demand deposits are relatively low funding cost vehicles for DTIs but can be withdrawn without notice.[4] By contrast, a five-year, fixed-term certificate of deposit may have a relatively high funding cost but can be

---

[3] See Chapter 17 for a discussion of the Large Value Transfer System (LVTS).

FIGURE 18–1   **Funding Risk versus Cost**

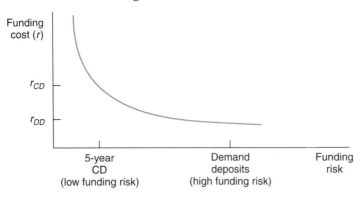

Source: CDIC, 2004 Annual
Report, www.cdic.ca,
http://www.cdic.ca/
bin/cdic_ar_e.pdf

withdrawn before the five-year maturity is up only after the deposit holder pays a substantial interest rate penalty.

Thus, in structuring the liability, or funding, side of the balance sheet, the DTI manager faces a trade-off along the lines suggested in Figure 18–1. That is, funding costs are generally inversely related to the period of time the liability is likely to remain on the DTI's balance sheet (i.e., to funding risk).

Although we have discussed deposit-taking institutions' funding risk, other FIs face a similar trade-off. For example, investment banks can finance through overnight funds (repurchase agreements and brokered deposits) or longer-term sources such as notes and bonds. Finance companies have a choice between commercial paper and longer-term notes and bonds.

In some respects, the management of funding risk and cost is similar to the treasury function of any other large corporation. However, the regulatory climate provides an added dimension to the "treasury" management of a large FI, particularly in those jurisdictions such as the U.S., which still have reserve requirements. The consequences for the FI of undershooting its liquidity needs and, as a result, being unable to meet any required reserve requirements, settle its payments through the clearing system, or meet its customer's deposit withdrawals are a loss of confidence by depositors and regulators, a potential for long-term damage to its reputation and, in a worst case scenario, insolvency. The next section looks at the spectrum of liabilities available to a DTI manager in seeking to actively impact liquidity risk exposure through the choice of liability structure.

**Concept
Questions**

1. How are liquidity and liability management related?
2. Describe the trade-off faced by an FI manager in structuring the liability side of the balance sheet.

CHOICE OF LIABILITY STRUCTURE

This section considers in more detail the withdrawal (or funding) risk and funding cost characteristics of the major liabilities available to a modern DTI manager.

Demand Deposits

Withdrawal Risk

Demand deposits issued by DTIs have a high degree of withdrawal risk. Withdrawals can be instantaneous and largely expected by the DTI manager, such as preweekend cash withdrawals, or unexpected, as occur during economic crisis situations (so-called bank runs; see Chapter 17).

---

[4] Depositors do not always exercise this option; therefore, some demand deposits behave like longer-term core deposits. In addition, many DTIs waive monthly fees when a depositor maintains a minimun monthly balance, creating an incentive to leave the funds on deposit.

Costs

Demand deposits pay the lowest interest rates, making them a low-cost source of funds for DTIs. In addition, DTIs can adjust the levels of interest rates and fees charged in order to partially control for the withdrawal risk associated with these contracts. For example, it is common for deposit accounts at FIs to pay a higher interest rate depending on the amount kept on balance in the account, or to provide no-fee chequing if a minimum monthly balance is maintained. Very few bank deposits in Canada are non-interest-bearing. For example, the Royal Bank's 2004 annual report shows total demand deposits (mainly chequing accounts for which the bank has no legal right to demand notice) of $59,738 million, total notice deposits (primarily savings accounts for which the bank can ask for notice of withdrawal) of $43,440 million, and total term deposits (paid on a fixed date) of $167,781 million. Of this total of $270,959 million, only $31,250 million (11.5 percent) was non-interest-bearing.

www.royalbank.com

Competition among DTIs and other FIs has resulted in the payment of implicit interest, or payments of interest in kind, on chequing accounts. Specifically, in providing demand deposits that are chequable accounts, a DTI must provide a whole set of associated services from providing cheque books, to clearing of cheques, to sending out statements with cleared cheques or cheque images. Because such services absorb real resources of labour and capital, they are costly for DTIs to provide. DTIs can recapture these costs by charging fees, such as 10 cents per cheque cleared. To the extent that these fees do not fully cover the DTI's cost of providing such services, the depositor receives a subsidy or an implicit interest payment.

The payment of implicit interest means that the DTI manager is not absolutely powerless to mitigate deposit withdrawals, especially if rates on competing instruments are rising. In particular, the DTI could lower cheque-clearing fees, which in turn raises implicit interest payments to depositors. Such payments are *payments in kind* or *subsidies* that are not paid in actual dollars and cents as is interest earned on competing instruments. Nevertheless, implicit payments of interest are tax-free to the depositor, but explicit interest payments are taxable.

EXAMPLE 18–1

Calculation of Average Implicit Interest Rate

Suppose a DTI pays 15 cents to clear a cheque but charges a fee of only 10 cents per cheque cleared. The customer receives a 5 cent subsidy per cheque. We can calculate implicit yields for each service, or an average implicit interest rate, for each demand deposit account. For example, an average implicit interest rate for a DI's demand deposits might be calculated as:

$$\begin{array}{c} \text{Average implicit} \\ \text{interest rate} \\ \text{(IIR)} \end{array} = \frac{\begin{array}{c}\text{Average management costs} \\ \text{per account per annum}\end{array} - \begin{array}{c}\text{Average fees earned per} \\ \text{account per annum}\end{array}}{\text{Average annual size of account}}$$

Suppose that:

$$\text{Average management costs per account per annum} = \$ \ 150$$
$$\text{Average fees earned per account per annum} = \$ \ 100$$
$$\text{Average annual size of account} = \$1,200$$

Then:

$$IIR = \frac{\$150 - \$100}{\$1,200} = 4.166\%$$

Interest-Bearing Chequing Accounts

Withdrawal Risk

Canadian FIs offer chequable deposits that pay interest and are withdrawable on demand. The major distinction between these instruments and traditional demand deposits is that these instruments require the depositor to maintain a minimum account balance to earn interest. If the minimum balance falls below some level, such as $500, the account formally converts to a status equivalent to demand deposits and earns no interest. The payment of explicit interest and the existence of minimum balance requirements make these accounts potentially less prone to withdrawal risk than demand deposits. Nevertheless, they are still highly liquid instruments from the depositor's perspective.

Costs

As with demand deposits, the FI can influence the potential withdrawability of chequing accounts by paying implicit interest or fee subsidies such as not charging the full cost of cheque clearance. However, the manager has two other ways to influence the yield paid to the depositor. The first is by varying the minimum balance requirement. If the minimum balance requirement is lowered—say, from $500 to $250—a larger portion of the account becomes subject to interest payments and thus the explicit return and attractiveness of these accounts increases. The second is to vary the explicit interest rate payment itself, such as increasing it from 5 to $5\frac{1}{4}$ percent. Thus, the FI manager has three pricing mechanisms to increase or decrease the attractiveness, and therefore impact the withdrawal rate, of chequing accounts: implicit interest payments, minimum balance requirements, and explicit interest payments.[5]

EXAMPLE 18–2 *Gross Interest Return*	Consider a depositor who holds on average $250 per month for the first three months of the year, $500 per month for the next three months, and $1,000 per month for the final six months of the year in a chequing account. The account pays 5 percent per annum if the minimum balance is $500 or more, and it pays no interest if the account falls below $500. The depositor writes an average of 50 cheques per month and pays a service fee of 10 cents for each cheque although it costs the bank 15 cents to process each cheque. The account holder's gross interest return, consisting of implicit plus explicit interest, is:

$$\text{Gross interest return} = \text{Explicit interest} + \text{Implicit interest} = \$500\,(.05)(.25)$$
$$+ \$1000\,(.05)(.5) + (\$.15 - \$.10)(50)(12)$$
$$= \$6.25 + \$25 + \$30 = \$61.25$$

Suppose the minimum balance was lowered from $500 to $250 and cheque service fees were lowered from 10 cents to 5 cents per cheque. Then:

$$\text{Gross interest return} = \$250(.05)(.25) + \$500(.05)(.25) + \$1000(.05)(.5)$$
$$+ (\$.15 - \$.05)(50)(12)$$
$$= \$3.125 + \$6.25 + \$25 + \$60$$
$$= \$94.375$$

---

[5] Recent research shows that customers are, in fact, fairly tolerant of such price changes. A 2001 market research study of more than 500 banking customers in the U.S. Southeast and Midwest suggests that few depositors actually change banks as a result of changes in the cost of the deposits. Chequing account customers, for instance, were surprisingly "sticky," citing convenience, the quality of service, and their relationships with bank personnel as reasons for not switching to other banks after price increases. In selecting a bank for CDs, customers said that interest rates accounted for 45 percent of their decision. Yet at renewal time, only a third of CD customers shopped around at all for a better rate and 85 percent of them renewed at the same bank. See V. Cvsa, A. M. Degeratu, and R. L. Ott-Wadhawan, "Bank Deposits Get Interesting," *The McKinsey Quarterly*, no. 2 (2002), pp. 1–5.

Savings Accounts

Withdrawal Risk

Savings accounts are generally less liquid than demand deposits and chequing accounts for two reasons. First, they are nonchequable and may involve physical presence at the institution for withdrawal. Second, the FI has the legal power to delay payment or withdrawal requests. This is rarely done and FIs normally meet withdrawal requests with immediate cash payment, but they have the legal right to delay, which provides important withdrawal risk control to FI managers.

Costs

Since these accounts are nonchequable, any implicit interest rate payments are likely to be small; thus, the principal costs to the FI are the explicit interest payments on these accounts. In recent years, FIs have normally paid slightly higher explicit rates on savings than on chequing accounts.

Retail Term Deposits and GICs

Withdrawal Risk

Retail term deposit
A fixed-maturity instrument offered to retail clients for a term of one to five years with a guaranteed interest payment that is usually semi-annual and carries an interest penalty for early withdrawal.

By contractual design, fixed-term deposits reduce the withdrawal risk to issuers. DTIs in Canada offer **term deposits**, which are redeemable prior to maturity subject to an interest penalty, and **Guaranteed Investment Certificates (GICs)**, which are generally not redeemable prior to maturity to retail investors. Term deposits are straightforward deposits whose rates are generally set to be competitive, but fixed over the term of the deposit. The size, maturity, and rate on term deposits are usually standardized. GICs, on the other hand, come in many variations to appeal to retail customers as an alternative to other sources of investment, particularly for Registered Retirement Savings Plans (RRSPs) or Registered Retirement Income Funds (RRIFs). For example, the rate on GICs may be tied to money market rates (e.g. the FI's rate for Banker's Acceptances), or, alternatively, may carry a rate tied to the S&P TSX 60 Index or other market indices, which may change over the term of the deposit. In a world of no early withdrawal requests, the DTI knows the exact scheduling of interest and principal payments to depositors holding such deposit claims, since these payments are contractually specified. As such, the FI manager can directly control fund inflows and outflows by varying the maturities of the deposits it offers to the public. In addition, since many GICs are held by depositors within an RRSP or RRIF, they may be less subject to withdrawal to another FI on rollover dates.

Guaranteed Investment Certificate (GIC)
A fixed-maturity instrument offered to retail clients that is non-redeemable, carries a term from 30 days to five years, and pays interest at a specified rate at the end of the term.

When depositors wish to withdraw before the maturity of a term deposit, FIs impose penalties on a withdrawing depositor such as the loss of a certain number of months' interest depending on the maturity of the deposit. Although this does impose a friction or transaction cost on withdrawals, it is unlikely to stop withdrawals of term deposits when the depositor has exceptional liquidity needs. Also, withdrawals may increase if depositors perceive the DTI to be insolvent, despite interest penalties and deposit insurance coverage up to $100,000. Nevertheless, under normal conditions, these instruments have low withdrawal risk compared with chequing accounts and can be used as an important liability management tool to control withdrawal/liquidity risk.

Costs

Similar to those of savings accounts, the major costs of these deposits are explicit interest payments. Short-term GICs are often competitive with money market instruments such as T-bills. Note that depositors who buy term deposits and GICs are subject to taxes on their interest payments, although those held within RRSPs are sheltered until withdrawn.

Wholesale Fixed-term Deposits and CDs

Withdrawal Risk

wholesale CDs
Time deposits with a face value above $100,000.

negotiable instrument
An instrument whose ownership can be transferred in the secondary market.

Wholesale CDs were innovated by U.S. banks in the early 1960s as a contractual mechanism to allow depositors to liquidate their positions in these CDs by selling them in the secondary market rather than settling up with the FI. Thus, a depositor can sell a relatively liquid instrument without causing adverse liquidity risk exposure for the FI. Thus, the unique feature of these wholesale CDs is not so much their large minimum denomination size of US$100,000 or more but the fact that they are **negotiable instruments.** That is, they can be resold by title assignment in a secondary market to other investors. This means, for example, that if IBM bought a US$1 million three-month CD from Citibank but for unexpected liquidity reasons needs funds after only one month has passed, it could sell this CD to another outside investor in the secondary market. This does not impose any obligation on Citibank in terms of an early funds withdrawal request. Thus, a depositor can sell a relatively liquid instrument without causing adverse withdrawal risk exposure for the FI. Essentially, the only withdrawal risk (which can be substantial) is that these wholesale CDs are not rolled over and reinvested by the holder of the deposit claim on maturity.[6]

Canadian FIs that operate in the United States are able to take advantage of the CD market. However, a similar active market does not exist in Canada. For Canadian FIs, most core wholesale deposits come from institutional investors (governments, other FIs) and corporate entities with which the FI may have a relationship. These wholesale fixed-term deposits are tailored to meet the cash management requirements of the customer with respect to the term, and the rates are higher than those on retail GICs.[7]

Costs

The rates that FIs pay on these instruments are competitive with other wholesale money market rates, especially those on commercial paper and T-bills. This competitive rate aspect is enhanced by the highly sophisticated nature of investors in CDs, such as money market mutual fund managers, and the fact that these deposits are covered by deposit insurance guarantees only up to the limit per investor, per institution ($100,000). To the extent that these CDs are offered by large FIs perceived as being too big to fail, the required credit risk premium on CDs is less than that required for similar-quality instruments issued by the nonbank private sector (e.g., commercial paper). In addition, required interest yields on CDs reflect investors' perceptions of the depth of the secondary market for CDs. In

---

[6] Wholesale dollar CDs are also offered in countries other than the United States, in which case they are called Eurodollar CDs. Eurodollar CDs may sell at slightly different rates from domestic CDs because of differences in demand and supply for CDs between the domestic market and the Euromarket and differences in credit risk perceptions of depositors buying a CD from a foreign branch (e.g., Citibank in London) rather than a domestic branch (Citibank in New York). To the extent that it is believed that banks are too big to fail, a guaranty that only extends to domestic branches, a higher risk premium may be required of overseas CDs. Indeed, FDICIA, passed in 1991, has severely restricted the ability of the FDIC to rescue overseas depositors of a failed U.S. bank.

[7] Many FIs rely on asset-backed commercial paper for short-term funding (See Chapter 27 on securitization). This market has grown from almost zero in 1985 to $63.7 billion in 2002. See P. Toovey and J. Kiff, "Developments and Issues in the Canadian Market for Asset-Backed Commercial Paper," *Financial System Review*, Bank of Canada, June 2003, pp. 43–49.

recent years, the liquidity of the secondary market in CDs appears to have diminished as dealers have withdrawn. This has increased FIs' relative cost of issuing such instruments.[8]

Inter-bank Funds

Withdrawal Risk

The liabilities just described are all deposit liabilities, reflecting deposit contracts issued by DTIs in return for cash. However, DTIs not only fund their assets by issuing deposits but also can borrow in various markets for purchased funds. Since the funds generated from these purchases are borrowed funds, not deposits, they are not subject to deposit insurance premium payments to the CDIC (as with all the domestic deposits described earlier).[9] The largest market available for purchased funds is the interbank market. While FIs with excess cash reserves can invest some of this excess in interest-earning liquid assets such as T-bills and short-term securities, an alternative is to lend excess cash for short intervals to other FIs seeking increased short-term funding. **Interbank funds** are short-term uncollateralized loans made by one FI to another; more than 90 percent of such transactions have maturities of one day. The FI that purchases funds shows them as a liability on its balance sheet, while the FI that sells them shows them as an asset.

For the liability-funding FIs, there is no risk that the interbank funds they have borrowed can be withdrawn within the day, although there is settlement risk at the end of each day (see Chapter 14). However, there is some risk that funds will not be rolled over by the lending bank the next day if rollover is desired by the borrowing FI. In reality, this has occurred only in periods of extreme crisis. Nevertheless, since interbank funds are uncollateralized loans, institutions selling interbank funds normally impose maximum bilateral limits or credit caps on borrowing institutions. This may constrain the ability of a bank to expand its interbank funds-borrowing position very rapidly if this is part of its overall liability management strategy.

Costs

The cost of interbank funds for the purchasing institution is the interbank rate. The rate is set by FIs (mostly banks) that trade in the market and can vary considerably both within the day and across days.[10, 11]

interbank funds
Short-term uncollateralized loans made by one FI to another.

---

[8] In addition, for all the liability instruments considered so far (with the exception of Euro CDs), the U.S. FI may have to pay an FDIC insurance premium depending on its perceived riskiness. For example, consider a bank issuing CDs at 3.26 percent, at which rate a depositor might just be indifferent to holding T-bills at 3.00 percent, given a local tax rate of 8 percent. However, the cost to the bank of the CD issue is not 3.26 percent but:

Effective CD cost = 3.26% + Insurance premium = 3.26% + .27% = 3.53%

where 27 basis points is the assumed size of the deposit insurance premium. Thus, deposit insurance premiums add to the cost of deposits as a source of funds. However, in 2004, the insurance premium was set by the FDIC at zero for most FIs, with only the very riskiest having to pay 27 basis points.

[9] Foreign deposits are not subject to deposit insurance premiums.

[10] See C. H. Furfine, "The Microstructure of the Federal Funds Market," *Financial Markets, Institutions and Instruments*, no. 5 (1999), pp. 24–44; and C. H. Furfine, "The Fed's New Discount Window and Interbank Borrowing," Federal Reserve Bank of Chicago, Working Paper, 2003.

[11] Another interbank source of funding is the London Interbank market (LIBOR). The LIBOR market provides a low-cost source of funds, often U.S. dollars, that FIs match with their borrowers who have LIBOR-based loans. The consolidated monthly balance sheet for all Canadian banks reported by OSFI as at March 31, 2005, showed fixed-term deposits from deposit-taking institutions that totalled $129,725.9 million. Of this total, $109,520.3 million or 84.4 percent were interbank deposits in foreign currency. See www.osfi-bsif.gc.ca for the latest quarterly report.

Repurchase Agreements (Repos)

Withdrawal Risk

repurchase agreements (repos)
Agreements involving the sale of securities by one party (i.e., a DTI) to another with a promise to repurchase the securities at a specified date and price in the future.

Repurchase agreements (RPs or repos) can be viewed as collateralized interbank transactions. The FI with excess cash sells overnight funds for one day to the purchasing FI. The next day, the purchasing FI returns the funds plus one day's interest reflecting the Bank of Canada's overnight rate. Since a credit risk exposure exists for the selling FI because the purchasing FI may be unable to repay the funds the next day, the seller may seek collateral backing for the one-day loan. In a repo transaction, the funds-selling FI receives government securities as collateral from the funds-purchasing FI. That is, the funds-purchasing FI temporarily exchanges securities for cash. The next day, this transaction is reversed. The funds-purchasing FI sends back the overnight funds it borrowed plus interest (the repo rate); it receives in return (or repurchases) its securities used as collateral in the transaction.

As with the interbank market, the repo market is a highly liquid and flexible source of funds for FIs needing to increase their liabilities and to offset deposit withdrawals. Moreover, these transactions can be rolled over each day. The major liability management flexibility difference between interbank funds and repos is that an interbank funds transaction can be entered into at any time in the business day. In general, it is difficult to transact a repo borrowing late in the day since the FI sending the funds must be satisfied with the type and quality of the securities collateral proposed by the borrowing institution. This collateral is normally in the form of T-bills, T-notes, T-bonds, and mortgage-backed securities, but their maturities and other features, such as callability and coupons, may be unattractive to the funds seller. Negotiations over the collateral package can delay repo transactions and make them more difficult to arrange than simple uncollateralized loans.[12]

Costs

Because of their collateralized nature, repo rates normally lie below interbank rates. Also, repo rates generally show less interday fluctuation than do interbank rates. This is partly due to the lesser intraday flexibility of repos relative to interbank transactions.

Other Borrowings

While interbank funds and repos have been a major sources of borrowed funds, FIs have utilized a host of other borrowing sources to supplement their liability management flexibility. We describe these briefly in the following sections.

Bankers Acceptances

Banks often convert off-balance-sheet letters of credit into on-balance-sheet bankers acceptances (BAs) by discounting the letter of credit the holder presents for acceptance (see Chapter 13). Further, these BAs may then be resold to money market investors. Thus, BA sales to the secondary market are an additional funding source.

---

[12] The Bank of Canada also participates in the overnight funds market via sale and repurchase agreements (SRAs) in order to enact monetary policy by influencing the overnight rate. When overnight funds are trading below the target rate, the Bank of Canada will offer to sell Government of Canada securities overnight and buy them back at a set price the next day. See the Bank of Canada's Web site at www.bankofcanada.ca. See also E. Lundrigan and S. Toll, "The overnight market in Canada," *Bank of Canada Review*, Winter 1997–98, pp. 27–42.

Commercial Paper

As noted previously, Canadian FIs are active issuers in the asset-backed commercial paper (ABCP) market. According to P. Toovey and J. Kiff (*Financial System Review*, Bank of Canada, June 2003), Canadian banks issued 90 percent of the $88.2 billion asset-backed securities outstanding in Canada in 2002. As well, Canadian banks are active in the U.S. and the European ABCP markets. ABCP is structured to reduce the credit risk for the purchaser and the cost for the issuer, and carry a credit rating assigned by Dominion Bond Rating Service (DBRS).

Medium-Term Notes

A number of DTIs in search of more stable sources of funds with low withdrawal risk have begun to issue medium-term notes, often in the five- to seven-year range. These notes are additionally attractive because they are subject to neither reserve requirements nor deposit insurance premiums.

Overnight Loans with the Bank of Canada

As discussed earlier, FIs facing temporary liquidity crunches can borrow from the central bank window at the overnight rate. Direct participants in the Large Value Transfer System may borrow directly from the Bank of Canada at the overnight rate through the Standing Liquidity Facility (SLF) as described in detail in Chapter 19.

Concept Questions

1. Describe the withdrawal risk and funding cost characteristics of some of the major liabilities available to a modern FI manager.
2. Since demand deposits are subject to deposit insurance premiums, whereas interbank funds are not, why should an FI not fund all its assets through interbank funds? Explain your answer.

LIQUIDITY AND LIABILITY STRUCTURES FOR CANADIAN DEPOSIT-TAKING INSTITUTIONS

We summarize the preceding discussion by considering some balance sheet data for Canadian banks. Table 18–1 shows the liquid asset–nonliquid asset composition of domestic Canadian banks in (March) 2005 versus 1996.

Although the level of cash and government securities has declined since 1996, total cash plus government securities plus other securities has increased from 28.3 percent of total assets in 1996 to 31.4 percent in 2005, making the banks marginally more liquid. Loans have also declined, which could be a reflection of the funding cost as well as the sale of loans and the securitization of mortgages (see Chapters 26 and 27).

Table 18–2 presents the liability composition of domestic Canadian banks at March 31 of 1996 and 2005. Although the level of notice deposits has stayed virtually the same, of interest is the shift from fixed-term deposits, over which the FI has some control to demand deposits, which have almost doubled from 5.8 percent to 10.6 percent in 2005. This could represent a decline in interest rates since 2002 that may not encourage depositors to lock up their funds in longer-term instruments.

On an individual basis, the Canadian banks reported that they manage their liquidity risk on an enterprise-wide scale in 2004. For example, Bank of Montreal (BMO) tracks cash and securities as a percentage of total assets over time, reporting a ratio of 25.8 percent in 2004. Canadian banks monitor their core deposits, and, as mentioned above, provide incentives such as the waiving of fees or interest rates based on deposit levels to encourage customers to leave their deposits in place.

www.bmo.com

TABLE 18–1
Liquid Assets versus Non-liquid Assets for Domestic Canadian Banks, as at March 31, 1996 and 2005 (in percentages)

Assets	1996	2005
Cash	9.2	5.2
Government securities	10.3	6.6
Other securities	8.9	19.6
Loans	67.4	55.2
Other assets	4.3	13.4
	100	100

Source: Office of the Superintendent of Financial Services, www.osfi-bsif.gc.ca

TABLE 18–2
Liability Structure of Domestic Canadian Banks, as at March 31, 1996 and 2005 (in percentages)

Liabilities	1996	2005
Demand deposits	5.8	10.6
Notice deposits	14.4	13.6
Fixed-term deposits	53.9	41.5
Borrowings and other liabilities	21.0	29.6
Bank capital	4.9	4.7
	100	100

Source: Office of the Superintendent of Financial Services, www.osfi-bsif.gc.ca

www.royalbank.com

www.cibc.com

BMO also monitors core deposits as a percentage of total deposits and reported a ratio of 58.2 percent in its 2004 Annual Report. Royal Bank of Canada (RBC) tracks its deposits on a global basis, and uses contingency risk planning to determine the impact of market disruptions on its liquidity needs. Similarly, Canadian Imperial Bank of Commerce (CIBC) monitors its core deposits and also securitizes its assets (e.g. credit card operations) to provide short-term funding.[13]

Finally, it should be noted that too heavy a reliance on borrowed funds can be a risky strategy in itself. Even though withdrawal risk may be reduced if lenders in the market for borrowed funds have confidence in the borrowing FI, perceptions that the FI is risky can lead to sudden nonrenewals of interbank and repo loans and the nonrollover of wholesale deposits and other purchased funds as they mature. The best example of an FI's failure as a result of excessive reliance on large CDs and purchased funds was Continental Illinois in 1984, with more than 80 percent of its funds borrowed from wholesale lenders. Consequently, excessive reliance on borrowed funds may be as bad an overall liability management strategy as excessive reliance on chequing and savings deposits. Thus, a well-diversified portfolio of liabilities may be the best strategy to balance withdrawal risk and funding cost considerations.

Concept Questions

1. Look at Table 18–1. How has the ratio of traditional liquid to illiquid assets changed over the 1996–2005 period?
2. Look at Table 18–2. How has the liability composition of banks changed over the 1996–2005 period?

---

[13] See Bank of Montreal 2004 Annual Report, pages 64–65, Royal Bank of Canada's 2004 Annual Report, pages 66–67, and Canadian Imperial Bank of Commerce's 2004 Annual Report, pages 87–90, for discussions of specific approaches to liquidity management.

LIABILITY AND LIQUIDITY RISK MANAGEMENT IN INSURANCE COMPANIES

Insurance companies use a variety of sources to meet liquidity needs. As discussed in Chapters 3 and 17, liquidity is required to meet claims on the insurance policies these FIs have written as well as unexpected surrenders of those policies. These contracts therefore represent a potential future liability to the insurance company. Ideally, liquidity management in insurance companies is conducted so that funds needed to meet claims on insurance contracts written can be met with premiums received on new and existing contracts. However, a high frequency of claims at a single point in time (e.g., an unexpectedly severe hurricane season) could force insurers to liquidate assets at something less than their fair market value.

Insurance companies can reduce their exposure to liquidity risk by diversifying the distribution of risk in the contracts they write. For example, property and casualty insurers can diversify across the types of disasters they cover.

Alternatively, insurance companies can meet liquidity needs by holding relatively marketable assets to cover claim payments. Assets such as government and corporate bonds and corporate stock usually can be liquidated quickly at close to their fair market values in financial markets to pay claims on insurance policies when premium income is insufficient. For example, in the first quarter of 2005, Canadian Life insurance companies reporting to OSFI had 73.9 percent of their assets in bonds and debentures and a further 8.3 percent in preferred and common shares. Similarly, Canadian P&C companies had 44.1 percent in bonds and debentures and 12 percent in preferred and common shares.

Concept Questions

1. Discuss two strategies insurance companies can use to reduce liquidity risk.
2. Why would property and casualty insurers hold more short-term liquid assets to manage liquidity risk than life insurers hold?

LIABILITY AND LIQUIDITY RISK MANAGEMENT IN OTHER FIs

Other FIs, such as securities firms, investment banks, and finance companies, may experience liquidity risk if they rely on short-term financing (such as commercial paper or bank loans) and investors become reluctant to roll those funds over. Remember from Chapter 4 that the main sources of funding for securities firms are repurchase agreements, bank call loans,[14] and short positions in securities. Liquidity management for these FIs requires the ability to have sufficient cash and other liquid resources at hand to underwrite (purchase) new securities from quality issuers before reselling these securities to other investors. Liability management also requires an investment bank or securities firm to be able to act as a market maker, which requires the firm to finance an inventory of securities in its portfolio. As discussed in Chapter 6, finance companies fund assets mainly with commercial paper and long-term debt. Liquidity management for these FIs requires the ability to fund loan requests and loan commitments of sufficient quality without delay.

---

[14] A bank call loan means that a lending bank can call in the loan from an investment bank with very little notice.

The experience of Drexel Burnham Lambert in 1989 in the United States is a good example of a securities firm being subjected to a liquidity challenge. Throughout the 1980s, Drexel Burnham Lambert captured the bulk of the junk bond market by promising investors that it would act as a dealer for junk bonds in the secondary market. Investors were, therefore, more willing to purchase these junk securities because Drexel provided an implied guarantee that it would buy them back or find another buyer at market prices should an investor need to sell. However, the junk bond market experienced extreme difficulties in 1989 as their prices fell, reflecting the economy's move into a recession. Serious concerns about the creditworthiness of Drexel's junk bond-laden asset portfolio led creditors to deny Drexel extensions of its vital short-term commercial paper financings. As a result, Drexel declared bankruptcy. Drexel's sudden collapse makes it very clear that access to short-term purchased funds is crucial to the health of securities firms.[15]

Concept Questions

1. What is a bank call loan?
2. Give two reasons an investment bank needs liquidity.

---

[15] For additional discussion of the failure of Drexel Burnham Lambert, see W. S. Haraf, "The Collapse of Drexel Burnham Lambert: Lessons for Bank Regulators," *Regulation,* Winter 1991, pp. 22–25.

Summary

Liquidity and liability management issues are intimately linked for the modern FI. Many factors, both cost and regulatory, influence an FI manager's choice of the amount of liquid assets to hold. An FI's choice of liquidity is something of a knife-edge situation, trading off the costs and benefits of undershooting or overshooting asset targets.

An FI can manage its liabilities in a fashion that affects the overall withdrawal risk of its funding portfolio and therefore the need for liquid assets to meet such withdrawals. However, reducing withdrawal risk often comes at a cost because liability sources that are easier to control from a withdrawal risk perspective are often more costly for the FI to utilize.

Questions and Problems

1. What are the benefits and costs to an FI of holding large amounts of liquid assets? Why are U.S. Treasury and government of Canada securities considered good examples of liquid assets?

2. How is an FI's liability and liquidity risk management problem related to the maturity of its assets relative to its liabilities?

3. Consider the assets (in millions) of two banks, A and B. Both banks are funded by $120 million in deposits and $20 million in equity. Which bank has the stronger liquidity position? Which bank probably has a higher profit?

Bank A Assets		Bank B Assets	
Cash	$ 10	Cash	$ 20
Govt. securities	40	Consumer loans	30
Commercial loans	90	Commercial loans	90
Total assets	$140	Total assets	$140

4. What concerns motivate regulators to require deposit-taking institutions to hold minimum amounts of liquid assets?

5. Rank these financial assets according to their liquidity: cash, corporate bonds, TSX-traded stocks, and T-bills.

6. What is the relationship between funding cost and funding or withdrawal risk?

7. An FI has estimated the following annual costs for its demand deposits: management cost per account = $140, average account size = $1,500, average number of cheques processed per account per month = 75, cost of clearing a cheque = $0.10, fees charged to customer per cheque = $0.05, and average fee charged per customer per month = $8.

   a. What is the implicit interest cost of demand deposits for the FI?

   b. What should be the cheque-clearing fees to reduce the implicit interest cost to 3 percent?

8. A chequing account requires a minimum balance of $750 for interest to be earned at an annual rate of 4 percent. An account holder has maintained an average balance of $500 for the first six months and $1,000 for the remaining six months. She writes an average of 60 cheques per month and pays $0.02 per cheque, although it costs the bank $0.05 to clear a cheque.

   a. What average return does the account holder earn on the account?

   b. What is the average return if the bank lowers the minimum balance to $400?

   c. What is the average return if the bank pays interest only on the amount in excess of $400? Assume that the minimum required balance is $400.

   d. How much should the bank increase its cheque clearing fee to ensure that the average interest it pays on this account is 5 percent? Assume that the minimum required balance is $750.

9. Rank the following liabilities with respect, first, to funding risk and, second, to funding cost.

   a. Demand deposits.
   b. GICs.
   c. Interbank funds.
   d. Bankers acceptances.
   e. Eurodollar deposits.
   f. Chequing accounts.
   g. Wholesale GICs.
   h. Savings accounts.
   i. Repos.
   j. Commercial paper.

10. How is the withdrawal risk different for interbank funds and repurchase agreements?

11. How does the cash balance, or liquidity, of an FI determine the types of repurchase agreements into which it will enter?

12. What characteristics of Bank of Canada funds may constrain a DTI's ability to use these funds to expand its liquidity quickly?

13. What trends have been observed between 1996 and 2005 in regard to liquidity and liability structures of commercial banks?

14. What are the primary methods that insurance companies can use to reduce their exposure to liquidity risk?

Deposit Insurance and Other Liability Guarantees

This chapter discusses

▸ deposit insurance for federally-regulated deposit-taking institutions, beginning with the history of these funds and including the problems experienced by these funds

▸ the methods available to reduce risk taking, thus reducing the probability that deposit holders must be paid off with deposit insurance

▸ the Bank of Canada's overnight funds as a (limited) alternative to deposit insurance

▸ other guarantee programs, including those for insurance companies, securities firms, and pension funds, and

▸ deposit insurance schemes for commercial banks in the EU and G-10 countries in Appendix 19B to the chapter (located at the book's Web site, www.mcgrawhill.ca/college/saunders)

INTRODUCTION

Chapter 17 discussed the liquidity risks faced by FIs and Chapter 18 described ways FIs can better manage that risk. Because of concerns about the asset quality or solvency of an FI, liability holders such as depositors and life insurance policyholders (and to a lesser extent, mutual fund shareholders) have incentives to engage in runs, that is, to withdraw all their funds from an FI. As we discussed in Chapter 17, the incentive to run is accentuated in banks, trusts, and insurance companies by the sequential servicing rule used to meet liability withdrawals. As a result, deposit and liability holders who are first in line to withdraw funds get preference over those last in line.

Although a run on an unhealthy FI is not necessarily a bad thing—it can discipline the performance of managers and owners—there is a risk that runs on bad FIs can become contagious and spread to good or well-run FIs. In contagious run or panic conditions, liability holders do not bother to distinguish between good and bad FIs but instead seek to turn their liabilities into cash or safe securities as quickly as possible. Contagious runs can have a major contractionary effect on the supply of credit as well as the money supply regionally, nationally, or even internationally.[1]

Moreover, a contagious run on FIs can have serious social welfare effects. For example, a major run on banks can have an adverse effect on the level of savings in all types of FIs and therefore can inhibit the ability of individuals to transfer wealth through time to protect themselves against major risks such as future ill health and falling income in old age.

Because of such wealth, money supply, and credit supply effects, government regulators of financial service firms have introduced guaranty programs to deter runs by offering liability holders varying degrees of failure protection. Specifically,

---

[1] For example, a run on Rhode Island state-chartered banks in the United States in 1990 had a major negative effect on the local (state) economy, but very little effect nationally.

if a liability holder believes a claim is totally secure even if the FI is in trouble, there is no incentive to run. The liability holder's place in line no longer affects getting his or her funds back. Regulatory guaranty or insurance programs for liability holders deter runs and thus deter contagious runs and panics.

www.cdic.ca

In Canada, insurance protection is provided by the Canada Deposit Insurance Corporation (CDIC) that was created in 1967 for eligible federally-regulated deposit-taking institutions (banks, trusts, and savings and loans) and federally-regulated cooperative credit associations (interprovincial associations of credit unions). Provincially incorporated credit unions and caisses populaires are covered by provincial stabilization funds or guarantee companies (e.g. Quebec Deposit Insurance Board). Assuris covers life insurance policies, accident and sickness policies and annuity contracts. The Property and Casualty Insurance Corporation (PACICC) provides coverage in the event of the failure of a property and casualty (P&C) insurance company. As noted previously in Chapter 4, the Canadian Investor Protection Fund (CIPF) provides coverage for investors through the Investment Dealers Association of Canada and the stock exchanges.

www.assuris.ca

www.pacicc.ca

www.cipf.ca

In this chapter we look at the Canadian guaranty funds, as well as the experience in the United States with the Federal Deposit Insurance Corporation (FDIC), which has a longer and more turbulent history since its creation in 1933.

www.fdic.gov

The Canadian Experience with Deposit Insurance

Despite the similarities between Canada and the United States, these two North American countries have different histories with respect to deposit insurance. The number of failures of Canadian FIs has been small relative to the experience covered below for the U.S. Canada managed to avoid both the major bank failures of the Great Depression (which resulted in the creation of U.S. deposit insurance in 1933) and the savings and loan failures of the 1980s. Thus, Canada Deposit Insurance Corporation (CDIC) was not formed until 1967 as support for the deposits of federally-regulated deposit-taking institutions. In fact, no Canadian bank failed from 1923 (the Home Bank) until 1985 (Canadian Commercial Bank and the Northland Bank of Canada). During that time period, when Canadian banks experienced financial difficulties, they were absorbed by other FIs, resulting in the concentrated banking system that Canada has today.

Although CDIC has not had extensive experience with bank failures, it has experienced trust and loan company failures, including Saskatchewan Trust Co. (1991, CDIC's total claim and loans of $64 million), Standard Loan Co./Standard Trust Co. (1991, $1.321 billion), Shoppers Trust Co. (1992, $492 million), Adelaide Capital Corp. (1992, $1.588 billion), Central Guaranty Trust Co. (1992, $500 million), Confederation Trust Co. (1994, $680 million), Income Trust Co. (1995, $193 million), and Security Home Mortgage Corp. (1996, $42 million). The failures in the 1990s were partly caused by a recession in the late 1980s, as well as consolidation in the financial industry as the four pillars (see Chapter 1) broke down. Only 43 members of CDIC have failed and no member has failed since 1996.

However, as we discuss in Chapter 22, Canada's financial system is smaller and more concentrated than that of the United States, which has roughly 100 times the number of deposit-taking institutions. At its largest in 1983, CDIC insured 188 deposit-taking institutions. Of these, 39 (20 percent) have since failed. Nevertheless, the government of the day in the 1980s was sufficiently alarmed by the failures of weaker deposit-taking institutions to form a Royal Commission chaired by W. Z. Estey to review deposit insurance and the regulatory structure. CDIC was

FIGURE 19–1

The Canadian Regulatory System

Source: CDIC, 2004 Annual Report, www.cdic.ca, http://www.cdic.ca/bin/cdic_ar_e.pdf

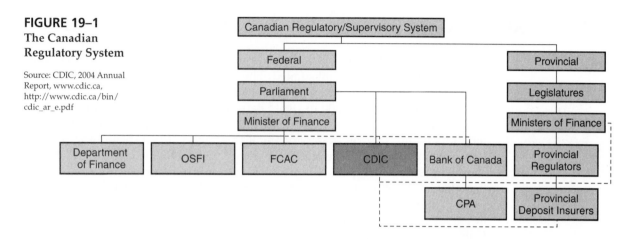

given new risk minimization and early intervention policies. As well, a new regulator, OSFI, was created to supervise federally-regulated trusts, insurance companies, and banks.[2] At April 30, 2005, CDIC insured over $425 billion in deposits at 81 banks, trust companies, loan companies, and cooperative credit associations.

www.bankofcanada.ca

www.osfi-bsif.gc.ca

www.fcac-acfc.gc.ca

www.fin.gc.ca

The Canadian regulatory system for financial institutions is shown schematically in Figure 19–1. The Bank of Canada does not directly supervise and audit federally-regulated FIs but it does have a mandate to ensure the safety and soundness of the financial system, and therefore its monetary policy affects both OSFI and CDIC, who jointly have powers to regulate FIs.[3] The Department of Finance, the Office of the Superintendent of Financial Institutions (OSFI), and the Financial Consumer Agency of Canada (FCAC) report to the Minister of Finance. CDIC and the Bank of Canada report to Parliament through the Minister of Finance. Under the Bank of Canada Act (amended in 1981) and the Canada Payments Act (1981), members of CDIC are eligible to operate in the Large Value Transfer System (see Chapter 17) and to borrow from the Bank of Canada. Banks who accept only wholesale deposits (greater than $150,000) may opt out of CDIC coverage, but remain members of the LVTS and eligible to borrow from the Bank of Canada. As well, the Bank of Canada has responsibility for Canada Payments Association (CPA).

Failures of weaker institutions in the 1980s, concerns that the strong were subsidizing the weak, and developments in other jurisdictions, such as the United States, led to CDIC's adoption of risk-based or differential premiums which is discussed in detail later in the chapter.

regulatory forbearance
Regulators' policy of allowing an FI to continue to operate even when it is in breach of regulations in hopes that the situation will correct itself over time.

---

[2] The difference in the Canadian and U.S. experiences of FI failures has been of interest to researchers. For example, see L. Kryzanowski and G. S. Roberts, "Canadian banking solvency, 1922–1940," *Journal of Money, Credit, and Banking*, August 1993, Vol. 25, Iss. 3, pp. 361–376 for a review of the literature and the proposal that **regulatory forbearance** played a role, along with the Canadian branch banking system in the stability of the Canadian financial system. For a detailed discussion of the bank failures of the 1980s, see W. Z. Estey, "Report of the Inquiry into the Collapse of the CCB and Northland Bank," 1986, Supply and Services Canada, Ottawa and also J. F. Dingle, "The Bank Failures of September 1985" in *Planning an Evolution: The Story of the Canadian Payments Association 1980–2002*, 2004, Bank of Canada and the Canadian Payments Association, pp. 25–30.

[3] The powers of OSFI and CDIC to examine, classify, and take action with respect to FIs are provided in detail in "Guide to Intervention for Federal Financial Institutions" at www.osfi-bsif.gc.ca.

[4] The FDIC is currently considering an increase in deposit insurance coverage to $130,000 and then indexing coverage to some major inflation or price index such as the CPI.

THE U.S. EXPERIENCE WITH BANK AND THRIFT GUARANTY FUNDS

The FDIC was created in 1933 in the wake of the banking panics of 1930–33, when some 10,000 commercial banks failed. The original level of individual depositor insurance coverage at commercial banks was US$2,500, which was increased (six times since 1934) to $100,000 in 1980.[4] Between 1945 and 1980, commercial bank deposit insurance clearly worked; there were no runs or panics, and the number of individual bank failures was very small (see Figure 19–2). Beginning in 1980, however, bank failures accelerated, with more than 1,039 failures in the decade ending in 1990, peaking at 221 in 1988. This number of failures was actually larger than that for the entire 1933–79 period. Moreover, the costs of each of these failures to the FDIC were often larger than the total costs for the mainly small bank failures in 1933–79. As the number and costs of these closures mounted in the 1980s, the FDIC fund, built up from premiums paid by banks (and the reinvestment income from those premiums), was rapidly drained. Any insurance fund becomes insolvent if the premiums collected and the reserves built up from investing premiums are insufficient to offset the cost of failure claims. The FDIC's resources were virtually depleted by early 1991, when it was given permission to borrow US$30 billion from the U.S. Treasury. Even then, it ended 1991 with a deficit of US$7 billion. In response to this crisis, Congress passed the FDIC Improvement Act (FDICIA) in December 1991 to restructure the bank insurance fund and prevent its potential insolvency.

Since 1991 there has been a dramatic turnaround in the fund's finances and a drop in bank failures—partially in response to record profit levels in banks. Specifically, as of January 2004, the FDIC's Bank Insurance Fund (BIF) had reserves of US$33.5 billion. In 2003, the number of bank failures had fallen to two. In 2002 there were 10 failures, in 2001 there were 3 failures, and in 2000 there were 6 failures. The largest of these recent failures was that of Superior Bank of Illinois in July 2001. The original expected loss to the FDIC from this failure was US$1 billion. However, in December 2001, the owners agreed to pay a fine of US$460 million to the FDIC to avoid being punished for mismanagement resulting in the failure. The final

FIGURE 19–2
Number of Failed U.S. Banks by Year, 1934–2003

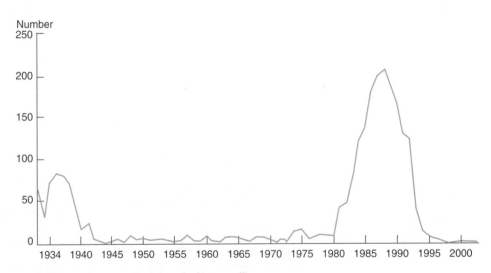

Source: FDIC annual reports and statistics on banking. *www.fdic.gov*

cost of this failure to the FDIC was US$428 million. The fund's reserves now exceed 1.31 percent of insured deposits.

The Federal Savings and Loan Insurance Corporation (FSLIC) covered savings associations (formerly called S&Ls); other thrifts, such as mutual savings banks, often chose to be insured under the FDIC rather than the FSLIC. Like the FDIC, this insurance fund was in relatively good shape until the end of the 1970s. Beginning in 1980, the fund's resources were rapidly depleted as more and more thrifts failed and had to be closed or merged. In August 1989, Congress passed the Financial Institutions Reform, Recovery, and Enforcement Act (FIRREA), largely in response to the deepening crisis in the thrift industry and the growing insolvency of the FSLIC. This act completely restructured the savings association fund and transferred its management to the FDIC.[5] At the same time, the restructured savings association insurance fund became the Savings Association Insurance Fund (SAIF). Currently, the FDIC manages the SAIF separately from the commercial bank fund, which is now called the Bank Insurance Fund (BIF).

INTERNET EXERCISE

Go to the Canada Deposit Insurance Corporation Web site and find the latest information available for the number of deposit-taking institutions insured by CDIC and the dollar value of insured deposits.

Go to the Canada Deposit Insurance Corporation Web site at www.cdic.ca. Find the figure for insured deposits on this home page. Then, click on "List of CDIC Members" to see the list of member institutions. Historical information about CDIC may be obtained by clicking on "Annual Report" and downloading the latest version.

DEPOSIT INSURANCE INSOLVENCY

Deposit insurance provides support for deposit-taking institutions and is therefore intended to contribute to the stability of the financial system. Canada has been fortunate that the impact of economic events in the 1980s and 1990s did not test the deposit insurance fund provided by CDIC beyond its strength, although, as discussed below, Assuris required re-funding after the collapse of Confederation Life in 1994. This means, however, that we need to look elsewhere for guidelines to failure. Therefore, the following discussion, though generalized for any deposit insurance system, draws heavily on the U.S. experience for examples and relevant research. There are at least two, not necessarily independent, views as to why deposit insurance funds become economically insolvent.

The Financial Environment

One view of the cause of insolvency is that a number of external events or shocks adversely affected U.S. banks and thrifts in the 1980s. The first was the dramatic rise in interest rates in the 1979–82 period. This rise in rates had a major negative effect on those thrifts funding long-term, fixed-rate mortgages with short-term deposits. The second event was the collapse in oil, real estate, and other commodity prices, which particularly harmed oil, gas, and agricultural loans in the

---

[5] At that time, the FSLIC ceased to exist.

southwestern United States. The third event was increased financial service firm competition at home and abroad, which eroded the value of bank and thrift charters during the 1980s.[6]

Moral Hazard

A second view is that these financial environment effects were catalysts for, rather than the causes of, the crisis in the U.S. At the heart of the crisis was deposit insurance itself, especially some of its contractual features. Although deposit insurance had deterred depositors and other liability holders from engaging in runs prior to 1980, in so doing it had also removed or reduced depositor discipline. Deposit insurance allowed insured FIs to borrow at rates close to the risk-free rate and, if they chose, to undertake high-risk asset investments. The FI owners and managers knew that insured depositors had little incentive to restrict such behaviour, either through fund withdrawals or by requiring risk premiums on deposit rates, since they were fully insured by the FDIC if the FI failed. Given this scenario, losses on oil, gas, and real estate loans in the 1980s are viewed as the outcome of bankers' exploiting underpriced or mispriced risk under the deposit insurance contract. The provision of insurance that encourages rather than discourages risk taking is called **moral hazard**.[7] This is because, with deposit insurance, a highly leveraged bank whose debt holders need not monitor the FI's (borrower's) actions has a strong incentive to undertake excessively risky investment decisions, such as in its loan-generating activities.[8]

In the absence of depositor discipline (as will be explained below), regulators could have priced risk taking either through charging explicit deposit insurance premiums linked to the FI's risk taking or by charging **implicit premiums** through restricting and monitoring the risky activities of FIs. This could potentially have substituted for depositor discipline; those FIs that took more risk would have paid directly or indirectly for this risk-taking behaviour. However, from 1933 until January 1, 1993, U.S. regulators based deposit insurance premiums on a deposit size rather than on risk. The 1980s were also a period of deregulation and capital adequacy forbearance rather than stringent activity regulation and tough capital requirements. Moreover, for the FSLIC, the number of bank examinations and examiners actually fell between 1981 and 1984.[9] Finally, prompt corrective action and closure for severely undercapitalized banks did not begin until the end of 1992.

moral hazard
The loss exposure faced by an insurer when the provision of insurance encourages the insured to take more risks.

implicit premiums
Deposit insurance premiums or costs imposed on a deposit-taking institution through activity constraints rather than direct monetary charges.

---

[6] The value of a bank or thrift charter is the present value of expected profits from operating in the industry. As expected profits fall, so does the value of a bank or thrift charter. See A. Saunders and B. Wilson, "An Analysis of Bank Charter Value and Its Risk-Constraining Incentives," *Journal of Financial Services Research,* April/June 2001, pp.185–96.

[7] The precise definition of moral hazard is the loss exposure of an insurer (the FDIC) that results from the character or circumstances of the insured (here, the bank).

[8] Recent research found that explicit deposit insurance tends to be detrimental to bank stability, more so when bank interest rates have been deregulated and moral hazard opportunities are great. In countries in which moral hazard opportunities are limited, regulation and supervision are more effective at offsetting the adverse incentives created by deposit insurance. See A. Demirgüç-Kunt and E. Detragiache, "Does Deposit Insurance Increase Banking System Stability? An Empirical Investigation," *Journal of Monetary Economics,* 2002, pp. 1373–1406.

[9] L. J. White points to a general weakness of thrift supervision and examination in the 1980s. The number of examinations fell from 3,210 in 1980 to 2,347 in 1984, and examinations per billion dollars of assets fell from 5.41 in 1980 to 2.4 in 1984. See L. J. White, *The S and L Debacle* (New York: Oxford University Press, 1991), p. 89.

Concept Questions

1. What two basic views are offered to explain why U.S.deposit insurance funds became insolvent during the 1980s?

PANIC PREVENTION VERSUS MORAL HAZARD

A great deal of attention has focused on the moral hazard reason for the collapse of the U.S. bank and thrift insurance funds in the 1980s. The less FI owners have to lose from taking risks, the greater are their incentives to take excessively risky asset positions. When asset investment risks or gambles pay off, FI owners make windfall gains in profits. If they fail, however, the insurer bears most of the costs, given that owners—like owners of regular corporations—have limited liability. It's a "heads I win, tails I don't lose (much)" situation.

Note that even without deposit insurance, the limited liability of FI owners or stockholders always creates incentives to take risk at the expense of fixed claimants such as depositors and debt holders.[10] The difference between deposit-taking institutions and other firms is risk-taking incentives induced by mispriced deposit insurance. That is, when risk taking is not **actuarially fairly priced** in deposit insurance premiums, this adds to the incentives to take additional risks.

Nevertheless, even though mispriced deposit insurance potentially accentuates risk taking, deposit insurance effectively deterred panics and runs of the 1930–33 kind in the postwar period (see Figure 19–2). That is, deposit insurance has ensured a good deal of stability in the U.S. credit and monetary system.

This suggests that, ideally, regulators should design the deposit insurance contract with the trade-off between moral hazard risk and panic or run risk in mind. For example, by providing 100 percent coverage of all depositors and reducing the probability of runs to zero, the insurer may be encouraging certain deposit-taking institutions to take a significant degree of moral hazard risk-taking behaviour.[11] On the other hand, a very limited degree of deposit insurance coverage might encourage runs and panics, although moral hazard behaviour itself would be less evident.

In the 1980s, extensive insurance coverage for deposit holders and the resulting lack of incentive for deposit holders to monitor and restrict owners' and managers' risk taking resulted in small levels of run risk but high levels of moral hazard

actuarially fairly priced insurance
Insurance pricing based on the perceived risk of the insured.

---

[10] Thus, one possible policy to reduce excessive bank risk taking would be to eliminate limited liability for bank stockholders. A study by L. J. White found that bank failures in private banking systems with unlimited liability, such as that which existed in 18th-century Scotland, were rare. Indeed, in the United States, double liability existed for bank stockholders prior to the introduction of deposit insurance; that is, on failure, the stockholders would lose their initial equity contribution and be assessed by the receiver an extra amount equal to the par value of their stock, which would be used to pay creditors (over and above the liquidation value of the bank's assets). See L. J. White, "Scottish Banking and Legal Restrictions Theory: A Closer Look," *Journal of Money Credit and Banking* 22 (1990), pp. 526–36. For a discussion of double liability in pre-1933 United States, see A. Saunders and B. Wilson, "If History Could Be Re-Run: The Provision and Pricing of Deposit Insurance in 1933," *Journal of Financial Intermediation* 4 (1995), pp. 396–413; and J. R. Macey and G. P. Miller, "Double Liability of Bank Shareholders: History and Implications," *Wake Forest Law Review* 27 (1992), pp. 31–62.

[11] Indeed, research on deposit insurance schemes in over 60 countries found that explicit deposit insurance tends to be detrimental to banking system stability, particularly when bank interest rates have been deregulated and where the regulatory environment is weak. In particular, deposit insurance encourages FIs to finance high-risk, high-return projects. However, when opportunities for moral hazard are more limited and more effective prudential regulation and supervision exist, the adverse incentives created by deposit insurance are limited. This, in turn, improves banking system stability. See A. Kunt and E. Detragiache, "Does Deposit Insurance Increase Banking System Stability? An Empirical Investigation," Working Paper, World Bank, June 2000.

risk.[12] By restructuring the deposit insurance contract, it may be possible to reduce moral hazard risk quite a bit without a very large increase in run risk.[13]

CONTROLLING RISK TAKING

There are three ways deposit insurance could be structured to reduce moral hazard behaviour:

1. Increase stockholder discipline.
2. Increase depositor discipline.
3. Increase regulator discipline.

Specifically, redesigning the features of the insurance contract can either directly or indirectly impact DI owners' and stockholders' risk-taking incentives by altering the behaviour of depositors and regulators.

Stockholder Discipline

Insurance Premiums

One approach toward making stockholders' risk taking more expensive is to link insurance premiums to the risk profile of the deposit-taking institution. Below we look at ways this might be done.

Theory A major feature of CDIC's deposit insurance contract from 1967–1998 was the flat deposit insurance premium levied on banks. Specifically, each year a bank paid a given sum or premium to the CDIC based on a fixed proportion of its deposits.[14]

To see why a flat or size-based premium schedule does not discipline risk taking, consider two banks of the same domestic deposit size, as shown in Table 19–1. Banks A and B have domestic deposits of $100 million and (in 1998) would pay the same premium to CDIC (.00167 × $100 million = $167,000 per annum). However, their risk-taking behaviour is completely different. Bank A is excessively risky, investing all its assets in real estate loans. Bank B is almost risk free, investing all its assets in government T-bills. We graph the insurance premium rates paid by the two banks compared with their asset risk in Figure 19–3.

---

[12] At this point, note that managers may not have the same risk-taking incentives as owners. This is especially true if managers are compensated through wage and salary contracts rather than through shares and share option programs. When managers are on fixed-wage contracts, their preferences in regard to risk lean toward being risk averse. That is, they are unlikely to exploit the same type of moral hazard incentives that stock owner–controlled banks would. This is because managers have little to gain if their banks do exceptionally well (their salaries are fixed) but probably will lose their jobs and human capital investments in a bank if they fail. A study by A. Saunders, E. Strock, and N. Travlos showed that stock owner–controlled banks tend to be more risky than manager-controlled banks. Thus, understanding the agency structure of the bank is important in identifying which banks are most likely to exploit risk-taking (moral hazard) incentives. See A. Saunders, E. Strock, and N. Travlos, "Ownership Structure, Deregulation, and Bank Risk Taking," *Journal of Finance* 45 (1989), pp. 643–54. Moreover, as pointed out by K. John, A. Saunders, and L. Senbet in "A Theory of Bank Regulation and Management Compensation," *Review of Financial Studies* (2000), pp. 95–126, deposit insurers might usefully take into account managerial compensation structures and incentives in setting deposit insurance premiums.

[13] E. Kane, "Three Paradigms for the Role of Capitalization Requirements in Insured Financial Institutions," *Journal of Banking and Finance* 19 (June 1995), pp. 431–60, models the trade-off between the level of risk taking eventually undertaken by banks, contractual features of deposit insurance, and capital regulation as the outcome of a "bargaining game" among three different groups of agents (with different preferences regarding risk taking) and the "agency conflicts" among these groups. The groups are bank stockholders, bank managers, and the providers of insurance guarantees (the FDIC).

[14] The premium was 1/30th of one percent per dollar of insured deposits from 1967–1985, increased to 1/10th of one percent from 1986–1992, and again to 1/8th of one percent in 1993 and 1/6th of one percent from 1994–1998, See www.cdic.ca.

TABLE 19–1
Flat Deposit
Insurance Premiums
and Risk Taking

Bank A				Bank B		
Assets		Liabilities		Assets		Liabilities
Real estate loans	100	Domestic deposits	100	T-bills 100	Domestic deposits	100

FIGURE 19–3
Premium Schedules
Relative to Risk

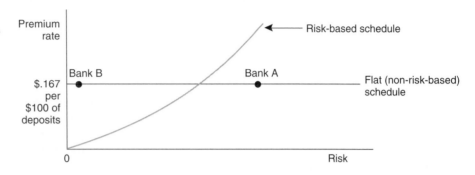

In Figure 19–3, note that under the flat premium schedule, banks A and B would have been charged the same deposit insurance premium based on a bank's domestic deposit size. Critics of flat premiums argue that a deposit insurance corporation should act more like a private property-casualty insurer. Under normal property & casualty insurance premium-setting principles, insurers charge those with higher risks higher premiums. That is, low-risk parties (such as bank B) do not generally subsidize high-risk parties (such as bank A). If premiums increased as bank risk increased, banks would have reduced incentives to take risks. Therefore, the ultimate goal might be to price risk in an actuarially fair fashion, similar to the process used by a private property & casualty insurer, so that premiums reflect the expected private costs or losses to the insurer from the provision of deposit insurance.

Note that there are arguments against imposing an actuarially fair risk-based premium schedule. If the deposit insurer's mandate is not to act as if it were a private cost-minimizing insurer such as a P & C insurance company because of social welfare considerations, some type of subsidy to banks and thrifts can be justified. Broader banking market stability concerns and savers' welfare concerns might arguably override private cost-minimizing concerns and require subsidies.[15] Other authors have argued that if an actuarially fair premium is imposed on a banking system that is fully competitive, banking itself cannot be profitable. That is, some subsidy is needed for banks to exist profitably.[16] However, while Canadian banking is competitive, it probably deviates somewhat from the perfectly competitive model.

Calculating the Actuarially Fair Premium[17]   Economists have suggested a number of approaches for calculating the fair deposit insurance premium that a cost-minimizing insurer such as the CDIC should charge. One approach would be to set

---

[15] Most of the deposit insurance literature, however, assumes that the objective should be to minimize cost; see S. Acharya and J. F. Dreyfus, "Optimal Bank Reorganization Policies and the Pricing of Federal Deposit Insurance," *Journal of Finance* 44 (1988), pp. 1313–34.

[16] See Y. S. Chan, S. I. Greenbaum, and A. V. Thakor, "Is Fairly Priced Deposit Insurance Possible?" *Journal of Finance* 47 (1992), pp. 227–46; and A. Buser, "Federal Deposit Insurance, Regulatory Policy, and Optimal Bank Capital," *Journal of Finance* 36 (1981), pp.51–60.

[17] This section, which contains more technical topics, may be included in or dropped from the chapter reading depending on the rigor of the course.

FIGURE 19–4
Deposit Insurance
as a Put Option
(0D = DI's deposits;
0A = DI's assets;
0P = premium
paid by DI)

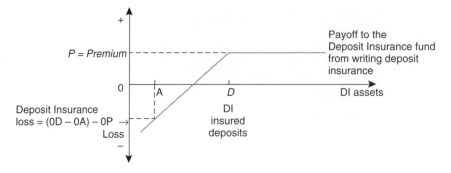

**option pricing
model of deposit
insurance**
A model for calculating
deposit insurance as
a put option on the
DI's assets.

the premium equal to the expected severity of loss times the frequency of losses due to failure plus some load or markup factor.[18] This would exactly mimic the approach toward premium setting in the property-casualty industry. However, the most common approach, the **option pricing model of deposit insurance** (OPM), has been to view the provision of deposit insurance as virtually identical to writing a put option on the assets of the FI that buys the deposit insurance.[19, 20] We depict the conceptual idea underlying the option pricing model approach in Figure 19–4.

In this framework, CDIC charges a premium 0P to insure the FI's deposits (0D). If the FI does well and the market value of the FI's assets is greater than 0D, its net worth is positive and it can continue in business. CDIC would face no charge against its resources and would keep the premium paid to it by the FI (0P). If the FI is insolvent, possibly because of a bad or risky asset portfolio, such that the value of the assets falls below 0D (say to 0A), and its net worth is negative, the owners will "put the bank" back to CDIC. If this happens, CDIC will pay out to the insured depositors an amount 0D and will liquidate the assets (0A). As a result, CDIC bears the cost of the insolvency (or negative net worth) equal to (0D − 0A) minus the insurance premiums paid by the FI (0P).

When valued in this fashion as a simple European put option, the cost of providing deposit insurance increases with the level of asset risk (σ_A^2) and with the FI's leverage (D/A). That is, the actuarially fair premium (0P) is equivalent to the premium on a put option and as such should be positively related to both asset risk (σ_A^2) and leverage risk (D/A).[21]

---

[18] D. Duffie, R. Jarrow, A. Purnanandam, and W. Yang develop a reduced-form model in which fair market deposit insurance rates can be inferred from market pricing of the credit risk in bank debt instruments. They find fair market deposit insurance rates to be much larger than actuarially calculated mean loss rates to the insurer. The fair market insurance rate of a given bank is the risk-neutral mean loss rate to the insurer, which is the product of (a) the annualized likelihood of failure during the period covered by the current contract and (b) the expected loss to the insurer given failure, as a fraction of assessed deposits. See "Market Pricing of Deposit Insurance," *Journal of Financial Services Research,* October/December 2003, pp. 93–119.

[19] See, for example, R. C. Merton, "An Analytic Derivation of the Cost of Deposit Insurance and Loan Guarantees: An Application of Modern Option Pricing Theory," *Journal of Banking and Finance* 1 (1977), pp. 3–11; and E. Ronn and A. K. Verma, "Pricing Risk-Adjusted Deposit Insurance: An Option-Based Model," *Journal of Finance* 41 (1986), pp. 871–96.

[20] There is a third approach that views deposit insurance premiums being set as the outcome of an agency conflict among three groups of self-interested parties: bank stockholders, bank managers, and bank regulators. See Kane, "Three Paradigms."

[21] In Merton, "An Analytic Derivation," the value of a deposit insurance guaranty is shown to be the same as the Black-Scholes model for a European put option of maturity T (where T is the time period until the next premium assessment):

$$0P(T) = De^{-rT}\phi(X_2) - A\phi(X_1)$$

where

$$X_1 = \{\log{(D/A)} - (r + \sigma_A^2/2)T\}/\sigma_A \sqrt{T}$$

$$X_2 = X_1 + \sigma_A \sqrt{T}$$

and ϕ is the standard normal distribution. *(continued on next page)*

Even though the option pricing model is a conceptually and theoretically elegant tool, it is difficult to apply in practice—especially because an FI's asset value (A) and its asset risks (σ^2_A) are not directly observable. However, values of these variables can be extracted from the equity value and the volatility of equity value of the FI (see the discussion on the KMV model in Chapter 11). Even so, the option model framework is useful because it indicates that both leverage and asset quality (or risk) are important elements that should enter into any deposit insurance pricing model.

Next, we look at the risk-based deposit insurance premium scheme introduced by CDIC in 1999.

Concept Questions

1. Bank A has a ratio of deposits to assets of 90 percent and a variance of asset returns of 10 percent. Bank B has a ratio of deposits to assets of 85 percent and a variance of asset returns of 5 percent. Which bank should pay the higher insurance premium?
2. If deposit insurance is similar to a put option, who exercises that option?

Implementing Risk-Based Premiums

risk-based deposit insurance program
A program that assesses insurance premiums on the basis of capital adequacy and supervisory judgments on FI quality.

As deposit-taking financial institutions were perceived to become more risky in the 1980s and 1990s, the FDIC adopted a **risk-based deposit insurance program** for U.S. FIs in 1993. CDIC established risk-based premiums for Canadian deposit-taking institutions in 1999. The level of premiums charged by CDIC is based its assessment of the deposit-taking institution's risk. The criteria are both quantitative and qualitative, and include capital adequacy (discussed in detail in Chapter 20) as well as risk-weighted assets, efficiency, impaired assets, asset growth, and loan concentration. Based on its score out of 100, the FI is placed into one of four categories, as shown in Table 19–2, and charged the appropriate premium based on its level of insured deposits. For example, an FI with a score greater than or equal to 80 was charged a premium of 1.4 basis points of insured deposits in 2005. So if the deposit-taking institution had $1 billion of insured deposits, it would pay $1,400,000 ($1,000,000,000 × .00014) for deposit insurance. If its score were below 50, it would pay $1,110,000 ($1,000,000,000 × .00111). Thus the incentive is to maintain a high score so that the cost to the FI is minimized, since, the insurance premium for deposits would be factored into an FI's cost of funds for loans and other services. The rates have declined from 2001 to 2005, in line with decreased risk and low claims on the insurance corporation. An insured institution is notified each year of the rate that it will pay, but CDIC does not permit the FI to disclose its risk category, its total score, the examiner's rating, the premium rate that has been assigned, or any other information related to its premiums.[22]

---

[21] *(continued)* Other authors have relaxed many of Merton's assumptions, including (1) allowing for partial deposit insurance coverage (Ronn and Verma, "Pricing Risk-Adjusted Deposit Insurance"), (2) closure taking place when $D < A$ (i.e., forbearance) rather than $D = A$ (Ronn and Verma; and Acharya and Dreyfus, "Optimal Bank Reorganization"), (3) surveillance and monitoring involving costs (R. C. Merton, "On the Cost of Deposit Insurance When There Are Surveillance Costs," *Journal of Business* 51 (1978), pp. 439–52), and (4) the option being American rather than European, that is, closure exercisable at any time during the insurance contract period rather than at the end (Merton, "On the Cost").

[22] Various researchers have examined the issue of moral hazard and the impact of deposit insurance on Canadian FIs. See for example, J. Gueyie and V. Son Lai, "Bank moral hazard and the introduction of official deposit insurance in Canada," *International Review of Economics and Finance* 12 (2003), pp. 247–273; J. So and J.Z. Wei, "Deposit insurance and forbearance under moral hazard," *Journal of Risk and Insurance*, December 2004, Vol. 71, Iss. 4, pp. 707–736; J. M. Hendrickson and M. W. Nichols, "How Does Regulation Affect the Risk Taking of Banks? A U.S. and Canadian Perspective," *Journal of Comparative Policy Analysis*, June 2003, 3,1, pp. 59–83; and E. J. Kane and B. Wilson, "Regression evidence of safety-net support in Canada and the U.S., 1893–1992," *The Quarterly Review of Economics and Finance* 42 (2002), pp. 649–671.

TABLE 19–2
Premium rates charged for deposit insurance, 2001–2005

Premium Categories and Rates						
Score	**Premium Category**	**Premium Rate (basis points % of insured deposits)**				
		2001	2002	2003	2004	2005
≥ 80	1	4	2	2	2	1.4
≥ 65 but < 80	2	8	4	4	4	2.8
≥ 50 but < 65	3	16	8	8	8	5.6
< 50	4	33	16	16	16	11.1

Source: Canada Deposit Insurance Corporation, www.cdic.ca

Increased Capital Requirements and Stricter Closure Rules

A second way to reduce stockholders' incentives to take excessive risks is to (1) require higher capital—lower leverage—ratios (so that stockholders have more at stake in taking risky investments) and (2) impose stricter closure rules. The moral hazard risk-taking incentives of FI owners increase as their capital or net worth approaches zero and their leverage increases. For those U.S. thrifts allowed to operate in the 1980s with virtually no book equity capital and with negative net worth, the risk-taking incentives of their owners were enormous.

capital forbearance
Regulators' policy of allowing an FI to continue operating even when its capital funds are fully depleted.

By failing to close such FIs, regulators exhibited excessive **capital forbearance.** In the short term, forbearance may save the insurance fund some liquidation costs. In the long run, owners of bad banks or thrifts have continuing incentives to grow and take additional risks in the hope of a large payoff that could turn the institution around. This strategy potentially adds to the future liabilities of the insurance fund and to the costs of liquidation. We now know that huge additional costs were the actual outcome of the regulators' policy of capital forbearance in the U.S. thrift industry in the 1980s.

As we discuss in Chapter 20, a system of risk-based capital requirements mandates that those FIs taking greater on- and off-balance-sheet, market, credit, operating, and interest rate risks must hold more capital. Thus, risk-based capital supports risk-based deposit insurance premiums by increasing the cost of risk taking for FI stockholders.[23]

To the extent that the book value of capital approximates true net worth or the market value of capital, this enhances stockholder discipline by imposing additional costs on FI owners for risk taking. It also increases the degree of coinsurance, in regard to risks taken, between FI owners and regulators such as the CDIC.

Concept Questions

1. If you are managing an FI that is technically insolvent but has not yet been closed by the regulators, would you invest in Treasury bonds or real estate development loans? Explain your answer.
2. Do we need both risk-based capital requirements and risk-based insurance premiums to discipline shareholders?

Depositor Discipline

An alternative, more indirect route to disciplining riskier FIs is to create conditions for a greater degree of depositor discipline. Depositors could either require higher interest rates and risk premiums on deposits or ration the amount of deposits they are willing to hold in riskier FIs.

---

[23] On the assumption that new equity is more costly to raise than deposits for banks.

Critics argue that under the current deposit insurance regulations, neither insured depositors nor uninsured depositors have sufficient incentives to discipline riskier deposit-taking institutions. To understand these arguments, we consider the risk exposure of both insured and uninsured depositors under the current deposit insurance contract.

Insured Depositors

As noted above, CDIC is a Crown corporation that was created in 1967 to protect deposits held at banks, trust companies, and savings and loans. The 2005 federal budget increased the level of coverage for a depositor from $60,000 to $100,000 effective February 2005 (coverage in the U.S. by FDIC is $100,000). The $100,000 cap concerns a depositor's beneficial interest and ownership of deposited funds that are made with an eligible member of CDIC, are in Canadian dollars payable in Canada, and are repayable within 5 years from the deposit date. The cap relates to deposits at a single member institution. In actuality, by structuring deposit funds in a CDIC-insured institution in a particular fashion, a depositor can achieve many times the $100,000 cap on deposits. To see this, consider the different categories of deposit fund ownership (defined as savings and chequing accounts, term deposits, debentures issued by loan companies, money orders, drafts, certified cheques, and travellers cheques) available to an individual, shown in Table 19–3. Each of these categories represents a distinct accumulation of funds towards the $100,000 deposit insurance cap, the coverage ceiling per financial institution. We give an example of how depositors can raise the coverage level by adopting certain strategies.

EXAMPLE 19–1

A married couple with one daughter, where both husband and wife had eligible funds in individual RRSPs, could accrue coverage at one CDIC-insured institution of $100,000 each for individual savings or chequing accounts ($300,000 total), $100,000 for each of 3 joint chequing accounts ($300,000), $100,000 each for trust deposits ($300,000), and $100,000 each for the husband and wife for five-year GICs in an RRSP ($200,000) for a total coverage cap of $1,100,000 as a family.

Note that this coverage ceiling is per institution, not per branch. Wealthy and institutional investors can spread their funds over many deposit-taking institutions up to the permitted cap insured by CDIC. In this way, all their deposits become explicitly insured. For example, a wealthy individual with $1 million in deposits could split the deposits between 10 of the CDIC's members. In the U.S., a wealthy individual might use a **deposit broker** such as Merrill Lynch to split US$1 million into parcels of US$100,000 and deposit those funds at 10 different banks. During the 1980s, the greatest purchasers of brokered deposits were the most risky banks that had no, or limited, access to the borrowed funds market. These risky banks attracted brokered deposits by offering higher interest rates than did relatively healthy banks. In fact, a high proportion of brokered deposits held by a bank became an early warning signal of its future failure risk. Neither the depositors nor the fund brokers were concerned about the risk of these funds because every parcel was including interest accrued up until the time of failure, was fully insured up to the US$100,000 ceiling.

deposit brokers
Brokers who break up large deposits into smaller units at different banks to ensure full coverage by deposit insurance.

Uninsured Depositors

The primary intention of deposit insurance is to deter runs and panics. A secondary and related objective has been to protect the smaller, less informed saver

TABLE 19–3
Deposit Ownership
Categories

Individual ownership, such as a simple chequing account.
Joint ownership, such as the savings account of a husband and wife.
Trust deposits that state the name of the trustees and the beneficiaries. Each beneficiary's portion is insured up to $100,000.
Registered plans, such as Registered Retirement Savings Plans (RRSPs) or Registered Retirement Income Funds (RRIFs) that are in Canadian currency and held in savings accounts or term deposits with maturities of less than 5 years.

Source: Canada Deposit Insurance Corporation, www.cdic.ca

against the reduction in wealth that would occur if that person were last in line when an FI fails. Under the current deposit insurance contract, the small, less informed depositor is defined by the $100,000 ceiling. Theoretically at least, larger, more informed depositors with more than $100,000 on deposit are at risk if an FI fails. As a result, these large uninsured depositors should be sensitive to risk and seek to discipline more risky FIs by demanding higher interest rates on their deposits or withdrawing their deposits completely.[24] Until recently, the manner in which failures have been resolved meant that both large and small depositors were often fully protected against losses. This was especially so where large banks got

too-big-to-fail banks
Banks that are viewed by regulators as being too big to be closed and liquidated without imposing a systemic risk to the banking and financial system.

into trouble and were viewed as **too big to fail.** That is, they were too big to be liquidated by regulators either because of the draining effects on the resources of the insurance fund or for fear of contagious or systemic runs spreading to other major banks. Thus, although uninsured depositors tended to lose in small-bank failures, in large-bank failures the failure resolution methods employed by regulators usually resulted in implicit 100 percent deposit insurance. As a result, for large banks in particular, neither small nor large depositors had sufficient incentives to impose market discipline on riskier banks.

In Canadian banking history, failing institutions have generally been absorbed by other institutions, such as the take over of Central Guaranty Trust's assets by TD Bank in the early 1990s. In an effort to prevent the failure of the Canadian Commercial Bank and the Northland Bank of Canada in 1985, the federal regulators at the time (the Inspector General of Banks along with the Bank of Canada and the Department of Finance) arranged for support from the six large banks and government to provide liquidity to replace the banks' wholesale deposits that were maturing and not being renewed. In the fallout, Continental Bank of Canada became unable to renew its wholesale deposits, despite being declared solvent by an examination of its loan portfolio by the Big Six banks, and was subsequently taken over by Hong Kong Bank of Canada. Next we look at three principal methods of failure resolution and their effect on depositors.

---

[24] L. G. Goldberg and S. C. Hudgins, in "Depositor Discipline and the Behavior of Uninsured Deposits: FSLIC vs. SAIF," *Journal of Financial Economics* 63 (2002), pp. 263–74, examine the behaviour of uninsured deposits at S&Ls from 1984–1995. They find that failed institutions exhibit declining levels of uninsured deposits prior to failure, that failing institutions attract fewer uninsured deposits prior to failure than do solvent institutions, and that factors indicating the well-being and aggressiveness of institutions affect the level of uninsured deposits. Further, M. S. M. Peria and S. L. Schmukler, in "Do Depositors Punish Banks for Bad Behavior? Market Discipline, Deposit Insurance, and Banking Crises," *Journal of Finance* 56 (2001), pp. 1029–52, find that (insured as well as uninsured) depositors in Argentina, Chile, and Mexico punish banks for risky behavior, both by withdrawing their deposits and by requiring higher interest rates. Market discipline is more significant after banking crises, suggesting that following bank interventions and failures, depositors become more aware of the risk of losing deposits; thus, they start exercising a stricter market discipline.

payoff method of closure
Failure resolution method in which the deposit insurance fund (CDIC) liquidates the FI and pays off the DI's depositors.

• *The payoff method (liquidation).* Historically, the **payoff method of closure** has resolved most small FI failures when a merger was unavailable or too costly or when the loss to the community would impose few local social costs. Under a payoff closure, regulators liquidate the assets of the FI and pay off the insured depositors in full (insured deposit payoff). They could also transfer these deposits in full to another local FI (insured deposit transfer).

EXAMPLE 19–2

Liquidation and Payoff of a Failed Bank Using the Payoff Method

To understand who gains and who potentially loses under the payoff (liquidation) method, consider the simple example of a failed bank in Table 19–4. The failed bank's liquidation value of assets is only $80 million. It has $50 million in outstanding claims held by small insured depositors whose claims individually are $100,000 or less and $50 million in uninsured domestic depositor claims that individually exceed $100,000. The net worth of the failed bank is negative $20 million.

On closure, the insured depositors receive a $50 million payoff in full.[25] CDIC liquidates the $80 million in assets and shares it on an equal, or pro rata, basis with the uninsured domestic depositors. Since CDIC owns 50 percent of deposit claims and the uninsured domestic depositors own the other 50 percent, each gets $40 million on the liquidation of the bank's assets.

TABLE 19–4
Failed Bank Balance Sheet (in millions of dollars)

Assets		Liabilities	
Asset (liquidation value)	$80	Insured deposits	$ 50
		Uninsured domestic deposits	50
	$80		$100

The allocation of the $20 million net worth loss of the bank among the three parties or the claimants follows:[26]

	Loss (in millions of dollars)
Insured depositors	$ 0
Deposit insurance fund	10
Uninsured domestic depositors	10
	$20

The negative $20 million net worth loss of the bank is shared pro rata by CDIC and the uninsured domestic depositors.[27]

From this example, it is clear that if the payoff method were always used to resolve FI failures, uninsured depositors would have very strong incentives to monitor FI risk taking. They would also discipline owners by requiring higher risk premiums on their deposits and/or withdrawing their deposits from riskier banks.

---

[25] Instead of a payoff in full, in an insured deposit transfer their deposits are transferred in full to another bank.

[26] We do not show the value of the equity holders' claims or those of foreign uninsured depositors and creditors in this example. Since they have junior claims to these three parties (CDIC, the insured depositors, and uninsured domestic depositors), their claims are reduced to zero on failure.

[27] In insured deposit transfers, when the insured deposits of the failed bank are transferred to another bank and its assets are liquidated, the acquirer of the insured deposits may pay a premium to CDIC reflecting the value of picking up new deposit customers. Any such premium would lower the costs of liquidation to CDIC.

Although regulators have frequently used the payoff method, this has been mostly for thrifts and small failing banks. The FDIC press release announcing the payoff of insured deposits of the failed Bank of Alamo in November 2002 is presented in Appendix 19A to the chapter (located at the book's Web site, www.mcgrawhill.ca/saunders. Regulators have used the second and third closure methods, described next, most often for large failing banks. As will become clear, these methods impose much less discipline on uninsured depositors.

purchase and assumption (P&A)
Merger of a failed deposit-taking institution with a healthy FI.

• *Purchase and assumption.* There are three types of **purchase and assumption (P&A)** resolutions. That most commonly used is the traditional "clean" P&A method. Under a traditional clean purchase and assumption, a stronger, healthy FI purchases and assumes both the insured and uninsured deposits of the failed FI as well as its remaining good assets, mostly securities. The difference between the total deposits of the failed FI and the market value of the failed FI's good assets is met by a cash infusion from CDIC minus any takeover premium the acquiring FI is willing to pay. The FDIC press release announcing the purchase and assumption of insured deposits of the failed Farmers Bank and Trust of Cheneyville in December 2002 is presented in Appendix 19A to the chapter (located at the book's Web site, **www.mcgrawhill.ca/saunders**.

EXAMPLE 19–3

Liquidation and Payoff of a Failed Bank Using the P & A Method

To understand the mechanics of a traditional clean P&A and who bears the losses, we look at a P&A of the same bank discussed in the *payoff* (liquidation) example earlier (see Table 19–4). The clean P&A transfers all depositors, insured and uninsured (both domestic and foreign), as well as other liabilities to the acquiring bank. Thus, neither the insured nor the uninsured depositors lose. The full $20 million loss is borne by CDIC through its cash injection to clean up the failed bank's bad assets prior to the merger with the acquiring bank minus any premium it can obtain from the acquiring bank.[28] For example, a Canadian bank may pay a premium to acquire a failing bank in Florida because Florida is a high-growth market and it is often cheaper to acquire a bank and its existing branches than to establish completely new branches.

To summarize the losses of the three parties in a traditional clean P&A:

Loss (in millions of dollars)		
Insured depositors	0	
Uninsured depositors	0	
Deposit insurance fund	$20	(minus any merger premium)
Total $20		

Clearly, with a clean P&A, large uninsured depositors are de facto insured depositors.

open assistance
Provision of loans or capital funds to keep a large failing FI open as part of a restructuring plan.

• *Open assistance.* The third main method of closure regulators used is **open assistance**. When very large FIs fail, such as Continental Illinois in 1984 with $36 billion in assets and First City Bancorporation of Texas in 1987 with US$11 billion in

---

[28] In recent years, U.S. regulators have held auctions to select the acquiring bank. However, the bank that bids the highest premium does not always win; the deposit insurance fund takes into account the quality of the bidder as well. For example, a low-quality bank that acquires a failed bank in an auction might become a bigger problem bank in the future.

assets, it is often difficult, if not impossible, to find an FI sound and big enough to engage in a P&A. Moreover, regulators fear that smaller FIs will be hurt by a large closure and that big depositors and investors might lose confidence if they used payoff and liquidation. Open assistance can take the form of promissory notes, net worth certificates, cash, infusions of equity, and so on. An example of open assistance was the commitment of US$870 million by the FDIC to an investor group headed by Robert Abboud to take over control of First City Bancorporation of Texas in September 1987. However, failure to close and liquidate a bad FI sends a strong and undesirable signal to large uninsured depositors at other big FIs that their deposits are safe and that regulators will not permit big FIs to fail. That is, all large uninsured depositors with big FIs are really implicitly 100 percent insured, thereby alleviating depositors from any monitoring/market discipline responsibilities.[29] Such an implicit guaranty to uninsured depositors at large FIs is often called the too-big-to-fail guaranty.[30]

Nevertheless, some concern has been raised about the continuance of the too-big-to-fail (TBTF) guarantee. With the growing wave of bank and financial service firm mergers, it is argued that more and more FIs are likely to be covered by TBTF guarantees.[31]

insured depositor transfer (IDT)
Method of resolution in which uninsured depositors take a loss, or haircut, on failure equal to the difference between their deposit claims and the estimated value of the failed FI's assets minus insured deposits.

The FDIC has been increasingly using an **insured depositor transfer (IDT)**, or "haircut," method to resolve a number of US post-1991 failures. Under the IDT method of resolution, the insured deposits of a closed FI are usually transferred in full to another local FI in the community to conduct a direct payoff of the depositors for the FDIC. By contrast, uninsured depositors must file a claim against the receiver of the failed FI and share with the FDIC in any receivership distributions from the liquidation of the closed FI's assets. This usually results in a loss for uninsured depositors (a so-called haircut). For example, in 60 out of 122 failures in 1992, the FDIC imposed initial losses, or haircuts, on uninsured depositors, ranging from 13 to 69 percent. The size of the haircut depends mostly on the FDIC-estimated value of the failed FI's assets. The total dollar size of 1992 haircuts taken by uninsured depositors was US$80 million. We describe a simplified form of the IDT, or haircut, method next. This allows us to compare the cost of this new approach to that of previous methods, such as the traditional P&A and payoff methods.

---

[29] For example, in the final restructuring arrangement for Continental Illinois, all depositors were protected; the FDIC assumed a large amount of problem loans and infused US$1 billion new capital into the bank with a part convertible into a direct ownership interest. By taking an equity stake in the failed bank, the FDIC stood to gain, with outside equity owners, from any improvement in the performance of the bank as well. Indeed, in a number of open assistance programs, the FDIC held (holds) long-term options or warrants that allow it to share in the upside of improved bank performance (if any). Nevertheless, the incentive to impose market discipline has still been eliminated for large uninsured depositors.

[30] O'Hara and Shaw and Mei and Saunders seek to calculate the value of such a too-big-to-fail guarantee. O'Hara and Shaw find significant value, while Mei and Saunders find little value from such guarantees. See M. O'Hara and W. Shaw, "Deposit Insurance and Wealth Effects: The Value of Being Too Big to Fail," *Journal of Finance* 45 (1990), pp. 1587–1600; and J. P. Mei and A. Saunders, "Bank Risk and Too Big to Fail Guarantees: An Asset Pricing Perspective," *Journal of Real Estate Finance and Economics* 10 (1995), pp. 199–224.

[31] Indeed, the US Federal Reserve–organized US$3.5 billion bank bailout of the Long-Term Capital Management (LTCM) hedge fund has been described by some as a TBTF bailout because the fund was allowed to continue operations largely on the basis of the size of its exposure both in capital market instruments and in derivatives of over US$1.25 trillion in nominal value. The fear here was that allowing LTCM to liquidate its positions at a massive loss could cause a number of banks that had lent money to the fund to fail or be significantly undercapitalized once losses were written off. Others have argued that this was not really a TBTF bailout in the conventional sense since no government money was directly involved.

EXAMPLE 19-4

Liquidation and Payoff of a Failed Bank Using the Insured Deposit Transfer (IDT) Method

In Table 19–5, the failed bank in panel (a) has only $80 million in good assets to meet the $50 million in deposit claims of insured depositors and the $50 million in claims of the uninsured depositors.[32] Under an IDT, in panel (b), the FDIC would transfer the $80 million in assets to an acquiring bank along with the full $50 million in small insured deposits but only $30 million of the $50 million in uninsured deposits.[33] Notice that the uninsured depositors get protection against losses only up to the difference between the estimated value of the failed bank's assets and its insured deposits. In effect, the uninsured depositors are subject to a haircut to their original deposit claims of $20 million (or, as a percentage, 40 percent of the value of their deposit claims on the failed bank). After the IDT, the uninsured depositors own $30 million in deposits in the acquiring bank and $20 million in receivership claims on the bad assets of the failed bank. Only if the FDIC as a receiver can recover some value from the $20 million in bad assets will the loss to the uninsured be less than $20 million.

To summarize the losses of the three parties under the IDT:

Loss (in millions of dollars)		
Insured depositors	=	0
FDIC	=	0
Uninsured depositors	=	$20

TABLE 19-5   **Insured Depositor Transfer Resolution (in millions of dollars)**

(a) Failed				(b) Insured Depositor Transfer				
Assets		**Liabilities**		**Assets**		**Liabilities**		
Good assets	$80	Insured deposits	$ 50	Good assets	$80	Insured deposits	$50	Merger with good bank →
		Uninsured deposits	50			Uninsured deposits	30	
	$80		$100		$80		$80	

As you can see from this simple example, the uninsured depositors bear all the losses and now have a much stronger incentive than before to monitor and control the actions of FI owners through imposing market discipline via interest rates and the amount of funds deposited.

Concept Questions

1. In Table 19–4, how would the losses of the FI be shared if insured deposits were $30m and uninsured deposits were $70m?
2. List four factors that might influence an acquirer to offer a large premium when bidding for a failed FI.
3. Make up a simple balance sheet example to show a case where a deposit insurance fund can lose even when it uses an IDT to resolve a failed FI.

Regulatory Discipline

In the event that stockholder and deposit holder discipline does not reduce moral hazard–induced risk taking, regulations can require regulators to act promptly and in a more consistent and predictable fashion to restrain FI risk-taking behaviour by: (1)

---

[32] That is, it has $20 million negative net worth.

[33] Unlike in a P&A, it would not inject cash into the failed bank prior to a merger with the acquiring bank.

the frequency and thoroughness of examinations and (2) the forbearance shown to weakly capitalized FIs.

Examinations

As shown in Figure 19–1, the joint oversight by OSFI and CDIC provides the regulatory discipline for federally-regulated banks, trusts, and loan companies in Canada. In addition to the monthly and quarterly reporting to OSFI, a federally-regulated FI is inspected annually by OSFI, which may also conduct special examinations if desired. As well, CDIC provides oversight for provincially-regulated deposit-taking FIs and may conduct annual or special examinations of these FIs. Since 1987, CDIC has been able to act as a liquidator or receiver in the event of the failure of a CDIC member. In the U.S., since 1992, every deposit-taking institution must be examined annually on-site and is also subject to an audit by an independent private accountant. This is similar to the situation in the United Kingdom, where the 1987 Bank Act required an enhanced role for private auditors as a backup for regulatory examiners.

Regulatory Forbearance

OSFI and CDIC jointly follow the "Guide to Intervention for Federal Financial Institutions" in dealing with a troubled FI which, it can be argued, gives them more discretionary powers as opposed to the strict rules-based approach that has been adopted in the United States, which mandates "prompt corrective action" symptomatic of a move toward a regulatory policy based on rules rather than on discretion. The weakness of such rules is that if a policy is bad, then bad policy becomes more effective.[34]

Concept Questions

1. What additional measures can be taken by regulators to bolster stockholder and depositor discipline?

DEPOSIT INSURANCE SYSTEMS GLOBALLY

Deposit insurance systems are increasingly being adopted worldwide. See Appendix 19B (located at the book's Web site, www.mcgrawhill.ca/college/saunders) for a description of systems in various countries. Many of these systems offer quite different degrees of protection to depositors compared with systems in Canada and the United States.[35] In response to the single banking and capital market in Europe, the EC established (at the end of 1999) a single deposit insurance system

---

[34] As mentioned previously, L. Kryzanowski and G. S. Roberts, "Canadian banking solvency, 1922–1940," *Journal of Money, Credit, and Banking*, (August 1993) Vol. 25, Iss.3, pp. 361–376 argues that regulatory forbearance allowed Sun Life to carry its securities at book value rather than at market value, keeping Sun Life from being declared insolvent and forcing the regulators to act to wind it up. J. So and J. Z. Wei, "Deposit insurance and forbearance under moral hazard," *Journal of Risk and Insurance*, (December 2004), Vol. 71. Iss. 4, pp. 707–735, use a real options model for a bank's assets and conclude that forbearance can help reduce a deposit fund's liability. Similar arguments have been made in the area of monetary policy, where proponents (such as monetarist Milton Friedman) have argued for a rules-based policy around a constant growth rate of the money supply. However, most central bankers prefer discretion in deciding on the timing and size of monetary policy actions such as their open market operations.

[35] A. Demirgüç-Kunt and E. J. Kane conclude that in institutionally weak environments, it is hard to design deposit insurance arrangements that will not increase the probability and depth of future banking crises. For countries with weak institutions, adopting explicit deposit insurance promises to spur financial development only in the very short run, if at all. Over longer periods, it is more likely to undermine market discipline in ways that reduce bank solvency, destroy real economic capital, increase financial fragility, and deter financial development. See "Deposit Insurance around the Globe: Where Does It Work?" *Journal of Economic Perspectives* 16 (2002), pp. 175–95.

covering all European Community-located banks. This directive requires the insurance of deposit accounts in EC countries up to 20,000 ECUs. However, depositors are subject to a 10 percent deductible in order to create incentives for them to monitor banks. The idea underlying the EC plan is to create a level playing field for banks across all European Community countries.

Japan also has a deposit insurance system that was established in 1971. In the late 1990s and early 2000s, the Japanese banking system was going through an experience similar to that of U.S. banks and thrifts in the 1930s and 1980s, with record bad debts and bank failures. Over the decade 1992–2002, Japanese banks had written off over US$650 billion in nonperforming loans. As of 2003, these banks still had over US$400 billion in bad loans on their balance sheets. The effect on Japan's deposit insurance fund has also been similar to that of the United States in the 1980s, with a rapidly declining reserve fund that has limited its ability to deal with the crisis. These problems have led to a government "bailout" to the tune of over US$500 billion and blanket, until April 2005, protection of all bank deposits.[36] Japanese regulators have stated that as of April 2005, only the first 10 million yen (US $91,000) in each savings account will be insured.

LENDER OF LAST RESORT

Deposit Insurance versus the Central Bank

The previous sections have described how a well-designed deposit insurance system might impose stockholder, depositor, and regulator discipline. Such a system can potentially stop runs and extreme liquidity problems arising in the banking system without introducing significant amounts of moral hazard risk-taking behaviour among insured institutions. However, deposit insurance is not the only mechanism by which regulators mitigate bank liquidity risk. A second mechanism has been the central banks' provision of a lender of last resort facility.

The Bank of Canada's Lender of Last Resort Policies

The Bank of Canada Act has the role of providing liquidity to the financial system. The Bank of Canada Act allows the bank to provide loans secured by acceptable collateral (e.g., government securities, bankers' acceptances, and commercial paper) to solvent banks and members of the Canada Payments Association. These functions come under the term "lender of last resort" activities. As a result of foreign bank branches setting up in Canada in 1999 and expansion of the membership of the Canadian Payments Association in 2002, as well as the need of Canadian FIs for foreign liquidity, the Bank recently reviewed its policies in light of its role in providing stability to the financial system, as shown in the Industry Perspectives Box.[37] The Bank provides funds to the payments system in three ways:

[36] See "Net Effect," *The Economist,* November 10, 2001, pp. 68–69.
[37] For a more detailed discussion of the Bank of Canada's role in ensuring the stability of the financial system, see F. Daniel, W. Engert, and D. Maclean, "The Bank of Canada as Lender of Last Resort," *Bank of Canada Review,* Winter 2004–2005, pp. 3–16 as well as "Bank of Canada Lender-of-Last-Resort Policies," *Bank of Canada Financial System Review,* December, 2004. Prior to this, the Bank of Canada's policies were last addressed in 1986 by the Estey Commission that was set up to investigate the failures of the Canadian Commercial Bank and the Northland Bank of Canada in 1985. See W. Z. Estey, "Report of the Inquiry into the Collapse of the CCB and Northland Bank," 1986, Supply and Services Canada. As noted by Dingle, it was the Bank of Canada's concerns for the stability of the payments system to handle the daily settlements process that led to the creation of the LVTS and its real time, irrevocable settlement method in Canada. See J. F. Dingle, "The Bank Failures of September 1985" in *Planning an Evolution: The Story of the Canadian Payments Association 1980–2002,* 2004, Bank of Canada and the Canadian Payments Association, pp. 25–30.

Industry Perspectives

THE BANK OF CANADA AND MORAL HAZARD

Moral hazard with regard to LLR occurs when an act or public policy reduces market discipline and provides incentive to DTIs to take excessive risks. In the case of the provision of ELA, moral hazard arises because such policies can encourage institutions that potentially have access to such advances from the central bank to be less cautious in managing their liquidity positions. Market discipline is reduced because unsecured creditors may also expect the central bank to provide these institutions with sufficient liquidity to pay their liabilities as they come due. Because unsecured creditors may be confident that they will be able to withdraw their funds from these institutions without incurring any losses, they will not monitor these institutions as closely as they might otherwise.

Moral hazard can be controlled by promoting market discipline through the creation of appropriate incentives, for institutions and investors, and establishing a strong prudential supervisory framework, including provisions for the management of liquidity risk. As well, policy-makers need to be careful not to extend the scope of their actions beyond what is necessary to achieve clear public policy objectives. The terms and conditions associated with the Bank of Canada's ELA are intended to reinforce the fact that the Bank is the lender of last resort, rather than the lender of preferred resort. Also, institutions have an incentive to avoid using ELA because they would be subject to heightened supervisory attention, and there could also be negative reputational effects from such borrowing.

One particular concern is that an insolvent institution might try to obtain ELA to buy time to develop a high-risk strategy ("a gamble for resurrection"). Thus, it is the Bank's policy to provide ELA only to those institutions that are judged to be solvent. The Bank relies primarily on OSFI to provide a judgment on solvency.

The regulatory and supervisory framework administered by OSFI is important in controlling moral hazard. The supervisory process focuses on having financial institutions implement policies and procedures that prudently manage risks. In addition OSFI's mandate emphasizes the importance of early intervention in the affairs of troubled institutions. In this regard, OSFI and the CDIC have developed the "Guide to Intervention for Federal Financial Institutons."[1] The guide provides a framework for responding effectively to circumstances that could threaten the solvency of a financial institution. With a formal process for early intervention and early resolution, there is greater likelihood of averting costly failures by discouraging institutions from taking excessive risks and by promptly dealing with troubled financial institutions.

---

[1] The guide is available on the OSFI Website at <http://www.osfi-bsif.gc.ca/eng/documents/practices/pages/index.ap?id=1995>, and on the CDIC Website at <http://www.cdic.ca/?id=26>.

Source: F. Daniel, W. Engert, and D. Maclean, "The Bank of Canada as Lender of Last Resort: Moral Hazard," *Bank of Canada Review*, Winter 2004–2005, page 9; The Bank of Canada's Lender of Last Resort Policies, www.bankofcanada.ca.

1. *The Standing Liquidity Facility (SLF)*: The SLF provides overnight, collateralized loans to those FIs who are direct participants in the Large Value Transfer System (LVTS, see Chapter 17) to handle temporary shortfalls in the day to day settlement of accounts. The borrowers must be solvent and the collateral limits the amounts that may be borrowed, providing a curb on moral hazard (see the Industry Perspectives Box), which would see a troubled FI transfer its risk to the central bank.

2. *Emergency Lending Assistance (ELA)*: Through the ELA, the Bank provides longer-term assistance to deposit-taking institutions that are solvent, but are illiquid. That is, they have illiquid assets supported by short-term highly liquid deposits.

3. *Forced LVTS Loans*: In order to protect the payments system from systemic risk that could cause the whole system to fail, the Bank of Canada could be forced to lend to an insolvent deposit-taking institution that failed to make its daily settlement. Since each LVTS participant pledges collateral (effectively co-insurance) in advance to cover its largest single expected daily settlement, the Bank of Canada's position would be protected.

As noted earlier in the chapter, the role of the Bank of Canada interconnects with the roles of OSFI and CDIC to provide a mechanism to ensure the safety and soundness of the Canadian financial system, including the payments system. Thus Canada may be viewed as a stable link in global financial markets that are increasingly connected.

The U.S. Federal Reserve's Discount Window

discount window
Central bank lender of last resort facility.

www.federalreserve. gov

Traditionally, central banks such as the Federal Reserve have provided a **discount window** facility to meet the short-term, nonpermanent liquidity needs of FIs.[38] For example, suppose an FI has an unexpected deposit drain close to the end of a reserve requirement period and cannot meet its reserve target. It can seek to borrow from the central bank's discount window facility. Alternatively, short-term seasonal liquidity needs due to crop planting cycles can also be met through discount window loans.[39] Normally, such loans are obtained by a discounting short-term high-quality paper such as Treasury bills and bankers acceptances with the central bank. The interest rate at which such securities are discounted is called the *discount rate* and is set by the central bank.

In the wake of the terrorist attacks of September 11, 2001, the Federal Reserve's discount window supplied funds to the banking system in unprecedented amounts. The magnitude of destruction resulting from the attacks caused severe disruptions to the U.S. banking system, particularly in FIs' abilities to send payments. The physical disruptions caused by the attacks included outages of telephone switching equipment in Lower Manhattan's financial district, impaired records processing and communications systems at individual banks, the evacuation of buildings that were the sites for the payment operations of several large FIs, and the suspended delivery of cheques by air couriers. These disruptions left some FIs unable to execute payments to other FIs through the Fed's Fedwire system, which in turn resulted in an unexpected shortfall for other FIs. The Federal Reserve took several steps to address the problems in the payments system on and after September 11, 2001. Around noon on the 11th, the Board of Governors of the Fed released a statement saying that the Fed was open and operating, and that the discount window was available to meet liquidity needs of all deposit-taking institutions. The Fed staff also contacted FIs often during the next few days, encouraging them to make payments and to consider the use of the discount window to cover unexpected shortfalls. Thus, the Fed's discount window was a primary tool used to restore payments coordination during this period.[40]

In the United States the central bank has traditionally set the discount rate below market rates, such as the overnight federal funds rates. The volume of outstanding discount loans was ordinarily small, however, because the Fed prohibited deposit-taking institutions from using discount window loans to finance sales of fed funds or to finance asset expansion. However, in January

---

[38] In times of extreme crisis, the discount window can meet the liquidity needs of securities firms as well (as was the case during the stock market crash of October 19, 1987, and the terrorist attacks on the United States on September 11, 2001).

[39] It has also been shown that, in normal economic conditions, the availability of the discount window induces banks to lend more than they would without the discount window. See S. Shaffer, "The Discount Window and Credit Availability," *Journal of Banking and Finance* 23 (1999), pp. 1383–1406.

[40] See J. J. McAndrews and S. M. Potter, "Liquidity Effect of the Events of September 11, 2001," *Economic Policy Review*, Federal Reserve Bank of New York, November 2002, pp. 59–79.

2003, the Fed implemented changes to its discount window lending that increased the cost of borrowing but eased the terms. Specifically, three lending programs are now offered through the Fed's discount window. *Primary credit* is available to generally sound depository institutions on a very short-term basis, typically overnight, at a rate above the Federal Open Market Committee's (FOMC) target rate for federal funds. Primary credit may be used for any purpose, including financing the sale of fed funds. Primary credit may be extended for periods of up to a few weeks to deposit-taking institutions in generally sound financial condition. *Secondary credit* is available to institutions that are not eligible for primary credit. It is extended on a very short-term basis, typically overnight, at a rate that is above the primary credit rate. Secondary credit is available to meet backup liquidity needs when its use is consistent with a timely return to a reliance on market sources of funding or the orderly resolution of a troubled institution. Secondary credit may not be used to fund an expansion of the borrower's assets. The Federal Reserve's seasonal credit program is designed to assist small institutions in managing significant seasonal swings in their loans and deposits. *Seasonal credit* is available to institutions that can demonstrate a clear pattern of recurring intrayearly swings in funding needs. Eligible institutions are usually located in agricultural or tourist areas.

With the changes, discount window loans to healthy banks would be priced at 1 percent above (rather than below) the fed funds rate. Loans to troubled banks would cost 1.5 percent above the fed funds rate. The changes were not intended to change the Fed's use of the discount window to implement monetary policy, but to significantly increase the discount rate while making it easier to get a discount window loan. By increasing banks' use of the discount window as a source of funding, the Fed hopes to reduce volatility in the fed funds market as well. The changes also allow healthy banks to borrow from the Fed regardless of the availability of private funds.

Despite the recent changes in the Fed's policy regarding discount window lending, there are a number of reasons why access to the discount window is unlikely to deter runs and panics to the extent deposit insurance does. The first reason is that to borrow from the discount window, an FI needs high-quality liquid assets to pledge as collateral. Failing, highly illiquid FIs are unlikely to have such assets available to discount. The second reason is that discount window borrowing, unlike deposit insurance coverage, is not automatic. That is, discount window loans are made at the discretion of the central bank. Third, discount window loans are meant to provide temporary liquidity for inherently solvent FIs, not permanent long-term support for otherwise insolvent FIs. Consequently, the discount window is a partial but not a full substitute for deposit insurance as a liquidity stabilizing mechanism.

Concept Questions

1. Is a deposit-taking institution's access to central bank funds likely to be as effective as deposit insurance in deterring bank runs and panics? Why or why not?

OTHER GUARANTY PROGRAMS

As discussed in Chapter 17, other FIs are also subject to liquidity crises and liability holder runs. To deter such runs and protect small claim holders, guaranty programs have appeared in other sectors of the financial services industry. We describe these programs and their similarities to and differences from deposit insurance next.

Quebec Deposit Insurance Board (QDIB)

www.radq.govv.qc.ca

CDIC provides protection for eligible members who are federally regulated (banks, trusts, and loan companies) as well as for eligible provincially-incorporated deposit-taking institutions (trusts and loan companies). The deposits of members of CDIC that are incorporated in the province of Quebec are covered by the Quebec Deposit Insurance Board for deposits in Quebec and by CDIC for deposits made elsewhere in Canada.

Credit Unions and Caisses Populaires

Since credit unions and caisses populaires are regulated at the provincial level in Canada, deposits are protected by the provincial deposit insurance fund or its equivalent. These funds have the ability to monitor their members and may levy premiums based on deposits, gross revenues, total assets, or some other measure. Because credit unions hold many of their assets in government securities, as well as in residential mortgages and small consumer loans, often for amounts less than $10,000, credit unions have a significant degree of risk diversification, which also lowers their risk of insolvency. Links to the funds for the different provinces and territories are provided at the Credit Union Central of Canada's Web site.

www.cucentral.ca

Assuris

www.assuris.ca

Although life insurers, like property and casualty (P&C) insurers, and securities firms, including mutual funds, are subject to regulation, they are not supported by government-run guaranty funds like the CDIC. These industries provide their own funds, supported by levies on their members.

Life insurance companies writing policies in Canada are required to become members of Assuris. If a life insurance company fails, Assuris covers policyholders for loss of benefits (e.g. health expenses, disability income, RRSPs, RRIFs, and death benefits). Assuris also covers savings benefits from policies. Details of the coverage provided by Assuris are shown in Table 19–6. The products covered reflect the range of consumer services provided by insurance companies in Canada, and is similar in scope to the deposit coverage provided by CDIC.

Assuris's current structure partially reflects a re-structuring subsequent to the failure of three insurance companies (Les Coopérants, January 1992, Sovereign Life, December, 1992, and Confederation Life, August, 1994) in the 1990s, which brought into question the stability of the insurance industry and caused companies with group life and health insurance coverage to re-consider the protection from liability provided by Assuris under these policies. The federal government threatened to create a Crown Corporation similar to CDIC for insurance companies, but Assuris increased its borrowing capabilities from members, established an independent board of directors, and put in place a plan for handling restructurings in order to keep control of its members out of government hands. Despite having to call on members for additional funds, Assuris provided 100 percent coverage in the case of Les Coopérants and Confederation Life, costing the industry $175 million and $5 million, respectively. Almost all of Sovereign Life's policyholders (96 percent) were covered 100 percent, with the remainder covered to 90 percent, costing the life insurance industry $25 million in the process. In the insurance company failures in Canada, the industry has worked to transfer policies to other insurers. For example, Confederation Life, which was the fourth largest group life insurer in 1994, got into trouble by concentrating its investments in commercial real estate. After its failure, many of its policies were eventually taken over by other life insurers (e.g., Manulife, Maritime Life, Canada Life, Sun Life, Empire Life, and others).[41]

Property and Casualty Insurance Compensation Corporation (PACICC)

www.pacicc.ca

Property and casualty insurance companies in Canada fund and operate a non-profit fund, the Property and Casualty Insurance Compensation Corporation (PACICC) since 1989, which, in the event of the failure of one of its members, will automatically cover policyholders and claims. In order to sell P & C insurance in Canada, a company must be a member of PACICC, so all Canadian insurance policies are automatically covered. Policyholders are covered to a maximum of $250,000 for claims on most P & C policies. The P & C industry, as noted in Chapter 3, relies heavily on investments in bonds and other securities which have suffered lower returns over the past few years. The incentives for insurance policyholders to engage in a run if they perceive that an insurer has asset quality problems or insurance underwriting problems may be quite strong despite the presence of private guaranty funds. However, P & C insurers regulated by OSFI file a "prudent person" investment strategy that provides a measure of comfort that the industry is being monitored.

Canadian Investor Protection Fund (CIPF)

www.cipf.ca

If an investment dealer becomes bankrupt, the Canadian Investor Protection Fund (CIPF), a private insurance fund founded in 1969, will cover the losses of eligible customers of the members of the Investment Dealers Association of Canada, the Bourse de Montréal, and the TSX Group of Companies. Since its inception, the fund has had 17 insolvent members for whom it has paid out $37 million. The coverage extends to securities, commodities and futures contracts, segregated insurance funds (the insurance industry's equivalent of mutual funds, as explained in Chapter 3), and cash, up to a total of $1 million per account when a member becomes insolvent and a liquidator is appointed. Coverage is provided for each separate account (e.g. Registered Retirement Plans, Registered Income Plans, Trusts), extending the coverage above the $1 million ceiling. Coverage may also exceed this amount if there are additional funds available upon liquidation. Only losses due to insolvency of a member of the CIPF are covered.

Concept Questions

1. How do industry-sponsored guaranty funds for insurance companies differ from deposit insurance?

[41] See F. Grossi, "Life after confed life," *Benefits Canada*, October 1994, Vol. 18, Iss. 9, pp. 27–20, L. Welsh, "PACIC and the fall of Confed," *Canadian Underwriter*, November 1994, 61, 11, p. 10, and B. Cox, "Canadian Guaranty Fund Revamped," *National Underwriter*, July 10, 1995, 99, 28, pp. 2 & 22, as well as Assuris's Web site at www.assuris.ca.

TABLE 19–6
Benefits and Product Coverage Provided by Assuris

The following benefits are fully covered by Assuris up to:

Monthly Income	$2,000
Death Benefit	$200,000
Health Expense	$60,000
Cash Value	$60,000

If total benefits exceed these amounts, Assuris covers **85%** of the promised benefits, but not less than these amounts.

Accumulated Value benefits are fully covered by Assuris up to $100,000. If accumulated value benefits are over $100,000, Assuris will ensure receipt of at least $100,000.

Coverage by Product

Assuris coverage applies to the benefits under a variety of products, including:

Individual Products

Life Insurance	Long Term Care Insurance
Critical Illness	RRIFs
Health Expense Insurance	RRSPs
Disability Income Insurance	Accumulation Annuities
Payout Annuities	Segregated Funds

Group Products

Group Insurance	Group Retirement Plans

Source: Benefits and Product Coverage Provided by Assuris

Summary

A contagious run on FIs can have serious social welfare effects. Because of adverse wealth, money supply, and credit supply effects, regulators of FIs in North America and around the world have introduced guaranty programs to deter runs by offering liability holders varying degrees of failure protection. Mispriced insurance or guarantee programs, however, can lead to moral hazard behaviour by FI owners. That is, since insurance guarantees result in little risk to FI owners with limited liability, they have an incentive to take excessively risk asset positions.

In recent years, deposit insurance and other financial industry guaranty programs have weakened (FDIC in the United States and Assuris in Canada, respectively). This chapter looked at the causes of the deposit insurance fund difficulties, including external economic events and moral hazard behaviour induced by the structure of the insurance plan itself. We discussed the establishment of deposit insurance in Canada and its restructuring in the 1990s, including the introduction of risk-related premiums, risk-based capital, and increased market and regulatory discipline on deposit-taking institutions and liability holders. As a result, the provision and cost of deposit insurance is currently more sensitive to a deposit-taking institution's risk exposure than previously. This chapter also examined liability guaranty programs for other FIs, including credit unions, life insurance and P & C insurance companies, as well as for investors.

Questions and Problems

1. What is a contagious run? What are some of the potentially serious adverse social welfare effects of a contagious run? Do all types of FIs face the same risk of contagious runs?

2. How does deposit insurance help mitigate the problem of bank runs? What other elements of the safety net are available to FIs in Canada?

3. What is moral hazard?

4. How does a risk-based insurance program solve the moral hazard problem of excessive risk taking by FIs? Is an actuarially fair premium for deposit insurance always consistent with a competitive banking system?

5. What are three suggested ways a deposit insurance contract could be structured to reduce moral hazard behaviour?

6. What are some ways of imposing stockholder discipline to prevent stockholders from engaging in excessive risk taking?

7. How is the provision of deposit insurance similar to writing a put option on the assets of an FI that buys the insurance? What two factors drive the premium of the option?

8. What is capital forbearance? How does a policy of forbearance potentially increase the costs of financial distress to the insurance fund as well as the stockholders?

9. Under what conditions may the implementation of minimum capital guidelines, either risk-based or non-risk-based, fail to impose stockholder discipline as desired by regulators?

10. What has happened to the level of deposit insurance premiums since the risk-based program was implemented? Why?

11. Why did the fixed-rate deposit insurance system fail to induce insured and uninsured depositors to impose discipline on risky banks in the 1980s?

    a. How is it possible to structure deposits in an FI to reduce the effects of the insured ceiling?

    b. What has been the effect on FIs in Canada of the deposit insurance ceiling increasing to $100,000?

12. What is the too-big-to-fail doctrine? What factors caused regulators to act in a way that caused this doctrine to evolve?

13. What steps are involved under the payoff method of failure resolution?

14. What are the three types of purchase and assumption failure resolution?

    a. How does the "clean" P&A differ from the "total bank" P&A?

    b. How are the uninsured depositors treated differently in a clean P&A as opposed to a payoff method of failure resolution?

    c. How does the open assistance process solidify the too-big-to-fail guaranty?

15. The following is a balance sheet of a commercial bank (in millions of dollars):

Assets		Liabilities and Equity	
Cash	$ 5	Insured deposits	$30
Loans	40	Uninsured deposits	10
		Equity	5
Total assets	$45	Total liabilities and equity	$45

The bank experiences a run on its deposits after it declares that it will write off $10 million of its loans as a result of nonpayment. The bank has the option of meeting the withdrawals by first drawing down its cash and then selling off its loans. A fire sale of loans in one day can be accomplished at a 10 percent discount. They can be sold at a 5 percent discount if they are sold in two days. The full market value will be obtained if they are sold after two days.

   a. What is the amount of loss to the insured depositors if a run on the bank occurs on the first day? On the second day?

   b. What amount do the uninsured depositors lose if the CDIC closes the bank immediately? The assets will be sold after the two-day period.

16. A bank with insured deposits of $55 million and uninsured deposits of $45 million has assets valued at only $75 million. What is the cost of failure resolution to insured depositors, uninsured depositors, and CDIC if the following occur?

   a. The payoff method is used.

   b. A purchase and assumption is arranged with no purchase premium.

   c. A purchase and assumption is arranged with a $5 million purchase premium.

   d. A purchase and assumption is arranged with a $25 million purchase premium.

   e. An insured depositor transfer method is used.

17. A bank has $150 million in assets at book value. The insured and uninsured deposits are valued at $75 and $50 million, respectively, and the book value of equity is $25 million. As a result of loan defaults, the market value of the assets has decreased to $120 million. What is the cost of failure resolution to insured depositors, uninsured depositors, shareholders, and the CDIC if the following occur?

   a. A payoff method is used to close the bank.

   b. A purchase and assumption method with no purchase premium paid is used.

   c. A purchase and assumption method is used with $10 million paid as a purchase premium.

   d. An insured depositor transfer method is used.

18. Match the following policies with their intended consequences:

   Policies:

   a. Lower CDIC insurance levels

   b. Stricter reporting standards

   c. Risk-based deposit insurance

   Consequences:

   1. Increased stockholder discipline

   2. Increased depositor discipline

   3. Increased regulator discipline

19. Why is access to the discount window of the U.S. Federal Reserve or the Standing Liquidity Facility of the Bank of Canada less of a deterrent to bank runs than deposit insurance?

20. How do insurance guaranty funds differ from deposit insurance? What impact do these differences have on the incentive for insurance policyholders to engage in a contagious run on an insurance company?

Web Questions

21. Go to the Canada Deposit Insurance Corporation's Web site at www.cdic.ca. Click on "CDIC & You." Click on "Quiz on Deposit Insurance" and answer the multiple choice questions. How well did you do relative to others who have taken the test?

22. Go to the Bank of Canada's Web site at www.bankofcanada.ca and click on "Target for the Overnight Rate." What is the percentage increase or decrease in this rate in the past 6 months? 12 months? Click on "Other Interest Rates." Click on "Selected Historical Interest Rates." Click on "Bank Rate B14006 (V122530)" to display a pdf file with the average monthly bank rate from 1935. In which year(s) was the bank rate the lowest? In which year(s) was the bank rate the highest?

Appendix 19A   FDIC Press Releases of Bank Failures

View Appendix 19A at the Web site for this textbook (**www.mcgrawhill.ca/college/saunders**).

Appendix 19B   Deposit Insurance Schemes for Commercial Banks in Various Countries

View Appendix 19B at the Web site for this textbook (**www.mcgrawhill.ca/college/saunders**).

Capital Adequacy

In this chapter, we examine:

▸ the different measures of capital adequacy used by FI owners, managers, and regulators and the arguments for and against each

▸ the current and proposed capital adequacy requirements for deposit-taking institutions, securities firms, and insurance companies set by Canadian (and in some cases, international) regulators such as the Bank for International Settlements (BIS), and

▸ the advanced approaches used to calculate adequate capital according to internal ratings-based models of measuring credit risk that proposed by the BIS (in Appendix 20A, on page 722 of this book)

INTRODUCTION

Chapters 7 to 17 examined the major areas of risk exposure facing a modern FI manager. These risks can emanate from both on- and off-balance-sheet (OBS) activities and can be either domestic or international in source. To ensure survival, an FI manager needs to protect the institution against the risk of insolvency, that is, shield it from risks sufficiently large to cause the institution to fail. The primary means of protection against the risk of insolvency and failure is an FI's capital. This leads to the first function of capital, namely:

1. To absorb unanticipated losses with enough margin to inspire confidence and enable the FI to continue as a going concern.

   In addition, capital protects nonequity liability holders—especially those uninsured by an external guarantor such as the CDIC—against losses. This leads to the second function of capital:

2. To protect uninsured depositors, bondholders, and creditors in the event of insolvency, and liquidation.

   When FIs fail, regulators have to intervene to protect insured claimants (see Chapter 19). The capital of an FI offers protection to insurance funds and ultimately the taxpayers who bear the cost of insurance fund insolvency. This leads to the third function of capital:

3. To protect FI insurance funds and the taxpayers.

   By holding capital and reducing the risk of insolvency, an FI protects the industry from larger insurance premiums. Such premiums are paid out of the net profits of the FI. Thus, a fourth function of capital is as follows:

4. To protect the FI owners against increases in insurance premiums.

Finally, just as for any other firm, equity or capital is an important source of financing for an FI. In particular, subject to regulatory constraints, FIs have a choice between debt and equity to finance new projects and business expansion. Thus, the traditional factors that affect a business firm's choice of a capital structure—for instance, the tax deductibility of the interest on debt or the private costs of failure or insolvency—also interpose on the FI's capital decision.[1] This leads to a fifth function of capital:

5. To fund the branch and other real investments necessary to provide financial services.[2]

In the following sections, we focus on the first four functions concerning the role of capital in reducing insolvency risk and in particular the adequacy of capital in attaining these functional objectives.

CAPITAL AND INSOLVENCY RISK

Capital

net worth
A measure of an FI's capital that is equal to the difference between the market value of its assets and the market value of its liabilities.

To see how capital protects an FI against insolvency risk, we must define *capital* more precisely. The problem is that there are many definitions of capital: an economist's definition of capital may differ from an accountant's definition, which, in turn, may differ from the definition used by regulators. Specifically, the economist's definition of an FI's capital or owners' equity stake in an FI is the difference between the market values of its assets and its liabilities. This is also called the **net worth** of an FI. Although this is the *economic* meaning of capital, regulators have found it necessary to adopt definitions of capital that depart by a greater or lesser degree from economic net worth. The concept of an FI's economic net worth is really a *market value accounting concept*. With the exception of the investment banking industry, regulatory-defined capital and required leverage ratios are based in whole or in part on historical or **book value** accounting concepts.

book value
Historical cost basis for asset and liability values.

We begin by looking at the role of economic capital or net worth as an insulation device against two major types of risk: credit risk and interest rate risk. We then compare this market value concept with the book value concept of capital. Because it can actually distort the true solvency position of an FI, the book value of capital concept can be misleading to managers, owners, liability holders, and regulators. We also examine some possible reasons why FI regulators continue to rely on book value concepts in the light of such economic value transparency problems.

The Market Value of Capital

market value or mark-to-market basis
Allowing balance sheet values to reflect current rather than historical prices.

To see how economic net worth or equity insulates an FI against risk, consider the following example. Table 20–1 presents a simple balance sheet where all the assets and liabilities of an FI are valued in **market value** terms at current prices on a **mark-to-market basis** (see Chapter 8). On a mark-to-market or market value basis, the economic value of the FI's equity is $10 million, which is the difference between the market value of its assets and liabilities. On a market value basis, the FI is economically solvent and imposes no failure costs on depositors or regulators if it were liquidated today. Let's consider the impact of two classic types of FI risk on this FI's net worth: credit risk and interest rate risk.

---

[1] See S. A. Ross, R. W. Westerfield, B. D. Jordan and G.S. Roberts, *Fundamentals of Corporate Finance* (Toronto: McGraw-Hill Ryerson, 2005).

[2] A sixth function might be added. This would focus on the role of capital regulation in restraining the rate of asset growth.

TABLE 20–1
An FI's Market
Value Balance Sheet
(in millions of
dollars)

Assets		Liabilities	
Long-term securities	$ 80	Liabilities (short-term, floating-rate deposits)	$ 90
Long-term loans	20	Net worth	10
	$100		$100

TABLE 20–2   **An FI's Market Value Balance Sheet after a Decline in the Value of Loans (in millions of dollars)**

Assets		Liabilities	
Long-term securities	$80	Liabilities	$90
Other assets	12	Net worth	2
	$92		$92

TABLE 20–3   **An FI's Balance Sheet after a Major Decline in the Value of the Loan Portfolio (in millions of dollars)**

Assets		Liabilities	
Long-term securities	$80	Liabilities	$90
Other assets	8	Net worth	−2
	$88		$88

Market Value of Capital and Credit Risk

In Table 20–1, an FI has $20 million in long-term loans. (For simplicity, we drop the $ sign and "million" notation in the rest of the example.) Suppose that, because of a recession, a number of these borrowers get into cash flow problems and are unable to keep up their promised loan repayment schedules. A decline in the current and expected future cash flows on loans lowers the market value of the loan portfolio held by the FI below 20. Suppose that loans are really worth only 12 (the price the FI would receive if it could sell these loans in a secondary market at today's prices). This means the market value of the loan portfolio has fallen from 20 to 12. Look at the revised market value balance sheet in Table 20–2.

The loss of 8 in the market value of loans appears on the liability side of the balance sheet as a loss of 8 to the FI's net worth. That is, the loss of asset value is charged against the equity owners' capital or net worth. As you can see, the liability holders (depositors) are fully protected in that the total market value of their claims is still 90. This is the case because debt holders legally are senior claimants and equity holders are junior claimants to an FI's assets. Consequently, equity holders bear losses on the asset portfolio first. In fact, in our example, liability holders are hurt only when losses on the loan portfolio exceed 10, the original net worth of the FI. Let's consider a larger credit risk shock such that the market value of the loan portfolio plummets from 20 to 8, a loss of 12 (see Table 20–3).

This larger loss renders the FI insolvent; the market value of its assets (88) is now less than the value of its liabilities (90). The owners' net worth stake has been completely wiped out (reduced from 10 to −2), making net worth negative. As a result, liability holders are hurt, but only a bit. Specifically, the first 10 of the 12 loss in value of the loan portfolio is borne by the equity holders. Only after the equity holders are wiped out do the liability holders begin to lose. In this example, the economic value of their claims on the FI has fallen from 90 to 88, or a loss of 2 (a percentage loss of 2.22 percent). After insolvency and the liquidation of the remaining 88 in assets, the depositors would get only 88/90 on the dollar, or 97.77 cents per $1 of deposits. Note here that we are ignoring deposit insurance.[3]

---

[3] In the presence of deposit insurance, the insurer, such as the CDIC, would bear some of the depositors' losses; for details, see Chapter 19.

TABLE 20–4   **An FI's Market Value Balance Sheet after a Rise in Interest Rates (in millions of dollars)**

Assets		Liabilities	
Long-term securities	$75	Liabilities	$90
Long-term loans	17	Net worth	2
	$92		$92

If the FI's net worth had been larger—say 15 rather than 10 in the previous example—the liability holders would have been fully protected against the loss of 12.[4] This example clearly demonstrates the concept of net worth or capital as an insurance fund protecting liability holders, such as depositors, against insolvency risk. The larger the FI's net worth relative to the size of its assets, the more insolvency protection or insurance there is for liability holders and liability guarantors such as CDIC. This is why regulators focus on capital requirements such as the ratio of net worth to assets in assessing the insolvency risk exposure of an FI and in setting risk–based deposit insurance premiums (see Chapter 19).

Market Value of Capital and Interest Rate Risk

Consider the market value balance sheet in Table 20–1 after a rise in interest rates. As we discuss in Chapter 8, rising interest rates reduce the market value of the FI's long-term fixed-income securities and loans whereas floating-rate instruments, if instantaneously repriced, find their market values largely unaffected. Suppose a rise in interest rates reduces the market value of the FI's long-term securities investments from 80 to 75 and the market value of its long-term loans from 20 to 17. Because all deposit liabilities are assumed to be short-term floating-rate deposits, their market values are unchanged at 90.

After the shock to interest rates, the market value balance sheet is represented in Table 20–4. The loss of 8 in the market value of the FI's assets is once again reflected on the liability side of the balance sheet by a fall in FI net worth from 10 to 2. Thus, as for increased credit risk, losses in asset values due to adverse interest rate changes are borne first by the equity holders. Only if the fall in the market value of assets exceeds 10 are the liability holders, as senior claimants to the FI's assets, adversely affected.

These examples show that market valuation of the balance sheet produces an economically accurate picture of the net worth, and thus, the solvency position of an FI. Credit risk and interest rate risk shocks that result in losses in the market value of assets are borne directly by the equity holders in the sense that such losses are charges against the value of their ownership claims in the FI. As long as the owners' capital or equity stake is adequate, or sufficiently large, liability holders (and, implicitly, regulators that back the claims of liability holders) are protected against insolvency risk. That is, if an FI were closed by regulators before its economic net worth became zero, neither liability holders nor those regulators guaranteeing the claims of liability holders would stand to lose. Thus, many academics and analysts have advocated the use of market value accounting and market value of capital closure rules for all FIs, especially in the light of the book value of capital rules associated with the U.S. savings and loan association disaster in the 1980s (see Chapter 19).[5]

For example, Canadian Generally Accepted Accounting Principles (GAAP) require securities to be classified as held for trading purposes (the trading book), or for investment (the banking book). Assets are reported as such in the financial statements of the major banks. Thus trading securities are carried at their settlement date

---

[4] In this case, the 12 loss reduces net worth to +3.

[5] See, for example, G. J. Benston and G. C. Kaufman, "Risk and Solvency Regulation of Depository Institutions: Past Policies and Current Options," Monograph Series in Finance and Economics, 1988–1 (New York University, Salomon Brothers Center, 1988); and L. J. White, *The S and L Debacle* (New York: Oxford University Press, 1991).

TABLE 20–5 Book Value of an FI's Assets and Liabilities (in millions of dollars)

Assets		Liabilities	
Long-term securities	$ 80	Short-term liabilities	$ 90
Long-term loans	20	Net worth	10
	$100		$100

price, which is their market value. Investments, on the other hand, are reported on the books at amortized cost and only declines in value that are not temporary are recorded in the income statement. Similarly, the U.S. Financial Accounting Standards Board (FASB) Statement No. 115 technically requires securities classified as "available for sale" to be marked to market.[6] By comparison, no similar market-to-market requirement exists on the liabilities side. In the absence of any contrary ruling by regulators, this would require FI capital (net worth) positions to be adjusted downward if interest rates rose.

The Book Value of Capital

We contrast market value or economic net worth with book value of capital or net worth. As we discuss in later sections, book value capital and capital rules based on book values are most commonly used by FI regulators. In Table 20–5, we use the same initial balance sheet we used in Table 20–1 but assume that assets and liabilities are now valued at their historical book values.

In Table 20–5, the 80 in long-term securities and the 20 in long-term loans reflect the historic or original book values of those assets. That is, they reflect the values when the loans were made and the bonds were purchased, which may have been many years ago. Similarly, on the liability side, the 90 in liabilities reflects their historical cost, and net worth or equity is now the book value of the stockholders' claims rather than the market value of those claims. For example, the book value of capital—the difference between the book values of assets and liabilities—may have the following components for an FI:

1. *Preferred shares*: Preferred shares rank ahead of common shares and may be considered the equivalent of fixed rate debt, but the dividends are not deductible for tax purposes. For regulatory capital, preferred shares may be included provided they meet certain criteria as we discuss later, but for market-to-book ratios, preferred shares are usually considered as debt and therefore are excluded.
2. *Common shares*: The book value of common shares is their issue price times the number of shares issued.
3. *Contributed surplus*: The difference between the price the public paid for common shares when originally offered (e.g., $5/share) and their par values (e.g., $1/share) times the number of shares outstanding. Common shares for the Big Six banks and other FIs are usually issued without a par (face) value.
4. *Retained earnings*: The accumulated value of past profits not yet paid out in dividends to shareholders. Since these earnings could be paid out in dividends, they are part of the equity owners' stake in the FI.
5. *Foreign currency translation adjustments*: These represent unrealized gains (losses) that arise from the translation of investments in foreign operations into Canadian dollars. When a gain (loss) is realized when the investment is sold, the gain (loss) is recorded on the income statement.

---

[6] Canadian banks that operate in the U.S. prepare their financial statements to meet Canadian as well as U.S. GAAP. Prior to fiscal year 2005, Royal Bank of Canada published both Canadian and U.S. GAAP statements. For a discussion of the differences between the two accounting frameworks, see 2004 Scotiabank Annual Report, pp. 121–122 available at www.scotiabank.ca.

TABLE 20–6

Effect of a Loan Loss Charge-Off against the Book Value of an FI's Equity (in millions of dollars)

Assets		Liabilities	
Long-term securities	$80	Liabilities	$90
Long-term loans less allowance for impairment	17	Equity (loss of 3 on loan loss allowance)	7
	$97		$97

Consequently, book value of capital equals the sum of preferred shares plus common shares plus contributed surplus plus retained earnings plus foreign currency translation adjustments.

As the example in Table 20–5 is constructed, the book value of capital equals 10. However, invariably, the *book value of equity does not equal the market value of equity* (the difference between the market value of assets and that of liabilities). This inequality in book and market value of equity can be understood by examining the effects of the same credit and interest rate shocks on the FI's capital position, but assuming book value accounting methods.

Book Value of Capital and Credit Risk

Suppose that some of the 20 in loans are in difficulty regarding repayment schedules. We assumed in Table 20–2 that the revaluation of cash flows leads to an immediate downward adjustment of the loan portfolio's market value from 20 to 12, a market value loss of 8. By contrast, under historic book value accounting methods such as generally accepted accounting principles (GAAP), FIs have greater discretion in reflecting or timing problem loan loss recognition on their balance sheets and thus in the impact of such losses on capital. Indeed, FIs may well resist writing down the values of bad assets as long as possible to try to present a more favourable picture to depositors and regulators. Such resistance may be expected if managers believe their jobs could be threatened when they recognize such losses. Only pressure from regulators such as bank or insurance examiners may force loss recognition and write-downs in the values of problem assets.[7] A good international example is the delay shown by Japanese banks in recognizing loan losses incurred over the 1996–2000 period, as a result of the Asian crisis and an economic recession domestically. As of year-end 2000 the collective bad debts of Japanese banks were conservatively estimated to exceed 32 trillion yen, most of which remained on their balance sheets at original book values. Moreover, even when loans are declared substandard by examiners, they may remain on the balance sheet at book value. A problem loan may require a write-down of only 50 percent, whereas only an outright loss requires a full 100 percent charge-off against the FI's equity position.

Suppose that in our example of historical book value accounting, the FI is forced to recognize a loss of 3 rather than 8 on its loan portfolio. Until the actual loan loss occurs, the amount would be recognized in a contra account and the total loans would be reported as "loans less allowance for impairment" on the balance sheet. When the loss is realized, the amount would be recognized on the income statement. The 3 is a charge against the 10 of the stockholders' book equity value. The new book value balance sheet is shown in Table 20–6.

---

[7] Canadian federally-regulated FIs (banks, co-operatives, property and casualty insurance companies, life insurance companies) are guided by OSFI's Guideline C-1 for impaired loans and Section 3025 of the Canadian Institute of Chartered Accountants (CICA) Handbook. See OSFI's Web site at www.osfi-bsif.gc.ca for the latest version of the guidelines.

Book Value of Capital and Interest Rate Risk

Although book value accounting systems do recognize credit risk problems, albeit only partially and usually with a long and discretionary time lag, their failure to recognize the impact of interest rate risk is more extreme.

In our market value accounting example in Table 20–4, a rise in interest rates lowered the market values of long-term securities and loans by 8 and led to a fall in the market value of net worth from 10 to 2. In a book value accounting world, when all assets and liabilities reflect their original cost of purchase, the rise in interest rates has no effect on the value of assets, liabilities, or the book value of equity. That is, the balance sheet remains unchanged; Table 20–5 reflects the position both before and after the interest rate rise. Consider the U.S. thrifts that, even though interest rates rose dramatically in the early 1980s, continued to report long-term fixed-rate mortgages at historical book values and, therefore, a positive book capital position. Yet, on a market value net worth basis, their mortgages were worth far less than the book values shown on their balance sheets. Indeed, more than half of the firms in the industry were economically insolvent—many massively so.[8]

The Discrepancy between the Market and Book Values of Equity

The degree to which the book value of an FI's capital deviates from its true economic market value depends on a number of factors, especially:

1. *Interest rate volatility.* The higher the interest rate volatility, the greater the discrepancy.

2. *Examination and enforcement.* The more frequent the on-site and off-site examinations and the stiffer the examiner/regulator standards regarding charging off problem loans, the smaller the discrepancy.

In actual practice, for large publicly traded FIs, we can get a good idea of the discrepancy between book values (*BV*) and market values (*MV*) of equity even when the FI itself does not mark its balance sheet to market. Specifically, in an efficient capital market, investors can value the shares of an FI by doing an as-if market value calculation of the assets and liabilities of the FI. This valuation is based on the FI's current and expected future net earnings or dividend flows. The stock price of the FI reflects this valuation and thus the market value of its shares outstanding. The market value of equity per share is therefore:

$$MV = \frac{\text{Market value of equity ownership shares outstanding}}{\text{Number of shares}}$$

By contrast, the historical or book value of the FI's common equity per share (*BV*) is equal to:

market to book ratio
Ratio showing the discrepancy between the stock market value of an FI's equity and the book value of its equity.

$$BV = \frac{\text{Common Shares} + \text{Contributed Surplus} + \text{Retained earnings} + \text{net unrealized foreign exchange gains (losses)}}{\text{Number of common shares outstanding}}$$

The ratio *MV/BV* is often called the **market to book ratio** and shows the degree of discrepancy between the market value of an FI's equity capital as perceived by investors in the stock market and the book value of capital on its balance sheet. The

---

[8] See White, *The S and L Debacle*, p. 89.

lower this ratio, the more the book value of capital *overstates* the true equity or economic net worth position of an FI as perceived by investors in the capital market.

Given such discrepancies, why do regulators and FIs continue to oppose the implementation of market value accounting?

Arguments against Market Value Accounting

The first argument against market value (*MV*) accounting is that it is difficult to implement. This may be especially true for smaller FIs with large amounts of nontraded assets such as small loans on their balance sheets. When it is impossible to determine accurate market prices or values for assets, marking to market may be done only with error. A counterargument to this is that the error resulting from the use of market valuation of nontraded assets is still likely to be less than that resulting from the use of original book or historical valuation since the market value approach does not require all assets and liabilities to be traded. As long as current and expected cash flows on an asset or liability and an appropriate discount rate can be specified, approximate market values can always be imputed (see CreditMetrics, described in Appendix 11A). Further, with the growth of loan sales and asset securitization (see Chapters 27 and 28), indicative market prices are available on an increasing variety of loans.[9]

The second argument against market value accounting is that it introduces an unnecessary degree of variability into an FI's earnings—and thus net worth—because paper capital gains and losses on assets are passed through the FI's income statement. Critics argue that reporting unrealized capital gains and losses is distortionary if the FI actually plans to hold these assets to maturity. Insurers and FI managers argue that in many cases they do hold loans and other assets to maturity and, therefore, never actually realize capital gains or losses. Further, regulators have argued that they may be forced to close FIs too early—especially if an interest rate spike is only temporary and capital losses on securities can be quickly turned into capital gains as rates fall again (e.g., if interest rates are mean reverting, as much empirical evidence shows). The counterargument is that FIs are increasingly trading, selling, and securitizing assets rather than holding them to maturity. Further, the failure to reflect capital gains and losses from interest rate changes means that the FI's equity position fails to reflect its true interest rate risk exposure.

The third argument against market value accounting is that FIs are less willing to accept longer-term asset exposures, such as mortgage loans and business loans, if these assets have to be continuously marked to market to reflect changing credit quality and interest rates. For example, as shown in Chapter 8, long-term assets are more interest rate sensitive than are short-term assets. The concern is that market value accounting may interfere with FIs' special functions as lenders and monitors (see Chapter 1) and may even result in (or accentuate) a major credit crunch. Of the three arguments against market value accounting, this one is probably the most persuasive to regulators concerned about small business finance and economic growth.

Having discussed the advantages and disadvantages of book- and market-based measures of an FI's capital, we should note that most FI regulators have chosen

---

[9] Angbazo, Mei, and Saunders (1998) analyze the pricing of loans in the secondary market by looking at highly leveraged transaction loans; see "Credit Spreads in the Market for Highly Leveraged Transaction Loans," *Journal of Banking and Finance* 22 (1998), pp. 1249–82.

www.sec.gov some form of book value accounting standard to measure an FI's capital adequacy. The major exception is the U.S. Securities and Exchange Commission (SEC). Along with the NYSE and other major stock exchanges, the SEC imposes on securities firms, retail brokers, and specialists a capital or net worth rule that is, for all intents and purposes, a market value accounting rule.[10]

Next, we examine the capital adequacy rules imposed in two key FI sectors: (1) deposit-taking institutions and (2) insurance companies. Because the capital adequacy rules currently differ considerably across these sectors, the current wave of consolidation in the U.S. financial industry into financial conglomerates (or universal banks) is likely to be more difficult than it would be if market value accounting rules were adopted across all sectors. Nevertheless, there is a clear trend toward similar risk-based capital rules in the banking and insurance (both P&C and life) industries. We discuss this trend in more detail in the remainder of the chapter.

Concept Questions

1. Why is an FI economically insolvent when its net worth is negative?
2. What are the major components of an FI's book equity?
3. Is book value accounting for loan losses backward looking or forward looking?
4. What does a market to book ratio that is less than 1 imply about an FI's performance?

CAPITAL ADEQUACY FOR DEPOSIT-TAKING INSTITUTIONS

Actual Capital Rules

Since 1988, Canadian banks and federally regulated trust and loan companies have faced two different capital requirements: an asset to capital multiple and a risk-based capital ratio that is in turn subdivided into a Tier I capital risk-based ratio and a total capital (Tier I plus Tier II capital) risk-based ratio. We describe these in more detail next.

The Assets to Capital Multiple

The assets to capital multiple applies to banks and federally-regulated trust and loan companies in Canada. It measures the ratio of the book value of assets to the book value of total capital. Total assets include off-balance sheet items as specified www.osfi-bsif.gc.ca by OSFI. Total capital is the FI's risk-based capital and includes common equity (book value) plus qualifying cumulative perpetual preferred stock plus minority interests in equity accounts of consolidated subsidiaries. The assets to capital multiple is calculated as follows:

$$\text{Assets to capital multiple} = \frac{\text{Total assets (including specified off-balance sheet items)}}{\text{Total Capital}}$$

---

[10] The Canadian securities industry is regulated provincially, but the formation of a national security regulator is under discussion (see Chapter 4) and therefore the regulations for securities firms are not discussed here. The provincial regulatory bodies and the Investment Dealers Association (IDA) require regulatory capital calculations of their members. The IDA's 207 members reported book value of shareholders equity to be $8,372 million compared to regulatory capital of $15,108 million at year-end 2004.

TABLE 20–7   Assets to Capital Multiples for Canadian Banks as at October 31, 2004

Name	Assets to Capital Multiple*
Bank of Montreal	17.0
Bank of Nova Scotia	13.8
CIBC	17.9
National Bank	16.8
Royal Bank	18.1
TD Bank	17.1

*Total risk-adjusted assets and off-balance sheet instruments as specified by OSFI, divided by Total Capital. Market risk from trading portfolios is included in the risk-adjusted assets. Unless otherwise specified by OSFI, total assets can be a maximum of 20 times capital.

Source: 2004 Annual Reports

The higher the assets to capital multiple, the greater is the leverage and therefore OSFI requires that the multiple be less than 20, but may set the multiple higher or lower for each deposit-taking institution based on "such factors as operating and management experience, strength of parent, earnings, diversification of assets and appetite for risk."[11] At year-end 2004, the assets to capital multiple for Canadian banks ranged from 13.8 for Bank of Nova Scotia to 18.1 for the Royal Bank as shown in Table 20–7. At the end of the second quarter of 2005, the ratio was 16.56 for all banks, 12.59 for federally-regulated trusts, and 16.13 for savings and loan companies. An individual FI trades off safety and soundness with the cost of holding capital (see the Industry Perspectives Box).

Unfortunately, the assets to capital multiple has three problems as a measure of capital adequacy:

1. *Market value.* Even if OSFI closed an FI before its multiple reached an astronomical level, the market value of the FI's assets could have resulted in a negative market value net worth. That is, there is no assurance that depositors and regulators (including taxpayers) are adequately protected against losses. Many U.S. thrifts that were closed with low book capital values in the 1980s had negative net worth on a market value basis exceeding 30 percent.

2. *Asset Risk.* By taking the numerator of the assets to capital multiple as total assets, the leverage ratio fails to take into account the different credit, interest rate, and other risks of the assets that constitute total assets.

3. *Off-balance-sheet activities.* Despite the massive growth in off-balance sheet activities, only off-balance sheet credit substitutes are included in the calculation. Thus, even though derivatives may contribute greatly to an FI's risk, for the purposes of the assets to capital multiple, no capital is required to be held to meet the potential insolvency risks involved with such contingent assets and liabilities.

Risk-Based Capital Ratios

www.bis.org

Basel Agreement
The requirement to impose risk-based capital ratios on banks in major industrialized countries.

In light of the weaknesses of the simple capital–assets ratio just described, Canadian and U.S. bank regulators formally agreed with other member countries of the Bank for International Settlements (BIS) to implement two new risk-based capital ratios for all commercial banks under their jurisdiction. The BIS phased in and fully implemented these risk-based capital ratios on January 1, 1993, under what has become known as the **Basel** (or Basle) **Agreement** (now called Basel I). The 1993 Basel Agreement explicitly incorporated the different credit risks of assets (both on and off the balance sheet) into capital adequacy measures. This was followed with a revision in 1998 in which market risk was incorporated into risk-based capital in the form of an add-on to the 7 percent ratio for credit risk exposure (see Chapter 11). In 2001, the BIS issued a Consultative Document, "The New Basel Capital Accord," that proposed the incorporation (effective by year-end 2006) of

---

[11] Office of Superintendent of Financial Services, "Guideline A—Part I: Capital Adequacy Requirements", January 2001, page 1–1. The detailed Guidelines, the reporting format, and the rationale used for the evaluation of the risk based capital of all federally-regulated FIs are available at OSFI's Web site at www.osfi-bsif.gc.ca

Industry Perspectives

CANADIAN BANKS: THIRD QUARTER 2004 PERFORMANCE

The major Canadian banks reported continued strong profitability through their first three fiscal quarters of 2004. Average return on equity in the third quarter was 19.3 per cent, compared with 18.7 per cent in the second quarter and 16.5 per cent for 2003 as a whole (Figure 20–2).

To date in 2004, the diversified business strategy of the major Canadian banks has been supportive of continued gains in profitability. Although there were some notable differences among the banks, in aggregate, the major segments of their diversified business strategy performed well. Credit performance continued to strengthen, as provisions for loan losses as a share of average assets declined to 0.04 per cent in the third quarter of 2004 (Figure 20–3). Results from foreign operations remained mixed, however.

The major Canadian banks continue to report high capital levels (Figure 20–1), well above minimum requirements. From a financial stability perspective, the strong capital position of the Canadian banking system may provide a buffer to absorb unexpected shocks that could negatively affect banks. These high levels of capital provide banks with the reserves from which

they may choose to carry out future acquisitions, as well as continuing to raise dividends and/or conduct common share repurchase programs. Indeed, TD Bank Financial Group announced the purchase of a $5 billion controlling interest in Banknorth Group in Maine. The deal, which is subject to approval by Banknorth's shareholders and by U.S. and Canadian regulatory authorities, is expected to close in February 2005.*

*Other, smaller foreign acquisitions by major Canadian banks have also taken place.

Source: "Canadian Banks: Third Quarter 2004 Performance," *Bank of Canada Financial System Review*, December 2004. www.bankofcanada.ca

FIGURE 20–2

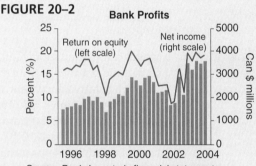

Bank Profits

Source: Banks' quarterly financial statements

FIGURE 20–1

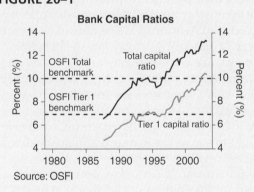

Bank Capital Ratios

Source: OSFI

FIGURE 20–3

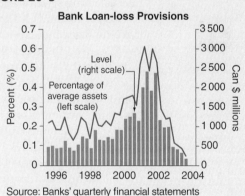

Bank Loan-loss Provisions

Source: Banks' quarterly financial statements

operational risk into capital requirements (see Chapter 14 and below) and updated the credit risk assessments in the 1993 agreement.[12]

The proposed new Basel Accord or Agreement (called Basel II) consists of three mutually reinforcing pillars (illustrated in Figure 20–4), which together contribute to the safety and soundness of the financial system. Pillar 1 covers regulatory minimum

[12] See Basel Committee on Banking Supervision, "The New Basel Capital Accord," January 2001; "Potential Modifications to the Committee's Proposals," November 2001; "The New Basel Capital Accord," April 2003; and "International Convergence of Capital Measurement and Capital Standards, June 2004. www.bis.org

FIGURE 20–4
Basel II Pillars of Capital Regulation

Pillar 1	**Pillar 2**	**Pillar 3**
Calculation of regulatory minimum capital requirements	Regulatory supervisory review so as to complement and enforce minimum capital requirements calculated under Pillar 1	Requirements on rules for disclosure of capital structure, risk exposures, and capital adequacy so as to increase FI transparency and enhance market/investor discipline
1. Credit risk: on-balance-sheet and off-balance-sheet (Standardized vs. Internal Ratings–Based Approach)		
2. Market risk (Standardized vs. Internal Ratings–Based Approach)		
3. Operational risk (Basic Indicator vs. Standardized vs. Advanced Measurement Approach)		

capital requirements for credit, market, and operational risk. The measurement of market risk did not change from that adopted in 1998 and is presented in Chapter 10. In the 2001 consultative document, the BIS proposed a range of options for addressing both credit and operational risk. Two options were proposed for the measurement of credit risk. The first is the Standardized Approach, discussed below, and the second is an Internal Ratings–Based (IRB) approach—see Appendix 20A on page 722 of this book. The Standardized Approach is similar to that of the 1993 agreement, but is more risk sensitive. Under the IRB approach, banks are allowed to use their internal estimates of borrower creditworthiness to assess credit risk in their portfolios (using their own internal rating systems and credit scoring models) subject to strict methodological and disclosure standards.[13] Three different approaches are available to measure operational risk: the Basic Indicator, Standardized, and Advanced Measurement approaches. We discussed these briefly in Chapter 14 and will do so in more detail below.

In Pillar 2, the BIS stressed the importance of the regulatory supervisory review process as a critical complement to minimum capital requirements. Specifically, the BIS proposed procedures through which regulators ensure that each bank has sound internal processes in place to assess the adequacy of its capital and set targets for capital that are commensurate with the bank's specific risk profile and control environment. In Pillar 3, the BIS sought to encourage market discipline by developing a set of requirements on the disclosure of capital structure, risk exposures, and capital adequacy. Such disclosure requirements allow market participants to assess critical information describing the risk profile and capital adequacy of banks.

OSFI and U.S. regulators currently enforce the Basel I risk-based capital ratios in North America. Unlike the simple assets to capital multiple ratio, the calculation

---

[13] Several papers have debated the ability and practicalities of implementing internal bank models. See, for example, B. J. Hirtle, M. Levonian, M. Saidenberg, S. Walter, and D. Wright, "Using Credit Risk Models for Regulatory Capital: Issues and Options," *FRBNY Economic Policy Review,* March 2001, pp. 19–36; M. Carey, "Dimensions of Credit Risk and Their Relationship to Economic Capital Requirements," NBER Working Paper 7629, March 2000; A. Garrett, "Insight on Basel II Loan Pricing," *International Treasurer,* July 2, 2001, pp. 10–11; and "Basel Gives Banks the Whip Hand," *Euromoney,* March 2001, pp. 48–53. See also A. Saunders and L. Allen, *Credit Risk Measurement: Value at Risk and Other New Paradigms,* 2nd ed. (New York: John Wiley and Sons, 2002). For an application to Canadian banks see M. Illing and G. Paulin, "The New Basel Accord and the cyclical Behaviour of Bank Capital," *Bank of Canada Working Paper No. 2004–30,* 2004.

of these risk-based capital adequacy measures is quite complex. Their major innovation is to distinguish among the different credit risks of assets on the balance sheet and to identify the credit risk inherent in instruments off the balance sheet by using a risk-adjusted assets denominator in these capital adequacy ratios. In a very rough fashion, these capital ratios mark to market a bank's on- and off-balance-sheet positions to reflect its credit risk. Further, additional capital charges must be held against market risk and operational risk.

In the measurement of a bank's risk-based capital adequacy, its capital is the standard by which each of these risks is measured.

Capital

OSFI requires all banks and federally-regulated trust and loan companies to report their components of capital and capital adequacy ratios quarterly. Table 20–8 shows this information for banks, trusts, and loan companies as compiled by OSFI at the end of the second quarter of 2005.

Basel I divides capital into Tier 1 and Tier 2. Tier 1 capital is primary or core capital; Tier 2 capital is supplementary capital. The total capital that the FI holds is defined as the sum of Tier 1 and Tier 2 capital, and it is this total capital that is used as the denominator in the assets to capital multiple as well as in the capital adequacy ratios discussed below.

Tier 1 Capital   Tier 1 capital is closely linked to an FI's book value of equity, reflecting the concept of the core capital contribution of an FI's owners. Basically, it includes the book value of common equity, non-cumulative perpetual preferred shares, innovative instruments as defined by OSFI, interests in subsidiaries, less intangible assets and goodwill. To be included as Tier 1 capital, an item must be intended to be permanent. As can be seen from Table 20–8, the types of Tier 1 capital used by banks, trusts, and loan companies differs.

Tier 2 Capital   Tier 2 capital is a broad array of secondary capital resources that includes non-perpetual preferred shares as well as subordinated debt and non-controlling interests in subsidiaries.

In addition, in order to ensure the stability of the capital provided by the FI, limitations are placed on the capital components as follows:

1. Strongly capitalized deposit-taking institutions will have innovative instruments and perpetual preferred shares less than 25 percent of net Tier 1 capital.
2. Innovative instruments will be less than 15 percent of net Tier 1 capital.
3. Tier 2 capital will be less than 100 percent of Tier 1 capital.
4. Limited life instruments will be lees than 50 percent of net Tier 1 capital.

We first look at how this capital is used as a cushion against credit risk using the BIS approach currently in operation (Basel I). We then examine its use as a cushion against credit risk using the BIS Standardized Approach described in Basel II and proposed to be effective in 2006. We also examine the required add-ons to capital under Basel II that cushion a bank against market and operational risk.

credit risk-adjusted assets
On- and off-balance-sheet assets whose values are adjusted for approximate credit risk.

Credit Risk-Adjusted Assets

Under both the current (Basel I) and proposed (Basel II) capital adequacy rules, risk-adjusted assets represent the denominator of the risk-based capital ratio. Two components make up **credit risk-adjusted assets:** (1) credit risk-adjusted on-balance-sheet assets, and (2) credit risk-adjusted off-balance-sheet assets.

TABLE 20–8   Components of Capital and Capital Adequacy Ratios for All Banks, Q2 2005 (thousands of dollars)

	Banks	Trusts	Loans
Tier 1			
Common shares	29,774,531	2,198,389	4,061,851
Contributed surplus	748,135	856,610	975,867
Retained earnings	59,937,251	2,760,719	3,309,211
Non-cumulative perpetual preferred shares	7,736,071	66,942	109,052
Innovative instruments included in tier 1 capital	8,672,054	0	0
Non-controlling tier 1 interests in subsidiaries	2,069,801	3,285	0
Gross Tier 1 Capital	105,242,192	5,885,945	8,455,981
Deduct: Intangible assets in excess of limits	803,957	58,702	0
Deduct: Goodwill	14,120,852	97,954	7,575
Tier 1 Capital	90,257,092	5,729,289	8,448,406
Tier 2A			
Preferred shares	255,042	88,250	141,460
Subordinated debt	2,008,927	95,650	235,000
Eligible general allowances	6,558,533	24,500	0
Non-controlling interests in subsidiaries (hybrid capital instruments)	0	612	0
Gross Tier 2A Capital	8,822,502	209,012	376,460
Tier 2B			
Preferred shares	305,750	0	8,151
Subordinated debt	23,677,168	864,157	872,235
Non-controlling interests in subsidiaries (subordinated term instruments)	0	536	0
Gross Tier 2B Capital	23,982,918	864,693	880,386
Tier 2 Capital	32,805,420	1,073,705	1,256,846
Tier 3 Capital			
Total Tier 1, 2 and 3 Capital	123,062,512	6,802,994	9,705,252
Deduct: Investments in unconsolidated subsidiaries/substantial investment	8,797,931	0	0
Deduct: Other facilities treated as capital	0	0	0
Deduct: Back-to-back inter-institutional placements of new capital issues	0	0	0
Deduct: First loss protection	753,997	23,295	35,032
Deduct: Other	79,525	0	0
Total Capital	113,431,059	6,779,699	9,670,220
Risk Weighted Assets			
Credit Risk Items			
On-balance sheet assets	681,526,955	25,879,872	41,997,364
Off-balance sheet exposure	147,480,474	409,516	208,809
Total Credit Risk Items	829,007,429	26,289,388	42,206,173
Market Risk Items	38,831,138	0	0
Total Adjusted Risk Weighted Assets	867,838,567	26,289,388	42,206,173
Risk Based Capital Ratios			
Tier 1 ratio	10.40	21.79	20.02
Total ratio	13.07	25.79	22.91
Assets To Capital Multiple	16.56	12.59	16.13

Source: OSFI at www.osfi-bsif.gc.ca

total risk-based capital ratio
The ratio of the total capital to the risk-adjusted assets of an FI.

To be adequately capitalized, a bank must hold a minimum ratio of total capital (Tier 1 core capital plus Tier 2 supplementary capital) to credit risk-adjusted assets of 10 percent; that is, its **total risk-based capital ratio** is calculated as:

$$\text{Total risk-based capital ratio} = \frac{\text{Total capital (Tier 1 + Tier 2)}}{\text{Credit risk} - \text{adjusted assets}} \geq 10\%$$

TABLE 20–9   OSFI's Assessment Criteria for Rating Capital Adequacy

ROLE OF CAPITAL
Capital is a source of financial support to protect an institution against unexpected losses, and is, therefore, a key contributor to its safety and soundness. Capital management is the on-going process of raising and maintaining capital at levels sufficient to support planned operations. For complex institutions, it also involves allocation of capital to recognize the level of risk in its various activities. The assessment is made in the context of the nature, scope, complexity, and risk profile of an institution.

ADEQUACY OF CAPITAL
The following statements describe the rating categories used in assessing capital adequacy and capital management policies and practices of an institution. Capital adequacy includes both the level and quality of capital. The assessment is made in the context of the nature, scope, complexity, and risk profile of an institution.

Strong
Capital adequacy is strong for the nature, scope, complexity, and risk profile of the institution, and meets OSFI's target levels. The trend in capital adequacy over the next 12 months is expected to remain positive. Capital management policies and practices are superior to generally accepted industry practices.

Acceptable
Capital adequacy is appropriate for the nature, scope, complexity, and risk profile of the institution and meets OSFI's target levels. The trend in capital adequacy over the next 12 months is expected to remain positive. Capital management policies and practices meet generally accepted industry practices.

Needs Improvement
Capital adequacy is not always appropriate for the nature, scope, complexity, and risk profile of the institution and, although meeting minimum regulatory requirements, may not meet, or is trending below, OSFI's target levels. The trend in capital adequacy over the next 12 months is expected to remain uncertain. Capital management policies and practices may not meet generally accepted industry practices.

Weak
Capital adequacy is inappropriate for the nature, scope, complexity, and risk profile of the institution and does not meet, or marginally meets, minimum regulatory requirements. The trend in capital adequacy over the next 12 months is expected to remain negative. Capital management polices and practices do not meet generally accepted industry practices.

Source: OSFI at www.osfi-bsif.gc.ca

Tier 1 (core) capital ratio
The ratio of core capital to the risk-adjusted assets of an FI.

In addition, the Tier 1 core capital component of total capital has its own minimum guideline. The **Tier 1 (core) capital ratio** is calculated as:

$$\text{Tier 1 (core) capital ratio} = \frac{\text{Core capital (Tier 1)}}{\text{Credit risk} - \text{adjusted assets}} \geq 7\%$$

That is, of the 10 percent total risk-based capital ratio, a minimum of 7 percent has to be held in core or primary capital.[14]

In addition to their use to define adequately capitalized FIs, risk-based capital ratios—along with the assets to capital multiple—also define the adequacy of capital in OSFIs assessment criteria. OSFI rates the adequacy of an FI's capital in four categories from "Strong" to "Weak" as summarized in Table 20–9. In applying these

[14] The difference between the 8 percent and the 4 percent can be made up with noncore or other capital sources; see the description in Table 20–8.

criteria, OSFI also looks at the specific institution and whether its capital management policies are appropriate and have sufficient senior management and Board of Directors oversight. OSFI's examination of the management of capital would short-circuit the incentive for an FI to increase its risk under certain circumstances as has been suggested by some research. [15]

Calculating Risk-Based Capital Ratios

Credit Risk-Adjusted On-Balance Sheet Assets under Basel I

Under the current BIS risk-based capital plan (Basel I), each bank assigns its assets to one of four categories of credit risk exposure: 0 percent, 20 percent, 50 percent, or 100 percent. In Table 20–10 we list the key categories and assets in these categories. The main feature is that cash assets and claims on **Organization for Economic Cooperation and Development (OECD)** governments are given a risk-free, i.e., 0 percent rating. The 20 percent weight category includes all claims on OECD banks and public sector entities, as well on Canadian deposit-taking institutions. Residential mortgages attract a weight of 50 percent and all other claims, that is, all business and personal loans, regardless of their risk, are given a 100 percent risk rating in the risk-based assets calculation. These risk weightings are reduced if collateral or security to support a loan is provided by an OECD government, central bank, or public sector entity. To calculate the credit risk-adjusted assets of the bank, trust, or loan company, we multiply the dollar amount of assets it has in each category by the appropriate risk weight.

Organization for Economic Cooperation and Development (OECD)
An international group of 30 developed countries in the world.

EXAMPLE 20–1
Calculation of On-Balance-Sheet Credit Risk-Adjusted Assets under Basel I

Consider the balance sheet in Table 20–11 as an example. The risk-adjusted value of the FI's on-balance-sheet assets (under Basel I) would be:

$$\sum_{i=1}^{n} w_i a_i$$

where

w_i = Risk weight of the ith asset

a_i = Dollar (book) value of the ith asset on the balance sheet

Thus,

Credit risk-adjusted on-balance-sheet assets = 0(8 m + 13 m + 60 m + 50 m + 42 m + 10 m) + .2(10 m + 10 m + 20 m) + .5(342 m) + 1(10 m + 55m + 75 m + 390 m + 10 m + 108 m + 22m) = $849 million

While the simple book value of on-balance-sheet assets is $1,235 million, its credit risk-adjusted value is $849 million.

[15] It has been argued that capital adequacy rules may induce a DI to make portfolio choices that actually increase the risk of the FI. The intuition behind the result is that under binding capital requirements, an additional unit of equity tomorrow is more valuable to a FI. If issuing new equity is excessively costly, the only possibility to increase equity tomorrow is to increase risk today in the hope that high-risk investments produce higher returns and thus boost the retained earnings component of equity tomorrow. Thus, some view higher minimum capital requirements as inducing a greater, not lesser, risk of FI insolvency (e.g., if the high-risk investments result in significant losses rather than profits). See J. Blum, "Do Capital Adequacy Requirements Reduce Risks in Banking?" *Journal of Banking and Finance* 23 (1999), pp. 755–71.

TABLE 20–10   Summary of the Risk-Based Capital Standards for On-Balance-Sheet Items under Basel I

Risk Categories	
Weight	**Details**
0%	Cash, gold bullion, claims on OECD* governments
	Claims guaranteed by OECD central governments (e.g. Export Development Corporation)
	NHA (National Housing Act) -insured residential mortgages mortgage-backed securities guaranteed by Canada Mortgage and Housing (CMHC)
	Deductions from capital (goodwill, investments in unconsolidated subsidiaries)
20%	Claims on Canadian deposit-taking institutions, OECD banks and non-domestic OECD public sector entities
	Claims on Canadian municipalities, school boards, universities, hospitals
	Claims on multi-lateral development banks (MDBs) (e.g. International Bank for Reconstruction and Development (IBRD))
	Cheques and cash items in transit
50%	Residential mortgages (one- to four-unit residential buildings)
100%	All other claims including business and personal loans, claims on United Nations entities, non-OECD banks, premises, plant and equipment, real estate

*The 30 OECD countries recognized by OSFI are Australia, Austria, Belgium, Canada, Czech Republic, Denmark, Finland, France, Germany, Greece, Hungary, Iceland, Ireland, Italy, Japan, Korea, Luxembourg, Mexico, The Netherlands, New Zealand, Norway, Poland, Portugal, Saudi Arabia, Spain, Sweden, Switzerland, Turkey, the United Kingdom and the United States. If a country has re-scheduled its external debt in the last five years, it is not granted the preferred risk treatment.
Source: OSFI, Capital Adequacy Requirements A-Part I, January 2001, page 1-4-1

Credit Risk-Adjusted On-Balance-Sheet Assets under Basel II

A major criticism of the original Basel Agreement is that individual risk weights depend on the broad categories of borrowers (i.e., sovereigns, banks, or corporates). For example, under Basel I all corporate loans have a risk weight of 100 percent regardless of the borrowing firm's credit risk. The Basel II Standardized Approach aligns regulatory capital requirements more closely with the key elements of banking risk by introducing a wider differentiation of credit risk weights. Specifically, the risk weights are refined by reference to a rating provided by an external credit rating agency (such as Standard & Poor's).[16] Accordingly, compared with the current accord (Basel I), the Standardized Approach of Basel II should produce capital ratios more in line with the actual economic risks that FIs are facing.

Under the Basel II risk-based capital plan proposed for implementation in 2006, each bank assigns its assets to one of seven categories of credit risk exposure: 0 percent, 20 percent, 35 percent, 50 percent, 75 percent, 100 percent, or 150 percent. Table 20–12 lists the key categories and assets in these categories. The main features are that in addition to those assets listed at zero percent under Basel I, loans to sovereigns with an S&P credit rating of AA− or better are zero risk based. The 20 percent class now includes loans to sovereigns with an S&P credit rating of A+ to A− and loans to banks and corporates with a credit rating of AA− or better. Uninsured

---

[16] Several recent papers have analyzed and critiqued the use of rating agency credit ratings in assigning risk weights. These include E. I. Altman and A. Saunders, "An Analysis and Critique of the BIS Proposal on Capital Adequacy and Ratings," *Journal of Banking and Finance* 25 (2001), pp. 25–46; G. Ferri, L. Liu, and D. Majnoni, "The Role of Rating Agency Assessments in Less Developed Countries: Impact of the Proposed Basel Guidelines," *Journal of Banking and Finance* 25 (2001), pp. 115–48; I. Linnell, "A Critical Review of the New Capital Adequacy Framework Paper Issued by the Basle Committee on Banking Supervision and Its Implications for the Rating Agency Industry," *Journal of Banking and Finance* 25 (2001), pp. 187–96; M. Carey and M. Hrycay, "Parameterizing Credit Risk Models with Rating Data," *Journal of Banking and Finance* 25 (2001), pp. 197–270; and E. Altman, S. Bharath, and A. Saunders, "Credit Ratings and the BIS Capital Adequacy Reform Agenda," *Journal of Banking and Finance*, 2002, pp. 909–22.

TABLE 20–11   Bank's Balance Sheet under Basel I (in millions of dollars)

Weight	Assets		Liabilities/Equity		Capital Class
0%	Cash, gold bullion	8	Demand deposits	$150	
	Deposits with the Bank of Canada	13	Notice deposits	500	
	Securities issued or guaranteed by the government of Canada	60	Fixed-term deposits	400	
	Securities issued or guaranteed by a Canadian province	50	Advances from the Bank of Canada	80	
	CMHC mortgage-backed securities	42			
	Goodwill and intangibles	10			
20	Items in process of collection	10	Non-controlling interests in subsidiaries (subordinated)	15	Tier 2
	Loan to multilateral development banks	10			
	Securities issued or guaranteed by a Canadian municipal or school corporation	20	Subordinated debt	15	Tier 2
			Preferred shares, non-perpetual	5	Tier 2
50	Residential one- to four-family mortgages	342			
100	Loans, less allowance for impairment:	10	Common shares	30	Tier 1
	AA+ rated loan to Manulife Financial		Contributed surplus	0	Tier 1
	Commercial loans, AAA− rated	55	Retained earnings	30	Tier 1
	Commercial loans, A rated	75	Non-cumulative perpetual preferred shares	10	Tier 1
	Commercial loans, BB+ rated	390			
	Commercial loans, CCC+ rated	10	Non-controlling Tier 1 interests in subsidiaries	0	Tier 1
	Loans to non-OECD countries, B+ rated	108			
	Premises, Equipment	22		$1235	
	Total assets	$1235			

Off-Balance-Sheet Items

	$80 m in two-year loan commitments to a large BB+ rated Canadian company
100%	$10 m direct credit substitute standby letters of credit issued to a BBB-rated Canadian company
	$50 million in commercial letters of credit issued to a BBB− rated Canadian company
50%	One fixed-floating interest rate swap for 4 years with notional dollar value of $100 m and replacement cost of $3 m
	One two-year Euro$ contract for $40 m with a replacement cost of −$1 m

residential mortgages are now weighted at 35 percent The 50 percent class now includes loans to sovereigns with an S&P credit rating of BBB+ to BBB− and loans to banks and corporates with a credit rating of A+ to A−. Claims on retail customers (personal loans) and small businesses are rated at 75 percent. Loans to sovereigns with an S&P credit rating of BB+ to B−, loans to banks with a credit rating of BBB+ to B−, and loans to corporates with a credit rating of BBB+ to BB− and loans to unrated entities are now the only loans included in the 100 percent class. Finally, loans to sovereigns and banks with a credit rating below B− and loans to corporates with a credit rating below BB− are in the 150 percent risk category.[17]

To figure the credit risk–adjusted assets of the bank, we again multiply the dollar amount of assets it has in each category by the appropriate risk weight.

[17] Using a sample of loans made by Spanish banks, J. Saurina and C. Trucharte find that changes in the weight on loans would detrimentally affect banks' patterns of financing to small and medium-sized firms; see "The Impact of Basel II on Lending to Small and Medium-Sized Firms," *Journal of Financial Services Research*, forthcoming. Lending for project financing is also likely to be reduced as a result of Basel II credit risk weighting. See "React or Die," *Project Finance*, February 2002, pp. 40–43; and "Basel II Discontent the Theme," *Project Finance*, June 2002, pp. 46–48.

TABLE 20–12   **Summary of the Risk-based Capital Standards for On-Balance-Sheet Items under Basel II**

Risk Categories	
Weight	**Details**
0%	Cash, gold bullion
	Claims on (or claims guaranteed by) sovereign governments and central banks with an external (e.g. S&P) credit rating of AAA to AA–.
	Claims on provincial and territorial governments
	Deductions from capital (goodwill, investments in unconsolidated subsidiaries)
20%	Claims on countries with credit ratings of A+ to A–
	Claims on banks and securities firms of countries with external credit ratings of AAA to AA–
	Claims on multi-lateral development banks (MDBs) and corporate entities with external credit ratings of AAA to AA–
	Cheques and cash items in transit
35%	Residential mortgages (uninsured, one- to four-unit residential buildings)
50%	Claims on countries with credit ratings of BBB+ to BBB–.
	Claims on banks and securities firms of countries with credit ratings of A+ to A–.
	Claims on MDBs with credit ratings from A+ to BBB–.
	Claims on corporate entities with credit ratings of A+ to A–.
75%	Claims on retail customers and small business
100%	Claims on countries with credit ratings of BB+ to B–.
	Claims on banks and securities firms of countries with credit ratings of BBB+ to B–.
	Claims on MDBs with credit ratings from BB+ to B–.
	Claims on corporate customers with credit ratings of BBB+ to BB–.
	Claims on governments, banks, securities firms, and corporate entities that are not rated.
150%	Claims on countries, multi-lateral development banks, banks and securities firms below B–, and corporate entities with credit ratings below BB–.

Source: OSFI, Presentation on the domestic implementation of the simpler approaches available under the new Basel framework, August 17, 2004; and Bank for International Settlements, "The New Basel Capital Accord," January 2001 (www.osfi-bsif.gc.ca, www.bis.org).

EXAMPLE 20–2

Calculation of On-Balance-Sheet Credit Risk-Adjusted Assets under Basel II

Consider our bank's balance sheet in Table 20–13, categorized according to the risk weights of Basel II. Under Basel II, the credit risk-adjusted value of the bank's on-balance-sheet assets would be:

Credit risk–adjusted on-balance-sheet assets = 0(8 m + 13 m + 60 m + 50 m + 42 m + 10 m) + .2(10 m + 10 m + 20 m + 10 m + 55 m) + .35 (342) + .5(75 m) + 1(390 m + 108 m + 22 m) + 1.5(10 m) = 675.7 million

The simple book value of on-balance-sheet assets is $1,215 million, its credit risk–adjusted value under Basel I is $849 million and under Basel II is $675.7 million. Basel II modifies the treatment of sovereign, bank, and corporate loans by using credit agency ratings of borrowers to improve the risk sensitivity of the Standardized Approach. The result, in our examples, is a decrease in the credit risk-weighted value of the bank's on-balance-sheet assets.

Credit Risk-Adjusted Off-Balance-Sheet Activities

The credit risk-adjusted value of on-balance-sheet assets is only one component of the capital ratio denominator; the other is the credit risk-adjusted value of the bank's

TABLE 20–13   Bank's Balance Sheet under Basel II (in millions of dollars)

Weight	Assets		Liabilities/Equity		Capital Class
0%	Cash, gold bullion	8	Demand deposits	$150	
	Deposits with the Bank of Canada	13	Notice deposits	500	
	Securities issued or guaranteed by the government of Canada	60	Fixed-term deposits	400	
	Securities issued or guaranteed by a Canadian province	50	Advances from the Bank of Canada	80	
	CMHC mortgage-backed securities	42			
	Goodwill and intangibles	10			
20	Items in process of collection	10	Non-controlling interests in subsidiaries (subordinated)	15	Tier 2
	Loan to multilateral development banks, AA– rated	10			
	Securities issued or guaranteed by a Canadian municipal or school corporation	20	Subordinated debt	15	Tier 2
			Preferred shares, non-perpetual	5	Tier 2
	Commercial loans, AAA– rated	55			
35	Residential one- to four-family mortgages (uninsured)	342	Common shares	30	Tier 1
			Contributed surplus	0	Tier 1
50	Commercial loans, A rated	75	Retained earnings	30	Tier 1
			Non-cumulative perpetual preferred shares	10	Tier 1
100	Commercial loans, BB+ rated	390			
	Loans to non-OECD countries, B+ rated	108	Non-controlling Tier 1 interests in subsidiaries	0	Tier 1
	Premises, Equipment	22			
150	Commercial loans, CCC+ rated	10		$1235	
	Total assets	$1235			

Off-Balance-Sheet Items

	$80 m in two-year loan commitments to a large BB+ rated Canadian company
100%	$10 m direct credit substitute standby letters of credit issued to a BBB– rated Canadian company
	$50 million in commercial letters of credit issued to a BBB– rated Canadian company
50%	One fixed-floating interest rate swap for 4 years with notional dollar value of $100 m and replacement cost of $3 m
	One two-year Euro$ contract for $40 m with a replacement cost of –$1 m

credit equivalent amount
The on-balance-sheet equivalent credit risk exposure of an off-balance-sheet item.

off-balance-sheet (OBS) activities. These OBS activities represent contingent rather than actual claims against deposit-taking institutions (see Chapter 14). Thus, regulations require that capital be held not against the full face value of these items, but against an amount equivalent to any eventual on-balance-sheet credit risk these securities might create for a deposit-taking institution. Therefore, in calculating the credit risk-adjusted asset values of these OBS items we must first convert them into **credit equivalent amounts**—amounts equivalent to an on-balance-sheet item. Further the calculation of the credit risk-adjusted values of the off-balance-sheet activities involves some initial segregation of these activities. In particular, the calculation of the credit risk exposure or the credit risk-adjusted asset amounts of contingent or guaranty contracts such as letters of credit differs from the calculation of the credit risk-adjusted asset amounts for foreign exchange and interest rate forward, option, and swap contracts. We consider the credit risk-adjusted asset value of OBS guaranty-type contracts and contingent contracts and then derivative or market contracts.

TABLE 20–14

Conversion Factors for Off-Balance-Sheet Contingent or Guaranty Contracts, Basel I and Basel II

Source: OSFI, CAR A-Part1, January, 2001; OSFI, Presentation on the domestic implementation of simpler approaches available under the New Basel framework, August 17, 2004

Sale and repurchase agreements and assets sold with recourse that are not included on the balance sheet (100%)
Direct-credit substitutes and standby letters of credit (100%)
Performance-related standby letters of credit (50%)
Unused portion of loan commitments with original maturity of *more than one year* (50%)*
Commercial letters of credit (20%)
Bankers acceptances conveyed (20%)
Other loan commitments (10%)
Commitments that are unconditionally cancellable (0%)

*Proposed for 2006, the unused portion of loan commitments with an original maturity of one year or less will be 20 percent. Under Basel I such commitments have a 0 percent risk weight.

The Credit Risk-Adjusted Asset Value of Off-Balance-Sheet Contingent Guaranty Contracts

Basel I.   Consider the appropriate conversion factors in Table 20–14.[18] Note that under Basel I, direct credit substitute standby letter of credit guarantees issued by banks have a 100 percent conversion factor rating. Similarly, sale and repurchase agreements and assets sold with recourse are also given a 100 percent conversion factor rating. Future performance-related SLCs and unused loan commitments of more that one year have a 50 percent conversion factor. Other loan commitments, those with one year or less to maturity, impose no credit risk on the bank and have a 0 percent credit conversion factor. However, under Base1 II, it is proposed that in 2006, this conversion factor will increase to 20 percent. Standard trade-related commercial letters of credit and bankers acceptances sold have a 20 percent conversion factor.

EXAMPLE 20–3

Calculating Off-Balance-Sheet Contingent or Guaranty Contracts' Credit Risk-Adjusted Assets

To see how OBS activities are incorporated into the risk-based ratio, we can extend Example 20–1 for the bank in Table 20–11. Assume that in addition to having $849 million in credit risk-adjusted assets on its balance sheet, the bank also has the following off-balance-sheet contingencies or guarantees:

1. $80 million two-year loan commitments to large BB+ rated Canadian company.
2. $10 million direct credit substitute standby letters of credit issued to a BBB-rated Canadian company.
3. $50 million commercial letters of credit issued to a BBB– rated Canadian company.

To find the risk-adjusted asset value for these OBS items, we follow a two-step process.

Step 1. Convert OBS Values into On-Balance-Sheet Credit Equivalent Amounts

In the first step we multiply the dollar amount outstanding of these items to derive the credit equivalent amounts using the conversion factors (CF) listed in Table 20–14.

OBS Item	Face Value		Conversion Factor		Credit Equivalent Amount
Two-year loan commitment	$80 m	×	.5	=	$40 m
Standby letter of credit	10 m	×	1.0	=	10 m
Commercial letter of credit	50 m	×	.2	=	10 m

---

[18] Appropriate here means those factors used by the regulators and required to be used by banks rather than being equal to conversion factors that might be calculated from a contingent asset valuation (option) model. Indeed, regulators used no such valuation model in deriving the conversion factors in Table 20–14.

Thus, the credit equivalent amounts of loan commitments, standby letters of credit, and commercial letters of credit are, respectively, $40, $10, and $10 million. These conversion factors convert an OBS item into an equivalent credit or on-balance-sheet item.

Step 2. Assign the OBS Credit Equivalent Amount to a Risk Category

In the second step we multiply these credit equivalent amounts by their appropriate risk weights. Under Basel I, the appropriate risk weight in each case depends on the underlying counterparty to the OBS activity, such as a municipality, a government, or a corporation. For example, if the underlying party being guaranteed is a municipality issuing bonds, and a bank issued an OBS standby letter of credit backing the credit risk of the municipal issue, then the risk weight is 0.2. However if, as in our example, the counterparty being guaranteed is a *private agent,* the appropriate risk weight in each case is 1. Note that if the counterparty had been the central government, the risk weight would have been zero. The appropriate risk weights for our example are:

OBS Item	Credit Equivalent Amount		Risk Weight (w_i)		Risk-Adjusted Asset Amount
Two-year loan commitment	$40 m	×	1.0	=	$40 m
Standby letter of credit	10 m	×	1.0	=	10 m
Commercial letter of credit	10 m	×	1.0	=	10 m
					$60 m

The bank's credit risk-adjusted asset value of its OBS contingencies and guarantees is $60 million.

Basel II. Under Basel II, except for loan commitments with an original maturity of one year or less (which will have a conversion factor of 20 percent), the conversion of OBS values to on-balance-sheet credit equivalent amounts is the same as under Basel I. However, risk weights assigned to OBS contingent guaranty contracts are the same as if the bank had entered into the transactions as a principal. Thus, the credit ratings used to assign a credit risk weight for on-balance-sheet assets (listed in Table 20–12) are also used to assign credit risk weights on these OBS activities (e.g., issuing a commercial letter of credit to a CCC-rated counterparty would result in a risk weight of 150 percent). In our example, because each of the contingent guarantee contracts involves a Canadian company with a credit rating between BBB+ and BB–, each is assigned a risk weight of 100 percent (the same weight as under Basel I). Thus, the bank's credit risk-adjusted value of its OBS contingencies and guarantees is again $60 million.

The Credit Risk-Adjusted Asset Value of Off-Balance-Sheet Market Contracts or Derivative Instruments   In addition to having OBS contingencies and guarantees, modern FIs engage heavily in buying and selling OBS futures, options, forwards, swaps, caps, and other derivative securities contracts for interest rate and foreign exchange management and hedging reasons, as well as buying and selling such products on behalf of their customers (see Chapter 13). Each of these positions potentially exposes FIs to **counterparty credit risk,** that is, the risk that the counterparty (or other side of a contract) will default when suffering large actual or potential losses on its position. Such defaults mean that an FI would have to go back to the market to replace such contracts at (potentially) less favourable terms.

Under the risk-based capital ratio rules, a major distinction is made between exchange-traded derivative security contracts (e.g., Chicago Board of Trade's exchange-

counterparty credit risk
The risk that the other side of a contract will default on payment obligations.

TABLE 20–15   Add-on Factors for Calculating Potential Future Credit Exposure

Residual Maturity	Interest Rate Contracts	Foreign Exchange and Gold Contracts	Equity	Precious Metals Except Gold	Other Commodities
Add-On Factors					
One year or less	0.0%	1.0%	6.0%	7.0%	10.0%
Over one year to five years	0.5%	5.0%	8.0%	7.0%	12.0%
Over five years	1.5%	7.5%	10.0%	8.0%	15.0%

Source: OSFI, Capital Adequacy Requirements A Part 1, January 2001, page 4-3-2

traded options) and over-the-counter–traded instruments (e.g., forwards, swaps, caps, and floors). The credit or default risk of exchange-traded derivatives is approximately zero because when a counterparty defaults on its obligations, the exchange itself adopts the counterparty's obligations in full. However, no such guarantees exist for bilaterally agreed, over-the-counter contracts originated and traded outside organized exchanges. Hence, most OBS futures and options positions have no capital requirements for a bank while most forwards, swaps, caps, and floors do.[19]

As with contingent or guaranty contracts, the calculation of the risk-adjusted asset values of OBS market contracts requires a two-step approach (under both Basel I and Basel II). First, we calculate a conversion factor to create credit equivalent amounts. Second, we multiply the credit equivalent amounts by the appropriate risk weights.

Step 1. Convert OBS Values into On-Balance-Sheet Credit Equivalent Amounts. We first convert the notional or face values of all non-exchange-traded swap, forward, and other derivative contracts into credit equivalent amounts. The credit equivalent amount itself is divided into a *potential exposure* element and a *current exposure* element. That is:

$$\begin{array}{l}\text{Credit equivalent amount} \\ \quad \text{of OBS derivative} \\ \quad \text{security items (\$)} \end{array} = \text{Potential exposure (\$)} + \text{Current exposure (\$)}$$

potential exposure
The risk that a counterparty to a derivative securities contract will default in the future.

The **potential exposure** component reflects the credit risk if the counterparty to the contract defaults in the *future*. The probability of such an occurrence depends on the future volatility of either interest rates for an interest rate contract or exchange rates for an exchange rate contract. The Bank of England and the Federal Reserve carried out an enormous number of simulations and found that FX rates were far more volatile than interest rates.[20] Thus, the potential exposure conversion factors in Table 20–15 are larger for foreign exchange contracts than for interest rate contracts. Also, note the larger potential exposure credit risk for longer-term contracts of all types.

current exposure
The cost of replacing a derivative securities contract at today's prices.

In addition to calculating the potential exposure of an OBS market instrument, a bank must calculate its **current exposure** with the instrument. This reflects the cost of replacing a contract if a counterparty defaults *today*. The bank calculates this *replacement cost* or *current exposure* by replacing the rate or price initially in the con-

---

[19] This may create some degree of preference among banks for using exchange-traded hedging instruments rather than over-the-counter instruments, because using the former may save a bank costly capital resources.

[20] The Bank of England and the Federal Reserve employed a Monte Carlo simulation approach in deciding on the size of the appropriate conversion factors. See C. W. Smith, C. W. Smithson, and D. S. Wilford, *Managing Financial Risk* (New York: Ballinger, 1990), pp. 225–56.

tract with the current rate or price for a similar contract and recalculates all the current and future cash flows that would have been generated under current rate or price terms.[21] The bank discounts any future cash flows to give a current present value measure of the contract's replacement cost. If the contract's replacement cost is negative (i.e., the bank profits on the replacement of the contract if the counterparty defaults), regulations require the replacement cost (current exposure) to be set to zero. If the replacement cost is positive (i.e., the bank loses on the replacement of the contract if the counterparty defaults), this value is used as the measure of current exposure. Since each swap or forward is in some sense unique, calculating current exposure involves a considerable computer processing task for the bank's management information systems. Indeed, specialized service firms are likely to perform this task for smaller banks.[22]

Step 2. Assign the OBS Credit Equivalent Amount to a Risk Category.   Once the current and potential exposure amounts are summed to produce the credit equivalent amount for each contract, we multiply this dollar number by a risk weight to produce the final credit risk-adjusted asset amount for OBS market contracts.

Basel I.   Under Basel I, the appropriate risk weight is generally .5, or 50 percent. That is:

$$\begin{matrix} \text{Credit risk-adjusted} \\ \text{value of OBS} \\ \text{market contracts} \end{matrix} = \text{Total credit equivalent amount} \times .5 \text{ (risk weight)}$$

EXAMPLE 20–4 *Calculating Off-Balance-Sheet Market Contract Credit Risk-Adjusted Assets*	Suppose the bank in Examples 20–1 and 20–3 had taken one interest rate hedging position in the fixed-floating interest rate swap market for four years with a notional dollar amount of $100 million and one two-year forward foreign exchange contract for $40 million (see Table 20–11). **Step 1** We calculate the credit equivalent amount for each item or contract as:

		Potential Exposure + Current Exposure				
Type of Contract (remaining maturity)	Notional Principal ×	Potential Exposure Conversion Factor =	Potential Exposure	Replacement Cost	Current Exposure =	Credit Equivalent Amount
Four-year fixed–floating interest rate swap	$100 m ×	.005 =	$0.5 m	$3 m	$3 m	$3.5 m
Two-year forward foreign exchange contract	$ 40 m ×	.050 =	$2 m	−$1 m	$0	$2 m

---

[21] For example, suppose a two-year forward foreign exchange contract was entered into in January 2006 at $1.55/£. In January 2007, the bank has to evaluate the credit risk of the contract, which now has one year remaining. To do this, it replaces the agreed forward rate $1.55/£ with the forward rate on current one-year forward contracts, $1.65/£. It then recalculates its net gain or loss on the contract if it had to be replaced at this price. This is the contract's replacement cost.

[22] One large New York money center bank has to calculate, on average, the replacement cost of more than 6,000 different forward contracts alone.

For the four-year fixed-floating interest rate swap, the notional value (contract face value) of the swap is $100 million. Since this is a long-term (one to five years to maturity) interest rate market contract, its face value is multiplied by .005 to get a potential exposure or credit risk equivalent value of $0.5 million (see row 2 of Table 20–15). We add this potential exposure to the replacement cost (current exposure) of this contract to the bank. The replacement cost reflects the cost of having to enter into a new four-year fixed-floating swap agreement at today's interest rates for the remaining life of the swap should the counterparty default. Assuming that interest rates today are less favourable, on a present value basis, the cost of replacing the existing contract for its remaining life would be $3 million. Thus, the total credit equivalent amount—current plus potential exposures—for the interest rate swap is $3.5 million.

Next, look at the foreign exchange two-year forward contract of $40 million face value. Since this is a foreign exchange contract with a maturity of one to five years, the potential (future) credit risk is $40 million $\times$ .05, or $2 million (see row 2 in Table 20–15). However, its replacement cost is *minus* $1 million. That is, in this example our bank actually stands to gain if the counterparty defaults. Exactly why the counterparty would do this when it is in the money is unclear. However, regulators cannot permit a bank to gain from a default by a counterparty since this might produce all types of perverse risk-taking incentives. Consequently, as in our example, current exposure has to be set equal to zero (as shown). Thus, the sum of potential exposure ($2 million) and current exposure ($0) produces a total credit equivalent amount of $2 million for this contract. Since the bank has just two OBS derivative contracts, summing the two credit equivalent amounts produces a total credit equivalent amount of $3.5 m + $2 m = $5.5 million for the bank's OBS market contracts.

Step 2

The next step is to multiply this credit equivalent amount by the appropriate risk weight. Specifically, to calculate the risk-adjusted asset value for the bank's OBS derivative or market contracts, we multiply the credit equivalent amount by the appropriate risk weight, which under Basel I is generally .5, or 50 percent:

$$\begin{array}{ccccc} \text{Credit risk-adjusted} & = & \$5.5 \text{ million} & \times & 0.5 & = \$2.75 \text{ million} \\ \text{asset value of} & & \text{(credit equivalent} & & \text{(risk weight)} & \\ \text{OBS derivatives} & & \text{amount)} & & & \end{array}$$

Basel II. As stated above, Basel I assigns a 50 percent weight to the total credit equivalent amount of these contracts. Basel II assigns these contracts a risk weight of 100 percent, assuming the OBS activities are more risky to the FI than assumed under Basel I. Under Basel II the risk weight assigned to the credit equivalent amount, $5.5 million, is 100 percent. Thus, the credit risk-adjusted value of the OBS derivatives is $5.5 million.

Total Credit Risk-Adjusted Assets under Basel I

From Examples 20–1 through 20–4, under the current Basel Agreement, Basel I, the total risk-adjusted assets for the bank are the sum of the credit risk-adjusted assets on the balance sheet ($849 million), the risk-adjusted value of OBS contingencies and guarantees ($60 million), and the risk-adjusted value of OBS derivatives ($2.75 million), or $911.75 million.

Total Credit Risk-Adjusted Assets under Basel II

Under Basel II, effective year-end 2006, the total credit risk-adjusted assets are $741.2 million ($675.7 million from on-balance-sheet activities, plus $60 million for the risk-adjusted value of OBS contingencies and guarantees, plus $5.5 million for the risk-adjusted value of OBS derivatives).

The Credit Risk-Adjusted Asset Value of Off-Balance-Sheet Derivative Instruments with Netting under Basel I[23,24]

One criticism of the above method is that it ignores the netting of exposures. In response, OSFI has adopted a proposal put forward by the BIS that allows netting of off-balance-sheet derivative contracts as long as the bank has a bilateral netting contract that clearly establishes a legal obligation by the counterparty to pay or receive a single net amount on the different contracts.[25] Provided that such written contracts are clearly documented by the bank, the new rules require the estimation of *net current exposure* and *net potential exposure* of those positions included in the bilateral netting contract. The sum of the net current exposure and the net potential exposure equals the total credit equivalent amount.

The rules define net current exposure as the net sum of all positive and negative replacement costs (or mark-to-market values of the individual derivative contracts). If the sum of the replacement costs is positive, then the net current exposure equals the sum. If it is negative, the net current exposure is zero. The net potential exposure is defined by a formula that adjusts the gross potential exposure estimated earlier:

$$A_{net} = (0.4 \times A_{gross}) + (0.6 \times NPR \times A_{gross})$$

where A_{net} is the net potential exposure (or adjusted sum of potential future credit exposures), A_{gross} is the sum of the potential exposures of each contract, and NPR is the ratio of net current exposure or net replacement cost (NR) to gross current exposure. The 0.6 is the amount of potential exposure that is reduced as a result of netting.

The same example used in the previous section (without netting) will be used to show the effect of netting on the total credit equivalent amount. *Here we assume that both contracts are with the same counterparty.*

$$A_{gross} = \$2.5 \text{ m} \quad \text{Net current exposure} = \$2 \text{ m} \quad \text{Current exposure} = \$3 \text{ m}$$

The net current exposure is the sum of the positive and negative replacement costs—that is, $\$+3$ m and $\$-1$ m $= \$2$ m. The gross potential exposure (A_{gross}) is the sum of the individual potential exposures $= \$2.5$ m. To determine the net potential exposure, the following formula is used:

$$A_{net} = (0.4 \times A_{gross}) + (0.6 \times NPR \times A_{gross})$$
$$NPR = \text{Net current exposure/Current exposure} = 2/3$$
$$A_{net} = (0.4 \times 2.5 \text{ m}) + (0.6 \times 2/3 \times 2.5 \text{ m})$$
$$= \$2 \text{ million}$$

$$\text{Total credit equivalent} = \text{Net potential exposure} + \text{Net current exposure}$$
$$= 2 \text{ m} + 2 \text{ m} = \$4 \text{ million}$$

$$\frac{\text{Risk-adjusted asset value}}{\text{of OBS market contracts}} = \text{Total credit equivalent amount} \times 0.5 \text{ (risk weight)}$$
$$= 4 \text{ m} \times 0.5 = \$2 \text{ million}$$

As can be seen, netting reduces the credit risk-adjusted asset value from $2.75 million to $2 million.

---

[23] This section, which involves more technical material, may be included in or dropped from the chapter reading depending on the rigor of the course without harming the continuity of the chapter.

[24] Under Basel II, off-balance-sheet netting of credit derivatives will be left to Pillar II (i.e., to the discretion of regulators). Originally, a specific netting formula had been proposed (the "w" factor).

[25] See OSFI, Capital Adequacy Requirements A-Part 1, January, 2001, pp. 4–4–1 to 4–4–4.

Calculating the Overall Risk-Based Capital Position

After calculating the risk-weighted assets for a deposit-taking institution, the final step is to calculate the Tier 1 and total risk–based capital ratios.

EXAMPLE 20–5

Calculating the Overall Risk-Based Capital Position of a Bank

From Tables 20–11 and 20–13, the bank's Tier 1 capital (common shares, retained earnings, non-cumulative perpetual preferred shares) less goodwill and intangible assets ($10) totals $60 million. Tier 2 capital (subordinated non-controlling interests in subsidiaries, subordinated debt, non-perpetual preferred shares) totals $35 million. The resulting total Tier 1 and Tier 2 capital is, therefore, $95 million.

We can now calculate our bank's overall capital adequacy in light of the current (Basel I) and proposed (Basel II) risk-based capital requirements as:

Basel I Basel II

$$\text{Tier I (core) capital} = \frac{\$60 \text{ m}}{\$911.75 \text{ m}} = 6.58\% \qquad \frac{\$60 \text{ m}}{\$741.2 \text{ m}} = 8.09\%$$

and

$$\text{Total risk–based capital ratio} = \frac{\$95 \text{ m}}{\$911.75 \text{ m}} = 10.42\% \qquad \frac{\$95 \text{ m}}{\$741.2 \text{ m}} = 12.82\%$$

The difference in these ratios under the two capital adequacy formulas is due to the modified treatment of sovereign, bank, and corporate loans under Basel II. Specifically, Basel II aligns regulatory capital requirements more closely with the key elements of banking risk by introducing a wider differentiation of credit risk weights. The risk weights are refined by reference to a rating provided by an external credit rating agency. The bank in our example held many low-risk, highly rated loans in its portfolio. Under Basel I these loans are all assigned a credit risk weight of 100 percent. Under Basel II, however, low-risk, highly rated loans are assigned a lower risk weight (20 and 50 percent) reflecting their decreased risk to the bank. Thus, the credit risk-adjusted assets for our bank are smaller under the proposed Basel II than under the currently used Basel I. Note that for a bank with a higher proportion of lower-quality loans, Basel II would likely result in higher credit risk-adjusted assets than under Basel I. Such a bank would be required to hold more capital to meet the required minimum risk-based ratios.

Since the minimum Tier I capital ratio required (see Table 20–7) is 7 percent and the minimum risk-based capital ratio required is 10 percent, the bank in our example has more than adequate capital under both capital requirement formulas.[26]

Interest Rate Risk, Market Risk, and Risk-Based Capital

From a regulatory perspective, a credit risk-based capital ratio is adequate only as long as a deposit-taking institution is not exposed to undue interest rate or market risk. The reason is that the risk-based capital ratio takes into account only the adequacy of a bank's capital to meet both its on- and off-balance-sheet credit risks. Not explicitly accounted for is the insolvency risk emanating from interest rate risk (duration mismatches) and market (trading) risk.

www.bis.org   To meet these criticisms, in 1993 the Bank for International Settlements) developed additional capital requirement proposals for interest rate risk (see Chapter 9)

---

[26] With netting, the total credit risk–adjusted assets ratio would have been $95 m/$911 m, or 10.43 percent, under Basel I and $95 m/$740.45 m, or 12.83 percent, under Basel II. Unlike Basel I, Basel II will distinguish between performing and nonperforming (impaired loans). Unsecured non-mortgage loans that are more than 90 days past due will be given a risk weight of 150 percent if specific loan loss provisions are less than 20 percent and 100 percent when specific provisions are more than 20 percent. Uninsured residential mortgages that are more than 90 days past due will be given a 100 percent risk weight. These new requirements will cause FIs to recognize and allow for impaired loans each reporting period.

and market risk (see Chapter 10). As is discussed in Chapter 10, since 1998 DIs have had to calculate an add-on to the 8 percent risk-based capital ratio to reflect their exposure to market risk. There are two approaches available to DIs to calculate the size of this add-on: (1) the standardized model proposed by regulators and (2) the DI's own internal market risk model. To date, no formal add-on has been required for interest rate risk, although in 2001 the BIS suggested a framework for a future capital ratio for interest rate risk similar to the original 1993 proposal and issued a final version in 2004.[27]

Operational Risk and Risk-Based Capital

In its 2001 proposed amendments to capital adequacy rules, the BIS proposed an additional add-on to capital for operational risk. Prior to this proposal, the BIS had argued that the operational risk exposures of banks were adequately taken care of by the 8 percent credit risk-adjusted ratio. But increased visibility of operational risks in recent years (see Chapter 14) has induced regulators to propose a separate capital requirement for credit and operational risks. As noted above, the BIS now believes that operational risks are sufficiently important for deposit-taking institutions to devote resources to quantify such risks and to incorporate them separately into their assessment of their overall capital adequacy. In the 2001 and 2003 Consultative Documents the Basel Committee proposed three specific methods (proposed for 2006) by which deposit-taking institutions would calculate capital to protect against operational risk: (1) the Basic Indicator Approach, (2) the Standardized Approach, and (3) the Advanced Measurement Approach.[28]

(1) *The Basic Indicator approach* is structured so that banks, on average, will hold 12 percent of their total regulatory capital for operational risk. This 12 percent target was based on a widespread survey conducted internationally of current practices by large banks. To achieve this target, the Basic Indicator Approach focuses on the gross income of the bank, that is, its net profits, or what Europeans called value added. This equals a bank's net interest income plus net noninterest income:

$$\text{Gross income} = \text{Net interest income} + \text{Net noninterest income}$$

According to BIS calculations, a bank that holds a fraction (alpha) of its gross income for operational risk capital, where alpha (α) is set between 17 and 20 percent, will generate enough capital for operational risk such that this amount will be 12 percent of its total regulatory capital holdings against all risks (i.e., credit, market, and operational risks). For example, under the Basic Indicator Approach:

$$\text{Operational capital} = \alpha \times \text{Gross income}$$

or

$$= .2 \times \text{Gross income}$$

The problem with the Basic Indicator Approach is that it is too aggregative, or "top-down," and does not differentiate at all among different areas in which operational

---

[27] The final version of the Basel Committee on Banking Supervision endorsed the Pillar 2 approach. Specifically, banks should have interest rate risk measurement systems that assess the effects of interest rate changes on both earnings and economic value. These systems should provide meaningful measures of a bank's current levels of interest rate risk exposure, and should be capable of identifying any excessive exposures that might arise. See Basel Committee on Banking Supervision, "Principles for the Management and Supervision of Interest Rate Risk," July 2004, www.bis.org and OSFI, "Guideline B-12, Interest Rate Risk Management-Sound Business and Financial Practices," February 2005, www.osfi-bsif.gc.ca

[28] See Basel Committee on Banking Supervision, "Working Paper on Regulatory Treatment of Operational Risk," September 2001 and Sound Practices for the Management and Supervision of Operational Risk,' February 2003. **www.bis.org**

TABLE 20–16
BIS Standardized
Approach Business
Units and Lines

Source: Bank for International
Settlements, "Working Paper
on the Regulatory Treatment
of Operational Risk," September 2001. www.bis.org

Business Line	Indicator	Capital Factors
Corporate finance	Gross income*	$\beta_1 = 18\%$
Trading and sales	Gross income	$\beta_2 = 18\%$
Retail banking	Gross income	$\beta_3 = 12\%$
Commercial banking	Gross income	$\beta_4 = 15\%$
Payment and settlement	Gross income	$\beta_5 = 18\%$
Agency services and custody	Gross income	$\beta_6 = 15\%$
Retail brokerage	Gross income	$\beta_7 = 12\%$
Asset management	Gross income	$\beta_8 = 12\%$

*The indicator relates to gross income reported for the particular line of business.

risks may differ (e.g., Payment and Settlement may have a very different operational risk profile from Retail Brokerage).[29]

(2) *The Standardized Approach* In an attempt to provide a finer differentiation of operational risks in a bank across different activity lines while still retaining a basically top-down approach, the BIS proposed a second method for operational capital calculation. The second method, the Standardized Approach, divides activities into eight major business units and lines (shown in Table 20–16). Within each business line, there is a specified broad indicator (defined as beta, β) that reflects the scale or volume of a deposit-taking institution's activities in that area. The indicator relates to the gross income reported for a particular line of business. It serves as a rough proxy for the amount of operational risk within each of these lines. A capital charge is calculated by multiplying the β for each line by the indicator assigned to the line and then summing these components. The βs reflect the importance of each activity in the average bank. The βs are set by regulators and are calculated from average industry figures from a selected sample of banks.

Suppose the industry β for Corporate Finance is 18% and gross income from the Corporate Finance line of business (the activity indicator) is $30 million for the bank. Then, the regulatory capital charge for this line for this year is:

$$\text{Capital}_{\text{Corporate Finance}} = \beta \times \text{Gross income from the Corporate Finance line of business for the bank}$$
$$= 18\% \times \$30 \text{ million}$$
$$= \$5,400,000$$

The total capital charge is calculated as the three-year average of the simple summation of the regulatory capital charge across each of the eight business lines.[30]

(3) *The Advanced Measurement Approach* The third method, the Advanced Measurement Approach, allows individual banks to rely on internal data for regulatory capital purposes. There are three broadly categorized methods currently under development: the Internal Measurement Approach (IMA), the Loss Distribution Approach (LDA), and the Scorecard Approach (SA).

The IMA calculations are based on a framework that separates a bank's operational risk exposures into lines of business and operational risk event types. As an

[29] A second issue is that the α term implies operational risk that is proportional to gross income. This ignores possible economies-of-scale effects that would make this relationship nonlinear (nonproportional); that is, α might fall as bank profits and/or size grows.

[30] The Basel Committee's Loss Data Collection Exercise for Operational Risk (March 2003), based on data provided by 89 banks from 19 countries, revealed that about 61 percent of operational loss events occurred in the retail area, with an average loss of $79,300. Also, only 0.9 percent of operational loss events occurred in the corporate finance area, but with an average loss of $646,600.

FIGURE 20–5 Internal Measurement Approach for Operational Risk as an Example of the Advanced Measurement Approach

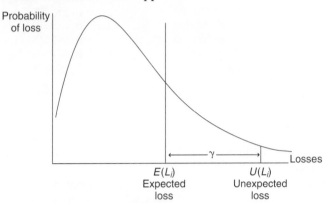

That is:

$$E(L_i) = EI_i \times PE_i \times LGE_i$$

where

$$i = \text{business activity area}$$

encouragement for banks to move toward the adoption of more advanced measures of operational risk, the target for operational risk capital is set at 75 percent of the level of that for the Basic Indicator and Standardized Models. That is, $.75 \times 12\% = 9\%$ of a bank's total regulatory capital. Banks will need three sets of data for a specified set of business lines and risk types: an operational risk exposure indicator (EI)—supplied by the regulator—plus data representing the probability that a loss event occurs (PE) and the losses given such events (LGE). The product of the three produces the expected loss, E(L), in an operational risk area (say, Corporate Finance). See Figure 20–2.

Since capital is meant to protect the bank against the risk of insolvency due to extreme or unexpected losses, $U(L_i)$, the $E(L_i)$ amount is multiplied by a factor defined as gamma (γ_i) that translates the estimate of expected losses for a business line into a capital charge (K_i) that covers losses at least up to the 99.9 percentile of likely losses based on average industry experience. Thus:

$$K_i = E(L_i) \times \gamma_i$$

To get the total operational risk capital requirement, the risks of the different activity areas are added using the same methodology. Unfortunately, doing this is difficult for the less quantitative areas of operational risk, such as fraud.[31]

The LDA method differs from the IMA method in one aspect: The LDA method assess unexpected losses at the 99.9 percentile directly rather than via an assumption about the relationship between expected loss and unexpected loss. Thus, there is no need for the determination of a gamma factor (γ_i) with the LDA method.

With the SA method, banks determine an initial level of operational risk capital at the firm or business line level and then modify these amounts over time on the basis of "scorecards" that attempt to capture the underlying risk profile and risk control environment of the various lines of business. The scorecards bring a forward-looking component to the capital calculations. That is, they reflect improvements in the risk control environment that will reduce both the frequency and severity of future operational risk losses.

The three methods involved are increasingly sophisticated in the measurement of operational risks. As the new standards are implemented (in 2006) deposit-taking institutions would start out using the Basic Indicator Approach and would be encouraged to move along the spectrum of approaches as they develop more sophisticated operational risk measurement systems because of the lower operational risk capital require-

---

[31] For a discussion of some of these models, see M. Cruz, R. Coleman, and G. Salkin, "Modeling and Measuring Operational Risk," *The Journal of Risk* 1 (1998), pp. 63–72; R. Ceski and J. Hernandez, "Where Theory Meets Practice," *Risk: Operational Risk Special Report,* November 1999, pp. 17–20; and L. Allen, J. Boudoukh, and A. Saunders, *Understanding Market, Credit, and Operational Risk: The Value at Risk Approach* (Malden, MA: Blackwell, 2004).

ment (8 percent) associated with the Advanced Measurement Approach compared with the requirement of the Standardized or Basic Indicator Approach (12 percent).

Criticisms of the Risk-Based Capital Ratio

The risk-based capital requirement seeks to improve on the simple assets to capital multiple by (1) incorporating credit, market, and operational risks into the determination of capital adequacy; (2) more systematically accounting for credit risk differences among assets; (3) incorporating off-balance-sheet risk exposures; and (4) applying a similar capital requirement across all the major deposit-taking institutions (and banking centers) in the world. Unfortunately, the requirements have a number of conceptual and applicability weaknesses in achieving these objectives:

1. *Risk weights.* It is unclear how closely the risk weight categories in Basel I (Basel II) reflect true credit risk. For example, commercial loans have risk weights between 20 and 150 percent under Basel II. Taken literally, these relative weights imply that some commercial loans are exactly four and a half times as risky as other loans.[32]

2. *Risk weights based on external credit rating agencies.* While Basel II proposed reforms to improve on Basel I in measuring credit risk, that is, by replacing the current single 100 percent risk weight for sovereign, bank, and commercial loans with different risk weights, depending on the loan's credit rating, it is unclear whether the risk weights accurately measure the relative (or absolute) risk exposures of individual borrowers. Moreover, Standard & Poor's and Moody's ratings are often accused of lagging behind rather than leading the business cycle. As a result required capital may peak during a recession, when banks are least able to meet the requirements.[33]

3. *Portfolio aspects.* The BIS plans largely ignore credit risk portfolio diversification opportunities. As we discuss in Chapter 12, when returns on assets have negative or less than perfectly positive correlations, an FI may lower its portfolio risk through diversification. As constructed, both Basel I and Basel II (standardized model) capital adequacy plans are essentially linear risk measures that ignore correlations or covariances among assets and asset group credit risks—such as between residential mortgages and commercial loans.[34] That is, the FI manager weights each asset separately by the appropriate risk weight and then sums those numbers to get an overall measure of credit risk. No account is taken of the covariances among asset risks between different counterparties (or risk weights).[35]

---

[32] R. B. Avery and A. Berger show evidence that these risk weights do a good job of distinguishing between failing and non-failing banks. See "Risk–Based Capital and Deposit Insurance Reform," *Journal of Banking and Finance* 15 (1991), pp. 847–74. However, D. S. Jones and K. K. King, in "The Implementation of Prompt Corrective Action: An Assessment," *Journal of Banking and Finance,* 1995, pp. 491–510, find that risk–based capital would have done a poor job in identifying failing banks over the 1981–89 period if it had been used for prompt corrective action purposes. P. S. Calem and M. LaCour-Little, in "Risk–Based Capital Requirements for Mortgage Loans, "*Journal of Banking and Finance*, 2004, pp. 647–72, find that risk–based capital requirements for mortgage loans offer little risk differentiation and result in significant divergence between regulatory and economic capital. L. Allen, "The Basel Capital Accords and International Mortgage Markets: A Survey of the Literature," Baruch College, CUNY Working Paper, 2003, surveys the literature to date on the impact of the Basel Accords on bank profitability, competitiveness, structure, and risk taking.

[33] E. I. Altman, S. T. Bharath, and A. Saunders, in "Credit Ratings and the BIS Reform Agenda," *Journal of Banking and Finance*, 2002, pp. 909–22, find that although the new BIS guidelines are an improvement over the original ones, several of the rating categories carry underweighted capital requirements, and that banks will continue to be motivated to skew their portfolios toward lower-rated loans. Moreover, relying on rating agencies to determine a borrower's credit risk questions the specialness of banks as monitors—see Chapter 1.

[34] In a portfolio context, it assumes that asset and OBS risks are independent of each other.

[35] However, the more advanced internal ratings–based approach (IRB—see Appendix 20A to this chapter) assumes a correlation among all loans of either 10 or 20 percent. Currently, it is estimated that only approximately 15 (the biggest) U.S. banks will use the IRB approach. Moreover, private sector models, such as KMV and CreditMetrics (see Chapters 11 and 12), generally find correlations of less than 10 percent. Most commonly, they find correlations in the 0 to 5 percent range—indicating a greater degree of diversification potential than implied by the IRB.

4. *FI specialness.* Giving private sector moderate- and high-risk commercial loans the highest credit risk weighting may reduce the incentive for deposit-taking institutions to make such loans relative to holding other assets. This may reduce the amount of loans to these businesses, as well as the degree of monitoring, and may have associated negative externality effects on the economy. That is, one aspect of banks' special functions—bank lending—may be muted.[36] This effect has been of great concern and controversy. Indeed, the high-risk weight given to commercial loans relative to securities has been blamed in part for inducing a credit crunch and a reorientation of bank portfolios away from commercial loans toward securities in the early 1990s.

5. *Excessive complexity.* Basel II will greatly raise the cost of regulation by adding new levels of complexity. The cost of developing and implementing new risk management systems will clearly be significant, and the benefits may turn out to be small. Initial calculations suggest that most banks using the IRB Approach for operational risk will end up with a higher capital charge than those using the Standardized Approach. In other words, not only is the most advanced approach extremely complex, it may also not deliver all the benefits that are generally expected. The U.S. Comptroller of the Currency said the "mind-numbing" complexity of the proposed accords underscores a number of voices that are uncomfortable with Basel II.[37]

6. *Other risks.* While market risk exposure was integrated into the risk-based capital requirements in 1998 and operational risk is proposed for 2006, the BIS plan does not yet account for other risks, such as interest rate and liquidity risk in the banking book, although these risks are accounted for in the market or trading book. A more complete risk-based capital requirement would include these risks.

7. *Impact on capital requirements.* A study of Canadian banks concluded that Basel II could cause the minimum required capital for exposure to corporate entities to be more volatile, depending on the method chosen by the FI for the internal ratings approach (IRB, see Appendix 20A on page 722 of this book) and could have an impact on lending. In December, 2003, the U.S. Federal Deposit Insurance Corporation issued a study making the case that the new rules would water down capital in place for U.S. banks instead of providing more protection against losses. However, the 2004 Annual Reports of several Canadian banks (e.g., Bank of Montreal, Bank of Nova Scotia) noted that Basel II would bring the capital requirements more in line with economic capital.[38]

8. *Competition.* In Canada, OSFI requires Basel II to apply to the Big Six Banks and other federally-regulated FIs. The U.S. Federal Reserve has stated that Basel II would be initially applied to internationally active banks. Thus, U.S. regulators will initially apply the new rules to fewer than a dozen U.S. banks. Further, in the United

---

[36] In addition, since many emerging-market countries have low credit ratings, under the Basel II plan, banks may have to hold considerably more capital against such loans than under Basel I. This may adversely affect the flow of bank financing to these less-developed countries—with major adverse effects on their economies. See C. Jacklin, "Bank Capital Requirements and Incentives for Lending," Working Paper, Stanford University, February 1993; and J. Haubich and P. Wachtel, "Capital Requirements and Shifts in Commercial Bank Portfolios," Federal Reserve Bank of Cleveland, *Economic Review* 29 (3rd quarter, 1994), pp. 2–15. However, A. Berger and G. Udell, "Did Risk–Based Capital Allocate Bank Credit and Cause a Credit Crunch in the U.S.?" *Journal of Money, Credit and Banking* 26 (August 1994), pp. 585–628, dispute these findings.

[37] See "Banking Talks Face Criticism," *The Wall Street Journal*, December 16, 2003, p. C15.[43] See "Rules on Bank Capital Draw Fire," *The Wall Street Journal*, December 8, 2003, p. B8.

[38] See "Rules on Bank Capital Draw Fire," *The Wall Street Journal*, December 8, 2003, p. B8 and M. Illing and G. Paulin, "Basel II and Required Bank Capital," Bank of Canada, *Financial System Review*, December 2004, pp. 61–65. See also the 2004 Bank of Montreal Annual Report, p. 60 and 2004 Scotiabank Annual Report, page 46 for insights into how two Canadian FIs are approaching the implementation of Basel II. OSFI will permit Canadian banks to choose their approach for operational risk with respect to regulatory capital. Basel I and Basel II are operating in tandem for two years with a final implementation date of October 31 2007.

States, Basel II will not apply to securities firms or investment banks. In Europe, Basel II is to be incorporated into European Union law and applied to all banks and investment firms, not just internationally active banks. Thus, different standards will apply to Canadian, U. S. and European banks, giving the American banks a theoretically lower (regulatory) cost of making loans. In addition, as a result of tax and accounting differences across banking systems and in safety net coverages, the 8 percent risk-based capital requirement has not created a level competitive playing field across banks. This is different from what proponents of the scheme claim. In particular, Japan and the United States have very different accounting, tax, and safety net rules that significantly affect the comparability of U.S. and Japanese bank risk-based capital ratios.[39]

9. *Pillar 2 may ask too much of regulators.* Pillar 2 of Basel II will require many very sensitive judgment calls from regulators who may be ill-equipped to make them. This will particularly be a problem for developing-country regulators. If Pillar 2 is taken seriously, supervisors may be exposed to a lot of criticism that most would rather avoid.

Concept Questions

1. What are the major strengths of the risk-based capital ratios?
2. You are a manager of a deposit-taking institution with a total risk-based capital ratio of 6 percent. Discuss four strategies to meet the required 8 percent ratio in a short period of time without raising new capital.
3. Why isn't a capital ratio levied on exchange-traded derivative contracts?
4. What are three problems with the simple assets to capital multiple measure of capital adequacy?
5. What is the difference between Tier 1 capital and Tier 2 capital?
6. Identify one asset in each of the four (five) credit risk weight categories for Basel I and Basel II.

CAPITAL REQUIREMENTS FOR OTHER FIS

Securities Firms

Canadian securities firms are governed by provincial and territorial governments, as well as self-regulatory organizations (SROs) such as the Investment Dealers Association (IDA) and the stock exchanges (e.g., the TSX and the Montréal Exchange). The implementation of a single national regulator which is currently under discussion would provide a standard calculation of regulatory capital across Canada.

Life Insurance Companies

Federally regulated life insurance companies (including branches of foreign life insurance companies operating in Canada) are required to maintain adequate levels of capital under the Insurance Companies Act (ICA). OSFI provides guidelines for the **minimum continuing capital and surplus requirements (MCCSR)** for life insurance companies that is risk-based, and uses the concepts of Tier 1 (core) and Tier 2 (supplementary) capital as for federally-regulated deposit-taking institutions. Two MCCSR Ratios apply. The Tier 1 ratio is calculated as

minimum continuing capital and surplus requirement (MCCSR)
The minimum capital required by OSFI for life insurance companies operating in Canada.

Tier 1 = Net Tier 1 Capital/Total Capital Required > 60 percent.

---

[39] H. S. Scott and S. Iwahara, "In Search of a Level Playing Field," Group of Thirty, Washington, D.C., 1994, argue that these distortions are so large that they render meaningful comparisons impossible. Indeed, many analysts have argued that a majority of the largest Japanese banks would have violated the 8 percent rule in 1998 under U.S. accounting and regulatory practices. This is one of the major reasons for the bailout plan announced by the Japanese government in October 1998. See "The Timid Japanese Bailout Just Might Do the Job," *New York Times,* October 22, 1998, p. C2.

TABLE 20–17
Minimum
Continuing
Capital and
Surplus
Requirements
(MCCSR) for
Canadian Life
Insurance
Companies as at
Quarter 2, 2005
(thousands of
dollars)

Source: Office of Superintendent of Financial Institutions
at www.osfi-bsif.gc.ca

Capital Available:	
Tier 1 Capital	
Common shares	13,293,590
Contributed surplus	839,580
Retained earnings	22,704,403
Non-cumulative perpetual preferred shares	293,108
Qualifying non-controlling interests	241,453
Innovative instruments	2,791,007
Other Tier 1 Capital Elements	3,766,180
Gross Tier 1 Capital	43,929,321
Deductions from Tier 1:	
Goodwill & intangibles in excess of limit	9,494,667
Other Deductions	5,956,322
Net Tier 1 Capital	28,478,332
Tier 2 Capital	
Tier 2A	1,068,900
Tier 2B allowed	3,364,538
Tier 2C	5,870,759
Total Tier 2 Capital Allowed	10,283,393
Total Tier 1 and Tier 2 Capital	38,761,725
Less Deductions/Adjustments	2,670,374
Total Capital Available	36,091,351
Capital Required:	
Assets Default & market risk	7,537,941
Insurance Risks	5,512,952
Interest Rate Risks	2,808,406
Other	127,336
Total Capital Required	15,986,635
MCCSR Ratios:	
Tier 1	178.14
Total	225.76

The Total Capital Ratio is calculated as

Total Capital Ratio = Total Capital Available/Total Capital Required > 120 percent.

Table 20–17 shows the components and the calculations of the MCCSR ratios for Canadian Life Insurance Companies as reported to OSFI at Quarter 2, 2005. Canadian life insurance companies regulated by OSFI are seen to be well above the minimum MCCSR ratios for Tier 1 and Total Capital.

As required for the banks under its jurisdiction, OSFI requires an estimate of risk-adjusted assets that encompass (1) default (credit) and market risk, (2) insurance risks, (3) interest rate risk, and (4) other risks. Default and market risk are similar to the credit-risk adjusted asset calculations for deposit-taking institutions. Insurance risk captures the risk of adverse changes in **mortality risk** and **morbidity risk**. Interest rate risk in part reflects the liquidity of liabilities and their probability or ease of withdrawal as interest rates change.[40]

mortality risk
The risk of death.

morbidity risk
The risk of ill health.

---

[40] For complete details, see Office of Superintendent of Financial Institutions, "Minimum Continuing Capital And Surplus Requirements (MCCSR) for Life Insurance Companies—A", October 2004 at www.osfi-bsif.gc.ca.

TABLE 20–18
Minimum Capital Test (MCT) for Canadian Property and Casualty Insurance Companies as at Quarter 2 2005 (thousands of dollars)

Source: Office of Superintendent of Financial Institutions at www.osfi-bsif.gc.ca

Capital Available	
Equity	15,725,207
Subordinated Indebtedness and Redeemable Preferred Shares	77,830
Investments—Adjustment to Market	1,169,732
Less: Assets with a Capital Requirement of 100%	1,034,066
Total Capital Available	**15,938,703**
Capital Required	
Balance Sheet Assets	2,334,896
Unearned Premiums/Unpaid Claims	3,914,093
Catastrophes	115,385
Reinsurance Ceded to Unregistered Insurers	263,446
Off-Balance Sheet Exposures	8,200
Minimum Capital Required	**6,636,020**
Excess Capital Available Over Capital Required	**9,302,683**
Total Capital Available as a % of Minimum Capital Required	**240.2**

minimum capital test (MCT)
The ratio of total capital available to minimum capital required for P & C companies regulated by OSFI in Canada.

Since 2003, federally-regulated property and casualty (P&C) companies have been required to meet a **minimum capital test (MCT)** which is defined as:

Total Capital Available/ Minimum Capital Required > 100 per cent.

The minimum ratio is 100 percent, but P&C companies are expected to maintain capital at or above 150 percent, the supervisory target, in order to have an amount to provide a buffer to deal with market volatility and other risks. Figure 20–18 shows the MCT calculation for all Canadian federally-regulated P&C companies as reported to OSFI as at Quarter 2, 2005. It can be seen that the ratio is simpler than that required under Basel I or Basel II for the internationally active banks, but does consider some of the same components for capital that can be included in the numerator of the MCT. The denominator of the MCT establishes the minimum capital required for on- and off- balance sheet assets, policy liabilities, accident and sickness insurance, as well as for catastrophes, unearned premiums and unearned claims, and reinsurance. As seen in Table 20–18, the ratio of 240.2 for all reporting companies is well above the 150 percent for individual companies. OSFI may set out different targets based on the risk profile of the individual institution. P&C companies must notify OSFI if they expect to fall below their target ratio, and must also provide a plan for returning above their minimum.[41]

Concept Questions

1. How do the capital requirements for life insurance firms differ from the book value capital rules employed by OSFI to deposit-taking institutions?
2. What types of risks are included in estimating the *MCCSR* of life insurance firms?
3. How does the MCT for P & C companies differ from the MCCSR for life insurance companies?

---

[41] For complete details, see Office of Superintendent of Financial Institutions, "Minimum Capital Test (MCT) for Federally Regulated Property and Casualty Insurance Companies—A," July 2003 at www.osfi-bsif.gc.ca

Summary

This chapter reviewed the role of an FI's capital in insulating it against credit, interest rate, and other risks. According to economic theory, capital or net worth should be measured on a market value basis as the difference between the market values of assets and liabilities. In actuality, regulators use book value accounting rules. While a book value capital adequacy rule accounts for credit risk exposure in a rough fashion, it overlooks the effects of interest rate changes and interest rate exposure on net worth. We analyzed the specific and proposed capital rules adopted by the regulators of federally-regulated banks and trust and loan companies, and, insurance companies, and discussed their problems and weaknesses. In particular, we looked at how regulators are now adjusting book value-based capital rules to account for different types of risk as part of their imposition of risk-based capital adequacy ratios. As a result, actual capital requirements are moving closer to market value-based net worth.

Questions and Problems

1. Identify and briefly discuss the importance of the five functions of an FI's capital.

2. Why are regulators concerned with the levels of capital held by an FI compared with those held by a nonfinancial institution?

3. What are the differences between the economic definition of capital and the book value definition of capital?

   a. How does economic value accounting recognize the adverse effects of credit and interest rate risk?

   b. How does book value accounting recognize the adverse effects of credit and interest rate risk?

4. A financial intermediary has the following balance sheet (in millions) with all assets and liabilities in market values.

   Assets

6 percent semiannual four-year notes (par value $12)	$10
7 percent annual three-year AA-rated bonds (par-$15)	15
9 percent annual five-year BBB-rated bonds (par-$15)	15
Total assets	$40

   Liabilities and Equity

5 percent two-year subordinated debt (par value $25)	$20
Equity capital	20
Total liabilities and equity	$40

   a. What would be the effect on equity capital (net worth) if interest rates increased by 30 basis points? The T-notes are held for trading purposes; the rest are all classified as held to maturity.

   b. How are the changes in the market value of assets adjusted in the income statements and balance sheets of FIs?

5. Why is the market value of equity a better measure of an FI's ability to absorb losses than book value of equity?

6. Provincial Bank has the following year-end balance sheet (in millions).

   Assets

Cash	$ 10
Loans	90
Total assets	$100

   Liabilities and Equity

Deposits	$ 90
Equity	10
Total liabilities and equity	$100

   The loans primarily are fixed-rate, medium-term loans, while the deposits are either short-term or variable-rate deposits. Rising interest rates have caused the failure of a key industrial company, and as a result, 3 percent of the loans are considered uncollectable and thus have no economic value. One-third of these uncollectable loans will be charged off. Further, the increase in interest rates has caused a 5 percent decrease in the market value of the remaining loans.

   a. What is the impact on the balance sheet after the necessary adjustments are made according to book value accounting? According to market value accounting?

   b. What is the new market to book value ratio if Provincial Bank has 1 million shares outstanding?

7. What are the arguments for and against the use of market value accounting for FIs?

8. How is the assets to capital multiple for an FI defined?

9. Identify and discuss the weaknesses of the assets to capital multiple as a measure of capital adequacy.

10. What is the Basel Agreement?

11. What is the major feature in the estimation of credit risk under Basel I capital requirements?

12. What is the total risk-based capital ratio?

13. What are the definitional differences between Tier 1 and Tier 2 capital?

14. What components are used in the calculation of risk-adjusted assets?

15. Explain the process of calculating risk-adjusted on-balance-sheet assets.

    a. What assets are included in the categories of credit risk exposure under Basel I (Basel II)?

    b. What are the appropriate risk weights for each category?

16. Halifax Bank has the following balance sheet (in millions) and has no off-balance-sheet activities.

Assets	
Cash	$ 20
Treasury bills	40
Residential mortgages	600
Other loans	430
Total assets	$1,090

Liabilities and Equity	
Deposits	$ 980
Subordinated debentures	40
Common stock	40
Retained earnings	30
Total liabilities and equity	$1,090

    a. What is the assets to capital multiple?

    b. What is the Tier 1 capital ratio?

    c. What is the total risk-based capital ratio?

    d. How would OSFI categorize this bank's capital? (Table 20–9)

17. Onshore Bank has $20 million in assets, with risk-adjusted assets of $10 million. Tier 1 capital is $500,000, and Tier 2 capital is $400,000. How will each of the following transactions affect the value of the Tier 1 and total capital ratios? What will be the new values of each ratio be?

    a. The bank repurchases $100,000 of common stock.

    b. The bank issues $2,000,000 of fixed-term deposits and uses the proceeds for loans to homeowners.

    c. The bank receives $500,000 in deposits and invests them in T-bills.

    d. The bank issues $800,000 in common stock and lends it to help finance a new shopping mall.

    e. The bank issues $1,000,000 in nonqualifying perpetual preferred stock and purchases provincial bonds.

    f. Homeowners pay back $4,000,000 of mortgages, and the bank uses the proceeds to build new ATMs.

18. Explain the process of calculating risk-adjusted off-balance-sheet contingent guaranty contracts.

    a. What is the basis for differentiating the credit equivalent amounts of contingent guaranty contracts?

    b. On what basis are the risk weights for the credit equivalent amounts differentiated?

19. Explain how off-balance-sheet market contracts, or derivative instruments, differ from contingent guaranty contracts.

    a. What is counterparty credit risk?

    b. Why do exchange-traded derivative security contracts have no capital requirements?

    c. What is the difference between the potential exposure and the current exposure of over-the-counter derivative contracts?

    d. Why are the credit conversion factors for the potential exposure of foreign exchange contracts greater than they are for interest rate contracts?

    e. Why do regulators not allow banks to benefit from positive current exposure values?

20. What is the process of netting off-balance-sheet derivative contracts under Basel I? What requirement is necessary to allow a bank to calculate this exposure? How is net current exposure defined? How does net potential exposure differ from net current exposure?

21. How does the risk-based capital measure attempt to compensate for the limitations of the static assets to capital multiple?

22. Identify and discuss the problems in the risk-based capital approach to measuring capital adequacy.

23. What is the contribution to the credit risk-adjusted asset base of the following items under the Basel I requirements? Under Basel II requirements?

    a. $10 million cash.

    b. $50 million 91-day U.S. Treasury bills.

    c. $25 million cash items in the process of collection.

    d. $5 million U.K. government bonds, AAA rated.

    e. $5 million Australian short-term government bonds, A− rated.

    f. $1 million provincial government bonds.

    g. $40 million repurchase agreements.

    h. $500 million one-to-four family home mortgages.

    i. $500 million commercial and industrial loans, BBB− rated.

    j. $100,000 performance-related standby letters of credit to a blue-chip corporation.

    k. $100,000 performance-related standby letters of credit to a municipality issuing bonds.

l. $7 million commercial letter of credit to a foreign, A rated corporation.

m. $3 million five-year loan commitment to an OECD government.

n. $8 million bankers acceptance conveyed to a Canadian, AA- rated corporation.

o. $17 million three-year loan commitment to a private agent.

p. $17 million three-month loan commitment to a private agent.

q. $30 million standby letter of credit to back a corporate issue of commercial paper.

r. $4 million five-year interest rate swap with no current exposure (the counterparty is a private agent).

s. $4 million five-year interest rate swap with no current exposure (the counterparty is a municipality).

t. $6 million two-year currency swap with $500,000 current exposure (the counterparty is a low-credit-risk entity).

The bank balance sheet information below is for questions 26 through 29.

24. What is the bank's risk-adjusted asset base under Basel I? Under Basel II?

25. What are the bank's Tier I and total risk-based capital requirements under Basel I? Under Basel II?

26. Using the assets to capital multiple requirement, what is the minimum regulatory capital required to keep the bank in the well-capitalized zone (below 20%)?

What is the bank's capital adequacy level (under Basel I and Basel II) if the par value of its equity is $150,000, the surplus value of equity is $200,000, and the qualifying perpetual preferred stock is $50,000? Does the bank meet Basel (Tier I) capital standards?

On-Balance-Sheet Items	Category	Face Value
Cash	1	$ 121,600
Short-term government securities (<92 days)	1	5,400
Long-term government securities (>92 days)	1	414,400
Bank of Canada Deposits	1	9,800
Repos secured by federal agencies	2	159,000
Claims on Canadian deposit-taking institutions	2	937,900
Short-term (<1 year) claims on foreign banks	2	1,640,000
Municipal bonds	2	170,000
Claims on or guaranteed by federal agencies	2	26,500
Municipal revenue bonds	3	112,900
Commercial loans, BB+ rated	4	6,645,700
Claims on foreign banks (>1 year)	4	5,800

Off-Balance-Sheet Items	Conversion Factor	Face Value
Canadian government counterparty		
Loan commitments, AAA rated:		
<1 year	0%	$ 300
1–5 years	50%	1,140
Standby letters of credit, AA rated:		
Performance-related	50%	200
Direct credit substitute	100%	100
Canadian deposit-taking institution counterparty (risk weight category 2)		
Loan commitments, BBB+ rated:		
<1 year	0%	1,000
>1 year	50%	3,000
Standby letters of credit, AA− rated:		
Performance-related	50%	200
Direct credit substitute	100%	56,400
Commercial letters of credit, BBB+ rated	20%	400
Provincial government counterparty (risk weight category 3)		
Loan commitments, BBB− rated:		
>1 year	50%	100
Standby letters of credit, AAA rated:		
Performance-related	50%	135,400
Corporate customer counterparty		
Loan Commitments, CCC rated:		
<1 year	0%	2,980,000
>1 year	50%	3,046,278
Standby letters of credit, BBB rated:		
Performance-related	50%	101,543
Direct credit substitute	100%	485,000
Commercial letters of credit, AA− rated	20%	78,978
Note issuance facilities	50%	20,154
Forward agreements	100%	5,900
Interest rate market contracts (Current exposure assumed to be zero)		
<1 year (notional amount)	0%	2,000
>1–5 years (notional amount)	.5%	5,000

27. Third Bank has the following balance sheet (in millions) with the risk weights in parentheses.

Assets	
Cash (0%)	$ 20
OECD interbank deposits (20%)	25
Mortgage loans (50%)	70
Consumer loans (100%)	70
Total assets	$185

Liabilities and Equity	
Deposits	$175
Subordinated debt (5 years)	3
Cumulative preferred stock	5
Equity	2
Total liabilities and equity	$185

The cumulative preferred stock is qualifying and perpetual. In addition, the bank has $30 million in performance-related standby letters of credit (SLCs), $40 million in two-year forward FX contracts that are currently in the money by $1 million, and $300 million in six-year interest rate swaps that are currently out of the money by $2 million. Credit conversion factors follow:

Performance-related standby LCs	50%
1- to 5-year foreign exchange contracts	5%
1- to 5-year interest rate swaps	0.5%
5- to 10-year interest rate swaps	1.5%

a. What are the risk-adjusted on-balance-sheet assets of the bank as defined under the Basel Accord?

b. What is the total capital required for both off- and on-balance-sheet assets?

c. Does the bank have enough capital to meet the Basel requirements? If not, what minimum Tier 1 or total capital does it need to meet the requirement?

28. Third Fifth Bank has the following balance sheet (in millions) with the risk weights in parentheses.

Assets	
Cash (0%)	$ 20
Mortgage loans (50%)	50
Consumer loans (100%)	70
Total assets	$140

Liabilities and Equity	
Deposits	$130
Subordinated debt (>5 years)	5
Equity	5
Total liabilities and equity	$140

In addition, the bank has $20 million in commercial standby letters of credit and $40 million in 10-year FX forward contracts that are in the money by $1 million.

a. What are the risk-adjusted on-balance-sheet assets of the bank as defined under the Basel Accord?

b. What is the total capital required for both off- and on-balance-sheet assets?

c. Does the bank have sufficient capital to meet the Basel requirements? How much in excess? How much short?

Web Question

29. Go to the Web site of the Bank for International Settlements at **www.bis.org.** Click on "Basel Committee." Click on "Basel II." This will bring the file onto your computer that contains information on the most recent set of capital requirements for deposit-taking institutions. How have these changed since 2003?

30. Go to the Web site of the Office of the Superintendent of Financial Institutions at www.osfi-bsif.gc.ca. Click on "Banks." Click on "Table of OSFI Guidelines and related advisories." Are all of the FIs under OSFI supervision subject to the same requirements? Why might the regulatory approach differ? Click on "Banks." Under the heading "Supervisory Practices" click on "Guide to Intervention." Compare the supervisory roles of OSFI and CDIC if an FI is rated No Problem/Normal Activities, Stage 1, Stage 2, Stage 3, and Stage 4.

31. Go to the Web site of the Office of the Superintendent of Financial Institutions at www.osfi-bsif.gc.ca. Click on "Banks" and then scroll down and click on "Financial Data—Banks." Click on "Quarterly." Click on the drop down menu and choose "Capital Adequacy—Components of Capital." Click "Submit" and then print the most recent quarterly report. Repeat the process by clicking on "Life Insurance and Fraternals." then clicking on "Financial Data—Life Insurance." From the drop down menu choose "MCCSR—Total capital required/available" and click "Submit." Print the MCCSR Report. Repeat the process

by clicking on "Property & Casualty Insurance Companies." Click on "Financial Data—Property and Casualty Insurance Companies." From the drop down menu, choose "Minimum Capital Test (effective Q1/03)" and click "Submit." Print the most recent quarterly report. How do the capital requirements of banks, life insurance companies, and property & casualty insurance companies compare? Why might the capital requirements differ? Are the companies in line with the requirements as set out by OSFI?

Appendix 20A Internal Ratings-Based Approach to Measuring Credit Risk-Adjusted Assets

View Appendix 20A on page 722 of this book.

Product Diversification: Universal Banking

This chapter examines the issue of universal banking and product diversification for FIs:

▸ first, we analyze the problems and risks that can arise and have arisen historically, for FIs constrained to limited financial service sectors or franchises, as well as the potential benefits from greater product expansion

▸ second, we analyze the laws and regulations that have restricted product expansions for banks, insurance companies and securities firms in North America and elsewhere, as well as the recent modifications of many of these laws and regulations

▸ third, we look at barriers to product expansion between the financial sector and the real or commercial sector of the economy

▸ fourth, we evaluate the advantages and disadvantages of allowing FIs to adopt more universal franchises, as appears to be the current global trend

INTRODUCTION

universal FI
An FI that can engage in a broad range of financial service activities.

The Canadian and U.S. financial systems have traditionally been structured along separatist or segmented product lines. Regulatory barriers and restrictions have often inhibited the ability of an FI operating in one area of the financial services industry to expand into other areas. This might be compared with FIs operating in Germany, where a more **universal FI** structure has traditionally allowed individual financial services organizations to offer a far broader range of banking, insurance, securities, and other financial services products.[1] Since the 1980s, both Canada and the United Kingdom have undergone "big bangs" that have revamped their regulatory systems and moved both countries towards universal banks. The revisions of the Bank Act in the 1980s and 1990s resulted in the Canadian banks absorbing and ultimately dominating the securities industry in Canada as well as eliminating the trust industry as a stand-alone function. The remaining Canadian issues to be resolved are the cross-pillar mergers with insurance companies, discussed in this chapter, as well as mergers within the banking pillar itself, discussed in detail in Chapter 22.

This chapter will look at developments in North America and the reasons why the U.S., while delayed in starting towards universal banking until the passage of the Financial Services Modernization Act of 1999, is now swiftly catching up, most notably with the bank-insurance company merger between Citicorp and Travelers to create Citigroup. Citigroup was the second largest universal bank in the world in 2004 as shown in Table 12–1. This is a sign that the importance of regulatory barriers continues to recede, and the globalization of financial services continues to move forward.

---

[1] For a thorough analysis of universal banking systems overseas, see A. Saunders and I. Walter, *Universal Banking in the U.S.?* (New York: Oxford University Press, 1994); and A. Saunders and I. Walter, eds., *Financial System Design: Universal Banking Considered* (Burr Ridge, IL: McGraw-Hill/Irwin, 1996).

TABLE 21–1   The 10 Largest Banks in the World
(in billions of US dollars)

	Total Assets
Mizuho Financial Group (Japan)	US$1,285.5
Citigroup (USA)	1,264.0
UBS (Switzerland)	1,120.5
Crédit Agricole Groupe (France)	1,105.4
HSBC Holdings (United Kingdom)	1,034.2
Deutsche Bank (Germany)	1,014.9
BNP Paribas (France)	989.0
Mitsubishi Tokyo Financial Group (Japan)	975.0
Sumitomo Mitsui Financial Group (Japan)	950.5
Royal Bank of Scotland (United Kingdom)	806.2

Source: *The Banker,* July 2004. www.thebanker.com

RISKS OF PRODUCT SEGMENTATION

Globally, banks have been evolving towards universal banks. In Canada, revisions to the Bank Act set off the process in the late 1980s that continued through the 1990s, a time which saw the mergers of banks with securities firms, the elimination of large trust companies, and the weakening of the four pillars (banks, trusts, insurance, and securities) which continues today. A Canadian issue still to be resolved is the merger of the Big Six banks with each other or with insurance companies, which would reduce competition within Canada, but which, it is argued, would make Canadian FIs better competitors in the global market. This argument has some credence, given that, as shown in Table 21–1, the top bank, Mizuho Financial Group, had total assets of US$1,285.5 billion in 2004 versus total Canadian bank assets of C$1,897.2 billion reported by the Bank of Canada for December, 2004.[2]

Since the U.S. financial market is one of the last large capital markets in the world that is going through a "Big Bang,"[3] the passage of the Financial Services Modernization Act of 1999 can be viewed as the start of the overhaul of the U.S. financial system. Because of its significance to world markets, and also its parallels with deregulation in Canada and elsewhere, we look more closely at the major laws and regulations segmenting the U.S. financial services industry and ways in which U.S. FIs have tried to overcome the effects of such regulations.

SEGMENTATION IN THE U.S. FINANCIAL SERVICES INDUSTRY

money market mutual funds (MMMFs)
Mutual funds that offer high liquidity, cheque-writing ability, and a money market return to smaller individual investors.

Historically, many U.S. financial services firms have faced return and risk problems due to constraints on product diversification, similar to Canada and then U.K. prior to 1990. Product and expansion restrictions have affected commercial banks the most. For example, regulations have limited the franchise of banks to traditional areas such as deposit-taking and commercial lending so that banks have been increasingly susceptible to nonbank competition on both the liability and asset sides of their balance sheets. For example, the growth of **money market mutual funds (MMMFs)** that offer chequing account-like deposit services with high liquidity, stability of value, and an attractive return has proven to be very

---

[2] Northcott argues that competition in the banking sector is complex and cannot be judged only by traditional factors such as the size and number of banks. See C. A. Northcott, "Competition in Banking," *Bank of Canada Financial System Review*, June 2004, pp.75 –77 and C. A. Northcott, "Competition in Banking: A Review of the Literature," *Bank of Canada Working Paper 2004–24.* See also R. Baltazar and M. Santos, "The Benefits of Banking Mega-Mergers: Event Study Evidence from the 1998 Failed Mega-Merger Attempts in Canada," *Canadian Journal of Administrative Sciences* 20(3), September 2003, pp. 196–208 who argue that the benefit expected to accrue to Canadian bank shareholders from the announcement of bank mega-mergers was market power rather than economies of scale.

[3] The deregulation of the financial markets in the United Kingdom was called the "Big Bang." The term has also been applied to the deregulation of Japan's foreign exchange markets in 1999 and the unification of European markets in the late 1990s. The term is now generally used to denote any significant deregulation of a financial market.

strong competition for bank deposit and transaction account products.[4] From virtually no assets in 1972, MMMFs had grown to more than US$2,072 billion by year-end 2003, compared to small time deposits and money market accounts of approximately US$2,291 billion in commercial banks.

On the asset side of the balance sheet, the commercial and industrial (C&I) loans of U.S. banks have faced increased competition from the dynamic growth of the commercial paper market as an alternative source of short-term financing for large- and middle-sized corporations. For example, in January 1988, C&I loans outstanding were US$565 billion versus US$380 billion of commercial paper; in December 2003, C&I loans were US$879 billion versus $1,265.4 billion of commercial paper outstanding. By comparison, in December 1988, Canadian business loans outstanding were $82.2 billion versus $7.96 billion of commercial paper, increasing to $132.1 billion of loans and $14.3 billion of commercial paper by 2004. In addition, relatively unregulated finance companies such as GE Credit, Ford Credit, and GMAC Corporation have been taking an increasing share of the credit market in North America, as shown in Chapter 5.

These trends mean that the economic value of narrowly defined bank franchises has declined since product line restrictions inhibit the ability of an FI to optimize the set of financial services it can offer, potentially forcing it to adopt a more risky set of activities than it would adopt if it could fully diversify.[5] Product restrictions also limit the ability of FI managers to adjust flexibly to shifts in the demand for financial products by consumers and to shifts in costs due to technology and related innovations. We analyze the advantages and disadvantages of increased product line diversification in more detail after we look more closely at the major laws and regulations segmenting the U.S. financial services industry.

Commercial and Investment Banking Activities

Since 1863 the United States has experienced several phases in regulating the links between the commercial and investment banking industries. Simply defined, **commercial banking** is the activity of deposit taking and commercial lending; **investment banking** is the activity of underwriting, issuing, and distributing securities. Early legislation such as the 1863 National Bank Act prohibited nationally chartered commercial banks from engaging in corporate securities activities such as underwriting and the distribution of corporate bonds and equities. However, as the United States industrialized and the demand for corporate finance grew, the largest banks, such as National City Bank (today's Citigroup), found ways around this restriction by establishing state-chartered affiliates to do the underwriting. By 1927 these bank affiliates were underwriting approximately 30 percent of the corporate securities being issued. In that year the Comptroller of the Currency, the regulator of national banks, relaxed the controls on national banks underwriting securities, thereby allowing them to pursue an even greater market share of securities underwritings.

After the 1929 stock market crash, the United States entered a major recession and some 10,000 banks failed between 1930 and 1933. A commission of inquiry (the Pecora Commission), established in 1932, began looking into the causes of the crash. The commission pointed to banks' securities activities and the inherent

commercial banking
Banking activity of deposit taking and lending.

investment banking
Banking activity of underwriting, issuing, and distributing securities.

---

[4] MMMFs collect small savers' funds and invest in a diversified portfolio of short-term money market instruments. This allows the small saver indirect access to the wholesale money market and to the relatively more attractive rates in those markets.

[5] Although it is true that banks earned very high profits in the 1993–2000 period, this was in large part due to relatively low interest rates for deposits and relatively high interest rates for loans. The increased profitability of banks in the 1990s and early 2000s may well be more cyclical than secular.

abuses and conflicts of interest that arise when commercial and investment banking activities were mixed as major causes.[6] The findings resulted in new legislation, the 1933 Banking Act, or the Glass-Steagall Act.

The Glass-Steagall Act sought to impose a rigid separation between commercial banking—taking deposits and making commercial loans—and investment banking—underwriting, issuing, and distributing stocks, bonds, and other securities. Sections 16 and 21 of the act limited the ability of banks and securities firms to engage directly in each other's activities, and Sections 20 and 32 limited the ability of banks and securities firms to engage indirectly in such activities through separately established affiliates. Nevertheless, the act defined three major securities underwriting exemptions. First, commercial banks were to continue to underwrite new issues of Treasury bills, notes, and bonds. Thus, the largest commercial banks today, such as J. P. Morgan Chase, actively compete with securities firms such as Goldman Sachs in government bond auctions. Second, commercial banks were allowed to continue underwriting municipal general obligation (GO) bonds.[7] Third, commercial banks were allowed to continue engaging in private placements of all

private placement
The placement of a whole issue of securities with a single or a few large investors by a bank acting as a placing agent.

types of bonds and equities, corporate and otherwise. In a **private placement,** a bank seeks to find a large institutional buyer or investor such as another FI for a new securities issue. As such, the bank acts as an agent for a fee. By comparison, in a public offering of securities, a bank normally acts as a direct principal and has an underwriting stake in the issue. This principal position, such as in **firm commitment underwriting,** involves buying securities from the issuer at one price and seeking to resell them to the public at a slightly higher price. Failure to sell these securities can result in a major loss to the underwriter of publicly issued securities. Thus, the act distinguished between the private placement of securities, which was allowed, and public placement, which was not.

firm commitment underwriting
An underwriter buys securities from an issuer and reoffers them to the public at a slightly higher price.

For most of the 1933–63 period, commercial banks and investment banks generally appeared to be willing to abide by the letter and spirit of the Glass-Steagall Act. However, between 1963 and 1987, banks challenged restrictions on municipal revenue bond underwriting, commercial paper underwriting, discount brokerage, managing and advising of open- and closed-end mutual funds, underwriting of mortgage-backed securities, and selling annuities.[8] In most cases, the courts have eventually upheld these activities.[9]

With this onslaught and de facto erosion of the Glass-Steagall Act by legal interpretation, in April 1987 the Federal Reserve Board allowed commercial bank

---

[6] Today, many question the Pecora Commission's findings, believing that the slow growth in bank reserves and the money supply by the Federal Reserve lay at the heart of the post-crash recession. For a major critique of the facts underlying the Pecora Commission's findings and the Glass-Steagall Act, see G. J. Benston, *The Separation of Commercial and Investment Banking: The Glass-Steagall Act Revisited and Reconsidered* (New York: St. Martins Press, 1989); and G. J. Benston, "Universal Banking," *Journal of Economic Perspectives* 8 (1994), pp. 121–43. For a monetary explanation of the 1930–33 contraction, see M. Freidman and A. J. Schwartz, *A Monetary History of the United States, 1867–1960* (Princeton, NJ: Princeton University Press, 1963).

[7] A municipal general obligation bond is a bond issued by a state, city, or local government whose interest and principal payments are backed by the full faith and credit of that local government, that is, its full tax and revenue base.

[8] Municipal revenue bonds are more risky than municipal GO bonds, since their interest and principal are guaranteed only by the revenue from the projects they finance. One example would be the revenue from road tolls if the bond funded the building of a new section of highway.

[9] To see the type of issues involved, discount brokerage was held to be legal since it was not viewed as being the same as full-service brokerage supplied by securities firms. In particular, a full-service brokerage combines both the agency function of securities purchase along with investment advice (e.g., hot tips). By contrast, discount brokers only carry out the agency function of buying and selling securities for clients; they do not give investment advice. For further discussion of these issues, see M. Clark and A. Saunders, "Judicial Interpretation of Glass-Steagall: The Need for Legislative Action," *The Banking Law Journal* 97 (1980), pp. 721–40; and "Glass-Steagall Revisited: The Impact on Banks, Capital Markets, and the Small Investor," *The Banking Law Journal* 97 (1980), pp. 811–40.

FIGURE 21–1 A U.S. Bank Holding Company
and Its Bank and Section 20 Subsidiary

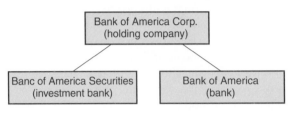

Section 20 affiliate

A securities subsidiary
of a U.S. bank holding
company through
which a banking
organization can
engage in investment
banking activities.

holding companies—such as Citigroup, the parent of
Citibank—to establish separate **Section 20 affiliates** as
investment banks. Through these Section 20 affiliates,
bank holding companies began to conduct all their
ineligible or gray area securities activities, such as
commercial paper underwriting, mortgage-backed
securities underwriting, and municipal revenue bond
underwriting.[10] Note the organizational structure of
Bank of America Corp., its bank, and the Section 20
subsidiary (or investment bank) in Figure 21–1.

Legally, these Section 20 subsidiaries did not violate Section 20 of the Glass-Steagall
Act, which restricts bank-securities firm affiliations as long as the revenue generated
from the securities underwriting activities restricted under the act amounted to less
than 50 percent of the total revenues they generated; that is, a majority of a Section 20
subsidiary's revenue does *not* come from ineligible security activities. To avoid legal
challenges, the Federal Reserve initially set the revenue limit at a very conservative
5 percent of total revenue (increased later to 10 percent, and then to 25 percent).

Significant changes occurred in 1997 as the Federal Reserve and the Office of the
Comptroller of the Currency (OCC) took actions to expand bank holding companies'
permitted activities. In particular, the Federal Reserve allowed commercial banks
to acquire existing investment banks directly rather than establish completely new
Section 20 investment banking subsidiaries.

The result was a number of mergers and acquisitions between commercial and
investment banks in 1997 through 2000. Some of the largest mergers included UBS's
US$12.0 billion purchase of Paine Webber in 2000, Credit Suisse First Boston's
purchase of Donaldson Lufkin Jenrette for US$11.5 billion in 2000, Deutsche
Bank's US$9.7 billion purchase of Banker's Trust in 1999, Citicorp's US$83 billion
merger with Travelers Group in April 1998, Banker's Trust's April 1997 acquisition
of Alex Brown for US$1.7 billion, NationsBank's 1997 purchase of Montgomery
Securities for more than US$1 billion, U.S. Bancorp's December 1997 acquisition of
Piper Jaffray for US$730 million, and Bank of America's June 1997 purchase of
Robertson Stephens for US$540 million (resold to Bank of Boston for US$800 million
in April 1998). In each case the banks stated that one motivation for the acquisition
was the desire to establish a presence in the securities business as laws separating
investment banking and commercial banking were changing. Also noted as a
motivation in these aquisitions was the opportunity to expand business lines, taking
advantage of economies of scale and scope to reduce overall costs and merge the
customer bases of the respective commercial and investment banks involved in the
acquisitions. The slumping stock market and U.S. economy in 2001–2003 resulted
in a reduction in these acquisitions.[11]

The erosion of the product barriers between the commercial and investment
banking industries was not one way.[12] Large investment banks such as Merrill

---

[10] In 1989 corporate bond and in 1990 corporate equities underwriting were added to the permitted list.

[11] K. P. Coyne, L. T. Mendonca, and G. Wilson, in "Can Banks Grow Beyond M&A?" *The McKinsey Quarterly* (2004),
conclude that for most large banks, further expansion will not necessarily yield dramatic scale-based savings in technology
and production development costs.

[12] J. P. Choi and C. Stefanadis, in "Financial Conglomerates, Informational Leverage, and Innovation: The Investment
Banking Connection," Michigan State University Working Paper, 2003, develop a model that shows that by expanding into
commercial banking and building lending relationships, an investment bank (IB) may erode the informational advantage
of rival IBs. In equilibrium, these financial conglomerates earn higher expected profits than pure investment banks.

Lynch increasingly sought to offer banking products. For example, in the late 1970s, Merrill Lynch introduced the cash management account (CMA), which allowed investors to own a money market mutual fund with cheque writing privileges into which bond and stock sale proceeds could be swept on a daily basis. This account allowed the investor to earn interest on cash held in a brokerage account. In addition, many investment banks acted as deposit brokers, who charge a fee to break large deposits into US$100,000 deposit units and place them in banks across the country. Further, investment banks have been major participants as traders and investors in the secondary market for LDC and other loans.

Finally, in recognition of the years of "homemade" deregulation by banks and securities firms described above, the U.S. Congress passed the Financial Services Modernization Act, which repealed the Glass-Steagall barriers between commercial banking and investment banking.[13] The bill, promoted as the biggest change in the regulation of financial institutions in nearly 70 years, allowed for the creation of "financial services holding companies" that could engage in banking activities *and* securities activities through a securities subsidiary (replacing the Section 20 subsidiary). The bill also allowed large national banks to place certain activities, including some securities underwritings, in direct bank subsidiaries regulated by the Office of the Comptroller of the Currency. Thus, after nearly 70 years of partial or complete separation between investment banking and commercial banking, the Financial Services Modernization Act of 1999 opened the door for the creation of full-service financial institutions in the United States similar to those that existed before 1933 and that exist in many other countries today.

Banking and Insurance

Prior to the passage of the Financial Services Modernization Act of 1999, very strong barriers restricted the entry of U.S. banks into insurance and vice versa. One notable exception was Travelers Corp.'s merger with Citicorp to form Citigroup in 1998, which to some extent proved to be a catalyst for the eventual passage of the 1999 act. Insurance activities can be either of the property & casualty kind (homeowners insurance, auto insurance) or of the life/health kind (term life insurance). Moreover, we must make a distinction between a bank selling insurance as an agent by selling other FIs' policies for a fee and a bank acting as an insurance underwriter and bearing the direct risk of underwriting losses. In general, the risks of insurance agency activities are quite low in loss potential compared to insurance underwriting. Certain types of insurance—for example, credit life insurance, mortgage insurance, and auto insurance—tend to have natural synergistic links to bank lending products.[14]

Prior to the Financial Services Modernization Act of 1999, banks were under very stringent restrictions when selling and underwriting almost every type of insurance. For example, national banks were restricted to offering credit-related

---

[13] The Financial Services Modernization Act also reduced the barriers between commercial banking, investment banking, and insurance (see below).

[14] See Saunders and Walter, *Universal Banking,* for an elaboration of these arguments. Further, D. Rule points out that bank/insurance company mergers produce portfolios that carry a mixture of insurance and banking exposure, which is likely to alter the diversification characteristics of the merged institutions; see "Risk Transfer Between Banks, Insurance Companies and Capital Markets," *Financial Stability Review,* December 2001. Canadian banks are permitted to sell some insurance products (e.g., travel insurance, and credit life insurance to support mortgages and loans) but since 2001, have been unable to provide information about property and casualty (P&C) insurance or referrals in their branches. This is primarily because of concerns about consumer privacy and protection and the potential for tied selling. Over the 1990s, Canadian life insurance companies have expanded from annuity-type offerings into a full range of mutual fund and investment offerings related to RRSPs, RRIFs, and pensions, etc.

life, accident, health, or unemployment insurance. Moreover, they could act as insurance agents only in small towns of less than 5,000 people (although they could sell insurance from these offices anywhere in the United States). Further, the Bank Holding Company Act of 1956 (and its 1970 amendments) and the Garn-St Germain Depository Institutions Act of 1982 placed severe restrictions on bank holding companies establishing separately capitalized insurance affiliates and on insurance companies acquiring banks.

One area where U. S. banks successfully survived legal challenges was in the area of annuities. In 1986, Nationsbank (which merged with Bank of America in 1997) started selling annuities and was aggressively challenged in court by the insurance industry. In the meantime, a large number of other banks began offering annuities as well. In 1995, the Supreme Court upheld the legality of banks' selling annuities, arguing they should be viewed more as investment products rather than as insurance products.[15] It is estimated that such sales add close to US$1 billion a year to bank profits.

Beginning in the early 1980s, several insurance companies and commercial firms found indirect ways to engage in banking activities. This was through the organizational mechanism of establishing **nonbank bank** subsidiaries. The 1956 Bank Holding Company Act legally defined a bank as an organization that both accepts demand deposits and makes commercial and industrial loans and severely limited the ability of an insurance company or commercial firm to acquire such a bank. An insurance company could get around this restrictive provision by buying a full-service bank and then divesting its demand deposits or commercial loans. This converted the bank into a nonbank bank. In 1987, the U.S. Congress passed the Competitive Equality Banking Act (CEBA), blocking the nonbank bank loophole. This essentially prevented the creation of any new nonbank banks by redefining a bank as any institution that accepts and is accepted for deposit insurance coverage. This meant that any new nonbank bank established after 1987 would have to forgo deposit insurance coverage, making it very difficult to raise deposits. Although nonbank banks established prior to 1987 were grandfathered by CEBA, their growth rates were capped.[16] Insurance companies found a way around this legislation as well by opening federally chartered thrifts. Indeed, under the Savings and Loan Holding Company Act of 1968 (and in direct contrast to the Bank Holding Company Act), any corporation or insurance firm can acquire one savings institution.

A great challenge to the Bank Holding Company Act's restrictions on bank-insurance company affiliations came from the 1998 merger between Citicorp and Travelers to create the largest financial services conglomerate in the United States. The primary activity of Travelers was insurance (life and property & casualty), while the primary activity of Citicorp was banking (both also were engaged in securities activities: Citicorp through its Section 20 subsidiary and Travelers through its

nonbank bank
A bank divested of its commercial loans and/or demand deposits.

[15] K. A. Carow, in "The Wealth Effects of Allowing Bank Entry into the Insurance Industry," Indiana University Working Paper, 1999, found that bank stock prices did not, on average, change significantly at the announcement of this act. However, life insurance companies' stock prices fell significantly. PC insurer stock prices dropped as well, but less significantly than life insurers. Around the Citicorp-Travelers Group merger, he found that life insurance companies and large banks had significant stock price increases, while small banks, health insurers, and PC insurers' stock price changes were not significantly affected. See "Citicorp-Travelers Group Merger: Challenging Barriers between Banking and Insurance," *Journal of Banking and Finance* 25 (2001), pp. 1553–71.

[16] Specifically, nonbank banks established before March 5, 1987, were allowed to continue in business but were limited to a maximum growth in assets of 7 percent during any 12-month period beginning one year after the act's passage. It also permitted those nonbank banks that were allowed to remain in business to engage only in the activities in which they were engaged as of March 1987 and limited the cross-marketing of products and services by nonbank banks and affiliated companies.

earlier acquisition of Smith-Barney and Salomon Brothers). Under the Bank Holding Company Act, the Federal Reserve had up to five years to formally approve the merger. The Federal Reserve gave initial approval in September 1998. (In a turnaround in strategy, Citigroup sold most of the Travelers Property/Casualty Insurance unit in 2002.)

The Financial Services Modernization Act of 1999 completely changed the landscape for insurance activities (and implicitly ratified the Citicorp-Travelers merger) as it allowed bank holding companies to open insurance underwriting affiliates and insurance companies to open commercial bank as well as securities firm affiliates through the creation of financial service holding companies (FSHC). With the passage of this act, banks no longer have to fight legal battles in states such as Texas and Rhode Island to overcome restrictions on their ability to sell insurance in these states. Indeed, by 2002 more than 50 percent of all U.S. banks sold insurance products, totalling a record US$3.49 billion in insurance commissions and premium income. The insurance industry applauded the act, as it forced banks that underwrite and sell insurance to operate under the same set of state regulations (pertaining to their insurance lines) as insurance companies. Under the new act, a financial services holding company that engages in commercial banking, investment banking, and insurance activities will be functionally regulated. This means that the holding company's banking activities will be regulated by bank regulators, its securities activities will be regulated by the SEC, and its insurance activities will be regulated by state insurance regulators (since insurance in the U.S. is not regulated at the federal level—see Chapter 3).

Commercial Banking and Commerce

The 1863 National Bank Act severely limited the ability of nationally chartered banks to expand into commercial activities by taking direct equity stakes in firms. Provisions of the National Bank Act limit participation by national banks in nonbank subsidiaries to those activities permitted by statute or regulation. Banks could engage only in commercial sector activities "incidental to banking" and even then, only through service or subsidiary corporations. However, broader powers to take equity stakes exist when a borrower is in distress. In this case, national banks have unlimited powers to acquire corporate stock and hold it for up to 10 years.

While the direct holding of equity by national banks has been constrained since 1863, restrictions on the commercial activities of bank holding companies are more recent phenomena. In particular, the 1970 amendments to the 1956 Bank Holding Company Act required bank holding companies to divest themselves of nonbank-related subsidiaries over a 10-year period following the amendment. When Congress passed the amendments, bank holding companies owned some 3,500 commercial sector subsidiaries ranging from public utilities to transportation and manufacturing firms. Nevertheless, prior to late 1999 bank holding companies could hold up to 4.9 percent of the voting shares in any commercial firm without regulatory approval.[17]

The Financial Services Modernization Act of 1999 changed restrictions on ownership limits imposed on financial services holding companies. Commercial banks belonging to a financial service holding company can now take a controlling interest in a nonfinancial enterprise provided that two conditions are met.

---

[17] Under the Bank Holding Company Act, *control* is defined as when a holding company has an equity stake exceeding 25 percent in a subsidiary bank or affiliate.

First, the investment cannot be made for an indefinite period of time. The act did not provide an explicit time limit and simply states that the investment can be "held for a period of time to enable the sale or disposition thereof on a reasonable basis consistent with the financial viability of the [investment]." Second, the bank cannot become actively involved in the management of the corporation in which it invests. Nevertheless, corporate stocks or equities are still conspicuously absent from most bank balance sheets (see Chapter 2).[18]

Nonbank Financial Service Firms and Commerce

In comparison with the barriers separating banking and either securities, insurance, or commercial sector activities, the barriers among nonbank financial service firms and commercial firms are generally much weaker. Indeed, in recent years, nonbank financial service firms and commercial firms have faced few barriers to entering into and exiting from various areas of nonbank financial service activity. For example, Travelers Group acquired Salomon Brothers in 1997, one year after acquiring Smith Barney.

Importantly, however, the passage of the Financial Services Modernization Act of 1999 standardized the relationship among financial service sectors (commercial banking, insurance, investment banking) and commerce. Specifically, a financial services holding company is now defined as holding a minimum of 85 percent of its assets in financial assets (i.e., a maximum of 15 percent in commercial sector or real assets).

Concept Questions

1. How has the Financial Services Modernization Act of 1999 opened the doors for the establishment of full-service financial institutions in the United States?

ACTIVITY RESTRICTIONS IN OTHER COUNTRIES

We have just described the barriers to product expansion and financial conglomeration in the United States. Appendix 21A, located at the book's Web site (www.mcgrawhill. ca/college/saunders), compares the range of activities permitted to U.S. commercial banks with the range of product activities permitted to banks in other major industrialized countries and financial centers.[19] Figure 21–2 shows the highly diversified product structure of the Swiss universal bank Credit Suisse First Boston. Universal banks offer not just investment banking services, but also commercial lending, foreign exchange, and custody and cash management services. Universal banks include Citigroup, J. P. Morgan Chase, UBS, Deutsche Bank, Credit Suisse First Boston, and to a lesser extent Bank of America. However, with the possible exception of Japan, U.S. banks are still among the most constrained of all the major industrialized countries in terms of the range of nonbank product activities permitted.[20]

---

[18] S. Park, in "Effects of the Affiliation of Banking and Commerce on the Firm's Investment and the Bank's Risk," *Journal of Banking and Finance* 24 (2000), pp. 1629–50, finds that a bank's holding of a borrowing firm's equity reduces the agency conflict between the firm and the bank, but increases the monitoring need of uninformed debtholders. The bank's risk exposure can increase in one of two ways. With a large equity share, the bank has more incentive to allow the firm to undertake risky projects. Further, when it has control over the bank, the firm may force the bank to finance its risky projects.

[19] See also J. R. Barth, R. D. Brumbaugh Jr., and J. A. Wilcox, "The Repeal of Glass-Steagall and the Advent of Broad Banking," Office of the Comptroller of the Currency, Economic and Policy Analysis Working Paper 2000–5, April 2000.

[20] Many of Japan's postwar regulations were modeled on those of the United States. Thus, Article 65 in Japan separates commercial banking from investment banking in a similar fashion to the Glass-Steagall Act. However, Japan has recently passed a major deregulation law that will considerably weaken the historic barriers between commercial and investment banking in that country. See T. Ito, T. Kiso, and H. Uchibori, "The Impact of the Big Bang on the Japanese Financial System," Fuji Research Paper No. 9, Fuji Research Institute Corporation, Tokyo, Japan, May 1998.

FIGURE 21–2   The Structure of a Universal Bank: CS Holding Group

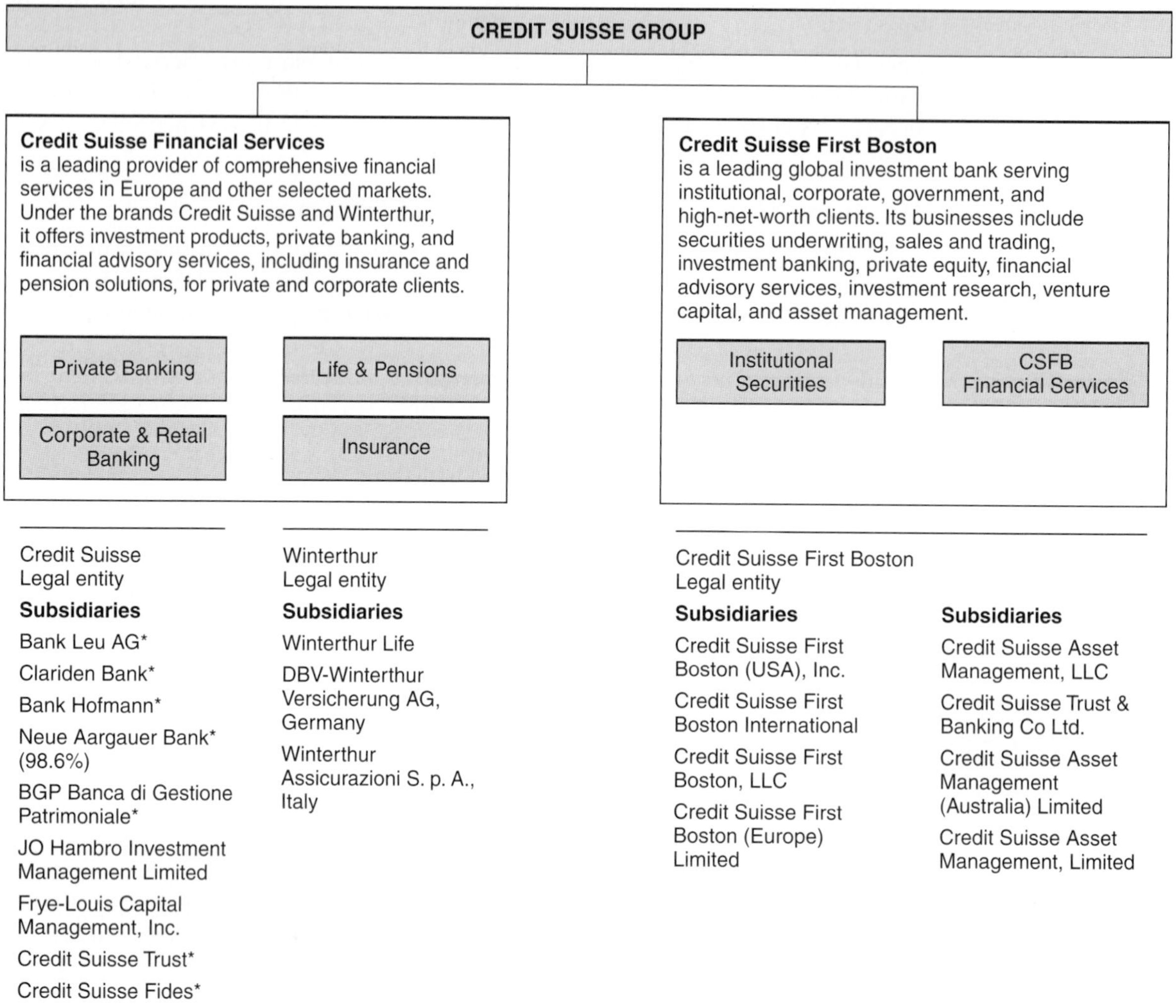

CREDIT SUISSE GROUP

Credit Suisse Financial Services
is a leading provider of comprehensive financial services in Europe and other selected markets. Under the brands Credit Suisse and Winterthur, it offers investment products, private banking, and financial advisory services, including insurance and pension solutions, for private and corporate clients.

| Private Banking | Life & Pensions |
| Corporate & Retail Banking | Insurance |

Credit Suisse First Boston
is a leading global investment bank serving institutional, corporate, government, and high-net-worth clients. Its businesses include securities underwriting, sales and trading, investment banking, private equity, financial advisory services, investment research, venture capital, and asset management.

| Institutional Securities | CSFB Financial Services |

Credit Suisse Legal entity	Winterthur Legal entity	Credit Suisse First Boston Legal entity	
Subsidiaries	**Subsidiaries**	**Subsidiaries**	**Subsidiaries**
Bank Leu AG*	Winterthur Life	Credit Suisse First Boston (USA), Inc.	Credit Suisse Asset Management, LLC
Clariden Bank*	DBV-Winterthur Versicherung AG, Germany	Credit Suisse First Boston International	Credit Suisse Trust & Banking Co Ltd.
Bank Hofmann*	Winterthur Assicurazioni S. p. A., Italy	Credit Suisse First Boston, LLC	Credit Suisse Asset Management (Australia) Limited
Neue Aargauer Bank* (98.6%)		Credit Suisse First Boston (Europe) Limited	Credit Suisse Asset Management, Limited
BGP Banca di Gestione Patrimoniale*			
JO Hambro Investment Management Limited			
Frye-Louis Capital Management, Inc.			
Credit Suisse Trust*			
Credit Suisse Fides*			

* Direct holding of Credit Suisse Group.

Source: Credit Suisse Group Web site, *www.credit-suisse.com*.

This has created continuing pressure to bring U.S. banks' activity powers in line with those of their global competitors and counterparts such as those in the EU and Switzerland.

In the next section, we look at the issues that have been raised in Canada and the U.S. and will continue to be raised whenever the question of expanded product (or more universal) powers for banks and other FIs arise.

Concept Questions

1. How does the range of product activities permitted for Canadian and U.S. commercial banks compare to that of banks in other major industrialized countries?

FIGURE 21–3 **Alternative Organizational Forms for Nonbank Product Expansions of Banking Organizations**

(a) Full Universal

Bank activities	Securities activities	Other activities

(b) Universal-Subsidiary

Bank parent

Other activities — Securities activities subsidiary

(c) Financial Services Holding Company (FSHC)

Financial services holding company

Bank subsidiary — Financial services subsidiary (securities) — Other activities

ISSUES INVOLVED IN THE DIVERSIFICATION OF PRODUCT OFFERINGS

Whether the debate concerns existing activities or expansion into securities, insurance, or commerce, similar issues arise. These include

1. Safety and soundness issues.
2. Economy of scale and scope issues.
3. Conflict of interest issues.
4. Deposit insurance issues.
5. Regulatory oversight issues.
6. Competition issues.

Canadian banks have dominated the investment banking and securities industry in Canada since their takeover of the independent securities firms in the late 1980s and early 1990s as discussed in Chapter 4. However, the regulation of banking functions is carried out by the Office of the Superintendent of Financial Institutions (OSFI), whereas securities regulation is in the hands of the provincial and territorial regulators. The six issues listed above are evaluated in the context of banks and securities firms, but can be extended to consider the last cross-pillar issue: the merger of banks and insurance companies.

www.osfi-bsif.gc.ca

Consider the three alternative organizational structures for linking banking and securities activities in Figure 21–3. The financial services holding company structure in panel (c) of the figure is the organizational form within which we will evaluate the six issues just identified.

In Figure 21–3, panel (a) shows the fully integrated universal bank, where banking and securities activities are conducted in different departments of a single organization. This is typical of the way in which large banks in Germany, such as Deutsche Bank, engage in securities activities. Panel (b) shows the universal subsidiary model where a bank engages in securities activities through a separately owned securities affiliate. This is typical of the way in which banks in Canada and in the United Kingdom conduct their securities activities. This is also the model adopted to allow U.S. nationally chartered banks to expand their nonbank activities.

Note that the degree of bank-nonbank integration is much less with the financial services holding company model [panel (c)] than with either the full or subsidiary universal banking model.[21] For example, in the universal subsidiary model, the bank holds a direct ownership stake in the securities subsidiary.

---

[21] For a comparative analysis of these three models, see Saunders and Walter, *Universal Banking.*

By comparison, in the financial services holding company model, the bank and securities subsidiary are separate companies with their own equity capital; the link is that their equity is held by the same parent company, the financial services holding company.[22]

Safety and Soundness Concerns

With respect to the securities activities of commercial banks and the possible effects on their safety and soundness, two key questions arise: How risky is securities underwriting? And if losses occur for a securities subsidiary, can this cause the affiliated bank to fail?

The Risk of Securities Underwriting

firm commitment offering
Securities offered from the issuing firm, purchased by an underwriter.

To understand the risk of securities underwriting, you must understand the mechanics of firm commitment securities offerings. In a **firm commitment offering,** the underwriter purchases securities directly from the issuing firm (say, at $99 per share) and then reoffers them to the public or the market at large at a slightly higher price, say, $99.50. The difference between the underwriter's buy price ($99) and the public offer price ($99.50) is the spread that compensates the underwriter for accepting the principal risk of placing the securities with outside investors as well as any administrative and distribution costs associated with the underwriting. In our simple example of a $0.50 spread, the maximum revenue the underwriter can gain from underwriting the issue is $0.50 times the number of shares issued. Thus, if 1 million shares were offered, the maximum gross revenue for the underwriting would be $0.50 times 1,000,000, or $500,000. Note that once the public offering has been made and the price specified in the prospectus, the underwriter cannot raise the price over the offering period. In this example, the underwriter could not raise the price above $99.50 even after determining that the market valued the shares more highly.[23]

The upside return from underwriting is normally capped, but the downside risk is not, and can be very large. The downside risk arises if the underwriter overprices the public offering, setting the public offer price higher than outside investors' valuations. As a result, the underwriter will be unable to sell the shares during the public offering period and will have to lower the price to get rid of the inventory of unsold shares, especially because this inventory is often financed through issuing commercial paper or repurchase agreements. In our example, if the underwriter has to lower the offering price to $99, the gross revenue from the underwriting will be zero, since this is the price paid to the issuing firm. Any price less than $99 generates a loss. For example, suppose that the issue can be placed only at $97; the underwriter's losses will be $2 times 1,000,000 shares, or $2 million.

There are a number of possible reasons why an underwriter may take a big loss or big hit on an underwriting. The first is simply overestimating the market's demand for the shares. The second is that in the short period between setting the public offering price and seeking to sell the securities to the public, there may be a major drop in security values in general.

---

[22] In general, the advantages of the full universal model is greater resource flexibility and integration of commercial bank and investment bank product lines. Its perceived disadvantages include greater monopoly power and greater potential conflicts of interest.

[23] The offering period is usually a maximum of 10 business days.

FIGURE 21–4   The Role of Firewalls in Protecting Banks

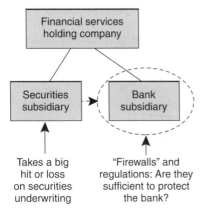

Takes a big hit or loss on securities underwriting

"Firewalls" and regulations: Are they sufficient to protect the bank?

If Underwriting Losses Occur for the Securities Affiliate, Can This Cause a Bank to Fail?

Proponents of allowing banking organizations to expand their securities activities argue that the answer to this question is no, as long as the bank subsidiary is sufficiently insulated from the risk problems of the securities affiliate. As noted earlier, in a financial services holding company structure, the bank is legally a separate corporation from the securities affiliate. As shown in Figure 21–4, its only link to its securities affiliate is indirect, through the holding company that owns a controlling equity stake in both the bank and securities affiliate. However, even this indirect link raises the concern that the effects of losses by the securities affiliate could threaten the safety of the bank unless firewalls or regulatory barriers are introduced to insulate the bank against such losses (see Figure 21–4).

There are at least three ways a bank could be harmed by losses of a securities affiliate in a holding company structure. First, a holding company might be tempted to drain capital and funds from the bank by requiring excessive dividends and fees from the bank (this is called *upstreaming*). The holding company could then *downstream* these funds to protect the failing securities affiliate from insolvency. As a result, the bank would be weakened at the expense (or because) of the securities affiliate.

A second way in which a bank could be harmed is through interaffiliate loans. For example, the holding company may induce the bank to extend loans to the securities affiliate to keep it afloat even though such loans are excessively risky.

The third way in which a bank may be affected is through a contagious confidence problem. Specifically, difficulty of a securities firm subsidiary may result in a negative information signal to financial service consumers and investors regarding the quality of the management of the holding company and its bank affiliate. Such negative information can create incentives for large depositors and investors to withdraw their money from the bank in the manner described in Chapter 19. This bank run possibility seems more likely to occur if the bank and its securities affiliate share similar names and logos, which in general they do.

Obviously, a big hit taken by the securities subsidiary can potentially threaten the safety and solvency of the affiliated bank, especially through the confidence effect.[24] However, at least two countervailing risk-reducing effects may enhance the safety and soundness of a bank indirectly linked to a securities subsidiary in a holding company framework. The first effect is a **product diversification benefit.** A well-diversified financial services firm (financial services holding company) potentially enjoys a far more stable earnings and profit stream over time than does

product diversification benefit
Stabilization of earnings and profits resulting from a well-diversified financial services holding company.

---

[24] For example, the investment banking activities of CIBC World Markets in New York in providing "loans" to special purpose entities (SPEs) of Enron led to CIBC agreeing to pay US$2.4 to settle an Enron shareholder's class-action lawsuit and an additional US$250 million to Enron in August, 2005, amounts which represented one-tenth of CIBC's market capitalization at the time. This seriously weakened its balance sheet, affecting future growth. Analysts downgraded the company's ratings and CIBC's shares dropped from $80.64 to $74.55 in one day. Although CIBC admitted no wrongdoing, the damage was done to its reputation, creating a difficult first day for its new Chairman, Gerry McCaughey, who took over from John Hunkin 24 hours before the announcement. See "A tough lesson learned," *Canadian Business*, August 15–August 28, 2005, Vol. 78., Iss. 16, p. 76 and K. Macklem, "A Bank's Enron Bomb," *Maclean's*, August 15, 2005, Vol. 118, Iss. 33, p. 39.

a product-specialized bank. As demand and cost shifts reduce earnings in one activity area, such as banking, offsetting demand and cost shifts may take place in other activity areas, such as securities or insurance, increasing the holding company's earnings. Advocates argue that a more stable and diversified earnings stream for the holding company enables it to act as a source of strength in keeping the affiliated bank well capitalized.

In the academic literature, a number of empirical studies have evaluated the gains from bank activity diversification by looking at the correlations of accounting earnings for segmented financial firms or industries and analyzing correlations between firms' stock market returns. Essentially, the lower these correlations, the greater the potential gains from activity diversification and the lower the coefficient of variation (COV)—the standard deviation divided by the mean—of a banking organization's earnings flows. Other studies have sought to evaluate the potential effects of activity diversification on the risk of failure (ROF) of banks and simulate the effects of bank-nonbank mergers (MS) on bank risk. We summarize the findings of a number of these COV, ROF, and MS studies in Table 21–2.

As you can see from Table 21–2, the majority of the studies find that a financial services holding company's risk could be reduced by diversification. However, the optimal proportion of investment in individual nonbank product lines often falls in the 5 to 25 percent range. This suggests that excessive product expansion in some nonbank lines could actually increase the total risk exposure of a banking organization.[25]

Economies of Scale and Scope

A second issue concerning the expansion of banks into securities and other nonbank activities is the potential for additional economies of scale and scope. However, most studies find cost-based economies of scope are negligible, although revenue-based economies of scope may arise for the largest FIs. Arguably, the pre-1997 restrictions between banks and their Section 20 investment banking affiliates covering finance, management and cross marketing severely limited economies of scope and related revenue and cost synergies. Post-1997, and more so, post-1999 U.S. financial service firms may realize greater economies of scope as restrictions are removed and the FSHCs become more universal in product scope.[26]

Conflicts of Interest

A third issue—the potential for conflicts of interest—lies at the very heart of opposition to an expansion of banking powers into other financial service areas. The two principal questions that arise are (1) the potential conflicts of interest arising from the expansion of banks' securities activities and (2) the type of incentive structures that change *potential* conflicts into *actual* conflicts.

---

[25] Much of the research has been conducted on U.S. financial services companies as shown in Table 21–2. For a review of the literature and its implications for the Canadian financial system, see C. A. Northcott, "Competition in Banking: A Review of the Literature," *Bank of Canada Working Paper 2004-24*.

[26] See T. F. Huertas, "Redesigning Regulation: The Future of Finance in the United States," Jackson Hole, Wyoming, August 22, 1987, mimeographed; and J. R. Barth, R. D. Brumbaugh Jr., and J. A. Wilcox, "The Repeal of Glass-Steagall and the Advent of Broad Banking," Office of the Comptroller of the Currency, Economic and Policy Analysis Working Paper 2000–5, April 2000. Nevertheless, Saunders and Walter, *Universal Banking,* could find no evidence of cost economies of scope for the world's 100 largest banks, many of which are universal banks.

TABLE 21–2   Review of Selected Studies of the Risk of Nonbank Activities*

Study	Time Period	Methodology[†]	Nonbank Activities Reduce BHC Risk
Johnson and Meinster (1974)	1954–69 (annual data)	COV	Yes. Impermissible activities: insurance agents and brokers, portfolio holding and investment companies, and real estate agents, analysis brokers and managers. Studies 13 activities. Portfolio analysis based on earnings and cash flow concludes there are diversification benefits into nonbank activities but that the benefits are sensitive to the percentage of assets in each activity.
Heggestad (1975)	1953–67	COV	Yes. Impermissible activities: insurance agents and brokers, and real estate agents, brokers, managers, holding, and investment companies, and lessors of R.R., oil, and mining properties. Banking is among the riskiest activities based on the coefficient of variation in profits. [Studies activities of one bank holding company (BHC) prior to 1970 BHC Act amendments.]
Eiseman (1976)	1961–68 (monthly data)	Industry (portfolio) selection model (COV)	Yes. Banking is minimum-risk activity. Lowest-risk BHC includes permissible activity of sales finance and impermissible activities of insurance and investment banking. Highest-risk BHC includes permissible activity of data processing. Studies 20 activities.
Jessee and Seelig (1977)		COV	No. Risk reduction is not related to share of nonbank investment.
Meinster and Johnson (1979)	1973–77	ROF	Yes. BHCs effectively diversified but slightly increased probability of capital impairment with debt financing. (Sample of only two BHCs in seven permissible activities of leasing, consumer finance, mortgage banking, bank management consulting, financial services, and foreign bank services.)
Boyd, Hanweek, and Pithyachanyakul (1980)	1971–77	COV/ROF	Yes, but limited. Permissible activities: mortgage banking, factoring, consumer finance, credit card, loan servicing, investment advisers, leasing (except auto), community welfare, data processing, credit life, accident and health insurance agents, and underwriters and management consulting.
			No (any investment increases probability of bankruptcy). Permissible activities: commercial and sales finance, industrial banks, trust services, auto leasing. (Study covered only permissible activities.)
Stover (1982)	1959–68	Wealth-maximization debt capacity	Yes. Impermissible activities: S&Ls, investment banking, land development, fire and casualty insurance. Measures equity returns and diversification benefits of 14 permissible and impermissible activities in wealth-maximization model.

(continued)

TABLE 21–2   Review of Selected Studies of the Risk of Nonbank Activities* (continued)

Study	Time Period	Methodology†	Nonbank Activities Reduce BHC Risk
Wall and Eisenbeis (1984)	1970–80	COV	Yes. Impermissible activities: S&Ls, security brokers and dealers, life insurance, general merchandise stores, lessor of R.R. property. Permissible activities personal and business credit agency. Banking neither highest nor lowest risk based on coefficient of variation. Results are sensitive to time period.
Wall (1984)	Select dates	Bond returns	No significant effect.
Wall and Eisenbeis (1984)	Select dates (monthly data)	Bond returns	No. (Study covered only permissible activity of discount brokerage.)
Litan (1985)	1978–83	COV	As likely to reduce volatility of BHC income as to increase it. (Sample of 31 large BHCs.)
Boyd and Graham (1986)	1971–83 (1971–77 and 1978–83)	ROF	Entire period: no significant relationship between nonbank activity and any risk or return measures. Less stringent policy period (1971–77): no nonbank activity is positively related to risk. More stringent policy period (1978–83): weak negative relationship between nonbank activity and risk.
Wall (1986)	1976–84	ROF	Nonbank activity either decreases BHC risk slightly or has no impact. The positive relationship between nonbank risk and BHCrisk, BHC leverage, and bank risk is consistent with the possibility that management preferences influence the riskiness of the BHC's subsidiaries and determine the use of leverage to influence overall risk.
Boyd and Graham (1988)	1971–84 (annual data)	COV/ROF/MS	Study covers six impermissible activities. Yes for life insurance. The standard deviation and bankruptcy risk measures indicate risk is likely to increase for real estate development, securities firms, and property-casualty insurance activities and increase slightly for other real estate and insurance agency and brokerage activities. BHC is lowest-risk activity.
Brewer (1988)	1979–85	COV	Yes. One standard deviation increase in investment in nonbank subsidiaries leads to 6-basis-point drop in BHC risk (approximately 7 percent).
Brewer (1988)	1979–83 (daily data)	COV	Yes. One standard deviation increase in investment in nonbank subsidiaries leads to an 8 to 11 percent basis point drop in BHC risk. Results are sensitive to the time period studied.
Brewer, Fortier, and Pavel (1988)	1980, 1982 and 1986 and 1979–83	COV/MS	Yes. Impermissible activities of insurance agents and brokers, property and casualty and life insurance underwriting. Investment of 5 percent or less for any of the tested activities would not increase the variance of the BHC significantly;

(continued)

TABLE 21–2   (continued)

Study	Time Period	Methodology[†]	Nonbank Activities Reduce BHC Risk
			the investment of 25 percent or more for all but the above-listed activities would increase the riskiness of the BHC significantly. Examination of the impact of total investment in nonbank activities regardless of the specific activities finds increases in nonbank activity tend to lower BHC risk significantly.
Wall, Reichart, and Mohanty (1993)	1981–89	COV	Yes, for insurance and real estate. The securities brokerage industry does not enter the efficient portfolio.
Saunders and Walter (1994)	1984–88	COV/MS	Yes. Looks at 250,000 possible merger combinations among the largest FIs in the United States. Finds that a full multiple activity universal bank with optimal investments in different financial service activities can lower risk by as much as one-third compared to specialized banks.
Berger, Demsetz, and Strahan (1999)	1985–97	MS	Yes. Looks at ability to diversify bank risk after a merger or acquisition.
Fields and Fraser (1999)	1992	ROF	Yes. Looks at moral hazard risk reduction as banks enter securities underwriting.
Cornett, Ors, and Tehranian (2002)	1987–97	COV	No significant effect. Looks at commercial bank entry into underwriting.
Roten and Mullineaux (2002)	1995–1998	MS	No. Finds only limited evidence that commercial bank Section 20 subsidiaries perform differently from investment banks.

*Permissible activities refer to those nonbank activities currently permissible, whether or not they were permissible at the time of the study. Impermissible activities also include activities not yet ruled upon by the Board at the time of the study.
[†]COV—analysis of coefficient of variation of rates of return of banking and nonbanking activities.
ROF—risk of failure (bankruptcy analysis).
MS—simulated merger analysis.

Source: From "Bank Risk from Nonbank Activities," by E. Brewer, D. Fortier, and C. Pavel, in *Economic Perspective,* July–August 1988, pp. 14–26; A. Saunders and I. Walter, *Universal Banking in the U.S.?* (New York: Oxford University Press, 1994), Chapter 6; and authors' research.

Six Potential Conflicts of Interest

Conflicts of interest that arise when commercial banks, investment banks, and insurance companies combine operations have been prominent in financial markets throughout the early 2000s. In this section, we discuss the six most common potential conflicts of interest identified by regulators and academics.[27]

Salesperson's Stake   Critics argue that when banks have the power to sell non-bank products, bank employees no longer dispense dispassionate advice to their customers about which product to buy. Instead, they have a salesperson's stake in

---

[27] See A. Saunders, "Conflicts of Interest: An Economic View," in *Deregulating Wall Street,* ed. I. Walter (New York: John Wiley & Sons, 1985), pp. 207–30; M. Puri, "Commercial Banks in Investment Banking: Conflict of Interest or Certification Role?" *Journal of Financial Economics* 40 (1996), pp. 373–401; I. Walter, "Conflicts of Interest in Merger Advisory Services," Working Paper, New York University, January 2004; L. Allen, J. Jagtiani, S. Peristiani, and A. Saunders, "The Role of Commercial Bank Advisors in Mergers and Acquisitions," *Journal of Money, Credit, and Banking,* forthcoming; S. Baharath, S. Dahiya, A. Saunders, and A. Srinivasan, "So What Do I Get? The Bank's View of Lending Relationships," Working Paper, New York University, 2004; and L. Allen and S. Peristiani, "Conflicts of Interest in Merger Advisory Services," Working Paper, Baruch College, CUNY, January 2004.

pushing the bank's own products, often to the disadvantage of the customer. For example, in 2002, Citigroup was under investigation from securities regulators, who were investigating whether Citigroup's stock research was tainted and whether its transactions with corporations and top corporate executives illegally helped the firm win lucrative underwriting contracts.

Stuffing Fiduciary Accounts   Suppose a bank is acting as a securities underwriter and is unable to place these securities in a public offering. To avoid being exposed to potential losses, the bank may "stuff" these unwanted securities in accounts managed by its own trust department and over which it has discretionary investment powers. For example, a U.S. judge threw money manager Alan Bond, CIO of Albriond Capital, in jail after he was convicted on charges of allocating winning trades to his own brokerage account and saddling his clients' accounts with losers.

Bankruptcy Risk Transference   Assume that a bank has a loan outstanding to a firm whose credit or bankruptcy risk has increased to the private knowledge of the banker. With this private knowledge, the banker may have an incentive to induce the firm to issue bonds underwritten by the bank's securities affiliate to an unsuspecting public. The proceeds of this bond issue could then be used to pay down the bank loan. As a result, the bank would have transferred the borrowing firm's credit risk from itself to less-informed outside investors, while the securities affiliate also earned an underwriting fee. For example, in 2002 CIBC, J. P. Morgan Chase and Citigroup faced several investor lawsuits over funding deals for high-profile bankruptcies such as Enron. Investors say that because of their lending relationships, the banks knew or should have known of the problems at these companies.

Third-Party Loans   To ensure that an underwriting goes well, a bank may make cheap loans to third-party investors on the implicit condition that this loan is used to purchase securities underwritten by its securities affiliate.

Tie-Ins   A bank may use its lending powers to coerce or "tie in" a customer to the products sold by its securities affiliate. For example, the bank may threaten to credit ration unless the customer agrees to let the bank's securities affiliate do its securities underwritings. In the early 2000s, CIBC's "loans" to Enron were in anticipation of other services the company might send its way.

Information Transfer   In acting as a lender, the bank may become privy to certain inside information about its customers or rivals that it can use to set the prices, or help the distribution of securities offerings by its affiliate. This information could also flow from the securities affiliate to the bank. Such conflicts are potentially present when M&A activity is involved along with new security issues and loan originations.[28] Such was the case with J. P. Morgan Chase and Citigroup, FIs involved as lead advisors *and* lead bankers in Enron's failed merger attempt with Dynegy in 2001. The two FIs had large balance sheets and boasted of their ability to provide both loans and advice in the merger. However, the FIs lost their bragging rights for pulling off a difficult deal as Dynegy pulled out of the merger stating they were deprived of enough information on the deal and then learning that Enron had been hiding billions of dollars in debt and had been reporting exaggerated profits for years. Enron ended up declaring bankruptcy in December 2001 and J. P. Morgan Chase and Citigroup ended up losing between US$800 million and US$900 million each on loans to Enron.

---

[28] L. Allen, J. Jagtiani, and A. Saunders, in "The Role of Bank Advisors in Mergers and Acquisitions," *Journal of Money, Credit, and Banking,* forthcoming, find that, in their merger and acquisition advisory function the certification effect of commercial banks dominates the conflict-of-interest effect. See also L. Allen and S. Peristiani, "Conflicts of Interest in Merger Advisory Services," 2004 Working Paper, for evidence on this type of conflict of interest.

Potential Conflicts of Interest and Their Actual Exploitation

On their own these conflicts appear to be extremely troublesome. Remember, however, that specific and general checks and balances limit their exploitation. Many of these conflicts are likely to remain potential rather than become actual conflicts of interest. Specifically, many of these conflicts, such as tie-ins and third-party loans, breach existing bank regulations and laws. Also, internal barriers or **Chinese walls** in most banks prohibit internal information transfers when they potentially conflict with the best interests of the customer. Further, sales of debt issues to a less-informed public to pay down bank loans may result in future lawsuits against the underwriter once investors discover their losses.[29]

More generally, conflicts of interest are exploitable only under three conditions. First, markets for bank services are uncompetitive so that banks have monopoly power over their customers, for example, in making loans. Second, information flows between the customer and the bank are imperfect or asymmetric so that the bank possesses an information advantage over its customers. Third, the bank places a relatively low value on its reputation. The discovery of having exploited a conflict can result in considerable market and regulatory penalties.[30]

Chinese wall
An internally imposed barrier within an organization that limits the flow of confidential client information among departments or areas.

Deposit Insurance

A traditional argument against expanded powers is that the explicit and implicit protection given to banks by deposit insurance coverage give banks a competitive advantage over other financial service firms (see Chapter 19). For example, because bank deposits up to $100,000 are covered by explicit deposit insurance, banks are able to raise funds at subsidized, lower-cost rates than are available to traditional securities firms. This may allow them to pass on these lower costs in cheaper loans to their affiliates. This advantage may result if bank regulators regard certain large banking organizations as being too-big-to-fail (TBTF), thereby encouraging these institutions to take excessive risks such as placing aggressive underwriting bids for new issues.

Regulatory Oversight

The regulation of integrated FIs in Canada is complex, involving both federal and provincial bodies as discussed in Chapter 2 and illustrated by Table 2–7. OSFI has been created as the primary prudential regulator for large federally-regulated FIs (banks, savings and loans, life insurance, property & casualty insurance), but the regulation of securities activities are handled provincially. The creation of a national regulatory body for securities firms such as the U.S. Securities and Exchange Commission is under discussion. As well, the regulatory issues regarding the deregulation of FI activities in individual countries is finding its way into the transnational regulations proposed by Basel II for internationally active banks, as discussed in Chapter 20. CIBC's Enron payouts, with their impact on CIBC's Tier 1 capital and thus the safety and soundness of the Canadian financial system, will also trigger discussions of securities operations risks for integrated banks even though the impact came from operations within the ambit of the SEC.

www.sec.gov

---

[29] In particular, the underwriter may be accused of lack of due diligence in not disclosing information in the new issue's prospectus.

[30] R. G. Rajan models these incentives in "A Theory of the Costs and Benefits of Universal Banking," C. R. S. P. Working Paper no. 346, University of Chicago, 1992. See also G. Kanatas and J. Qi, "Underwriting by Commercial Banks: Conflicts of Interest vs. Scope Economics," *Journal of Money, Credit, and Banking*, February 1998, pp. 119–133. For an assessment of the reputational costs of exploiting conflicts of interest, see R. Smith and I. Walter, *Street Smarts: Leadership, Conduct and Shareholder Value in the Securities Industry* (Boston: Harvard Business School Press, 1997).

Competition

The final issue concerns the effects of bank activity expansions on competition in investment banking product lines. Since the Bank Act revisions of the 1980s, banks have come to dominate investment banking activities in Canada, as we discussed in Chapter 4. It could be argued that the banks have had greater monopoly power over capital markets in Canada, but this has been mitigated by the globalization of the investment banking industry which allows Canadian companies to access international markets through cross-listing of shares on U.S. markets. In addition, large U.S. investment banking firms have entered the Canadian market, providing:

Increased capital market access for large and small Canadian firms;[31]

Lowered commissions and fees as both Canadian bank-owned firms and international investment bankers compete for large securities issues such as TD Canada Trust's acquisition of BankNorth and the Molson and Coors breweries merger in 2004;[32]

A Reduction in the degree of underpricing of new issues.

The greatest risk to the underwriter is to price a new issue too high relative to the market's valuation of that security. That is, underwriters stand to lose when they overprice new issues. Given this, underwriters have an incentive to underprice new issues by setting the public offer price (OP) below the price established for the security in the secondary market once trading begins (P). The investment banker stands to gain by underpricing as it increases the probability of selling out the issue without affecting the fixed underwriting spread. That is, a spread of $.50 at a bid-offer price spread of $93 and $93.50 produces the same gross revenue (spread) of $.50 per share to the underwriter as a bid-offer price spread of $97 and $97.50. The major difference is that a lower offer price (i.e., $93 rather than $97) increases the demand for the shares by investors and the probability of selling the whole issue to the public very quickly. Both the underwriter and the outside investor may benefit from underpricing; the loser is the firm issuing the securities because it obtains lower proceeds than if the offer price had been set at a higher price reflecting a more accurate market valuation. In this example, the issuer receives only $93 per share rather than $97. Consequently, underpricing new issues is an additional cost of securities issuance borne by issuing firms. Most empirical research on the underpricing of U.S. new issues, or **initial public offerings (IPOs),** has found that they are underpriced in the range of 8 to 48 percent depending on the sample and time period chosen.[33] In contrast, **secondary issues** tend to be underpriced by less than 3 percent.[34]

IPO (initial public offering)
A corporate equity or debt security offered to the public for the first time through an underwriter.

secondary issues
A new issue of equity or debt of firms whose securities are already traded in the market.

---

[31] See A. Gande, M. Puri, A. Saunders, and I. Walter, "Bank Underwriting of Debt Securities: Modern Evidence," *Review of Financial Studies* 10, no. 4 (1997), pp. 1175–1201. More recent studies, e.g., I. C. Roten and D. J. Mullineaux, question the persistence of such benefits over the more recent 1995–1998 period ("Debt Underwriting by Commercial Bank-Affiliated Firms and Investment Banks: More Evidence," *Journal of Banking and Finance*, 2002, pp. 689–718). For Canadian evidence, see G. M. Hebb and D. R. Fraser, "Conflict of Interest in Commercial Bank Security Underwriting: Canadian Evidence," *Journal of Banking and Finance*, 2002, pp. 1935–49.

[32] See A. Gande, M. Puri, and A. Saunders, "Bank Entry, Competition and the Market for Corporate Securities Underwriting," *Journal of Financial Economics* 54 (1999), pp. 165–95. See also "Banks Push into Securities Squeezes Fees," *The Wall Street Journal,* December 16, 1997.

[33] See the review of some 20 studies of underpricing by A. Saunders, "Why Are So Many Stock Issues Underpriced?" Federal Reserve Bank of Philadelphia, *Business Review,* March–April 1990, pp. 3–12.

[34] See C. F. Loderer, D. P. Sheehan, and G. B. Kadler, "The Pricing of Equity Offerings," *Journal of Financial Economics,* 1991, pp. 35–37.

If a major cause of IPO underpricing is a lack of competition among existing investment banks, then bank entry and competition should lower the degree of underpricing and increase the new issue proceeds for firms. Nevertheless, many economists argue that monopoly power is not the primary reason for the underpricing of new issues; in their view, underpricing reflects a risk premium that must be paid to investors and investment bankers for information imperfections. That is, underpricing is a risk premium for the information advantage possessed by issuers who better know the true quality of their firm's securities and its assets.[35] If this is so, bank entry into securities underwriting may only reduce the degree of underpricing to the extent that it reduces the degree of information imperfection among issuers and investors. This might reasonably be expected given the specialized role of banks as delegated monitors (see Chapter 1).[36]

Anticompetitive Effects

With the revision of the Bank Act, the biggest Canadian banking organizations, measured by either capital or assets, were many times larger than the biggest securities firms. The Big Six Canadian banks, aided by the stock market crash of 1987,which weakened securities firms, particularly those which had underwritten the IPO of British Petroleum, absorbed the independent securities firms. The banks thus assumed quasi-oligopoly positions, causing market concentration to rise and perhaps long-run prices for investment banking services to rise also.[37]

Cross-Pillar Mergers: Banks and Insurance Companies

A cross-pillar issue in Canada that has yet to be resolved is the merger of banks and insurance companies. Banks and insurance companies have been presenting briefs to the federal government since the MacKay Commission Report in 1998, and a review of the financial services legislation in Canada is conducted every 5 years, most recently in October, 2005. The six issues discussed with respect to banks and securities mergers are relevant to the insurance discussion and are briefly discussed briefly below:

Safety and soundness issues   Both the banks and federally-regulated life insurance companies and property and casualty (P&C) insurance companies in Canada are already regulated by OSFI. It can be argued that the regulations for these FIs are converging since OSFI provides guidelines on capital adequacy, large exposure limits, and risk management for all of the FIs under its jurisdiction. Therefore, unlike the securities industry, which is regulated by self-regulatory organizations

---

[35] See F. Beatty and J. Ritter, "Investment Banking, Reputation, and the Underpricing of Initial Public Offerings," *Journal of Financial Economics* 15 (1986), pp. 213–32; and K. Rock, "Why New Issues Are Underpriced," *Journal of Financial Economics* 15 (1986), pp. 187–212.

[36] However, firewalls limited the efficiency with which the delegated monitor can transfer information to its affiliate. See M. Puri, "Conflicts of Interest, Intermediation and the Pricing of Underwritten Securities," *Journal of Financial Economics*, October 1999, pp. 133–64.

[37] One possible reason for the slow development of the German corporate bond market is that Germany universal banks wish to preserve their monopoly power over corporate debt. This may best be done by encouraging corporate loans rather than bond issues. This may be ascribed to the structure of the financial system in Germany, which historically did not have the strict separation of banking and securities functions found in Canada, the United Kingdom and the United States. For a discussion of the historical differences in the financial system structures in different countries and its effect on banking and corporate financing, see M. Roe, *Strong Managers, Weak Owners The Political Roots of American Corporate Finance*, 1996, Princeton University Press.

www.ida.ca (SROs) such as the exchanges and the Investment Dealers Association of Canada (IDA), the regulatory oversight is already in place for cross-pillar mergers of insurance companies and banks and the safety and soundness of the financial system will not be threatened.

Economy of scale and scope issues   The banks already possess a branch network that gives them the ability to sell mutual fund and other investment products in their branches. Therefore, the availability of insurance products, along with the banks' experience in creating innovative savings products, could allow them to offer insurance products at a competitive price to existing customers and to generate more profits for their investment in branches, savings that could be passed on to the consumer. To the extent that insurance products could be offered on line through existing bank Web sites could mean additional cost savings for consumers.[38]

Conflict of interest issues   Both banks and insurance companies already sell mutual fund and mutual fund-type (segregated funds) products by employees licensed to sell such products. The issue of tied product selling and other legal and ethical issues are already addressed by such organizations as the Mutual Fund www.mfda.ca Dealers Association of Canada (MFDA).

Deposit insurance issues   To the extent that insurance companies would accept deposits similar to other deposit-taking FIs, they would be eligible for membership in the Canada Deposit Insurance Corporation and able to pay the risk-based premiums. This would add another layer of regulation to insurance based companies and may increase their costs along with the additional annual regulatory evaluation that CDIC conducts to establish the insurance premiums (see Chapter 19). www.cdic.ca

Regulatory oversight issues   Regulation of insurance companies as part of a bank-insurance conglomerate should not be an issue for OSFI since banks already report their assets based on banking, trading, and insurance. No doubt there would be more discussion of the regulation of financial conglomerates, particularly those holding companies outside of the banking sphere, such as Power Financial, which controls significant Canadian insurance (Great West Life, London Life, Canada Life) and mutual fund assets (IGM Financial that includes Investors Group and Mackenzie Financial, see Figure 5–1).

Competition issues   The biggest barrier to bank-insurance mergers is the issue of competition in Canada. The banks hold in excess of $1.9 trillion assets in Canada in 2005, and dwarf the remaining FIs, including the insurance companies, even with the $7.3 billion merger of Sun Life and Clarica Life Insurance in 2003 and the Manulife and John Hancock of Boston $11 billion deal completed in 2004. There were rumours that Manulife was to merge with CIBC in 2003, but the department of finance was not open to that possibility. Since the template for bank-insurance mergers has not been established, it is difficult to speculate as to whether a cross-pillar merger would reduce competition and services for consumers. For example, sale of insurance products in bank branches might still be

---

[38] B. Amoako-Adu and B. F. Smith, "The wealth effects of deregulation of Canadian financial institutions," *Journal of Banking & Finance* 19 (1995), pp. 1211–1236, studied the early deregulation and Canadian FIs for the period from 1984 to 1991 and found that there was a significant gain for insurance companies but no evidence to support the transfer of wealth among institutions.

prohibited in order to protect the small insurance brokers. Similarly, banks could be required to keep branches open and staff levels up as a condition of mergers, either cross-pillar or bank-bank.[39]

Concept Questions

1. What are some of the issues that arise in response to bank expansion into securities, insurance, and commercial activities?
2. Explain how firm commitment underwriting of securities is similar to writing put options on assets.
3. Describe ways in which the losses of a securities affiliate in a holding company structure could be transmitted to a bank.
4. In addition to the potential conflicts of interest discussed in this section, can you think of any additional possible conflicts that might arise when commercial banks are allowed to expand their investment banking or insurance activities?

---

[39] In 2001, a review of the financial services contained a clause that required new legislation to be put into place by October 26 2006. Since 2001, and particularly throughout 2004 and 2005, various FIs have filed briefs with the federal Department of Finance outlining their positions. See for example, R. Trichur, "Bank executive calls for sweeping regulatory changes in Canada," *The Vancouver Sun*, July 19, 2005, p. D.4 and R. Maurino, "Canadian banks look to grow via U.S. expansion, insurance and other avenues", *Canadian Press NewsWire*, September 13, 2005, as well as S. Stewart, "A case for allowing bank-insurance mergers: shareholder value," *The Globe and Mail Report on Business*, September 15, 2003, p. B1. For a taste of the insurance industry's views on the matter, see C. Harris, "Financial Reform Redux," *Canadian Underwriter*, July 2005, 72, 7, pp. 16–17 and F. Iacurto, "Bill C-8: A time to rejoice?," *Canadian Underwriter*, October 2001, 68, 10, pp. 50–51. In addition, Power Financial's written submission to the Department of Finance did not support cross-pillar mergers. See K. Kalawsky, "To kill a bank merger: First there was Chretien. Now banks have a new enemy—Power Financial," *National Post*, January 24, 2004, p. FP01.

Summary

Traditionally, the financial systems of Canada, the United Kingdom, and the United States have been structured on segmented product lines. These restrictions on product or activity expansion have had some significant costs. Most important has been the loss of potential risk-reducing gains that arise from product diversification, as well as gains from the potential generation of cost and revenue synergies. However, a set of important public policy or social welfare concerns relate to conflicts of interest, safety and soundness, competition, and regulation. Although Canada and the U.K. started deregulating in the early 1990s, the U.S. lagged behind. Nevertheless, in recent years, there has been a dramatic breakdown in many of the regulatory barriers to financial service conglomeration in the U.S. culminating with the Financial Services Modernization Act of 1999. The act allowed the creation of a financial service holding company that could engage in banking activities *and* securities underwriting and insurance. As a result, the Canadian and the U.S. financial systems are rapidly converging toward a "universal banking" system. In such a system, bank, insurance, and securities products are increasingly cross-sold by large conglomerate (universal) financial service firms with the objective of maximizing revenue and cost synergies and reducing risk through diversification.

Questions and Problems

1. How does product segmentation reduce the risks of FIs? How does it increase the risks of FIs?

2. In what ways have other FIs taken advantage of the restrictions on product diversification imposed on commercial banks?

3. How does product segmentation reduce the profitability of FIs? How does product segmentation increase the profitability of FIs?

4. What are the differences in the risk implications of a firm commitment securities offering versus a best-efforts offering?

5. An FI is underwriting the sales of 1 million shares of Ultrasonics, Inc., and is quoting a bid–ask price of $6.00–6.50.

a. What are the fees earned by the FI if a firm commitment method is used to underwrite the securities?

b. What are the fees if it uses the best-efforts method and a commission of 50 basis points is charged?

c. How would your answer be affected if it manages to sell the shares only at $5.50 using the firm commitment method? The commission for best efforts is still 50 basis points.

6. What is the maximum possible underwriter's fee on both the best-efforts and firm commitment underwriting contracts on an issue of 12 million shares at a bid price of $12.45 and an offer price of $12.60? What is the maximum possible loss? The best-efforts underwriting commission is 75 basis points.

7. The investment arm of a large Canadian bank agrees to underwrite a debt issue for one of its clients. It has suggested a firm commitment offering for issuing 100,000 shares of stock. The bank quotes a bid-ask spread of $97–$97.50 to its customers on the issue date.

a. What are the total underwriting fees generated if all the issue is sold? If only 60 percent is sold?

b. Instead of taking a chance that only 60 percent of the shares will be sold on the issue date, a bank suggests a price of $95 to the issuing firm. It expects to quote a bid-ask spread of $95–$95.40 and sell 100 percent of the issue. From the FI's perspective, which price is better if it expects to sell the remaining 40 percent at the bid price of $97 under the first quote?

8. What are the reasons why the upside returns from firm commitment securities offerings are not symmetrical in regard to the downside risk? How is underwriting on a firm commitment basis similar to writing a put option on a firm's assets?

9. How could the failure of a securities affiliate organizational form negatively affect a bank?

10. What are two operational strategies to reduce the risk to the safety and soundness of a bank resulting from the failure of a securities affiliate or many other types of financial distress?

11. What do empirical studies reveal about the effect of activity diversification on the risk of failure of banks?

12. What role does bank activity diversification play in the ability of a bank to exploit economies of scale and scope? What remains as the limitation to creating potentially greater benefits?

13. What conflicts of interest have been identified as potential roadblocks to the expansion of banking powers into the financial services area?

14. What are some of the legal, institutional, and market conditions that lessen the likelihood that an FI can exploit conflicts of interest from the expansion of commercial banks into other financial service areas?

15. Under what circumstances could the existence of deposit insurance provide an advantage to banks in competing with other traditional securities firms?

16. In what ways does the current regulatory structure argue against providing additional insurance powers to the banking industry? Does this issue just concern banks?

17. What are the potential procompetitive effects of allowing banks to enter more fully into insurance sales and underwriting? What is the anticompetitive argument or position?

Web Question

18. Go to the Board of Governors of the Federal Reserve Web site at **www.federalreserve.gov**. Locate the organizational structure of the two largest U.S. commercial bank holding companies using the following steps. Click on "Banking Information and Regulation." Click on "National Information Center." Click on "Top 50 BHCs/Banks." Click on the top listed (largest) bank holding company. Click on "Institution Organization Hierarchy." Click on "Submit." Click on "Display *Complete Summary Hierarchy Report* for the selected institution." This will download a file onto your computer that will contain the most recent information on the organizational structure of the largest bank. Repeat these steps for the second listed (largest) bank holding company. Compare the organizational structure of the two institutions. How do they differ from the large Canadian banks, e.g., Royal Bank of Canada or CIBC?

Appendix 21A EU and G-10 Countries: Regulatory Treatment of the Mixing of Banking, Securities, and Insurance Activities and the Mixing of Banking and Commerce

View Appendix 21A at the Web site for this textbook (**www.mcgrawhill.ca/college/saunders**).

Geographic Diversification: Domestic and International

This chapter examines the issue of geographic diversification, both international and domestic, for FIs and:

▸ traces the potential benefits and costs to the risk management strategies considered by FI managers from geographic expansion, especially from mergers and acquisitions

▸ discusses the reasons underlying the current pressure for mergers among financial services firms that is dramatically changing and consolidating the structure of the North American and global financial systems

▸ presents some evidence on the cost and revenue synergies as well as other market and firm-specific factors affecting geographic expansion

INTRODUCTION

Just as product expansion (see Chapter 21) may enable an FI to reduce risk and increase returns, so may geographic expansion. Geographic expansions can have a number of dimensions. In particular, they can be either domestic or international. For example, Sun Life acquired Celestica in 2002, a domestic insurance firm, whereas Manulife merged with John Hancock of Boston, an "international" expansion, in 2003. Expansions also occur through opening a new office or branch or by acquiring another FI through a merger or acquisition. Insurance companies are able to merge with each other, as noted in chapter 21, but cross-pillar mergers of banks and insurance companies have yet to occur. Bank-bank mergers are permitted by existing legislation, but are subject to the approval of the Minister of Finance.

www.cibc.com
www.td.com
www.royalbank.com
www.bmo.com

However, since the proposed mergers of Canadian Imperial Bank of Commerce (CIBC) with Toronto-Dominion Bank (TD), and Royal Bank of Canada (RBC) with Bank of Montreal (BMO) were disallowed in 1998, the Minister of Finance has promised guidelines on bank mergers. As of late 2005, and after considerable public consultation, the decision on large bank mergers was postponed until after the next federal election in Canada.[1]

DOMESTIC EXPANSIONS: CANADA AND THE UNITED STATES

Historically, the ability of FIs to expand domestically has been constrained by regulation. By comparison, no special regulations have inhibited the ability of commercial firms such as General Motors, IBM, and Sears from establishing new or **de novo offices,**

de novo office
A newly established office.

---

[1] The election of a minority federal government in 2004 caused Ralph Goodale, the Minister of Finance, to defer a decision on this highly political issue. See S. Chase, "No Bank merger rules before election: Goodale," *Globe and Mail*, September 27, 2005, p. B8. Public consultations on the merger issue have been conducted. The public responses to the large bank merger issue submitted to the Department of Finance Canada from June to December 2003 are available at www.fin.gc.ca.

factories, or branches anywhere in the country. Nor have commercial firms been prohibited from acquiring other firms—as long as they are not banks. Though securities firms and insurance companies have faced relatively few restrictions in expanding their business domestically, other FIs, especially banks, have faced a complex and changing network of rules and regulations. Such regulations may inhibit expansions, but they also create potential opportunities to increase an FI's returns. In particular, regulations may create locally uncompetitive markets with monopoly economic rents that new entrants can potentially exploit. Thus, for the most innovative FIs, regulation can provide profit opportunities as well as costs. As a result, regulation both inhibits and creates incentives to engage in geographic expansions.[2]

In addition, the economic factors that affect commercial firm expansion and acquisition decisions are likely to influence the decisions of FIs as well. Two major groups of factors are cost and revenue synergies and firm/market-specific attractions, such as the specialized skills of an acquired firm's employees and the markets of the firm to be acquired. Thus, the attractiveness of a geographic expansion, whether through acquisition, branching, or opening a new office, depends on a broad set of factors encompassing

1. Regulation and the regulatory framework.
2. Cost and revenue synergies.
3. Firm- or market-specific factors.

We start by considering how the first factor—regulation—influences an FI's geographic expansion decision.

Concept Questions

1. Explain why regulation both inhibits and provides incentives to an FI to engage in geographic expansion.
2. What three basic factors influence the attractiveness of geographic expansion to an FI?

REGULATORY FACTORS IMPACTING GEOGRAPHIC EXPANSION

Insurance Companies

As discussed in Chapter 3, with the exception of the federally-regulated life and property and casualty (P&C) companies insurance companies are provincially-regulated firms. By establishing a subsidiary in one province, an insurance company normally has the opportunity to sell insurance anywhere in that province and often to market the product nationally by telemarketing and direct sales. To deliver a financial service effectively, however, it is often necessary to establish a physical presence in a local market. To do this, insurance companies establish offices in other provinces. Thus, most large insurance companies have a physical presence in virtually every Canadian province and territory.

---

[2] E. Kane has called this interaction between regulation and incentives the regulatory dialectic. See "Accelerating Inflation, Technological Innovation, and the Decreasing Effectiveness of Banking Regulation," *Journal of Finance* 36 (1981), pp. 335–67. Expansions that are geographic market extensions involving firms in the same product areas are part of a broader set of horizontal mergers.

Banks

Canadian banks can only be chartered federally and thus the industry is controlled by one federal regulator. This means that Canadian banks and Canadian consumers take the "sea-to-sea" nature of their banking system for granted. It can be argued that the absence of branching restrictions for domestic banks accelerated the introduction of the technology for interbranch banking and, as well, facilitated the development of the Large Value Transfer System (LVTS) for payments settlements (see Chapters 17 and 20). In a Canadian market that is roughly one-tenth the size of the U.S. market, the major considerations for a domestic expansion are cost and revenue synergies, as discussed below. Regulatory restrictions on branches have been applied to Schedule II and Schedule III banks as discussed in Chapter 2 in an effort to protect the Canadian control of financial services.

U.S. Commercial Banks

The United States market has provided many opportunities for growth and expansion for Canadian banks (e.g. Bank of Montreal's acquisition of Harris Bank of Chicago in the 1990s and Toronto Dominion's acquisition of BankNorth in 2004). We next consider the U.S. situation in order to provide a North American perspective on the merger wave that has been ongoing since the passage of the Riegle-Neal Interstate Branching and Efficiency Act of 1994.

U.S. Restrictions on Intrastate Banking

unit bank
A bank with a single office.

At the beginning of the century most U.S. banks were **unit banks** with a single office. Improving communications and customer needs resulted in a rush to branching in the first two decades of the 20th century. Increasingly, this movement ran into opposition from the smallest unit banks and the largest money center banks. The smallest unit banks perceived a competitive threat to their retail business from the larger branching banks; money center banks feared a loss of valuable correspondent business such as cheque clearing and other payment services. As a result, several states restricted the ability of banks to branch within the state.

U.S. Restrictions on Interstate Banking

The defining piece of legislation affecting interstate branching until 1997 was the McFadden Act, passed in 1927 and amended in 1933. The McFadden Act and its amendments restricted nationally chartered banks' branching abilities to the same extent allowed to state-chartered banks. Because states prohibit interstate banking for state-chartered banks in general, nationally chartered banks were similarly prohibited.

multibank holding company (MBHC)
A parent banking organization that owns a number of individual bank subsidiaries.

Between 1927 and 1997 bank organizations expanding across state lines largely relied on establishing subsidiaries rather than branches. Some of the biggest banking organizations established **multibank holding companies** for that purpose. A multibank holding company (MBHC) is a parent company that acquires more than one bank as a direct subsidiary. While MBHCs had been around in the early part of the 20th century, the 1927 restrictions on interstate branching gave the bank acquisition movement an added impetus.

Riegle-Neal Interstate Banking and Branching Efficiency Act of 1994   It had long been recognized that nationwide banking expansion through multibank holding companies was potentially far more expensive than through branching. Separate corporations and boards of directors must be established for each bank in an MBHC, and it is hard to achieve the same level of economic and financial integration as

TABLE 22–1   **Key Dates for the Riegle-Neal Interstate Banking and Branching Efficiency Act of 1994**

Date	Event	Summary
September 24, 1994, to May 31, 1997	Interstate bank merger and branch acquisition early opt-in	A state may "opt in early" to allow interstate merger transactions, including branch acquisitions, to occur prior to June 1, 1997.
	Interstate bank merger opt-out	A state may "opt out" to prohibit interstate merger transactions entirely.
Any time after date of enactment	Interstate de novo branching opt-in	A state may expressly permit out-of-state banks to establish de novo branches within its limits.
One year after date of enactment and thereafter	Interstate banking	A bank holding company may acquire banks located in any state. States do not have the ability to opt out. However, the acquiring institution is not permitted to control more than 10 percent of nationwide deposits or 30 percent of deposits in the state entered.
June 1, 1997, and thereafter	Interstate bank mergers	Banks in different states may merge unless one of the states has opted out of interstate merger transactions by June 1, 1997.
	Interstate branching acquisitions	Banks may acquire an existing branch in another state if the law of that state permits it.

Source: Office of the Comptroller of the Currency. www.occ.treas.gov

with branches. Moreover, most major banking countries, such as Canada, Japan, Germany, France, and the United Kingdom, have nationwide branching.

In the fall of 1994, the U.S. Congress passed an interstate banking law that allows U.S. and nondomestic banks to branch interstate by consolidating out-of-state bank subsidiaries into a branch network and/or acquiring banks or individual branches of banks by merger and acquisition. (The effective date for these new branching powers was June 1, 1997.) Although the act is silent on the ability of banks to establish de novo (new) branches in other states—essentially leaving it to individual states to pass laws allowing de novo branching—it became possible under the new law for a New York bank such as Citibank to purchase a single branch of a California bank such as a branch of Bank of America in San Francisco.

The implication of the Riegle-Neal Act is that full interstate banking—with the exception of de novo branching—became a reality in the United States in 1997. Further details of the Riegle-Neal Act are provided in Table 22–1.[3] The relaxation of the branching restrictions, along with recognition of the potential cost, revenue, and risk benefits from geographic expansions (discussed next), set off a wave of consolidation in the U.S. banking system. This consolidation trend has been particularly evident among the largest U.S. banks in a wave of "megamergers." Table 22–2 shows some of the biggest mergers between 1995 and 2004 that are reshaping the U.S. banking industry into a nationwide banking system along Canadian and European lines. Many of these mergers are discussed below.

For comparison with the U.S. powerhouses being created, the domestic, U.S. and other international assets of the five major Canadian banks is shown in Table 22-3. Bank of Montreal has the highest concentration of U.S. assets, with C$68.8 billion, 25 percent of their total assets. CIBC ranks second at 18.4 percent, followed by TD at 13.3 percent. However, these asset exposures are dwarfed by the financial

---

[3] The reason for the restriction on de novo branching is to protect smaller community banks' franchise values. If you can branch only by acquisition, the franchise values of small banks will be greater than when larger banks have the alternative of branching de novo.

TABLE 22-2   The New Shape of U.S. Banking Major Mergers, 1995-2004

	1995-1996		1996-1997		1997-1998		1998-1999	
	Capital, US$million	Assets, US$million	Capital, US$million	Assets, US$million	Capital, US$million	Assets, US$million	Capital, US$million	Assets, US$million
Chemical	11,436	82,296	(Chase Manhattan Corp.)					
Chase	8,444	121,173	21,095	336,099	22,594	365,521	23,617	406,105
J. P. Morgan	11,432	222,026	11,404	262,159	11,261	261,067	11,439	260,898
Banc One	7,824	90,176	8,107	102,034	8,701	115,901	(Bank One)	
First Chicago NBD	7,890	122,002	9,318	104,619	8,541	114,096	19,900	269,425
Citicorp	19,239	256,853	20,109	281,018	21,096	310,897	(Citigroup)	
Travelers	15,853	302,344	17,942	345,948	20,893	386,555	58,290	795,584
BankAmerica	14,820	232,446	17,181	250,753	17,200	260,159		
NationsBank	11,074	187,298	12,662	185,794				
Boatmen's	2,666	33,704						
Fourth Financial	592	7,456	3,359	41,200			(Bank of America)	
Barnett Banks	2,491	41,631	3,289	41,456	13,593	310,602	44,432	632,574
FleetFinancial	7,415	85,518	8,452	91,047	9,409	104,382	(Fleet Boston)	
Bank Boston	4,934	62,306	4,610	69,268	4,817	73,513	18,074	226,817
First Union	4,479	96,740						
First Fidelity	2,301	35,366	7,790	140,127	10,215	157,274		
CoreStates	2,165	29,729						
Meridian	1,191	14,740	3,725	45,651			(First Union)	
Signet	779	11,100	857	11,751	3,756	48,461	15,347	253,024
Wachovia	3,625	44,964	3,963	46,886	(Wachovia)			
Central Fidelity	739	10,822	778	10,556	5,465	65,397	5,658	67,352
Wells Fargo	3,505	50,316	(Wells Fargo)					
First Interstate	3,431	58,071	6,572	108,888	20,759	202,475	23,871	241,053
Norwest	5,875	80,175	6,834	88,540				
First Security	1,217	15,457	1,400	18,152	1,595	21,689	1,770	22,993

Source: *The Banker*, May 1998, p. 5, and authors' research.

conglomerates being created in the U.S. and the rest of the world. Based on asset size, Citicorp ranked second in the world at US$1.264 trillion behind Mizuho Financial Group of Japan at US$1.285 trillion in assets.

COST AND REVENUE SYNERGIES INFLUENCING GEOGRAPHIC EXPANSION BY MERGER AND ACQUISITION

One reason for an FI deciding to expand (or not to expand) geographically by acquisition relates to the regulations defining its merger opportunities. Other reasons relate to the exploitation of potential cost and revenue synergies from merging (as well as the associated diversification of risk benefits). We look at these potential gains next.

Cost Synergies

A common reason given for bank mergers is the potential cost synergies that may result from economies of scale, economies of scope, or managerial efficiency sources

TABLE 22–2   (concluded)

1999–2000		2000–2001		2001–2002		2002–2003		2003–2004	
Capital, US$million	Assets, US$million	Capital, US$million	Assets, US$million	Capital, US$million	Assets, US$million	Capital, US$million	Assets, US$million	Capital, US$million	Assets, US$million
(J. P. Morgan Chase)									
42,338	715,348	41,099	693,575	42,306	758,800	46,154	770,912	(J. P. Morgan Chase)	
18,635	269,300	20,226	268,954	22,440	277,985	23,419	326,563		
66,206	902,210	81,247	1,051,450	86,718	1,097,190	98,014	1,264,032		
47,628	642,191	48,520	621,764	47,980	660,951	50,319	736,445	(Bank of America)	
19,361	219,095	17,608	203,744	16,833	190,453	18,280	200,235		
		(Wachovia)							
16,709	254,170	28,455	330,452	32,078	341,834	32,428	401,032		
6,285	74,032								
(Wells Fargo)									
26,488	272,426	27,214	307,569	30,358	349,259	32,372	390,813		

X efficiency
Cost savings due to the greater managerial efficiency of the acquiring bank.

(often called **X efficiencies**[4] because they are difficult to pin down in a quantitative fashion). For example, in 1996, Chase Manhattan and Chemical Bank merged, creating the (then) largest banking organization in the United States, with assets of US$300 billion. It was estimated that annual cost savings from the merger would be US$1.5 billion, to be achieved by consolidating certain operations and eliminating redundant costs, including the elimination of some 12,000 positions from a combined staff of 75,000 in 39 states and 51 countries. In 2001 First Union acquired Wachovia for US$14.6 billion. The merger of these two North Carolina banks was expected to reduce annual expenses by US$890 million through the consolidation of 250 to 300 branches and cutting of some 7,000 jobs.

megamerger
The merger of two large banks.

Through the mergers discussed above are interesting examples of **megamergers,** they are still essentially mergers in the same or closely related banking markets. By comparison, the two largest pure bank mergers in 1998—those between BancOne (now Bank One) and First Chicago and between NationsBank and Bank of America—were clearly geographic extension mergers with little or no geographic overlap.

---

[4] X efficiencies are those cost savings not directly due to economies of scope or economies of scale. As such, they are usually attributed to superior management skills and other difficult-to-measure managerial factors. To date, the explicit identification of what composes these efficiencies remains to be established in the empirical banking literature.

TABLE 22–3   Canadian Banks' Domestic, U.S., and international income and assets, 2004 (millions of Canadian dollars, for year ended October 31)

	Canada	United States	Other Countries	Total
Bank of Montreal:				
Net Interest Income	3,441	1,450	170	5,061
Non-interest Income	3,199	1,200	152	4,551
Net Income	1,693	436	152	2,351
Average Assets	177,306	68,758	23,728	269,792
Bank of Nova Scotia:				
Net Interest Income	3,686	354	2,088	6,128
Non-Interest Income	2,495	513	1,058	4,066
Net Income	1,679	351	956	2,986
Average Assets	188,000	21,000	73,000	282,000
CIBC:				
Net Interest Income	4,604	487	276	5,366
Non-interest Income	4,974	1,204	519	6,517
Net Income	1,802	45	352	2,199
Average Assets	195,263	51,545	34,002	280,810
Royal Bank of Canada:				
Net Interest Income	5,183	1,116	394	6,693
Non-Interest Income	6,121	3,699	1,608	11,428
Net Income	2,155	16	646	2,817
Average Assets	238,000	95,500	95,300	429,200
Toronto Dominion Bank:				
Net Income	1,446	259	605	2,310
Average Assets	216,110	41,506	53,411	311,027

Source: 2004 Annual Reports

Their merger created the then second largest credit card bank (behind Citigroup), with 40 million accounts and over US$56 billion in loans outstanding. It is also perceived that the enhanced scale of the new bank's credit card business allows it to invest in even more innovative computer technology.

Another example of a market extension megamerger that has both geographic and cost synergy dimensions was North Carolina-based NationsBank's acquisition of Boatmen's Bancshares of St. Louis, Missouri, in 1997. Then, Bank of America and NationsBank became the first truly nationwide bank when they merged in 1998, a transaction valued at US$60 billion. The banks estimated the merger would cut their combined expenses by US$1.3 billion and would eliminate between 5,000 and 8,000 jobs (3 to 4 percent of their workforce).

Finally, the most recent examples of these types of mergers are those by Bank of America and J. P. Morgan Chase. By acquiring FleetBoston for US$43 billion, Bank of America added nearly 1,500 branches and 3,400 ATM machines in the New England area. The combined banks projected annual cost savings to be US$1.1 billion, including consolidation of redundant technology systems. This was followed in 2004 by J. P. Morgan Chase's US$60 billion merger with Bank One to form the second largest bank in the United States. With this merger J. P. Morgan Chase (which had been operating in only four states) acquired Bank One's First USA credit card operations and a massive retail network of about 1,800 branches concentrated in the Midwest. Together the merged bank would hold about US$125 billion in credit card balances, giving the combined company an almost 20 percent share of the credit card market. Further, the combined bank was projecting before-tax savings of US$2.2 billion in the three years after the merger with job cuts estimated to total 10,000 of a combined 140,000 workers.

In a comprehensive study, Berger and Humphrey used data from 1981 to 1989 to analyze the cost savings from megamergers, which they defined as a merger in which the acquirer's and the target bank's assets combined exceeded US$1 billion. They could find very little evidence of potential gains from economies of scale and scope. Indeed, the cost savings they could find were related to improved managerial efficiency (X efficiency). Their study had three major findings. First, the managerial efficiency of the acquirer tended to be superior to that of the acquired bank. Second, the 57 megamergers analyzed produced small but significant X efficiency gains. Third (and perhaps surprisingly), the degree of cost savings in market overlap mergers (e.g., as in the Chase/Chemical case) was apparently no greater than for geographic extension mergers (as in the Bank of America/NationsBank case). Overall, they could not find the sizable cost synergies of 30 percent or so that are often given as the motivational forces behind such mergers.[5]

In a more recent study of nine megamergers by Rhoades (seven of the nine occurring since 1990), large cost savings were found. Specifically, four of the nine mergers showed significant cost efficiency gains relative to a peer group of nonmerged banks and seven of the nine showed a significant improvement in their return on assets. Interestingly, where cost efficiency gains were *not* realized, the major problems came from integrating data processing and operating systems. Houston, James, and Ryngaert examined large bank mergers over the period 1985 through 1996. They found that cost savings represented the primary source of gains in the large majority of recent mergers and that managerial cost savings projections have significant capital market credibility.[6]

Berger and DeYoung examined the effects of geographic expansion on bank efficiency using cost and profit efficiencies estimates for over 7,000 U.S. banks from 1993 to 1998. They found both positive and negative links between geographic scope and bank efficiency. Parent organizations exercised some control over the efficiency of their affiliates, although the control dissipated with physical distance to the affiliate. On average, the distance-related effect was small, and thus results suggested that the more efficient banks could export efficient practices to their affiliates and overwhelm any effects of distance. The results suggested that some banks may operate efficiently only within a single region, whereas others may operate efficiently on a nationwide or even international basis.[7]

Finally, G. DeLong and M. M. Cornett et al. find that mergers of banks that are activity or geographically focused earn significantly higher abnormal returns (ARs) than those that are activity or geographically diversifying. Thus, they increase opportunities for greater cost efficiency or for concentrating the bidder's existing market power and brand recognition. In contrast, diversifying mergers are those in which the bidder bank has lines of business that are not

---

[5] A. Berger and D. B. Humphrey, "Megamergers in Banking and the Use of Cost Efficiency as an Antitrust Defense," *The Antitrust Bulletin* 37 (1992), pp. 541–600.

[6] S. A. Rhoades, "The Efficiency Effects of Bank Mergers: An Overview of Case Studies of Nine Mergers," *Journal of Banking and Finance* 22, no. 3 (1998), pp. 273–92; and J. F. Houston, C. M. James, and M. D. Ryngaert, "Where Do Merger Gains Come From? Bank Mergers from the Perspective of Insiders and Outsiders," *Journal of Financial Economics* 60 (2001), pp. 285–331.

[7] A. N. Berger and R. DeYoung, "The Effects of Geographic Expansion on Bank Efficiency," *Journal of Financial Services Research* 19 (2001), pp. 163–84.

common to those of the target bank. These mergers required the bidder bank to extend operations into new areas and devote additional resources beyond the current operations.[8]

Revenue Synergies

The revenue synergies argument has three dimensions. First, revenues may be enhanced by acquiring a bank in a growing market. For example, although the 2000 merger of J. P. Morgan and Chase Manhattan to form J. P. Morgan Chase was estimated to produce a cost savings of US$1.5 billion, the CEOs of both companies stated that the success of the merger was pinned on revenue growth. The merger combined J. P. Morgan's greater array of products with Chase's broad client base. The merger added substantially to many businesses (such as equity underwriting, equity derivatives, and asset management) that Chase had been trying to build on its own through smaller deals and gave it a bigger presence in Europe where investment and corporate banking were fast-growing businesses. When J. P. Morgan Chase then acquired Bank One, analysts praised the combination as one that offered revenue growth potential, the result of the combination of two different business models as well as expense reduction.

Second, the acquiring bank's revenue stream may become more stable if the asset and liability portfolio of the target institution exhibits different credit, interest rate, and liquidity risk characteristics from the acquirer.[9] For example, real estate loan portfolios showed very strong regional cycles in the 1980s. Specifically, U.S. real estate declined in value in the Southwest, then in the Northeast, and then in California with a long and variable lag. Thus, a geographically diversified real estate portfolio may be far less risky than one in which both acquirer and target specialize in a single region.[10] Studies confirm risk diversification gains from geographic expansions.[11]

Third, there is an opportunity for revenue enhancement by expanding into markets that are less than fully competitive. That is, banks may be able to identify and expand geographically into those markets where *economic rents* potentially exist, but where such entry will not be viewed as being potentially anticompetitive by regulators. Arguably, one of the great potential benefits of the J. P. Morgan Chase and Bank One merger was the potential for enhanced revenue diversification due to the lack of overlap of the branch networks of the two systems due to the merger.

Merger Guidelines for Acceptability

To the extent that geographic expansions are viewed as enhancing the monopoly power of an FI, regulators and governments may act to prevent a merger unless it produces potential efficiency gains that cannot be reasonably achieved by other

---

[8] G. L. DeLong, "Gains from Focusing versus Diversifying Bank Mergers," *Journal of Financial Economics* 59 (2001), pp. 221–52; G. L. DeLong, "Does Long-Term Performance of Mergers Match Market Expectations? Evidence from the U. S. Banking Industry," Working Paper, City University of New York, 2002; and M. M. Cornett, G. Hovakimian, D. Palia, and H. Tehranian, "The Impact of the Manager-Shareholder Conflict on Acquiring Bank Returns," *Journal of Banking and Finance* 27 (2003), pp. 103–31.

[9] See B. Esty et al., "Interest Rate Exposure and Bank Mergers," *Journal of Banking and Finance* 23 (February 1999), pp. 255–85, for evidence on the opposing interest rate risk exposures of acquirers and targets.

[10] As a result, the potential revenue diversification gains for more geographically concentrated mergers are likely to be relatively low. As noted in Chapter 20, the failures of the Canadian Commercial Bank and the Northland Bank of Canada in 1985 were related to their undiversified loan portfolios that concentrated on oil and gas and real estate loans in Western Canada.

[11] M. Levonian, "Interstate Banking and Risk," Federal Reserve Bank of San Francisco, *Weekly Letter* 94–26 (1994); W. Lee, "The Value of Risk Reduction to Investors," unpublished Research Paper 9312, Federal Reserve Bank of New York, 1993; and P. S. Rose, "The Diversification and Cost Effects of Interstate Banking," *The Financial Review* 13 (May 1996), pp. 431–51.

means. In Canada, mergers of large FIs require the approval of the Minister of Finance. In 1998, Royal Bank of Canada and Bank of Montreal were set to merge, as were Canadian Imperial Bank of Commerce and Toronto-Dominion Bank, but the mergers were not approved. Shortly after, the federal government started public

www.fin.gc.ca

consultations regarding large bank mergers in Canada and accepted submissions up until December 31, 2003. A policy paper on bank mergers was promised, but as of late 2005, its release had been postponed until after the next federal election.[12]

However, as previously discussed, there is a wealth of information regarding mergers in the U.S. which may be of use to the Canadian situation. In recent years, the enforcement of antimonopoly laws and guidelines has fallen to the U.S.

www.usdoj.gov

Department of Justice which has laid down guidelines regarding the acceptability or unacceptability of acquisitions based on the potential increase in concentration in the market in which an acquisition takes place.[13]

Herfindahl-Hirschman Index (HHI)

An index or measure of market concentration based on the squared market shares of market participants.

These merger guidelines are based on a measure of market concentration called the **Herfindahl-Hirschman Index (HHI)**. This index is created by taking the percentage market shares of each firm in a market, squaring them, and then adding these squared shares. Thus, in a market where a single firm had a 100 percent market share, the HHI would be

$$HHI = (100)^2 = 10,000$$

Alternatively, in a market in which there were an infinitely large number of firms of equal size, then

$$HHI = 0$$

Thus, the HHI must lie between 0 and 10,000.

Whether a merger will be challenged under the U.S. Department of Justice guidelines depends on the postmerger HHI level. As you can see in Table 22–4, the Department of Justice defines a *concentrated* market as having a postmerger HHI ratio of 1,800, a moderately concentrated market as having a ratio of 1,000 to 1,800, and an unconcentrated market as having a ratio of less than 1,000. In either a concentrated or a moderately concentrated market, postmerger HHI increases of 100 or more may be challenged.[14]

---

[12] The consultation documents and the public responses are available at the Department of Finance Web site at www.fin.gc.ca. David Dodge, the Governor of the Bank of Canada, speaking before the Senate Banking Committee in Ottawa, indicated that economic research has shown that mergers can produce efficiencies that would benefit consumers and FIs. See "Research backs case for bank mergers: Dodge," CBC News, Wednesday, 20 April 2005 at www.cbc.ca, as well as C. A. Northcott, "Competition in Banking: A Review of the Literature," 2004, *Bank of Canada Working Paper 2004-24*, available at www.bankofcanada.ca for a summary of the issues related to banking and a review of the international and U.S. evidence on banking mergers. As well, the Bank for International Settlements has published a report on consolidation of the global financial services sector that includes trends to 2000 which of course, has been eclipsed by the developments discussed above. See Bank for International Settlements, "Group of Ten Report on Consolidation in the Financial Sector," January 2001, available at www.bis.org.

[13] The Federal Reserve also has the power to approve or disapprove mergers among state member banks and bank holding companies. The Comptroller of the Currency has similar powers over nationally chartered banks. The Federal Reserve's criteria are similar to those of the Department of Justice in that they take into account the HHI (market concentration index). However, it also evaluates the risk effects of the merger. The Department of Justice has powers to review the decisions made by the bank regulatory agencies. For example, in 1990 and 1991, the Department of Justice successfully challenged two mergers approved by the Federal Reserve Board. These two mergers eventually went ahead only after the acquiring bank had divested some branches and offices. The two mergers were First Hawaiian's acquisition of First Interstate of Hawaii and the Society-Ameritrust merger. See D. Palia, "Recent Evidence of Bank Mergers," *Financial Markets, Instruments, and Institutions* 3, no. 5 (1994), pp. 36–59, for further details.

[14] In practice, it is only when the change exceeds 200 in banking that a challenge may occur. This is the case because banking is generally viewed as being more competitive than most industries. See U.S. Department of Justice, "Horizontal Merger Guidelines", April 2, 1982.

TABLE 22–4
1982 U.S. Department of Justice Horizontal Merger Guidelines

Source: Department of Justice, Merger Guidelines, 1982.

Postmerger Market Concentration	Level of Herfindahl-Hirschman Index	Percentage Change in Herfindahl-Hirschman Index and Likelihood of a Challenged Merger
Highly concentrated	Greater than 1,800	Greater than 100—likely to be challenged 50 to 100—depends on other factors* Less than 50—unlikely to be challenged
Moderately concentrated	1,000–1,800	Greater than 100—likely to be challenged; other factors considered* Less than or equal to 100—unlikely to be challenged
Unconcentrated	Less than 1,000	Any increase—unlikely to be challenged

*In addition to the postmerger concentration of the market and the size of the resulting increase in concentration, the department will consider the presence of the following factors in deciding whether to challenge a merger: ease of entry; the nature of the product and its terms of sale; market information about specific transactions; buyer market characteristics; conduct of firms in the market; and market performance. [For a detailed explanation of these factors see Sections III(B) and III(C) of the 1982 Department of Justice Merger Guidelines.]

EXAMPLE 22–1

Calculation of Change in the HHI Associated with a Merger

Consider a market that has three banks with the following market shares:

Bank A = 50%

Bank B = 46%

Bank C = 4%

The premerger HHI for the market is

$$HHI = (50)^2 + (46)^2 + (4)^2 = 2,500 + 2,116 + 16 = 4,632$$

Thus, the market is highly concentrated according to the Department of Justice guidelines.

Suppose Bank A wants to acquire Bank C so that the postacquisition market would exhibit the following shares:[15]

$$A + C = 54\%$$
$$B = 46\%$$

The postmerger HHI would be

$$HHI = (54)^2 + (46)^2 = 2,916 + 2,116 = 5,032$$

Thus, the increase or change in the HHI (ΔHHI) postmerger is

$$\Delta HHI = 5,032 - 4,632 = 400$$

Since the increase is 400, which is more than the 100 benchmark defined in the Department of Justice guidelines, the market is heavily concentrated and the merger could be challenged.

There are two problems of interpretation of the HHI in the context of banking and financial services. First, what is the relevant geographic scope of the market for financial services—national, regional, or city?[16] Second, once that market is defined, do we view banks, savings and loan companies, and insurance companies as separate or

---

[15] Here we consider the effect on the HHI of a within-market acquisition; similar calculations can be carried out for between-market acquisitions.

[16] K. A. Gilbert and A. M. Zaretsky, in "Banking Antitrust: Are the Assumptions Still Valid?" *Review*, The Federal Reserve Bank of St. Louis, November/December 2003, pp. 29–52, review the literature on anti-trust analysis of bank M&As and conclude that the evidence is consistent with the view that the relevant market areas for banking antitrust actions are local communities.

unique lines of business, or are they competing in the same financial market? That is, what defines the institutional scope of the market? In the case of financial services, it has been traditional to define markets on functional, or line of business, criteria, so that commercial banking is a separate market from savings (thrift) banking and other financial services. Further, the relevant market area has usually been defined as highly localized: the standard metropolitan statistical areas (SMSAs) or rural areas (non-SMSAs). Unfortunately, such definitions become increasingly irrelevant in a world of greater geographic and product expansions. Indeed, the use of HHIs should increasingly be based on regional or national market lines and include a broad financial service firm definition of the marketplace. Consequently, in recent years the Federal Reserve has often included one-half of thrift deposits in calculating bank market HHIs.

Interestingly, comparing asset concentrations by bank size, the merger wave in banking appears to have decreased the national asset share of the very smallest banks (under US$100 million) from 16.1 percent in 1984 to 2.6 percent in 2003 while the relative size of the very biggest banks (over US$10 billion) has increased from 34.5 percent in 1984 to 72.9 percent in 2003. The relative market shares of intermediate-sized banks (US$100 million to US$10 billion) have decreased as well, falling from 49.4 percent in 1984 to 24.5 percent in 2003. However, even though the degree of concentration of assets among the largest banks has increased, the percentage share exhibited by the largest U.S. banks is still well below the shares attained by the largest Canadian[17] and European banks in their domestic markets. Thus, mergers involving the largest U.S. banks will likely continue to be approved by the Department of Justice as well as other regulatory bodies.

S. Claessens and L. Laeven evaluated the concentration of banking assets for 50 different countries using an H-statistic which has a value from 0 to 1, with 1 being the highest level of concentration. Table 22–5 summarizes H-statistic data for eight countries from their sample for the period from 1994-2001. As can be seen, Canada's H-statistic is 0.83 while the U.S. has the lowest H-statistic at 0.47, an indication of the difference in the level of banking concentration between Canada and its closest neighbour.[18]

Concept Questions

1. What recent bank mergers have been motivated by cost synergies?
2. What are the three dimensions of revenue synergy gains?
3. Suppose each of five firms in a banking market has a 20 percent share. What is the HHI?
4. What factors might sway Canada's Minister of Finance to allow large bank mergers?

OTHER MARKET- AND FIRM-SPECIFIC FACTORS IMPACTING GEOGRAPHIC EXPANSION DECISIONS

In addition to regulation and cost and revenue synergies, other factors may impact an acquisition decision. For example, an acquiring FI may be concerned about the solvency and asset quality of a potential target FI in another region.

---

[17] The Big Six Canadian banks account for more than 90 percent of the assets of Canadian banks.

[18] For details of the calculation of the H-statistic, see S. Claessens and L. Laeven, "What Drives Bank Competition? Some International Evidence," Presented at the Conference on Bank Concentration and Competition at the World Bank, April 3–4, 2003 available at www.worldbank.org/research/interest/confs/042003/papers042003.htm. Northcott (2004) compares and summarizes this study with others from a Canadian perspective on competition. S. Shaffer, "A Test of Competition in Canadian Banking," 1993, *Journal of Money, Credit, and Banking* 25(1), pp. 49–61 studied the Canadian banking system between 1965–1989 and concluded that the Canadian banking system was concentrated, but still competitive over that time.

TABLE 22–5 H-statistic Measures of Concentration for Selected Countries

	H-statistic	Number of Banks
Australia	0.94	26
Canada	0.83	49
Germany	0.65	2,226
France	0.81	355
Japan	0.53	44
Switzerland	0.74	227
United Kingdom	0.78	106
United States	0.47	1135

Source: S. Claessens and L. Laeven, (2003), www.worldbank.org/research/interest/confs/042003/papers042003.htm

merger premium
The ratio of the purchase price of a target bank's equity to its book value.

Thus, important factors influencing the acquisition decision may include the target FI's leverage or capital ratio, and the amount of nonperforming loans in its portfolio.

An early study by Beatty, Santomero, and Smirlock is indicative of the type of tests conducted. They analyzed the factors potentially affecting the attractiveness of bank mergers and identified some 13 factors or variables, many of them bank specific. In particular, they analyzed 149 bank acquisitions over the period 1984–85; they measured the attraction of the merger by the size of the **merger premium** the acquiring bank was willing to pay for a target bank. Analytically, we measure this premium by the ratio of the purchase price of the target bank's equity to its book price or the market to book ratio (see Chapter 20).

The variables analyzed, their average values, and the expected direction of their effect on the merger premium appear in Table 22–6, panel (a), with the regression results in panel (b). As you can see, 6 of the 13 variables are bank-specific variables measuring the quality of the bank and 3 variables are regulatory variables reflecting the degree of barriers to entry into the market of the target bank. Two variables are market structure variables reflecting the possibilities of revenue synergies and rents from entry as measured by the market HHI and the deposit share of the target bank. Panel (b) indicates that the highest merger premiums are paid for well-managed banks in relatively uncompetitive environments.[19]

In a review of a number of studies that analyzed the determinants of merger bid premiums (the ratio of the purchase price of a target bank's equity to its book value), Darius Palia found some support for the Beatty, Santomero, and Smirlock findings.[20] Specifically, other empirical studies appear to confirm that premiums are higher (1) in states with the most restrictive regulations and (2) for target banks with high-quality loan portfolios. Palia also concludes that the growth rate of the target bank has little effect on bid premiums, whereas the results for the effects on bid premiums of target bank profitability and capital adequacy are rather mixed. More recently, Brewer, Jackson, Jagtiani, and Nguyen find that, in the 1990s, higher-performing targets (as measured by both return on equity and return on assets) receive higher bids; the lower the capital-to-deposit ratio, the larger the bid the acquiring bank is willing to offer; larger targets' loan-to-assets ratios and bank size are positively related to bid premiums.

Concept Questions

1. Suppose you are a manager of an FI looking at another FI as a target for acquisition. What three characteristics of the target FI would most attract you?
2. Given the same scenario as in question (1), what three characteristics would most discourage you?

---

[19] R. P. Beatty, A. M. Santomero, and M. L. Smirlock, "Bank Merger Premiums: Analysis and Evidence," *The Salomon Center Monograph Series on Economics and Finance,* New York University, 1987.

[20] D. Palia, "Recent Evidence of Bank Mergers," *Financial Markets, Instruments, and Institutions* 3, no. 5 (1994), pp. 36–59; and E. Brewer II, W. E. Jackson III, J. A. Jagtiani, and T. Nguyen, "The Price of Bank Mergers in the 1990s," Federal Reserve Bank of Chicago, *Economic Perspectives* 24, no. 1 (2000), pp. 2–24.

TABLE 22–6   Determinants of Bank Merger Premiums

(a) Variable Definitions and Expected Coefficient Signs

	Variable	Definition	Average	Expected Sign
Bank Variables	TREAS	Ratio of U.S. Treasury investments to total assets	.203	−
	LNTOAST	Ratio of net loans to total assets	.482	?
	PROV	Ratio of loan loss provision to net loans	.007	+
	CHARGOFF	Ratio of loan write-offs to net loans	.008	−
	ROEQ	Ratio of net income to equity capital	.091	+
	CAPDEV	(Ratio of loan loss allowance plus equity capital to assets) − .06	.030	−
Regulatory Variables	UNIT	Equals 1 if acquired bank located in unit bank state and zero otherwise	.276	+
	MULTI	Equals 1 if state law permits multibank holding companies and zero otherwise	.002	?
	ELECT	Equals 1 if state law permits statewide electronic banking and zero otherwise	.397	−
Market Structure Variables	MS	Ratio of bank's total deposits to those of the market; its market share	.179	+
	HERF	The Herfindahl index of the target bank's market	.253	+
Other Variables	PURCH	Equals 1 if the acquisition was a purchase of the acquired bank	.609	?
	COMB	Equals 1 if the acquisition involved a combination of cash and equity shares	.166	?

(b) Bank Merger Premium Regression Equation Results*

$$\text{Premium} = 1.927^\dagger - .771\ \text{TREAS}^\dagger - .574\ \text{LNTOAST}^\dagger + 10.438\ \text{PROV}$$
$$(9.27) \quad (-2.76) \quad (-1.96) \quad (1.41)$$

$$- 6.684\ \text{CHARGOFF} - 1.786\ \text{CAPDEV}^\dagger + .510\ \text{ROEQ}^\dagger + .096\ \text{UNIT}^\dagger$$
$$(-1.08) \quad (-1.76) \quad (2.10) \quad (1.66)$$

$$- .506\ \text{MULTI} - .061\ \text{ELECT} - .306\ \text{MS}^\dagger + .392\ \text{HERF}^\dagger$$
$$(-1.26) \quad (-1.19) \quad (-1.66) \quad (1.70)$$

$$- .176\ \text{PURCH}^\dagger - .171\ \text{COMB}^\dagger$$
$$(-2.85) \quad (-2.2)$$

$R^2 = .121$ Number of observations = 264   F-statistic = $2.68^{*\dagger}$

*T-statistics in parentheses below estimated coefficients.
†Coefficient on variable or test statistic significant at the 10 percent level.

Source: R. P. Beatty, A. M. Santomero, and M. L. Smirlock, "Bank Merger Premiums: Analysis and Evidence," *The Salomon Center Monograph Series on Economics and Finance*, New York University, 1987. Reprinted by permission.

THE SUCCESS OF GEOGRAPHIC EXPANSIONS

A variety of regulatory and economic factors affect the attractiveness of geographic expansions to an FI manager. This section evaluates some of the empirical evidence on the success of market extension mergers. There are at least two levels at which such an evaluation can be done: First, how do investors react when a bank merger is announced? Second, once bank mergers have taken place, do they produce, in aggregate, the expected gains in efficiency and profitability? Both the announcement effect studies and the postmerger performance studies generally support the existence of gains from domestic geographic expansions by U.S. commercial banks.

Investor Reaction

An event study of the 1998 failed Canadian bank mergers (Royal Bank and Bank of Montreal; Canadian Imperial Bank of Commerce and Toronto-Dominion Bank) by Baltazar and Santos found that market power rather than scale, scope, or X-efficiency economies was important to shareholders and that event studies would be useful to regulators in discerning societal benefits.[21] Investors do not necessarily react positively to the news of an acquisition or merger between financial institutions. For example, at the announcement of the merger of J. P. Morgan and Chase, shares of J. P. Morgan Chase fell from US$3.46 in 1999 to US$1.67 per share in 2002. Researchers have conducted a number of studies on both nonbank and bank mergers, looking at the announcement effects of mergers on both bidding and target firms' share values. The studies measure the announcement effect by the reaction of investors in the stock market to the news of a merger event. In particular, economists have been interested in whether a merger announcement generates positive **abnormal returns**—risk-adjusted stock returns above normal levels—for the bidding and/or target firms. Unlike the situation with commercial firms, where the typical study finds that only target firms' shareholders gain from merger announcements through significantly positive abnormal returns, studies in banking find that occasionally both the acquiring bank and the target bank gain.[22] For example, Cornett and De studied interstate merger proposals during the period 1982–86. They found that on the day of the merger announcement, bidding bank stockholders enjoyed positive abnormal returns of 0.65 percent while target bank shareholders enjoyed 6.08 percent abnormal returns. They also found that bidding bank returns were higher for those banks seeking to acquire targets in states with more restrictive banking pact laws that prohibited nationwide entry and where the target bank was not a failed bank. Studies by Desai and Stover and James and Weir also report significant abnormal returns for bidding bank stockholders even for intrastate mergers. More recently, Becher finds that bank mergers from 1990 through 1997 produce positive abnormal returns for targets and bidders. Kane examines bank megamergers in the mid-1990s. He finds that large bank bidders gain value when a target is large and when the large target is headquartered in the same state as the bidder. The gain is likely due to the fact that megamergers are more likely to create a bank that regulators would find too big to fail. Nevertheless, other studies—for example, by Hawawini and Swary—find negative returns for bidding banks.[23] Table 22–7 summarizes these and other findings.

abnormal returns
Risk-adjusted stock returns above expected levels.

---

[21] See R. Baltazar and M.Santos, "The Benefits of Banking Mega-Mergers: Event Study Evidence from the 1998 Failed Mega-Merger Attempts in Canada," *Canadian Journal of Administrative Sciences* 20(2), September 2003, pp. 196–208.

[22] See, for example, N. Travlos, "Corporate Takeover Bids, Methods of Payment, and Bidding Firm Stock Returns," *Journal of Finance* 42 (1987), pp. 943–63.

[23] M. M. Cornett and S. De, "Common Stock Returns in Corporate Takeover Bids: Evidence of Interstate Bank Mergers," *Journal of Banking and Finance* 15 (1991), pp. 273–95; A. Desai and R. Stover, "Bank Holding Company Acquisitions, Stockholders Returns, and Regulatory Uncertainty," *Journal of Financial Research* 8 (1985), pp. 145–56; C. James and P. Weir, "Returns to Acquirers and Competition in the Acquisition Market: The Case of Banking," *Journal of Political Economy* 95 (1983), pp. 355–70; G. Hawawini and I. Swary, *Mergers and Acquisitions in the U.S. Banking Industry* (Amsterdam: North Holland, 1990), p. 211; D. A. Becher, "The Valuation Effects of Bank Mergers," *Journal of Corporate Finance,* 2000, pp. 189–214; and E. J. Kane, "Incentives for Banking Megamergers: What Motives Might Regulators Infer from Event-Study Evidence?" *Journal of Money, Credit, and Banking,* 2000, pp. 671–701.

TABLE 22–7 Summary of Event Studies

Study	Sample	Definition of Event*	Definition of Market†	Target's Excess Returns‡	Acquirer's Excess Returns
Baradwaj, Dubofsky, and Fraser, 1991	108 interstate (July 1981–87)	1	Nasdaq value weighted	N/A	Negative
Baradwaj, Fraser, and Furtado, 1990	23 hostile 30 nonhostile (1980–87)	1	OTC equally weighted	Positive	Negative
Becher, 2000	558 mergers (1960–97)	1, 2	Value weighted	Positive	Positive
Cornett and De, 1991a	152 interstate 152 acquirers 37 targets (1982–86)	1, 4 5	Equally weighted, value weighted	Positive	Positive
Cornett and De, 1991b	132 interstate 132 acquirers 36 targets (1982–86)	1, 4 5	Equally weighted, value weighted	Positive	Positive
Cornett and Tehranian, 1992	30 mergers (1982–87)	7	Equally weighted	Positive	Negative
Cornett, Hovakimian, Palia, and Tehranian, 2001	423 acquirers (1988–95)	1, 8	Equally weighted	N/A	Focusing, no change Diversifying, negative
Cornett, McNutt, and Tehranian, 2004	193 mergers (1990–2000)	1, 2, 9	Value weighted	Positive	Negative
DeLong, 2001	280 mergers (1988–1995)	1, 9	Value weighted	Positive	Focusing, negative Diversifying, more negative
Desai and Stover, 1985	18 BHCs (1976–82)	1,2 3	Equally weighted	N/A	Positive
Dubofsky and Fraser, 1989	101 mergers (1973–83)	1	Equally weighted, value weighted	N/A	Positive (before June 1981), negative (after June 1981)
Hannan and Wolken, 1989	43 acquirers 69 targets (1982–87)	1	Wilshire Index	Positive	Negative
Hawawini and Swary, 1990	78 acquirers 123 targets (1971–86)	1, 2	Nasdaq value weighted	Positive	Negative
James and Weir, 1987a	60 mergers (1972–83)	1	Equally weighted	N/A	Positive
Kane and Tehranian, 1989	33 New Hampshire mergers (June 1979–87)	1, 6 9	Nasdaq equally weighted bank index	N/A	Zero
Kane, 2000	110 megamergers (1991–98)	9	Value weighted	Positive	Giant banks, positive
Lobue, 1984	37 BHCs (N/A)	3	OTC general market index and OTC banking index	N/A	Positive
Neely, 1987	26 mergers (1979–85)	1, 5	Creates bank index from S&P	Positive	Negative
Palia, 1994	48 mergers (1984–87)	1	Nasdaq value weighted	N/A	Negative
Sushka and Bendeck, 1988	41 mergers (1972–85)	2	Uses mean adjusted returns model	N/A	Negative

TABLE 22–7   (*concluded*)

Study	Sample	Definition of Event*	Definition of Market†	Target's Excess Returns‡	Acquirer's Excess Returns
Trifts and Scanlon, 1987	21 interstate 14 acquirers 17 targets (1982–85)	1	S&P 500 index	Positive	Negative
Wall and Gup, 1989	23 mergers (June 1981–83)	1	Value weighted	N/A	Negative

*The event dates among the various studies are coded (for easy presentation) as follows: 1 = *Wall Street Journal* announcement date; 2 = Federal Reserve Board approval date; 3 = acquisition completion date; 4 = Dow Jones News Wire announcement date; 5 = *New York Times* announcement date; 6 = Cates MergerWatch announcement date; 7 = Shearson Lehman Brothers' Bank Merger and Acquisition study announcement date; 8 = LEXIS/NEXIS; 9 = Securities Data Company.
†Whenever the study specifies that Nasdaq stocks have been included in the market portfolio, we explicitly specify so. Otherwise, we present the market portfolio as an equally weighted and/or value weighted portfolio. Other market portfolios (such as the Standard & Poor's 500 Index) are also presented.
‡We do not present the actual excess returns earned because many studies provide results for a larger number of differing event windows (which are not comparable). Accordingly, we present whether the excess returns were positive or negative. N/A stands for not available or not examined.

Source: D. Palia, "Recent Evidence of Bank Mergers," *Financial Markets, Instruments, and Institutions* 3, no. 5 (1994), pp. 36–59, and authors' research.

Postmerger Performance

Even though the expectation, on announcement, might be favourable for enhanced profitability and performance as a result of an interstate geographic expansion, are such mergers actually proving successful in the postmerger period? For example, after its acquisition of First Chicago, profits of Bank One fell from US$3.45 per share in 1999 to US$2.77 in 2002. Cornett and Tehranian studied the postacquisition performance of large bank mergers between 1982 and 1987 and again from 1990 through 2000. Using operating cash flows (defined as earnings before depreciation, goodwill, interest on long-term debt, and taxes) divided by assets as a performance measure, they found that merged banks tended to outperform the banking industry. They found that superior performance resulted from improvements in these banks' ability to (1) attract loans and deposits, (2) increase employee productivity, and (3) enhance asset growth. Further, for 1990 through 2000, they found that large bank mergers produced greater performance gains than small bank mergers, activity-focusing mergers produced greater performance gains than diversifying mergers, geographically focusing mergers produced greater performance gains than geographically diversifying mergers, and performance gains were larger after the implementation of nationwide banking in 1997. Finally, they found improved performance of a merged bank is the result of both revenue enhancements and cost-reduction activities. However, revenue enhancements are most significant in those mergers that also experience reduced costs. Both studies find that the announcement period abnormal stock returns are significantly related to the changes in operating performance after the merger. Stiroh and Strahan studied the performance of banks that merged as their home state passed regulations allowing intrastate and interstate banking. They show that after deregulation, poor-performing banks come under increased pressure as well-run banks entered their previously shielded markets. They found a large and significant change in the control of bank assets (from poor- to high-performing banks) after deregulation. They concluded that the transfer of assets to better banks represents a clear benefit from the deregulation.[24]

---

[24] M. M. Cornett and H. Tehranian, "Changes in Corporate Performance Associated with Bank Acquisitions," *Journal of Financial Economics* 31 (1992), pp. 211–34; K. J. Stiroh and P. E. Strahan, "Competitive Dynamics of Deregulation: Evidence from U. S. Banking, "*Journal of Money, Credit, and Banking* 35, no. 5 (2003), pp. 801–28; and M. M. Cornett, J. J. McNutt, and H. Tehranian, "Performance Changes Around Bank Mergers: Revenue Enhancements versus Cost Reductions," Working Paper, 2004.

Boyd and Graham studied small bank mergers (with combined total deposits less than US$400 million) from 1989 through 1991. Comparing industry-adjusted return on assets (ROA) before versus after a merger, they found that 1989 mergers saw large ROA increases, 1991 mergers resulted in decreases, and 1990 mergers had results somewhere in the middle. However, for all years the merged banks outperformed the banking industry. DeLong found that mergers that "focused" activities over the 1988–95 period improved the performance of the merging firms while those that diversified activities did not.[25] Finally, using 1994 data, Hughes et al. found that banks that engage in interstate expansion outperform banks that do not. Not only do these banks experience gains in financial performance, but society also benefits from enhanced bank safety that follows from improved performance.[26]

Concept Questions

1. If the abnormal returns for target banks are usually positive, does this mean that managers of acquiring banks tend to overpay the shareholders of the target bank?
2. In general, what do studies of the announcement effect and postmerger performance conclude?

GLOBAL AND INTERNATIONAL EXPANSIONS

Many FIs can diversify domestically, but only the very largest can aspire to diversify beyond national frontiers. This section analyzes recent trends toward the globalization of FI franchises and examines the potential return-risk advantages and disadvantages of such expansions. While FIs from some countries, such as Canada and the United States, are currently seeking to expand internationally as fast as possible, others, most notably those from Japan, are contracting their international operations. The extent to which an FI expands internationally is thus part of the overall risk management of the FI.

There are at least three ways an FI can establish a global or international presence: (1) selling financial services from its domestic offices to foreign customers, such as a loan originating in the Toronto office of the Bank of Nova Scotia (BNS) made to a Mexican manufacturer; (2) selling financial services through a branch, agency, or representative office established in the foreign customer's country, such as making a loan to the Mexican customer through BNS's branch in Mexico; and (3) selling financial services to a foreign customer through subsidiary companies in the foreign customer's country, such as BNS buying a Mexican bank and using that wholly-owned bank to make loans to the Mexican customer. Note that these three methods of global activity expansion are not mutually exclusive; an FI could use all three simultaneously to expand the scale and scope of its operations.

---

[25] While most research has found bank acquisitions improve financial performance of the combined bank, results to the contrary have been found in some papers. See B. G. Baradwaj, D. A. Dubofsky, and D. R. Fraser, "Bidder Returns in Interstate and Intrastate Bank Acquisitions," *Journal of Financial Services Research* 5 (1992), pp. 261–73; D. Palia, "Recent Evidence of Bank Mergers," *Financial Markets, Instruments, and Institutions* 3, no. 5 (1994), pp. 36–59; Hawawini and I. Swary, *Mergers and Acquisitions in the U.S. Banking Industry* (New York: Elsevier Science, 1990); and M. F. Toyne and J. D. Tripp, "Interstate Bank Mergers and Their Impact on Shareholder Return: Evidence from the 1990's," *Quarterly Journal of Business and Economics* 37, no. 4 (1998), pp. 48–58.

[26] J. D. Boyd and S. L. Graham, "Consolidation in U.S. Banking: Implications for Efficiency and Competitive Risk, "*Bank Mergers and Acquisitions,* eds. T. Amihud and G. Miller (Amsterdam: Kluwer, 1998); G. DeLong, "Domestic and International Bank Mergers: The Gains from Focusing versus Diversifying," *Journal of Financial Economics* 59 (2001), pp. 221–52; G. DeLong, "Does Long-Term Performance of Mergers Match Market Expectations? Evidence from the U. S. Banking Industry," *Financial Management,* 2003, pp. 5–25; and J. P. Hughes, W. W. Lang, L. J. Mester, and C. Moon, "The Dollars and Sense of Bank Consolidation," *Journal of Banking and Finance* 23 (1999), pp. 291–324.

TABLE 22–8
Top Global Banks

Source: "Top 50 Global
Banks," *The Banker,* February
2003. www.thebanker.com

Banks	Home Country	Percentage of Overseas Business*
1. American Express Bank	United States	80.9%
2. Standard Chartered	United Kingdom	79.2
3. UBS	Switzerland	76.8
4. Investec	South Africa	74.2
5. Credit Suisse Group	Switzerland	72.9
6. Deutsche Bank	Germany	64.4

*Overseas business refers to the percentage of assets banks hold outside their home country.

Canadian and U.S. banks, insurance companies, and securities firms have all expanded abroad in recent years, often through branches and subsidiaries; this has been reciprocated by the entrance and growth until recently of foreign FIs in Canadian and U.S. financial service markets. At the end of 2002, 15 banks in the world had more than 50 percent of their bank assets held in foreign countries. Table 22–8 lists the top six banks in terms of global activity. Of the top 30 global banks, no single country dominated the list. Canada had five banks in the top 30; Ireland, the Netherlands, and the United States all had three banks, while Austria, Germany, Spain, Switzerland, and the United Kingdom each had two banks. A severe economic recession and burgeoning bad debts in their loan portfolios have left Japanese banks noticeably absent even though, based on size of assets, they are among the largest in the world.

The next section concentrates on the growth of global banking. It begins with Canadian and U.S. bank expansions into foreign countries and the factors motivating these expansions and then discusses foreign bank expansions into Canada and the United States.

Canadian and U.S. Banks Abroad

Serving an exporting nation, particularly in the resource sector, Canadian banks have a long history of international activities, maintaining representative offices for their Canadian clients abroad and networks of correspondent banks to support their exports. As well, Canadian banks are strong participants in the global loan syndication markets (see Chapters 12, 15, and 26). However, the level of international diversification varies among the largest banks, ranging from the National Bank of Canada with just 28.9 percent of its total earning assets outside of Canada to the Bank of Nova Scotia with 55.1 percent in 2004. As well as billing itself as "a local bank in 50+ countries" in its 1997 Annual Report, Bank of Nova Scotia owned 10 percent of Mexico's Grupo Financiero Inverlat, increasing the stake to 97 percent by 2004 and changing the name of the bank to Scotiabank Inverlat. Table 22–9 shows the foreign assets of Canadian banks in 2004. As can be seen, a significant portion of the foreign assets of Canadian banks are located in the United States. This is particularly true for Bank of Montreal, with Harris Bank in Chicago, and CIBC World Capital Markets, with a strong presence in New York. Though some U.S. banks, such as J. P. Morgan Chase, have had offices abroad since the beginning of the twentieth century, the major phase of growth began in the early 1960s after the passage of the Overseas Direct Investment Control Act of 1964. This law restricted domestic U.S. banks' ability to lend to U.S. corporations that wanted to make foreign investments. The law was eventually repealed, but it created

TABLE 22–9
Average assets of the Big Six Canadian Banks by geographic location 2004 (in billions of dollars)

Source: Company Annual Reports, 2004

	Canada	United States	Other Countries	Total
Bank of Montreal	177.3	68.8	23.7	269.8
Bank of Nova Scotia	165.0	44.0	83.0	292.0
CIBC	199.4	54.4	38.7	292.5
National Bank of Canada*	63.1	6.1	4.6	73.9
Royal Bank	238.0	95.5	95.7	429.2
Toronto-Dominion Bank	216.1	41.5	53.4	311.0

*Earning assets

Eurocurrency transaction
Any transaction in a currency that takes place outside of the country of origin.

Eurodollar transaction
Any transaction involving U.S. dollars that takes place outside the United States.

incentives for U.S. banks to establish foreign offices to service the funding and other business needs of their U.S. clients in other countries. This offshore funding and lending in dollars created the beginning of a market we now call the *Eurodollar market*. The term **Eurocurrency transaction** denotes any transaction in a currency that takes place outside of the country of origin. For example, a banking transaction booked externally to the boundaries of the United States, often through an overseas branch or subsidiary, is called a **Eurodollar transaction**.[27]

Table 22–10 shows the aggregate size of U.S. bank activities abroad between 1980 and 2003 as well as the different types of loan activities those subsidiaries engage in. As reported in Table 22–10, assets in U.S. bank foreign offices increased from US$353.8 billion in 1980 to US$804.4 billion in 2003. However, as a percent of these banks' total assets, assets in foreign offices fell from 32.4 percent in 1980 to 16.2 percent in 2003. The same trend is found for much of the loan portfolio. The majority of loans (in dollar terms) in foreign offices of U.S. banks are commercial and industrial (C&I) loans at US$127.6 billion in 2003. In 1980, 38.6 percent of these banks' C&I loans were in foreign offices, compared to 19.9 percent in 2003. In 1980, 5.8 percent of these banks' real estate loans were in foreign offices compared to 2.7 percent in 2003. In contrast to C&I and mortgage loans, in 1980 8.7 percent of the loans to individuals in these banks were in foreign offices compared to 16.3 percent in 2003.

U.S. Bank Expansions Abroad

While regulation of foreign lending was the original impetus for the early growth of the Eurodollar market and the associated establishment of U.S. branches and subsidiaries outside the United States, other regulatory and economic factors also have impacted the growth of U.S. offshore banking. These factors are discussed next.

The US Dollar as an International Medium of Exchange The growth of international trade after World War II and the use of the dollar as an international medium of exchange encouraged foreign corporations and investors to demand dollars. A convenient way to do this was by using U.S. banks' foreign offices to intermediate such fund flows between the United States and foreigners wishing to hold dollars. Today, trade-related transactions underlie much of the activity in the Eurodollar market.[28] However, with the creation of the new euro currency in January 2002, the importance of the dollar as the "international medium of exchange" may well decline, especially among major European corporations.

---

[27] That is, the definition of a Eurodollar transaction is more general than "a transaction booked in Europe." In fact, any deposit in dollars taken externally to the United States normally qualifies that transaction as a Eurodollar transaction. The definition may be generalized to all currencies. e.g. Euroyen, etc.

[28] The decline in the dollar relative to the Euro, yen and mark in recent years has weakened the role of the dollar as the international medium of exchange.

TABLE 22–10
Assets of U.S. Banks with Foreign Offices, 1980–2003 (in billions of U.S. dollars)

Source: *Federal Reserve Bulletin,* various issues, Table 4–20.

	1980	1990	1995	2000	2003
Total assets	1,091.4	1,901.5	2,530.1	4,311.4	4,961.7
Domestic assets	768.7	1,559.3	1,962.8	3,576.3	4,157.3
Foreign assets	353.8	410.7	666.3	735.1	804.4
C&I loans (domestic)*	173.8	326.1	356.8	647.2	514.3
C&I loans (foreign)	109.4	103.6	125.5	189.8	127.6
Real estate loans (domestic)	108.9	387.2	486.1	955.5	1,211.2
Real estate loans (foreign)	6.7	26.6	27.2	32.0	33.4
Individual loans (domestic)	67.1	151.9	207.0	302.1	329.1
Individual loans (foreign)	6.4	17.2	30.6	44.3	64.1

*Commercial and Industrial loans.

Political Risk Concerns   Political risk concerns among savers in emerging market countries have led to enormous outflows of dollars from those countries, often to U.S. branches and subsidiaries in the Cayman Islands and the Bahamas, where there are very stringent bank secrecy rules. Because of the secrecy rules in some foreign countries and the possibility that these rules may result in money laundering and the financing of terrorist activities, the U.S. government enacted the USA Patriot Act of 2001. The act prohibits U.S. banks from providing banking services to foreign banks that have no physical presence in any country (so-called shell banks). The bill also added foreign corruption offenses to the list of crimes that can trigger a U.S. money-laundering prosecution. Also, federal authorities have the power to subpoena the records of a foreign bank's U.S. correspondent account. Further, the bill makes a depositor's funds in a foreign bank's U.S. correspondent account subject to the same civil forfeiture rules that apply to depositors' funds in other U.S. accounts. Finally, the act requires U.S. banks to improve their due diligence reviews in order to guard against money laundering. The Office of the Superintendent of Financial Institutions (OSFI) maintains a list of suspected terrorist organizations and, under the *United Nations Suppression of Terrorism Regulations (UNSTR)* requires all Canadian banks and foreign bank subsidiaries to provide monthly reports of accounts held for suspect individuals. Also, under the *Proceeds of Crime (Money Laundering) and Terrorist Financing Act* reports must be sent to the Financial Transactions and Reports Analysis Centre of Canada (FINTRAC).

www.osfi-bsif.gc.ca

www.fintrac.gc.ca

Violations of the USA Patriot Act have resulted in large fines and actions taken against violating banks. For example, in 2004 Hudson United Bank agreed to pay US$5 million to settle a probe into whether a branch failed to monitor accounts in its correspondent banking business. Investigators discovered that more than US$1 billion flowed through suspicious accounts used by customers from South America and the Caribbean at a Hudson United Bank branch over a 16-month period ending in November 2003, when the bank shut down the correspondent business dealing with international customers. The branch was not following required "know your customer" rules set out in the Patriot Act. More recently, in April 2004, federal officials intensified their inquiry into Riggs Bank's handling of large amounts of cash for foreign accounts, and a central focus was on the bank's failure to report properly dozens of substantial withdrawals from the personal accounts of Saudi Arabia's longtime ambassador to Washington. The Saudi accounts and other international transactions at Riggs were being investigated by the Federal Bureau of Investigation and two Treasury Department agencies, the Office of the Comptroller of the Currency and the Financial Crimes Enforcement Network. Further, regulators threatened to impose new requirements and other penalties on Riggs.

Domestic Regulatory Restrictions/Foreign Regulatory Relaxations   As discussed in Chapter 21, prior to the 1999 Financial Services Modernization Act, U.S. banks faced considerable activity restrictions at home regarding their securities, insurance, and commercial activities. However, with certain exceptions, Federal Reserve regulations have allowed U.S. banking offices in other countries to engage in the permitted banking activities of the foreign country even if such activities were not permitted in the United States. For example, U.S. banks setting up foreign subsidiaries can lease real property, act as general insurance agents, and underwrite and deal in foreign corporate securities (up to a maximum commitment of US$2 million). Foreign activity regulations also encourage U. S. bank expansion abroad. For example, in late 2003 the Chinese Banking Regulatory Commission signaled a shift in policy away from restricting overseas competition to one of cautiously embracing it when it announced a comprehensive plan to overhaul the country's shaky banking system. The plan gave foreign banks greater scope to operate in China, including increasing the ceiling on foreign ownership in Chinese financial institutions from 15 percent to 20 percent for a single investor, expanding the number of cities where foreign branches could do local currency business, and easing capital requirements for foreign branches.[29] In a recent study Whalen[30] has shown that many of these nonbanking activities produce revenue flows that have a low or negative correlation with the revenues from domestic (U.S.) banking. That is, international expansions appear to produce important revenue-risk diversification benefits for U.S. banks.

Technology and Communications Improvements   The improvements in telecommunications and other communications technologies such as CHIPS (the international payment system, see Chapter 14) and the development of proprietary communication networks by large FIs have allowed U.S. parent FIs to extend and maintain real-time control over their foreign operations at a decreasing cost. The decreasing operating costs of such expansions have made it feasible to locate offices in an even wider array of international locations.[31]

Factors Deterring Expansions Abroad

A number of potential factors deter international expansion, as discussed next.

Capital Constraints   The proposed (2006) reforms of the Bank for International Settlements (BIS) capital requirements will raise the required capital needed to back loans to sovereign countries outside of the OECD rated below B− as well as any loans to OECD countries who are rated below AA− (i.e., it is only the OECD countries rated above AA− that will have zero risk weight as under the current BIS risk-based capital system—see Chapter 20).

---

[29] C. M. Buch and G. DeLong find that as countries increase regulatory transparency, their banks become more attractive targets of international bank mergers. At the same time, they find some evidence that increased supervisory power reduces the incentives of banks to engage as acquirers in international mergers. In addition, banks from more developed countries tend to take over banks in less developed countries. See "Cross-Border Bank Mergers: What Lures the Rare Animal?" Working Paper, Baruch College, CUNY, 2003.

[30] See G. Whalen, "The Securities Activities of the Foreign Subsidiaries of U.S. Banks: Evidence of Risk and Returns," White Paper 98–2, OCC, Washington, D.C., February 1998.

[31] M. E. Chaffai, M. Dietsch, and A. Lozano-Vivas, in "Technological and Environmental Differences in the European Banking Industries," *Journal of Financial Studies Research* 19 (2001), pp. 147–62, break bank productivity into technological differences and environmental differences. They find that while technology improves bank productivity, differences due to environmental conditions are larger than those due to technology. Even if the banking industry in a country uses better technology, it could be less productive in a hostile environment.

TABLE 22–11
The NAFTA Agreement and Banks

Source: Institute of International Bankers, *1994 Global Survey of Regulatory and Market Developments in Banking, Securities and Insurance,* September 1994, p. 17.

- Any bank chartered in Canada or the United States, including Canadian or U.S. banks owned by nondomestic banks, may establish a bank subsidiary in Mexico that may expand in Mexico without geographic restriction. Canadian and U.S. banks, however, may not branch directly into Mexico.
- Banks from Mexico and Canada may establish direct branches and subsidiaries in the United States subject to the same geographic restrictions imposed on direct branches of other nondomestic banks and on other U.S. chartered banks, respectively.
- Banks from the United States and Mexico that are not controlled by investors from other countries may establish Schedule II bank subsidiaries in Canada, which subsidiaries enjoy nationwide branching powers. Mexican and U.S. banks may not branch directly into Canada.

Notes:
1. Nondomestic banks cannot open branches but are allowed to establish Schedule II subsidiary banks in Canada. Schedule II subsidiary banks owned by banks from the United States or Mexico have the same nationwide branching privileges as domestic Canadian banks. Schedule II banks owned by banks from other countries must seek government approval to open additional branches. This geographic restriction on Schedule II subsidiaries will be eliminated when the latest round of GATT comes into effect.
2. Mexico does not permit nondomestic banks to establish domestic branches. However, nondomestic banks can establish representative offices and offshore branches and take minority interests in local banking institutions. In addition, under NAFTA, banks from the United States and Canada, including U.S. and Canadian banks owned by banks from other countries, are allowed to establish bank subsidiaries with the same nationwide branching privileges as Mexican banks.

Emerging Market Problems

The problems of other emerging market countries such as Korea, Thailand, and Indonesia in 1997 and 1998 and more recently (in the early 2000s) in Argentina have made many Canadian and U.S. banks more cautious in expanding outside traditional foreign markets.[32] This is despite the existence of increasingly favorable regulatory environments. For example, the 1994 **NAFTA** agreement has given U.S. and Canadian banks greater powers to expand into Mexico. See Table 22–11 for details on the NAFTA agreement.[33] The December 1997 agreement by 100 countries, reached under the auspices of the World Trade Organization (WTO), is also an important step toward dismantling the regulatory barriers inhibiting the entry of North American FIs into emerging market countries.[34]

NAFTA
The North American Free Trade Agreement.

Competition   During the 1990s, global banks faced extensive competition from Japanese banks for overseas business. Aiding the Japanese banks was their access to a large domestic savings base at a relatively low funding cost, the relatively slow pace of deregulation in the Japanese domestic financial markets, and their size. For example, for most of the 1990s, Japan had 9 of the 10 largest banks, measured by asset size, in the world. Though large size does not necessarily mean high profits,[35] it gives a bank a greater ability to diversify across borders (and products) and to attract business by aggressively cutting fees and spreads in selected areas.

[32] Notable exceptions are Bank of Nova Scotia, as previously noted, and Citigroup. Citigroup purchased Mexico's second largest bank, Grupo Financiero Banamex-Accival in 2000. Citing Citigroup's faith in the recovery of Mexico's economy and banking system, the company hoped to use the Banamex brand name to serve the fast-growing Hispanic population in the United States as well.

[33] For an excellent discussion of the effects of NAFTA on banks, securities firms, and insurance companies, see R. S. Sczudio, "NAFTA: Opportunities Abound for U.S. and Canadian Financial Institutions," *Bankers Magazine,* July–August 1993, pp. 28–32.

[34] See "Accord Is Reached to Lower Barriers in Global Finance," *New York Times,* December 12, 1997, p. A1.

[35] In fact, Credit Lyonnais is a good example of why large size does not necessarily correlate with high profitability. In spring 1995, the French government had to bail out the bank by shifting its bad loans into a newly created entity. In addition, most Japanese banks have had severe problems with bad loans in recent years, which has meant a reduced tendency to expand abroad further.

However, in the late 1990s and early 2000s, as the Japanese economy moved into recession and the bad debts of Japanese banks mounted, the main competitive threat to U.S. banks has come from European banks.

Aiding the competitive position of European banks has been the passage of the European Community (EC) Second Banking Directive, which has created a single banking market in Europe as well as the introduction of a single currency for much of Europe (the euro). Under the Directive, European banks are allowed to branch and acquire banks throughout the European Community—that is, they have a single EC passport.[36] Although the Second Banking Directive did not come fully into effect until the end of 1992, it was announced as early as 1988. As a result, there has been a cross-border merger wave among European banks that has paralleled the U.S. domestic merger and acquisition wave that followed the dismantling of interstate branching restrictions after the passage and implementation of the Reigle-Neal Act in 1994 (see Chapter 22).[37] In addition, a number of European banks have formed strategic alliances that will enable retail bank customers to open new accounts, access account information, and make payments to third parties through any of the branches of the member banks in the alliance. This greater consolidation in European banking has created more intense competition for U.S. and other foreign banks in European wholesale markets and has made it more difficult for them to penetrate European retail markets.

Foreign Banks in North America

As shown in Table 22–11 and also discussed in Chapter 2, foreign banks in Canada are called Schedule II banks, are regulated by OSFI, and are subsidiaries of international FIs such as Citibank, the U.K.'s HSBC, and Germany's Deutsche Bank. OSFI lists 25 foreign bank branches in Canada in 2005, with total assets of $36.2 billion at the end of the first quarter of 2005. Canadian banks, as shown in Table 22–9, hold many of their assets in the United States. Just as U.S. banks can profitably expand into foreign markets, foreign banks have historically viewed the United States as an attractive market for entry. The following sections discuss foreign banks in the United States.

Organizational Form

Foreign banks use five primary forms of entry into the U.S. market. The choice of which organizational form to use is a function of regulations in the bank's home country as well as the risk management strategies followed by the bank.

Subsidiary   A foreign bank subsidiary has its own capital and charter; it operates in the same way as any U.S. domestic bank, with access to both retail and wholesale markets.

---

[36] Direct branching by non-EC banks into member states was not governed by the Second Banking Directive but the laws of each member state. Currently, all EC countries allow foreign banks to branch.

[37] See A. Cybo-Ottone and M. Murgia, "Mergers and Acquisitions in the European Banking Markets," *Journal of Banking and Finance* 24 (2000), pp. 831–59; A. W. A. Boot, "European Lessons on Consolidation in Banking," *Journal of Banking and Finance* 23 (1999), pp. 609–13; C. M. Buch, "Why Do Banks Go Abroad? Evidence from German Data," *Financial Markets, Institutions, and Instruments* 9 (2000), pp. 33–67; C. M. Buch and G. DeLong, "Determinants of Cross-Border Bank Mergers: Is Europe Different?" in *Foreign Direct Investment in the Real and Financial Sector of Industrial Countries*, ed. H. Herrmann and R. Lipsey (Berlin: Springer, 2003); and P. Angelini and N. Citorellis. "The Effects of Regulatory Reform on Competition in the Banking Industry," *Journal of Money, Credit, and Banking*, October 2003, pp. 663–84. The largest European cross-border deal in progress at the time of writing is the takeover of Germany's second largest lender, HVB Group AG by Italy's Unicredito Italiano SpA for €15 billion. See S. Graham, "HVB accepts Unicredito's €15-billion takeover offer," *Globe and Mail*, Monday, June 13, 2005, p. B5.

TABLE 22–12 U.S. and Foreign Bank Assets, 1980–2003

	Bank Assets Held in United States (billions of US dollars)	
	U.S.-Owned	Foreign-Owned
1980	1,537.0	166.7
1985	2,284.8	175.5
1990	3,010.3	389.6
1992	3,138.4	514.3
1994	3,409.9	471.1
1995	3,660.6	530.1
2000	6,088.2	984.3
2003	7,385.4	1,069.6

Source: *Federal Reserve Bulletin*, various issues, Tables 1.26 and 4.30.

Branch A branch bank is a direct expansion of the parent bank into a foreign or U.S. banking market. As such, it is reliant on its parent bank, such as Sumitomo Mitsui Banking Corporation in Japan, for capital support; normally, it has access to both wholesale and retail deposit and funding markets in the United States.

Agency An agency is a restricted form of entry; this organizational form restricts access of funds to those funds borrowed on the wholesale and money markets (i.e., an agency cannot accept deposits). A special case of an agency is a New York Agreement Company that has both agency functions and limited investment banking functions.

Edge Act Corporation
Specialized organizational form open to U.S. domestic banks that specialize in international trade-related banking transactions or investments.

Edge Act Corporation An **Edge Act Corporation** is a specialized organizational form open to U.S. domestic banks since 1919 and to foreign banks since 1978. These banks specialize in international trade-related banking transactions or investments.

Representative Office Even though a representative office books neither loans nor deposits in the United States, it acts as a loan production office, generating loan business for its parent bank at home. This is the most limited organizational form for a foreign bank entering the United States.[38]

Trends and Growth

Table 22–12 shows the expansion of foreign banks in the United States between 1980 and 2003. In 1980 foreign banks had US$166.7 billion in assets (10.8 percent of the size of total U.S. bank assets). This activity grew through 1992, when foreign banks had US$514.3 billion in assets (16.4 percent of the size of U.S. assets). In the mid-1990s, there was a modest retrenchment in the asset share of foreign banks in the United States. In 1994, their U.S. assets totaled US$471.1 billion (13.8 percent of the size of U.S. assets). This retrenchment reflected a number of factors, including the highly competitive market for wholesale banking in the United States, a decline in average U.S. loan quality, capital constraints on Japanese banks at home, and their poor lending performance at home, and the introduction of the Foreign Bank Supervision and Enhancement Act (FBSEA) of 1991, which tightened regulations on foreign banks in the United States (discussed below).[39] However, as foreign banks adjusted to these developments and because of the strong U.S. economy in the late 1990s, activity of foreign banks in the United States has grown again, reaching 16.1 percent in 2000. The worldwide economic recession in the early 2000s again depressed the level of international activity in the United States. For example, in 2003 the percent of foreign bank assets in the United States dipped to 14.5 percent.

[38] Also note the existence of International Banking Facilities (IBF) in the United States since 1981. These are specialized vehicles that are allowed to take deposits from and make loans to foreign (non-U.S.) customers only. As such, they are essentially offshore banking units that operate onshore. Most are located in New York, Illinois, and California and are generally free of U.S. bank regulation and taxes.

[39] J. Peek, E. Rosengren, and F. Kasirye, "The Poor Performance of Foreign Subsidiaries: Were the Problems Acquired or Created?" *Journal of Banking and Finance* 23 (2000), pp. 579–604, find that many foreign banks acquiring U.S. banks have been hurt by the fact that the target banks already had problems at the time of acquisition. Moreover, they find that the changes in strategy introduced by foreign owners were generally insufficient in raising the performance of foreign banks relative to U.S. domestically owned peer banks.

Regulation of Foreign Banks in the United States

Before 1978, foreign branches and agencies entering the United States were licensed mostly at the state level. As such, their entry, regulation, and oversight were almost totally confined to the state level. Beginning in 1978 with the passage of the International Banking Act (IBA) and the more recent passage of the Foreign Bank Supervision Enhancement Act (FBSEA), Title II of the FDICIA of December 1991, federal regulators have exerted increasing control over foreign banks operating in the United States.

The International Banking Act of 1978

Pre-IBA. Before the passage in 1978 of the IBA, foreign agencies and branches entering the United States with state licenses had some competitive advantages and disadvantages relative to most domestic banks. On the one hand, as state-licensed organizations, they were not subject to the Federal Reserve's reserve requirements, audits, and exams; interstate branching restrictions (the McFadden Act); or restrictions on corporate securities underwriting activities (the Glass-Steagall Act). However, they had no access to the Federal Reserve's discount window (i.e., lender of last resort); no direct access to Fedwire, and, thus, the fed funds market; and no access to FDIC deposit insurance.

www.fdic.gov

Their inability to gain access to deposit insurance effectively precluded them from the U.S. retail banking market and its deposit base. As a result, prior to 1978, foreign banks in the United States largely concentrated on wholesale banking.

www.federalreserve. gov

Post-IBA. The unequal treatment of domestic and foreign banks regarding federal regulation and lobbying by domestic banks regarding the unfairness of this situation provided the impetus for Congress to pass the International Banking Act in 1978. The fundamental regulatory philosophy underlying the IBA was one of **national treatment**, a philosophy that attempted to create a level playing field for both domestic and foreign banks in U.S. banking markets. As a result of this act, foreign banks were required to hold Federal Reserve-specified reserve requirements if their worldwide assets exceeded US$1 billion, were subjected to Federal Reserve examinations, and were subjected to both the McFadden and Glass-Steagall Acts. With respect to the latter, an important grandfather provision in the act allowed foreign banks established in the United States prior to 1978 to keep their "illegal" interstate branches and securities-activity operations. That is, interstate and security-activity restrictions were applied only to new foreign banks entering the United States after 1978.[40]

national treatment
Regulating foreign banks in the same fashion as domestic banks or creating a level playing field.

If anything, the passage of the IBA accelerated the expansion of foreign bank activities in the United States. A major reason for this was that for the first time, the IBA gave foreign banks access to the Federal Reserve's discount window, Fedwire, and FDIC insurance. In particular, access to FDIC insurance allowed entry into retail banking. For example, in 1979 alone foreign banks acquired four large U.S. banks (Crocker, National Bank of North America, Union Planters, and Marine Midland). In addition, in the early 1980s the Bank of Tokyo, Mitsubishi Bank, and Sanwa Bank invested US$1.3 billion in California bank acquisitions. Overall, Japanese banks owned over 25 percent of California bank assets at the end of the 1980s. (By the end of the 1990s, many of these Japanese-owned California bank assets were up for sale.)

---

[40] For example, in 1978, some 60 foreign banks had branches in at least three states. As noted earlier, the McFadden Act prevented domestic banks from engaging in interstate branching.

FIGURE 22–1   **The Bank of Credit and Commerce International's Organizational Structure**

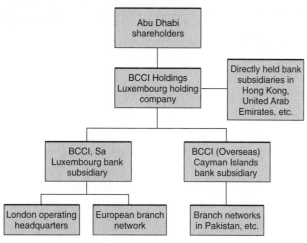

Source: U.S. General Accounting Office, *International Banking,* GAO/GGD–94–68 (1994), p. 17.

The Foreign Bank Supervision Enhancement Act (FBSEA) of 1991   Along with the growth of foreign bank assets in the United States came concerns about foreign banks' rapidly increasing share of U.S. banking markets as well as about the weakness of regulatory oversight of many of these institutions. Three events focused attention on the weaknesses of foreign bank regulation. The first event was the collapse of the Bank of Credit and Commerce International (BCCI), which had a highly complex international organizational structure based in the Middle East, the Cayman Islands, and Luxembourg and had undisclosed ownership stakes in two large U.S. banks (see Figure 22–2). BCCI was not subject to any consolidated supervision by a home country regulator; this quickly became apparent after its collapse, when massive fraud, insider lending abuses, and money-laundering operations were discovered. The second event was the issuance of more than US$1 billion in unauthorized letters of credit to Saddam Hussein's Iraq by the Atlanta agency of the Italian Banca Nazionale del Lavoro. The third event was the unauthorized taking of deposit funds by the U.S. representative office of the Greek National Mortgage Bank of New York.

These events and related concerns led to the passage of the FBSEA of 1991. The objective of this act was to extend federal regulatory authority over foreign banking organizations in the United States, especially where these organizations have entered using state licenses. The act's five main features have significantly enhanced the powers of federal bank regulators over foreign banks in the United States.[41]

1. *Entry.* Under FBSEA, a foreign banking organization must now have the Fed's approval to establish a subsidiary, branch, agency, or representative office in the United States. The approval applies to both a new entry and an entry by acquisition. To get Fed approval, the organization must meet a number of standards, two of which are mandatory. First, the foreign bank must be subject to comprehensive supervision on a consolidated basis by a home country regulator.[42] Second, that regulator must furnish all the information needed by the Federal Reserve to evaluate the application. Both standards are aimed at avoiding the lack of disclosure and lack of centralized supervision associated with BCCI's failure.

2. *Closure.* The act also gives the Federal Reserve authority to close a foreign bank if its home country supervision is inadequate, if it has violated U.S. laws, or if it is engaged in unsound and unsafe banking practices.

3. *Examination.* The Federal Reserve has the authority to examine each office of a foreign bank, including its representative offices. Further, each branch or agency must be examined at least once a year.

[41] See S. Bellanger, "Stormy Weather: The FBSEA's Impact on Foreign Banks," *Bankers Magazine,* November–December 1992, pp. 25–31; and GAO, "Foreign Banks: Implementation of the Foreign Bank Supervision and Enhancement Act of 1991," GAO/GGD–96–187, September 1996, Washington, D.C.

[42] A requirement for consolidated supervision also has been proposed by the Bank for International Settlements in its "Minimum Standards for the Supervision of International Banking Groups and Their Cross Border Establishments," Basel, Switzerland, June 1992.

4. *Deposit taking.* Only foreign subsidiaries with access to FDIC insurance can take retail deposits under US$100,000. This effectively rolls back the provision of the IBA that gave foreign branches and agencies access to FDIC insurance.

5. *Activity powers.* Beginning on December 19, 1992, state-licensed branches and agencies of foreign banks could not engage in any activity that was not permitted to a federal branch.[43]

Overall, the FBSEA considerably increased the Federal Reserve's authority over foreign banks and added to the regulatory burden or costs of entry into the United States. Indeed, in the two years after the passage of the FBSEA, federal bank supervisors issued 40 formal enforcement actions against foreign banks operating in the United States. In the most serious case, the Japanese Daiwa bank was ordered to cease its U.S. banking operations. Underlying its forced closure were losses by a single bond trader that had been concealed by Daiwa's management from U.S. regulators for over six weeks, and that amounted to over US$1 billion. In January 1996 Daiwa's U.S. bank assets were sold to Sumitomo Bank of Japan, and in February 1996 Daiwa paid a fine of US$340 million to the U.S. authorities for settlement of charges against the bank. This sent a strong signal regarding the willingness of the authorities to take a tough stand against errant foreign banks. More recently, in November 2001, the State Bank of India was ordered by U.S. federal and state banking regulators to pay US$7.5 million in fines resulting from the bank's apparent engagement in unsafe and unsound practices in its branches in New York, Chicago, and Los Angeles.

Concept Questions

1. What regulatory and economic factors have encouraged the growth of offshore banking? What factors have deterred offshore banking?
2. What were the major policy changes pertaining to bank expansion introduced by NAFTA?
3. What are the primary forms of entry by foreign banks into the U.S. market?
4. What impact did the passage of the International Banking Act of 1978 have on foreign bank activities in the United States?

ADVANTAGES AND DISADVANTAGES OF INTERNATIONAL EXPANSION

Historical and recent trends affecting the geographic expansion of FIs both into and outside North America have been discussed above. Here we summarize the advantages and disadvantages of international expansions to the individual FI seeking to generate additional returns or better diversify its risk.

Advantages

These are the six major advantages of international expansion:[44]

Revenue and Risk Diversification

As with domestic geographic expansions, an FI's international activities potentially enhance its opportunity to diversify the risk of its revenue flows. Often, domestic revenue flows from financial services are strongly linked to the state of that economy. Therefore, the less integrated the economies of the world are, the greater

---

[43] See M. Gruson, "Non-Banking Investments and Activities of Foreign Banks in the United States," paper presented at the Salomon Center, New York University, Conference on Universal Banking, February 23–24, 1995.

[44] See, for example, L. Goldberg and A. Saunders, "The Determinants of Foreign Banking Activity in the United States," *Journal of Banking and Finance* 5 (1981), pp. 17–32; and C. W. Hultman and L. R. McGee, "Factors Affecting the Foreign Banking Presence in the United States," *Journal of Banking and Finance* 13 (1989), pp. 383–96.

is the potential for revenue diversification through international expansions.[45] For example, operating in Malaysia with just three branches but a strong marketing program, Citigroup became one of the country's largest mortgage lenders in the early 2000s. Despite protectionist laws that bar foreign banks from opening new branches, Citigroup countered with aggressive marketing, strong customer service, and an assertive sales force that made house calls. The result was that, as the U.S. economy experienced a recession, Citigroup grew to hold 8 percent of Malaysia's fast-growing mortgage market. Indeed, in the early 2000s, while its biggest U.S. rivals, J. P. Morgan and Bank of America, grabbed headlines with megamergers, Citigroup undertook a strategy of projecting products and services globally. Citigroup's goal during the early 2000s was to aggressively expand its consumer banking presence outside the United States to boost profits and to leave behind rival U.S. banks who were just starting to take steps to combine corporate and consumer banking as a strategy.[46] International expansions also can reduce risk if the FI can undertake activities that are not permitted domestically but that have a low, or negative, correlation with domestic activities.

Economies of Scale

To the extent that economies of scale exist, an FI can potentially lower its average operating costs by expanding its activities beyond domestic boundaries.

Innovations

An FI can generate extra returns from new product innovations if it can sell such services internationally rather than just domestically. For example, consider complex financial innovations, such as securitization, caps, floors, and options, that FIs have innovated in North America and sold to new foreign markets with few domestic competitors. It has been argued that the increasing dominance of foreign securities firms in Japan is attributable to their comparative advantage and knowledge of risk management techniques and the use of derivatives compared to domestic Japanese securities firms.[47] However, the large losses incurred by many of these U.S. securities firms from trading in Asian and Russian markets in the late 1990s raise doubts about the size of any such comparative advantage.

Funds Source

International expansion allows an FI to search for the cheapest and most available sources of funds. This is extremely important given the very thin profit margins in

---

[45] G. Whalen, in "The Securities Activities," provides empirical evidence on the benefits of international expansions as a mechanism of reducing risk. For example, he finds that for 1987–96 domestic bank and foreign insurance underwriting had a return correlation that was highly negative: −0.56. S. Claessens, A. Demirguc-Kunt, and H. Hisizinga, in "How Does Foreign Entry Affect Domestic Banking Markets?" *Journal of Banking and Finance* 25 (2001), pp. 891–911, find that foreign banks have higher profits than domestic banks in developing countries. However, they also show that domestic banks have higher profits than foreign banks in developed countries. Finally, Y. Amihud, G. DeLong, and A. Saunders, in "The Effects of Cross-Border Mergers on Bank Risk and Values," *Journal of International Money and Finance* 21, (2002), pp. 857–77, find that overall, in cross-border bank mergers, the acquirers' risk neither increases nor decreases.

[46] See "In Malaysia, Citibank Shows the Difference Marketing Makes," *The Wall Street Journal*, December 12, 2002, p. A20, and "Citigroup Looks Abroad for Its Future Growth," *The Wall Street Journal*, March 15, 2004, p. C1.

[47] In 1998, Merrill Lynch absorbed 30 branches and 2,000 employees of the defunct Yamaichi Securities (traditionally the fourth largest domestic securities firm in Japan). In the same year Travelers (and its Salomon Securities subsidiary) bought a 25 percent share in Nikko Securities (traditionally the third largest securities firm in Japan). The comparative advantage of U.S. FIs over Japanese FIs in risk management is discussed in "Rich Pickings for the Gaijin," *The Economist,* May 16, 1998, p. 83.

domestic and international wholesale banking. Also, it reduces the risk of fund shortages (credit rationing) in any one market.

Customer Relationships

International expansions also allow an FI to maintain contact with and service the needs of domestic multinational corporations. Indeed, one of the fundamental factors determining the growth of FIs in foreign countries has been the parallel growth of foreign direct investment and foreign trade by globally oriented multinational corporations from the FI's home country.[48]

Regulatory Avoidance

To the extent that domestic regulations such as activity restrictions and reserve requirements impose constraints or taxes on the operations of an FI, seeking out low regulatory tax countries can allow an FI to lower its net regulatory burden and to increase its potential net profitability.

Disadvantages

These are the three major disadvantages of international expansion:

Information/Monitoring Costs

Although global expansions give an FI the potential to better diversify its geographic risk, the absolute level of exposure in certain areas such as lending can be high, especially if the FI fails to diversify in an optimal fashion. For example, the FI may fail to choose a loan portfolio combination on the efficient lending frontier (see Chapter 12). Foreign activities may also be riskier for the simple reason that monitoring and information collection costs are often higher in foreign markets. For example, Japanese and German accounting standards differ significantly from the generally accepted accounting principles (GAAP) used by U.S. firms. In addition, language, legal, and cultural issues can impose additional transaction costs on international activities. Finally, because the regulatory environment is controlled locally and regulation imposes a different array of net costs in each market, a truly global FI must master the various rules and regulations in each market.[49]

Nationalization/Expropriation

To the extent that an FI expands by establishing a local presence through investing in fixed assets such as branches or subsidiaries, it faces the political risk that a change in government may lead to the nationalization of those fixed assets.[50] Further, if foreign FI depositors take losses following a nationalization, they may seek legal recourse from the FI in North American courts rather than from the nationalizing

---

[48] R. Seth et al., "Do Banks Follow Their Customers Abroad?" *Financial Markets, Institutions, and Instruments* no. 4 (1998), find that the customer relationships are getting weaker as banks and firms become more global. For example, they find that foreign banks in the United States from Japan, Canada, the Netherlands, and the United Kingdom allocated a majority of their loans to non–home country borrowers over the 1981–92 period. Further, B. Williams, in "The Defensive Expansion Approach to Multinational Banking: Evidence to Date," *Financial Markets, Institutions, and Instruments*, May 2002, pp. 127–203, concludes that defensive expansion (in which banks follow their customers abroad) increases multinational bank size but has little impact upon these banks' profit.

[49] C. M. Buch and G. DeLong find that high information costs, as proxied by distance and common cultural factors (measured by geographic distance and language differences), tend to hold back merger activity. Moreover, information costs have larger effects on the number of bank mergers than regulatory variables. See "Cross-Border Bank Mergers: What Lures the Rare Animal?" Working Paper, Baruch College, CUNY, 2003.

[50] Such nationalizations have occurred with some frequency in African countries.

government. For example it took many years to resolve the outstanding claims of depositors in Citicorp's branches in Vietnam following the Communist takeover and expropriation of those branches.[51]

Fixed Costs

The fixed costs of establishing foreign organizations may be extremely high. For example, a North American FI seeking an organizational presence in the Tokyo banking market faces real estate prices significantly higher than those in Toronto, Vancouver or New York. Such relative costs can be even higher if an FI chooses to enter by buying an existing Japanese bank rather than establishing a new operation because of the considerable cost of acquiring Japanese equities measured by price-earnings ratios (despite significant loan problems in Japanese banks and recent falls in the Nikkei Index). These relative cost considerations become even more important if there is uncertainty about the expected volume of business to be generated and thus revenue flows from foreign entry. The failure of foreign acquisitions to realize expected profits following the 1986 "big bang" deregulation in the United Kingdom is a good example of unrealized revenue expectations vis-à-vis the high fixed costs of entry and the costs of maintaining a competitive position.[52]

Concept Questions

1. What are the major advantages of international expansion to an FI?
2. What are the major disadvantages of international expansion to an FI?
3. Comparing the advantages and disadvantages discussed above, why do you think so few North American banks have established branches in the Ukraine?

---

[51] See G. Dufey and I. Giddy, "Eurocurrency Deposit Risk," *Journal of Banking and Finance* 8 (1984), pp. 567–89.

[52] For example, the return on US. banks' foreign subsidiaries securities activities (assets) in 1987 were –0.96 percent. However, U.S. banks and securities firms have fared better in the Canadian "big bang" deregulation of securities business (see "Canada's Borrowing with Its Fat Fees Lures Wall Street," *New York Times,* April 15, 1995, p. D1).

Summary

In this chapter, we examined the potential return-risk advantages and disadvantages to FIs from domestic and international geographic expansion. Domestic expansions are one way in which an FI can improve its return-risk performance. U.S. commercial banks have faced the most restrictions on their geographic expansions (especially in their branching activities), these restrictions have recently been removed. Partly as a result of this and other factors relating to cost and revenue synergies, the U.S. financial system is now in a dramatic period of consolidation. This consolidation has resulted in a number of megamergers among large FIs and the movement of the United States toward a nationwide banking system similar to those that exist in Canada and major European countries.

Although regulatory considerations and costs are fundamental to international expansion decisions, several other economic factors play an important role in the net return or benefit-cost calculus for any given FI. For example, considerations such as earnings diversification, economies of scale and scope, extension of customer relationships, and better exploiting of financial service innovations add to the potential benefits from international geographic expansions. However, there are also costs or risks of such expansions such as monitoring costs, expropriation of assets, and the fixed costs of market entry. Managers need to carefully weigh each of these factors before making a geographic expansion decision, whether international or domestic.

Questions and Problems

1. How do limitations on geographic diversification affect an FI's profitability?

2. Bank mergers often produce hard-to-quantify benefits called X efficiencies and costs called X inefficiencies. Give an example of each.

3. What does the Berger and Humphrey study reveal about the cost savings from bank mergers? What differing results are revealed by the Rhoades study?

4. What are the three revenue synergies that may be obtained by an FI from expanding geographically?

5. What is the Herfindahl-Hirschman Index? How is it calculated and interpreted?

6. City Bank currently has a 60 percent market share in banking services, followed by NationsBank with 20 percent and State Bank with 20 percent.

   a. What is the concentration ratio as measured by the Herfindahl-Hirschman Index (HHI)?

   b. If City Bank acquires State Bank, what will be the new HHI?

   c. Assume that the government will allow mergers as long as the changes in HHI do not exceed 1,400. What is the minimum amount of assets that City Bank will have to divest after it merges with State Bank?

7. The government has been asked to review a merger request for a market with the following four FIs:

Bank	Assets
A	$ 12 million
B	25 million
C	102 million
D	3 million

   a. What is the HHI for the existing market?

   b. If bank A acquires bank D, what will be the effect on the market's level of concentration?

   c. If bank C acquires bank D, what will be the effect on the market's level of concentration?

   d. What is likely to be the government's response to the two merger applications?

8. A government measures market concentration using the HHI of market share. What problems does this measure have for (a) multiproduct FIs and (b) FIs with global operations?

9. What factors other than market concentration should a government consider in determining the acceptability of a merger?

10. According to empirical studies, what factors have the highest impact on merger premiums as defined by the ratio of a target bank's purchase price to book value?

11. What are the results of studies that have examined the mergers of banks, including postmerger performance? How do they differ from the studies examining mergers of nonbanks?

12. What are some of the important firm-specific financial factors that influence the acquisition of an FI?

13. How has the performance of merged banks compared to that of bank industry averages?

14. What are some of the benefits for banks engaging in geographic expansion?

15. What are three ways in which an FI can establish a global or international presence?

16. What is a Eurodollar transaction? What are Eurodollars?

17. Identify and explain the impact of at least four factors that have encouraged global bank expansion.

18. What is the expected impact of the implementation of the revised BIS risk-based capital requirements on the international activities of major banks?

19. What effect have the problems of emerging-market economies in the late 1990s had on the global expansion of traditional banking activities by banks?

20. What factors gave Japanese banks significant advantages in competing for international business for an extended period through the mid-1990s? What are the advantages of size in a competitive market? Does size necessarily imply high profitability?

21. What is the European Community (EC) Second Banking Directive? What impact has the Second Banking Directive had on the competitive banking environment in Europe?

22. Identify and discuss the various ways in which foreign banks can enter the U.S. market. What are international banking facilities?

23. What are the major advantages of international expansion to FIs? Explain how each advantage can affect the operating performance of FIs.

24. What are the difficulties of expanding globally? How can each of these difficulties create negative effects on the operating performance of FIs?

Web Question

25. Go to the Department of Finance Web site at www.fin.gc.ca. Click on "Consultations" and then scroll down and click on "Large Bank Mergers." Scroll down and click on "Response of the Government to Commons and Senate Committee Reports on Bank Mergers and the Public Interest" to download the June 23, 2003 report to understand the parameters establishing the public consultation on large bank mergers. Then browse the documents labeled "Responses from the public:" and answer the following questions:

The Canadian Minister of Finance has asked you to provide a recommendation regarding the merger of large financial institutions in Canada. Using the experience of U.S. bank mergers, answer the following questions:

a. What factors should be considered in evaluating the benefits of a merger?

b. Should bank-bank and bank-insurance mergers be allowed in Canada?

c. How would your response differ if you were preparing this report for the Board of Directors of a large Canadian bank or insurance company?

In this chapter, we look at the role futures and forward contracts play in managing an FI's risk and:

▸ compare futures and forwards contracts to spot contracts

▸ examine how futures and forward can be used to hedge an FI's:

  ▸ interest rate risk

  ▸ foreign exchange (FX) risk

  ▸ credit risk, and

  ▸ catastrophe risk

INTRODUCTION

**notional value
of an OBS item**
The face value of
an off-balance-
sheet contract.

Chapter 13 describes the growth in FIs' off-balance-sheet activities. A major component of this growth has been in futures and forward contracts. Although a significant amount of derivatives reflects the trading activity of large banks, FIs of all sizes have used these instruments to hedge their asset-liability risk exposures and thus reduce the value of their net worth at risk due to adverse events. As will be discussed in this chapter, derivative contracts—such as futures and forwards—potentially allow an FI to manage (or hedge) its interest rate, foreign exchange (FX), and credit risk exposures, and even its exposure to catastrophes such as hurricanes.[1]

Table 23–1 lists the derivative holdings of the six major Canadian banks at October 31, 2004. Table 23–2 provides similar data for U.S. commercial banks in September 2003 (in US dollars). The tables show the breakdown of the derivatives positions into futures and forwards, swaps, options, and credit derivatives. The tables show that the **notional value** (dollar) contract volumes for the Canadian banks was equal to C$8.9 trillion, whereas the total for the top 25 U.S. banks, reflecting the size of the broader North American market for derivatives, was in excess of US$67 trillion. As can be seen, both in Canada and in the United States, swaps dominate, representing 49.5 and 61.4 percent, respectively, of the total notional amount. Futures and forwards are in second place in Canada (28.9 percent) but options are the second largest notional amount for U.S. banks (21.2 percent). The replacement cost of these derivative contracts (bilaterally netted current exposure) for the Canadian banks is C$56.6 billion and the credit equivalent amount is C$115.9 billion compared with US$202.1 and US$709.8 billion for the top 25 U.S. banks.[2]

---

[1] In fact, a survey of financial institutions, foundations, and university endowments conducted by New York University's Stern School of Business, CIBC World Markets, and KPMG Investment Consulting Group found that the most commonly cited reason for using derivatives was risk reduction and hedging. Among large institutions, 41 percent had a designated risk manager or risk management committee and, among derivatives users, 68 percent had a written policy on risk management. See 1998 Survey of Derivative and Risk Management Practices by U.S. Institutional Investors, 1999, NYU Stern School of Business, CIBC World Markets, and KPMG.

[2] See Chapter 20 for a discussion of how the credit exposure of derivatives is calculated for regulatory reporting.

TABLE 23–1   Derivative Contracts: Notional Amount, Credit Equivalent Amount, and Risk-Weighted Amount of the Six Major Canadian Banks, October 31, 2004 (billions of dollars)

Bank	Total Assets	Derivative Contracts						Replacement Cost of All Contracts	Credit Equivalent Amount	Risk-Weighted Amount
		Futures & Forwards	Total Swaps	Total Options	Credit Derivatives	Other Contracts	Total Derivatives			
BMO	265.2	582.3	802.9	293.5	26.4	24.7	1,729.9	12.2	23.7	6.9
BNS	279.2	306.1	524.9	101.6	18.8	25.9	977.3	7.9	13.2	3.9
CIBC	278.8	185.8	737.2	118.9	45.9	85.5	1,173.3	7.0	14.2	3.7
National	88.8	47.5	146.3	80.3	n.a.	17.7	291.8	1.5	2.7	0.6
RBC	447.7	699.2	1,169.8	453.1	112.3	88.0	2,522.3	16.0	34.0	8.7
TD Bank	311.0	738.2	1,004.0	238.8	83.6	105.2	2,169.8	12.0	28.1	6.3
Total	1,670.7	2,559.1	4,385.2	1,286.2	287.1	346.9	8,864.4	56.6	115.9	30.1
% of Total Derivatives		28.9%	49.5%	14.5%	3.2%	3.9%	100.0%			

Note: Replacement cost of all contracts, credit equivalent amount, and risk-weighted amount reported after master netting agreements. Master netting agreements close out and net all contracts with a counterparty in the event of a default.

Source: Bank Annual Reports, 2004

TABLE 23–2 Derivative Contracts: Notional Amount and Credit Equivalent Exposure of the 25 Commercial Banks and Trust Companies with the Most Derivative Contracts, September 2003 (in millions of US dollars)

| Rank | Bank Name | Total Assets | Derivative Contracts | | | | | Total Derivatives | Replacement Cost of All Contracts | Future Exposure RBC* Add-On | Credit Exposure from All Contracts | Credit Exposure to Capital Ratio |
			Futures & Forwards	Total Swaps	Total Options	Credit Derivatives	Spot FX					
1.	J. P. Morgan Chase Bank	$638,120	$4,228,366	$22,459,088	$6,967,128	$496,561	$193,596	$34,151,143	$66,134	$288,707	$354,841	783.0
2.	Bank of America NA	624,723	2,638,710	8,654,660	2,385,906	123,939	95,294	13,803,216	35,184	90,335	125,518	237.1
3.	Citibank NA	554,540	2,022,072	6,731,694	1,912,884	145,976	214,854	10,812,626	42,388	84,711	127,340	240.8
4.	Wachovia Bank NA	344,056	337,622	865,446	1,117,400	30,236	32,544	2,350,704	16,946	11,356	28,302	91.5
5.	Bank One National Assn.	216,452	265,042	730,626	196,972	16,645	16,598	1,209,285	5,913	7,180	13,093	57.5
6.	HSBC Bank USA	90,157	255,176	540,347	378,434	25,678	27,995	1,199,636	6,207	9,448	15,655	219.9
7.	Wells Fargo Bank NA	224,376	302,367	86,933	341,368	2,889	8,027	733,557	6,683	1,225	7,908	37.9
8.	Bank of New York	92,203	124,129	181,121	224,829	1,659	10,662	531,738	3,800	2,615	6,414	77.8
9.	Fleet National Bank	188,775	41,511	115,660	305,223	11,739	4,561	474,133	2,783	1,591	4,374	22.0
10.	State Street Bank & TC	74,100	290,254	37,243	3,529	0	30,283	331,026	3,692	2,279	5,972	140.7
11.	National City Bank	45,799	41,041	92,037	124,059	0	499	257,137	2,210	860	3,071	65.2
12.	National City Bank of IN	50,104	59,152	32,860	75,478	0	0	167,489	1,112	1,252	2,364	74.1
13.	Mellon Bank NA	20,830	56,314	15,274	29,820	410	7,377	101,818	1,072	761	1,833	67.8
14.	Standard Federal Bank NA	50,489	23,944	55,985	11,751	4,207	0	95,887	59	558	617	10.9
15.	Keybank National Assn.	73,939	20,308	68,054	1,930	0	842	90,292	2,105	471	2,575	30.8
16.	LaSalle Bank NA	62,830	8,230	70,031	2,944	0	0	81,206	174	716	890	16.8
17.	SunTrust Bank	125,027	16,502	47,440	13,030	398	805	77,370	1,928	522	2,450	20.6
18.	Merrill Lynch Bank NA	66,735	20,100	35,640	320	2,608	0	58,667	148	166	314	6.7
19.	PNC Bank NA	65,167	3,557	40,045	5,266	225	711	49,092	1,100	327	1,427	20.5
20.	Deutsche Bank Tr. Co. American	35,838	662	37,987	7,711	3,140	43	49,500	868	1,938	2,806	40.3
21.	U.S. Bank National Assn.	186,464	6,257	36,474	2,280	2	189	45,014	764	210	974	5.4
22.	First Tennessee Bank NA	24,984	13,290	6,028	14,811	0	1	34,129	393	55	449	19.8
23.	Capital One Bank	22,510	804	24,224	0	0	0	25,027	0	172	172	4.3
24.	Northern Trust Co.	33,026	22,621	1,086	34	99	4,706	23,840	427	203	631	23.5
25.	Irwin Union B&T Co.	4,727	13,847	25	6,477	0	0	20,350	1	2	3	0.5
	Total 25 commercial banks	**$3,915,971**	**$10,811,876**	**$40,966,009**	**$14,179,676**	**$866,411**	**$649,587**	**$66,773,883**	**$202,091**	**$507,660**	**$709,851**	**92.6†**
	Other 547 commercial banks	**$2,110,959**	**$47,436**	**$239,442**	**$50,089**	**$2,362**	**$2,888**	**$339,514**	**$5,397**	**$2,481**	**$7,878**	**N/A**
	Total for all banks	**$6,026,930**	**$10,859,331**	**$41,205,451**	**$14,229,765**	**$868,773**	**$652,475**	**$67,113,397**	**$207,488**	**$510,141**	**$717,629**	**5.6**

* Risk-based capital
† Average

Source: Office of the Comptroller of the Currency Web site, September 2003. www.occ.treas.gov

Not only do FIs hold these contracts to hedge their own risk (interest rate, credit, etc.), but FIs also serve as the counterparty (for a fee) in these contracts for other (financial and nonfinancial) firms wanting to hedge risks on their balance sheets.

The rapid growth of derivatives use by both FIs and nonfinancial firms has been controversial. Critics charge that derivatives contracts contain potential losses that can materialize to haunt their holders, particularly banks and insurance companies that deal heavily in these instruments. As will be discussed in this chapter and the following two chapters, when employed appropriately, derivatives can be used to hedge (or reduce) an FI's risk.[3] However, when misused, derivatives can increase the risk of an FI's insolvency. A number of recent scandals involving FIs, firms, and municipalities (such as Bankers Trust and the Allied Irish Bank) have led to a tightening of the accounting (reporting) requirements for derivative contracts.[4] Specifically, beginning in 2000, the Financial Accounting Standards Board (FASB) in the U.S. required all derivatives to be marked to market and mandated that losses and gains be immediately transparent on FIs' and other firms' financial statements.

www.fasb.org

www.acsb.org

In Canada, the Accounting Standards Board (AcSB), aware of the experience with derivative losses elsewhere in the world, has produced new regulations for derivative instruments that meld U.S. Generally Accepted Accounting Principles (GAAP) and international accounting standards. These new regulations will become mandatory for all companies, including FIs, who use derivative products after October 1, 2006.

www.bmo.com

The use of derivatives for trading as opposed to hedging dominates the derivatives activities of FIs. For example, Bank of Montreal (BMO) reports that of a total notional amount of derivatives contracts of $1,729 billion in 2004, just $58.8 billion, or 3.4 percent was used for hedging. The type of risk hedged, as well as the type of contract used to hedge a specific risk, varies across FIs. For example, Bank of Nova Scotia (BNS) notes in its 2004 Annual Report that it uses spot and forward transactions and options as hedging instruments for foreign currency risk, but BMO hedges both interest rate risk and foreign currency risk using interest rate swaps and options, and cross-currency swaps. The Industry Perspectives box demonstrates how the uncertainty regarding the strengthening of the Canadian dollar relative to the U.S. dollar affected BNS and its hedging strategy in 2004.

www.scotiabank.com

FORWARD AND FUTURES CONTRACTS

To understand the essential nature and characteristics of forward and futures contracts, we can compare them with spot contracts. We show appropriate time lines for each of the three contracts using a bond as the underlying financial security to the derivative contract in Figure 23–1.

---

[3] E. Brewer III, B. A. Minton, and J. T. Moser, in "Interest-Rate Derivatives and Bank Lending," *Journal of Banking and Finance* 24 (2000), pp. 353–79, find that US banks using interest rate derivatives experience greater growth in their commercial and industrial loan portfolios than banks that do not use these financial instruments. Their results suggest that FIs' use of derivatives enables increased reliance on their comparative advantage as delegated monitors (see Chapter 1).

[4] From March through May 1994, several large nonfinancial firms announced millions of dollars in losses from derivatives deals, especially those arranged by Bankers Trust. Accompanying these announcements and related new stories were allegations that Bankers Trust had either misrepresented, lied, or deceived its clients. J. F. Sinkey Jr. and D. A. Carter, in "The Reaction of Bank Stock Prices to News of Derivatives Losses by Corporate Clients," *Journal of Banking and Finance* 23 (1999), pp. 1725–43, investigated how these announcements affected Bankers Trust and three portfolios of banks' stock returns: dealers, nondealers, and nonusers. They report significant negative cumulative abnormal returns of −12.14 percent for Bankers Trust, −5.56 percent for dealer banks, and −2.45 percent for nondealer, user banks, indicating that banks were adversely affected by these news stories.

Industry Perspectives

SCOTIABANK'S FOREIGN CURRENCY RISK, 2004

Foreign currency risk arising from the Bank's funding and investment activities includes that from the Bank's net corporate foreign currency positions (loans, investments and other assets less deposits and other funding) and from its net investments in self-sustaining foreign operations (both subsidiaries and branches). The Bank's exposure is subject to a Board-approved limit and is reviewed quarterly by the Liability Committee. To mitigate the foreign currency exposure in its corporate position, the Bank customarily funds assets with liabilities in the same currency. When economically feasible, the Bank will hedge the foreign currency exposure with respect to its net investments in self-sustaining foreign operations primarily by funding the investments in the same currency.

In accordance with GAAP, foreign currency translation gains and losses from corporate positions are recorded in earnings, while foreign currency translation gains and losses from net investments in self-sustaining operations are recorded in the cumulative foreign currency translation account within share-holders' equity. While gains/losses on net investments may increase/reduce the Bank's capital, depending on the strength or weakness of the Canadian dollar against other currencies, the Bank's regulatory capital ratios are not materially affected, since the risk-weighted assets of the foreign operations rise or fall in about the same proportion as the change in capital.

The Bank is also subject to foreign currency translation risk on the earnings of its foreign operations. The Bank projects its foreign currency revenues and expenses, which are primarily denominated in U.S. dollars, out over a number of future fiscal quarters. The Liability Committee assesses economic data and forecasts and decides on the portion of the estimated future foreign currency revenues and expenses to hedge. Hedging instruments would normally include foreign currency spot and forward contracts, as well as foreign currency options.

The translation effect of the strengthening of the Canadian dollar on the Bank's earnings is summarized below. In the absence of hedging activity, a one per cent increase (decrease) in the Canadian dollar against all the currencies in which we operate, decreases (increases) our earnings by approximately $23 million before tax. A similar change in the Canadian dollar would decrease (increase) the foreign currency translation account in shareholder's equity by approximately $70 million.

Impact of Foreign Currency Translation

Foreign currency translation had a significant negative effect on the Bank's earnings in 2004. This arose from the ongoing strengthening of the Canadian dollar by 9% versus the U.S. dollar, 17% versus the Mexican peso and against many other currencies in which the Bank conducts its business.

Changes in the average exchange rates between 2003 and 2004 affected 2004 net income as follows:

Average exchange rate	2004	2003
U.S. dollar/Canadian dollar	0.7586	0.6936
Mexican peso/Canadian dollar	8.5968	7.3388

Impact on Income ($ millions)	2004 vs. 2003
Net interest income	$ (321)
Other income	(212)
Non-interest expenses	227
Other items (net of tax)	96
Net income	$ (210)

The above-noted impact on net income was moderated somewhat by actions taken by management

However, recent changes to hedge accounting standards, effective November 1, 2003, have made it more difficult to achieve hedge accounting treatment for these economic hedges. Consequently, this has the potential for a mismatch in the timing of the recognition of economic hedge gains/losses with the underlying foreign earnings translation losses/gains.

Source: Bank of Nova Scotia 2004 Annual Report, pp. 58–59, page 33.

Spot Contracts

spot contract
An agreement involving the immediate exchange of an asset for cash.

A **spot contract** is an agreement between a buyer and a seller at time 0, when the seller of the asset agrees to deliver it immediately and the buyer of the asset agrees to pay for that asset immediately.[5] Thus, the unique feature of a spot market

---

[5] Technically, physical settlement and delivery may take place one or two days after the contractual spot agreement in bond markets. In equity markets, delivery and cash settlement normally occur three business days after the spot contract agreement.

FIGURE 23–1
Contract Time Lines

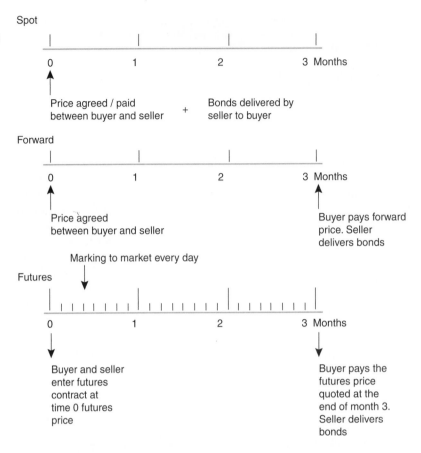

contract is the immediate and simultaneous exchange of cash for securities, or what is often called *delivery versus payment*. A spot bond quote of $97 for a 20-year maturity bond is the price the buyer must pay the seller, per $100 of face value, for immediate (time 0) delivery of the 20-year bond.

Forward Contracts

forward contract
An agreement involving the exchange of an asset for cash at a fixed price in the future.

A **forward contract** is a contractual agreement between a buyer and a seller at time 0 to exchange a prespecified asset for cash at a later date. For example, in a three-month forward contract to deliver 20-year bonds, the buyer and seller agree on a price and quantity today (time 0) but the delivery (or exchange) of the 20-year bond for cash does not occur until three months hence. If the forward price agreed to at time 0 was $97 per $100 of face value, in three months' time the seller delivers $100 of 20-year bonds and receives $97 from the buyer. This is the price the buyer must pay and the seller must accept no matter what happened to the spot price of 20-year bonds during the three months between the time the contract was entered into and the time the bonds are delivered for payment.

Futures Contracts

futures contract
An agreement involving the future exchange of an asset for cash at a price that is determined daily.

A **futures contract** is normally arranged through an organized exchange (in Canada, the Montréal Exchange, www.m-x.ca). It is an agreement between a buyer and a seller at time 0 to exchange a standardized, prespecified asset for cash at a later date. As such, a futures contract is very similar to a forward contract.

marked to market
The process by which the prices on outstanding futures contracts are adjusted each day to reflect current futures market conditions.

The difference relates to the price, which in a forward contract is fixed over the life of the contract ($97 per $100 of face value for three months), but in a futures contract is **marked to market** daily. This means the contract's price is adjusted each day as the futures price for the contract changes. Therefore, actual daily cash settlements occur between the buyer and seller in response to this marking-to-market process. This can be compared to a forward contract, where the whole cash payment from buyer to seller occurs at the end of the contract period.[6]

Concept Questions

1. What is the difference between a futures contract and a forward contract?
2. What are the major differences between a spot contract and a forward contract?

FORWARD CONTRACTS AND HEDGING INTEREST RATE RISK

naive hedge
When a cash asset is hedged on a direct dollar-for-dollar basis with a forward or futures contract.

To see the usefulness of forward contracts in hedging the interest rate risk of an FI, consider a simple example of a **naive hedge** (the hedge of a cash asset on a direct dollar-for-dollar basis with a forward or futures contract). Suppose an FI portfolio manager holds a 20-year, $1 million face value bond on the balance sheet. At time 0, these bonds are valued by the market at $97 per $100 face value, or $970,000 in total. Assume the manager receives a forecast that interest rates are expected to rise by 2 percent from their current level of 8 to 10 percent over the next three months. Knowing that rising interest rates mean that bond prices will fall, the manager stands to make a capital loss on the bond portfolio. Having read Chapters 8 and 9, the manager is an expert in duration and has calculated the 20-year maturity bonds' duration to be exactly 9 years. Thus, the manager can predict a capital loss, or change in bond values (ΔP) from the duration equation of Chapter 9:[7]

$$\frac{\Delta P}{P} = -D \times \frac{\Delta R}{1 + R}$$

where

ΔP = Capital loss on bonds = ?

P = Initial value of bond position = $970,000

D = Duration of the bonds = 9 years

ΔR = Change in forecast yield = .02

$1 + R$ = 1 plus the current yield on 20-year bonds = 1.08

$$\frac{\Delta P}{\$970,000} = -9 \times \left[\frac{.02}{1.08}\right]$$

$$\Delta P = -9 \times \$970,000 \times \left[\frac{.02}{1.08}\right] = -\$161,666.67$$

As a result, the FI portfolio manager expects to incur a capital loss on the bond portfolio of $161,666.67 (as a percentage loss ($\Delta P/P$) = 16.67%) or as a drop in price from $97 per $100 face value to $80.833 per $100 face value. To offset this loss—in fact, to reduce the risk of capital loss to zero—the manager may hedge this position by taking an off-balance-sheet hedge, such as selling $1 million face value

---

[6] Aside from the marking-to-market process, the two major differences between forwards and futures are that (1) forwards are tailor-made contracts whereas futures are standardized contracts and (2) forward contracts are bilateral contracts subject to counterparty default risk, whereas the default risk on futures is significantly reduced by the futures exchange guaranteeing to indemnify counterparties against credit or default risk.

[7] For simplicity, we ignore issues relating to convexity here.

of 20-year bonds for forward delivery in three months' time.[8] Suppose at time 0 the portfolio manager can find a buyer willing to pay $97 for every $100 of 20-year bonds delivered in three months' time.

Now consider what happens to the FI portfolio manager if the gloomy forecast of a 2 percent rise in interest rates proves to be true. The portfolio manager's bond position has fallen in value by 16.67 percent, equal to a capital loss of $161,667. After the rise in interest rates, the manager can buy $1 million face value of 20-year bonds in the spot market at $80.833 per $100 of face value, a total cost of $808,333, and deliver these bonds to the forward contract buyer. Remember that the forward contract buyer agreed to pay $97 per $100 of face value for the $1 million of face value bonds delivered, or $970,000. As a result, the portfolio manager makes a profit on the forward transaction of:

$$\underset{\substack{\text{(price paid by}\\\text{forward buyer to}\\\text{forward seller)}}}{\$970,000} \quad - \quad \underset{\substack{\text{(cost of purchasing}\\\text{bonds in the spot market}\\\text{at } t = \text{month 3 for delivery}\\\text{to the forward buyer)}}}{\$808,333} \quad = \quad \$161,667$$

As you can see, the on-balance-sheet loss of $161,667 is exactly offset by the off-balance-sheet gain of $161,667 from selling the forward contract. In fact, for any change in interest rates, a loss (gain) on the balance sheet is offset by a gain (loss) on the forward contract. Indeed, the success of a hedge does not hinge on the manager's ability to accurately forecast interest rates. Rather, the reason for the hedge is the lack of ability to perfectly predict interest rate changes. The hedge allows the FI manager to protect against interest rate changes even if they are unpredictable. Thus, the FI's net interest rate exposure is zero; in the parlance of finance, it has **immunized** its assets against interest rate risk.

immunized
Describes an FI that is fully hedged or protected against adverse movements in interest rates (or other asset prices).

Concept Questions

1. Explain how a naive hedge works.
2. What does it mean to say that an FI has immunized its portfolio against a particular risk?

HEDGING INTEREST RATE RISK WITH FUTURES CONTRACTS

Even though some hedging of interest rate risk does take place using forward contracts—such as forward rate agreements commonly used by insurance companies and banks prior to mortgage loan originations—most FIs hedge interest rate risk either at the micro level (called *microhedging*) or at the macro level (called *macrohedging*) using futures contracts. Before looking at futures contracts, we explain the difference between microhedging and macrohedging and between routine hedging and selective hedging.

Microhedging

microhedging
Using a futures (forward) contract to hedge a specific asset or liability.

An FI is **microhedging** when it employs a futures or a forward contract to hedge a particular asset or liability risk. For example, earlier we considered a simple example of microhedging asset-side portfolio risk, where an FI manager wanted to insulate the value of the institution's bond portfolio fully against a rise in

---

[8] Since a forward contract involves delivery of bonds in a future time period, it does not appear on the balance sheet, which records only current and past transactions. Thus, forwards are one example of off-balance-sheet items (see Chapter 13).

interest rates. An example of microhedging on the liability side of the balance sheet occurs when an FI, attempting to lock in a cost of funds to protect itself against a possible rise in short-term interest rates, takes a short (sell) position in futures contracts on CDs or T-bills. In microhedging, the FI manager often tries to pick a futures or forward contract whose underlying deliverable asset is closely matched to the asset (or liability) position being hedged. The earlier example, where we had an exact matching of the asset in the portfolio with the deliverable security underlying the forward contract (20-year bonds) was unrealistic. Such exact matching cannot be achieved often, and this produces a residual unhedgable risk termed **basis risk.** We discuss basis risk in detail later in this chapter; it arises mainly because the prices of the assets or liabilities that an FI wishes to hedge are imperfectly correlated over time with the prices on the futures or forward contract used to hedge risk.

basis risk
A residual risk that arises because the movement in a spot (cash) asset's price is not perfectly correlated with the movement in the price of the asset delivered under a futures or forward contract.

Macrohedging

Macrohedging occurs when an FI manager wishes to use futures or other derivative securities to hedge the entire balance sheet duration gap. This contrasts to micro-hedging, where an FI manager identifies specific assets and liabilities and seeks individual futures and other derivative contracts to hedge those individual risks. Note that macrohedging and microhedging can lead to quite different hedging strategies and results. In particular, a macrohedge takes a whole portfolio view and allows for individual asset and liability interest sensitivities or durations to net each other out. This can result in a very different aggregate futures position than when an FI manager disregards this netting or portfolio effect and hedges individual asset and liability positions on a one-to-one basis.[9]

macrohedging
Hedging the entire duration gap of an FI.

Also, to dynamically hedge the entire portfolio, the assets must be marked-to-market on a daily basis, and the portfolio rebalanced. The futures and forwards markets may not be sufficiently liquid to permit this or a Canadian FI may resort to using U.S. contracts to achieve its goal of being fully hedged.

Routine Hedging versus Selective Hedging

Routine hedging occurs when an FI reduces its interest rate or other risk exposure to the lowest possible level by selling sufficient futures to offset the interest rate risk exposure of its whole balance sheet or cash positions in each asset and liability. For example, this might be achieved by macrohedging the duration gap, as described next. However, since reducing risk also reduces expected return and thus shareholder wealth, not all FI managers seek to do this. Indeed, a manager would follow this strategy only if the direction and size of interest rate changes are extremely unpredictable to the extent that the manager is willing to forgo return to hedge this risk. Figure 23–2 shows the trade-off between expected return and risk and the minimum-risk fully hedged portfolio.[10]

routine hedging
Seeking to hedge all interest rate risk exposure.

Rather than a fully hedged position, most FIs choose to bear some interest rate risk as well as credit and FX risks because of their comparative advantage as FIs (see Chapter 1). One possibility is that an FI may choose to **hedge selectively** its portfolio. For example, an FI manager may generate expectations regarding future interest rates

hedging selectively
Only partially hedging the gap or individual assets and liabilities.

---

[9] P. H. Munter, D. K. Clancy, and C. T. Moores found that macrohedges provided better hedge performance than microhedges in a number of different interest rate environments. See "Accounting for Financial Futures: A Question of Risk Reduction," *Advances in Accounting* 3 (1986), pp. 51–70. See also R. Stoebe, "Macrohedging Bank Investment Portfolios," *Bankers Magazine*, November–December 1994, pp. 45–48.

[10] The minimum-risk portfolio is not shown as zero here because of basis risk that prevents perfect hedging. In the absence of basis risk, a zero-risk position becomes possible.

FIGURE 23–2 The Effects of Hedging on Risk and Expected Return

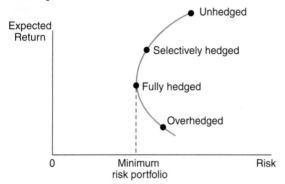

before deciding on a futures position. As a result, the manager may selectively hedge only a proportion of its balance sheet position. Alternatively, the FI manager may decide to remain unhedged or even to overhedge by selling more futures than required by the cash position, although regulators may view this as speculative. Thus, the fully hedged position—and the minimum risk portfolio—becomes one of several choices depending, in part, on managerial interest rate expectations, managerial objectives, and the nature of the return-risk trade-off from hedging. Finally, an FI may selectively hedge in an attempt to arbitrage profits between a spot asset's price movements and movements in a futures price.

Macrohedging with Futures

The number of futures contracts that an FI should buy or sell in a macrohedge depends on the size and direction of its interest rate risk exposure and the return-risk trade-off from fully or selectively hedging that risk. Chapter 9 showed that an FI's net worth exposure to interest rate shocks was directly related to its leverage-adjusted duration gap as well as its asset size. Again, this is

$$\Delta E = -[D_A - kD_L] \times A \times \frac{\Delta R}{1 + R}$$

where

ΔE = Change in an FI's net worth

D_A = Duration of its asset portfolio

D_L = Duration of its liability portfolio

k = Ratio of an FI's liabilities to assets (L/A)

A = Size of an FI's asset portfolio

$\dfrac{\Delta R}{1 + R}$ = Shock to interest rates

EXAMPLE 23–1

Calculation of Change in FI Net Worth as Interest Rates Rise

To see how futures might fully hedge a positive or negative portfolio duration gap, consider the following FI where

$$D_A = 5 \text{ years}$$
$$D_L = 3 \text{ years}$$

Suppose the FI manager receives information from an economic forecasting unit that interest rates are expected to rise from 10 to 11 percent over the next year. That is:

$$\Delta R = 1\% = .01$$
$$1 + R = 1.10$$

The FI's initial balance sheet is

Assets (in millions)	Liabilities (in millions)
$A = \$100$	$L = \$\ 90$
	$E = \ \ \ 10$
$\overline{\$100}$	$\overline{\$100}$

so that *k* equals *L/A* equals 90/100 equals 0.9.

The FI manager wants to calculate the potential loss to the FI's net worth (E) if the forecast of rising rates proves to be true. As we showed in Chapter 9:

$$\Delta E = -(D_A - kD_L) \times A \times \frac{\Delta R}{1 + R}$$

so that

$$\Delta E = -(5 - (.9)(3)) \times \$100 \times \frac{.01}{1.1} = -\$2.091 \text{ million}$$

The FI could expect to lose \$2.091 million in net worth if the interest rate forecast turns out to be correct. Since the FI started with a net worth of \$10 million, the loss of \$2.091 million is almost 21 percent of its initial net worth position. Clearly, as this example illustrates, the effect of the rise in interest rates could be quite threatening to the FI and its insolvency risk exposure.

The Risk-Minimizing Futures Position

The FI manager's objective to fully hedge the balance sheet exposure would be fulfilled by constructing a futures position such that if interest rates do rise by 1 percent to 11 percent, as in the prior example, the FI will make a gain on the futures position that just offsets the loss of balance sheet net worth of \$2.091 million.

When interest rates rise, the price of a futures contract falls since its price reflects the value of the underlying bond that is deliverable against the contract. The amount by which a bond price falls when interest rates rise depends on its duration. Thus, we expect the price of the 20-year T-bond futures contract to be more sensitive to interest rate changes than the price of the 3-month T-bill futures contract since the former futures price reflects the price of the 20-year T-bond deliverable on contract maturity. Thus, the sensitivity of the price of a futures contract depends on the duration of the deliverable bond underlying the contract, or

$$\frac{\Delta F}{F} = -D_F \frac{\Delta R}{1 + R}$$

where

$\quad \Delta F$ = Change in dollar value of futures contracts

$\quad\quad F$ = Dollar value of the initial futures contracts

$\quad\; D_F$ = Duration of the bond to be delivered against the futures contracts such as a 20-year, 8 percent coupon T-bond

$\quad \Delta R$ = Expected shock to interest rates

$1 + R$ = 1 plus the current level of interest rates

This can be rewritten as

$$\Delta F = -D_F \times F \times \frac{\Delta R}{1 + R}$$

The left side of this expression (ΔF) shows the dollar gain or loss on a futures position when interest rates change.

To see this dollar gain or loss more clearly, we can decompose the initial dollar value position in futures contracts, F, into its two component parts:

$$F = N_F \times P_F$$

The dollar value of the outstanding futures position depends on the number of contracts bought or sold (N_F) and the price of each contract (P_F). N_F is positive when the futures contracts are bought and is assigned a negative value when contracts are sold.

FIGURE 23–3
U.S. Futures
Contracts on
Interest Rates

Source: *The Wall Street Journal*, March 18, 2004, p. B6. Reprinted by permission of The Wall Street Journal, © 2004 Dow Jones & Company, Inc. All Rights Reserved Worldwide.

Interest Rate Futures

	OPEN	HIGH	LOW	SETTLE	CHG	LIFETIME HIGH	LIFETIME LOW	OPEN INT
Treasury Bonds (CBT)-$100,000; pts 32nds of 100%								
Mar	117-04	117-10	116-15	116-25	-21	117-26	101-00	28,546
June	115-23	115-31	114-31	115-10	-21	116-15	104-00	522,017
Sept	113-28	114-15	113-19	113-29	-21	114-30	101-25	11,850
Est vol 216,969; vol Wed 258,838; open int 562,788, -2,710.								
Treasury Notes (CBT)-$100,000; pts 32nds of 100%								
Mar	117-18	117-22	117-05	117-08	-15.5	117-31	106-29	47,574
June	116-045	116-09	115-20	15-255	-16.0	16-185	107-13	1,257,280
Est vol 680,136; vol Wed 732,007; open int 1,318,731, +13,896.								
5 Yr. Treasury Notes (CBT)-$100,000; pts 32nds of 100%								
Mar	115-02	15-035	114-25	114-27	-10.5	19-215	09-145	45,394
Est vol 254,899; vol Wed 286,275; open int 1,005,955, +13,094.								
2 Yr. Treasury Notes (CBT)-$200,000; pts 32nds of 100%								
Mar	08-022	08-022	08-005	08-012	-2.0	08-045	106-02	25,304
Est vol 20,836; vol Wed 25,977; open int 176,294, -1,371.								
30 Day Federal Funds (CBT)-$5,000,000; 100 - daily avg.								
Mar	...	...	...	98.995	...	99.160	98-47	46,584
Apr	99.00	99.00	99.00	99.00	...	99.17	89.96	95,607
May	99.00	99.00	99.00	99.00	...	99.79	98.40	58,336
July	98.98	98.98	98.97	98.98	...	98.98	98.20	64,430
Aug	98.94	98.95	98.94	98.95	...	98.95	98.24	15,103
Sept	98.90	98.92	98.90	98.92	...	98.93	98.22	19,557
Oct	98.88	98.88	98.86	98.88	...	98.88	98.58	12,092
Nov	98.79	98.82	98.79	98.81	...	98.83	98.37	8,552
Dec	98.73	98.75	98.73	98.73	-.01	98.75	98.63	201
Est vol 15,968; vol Wed 16,471; open int 367,835, +494.								
10 Yr. Interest Rate Swaps (CBT)-$100,000; pts 32nds of 100%								
June	114-13	114-22	114-03	114-06	-19	115-04	109-06	38,871
Est vol 833; vol Wed 835; open int 38,872, +543.								
10 Yr. Muni Note Index (CBT)-$1,000 x index								
Mar	107-07	107-11	107-04	107-05	-13	107-24	99-21	1,162
Est vol 124; vol Wed 163; open int 3,004, -15.								
Index: Close 107-05; Yield 4.118.								

	OPEN	HIGH	LOW	SETTLE	CHG	YIELD	CHG	OPEN INT
1 Month Libor (CME)-$3,000,000; pts of 100%								
Apr	98.90	98.90	98.90	98.90	...	1.10	...	21,868
May	98.90	98.90	98.90	98.90	...	1.10	...	11,457
June	98.88	98.88	98.88	98.88	...	1.12	...	23,235
July	98.86	98.87	98.86	98.86	...	1.14	...	31,776
Aug	98.82	98.82	98.82	98.82	-.01	1.18	.01	87,903
Est vol 4,093; vol Wed 4,541; open int 349,461, +664.								
Eurodollar (CME)-$1,000,000; pts of 100%								
Apr	98.87	98.88	98.87	98.88	...	1.12	...	85,224
May	98.86	98.87	98.86	98.86	...	1.14	...	35,817
June	98.83	98.85	98.83	98.84	...	1.16	...	876,378
July	98.80	98.80	98.80	98.80	-.01	1.20	.01	14,001
Sept	98.70	98.74	98.68	98.70	-.01	1.30	.01	881,589
Dec	98.46	98.49	98.44	98.46	-.03	1.54	.03	738,811
Mr05	98.19	98.21	98.13	98.16	-.04	1.84	.04	541,141
June	97.86	97.87	97.80	97.82	-.05	2.18	.05	398,581
Sept	97.54	97.55	97.47	97.49	-.05	2.51	.05	337,331
Dec	97.26	97.25	97.19	97.20	-.06	2.80	.06	241,323
Mr06	97.04	97.04	96.95	96.96	-.07	3.04	.07	211,567
June	96.78	96.79	96.72	96.74	-.07	3.26	.07	147,497
Sept	96.57	96.58	96.51	96.53	-.07	3.47	.07	154,596
Dec	96.37	96.38	96.31	96.32	-.08	3.68	.08	123,503
Mr07	96.20	96.21	96.14	96.15	-.08	3.85	.08	103,626
June	96.03	96.05	95.97	95.99	-.08	4.01	.08	79,357
Sept	95.88	95.90	95.81	95.83	-.08	4.17	.08	73,086
Dec	95.69	95.74	95.65	95.67	-.08	4.33	.08	60,833
Mr08	95.54	95.61	95.52	95.54	-.07	4.46	.07	45,208
June	95.41	95.47	95.38	95.41	-.08	4.59	.08	50,190
Sept	95.29	95.34	95.26	95.28	-.08	4.72	.08	35,215
Dec	95.17	95.22	95.13	95.15	-.08	4.85	.08	34,646
Mr09	95.08	95.08	95.02	95.04	-.08	4.96	.08	15,403
Dec	94.72	94.73	94.70	94.73	-.07	5.27	.07	5,844
Dc10	94.39	94.42	94.35	94.39	-.07	5.61	.07	3,852
Est vol 793,815; vol Wed 944,786; open int 5,347,589, +49,467.								

Futures contracts are homogeneous in size. Thus, futures exchanges sell T-bond futures in minimum units of $100,000 of face value; that is, one T-bond future ($N_F = 1$) equals $100,000. T-bill futures are sold in larger minimum units: one T-bill future ($N_F = 1$) equals $1,000,000. The price of each contract quoted in the newspaper is the price per $100 of face value for delivering the underlying bond. Looking at Figure 23–3, a price quote of $115^{10}/_{32}$ on March 18, 2004, for the T-bond futures contract maturing in June 2004 means that the buyer is required to pay $115,312.50 for one contract.[11] The subsequent profit or loss from a position in the June 2004 T-bond taken on March 18, 2004, is graphically described in Figure 23–4. A short position in the futures contract will produce a profit when interest rates rise (meaning that the value of the underlying T-bond decreases). Therefore, a short position in the futures market is the appropriate hedge when the FI stands to lose on the balance sheet if interest rates are expected to rise (e.g., the FI has a positive duration gap). A long position in the futures market produces a profit when interest rates fall (meaning that the value of the underlying T-bond increases).[12] Therefore, a long position is the appropriate hedge when the FI stands to lose on the balance sheet if interest rates are expected to fall (e.g., has a negative duration gap).

If, at maturity (in June 2004), the price quote on the T-bond futures contract was $115^{10}/_{32}$, the buyer would pay $115,312.50 to the seller and the futures seller would

---

[11] In practice, the futures price changes day to day and gains or losses would be generated for the seller/buyer over the period between when the contract is entered into and when it matures. See our later discussion of this unique marking-to-market feature. Note that the FI could sell contracts in T-bonds maturing at later dates. However, although contracts exist for up to two years into the future, longer-term contracts tend to be infrequently traded and therefore relatively illiquid.

[12] Notice that if rates move in an opposite direction from that expected, losses are incurred on the futures position. That is, if rates rise and futures prices drop, the long hedger loses. Similarly, if rates fall and futures prices rise, the short hedger loses. However, such losses are offset by gains on their cash market positions. Thus, the hedger is still protected.

FIGURE 23–4
Profit or Loss on a Futures Position in Treasury Bonds Taken on March 18, 2004

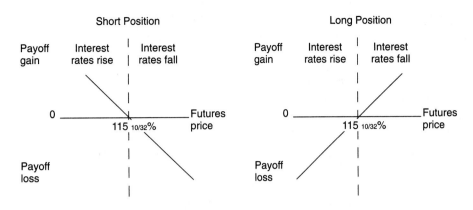

deliver one $100,000, 20-year, 8 percent T-bond to the futures buyer. In actuality, the seller of the futures contract has a number of alternatives other than an 8 percent coupon 20-year bond that can be delivered against the T-bond futures contract. If only one type of bond could be delivered, a shortage or squeeze might develop, making it very hard for the short side or seller to deliver. In fact, the seller has quite flexible delivery options; apart from delivering the 20-year, 8 percent coupon bond, the seller can deliver bonds that range in maturity from 15 years upward. Often, up to 25 different bonds may qualify for delivery. When a bond other than the 20-year benchmark bond is delivered, the buyer pays a different invoice price for the futures contract based on a **conversion factor** that calculates the price of the deliverable bond if it were to yield 8 percent divided by face value. Suppose $100,000 worth of 18-year, 6 percent semiannual coupon Treasury bonds were valued at a yield of 5.5 percent. This would produce a fair present value of the bond of approximately $105,667. The conversion factor for the bond would be 1.057 (or $105,667/$100,000). This means the buyer would have to pay the seller the conversion factor of 1.057 times the published futures price of $115,312.50. That is, the futures price would be $121,885.31.[13]

conversion factor
A factor used to figure the invoice price on a futures contract when a bond other than the benchmark bond is delivered to the buyer.

We can now solve for the number of futures contracts to buy or sell to fully macro-hedge an FI's on-balance-sheet interest rate risk exposure. We have shown that:

1. *Loss on balance sheet.* The loss of net worth for an FI when rates rise is equal to:

$$\Delta E = -(D_A - kD_L)A\frac{\Delta R}{1 + R}$$

2. *Gain off balance sheet on futures.* The gain off balance sheet from selling futures is equal to[14]

$$\Delta F = -D_F(N_F \times P_F)\frac{\Delta R}{1 + R}$$

Fully hedging can be defined as buying or selling a sufficient number of futures contracts (N_F) so that the loss of net worth on the balance sheet (ΔE) when interest rates change is just offset by the gain from off-balance-sheet buying or selling of futures (ΔF), or

$$\Delta F = \Delta E$$

---

[13] In practice, the seller exploits the delivery option by choosing the cheapest bond to deliver, that is, bonds whose conversion factor is most favorable (being based on an 8 percent yield) relative to the true price of the bond to be delivered (which reflects the actual level of yields). See S. Figlewski, *Hedging with Financial Futures for Institutional Investors: From Theory to Practice* (Cambridge, MA: Ballinger, 1986).

[14] When futures prices fall, the buyer of the contract compensates the seller, here the FI. Thus, the FI gains when the prices of futures fall.

Substituting in the appropriate expressions for each:

$$-D_F(N_F \times P_F)\frac{\Delta R}{1 + R} = -(D_A - kD_L)A\frac{\Delta R}{1 + R}$$

Canceling $\Delta R/(1 + R)$ on both sides:[15]

$$D_F (N_F \times P_F) = (D_A - kD_L) A$$

Solving for N_F (the number of futures to sell):

$$N_F = \frac{(D_A - kD_L)A}{D_F \times P_F}$$

Appendix 23A (located at the book's Web site, **www.mcgrawhill.ca/college/saunders**) derives the equation for the number of futures contracts to buy or sell for a microhedge.[16]

Short Hedge

An FI takes a short position in a futures contract when rates are expected to rise; that is, the FI loses net worth on its balance sheet if rates rise, so it seeks to hedge the value of its net worth by selling an appropriate number of futures contracts.

EXAMPLE 23–2

Macrohedge of Interest Rate Risk Using a Short Hedge

From the equation for N_F, we can now solve for the correct number of futures positions to sell (N_F) in the context of Example 23–1 where the FI was exposed to a balance sheet loss of net worth (ΔE) amounting to $2.091 million when interest rates rose. In that example:

$$D_A = 5 \text{ years}$$
$$D_L = 3 \text{ years}$$
$$k = .9$$
$$A = \$100 \text{ million}$$

Suppose the current futures price quote is $97 per $100 of face value for the benchmark 20-year, 8 percent coupon bond underlying the nearby futures contract, the minimum contract size is $100,000, and the duration of the deliverable bond is 9.5 years. That is:

$$D_F = 9.5 \text{ years}$$
$$P_F = \$97,000$$

Inserting these numbers into the expression for N_F, we can now solve for the number of futures to sell:[17]

$$N_F = \frac{(5 - (.9)(3)) \times \$100 \text{ million}}{9.5 \times \$97,000}$$

$$= \frac{\$230,000,000}{\$921,500}$$

$$= 249.59 \text{ contracts to be sold}$$

---

[15] This amounts to assuming that the interest changes of the cash asset position match those of the futures position; that is, there is no basis risk. This assumption is relaxed later.

[16] For a microhedge, this equation becomes $N_F = \frac{D \times P}{D_F \times P_F}$

where P is the price of the asset or liability being hedged and D is its duration.

[17] For further discussions of this formula, see Figlewski, *Hedging with Financial Futures*, and E. Brewer, "Bank Gap Management and the Use of Financial Futures," Federal Reserve Bank of Chicago, *Economic Perspectives*, March–April 1985. Also note that if the FI intends to deliver any bond other than the 20-year benchmark bond, the P_F has to be multiplied by the appropriate conversion factor (c). If c = 1.19, then P_F = 97 × 1.19 = $115.43 per $100 of face value and the invoice price per contract would be $115,430.

Since the FI cannot sell a part of a contract, the number of contracts should be rounded down to the nearest whole number, or 249 contracts.[18]

Next, we verify that selling 249 T-bond futures contracts will indeed hedge the FI against a sudden increase in interest rates from 10 to 11 percent, or a 1 percent interest rate shock.

On Balance Sheet
As shown above, when interest rates rise by 1 percent, the FI loses $2.091 million in net worth (ΔE) on the balance sheet:

$$\Delta E = -(D_A - kD_L) A \frac{\Delta R}{1 + R}$$

$$-\$2.091 \text{ million} = -(5 - (.9)(3)) \times \$100 \text{ million} \times \left(\frac{.01}{1.1}\right)$$

Off Balance Sheet
When interest rates rise by 1 percent, the change in the value of the futures position is:

$$\Delta F = -D_F (N_F \times P_F) \frac{\Delta R}{1 + R}$$

$$= -9.5 (-249 \times \$97,000)\left(\frac{.01}{1.1}\right)$$

$$= \$2.086 \text{ million}$$

The value of the off-balance-sheet futures position (ΔF) falls by $2.086 million when the FI sells 249 futures contracts in the T-bond futures market. Such a fall in value of the futures contracts means a positive cash flow to the futures seller as the buyer compensates the seller for a lower futures price through the marking-to-market process. This requires a cash flow from the buyer's margin account to the seller's margin account as the price of a futures contract falls.[19] Thus, as the seller of the futures, the FI makes a gain of $2.086 million. As a result, the net gain/loss on and off the balance sheet is

$$\Delta E + \Delta F = -\$2.091 \text{ m} + \$2.086 \text{ m} = -\$0.005 \text{ million}$$

This small remaining net loss of $.005 million to equity or net worth reflects the fact that the FI could not achieve the perfect hedge—even in the absence of basis risk—as it needed to round down the number of futures to the nearest whole contract from 249.59 to 249 contracts. Table 23–3 summarizes the key features of the hedge (assuming no rounding of futures contracts).

(continued)

---

[18] The reason for rounding down rather than rounding up is technical. The target number of contracts to sell is that which minimizes interest rate risk exposure. By slightly underhedging rather than overhedging, the FI can generate the same risk exposure level but the underhedging policy produces a slightly higher return (see Figure 23–2).

[19] An example of marking to market might clarify how the seller gains when the price of the futures contract falls. Suppose on day 1 the seller entered into a 90-day contract to deliver 20-year T-bonds at $P = \$97$. The next day, because of a rise in interest rates, the futures contract, which now has 89 days to maturity, is trading at $96 when the market closes. Marking to market requires the prices on all contracts entered into on the previous day(s) to be marked to market at each night's closing (settlement) price. As a result, the price of the contract is lowered to $96 per $100 of face value, but in return for this lowering of the price from $97 to $96, the buyer has to compensate the seller to the tune of $1 per $100 of face value. Thus, given a $100,000 contract, there is a cash flow payment of $1,000 on that day from the buyer to the seller. Note that if the price had risen to $98, the seller would have had to compensate the buyer $1,000. The marking-to-market process goes on until the futures contract matures. If, over the period, futures prices have mostly fallen, then the seller accumulates positive cash flows on the futures position. It is this accumulation of cash flows that can be set off against losses in net worth on the balance sheet.

TABLE 23–3 On- and Off-Balance-Sheet Effects of a Microhedge Hedge

	On Balance Sheet	**Off Balance Sheet**
Begin hedge t = 0	Equity value of $10 million exposed to impact of rise in interest rates.	Sell 249.59 T-bond futures contracts at $97,000. Underlying T-bond coupon rate is 8%.
End *hedge t = 1 day*	Interest rates rise on assets and liabilities by 1%	Buy 249.59 T-bond futures (closes out futures position)
	Opportunity loss on-balance-sheet: $$\Delta E = [5 - .9(3)] \times \$100m \times \frac{.01}{1.1}$$ $$= -\$2.091 \text{ million}$$	Real gain on futures hedge: $$\Delta F = 9.5 \times (-249.59 \times \$97,000) \times \frac{.01}{1.1}*$$ $$= \$2.091 \text{ million}$$

*Assuming no basis risk and no contract "rounding."

Suppose instead of using the 20-year T-bond futures to hedge, it had used the three-month Eurodollar futures.[20] We can use the same formula to solve for N_F in the case of Eurodollar futures:

$$N_F = \frac{(D_A - kD_L)A}{D_F \times P_F}$$

$$= \frac{(5 - (.9)(3))\,\$100 \text{ million}}{D_F \times P_F}$$

Assume that $P_F = \$97$ per $100 of face value or $970,000 per contract (the minimum contract size of a Eurodollar future is $1,000,000) and $D_F = .25$ (the duration of a three-month Eurodollar deposit that is the discount instrument deliverable under the contract).[21] Then:

$$N_F = \frac{(5 - (.9)(3))\$100 \text{ million}}{.25 \times \$970,000} = \frac{\$230,000,000}{\$242,500}$$

$$N_F = 948.45 \text{ contracts to be sold}$$

Rounding down to the nearest whole contract, $N_F = 948$.

As this example illustrates, we can hedge an FI's on-balance-sheet interest rate risk when its $D_A > kD_L$ by shorting or selling either T-bond or Eurodollar futures. In general, fewer T-bond than Eurodollar contracts need to be sold—in our case, 948 Eurodollar versus 249 T-bond contracts. This suggests that on a simple transaction cost basis, the FI might normally prefer to use T-bond futures. However, other considerations can be important, especially if the FI holds the futures contracts until the delivery date. The FI needs to be concerned about the availability of the deliverable set of securities and any possible supply shortages or squeezes. Such liquidity concerns may favour Eurodollars.[22]

The Problem of Basis Risk

Because spot bonds and futures on bonds are traded in different markets, the shift in yields, $\Delta R/(1 + R)$, affecting the values of the on-balance-sheet cash portfolio may

---

[20] As Figure 23–3 shows, three-month Eurodollar futures are an alternative interest rate futures contract to the long-term bond futures contract.

[21] We assume the same futures price ($97) here for purposes of comparison. Of course, the actual prices of the two futures contracts are very different (see Figure 23–3).

[22] However, when rates change, the loss of net worth on the balance sheet and the gain on selling the futures are instantaneous; therefore, delivery need not be a concern. Indeed, because of the daily marking-to-market process, an FI manager can close out a futures position by taking an exactly offsetting position. That is, a manager who had originally sold 100 futures contracts could close out a position on any day by buying 100 contracts. Because of the unique marking-to-market feature, the marked-to-market price of the contracts sold equals the price of any new contracts bought on that day.

differ from the shift in yields, $\Delta R_F/(1 + R_F)$, affecting the value of the underlying bond in the futures contract; that is, changes in spot and futures prices or values are not perfectly correlated. This lack of perfect correlation is called *basis risk.* In the previous section, we assumed a simple world of no basis risk in which $\Delta R/(1 + R) = \Delta R_F/(1 + R_F)$.

Basis risk occurs for two reasons. First, the balance sheet asset or liability being hedged is not the same as the underlying security on the futures contract. For instance, in Example 23–2 we hedged interest rate changes on the FI's entire balance sheet with T-bond futures contracts written on 20-year maturity bonds with a duration of 9.5 years. The interest rates on the various assets and liabilities on the FI's balance sheet and the interest rates on 20-year T-bonds do not move in a perfectly correlated (or one-to-one) manner. The second source of basis risk comes from the difference in movements in spot rates versus futures rates. Because spot securities (e.g., government bonds) and futures contracts (e.g., on the same bonds) are traded in different markets, the shift in spot rates may differ from the shift in futures rates (i.e., they are not perfectly correlated).

To solve for the risk-minimizing number of futures contracts to buy or sell, N_F, while accounting for greater or less rate volatility and hence price volatility in the futures market relative to the spot or cash market, we look again at the FI's on-balance-sheet interest rate exposure:

$$\Delta E = -(D_A - kD_L) \times A \times \Delta R/(1 + R)$$

and its off-balance-sheet futures position:

$$\Delta F = -D_F(N_F \times P_F) \times \Delta R_F/(1 + R_F)$$

Setting:

$$\Delta E = \Delta F$$

and solving for N_F, we have

$$N_F = \frac{(D_A - kD_L) \times A \times \Delta R/(1 + R)}{D_F \times P_F \times \Delta R_F/(1 + R_F)}$$

Let *br* reflect the relative sensitivity of rates underlying the bond in the futures market relative to interest rates on assets and liabilities in the spot market, that is, $br = (\Delta R_F/(1 + R_F))/(\Delta R/(1 + R))$. Then the number of futures contracts to buy or sell is

$$N_F = \frac{(D_A - kD_L)A}{D_F \times P_F \times br}$$

The only difference between this and the previous formula is an adjustment for basis risk (*br*), which measures the degree to which the futures price (yield) moves more or less than spot bond price (yield).

EXAMPLE 23–3

Macrohedging Interest Rate Risk When Basis Risk Exists

From Example 23–2, let *br* = 1.1. This means that for every 1 percent change in discounted spot rates ($\Delta R/(1 + R)$), the implied rate on the deliverable bond in the futures market moves by 1.1 percent. That is, futures prices are more sensitive to interest rate shocks than are spot market prices. Solving for N_F we have

$$N_F = \frac{(5 - (.9)(3))\$100 \text{ million}}{9.5 \times \$97,000 \times 1.1}$$

$$= 226.9 \text{ contracts}$$

(continued)

or 226 contracts, rounding down. This compares to 249 when we assumed equal rate shocks in both the cash and futures markets ($\Delta R/(1 + R) = \Delta R_F/(1 + R_F)$). Here we need fewer futures contracts than was the case when we ignored basis risk because futures rates and prices are more volatile, so that selling fewer futures would be sufficient to provide the same change in ΔF (the value of the futures position) than before when we implicitly assumed $br = 1$. Note that if futures rates or prices had been less volatile than spot rates or prices, we would have had to sell more than 249 contracts to get the same dollar gain in the futures position as was lost in net worth on the balance sheet so that $\Delta E = \Delta F$.

An important issue FIs must deal with in hedging interest rate and other risks is how to estimate the basis risk adjustment in the preceding formula. One method is to look at the ratio between $\Delta R/(1 + R)$ and $\Delta R_F/(1 + R_F)$ today. Since this is only one observation, the FI might better analyze the relationship between the two interest rates by investigating their relative behavior in the recent past. We can do this by running an ordinary least squares linear regression of implied futures rate changes on spot rate changes with the slope coefficient of this regression giving an estimate of the degree of comovement of the two rates over time. We discuss this regression procedure in greater detail next in connection with calculating basis risk when hedging with FX futures.[23]

Concept Questions

1. What is the difference between microhedging and macrohedging and between routine hedging and selective hedging?
2. In Example 23–2, suppose the FI had the reverse duration gap; that is, the duration of its assets was shorter ($D_A = 3$) than the duration of its liabilities ($D_A = 5$). (This might be the case of a bank that borrows with long-term notes or time deposits to finance floating-rate loans.) How should it hedge using futures?
3. In Example 23–3, how many futures contracts should have been sold using the 20-year bond and 3-month Eurodollar contracts, if the basis risk measure $br = .8$?

HEDGING FOREIGN EXCHANGE RISK

Just as forwards and futures can hedge an FI against losses due to interest rate changes, they also can hedge against foreign exchange risk.

Forwards

Chapter 15 analyzed how an FI uses forward contracts to reduce the risks due to FX fluctuations when it mismatches the sizes of its foreign asset and liability portfolios. That chapter considered the simple case of an FI that raised all its liabilities in dollars while investing half of its assets in British pound sterling-denominated loans and the other half in dollar-denominated loans. Its balance sheet looks as follows:

Assets	Liabilities
Cdn loans ($) $100 million	Cdn CDs $200 million
U.K. loans (£) $100 million	

---

[23] Another problem with the simple duration gap approach to determining N_F is that it is assumed that yield curves are flat. This could be relaxed by using duration measures that allow for nonflat yield curves (see Chapter 9).

FIGURE 23–5
Hedging a Long Position in Pound Assets through Sale of Pound Forwards

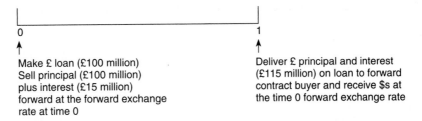

0

Make £ loan (£100 million)
Sell principal (£100 million)
plus interest (£15 million)
forward at the forward exchange
rate at time 0

1

Deliver £ principal and interest
(£115 million) on loan to forward
contract buyer and receive $s at
the time 0 forward exchange rate

All assets and liabilities are of a one-year maturity and duration. Because the FI is net long in pound sterling assets, it faces the risk that over the period of the loan, the pound will depreciate against the dollar so that the proceeds of the pound loan (along with the dollar loan) will be insufficient to meet the required payments on the maturing dollar CDs. Then the FI will have to meet such losses out of its net worth; that is, its insolvency risk will increase.

Chapter 15 showed that by selling both the pound loan principal and interest forward one year at the known forward exchange rate at the beginning of the year, the FI could hedge itself against losses on its pound loan position due to changes in the dollar/pound exchange rate over the succeeding year. Note the strategy for hedging (£100 million) of British pound sterling loans with forwards in Figure 23–5.

Futures

Instead of using FX forward contracts to hedge foreign exchange risk, the FI could use FX futures contracts. Consider an FI wishing to hedge a one-year British pound loan of £100 million principal plus £15 million interest (or £115 million) against the risk of the pound falling in value against the dollar over the succeeding year. Suppose the FI wished to hedge this loan position on March 18, 2006. On that day, there were two British pound futures contracts outstanding: a contract expiring in June 2006 (the "nearby" contract) and a contract expiring in December 2006. Thus, the futures market did not allow the FI to institute a long-term one-year hedge that day. The longest maturity contract available matured in just over five months (December 2006). Thus, the FI could use futures only by rolling over the hedge into a new futures contract on maturity. Considerations such as the transactions costs from having to roll over the hedge and uncertainty regarding the prices of new futures contracts may make hedging through forwards or swaps relatively more attractive to those FIs that want to lock in a longer-term hedge (see Chapter 25).

However, suppose the FI still wants to hedge fully via the futures markets. How many futures should it sell? The answer to this question is that it should sell the amount that produces a sufficient profit on the pound futures contracts to just offset any exchange rate losses on the pound loan portfolio should the pound fall in value relative to the dollar. There are two cases to consider:

1. The futures dollar/pound price is expected to change in exactly the same fashion as the spot dollar/pound price over the course of the year. That is, futures and spot price changes are perfectly correlated; there is no basis risk.

2. Futures and spot prices, though expected to change in the same direction, are not perfectly correlated (there is basis risk).

EXAMPLE 23–4

Hedging Foreign Exchange Risk Assuming Perfect Correlation between Spot and Futures Prices

Suppose on March 18, 2006,

$$S_t = \text{Spot exchange rate (\$/£): \$1.8057 per £1}$$

$$f_t = \text{Futures price (\$/£) for the nearby contract (June 2006): \$1.7916 per £1}$$

Suppose the FI made a £100 million loan at 15 percent interest and wished to hedge fully the risk that the dollar value of the proceeds would be eroded by a declining British pound sterling over the year. Also suppose that the FI manager receives a forecast that in one year's time the spot and futures will be

$$S_{t+1} = \$1.7557 \text{ per £1}$$

$$f_{t+1} = \$1.7416 \text{ per £1}$$

so that over the year,

$$\Delta S_t = -5 \text{ cents}$$

$$\Delta f_t = -5 \text{ cents}$$

For a manager who believes this forecast of a depreciating pound against the dollar, the correct full-hedge strategy is to cover the £115 million of expected earnings on the British loan by selling, or shorting, £115 million of British pound futures contracts on March 18, 2006. We assume here that the FI manager continuously rolls over the futures position into new futures contracts and will get out of futures on March 18, 2007.

The size of each British pound futures contract is £62,500. Therefore, the number (N_F) of futures to be sold is

$$N_F = \frac{£115,000,000}{£62,500} = \frac{\text{Size of long position}}{\text{Size of a pound futures contract}}$$

$$= 1,840 \text{ contracts to be sold}$$

Next, we consider whether losses on the long asset position (the British loan) would just offset gains on the futures should the FI sell 1,840 British pound futures contracts should spot and futures prices change in the direction and amount expected.

Loss on British Pound Loan

The loss on the British pound loan in dollars would be

$$[£ \text{ Principal} + \text{Interest}] \times \Delta S_t$$

$$[£115 \text{ million}] \times [\$1.8057/£ - \$1.7557/£] = \$5.75 \text{ million}$$

That is, the dollar value of the British pound loan proceeds would be $5.75 million less should the pound depreciate from $1.8057/£ to $1.7557/£ in the spot market over the year.

Gain on Futures Contracts

The gain on the futures contracts would be

$$[N_F \times £62,500] \times \Delta f_t$$

$$[1,840 \times £62,500] \times [\$1.7916/£ - \$1.7416/£] = \$5.75 \text{ million}$$

By selling 1,840 futures contracts of 62,500 each, the seller makes $5.75 million as the futures price falls from $1.7916/£ at the contract initiation on March 18, 2006, to $1.7416/£

at the futures position termination on March 18, 2007. This cash flow of $5.75 million results from the marking to market of the futures contract. As the futures price falls, due to the daily marking to market, the pound futures contract buyer has the contract repriced to a lower level in dollars to be paid per pound. But the seller must be compensated from the buyer's margin account for the difference between the original contract price and the new lower marked-to-market contract price. Thus, over the one year, the buyer compensates the seller by a net of 5 cents per £1 of futures purchased: that is, $1.7916/£1 minus $1.7416/£1 as the futures price falls, or a total of 5 cents $\times$ the number of contracts (1,840) $\times$ the pound size of each contract (62,500). Note that on March 18, 2007, when the principal and interest on the pound loan are paid by the borrower, the FI seller of the pound futures terminates its position in 1,840 short contracts by taking an opposing position of 1,840 long in the same contract. This effectively ends any net cash flow implications from futures positions beyond this date.

tail the hedge
Reducing the number of futures contracts that are needed to hedge a cash position because of the interest income that is generated from reinvesting the marked-to-market cash flows generated by the futures contract.

Finally, in this example we have ignored the interest income effects of marking to market. In reality, the $5.75 million from the futures position would be received by the FI seller over the course of the year. As a result, this cash flow can be reinvested at the current short-term dollar interest rate to generate a cash flow of more than $5.75 million. Given this, an FI hedger can sell slightly fewer contracts in anticipation of this interest income. The number of futures that could be sold, below the 1,840 suggested, would depend on the level and pattern of short-term rates over the hedging horizon as well as the precise expected pattern of cash flows from marking to market. In general, the higher the level of short-term interest, the more an FI manager could **tail the hedge** in this fashion.[24]

EXAMPLE 23–5

Hedging Foreign Exchange Risk Assuming Imperfect Correlation between Spot and Futures Prices (Basis Risk)

Suppose, instead, the FI manager did not believe that the spot exchange rate and futures price on the dollar/pound contract would fall by exactly the same amount. Instead, let the forecast for one year's time be:

$$S_{t+1} = 1.7557/£1$$

$$f_{t+1} = \$1.7616/£1$$

Thus, in expectation, over the succeeding year:

$$\Delta S_t = -5 \text{ cents}$$

$$\Delta f_t = -3 \text{ cents}$$

This means that the dollar/pound futures price is expected to depreciate less than the spot dollar/pound. This basis risk arises because spot and futures contracts are traded in different markets with different demand and supply functions. Given this, even though futures and spot prices are normally highly correlated, this correlation is often less than 1.

Because futures prices and spot prices do not always move exactly together, this can create a problem for an FI manager seeking to hedge the long position of £115 million with pound futures. Suppose the FI manager ignored the fact that the spot pound is expected to depreciate faster against the dollar than the futures price for pounds and continued to believe that selling 1,840 contracts would be the best hedge. That manager could be in for a big (and nasty) surprise in one year's time. To see this, consider the loss on the cash asset position and the gain on the futures position under a new scenario where the dollar/pound spot rate falls by 2 cents more than dollar/pound futures over the year.

(continued)

---

[24] See Figlewski, *Hedging with Financial Futures*, for further discussion. One way to do this is to discount the calculated hedge ratio (the optimal number of futures to sell per $1 of cash position) by a short-term interest rate such as the Bank of Canada's Overnight Rate.

Loss on British Pound Loan

The expected fall in the spot value of the pound by 5 cents over the year results in a loss of

$$[\text{£}115 \text{ million}] \times [\$1.8057/\text{£} - \$1.7557/\text{£}] = \$5.75 \text{ million}$$

Gain on Futures Position

The expected gain on the futures position is

$$[1,840 \times \text{£}62,500] \times [\$1.7916/\text{£} - \$1.7616/\text{£}] = \$3.45 \text{ million}$$

Thus, the net loss to the FI is

Net loss = Loss on British pound loan − Gain on British pound futures

Net loss = $5.75 − $3.45

Net loss = $2.3 million

Such a loss would have to be charged against the FI's profits and implicitly its net worth or equity. As a result, the FI manager needs to take into account the lower sensitivity of futures prices relative to spot exchange rate changes by selling more than 1,840 futures contracts to hedge fully the British pound loan risk.

To see how many more contracts are required, we need to know how much more sensitive spot exchange rates are relative to futures prices. Let h be the ratio of ΔS_t to Δf_t:

$$h = \frac{\Delta S_t}{\Delta f_t}$$

Then, in our example:

$$h = \frac{\$.05}{\$.03} = 1.66$$

That is, spot rates are 66 percent more sensitive than futures prices, or—put slightly differently—for every 1 percent change in futures prices, spot rates change by 1.66 percent.[25]

hedge ratio
The dollar value of futures contracts that should be sold per $ of cash position exposure.

An FI manager could use this ratio, h, as a **hedge ratio** to solve the question of how many futures should be sold to hedge the long position in the British pound when the spot and futures prices are imperfectly correlated. Specifically, the value of h means that for every £1 in the long asset position, £1.66 futures contracts should be sold. To see this, look at the FI's losses on its long asset position in pound loans relative to the gains on its selling pound futures.

Loss on British Pound Loans

As before, its losses are

$$[\text{£}115 \text{ million}] \times [\$1.8057/\text{£} - \$1.7557/\text{£}] = \$5.75 \text{ million}$$

Gains on British Pound Futures Position

Taking into account the degree to which spot exchange rates are more sensitive than futures prices—the hedge ratio (h)— we can solve for the number of futures (N_F) to sell as

$$N_F = \frac{\text{Long asset position} \times h}{\text{Size of one futures contract}}$$

$$N_F = \frac{\text{£}115 \text{ million} \times 1.66}{\text{£}62,500} = 3,054.4 \text{ contracts}$$

or, rounding down to the nearest whole contract, 3,054 contracts. Selling 3,054 British pound futures results in expected profits of

$$[3,054 \times \text{£}62,500] \times [\$1.7916/\text{£} - \$1.7616/\text{£}] = \$5.73 \text{ million}$$

The difference of $0.02 million between the loss on British pound loans and the gain on the pound futures is due to rounding.

---

[25] Of course, this can always be expressed the other way around: a 1 percent change in spot prices leads, on average, to only a 0.6 percent change in futures prices.

Estimating the Hedge Ratio[26]

The previous example showed that the number of FX futures that should be sold to hedge fully foreign exchange rate risk exposure depends crucially on expectations regarding the correlation between the change in the dollar/pound spot rate (ΔS_t) and the change in its futures price (Δf_t). When:

$$h = \frac{\Delta S_t}{\Delta f_t} = \frac{\$.05}{\$.05} = 1$$

there is no basis risk. Both the spot and futures are expected to change together by the same absolute amount, and the FX risk of the cash position should be hedged dollar for dollar by selling FX futures. When basis risk is present, the spot and future exchange rates are expected to move imperfectly together:

$$h = \frac{\Delta S_t}{\Delta f_t} = \frac{\$.05}{\$.03} = 1.66$$

The FI must sell a greater number of futures than it has to when basis risk is absent.

Unfortunately, without perfect foresight, we cannot know exactly how exchange rates and futures prices will change over some future time period. If we did, we would have no need to hedge in the first place! Thus, a common method to calculate h is to look at the behavior of ΔS_t relative to Δf_t over the *recent past* and to use this past behavior as a prediction of the appropriate value of h in the future. One way to estimate this past relationship is to run an ordinary least squares regression of recent changes in spot prices on recent changes in futures prices.[27]

Consider Figure 23–6, where we plot hypothetical monthly changes in the spot pound/dollar exchange rate (ΔS_t) against monthly changes in the futures pound/dollar price (Δf_t) for the year 200X. Thus, we have 12 observations from January through December. For information purposes, the first observation (January) is labeled in Figure 23–6. In January, the dollar/pound spot rate rose by 4.5 cents and the dollar/pound futures price rose by 4 cents. Thus, the pound appreciated in value over the month of January but the spot exchange rate rose by more than the futures price did. In some other months, as implied by the scatter of points in Figure 23–6, the futures price rose by more than the spot rate did.

An ordinary least squares (OLS) regression fits a line of best fit to these monthly observations such that the sum of the squared deviations between the observed values of ΔS_t and its predicted values (as given by the line of best fit) is minimized. This line of best fit reflects an intercept term α and a slope coefficient β. That is:

$$\Delta S_t = \alpha + \beta \, \Delta f_t + u_t$$

where the u_t are the regression's residuals (the differences between actual values of ΔS_t and its predicted values based on the line of best fit).

Definitionally, β, or the slope coefficient, of the regression equation is equal to

$$\beta = \frac{\text{Cov}(\Delta S_t, \Delta f_t)}{\text{Var}(\Delta f_t)}$$

---

[26] The material in this section is more technical in nature. It may be included or dropped from the chapter reading depending on the rigor of the course without harming the continuity of the chapter.

[27] When we calculate h (the hedge ratio), we could use the ratio of the most recent spot and futures price changes. However, this would amount to basing our hedge ratio estimate on *one* observation of the change in S_t and f_t. This is why the regression model, which uses many past observations, is usually preferred by market participants.

FIGURE 23–6
Monthly Changes in ΔS_t and Δf_t in 200X

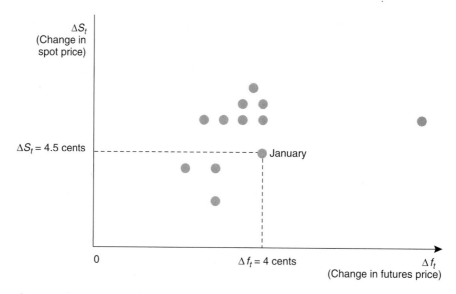

that is, the covariance between the change in spot rates and change in futures prices divided by the variance of the change in futures prices. Suppose ΔS_t and Δf_t moved perfectly together over time. Then:

$$\text{Cov}(\Delta S_t, \Delta f_t) = \text{Var}(\Delta f_t)$$

$$\text{and } \beta = 1$$

If spot rate changes are greater than futures price changes, then $\text{Cov}(\Delta S_t, \Delta f_t) > \text{Var}(\Delta f_t)$ and $\beta > 1$. Conversely, if spot rate changes are less sensitive than futures price changes over time, then $\text{Cov}(\Delta S_t, \Delta f_t) < \text{Var}(\Delta f_t)$ and $\beta < 1$.

Moreover, the value of β, or the estimated slope of the regression line, has theoretical meaning as the hedge ratio (h) that minimizes the risk of a portfolio of spot assets and futures contracts.[28] Put more simply, we can use the estimate of β from the regression model as the appropriate measure of h (the hedge ratio) to be used by the FI manager. For example, suppose we used the 12 observations on ΔS_t and Δf_t in 200X to estimate an OLS regression equation (the equation of the line of best fit in Figure 23–6). This regression equation takes the form:

$$\Delta S_t = 0.15 + 1.2\,\Delta f_t$$

Thus:

$$\alpha = 0.15$$

$$\beta = 1.2$$

Using $\beta = 1.2$ as the appropriate risk minimizing hedge ratio h for the portfolio manager, we can solve our earlier problem of determining the number of futures contracts to sell to protect the FI from FX losses on its £115 million loan:

$$N_F = \frac{\text{Long position in £ assets} \times \beta \text{ (the estimated value of the hedge ratio } h \text{ using past data)}}{\text{Size of one £ futures contract}}$$

$$N_F = \frac{£115 \text{ million} \times 1.2}{£62,500} = 2,208 \text{ contracts}$$

---

[28] For proof of this, see L. H. Ederington, "The Hedging Performance of the New Futures Markets," *Journal of Finance* 34 (1979), pp. 157–70.

Thus, using the past relationship between ΔS_t and Δf_t as the best predictor of their future relationship over the succeeding year dictates that the FI manager sell 2,208 contracts.

The degree of confidence the FI manager may have in using such a method to determine the appropriate hedge ratio depends on how well the regression line fits the scatter of observations. The standard measure of the goodness of fit of a regression line is the R^2 value of the equation, where the R^2 is the square of the correlation coefficient between ΔS_t and Δf_t:

$$R^2 = \rho^2 = \left[\frac{(\text{Cov}(\Delta S_t, \Delta f_t))}{\sigma_{\Delta S_t} \times \sigma_{\Delta f_t}} \right]^2$$

The term in brackets is the statistical definition of a correlation coefficient. If changes in the spot rate (ΔS_t) and changes in the futures price (Δf_t) are perfectly correlated, then:

$$R^2 = \rho^2 = (1)^2 = 1$$

and all observations between ΔS_t and Δf_t lie on a straight line. By comparison, an $R^2 = 0$ indicates that there is no statistical association at all between ΔS_t and Δf_t.

hedging effectiveness
The (squared) correlation between past changes in spot asset prices and futures prices.

Since we are using futures contracts to hedge the risk of loss on spot asset positions, the R^2 value of the regression measures the degree of **hedging effectiveness** of the futures contract. A low R^2 means that we might have little confidence that the slope coefficient β from the regression is actually the true hedge ratio. As the value of R^2 approaches 1, the degree of confidence increases in the use of futures contracts, with a given hedge ratio (h) estimate, to hedge our cash asset-risk position.

Concept Questions

1. Circle an observation in Figure 23–6 that shows futures price changes exceeding spot price changes.
2. Suppose that $R^2 = 0$ in a regression of ΔS_t on Δf_t. Would you still use futures contracts to hedge? Explain your answer.
3. In running a regression of ΔS_t on Δf_t, the regression equation is $\Delta S_t = .51 + .95\Delta f_t$ and $R^2 = .72$. What is the hedge ratio? What is the measure of hedging effectiveness?

HEDGING CREDIT RISK WITH FUTURES AND FORWARDS

Chapter 12 demonstrated that by diversifying their loan portfolios across different borrowers, sectors, and regions, FIs can diversify away much of the borrower-specific or unsystematic risk of the loan portfolio. Of course, the ability of an FI manager to diversify sufficiently depends in part on the size of the loan portfolio under management. Thus, the potential ability to diversify away borrower-specific risk increases with the size of the FI.

In recent years, however, new types of derivative instruments have been developed (including forwards, options, and swaps) to better allow FIs to hedge their credit risk. Credit derivatives can be used to hedge the credit risk on individual loans or bonds or on portfolios of loans and bonds. The credit derivative market, while still relatively young, has already gained a reputation as an early warning signal for spotting corporate debt problems. As shown in Table 23–1, at October 31, 2004, the notional amount of credit derivatives reported by the Big Six Canadian banks was equal to $287.1 billion, 3.2 percent of the total notional amount of $8,864.4 billion reported. As shown in Table 23–2, U.S. banks had over US$868 billion of notional value in credit derivatives outstanding in September 2003, and there were an estimated US$2 trillion outstanding worldwide. The emergence of these new derivatives is important since more FIs fail due to credit risk exposure (e.g. Canadian Commercial Bank, Northlands Bank in 1985) than to either interest rate or FX risk exposures. We discuss credit forward contracts below. In Chapter 24 we discuss credit options, and in Chapter 25 we discuss credit swaps.

Credit Forward Contracts and Credit Risk Hedging

credit forward

An agreement that hedges against an increase in default risk on a loan after the loan terms have been determined and the loan has been issued.

A **credit forward** is a forward agreement that hedges against an increase in default risk on a loan (a decline in the credit quality of a borrower) after the loan rate is determined and the loan is issued. Common buyers of credit forwards are insurance companies and common sellers are banks. The credit forward agreement specifies a credit spread (a risk premium above the risk-free rate to compensate for default risk) on a benchmark bond issued by an FI borrower. For example, suppose the benchmark bond of a bank borrower was rated BBB at the time a loan was originated. Further, at the time the loan was issued, the benchmark bonds had a 2 percent interest rate or credit spread (representing default risk on the BBB bonds) over a government security (bond) of the same maturity. To hedge against an increase in the credit risk of the borrower, the bank enters into (sells) a credit forward contract when the loan is issued. We define CS_F as the credit spread over the government security (bond) rate on which the credit forward contract is written (equals 2 percent in this example). Table 23–4 illustrates the payment pattern resulting from this credit forward. In Table 23–4, CS_T is the actual credit spread on the bond when the credit forward matures, for example, one year after the loan was originated and the credit forward contract was entered into, MD is the modified duration on the benchmark BBB bond, and A is the principal amount of the forward agreement.

From the payment pattern established in the credit forward agreement, Table 23–4 shows that the credit forward buyer (an insurance company) bears the risk of an increase in default risk on the benchmark bond of the borrowing firm, while the credit forward seller (the bank lender) hedges itself against an increase in the borrower's default risk. That is, if the borrower's default risk increases so that when the forward agreement matures the market requires a higher credit spread on the borrower's benchmark bond, CS_T, than that originally agreed to in the forward contract, CS_F, (i.e., $CS_T > CS_F$), the credit forward buyer pays the credit forward seller, which is the bank, $(CS_T - CS_F) \times MD \times A$. For example, suppose the credit spread between BBB bonds and government bonds widened to 3 percent from 2 percent over the year, the modified duration (MD) of the benchmark BBB bond was five years, and the size of the forward contract A was $10,000,000. Then the gain on the credit forward contract to the seller (the bank) would be $500,000 [$(3\% - 2\%) \times 5 \times \$10,000,000$]. This amount could be used to offset the loss in mar-

TABLE 23–4
Payment Pattern on a Credit Forward

Credit Spread at End of Forward Agreement	Credit Spread Seller (Bank)	Credit Spread Buyer (Counterparty)
$CS_T > CS_F$	Receives $(CS_T - CS_F) \times MD \times A$	Pays $(CS_T - CS_F) \times MD \times A$
$CS_F > CS_T$	Pays $(CS_F - CS_T) \times MD \times A$	Receives $(CS_F - CS_T) \times MD \times A$

FIGURE 23–7
Effect on a Bank of Hedging a Loan with a Credit Forward Contract

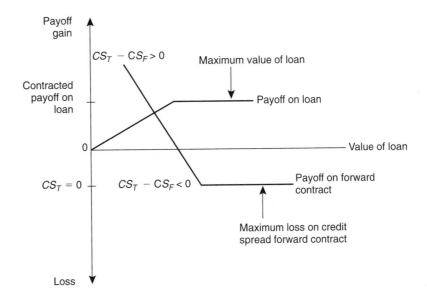

ket value of the loan due to the rise in the borrower's default risk. However, if the borrower's default risk and credit spread decrease over the year, the credit forward seller pays the credit forward buyer $(CS_F - CS_T) \times MD \times A$. [However, the maximum loss on the forward contract (to the bank seller) is limited, as will be explained below.]

Figure 23–7 illustrates the effect on the bank of hedging the loan.[29] If the default risk on the loan increases, the market or present value of the loan falls below its value at the beginning of the hedge period. However, the bank hedged the change in default risk by selling a credit forward contract. Assuming the credit spread on the borrower's benchmark bond also increases (so that $CS_T > CS_F$), the bank receives $(CS_T - CS_F) \times MD \times A$ on the forward contract. If the characteristics of the benchmark bond (i.e., change in credit spread, modified duration, and principal value) are the same as those of the bank's loan to the borrower, the loss on the balance sheet is offset completely by the gain (off the balance sheet) from the credit forward (i.e., in our example a $500,000 market value loss in the loan would be offset by a $500,000 gain from selling the credit forward contract).

If the default risk does not increase, or actually decreases (so that $CS_T < CS_F$), the bank selling the forward contract will pay $(CS_F - CS_T) \times MD \times A$ to the credit forward buyer (the insurance company). However, importantly, this payout by the bank is limited to a maximum. This is when CS_T falls to zero, that is, the default spread on BBB bonds falls to zero or the original BBB bonds of the borrower are viewed as having the same default risk as government bonds (in other words, the credit spread or rate on the benchmark bond cannot fall below the risk-free rate). In this case the maximum loss on the credit forward $[CS_F - (0)] \times MD \times A$ mirrors (offsets) the maximum and limited upside gain (return) on the loan. Anyone familiar with options will recognize that (as was discussed in Chapter 11) when the bank makes a loan, it is similar to writing a put option. In selling a credit forward, the payoff is similar to buying a put option (see Chapter 24 as well).

---

[29] For additional discussion, see J. D. Finnerty, "Credit Derivatives, Infrastructure Finance, and Emerging Market Risk," *The Financier,* ACMT, February 1996, pp. 64–75.

Futures Contracts and Catastrophe Risk

www.cbot.com

In recent years, the Chicago Board of Trade (CBOT) has introduced futures and options for catastrophe insurance. This chapter discusses catastrophe insurance futures, and the next chapter discusses catastrophe insurance options. The essential idea of catastrophe futures is to allow property-casualty insurers to hedge the extreme losses that occur after major hurricanes, such as the series of hurricanes that hit Florida in September 2004 and the U.S. Gulf Coast in August and September 2005, which resulted in damage of over US$25 and US$35 billion (insured value), respectively. Since in a catastrophe the ratio of insured losses to premiums rises (i.e., the so-called loss ratio increases), the payoff on a catastrophe futures contract is directly linked to the loss ratio. Specifically, on settlement, the payoff to the buyer of the futures is equal to the nominal value of the futures contract (which is US$25,000) times the actual loss ratio incurred by insurers. Suppose that on maturity of the futures contract the loss ratio was 1.5. This means that the payoff to the insurance company futures hedger would be 1.5 × US$25,000 = US$37,500. Also suppose that three months earlier (before the catastrophe occurred) the market expected the loss ratio to be only 0.8. Thus, the insurer would have been able to pay 0.8 × US$25,000 = US$20,000 to buy the futures contract. Because actual losses exceeded expected losses, the insurer makes a profit of US$37,500 − $20,000 = US$17,500 on each contract. These profits on futures contracts can be used to help offset the huge payouts on hurricane insurance contracts.[30]

Futures and Forward Regulation

www.m-x.ca

In Canada, derivatives contracts are traded on the Montréal Exchange (ME), which is responsible for the regulation of trading. The ME determines which contracts will trade as well as who may trade. The ME also establishes other rules regarding futures contracts such as price reporting requirements, anti-manipulation regulations, position limits, audit trail requirements, and margin requirements.

www.osfi-bsif.gc.ca

The Office of the Superintendent of Financial Services (OSFI) requires federally regulated financial institutions (domestic and foreign banks, trust & loans, co-operatives, life insurance companies, and property & casualty insurance companies) to follow its "Derivatives Best Practices Guideline B-7" effective May 1995. Banks are required to report on their derivatives positions quarterly as well as to follow the guidelines for best practices regarding capital adequacy, innovative instruments, large exposure limits, and derivative best practices, as well as specific guidelines with respect to interest rate risk, and accounting guidelines regarding the disclosure of derivative positions. Overall, the policy of OSFI is to encourage appropriate risk management practices at the FIs under its jurisdiction.

www.acsbcanada.org

As noted previously, as of October 1, 2006, the main regulator of accounting standards, the AcSB will require all FIs (and non-financial firms) to reflect the marked-to-market value of their derivative positions in their financial statements.

In the United States, derivatives contracts are subject to three levels of institutional regulation. First, regulators of derivatives specify "permissible activities" that institutions may engage in. Second, once permissible activities have been specified, institutions engaging in those activities are subjected to supervisory oversight. Third, regulators attempt to judge the overall integrity of each institution engaging

---

[30] For more details on catastrophe insurance, see J. D. Cummins and H. Geman, "Pricing Catastrophe Insurance Futures and Call Spreads: An Arbitrage Model," *Journal of Fixed Income*, March 1995, pp. 46–57; K. K. Aase, "A Markov Model for the Pricing of Catastrophe Insurance Futures and Spreads," *Journal of Risk and Insurance*, March 2001, pp. 25–49; and G. Zanjani, "Pricing and Capital Allocation in Catastrophe Insurance," *Journal of Financial Economics*, August 2002, pp. 283–305.

www.sec.gov
www.cftc.gov

in derivative activities by assessing the capital adequacy of the institutions and by enforcing regulations to ensure compliance with those capital requirements. The Securities and Exchange Commission (SEC) and the Commodities Futures Trading Commission (CFTC) are often viewed as "functional" regulators. The SEC regulates all securities traded on national securities exchanges, including several exchange-traded derivatives. The CFTC has exclusive jurisdiction over all exchange-traded derivative securities. It therefore regulates all national futures exchanges, as well as all futures and options on futures. This means that FIs must immediately recognize all gains and losses on such contracts and disclose those gains and losses to shareholders and regulators. Further, firms must show whether they are using derivatives to hedge risks connected to their business or whether they are just taking an open (risky) position.

Finally, as noted in Chapter 20, exchange-traded futures contracts are not subject to risk-based capital requirements; by contrast, OTC forward contracts are potentially subject to capital requirements. Other things being equal, the risk-based capital requirements favor the use of futures over forwards.

Concept Questions

1. Why are credit forwards useful for hedging the credit risk of an FI's portfolio?
2. Manulife Financial Corporation estimated after-tax losses of US$165 million on reinsurance contracts related to Hurricane Katrina that devastated New Orleans (see J. Partridge, "Manulife to take $165-million charge because of Katrina," *The Globe and Mail*, Tuesday, September 20, 2005, p. B5). What are some of the practical problems an FI manager may face when using catastrophe futures to hedge losses on insurance lines?

Summary

This chapter analyzed the risk-management role of futures and forwards. We saw that although they are close substitutes, they are not perfect substitutes. A number of characteristics, such as maturity, liquidity, flexibility, marking to market, and capital requirements, differentiate these products and make one or the other more attractive to any given FI manager. These products might be used to partially or fully hedge at least four types of risk commonly faced by an FI: interest rate risk, foreign exchange risk, credit risk, and catastrophe risk. An FI can engage in microhedging or macrohedging as well as engage in selective or routine hedging. In all cases, perfect hedging is shown to be difficult because of basis risk. Finally, accounting rules require FIs to disclose the market values of their (off-balance-sheet) derivatives positions.

Questions and Problems

1. What are derivative contracts? What is the value of derivative contracts to the managers of FIs? Which type of derivative contracts had the highest volume among Canadian banks as of October 2004?
2. What has been the regulatory result of some of the misuses by FIs of derivative products?
3. What are some of the major differences between futures and forward contracts? How do these contracts differ from spot contracts?
4. What is a naive hedge? How does a naive hedge protect an FI from risk?
5. An FI holds a 15-year, par value, $10,000,000 bond that is priced at 104 with a yield to maturity of 7 percent. The bond has a duration of eight years, and the FI plans to sell it after two months. The FI's market analyst predicts that interest rates will be 8 percent at the time of the desired sale. Because most other analysts are predicting no change in rates, two-month forward contracts for 15-year bonds are available at 104. The FI would like to hedge against the expected change in interest rates with an appropriate position in a forward contract. What will this position be? Show that if rates rise 1 percent as forecast, the hedge will protect the FI from loss.

www.mcgrawhill.ca/college/saunders

6. Contrast the position of being short with that of being long in futures contracts.

7. Suppose an FI purchases a bond futures contract at 95.

   a. What is the FI's obligation at the time the futures contract is purchased?

   b. If an FI purchases this contract, in what kind of hedge is it engaged?

   c. Assume that the bond futures price falls to 94. What is the loss or gain?

   d. Assume that the bond futures price rises to 97. Mark to market the position.

8. Long Bank has assets that consist mostly of 25-year mortgages and liabilities that are short-term time and demand deposits. Will an interest rate futures contract the bank buys add to or subtract from the bank's risk?

9. In each of the following cases, indicate whether it would be appropriate for an FI to buy or sell a forward contract to hedge the appropriate risk.

   a. A bank plans to issue CDs in three months.

   b. An insurance company plans to buy bonds in two months.

   c. A credit union is going to sell Government of Canada securities next month.

   d. A U.S. bank lends to a French company: the loan is payable in euros.

   e. A finance company has assets with a duration of six years and liabilities with a duration of 13 years.

10. The duration of a 20-year, 8 percent coupon government bond selling at par is 10.292 years. The bond's interest is paid semiannually, and the bond qualifies for delivery against a government bond futures contract.

    a. What is the modified duration of this bond?

    b. What is the effect on the bond price if market interest rates increase 50 basis points?

    c. If you sold a bond futures contract at 95 and interest rates rose 50 basis points, what would be the change in the value of your futures position?

    d. If you purchased the bond at par and sold the futures contract, what would be the net value of your hedge after the increase in interest rates?

11. What are the differences between a microhedge and a macrohedge for an FI? Why is it generally more efficient for FIs to employ a macrohedge than a series of microhedges?

12. What are the reasons why an FI may choose to selectively hedge its portfolio?

13. Hedge Row Bank has the following balance sheet (in millions):

Assets	$150	Liabilities	$135
		Equity	$ 15
Total	$150	Total	$150

The duration of the assets is six years, and the duration of the liabilities is four years. The bank is expecting interest rates to fall from 10 percent to 9 percent over the next year.

   a. What is the duration gap for Hedge Row Bank?

   b. What is the expected change in net worth for Hedge Row Bank if the forecast is accurate?

   c. What will be the effect on net worth if interest rates increase 100 basis points?

   d. If the existing interest rate on the liabilities is 6 percent, what will be the effect on net worth of a 1 percent increase in interest rates?

14. For a given change in interest rates, why is the sensitivity of the price of a government bond futures contract greater than the sensitivity of the price of a government t-bill futures contract?

15. What is the meaning of the government bond futures price quote 101–13?

16. What is meant by fully hedging the balance sheet of an FI?

17. Tree Row Bank has assets of $150 million, liabilities of $135 million, and equity of $15 million. The asset duration is six years, and the duration of the liabilities is four years. Market interest rates are 10 percent. Tree Row Bank wishes to hedge the balance sheet with government bond futures contracts, which currently have a price quote of $95 per $100 face value for the benchmark 20-year, 8 percent coupon bond underlying the contract.

   a. Should the bank go short or long on the futures contracts to establish the correct macrohedge?

   b. How many contracts are necessary to fully hedge the bank?

   c. Verify that the change in the futures position will offset the change in the cash balance sheet position for a change in market interest rates of plus 100 basis points and minus 50 basis points.

   d. If the bank had hedged with Treasury bill futures contracts that had a market value of $98 per $100 of face value, how many futures contracts would have been necessary to fully hedge the balance sheet?

e. What additional issues should be considered by the bank in choosing between T-bond and T-bill futures contracts?

18. Reconsider Tree Row Bank in problem 17 but assume that the cost rate on the liabilities is 6 percent.

   a. How many contracts are necessary to fully hedge the bank?

   b. Verify that the change in the futures position will offset the change in the cash balance sheet position for a change in market interest rates of plus 100 basis points and minus 50 basis points.

   c. If the bank had hedged with Treasury bill futures contracts that had a market value of $98 per $100 of face value, how many futures contracts would have been necessary to fully hedge the balance sheet?

19. What is basis risk? What are the sources of basis risk?

20. How would your answers for part (b) in problem 17 change if the relationship of the price sensitivity of futures contracts to the price sensitivity of underlying bonds were $br = 0.92$?

21. A mutual fund plans to purchase $500,000 of 30-year government bonds in four months. These bonds have a duration of 12 years and are priced at 96–08 (32nds). The mutual fund is concerned about interest rates changing over the next four months and is considering a hedge with government bond futures contracts that mature in six months. The bond futures contracts are selling for 98–24 (32nds) and have a duration of 8.5 years.

   a. If interest rate changes in the spot market exactly match those in the futures market, what type of futures position should the mutual fund create?

   b. How many contracts should be used?

   c. If the implied rate on the deliverable bond in the futures market moves 12 percent more than the change in the discounted spot rate, how many futures contracts should be used to hedge the portfolio?

   d. What causes futures contracts to have a different price sensitivity than assets in the spot markets?

22. Consider the following balance sheet (in millions) for an FI:

Assets		Liabilities	
Duration = 10 years	$950	Duration = 2 years	$860
		Equity	90

   a. What is the FI's duration gap?

   b. What is the FI's interest rate risk exposure?

   c. How can the FI use futures and forward contracts to put on a macrohedge?

   d. What is the impact on the FI's equity value if the relative change in interest rates is an increase of 1 percent? That is $\Delta R/(1 + R) = 0.01$.

   e. Suppose that the FI in part (c) macrohedges using government bond futures that are currently priced at 96. What is the impact on the FI's futures position if the relative change in all interest rates is an increase of 1 percent? That is, $\Delta R/(1 + R) = 0.01$. Assume that the deliverable government bond has a duration of nine years.

   f. If the FI wants a perfect macrohedge, how many government bond futures contracts does it need?

23. Refer again to problem 22. How does consideration of basis risk change your answers to problem 22?

   a. Compute the number of futures contracts required to construct a perfect macrohedge if

   $$[\Delta R_f/(1 + R_f)/\Delta R/(1 + R)] = br = 0.90$$

   b. Explain what is meant by $br = 0.90$.

   c. If $br = 0.90$, what information does this provide on the number of futures contracts needed to construct a perfect macrohedge?

24. An FI is planning to hedge its US$100 million bond instruments with a cross hedge using Eurodollar interest rate futures. How would the FI estimate

   $$br = [\Delta R_f/(1 + R_f)/\Delta R/(1 + R)]$$

   to determine the exact number of Eurodollar futures contracts to hedge?

25. Village Bank has $240 million worth of assets with a duration of 14 years and liabilities worth $210 million with a duration of 4 years. In the interest of hedging interest rate risk, Village Bank is contemplating a macrohedge with interest rate futures contracts now selling for 102–21 (32nds). If the spot and futures interest rates move together, how many futures contracts must Village Bank sell to fully hedge the balance sheet?

26. Assume that an FI has assets of $250 million and liabilities of $200 million. The duration of the assets is six years, and the duration of the liabilities is three years. The price of the futures contract is $115,000, and its duration is 5.5 years.

   a. What number of futures contracts is needed to construct a perfect hedge if $br = 1.10$?

   b. If $\Delta R_f/(1 + R_f) = 0.0990$, what is the expected $\Delta R/(1 + R)$?

27. Suppose an FI purchases a US$1 million 91-day Eurodollar futures contract trading at 98.50.

    a. If the contract is reversed two days later by purchasing the contract at 98.60, what is the net profit?

    b. What is the loss or gain if the price at reversal is 98.40?

28. What factors may make the use of swaps or forward contracts preferable to the use of futures contracts for the purpose of hedging long-term foreign exchange positions?

29. An FI has an asset investment in euros. The FI expects the exchange rate of $/€ to increase by the maturity of the asset.

    a. Is the dollar appreciating or depreciating against the euro?

    b. To fully hedge the investment, should the FI buy or sell euro futures contracts?

    c. If there is perfect correlation between changes in the spot and futures contracts, how should the FI determine the number of contracts necessary to hedge the investment fully?

30. What is meant by tailing the hedge? What factors allow an FI manager to tail the hedge effectively?

31. What does the hedge ratio measure? Under what conditions is this ratio valuable in determining the number of futures contracts necessary to hedge fully an investment in another currency? How is the hedge ratio related to basis risk?

32. What technique is commonly used to estimate the hedge ratio? What statistical measure is an indicator of the confidence that should be placed in the estimated hedge ratio? What is the interpretation if the estimated hedge ratio is greater than one? Less than one?

33. An FI has assets denominated in British pounds sterling of $125 million and sterling liabilities of $100 million.

    a. What is the FI's net exposure?

    b. Is the FI exposed to a dollar appreciation or depreciation?

    c. How can the FI use futures or forward contracts to hedge its FX rate risk?

    d. What is the number of futures contracts that must be utilized to fully hedge the FI's currency risk exposure?

    e. If the British pound falls from $1.60/£ to $1.50/£, what will be the impact on the FI's cash position?

    f. If the British pound futures price falls from $1.55/£ to $1.45/£, what will be the impact on the FI's futures position?

    g. Using the information in parts (e) and (f), what can you conclude about basis risk?

34. Refer to problem 33, part (f).

    a. If the British pound futures price fell from $1.55/£ to $1.43/£, what would be the impact on the FI's futures position?

    b. Does your answer to part (a) differ from your answer to part (f) in problem 33? Why or why not?

    c. How would you fully hedge the FX risk exposure in problem 33 using the new futures price change?

35. An FI is planning to hedge its one-year $100 million Swiss francs (Sf)–denominated loan against exchange rate risk. The current spot rate is $0.60/Sf. A 1-year Sf futures contract is currently trading at $0.58/Sf. Sf futures are sold in standardized units of Sf125,000.

    a. Should the FI be worried about the Sf appreciating or depreciating?

    b. Should it buy or sell futures to hedge against exchange rate exposure?

    c. How many futures contracts should it buy or sell if a regression of past changes in spot prices on changes in future prices generates an estimated slope of 1.4?

    d. Show exactly how the FI is hedged if it repatriates its principal of Sf100 million at year end, the spot price of Sf at year end is $0.55/Sf, and the forward price is $0.5443/Sf.

36. An FI has made a loan commitment of Sf10 million that is likely to be taken down in six months. The current spot rate is $0.60/Sf.

    a. Is the FI exposed to the dollar's depreciating or appreciating? Why?

    b. If the spot rate six months from today is $0.64/Sf, what amount of dollars is needed if the loan is taken down and the FI is unhedged?

    c. If it decides to hedge using Sf futures, should the FI buy or sell Sf futures?

    d. A six-month Sf futures contract is available for $0.61/Sf. What net amount would be needed to fund the loan at the end of six months if the FI had hedged using the Sf10 million futures contract? Assume that futures prices are equal to spot prices at the time of payment (i.e., at maturity).

37. An FI has assets denominated in Swiss francs (Sf) of 75 million and liabilities of 125 million. The spot rate is $0.6667/Sf, and one-year futures are available for $0.6579/Sf.

a. What is the FI's net exposure?

b. Is the FI exposed to dollar appreciation or depreciation?

c. If the Sf spot rate changes from $0.6667/Sf to $0.6897/Sf, how will this affect the FI's currency exposure? Assume no hedging.

d. What is the number of futures contracts necessary to fully hedge the currency risk exposure of the FI? The contract size is Sf125,000 per contract.

e. If the Sf futures price falls from $0.6579/Sf to $0.6349/Sf, what will be the effect on the FI's futures position?

38. What is a credit forward? How is it structured?

39. What is the gain on the purchase of a $20,000,000 credit forward contract with a modified duration of seven years if the credit spread between a benchmark government bond and a borrowing firm's debt decreases 50 basis points?

40. How is selling a credit forward similar to buying a put option?

41. A property and casualty (P&C) insurance company purchased catastrophe futures contracts to hedge against loss during the hurricane season. At the time of purchase, the market expected a loss ratio of 0.75. After processing claims from a severe hurricane, the P&C actually incurred a loss ratio of 1.35. What amount of profit did the P&C make on each US$25,000 futures contract?

42. What is the primary goal of regulators in regard to the use of futures by FIs? What guidelines have regulators given to banks for trading in futures and forwards?

Web Questions

43. Go to the Web site of any one of the six major banks in Canada and download the latest version of the annual report. Use the search function in Adobe Acrobat to find the term "notional amount." How have the notional amounts of each type of derivative contract changed since the results reported in Table 23–1 for October 31, 2004? Conduct a second search using the term "hedging." Does this FI report the amount of derivatives held for trading and the amount held for hedging? Repeat the process for a second bank. How does the use of derivatives used for hedging and trading differ between the two FIs?

44. Go to the Office of the Comptroller of the Currency Web site at **www.occ.treas.gov.** Find the most recent levels of futures, forwards, options, swaps, and credit derivatives using the following steps. Click on "Publications." From there click on "Qrtrly. Derivative Fact Sheet." Click on the most recent date. This will bring the files up on your computer that contain the relevant data. The tables containing the data are at the bottom of this document. How have these values increased since September 2003 (as reported in Table 23–2)?

www.mcgrawhill.ca/college/saunders

Appendix 23A Microhedging with Futures

View Appendix 23A at the Web site for this textbook (**www.mcgrawhill.ca/college/saunders**).

CHAPTER 24

Options, Caps, Floors, and Collars

In this chapter, we:

▸ review the four basic options strategies:
  ▸ buying a call
  ▸ writing a call
  ▸ buying a put, and
  ▸ writing a put[1]
▸ look at economic and regulatory reasons FIs choose to buy versus write (sell) options
▸ discuss the use of fixed-income or interest rate options to hedge interest rate risk
▸ discuss the role of options in hedging:
  ▸ foreign exchange risk
  ▸ credit risks, and
  ▸ catastrophe risks
▸ conclude with an examination of caps, floors, and collars

INTRODUCTION

Just as there is a wide variety of forward and futures contracts available for an FI to use in hedging, there is an even wider array of option products, including exchange-traded options, over-the-counter options, options embedded in securities, and caps, collars, and floors. As we saw with futures contracts (in Chapter 23), the use of options can protect an FI against a loss of net worth due to unexpected changes in interest rates, credit risk, foreign exchange risk, and so forth. Not only has the range of option products increased in recent years, but the use of options has increased as well. However, options can also lead to huge losses for FIs (see the Ethical Dilemmas box).

As with futures and forwards, discussed in Chapter 23, options, caps, floors, and collars are held by FIs not only to hedge their own risk, but also to serve as counterparties (for a fee) for other (financial and nonfinancial) firms wanting to hedge risk on their own balance sheets.

BASIC FEATURES OF OPTIONS

In describing the features of the four basic option strategies FIs might employ to hedge interest rate risk, we discuss their return payoffs in terms of interest rate movements. Specifically, we consider bond options whose payoff values are inversely linked to interest rate movements in a manner similar to bond prices and interest rates in general (see Chapter 8).

---

[1] There are two basic option contracts: puts and calls. However, an FI could potentially be a buyer or seller (writer) of each.

Widening its investigation into a rogue-trading scandal, National Australia Bank Ltd. said foreign-currency trading losses could rise to as much as 600 million Australian dollars (US$485 million). The big Australian bank's Chief Executive Frank Cicutto ordered that a probe into unauthorized trading of foreign-currency options be expanded into other market operations, such as commodities, spot currency, and interest rates. While the focus continues to be on bogus trades from its foreign-currency options desk, NAB hopes the broader review of its entire trading floor will inject confidence into its market operation.

Details of the wider investigation emerged as NAB raised its estimate of a pretax loss arising from unauthorized foreign-currency options trades since October by A$5 million to A$185 million. Analysts already expect known losses to wipe out the bank's entire fiscal 2004 earnings growth. . . . Four NAB employees were suspended last week in connection with the allegations of unauthorized trading. The federal police and bank-sector regulators also are investigating. . . .

Source: Excerpt from Erick Johnston, "Big Australian Bank Widens Probe," *The Wall Street Journal*, January 20, 2004, p. A12. www.wsj.com. Reprinted by permission of *The Wall Street Journal*, copyright © 2004 Dow Jones & Company, Inc. All Rights Reserved Worldwide. License number 1395940073119

Buying a Call Option on a Bond

call option

Gives a purchaser the right (but not the obligation) to buy the underlying security from the writer of the option at a prespecified exercise price on a prespecified date.

The first strategy of buying (or taking a long position in) a call option on a bond is shown in Figure 24–1. A **call option** gives the purchaser the right (but not the obligation) to buy the underlying security—a bond—at a prespecified *exercise* or *strike price* (X). In return, the buyer of the call option must pay the writer or seller an up-front fee known as a *call premium* (C). This premium is an immediate negative cash flow for the buyer of the call, who potentially stands to make a profit if the underlying bond's price rises above the exercise price by an amount exceeding the premium. If the price of the bond never rises above X, the buyer of the call never exercises the option (i.e., buying the bond at X when its market value is less than X). In this case, the option matures unexercised. The call buyer incurs a cost, C, for the option, and no other cash flows result.

As shown in Figure 24–1, if the price of the bond underlying the option rises to price B, the buyer makes a profit of π, which is the difference between the bond price (B) and the exercise price of the option (X) minus the call premium (C). If the bond price rises to A, the buyer of the call has broken even in that the profit from exercising the call ($A - X$) just equals the premium payment for the call (C).

Notice two important things about bond call options in Figure 24–1:

1. As interest rates fall, bond prices rise and the call option buyer has large profit potential; the more that rates fall, the higher bond prices rise and the larger the profit on the exercise of the option.

2. As interest rates rise, bond prices fall and the potential for a negative payoff (loss) for the buyer of the call option increases. If rates rise so that bond prices fall below the exercise price X, the call buyer is not obliged to exercise the option. Thus, the losses of the buyer are truncated by the amount of the up-front premium payment (C) made to purchase the call option.

Thus, buying a call option is a strategy to take when interest rates are expected to fall. Notice that unlike interest rate futures, whose prices and payoffs move symmetrically with changes in the level of rates, the payoffs on bond call options move asymmetrically with interest rates (see Chapter 23).

Writing a Call Option on a Bond

The second strategy is writing (or taking a short position in) a call option on a bond. In writing a call option on a bond, the writer or seller receives an up-front fee or

FIGURE 24–1
Payoff Function for the Buyer of a Call Option on a Bond

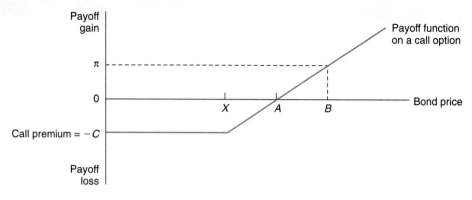

FIGURE 24–2
Payoff Function for the Writer of a Call Option on a Bond

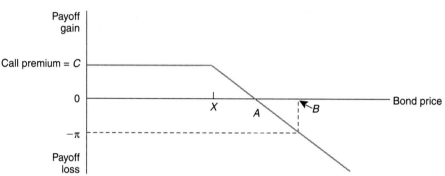

premium (C) and must stand ready to sell the underlying bond to the purchaser of the option at the exercise price, X. Note the payoff from writing a call option on a bond in Figure 24–2.

There are two important things to notice about this payoff function:

1. When interest rates rise and bond prices fall, there is an increased potential for the writer of the call to receive a positive payoff or profit. The call buyer is less likely to exercise the option, which would force the option writer to sell the underlying bond at the exercise price. However, this profit has a maximum equal to the call premium (C) charged up front to the buyer of the option.

2. When interest rates fall and bond prices rise, the writer has an increased potential to take a loss. The call buyer will exercise the option, forcing the option writer to sell the underlying bonds. Since bond prices are theoretically unbounded in the upward direction, although they must return to par at maturity, these losses could be very large.

Thus, writing a call option is a strategy to take when interest rates are expected to rise. Caution is warranted, however, because profits are limited but losses are potentially large if rates fall. In Figure 24–2, a fall in interest rates and a rise in bond prices to B results in the writer of the option losing π.

put option
Gives a purchaser the right (but not the obligation) to sell the underlying security to the writer of the option at a prespecified exercise price on a prespecified date.

Buying a Put Option on a Bond

The third strategy is buying (or taking a long position in) a put option on a bond. The buyer of a **put option** on a bond has the right (but not the obligation) to sell the underlying bond to the writer of the option at the agreed exercise price (X). In return for this option, the buyer of the put option pays a premium to the writer (P).

FIGURE 24–3
Payoff Function for
the Buyer of a Put
Option on a Bond

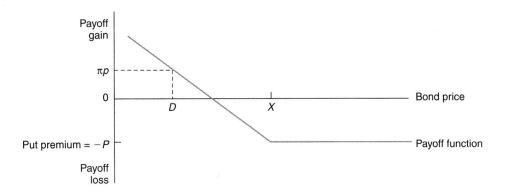

We show the potential payoffs to the buyer of the put option in Figure 24–3. Note that

1. When interest rates rise and bond prices fall, the buyer of the put has an increased probability of making a profit from exercising the option. Thus, if bond prices fall to D, the buyer of the put option can purchase bonds in the bond market at that price and put them (sell them) back to the writer of the put at the higher exercise price (X). As a result, the buyer makes a profit, after deducting the cost of the put premium (P), of πp in Figure 24–3.
2. When interest rates fall and bond prices rise, the probability that the buyer of a put will lose increases. If rates fall so that bond prices rise above the exercise price X, the put buyer does not have to exercise the option. Thus, the maximum loss is limited to the size of the up-front put premium (P).

Thus, buying a put option is a strategy to take when interest rates are expected to rise.

Writing a Put Option on a Bond

The fourth strategy is writing (or taking a short position in) a put option on a bond. In writing a put option on a bond, the writer or seller receives a fee or premium (P) in return for standing ready to buy bonds at the exercise price (X) if the buyer of the put chooses to exercise the option to sell. See the payoff function for writing a put option on a bond in Figure 24–4. Note that

1. If interest rates fall and bond prices rise, the writer has an enhanced probability of making a profit. The put buyer is less likely to exercise the option, which would force the option writer to buy the underlying bond. However, the writer's maximum profit is constrained to be equal to the put premium (P).
2. If interest rates rise and bond prices fall, the writer of the put is exposed to potentially large losses (e.g., $-\pi p$, if bond prices fall to D in Figure 24–4).

Thus, writing a put option is a strategy to take when interest rates are expected to fall. However, profits are limited and losses are potentially unlimited.

Concept Questions

1. How do interest rate increases affect the payoff from buying a call option on a bond? How do they affect the payoff from writing a call option on a bond?
2. How do interest rate increases affect the payoff from buying a put option on a bond? How do they affect the payoff from writing a put option on a bond?

FIGURE 24–4
Payoff Function for the Writer of a Put Option on a Bond

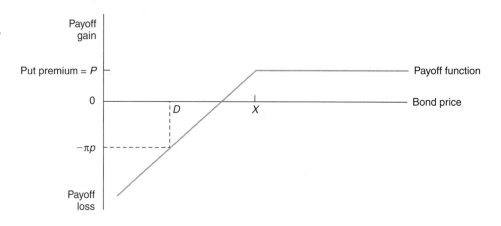

FIGURE 24–5
Writing a Call Option to Hedge the Interest Rate Risk on a Bond

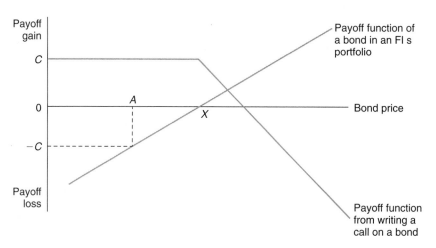

WRITING VERSUS BUYING OPTIONS

Many small FIs are restricted to buying rather than writing options. There are two reasons for this, one economic and the other regulatory. However, as we note later, large FIs often both write and buy options including caps, floors, and collars, which are complex forms of interest rate options.

Economic Reasons for Not Writing Options

In writing an option, the upside profit potential is truncated, but the downside losses are not. While such risks may be offset by writing a large number of options at different exercise prices and/or hedging an underlying portfolio of bonds, the downside risk exposure of the writer may still be significant. To see this, look at Figure 24–5, where an FI is long in a bond in its portfolio and seeks to hedge the interest rate risk on that bond by writing a bond call option.

Note that writing the call may hedge the FI when rates fall and bond prices rise; that is, the increase in the value of the bond is offset by losses on the written call. When the reverse occurs and interest rates rise, the FI's profits from writing the call may be insufficient to offset the loss on its bonds. This occurs because the upside profit (per call written) is truncated and is equal to the premium income (C).

FIGURE 24–6
**Buying a Put
Option to Hedge
the Interest Rate
Risk on a Bond**

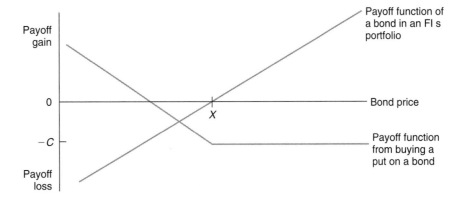

FIGURE 24–7
**Net Payoff of
Buying a Bond
Put and Investing
in a Bond**

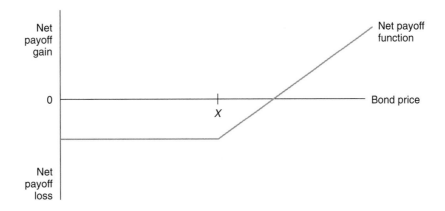

If the decrease in the bond value is larger than the premium income (to the left of point A in Figure 24–5), the FI is unable to offset the associated capital value loss on the bond with profits from writing options.

By contrast, hedging the FI's risk by buying a put option on a bond offers the manager a much more attractive alternative. Figure 24–6 shows the gross payoff of the bond and the payoff from buying a put option on a bond. In this case, any losses on the bond (as rates rise and bond values fall) are offset with profits from the put option that was bought (points to the left of point X in Figure 24–6). If rates fall, the bond value increases, yet the accompanying losses on the purchased put option positions are limited to the option premiums paid (points to the right of point X). Figure 24–7 shows the net payoff or the difference between the bond and option payoff.

Note that

1. Buying a put option truncates the downside losses on the bond following interest rate rises to some maximum amount and scales down the upside profits by the cost of bond price risk insurance—the put premium—leaving some positive upside profit potential.

2. The combination of being long in the bond and buying a put option on a bond mimics the payoff function of buying a call option (compare Figures 24–1 and 24–7).

Regulatory Reasons

naked options
Option positions that do not identifiably hedge an underlying asset or liability.

There are also regulatory reasons why FIs buy options rather than write options. Regulators view writing options, especially **naked options** that do not identifiably hedge an underlying asset or liability position, to be risky because of the large loss potential. Indeed, in some countries, bank regulators prohibit banks from writing puts or calls in certain areas of risk management.

Futures versus Options Hedging

To understand the differences between using futures versus options contracts to hedge interest rate risk, compare the payoff gains illustrated in Figure 24–8 (for futures contracts) with those in Figure 24–6 (for buying put option contracts). A hedge with futures contracts reduces volatility in payoff gains on both the upside and downside of interest rate movements. That is, if the FI in Figure 24–8 loses value on the bond resulting from an interest rate increase (to the left of point X), a gain on the futures contract offsets the loss. If the FI gains value on the bond due to an interest rate decrease (to the right of point X), however, a loss on the futures contract offsets the gain.

In comparison, the hedge with the put option contract completely offsets losses but only partly offsets gains. That is, in Figure 24–6, if the FI loses value on the bond due to an interest rate increase (to the left of point X), a gain on the put option contract offsets the loss. However, if the FI gains value on the bond due to an interest rate decrease (to the right of point X), the gain is offset only to the extent that the FI loses the put option premium (because it never exercises the option). Thus, the put option hedge protects the FI against value losses when interest rates move against the on-balance-sheet securities but, unlike futures hedging, does not reduce value when interest rates move in favor of on-balance-sheet securities.

Concept Questions

1. What are some of the economic reasons for an FI not to write options?
2. What are some regulatory reasons why an FI might choose to buy options rather than write options?

THE MECHANICS OF HEDGING A BOND OR BOND PORTFOLIO[2]

You have seen how buying a put option on a bond can potentially hedge the interest rate risk exposure of an FI that holds bonds as part of its investment portfolio. In this section, we use a simple example to demonstrate the mechanics of buying a put option as a hedging device and how an FI manager can calculate the fair premium value for a put option on a bond.

In calculating the fair value of an option, two alternative models can be used: the binomial model and the Black-Scholes model. The Black-Scholes model produces a closed-form solution to the valuation of call and put options. Appendix 24A to this chapter (located at the book's Web site, www.mcgrawhill.ca/college/saunders) shows how to calculate the value of an option using the Black-Scholes model. Although it works well for stocks, the Black-Scholes model has two major problems when employed to

---

[2] The material in this section is more technical in nature. It may be included or dropped from the chapter reading depending on the rigor of the course without harming the continuity of the chapter.

FIGURE 24–8
Buying a Futures Contract to Hedge the Interest Rate Risk on a Bond

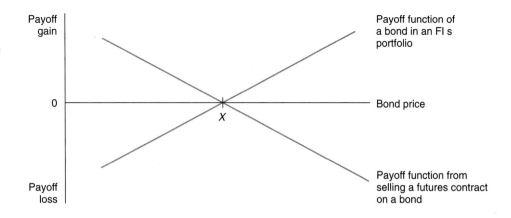

Payoff gain

0

Payoff loss

Payoff function of a bond in an FI s portfolio

Bond price

X

Payoff function from selling a futures contract on a bond

value bond options. First, it assumes that short-term interest rates are constant, which they generally are not. Second, it assumes a constant variance of returns on the underlying asset.[3] The application of the Black-Scholes formula to bonds is problematic because of the way bond prices behave between issuance and maturity.[4] This is shown in Figure 24–9, where a bond is issued at par, that is, the price of the bond is 100 percent times its face value at time of issue. If interest rates fall, its price may rise above 100 percent, and if interest rates rise, its price may fall below 100 percent. However, as the bond approaches maturity, all price paths must lead to 100 percent of the face value of the bond or principal paid by the issuer on maturity. Because of this **pull-to-par,** the variance of bond prices is nonconstant over time, rising at first and then falling as the bond approaches maturity. We evaluate the mechanics of hedging using bond put options in a simple binomial framework next.

pull-to-par
The tendency of the variance of a bond's price or return to decrease as maturity approaches.

Hedging with Bond Options Using the Binomial Model

Suppose that an FI manager has purchased a $100 zero-coupon bond with exactly two years to maturity. A zero-coupon bond, if held to maturity, pays its face value

---

[3] The Black-Scholes formulas for a put and a call are

$$P = Xe^{-rT}N[-D + \sigma\sqrt{T}] - SN[-D]$$
$$C = SN[D] - Xe^{-rT}N[D - \sigma\sqrt{T}]$$

where

S = Price of the underlying asset

X = Exercise price

T = Time to option expiration

r = Instantaneous riskless interest rate

$$D = \frac{\ln(S/X) + (r + \sigma^2/2)T}{\sigma\sqrt{T}}$$

$\ln[\,.\,]$ = Natural logarithm

σ = Volatility of the underlying asset

$N[\,.\,]$ = Cumulative normal distribution function, that is, the probability of observing a value less than the value in brackets when drawing randomly from a standardized normal distribution

[4] There are models that modify Black-Scholes to allow for nonconstant variance. These include Merton, who allows variance to be time dependent; Ball and Tourous, who allow bond prices to change as a stochastic process with a variance that first increases and then decreases (the Brownian bridge process); and the Schaefer-Schwartz model, which assumes that the standard deviation of returns is proportional to a bond's duration. See R. C. Merton, "On the Pricing of Corporate Debt: The Risk Structure of Interest Rates," *Journal of Finance* 29 (1974), pp. 449–70; C. Ball and W. N. Tourous, "Bond Price Dynamics and Options," *Journal of Financial and Quantitative Analysis* 18 (1983), pp. 517–31; and S. Schaefer and E. S. Schwartz, "Time Dependent Variance and the Pricing of Bond Options," *Journal of Finance* 42 (1987), pp. 1113–28.

FIGURE 24–9
The Variance of
a Bond's Price

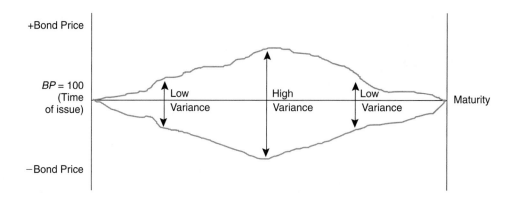

of $100 on maturity in two years. Assume that the FI manager pays $80.45 per $100 of face value for this zero-coupon bond. This means that if held to maturity, the FI's annual yield to maturity (R_2) from this investment would be

$$BP_2 = \frac{100}{(1 + R_2)^2}$$

$$80.45 = \frac{100}{(1 + R_2)^2}$$

$$(1 + R_2)^2 = \frac{100}{80.45}$$

$$1 + R_2 = \sqrt{\frac{100}{80.45}}$$

$$R_2 = \sqrt{\frac{100}{80.45}} - 1 = .115 = 11.5\%$$

Suppose also that, at the end of the first year, interest rates rise unexpectedly. As a result, depositors, seeking higher returns on their funds, withdraw deposits. To meet these unexpected deposit withdrawals, the FI manager is forced to liquidate (sell) the two-year bond before maturity, at the end of year one. As we discuss in Chapter 17, government securities are important liquidity sources for an FI. Because of the unexpected rise in interest rates at the end of year one, the FI manager must sell the bond at a low price.

Assume when the bond is purchased, the current yield on one-year discount bonds (R_1) is $R_1 = 10$ percent. Also, assume that at the end of year one, the one-year interest rate (r_1) is forecasted to rise to either 13.82 percent or 12.18 percent. If one-year interest rates rise from $R_1 = 10$ percent when the bond is purchased to $r_1 = 13.82$ percent at the end of year one, the FI manager will be able to sell the zero-coupon bond with one year remaining to maturity for a bond price, BP, of

$$BP_1 = \frac{100}{(1 + r_1)} = \frac{100}{(1.1382)} = \$87.86$$

If, on the other hand, one-year interest rates rise to 12.18 percent, the manager can sell the bond with one year remaining to maturity for

$$BP_1 = \frac{100}{(1 + r_1)} = \frac{100}{(1.1218)} = \$89.14$$

In these equations, r_1 stands for the two possible one-year rates that might arise one year into the future.[5] That is,

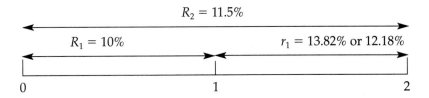

Assume the manager believes that one-year rates (r_1) one year from today will be 13.82 percent or 12.18 percent with an equal probability. This means that the expected one-year rate one year from today would be

$$[E(r_1)] = .5(.1382) + .5(.1218) = .13 = 13\%$$

Thus, the expected price if the bond has to be sold at the end of the first year is[6]

$$E(P_1) = \frac{100}{(1.13)} = \$88.5$$

Assume that the FI manager wants to ensure that the bond sale produces at least $88.5 per $100; otherwise the FI has to find alternative and very costly sources of liquidity (for example, the FI might have to borrow from the central bank's discount window and incur the direct and indirect penalty costs involved, see Chapter 19). One way for the FI to ensure that it receives at least $88.5 on selling the bond at the end of the year is to buy a put option on the bond at time 0 with an exercise price of $88.5 at time (year) 1. If the bond is trading below $88.5 at the end of the year—say, at $87.86—the FI can exercise its option and put the bond back to the writer of the option, who will have to pay the FI $88.5. If, however, the bond is trading above $88.5—say, at $89.14—the FI does not have to exercise its option and instead can sell the bond in the open market for $89.14.

The FI manager will want to recalculate the fair premium to pay for buying this put option or bond insurance at time 0. Figure 24–10 shows the possible paths (i.e., the binomial tree or lattice) of the zero-coupon bond's price from purchase to maturity over the two-year period.[7] The FI manager purchased the bond at $80.45 with two years to maturity. Given expectations of rising rates, there is a 50 percent probability that the bond with one year left to maturity will trade at $87.86 and a 50 percent probability that it will trade at $89.14. Note that between $t = 1$, or one year left to maturity, and maturity ($t = 2$), there must be a pull to par on the bond; that is, all paths must lead to a price of $100 on maturity.

---

[5] If one-year bond rates next year equaled the one-year bond rate this year, $R_1 = r_1 = 10$ percent, then the bond could be sold for $BP_1 = \$90.91$.

[6] The interest rates assumed in this example are consistent with arbitrage-free pricing under current term structure conditions. [See T. S. Y. Ho and S. B. Lee, "Term Structure Movements and Pricing Interest Rate Contingent Claims," *Journal of Finance* 61 (1986), pp. 1001–29.] That is, the expectations theory of interest rates implies that the following relationship must hold:

$$(1 + R_2)^2 = (1 + R_1) \times (1 + E(r_1))$$

As you can easily see, when the interest rates from our example are inserted, $R_1 = 10\%$, $R_2 = 11.5\%$, $E(r_1) = 13\%$, this equation holds. Also, the two interest rates (prices) imply that the current volatility of one-year interest rates is 6.3 percent. That is, from the binomial model, $\sigma = 1/2 ln[r_u/r_d]$, such that $\sigma = 1/2 ln[13.82/12.18] = .063$ or 6.3%.

[7] This example is based on R. Litterman and T. Iben, "Corporate Bond Valuation and the Term Structure of Credit Spreads," *Journal of Portfolio Management,* 1989, pp. 52–64.

FIGURE 24–10
Binomial Model
of Bond Prices:
Two-Year Zero-
Coupon Bond

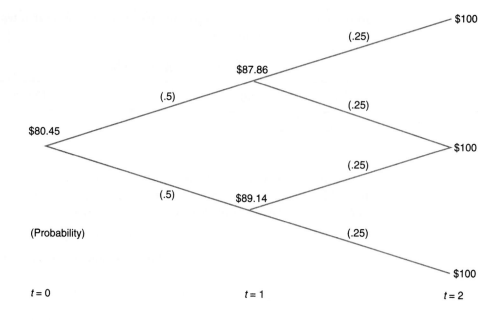

The value of the option is shown in Figure 24–11. The option in Figure 24–11 can be exercised only at the end of year 1 ($t = 1$). If the zero-coupon bond with one year left to maturity trades at $87.86, the option is worth $88.5 − $87.86 in time 1 dollars, or $0.64. If the bond trades at $89.14, the option has no value since the bond could be sold at a higher value than the exercise price of $88.5 on the open market. This suggests that in time 1 dollars, the option is worth

$$.5(0.64) + .5(0) = \$0.32$$

However, the FI is evaluating the option and paying the put premium at time $t = 0$, that is, one year before the date when the option might be exercised. Thus, the fair value of the put premium (P) the FI manager should be willing to pay is the discounted present value of the expected payoff from buying the option. Since one-year interest rates (R_1) are currently 10 percent, this implies

$$P = \frac{\$0.32}{1 + R_1} = \frac{\$0.32}{(1.1)} = \$0.29$$

or a premium, P, of approximately 29 cents per $100 bond option purchased.

Further, as you can easily see, the option becomes increasingly valuable as the variability of interest rates increases. Conceptually, the branches of the binomial tree diagram become more widely dispersed as variability increases. For example, suppose one-year interest rates on the upper branch were expected to be 14.82 percent instead of 13.82 percent. Then, the price on a one-year, zero-coupon bond associated with a one-year yield of 14.82 percent is $87.09 and the option is worth $88.5 − $87.09 in time 1 dollars, or $1.41. Thus, the value of the put option (P) with the same exercise price of $88.5 is

$$P = \frac{.5(1.41) + .5(0)}{1.1}$$

$$= 64 \text{ cents}$$

FIGURE 24–11
The Value of a
Put Option on the
Two-Year Zero-
Coupon Bond

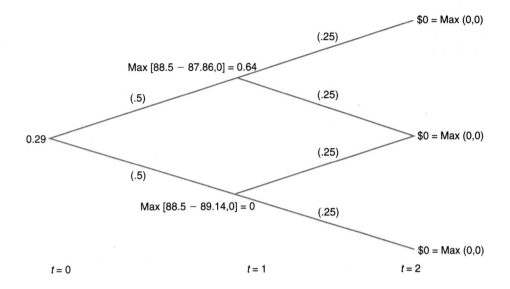

Notice the familiar result from option pricing theory holds

$$\frac{\delta P}{\delta \sigma} > 0$$

That is, the value of the put option increases with an increase in underlying variance of asset returns.

Concept Questions

1. What are two common models used to calculate the fair value of a bond option? Which is preferable, and why?
2. In the example above, calculate the value of the option if the exercise price (X) = $88. ($P$ = $0.064)

BOND FUTURES OPTIONS FOR HEDGING INTEREST RATE RISK

www.m-x.ca
www.cboe.com

open interest
The outstanding stock of put or call contracts.

futures option
An option contract that, when exercised, results in the delivery of a futures contract as the underlying asset.

We have presented a simple example of how FIs may use bond options to hedge exposure to liability withdrawal and forced liquidation of assets in a world of interest rate variability. In actuality, FIs have a wide variety of over-the-counter (OTC) and exchange-traded options available. Interest rate options are listed on the Montréal exchange in Canada and on the Chicago Board Options Exchange (CBOE). However, these contracts are rarely traded. For example, on March 18, 2004, **open interest** (the outstanding stock of put or call contracts) in short-term interest rate options was 217 contracts. In actual practice, most pure bond options trade over-the-counter. This is not because interest rate or bond options are not used, although the open interest is relatively small, but because the preferred method of hedging is an option on an interest rate futures contract. See these **futures options** (i.e., an option contract that, when exercised, results in the delivery of a futures contract as the underlying asset) on bonds in Figure 24–12 for trading on Thursday, March 18, 2004. Bond or interest rate futures options are generally preferred to options on the underlying bond because they combine the favourable liquidity, credit risk, homogeneity, and marking-to-market features of futures with the same asymmetric payoff functions as regular puts and calls (see Chapter 23).

FIGURE 24–12
Futures Options on Interest Rates, March 18, 2004

Interest Rate

STRIKE	CALLS-SETTLE	PUTS-SETTLE

T-Bonds (CBT)
$100,000; points and 64ths of 100%

Price	Apr	May	Jun	Apr	May	Jun
115	0-54	1-46	2-13	0-34	1-26	1-57
116	0-24	1-14	1-45	1-04	1-58	2-25
117	0-09	0-53	1-18	1-53	2-33	2-62
118	0-03	0-35	0-61	2-47	3-14	3-40
119	0-01	0-22	0-44	...	...	...
120	0-01	0-13	0-31	...	...	5-10

Est vol 43,594;
Wd vol 42,376 calls 21,923 puts
Op int Wed 357,398 calls 413,632 puts

T-Notes (CBT)
$100,000; points and 64ths of 100%

Price	Apr	May	Jun	Apr	May	Jun
115	1-00	1-34	1-54	0-13	0-47	1-03
116	0-24	0-61	1-17	0-37	1-09	1-30
117	0-06	0-34	0-53	1-19	1-47	2-02
118	0-01	0-17	0-32	2-14	...	2-45
119	0-01	0-08	0-18	...	...	3-30
120	...	0-04	0-10	...	...	...

Est vol 158,759 Wd 158,543 calls 120,182 puts
Op int Wed 1,166,258 calls 1,222,764 puts

5 Yr Treas Notes (CBT)
$100,000; points and 64ths of 100%

Price	Apr	May	Jun	Apr	May	Jun
11400	0-09	0-31	0-46	0-31	0-54	1-04
11450	0-02	0-20	0-33	...	...	...
11500	0-01	0-11	0-23	...	...	...
11550	0-01	0-06	0-15	...	...	...
11600	...	0-03	0-09	...	...	...
11650	...	0-02	0-06	...	...	...

Est vol 34,573 Wd 10,626 calls 19,813 puts
Op int Wed 172,925 calls 518,654 puts

30 Day Federal Funds (CBT)
$5,000,000; 100 minus daily average

Price	Mar	Apr	May	Mar	Apr	May
988750	.122	.127	.122	.002	.002	.002
989375	.062	.065	.065	.002	.002	.005
990000	.002	.007	.010	.007	.007	.015
990625	.002	.002	...	...	...	...
991250	.002	...	.002	...	...	.132
991875	...	...	...	...	...	...

Est vol 410 Wd 11,175 calls 300 puts
Op int Wed 163,010 calls 161,971 puts

STRIKE	CALLS-SETTLE	PUTS-SETTLE

Eurodollar (CME)
$ million; pts. of 100%

Price	Apr	May	Jun	Apr	May	Jun
9850	3.40	...	3.47	0.00	0.05	0.07
9875	1.00	1.10	1.17	0.10	0.20	0.27
9900	0.02	0.07	0.10	...	...	1.70
9925	...	0.02	...	...	...	4.12
9950	...	...	0.00	...	...	...
9975	...	...	0.00	...	...	...

Est vol 276,654;
Wd vol 134,553 calls 520,901 puts
Op int Wed 3,568,321 calls 3,950,481 puts

1 Yr. Mid-Curve Eurodlr (CME)
$1,000,000 contract units; pts. of 100%

Price	Apr	May	Jun	Apr	May	Jun
9725	5.85	...	6.52	0.15	0.47	0.85
9750	3.60	4.15	4.60	0.40	0.95	1.40
9775	1.80	2.40	2.92	1.10	1.70	2.22
9800	0.62	1.17	1.62	2.42	...	3.42
9825	0.17	...	0.72	...	...	...
9850	0.05	...	0.27	...	...	7.05

Est vol 71,710 Wd 28,000 calls 37,835 puts
Op int Wed 730,247 calls 727,189 puts

2 Yr. Mid-Curve Eurodlr (CME)
$1,000,000 contract units; pts. of 100%

Price	Jun	Sep	Dec	Jun	Sep	Dec
9625	6.05	5.72	5.50	1.15	2.95	4.75
9650	4.20	4.20	4.15	1.80	3.90	5.90
9675	2.65	2.90	...	2.75	5.10	...
9700	1.52	...	2.20	...	...	...
9725	...	1.20	...	...	...	...
9750	...	...	0.92	...	...	...

Est vol 2,350 Wd 6,530 calls 3,080 puts
Op int Wed 60,547 calls 20,705 puts

Euribor (LIFFE)
Euro 1,000,000

Price	Apr	May	Jun	Apr	May	Jun
97750	0.32	0.32	0.32	...	...	0.00
97875	0.19	0.20	0.20	...	0.00	0.01
98000	0.08	0.09	0.11	0.01	0.02	0.04
98125	0.02	0.04	0.05	0.07	0.09	0.10
98250	0.00	0.02	0.02	0.18	0.20	0.20
98375	...	0.00	0.01	0.30	0.31	0.31

Vol Th 270,614 calls 46,921 puts
Op int Wed 5,303,386 calls 1,809,827 puts

Euro-BUND (EUREX)
100,000; pts. in 100%

Price	Apr	May	Jun	Apr	May	Jun
11500	1.26	1.52	1.75	0.02	0.28	0.51
11550	0.81	1.16	1.40	0.07	0.42	0.66
11600	0.43	0.85	1.10	0.19	0.61	0.86
11650	0.18	0.59	0.84	0.44	0.85	1.10
11700	0.06	0.38	0.62	0.82	1.14	1.38
11750	0.01	0.24	0.45	1.27	1.50	1.71

Vol Th 48,047 calls 34,758 puts
Op int Wed 505,506 calls 589,281 puts

Currency

Japanese Yen (CME)
12,500,000 yen; cents per 100 yen

Price	Apr	May	Jun	Apr	May	Jun
9300	1.51	1.94	2.24	0.59	1.02	1.32
9350	1.23	1.68	1.97	0.81	1.26	1.55
9400	1.00	1.44	1.72	1.08	1.52	1.80
9450	0.79	...	1.52	1.37	...	2.10
9500	0.61	...	1.34	1.69	...	2.42
9550	0.48	0.90	1.18	2.06	...	2.75

Est vol 1,940 Wd 1,596 calls 1,006 puts
Op int Wed 21,813 calls 17,559 puts

Canadian Dollar (CME)
100,000 Can.$, cents per Can.$

Price	Apr	May	Jun	Apr	May	Jun
7400	...	...	1.84	0.30	...	0.81
7450	0.98	...	1.53	0.45	...	1.00
7500	0.69	1.01	1.25	0.66	0.98	1.22
7550	0.48	0.80	1.03	0.95	1.27	1.50
7600	0.34	...	0.85	1.31	...	1.82
7650	0.24	...	0.69	...	...	2.15

Est vol 188 Wd 127 calls 175 puts
Op int Wed 9,077 calls 4,985 puts

British Pound (CME)
62,500 pounds; cents per pound

Price	Apr	May	Jun	Apr	May	Jun
1800	3.08	4.09	4.63	1.16	2.17	2.72
1810	2.50	...	...	1.58	...	...
1820	2.00	3.00	3.56	2.08	3.08	3.64
1830	1.64	2.55	3.10	2.72	...	4.18
1840	1.28	2.17	2.69	3.36	4.25	4.76
1850	1.00	1.83	2.31	4.08	...	5.38

Est vol 1,559 Wd 377 calls 53 puts
Op int Wed 9,050 calls 3,590 puts

Swiss Franc (CME)
125,000 francs; cents per franc

Price	Apr	May	Jun	Apr	May	Jun
7850	1.57	...	2.29	0.47	...	1.19
7900	1.25	1.69	2.00	0.65	1.09	1.40
7950	0.96	1.42	...	0.86	1.32	...
8000	0.73	1.19	1.50	1.13	1.59	1.90
8050	0.55	...	...	1.45	...	...
8100	0.40	...	1.10	1.80	...	2.49

Est vol 145 Wd 9 calls 7 puts
Op int Wed 1,010 calls 2,094 puts

Euro Fx (CME)
125,000 euros; cents per euro

Price	Apr	May	Jun	Apr	May	Jun
12250	1.92	...	3.10	0.96	...	2.14
12300	1.63	2.31	2.83	1.17	1.85	2.37
12350	1.37	...	...	1.41	...	...
12400	1.14	1.83	2.35	1.68	2.37	2.89
12450	0.94	...	2.13	1.98	...	3.17
12500	0.76	1.42	1.92	2.30	2.96	3.45

Est vol 7,717 Wd 1,551 calls 2,278 puts
Op int Wed 28,166 calls 28,727 puts

Specifically, when the FI hedges by buying put options on bond futures, if interest rates rise and bond prices fall, the exercise of the put causes the FI to deliver a bond futures contract to the writer at an exercise price higher than the cost of the bond future currently trading on the futures exchange. The futures price itself reflects the price of the underlying deliverable bond such as a 20-year, 8 percent coupon T-bond; see Figure 24–12. As a result, a profit on futures options may be made to offset the loss on the market value of bonds held directly in the FI's portfolio. If interest rates fall and bond and futures prices rise, the buyer of the futures option will not exercise the put, and the losses on the futures put option are limited to the put premium. Thus, if on March 18, 2004, the FI had bought one US$100,000 June 2004 T-bond futures put option at a strike price of US$117 but did not exercise the option, the FI's loss equals the put premium of $2^{62}/_{64}$ per US$100, or $2,968.75 per US$100,000 contract. Offsetting these losses, however, would be an increase in the market value of the FI's underlying bond portfolio. Unlike futures positions in Chapter 23, an upside profit potential remains when interest rates fall and FIs use put options on futures to hedge interest rate risk. We show this in the next section.

Concept Questions

1. Why are bond or interest rate futures options generally preferred to options on the underlying bond?
2. If an FI hedges by buying put options on futures and interest rates rise (i.e., bond prices fall), what is the outcome?

USING OPTIONS TO HEDGE INTEREST RATE RISK ON THE BALANCE SHEET

Our previous simple example showed how a bond option could hedge the interest rate risk on an underlying bond position in the asset portfolio. Next, we determine the put option position that can hedge the interest rate risk of the overall balance sheet; that is, we analyze macrohedging rather than microhedging.

Chapter 8 showed that an FI's net worth exposure to an interest rate shock could be represented as

$$\Delta E = -(D_A - kD_L) \times A \times \frac{\Delta R}{1 + R}$$

where

$$\Delta E = \text{Change in the FI's net worth}$$

$$(D_A - kD_L) = \text{FI's duration gap}$$

$$A = \text{Size of the FI's assets}$$

$$\frac{\Delta R}{1 + R} = \text{Size of the interest rate shock}$$

$$k = \text{FI's leverage ratio } (L/A)$$

Suppose the FI manager wishes to determine the optimal number of put options to buy to insulate the FI against rising rates. An FI with a positive duration gap (see Figure 24–13) would lose on-balance-sheet net worth when interest rates rise. In this case, the FI manager would buy put options.[8] That is, the FI manager

---

[8] Conversely, an FI with a negative duration gap would lose on-balance-sheet net worth when interest rates fall. In this case, the FI manager wants to buy call options to generate profits to offset the loss in net worth due to an interest rate shock.

FIGURE 24–13
Buying Put Options to Hedge the Interest Rate Risk Exposure of the FI

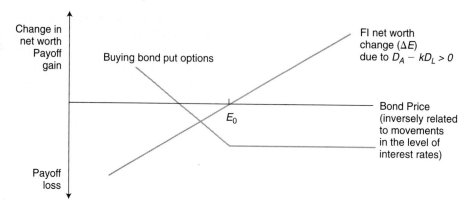

wants to adopt a put option position to generate profits that just offset the loss in net worth due to an interest rate shock (where E_0 is the FI's initial equity (net worth) position in Figure 24–13).

Let ΔP be the total change in the value of the put option position in T-bonds. This can be decomposed into

$$\Delta P = (N_p \times \Delta p) \qquad \textbf{(24.1)}$$

where N_p is the number of \$100,000 put options on T-bond contracts to be purchased (the number for which we are solving) and Δp is the change in the dollar value for each \$100,000 face value T-bond put option contract.

The change in the dollar value of each contract (Δp) can be further decomposed into

$$\Delta p = \frac{dp}{dB} \times \frac{dB}{dR} \times \Delta R \qquad \textbf{(24.2)}$$

This decomposition needs some explanation. The first term (dp/dB) shows the change in the value of a put option for each \$1 change in the underlying bond. This is called the *delta of an option* (δ) and lies between 0 and 1. For put options, the delta has a negative sign since the value of the put option falls when bond prices rise.[9] The second term (dB/dR) shows how the market value of a bond changes if interest rates rise by one basis point. This value of one basis point term can be linked to duration. Specifically, we know from Chapter 9 that

$$\frac{dB}{B} = -MD \times dR \qquad \textbf{(24.3)}$$

That is, the percentage change in the bond's price for a small change in interest rates is proportional to the bond's modified duration (*MD*). Equation (3) can be rearranged by cross multiplying as

$$\frac{dB}{dR} = -MD \times B \qquad \textbf{(24.4)}$$

Thus, the term dB/dR is equal to minus the modified duration on the bond (*MD*) times the current market value of the T-bond (*B*) underlying the put option contract. As a result, we can rewrite equation (2) as

$$\Delta p = [(-\delta) \times (-MD) \times B \times \Delta R] \qquad \textbf{(24.5)}$$

[9] For call options, the delta has a positive sign since the value of the call rises when bond prices rise. As we proceed with the derivation, we examine only the case of a hedge using a put option contract (i.e., the FI has a positive duration gap and expects interest rates to rise). For a hedge with a call option contract (i.e., the FI has a negative duration gap), the derivation below changes only in that the sign on the delta is reversed (from negative to positive).

where ΔR is the shock to interest rates (i.e., the number of basis points by which rates change). Since from Chapter 9 we know that $MD = D/(1 + R)$, we can rewrite equation (5) as

$$\Delta p = \left[(-\delta) \times (-D) \times B \times \frac{\Delta R}{1 + R} \right] \qquad \textbf{(24.6)}$$

Thus, the change in the total value of a put position[10] (ΔP) is

$$\Delta P = N_p \times \left[\delta \times D \times B \times \frac{\Delta R}{1 + R} \right] \qquad \textbf{(24.7)}$$

The term in brackets is the change in the value of one $100,000 face-value T-bond put option as rates change, and N_p is the number of put option contracts.

To hedge net worth exposure, we require the profit on the off-balance-sheet put options (ΔP) to just offset the loss of on-balance-sheet net worth ($-\Delta E$) when interest rates rise (and thus, bond prices fall). That is,[11]

$$\Delta P = -\Delta E$$

$$N_p \times \left[\delta \times D \times B \times \frac{\Delta R}{1 + R} \right] = [D_A - kD_L] \times A \times \frac{\Delta R}{1 + R}$$

Canceling $\Delta R/(1 + R)$ on both sides, we get

$$N_p \times [\delta \times D \times B] = [D_A - kD_L] \times A$$

Solving for N_p—the number of put options to buy—we have[12]

$$N_P = \frac{[D_A - kD_L] \times A}{[\delta \times D \times B]} \qquad \textbf{(24.8)}$$

Appendix 24B (located at the book's Web site, www.mcgrawhill.ca/college/saunders) derives the equation for the number of option contracts to buy or sell for a microhedge.[13]

EXAMPLE 24–1

Macrohedge of Interest Rate Risk Using a Put Option

Suppose, as in Chapter 23, an FI's balance sheet is such that $D_A = 5$, $D_L = 3$, $k = .9$, and $A = 100 million. Rates are expected to rise from 10 to 11 percent over the next six months, which would result in a $2.09 million loss in net worth to the FI. Suppose also that δ of the put option is .5, which indicates that the option is close to being in the money, $D = 8.82$ for the bond underlying the put option contract, and the current market value of $100,000 face value of long-term Treasury bonds underlying the option contract, B, equals $97,000. Solving for N_p, the number of put option contracts to buy:

$$N_p = \frac{\$230,000,000}{[.5 \times 8.82 \times \$97,000]} = \frac{\$230,000,000}{\$427,770}$$

$$= 537.672 \text{ contracts}$$

(continued)

---

[10] Note that since both the delta and D values of the put option and bond have negative signs, their product will be positive. Thus, these negative signs are not shown in the equation to calculate N_p.

[11] Note that $\quad \Delta E = -(D_A - kD_L) \times A \times \dfrac{\Delta R}{1 + R}$

Thus: $\quad -\Delta E = +(D_A - kD_L) \times A \times \dfrac{\Delta R}{1 + R}$

[12] For a hedge involving a call option, the formula is

$$N_C = \frac{[D_A - kD_L] \times A}{-[\delta \times D \times B]}$$

[13] For a microhedge, this equation becomes

$$N_O = \frac{D \times P}{\delta \times D \times B}$$

where P is the price of the asset or liability being hedged and D is its duration.

If the FI slightly underhedges, this will be rounded down to 537 contracts. If rates increase from 10 to 11 percent, the value of the FI's put options will change by

$$\Delta P = 537 \times \left[.5 \times 8.82 \times \$97,000 \times \frac{.01}{1.1} \right] = \$2.09 \text{ million}$$

just offsetting the loss in net worth on the balance sheet.

The total premium cost to the FI of buying these puts is the price (premium) of each put times the number of puts:

$$\text{Cost} = N_p \times \text{Put premium per contract}$$

Suppose that T-bond put option premiums are quoted at $2\frac{1}{2}$ per $100 of face value for the nearby contract or $2,500 per $100,000 put contract; then the cost of macrohedging the gap with put options will be

$$\text{Cost} = 537 \times \$2,500 = \$1,342,500$$

or just over $1.3 million. Remember, the total assets of the FI were assumed to be $100 million.

Figure 24–14 summarizes the change in the FI's overall value from a one percent increase in interest rates and the offsetting change in value from the hedge in the put option market. If rates increase as predicted, the FI's gap exposure results in a decrease in net worth of $2.09 million. This decrease is offset with a $2.09 million gain on the put option position held by the FI. Should rates decrease, however, the resulting increase in net worth is not offset by a decrease in an out-of-the-money put option.

Appendix 24B to this chapter (located at the book's Web site, www.mcgrawhill.ca/college/saunders) illustrates how these options can be used to microhedge a specific asset or liability on an FI's balance sheet against interest rate risk.

Basis Risk

It is again important to recognize that in the previous examples, the FI hedged interest rate risk exposure perfectly because basis risk was assumed to be zero. That is, we assumed the change in interest rates on the balance sheet is equal to the change in the interest rate on the bond underlying the option contract (i.e., $\Delta R/(1 + R) = \Delta R_b/(1 + R_b)$). As discussed in Chapter 23, the introduction of basis risk means that

FIGURE 24–14   **Buying Put Options to Hedge an FI's Interest Rate Gap Risk Exposure**

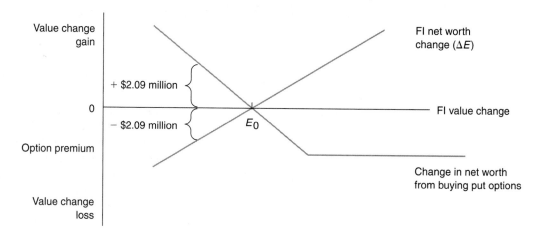

the FI must adjust the number of option contracts it holds to account for the degree to which the rate on the option's underlying security (i.e., T-bond) moves relative to the spot rate on the asset or liability the FI is hedging.

Allowing basis risk to exist, the equation used to determine the number of put options to buy to hedge interest rate risk becomes

$$N_p = \frac{(D_A - kD_L) \times A}{\delta \times D \times B \times br}$$

where br is a measure of the volatility of interest rates (R_b) on the bond underlying the options contract relative to the interest rate that impacts the bond on the FI's balance sheet (R). That is,

$$br = \frac{\dfrac{\Delta R_b}{1 + R_b}}{\dfrac{\Delta R}{1 + R}}$$

EXAMPLE 24–2

Put Option Macrohedge with Basis Risk

Refer to Example 24–1. Suppose that basis risk, br, is 0.92 (i.e., the rate on the option's underlying bond changes by 92 percent of the spot rate change on the balance sheet being hedged). In Example 24–1, with no basis risk, the number of options needed to hedge interest rate risk on the bond position is 537.672 put option contracts. Introducing basis risk, $br = 0.92$:

$$N_p = \frac{\$230,000,000}{.5 \times 8.82 \text{ years} \times \$97,000 \times 0.92} = 584.4262 \text{ put option contracts}$$

Additional put option contracts are needed to hedge interest rate risk because interest rates on the bond underlying the option contract do not move as much as interest rates on the bond held as an asset on the balance sheet.

Concept Questions

1. If interest rates fall, are you better off purchasing call or put options on bonds, and why?
2. In the example above, what number of put options should you purchase if $\delta = .25$ and $D = 6$? ($N_p = 1,718.213$)

USING OPTIONS TO HEDGE FOREIGN EXCHANGE RISK

Just as an FI can hedge a long position in bonds against interest rate risk through bond options or futures options on bonds, a similar opportunity is available to microhedge long or short positions in a foreign currency asset against foreign exchange rate risk. To see this, suppose that a U.S. based FI bought, or is long in, a Canadian dollar (C$) asset in March 2004. This C$ asset is a one-month T-bill paying C$100 million in April 2004. Since the FI's liabilities are in U.S. dollars, it may wish to hedge the FX risk that the Canadian dollar will depreciate over the forthcoming month. Suppose that if the C$ were to fall from the current exchange rate of US$0.7531/C$1, the FI would make a loss on its Canadian T-bill investment when measured in U.S. dollar terms. For example, if the C$ depreciated from US$0.7531/C$ in March 2004 to US$0.7350/C$1 in April 2004, the C$100 million asset would be worth only US$73.50 million on maturity instead of the expected US$75.31 million

FIGURE 24–15

Hedging FX Risk by Buying a Put Option on Canadian Dollars

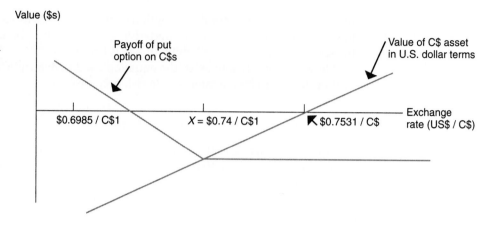

when it was purchased in March. If the foreign exchange rate depreciation is sufficiently severe, the FI might be unable to meet its dollar liability commitments used to fund the T-bill purchase. To offset this exposure, the FI may buy one-month put options on Canadian dollars at an exercise price of US$0.740/C1$. Thus, if the exchange rate does fall to US$0.7350/C$1 at the end of the month, the FI manager can put the C$100 million proceeds from the T-bill on maturity to the writer of the option. Then the FI receives US$74 million instead of the US$73.50 million if the Canadian dollars were sold at the open market spot exchange rate at the end of the month. If the C$ actually appreciates in value, or does not depreciate below US$0.74/C$1, the option expires unexercised and the proceeds of the C$100 million asset will be realized by the FI manager by a sale of Canadian dollars for U.S. dollars in the spot foreign exchange market one month into the future (see Figure 24–15).

As with bonds, the FI can buy put options on foreign currency futures contracts to hedge this currency risk. The futures option contracts for foreign currencies traded on the Chicago Mercantile Exchange (CME) are shown in Figure 24–12. A put position in one foreign currency futures contract with expiration in April 2004 and exercise price of US$0.74/C$1 would have cost the FI a premium of US$.0030 per C$1 on March 18, 2004. Since each Canadian dollar futures option contract is C$100,000 in size, the cost would have been US$300 per contract. If we ignore the question of basis risk—that is, the imperfect correlation between the U.S.$/C$ exchange rate on the spot and futures in options markets—the optimal number of futures options purchased would be

www.cme.com

$$\frac{C\$100,000,000}{C\$100,000} = 1,000 \text{ contracts}$$

with a total premium cost of US$300,000.

Concept Questions

1. What is the difference between options on foreign currency and options on foreign currency futures?
2. If an FI has to hedge a US$5,000,000 liability exposure in Swiss francs (SF), what options should it purchase to hedge this position? Using Figure 24–12, how many contracts of Swiss franc futures options should it purchase (assuming no basis risk) if it wants to hedge against the SF falling in value against the dollar given a current exchange rate of US$0.7957/SF1 (or 1.2568 SF/US$1). (Buy 50.272 call options on SF futures)

FIGURE 24–16
Buying Credit Spread Call Options to Hedge Credit Risk

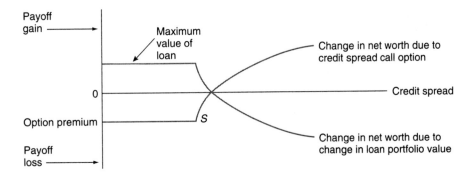

HEDGING CREDIT RISK WITH OPTIONS

Options also have a potential use in hedging the credit risk of an FI. Relative to their use in hedging interest rate risk, option use to hedge credit risk is a relatively new phenomenon. Although FIs are always likely to be willing to bear some credit risk as part of the intermediation process (i.e., exploit their comparative advantage to bear such risk), options may allow them to modify that level of exposure selectively. In Chapter 23 we stated that an FI could seek an appropriate credit risk hedge by selling credit forward contracts. Rather than using credit forwards to hedge, an FI has at least two alternative credit option derivatives with which it can hedge its on-balance-sheet credit risk.

credit spread call option
A call option whose payoff increases as a yield spread increases above some stated exercise spread.

A **credit spread call option** is a call option whose payoff increases as the (default) risk premium or yield spread on a specified benchmark bond of the borrower increases above some exercise spread, S. An FI concerned that the risk on a loan to that borrower will increase can purchase a credit spread call option to hedge the increased credit risk.

Figure 24–16 illustrates the change in the FI's capital value and its payoffs from the credit spread call option as a function of the credit spread. As the credit spread increases on an FI's loan to a borrower, the value of the loan, and consequently the FI's net worth, decreases. However, if the credit risk characteristics of the benchmark bond (i.e., change in credit spread) are the same as those on the FI's loan, the loss of net worth on the balance sheet is offset with a gain from the credit spread call option. If the required credit spread on the FI's loan decreases (perhaps because the credit quality of the borrower improves over the loan period), the value of the FI's loan and net worth increases (up to some maximum value), but the credit spread call option will expire out of the money. As a result, the FI will suffer a maximum loss equal to the required (call) premium on the credit option, which will be offset by the market value gain of the loan in the portfolio (which is reflected in a positive increase in the FI's net worth).[14]

digital default option
An option that pays the par value of a loan in the event of default.

A **digital default option** is an option that pays a stated amount in the event of a loan default (the extreme case of increased credit risk). As shown in Figure 24–17, the FI can purchase a default option covering the par value of a loan (or loans) in its portfolio. In the event of a loan default, the option writer pays the FI the par value of the defaulted loans. If the loans are paid off in accordance with the loan

---

[14] For additional discussion, see J. D. Finnerty, "Credit Derivatives, Infrastructure Finance, and Emerging Market Risk," *The Financier, ACMT,* February 1996, pp. 64–75.

FIGURE 24–17
Buying a Digital Default Option to Hedge Credit Risk

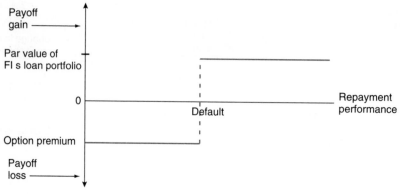

FIGURE 24–18
Catastrophe Call Spread Options

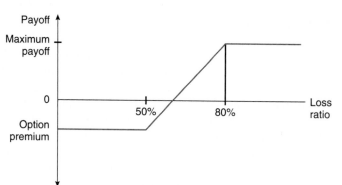

agreement, however, the default option expires unexercised. As a result, the FI will suffer a maximum loss on the option equal to the premium (cost) of buying the default option from the writer (seller).

HEDGING CATASTROPHE RISK WITH CALL SPREAD OPTIONS

catastrophe (CAT) call spread
A call option on the loss ratio incurred in writing catastrophe insurance with a capped (or maximum) payout.

www.cbot.com

In 1993 the Chicago Board of Trade (CBOT) introduced **catastrophe (CAT) call spread** options to hedge the risk of unexpectedly high losses being incurred by property-casualty insurers as a result of catastrophes such as hurricanes. The basic idea can be seen in Figure 24–18. For an option premium, the insurer can hedge a range of loss ratios that may occur (remember that the loss ratio is the ratio of losses incurred divided by premiums written). In Figure 24–18, the insurer buys a call spread to hedge the risk that the loss ratio on its catastrophe insurance may be anywhere between 50 percent and 80 percent. If the loss ratio ends up below 50 percent (perhaps because of a mild hurricane season), the insurance company loses the option premium. For loss ratios between 50 percent and 80 percent, it receives an increasingly positive payoff. For loss ratios above 80 percent, the amount paid by the writers of the option to the buyer (the insurer) is capped at the 80 percent level. Cummins, Lalonde, and Phillips examined catastrophe loss index options in hedging hurricane losses in Florida. Using data from 255 of 264 property insurers operating in Florida in 1998, they found that these options can be used effectively by insurers to hedge catastrophe risk.[15]

---

[15] For more information, see J. D. Cummins and H. Geman, "Pricing Catastrophe Insurance Futures and Call Spreads: An Arbitrage Approach," ibid.; and J. D. Cummins, D. Lalonde, and R. D. Phillips, "The Basis Risk of Catastrophe-Loss Index Securities," *Journal of Financial Economics*, January 2004, pp. 77–111.

Concept Questions	1. What is the difference between a credit spread call option and a digital default option?
	2. What is the difference between the payoff on the catastrophe call spread option in Figure 24–18 and the payoff of a standard call option on a stock?

CAPS, FLOORS, AND COLLARS

cap
A call option on interest rates, often with multiple exercise dates.

floor
A put option on interest rates, often with multiple exercise dates.

collar
A position taken simultaneously in a cap and a floor.

Caps, floors, and collars are derivative securities that have many uses, especially in helping an FI hedge interest rate risk exposure as well as risk unique to its individual customers. Buying a **cap** means buying a call option or a succession of call options on interest rates. Specifically, if interest rates rise above the cap rate, the seller of the cap—usually a bank—compensates the buyer—for example, another FI—in return for an up-front premium. As a result, buying an interest rate cap is like buying insurance against an (excessive) increase in interest rates. A cap agreement can have one or many exercise dates.

Buying a **floor** means buying a put option on interest rates. If interest rates fall below the floor rate, the seller of the floor compensates the buyer in return for an up-front premium. As with caps, floor agreements can have one or many exercise dates.

A **collar** occurs when an FI takes a simultaneous position in a cap and a floor, such as buying a cap and selling a floor. The idea here is that the FI wants to hedge itself against rising rates but wants to finance the cost of the cap. One way to do this is to sell a floor and use the premiums on the floor to pay the premium on the purchase of the cap. Thus, these three over-the-counter instruments are special cases of options; FI managers use them like bond options and bond futures options to hedge the interest rate risk of an FI's portfolios.

In general, FIs purchase interest rate caps if they are exposed to losses when interest rates rise. Usually, this happens if they are funding assets with floating-rate liabilities such as notes indexed to LIBOR (or some other cost of funds) and they have fixed-rate assets or they are net long in bonds, or—in a macrohedging context—their duration gap is $D_A - kD_L > 0$. By contrast, FIs purchase floors when they have fixed costs of debt and have variable rates (returns) on assets, are net short in bonds, or $D_A - kD_L < 0$. Finally, FIs purchase collars when they are concerned about excessive volatility of interest rates and to finance cap or floor positions.

Example: Buying An Interest Rate Cap

For simplicity, assume that an FI buys a 9 percent cap at time 0 from another FI with a notional face value of $100 million. In return for paying an up-front premium, the seller of the cap stands ready to compensate the buying FI whenever the interest rate index defined under the agreement is above the 9 percent cap rate on the dates specified under the cap agreement. This effectively converts the cost of the FI's floating-rate liabilities into fixed-rate liabilities. In this example, we assume that the purchasing FI buys a cap at time 0 with cap exercise dates at the end of the first year and the end of the second year. That is, the cap has a three-year maturity from initiation until the final exercise dates, with exercise dates at the end of year 1 and year 2.[16]

---

[16] There is no point exercising the option at the end of year 0 (i.e., having three exercise dates) since interest rates for year 0 are set at the beginning of that year and are contractually set throughout. As a result, the FI does not bear interest rate uncertainty until the end of year 0 (i.e., interest uncertainty exists only in years 1 and 2).

FIGURE 24–19
Hypothetical Path
of Interest Rates

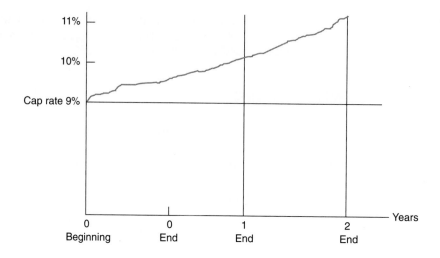

TABLE 24–1
Payments under
the Cap

End of Year	Cap Rate	Actual Interest Rate	Interest Differential	Payment by Seller to Buyer
1	9%	10%	1%	$1 million
2	9	11	2	$2 million
Total				$3 million

Thus, the buyer of the cap would demand two cash payments from the seller of the cap if rates lie above 9 percent at the end of the first year and at the end of the second year on the cap exercise dates. In practice, cap exercise dates usually closely correspond to payment dates on liabilities, for example, coupon dates on floating-rate notes. Consider one possible scenario in Figure 24–19.

In Figure 24–19, the seller of the cap has to pay the buyer of the cap the amount shown in Table 24–1. In this scenario, the cap-buying FI would receive $3 million (undiscounted) over the life of the cap to offset any rise in the cost of liability funding or market value losses on its bond/asset portfolio. However, the interest rates in Figure 24–19 are only one possible scenario. Consider the possible path to interest rates in Figure 24–20. In this interest scenario, rates fall below 9 percent at the end of the first year to 8 percent and at the end of the second year to 7 percent on the cap exercise dates. Thus, the cap seller makes no payments. This example makes it clear that buying a cap is similar to buying a call option on interest rates in that when the option expires out of the money, because the interest rate is below the cap level, the cap seller makes no payments to the buyer. Conceptually, buying this cap is like buying a complex call option on an interest rate or a put option on a bond price with a single exercise price or interest rate and two exercise dates: the end of year 1 and the end of year 2.

The problem for the FI manager is to calculate the fair value of this 9 percent cap in the face of interest rate uncertainty. In particular, the FI manager does not know whether interest rates will be 10 percent at the end of year 1 or 8 percent. Similarly, the manager does not know whether interest rates will be 11 percent or 7 percent at the end of year 2. Nevertheless, to buy interest rate risk insurance in the form of a cap, the manager has to pay an up-front fee or premium to the seller

FIGURE 24–20
Hypothetical Path
of Interest Rates

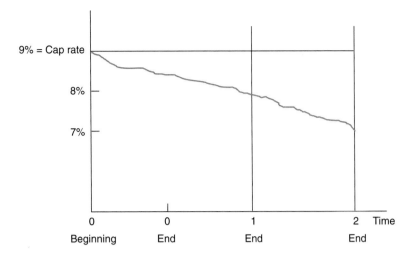

FIGURE 24–21
Interest Rate Cap
with a 9 Percent
Cap Rate

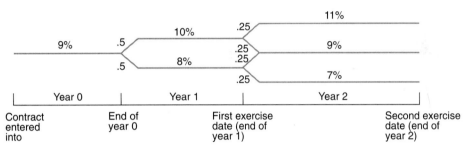

of the cap. Next, we solve for the fair value of the cap premium in the framework of the binomial model introduced earlier to calculate the premium on a bond option.[17]

Consider Figure 24–21, the binomial tree for the cap contract entered into at the beginning of year 0. The cap can be exercised at the end of the first year and the end of the second year.[18] The current (time 0) value of the cap or the fair cap premium is the sum of the present value of the cap option exercised at the end of year 1 plus the present value of the cap option exercised at the end of year 2:

$$\text{Fair premium} = P = PV \text{ of year 1 option} + PV \text{ of year 2 option}$$

EXAMPLE 24–3

Calculating the
Premium on
an Interest
Rate Cap

PV of Year 2 Option
At the end of year 2, there are three possible interest rate scenarios: 11 percent, 9 percent, and 7 percent. With a cap exercise price of 9 percent and the 9 percent or 7 percent scenarios realized, the cap would have no value to the buyer. In other words, it would expire out of the money. The only interest rate scenario where the cap has exercise value to the buyer at the end of the second year is if rates rise to 11 percent. With rates at 11 percent, the interest differential would be 11 percent minus 9 percent, or 2 percent. But since there is only a 25 percent probability that interest rates will rise to 11 percent at the end of the second year, the expected value of this interest differential is

$$.25 \times 2\% = 0.5\%$$

(continued)

---

[17] For more details and examples, see R. C. Stapleton and M. Subrahmanyam, "Interest Rate Caps and Floors," in *Financial Options: From Theory to Practice,* ed. S. Figlewski (Homewood, IL: Business One-Irwin, 1990), pp. 220–80.

[18] Interest rates are normally set at the *beginning* of each period and paid at the *end* of each period.

With a $100 million cap, therefore, the expected cash payment at the end of year 2 would be $0.5 million. However, to calculate the fair value of the cap premium in current dollars, the expected cash flow at the end of year 2 has to be discounted back to the present (time 0):

$$PV_2 = \frac{0.5}{(1.09)(1.1)(1.11)} = .3757$$

where 9 percent, 10 percent, and 11 percent are the appropriate one-year discount rates for payments in years 0, 1, and 2. Thus, the fair present value of the option at the end of year 2 is .3757, or $375,700, given the $100 million face value of the cap.

PV of Year 1 Option

At the end of year 1, there are two interest rate scenarios: Interest rates could rise to 10 percent or fall to 8 percent. If rates fall to 8 percent, the 9 percent cap has no value to the buyer. However, if rates rise to 10 percent, this results in a positive interest differential of 1 percent at the end of year 1. However, the expected interest differential is only .5 of 1 percent since this is the probability that rates will rise from 9 percent to 10 percent between the beginning of year 0 and end of year 1:

$$.5 \times 1\% = 0.5\%$$

In dollar terms, with a $100 million cap, the expected value of the cap at the end of year 1 is $0.5 million. To evaluate the time 0 or present value of a cap exercised at the end of time period 1, this expected cash flow has to be discounted back to the beginning of time 0 using the appropriate one-year discount rates. That is:

$$PV_1 = \frac{0.5}{(1.09)(1.1)} = .417$$

or $417,000, given the $100 million face value of the cap. As a result, the fair value of the premium the FI should be willing to pay for this cap is:

$$\text{Cap premium} = PV_1 + PV_2$$

$$= \$417,000 + \$375,700$$

$$= \$792,700$$

That is, under the interest rate scenarios implied by this simple binomial model, the FI should pay no more than $792,700, or 0.7927 percent of notional face value, in buying the cap from the seller.

Floors

A floor is a put option or a collection of put options on interest rates. Here the FI manager who buys a floor is concerned about falling interest rates. Perhaps the FI is funding liabilities at fixed rates and has floating-rate assets, or maybe it is short in some bond position and will lose if it has to cover the position with higher-priced bonds after interest rates fall. In a macrohedging sense, the FI could face a duration gap where the duration of assets is less than the leverage-adjusted duration of liabilities $(D_A - kD_L < 0)$. For an example of the payoff from buying a floor, see Figure 24–22.

In this simple example, the floor is set at 4 percent and the buyer pays an up-front premium to the seller of the floor. Whereas caps can be viewed as buying a complex call option on interest rates, a floor can be viewed as buying a complex put option on interest rates. In our example, the floor has two exercise dates: the end of year 1 and the end of year 2.

FIGURE 24–22
Interest Rate Floor with a 4 Percent Floor

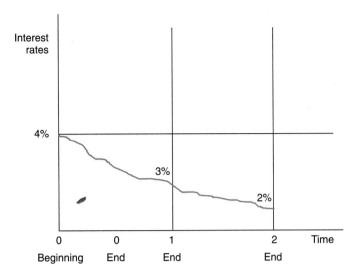

TABLE 24–2
Hypothetical Floor Payments

End of Year	Cap Rate	Actual Interest Rate	Interest Differential	Payment by Seller to Buyer
1	4%	3%	1%	$1 million
2	4	2	2	$2 million
Total				$3 million

If the interest scenario in Figure 24–22 is the actual interest rate path, the payments from the seller to the buyer would be as shown in Table 24–2. However, since the buyer of the cap is uncertain about the actual path of interest rates—rates could rise and not fall—such profits are only probabilistic. That is, the buyer would have to use a model similar to the binomial model for caps to calculate the fair up-front premium to be paid for the floor at time 0.

Collars

FI managers who are very risk averse and overly concerned about the exposure of their portfolios to increased interest rate volatility may seek to protect the FI against such increases. One method of hedging this risk is through buying a cap and a floor together. This is usually called a collar. Figure 24–23 illustrates the essential risk-protection features of a collar when an FI buys a 9 percent cap and a 4 percent floor.

The shaded areas in Figure 24–23 show the interest rate payment regions (>9 percent or < 4 percent) where the cap or floor is in the money and the buyer potentially receives either a cap or a floor payment from the seller. If interest rates stay in the 4 through 9 percent range, the buyer of the collar receives no compensation from the seller. In addition, the buyer has to pay two up-front premiums: one for the cap and one for the floor to the cap and floor sellers. As is clear, buying a collar is similar to simultaneously buying a complex put and call bond option, or straddle.

An alternative and more common use of a collar is to finance the cost of purchasing a cap. In our earlier example of the $100 million cap, the fair cap premium (*pc*) was

FIGURE 24–23
Payoffs from a Collar

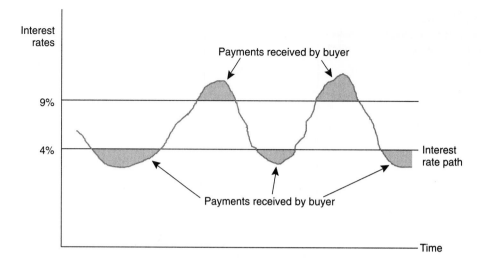

$792,700, or 0.7927 percent of the notional face value (NV_c) of the cap. That is, the cost (C) of the cap is

$$C = NV_c \times pc$$
$$= \$100 \text{ million} \times .007927$$
$$= \$792,700$$

To purchase the cap, the FI must pay this premium to the cap seller in up-front dollars.

Many large FIs, more exposed to rising interest rates than falling interest rates—perhaps because they are heavily reliant on interest-sensitive sources of liabilities—seek to finance a cap by selling a floor at the same time.[19] In so doing, they generate up-front revenues; this floor premium can finance the cost of the cap purchase or the cap premium. Nevertheless, they give up potential profits if rates fall rather than rise. Indeed, when rates fall, the floor is more likely to be triggered and the FI must compensate the buyer of the floor.

After an FI buys a cap and sells a floor, its net cost of the cap is[20]

$$C = (NV_c \times pc) - (NV_f \times pf)$$
$$C = \text{Cost of cap} - \text{Revenue on floor}$$

where

NV_f = Notional principal of the floor

pf = Premium rate on the floor

Example: Calculating the Cost of a Collar

Suppose that, in the example above, while buying the cap the FI sold a two-year $100 million notional face value floor at a premium of .75 percent. The net up-front cost of purchasing the cap is reduced to

$$C = (\$100 \text{ million} \times .007927) - (\$100 \text{ million} \times .0075) = \$42,700$$

---

[19] In this context, the sale of the floor is like the sale of any revenue-generating product.

[20] See K. C. Brown and D. J. Smith, "Recent Innovations in Interest Rate Risk Management and the Reintermediation of Commercial Banking," *Financial Management* 17 (1988), pp. 45–58.

FIGURE 24–24
In-the-Money Floor and Out-of-the-Money Cap

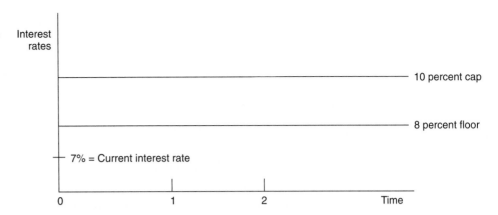

Note that if the FI is willing to raise the floor exercise interest rate, thereby exposing itself to increasing losses if rates fall, it can generate higher premiums on the floor it sells. Like any option, as the exercise price or rate moves from being out of the money, when current rates are above the floor, to being in the money, when current rates are below the floor, the floor buyer would be willing to pay a higher premium to the writer (the FI). Given this, the buyer of the cap could set the floor rate with notional face values of $100 million each so that the floor premium earned by the FI just equals the cap premium paid:

$$C = (\$100 \text{ million} \times .007927) - (\$100 \text{ million} \times .007927)$$

$$C = 0$$

When $pc = pf$, the cap buyer–floor seller can reduce the cap's net cost of purchase to zero.

Indeed, if the cap buyer bought a very out-of-the-money cap and sold a very in-the-money floor, as shown in Figure 24–24, the net cost of the cap purchase could actually be negative. In Figure 24–24, the current interest rate is 7 percent while the cap rate is 10 percent. Thus, rates would have to rise at least 3 percent for the cap buyer to receive a payment at the end of year 1. By contrast, the 8 percent floor is already 1 percent above the current 7 percent rate. If rates stay at 7 percent until the end of year 1, the FI seller of the floor is already exposed to a 1 percent notional face value loss in writing the floor.

If the out-of-the-money cap can be bought at a premium of .7927 percent, but the in-the-money floor is sold at a premium of .95 percent, the (net) cost of the cap purchase is

$$C = (NV_c \times pc) - (NV_f \times pf)$$

$$= \$792,700 - \$950,000$$

$$= -\$157,300$$

Raising the floor exercise rate and thus the floor premium also can be combined with mismatching the notional principal amounts of the cap and the floor to produce a zero net cost financing for the cap. That is, there is no reason why both the floor and cap agreements have to be written against the same notional face values ($NV_c = NV_f = \$100$ million).

Suppose the out-of-the-money cap can be bought at a premium of .7927 percent and the in-the-money floor can be sold at a .95 percent premium. An FI manager might want to know what notional principal on the floor (or contract size) is necessary to finance a $100 million cap purchase at zero net up-front cost. That is,

$$C = (NV_c \times pc) - (NV_f \times pf) = 0$$
$$= (\$100 \text{ million} \times .007927) - (NV_f \times .0095) = 0$$

Solving for NV_f:

$$NV_f = \frac{(\$100 \text{ million} \times .007927)}{.0095} = \frac{(NV_c \times pc)}{pf}$$

$$= \$83.44 \text{ million}$$

Clearly, the higher premium rate on the floor requires a lower notional face value floor amount to generate sufficient premium income up front to finance the cap's purchase. In general, to fund fully the cap purchase ($C = 0$), the relationship between premium rates and notional value should be:[21]

$$\frac{NV_f}{NV_c} = \frac{pc}{pf}$$

Caps, Floors, Collars, and Credit Risk

One important feature of buying caps, collars, and floors for hedging purposes is the implied credit risk exposure involved that is absent for exchange-traded futures and options. Since these are multiple exercise over-the-counter contracts, the buyer of these instruments faces a degree of counterparty credit risk. To see this, consider the cap example just discussed. Suppose the writer of the cap defaulted on the $1 million due at the end of the first year if interest rates rose to 10 percent. The buyer not only would fail to collect on this in-the-money option but also would lose a potential payment at the end of year 2. In general, a default in year 1 would mean that the cap buyer would have to find a replacement contract for year 2 (and any succeeding years thereafter) at the cap rate terms or premiums prevailing at the end of year 1 rather than at the beginning of year 0. These cap rates may be far less favorable than those under the original cap contract (reflecting the higher interest rate levels of time 1). In addition, the buyer could incur further transaction and contracting costs in replacing the original contract. Because of the often long-term nature of cap agreements, occasionally extending up to 10 years, only FIs that are the most creditworthy are likely to be able to write and run a large cap/floor book without the backing of external guarantees such as standby letters of credit. As we discuss in the next chapter, swaps have similar credit risk exposures due to their long-run contractual nature and their OTC origination.

---

[21] As shown earlier in this chapter, it is possible to macrohedge a gap position of an FI using put options. A cap is economically equivalent to a call option on an interest rate or a put option on a bond. However, the major difference is that the cap is a complex option in that there are multiple exercise dates. For example, in our simple model of the determination of the fair cap premium, there were two exercise dates: the end of year 1 and the end of year 2. However, we showed that we could decompose the value of the cap as a whole into the value of the (end of) year 1 option and the value of the (end of) year 2 option. Both of these options would have their own deltas (δ) because of the different maturity of these options. Thus, the change in the total value of the cap (ΔC) position would equal

$$\Delta C = N_c \times \{[\delta_1 \times (D_1 \times B)] + [\delta_2 \times (D_2 \times B)]\} \times \Delta R/(1 + R)$$

where N_c—the number of $100,000 cap contracts—is calculated by solving

$$N_c = \frac{[D_A - kD_L] \times S}{\{[\delta_1 \times (D_1 \times B)] + [\delta_2 \times (D_2 \times B)]\}}$$

Concept Questions

1. In Example 24–3 suppose that in year 2 the highest and lowest rates were 12 percent and 6 percent instead of 11 percent and 7 percent. Calculate the fair premium on the cap. ($980,500)

2. Assume two exercise dates at the end of year 1 and the end of year 2. Suppose the FI buys a floor of 4 percent at time 0. The binomial tree suggests that rates at the end of year 1 could be 3 percent ($p = .5$) or 5 percent ($p = .5$) and at the end of year 2 rates could be 2 percent ($p = .25$), 4 percent ($p = .5$), or 6 percent ($p = .25$). Calculate the fair value of the floor premium. Assume the one-year discount rates for payments in years 0, 1, and 2 are 9 percent, 10 percent, and 11 percent, respectively. ($792,700)

3. An FI buys a $100 million cap at a premium of .75 percent and sells a floor at a .85 percent premium. What size floor should be sold so that the net cost of the cap purchase is zero? ($88,235,394)

4. Why are only the most creditworthy FIs able to write a large cap/floor book without external guarantees?

Industry Perspectives

As noted in Chapter 22, the level of involvement in derivatives products varies from one FI to the next. The large Canadian FIs provide risk management services to their clients, including commodity, credit, equity, foreign exchange, and interest rate derivatives. Bank of Montreal (BMO) is one Canadian FI that actively creates and markets derivatives products to its customers, focusing on trading rather than on actively hedging its own exposure. BMO used their expertise in derivatives trading to expand internationally, becoming the first Canadian bank to be authorized to sell derivative products in China in 2004.

BMO & Derivatives 2004

We structure and market derivative products to customers to enable them to transfer, modify or reduce current or expected risks. We may also take proprietary trading positions in various capital markets instruments and derivatives that, taken together, are designed to profit from anticipated changes in market factors. We also use derivatives as hedges of our own positions.

In most cases, we act as an intermediary. As a result, for each derivative liability we usually have an offsetting derivative asset. Therefore, at any point in time our net derivative assets, together with associated capital markets instruments, are not significant.

Trading derivatives are fully recognized on our Consolidated Balance sheet at their fair values. These trading derivatives represent over 95% of our total outstanding derivatives.

Only our hedging derivatives represent off-balance sheet items, since these derivatives are not recorded at fair value on our Consolidated Balance Sheet. We follow accrual accounting for these derivatives, since they are expected to be highly effective in hedging certain risks associated with on-balance sheet financial instruments or future cash flows. Any ineffectiveness in a hedging derivative is recognized in income over the term of the derivative contract.

Fair values of our derivative financial instruments are as follows:

(continued)

(Canadian $ in millions)			2004
	Gross Assets	Gross liabilities	Net
Trading			
Interest Rate Contracts			
Swaps	$10,655	$(10,485)	$170
Forward rate agreements	105	(109)	(4)
Futures	4	(10)	(6)
Purchased options	1,548	(2)	(1,546)
Written options		(1,295)	(1,295)
Foreign Exchange Options			
Cross-currency swaps	940	(622)	318
Cross-currency interest rate swaps	3,341	(2,677)	664
Forward current exchange contracts	2,028	(3,023)	(995)
Purchased options	157	–	157
Written options	–	(156)	(156)
Community Contracts			
Swaps	3,514	(2,979)	535
Purchases options	2,156	–	2,156
Written options	–	(1,994)	(1,994)
Equity contracts	391	(300)	91
Credit contracts	75	(89)	(14)
Total fair value/book value—trading derivatives	$24,914	($23,741	$1,173
Average fair value(1)	$21,556	$(20,637)	$919
Hedging			
Interest rate contracts			
Swaps	$437	$(284)	$153
Forward rate agreements	1	(1)	–
Purchased options	20	–	20
Foreign Exchange Contracts			
Cross-currency interest rate swaps	394	(118)	276
Forward foreign exchange contracts	15	(59)	(44)
Equity Contracts	–	–	–
Total fair value – hedging derivatives (2)	$867	$462	$405
Total book value – hedging derivatives	$534	$(232)	$302
Average fair value (1)	$850	$(558)	$292

Source: BMO Financial Group Annual Report 2004, pp. 53 and 99.

(1) Average fair value amounts are calculated using a five-quarter rolling average.

(2) The fair values of hedging derivatives wholly or partially offset the changes in fair values of the related on-balance sheet financial instruments.

   Assets are shown net of liabilities to customers where we have an enforceable right to offset amounts and we intend to settle contracts on a net basis.

Summary

In this chapter we evaluated a wide range of option-type contracts that are available to FI managers to hedge the risk exposures of individual assets, portfolios of assets, and the balance sheet gap itself. We illustrated how these options—some of which are exchange traded and some of which are sold OTC—can hedge the interest rate, credit, FX, and catastrophe risks of FIs. In particular, we described how the unique nature of the asymmetric payoff function of option-type contracts often makes them more attractive to FIs than other hedging instruments, such as forwards and futures.

However, the hedging of on balance sheet exposures is a small portion of the risk management activities of FIs. As their expertise has increased in the area of derivatives, FIs have expanded their risk transference expertise to trading, creating complex contracts that enhance the traditional asset transformation function of FIs to accomplish global risk transference. The focus of regulators such as the Office of the Superintendent of Financial Institutions on the risk management activities of FIs has also expanded to ensure the safety and soundness of the financial system and to capture the increased focus of FIs on trading activities rather than hedging activities.

Questions and Problems

1. How does using options differ from using forward or futures contracts?

2. What is a call option?

3. What must happen to interest rates for the purchaser of a call option on a bond to make money? How does the writer of the call option make money?

4. What is a put option?

5. What must happen to interest rates for the purchaser of a put option on a bond to make money? How does the writer of the put option make money?

6. Consider the following:

   a. What are the two ways to use call and put options on government bonds to generate positive cash flows when interest rates decline? Verify your answer with a diagram.

   b. Under what balance sheet conditions can an FI use options on government bonds to hedge its assets and/or liabilities against interest rate declines?

   c. Is it more appropriate for FIs to hedge against a decline in interest rates with long calls or short puts?

7. In each of the following cases, identify what risk the manager of an FI faces and whether that risk should be hedged by buying a put or a call option.

   a. A commercial bank plans to issue CDs in three months.

   b. An insurance company plans to buy bonds in two months.

   c. A credit union plans to sell Government of Canada securities next month.

   d. A U.S. bank lends to a French company with a loan payable in euros.

   e. A mutual fund plans to sell its holding of stock in a British company.

   f. A finance company has assets with a duration of six years and liabilities with a duration of 13 years.

8. Consider an FI that wishes to use bond options to hedge the interest rate risk in the bond portfolio.

   a. How does writing call options hedge the risk when interest rates decrease?

   b. Will writing call options fully hedge the risk when interest rates increase? Explain.

   c. How does buying a put option reduce the losses on the bond portfolio when interest rates rise?

   d. Diagram the purchase of a bond call option against the combination of a bond investment and the purchase of a bond put option.

9. What are the regulatory reasons why FIs seldom write options?

10. What are the problems of using the Black-Scholes option pricing model to value bond options? What is meant by the term *pull-to-par*?

11. An FI has purchased a two-year, $1,000 par value zero-coupon bond for $867.43. The FI will hold the bond to maturity unless it needs to sell the bond at the end of one year for liquidity purposes. The current one-year interest rate is 7 percent, and the one-year rate in one year is forecast to be either 8.04 percent or 7.44 percent with equal likelihood. The FI wishes to buy a put option to protect itself against a capital loss if the bond needs to be sold in one year.

    a. What was the yield on the bond at the time of purchase?

    b. What is the market-determined, implied one-year rate one year before maturity?

c. What is the expected sale price if the bond has to be sold at the end of one year?

d. Diagram the bond prices over the two-year horizon.

e. If the FI buys a put option with an exercise price equal to your answer in part (c), what will be its value at the end of one year?

f. What should be the premium on the put option today?

g. Diagram the values of the put option on the two-year, zero-coupon bond.

h. What would have been the premium on the option if the one-year interest rates at the end of one year were expected to be 8.14 percent and 7.34 percent?

12. A pension fund manager anticipates the purchase of a 20-year, 8 percent coupon U.S. Treasury bond at the end of two years. Interest rates are assumed to change only once every year at year-end, with an equal probability of a 1 percent increase or a 1 percent decrease. The Treasury bond, when purchased in two years, will pay interest semiannually. Currently the Treasury bond is selling at par.

a. What is the pension fund manager's interest rate risk exposure?

b. How can the pension fund manager use options to hedge that interest rate risk exposure?

c. What prices are possible on the 20-year T-bonds at the end of year 1 and year 2?

d. Diagram the prices over the two-year period.

e. If options on US$100,000, 20-year, 8 percent coupon Treasury bonds (both puts and calls) have a strike price of 101, what are the possible (intrinsic) values of the option position at the end of year 1 and year 2?

f. Diagram the possible option values.

g. What is the option premium? (Use an 8 percent discount factor.)

13. Why are options on interest rate futures contracts preferred to options on cash instruments in hedging interest rate risk?

14. Consider Figure 24–12. What are the prices paid for the following futures option?

a. June T-bond calls at 116.

b. June five-year T-note puts at 116.

c. June Eurodollar calls at 9900 (99.00).

15. Consider Figure 24–12 again. What happens to the price of the following?

a. A call when the exercise price increases.

b. A call when the time until expiration increases.

c. A put when the exercise price increases.

d. A put when the time to expiration increases.

16. An FI manager writes a call option on a T-bond futures contract with an exercise price of 114 at a quoted price of 0–55.

a. What type of opportunities or obligations does the manager have?

b. In what direction must interest rates move to encourage the call buyer to exercise the option?

17. What is the delta of an option (δ)?

18. An FI has a US$100 million portfolio of six-year Eurodollar bonds that have an 8 percent coupon. The bonds are trading at par and have a duration of five years. The FI wishes to hedge the portfolio with T-bond options that have a delta of -0.625. The underlying long-term Treasury bonds for the option have a duration of 10.1 years and trade at a market value of US$96,157 per US$100,000 of par value. Each put option has a premium of US$3.25.

a. How many bond put options are necessary to hedge the bond portfolio?

b. If interest rates increase 100 basis points, what is the expected gain or loss on the put option hedge?

c. What is the expected change in market value on the bond portfolio?

d. What is the total cost of placing the hedge?

e. Diagram the payoff possibilities.

f. How far must interest rates move before the payoff on the hedge will exactly offset the cost of placing the hedge?

g. How far must interest rates move before the gain on the bond portfolio will exactly offset the cost of placing the hedge?

h. Summarize the gain, loss, and cost conditions of the hedge on the bond portfolio in terms of changes in interest rates.

19. Corporate Bank has US$840 million of assets with a duration of 12 years and liabilities worth US$720 million with a duration of 7 years. The bank is concerned about preserving the value of its equity in the event of an increase in interest rates and is contemplating a macrohedge with interest rate options. The call and put options have a delta (δ) value of 0.4 and -0.4, respectively. The price of an underlying T-bond is 104–34, and its modified duration is 7.6 years.

a. What type of option should Corporate Bank use for the macrohedge?

b. How many options should be purchased?

c. What is the effect on the economic value of the equity if interest rates rise 50 basis points?

d. What will be the effect on the hedge if interest rates rise 50 basis points?

e. What will be the cost of the hedge if each option has a premium of US$0.875?

f. Diagram the economic conditions of the hedge.

g. How much must interest rates move against the hedge for the increased value of the bank to offset the cost of the hedge?

h. How much must interest rates move in favour of the hedge, or against the balance sheet, before the payoff from the hedge will exactly cover the cost of the hedge?

i. Formulate a management decision rule regarding the implementation of the hedge.

20. An FI has a US$200 million asset portfolio that has an average duration of 6.5 years. The average duration of its US$160 million in liabilities is 4.5 years. The FI uses put options on T-bonds to hedge against unexpected interest rate increases. The average delta (δ) value of the put options has been estimated at -0.3, and the average duration of the T-bonds is 7 years. The current market value of the T-bonds is US$96,000.

a. What is the modified duration of the T-bonds if the current level of interest rates is 10 percent?

b. How many put option contracts should it purchase to hedge its exposure against rising interest rates? The face value of the T-bonds is US$100,000.

c. If interest rates increase 50 basis points, what will be the change in value of the equity of the FI?

d. What will be the change in value of the T-bond option hedge position?

e. If put options on T-bonds are selling at a premium of US$1.25 per face value of US$100, what is the total cost of hedging using options on T-bonds?

f. Diagram the spot market conditions of the equity and the option hedge.

g. What must be the change in interest rates before the change in value of the balance sheet (equity) will offset the cost of placing the hedge?

h. How much must interest rates change before the payoff of the hedge will exactly cover the cost of placing the hedge?

i. Given your answer in part (g), what will be the net gain or loss to the FI?

21. A mutual fund plans to purchase US$10,000,000 of 20-year T-bonds in two months. These bonds have a duration of 11 years. The mutual fund is concerned about interest rates changing over the next four months and is considering a hedge with a two-month option on a T-bond futures contract. Two-month calls with a strike price of 105 are priced at 1–25, and puts of the same maturity and exercise price are quoted at 2–09. The delta of the call is .5 and the delta of the put is $-.7$. The current price of a deliverable T-bond is US$103–08 per US$100 of face value, and its modified duration is nine years.

a. What type of option should the mutual fund purchase?

b. How many options should it purchase?

c. What is the cost of those options?

d. If rates change $+/-$ 50 basis points, what will be the effect on the price of the desired T-bonds?

e. What will be the effect on the value of the hedge if rates change $+/-$ 50 basis points?

f. Diagram the effects of the hedge and the spot market value of the desired T-bonds.

g. What must be the change in interest rates to cause the change in value of the hedge to exactly offset the change in value of the T-bonds?

22. An FI must make a single payment of 500,000 Swiss francs in six months at the maturity of a CD. The FI's in-house analyst expects the spot price of the franc to remain stable at the current $0.80/Sf. But as a precaution, the analyst is concerned that it could rise as high as $0.85/Sf or fall as low as $0.75/Sf. Because of this uncertainty, the analyst recommends that the FI hedge the CD payment using either options or futures. Six-month call and put options on the Swiss franc with an exercise price of $0.80/Sf are trading at 4 cents and 2 cents, respectively. A six-month futures contract on the Swiss franc is trading at $0.80/Sf.

a. Should the analysts be worried about the dollar depreciating or appreciating?

b. If the FI decides to hedge using options, should the FI buy put or call options to hedge the CD payment? Why?

c. If futures are used to hedge, should the FI buy or sell Swiss franc futures to hedge the payment? Why?

d. What will be the net payment on the CD if the selected call or put options are used to hedge the payment? Assume the following three scenarios: the spot price in six months will be $0.75, $0.80, or $0.85/Sf. Also assume that the options will be exercised.

www.mcgrawhill.ca/college/saunders

e. What will be the net payment if futures had been used to hedge the CD payment? Use the same three scenarios as in part (a).

f. Which method of hedging is preferable after the fact?

23. An American insurance company issued $10 million of one-year, zero-coupon GICs (guaranteed investment contracts) denominated in Swiss francs at a rate of 5 percent. The insurance company holds no Sf-denominated assets and has neither bought nor sold francs in the foreign exchange market.

   a. What is the insurance company's net exposure in Swiss francs?

   b. What is the insurance company's risk exposure to foreign exchange rate fluctuations?

   c. How can the insurance company use futures to hedge the risk exposure in part (b)? How can it use options to hedge?

   d. If the strike price is US$0.6667/Sf and the spot price is US$0.6452/Sf, what is the intrinsic value (on expiration) of a call option on Swiss francs? What is the intrinsic value (on expiration) of a Swiss franc put option? (*Note:* Swiss franc futures options traded on the Chicago Mercantile Exchange are set at Sf125,000 per contract.)

   e. If the June delivery call option premium is US0.32 cent per franc and the June delivery put option is US10.7 cents per franc, what is the dollar premium cost per contract? Assume that today's date is April 15.

   f. Why is the call option premium lower than the put option premium?

24. An FI has made a loan commitment of Sf10 million that is likely to be taken down in six months. The current spot rate is $0.60/Sf.

   a. Is the FI exposed to the dollar depreciating or the dollar appreciating? Why?

   b. If it decides to hedge using Sf futures, should it buy or sell Sf futures?

   c. If the spot rate six months from today is $0.64/Sf, what dollar amount is needed in six months if the loan is drawn?

   d. A six-month Sf futures contract is available for $0.61/Sf. What is the net amount needed at the end of six months if the FI has hedged using the Sf10 million of futures contracts? Assume that futures prices are equal to spot prices at the time of payment, that is, at maturity.

   e. If it decides to use options to hedge, should it purchase call or put options?

   f. Call and put options with an exercise price of $0.61/Sf are selling for $0.02 and $0.03, respectively. What would be the net amount needed by the FI at the end of six months if it had used options instead of futures to hedge this exposure?

25. What is a credit spread call option?

26. What is a digital default option?

27. How do the cash flows to the lender differ for a credit spread call option hedge from the cash flows for a digital default option?

28. What is a catastrophe call option? How do the cash flows of this option affect the buyer of the option?

29. What are caps? Under what circumstances would the buyer of a cap receive a payoff?

30. What are floors? Under what circumstances would the buyer of a floor receive a payoff?

31. What are collars? Under what circumstances would an FI use a collar?

32. How is buying a cap similar to buying a call option on interest rates?

33. Under what balance sheet circumstances would it be desirable to sell a floor to help finance a cap? When would it be desirable to sell a cap to help finance a floor?

34. Use the following information to price a three-year collar by purchasing an in-the-money cap and writing an out-of-the-money floor. Assume a binomial options pricing model with an equal probability of interest rates increasing 2 percent or decreasing 2 percent per annum. Current rates are 7 percent, the cap rate is 7 percent, and the floor rate is 4 percent. The notional value is $1 million. All interest payments are annual payments as a percent of notional value, and all payments are made at the end of year 1 and the end of year 2.

35. Use the following information to price a three-year collar by purchasing an out-of-the-money cap and writing an in-the-money floor. Assume a binomial options pricing model with an equal probability of interest rates increasing 2 percent or decreasing 2 percent per annum. Current rates are 4 percent, the cap rate is 7 percent, and the floor rate is 4 percent. The notional value is $1 million. All interest payments are annual payments as a percent of notional value, and all payments are made at the end of year 1 and the end of year 2.

36. Contrast the total cash flows associated with the collar position in question 34 against the collar in question 35. Do the goals of FIs that utilize the collar in question 34 differ from those that put on the collar in question 35? If so, how?

37. An FI has purchased a $200 million cap (i.e., call options on interest rates) of 9 percent at a premium of 0.65 percent of face value. A $200 million floor (i.e., put options on interest rates) of 4 percent is also available at a premium of 0.69 percent of face value.

   a. If interest rates rise to 10 percent, what is the amount received by the FI? What are the net savings after deducting the premium?

   b. If the FI also purchases a floor, what are the net savings if interest rates rise to 11 percent? What are the net savings if interest rates fall to 3 percent?

   c. If, instead, the FI sells (writes) the floor, what are the net savings if interest rates rise to 11 percent? What if they fall to 3 percent?

   d. What amount of floors should it sell to compensate for its purchase of caps, given the above premiums?

38. What credit risk exposure is involved in buying caps, floors, and collars for hedging purposes?

Web Questions

39. Go to the Chicago Board Options Exchange Web site at **www.cboe.com**. Find the most recent data on 10-Year Treasury Yield Options (TNX) by clicking on "CBOE Daily Market Statistics" under "Data." Clicking on the current date on the calendar at the top of the page will allow the user to retrieve data on any particular day. What is the reported Volume, Open Interest, and Level of trading for calls and puts on these options? What is the percent change in the most recent data from that of one year earlier?

Appendix 24A Black-Scholes Option Pricing Model

View Appendix 24A at the Web site for this textbook (**www.mcgrawhill.ca/college/saunders**).

Appendix 24B Microhedging with Options

View Appendix 24B at the Web site for this textbook (**www.mcgrawhill.ca/college/saunders**).

In this chapter, we discuss three types of swaps:

▸ interest rate swaps

▸ currency swaps

▸ credit swaps, the newest and fastest growing type of swap, and

▸ conclude with a discussion of credit risk concerns related to swaps

INTRODUCTION

Conceptually, swaps are a succession of forward contracts arranged by two parties. For example, a four-year swap with annual swap dates involves four net cash flows between the parties to a swap. This is essentially similar to arranging four forward contracts (see Chapter 23): a one-year, a two-year, a three-year, and a four-year contract.[1] Though the instrument underlying the swap may change, the basic principle of a swap agreement is the same in that there is a restructuring of asset or liability cash flows in a preferred direction by the transacting parties.

The global market for swaps has grown enormously in recent years, driven by five generic types of swaps: interest rate swaps, currency swaps, credit swaps, commodity swaps, and equity swaps.[2] The notional amount of over the counter (OTC) interest rate swaps reported by the Bank for International Settlements (BIS) globally was US$137,277 billion at the end of June 2004, 2.4 times the US$57,220 billion reported at the end of June, 2001. Similarly, the notional global amount of currency swaps reported at the end of June 2004 was US$7,939 billion, up from US$4,302 billion at the end of June 2001. Credit-linked forwards and swaps, equity-linked forwards and swaps, and commodity forwards and swaps were US$4,664 billion, US$773 billion, and US$541 billion, respectively. Credit-linked contracts were the fastest-growing, increasing from US$698 billion in 2001, a 568 percent increase. The amount reported to the Bank of Canada's Triennial Survey by Canadian financial institutions was a small fraction of the global numbers: interest rate swaps were US$2,973.9 billion, currency swaps were US$398.8 billion, credit swaps were US$216.5, forwards and swaps on commodities and precious metals were US$64.0 billion, and equity-linked forwards and swaps were US$52.6 billion at June 30, 2004.[3]

Commercial banks and investment banks are major participants in the market as dealers, traders, and users for proprietary hedging purposes. Insurance companies have only recently adopted hedging strategies using swaps, but their interest in this market is growing quickly. A swap dealer can act as an intermediary or third

---

[1] See C. W. Smith, C. W. Smithson, and D. S. Wilford, *Managing Financial Risk* (Cambridge, MA: Ballinger Publishing, 1990).

[2] There are also *swaptions,* which are options to enter into a swap agreement at some preagreed contract terms (e.g., a fixed rate of 10 percent) at some time in the future in return for the payment of an up-front premium.

[3] BIS Triennial Central Bank Survey 2004, Final Report, March 2005, page 22 available at www.bis.org and Bank of Canada Triennial Central Bank Survey of Foreign Exchange and Over-the-Counter (OTC) Derivatives Markets, March 2005, Tables 16 and 17 available at www.bankofcanada.ca.

party by putting a swap together and/or creating an over-the-counter (OTC) secondary market for swaps for a fee. The massive growth of the swap market has raised regulatory concerns regarding the credit risk exposures of banks engaging in this market. This growth was one of the motivations behind the introduction of the Bank for International Settlements (BIS)–sponsored risk-based capital adequacy reforms described in Chapter 20. In addition, in recent years there has been a growth in exotic swap products such as "inverse floater" swaps that have raised considerable controversy—especially since the bankruptcy in the United States of Orange County and the legal suits filed against swap-selling banks and investment banks. Indeed, the legal costs and reputational damage emanating from the Orange County bankruptcy have been huge.

INTEREST RATE SWAPS

interest rate swap
An exchange of fixed interest payments for floating interest payments by two counterparties.

By far the largest segment of the global swap market is comprised of **interest rate swaps.** An interest rate swap is a succession of forward contracts on interest rates arranged by two parties. As such, it allows an FI to put in place a long-term hedge sometimes for as long as 15 years. This hedge reduces the need to roll over contracts if reliance had been placed on futures or forward contracts to achieve such long-term hedges.

swap buyer
By convention, makes the fixed-rate payments in an interest rate swap transaction.

swap seller
By convention, makes the floating-rate payments in an interest rate swap transaction.

In a swap, the **swap buyer** agrees to make a number of fixed interest rate payments on periodic settlement dates to the **swap seller.** The seller of the swap in turn agrees to make floating-rate payments to the swap buyer on the same periodic settlement dates. The fixed-rate side—by convention, the swap buyer—generally has a comparative advantage in making fixed-rate payments, whereas the floating-rate side—by convention, the swap seller—generally has a comparative advantage in making variable or floating-rate payments. In undertaking this transaction, the FI that is the fixed-rate payer is seeking to transform the variable-rate nature of its liabilities into fixed-rate liabilities to better match the fixed returns earned on its assets. Meanwhile, the FI that is the variable-rate payer seeks to turn its fixed-rate liabilities into variable-rate liabilities to better match the variable returns on its assets.[4]

To explain the role of a swap transaction in hedging FI interest rate risk, we use a simple example. Consider two FIs: The first is a bank that has raised $100 million of its funds by issuing four-year, medium-term notes with 10 percent annual fixed coupons rather than relying on short-term deposits to raise funds (see Table 25–1). On the asset side of its portfolio, the bank makes business loans whose rates are indexed to annual changes in the London Interbank Offered Rate (LIBOR). As we discussed in Chapter 11, banks currently index most large business loans to LIBOR.

As a result of having floating-rate loans and fixed-rate liabilities in its asset-liability structure, the bank has a negative duration gap; the duration of its assets is shorter than that of its liabilities:

$$D_A - kD_L < 0$$

One way for the bank to hedge this exposure is to shorten the duration or interest rate sensitivity of its liabilities by transforming them into short-term floating-rate liabilities that better match the duration characteristics of its asset portfolio. The

---

[4] In the early 2000s, record low interest rates and depressed equity values reduced the value of many defined benefit pension plan surpluses. To protect their surplus values from declining further, many pension plans entered into interest rate swaps that protected them from further falls in interest rates. See "Solving the Pension Puzzle," *Risk,* March 2002, pp. 23–25.

TABLE 25–1
Bank Balance Sheet

Assets	Liabilities
Business loans (rate indexed to LIBOR) = $100 million	Medium-term notes (coupons fixed) = $100 million

TABLE 25–2
Credit Union Balance Sheet

Assets	Liabilities
Fixed-rate mortgages = $100 million	Short-term CDs (one year) = $100 million

bank can make changes either on or off the balance sheet. On the balance sheet, the bank could attract an additional $100 million in short-term deposits that are indexed to the LIBOR rate (say, LIBOR plus 2.5 percent) in a manner similar to its loans. The proceeds of these deposits can be used to pay off the medium-term notes. This reduces the duration gap between the bank's assets and liabilities. Alternatively, the bank could go off the balance sheet and sell an interest rate swap—that is, enter into a swap agreement to make the floating-rate payment side of a swap agreement.

The second party in the swap is a credit union that has invested $100 million in fixed-rate residential mortgages of long duration. To finance this residential mortgage portfolio, the credit union has had to rely on short-term certificates of deposit with an average duration of one year (see Table 25–2). On maturity, these CDs have to be rolled over at the current market rate.

Consequently, the credit union's asset-liability balance sheet structure is the reverse of the bank's; that is,

$$D_A - kD_L > 0$$

The credit union could hedge its interest rate risk exposure by transforming the short-term floating-rate nature of its liabilities into fixed-rate liabilities that better match the long-term maturity/duration structure of its assets. On the balance sheet, the credit union could issue long-term notes with a maturity equal or close to that on the mortgages (at, say, 12 percent). The proceeds of the sale of the notes can be used to pay off the CDs and reduce the duration gap. Alternatively, the credit union can buy a swap—take the fixed payment side of a swap agreement.

The opposing balance sheet and interest rate risk exposures of the bank and the credit union provide the necessary conditions for an interest rate swap agreement between the two parties. This swap agreement can be arranged directly between the parties. However, it is likely that an FI—another bank or an investment bank—would act as either a broker or an agent, receiving a fee for bringing the two parties together or intermediating fully by accepting the credit risk exposure and guaranteeing the cash flows underlying the swap contract. By acting as a principal as well as an agent, the FI can add a credit risk premium to the fee. However, the credit risk exposure of a swap to an FI is somewhat less than that on a loan (this is discussed later in this chapter). Conceptually, when a third-party FI fully intermediates the swap, that FI is really entering into two separate swap agreements: one with the bank and one with the credit union.

plain vanilla
Standard agreement without any special features.

For simplicity, we consider a **plain vanilla** fixed-floating rate swap where a third-party intermediary acts as a simple broker or agent by bringing together two FIs with opposing interest rate risk exposures to enter into a swap agreement or contract.

EXAMPLE 25–1

Expected Cash Flows on an Interest Rate Swap

Suppose the notional value of a swap is $100 million—equal to the assumed size of the bank's medium-term note issue—and the maturity of four years is equal to the maturity of the bank's note liabilities. The annual coupon cost of these note liabilities is 10 percent, and the bank's problem is that the variable return on its assets may be insufficient to cover the cost of meeting these coupon payments if market interest rates, and therefore asset returns, *fall*. By comparison, the fixed returns on the credit union's mortgage asset portfolio may be insufficient to cover the interest cost of its CDs if market rates *rise*. As a result, a feasible swap agreement might dictate that the credit union send fixed payments of 10 percent per annum of the notional $100 million value of the swap to the bank to allow the bank to cover fully the coupon interest payments on its note issue. In return, the bank sends annual payments indexed to one-year LIBOR to help the credit union cover the cost of refinancing its one-year renewable CDs. Suppose that one-year LIBOR is currently 8 percent and the bank agrees to send annual payments at the end of each year equal to one-year LIBOR plus 2 percent to the credit union[5] We depict this fixed–floating rate swap transaction in Figure 25–1; the expected net financing costs for the FIs are listed in Table 25–3.

As a result of the swap, the bank has transformed its four-year, fixed-rate interest payments into variable-rate payments, matching the variability of returns on its assets. Further, through the interest rate swap, the bank effectively pays LIBOR plus 2 percent for its financing. Had it gone to the debt market, we assumed (on page 762) that the bank would pay LIBOR plus 2.5 percent (a savings of 0.5 percent with the swap). Further, the credit union has transformed its variable-rate interest payments into fixed-rate payments, plus a "small" variable component (CD rate − LIBOR), similar to those received on its assets. Had it gone to the debt market, we assumed (on page 763) that the credit union would pay 12 percent (a savings of 4 percent + CD rate − LIBOR with the swap).

FIGURE 25–1
Fixed–Floating Rate Swap

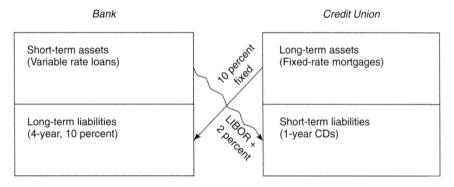

TABLE 25–3
Financing Cost Resulting from Interest Rate Swap (in millions of dollars)

	Bank	Credit Union
Cash outflows from balance sheet financing	−10% × $100	−(CD) × $100
Cash inflows from swap	10% × $100	(LIBOR + 2%) × $100
Cash outflows from swap	−(LIBOR + 2%) × $100	−10% × $100
Net cash flows	−(LIBOR + 2%) × $100	−(8% + CD Rate − LIBOR) × $100
Rate available on:		
Variable-rate debt	LIBOR + 2½%	
Fixed-rate debt		12%

---

[5] These rates implicitly assume that this is the cheapest way each party can hedge its interest rate exposure. For example, LIBOR + 2 percent is the lowest-cost way in which the money center bank can transform its fixed-rate liabilities into floating-rate liabilities.

Note in Example 25–1 that in the absence of default/credit risk, only the bank is really fully hedged. This happens because the annual 10 percent payments it receives from the credit union at the end of each year allow it to meet the promised 10 percent coupon rate payments to its note holders regardless of the return it receives on its variable-rate assets. By contrast, the credit union receives variable-rate payments based on LIBOR plus 2 percent. However, it is quite possible that the CD rate the credit union has to pay on its deposit liabilities does not exactly track the LIBOR-indexed payments sent by the bank. That is, the credit union is subject to basis risk exposure on the swap contract. There are two possible sources of this basis risk. First, CD rates do not exactly match the movements of LIBOR rates over time since the former are determined in the domestic money market and the latter in the Eurodollar market. Second, the credit/default risk premium on the credit union's CDs may increase over time; thus, the +2 percent add-on to LIBOR may be insufficient to hedge the credit union's cost of funds. The credit union might be better hedged by requiring the bank to send it floating payments based on domestic CD rates rather than LIBOR. To do this, the bank would probably require additional compensation since it would then be bearing basis risk. Its asset returns would be sensitive to LIBOR movements while its swap payments were indexed to CD rates.

Pricing A Swap

In analyzing this swap, one has to distinguish between how it should be priced at time 0 (now); that is, how the exchange rate of fixed (10 percent) for floating (LIBOR + 2 percent) is set when the swap agreement is initiated and the actual realized cash flows on the swap. As we discuss in Appendix 25A (on page 724 of this book), *fair pricing* on initiation of the swap depends on the market's expectations of future short-term rates, while realized cash flows on the swap depend on the actual market rates (here, LIBOR) that materialized over the life of the swap contract.

Realized Cash Flows on an Interest Rate Swap

EXAMPLE 25–2

Calculation of Realized Cash Flows

We assume that the realized or actual path of interest rates (LIBOR) over the four-year life of the contract would be

End of Year	LIBOR
1	9%
2	9
3	7
4	6

The bank's variable payments to the credit union were indexed to these rates by the formula

(LIBOR + 2%) × $100 million

By contrast, the fixed annual payments the credit union made to the bank were the same each year: 10% × $100 million. We summarize the actual or realized cash flows among the two parties over the four years in Table 25–4. The credit union's net gains from the swap in years 1 and 2 are $1 million per year. The enhanced cash flow offsets the increased cost of refinancing its CDs in a higher interest rate environment—that is, the credit union is hedged against rising rates. By contrast, the bank makes net gains on the swap in years 3 and 4 when rates fall; thus, it is hedged against falling rates. The positive cash flow from the swap offsets the decline in the variable returns on the bank's asset portfolio. Overall, the bank made a net dollar gain of $1 million in nominal dollars; its true realized gain would be the present value of this amount.

TABLE 25–4
Realized Cash Flows on the Swap Agreement (in millions of dollars)

End of Year	One-Year LIBOR	One-Year LIBOR +2 percent	Cash Payment by Bank	Cash Payment by Credit Union	Net Payment Made by MCB
1	9%	11%	$11	$10	$+1
2	9	11	11	10	+1
3	7	9	9	10	−1
4	6	8	8	10	−2
Total			$39	$40	$−1

FIGURE 25–2
Inverse Floater Swap–Structured Note

Swaps can always be molded or tailored to the needs of the transacting parties as long as one party is willing to compensate the other party for accepting nonstandard terms or **off-market swap** arrangements, usually in the form of an up-front fee or payments. Relaxing a standardized swap can include special interest rate terms and indexes as well as allowing for varying notional values underlying the swap.

off-market swaps
Swaps that have nonstandard terms that require one party to compensate another.

For example, in the case we just considered, the notional value of the swap was fixed at $100 million for each of the four annual swap dates. However, swap notional values can be allowed either to decrease or to increase over a swap contract's life. This flexibility is useful when one of the parties has heavy investments in mortgages (in our example, the credit union) and the mortgages are **fully amortized,** meaning that the annual and monthly cash flows on the mortgage portfolio reflect repayments of both principal and interest such that the periodic payment is kept constant (see Chapter 27). Fixed-rate mortgages normally have larger payments of interest than principal in the early years, with the interest component falling as mortgages approach maturity. One possibility is for the credit union to enter into a mortgage swap to hedge the amortizing nature of the mortgage portfolio or alternatively to allow the notional value of the swap to decline at a rate similar to the decline in the principal component of the mortgage portfolio.[6]

fully amortized mortgages
Mortgage portfolio cash flows that have a constant payment.

Another example of a special type of interest rate swap is the inverse floater swap, which was engineered by major FIs as part of structured note financing deals to lower the cost of financing to various government agencies. Such arrangements have resulted in enormous problems for investor groups such as municipal authorities and corporations that are part of the overall swap deal.

A structured note-inverse floater swap arrangement is shown in Figure 25–2. In this arrangement, a government agency issues notes (say, $100 million) to investors with a coupon that is equal to 7 percent minus LIBOR—that is, an (inverse) floating coupon. The novel feature of this coupon is that when market rates fall (and thus LIBOR is low), the coupon received by the investor is large. The government agency then converts this spread liability (7 percent − LIBOR) into a LIBOR liability by entering into a swap with an FI dealer (e.g., a bank). In effect, the cost of the $100 million note issue is LIBOR to the agency plus any fees relating to the swap.

---

[6] For further details of nonstandard swaps, see P. A. Abken, "Beyond Plain Vanilla: A Taxonomy of Swaps," *Federal Reserve Bank of Atlanta, Economic Review,* March–April 1991, pp. 21–29; and C. James and C. Smith, "The Use of Index Amortizing Swaps by Banc One," *Journal of Applied Corporate Finance* 7, No. 5 (Fall 1994), pp. 54–59.

The risk of these notes to the investor is very clear. If LIBOR is 2 percent, then the investor will receive coupons of 7 percent − 2 percent = 5 percent, which is an excellent spread return if the investor can borrow at close to LIBOR (or 2 percent in this case). However, consider what happens if interest rates rise. If LIBOR rises from 2 to 8 percent, the promised coupon becomes 7 percent − 8 percent = −1 percent. Since negative coupons cannot be paid, the actual coupon paid to the investor is 0 percent. However, if the investor borrowed funds to buy the notes at LIBOR, the cost of funds is 8 percent in this case. Thus, the investor is facing an extremely large negative spread and loss.

Macrohedging with Swaps

The duration model shown in Chapters 23 and 24 to estimate the optimal number of futures and options contracts to hedge an FI's duration gap also can be applied to estimate the optimal number of swap contracts. For example, an FI manager might wish to know how many 10-year (or 5-year) swap contracts are needed to hedge its overall risk exposure. The optimal notional value of swap contracts should be set so that the gain on swap contracts entered into off the balance sheet just offsets any loss in net worth on the balance sheet when interest rates change.

Assume that an FI has a positive duration gap so that it has positive net worth exposure to rising interest rates:

$$\Delta E = -(D_A - kD_L)A\,\frac{\Delta R}{1 + R} > 0$$

As discussed above, the FI can seek to hedge by paying fixed and receiving floating payments through an interest rate swap. However, many different maturity swaps are available. As will be shown below, the size of the notional value of the interest rate swaps entered into will depend on the maturity (duration) of the swap contract. Suppose the FI manager chooses to hedge with 10-year swaps.

In terms of valuation, a 10-year swap arrangement can be considered in terms of bond equivalent valuation. That is, the fixed-rate payments on a 10-year swap are formally equivalent to the fixed payments on a 10-year government bond. Similarly, the floating-rate payments on a 10-year swap with *annual* payments can be viewed as equivalent to floating coupons on a bond where coupons are repriced (to LIBOR) every year. That is, the change in the value of the swap (ΔS) when interest rates ($\Delta R/(1 + R)$) rise will depend on the relative interest sensitivity of 10-year bonds to 1-year bonds, or in duration terms, $(D_{10} - D_1)$.[7] In general,

$$\Delta S = -(D_{fixed} - D_{float}) \times N_S \times \frac{\Delta R}{1 + R}$$

where

$$\Delta S = \text{Change in the market value of the swap contract}$$

$(D_{fixed} - D_{float}) = $ Difference in durations between a government bond that has the same maturity and coupon as the fixed-payment side of the swap and a government bond that has the same duration as the swap-payment interval (e.g., annual floating payments)

---

[7] Although principal payments on bonds are not swapped on maturity, this does not matter since the theoretical payment and receipt of principal values cancel each other out.

$$N_S = \text{Notional value of swap contracts}$$

$$\frac{\Delta R}{1 + R} = \text{Shock to interest rates}$$

Note that as long as $D_{fixed} > D_{float}$, when interest rates rise, the market (present) value of fixed-rate payments will fall by more than the market (present) value of floating-rate payments; in market (or present) value terms, the fixed-rate payers gain when rates rise and lose when rates fall.

To solve for the optimal notional value of swap contracts,[8] we set

$$\Delta S = \Delta E$$

The gain on swap contracts entered into off the balance sheet just offsets the loss in net worth on the balance sheet when rates rise. Substituting values for ΔS and ΔE

$$-(D_{fixed} - D_{float}) \times N_S \times \frac{\Delta R}{1 + R} = -(D_A - kD_L) \times A \times \frac{\Delta R}{1 + R}$$

Canceling out the common terms

$$(D_{fixed} - D_{float}) \times N_S = (D_A - kD_L) \times A$$

Solving for N_S

$$N_S = \frac{(D_A - kD_L) \times A}{D_{fixed} - D_{float}}$$

EXAMPLE 25–3

Calculating the Notional Value of Swaps in a Macrohedge

Suppose $D_A = 5$, $D_L = 3$, $k = .9$, and $A = \$100,000,000$. Also, assume the duration of a current 10-year, fixed-rate bond with the same coupon as the fixed rate on the swap is seven years, while the duration of a floating-rate bond that reprices annually is one year:[9]

$$D_{fixed} = 7 \quad \text{and} \quad D_{float} = 1$$

Then:

$$N_S = \frac{(D_A - kD_L) \times A}{D_{fixed} - D_{float}} = \frac{\$230,000,000}{(7 - 1)} = \$38,333,333$$

If each swap contract is \$100,000 in size,[10] the number of swap contracts into which the FI should enter will be \$38,333,333/\$100,000 = 383.33, or 383 contracts, rounding down. Table 25–5 summarizes the key features of the hedge assuming that the initial rate on the T-bond is 10 percent and is expected to rise by 1 percent. As shown in Table 25–5, the loss of \$2.09 million in net worth on the balance sheet is exactly offset by a gain off the balance sheet on the swap hedge.

If the FI engaged in a longer-term swap—for example, 15 years—such that $D_{fixed} = 9$ and $D_{float} = 1$, then the notional value of swap contracts would fall to \$230,000,000/(9 − 1) = \$28,750,000. If each swap contract is \$100,000 in size, the FI should enter into 287 swap contracts.

---

[8] Note that the FI wants to enter swaps to protect itself against rising rates. Thus, it will pay fixed and receive floating. In the context of swap transactions, when an FI pays fixed, it is said to be "buying swaps." Thus, we are solving for the optimal number of swaps contracts the FI should buy in this example.

[9] See Chapter 8 for a discussion of the duration on floating-rate bonds.

[10] The notional value of swap contracts can take virtually any size since they are individually tailored OTC contracts.

TABLE 25–5
On- and Off-Balance-Sheet Effects of a Swap Hedge

		Bank	Credit Union
Begin hedge, $t = 0$		Equity exposed to impact of rise in interest rates	Sell interest rate swap
End hedge, $t = 1$		Interest rates rise on assets and liabilities by 1%	Buy interest rate swap

Opportunity loss on balance sheet:
$$\Delta E = -[5 - .9(3) \times \$100m \times (.01/(1.1))]$$
$$= -\$2.09 \text{ million}$$

Gain on interest rate swap:
$$\Delta S = [(7 - 1) \times \$38{,}333{,}333 \times (.01/(1.1))]$$
$$= \$2.09 \text{ million}$$

Although it may seem logical that fewer contracts are preferable in the sense of saving on fees and other related costs of hedging, this advantage is offset by the fact that longer-term swaps have greater counterparty default or credit risk (discussed later in this chapter).

Concept Questions

1. In Example 25–2, which of the two FIs has its liability costs fully hedged and which is only partially hedged? Explain your answer.
2. What are some nonstandard terms that might be encountered in an off-market swap?
3. In Example 25–3, what is the notional size of swap contracts if $D_{fixed} = 5$ and swap contracts require payment every six months? ($N_s = \$51{,}111{,}111$)

CURRENCY SWAPS

currency swap
A swap used to hedge against exchange rate risk from mismatched currencies on assets and liabilities.

Just as swaps are long-term contracts that can hedge interest rate risk exposure, they can also be used to hedge currency risk exposures of FIs. The following section considers a simple plain vanilla example of how **currency swaps** can immunize FIs against exchange rate risk when they mismatch the currencies of their assets and liabilities.

Fixed-Fixed Currency Swaps

Consider an FI with all of its fixed-rate assets denominated in dollars. It is financing part of its asset portfolio with a £50 million issue of four-year, medium-term British pound sterling notes that have a fixed annual coupon of 10 percent. By comparison, there is a U.K. FI that has all its assets denominated in sterling; it is partly funding those assets with a $100 million issue of four-year, medium-term dollar notes with a fixed annual coupon of 10 percent.

These two FIs are exposed to opposing currency risks. The Canadian FI is exposed to the risk that the dollar will depreciate against the pound over the next four years, making it more costly to cover the annual coupon interest payments and the principal repayment on its pound-denominated notes. On the other hand, the U.K. FI is exposed to the dollar appreciating against the pound, making it more difficult to cover the dollar coupon and principal payments on its four-year $100 million note issue out of the sterling cash flows on its assets.

The FIs can hedge the exposures either on or off the balance sheet. Assume that the dollar/pound exchange rate is fixed at $2/£1. On the balance sheet, the Canadian FI can issue $100 million in four-year, medium-term dollar notes (at, say, 10.5 percent). The proceeds of the sale can be used to pay off the £50 million of four-year, medium-term sterling notes. Similarly, the U.K. FI can issue £50 million in four-year, medium-term sterling notes (at, say, 10.5 percent), using the proceeds to pay off the $100 million of four-year, medium-term dollar notes. Both FIs have taken actions on the balance sheet so that they are no longer exposed to movements in the exchange rate between the two currencies.

EXAMPLE 25–4

Expected Cash Flows on Fixed-Fixed Currency Swap.

Rather than make changes on the balance sheet, a feasible currency swap in which the U.K. and Canadian FIs can enter is one under which the U.K. FI sends annual payments in pounds to cover the coupon and principal repayments of the Canadian FI's pound sterling note issue, and the Canadian FI sends annual dollar payments to the U.K. FI to cover the interest and principal payments on its dollar note issue.[11] We summarize the currency swap in Figure 25–3 and Table 25–6. As a result of the swap, the U.K. FI transforms fixed-rate dollar payments into fixed-rate sterling payments that better match the sterling fixed-rate cash flows from its asset portfolio. Similarly, the Canadian FI transforms fixed-rate sterling payments into fixed-rate dollar payments that better match the fixed-rate dollar cash flows from its asset portfolio. Further, both FIs transform the pattern of their payments at a lower rate than if they had made changes on the balance sheet. Both FIs effectively obtain financing at 10 percent while hedging against exchange rate risk. Had they gone to the market, we assumed above that they would have paid 10.5 percent to do this. In undertaking this exchange of cash flows, the two parties normally agree on a fixed exchange rate for the cash flows at the beginning of the period.[12] In this example, the fixed exchange rate would be $2/£1.

FIGURE 25–3
Fixed-Fixed Pound/Dollar Currency Swap

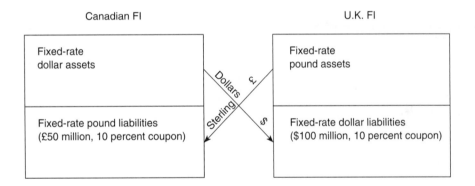

TABLE 25–6
Financing Costs Resulting from the Fixed-Fixed Currency Swap Agreement (in millions of $ and £)

	Canadian FI	U.K. FI
Cash outflows from balance sheet financing	−10% × £50	−10% × $100
Cash inflows from swap	10% × £50	10% × $100
Cash outflows from swap	−10% × $100	−10% × £50
Net cash flows	−10% × $100	−10% × £50
Rate available on		
Dollar-denominated notes	10.5%	
Pound-denominated notes		10.5%

---

[11] In a currency swap, it is usual to include both principal and interest payments as part of the swap agreement. For interest rate swaps, it is usual to include just interest rate payments. The reason for this is that both principal and interest are exposed to FX risk.

[12] As with interest rate swaps, this exchange rate reflects the contracting parties' expectations in regard to future exchange rate movements.

In this example, both liabilities bear a fixed 10 percent interest rate. This is not a necessary requirement for the fixed-fixed currency swap agreement. For example, suppose that the Canadian FI's note coupons were 5 percent per annum, while the U.K. FI's note coupons were 10 percent. The swap dollar payments of the Canadian FI would remain unchanged, but the U.K. FI's sterling payments would be reduced by £2.5 million (or $5 million) in each of the four years. This difference could be met either by some up-front payment by the U.K. FI to the Canadian FI, reflecting the difference in the present value of the two fixed cash flows, or by annual payments that result in zero net present value differences among the fixed-fixed currency swap participants' payments. Also note that if the exchange rate changed from the rate agreed in the swap ($2/£1), either one or the other side would be losing in the sense that a new swap might be entered into at an exchange rate more favourable to one party. Specifically, if the dollar were to appreciate (rise in value) against the pound over the life of the swap, the agreement would become more costly for the Canadian FI. If, however, the dollar were to depreciate (fall in value), the U.K. FI would find the agreement increasingly costly over the swap's life.

By combining an interest rate swap of the fixed-floating type described earlier with a currency swap, we can also produce a fixed-floating currency swap that is a hybrid of the two plain vanilla swaps we have considered so far.

Fixed-Floating Currency Swaps

EXAMPLE 25–5

Financing Costs Associated with a Fixed-Floating Currency Swap

Consider a Canadian FI that primarily holds floating-rate, short-term dollar–denominated assets. It has partly financed this asset portfolio with a £50 million, four-year note issue with fixed 10 percent annual coupons denominated in sterling. By comparison, a U.K. FI that primarily holds long-term, fixed-rate assets denominated in sterling has partly financed this portfolio with $100 million short-term dollar-denominated Euro CDs whose rates reflect changes in one-year LIBOR plus a 2 percent premium. As a result, the Canadian FI is faced with both an interest rate risk and a foreign exchange risk. Specifically, if dollar short-term rates fall and the dollar depreciates against the pound, the FI may face a problem in covering its promised fixed-coupon and principal payments on the pound-denominated note. Consequently, it may wish to transform its fixed-rate, pound-denominated liabilities into variable-rate, dollar-denominated liabilities. The U.K. FI also faces interest rate and foreign exchange rate risk exposures. If Canadian interest rates rise and the dollar appreciates against the pound, the U.K. FI will find it more difficult to cover its promised coupon and principal payments on its dollar-denominated CDs out of the cash flows from its fixed-rate pound asset portfolio. Consequently, it may wish to transform its floating-rate, short-term, dollar-denominated liabilities into fixed-rate pound liabilities.

Both FIs can make changes on the balance sheet to hedge the interest rate and foreign exchange rate risk exposure. The Canadian FI can issue $100 million dollar-dominated, floating-rate, short-term debt (at, say, LIBOR plus 2.5 percent), the proceeds of which can be used to pay off the existing £50 million four-year note. The U.K. FI can issue £50 million in four-year notes (at, say, 11 percent) and use the proceeds to pay off the $100 million in short-term Euro CDs. Both FIs, by changing the financing used on the balance sheet, hedge both the interest rate and foreign exchange rate risk. We again assume that the dollar/pound exchange rate is $2/£1.

Alternatively, each FI can achieve its objective of liability transformation by engaging in a fixed-floating currency swap. A feasible swap would be one in which each year, the two FIs swap payments at some prearranged dollar/pound exchange rate, assumed to be $2/£1. The U.K. FI sends fixed payments in pounds to cover the cost of the Canadian FI's pound-denominated note issue, while the Canadian FI sends floating payments in dollars to cover the U.K. FI's floating-rate

(continued)

TABLE 25–7   Financing Costs Resulting from the Fixed-Floating Currency Swap (in millions of $ and £)

	Canadian FI	U.K. FI
Cash outflows from balance sheet financing	$-10\% \times £50$	$-(LIBOR + 2\%) \times \$100$
Cash inflows from swap	$10\% \times £50$	$(LIBOR + 2\%) \times \$100$
Cash outflows from swap	$-(LIBOR + 2\%) \times \$100$	$-10\% \times £50$
Net cash outflows	$-(LIBOR + 2\%) \times \$100$	$-10\% \times £50$
Rate available on		
Dollar-denominated variable-rate debt	LIBOR + 2½%	
Pound-denominated fixed-rate debt		11%

TABLE 25–8   Realized Cash Flows on a Fixed-Floating Currency Swap (in millions of $ and £)

Year	LIBOR	LIBOR +2 percent	Floating Rate Payment by Canadian Bank ($)	Fixed Rate Payment by U.K. FI (£s)	Fixed Rate Payment by U.K. FI ($ at $2/£1)	Net Payment by Canadian. FI ($s)
1	9%	11%	$ 11	£5	$ 10	$+1
2	7	9	9	5	10	−1
3	8	10	10	5	10	0
4	10	12	112	55	110	+2
Total net payment						$+2

dollar CD costs. The resulting expected financing costs are calculated in Table 25–7. As a result of the fixed-floating currency swap, both FIs have hedged interest rate and foreign exchange rate risk and have done so at a rate below what they could have achieved by making on-balance-sheet changes. The Canadian FI's net financing cost is LIBOR plus 2 percent with the swap, compared to LIBOR plus 2.5 percent in the debt market. The U.K. FI's financing cost is 10 percent with the swap, compared to 11 percent had it refinanced on the balance sheet.

Given the realized LIBOR rates in column (2), we show the relevant payments among the contracting parties in Table 25–8. The realized cash flows from the swap result in a net nominal payment of $2 million by the Canadian FI to the U.K. FI over the life of the swap.

Concept Questions

1. Referring to the fixed-fixed currency swap in Table 25–6, if the net cash flows on the swap are zero, why does either FI enter into the swap agreement?
2. Referring to Table 25–8, suppose that the Canadian FI had agreed to make floating payments of LIBOR + 1 percent instead of LIBOR + 2 percent. What would its net payment have been to the U.K. FI over the four-year swap agreement?

CREDIT SWAPS

In recent years the fastest growing types of swaps have been those developed to better allow FIs to hedge their credit risk. This is important for two reasons. First, credit risk is still more likely to cause an FI to fail than is either interest rate risk or FX risk. Second, credit swaps allow FIs to maintain long-term customer lending relationships without bearing the full credit risk exposure from those relationships. The Industry Perspectives Box shows how Federal Reserve Board Chairman Alan Greenspan has credited this market with helping the U.S. banking system maintain its strength through an economic recession in the early 2000s. He argued that credit swaps were effectively used to shift a significant part of banks' risk from their corporate loan portfolios.[13] For example, significant exposures to telecommunication firms were hedged by banks through credit swaps. However, the Fed chairman also commented that these derivative securities are prone to induce speculative excesses that need to be contained through regulation, supervision, and private sector action.[14]

Below we look at two types of credit swaps: (1) the total return swap and (2) the pure credit swap. We then look at credit risk concerns with the swaps themselves.

Industry Perspectives

THE ECONOMY: DERIVATIVES GROWTH HAS HELPED BANKS, GREENSPAN SAYS

WASHINGTON—Proliferating financial derivatives have helped banks withstand rising corporate defaults, but they also can fuel speculative excess, Federal Reserve Chairman Alan Greenspan said.

"Financial derivatives . . . have grown at a phenomenal pace over the past fifteen years," Mr. Greenspan said in prepared remarks to the American Bankers Association convention in Phoenix. "Banks appear to have effectively used such instruments to shift a significant part of the risk from their corporate loan portfolios" to other institutions. For example, significant exposures to telecommunications firms were laid off through credit-default swaps and collateralized debt obligations.

"These transactions represent a new paradigm of active credit management and are a major part of the explanation of the banking system's strength during a period of stress," the Fed chairman said.

But more-sophisticated risk-management techniques and "especially the various forms of derivatives, are, by construction, highly leveraged. They are thus prone to induce speculative excesses, not only in the U.S. financial system but also through the rest of the world." This potential for systemic risk can be contained through a combination of regulation, supervision and private-sector action, including better public disclosure, Mr. Greenspan said. But ultimately, some of that systemic risk must also be absorbed by central banks, he said.

A derivative is a financial contract derived from an underlying security, commodity, interest rate or currency. It can be as simple as an option to buy or sell a stock or bond, or a way of profiting from changes in interest rates, or even a kind of complex insurance that banks can obtain against the possibility that a loan will default. The volume of derivatives has exploded in recent years, with trillions of dollars of derivatives now in existence; most cancel each other out.

A key element of some derivatives is that they allow an investor to protect large investments with relatively little capital, but the resulting leverage makes outsized gains and losses possible. Mr. Greenspan has long been a fan of derivatives, as well as a leading opponent of moves to impose new regulations on them. He has opposed a recent proposal by Sens. Tom Harkin (D., Iowa) and Richard Lugar (R., Ind.) to regulate some energy derivatives. That proposal was sparked by alleged abuses by Enron Corp.

Mr. Greenspan said the Asian and Russian financial crises in 1998 sent a "strong and timely message" to the U.S. financial system to raise its credit standards and work harder to manage risk. This led to a far stronger position heading into recession. "Our banks have been able to retain their strength in this business cycle, in contrast to the early 1990s when so many either failed or had near-death experiences," he said. He urged banks to take careful note of the current problems. Many banks didn't keep proper records during the early 1990s and are now regretting it, he said.

---

[13] Much of this risk exposure was absorbed by domestic and foreign insurance and reinsurance companies.

[14] See G. IP and R. Christie, "Derivatives Growth Has Helped Banks, Greenspan Says," *The Wall Street Journal*, October 8, 2002, p. A2.

Total Return Swaps

total return swap
A swap involving an obligation to pay interest at a specified fixed or floating rate for payments representing the total return on a specified amount.

Although FIs spend significant resources attempting to evaluate and price expected changes in a borrower's credit risk over the life of a loan, a borrower's credit situation (credit quality) sometimes deteriorates unexpectedly after the loan terms are determined and the loan is issued. A lender can use a total return swap to hedge this possible change in credit risk exposure. A **total return swap** involves swapping an obligation to pay interest at a specified fixed or floating rate for payments representing the total return on a loan or a bond (interest and principal value changes) of a specified amount.

EXAMPLE 25–6

Calculation of Cash Flows on a Total Return Swap

Suppose that an FI lends $100 million to a Brazilian manufacturing firm at a fixed rate of 10 percent. If the firm's credit risk increases unexpectedly over the life of the loan, the market value of the loan and consequently the FI's net worth will fall. The FI can hedge an unexpected increase in the borrower's credit risk by entering into a total return swap in which it agrees to pay a total return based on an annual fixed rate (f) plus changes in the market value of Brazilian (dollar-denominated) government debt (changes in the value of these bonds reflect the political and economic events in the firm's home country and thus will be correlated with the credit risk of the Brazilian borrowing firm). Also, the bonds are in the same currency (dollars) as the loans. In return, the FI receives a variable market rate payment of interest annually (e.g., one-year LIBOR rate). Figure 25–4 and Table 25–9 illustrate the cash flows associated with the typical total return swap for the FI.

Using the total return swap, the FI agrees to pay a fixed rate of interest annually and the capital gain or loss on the market value of the Brazilian (dollar) bond over the period of the hedge. In Figure 25–4, P_0 denotes the market value of the bond at the beginning of the swap period and P_T represents the market value of the bond at the end of the swap period. If the Brazilian bond decreases in value over the period of the hedge ($P_0 > P_T$), the FI pays a relatively small (possibly negative) amount to the counterparty equal to the fixed payment on the swap minus the capital loss[15] on the bond. For example, suppose the Brazilian (U.S. dollar) bond was priced at par ($P_0 = 100$) at the beginning of the swap period. At the end of the swap period or the payment date, the Brazilian bond had a secondary market value of 90 ($P_T = 90$) due to an increase in Brazilian country risk. Suppose that the fixed-rate payment ($\bar{f}$) as part of the total return swap was 12 percent; then the FI would send to the swap counterparty the fixed rate of 12 percent minus 10 percent (the capital loss on the Brazilian bond), or a total of 2 percent, and would receive in return a floating payment (e.g., LIBOR = 11 percent) from the counterparty to the swap. Thus, the net profit on the swap to the FI lender is 9 percent (11 percent minus 2 percent) times the notional amount of the swap contract. This gain can be used to offset the loss of market value on the loan to the Brazilian firm. This example is illustrated in Table 25–9.[16]

Thus, the FI benefits from the total return swap if the Brazilian bond value deteriorates as a result of a political or economic shock. Assuming that the Brazilian firm's credit risk deteriorates along with the local economy, the FI will offset some of this loss of the Brazilian loan on its balance sheet with a gain from the total return swap.

Note that hedging credit risk in this fashion allows the FI to maintain its customer relationship with the Brazilian firm (and perhaps earn fees from selling other financial services to that firm) without bearing a large amount of credit risk exposure.

---

[15] Total return swaps are typically structured so that the capital gain or loss is paid at the end of the swap. However, an alternative structure does exist in which the capital gain or loss is paid at the end of each interest period during the swap.

[16] For additional discussion, see J. D. Finnerty, "Credit Derivatives, Infrastructure Finance, and Emerging Market Risk," *The Financier, ACMT,* February 1996, pp. 64–75.

FIGURE 25–4
Cash Flows on a
Total Return Swap

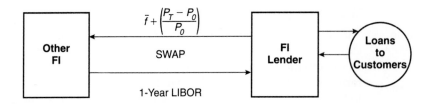

TABLE 25–9   Cash Flows on a Total Return Swap

	Annual Cash Flow for Year 1 through Final Year	Additional Payment by FI	Total Return
Cash inflow on swap to FI lender	1-year LIBOR (11%)	—	1-year LIBOR (11%)
Cash outflow on swap to other FI	Fixed rate ($\bar{f}$) (12%)	$P_T - P_0$ (90 2 100)	$\left[\bar{f} + \dfrac{P_T - P_0}{P_0}\right]$
			$(12\% + \dfrac{90 - 100}{100} = 12\% - 10\% = 2\%)$
	Net profit		9%

Moreover, since the Brazilian loan remains on the FI's balance sheet, the Brazilian firm may not even know its loan is being hedged. This would not be the case if the FI sought to reduce its risk by selling all or part of the loan (see Chapter 26). Finally, the swap does not completely hedge credit risk in this case. Specifically, basis risk is present to the extent that the credit risk of the Brazilian firm's dollar loan is imperfectly correlated with Brazilian country risk reflected in the price of the Brazilian (dollar) bonds.[17]

Pure Credit Swaps

Total return swaps can be used to hedge credit risk exposure, but they contain an element of interest rate risk as well as credit risk. For example, in Table 25–9, if the LIBOR rate changes due to changes in monetary policy, the *net* cash flows on the total return swap also will change—even though the credit risks of the underlying loans (and bonds) have not changed.

pure credit swap
A swap by which an FI receives the par value of the loan on default in return for paying a periodic swap fee.

To strip out the "interest rate" sensitive element of total return swaps, an alternative swap has been developed called a **"pure" credit swap.** In this case, as shown in Figure 25–5, the FI lender will send (each swap period) a fixed fee or payment (like an insurance premium) to the FI counterparty. If the FI lender's loan or loans do not default, it will receive nothing back from the FI counterparty. However, if the loan or loans default, the FI counterparty will cover the default loss by making a default payment that is often equal to the par value of the original loan (e.g., $P_0 = \$100$) minus the secondary market value of the defaulted loan (e.g., $P_T = \$40$); that

---

[17] In many swaps, the total return on a loan (rather than a bond as in this example) is swapped for a floating payment such as LIBOR. In this case, $\bar{f}$ would equal any fees paid for loan origination and $((P_T - P_0)/P_0)$ would reflect the estimated change in market value of the loan as perceived by brokers/traders in the secondary market for loan sales. The secondary market for loans is described in Chapter 26.

FIGURE 25–5
A Pure Credit Swap

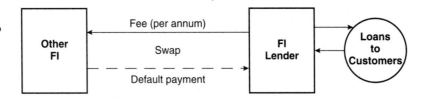

is, the FI counterparty will pay $P_0 - P_T$ (or \$60, in this example).[18] Thus, a pure credit swap is like buying credit insurance and/or a multiperiod credit option.

SWAPS AND CREDIT RISK CONCERNS

The growth of the over-the-counter (OTC) swap market was one of the major motivating factors underlying the imposition of the BIS risk-based capital requirements in January 1993 (see Chapter 20). The fear was that in a long-term OTC swap-type contract, the out-of-the-money counterparty would have incentives to default to deter future and current losses. Consequently, the BIS requirements imposed a required capital ratio for deposit-taking institutions against their holdings of both interest rate and currency swaps (and, more recently, other types of swaps, including credit swaps). Many analysts have argued that these capital requirements work against the growth of the swap market since they can be viewed as a cost or tax on market participants.

www.bis.org

Both regulators and market participants have a heightened awareness of credit risks. If the transaction is not structured carefully, it may pass along unintended risks to participants, exposing them to higher frequency and severity of losses than if they had held an equivalent cash position.[19] As defined by Moody's Investor Service, default risk on swaps comes from three sources: (1) any missed or delayed payment of interest and/or principal; (2) bankruptcy or receivership; and (3) distressed exchange, where the borrower offers debtholders a new security that amounts to a diminished financial obligation, or the swap dealer has the apparent purpose of helping the borrower avoid default. Both Merrill Lynch and J. P. Morgan Chase are heavy participants as intermediaries in the swap market; for example, they act as counterparty guarantors to both the fixed and floating sides in swaps. To do this successfully and to maintain market share, a high if not the highest credit rating is increasingly required.

www.moodys.com

This raises a question: Is credit or default risk on swaps the same as or different from the credit or default risk on loans? In fact, there are three major differences between the credit risk on swaps and the credit risk on loans. As a result, the credit risk on a swap is generally much less than that on a loan.[20] We discuss these differences next.[21]

---

[18] While a pure credit swap is like a default option (e.g., the digital default option in Chapter 24), a key difference is that the fee (or premium) payments on the swap are paid over the life of the swap, whereas for a default option the whole fee (premium) is paid up front.

[19] See J. S. Tolk, "Understanding the Risks in Credit Default Swaps," *The Financier,* Spring 2002, pp. 87–100.

[20] As with loans, swap participants deal with the credit risk of counterparties by setting bilateral limits on the notional amount of swaps entered into (similar to credit rationing on loans) as well as adjusting the fixed and/or floating rates by including credit risk premiums. For example, a low-credit-quality fixed-rate payer may have to pay an additional spread to a high-credit-quality floating-rate payer. For a discussion on pricing swap default risk, see E. H. Sorensen and T. F. Bollier, "Pricing Swap Default Risk," *Financial Analyst's Journal,* May–June 1994, pp. 23–33.

[21] See also A. Saunders and L. Allen, *Credit Risk Measurement, New Approaches to Value at Risk and Other Paradigms,* 2nd ed. (New York: John Wiley & Sons, 2002), Chapters 14 and 15; and C. Finger, "Credit Derivatives in Credit Metrics," *The Financier,* Winter 1999, pp. 18–27.

Netting and Swaps

One factor that mitigates the credit risk on swaps is the netting of swap payments. On each swap payment date, a fixed payment is made by one party and a floating payment is made by the other. However, in general, each party calculates the net difference between the two payments, and a single payment for the net difference is made by one party to the other. This netting of payments implies that the default exposure of the in-the-money party is limited to the net payment rather than either the total fixed or floating payment. Further, when two parties have large numbers of contracts outstanding against each other, they tend to net across contracts. This process, called *netting by novation*—often formalized through a master netting agreement—further reduces the potential risk of loss if some contracts are in the money and other are out of the money to the same counterparty.[22] However, note that netting by novation has not been fully tested in all international courts of law. For example, in the 1990s a number of U.K. municipal authorities engaged in swaps with U.S. and U.K. banks and investment banks. These municipal authorities, after taking major losses on some swap contracts, defaulted on further payments. The U.K. High Court supported the municipal authorities' right to default by stating that their entering into such swaps had been outside their powers of authority in the first place. This still did not stop these municipal authorities from seeking to collect on in-the-money swaps.

Payment Flows Are Interest and Not Principal

While currency swaps involve swaps of interest and principal, interest rate swaps involve swaps of interest payments only measured against some notional principal value. This suggests that the default risk on such swaps is less than that on a regular loan, where both interest and principal are exposed to credit risk.

Standby Letters of Credit

In cases where swaps are made between parties of different credit standing, such that one party perceives a significant risk of default by the other party, the poor-quality credit risk party may be required to buy a standby letter of credit (or another form of performance guaranty) from a third-party high-quality (AA) FI such that if default occurs, the standby letter of credit will provide the swap payments in lieu of the defaulting party. Further, low-quality counterparties are increasingly required to post collateral in lieu of default. This collateral is an incentive mechanism working to deter swap defaults.[23]

Concept Questions

1. What is the link between preserving "customer relationships" and credit derivatives such as total return swaps?
2. Is there any difference between a digital default option (see Chapter 24) and a pure credit swap?
3. Are swaps as risky as equivalent-sized loans?

---

[22] In January 1995, FASB Interpretation No. 39 (FIN 39) established the right of setoff under a master netting agreement. Also, since 1995, the BIS has allowed banks to use bilateral netting of swap contracts in calculating their risk-based capital requirements (see Chapter 20). It is estimated that this reduces banks' capital requirements against swaps by up to 40 percent. See also D. Hendricks, "Netting Agreements and the Credit Exposures of OTC Derivatives Portfolios," Federal Reserve Bank of New York, *Quarterly Review,* Spring 1994.

[23] One solution being considered by market participants (such as the International Association of Swap Dealers) is to use collateral to mark to market a swap contract in a way similar to that in which futures are marked to market to prevent credit risk building up over time. Remember, a swap contract is like a succession of forwards. A survey by Arthur Andersen showed that approximately US$6.9 billion was posted as collateral against a net replacement value of US$77.9 billion of swaps. (See "A Question of Collateral," *Euromoney,* November 1995, pp. 46–49.)

Summary

This chapter evaluated the role of swaps as risk-management vehicles for FIs. We analyzed the major types of swaps: interest rate and currency swaps as well as credit swaps. Swaps have special features of long maturity, flexibility, and liquidity that make them attractive alternatives relative to shorter-term hedging vehicles such as the futures, forwards, options, and caps discussed in Chapters 23 and 24. However, even though the credit risk of swaps is less than that of loans, because of their OTC nature and long maturities, their credit risk is still generally greater than that for other OTC derivative instruments such as floors and caps. Also, the credit risk on swaps compares unfavourably with that on exchange-traded futures and options, whose credit risk is approximately zero.

Questions and Problems

1. Explain the similarity between a swap and a forward contract.

2. Forwards, futures, and options contracts had been used by FIs to hedge risk for many years before swaps were invented. If FIs already had these hedging instruments, why did they need swaps?

3. Distinguish between a swap buyer and a swap seller. In which markets does each have the comparative advantage?

4. An insurance company owns $50 million of floating-rate bonds yielding LIBOR plus 1 percent. These loans are financed by $50 million of fixed-rate guaranteed investment contracts (GICs) costing 10 percent. A finance company has $50 million of auto loans with a fixed rate of 14 percent. The loans are financed by $50 million in CDs at a variable rate of LIBOR plus 4 percent.
   a. What is the risk exposure of the insurance company?
   b. What is the risk exposure of the finance company?
   c. What would be the cash flow goals of each company if they were to enter into a swap arrangement?
   d. Which company would be the buyer and which company would be the seller in the swap?
   e. Diagram the direction of the relevant cash flows for the swap arrangement.
   f. What are reasonable cash flow amounts, or relative interest rates, for each of the payment streams?

5. In a swap arrangement, the variable-rate swap cash flow streams often do not fully hedge the variable-rate cash flow streams from the balance sheet due to basis risk.
   a. What are the possible sources of basis risk in an interest rate swap?
   b. How could the failure to achieve a perfect hedge be realized by the swap buyer?
   c. How could the failure to achieve a perfect hedge be realized by the swap seller?

6. A bank has $200 million of floating-rate loans yielding the T-bill rate plus 2 percent. These loans are financed by $200 million of fixed-rate deposits costing 9 percent. A credit union has $200 million of mortgages with a fixed rate of 13 percent. They are financed by $200 million in CDs with a variable rate of the T-bill rate plus 3 percent.
   a. Discuss the type of interest rate risk each FI faces.
   b. Propose a swap that would result in each FI having the same type of asset and liability cash flows.
   c. Show that this swap would be acceptable to both parties.
   d. What are some of the practical difficulties in arranging this swap?

7. Bank 1 can issue five-year CDs at an annual rate of 11 percent fixed or at a variable rate of LIBOR plus 2 percent. Bank 2 can issue five-year CDs at an annual rate of 13 percent fixed or at a variable rate of LIBOR plus 3 percent.
   a. Is a mutually beneficial swap possible between the two banks?
   b. Where is the comparative advantage of the two banks?
   c. What is the net quality spread?
   d. What is an example of a feasible swap?

8. First Bank can issue one-year floating-rate CDs at prime plus 1 percent or fixed-rate CDs at 12.5 percent. Second Bank can issue one-year floating-rate CDs at prime plus 0.5 percent or fixed-rate CDs at 11 percent.
   a. What is a feasible swap with all the benefits going to First Bank?
   b. What is a feasible swap with all the benefits going to Second Bank?
   c. Diagram each situation.
   d. What factors will determine the final swap arrangement?

9. Two multinational corporations enter their respective debt markets to issue $100 million of two-year notes. Firm A can borrow at a fixed annual rate of 11 percent or a floating rate of LIBOR plus 50 basis points, repriced at the end of the year. Firm B can borrow at a fixed annual rate of 10 percent or a floating rate of LIBOR, repriced at the end of the year.

   a. If firm A is a positive duration gap insurance company and firm B is a money market mutual fund, in what market(s) should each firm borrow to reduce its interest rate risk exposure?

   b. In which debt market does firm A have a comparative advantage over firm B?

   c. Although firm A is riskier than firm B and therefore must pay a higher rate in both the fixed-rate and floating-rate markets, there are possible gains to trade. Set up a swap to exploit firm A's comparative advantage over firm B. What are the total gains from the swap trade? Assume a swap intermediary fee of 10 basis points.

   d. The gains from the swap trade can be apportioned between firm A and firm B through negotiation. What terms of trade would give all the gains to firm A? What terms of trade would give all the gains to firm B?

   e. Assume swap pricing that allocates all the gains from the swap to firm A. If A buys the swap from B and pays the swap intermediary's fee, what are the end-of-year net cash flows if LIBOR is 8.25 percent?

   f. If A buys the swap in part (e) from B and pays the swap intermediary's fee, what are the end-of-year net cash flows if LIBOR is 11 percent? Be sure to net swap payments against cash market payments for both firms.

   g. If all barriers to entry and pricing inefficiencies between firm A's debt markets and firm B's debt markets were eliminated, how would that affect the swap transaction?

10. What are off-market swap arrangements? How are these arrangements negotiated?

11. Describe how an inverse floater works to the advantage of an investor who receives coupon payments of 10 percent minus LIBOR if LIBOR is currently at 4 percent. When is it a disadvantage to the investor? Does the issuing party bear any risk?

12. An FI has $500 million of assets with a duration of nine years and $450 million of liabilities with a duration of three years. The FI wants to hedge its duration gap with a swap that has fixed-rate payments with a duration of six years and floating-rate payments with a duration of two years. What is the

optimal amount of the swap to effectively macro-hedge against the adverse effect of a change in interest rates on the value of the FI's equity?

13. A Swiss bank issues a $100 million, three-year Eurodollar CD at a fixed annual rate of 7 percent. The proceeds of the CD are lent to a Swiss company for three years at a fixed rate of 9 percent. The spot exchange rate is Sf1.50/$.

   a. Is this expected to be a profitable transaction?

   b. What are the cash flows if exchange rates are unchanged over the next three years?

   c. What is the risk exposure of the bank's underlying cash position?

   d. How can the Swiss bank reduce that risk exposure?

   e. If the dollar is expected to appreciate against the Sf to Sf1.65/$, Sf1.815/$, and Sf2.00/$ over the next three years, what will be the cash flows on this transaction?

   f. If the Swiss bank swaps $ payments for Sf payments at the current spot exchange rate, what are the cash flows on the swap? What are the cash flows on the entire hedged position? Assume that the $ appreciates at the rates in part (e).

   g. What are the cash flows on the swap and the hedged position if actual spot exchange rates are as follows:

   End of year 1: Sf1.55/$

   End of year 2: Sf1.47/$

   End of year 3: Sf1.48/$

   h. What would be the bank's risk exposure if the fixed-rate Swiss loan was financed with a floating-rate $100 million, three-year Eurodollar CD?

   i. What type(s) of hedge is appropriate if the Swiss bank in part (h) wants to reduce its risk exposure?

   j. If the annual Eurodollar CD rate is set at LIBOR and LIBOR at the end of years 1, 2, and 3 is expected to be 7 percent, 8 percent, and 9 percent, respectively, what will be the cash flows on the bank's unhedged cash position? Assume no change in exchange rates.

   k. What are the cash flows on the bank's unhedged cash position if exchange rates are as follows:

   End of year 1: Sf1.55/$

   End of year 2: Sf1.47/$

   End of year 3: Sf1.48/$

   l. What are both the swap and the total hedged position cash flows if the bank swaps out its floating rate $ CD payments in exchange for 7.75 percent fixed-rate Sf payments at the current spot exchange rate of Sf1.50/$?

m. Use the following spot rates for par value coupon bonds to forecast expected future spot rates. (*Hint:* Forecast expected future spot rates using implied forward rates.)

One-year 7.0 percent
Two-year 8.5 percent
Three-year 9.2 percent

n. Use the rate forecasts in part (m) to calculate the cash flows on an 8.75 percent fixed-floating rate swap of dollars to Swiss francs at Sf1.50/$.

14. Use the following balance sheet information (in millions) to construct a swap hedge against interest rate risk exposure.

Assets	
Rate-sensitive assets	$ 50
Fixed-rate assets	150
Total assets	$200
Liabilities and Equity	
Rate-sensitive liabilities	$ 75
Fixed-rate liabilities	100
Net worth	25
Total liabilities and equity	$200

Rate-sensitive assets are repriced quarterly at the 91-day Treasury bill rate plus 150 basis points. Fixed-rate assets have five years until maturity and are paying 9 percent annually. Rate-sensitive liabilities are repriced quarterly at the 91-day Treasury bill rate plus 100 basis points. Fixed-rate liabilities have two years until maturity and are paying 7 percent annually. Currently, the 91-day Treasury bill rate is 6.25 percent.

a. What is the bank's current net interest income? If Treasury bill rates increase 150 basis points, what will be the change in the bank's net interest income?

b. What is the bank's repricing or funding gap? Use the repricing model to calculate the change in the bank's net interest income if interest rates increase 150 basis points.

c. How can swaps be used as an interest rate hedge in this example?

15. Use the following information to construct a swap of asset cash flows for the bank in problem 14. The bank is a price taker in both the fixed-rate market at 9 percent and the rate-sensitive market at the T-bill rate plus 1.5 percent. A securities dealer has a large portfolio of rate sensitive assets funded with fixed rate liabilities. The dealer is a price taker in a fixed-rate asset market paying 8.5 percent and a floating-rate asset market paying the 91-day T-bill rate plus 1.25 percent. All interest is paid annually.

a. What is the interest rate risk exposure to the securities dealer?

b. How can the bank and the securities dealer use a swap to hedge their respective interest rate risk exposures?

c. What are the total potential gains to the swap trade?

d. Consider the following two-year swap of asset cash flows: An annual fixed-rate asset cash flow of 8.6 percent in exchange for a floating-rate asset cash flow of T-bill plus 125 basis points. The total swap intermediary fee is 5 basis points. How are the swap gains apportioned between the bank and the securities dealer if they each hedge their interest rate risk exposures using this swap?

e. What are the swap net cash flows if T-bill rates at the end of the first year are 7.75 percent and at the end of the second year 5.5 percent? Assume that the notional value is $107.14 million.

f. What are the sources of the swap gains to trade?

g. What are the implications for the efficiency of cash markets?

16. Consider the following currency swap of coupon interest on the following assets:

5 percent (annual coupon) fixed-rate $1 million bond

5 percent (annual coupon) fixed-rate bond denominated in Swiss francs (Sf)

Spot exchange rates: Sf1.5/$

a. What is the face value of the Sf bond if the investments are equivalent at spot rates?

b. What are the end-of-year cash flows, assuming no change in spot exchange rates? What are the net cash flows on the swap?

c. What are the cash flows if spot exchange rates fall to Sf0.50/$? What are the net cash flows on the swap?

d. What are the cash flows if spot exchange rates rise to Sf 2.25/$? What are the net cash flows on the swap?

e. Describe the underlying cash position that would prompt the FI to hedge by swapping dollars for Swiss Francs.

17. Consider the following fixed–floating rate currency swap of assets: 5 percent (annual coupon) fixed-rate $1 million bond and floating-rate Sf1.5 million bond set at LIBOR annually. Currently LIBOR is 4 percent. The face value of the swap is Sf1.5 million. Spot exchange rate: Sf1.5/$.

a. What are the end-of-year cash flows assuming no change in the spot exchange rate? What are the net cash flows on the swap at the spot exchange rate?

b. If the 1-year forward rate is Sf1.538 per $, what are the end-of-year net cash flows on the swap? Assume LIBOR is unchanged.

c. If LIBOR increases to 6 percent, what are the end-of-year net cash flows on the swap? Evaluate at the forward rate.

18. What is a total return swap?

19. Give two reasons why credit swaps have been the fastest growing form of swaps in recent years.

20. How does a pure credit swap differ from a total return swap? How does it differ from a digital default option?

21. Why is the credit risk on a swap lower than the credit risk on a loan?

22. What is netting by novation?

23. A Canadian FI has most of its assets in the form of Swiss franc–denominated floating-rate loans. Its liabilities consist mostly of fixed-rate dollar-denominated CDs. What type of currency risk and interest rate risk does this FI face? How might it use a swap to eliminate some of those risks?

The following, problem refers to material in Appendix 25A.

24. The following information is available on a three-year swap contract. One-year maturity notes are currently priced at par and pay a coupon rate of 5 percent annually. Two-year maturity notes are currently priced at par and pay a coupon rate of 5.5 percent annually. Three-year maturity notes are currently priced at par and pay a coupon rate of 5.75 percent annually. The terms of a three-year swap of $100 million notional value are 5.45 percent annual fixed-rate payments in exchange for floating-rate payments tied to the annual discount yield.

a. If an insurance company buys this swap, what can you conclude about the interest rate risk exposure of the company's underlying cash position?

b. What are the end-of-year cash flows expected over the three-year life of the swap? (*Hint*: Be sure to convert par value coupon yields to discount yields and then solve for the implied forward rates.)

c. What are end-of-year actual cash flows that occur over the three-year life of the swap if $d_2 = 4.95$ percent and $d_3 = 6.1$ percent (where d_i are discount yields)?

Appendix 25A Pricing an Interest Rate Swap

View Appendix 25A on page 724 of this book.

Credit Risk Management Techniques: Loan Sales

In this chapter, we consider the growing role of loan sales in managing credit risk and:

▸ provide an overview of the loan sales market

▸ define and look at types of loan sales

▸ summarize who are the buyers and sellers of loans

▸ discuss why banks and other FIs would sell loans

▸ evaluate the factors that deter and encourage loan sales, and

▸ conclude with a review of the purchase and sale of foreign loans

INTRODUCTION

Traditionally, banks and other FIs have relied on a number of contractual mechanisms to control the credit risks of lending. These have included (1) requiring higher interest rate spreads and fees on loans to more risky borrowers, (2) restricting or rationing loans to more risky borrowers, (3) requiring enhanced seniority (collateral) for the bank over the assets of risky borrowers, (4) diversifying across different types of risky borrowers, and (5) placing more restrictive covenants on risky borrowers' actions, such as restrictions on the use of proceeds from asset sales, new debt issues, and dividend payments. These traditional mechanisms for controlling or managing credit risk were described in Chapters 11 and 12.

Additionally, in Chapters 23 through 25 we discussed the increasing use of credit derivatives in the forward, options, and swaps markets to manage credit risk—for example, the use of digital put options to control the credit risk of an individual loan or portfolio of loans. In addition, FIs are increasingly requiring borrowers to hedge their own risks, especially when the FI makes floating-rate loans to borrowers. When interest rates rise, the borrower of a floating-rate loan may have greater difficulty meeting interest rate payments. However, if the borrower has hedged the risk of rising rates in the derivatives market (e.g., by selling interest rate futures or receiving floating payments—paying fixed payments in an interest rate swap), the borrower is in a far better position to meet its contractual payments to the FI. As a result, the credit risk exposure of the FI is reduced.[1]

This and the following chapter on securitization describe the growing role of loan sales and other newer types of techniques (such as the good bank-bad bank structure) increasingly used by FI managers to control credit risk. Although loan sales have been in existence for many years, the use of loan sales (by removing existing loans from the balance sheet) is increasingly being recognized as a valuable additional tool in an FI manager's portfolio of credit risk management techniques (see the Industry Perspectives box).

---

[1] In addition, the floating-rate loans may enable the FI to better hedge its own duration gap exposure.

Industry Perspectives

SUDDENLY, BANKS ARE ACTING A LOT LIKE BOND MARKETS

When numerous companies suddenly found investors unwilling to buy their debt this year, amid a rocky economy and accounting scandals, many turned to their lenders of last resort, their banks. They discovered banking has changed a lot. And some discovered that loans cost them a good deal more. Banks traditionally have been the institutions that take a long-term view of a company's prospects, management and ability to repay a debt. By contrast, the fast-paced, fickle bond market can change its mind in an instant about a company's creditworthiness and how much to charge. But many borrowers are finding that banks' loan business had come to look a lot like the markets. . . .

Scarred by their early-1990s experience, they often don't hold onto loans, especially those to lower quality companies. Increasingly, banks sell pieces of their loans to other banks, to specialized investment funds, insurance companies or to other institutional investors. As a result, the loans are subject to all the pricing and other tactics of the markets. And the banks are acting less like lenders and more like middlemen between borrowers and investors.

Although this shift means painfully high interest rates for some, it has benefits to the overall economy in making credit available. Even if a bank considers a particular borrower too risky, it can usually find someone willing to share the risk. And the capital mar-

kets help it find out what interest rate is needed to compensate for the risk. "The actual creditworthiness of borrowers had come down," Fed Chairman Alan Greenspan observed earlier this year. "There has, however, been no evidence of anything remotely resembling the credit crunch that we had a decade ago, where you just could not get a loan out of a commercial bank no matter what your creditworthiness was, at least in some cases." . . .

Bank loans and pieces of them now change hands in an increasingly active secondary market. Its daily turnover of about $500 million is puny next to the stock and bond markets but up 15-fold from a decade earlier, according to Credit Suisse First Boston. When a company sets out to borrow now, its lenders can see how this secondary market is valuing its old loans, and adjust terms of this new borrowing accordingly. Initially, many companies weren't happy that banks were selling off their loans. "Today everyone accepts that if you want a noninvestment-grade loan, it's very similar to a bond deal," says Scott Page, co-manager of senior debt portfolios at Eaton Vance Management in Boston. "You're not doing a handshake deal on the golf course with a handful of banks. But ultimately you have a more reliable source of capital." . . .

Source: Greg Ip, *The Wall Street Journal*, September 17, 2002, p. A1. www.wsj.com

LOAN SALES

correspondent banking
A relationship entered into between a small bank and a big bank in which the big bank provides a number of deposit, lending, and other services.

project finance loan
A loan made to a single purpose entity where principal and interest are paid from the cash flows of the project.

Banks and other FIs have sold loans among themselves for over 100 years. In fact, a large part of **correspondent banking** involves small banks making loans that are too big for them to hold on their balance sheets—for lending concentration, risk, or capital adequacy reasons—and selling parts of these loans to large banks with whom they have a long-term deposit-lending correspondent relationship. In turn, the large banks often sell parts of their loans called *participations* to smaller banks. Even though this market has existed for many years, it grew slowly until the early 1980s, when it entered a period of spectacular growth, largely due to expansion in **project finance loans** as well as **highly leveraged transaction (HLT) loans** to finance leveraged buyouts (LBOs) and mergers and acquisitions (M&As). Specifically, the volume of loans sold by North American banks grew from less than US$20 billion in 1980 to US$285 billion in 1989. Between 1990 and 1994 the volume of loan sales fell almost equally dramatically, along with the decline in LBOs and M&As as a result of the credit crunch associated with the 1990–91 recession. In 1994, the volume of loan sales had fallen to approximately US$20 billion.

FIGURE 26–1
Recent Trends in the Loan Sales Market, Secondary loan volume, (1994–3Q2003)

Source: Loan Pricing Corporation Web site, April 2004. www.loanpricing.com

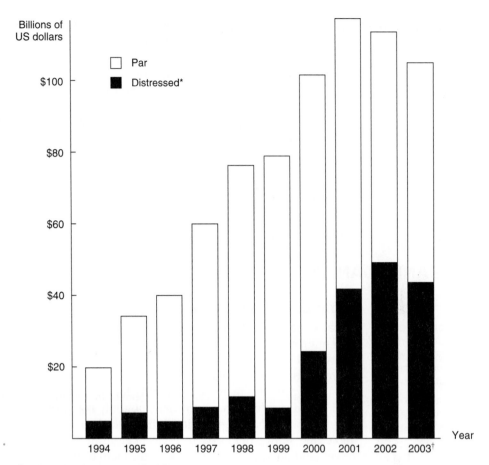

*Trading at less than 90 cents on the dollar.
†As of September.

highly leveraged transaction (HLT) loan
A loan made to finance a merger and acquisition: a leveraged buyout results in a high leverage ratio for the borrower.

In the late 1990s, the volume of loan sales expanded again, partly due to an expanding economy and a resurgence in M&As. For example, the loan market research firm, Loan Pricing Corporation, reported secondary trading volume in 1999 was more than US$79 billion. Loan sales continued to grow to almost US$120 billion in the early 2000s as FIs sold distressed loans (loans trading below 90 cents on the dollar). Triggered by an economic slowdown, distressed loan sales jumped from 11 percent of total loan sales in 1999 to 35 percent in 2001, and 42 percent in 2002. As the U.S. economy improved in 2003, the percent of distressed loan sales fell to 40 percent. Figure 26–1 shows the growth in loan sales over the 1994–2003 (third quarter) period.

Many of these loans are syndicated, involving many sponsoring banks. For example, in 2003 the Loan Pricing Corporation reported that J. P. Morgan Chase was the leading loan syndicator in the worldwide secondary loan market sponsoring 620 deals worth US$567 billion. Yet J. P. Morgan Chase retained risk for only US$283 billion of these loans. Along with J. P. Morgan Chase, Citigroup (US$496 billion), Bank of America (US$292 billion), Barclays Bank (US$263 billion), and HSBC (US$242 billion) were the top five secondary-market loan syndicators in 2003.

The Canadian debt market, dominated by the top five banks, plays a very small role in loan sales in North America. Recent figures estimate that $100 million (Canadian) bad debt loans were sold in 2000 and only $300 to $400 million were

www.cibc.com

www.scotiabank.com

forecast to be sold in 2005. In 2001, Canadian Imperial Bank of Commerce (CIBC) sold $848 million in U.S. corporate loans to Ark II LLC, a U.S. based firm, in order to reduce its exposure to credit risk. More recently, Bank of Nova Scotia (BNS) sold some of its US$825 million bridge financing to Masonite to U.S. hedge funds. However, when loan defaults are low and banks have sufficient capital, there is little need for a bank to sell its loans. The major Canadian banks consider loan sales to be a credit management technique and part of their risk management strategy. U.S. companies such as Allied Interstate Inc., Cerberus Capital Management LP (who purchased Air Canada debt during their restructuring in 2003), Portfolio Management Canada Inc., and Portfolio Recovery Associates operate in Canada, but concerns about privacy issues related to the U.S. Patriot Act and banks' concerns about their reputation appear to have so far limited sales of loans extended to Canadian customers to U.S. buyers. However, Basel II may provide an opportunity for loan sales as global banks re-adjust their capital levels (Chapter 20).[2]

THE BANK LOAN SALES MARKET

Definition of a Loan Sale

bank loan sale
Sale of a loan originated by an FI with or without recourse to an outside buyer.

A **bank loan sale** occurs when an FI originates a loan and sells it either with or without recourse to an outside buyer. Many loan agreements contain a clause that allows an FI to sell the loan to another buyer, sometimes without having to notify the borrower of the sale. This facilitates the legal transfer of ownership of the financial asset, and provides increased flexibility for an FI to adjust its balance sheet.

If a loan is sold without recourse, not only is it removed from the FI's balance sheet but the FI has no explicit liability if the loan eventually goes bad. Panel A of Table 26–1 shows an FI's balance sheet before and after a $20 million loan sale. The buyer (and not the FI that originated the loan) bears all the credit risk. If, however, the loan is sold with **recourse**, under certain conditions the buyer can put the loan back to the selling FI; therefore, the FI retains a contingent credit risk liability. Panel B of Table 26–1 shows the FI's balance sheet, including the contingent liability from the loan sale held off the balance sheet. In practice, most loans are sold without recourse because a loan sale is technically removed from the balance sheet only when the buyer has no future credit risk claim on the FI. Importantly, loan sales involve no creation of new types of securities such as the pass-throughs, CMOs, and MBSs described in Chapter 27. As such, loan sales are a primitive form of securitization in that loan selling creates a secondary market for loans in which ownership of the loan is simply transferred to the loan buyer.

recourse
The ability of a loan buyer to sell the loan back to the originator if it goes bad.

Types of Loan Sales

The loan sales market has three segments: two involve the sale and trading of domestic loans, while the third involves emerging-market loan sales and trading. Since we fully described emerging-market loan sales in Chapter 16 on sovereign risk, we concentrate on the North American loan sales market here.

---

[2] For a discussion of bad debt sales in Canada, see D. Waggoner, "Buyers Bank on Canada's Debt," *Collections and Credit Risk*, June 2005, 10, 6, pp. 46, 48 & 50. See also Canada NewsWire, Ottawa, "CIBC completes sale of $848 million in corporate loans," October 30, 2001, p. 1 and K. Tully, "Private equity takes the supersize option," *Euromoney*, May 2005, p. 1. K. Kalawsky's article, "Investor eager to take banks' shaky loans: Recovery Partners," *National Post*, January 14, 2005, pp. IN1–IN2, suggests that the implementation of Basel II could cause North American and European banks to sell off as much as US$1 trillion in loans.

TABLE 26–1   FI Balance Sheet before and after a $20 Million Loan Sale (in millions)

Panel A Loan Sale without Recourse

	Before Loan Sale			After Loan Sale			
Assets		**Liabilities/Equity**		**Assets**		**Liabilities/Equity**	
Cash assets	$ 10	Deposit	$ 90	Cash assets	$ 10	Deposits	$ 90
				Loans	70		
Loans	90	Equity	10	New investments	20	Equity	10
	$100		$100		$100		$100

Panel B Loan Sale with Recourse

	Before Loan Sale			After Loan Sale			
Assets		**Liabilities/Equity**		**Assets**		**Liabilities/Equity**	
Cash assets	$ 10	Deposit	$ 90	Cash assets	$ 10	Deposits	$ 90
				Loans	70		
Loans	90	Equity	10	New investments	20	Equity	10
	$100		$100		$100		$100
				Off balance sheet: Loan sale (contingent liability)			$20

Traditional Short Term

In the traditional short-term segment of the market, FIs sell loans with short maturities, often one to three months. This market has characteristics similar to those of the market for commercial paper issued by corporations in that loan sales have similar maturities and issue size. Loan sales, however, usually have yields that are 1 to 10 basis points above those of commercial paper of a similar rating. In particular, the loan sales market in which an FI originates and sells a short-term loan of a corporation is a close substitute for the issuance of commercial paper The key characteristics of the short-term loan sales market are

Secured by assets of the borrowing firm.

Made to investment grade borrowers or better.

Issued for a short term (90 days or less).

Has yields closely tied to the commercial paper rate.

Sold in units of $1 million and up.

Until 1984 and the emergence of the HLT and emerging market loan markets, traditional short-term loan sales dominated the loan sales market. The growth of the commercial paper market, as well as the increased ability of banks to underwrite commercial paper (see Chapter 21), also has reduced the importance of this market segment.

HLT Loan Sales

With the growth in M&As and LBOs via highly leveraged transactions (HLTs), especially during the period 1985–89, a new segment in the loan sales market appeared. One measure of the increase in HLTs is that between January 1987 and September 1994, **www.loanpricing. com** the Loan Pricing Corporation reported 4,122 M&A deals with a combined dollar amount of new-issue HLT loans estimated at US$593.5 billion.

What constitutes an HLT loan has often caused dispute. However, in October 1989 the three U.S. federal bank regulators adopted a definition of an HLT loan as one that (1) involves a buyout, acquisition, or recapitalization and (2) doubles the company's liabilities and results in a leverage ratio higher than 50 percent, results in a leverage ratio higher than 75 percent, or is designated as an HLT by a syndication agent. HLT loans mainly differ according to whether they are nondistressed (bid price exceeds 90 cents per $1 of loans) or distressed (bid price is less than 90 cents per $1 of loans or the borrower is in default).[3]

Virtually all HLT loans have the following characteristics:

They are term loans (TLs).

They are secured by assets of the borrowing firm (usually given senior secured status).

They have a long maturity (often three- to six-year maturities).

They have floating rates tied to LIBOR, the prime rate, or a CD rate (normally 200 to 275 basis points above these rates).

They have strong covenant protection.

Nevertheless, HLTs tend to be quite heterogeneous with respect to the size of the issue, the interest payment date, interest indexing, and prepayment features. After origination, some HLT borrowers, such as Macy's and El Paso Electric, suffered periods of **financial distress.** As a result, a distinction is usually made between the markets for distressed and nondistressed HLTs.

Approximately 100 banks and securities firms make a market in this debt either as brokers or (less commonly) as broker-dealers, including Bear Stearns, CIBC, Prudential Securities, and Goldman Sachs. Most of these FIs view trading in this debt as similar to trading in junk bonds.[4]

financial distress
A period when a borrower is unable to meet a payment obligation to lenders and other creditors.

Types of Loan Sales Contracts

There are two basic types of loan sale contracts or mechanisms by which loans can be transferred between seller and buyer: participations and assignments. Currently, assignments comprise the bulk of loan sales trading.

Participations

participation in a loan
Buying a share in a loan syndication with limited, contractual control and rights over the borrower.

The unique features of **participations in loans** are

- The holder (buyer) is not a party to the underlying credit agreement so that the initial contract between loan seller and borrower remains in place after the sale.
- The loan buyer can exercise only partial control over changes in the loan contract's terms. The holder can only vote on material changes to the loan contract, such as the interest rate or collateral backing.

---

[3] See Walter J. Blumenthal, "Loan Trading: A New Business Opportunity for Your Bank," *Commercial Lending Review,* Winter 1997–1998, pp. 26–31.

[4] In a study comparing the determinants of the yield spreads on HLT loans versus those on high-yield (junk) bonds, it was found that the spreads on HLT loans behaved more like investment grade bonds than like high-yield bonds. A possible reason for this is that HLT loans tend to be more senior in bankruptcy and to have greater collateral backing than do high-yield bonds. See L. Angbazo, Jianping Mei, and Anthony Saunders, "Credit Spreads in the Market for Highly Leveraged Transaction Loans," *Journal of Banking and Finance* 22 (1998), pp. 1249–82. Also, E. Altman, A. Gande, and A. Saunders, in "Informational Efficiency of Loans versus Bonds: Evidence from Secondary Market Prices," Working Paper, Department of Finance, New York University, 2004, find that the correlations among loan and bond prices of the same company are generally quite low, except in periods approaching distress.

The economic implication of these features is that the buyer of the loan participation has a double risk exposure: a risk exposure to the borrower and a risk exposure to the loan selling FI. Specifically, if the selling FI fails, the loan participation bought by an outside party may be characterized as an unsecured obligation of the FI rather than as a true sale if there are grounds for believing that some explicit or implicit recourse existed between the loan seller and the loan buyer. Alternatively, the borrower's claims against a failed selling FI may be set off against its loans from that FI, reducing the amount of loans outstanding and adversely impacting the buyer of a participation in those loans. As a result of these exposures, the buyer bears a double monitoring cost as well.

Assignments

Because of the monitoring costs and risks involved in participations, loans are sold on an assignment basis in more than 90 percent of the cases on the North American market. The key features of an **assignment** are

assignment
Buying a share in a loan syndication with some contractual control and rights over the borrower.

- All rights are transferred on sale, meaning the loan buyer now holds a direct claim on the borrower.

- Transfer is normally associated with proof that a change of ownership has occurred.

Although ownership rights are generally much clearer in a loan sale by assignment, frequently contractual terms limit the seller's scope regarding to whom the loan can be sold. In particular, the loan contract may require either the FI agent or the borrower to agree to the sale. The loan contract may also restrict the sale to a certain class of institutions, such as those that meet certain net worth/net asset size conditions. (An *FI agent* is an FI that distributes interest and principal payments to lenders in loan syndications with multiple lenders.)

Currently, the trend appears to be toward loan contracts being originated with very limited assignment restrictions. This is true in both the North American domestic and the emerging-market loan sales markets. The most tradable loans are those that can be assigned without buyer restrictions. Even so, one has to distinguish between floating-rate and fixed-rate assignment loans. For floating-rate loans, most loan sales by assignment occur on the loan's repricing date (which may be two or four times a year), due to complexities for the agent FI in calculating and transferring accrued interest—especially given the heterogeneous nature of floating-rate loan indexes such as LIBOR. In addition, the nonstan-

accrued interest
The loan seller's claim to part of the next interest payment on the loan.

dardization of **accrued interest** payments in fixed-rate loan assignments (trade date, assignment date, coupon payment date) adds complexity and friction to this market. Moreover, while the FI agent may have a full record of the initial owners of the loans, it does not always have an up-to-date record of loan ownership changes and related transfers following trades. This means that great difficulties often occur for the borrower, FI agent, and loan buyer in ensuring that the current holder of the loan receives the interest and principal payments due. Finally, the buyer of the loan often needs to verify the original loan contract and establish the full implications of the purchase regarding the buyer's rights to collateral if the borrower defaults.

Because of these contractual problems, trading frictions, and costs, some loan sales take as long as three months to complete; reportedly, up to 50 percent eventually fail to be completed at all. In many cases, the incentive to renege on a contract arises because market prices move away from those originally agreed so that the counterparty finds reasons to delay the completion of a loan sale and/or eventually refuses to complete the transaction.[5]

The Buyers and the Sellers

The Buyers

Of the wide array of potential buyers, some are concerned with only a certain segment of the market for regulatory and strategic reasons. In particular, an increasingly specialized group of buyers of distressed HLT loans includes investment banks, hedge funds, and **vulture funds.**

vulture fund
A specialized fund that invests in distressed loans.

Investment Banks   Investment banks are predominantly buyers of HLT loans because (1) analysis of these loans utilize investment skills similar to those used in junk bond trading and (2) investment banks were often closely associated with the HLT distressed borrower in underwriting the original junk bond/HLT deals. As such, large investment banks—for example, CSFB, Merrill Lynch, and Goldman Sachs—are relatively more informed agents in this market, either by acting as market makers or in taking short-term positions on movements in the discount from par.

Vulture Funds   Vulture funds are specialized hedge funds established to invest in distressed loans, often with an agenda that may not include helping the distressed firm to survive (see Chapter 5 for a discussion of hedge funds). They include funds run by entrepreneurs such as George Soros and Sam Zell. These investments can be active, especially for those seeking to use the loans purchased for bargaining in a restructuring deal; this generates restructuring returns that strongly favour the loan purchaser. Alternatively, such loans may be held as passive investments, such as high-yield securities in a well-diversified portfolio of distressed securities. Many vulture funds are in fact managed by investment banks.

The common perception of vulture funds is that after picking up distressed loans at a discount, they force firms to restructure or are quick to realize the breakup value of the firm: turning their 50-cent-on-the-dollar investment to a fast 70-cent-on-the-dollar profit. Thus, a vulture fund's reputation is often not a congenial one. A possible reason for this adverse reputation is that while banks are looking for a return of loan principal in a restructuring, vulture funds are looking for a return on capital invested. That is, vulture funds are transaction driven, not relationship based. Unlike banks, vulture funds are far less interested in making decisions based on developing and maintaining long-term relationships with the corporation in question. Nevertheless, they provide an exit strategy for investors and creditors, and enable assets to be liquidated in an orderly manner.

For the nondistressed HLT market and the traditional loan sales market, the major buyers are other domestic or foreign banks, insurance companies and pension funds, closed-end bank loan mutual funds, and nonfinancial corporations.

Other Banks   Interbank loan sales are at the core of the traditional market and have historically revolved around correspondent banking relationships and, in the United States, regional banking/branching restrictions. Restrictions on nationwide banking have often led U.S. banks to originate regionally undiversified and borrower-undiversified loan portfolios. Small U.S. banks often sell loan participations to their large correspondents to improve regional/borrower diversification and to

---

[5] See "In Distress but Booming," *The Independent*, February 19, 1993. However, in recent years, completion of a trade within 10 days (or *T* + 10) has become an increasing convention.

www.osfi-bsif.gc.ca

avoid regulatory-imposed single-borrower loan concentration ceilings. In Canada, FIs (banks, authorized foreign banks, and trust and loan companies) regulated by the Office of the Superintendent of Financial Services (OSFI) are subject to the "Prudent Person Approach" and so must have written internal policies regarding large exposures to any one customer, country, or other FI. These FIs are limited to 25 percent of capital to any one entity and, in the normal course of business, are expected to be below this limit. Thus large loans may be originated with the intention of syndication to other banks. Foreign bank subsidiaries are limited to 100 percent of their total capital to any one entity, and so may be both buyers and sellers of loans. Foreign banks thus are able to diversify their North American loan portfolios without having a banking network in either Canada or the U.S. and so, in recent years, have purchased over 40 percent of the loans sold in the U.S. However, asset **downsizing**, particularly in Japan, has caused this source of demand for loan sales to contract.

downsizing
Shrinking the asset size of an FI.

Insurance Companies and Pension Funds   Subject to meeting liquidity and quality or investment grade regulatory restrictions, insurance companies (such as Aetna) and pension funds are important buyers of long-term maturity loans.

Closed- and Open-End Bank Loan Mutual Funds   First established in the United States in 1988, these leveraged mutual funds, such as Merrill Lynch Prime Fund, invest in domestic U.S. bank loans. Although they purchase loans on the secondary market, such as loan resales, the largest funds also have moved into primary loan syndications because of the attractive fee income available. That is, these mutual funds participate in funding loans originated by commercial banks. The mutual fund, in turn, receives a fee or part of the interest payment. Indeed, some money center banks, such as J. P. Morgan Chase, have actively encouraged closed-end fund participation in primary loan syndications.

There is no track record for this type of loan purchaser in Canada since the first bank loan mutual fund (Trimark Floating Rate Income Fund) was created by AIM Trimark in 2005. It is estimated that U.S.-based bank loan mutual funds (e.g. Eaton Vance Floating Rate, Fidelity Floating Rate Income) have total assets of US$38.5 billion.[6]

Nonfinancial Corporations   There are some corporations that buy loans, but this activity is limited mostly to the financial services arms of the very largest U.S. and European companies (e.g., GE Capital and ITT Finance) and amounts to no more than 5 percent of total U.S. domestic loan sales.[7]

The Sellers

The sellers of domestic loans and HLT loans are major banks, foreign banks, investment banks, and the U.S. government and its agencies.

Major Banks   In the United States, loan selling has been dominated by the largest money center banks. In recent years, market concentration on the loan-selling side has been accentuated by the growth of HLTs (and the important role major money center banks have played in originating loans in HLT deals) as well as the growth in real estate loan sales. In recent years, large money center banks have engaged in large (real estate) loan sales directly or have formalized such sales through the mechanism of a "good bank-bad bank" structure.

---

[6] See Luukko, Rudy, "AIM Trimark becomes pioneer of bank-loan funds in Canada," Morningstar Research Inc., February 8, 2005, www.morningstar.ca.

[7] Nonfinancial corporations are bigger buyers in the emerging-market loan sales market as part of debt-equity swaps (see Chapter 16).

TABLE 26–2   Good Bank–Bad Bank Balance Sheets before and after a Loan Sale (in millions)

Panel A: Good Bank

Before Loan Sale				After Loan Sale			
Assets		**Liabilities/Equity**		**Assets**		**Liabilities/Equity**	
Cash assets	$ 500	Deposits	$2,500	Cash assets	$ 500	Deposits	$2,500
Loans		Purchased		Loans		Purchased	
Performing	2,500	funds	750	Performing	2,500	funds	170
Nonperforming	950	Equity	700	Nonperforming	0	Equity	330
	$3,950		$3,950		$3,000		$3,000

Panel B: Bad Bank

Before Loan Sale				After Loan Sale			
Assets		**Liabilities/Equity**		**Assets**		**Liabilities/Equity**	
Cash assets	$ 600	Bonds	$300	Cash assets	$ 20	Bonds	$300
Loans	0	Preferred		Loans	580	Preferred	
		stock	100			stock	100
		Common				Common	
		stock	200			stock	200
	$ 600		$600		$600		$600

Good Bank-Bad Bank   Bad banks are special-purpose vehicles organized to liquidate portfolios of nonperforming loans. The principal objective in their creation is to maximize asset values by separating good loans (in the "good bank") from bad loans (in the "bad bank"). Past examples of bad banks include Grant Street National Bank (established by Mellon bank), National Loan Bank (established by Chemical), and National Asset Bank (established by First Interstate).[8] For example, Mellon Bank wrote down the face value of US$941 million in real estate loans and sold them to a specially created bad bank subsidiary—Grant Street National Bank—for US$577 million. This special-purpose bad bank was funded by bond issues and common and preferred stock. Managers of the bad bank were given equity (junior preferred stock) as an incentive mechanism to generate maximum values in liquidating the loans purchased from Mellon (i.e., achieving a market resale value greater than US$577 million).

Table 26–2 illustrates the sale of nonperforming loans from a good bank to a subsidiary bad bank. In panel A of Table 26–2, the good bank has $950 million of nonperforming loans along with $2,500 million in performing loans and $500 million in cash assets on its balance sheet before the loan sale. The assets are financed with $2,500 million in deposits, $750 million in purchased funds, and $700 million in equity. If the bad bank, in panel B, buys the nonperforming loans (with the proceeds of a bond, preferred stock, and common stock financing) for $580 million, the good bank gets these loans off of its balance sheet, incurring a $370 million loss in equity (i.e., $950 million face value of loans minus $580 million received in their purchase). The proceeds of the loan sale are then used to pay off purchased funds, bringing

---

[8] This technique also has been used outside the United States. For example, in 1998 the good bank-bad bank structure was adopted by the Indonesian government as a way of resolving the bad debt crisis in the domestic banking industry. In the early 2000s, this format was adopted in Japan as a way to separate nonperforming loans from other bank assets.

their balance down to $170 million, or $750 million minus $580 million. The bad bank now has the $950 million face value loans (for which it paid $580 million) on its balance sheet. These loans can be restructured or disposed of. If the loans realize more than $580 million, additional returns can be passed through to the bad bank common stockholders in dividends or used to repurchase bonds or preferred stock.

There are at least five reasons for believing that loan sales through a bad bank vehicle will be value enhancing compared to the originating bank itself retaining (and eventually selling) these loans:

1. The bad bank enables bad assets to be managed by loan workout specialists.
2. The good bank's reputation and access to deposit and funding markets tend to be improved once bad loans are removed from the balance sheet.
3. Because the bad bank does not have any short-term deposits (i.e., is a self-liquidating entity), it can follow an optimal disposition strategy for bad assets, as it is not overly concerned with liquidity needs.
4. As in the case of Mellon's bad bank, contracts for managers can be created to maximize their incentives to generate enhanced values from loan sales.
5. The good bank-bad bank structure reduces information asymmetries about the value of the good bank's assets (the so-called lemons problem), thus potentially increasing its attractiveness to risk-averse investors.

The good bank-bad bank solution is relatively new and, given the stability of the banking system, has not been employed in Canada as yet. The major banks in Canada use loan sales along with credit derivatives to manage their credit exposure. For example, Bank of Montreal reported sales of $440 million of non-performing loans in 2004, up from $288 million in 2003. In 2004, Bank of Nova Scotia sold $630 million in loans ($660 million in 2003) while CIBC sold $1.3 billion in 2004 and $493 million in 2003.

www.bmo.com
www.scotiabank.com
www.cibc.com

Foreign Banks   To the extent that foreign banks are sellers rather than buyers of loans, these loans come out of branch networks such as Japanese-owned banks in California or through their market-making activities selling loans originated in their home country in the North American loan sales markets. One of the major market makers in the North American loan sales market (especially the HLT market) is the Dutch FI, ING Bank.

Investment Banks   Investment banks, such as Bear Stearns, act as loan sellers either as part of their market-making function (selling loans they have originated) or as active traders. Again, these loan sales are generally confined to large HLT transactions.

The U.S. Government and Its Agencies.   In recent years the U.S. government and its agencies have shown an increased willingness to engage in loan sales. This has been aided by the passage of the 1996 Federal Debt Collection Improvements Act, which authorizes federal agencies to sell delinquent and defaulted loan assets. Figure 26–2 shows an advertisement by the FDIC of a sale of assets in November 2001. The Department of Housing and Urban Development also has been an increasingly large seller of mortgage loans on multifamily apartment properties. However, the largest loan sales by a government agency to date were made by the Resolution Trust Corporation (RTC). Established in 1989, and disbanded at the end of 1995, the RTC had to resolve more than 700 problem savings institutions through merger, closure, or conservatorship. With respect to the U.S. commercial and industrial loan sale market, RTC dispositions had a relatively moderate supply-side effect

www.fdic.gov
www.hud.gov

FIGURE 26–2
Loan Sale
Announcement
by the FDIC

FDIC

Special Sales Announcement - 4th Quarter Performing/Non-Performing
Loan Sale

The Dallas Field Operations Branch of the FDIC is offering for sale the following Loan Sale Pools. Loans in these packages are stratified as listed below.

Pool Number	Description	# of Loans	Book Value
1152MC	Primarily Performing SFR's	88	3,138,914
1180DJ	Non-Performing Chapter 11 Bankruptcy	1	748,556
1185CF	Performing Auto / SFR / Manufactured Housing	10	171,984
1191CW	Non-Performing / Performing Autos / Real Estate / Unsecured	10	90,774
1195RK	Charge-offs	64	177,392
SNB175RK	Non-Performing Automobile Retail Installment Contracts	35	140,798
SNB200RK	Non-Performing Manufactured Housing Contracts	14	604,788
SNB250RK	Non-Performing Real Estate Mortgages	18	1,129,402
SNB275RK	Non-Performing Consumer Loans	17	559,293
SNB415RK	Performing Automobile Retail Installment Contracts	791	2,622,463
SNB425RK	Performing Manufactured Housing Contracts	130	6,078,566

The size of these packages may change without notice

Bid Package information and package updates will be available via a secured Internet site at IntraLinks.com. If you would like access to the secured website, please fax a signed Confidentiality Agreement to 972-761-8241.
Confidentiality Agreement for 4th Quarter Loan Sale

Please make sure to include your phone number and e-mail address on the Confidentiality Agreement. This information will be required to give you access to the secured website and bid package. Hard copy Bid Packages will be available by contacting Twila Tedder (ttedder@fdic.gov) at 1-800-568-9161, Ext. 8232 or Beatrice Culley (bculley@fdic.gov) at Ext. 8228.

Interested bidders may schedule on-site due diligence, which will commence on Monday, October 22, 2001 through Friday, November 9, 2001. Due diligence will be held at the FDIC - Dallas Field Operations Branch, Pacific Place, 1910 Pacific Avenue, Dallas, Texas 75201 from 7:30 a.m. to 5:00 p.m. Monday through Friday. Access to the files will be granted by appointment only. A Confidentiality Agreement is required prior to viewing.

To schedule an appointment for due diligence please e-mail or call 1-800-568-9161 and ask for one of the following individuals: Edith Allen, ext. 2326 (eallen@fdic.gov), or Beatrice Culley, ext. 8228 (bculley@fdic.gov).

BID DEADLINE: 1:00 P.M. (CST) WEDNESDAY, NOVEMBER 14, 2001

largely because the bulk of RTC's asset sales were real estate assets (such as multifamily mortgages). The tendency of the RTC was to combine good and bad loans into loan packages and sell them at auction to bidders. For example, in an April 21, 1995, auction, it offered the highest bidder a package of 29 different commercial assets for sale—located in New Jersey, New York, and Pennsylvania— with aggregate estimated market values of US$7.5 million. Bidders had only four days to enter bids on this asset package.

Concept Questions

1. Which loans should have the highest yields: (*a*) loans sold with recourse or (*b*) loans sold without recourse?
2. Which have higher yields, junk bonds or HLT loans? Explain your answer.
3. Describe the two basic types of loan sale contracts by which loans can be transferred between seller and buyer.
4. What institutions are the major buyers in the traditional North American loan sales market? What institutions are the major sellers in this market?

WHY BANKS AND OTHER FIs SELL LOANS

The introduction to this chapter stated that one reason that FIs sell loans is to manage their credit risk better. Loan sales remove assets (and credit risk) from the balance sheet and allow an FI to achieve better asset diversification. However, other than credit risk management, there are a number of economic and regulatory reasons that encourage FIs to sell loans. These are discussed below.

Fee Income

An FI can often report any fee income earned from originating (and then selling) loans as current income, whereas interest earned on direct lending can be accrued (as income) only over time. As a result, originating and quickly selling loans can boost an FI's reported income under current accounting rules.

Capital Costs

Like reserve requirements, the capital adequacy requirements imposed on FIs are a burden as long as required capital exceeds the amount the FI believes to be privately beneficial. For tax reasons, debt is a cheaper source of funds than equity capital. Thus, FIs struggling to meet a required assets (A) to capital (K) ratio can reduce this ratio by reducing assets (A) rather than boosting capital (K) (see Chapter 20). One way to downsize or reduce A and reduce the A/K ratio is through loan sales.

Liquidity Risk

In addition to credit risk and interest rate risk, holding loans on the balance sheet can increase the overall illiquidity of an FI's assets. This illiquidity is a problem because FI liabilities tend to be highly liquid. Asset illiquidity can expose an FI to harmful liquidity squeezes whenever liability holders unexpectedly liquidate their claims. To mitigate a liquidity problem, an FI's management can sell some of its loans to outside investors. Thus, the loan sales market has created a secondary market in loans that has significantly reduced the illiquidity of FI loans held as assets on the balance sheet.

Concept Questions

1. What are some of the economic and regulatory reasons why FIs choose to sell loans?
2. How can an FI use its loans to mitigate a liquidity problem?

FACTORS DETERRING LOAN SALES GROWTH IN THE FUTURE

The loan sales market has gone through a number of up and down phases in recent years (as discussed above). However, notwithstanding the value of loan sales as a credit risk management tool, there remain a number of factors that will both spur and deter the market's growth and development in future years. We first discuss factors that may deter the market's growth.

Customer Relationship Effects

As the financial institutions industry consolidates and expands the range of financial services sold, customer relationships are likely to become even more important than they are today. To the extent that a loan customer (borrower) views the sale of its loan by its FI as an adverse statement about the customer's value to the FI,[9] loan sales can harm revenues generated by the FI as current and potential future customers take their business elsewhere.

Legal Concerns

fraudulent conveyance
When a transaction such as a sale of securities or transference of assets to a particular party is ruled illegal.

A number of legal concerns hamper the loan sale market's growth, especially for distressed HLT loans. In particular, while banks are normally secured creditors, this status may be attacked by other creditors if the firm enters bankruptcy. For example, **fraudulent conveyance** proceedings have been brought against the secured lenders to Revco, Circle K, Allied Stores, and RJR Nabisco in the United States. If such legal moves are upheld, then the sale of loans to a particular party may be found to be illegal. Such legal suits represent one of the factors that have slowed the growth of the distressed loan market. Indeed, in many of the most recent HLT sales, loan buyers have demanded a put option feature that allows them to put the loan back to the seller at the purchase price if a transaction is proved to be fraudulent under the Uniform Fraudulent Conveyance Act. Further, a second type of distressed-firm risk may result if, in the process of a loan workout, the FI lender acts more like an equity owner than an outside debtor. For example, the FI may get involved in the day-to-day running of the firm and make strategic investment and asset sales decisions. This could open up claims that the FI's loans should be treated like equity rather than secured debt. That is, the FI's loans may be subordinated in the claims priority ranking or be subject to lender liability.[10]

Concept Questions

1. What are some of the factors that are likely to deter the growth of the loan sales market in the future?
2. What are some specific U.S. legal concerns that have hampered the growth of the North American loan sales market?

FACTORS ENCOURAGING LOAN SALES GROWTH IN THE FUTURE

There are at least six factors that point to an increasing volume of loan sales in the future. These are in addition to the credit risk "hedging" value of loan sales.

BIS Capital Requirements

www.bis.org

The Bank for International Settlements (BIS) risk-based capital rules and the proposed reforms to those rules (see Chapter 20) mean that bankers will continue to have strong incentives to sell commercial loans to other FIs and investors to downsize their balance sheets and boost bank capital ratios.

Market Value Accounting

www.sec.gov
www.fasb.org

The U.S. Securities and Exchange Commission and the Financial Accounting Standards Board (FASB) have advocated the replacement of book value accounting with market value accounting for financial services firms (see Chapter 20). In addition,

---

[9] S. Dahiya, M. Puri, and A. Saunders, in "Bank Borrowers and Loan Sales: New Evidence on the Uniqueness of Bank Loans," *Journal of Business,* 2003, pp. 563–82, find that stock returns of borrowers are significantly negatively impacted in the period surrounding the announcement of a loan sale. Further, the post-loan sale period is also marked by a large incidence of bankruptcy filings by those borrowers whose loans are sold. The results support the hypothesis that news of a bank loan sale has a negative certification impact.

[10] See C. James, "When Do Banks Take Equity in Debt Restructurings," *Review of Financial Studies,* 1995, pp. 1209–34. See also "P. McGraw and G. Roberts, "Lender Liability as a Contract Alteration," *Banking and Finance Law Review,* 12(1), 1996, pp. 1–14.

capital requirements for interest rate risk and market risk have moved banks toward a market value accounting framework (see Chapter 10). The trend towards the marking to market of assets will make bank loans look more like securities and thus make them easier to sell and/or trade.

Asset Brokerage and Loan Trading

The increased emphasis of large banks as well as investment banks on trading and trading income suggests that significant attention will still be paid to those segments of the loan sales market where price volatility is high and thus potential trading profits can be made. Most HLT loans have floating rates so that their underlying values are in large part insulated from swings in the level of interest rates (unlike fixed-income securities such as government bonds). Nevertheless, the low credit quality of many of these loans and their long maturities create an enhanced potential for credit risk volatility. As a result, a short-term, three-month secured loan to a AAA-rated company is unlikely to show significant future credit risk volatility compared to an eight-year HLT loan to a distressed company. This suggests that trading in loans to below-investment-grade companies will always be attractive for FIs that use their specialized credit monitoring skills as asset traders rather than as asset transformers in participating in the market.

Credit Ratings

There is a growing trend toward the "credit rating" of loans offered for sale. Unlike bonds, a loan credit rating reflects more than the financial soundness of the underlying borrowing corporation. In particular, the value of the underlying collateral can change a loan's credit rating up to one full category above a standard bond rating.[11] As more loans are rated, their attractiveness to secondary market buyers is likely to increase.

Purchase and Sale of Foreign Bank Loans

With over US$1,200 billion in doubtful and troubled loans on their books in the early 2000s, Japanese banks present a huge potential market for the sale of distressed loans. Indeed, a number of commercial banks and investment banks have established funds to buy up some of these bad loans. For example, in 2003 Goldman Sachs announced a US$9.3 billion fund to buy troubled loans from Japan's second largest bank, SMFG. This fund represented the first transfer of a bad loan package of this size to a non-government-affiliated entity in Japan. This deal was watched closely as it provided banks with a way of removing bad loans from their balance sheets while still retaining control over the corporate restructuring process.[12]

Concept Questions

1. What are some of the factors that are likely to encourage loan sales growth in the future?

---

[11] See L. S. Alex, "How S and P Rates Commercial Loans: Implications for Bank Portfolios," *Commercial Lending Review,* Winter 1997–1998, pp. 32–37.

[12] See "SMFG Links with Goldman to Tackle Bad Loans," *Financial Times,* October 9, 2003, p. 32.

Summary

Loan sales provide a primitive alternative to the full securitization of loans through bond packages. In particular, they provide a valuable off-balance-sheet tool to an FI that wishes to manage its credit risk exposure better. The new loan sales market grew rapidly in the 1980s and allowed FIs to sell off short-term and long-term loans of both high and low credit quality. There are a number of important factors that suggest that the loan sales market will continue to grow.

Questions and Problems

1. What is the difference between loans sold with recourse and loans sold without recourse from the perspective of both sellers and buyers?

2. A bank has made a three-year $10 million loan that pays annual interest of 8 percent. The principal is due at the end of the third year.

   a. The bank is willing to sell this loan with recourse at an interest rate of 8.5 percent. What price should it receive for this loan?

   b. The bank has the option to sell this loan without recourse at a discount rate of 8.75 percent. What price should it receive for this loan?

   c. If the bank expects a 0.5 percent probability of default on this loan, is it better to sell this loan with or without recourse? It expects to receive no interest payments or principal if the loan is defaulted.

3. What are some of the key features of short-term loan sales?

4. Why are yields higher on loan sales than on commercial paper issues with similar maturity and issue size?

5. What are highly leveraged transactions? What constitutes the regulatory definition of an HLT?

6. How do the characteristics of an HLT loan differ from those of a short-term loan that is sold?

7. What is a possible reason why the spreads on HLT loans perform differently than do the spreads on junk bonds?

8. City Bank has made a 10-year, $2 million HLT loan that pays an annual interest of 10 percent. The principal is expected at maturity.

   a. What should City Bank expect to receive from the sale of this loan if the current market interest rate on loans of this risk is 12 percent?

   b. The price of loans of this risk is currently being quoted in the secondary market at bid-offer prices of 88–89 cents (on each dollar). Translate these quotes into actual prices for the above loan.

   c. Do these prices reflect a distressed or nondistressed loan? Explain.

9. What is the difference between loan participations and loan assignments?

10. What are the difficulties in completing a loan assignment?

11. Who are the buyers of loans, and why do they participate in this activity?

    a. What are vulture funds?

    b. What are three reasons why the interbank market has been shrinking?

    c. What are reasons why a small FI would be interested in participating in a loan syndication?

12. Who are the sellers of loans, and why do they participate in this activity?

    a. What is the purpose of a bad bank?

    b. What are the reasons why loan sales through a bad bank will be value enhancing?

    c. What impact has the 1996 U.S. Federal Debt Collection Improvements Act had on the loan sale market?

13. In addition to managing credit risk, what are some other reasons for the sale of loans by FIs?

14. What are factors that may deter the growth of the loan sales market in the future? Discuss.

15. An FI is planning the purchase of a $5 million loan to raise the existing average duration of its assets from 3.5 years to 5 years. It currently has total assets worth $20 million, $5 million in cash (0 duration) and $15 million in loans. All the loans are fairly priced.

    a. Assuming it uses the cash to purchase the loan, should it purchase the loan if its duration is seven years?

    b. What asset duration loans should it purchase to raise its average duration to five years?

16. In addition to hedging credit risk, what are five factors that are expected to encourage loan sales in the future? Discuss the effect of each factor.

In this chapter, we consider the growing role of securitization in improving the risk-return tradeoff for FIs and:

▸ provide an overview of the Canadian market for asset-backed securities (ABS)

▸ describe the major forms, or vehicles used for asset securitization

▸ analyze the characteristics of asset-backed securities, and

▸ discuss how the techniques are being applied to loans other than mortgages such as credit card loans, car loans, and business loans

INTRODUCTION

asset securitization
The packaging and selling of loans and other assets backed by securities.

Along with futures, forwards, options, swaps, and loan sales, **asset securitization**—the packaging and selling of loans and other assets backed by securities—is a mechanism that FIs use to hedge their interest rate exposure gaps. In addition, the process of securitization allows FI asset portfolios to become more liquid, provides an important source of fee income (with FIs acting as servicing agents for the assets sold), and helps reduce the effects of regulatory "taxes" such as capital requirements and deposit insurance premiums.

The Canadian and U.S. securitization markets have evolved differently. Thus, while mortgage-back securities have become a big market in the United States, a small amount, (just over 11 percent) of Canadian residential mortgages were securitized in 2003. In Canada, short-term commercial borrowing dominates the market led by automobile leases and loans, then credit card receivables, residential mortgages, and commercial mortgages.[1] We first discuss the market for asset-backed commercial paper and asset-backed term notes in Canada followed by a discussion of mortgage-backed securities in a North American context.

THE CANADIAN MARKET FOR ASSET-BACKED SECURITIES (ABS)

www.dbrs.com

Dominion Bond Rating Service (DBRS) assigns credit ratings for asset-backed securities in Canada, which help to determine their price and marketability. DBRS also provides an annual review of the market, which is the source for many of the Canadian statistics quoted in this section. Figure 27–1 shows the total dollar amount of ABS outstanding in Canada at year-end 2004. The amounts are divided into two types: term notes for longer maturities and asset-backed commercial paper (ABCP) for shorter maturities. As can be seen from Figure 27–1, ABCP has grown

---

[1] See C. Freedman and W. Engert, "Financial Developments in Canada: Past Trends and Future Challenges," *The Bank of Canada Review*, Summer 2003, pp. 3–16 for an analysis of the difference between the Canadian and U.S. securitization history. In addition to attributing Canadian market development to FIs who were more risk-averse, the authors cite "luck" as one of the reasons why the Canadian market had only 11 percent of Canadian residential mortgages securitized in 2003.

FIGURE 27–1
Asset-Backed
Commercial Paper
and Asset-Backed
Term Notes Out-
standing in Canada,
December 1995 to
December 2004

Source: Dominion Bond
Rating Service, 2005.
www.dbrs.com

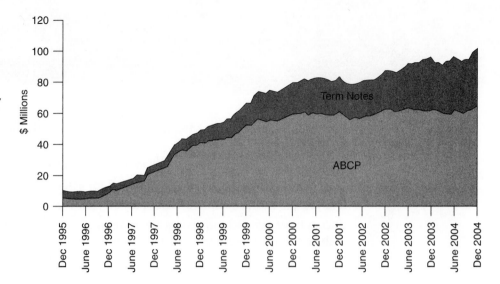

FIGURE 27–2
Asset composition
of the ABS Market
in Canada,
December 31, 2004

Source: Dominion Bond
Rating Service, 2005.
www.dbrs.com

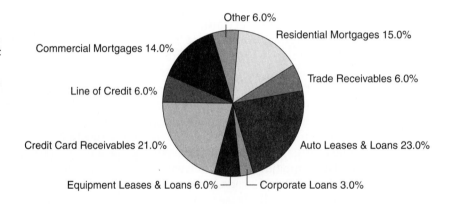

from less than $10 billion in December 1995 to $67 billion at December 31, 2004. ABCP has exceeded corporate commercial paper outstanding ($47 billion at year-end 2004) since 2001 and now represents approximately 40 percent of the total short-term paper market (bankers' acceptances, commercial paper, ABCP) in Canada.[2] Nevertheless, despite its growth over the 9-year period, the securitization market in Canada is in its infancy, reaching just $101.7 billion at the end of 2004 compared to the United States market, which has been in a growth mode since the 1980s, largely driven by residential mortgage funding. In the United States, total outstanding mortgage pools stood at US$4.3 trillion in 2003. The Canadian ABS

---

[2] For additional statistics and detailed analysis of the ABS market in Canada, see H. Loke and S. Bridges, "2004 Year-End Review of Canadian Asset-Backed Securities," March 2005, Dominion Bond Rating Service; E. Stafford, A. Fitzgerald and T. Westlake, "Historical Performance of Canadian CMBS, 1998–2004," March 2005, Dominion Bond Rating Service; J. Kiff, "Recent Developments in Markets for Credit-Risk Transfer," *Bank of Canada Financial System Review*, June 2003, pp. 33–41; and P. Toovey and J. Kiff, "Developments and Issues in the Canadian Market for Asset-Backed Commercial Paper," *Bank of Canada Financial System Review*, June 2003, pp. 43–49.

TABLE 27–1
Outstanding
Canadian Non-MBS
Asset-Backed
Securities,
December 31, 2004
(all outstandings in
millions of dollars,
investment dealers
listed alphabetically)

Source: Dominion Bond
Rating Service, 2005,
www.dbrs.com

Investment Dealer	Total Non-MBS ABS	
	Outstanding	Market Share
BMO Nesbitt Burns Inc.	21,978	21.6%
CIBC World Markets Inc.	17,676	17.4%
Merrill Lynch	5,435	5.3%
National Bank	3,982	3.9%
RBC Capital Markets	13,182	13.0%
Scotia Capital	9,042	8.9%
TD Securities	17,591	17.3%
Coventree Capital Group, Inc.	7,825	7.7%
Other	4,930	4.9%
Total	101,641	100.0%

market, on the other hand, consisted of auto leases and loans (23 percent), followed by credit card receivables (21 percent), residential mortgages (15 percent), and commercial mortgages (14 percent) in 2004 as shown in Figure 27–2.

Canadian banks have been active in securitizing their own credit card receivables as a means of managing their capital and as a source of funding. In addition, Canadian Tire Corporation formed Canadian Tire Bank and Sears Canada Inc. created Sears Canada Bank, both of which are regulated by OSFI and whose purpose is to manage these retail firms' credit card receivables via securitization vehicles. In addition, Canadian banks manage the securitizations of the trade receivables, credit cards, and mortgages of other firms via special purpose entities (SPEs) or variable interest entities (VIEs) and receive a fee to administer them. Along with residential MBS, Canadian FIs also create commercial mortgage-backed securities (CMBS).

As they develop, the North American and the global markets for securitizations are undergoing a convergence in regulations in order to increase the transparency of the deals for investors, and, through standardization of these transactions, to reduce the costs for FIs who originate these securities. As noted in Chapter 20, global regulators are concerned with credit risk transfer mechanisms and their effects on the stability of global capital markets, and Basel II addresses these risk issues. An example of cross-border harmonization of regulations is presented in the Industry Perspectives Box. The Office of the Superintendent of Financial Insti-

www.osfi-bsif.gc.ca

tution's (OSFI's) Guideline B-5 considers the differences in the Canadian and U.S. ABCP markets and in the process, makes Canadian markets more transparent and attractive to investors.

The harmonization of regulations is important for the major Canadian dealers since in addition to being the major source of ABS, mortgage- and non-mortgage-backed securities (as shown in Table 27–1), the Canadian bank-owned dealers generate additional fee income as active participants in the U.S. markets. For example, Bank

www.bmo.com

of Montreal Financial Group, which had a 29.3 percent market share of outstanding securitizations in Canada at year-end December, 2004, maintains a Securitization Group at its U.S. subsidiary, Harris Nesbitt Corp. Thus, while securitization serves as a risk-transfer technique for Canadian FIs, it is also a source of new product development and fee income.

Industry Perspectives

OSFI'S NEW GUIDELINE B-5 AND THE CANADIAN ABCP MARKET

On 23 November, the Office of the Superintendent of Financial Institutions (OSFI) published a revision to its Guideline B-5 for asset securitization transactions. Many of the changes aim to align Canada's regulatory treatment of securitization with that of other countries. The revision also clarifies a number of old B-5 provisions.

The revisions that may have the most significant impact on the Canadian financial system are those pertaining to facilities for enhancing the liquidity of asset-backed commercial paper (ABCP). They remove a major impediment to the potential growth of the Canadian ABCP market. This should impart greater efficiency to Canadian-dollar capital markets.

Because the assets that comprise the collateral are typically of longer maturity than the ABCP financing them, some sort of liquidity buffer is needed to protect against rollover risk and timing mismatches. Hence, ABCP issuance programs purchase liquidity protection. At a minimum, in the old B-5 such protection should have safeguarded against what it called a "general market disruption" (GMD), which was never defined but was interpreted by market participants to mean a situation in which "not a single dollar of corporate or asset-backed commercial paper can be placed in the market at any price."

Because Standard & Poor's and Moody's viewed Canadian liquidity enhancements as too restrictive, they have been reluctant to give their highest investment-grade ratings to Canadian ABCP. But if a Canadian bank provided less-restrictive liquidity, it would, at a minimum, incur increased regulatory capital charges that would make the ABCP less economical.

The new B-5 defines a GMD as a "disruption in the Canadian commercial paper market resulting in the inability of Canadian paper issuers, including the SPE, to issue any commercial paper, and where the inability does not result from a diminution in the creditworthiness of the SPE or any originator or from a deterioration in the performance of the assets of the SPE."[1] This would allow the liquidity facility to be tapped in the event of any non-credit disruptions, satisfying Moody's and Standard & Poor's standards to provide their highest investment-grade ratings to Canadian ABCP, while still retaining a zero capital charge.

Furthermore, the new B-5 acknowledges that the liquidity facility might not even need to include GMD as a restriction, leading to the type of liquidity support common in other markets. However the use of this alternative would also come at the cost of capital charges, as outlined in the Basel II Framework. Moody's and Standard & Poor's have both suggested that this approach might also meet their highest short-term rating standards.

Hence, with the new B-5 it will be possible for Canadian banks to offer expanded liquidity protection to Canadian ABCP programs on a cost-effective basis. Although it is premature to speculate which, if any, of the new liquidity options the banks will adopt, and therefore whether Moody's or Standard & Poor's will be able to give Canadian ABCP their highest short-term ratings, it appears that the Canadian market will at least have that option.

Although Canada's Dominion Bond Rating Service (DBRS) already gives Canadian ABCP their highest short-term rating, many institutional investors require two ratings for investments to be acceptable. Hence, the new B-5 could significantly broaden demand for Canadian ABCP and give corporate borrowers expanded and lower-cost access to financing.

---

[1] An ABCP program bundles together numerous assets into a "special-purpose entity" (SPE), which in turn, issues marketable securities.

Source: "OSFI's New Guideline B-5 and the Canadian ABCP Market," *Bank of Canada Financial System Review*, December 2004, page 24. www.bankofcanada.ca

THE PASS-THROUGH SECURITY

FIs frequently pool mortgages and other assets they originate and offer investors an interest in the pool in the form of *pass-through securities*. While many different types of loans and assets on FIs' balance sheets are currently being securitized, the original use of securitization was a result of U.S. government-sponsored programs designed to enhance the liquidity of the residential mortgage market, creating residential MBS. They are called pass-through securities because collections of interest and principal, including prepayments allowed under the mortgage agreements, are passed on to the holder of the securities on a monthly basis.

Most of the residential MBS in Canada are sold by Canada Mortgage and Housing **www.cmhc.ca** Corporation (CMHC), a Crown Corporation. In addition to being fully-insured, CMHC guarantees all payments to the security holders under the National Housing Act (NHA), and so an NHA MBS is the equivalent of a Government of Canada bond that is also secured by residential property. These securities are thus default-free for the purchasers and have, in recent years, with the decrease in the issuance of Canadian government securities, served as substitutes for fixed income securities. As well, they are eligible for the Registered Retirement Savings Plans (RRSPs) and Registered Retirement Income Funds (RRIFs) of individual investors and so are sold by Canadian banks and trusts for this purpose. Issuers of NHA MBS are FIs who are approved lenders of NHA-insured mortgages. These include insurance companies, banks, trust and loan companies, credit unions, and caisses populaires, as well as investment dealers who are not originators of mortgages, but who may be approved by CMHC. The issuer pays a fee for the NHA guarantee and generally lists the security in the name of the issuer, or 'street name' so that they are liquid and may be sold by the investor at any time.

The markets for mortgage-backed securities have developed differently in the United States and Canada. In the U.S., savings and loan companies (S&Ls) were the chief supplier of mortgages which, in the 1980s, were based on fixed rate, 25 or 30-year terms. Because of ceilings on the rates that the S&Ls could pay on their deposits, these FIs mis-matched their long-term mortgage assets with short-term deposits. The creation of MBS resolved this issue, and, in the process, created three **www.ginniemae.gov** large government agencies, "Ginnie Mae" (Government National Mortgage Asso-**www.fanniemae.com** ciation, GNMA), "Fannie Mae" (Federal National Mortgage Association) and **www.freddiemac.com** "Freddie Mac" (Federal Home Loan Mortgage Corporation, FHLMC) to provide funding for the housing industry These three organizations provide residential mortgage-backed securities in the U.S. They have grown so that Fannie Mae is the third-largest FI by asset size in the U.S. Over 63 percent of all residential mortgages in the U.S. were securitized in 2003 compared with less than 15 percent in 1980. The same level of MBS market development did not occur in Canada because by the 1960s Canadian fixed-rate mortgages, while amortized over 25-year periods, had their rates re-set every five years or less and so could be matched more easily with 5-year deposits. Nevertheless, in 2004 there were approximately $100 billion mortgage-backed securities outstanding. Canada Mortgage Bonds, whose first issue by CMHC in June 2001 was $1.5 billion, has total new issues of $19.3 billion in 2003, $17.25 billion in 2004, and an estimated $20 billion in 2005.[3]

Together FNMA and FHLC represent a huge presence in the U.S. financial system as they have over 63 percent of the single-family mortgage pools. In the early 2000s, their credit losses increased, as did their debt-to-equity ratios, ranging from 30 to 97 percent depending on the assumptions made about off-balance sheet exposures. In 2003, Fannie Mae announced that it miscalculated the value of its mortgages, forcing it to make a US$1.1 billion restatement of its stockholders' equity and Freddie Mac announced a US$4.5 billion restatement of its earnings. While both were claimed to be computational errors, the episodes reinforced fears that Fannie Mae and Freddie Mac lack the necessary skills to operate their complex businesses. Finally, in February 2004, Federal Reserve Chairman Alan

---

[3] See C. Freedman and W. Engert, "Financial Developments in Canada: Past Trends and Future Challenges," *The Bank of Canada Review*, Summer 2003, pp. 3–16; W. Dabrowski, "Lenders find security in mortgage bond plan," *National Post*, October 3, 2005, p. FP4; and D. Mavin," CMHC offers major backstop to ownership," *National Post*, October 7, 2005, p. FP6.

Greenspan stated that Fannie Mae and Freddie Mac pose very serious risks to the U.S. financial system.

The potential for "spillover effects" on Canadian markets of a failure of either Fannie Mae or Freddie Mac, while deemed "highly unlikely", was raised in the Bank of Canada's *Financial System Review* of June and December 2004. Some of these concerns might be mitigated should the United States create a single independent regulator of Fannie Mae and Freddie Mac who would have broad authority to determine the companies' safety and soundness, capital standards, and new lines of business, and to spell out how Fannie Mae and Freddie Mac would be wound down should they ever get into trouble. These actions would send a strong signal to investors that the two agencies are not fully guaranteed by the U.S. government and not immune from market forces.[4]

The Incentives and Mechanics of Pass-Through Security Creation

In order to analyze the securitization process, we trace through the mechanics of an NHA-MBS securitization to provide insights into the risk-return benefits of this process to the originating FI in enhancing ROE, as well as the attractiveness of these securities to investors. The focus for an FI in creating an ABS is to forecast the projected cash flow which determines the yield and depends on the prepayment model assumed. For an MBS security, contraction risk arises when mortgage rates decline and borrowers speed up their prepayments. Similarly, extension risk arises when mortgage rates rise and prepayments slow down, leading to a decline in market price of the security. This instability in the cash flows makes pass-through securities unsuitable as an investment vehicle for asset-liability management for certain FIs such as pension funds, which have long-term liabilities. Thus, our discussion focuses on the prepayment models used to structure an ABS followed by a discussion of collateralized mortgage obligations (CMOs) and other innovations in securitization.[5]

Suppose a bank has just originated 1,000 new residential mortgages. The average size of each mortgage is $100,000. Thus, the total size of the new mortgage pool is

$$1,000 \times \$100,000 = \$100 \text{ million}$$

Each mortgage qualifies for CMHC mortgage insurance. In addition, each of these new mortgages has an initial stated maturity of 25 years and a mortgage rate—

[4] See Bank of Canada, *Financial System Review* June 2004, pp. 4–8 and Bank of Canada, *Financial System Review* December 2004, pp. 24–27; "Fannie, Freddie Face a Tough Plan," *Wall Street Journal*, March 29, 2004, p. A2; and "Regulators Hit Fannie, Freddie with New Assault," *Wall Street Journal*, April 28, 2004, p. A1. The convergence of regulations and regulators will continue as long as new FIs are created and existing FIs expand their functions. OSFI supervises federally-regulated institutions in Canada and a national securities regulator for Canada is discussed in Chapter 3. Elizabeth Brown considers a single financial services regulator in the U.S. See E. F. Brown, "E Pluribus Unum—Out of Many, One: Why the United States Needs a Single Financial Services Agency," *University of Miami Business Law Review*, forthcoming available at http://papers.ssrn.com/paper.taf?abstract_id=757010.

[5] We assume CMHC mortgage insurance in the discussion that follows, but it is not required. By law, all high ratio mortgages in Canada (loan to value greater than 75 percent) must carry CMHC mortgage insurance. Low ratio mortgages are not required to carry mortgage insurance but on April 22, 2005, CMHC announced that it was eliminating Application Fees and that it would provide Portfolio Insurance for three categories of low-ratio mortgages (loan to value less than 75 percent) in order to facilitate securitization for the FI and to make the NHA MBS essentially risk-free for the investor. Insurance fees range from 0.25 percent to 0.45 percent. Private insurance may also be provided. See www.cmhc.ca for up-to-date regulations. See also R. D. Quick, "Standard Terminology and Calculations" at CMHC's Web site for sample calculations on prices and prepayment assumptions for Canadian MBS. Non-NHA MBS securitizations are rated by a bond rating agency such as DBRS, so other mechanisms may be put in place to improve the quality of the credit to make it marketable and to protect the investor from default. F. J. Fabozzi, *Handbook of Mortgage Backed Securities*, 2006, McGraw-Hill is a detailed reference for all aspects of asset securitization.

TABLE 27–2
Bank Balance Sheet (in millions of dollars)

Assets		Liabilities	
Cash	$ 0.00	Demand deposits	$ 96.50
Long-term mortgages	100.00	Capital	3.50
	$100.00		$100.00

often called the mortgage coupon—of 12 percent per annum. Suppose the bank originating these loans relies mostly on liabilities such as demand deposits as well as its own capital or equity to finance its assets. Under current capital adequacy requirements, each $1 of new residential mortgage loans has to be backed by some capital. Since residential mortgages fall into Category 3 [50 percent risk weight in the risk-based capital standards (see Chapter 20)], and the risk-based capital requirement is 7 percent, the bank capital needed to back the $100 million mortgage portfolio would be

Capital requirement = $100 million × .5 × .07 = $3.5 million

We assume that the remaining $96.5 million needed to fund the mortgages come from the issuance of demand deposits.

Given these considerations, the bank's initial postmortgage balance sheet may look like that in Table 27–2. In addition to the capital requirement, the bank has to pay an annual insurance premium to CDIC based on the risk of the bank. Assuming a deposit insurance premium of 11.1 basis points (for the lowest-quality FI), the fee would be[6]

$100.00 million × .00111 = $111,000

Although the bank is earning a 12 percent mortgage coupon on its mortgage portfolio, it is facing two levels of regulatory costs.

1. Capital requirements.
2. CDIC insurance premiums.

Thus, one incentive to securitize is to reduce the regulatory burden on the FI to increase its after-tax return.[7] In addition to facing regulatory costs on its residential mortgage portfolio earnings, the bank in Table 27–2 has two risk exposure problems.

Gap Exposure or $D_A > kD_L$

The FI funds the 25-year mortgage portfolio with short-term demand deposits; thus, it has a duration mismatch.[8] This is true even if the mortgage assets have been funded with short-term CDs, time deposits, or other purchased funds.

Illiquidity Exposure

The bank is holding a very illiquid asset portfolio of long-term mortgages and no excess reserves; as a result, it is exposed to the potential liquidity shortages discussed in Chapter 17, including the risk of having to conduct mortgage asset fire sales to meet large unexpected demand deposit withdrawals.

---

[6] In 2005 the deposit insurance premium was 1.4 basis points for the highest-quality banks (see Chapter 19).

[7] Other reasons for securitization include greater geographic diversification of the loan portfolio. Specifically, many FIs originate mortgages from the local community; the ability to securitize facilitates replacing them with MBSs based on mortgages from other cities and regions.

[8] As we discuss in Chapters 8 and 9, core demand deposits usually have a duration of less than three years. Depending on prepayment assumptions, mortgages normally have durations of at least 4.5 years.

One possible solution to these duration mismatch and illiquidity risk problems is to lengthen the bank's on-balance-sheet liabilities by issuing longer-term deposits or other liability claims, such as medium-term notes. Another solution is to engage in interest rate swaps to transform the bank's liabilities into those of a long-term, fixed-rate nature (see Chapter 25). These techniques do not resolve the problem of regulatory costs and the burden they impose on the FI's returns.

By contrast, creating NHA pass-through securities can largely resolve the duration and illiquidity risk problems on the one hand and reduce the burden of regulatory costs on the other. This requires the bank to securitize the $100 million in residential mortgages by issuing NHA pass-through securities. In our example, the bank can do this since the 1,000 underlying mortgages each has NHA mortgage insurance, the same stated mortgage maturity of 25 years, and coupons of 12 percent. Therefore, they are eligible for securitization under the NHA program if the bank is an approved lender (which we assume it is).

The bank begins the securitization process by packaging the $100 million in mortgage loans and removing them from the balance sheet by placing them with a third-party trustee, in a special-purpose vehicle (SPV) off the balance sheet. This third-party trustee may be another bank of high creditworthiness or a legal trustee.[9] Next, the bank determines that (1) CMHC will guarantee, for a fee, the timing of interest and principal payments on the securities issued to back the mortgage pool and (2) the bank itself will continue to service the pool of mortgages for a fee, even after they are placed in trust. Then CMHC issues pass-through securities backed by the underlying $100 million pool of mortgages. These NHA CMHC securities MBS are sold to outside investors in the capital market and the proceeds (net of any underwriting fees) go to the originating bank. Large purchasers of these securities include insurance companies and pension funds.

Before we examine the mechanics of the repayment on a pass-through security, we consider the attractiveness of these bonds to investors. In particular, investors in these bonds are protected against two levels or types of default risk.

Default Risk by the Mortgagees

Suppose that because of rapidly falling house prices, a homeowner walked away from a mortgage, leaving behind a low-valued house to be foreclosed at a price below the outstanding mortgage. This might expose the MBS to losses unless there are external guarantors. Through CMHC housing insurance, government agencies bear the risk of default, thereby protecting the NHA MBS holders against such losses.

Default Risk by Bank/Trustee

Suppose the bank that had originated the mortgages went bankrupt or the trustee absconded with the mortgage interest and principal due to the MBS holders. Because it guaranteed the prompt timing of interest and principal payments on NHA CMHC securities, CMHC would bear the cost of making the promised payments in full and on time to MBS holders.

Given this default protection, investors' returns from holding these securities would be the monthly repayments of interest and principal on the 1,000 mortgages in the pool, after the deduction of a mortgage-servicing fee by the mortgage-originating bank and a monthly timing insurance fee to be paid to CMHC. If we assume that the total of these fees is around 50 basis points, or $\frac{1}{2}$ percent, the

---

[9] For Canada Mortgage Bonds, which are AAA-rated, the trustee is Canada Housing Trust.

stated coupons on the NHA MBS bonds would be set at approximately $\frac{1}{2}$ percent below the coupon rate on the underlying mortgages. In our example:

Mortgage coupon rate	=	12.00%
minus		
Servicing fee	=	0.50
NHA MBS coupon	=	11.50%

Suppose that CMHC issues $100 million face value NHA MBS at par to back the pool of mortgage loans. The minimum size of a single MBS is $5,000; each investor gets a pro rata monthly share of all the interest and principal received by the bank minus servicing costs and insurance fees. Thus, if a life insurance company bought 25 percent of the NHA MBS issue (or 1,000 bonds × $5,000 each = $5 million), it would get a 25 percent share of the 300 promised monthly payments from the mortgages comprising the mortgage pool.

Every month, each mortgagee makes a payment to the bank. The bank aggregates these payments and passes the funds through to NHA MBS investors via the trustee net of servicing fee. To make things easy, most fixed-rate mortgages are **fully amortized** over the mortgage's life. This means that as long as the mortgagee does not seek to prepay the mortgage early within the 25 year period, either to buy a new house or to refinance the mortgage should interest rates fall, investors can expect to receive a constant stream of payments each month analogous to the stream of income on other fixed-coupon, fixed-income bonds. In reality, however, mortgagees do not act in such a predictable fashion. For a variety of reasons, they relocate (sell their house) or refinance their mortgages (especially when current mortgage rates are below mortgage coupon rates). This propensity to **prepay** early, before a mortgage matures, and then refinance with a new mortgage means that *realized* coupons/cash flows on pass-through securities can often deviate substantially from the stated or expected coupon flows in a no-prepayment world. This unique prepayment risk provides the attraction of pass-throughs to some investors but leads other, more risk-averse, investors to avoid these instruments. Before we analyze in greater detail the unique nature of prepayment risk, we summarize the steps followed in the creation of a pass-through in Figure 27–3. Then we analyze how this securitization has helped solve the duration, illiquidity, and regulatory cost problems of the FI manager.

In the previous discussion we traced the securitization process, the origination of mortgages on the balance sheet (Figure 27–3, Box 1) through to the sale of NHA MBS to outside investors (Box 4). To close the securitization process, the cash proceeds of the sale of NHA MBS (Box 5) net of any underwriting fees go to the originating bank. As a result, the bank has substituted cash for long-term mortgages by using the securitization mechanism. Abstracting from the various fees and underwriting costs in the securitization process, the balance sheet of the bank might look like the one in Table 27–3 immediately after the securitization has taken place.

There has been a dramatic change in the balance sheet exposure of the bank. First, $100 million illiquid mortgage loans have been replaced by $100 million cash. Second, the duration mismatch has been reduced since both D_A and D_L are now low. Third, the bank has an enhanced ability to deal with and reduce its regulatory costs. Specifically, it can reduce its capital since capital standards require none be held against cash on the balance sheet compared to residential

fully amortized
An equal periodic repayment on a loan that reflects part interest and part principal over the life of the loan.

prepay
A borrower pays back a loan before maturity to the FI that originated the loan.

FIGURE 27–3
Summary of an
NHA MBS

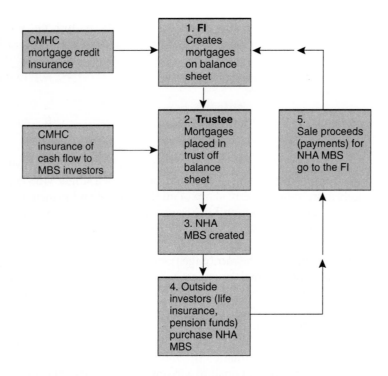

TABLE 27–3
The Bank's Balance
Sheet after
Securitization (in
millions of dollars)

Assets		Liabilities	
Cash (proceeds from mortgage securitization)	$100.00	Demand deposits	$ 96.50
		Capital	3.50
Mortgages	0.00		
	$100.00		$100.00

mortgages. Deposit insurance premiums are also reduced if the bank uses part of the cash proceeds from the NHA MBS sale to pay off or retire demand deposits and downsize its balance sheet.

Of course, keeping a highly liquid asset portfolio and/or downsizing is a way to reduce regulatory costs, but these strategies are hardly likely to enhance an FI's profits. The real logic of securitization is that the cash proceeds from the mortgage/NHA MBS sale can be reused to create or originate new mortgages, which in turn can be securitized. In so doing, the FI is acting more like an asset (mortgage) broker than a traditional asset transformer, as we discussed in Chapter 1. The advantage of being an asset broker is that the FI profits from mortgage pool servicing fees plus up-front points and fees from mortgage origination. At the same time, the FI no longer has to bear the illiquidity and duration mismatch risks and regulatory costs that arise when it acts as an asset transformer and holds mortgages to maturity on its balance sheet. Put more simply, the FI's profitability becomes more fee dependent than interest rate spread dependent.

The limits of this securitization process clearly depend on the supply of mortgages (and other assets such as credit card receivables, car loans, business loans, etc.) that can be securitized and the demand by investors for pass-through securities.

As was noted earlier, the unique feature of pass-through securities from the demand-side perspective of investors is prepayment risk. To understand the unique nature of this risk and why it might deter or limit investments by other FIs and investors, we next analyze the characteristics of pass-through securities more formally.

Concept Questions	1. What is a pass-through security?
	2. Should an FI with $D_A > kD_L$ seek to securitize its assets? Why or why not?

Prepayment Risk on Pass-Through Securities

To understand the effects of prepayments on pass-through security returns, it is necessary to understand the nature of the cash flows received by investors from the underlying portfolio of mortgages. Most conventional mortgages are fully amortized. This means that the mortgagee pays back to the mortgage lender (mortgagor) a constant amount each month that contains some principal and some interest. While the total monthly promised payment remains unchanged, the interest component declines throughout the life of the mortgage contract and the principal component increases.

Although 12 percent is the coupon or interest rate the housebuyers pay on the mortgages, the rate passed through to NHA MBS investors is $11\frac{1}{2}$ percent, reflecting an average 50-basis-point fee paid to the originating bank. The servicing fees are normally paid monthly rather than as lump-sum single payments up front to create the appropriate collection/servicing incentives over the life of the mortgage for the originating bank. For example, the bank's incentive to act as an efficient collection/servicing agent over 300 months would probably decline if it received a single large up-front fee in month 1 and nothing thereafter. The effect of the $\frac{1}{2}$ percent fee is to reduce the cash flows passed through to the MBS investors from \$1,053,224 (\$100,000,000 amortized at 12%) to \$1,016,469 (11.5% amortization).

As we have shown so far, the cash flows on the pass-through directly reflect the interest and principal cash flows on the underlying mortgages minus service fees. However, over time, mortgage rates change. Let Y be the current annual mortgage coupon rate, which could be higher or lower than 12 percent, and let y be the yield on newly issued par value NHA MBS. With no prepayments, the market value of the 12 percent mortgage coupon pool ($11\frac{1}{2}$ percent actual coupons) could be calculated as

$$V = \frac{\$1,016,469}{\left(1 + \frac{y}{12}\right)^1} + \frac{\$1,016,469}{\left(1 + \frac{y}{12}\right)^2} + \cdots + \frac{\$1,016,469}{\left(1 + \frac{y}{12}\right)^{300}}$$

If y is less than $11\frac{1}{2}$ percent, the market value of the pool will be greater than its original value; if y is greater than $11\frac{1}{2}$ percent, the pool will decrease in value. However, valuation is more complex than this since we have ignored the prepayment behaviour of the 1,000 mortgages. In effect, prepayment risk has two principal sources: refinancing and housing turnover.

Refinancing

As coupon rates on new mortgages fall, there is an increased incentive for individuals in the pool to pay off old, high-cost mortgages and refinance at lower rates. However, refinancing involves transaction costs and recontracting costs. Many FIs charge prepayment penalty fees on the outstanding mortgage balance prepaid. In addition,

FIGURE 27–4
The Prepayment Relationship

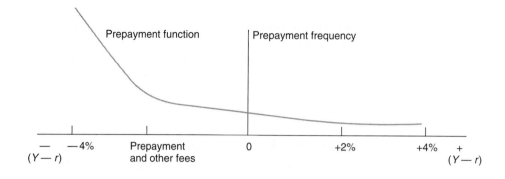

there are often origination costs for new mortgages to consider along with the cost of appraisals and credit checks. As a result, mortgage rates may have to fall by some amount below the current coupon rate before there is a significant increase in prepayments in the pool.[10]

Housing Turnover

The other factor that affects prepayments is the propensity of the mortgagees in the pool to move before their mortgages reach maturity. The decision to move or turn over a house may be due to a complex set of factors, such as the level of house prices, the size of the underlying mortgage, the general health of the economy, and even the season (e.g., spring is a good time to move). In addition, if the existing mortgage is an **assumable mortgage,** the buyer of the house takes over the outstanding mortgage's payments. Thus, the sale of a house in a pool does not necessarily imply that the mortgage has to be prepaid. By contrast, nonassumability means a one-to-one correspondence between sale of a house and mortgage prepayment.

Figure 27–4 plots the prepayment frequency of a pool of mortgages in relation to the spread between the current mortgage coupon rate (Y) and the mortgage coupon rate (r) in the existing pool (12 percent in our example). Notice when the current mortgage rate (Y) is above the rate in the pool ($Y > r$), mortgage prepayments are small, reflecting monthly forced turnover as people have to relocate because of jobs, divorces, marriages, and other considerations. Even when the current mortgage rate falls below r, those remaining in the mortgage pool do not rush to prepay because up-front refinancing, contracting, and penalty costs are likely to outweigh any present value savings from lower mortgage rates. However, as current mortgage rates continue to fall, the propensity for mortgage holders to prepay increases significantly. Conceptually, mortgage holders have a very valuable call option on the mortgage when this option is in the money.[11] That is, when current mortgage rates fall sufficiently low so that the present value savings of refinancing outweigh the exercise price (the cost of prepayment penalties and other fees and costs), the mortgage will be called.

assumable mortgage
The mortgage contract is transferred from the seller to the buyer of a house.

---

[10] J. R. Follian and D. Tzang, in "The Interest Rate Differential and Refinancing a Home Mortgage," *Appraisal Journal* 56, no. 2 (1988), pp. 243–51, found that only when the mortgage rate fell below the coupon rate by 60 basis points was there an incentive to refinance a mortgage with an average of 10 years left to maturity. As might be expected, this required differential declined as the holding period increased.

[11] The option is a call option on the value of the mortgage since falling rates increase the value of calling the old mortgage and refinancing a new mortgage at lower rates for the owner of the call option, who is the mortgagee. See M. J. Brennan and E. S. Schwartz, "Savings Bonds, Retractable Bonds, and Callable Bonds," *Journal of Financial Economics* 5 (1977), pp. 67–88. This option also can be viewed as a put option on interest rates.

FIGURE 27–5
The Effects of Prepayments on Pass-Through Cash Flows

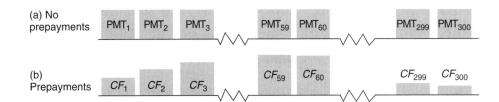

Since the bank has sold the mortgage cash flows to investors and must by law pass through all payments received (minus servicing fees), investors' cash flows directly reflect the rate of prepayment. As a result, instead of receiving an equal monthly cash flow, *PMT*, as is done under a no-prepayment scenario, the actual cash flows (*CF*) received on these securities by investors fluctuate monthly with the rate of prepayments (see Figure 27–5).

In a no-prepayment world, each month's cash flows are the same: $PMT_1 = PMT_2 = \cdots = PMT_{300}$. However, in a world with prepayments, each month's realized cash flows from the mortgage pool can differ. In Figure 27–5 we show a rising level of cash flows from month 2 onward peaking in month 60, reflecting the effects of early prepayments by some of the 1,000 mortgagees in the pool. This leaves less outstanding principal and interest to be paid in later years. For example, if 300 mortgagees fully prepay by month 60, only 700 mortgagees will remain in the pool at that date. The effect of prepayments is to lower dramatically the principal and interest cash flows received in the later months of the pool's life. For instance, in Figure 27–5, the cash flow received by MBS holders in month 300 is very small relative to month 60 and even months 1 and 2. This reflects the decline in the pool's outstanding principal.

The lowering of current mortgage interest rates and faster prepayments have some good news and bad news effects on the current market valuation of the 12 percent mortgage pool, that is, the $11\frac{1}{2}$ percent NHA MBS.

Good News Effects   First, lower market yields reduce the discount rate on any mortgage cash flow and increase the present value of any given stream of cash flows. This would also happen for any fixed-income security. Second, lower yields lead to faster prepayment of the mortgage pool's principal. As a result, instead of principal payments being skewed toward the end of the pool's life, the principal is received (paid back) much faster.

Bad News Effects   First, with early prepayment comes fewer interest payments in absolute terms. Thus, instead of receiving scheduled interest payments over 300 months, some of these payments are irrevocably lost as principal outstanding is paid early; that is, mortgage holders are not going to pay interest on mortgage loans they no longer have outstanding. Second, faster cash flow due to prepayments induced by interest rate falls can only be reinvested at lower interest rates when they are received. That is, instead of reinvesting monthly cash flows at 12 percent, investors may reinvest only at lower rates such as 8 percent.

Concept Questions

1. What are the two sources of cash flows on a pass-through security?
2. What two factors can cause prepayments on the mortgages underlying pass-through securities?

Prepayment Models

Clearly, managers running FI investment portfolios need to factor in assumptions about the prepayment behaviour of mortgages before they can assess the fair value

FIGURE 27–6
PSA Prepayment
Model

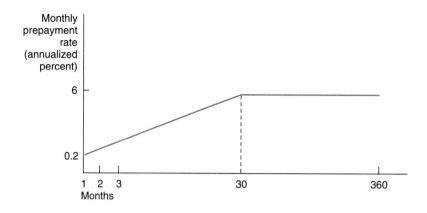

www.psa.com

and risk of their MBS portfolios. Next, we consider three alternative ways to model prepayment effects using the Public Securities Association (PSA) prepayment model, other empirical models, and option valuation models.

To begin, we look carefully at the results of one prepayment model. The weighted-average life of an MBS reflects an assumed prepayment schedule. This weighted-average life is not the same as duration, which measures the weighted-average time to maturity based on the relative present values of cash flows as weights. Instead, it is a significant simplification of the duration measure seeking to concentrate on the expected timing of payments of principal. Technically, **weighted-average life (WAL)** is measured by

weighted-average life (WAL)
The sum of the products of the time when principal payments are received and the amount of principal received all divided by total principal outstanding.

$$WAL = \frac{\Sigma \, (\text{Time} \times \text{Expected principal received})}{\text{Total principal outstanding}}$$

For example, consider a loan with two years to maturity and $100 million in principal. Investors expect $40 million of the principal to be repaid at the end of year 1 and the remaining $60 million to be repaid at maturity.

Time	Expected Principal Payments	Time × Principal
1	$40	$40
2	60	120
	$100	$160

$$WAL = \frac{160}{100} = 1.6 \text{ years}$$

PSA Model

The prepayment model developed by the Public Securities Association is an empirically based model that reflects an average rate of prepayment based on past experience. Essentially, the PSA model assumes that the prepayment rate starts at 0.2 percent (per annum) in the first month, increasing by 0.2 percent per month for the first 30 months, until the annualized prepayment rate reaches 6 percent. This model assumes that the prepayment rate then levels off at a 6 percent annualized rate for the remaining life of the pool[12] (see Figure 27–6). Issuers or investors who

---

[12] Or, after month 30, prepayments are made at approximately ½ percent per *month*.

FIGURE 27–7
Deviations from 100 Percent PSA

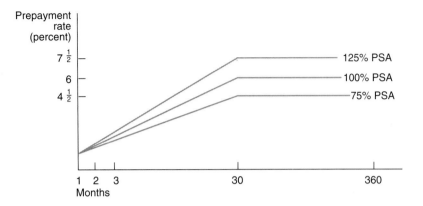

assume that their mortgage pool prepayments exactly match this pattern are said to assume 100 percent PSA behaviour. Realistically, the actual prepayment rate on any specific mortgage pool backing a specific pass-through security may differ from PSA's assumed pattern for general and economic reasons, including

1. The level of the pool's coupon relative to the current mortgage coupon rate (the weighted-average coupon).
2. The age of the mortgage pool.
3. Whether the payments are fully amortized.
4. Assumability of mortgages in the pool.
5. Size of the pool.
6. Conventional or nonconventional mortgages.
7. Geographic location.
8. Age and job status of mortgagees in the pool.

One approach would be to approximately control for these factors by assuming some fixed deviation of any specific pool from PSA's assumed average or benchmark pattern. For example, one pool may be assumed to be 75 percent PSA, and another 125 percent PSA. The former has a slower prepayment rate than historically experienced; the latter, a faster rate. Note these values in Figure 27–7 relative to 100 percent PSA.

Other Empirical Models

FIs that are trading, dealing, and issuing pass-throughs have also developed their own proprietary empirical models of prepayment behaviour to get a pricing edge on other issuers/investors. Clearly, the FI that can develop the best, most accurate, prepayment model stands to make large profits either in originating and issuing such securities or in trading such instruments in the secondary market. As a wide variety of empirical models have been developed, we briefly look at the types of methodology followed.

Specifically, most empirical models are proprietary versions of the PSA model in which FIs make their own estimates of the pattern of monthly prepayments. From this modeling exercise, an FI can estimate either the fair price or the fair yield on the pass-through. Of course, those FIs that make the most profits from buying and selling pass-throughs over time are the ones that have most accurately predicted actual prepayment behaviour.

FIGURE 27–8
Estimated
Prepayment
Function for
a Given Pool

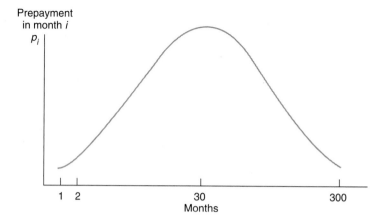

In constructing an empirical valuation model, FIs begin by estimating a prepayment function from observing the experience of mortgage holders prepaying during any particular period on mortgage pools similar to the one to be valued. This is conditional, of course, on the mortgages not having been prepaid prior to that period. These conditional prepayment rates in month i (p_i) for similar pools would be modeled as functions of the important economic variables driving prepayment—for example, $p_i = f$ (mortgage rate spread, age, collateral, geographic factors, **burn-out factor**).[13] This modeling should take into account the idiosyncratic factors affecting this specific pool, such as its age and burn-out factor, as well as market factors affecting prepayments in general, such as the mortgage rate spread. Once the frequency distribution of the p_i's is estimated, as shown in Figure 27–8, the FI can calculate the expected cash flows on the mortgage pool under consideration and estimate its fair yield given the current market price of the pool.[14]

burn-out factor
The aggregate percent of the mortgage pool that has been prepaid prior to the month under consideration.

Option Models[15]

The third class of models uses option pricing theory to figure the fair yield on pass-throughs. These so-called option-adjusted spread (OAS) models focus on the prepayment risk of pass-throughs as the essential determinant of the required yield spread of pass-through bonds over Treasuries. As such, they are open to the criticism that they fail to properly include nonrefinancing incentives to prepay and the variety of transaction costs and recontracting costs involved in refinancing. Recent research has tried to integrate the option model approach with the empirical model approach.[16]

---

[13] A burn-out factor is a summary measure of a pool's prepayments in total prior to month i. As such, it is meant to capture heterogeneity of prepayment behavior within any given pool rather than between pools. See E. S. Schwartz and W. N. Tourous, "Prepayment and the Valuation of Mortgage-Backed Securities," *Journal of Finance* 44 (1989), pp. 375–92.

[14] A commonly used empirical model is the proportional hazards model. This model produces a prepayment function similar to that in Figure 27–8 where, other things being equal, conditional prepayment rates are typically low in the early years of a mortgage, increase as the age of the mortgage increases, and then diminish with further seasoning (see Schwartz and Tourous, "Prepayment").

[15] This section contains material that is relatively technical. It may be included or dropped from the chapter reading depending on the rigor of the course without harming the continuity of the chapter.

[16] See J. P. Kau et al., "A Generalized Valuation Model for Fixed-Rate Residential Mortgages," *Journal of Money, Credit and Banking* 24 (1992); W. Archer and D. C. Ling, "Pricing Mortgage-Backed Securities: Should Contingent-Claim Models Be Abandoned for Empirical Models of Prepayments?" paper presented at the AFA Conference, Anaheim, California, January 1993; and M. LaCour-Little, "Another Look at the Role of Borrower Characteristics in Predicting Mortgage Prepayments," *Journal of Housing Research* 10 (1999), pp. 45–60.

Stripped to its basics, the option model views the fair price on a pass-through such as an MBS as being decomposable into two parts:[17]

$$P_{MBS} = P_{TBOND} - P_{PREPAYMENT\ OPTION}$$

That is, the value of an MBS to an investor (P_{MBS}) is equal to the value of a standard noncallable Treasury bond of the same duration (P_{TBOND}) minus the value of the mortgage holder's prepayment call option ($P_{PREPAYMENT\ OPTION}$). Specifically, the ability of the mortgage holder to prepay is equivalent to the bond investor writing a call option on the bond and the mortgagee owning or buying the option. If interest rates fall, the option becomes more valuable as it moves into the money and more mortgages are prepaid early by having the bond called or the prepayment option exercised. This relationship can also be thought of in the yield dimension:

$$Y_{MBS} = Y_{TBOND} + Y_{OPTION}$$

The investors' required yield on an MBS should equal the yield on a similar duration T-bond plus an additional yield for writing the valuable call option. That is, the fair yield spread or **option-adjusted spread (OAS)** between MBS and T-bonds should reflect the value of this option.

option-adjusted spread (OAS)

The required interest spread of a pass-through security over a Treasury when prepayment risk is taken into account.

To gain further insights into the option model approach and the OAS, we can develop an example along the lines of S. D. Smith showing how to calculate the value of the option-adjusted spread on MBS.[18] To do this, we make a number of simplifying assumptions indicative of the restrictive nature of many of these models:

1. The only reasons for prepayment are due to refinancing mortgages at lower rates; there is no prepayment for turnover reasons.
2. The current discount (zero-coupon) yield curve for T-bonds is flat (this could be relaxed).
3. The mortgage coupon rate is 10 percent on an outstanding pool of mortgages with an outstanding principal balance of $1,000,000.
4. The mortgages have a three-year maturity and pay principal and interest only once at the end of each year. Of course, real-world models would have 15- or 25-year maturities and pay interest and principal monthly. These assumptions are made for simplification purposes only.
5. Mortgage loans are fully amortized, and there is no servicing fee (again, this could be relaxed). Thus, the annual fully amortized payment under no prepayment conditions is

$$PMT = \frac{1,000,000}{\left[\dfrac{1 - \dfrac{1}{(1 + .10)^3}}{.1}\right]} = \frac{1,000,000}{2.48685} = \$402,114$$

In a world without prepayments, no default risk, and current mortgage rates (y) of 9 percent, we would have the MBS selling at a premium over par:

$$P_{MBS} = \frac{PMT}{(1 + y)} + \frac{PMT}{(1 + y)^2} + \frac{PMT}{(1 + y)^3}$$

---

[17] For an excellent review of these option models, see Spahr and Sunderman, "The Effect of Prepayment Modeling."

[18] S. D. Smith, "Analyzing Risk and Return for Mortgage-Backed Securities," Federal Reserve Bank of Atlanta, *Economic Review,* January–February 1991, pp. 2–11.

FIGURE 27–9
Mortgage Rate Changes: Assumed Time Path

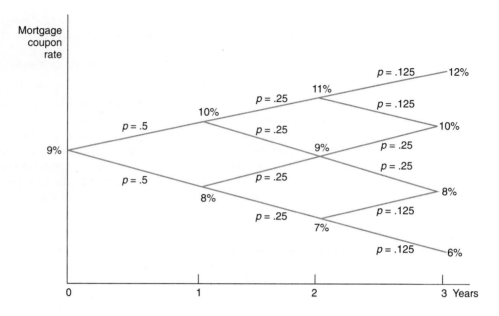

$$P_{MBS} = \frac{\$402{,}114}{(1.09)} + \frac{\$402{,}114}{(1.09)^2} + \frac{\$402{,}114}{(1.09)^3}$$

$$P_{MBS} = \$1{,}017{,}869$$

6. Because of prepayment penalties and other refinancing costs, mortgagees do not begin to prepay until mortgage rates, in any year, fall 3 percent or more below the mortgage coupon rate for the pool (the mortgage coupon rate is 10 percent in this example).

7. Interest rate movements over time change a maximum of 1 percent up or down each year. The time path of interest rates follows a binomial process.

8. With prepayments present, cash flows in any year can be the promised payment $PMT = \$402{,}114$, the promised payment ($PMT$) plus repayment of any outstanding principal, or zero if all mortgages have been prepaid or paid off in the previous year.

In Figure 27–9 we show the assumed time path of interest rates over the three years with associated probabilities (p).

End of Year 1   Since rates can change up or down by only 1 percent per annum, the farthest they can be expected to fall in the first year is to 8 percent. At this level, no mortgage holder would prepay since any mortgage rate savings would be offset by the penalty costs of prepayment, that is, by the assumption it is worth prepaying only when the mortgage rate falls at least 3 percent below its 10 percent coupon rate. As a result, the MBS pass-through investor could expect to receive $PMT = \$402{,}114$ with certainty. Thus, $CF_1 = \$402{,}114$.

End of Year 2   In year 2, there are three possible mortgage interest rate scenarios. However, the only one that triggers prepayment is when mortgage rates fall to 7 percent (3 percent below the 10 percent mortgage coupon rate of the pool). According to Figure 27–9, this occurs with only a 25 percent probability. If prepayment does not occur with 75 percent probability, the investor receives $PMT = \$402,114$. If prepayment occurs with 25 percent probability, the investor receives

$$PMT + \text{Principal balance remaining at end of year 2}$$

We can calculate the principal balance remaining at the end of year 2 as follows. At the end of the first year, we divide the amortized payment, $PMT = \$402,114$, into a payment of interest and a payment of principal. With a 10 percent mortgage coupon rate, the payment of interest component would be $.10 \times \$1,000,000 = \$100,000$, and the repayment of principal component $= \$402,114 - \$100,000 = \$302,114$. Thus, at the beginning of the second year, there would be $\$1,000,000 - \$302,114 = \$697,886$ principal outstanding. At the end of the second year, the promised amortized payment of $PMT = \$402,114$ can be broken down to an interest component of 10 percent $\times \$697,886 = \$69,788.6$, and a principal component amount of $\$402,114 - \$69,788.6 = \$332,325.4$, leaving a principal balance at the end of year 2 of $\$1,000,000 - \$302,114 - \$332,325.4 = \$365,560.6$.

Consequently, if yields fall to 7 percent, the cash flow received by the investor in year 2 would be

$$PMT + \text{Principal balance outstanding at end of year 2}$$
$$= \$402,114 + \$365,560.6 = \$767,674.6$$

Thus, expected cash flows at the end of year 2 would be

$$CF_2 = .25(\$767,674.6) + .75(\$402,114)$$
$$= \$191,918.64 + \$301,585.5$$
$$= \$493,504.15$$

End of Year 3   Since there is a 25 percent probability that mortgages will be prepaid in year 2, there must be a 25 percent probability that the investor will receive no cash flows at the end of year 3 since mortgage holders owe nothing in this year if all mortgages have already been paid off early in year 2. However, there is also a 75 percent probability that mortgages will not be prepaid at the end of year 2. Thus, at the end of year 3 (maturity), the investor has a 75 percent probability of receiving the promised amortized payment $PMT = \$402,114$. The expected cash flow in year 3 is

$$CF_3 = .25(0) + .75(\$402,114) = \$301,585.5$$

Derivation of the Option-Adjusted Spread   As just discussed, we conceptually divide the required yield on an MBS, or other pass-throughs, with prepayment risk, into the required yield on T-bonds plus a required spread for the prepayment call option given to the mortgage holders:

$$P = \frac{E(CF_1)}{(1 + d_1 + O_S)} + \frac{E(CF_2)}{(1 + d_2 + O_S)^2} + \frac{E(CF_3)}{(1 + d_3 + O_S)^3}$$

where

$P = $ Price of MBS

$d_1 = $ Discount rate on one-year, zero-coupon Treasury bonds

$d_2 = $ Discount rate on two-year, zero-coupon Treasury bonds

d_3 = Discount rate on three-year, zero-coupon Treasury bonds

O_S = Option-adjusted spread on MBS

Assume that the T-bond yield curve is flat, so that

$$d_1 = d_2 = d_3 = 8\%$$

We can now solve for O_S:

$$1,017,869 = \frac{\$402,114}{(1+.08+O_S)} + \frac{\$493,504.15}{(1+.08+O_S)^2} + \frac{\$301,185.5}{(1+.08+O_S)^3}$$

Solving for O_S, we find that

$$O_S = 0.96\% \text{ (to two decimal places)}$$
$$Y_{MBS} = Y_{TBOND} + O_S$$
$$= 8\% + 0.96\%$$
$$= 8.96\%$$

Notice that when prepayment risk is present, the expected cash flow yield at 8.96 percent is 4 basis points less than the required 9 percent yield on the MBS when no prepayment occurs. The slightly lower yield results because the positive effects of early prepayment (such as earlier payment of principal) dominate the negative effects (such as loss of interest payments). Note, however, that this result might well be reversed if we altered our assumptions by allowing a wider dispersion of possible interest rate changes and having heavier penalties for prepayment.

Nevertheless, the option-adjusted spread approach is useful for FI managers in that they can place lower bounds on the yields they are willing to accept on MBS and other pass-through securities before they place them in their portfolios. Realistically, some account has to be taken of nonrefinancing prepayment behaviour and patterns; otherwise significant mispricing may occur.

Concept Questions

1. Should an FI with $D_A < kD_L$ seek to securitize its assets? Why or why not?
2. In general terms, discuss the three approaches developed by analysts to model prepayment behaviour.
3. In the context of the option model approach, list three ways in which transaction and other contracting costs are likely to interfere with the accuracy of its predictions regarding the fair price or interest spread on a pass-through security.

NHA Mortgage-Backed Securities Pools

All NHA MBS issues are pooled according to mortgage type and prepayment provisions of the original mortgages. Table 27–4 lists the numbers and the definition of some of the pool types available. New pools have been created to allow for the types of mortgages that are issued in Canada and the conditions that they must meet in order to be eligible for mortgage insurance. For example, the 970 pool type allows for prepayments up to the third anniversary of the mortgage and the 975 type up to the fifth anniversary. As can be seen in Table 27–5, which shows the percentage share of the market by pool type outstanding in September 2005, the largest pools dollar-wise and in total are the 970 and 975 types, which are single-family mortgages issued according to the standard NHA mortgage provisions. The 966 and 990 pools are backed by non-repayable mortgages and make up less than 10 percent of the total MBS outstanding.

TABLE 27–4
NHA MBS
Mortgage Pool
Classifications

a) Homeowner:

964—exclusive homeowner mortgage pools which are classified as prepayable because the borrowers within this type of pool have the option to prepay their mortgage (often at a penalty) in accordance with the specific terms of the mortgage. The appropriate Penalty Interest Payment (PIP) is passed through to the investors.
967—exclusive homeowner mortgage pools which are classified as prepayable because the borrowers within this type of pool have the option to prepay their mortgage. However, the PIP is not passed through to the investor.
970—offers investors an indemnity where mortgages are renegotiated during the closed period of the loan. Penalty Interest Payments (PIP) are retained by the issuer. For all prepayments in circumstances other than those permitted in the Information Circular, an indemnity is passed through.

b) Multiples:

966—multi-family pool type which is comprised exclusively of multiple family loans, and are not prepayable.

c) Social housing:

These NHA-insured mortgages are issued to finance low-cost housing for senior citizens, the disabled and the economically disadvantaged. Typically, such housing is sponsored by government housing agencies, other social service organizations and private non-profit organizations.
99—special category of NHA MBS pool created to allow exclusive pools of "Social Housing mortgages". The key feature of Social Housing pools is the absence of prepayment at the option of the borrower on the underlying mortgages; this makes them more attractive to investors who seek predictable cash flow.

d) Mixed

965—mixed pools which are comprised of a combination of homeowner, multiple or social housing mortgages. These also consist of prepayable multifamily pools.

Other:

975—similar to 970 but with prepayments allowed up to five years, introduced December 29, 2000
985—backed by variable rate mortgages, introduced November 26, 2004
980—backed by adjustable rate mortgages with a one month interest rate reset, introduced May 31, 2005
987—backed by floating rate mortgages with a coupon rate that is a weighted average of the pooled mortgages, introduced September 1, 2005
990—non-repayable mortgages

The NHA MBS provide a cheaper source of funds for FIs and the benefits are passed on to home buyers in lower mortgage rate. There were thirty different issuers by 2005, including insurance companies (Manulife, Sun Life), trust companies (Equitable Trust, Home Trust), credit unions and caisses populaires (Vancouver City Savings, Caisse Centrale Desjardins du Québec) and investment firms (Merrill Lynch Canada Inc.). As might be expected, the largest issuers of these types of securities were the major banks, with Bank of Nova Scotia having 47.71 percent market share of the 970 pool ($7.61 billion, 82 pools) and Toronto-Dominion Bank with 41.35 percent of the 975 pool ($22.26 billion, 294 pools).

Pool Type	No. of Pools	Amount	Market Share
964	146	$1,499,930,586.51	1.60
965	190	$2,689,091,982.50	2.87
966	142	$2,124,356,368.23	2.27
967	31	$11,992,161.10	0.01
970	384	$15,952,548,809.91	17.03
975	911	$53,829,827,253.84	57.48
980	17	$252,196,765.20	0.27
985	133	$12,162,870,941.12	12.99
987	13	$1,067,579,800.56	1.14
990	81	$4,057,180,903.43	4.33
Grand Total	2,048	$93,647,575,572.40	100.00

THE COLLATERALIZED MORTGAGE OBLIGATION (CMO)

While pass-throughs are still the primary mechanism for securitization, the CMO is a second and growing vehicle for securitizing FI assets. Innovated in 1983 by the U.S. FHLMC and First Boston, the CMO is a device for making mortgage-backed securities more attractive to investors. The CMO does this by repackaging the cash flows from mortgages and pass-through securities in a different fashion to attract different types of investors. While a pass-through security gives each investor a pro rata share of any promised and prepaid cash flows on a mortgage pool, the CMO is a multiclass pass-through with a number of different investor classes or tranches. Unlike a pass-through, each class has a different guaranteed coupon just like a regular T-bond; but more importantly, the allocation of early cash flows due to mortgage prepayments is such that at any one time, all prepayments go to retiring the principal outstanding of only one class of bondholders at a time, leaving the other classes' prepayment protected for a period of time. Thus, a CMO serves as a way to mitigate or reduce prepayment risk.

Creation of CMOs

CMO (Collateralized mortgage obligation)
A mortgage-backed bond issued in multiple classes or tranches.

CMOs can be created either by packaging and securitizing whole mortgage loans or, more usually, by placing existing pass-throughs in a trust off the balance sheet. The trust or third-party FI holds the pass-through as collateral against issues of new CMO securities. The trust issues these CMOs in three or more different classes. We show a three-class or tranche CMO in Figure 27–10.

Issuing CMOs is often equivalent to double securitization. Mortgages are packaged, and a pass-through is issued. An investment bank or a savings institution may buy this whole issue or a large part of the issue and would then place these MBS securities as collateral with a trust and issue three new classes of bonds backed by the MBS securities as collateral. As a result, the investors in each CMO class have a sole claim to the MBS collateral if the issuer fails. The investment bank or other issuer creates the CMO to make a profit by repackaging the cash flows from the single-class MBS pass-through into cash flows more attractive to different groups of investors. The sum of the prices at which the three CMO bond classes can be sold normally exceeds that of the original pass-through:

FIGURE 27–10
The Creation of a CMO

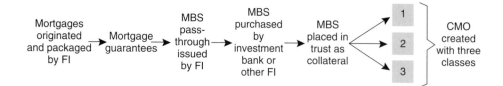

$$\sum_{i=1}^{3} P_{i, CMO} > P_{MBS}$$

To understand the gains from repackaging, it is necessary to understand how CMOs restructure prepayment risk to make it more attractive to different classes of investors. We explain this in the following simple example.

EXAMPLE 27–1

The Value Additivity of CMOs

Suppose an investment bank buys a $150 million issue of MBS and places them in trust as collateral. It then issues a CMO with these three classes:

Class A: Annual fixed coupon 7 percent, class size $50 million
Class B: Annual fixed coupon 8 percent, class size $50 million
Class C: Annual fixed coupon 9 percent, class size $50 million

Under the CMO, each class has a guaranteed or fixed coupon.[19] By restructuring the MBS as a CMO, the investment bank can offer investors who buy bond class C a higher degree of mortgage prepayment protection compared to a pass-through. Those who buy bond class B receive an average degree of prepayment protection, and those who take class A receive virtually no prepayment protection.

Each month, mortgagees in the pool pay principal and interest on their mortgages; each payment includes the promised amortized amount (*PMT*) plus any additional payments as some of the mortgage holders prepay principal to refinance their mortgages or because they have sold their houses and are relocating. These cash flows are passed through to the owner of the MBS. The CMO issuer uses the cash flows to pay promised coupon interest to the three classes of CMO bondholders. Suppose that in month 1 the promised amortized cash flows (PMT) on the mortgages underlying the pass-through collateral are $1 million, but an additional $1.5 million cash flow results from early mortgage prepayments. Thus, the cash flows in the first month available to pay promised coupons to the three classes of investors would be

PMT + Prepayments = $1 million + $1.5 million = $2.5 million

This cash flow is available to the trustee, who uses it in the following fashion.

1. *Coupon payments.* Each month (or more commonly, each quarter or half year), the trustee pays out the guaranteed coupons to the three classes of investors at annualized coupon rates of 7 percent, 8 percent, and 9 percent, respectively. Given the stated principal of $50 million for each class, the class A (7 percent coupon) investors receive approximately $291,667 in coupon payments in month 1, the class B (8 percent coupon) receive approximately $333,333 in month 1, and the class C (9 percent coupon) receive approximately $375,000 in month 1. Thus, the total promised coupon payments to the three classes amount to $1,000,000 (equal to *PMT*, the no-prepayment cash flows in the pool).

2. *Principal payments.* The trustee has $2.5 million available to pay out as a result of promised mortgage payments plus early prepayments, but the total payment of coupon interest amounts to $1 million. The remaining $1.5 million has to be paid out to the CMO investors. The unique feature of the CMO is that the trustee would pay this remaining

---

[19] In some cases, coupons are paid monthly, in others quarterly, and in still others semiannually.

Figure 27–11   **Allocation of Cash Flows to Owners of CMO Tranches**

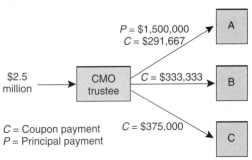

FIGURE 27–12   **Allocation of Cash Flows to Remaining Tranches of CMO Bonds**

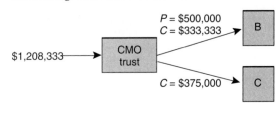

$1.5 million only to class A investors to retire these investors' principal. This retires early some of these investors' principal outstanding. At the end of month 1, only $48.5 million ($50 million − $1.5 million) of class A bonds remains outstanding, compared to $50 million class B and $50 million class C. These payment flows are shown graphically in Figure 27–11.

Let's suppose that in month 2 the same thing happens. The cash flows from the mortgage pool exceed the promised coupon payments to the three classes of bondholders. Again, the trustee uses any excess cash flows to pay off or retire the principal of class A bondholders. If the excess cash flows again amount to $1.5 million, at the end of month 2 there will be only $47 million ($48.5 million—$1.5 million) of class A bonds outstanding.

Given any positive flow of prepayments, it is clear that within a few years the class A bonds will be fully retired. In practice, this often occurs between 1.5 and 3 years after issue. After the trustee retires class A, only classes B and C remain.

As before, out of any cash flows received from the mortgage pool, the trustee pays the bondholders their guaranteed coupons, $C_B = \$333,333$ and $C_C = \$375,000$ for a total of $708,333. Suppose that total cash flows received by the trustee are $1,208,333 in the first month after the total retirement of class A bonds, reflecting amortized mortgage payments by the remaining mortgagees in the pool plus any new prepayments. The excess cash flows of $500,000 ($1,208,333 − $708,333) then go to retire the principal outstanding of CMO bond class B. At the end of that month, there are only $49.5 million class B bonds outstanding. This is shown graphically in Figure 27–12.

As the months pass, the trustee will use any excess cash flows over and above the promised coupons to investors of class B and C bonds to retire bond class B's principal. Eventually, all of the $50 million principal on class B bonds will be retired—in practice, five to seven years after the CMO issue. After class B bonds are retired, all remaining cash flows will be dedicated to paying the promised coupon of investors of class C bonds and retiring the $50 million principal on class C bonds. In practice, class C bonds can have an average life as long as 20 years.

Class A, B, and C Bond Buyers

Class A

These bonds have the shortest average life with a minimum of prepayment protection. They are, therefore, of great interest to investors seeking short-duration mortgage-backed assets to reduce the duration of their mortgage-related asset portfolios.

Class B

These bonds have some prepayment protection and expected durations of five to seven years depending on the level of interest rates. Pension funds and life insurance companies would purchase these bonds, although some deposit-taking institutions would buy this bond class as well.

Class C

Because of their long expected duration, Class C bonds are highly attractive to insurance companies and pension funds seeking long-term duration assets to match their long-term duration liabilities. Indeed, because of their failures to offer prepayment protection, regular pass-throughs may not be very attractive to these institutions. Class C CMOs, with their high but imperfect degree of prepayment protection, may be of greater interest to the FI managers of these institutions.

In summary, by splitting bondholders into different classes and by restructuring cash flows into forms more valued by different investor clienteles, the CMO issuer stands to make a profit.

INNOVATIONS IN SECURITIZATION

We now turn our attention to the growing innovations in FIs' asset securitization. We discuss two major innovations and their use in return-risk management by FIs: mortgage pass-through strips and the extension of the securitization concept to other assets.

Mortgage Pass-Through Strips

The mortgage pass-through strip is a special type of a CMO with only two classes. The fully amortized nature of mortgages means that any given monthly payment, *PMT*, contains an interest component and a principal component. Beginning in 1987, investment banks and other FI issuers stripped out the interest component from the principal component and sold each payment stream separately to different bond class investors. They sold an interest only (IO) class and a principal only (PO) class; these two bond classes have very special cash flow characteristics, especially regarding the interest rate sensitivity of these bonds. We show this stripping of the cash flows in Figure 27–13 and consider the effects of interest rate changes on the value of each of these stripped instruments below.

IO Strips

IO strip
A bond sold to investors whose cash flows reflect the monthly interest payments received from a pool of mortgages.

The owner of an **IO strip** has a claim to the present value of interest payments made by the mortgageholders in the pool—that is, to the IO segments of each month's cash flow received from the underlying mortgage pool:

$$P_{IO} = \frac{IO_1}{\left(1 + \frac{y}{12}\right)} + \frac{IO_2}{\left(1 + \frac{y}{12}\right)^2} + \frac{IO_3}{\left(1 + \frac{y}{12}\right)^3} + \ldots + \frac{IO_{300}}{\left(1 + \frac{y}{12}\right)^{300}}$$

When interest rates change, they affect the cash flows received on mortgages. We concentrate on two effects: the discount effect and the prepayment effect on the price or value of IOs, denoted by P_{IO}.

Discount Effect   As interest rates (y) fall, the present value of any cash flows received on the strip—the IO payments—rises, increasing the value (P_{IO}) of the bond.

Prepayment Effect   As interest rates fall, mortgagees prepay their mortgages. In absolute terms, the number of IO payments the investor receives is likely to shrink. For example, the investor might receive only 100 monthly IO payments instead of the expected 300 in a no-prepayment world. The shrinkage in the size and value of IO payments reduces the value (P_{IO}) of the bond.

FIGURE 27–13 **IO/PO Strips**

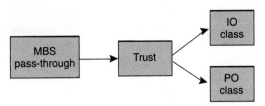

Specifically, one can expect that as interest rates continue to fall below the mortgage coupon rate of the bonds in the pool, the prepayment effect gradually dominates the discount effect, so that over some range the price or value of the IO bond falls as interest rates fall. Note the price-yield curve in Figure 27–14 for an IO strip on a pass-through bond with 10 percent mortgage coupon rates. The price-yield curve slopes upward in the interest rate range below 10 percent. This means that as current interest rates rise or fall, IO values or prices rise or fall. As a result, the IO is a rare example of a **negative duration** asset that is very valuable as a portfolio-hedging device for an FI manager when included with regular bonds whose price-yield curves show the normal inverse relationship. That is, even though as interest rates rise the value of the regular bond portfolio falls, the value of an IO portfolio may rise. Note in Figure 27–14 that at rates above the pool's mortgage coupon of 10 percent, the price-yield curve changes shape and tends to perform like any regular bond. In recent years, thrifts have been major purchasers of IOs to hedge the interest rate risk on the mortgages and other bonds held as assets in their portfolios. We depict the hedging power of IOs in Figure 27–15.

negative duration
When the price of a bond increases or decreases as yields increase or decrease.

PO Strips

PO strip
A bond sold to investors whose cash flows reflect the monthly principal payments received from a pool of mortgages.

The value of the **PO strip** (P_{PO}) is defined by

$$P_{PO} = \frac{PO_1}{\left(1 + \frac{y}{12}\right)} + \frac{PO_2}{\left(1 + \frac{y}{12}\right)^2} + \frac{PO_3}{\left(1 + \frac{y}{12}\right)^3} + \ldots + \frac{PO_{300}}{\left(1 + \frac{y}{12}\right)^{300}}$$

where the PO_i represents the mortgage principal components of each monthly payment by the mortgage holders. This includes both the monthly amortized payment component of *PMT* that is principal and any early prepayments of principal by the mortgagees. Again, we consider the effects on a PO's value (P_{PO}) of a change in interest rates.

Discount Effect   As yields (*y*) fall, the present value of any principal payments must increase and the value of the PO strip rises.

FIGURE 27–14
Price-Yield Curve of an IO Percent Strip

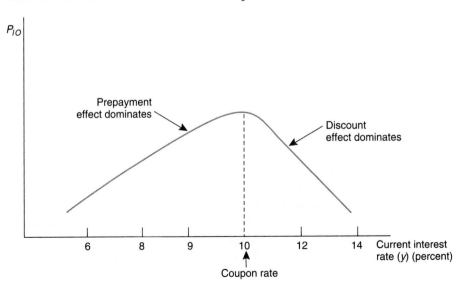

FIGURE 27–15
Hedging with IOs

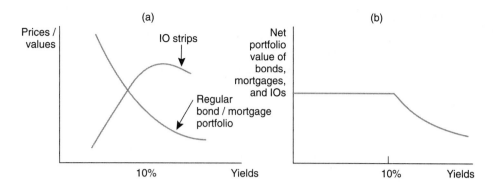

FIGURE 27–16
Price-Yield Curve
of a PO Strip

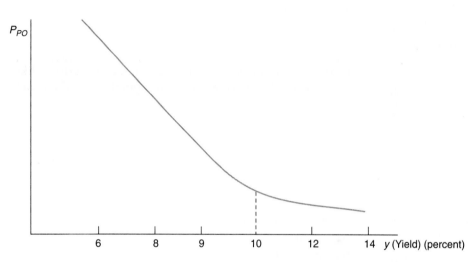

Prepayment Effect As yields fall, the mortgage holders pay off principal early. Consequently, the PO bondholder receives the fixed principal balance outstanding on the pool of mortgages earlier than stated. Thus, this prepayment effect must also work to increase the value of the PO strip.

As interest rates fall, both the discount and prepayment effects point to a rise in the value of the PO strip. The price-yield curve reflects an inverse relationship, but with a steeper slope than for normal bonds; that is, PO strip bond values are very interest rate sensitive, especially for yields below the stated mortgage coupon rate. We show this in Figure 27–16 for a 10 percent PO strip. (Note that a regular coupon bond is affected only by the discount effect.) As you can see, when yields fall below 10 percent, the market value or price of the PO strip can increase very fast. At rates above 10 percent, it tends to behave like a regular bond (as the incentive to prepay disappears).

The IO–PO strip is a classic example of financial engineering. From a given pass-through bond, two new bonds have been created: the first with an upward-sloping price-yield curve over some range and the second with a steeply downward-sloping price-yield curve over some range. Each class is attractive to different investors and investor segments. The IO is attractive to deposit-taking institutions as an on-balance-sheet hedging vehicle. The PO is attractive to FIs that wish to increase the interest rate sensitivity of their portfolios and to investors or traders who wish to take a naked or speculative position regarding the future course of interest

TABLE 27–6
Asset-Backed
Commercial Paper
Conduits in Canada,
December 2004

Source: Dominion Bond Rating Service. www.dbrs.com

Investment Dealer	ABCP Outstanding	ABCP Marker Share
BMO Nesbitt Burns Inc.	$18,424	29.3%
CIBC World Markets Inc.	10,909	17.3%
RBC Capital Markets	7,549	12.0%
Scotia Capital	3,402	5.4%
TD Securities Inc.	7,964	12.7%
Coventree Capital Group ,Inc.	7,825	12.4%
National Bank Financial	2,283	3.6%
Other (includes some estimates)	4,550	7.2%
Total	$62,906	100.0%

FIGURE 27–17
The Structure of
a Credit Card
Securitization

rates. This high and complex interest sensitivity has resulted in major traders such as J. P. Morgan Chase and Merrill Lynch, as well as many investors such as hedge funds, suffering considerable losses on their investments in these instruments when interest rates have moved unexpectedly against them.

Securitization of Other Assets

Although a major use of securitization vehicles has been for packaging residential mortgages, the techniques have been adapted and used for FIs' other assets such as automobile loans and leases, credit card receivables, commercial mortgages, equipment leases and loans, lines of credit, trade receivables, and corporate loans (Figure 27–2).

In addition to securitizing their residential mortgages, Canadian banks as well as retail stores Canadian Tire (Canadian Tire Bank) and Sears Canada (Sears Canada Bank) have been active in securitizing their credit card receivables. Credit card securitization is very similar in technology to pass-through mortgage securities. As shown in Figure 27–17, the credit card receivables are sold to a trust company and then asset-backed securities are issued in the form of notes, which are rated and are tradable. For example, in 2004, in addition to securitizing $7.9 billion in residential mortgages, CIBC issued $1.4 billion in term ABS notes rated AAA by DBRS through CARDS-II Trust. CIBC continues to service these receivables. Bank of Nova Scotia, on the other hand, wound up its credit card securitization program in 2004.[20]

FIs have also implemented the securitization technology for their customers for a fee. These third-party assets are securitized by creating **variable interest entities (VIEs)** (also called **multi-seller conduits**) that create asset-backed commercial paper (ABCP) that is rated and then sold in the capital markets. Table 27–6 shows the top seven investment dealers and their share of the ABCP in December 2004, as well as the names of the conduits.

variable interest entities (VIEs)/ multi-seller conduits
Special purpose entities created by FIs for the securitization and sale of customer's assets.

---

[20] See CIBC Annual Accountability Report 2004, p. 88–89 and H. Loke and S. Bridges, 2004 Year-End Review of Canadian Asset-Backed Securities, Dominion Bond Rating Services, March 2005, pp. 8–10.

TABLE 27–7
Benefits versus
Costs of
Securitization

Benefits	Costs
1. New funding source (bonds versus deposits) 2. Increased liquidity of FI loans 3. Enhanced ability to manage the duration gap of $(D_A - kD_L)$ 4. If off balance sheet, the issuer saves on deposit insurance premiums, and capital adequacy requirements	1. Cost of public/private credit risk insurance and guarantees 2. Cost of overcollateralization 3. Valuation and packaging costs (the cost of asset heterogeneity)

CAN ALL ASSETS BE SECURITIZED?

The extension of securitization technology to other assets raises questions about the limits of securitization and whether all assets and loans can be securitized. Conceptually the answer is that they can, so long as it is profitable to do so or the benefits to the FI from securitization outweigh the costs of securitization.[21] In Table 27–7, we summarize the benefits versus the costs of securitization.

From Table 27–7, given any set of benefits, the more costly and difficult it is to find asset packages of sufficient size and homogeneity, the more difficult and expensive it is to securitize. For example, corporate loans have maturities running from a few months up to eight years; further, they have varying interest rate terms (fixed, LIBOR floating, prime rate floating) and fees. In addition, they contain differing covenants and are made to firms in a wide variety of industries. Despite this, FIs have still been able to issue securitization packages called CLOs (collateralized loan obligations) containing high-quality low-default-risk loans and CDOs (collateralized debt obligations) containing a diversified collection of loans and other assets. The interest and principal payments on a CDO are linked to the timing of default losses and repayments on a pool of underlying loans or bonds. The riskiest of the CDOs, sometimes called toxic waste, pay out only if everything goes right. The best CDOs will pay out unless the entire portfolio defaults. Generally, it has been much harder to securitize low-quality loans into CDOs. Specifically, the harder it is to value a loan or asset pool, the greater the costs of securitization due to the need for overcollateralization or credit risk insurance. Further, given the economic recession of the early 2000s and some large defaults and frauds at once highly rated companies (such as Enron and Worldcom), many CDOs debt pools have suffered large value losses. For example, American Express discovered the risk of CDOs in the early 2000s. In 1997 and 1998, American Express took a US$3.5 billion position in CDOs based on an assumed default rate of 2 percent on the underlying assets. In early 2001, the actual default rate was 8 percent and American Express was forced to take an US$830 million charge for losses on their CDOs. Similarly, Barclay's issued over US$3.5 billion of CDO bonds between 1999 and 2001, of which US$2.9 billion were rated AAA by Fitch Investors Services. By March 2003 only US$128 million of the bonds were still AAA rated and the underlying debtors had defaulted on over US$120 million face value of bonds. [22]

---

[21] See C. Pavel, "Securitization," Federal Reserve Bank of Chicago, *Economic Perspectives,* 1985, pp. 16–31.

[22] See "CDO—Not Cash on Delivery," *The Economist,* July 28, 2001, p. 68.

The potential boundary to securitization may well be defined by the relative degree of heterogeneity and credit quality of an asset type or group. It is not surprising that fixed-rate residential mortgages were the first assets to be securitized since they are the most homogeneous of all assets on FI balance sheets. For example, the existence of secondary markets for houses provides price information that allows reasonably accurate market valuations of the underlying asset to be made, and extensive data are available on mortgage default rates by locality.

Concept Questions

1. Can all assets and loans be securitized? Explain your answer.

Summary

In Chapter 1 we distinguished between FIs that are asset transformers and those that are asset brokers. By becoming increasingly reliant on securitization, banks are moving away from being asset transformers that originate and hold assets to maturity; they are becoming asset brokers more reliant on servicing and other fees. This makes banks look more similar to securities firms. Thus, over time, we can expect the traditional financial technology differences between commercial banking and investment banking to diminish as more loans and assets are securitized. The major forms of securitization—pass-through securities, collateralized mortgage obligations (CMOs)—were discussed. Also, the impact of prepayment behaviour on MBS valuation was discussed. Finally, recent innovations in securitization were described and a summary of the Canadian ABS market provided.

Questions and Problems

1. What has been the effect of securitization on the asset portfolios of financial institutions?

2. What regulatory costs do FIs face when making loans? How does securitization reduce the levels of cost?

3. An FI is planning to issue $100 million in commercial loans. The FI will finance the loans by issuing demand deposits.

   a. What is the minimum amount of capital required by the Basel accord?

   b. What is the amount of demand deposits needed to fund this loan assuming there are no reserve requirement on demand deposits?

   c. Show a simple balance sheet with total assets, total liabilities, and equity if this is the only project funded by the bank.

4. Consider the FI in problem 4.

   a. What additional risk exposure problems does the FI face?

   b. What is the duration of a 25-year, 12 percent annual $100,000 monthly amortizing mortgage loan if the yield to maturity is 12 percent? *Hint:* Use a spreadsheet for calculations.

   c. What are some possible solutions to the duration mismatch and the illiquidity problems?

   d. What advantages does securitization have in dealing with the FI's risk exposure problems?

5. How are investors in pass-through securities protected against default risk?

6. What specific changes occur on the balance sheet at the completion of the securitization process? What adjustments occur to the risk profile of the FI?

7. Consider a mortgage pool with principal of $20 million. The maturity is 25 years with a monthly mortgage payment of 10 percent per annum. Assume no prepayments.

   a. What is the monthly mortgage payment (100 percent amortizing) on the pool of mortgages?

   b. If the servicing fee is 45 basis points, what is the yield on the MBS pass-through?

   c. What is the monthly payment on the MBS in part (b)?

   d. Calculate the first monthly servicing fee paid to the originating FIs.

8. Calculate the value of (a) the mortgage pool and (b) the MBS pass-through in question 9 if market

interest rates increase 50 basis points. Assume no prepayments.

9. What would be the impact on MBS pricing if the pass-through was not fully amortized? What is the present value of a $10 million pool of 15-year mortgages with an 8.5 percent per annum monthly mortgage coupon if market rates are 5 percent? The FI servicing fee is 44 basis points.

   a. Assume that the MBS is fully amortized.

   b. Assume that the MBS is only half amortized. There is a lump-sum payment at the maturity of the MBS that equals 50 percent of the mortgage pool's face value.

10. What is prepayment risk? How does prepayment risk affect the cash flow stream on a fully amortized mortgage loan? What are the two primary factors that cause early payment?

11. Under what conditions do mortgage holders have a call option on their mortgages? When is the call option in the money?

12. What are the benefits of market yields that are less than the average rate in the NHA MBS mortgage pool? What are the disadvantages of this rate inversion? To whom do the good news and the bad news accrue?

13. What is the weighted-average life (WAL) of a mortgage pool supporting pass-through securities? How does WAL differ from duration?

14. If 150 $200,000 mortgages are expected to be prepaid in three years and the remaining 150 $200,000 mortgages in a $60 million 15-year mortgage pool are to be prepaid in four years, what is the weighted-average life of the mortgage pool? Mortgages are fully amortized, with mortgage coupon rates set at 10 percent to be paid annually.

15. A FI originates a pool of 500 25-year mortgages, each averaging $150,000 with an annual mortgage coupon rate of 8 percent. Assume that the FI's servicing fee is 55 basis points.

   a. What is the present value of the mortgage pool?

   b. What is the monthly mortgage payment?

   c. For the first two payments, what portion is interest and what portion is principal repayment?

   d. What are the expected monthly cash flows to each MBS investor?

   e. What is the present value of the MBS? Assume that the risk-adjusted market annual rate of return is 8 percent compounded monthly.

   f. Would actual cash flows to MBS investors deviate from expected cash flows as in part (d)? Why or why not?

   g. What are the expected monthly cash flows for the FI?

   h. If all the mortgages in the pool are completely prepaid at the end of the second month, what is the pool's weighted-average life? *Hint:* Use your answer to part (c).

   i. What is the price of the pass-through security if its weighted-average life is equal to your solution for part (h)? Assume no change in market interest rates.

   j. What is the price of the MBS with a weighted-average life equal to your solution for part (h) if market yields decline 50 basis points?

16. What is the difference between the yield spread to average life and the option-adjusted spread on mortgage-backed securities?

17. What factors may cause the actual prepayment pattern to differ from the assumed pattern? How would an FI adjust for the presumed occurrence of some of these factors?

18. What is the burnout factor? How is it used in modeling prepayment behavior? What other factors may be helpful in modeling the prepayment behavior of a given mortgage pool?

19. What is the goal of prepayment models that use option pricing theory? How do these models differ from the PSA or empirical models? What criticisms often are directed toward these models?

20. How does the price on an MBS relate to the yield on an MBS option from the perspective of the investor? What is the option-adjusted spread (OAS)?

21. Use the options prepayment model to calculate the yield on a $30 million three-year fully amortized mortgage pass-through where the mortgage coupon rate is 6 percent paid annually. Market yields are 6.4 percent paid annually. Assume that there is no servicing or guarantee fee.

   a. What is the annual payment on the MBS?

   b. What is the present value of the MBS?

   c. Interest rate movements over time are assumed to change a maximum of 0.5 percent per year. Both an increase of 0.5 percent and a decrease of 0.5 percent in interest rates are equally probable. If interest rates fall 1.0 percent below the current mortgage coupon rates, all of the mortgages in the pool will be completely prepaid. Diagram the interest-rate tree and indicate the probabilities of each node in the tree.

   d. What are the expected annual cash flows for each possible situation over the three-year period?

e. The Treasury yield curve is flat at a discount yield of 6 percent. What is the option-adjusted spread on the MBS?

22. Use the options prepayment model to calculate the yield on a $12 million, five-year, fully amortized mortgage pass-through where the mortgage coupon rate is 7 percent paid annually. Market yields are 8 percent paid annually. Assume that there is no servicing or guarantee fee.

    a. What is the annual payment on the MBS?

    b. What is the present value of the MBS?

    c. Interest rate movements over time are assumed to change a maximum of 1 percent per year. Both an increase of 1 percent and a decrease of 1 percent in interest rates are equally probable. If interest rates fall 3 percent below the current mortgage coupon rates, all mortgages in the pool will be completely prepaid. Diagram the interest rate tree and indicate the probabilities of each node in the tree.

    d. What are the expected annual cash flows for each possible situation over the five-year period?

    e. The Treasury yield curve is flat at a discount yield of 6 percent. What is the option-adjusted spread on the MBS?

23. What conditions would cause the yield on pass-through securities with prepayment risk to be less than the yield on pass-through securities without prepayment risk?

24. What is a collateralized mortgage obligation (CMO)? How is it similar to a pass-through security? How does it differ? In what way does the creation of a CMO use market segmentation to redistribute prepayment risk?

25. Consider $200 million of 25-year mortgages with a coupon of 10 percent per annum paid quarterly.

    a. What is the quarterly mortgage payment?

    b. What are the interest repayments over the first year of life of the mortgages? What are the principal repayments?

    c. Construct a 25-year CMO using this mortgage pool as collateral. The pool has three tranches, where tranche A offers the least protection against prepayment and tranche C offers the most protection against prepayment. Tranche A of $50 million receives quarterly payments at 9 percent per annum, tranche B of $100 million receives quarterly payments at 10 percent per annum, and tranche C of $50 million receives quarterly payments at 11 percent per annum. Diagram the CMO structure.

    d. Assume nonamortization of principal and no prepayments. What are the total promised coupon payments to the three classes? What are the principal payments to each of the three classes for the first year?

    e. If, over the first year, the trustee receives quarterly prepayments of $10 million on the mortgage pool, how are these funds distributed?

    f. How are the cash flows distributed if prepayments in the first half of the second year are $20 million quarterly?

    g. How can the CMO issuer earn a positive spread on the CMO?

26. What is an interest-only (IO) strip? How do the discount effect and the prepayment effect of an IO create a negative duration asset? What macroeconomic effect is required for this negative duration effect to be possible?

27. What is a principal-only (PO) strip? What causes the price-yield profile of a PO strip to have a steeper slope than a normal bond?

28. An FI originates a pool of short-term real estate loans worth $20 million with maturities of five years and paying interest rates of 9 percent per annum.

    a. What is the average payment received by the FI, including both principal and interest, if no prepayment is expected over the life of the loan?

    b. If the loans are converted into pass-through certificates and the FI charges a servicing fee of 50 basis points, what is the payment amount expected by the holders of the pass-through securities if no prepayment is expected?

    c. Assume that the payments are separated into interest-only (IO) and principal-only (PO) payments, that prepayments of 5 percent occur at the end of years 3 and 4, and that the payment of the remaining principal occurs at the end of year 5. What are the expected annual payments for each instrument? Assume discount rates of 9 percent.

    d. What is the market value of IOs and POs if the market interest rates for instruments of similar risk decline to 8 percent?

29. What are the factors that, in general, allow assets to be securitized? What are the costs involved in the securitization process?

30. How does an FI use loan sales and securitization to manage interest rate, credit, and liquidity risks? Summarize how each of the possible methods of securitization affects the balance sheet and profitability of an FI in the management of these risks.

Web Question

31. Go to Canada Mortgage and Housing Corporation's Web site at www.cmhc.ca. Click on "Mortgage insurance & securitization." Click on "Mortgage-backed Securities," then on "Mortgage-backed Securities Community," and finally on "Standard Terminology and Calculations" to view the report by Roger D. Quick provided by Scotia McLeod. What prepayment model is used as an example in determining the prepayment rates on NHA mortgage-backed securities? How does this model compare to the models presented in this textbook?

32. Go to the Bank of Canada's Web site at www.bankofcanada.ca. Click on "Research and Publications." Click on "Financial System Review." Download the latest copy of the Review. Using the search feature in Adobe Acrobat, search for "U.S." What are the cross-border issues currently of concern to the Bank of Canada? What short-term and long-term effects are they expected to have on Canadian financial markets? Search the document using the term "global." What current global financial market issues are of concern to the Bank of Canada?

Chapter Appendixes

Financial Statement Analysis Using a Return on Equity (ROE) Framework

Despite record profits, many FIs have areas of weakness and inefficiency that need to be addressed. One way of identifying weaknesses and problem areas is through an analysis of financial statements. In particular, an analysis of selected accounting ratios—ratio analysis—allows FI managers to evaluate the current performance of an FI, the change in an FI's performance over time (*time series analysis* of ratios over a period of time), and the performance of an FI relative to competitor FIs (*cross-sectional analysis* of ratios across a group of FIs).

Figure 2A–1 provides a summary of the breakdown of the return on equity (ROE) framework. This framework is similar to the DuPont analysis frequently used by managers of nonfinancial institutions. The ROE framework starts with a frequently used measure of profitability—return on equity (ROE)—and then decomposes ROE to identify strengths and weaknesses in an FI's performance.[1] Such a decomposition provides a convenient and systematic method for identifying the strengths and weaknesses of an FI's performance.

FIGURE 2A–1
**Breakdown of ROE
into Various
Financial Ratios**

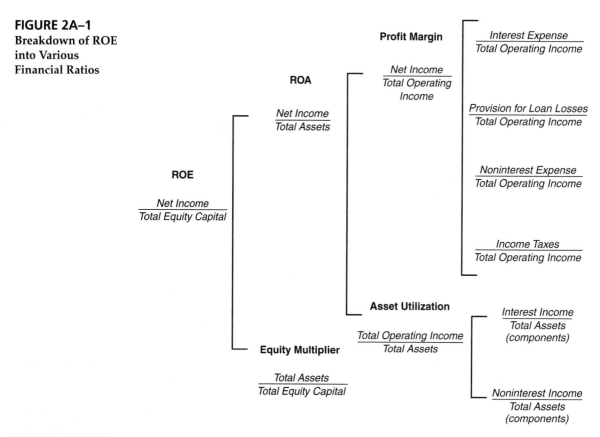

---

[1] Many large banks also use a risk-adjusted return on capital (RAROC) measure to evaluate the impact of credit risk on bank performance. ROE does not consider the bank's risk in lending as does RAROC. RAROC is described in Chapter 11.

Identification of strengths and weaknesses and the reasons for them provide a useful tool for FI managers as they look for ways to improve performance. Table 2A–1 summarizes the role of ROE and the first two levels (from Figure 2A–1) of its decomposition in analyzing an FI's performance.

These ratios are related as follows (see Figure 2A–1):

$$ROE = ROA \times EM$$
$$ROA = PM \times AU$$

In turn, the PM and AU ratios can also be broken down and shown to depend on key financial ratios (see Figure 2A–1).

TABLE 2A–1
Role of ROE, ROA, EM, PM, and AU in Analyzing an FI's Performance

> **Return on Equity (ROE):** measures overall profitability of the FI per dollar of equity.
> **Return on Assets (ROA):** measures profit generated relative to the FI's assets.
> **Equity Multiplier (EM):** measures the extent to which assets of the FI are funded with equity relative to debt.
> **Profit Margin (PM):** measures the ability to pay expenses and generate net income from interest and noninterest income.
> **Asset Utilization (AU):** measures the amount of interest and noninterest income generated per dollar of total assets.

Appendix 2B   Technology in Commercial Banking

Technology is important because well-chosen technological investments have the potential to increase both the FI's net interest margin—or the difference between interest income and interest expense—and other net income. Therefore, technology can directly improve profitability. The following subsections focus on some specific technology-based products found in modern wholesale and retail banking.

WHOLESALE BANKING SERVICES

Probably the most important area on which technology has impacted wholesale or business customer services is a bank's ability to provide cash management or working capital services. Cash management service needs have largely resulted from (1) recognition that excess cash balances result in a significant opportunity cost for business firms due to lost or forgone interest and (2) business firms' need-to-know cash or working capital positions on a real-time basis. Among the services that modern banks provide to improve the efficiency with which business clients manage their financial positions are these:

1. *Cheque clearing services.* Also called *controlled disbursement accounts* for businesses operating in the U.S. An account feature that allows almost all payments to be made in a given day to be known in the morning. The bank informs the business client, usually electronically, of the total funds it needs to meet disbursements and the client electronically transfers the amount needed. These chequing accounts are debited early each day so that businesses can obtain an early insight into their net cash positions.

2. *Account Reconciliation.* A chequing account that captures the data of all of the firm's cheques that have cleared during the day. The data is delivered to the firm electronically, usually by 9 a.m. the next morning, and the firm is able to generate cash management reports for its own use. As well, the paper cheques are returned to the business for internal verification.

3. *Lockbox services.* A centralized collection service for business payments to reduce the delay in paper-based cheque clearing, or the **float**. In a typical lockbox arrangement, a bank sets up a lockbox at the post office for a business client located outside the area. Customers mail payments to the lockbox and the bank collects these cheques several times per day and deposits them directly into the customer's account. Details are provided electronically to the business customer. Canadian banks provide lockbox services for customers in both Canada and the United States.

4. *Electronic lockbox.* Same as item 3 but the customer receives on line payments. The bank provides the security and encryption services needed to protect the electronic transfers.

5. *Concentration Accounts.* A service that redirects funds from accounts in a large number of branches or even from different financial institutions to a centralized account at one bank. The account balance is provided to the firm early in the morning so that the firm can make decisions about investing excess funds, or borrowing against its line of credit.

6. *Electronic funds transfer.* Includes automated receipt of customer's payments as well as payments of payrolls or dividends, and electronic submission of business taxes.

7. *Cheque deposit services.* Encoding, endorsing, microfilming, and handling customers' cheques.

8. *Electronic initiation of letters of credit.* Allows customers in a network to access bank computers to initiate letters of credit.

9. *Treasury management software.* Allows efficient management of multiple currency and security portfolios for trading and investment purposes.

10. *Electronic data interchange.* A specialized application of electronic mail, allowing businesses to transfer and transact invoices, purchase orders, and shipping notices automatically, using banks as clearinghouses.

11. *Facilitating business-to-business e-commerce.* The largest banks offer firms the technology for electronic business-to-business commerce. The banks are essentially automating the entire information flow associated with the procurement and distribution of goods and services among businesses.

12. *Electronic billing.* Provides the presentment and collection services for companies that send out substantial volumes of recurring bills. Banks combine the e-mail capability of the Internet to send out bills with their ability to process payments electronically through the payment networks.

13. *Verifying identities.* Using encryption technology a bank certifies the identities of its own account holders and serves as the intermediary through which its business customers can verify the identities of account holders at other banks.

14. *Assisting small business entries in e-commerce.* Helps smaller firms in setting up the infrastructure—interactive Web site and payment capabilities—for engaging in e-commerce.

RETAIL BANKING SERVICES

Retail customers have demanded efficiency and flexibility in their financial transactions. Using only cheques or holding cash is often more expensive and time-consuming than using retail-oriented electronic payment technology, and increasingly, the Internet. Some of the most important retail payment product innovations include the following:

1. *Automated teller machines (ATMs).* Also called Automated Banking Machines (ABMs). Allow customers 24-hour access to their chequing accounts. They can pay bills as well as withdraw cash from these machines. In addition, if the bank's ATMs are part of a bank network (such as Interac), retail depositors can gain direct nationwide—and in many cases international—access to their deposit accounts by using the ATMs of other banks in the network to draw on their accounts.

2. *Point-of-sale (POS) debit cards.* Allow customers who choose not to use cash, cheques, or credit cards for purchases to buy merchandise using debit card/point-of-sale (POS) terminals. The merchant avoids the cheque float and any delay in payment associated with credit card receivables since the bank offering the debit card/POS service immediately and directly transfers funds from the customer's deposit account to the merchant's deposit account at the time of card use. Unlike cheque or credit card purchases, the use of a debit card results in an immediate transfer of funds from the customer's account to the merchant's account.[1] Moreover, the customer never runs up a debit to the card issuer as is common with a credit card.

3. *Home banking.* Connects customers to their deposit and brokerage accounts and provides such services as electronic securities trading and bill-paying service via personal computers.

---

[1] In the case of bank-supplied credit cards, the merchant normally is compensated very quickly but not instantaneously (usually one or two days) by the credit card issuer. The bank then holds an account receivable against the card user. However, even a short delay can represent an opportunity cost for the merchant.

4. *Preauthorized debits/credits.* Includes direct deposit of payroll cheques into bank accounts and direct payments of mortgage and utility bills.

5. *Paying bills via telephone.* Allows direct transfer of funds from the customer's bank account to outside parties either by voice command or by touch-tone telephone.

6. *E-mail billing.* Allows customers to receive and pay bills by using the Internet, thus saving postage and paper.

7. *On-line banking.* Allows customers to conduct retail banking and investment services offered via the Internet.[2] In some cases this involves building a new on-line Internet-only bank, such as ING Direct.

8. *Smart cards (stored-value cards).* Allow the customer to store and spend money for various transactions using a card that has a chip storage device, usually in the form of a strip. These have become increasingly popular at universities.

---

[2] A survey conducted by the Canadian Bankers Association (CBA) in 2004 found that 23 percent of the survey's participants banked primarily through the Internet, almost triple the 8 percent of participants reported in the 2000 survey. See "Taking a Closer Look: Electronic Banking", May 2005, available at www.cba.ca. In addition, electronic banking and debit cards raise concerns about security and that have led to the formation of the Working Group on Electronic Commerce and Consumers whose report, "Principles of Consumer Protection for Electronic Commerce: A Canadian Framework" provides guidelines for merchants and consumers to protect their electronic information. This report is available at http://strategis.ic.gc.ca/oca, as well as on the CBA's web site.

Appendix 8A   Term Structure of Interest Rates

To explain the process of estimating the impact of an unexpected shock in short-term interest rates on the entire term structure of interest rates, FIs use the theory of the term structure of interest rates or the yield curve. The *term structure of interest rates* compares the market yields or interest rates on securities, assuming that all characteristics (default risk, coupon rate, etc.) except maturity are the same. The yield curve for U.S. Treasury securities is the most commonly reported and analyzed yield curve. The shape of the yield curve on Treasury securities has taken many forms over the years. Figure 8A–1 presents the Treasury yield curve as of October 3, 2003. As can be seen, the yield curve on this date reflected the normal upward-sloping relationship between yield and maturity. Explanations for the shape of the yield curve fall predominantly into three theories: the unbiased expectations theory, the liquidity premium theory, and the market segmentation theory.

UNBIASED EXPECTATIONS THEORY

According to the unbiased expectations theory for the term structure of interest rates, at a given point in time the yield curve reflects the market's current expectations of future short-term rates. Thus, an upward-sloping yield curve reflects the market's expectation that short-term rates will rise throughout the relevant time period (e.g., the Fed-

eral Reserve is expected to tighten monetary policy in the future). Similarly, a flat yield curve reflects the expectation that short-term rates will remain constant over the relevant time period.

The intuition behind the unbiased expectations theory is that if investors have a 30-year investment horizon, they could either buy a current 30-year bond and earn the current yield on a 30-year bond (R_{30}, if held to maturity) each year, or could invest in 30 successive one-year bonds (of which they know only the current one-year rate, R_1, but form expectations of the unknown future one-year rates). In equilibrium, the return to holding a 30-year bond to maturity should equal the expected return to investing in 30 successive one-year bonds. Similarly, the return on a 29-year bond should equal the expected return on investing in 29 successive one-year bonds. If future one-year rates are expected to rise each successive year into the future, then the yield curve will slope upward. Specifically, the current 30-year T-bond rate or return will exceed the 29-year bond rate, which will exceed the 28-year bond rate, and so on. Similarly, if future one-year rates are expected to remain constant each successive year into the future, then the 30-year bond rate will be equal to the 29-year bond rate; that is, the term structure of interest rates will remain constant over the relevant time period. Specifically, the unbiased expectations theory posits that long-term rates are a geometric average of current and expected short-term interest rates. That is, the interest rate that equates the return on a series of short-term security investments with the return on a long-term security with an equivalent maturity reflects the market's forecast of future interest rates. The mathematical equation representing this relationship is:

$$(1 + {}_1R_N)^N = (1 + {}_1R_1)(1 + E({}_2r_1)) \ldots (1 + E({}_Nr_1))$$

where

$$
\begin{aligned}
{}_1R_N &= \text{Actual N-period rate} \\
N &= \text{Term to maturity} \\
{}_1R_1 &= \text{Current one-year rate} \\
E({}_tr_1) &= \text{Expected one-year (forward) yield} \\
&\qquad \text{during period } t
\end{aligned}
$$

FIGURE 8A–1
Treasury Yield Curve, October 3, 2003

Source: Board of Governors of the Federal Reserve, "Selected Interest Rates," October 2003. *www.federalreserve.gov*

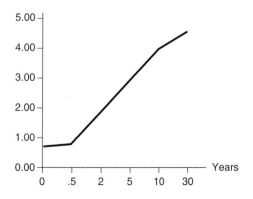

% Rate of Interest

Notice that uppercase interest rate terms $_1R_t$ are the actual current interest rates on securities purchased today with a maturity of t years. Lowercase interest rate terms $_tr_1$ are estimates of future one-year interest rates starting t years into the future. For example, suppose the current one-year spot rate and expected one-year Treasury bill rates over the following three years (i.e., years 2, 3, and 4, respectively) are as follows:

$$_1R_1 = 6\%, \quad E(_2r_1) = 7\%,$$
$$E(_3r_1) = 7.5\%, \quad E(_4r_1) = 7.85\%$$

This would be consistent with the market's expecting the Federal Reserve to increasingly tighten monetary policy. With the unbiased expectations theory, current long-term rates for one-, two-, three-, and four-year maturity Treasury securities should be:

$$_1R_1 = 6\%$$
$$_1R_2 = [(1+.06)(1+.07)]^{1/2} - 1 = 6.499\%$$
$$_1R_3 = [(1+.06)(1+.07)(1+.075)]^{1/3} - 1 = 6.832\%$$
$$_1R_4 = [(1+.06)(1+.07)(1+.075)(1+.0785)]^{1/4} - 1$$
$$= 7.085\%$$

And the yield curve should look like this:

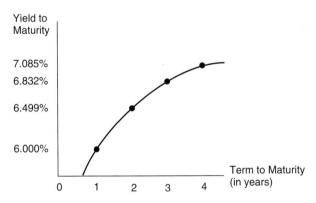

Thus, the upward-sloping yield curve reflects the market's expectation of consistently rising one-year (short-term) interest rates in the future.

LIQUIDITY PREMIUM THEORY

The unbiased expectations theory has the shortcoming that it neglects to recognize that forward rates are not perfect predictors of future interest rates. If forward rates were perfect predictors of future interest rates, future prices of Treasury securities would be known with certainty. The return over any investment period would be certain and independent of the maturity of the instrument initially purchased and of the time at which the investor needs to liquidate the security. However, with uncertainty about future interest rates (and future monetary policy actions) and hence about future security prices, these instruments become risky in the sense that the return over a future investment period is unknown. In other words, because of future uncertainty of return, there is a risk in holding long-term securities, and that risk increases with the security's maturity.

The liquidity premium theory of the term structure of interest rates allows for this future uncertainty. It is based on the idea that investors will hold long-term maturities only if they are offered a premium to compensate for the future uncertainty in a security's value, which increases with an asset's maturity. In other words, the liquidity premium theory states that long-term rates are equal to the geometric average of current and expected short-term rates plus a liquidity or risk premium that increases with the maturity of the security. Figure 8A–2 illustrates the difference in the shape of the yield curve under the unbiased expectations theory versus the liquidity premium theory. For example, according to the liquidity premium theory, an upward-sloping yield curve may reflect the investor's expectations that future short-term rates will rise, be flat, or fall, but because the liquidity premium increases with maturity, the yield curve will nevertheless increase with the term to maturity. The liquidity premium theory may be mathematically represented as:

$$_1R_N = [(1 + {_1R_1})(1 + E(_2r_1) + LP_2) \cdots$$
$$(1 + E(_Nr_1) + LP_N)]^{1/N} - 1$$

where

LP_t = liquidity premium for a period t and $LP_2 < LP_3 < \cdots < LP_N$.

MARKET SEGMENTATION THEORY

Market segmentation theory argues that individual investors have specific maturity preferences. Accordingly, securities with different maturities are not seen as perfect substitutes under the market segmentation theory. Instead, individual investors have

FIGURE 8A–2   Yield Curve under the Unbiased Expectations Theory (UET) versus the Liquidity-Premium Theory (LPT)

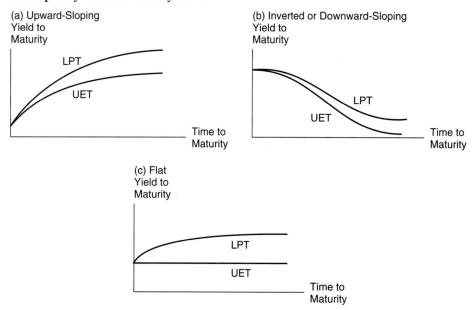

(a) Upward-Sloping
Yield to
Maturity

LPT

UET

Time to
Maturity

(b) Inverted or Downward-Sloping
Yield to
Maturity

LPT

UET

Time to
Maturity

(c) Flat
Yield to
Maturity

LPT

UET

Time to
Maturity

preferred investment horizons dictated by the nature of the assets and liabilities they hold. For example, banks might prefer to hold relatively short-term U.S. Treasury bills because of the short-term nature of their deposit liabilities, while insurance companies might prefer to hold long-term U.S. Treasury bonds because of the long-term nature of their life insurance contractual liabilities. As a result, interest rates are determined by distinct supply and demand conditions within a particular maturity bucket or market segment (e.g., the short end and the long end of the market). The market segmentation theory assumes that neither investors nor borrowers are willing to shift from one maturity sector to another to take advantage of opportunities arising from changes in yields. Figure 8A–3 demonstrates how changes in the supply curve for short-versus long-term bonds result in changes in the shape of the yield curve. Such a change may occur if the U.S. Treasury decides to issue fewer short-term bonds and more long-term bonds (i.e., to lengthen the average maturity of government debt outstanding). Specifically in Figure 8A–3, the higher the yield on securities, the higher the demand for them. Thus, as the supply of securities decreases in the short-term market and increases in the long-term market, the slope of the yield curve becomes steeper. If the supply of short-term securities had increased while

the supply of long-term securities had decreased, the yield curve would have become flatter (and may even have sloped downward). Indeed, the large-scale repurchases of long-term Treasury bonds (i.e., reductions in supply) by the U.S. Treasury in 2000 have been viewed as the major cause of the inverted yield curve that appeared in February 2000.

FORECASTING INTEREST RATES

As interest rates change, so do the values of financial securities. Accordingly, the ability to predict or forecast interest rates is critical to the profitability of FIs. For example, if interest rates rise, the value of investment portfolios of FIs will fall, resulting in a loss of wealth. Thus, interest rate forecasts are extremely important for the financial wealth of FIs. The discussion of the unbiased expectations theory above indicated that the shape of the yield curve is determined by the market's current expectations of future short-term interest rates. For example, an upward-loping yield curve suggests that the market expects future short-term interest rates to increase. Given that the yield curve represents the market's current expectations of future short-term interest rates, the unbiased expectations theory can be used to forecast (short-term) interest rates in the future (i.e., forward one-year interest

FIGURE 8A-3 Market Segmentation and Determination of the Slope of the Yield Curve

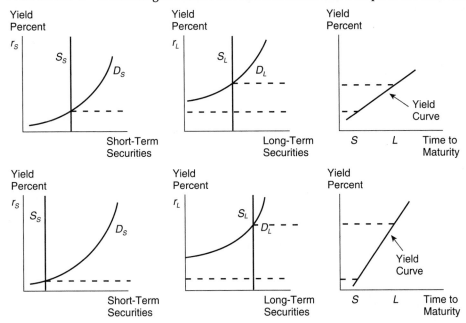

rates). A forward rate is an expected or implied rate on a short-term security that is to be originated at some point in the future. With the equations representing unbiased expectations theory, the market's expectation of forward rates can be derived directly from existing or actual rates on securities currently traded in the spot market.

To find an implied forward rate on a one-year security to be issued one year from today, we can rewrite the unbiased expectation theory equation as follows:

$$_1R_2 = [(1 + {}_1R_1)(1 + ({}_2f_1))]^{1/2} - 1$$

where

$_2f_1$ = Expected one-year rate for year 2, or the implied forward one-year rate for next year

Therefore, $_2f_1$ is the market's estimate of the expected one-year rate for year 2. Solving for $_2f_1$, we get:

$$_2f_1 = [(1 + {}_1R_2)^2/(1 + ({}_1R_1)] - 1$$

In general, we can find the one-year forward rate for any year, N years into the future using the following equation:

$$_Nf_1 = [(1 + {}_1R_N)^N/(1 + ({}_1R_{N-1}))^{N-1}] - 1$$

For example, on October 3, 2003, the existing or current (spot) one-year, two-year, three-year, and four-year zero-coupon Treasury security rates were as follows:

$$_1R_1 = 2.47\%, \quad _1R_2 = 3.66\%,$$
$$_1R_3 = 4.29\%, \quad _1R_4 = 4.69\%$$

With the unbiased expectation theory, one-year forward rates on zero-coupon Treasury bonds for years 2, 3, and 4 as of October 3, 2003, were:

$$_2f_1 = [(1.0366)^2/(1.0247)] - 1 = 4.864\%$$
$$_3f_1 = [(1.0429)^3/(1.0366)^2] - 1 = 5.561\%$$
$$_4f_1 = [(1.0469)^4/(1.0429)^3] - 1 = 5.900\%$$

Thus, the expected one-year rate one year into the future was 4.864 percent; the expected one-year rate two years into the future was 5.561 percent; and the expected one-year rate three years into the future was 5.900 percent.

Appendix 9A   Incorporating Convexity into the Duration Model[1]

In the main body of the chapter, we established these three characteristics of convexity:

1. *Convexity is desirable.* The greater the convexity of a security or a portfolio of securities, the more insurance or interest rate protection an FI manager has against rate increases and the greater the potential gains after interest rate falls.

2. *Convexity and duration.* The larger the interest rate changes and the more convex a fixed-income security or portfolio, the greater the error the FI manager faces in using just duration (and duration matching) to immunize exposure to interest rate shocks.

3. *All fixed-income securities are convex.*[2] To see this, we can take the six-year, 8 percent coupon, 8 percent yield bond and look at two extreme price-yield scenarios. What is the price on the bond if yields falls to zero, and what is its price if yields rise to some very large number?

When $R = 0$:

$$P = \frac{80}{(1+0)} + \ldots + \frac{1,080}{(1+0)^6} = 1,480$$

The price is just the simple undiscounted sum of the coupon values and the face value. Since yields can never go below zero, $1,480 is the maximum possible price for the bond.

When R is very large:

$$P \simeq 0$$

As the yield goes to infinity, the bond price falls asymptotically toward zero, but by definition a bond's price can never be negative. Thus, zero must be the minimum bond price (see Figure 9A–1).

Since convexity is a desirable feature for assets, the FI manager might ask: Can we measure convexity? And can we incorporate this measurement in the duration model to adjust for or offset the error in prediction due to its presence? The answer to both questions is yes.

Theoretically speaking, duration is the slope of the price-yield curve, and convexity, or curvature, is the change in the slope of the price-yield curve. Consider the total effect of a change in interest rates on a bond's price as being broken into a number of separate effects. The precise mathematical derivation of these separate effects is based on a Taylor series expansion that you might remember from your math classes. Essentially, the first-order effect (dP/dR) of an interest rate change on the bond's price is the price-yield curve slope effect, which is measured by duration. The second-order effect (d^2P/dR^2) measures the change in the slope of the price-yield curve; this is the curvature, or convexity, effect. There are also third-, fourth-, and higher-order effects from the Taylor series expansion, but for all practical purposes these effects can be ignored.

We have noted that overlooking the curvature of the price-yield curve may cause errors in predicting the interest sensitivity of a portfolio of assets and liabilities, especially when yields change by large amounts. We can adjust for this by explicitly recognizing the second-order effect of yield changes by measuring the change in the slope of the price-yield curve around a given point. Just as D (duration) measures the slope effect (dP/dR), we introduce a new parameter (CX) to measure the curvature effect (d^2P/dR^2) of the price-yield curve.

The resulting equation, predicting the change in a security's price $(\Delta P/P)$, is:

$$\frac{\Delta P}{P} = -D\frac{\Delta R}{(1+R)} + \frac{1}{2}CX(\Delta R)^2 \quad \textbf{(9A.1)}$$

or:

$$\frac{\Delta P}{P} = -MD\Delta R + \frac{1}{2}CX(\Delta R)^2 \quad \textbf{(9A.2)}$$

The first term in equation (1) is the simple duration model that over- or underpredicts price changes for large changes in interest rates, and the second term is the second-order effect of interest rate changes, that is, the convexity or curvature adjustment. In equation (1), the first term D can be divided by $1 + R$ to produce what we called earlier

[1] This section contains more technical details, which may be included or dropped from the chapter reading depending on the rigour of the course.
[2] This applies to fixed-income securities without special option features such as calls and puts.

FIGURE 9A–1
The Natural Convexity of Bonds

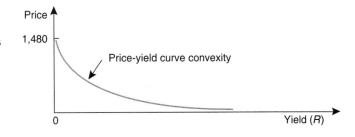

FIGURE 9A–2
Convexity and the Price-Yield Curve

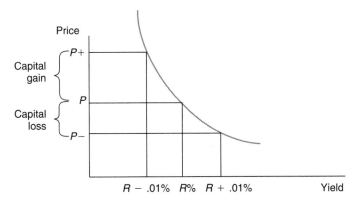

modified duration (MD). You can see this in equation (2). This form is more intuitive because we multiply MD by the simple change in R (ΔR) rather than by the discounted change in R ($\Delta R/(1 + R)$). In the convexity term, the number 1/2 and ($\Delta R)^2$ result from the fact that the convexity effect is the second-order effect of interest rate changes while duration is the first-order effect. The parameter CX reflects the degree of curvature in the price-yield curve at the current yield level, that is, the degree to which the *capital gain effect* exceeds the *capital loss effect* for an equal change in yields up or down. At best, the FI manager can only approximate the curvature effect by using a parametric measure of CX. Even though calculus is based on infinitesimally small changes, in financial markets the smallest change in yields normally observed is one basis point, or a 1/100th of 1 percent change. One possible way to measure CX is introduced next.

As just discussed, the convexity effect is the degree to which the capital gain effect more than offsets the capital loss effect for an equal increase and decrease in interest rates at the current interest rate level. In Figure 9A–2 we depict yields changing upward by one basis point ($R + .01\%$) and downward by one basis point ($R - .01\%$). Because convexity measures the curvature of the price-yield curve around the rate level R percent, it intuitively

measures the degree to which the capital gain effect of a small yield decrease exceeds the capital loss effect of a small yield increase.[3] Definitionally, the CX parameter equals:

$$CX = \frac{\text{Scaling}}{\text{factor}} \left[\begin{array}{c} \text{Capital} \\ \text{loss from a} \\ \text{one-basis-point} \\ \text{rise in yield} \\ \text{(negative effect)} \end{array} + \begin{array}{c} \text{Capital} \\ \text{gain from a} \\ \text{one-basis-point} \\ \text{fall in yield} \\ \text{(positive effect)} \end{array} \right]$$

The sum of the two terms in the brackets reflects the degree to which the capital gain effect exceeds the capital loss effect for a small one-basis-point interest rate change down and up. The scaling factor normalizes this measure to account for a larger 1 percent change in rates. Remember, when interest rates change by a large amount, the convexity effect is important to measure. A commonly used scaling factor is 10^8 so that:[4]

$$CX = 10^8 \left[\frac{\Delta P-}{P} + \frac{\Delta P+}{P} \right]$$

---

[3] We are trying to approximate as best we can the change in the slope of the price-yield curve at R percent. In theory, the changes are infinitesimally small (dR), but in reality, the smallest yield change normally observed is one basis point (ΔR).

[4] This is consistent with the effect of a 1 percent (100 basis points) change in rates.

TABLE 9A–1   Properties of Convexity

1. Convexity Increases with Bond Maturity			2. Convexity Varies with Coupon		3. For Same Duration, Zero-Coupon Bonds Are Less Convex Than Coupon Bonds	
Example			Example		Example	
A	B	C	A	B	A	B
$N = 6$	$N = 18$	$N = \infty$	$N = 6$	$N = 6$	$N = 6$	$N = 5$
$R = 8\%$	$R = 8\%$	$R = 8\%$	$R = 8\%$	$R = 8\%$	$R = 8\%$	$R = 8\%$
$C = 8\%$	$C = 8\%$	$C = 8\%$	$C = 8\%$	$C = 0\%$	$C = 8\%$	$C = 0\%$
$D = 5$	$D = 10.12$	$D = 13.5$	$D = 5$	$D = 6$	$D = 5$	$D = 5$
$CX = 28$	$CX = 130$	$CX = 312$	$CX = 28$	$CX = 36$	$CX = 28$	$CX = 25.72$

Calculation of CX

To calculate the convexity of the 8 percent coupon, 8 percent yield, six-year maturity Eurobond that had a price of $1,000:[5]

$$CX = 10^8 \left[\frac{999.53785 - 1,000}{1,000} + \frac{1,000.46243 - 1,000}{1,000} \right]$$

$$\underbrace{\text{Capital loss from a one-basis-point increase in rates}}_{} + \underbrace{\text{Capital gain from a one-basis-point decrease in rates}}_{}$$

$$CX = 10^8 [0.00000028]$$

$$CX = 28$$

This value for CX can be inserted into the bond price prediction equation (2) with the convexity adjustment:

$$\frac{\Delta P}{P} = -MD\Delta R + \frac{1}{2}(28)\Delta R^2$$

Assuming a 2 percent increase in R (from 8 to 10 percent),

$$\frac{\Delta P}{P} = -\left[\frac{4.993}{1.08} \right].02 + \frac{1}{2}(28)(.02)^2$$

$$= -.0925 + .0056$$

$$= -.0869 \text{ or } -8.69\%$$

The simple duration model (the first term) predicts that a 2 percent rise in interest rates will cause the bond's price to fall 9.25 percent. However, for large changes in yields, the duration model overpredicts the price fall. The duration model with the second-order convexity adjustment predicts a price fall of 8.69 percent; it adds back 0.56 percent because of the convexity effect. This is much closer to the true fall in the six-year, 8 percent coupon bond's price if we calculated this using 10 percent to discount the coupon and face value cash flows on the bond. The true value of the bond price fall is 8.71 percent. That is, using the convexity adjustment reduces the error between predicted value and true value to just a few basis points.[6]

In Table 9A–1 we calculate various properties of convexity, where

N = Time to maturity

R = Yield to maturity

C = Annual coupon

D = Duration

CX = Convexity

Part 1 of Table 9A–1 shows that as the bond's maturity (N) increases, so does its convexity (CX). As a result, long-term bonds have more convexity—which is a desirable property—than do short-term bonds. This property is similar to that possessed by duration.[7]

---

[5] You can easily check that $999.53785 is the price of the six-year bond when rates are 8.01 percent and $1,000.46243 is the price of the bond when rates fall to 7.99 percent. Since we are dealing in small numbers and convexity is sensitive to the number of decimal places assumed, we use at least five decimal places in calculating the capital gain or loss. In fact, the more decimal places used, the greater the accuracy of the CX measure.

[6] It is possible to use the third moment of the Taylor series expansion to reduce this small error (8.71 percent versus 8.69 percent) even further. In practice, few people do this.

[7] Note that the CX measure differs according to the level of interest rates. For example, we are measuring CX in Table 9A–1 when yields are 8 percent. If yields were 12 percent, the CX number would change. This is intuitively reasonable, as the curvature of the price-yield curve differs at each point on the price-yield curve. Note that duration also changes with the level of interest rates.

FIGURE 9A–3
Convexity of a
Coupon versus a
Discount Bond with
the Same Duration

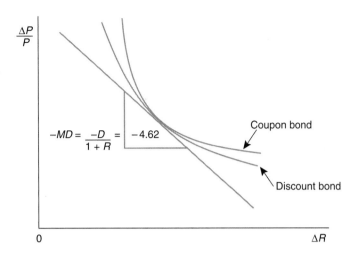

$$-MD = \frac{-D}{1+R} = -4.62$$

Coupon bond

Discount bond

Part 2 of Table 9A–1 shows that coupon bonds of the same maturity (N) have less convexity than do zero-coupon bonds. However, for coupon bonds and discount or zero-coupon bonds of the same duration, part 3 of the table shows that the coupon bond has more convexity. We depict the convexity of both in Figure 9A–3.

Finally, before leaving convexity, we might look at one important use of the concept by managers of insurance companies, pension funds, and mutual funds. Remembering that convexity is a desirable form of interest rate risk insurance, FI managers could structure an asset portfolio to maximize its desirable effects. Consider a pension fund manager with a 15-year payout horizon. To immunize the risk of interest rate changes, the manager purchases bonds with a 15-year duration. Consider two alternative strategies to achieve this:

Strategy 1: Invest 100 percent of resources in a 15-year deep-discount bond with an 8 percent yield.

Strategy 2: Invest 50 percent in the very short-term money market and 50 percent in 30-year deep-discount bonds with an 8 percent yield.

The duration (D) and convexities (CX) of these two asset portfolios are:

Strategy 1: $D = 15, CX = 206$
Strategy 2:[8] $D = \frac{1}{2}(0) + \frac{1}{2}(30) = 15, CX = \frac{1}{2}(0) + \frac{1}{2}(797) = 398.5$

Strategies 1 and 2 have the same durations, but strategy 2 has a greater convexity. Strategy 2 is often called a barbell portfolio, as shown in Figure 9A–4 by the shaded bars.[9] Strategy 1 is the unshaded bar. To the extent that the market does not price (or fully price) convexity, the barbell strategy dominates the direct duration-matching strategy (strategy 1).[10]

More commonly, an FI manager may seek to attain greater convexity in the asset portfolio than in the liability portfolio, as shown in Figure 9A–5. As a result, both positive and negative shocks to interest rates would have beneficial effects on the FI's net worth.[11]

---

[8] The duration and convexity of one-day funds are approximately zero.

[9] This is called a barbell because the weights are equally loaded at the extreme ends of the duration range, or bar, as in weight lifting.

[10] In a world in which convexity is priced, the long-term 30-year bond's price would rise to reflect the competition among buyers to include this more convex bond in their barbell asset portfolios. Thus, buying bond insurance—in the form of the barbell portfolio—would involve an additional cost to the FI manager. In addition, for the FI to be hedged in both a duration sense and a convexity sense, the manager should not choose the convexity of the asset portfolio without seeking to match it to the convexity of the liability portfolio. For further discussion of the convexity trap that results when an FI mismatches its asset and liability convexities, see J. H. Gilkeson and S. D. Smith, "The Convexity Trap: Pitfalls in Financing Mortgage Portfolios and Related Securities," Federal Reserve Bank of Atlanta, *Economic Review,* November–December 1992, pp. 17–27.

[11] Another strategy would be for the FI to issue callable bonds as liabilities. Callable bonds have limited upside capital gains because if rates fall to a low level, then the issuer calls the bond in early (and reissues new lower coupon bonds). The effect of limited upside potential for callable bond prices is that the price-yield curve for such bonds exhibits negative convexity. Thus, if asset investments have positive convexity and liabilities negative convexity, then yield shocks (whether positive or negative) are likely to produce net worth gains for the FI.

FIGURE 9A–4
Barbell Strategy

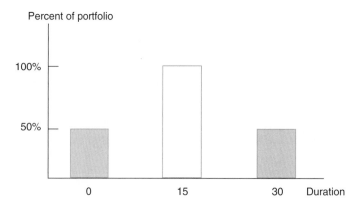

FIGURE 9A–5
Assets Are More
Convex Than
Liabilities

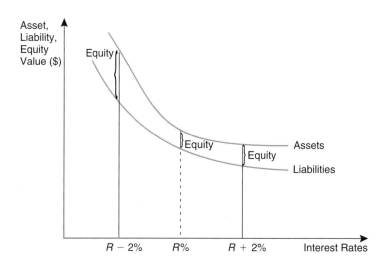

THE PROBLEM OF THE FLAT TERM STRUCTURE

We have been calculating simple, or Macauley, duration, which was named after an economist who was among the first to develop the *duration* concept. A key assumption of the simple duration model is that the yield curve or the term structure of interest rates is flat and that when rates change, the yield curve shifts in a parallel fashion. We show this in Figure 9A–6.

In the real world, the yield curve can take many shapes and at best may only approximate a flat yield curve. If the yield curve is not flat, using simple duration could be a potential source of error in predicting asset and liability interest rate sensitivities. Many models can deal with this problem. These models differ according to the shapes and shocks to the yield curve that are assumed.

Suppose the yield curve is not flat but shifts in such a manner that the yields on different maturity discount bonds change in a proportional fashion.[12] Consider calculating the duration of a six-year Eurobond when the yield curve is not flat at 8 percent. Instead, the yield curve looks like the one in Figure 9A–7.

Suppose the yield on one-year discount bonds rises. Assume also that the discounted changes in longer-maturity discount bonds yields are just proportional to the change in the one-year discount bond yield:

$$\frac{\Delta R_1}{1 + R_1} = \frac{\Delta R_2}{1 + R_2} = \cdots = \frac{\Delta R_6}{1 + R_6}$$

---

[12] We are interested in the yield curve on discount bonds because these yields reflect the time value of money for single payments at different maturity dates. Thus, we can use these yields as discount rates for cash flows on a security to calculate appropriate present values of its cash flows and its duration.

FIGURE 9A–6
Yield Curve
Underlying
Macauley Duration

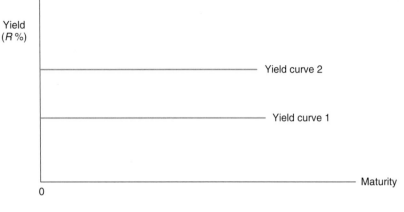

FIGURE 9A–7
Nonflat Yield Curve

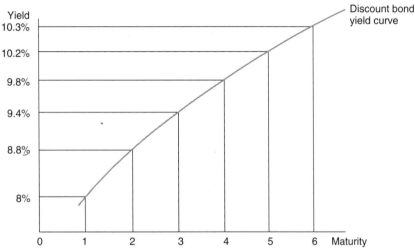

Given this quite restrictive assumption, it can be proved that the appropriate duration measure of the bond—call it D^*—can be derived by discounting the coupons and principal value of the bond by the discount rates or yields on appropriate maturity zero-coupon bonds. Given the discount bond yield curve plotted in Figure 9A–7, D^* is calculated in Table 9A–2.[13]

Notice that D^* is 4.916 years, while simple Macauley duration (with an assumed flat 8 percent yield curve) is 4.993 years. D^* and D differ because, by taking into account the upward-sloping yield curve in Figure 9A–7, the later cash flows are discounted at higher rates than they are under the flat yield curve assumption underlying Macauley's measure D.

With respect to the FI manager's problem, choosing to use D^* instead of D does not change the basic problem except for a concern with the gap between the D^* on assets and leverage-weighted liabilities:

$$D_A^* - kD_L^*$$

However, remember that the D^* was calculated under very restrictive assumptions about the yield curve. If we change these assumptions in any way, the measure of D^* changes.[14]

---

[13] For more details, see Hawawini, "Controlling the Interest Rate Risk;" and G. O. Bierwag, G. G. Kaufman, and A. Toevs, "Duration: Its Development and Use in Bond Portfolio Management," *Financial Analysts Journal* 39 (1983), pp. 15–35.

[14] A number of authors have identified other nonstandard measures of duration for more complex yield curve shapes and shifts. See, for example, Bierwag, Kaufman, and Toevs, "Duration: Its Development and Use." *Financial Analysts Journal* 39 (1983), pp. 15–35. See also I. J. Fooladi and G. S. Roberts, "Macrohedging for Financial Institutions: Beyond Duration," *Journal of Applied Finance*, Spring 2004, Vol. 14, Iss. 1, pp. 11–19 for a discussion of adjustments for convexity as well as adjustments for the default risk of FI assets. K. C. Ahlgrim, S. P. D'Arcy, and R. W. Gorvett, "The Effective Duration and Convexity of Liabilities for Property-Liability Insurers Under Stochastic Interest Rates, The Geneva Papers on Risk and Insurance Theory, 29, 2004, pp. 75–108 provides modeling techniques applicable to property and casualty insurers.

TABLE 9A–2
Duration with an
Upward-Sloping
Yield Curve

t	CF	DF	CF × DF	CF × DF × t
1	80	$\frac{1}{(1.08)} = 0.9259$	74.07	74.07
2	80	$\frac{1}{(1.088)^2} = 0.8448$	67.58	135.16
3	80	$\frac{1}{(1.094)^3} = 0.7637$	61.10	183.30
4	80	$\frac{1}{(1.098)^4} = 0.6880$	55.04	220.16
5	80	$\frac{1}{(1.102)^5} = 0.6153$	49.22	246.10
6	1,080	$\frac{1}{(1.103)^6} = 0.5553$	599.75	3,598.50
			906.76	4,457.29

$$D^* = \frac{4,457.29}{906.76} = 4.91562$$

TABLE 9A–3
Duration and
Rescheduling

t	CF	DF	CF × DF	CF × DF × t
1	0	.9259	0	0
2	160	.8573	137.17	274.34
3	80	.7938	63.51	190.53
4	80	.7350	58.80	235.21
5	80	.6806	54.45	272.25
6	1,080	.6302	680.58	4,083.48
			994.51	5,055.81

$$D = \frac{5,055.81}{994.51} = 5.0837 \text{ years}$$

THE PROBLEM OF DEFAULT RISK

The models and the duration calculations we have looked at assume that the issuer of bonds or the borrower of a loan pays the promised interest and principal with a probability of 1; we assume no default or delay in the payment of cash flows. In the real world, problems with principal and interest payments are common and lead to restructuring and workouts on debt contracts as bankers and bond trustees renegotiate with borrowers; that is, the borrower reschedules or recontracts interest and principal payments rather than defaulting outright. If we view default risk as synonymous with the rescheduling of cash flows to a later date, this is quite easy to deal with in duration models.

Consider the six-year, 8 percent coupon, 8 percent yield Eurobond. Suppose the issuer gets into difficulty and cannot pay the first coupon. Instead, the borrower and the FI agree that the unpaid interest can be paid in year 2. This alleviates part of the cash flow pressure on the borrower while lengthening the duration of the bond from the FI's perspective (see Table 9A–3). The effect of rescheduling the first interest payment is to increase duration from approximately 5 years to 5.08 years.

More commonly, an FI manager unsure of the future cash flows because of future default risk might multiply the promised cash flow (CF_t) by the probability of repayment (p_t) in year t to generate expected cash flows in year t—$E(CF_t)$.[15]

$$E(CF_t) = p_t \times CF_t$$

---

[15] The probability of repayment is between 0 and 1.

FIGURE 9A–8
Floating-Rate Note

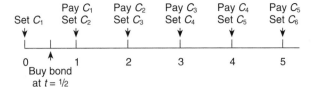

Chapter 11 suggests a number of ways to generate these repayment probabilities. Once the cash flows have been adjusted for default risk, a duration measure can be directly calculated in the same manner as the Macauley formula (or D^*) except that $E(CF_t)$ replaces CF_t.[16]

FLOATING-RATE LOANS AND BONDS

The duration models we have looked at assume that the interest rates on loans or the coupons on bonds are fixed at issue and remain unchanged until maturity. However, many bonds and loans carry floating interest rates. Examples include loan rates indexed to LIBOR (London Interbank Offered Rate) and adjustable rate mortgages (ARMs) whose rates can be indexed to government bonds or other securities yields. Moreover, in the 1980s, many banks and security firms either issued or underwrote perpetual floating-rate notes (FRNs). These are like consol bonds in that they never mature; unlike consols, their coupons fluctuate with market rates. The FI manager, who wants to analyze overall gap exposure, may ask: What are the durations of such floating-rate securities? The duration of a floating-rate instrument is generally the time interval between the purchase of the security and the time when the next coupon or interest payment is readjusted to reflect current interest rate conditions. We call this the time to repricing of the instrument.

For example, suppose the investor bought a perpetual floating-rate note. These floating-rate notes never mature. At the beginning of each year, the FI sets the coupon rate, which is paid at the end of that year. Suppose the investor buys the bond in the middle of the first year ($t = \frac{1}{2}$) rather than at the beginning (see Figure 9A–8).

The present value of the bond from time of purchase is:[17]

$$P = \frac{C_1}{(1 + \frac{1}{2}R)} + \frac{C_2}{(1 + \frac{1}{2}R)(1 + R)}$$

$$+ \frac{C_3}{(1 + \frac{1}{2}R)(1 + R)^2} + \frac{C_2}{(1 + \frac{1}{2}R)(1 + R)^3}$$

$$+ \frac{C_5}{(1 + \frac{1}{2}R)(1 + R)^4} + \dots$$

Note three important aspects of this present value equation. First, the investor has to wait only a half year to get the first coupon payment—hence, the discount rate is $(1 + \frac{1}{2}R)$. Second, the investor knows with certainty only the size of the first coupon C_1, which was preset at the beginning of the first coupon period to reflect interest rates at that time. The FI set the first coupon rate six months before the investor bought the bond. Third, the other coupons on the bond, C_2, C_3, C_4, C_5, . . ., are unknown at the time the bond is purchased because they depend on the level of interest rates at the time they are reset (see Figure 9A–8).

To derive the duration of the bond, rewrite the cash flows at one-half year onward as:

$$P = \frac{C_1}{(1 + \frac{1}{2}R)} + \frac{1}{(1 + \frac{1}{2}R)}$$

$$\left[\frac{C_2}{(1 + R)} + \frac{C_3}{(1 + R)^2} + \frac{C_4}{(1 + R)^3} + \frac{C_5}{(1 + R)^4} + \dots \right]$$

where P is the present value of the bond (the bond price) at one-half year, the time of purchase.

---

[16] Alternatively, the promised cash flow could be discounted by the appropriate discount yield on a risk-free government security plus an appropriate credit-risk spread; that is, $CF_t / (1 + d_t + S_t)t$, where CF_t is the promised cash flow in year t, d_t is the yield on a t-period zero-coupon government bond, and S_t is a credit-risk premium.

[17] This formula follows the Eurobond convention that any cash flows received in less than one full coupon period's time are discounted using simple interest. Thus, we use $1 + \frac{1}{2}R$ rather than $(1 + R)^{1/2}$ for the first coupon's cash flow in the example above. Also see R. A. Grobel, "Understanding the Duration of Floating Rate Notes," MIMED (New York: Salomon Brothers, 1986).

The term in brackets is the present value or fair price (P_1) of the bond if it were sold at the end of year 1, the beginning of the second coupon period. As long as the variable coupons exactly match fluctuations in yields or interest rates, the present value of the cash flow in the square brackets is unaffected by interest rate changes. Thus,

$$P = \frac{C_1}{(1 + \frac{1}{2}R)} + \frac{P_1}{(1 + \frac{1}{2}R)}$$

Since C_1 is a fixed cash flow preset before the investor bought the bond and P_1 is a fixed cash flow in present value terms, buying this bond is similar to buying two single-payment deep-discount bonds each with a maturity of six months. Because the duration of a deep-discount bond is the same as its maturity, this FRN bond has:

$$D = \frac{1}{2} \text{ year}$$

As indicated earlier, a half year is exactly the interval between the time when the bond was purchased and the time when it was first repriced.[18]

DEMAND DEPOSITS AND SAVINGS ACCOUNT LIABILITIES

Many banks and other deposit-taking institutions hold large amounts of chequing and savings account liabilities. The problem in assessing the duration of such claims is that their maturities are open-ended and many demand deposit accounts do not turn over very frequently. Although demand deposits allow holders to demand cash immediately—suggesting a very short maturity—many customers tend to retain demand deposit balances for lengthy periods. In the parlance of

banking, they behave as if they were a bank's core deposits. A problem arises because defining the duration of a security requires defining its maturity. Yet demand deposits have open-ended maturities. One way for an FI manager to get around this problem is to analyze the runoff, or the turnover characteristics, of the FI's demand and savings account deposits. For example, suppose the manager learned that on average each dollar in demand deposit accounts turned over five times a year. This suggests an average turnover or maturity per dollar of around 73 days.[19]

A second method is to consider demand deposits as bonds that can be instantaneously put back to the bank in return for cash. As instantaneously putable bonds, the duration of demand deposits is approximately zero.

A third approach is more directly in line with the idea of duration as a measure of interest rate sensitivity. It looks at the percentage change of demand deposits ($\Delta DD/DD$) to interest rate changes (ΔR). Because demand deposits and, to a lesser extent, savings deposits pay either low explicit or implicit interest—where implicit interest takes forms such as subsidized chequing fees—there tend to be enhanced withdrawals and switching into higher-yielding instruments as rates rise. You can use a number of quantitative techniques to test this sensitivity, including linear and nonlinear time series regression analysis.

A fourth approach is to use simulation analysis. This is based on forecasts of future interest rates and the net withdrawals by depositors from their accounts over some future time period. Taking the discounted present values of these cash flows allows a duration measure to be calculated.[20]

MORTGAGES AND MORTGAGE-BACKED SECURITIES

Calculating the durations of mortgages and mortgage-backed securities is difficult because of prepayment risk. Essentially, as the level of interest rates falls, mortgage holders have the option to prepay their old mortgages and refinance with a

---

[18] In another case an FI manager might buy a bond whose coupon floated but repaid fixed principal (many loans are priced like this). Calculating the duration on this bond or loan is straightforward. First, we have to think of it as two bonds: a floating-rate bond that pays a variable coupon (C) every year and a deep-discount bond that pays a fixed amount (F) on maturity. The duration of the first bond is the time between purchase and the first coupon reset date; $D = \frac{1}{2}$ year in the preceding example. While the duration of the deep-discount bond equals its maturity, $D =$ three years for a three-year bond. The duration of the bond as a whole is the weighted average of a half year and three years, where the weights (w_1) and ($1 - w_1$) reflect the present values of, respectively, the coupon cash flows and face value cash flow to the present value of the total cash flows (the sum of the two present values). Thus,

$$D = w_1(\tfrac{1}{2}) + (1 - w_1)(3)$$

[19] That is, 365 days/5 = 73 days.

[20] For a very sophisticated model along these lines, see E. W. Irmler, "The OTS Net Portfolio Value Model" (Washington, DC: OTS, 1994).

new mortgage at a lower interest rate. In the terminology of finance, fixed-rate mortgages and mortgage-backed securities contain an embedded option. Calculating duration requires projecting the future cash flows of an asset. Consequently, to calculate the duration of mortgages, we need to model the prepayment behaviour of mortgage holders. Possible ways to do this are left to Chapter 27 on mortgage asset securitization.

FUTURES, OPTIONS, SWAPS, CAPS, AND OTHER CONTINGENT CLAIMS

When interest rates change, so do the values of (off-balance-sheet) derivative instruments such as futures, options, swaps, and caps (see Chapter 13). Market value gains and losses on these instruments can also have an impact on the net worth (E) of an FI. The calculation of the durations of these instruments is left to Chapters 23 to 25. However, it should be noted that a fully fledged duration gap model of an FI should take into account the durations of its derivatives portfolio as well as the duration of its on-balance-sheet assets and liabilities. This is especially so today as more and more FIs take positions in derivative contracts.

Appendix 11A[1]   CreditMetrics

CreditMetrics was introduced in 1997 by J. P. Morgan and its co-sponsors (Bank of America, Bank of Montreal, et al.) as a value at risk (VAR) framework to apply to the valuation and risk of nontradable assets such as loans and privately placed bonds.[2] Thus, while RiskMetrics seeks to answer the question, if tomorrow is a bad day, how much will I lose on tradable assets such as stocks, bonds, and equities? CreditMetrics asks, if next year is a bad year, how much will I lose on my loans and loan portfolio?[3]

With RiskMetrics (see Chapter 10) we answer this question by looking at the market value or price of an asset and the volatility of that asset's price or return in order to calculate a probability (e.g., 5 percent) that the value of that asset will fall below some given value tomorrow. In the case of RiskMetrics, this involves multiplying the estimated standard deviation of returns on that asset by 1.65 and then revaluing the current market value of the position (P) downward by 1.65σ. That is, VAR for one day (or DEAR) is:

$$VAR = P \times 1.65 \times \sigma$$

Unfortunately, since loans are not publicly traded, we observe neither P (the loan's market value) nor σ (the volatility of loan value over the horizon of interest—assumed to be one year for loans and bonds under CreditMetrics). However, using (1) available data on a borrower's credit rating, (2) the probability of that rating changing over the next year (the rating transition matrix), (3) recovery rates on defaulted loans, and (4) yield spreads in the bond market, it is possible to calculate a hypothetical P and σ for any nontraded loan or bond and thus a VAR figure for individual loans and the loan portfolio.

Consider the example of a five-year, fixed-rate loan of $100 million made at 6 percent annual interest.[4] The borrower is rated BBB.

RATING MIGRATION

On the basis of historical data collected by S&P, Moody's, and other bond analysts, it is estimated that the probability of a BBB borrower's staying at BBB over the next year is 86.93 percent. There is also some probability that the borrower of the loan will be upgraded (e.g., to A), and there is some probability that it will be downgraded (e.g., to CCC) or even default. Indeed, there are eight possible transitions the borrower can make over the next year, seven of which involve upgrades, downgrades, and no rating changes and one which involves default. The estimated probabilities are shown in Table 11A–1.

TABLE 11A–1   One-Year Transition Probabilities for BBB-Rated Borrower

Rating	Transition Probability, %	
AAA	0.02	
AA	0.33	
A	5.95	
BBB	86.93	← Most likely to stay
BB	5.30	in same class
B	1.17	
CCC	0.12	
Default	0.18	

VALUATION

The effect of rating upgrades and downgrades is to impact the required credit risk spreads or premiums on loans and thus the implied market value (or present value) of the loan. If a loan is downgraded, the required credit spread premium should rise (remember, the loan rate in our example is fixed at 6 percent) so that the present value of the loan to the FI should fall; the reverse is true for a credit rating upgrade.

---

[1] This Appendix, which contains more technical topics, may be included in or dropped from the chapter reading depending on the rigor of the course.

[2] See CreditMetrics, *Technical Document*, New York, April 2, 1997; and Saunders and Allen, *Credit Risk Measurement,* Chapter 6.

[3] In 2002, J. P. Morgan introduced a third measure of credit risk, Credit-Grades. The CreditGrades model establishes a framework linking the credit and equity markets. The model employs approximations for the asset value, volatility, and drift, which are used to value credit as an exotic equity derivative. This model is similar in approach to the KMV model described in the chapter. See "CreditGrades: Technical Documents," RiskMetrics Group, Inc., May 2002.

[4] This example is based on the one used in the CreditMetrics, *Technical Document*, April 2, 1997.

Technically, since we are revaluing the five-year $100 million, 6 percent loan at the end of the first year after a credit event has occurred during that year, then (measured in millions of dollars):

$$P = 6 + \frac{6}{(1 + r_1 + s_1)} + \frac{6}{(1 + r_2 + s_2)^2}$$
$$+ \frac{6}{(1 + r_3 + s_3)^3} + \frac{106}{(1 + r_4 + s_4)^4}$$

where the r_i are the risk-free rates on T-bonds expected to exist one year, two years, and so on, into the future (i.e., they reflect forward rates from the current Treasury yield curve—see discussion in the main body of this chapter) and s_i are annual credit spreads for loans of a particular rating class of one year, two years, three years, and four years to maturity (the latter are derived from observed spreads in the corporate bond market over Treasuries). The first coupon or interest payment of $6 million in the above example is undiscounted and can be viewed as being similar to the accrued interest earned on a bond or a loan since we are revaluing the loan at the end (not the beginning) of the first year of its life.

Suppose the borrower gets upgraded during the first year from BBB to A. Then the present value or market value of the loan to the FI at the end of the one-year risk horizon (in millions of dollars) is:

$$P = 6 + \frac{6}{(1.0372)} + \frac{6}{(1.0432)^2} + \frac{6}{(1.0493)^3} + \frac{106}{(1.0532)^4}$$
$$= \$108.66$$

That is, at the end of the first year, if the loan borrower is upgraded from BBB to A, the $100 million (book value) loan has a market value to the FI of $108.66 million. (This is the value the FI would theoretically be able to obtain if it "sold" the loan, with the accrued first year coupon of 6, to another FI at the end of year 1 horizon at the fair market price or value.) Table 11A–2 shows the value of the loan if other credit events occur. Note that the loan has a maximum market value of $109.37 (if the borrower is upgraded to AAA) and a minimum value of $51.13 if the borrower defaults. The minimum value is the estimated recovery value of the loan if the borrower declares bankruptcy.

The probability distribution of loan values is shown in Figure 11A–1. As can be seen, the value of the loan has a fixed upside and a long downside

TABLE 11A–2 Value of the Loan at the End of One Year under Different Ratings

Year-End Rating	Loan Value ($) (including first-year coupon)
AAA	109.37
AA	109.19
A	108.66
BBB	107.55
BB	102.02
B	98.10
CCC	83.64
Default	51.13

FIGURE 11A–1 Distribution of Loan Values on a Five-Year BBB Loan at the End of Year 1

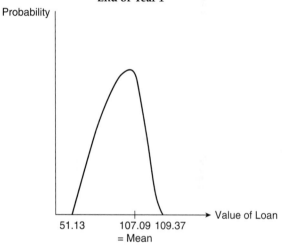

(i.e., a negative skew). It is clear that the value of the loan is not symmetrically (or normally) distributed. Thus CreditMetrics produces two VAR measures:

1. Based on the normal distribution of loan values.
2. Based on the actual distribution of loan values.

CALCULATION OF VAR

Table 11A–3 shows the calculation of the VAR based on each approach for both the 5 percent worst-case and the 1 percent worst-case scenarios.

The first step in calculating VAR is to calculate the mean of the loan's value, or its expected value, at year 1, which is the sum of each possible loan value at the end of year 1 times its transition prob-

TABLE 11A–3   VAR Calculations for the BBB Loan

Year-End Rating	Probability of State, %	New Loan Value plus Coupon, $	Probability Weighted Value, $	Difference of Value from Mean, $	Probability Weighted Difference Squared
AAA	0.02	109.37	0.02	2.28	0.0010
AA	0.33	109.19	0.36	2.10	0.0146
A	5.95	108.66	6.47	1.57	0.1474
BBB	86.93	107.55	93.49	0.46	0.1853
BB	5.30	102.02	5.41	(5.06)	1.3592
B	1.17	98.10	1.15	(8.99)	0.9446
CCC	0.12	83.64	1.10	(23.45)	0.6598
Default	0.18	51.13	0.09	(55.96)	5.6358

Mean = $107.09

Variance = 8.94777

σ = Standard deviation = $2.99

Assuming Normal Distribution
$$\begin{cases} 5\% \text{ VAR } = 1.65 \times \sigma = \$4.93 \\ 1\% \text{ VAR } = 2.33 \times \sigma = \$6.97 \end{cases}$$

Assuming Actual Distribution*
$$\begin{cases} 5\% \text{ VAR } = 95\% \text{ of actual distribution } = \$107.09 - \$102.02 = \$5.07 \\ 1\% \text{ VAR } = 99\% \text{ of actual distribution } = \$107.09 - \$98.10 = \$8.99 \end{cases}$$

*5% VAR approximated by 6.77% VAR (i.e., 5.3% + 1.17% + 0.12% + 0.18%) and 1% VAR approximated by 1.47% VAR (i.e., 1.17% + 0.12% + 0.18%).

ability. As can be seen, the mean value of the loan is $107.09 (also see Figure 11A–1). However, the FI is concerned about losses or volatility in value. In particular, if next year is a bad year, how much can it expect to lose? We could define a bad year as occurring once every 20 years (the 5 percent VAR) or once every 100 years (the 1 percent VAR)—this is similar to market risk VAR except that for credit risk the horizon is longer: 1 year rather than 1 day as under market risk DEAR.

Assuming that loan values are normally distributed, the variance of loan value around its mean is $8.9477 (squared) and its standard deviation or volatility is the square root of the variance equal to $2.99. Thus the 5 percent VAR for the loan is 1.65 × $2.99 = $4.93 million, while the 1 percent VAR is 2.33 × $2.99 = $6.97 million. However, this is likely to underestimate the actual or true VAR of the loan because, as shown in Figure 11A–1, the distribution of the loan's value is clearly nonnormal. In particular, it demonstrates a negative skew or a long-tail downside risk. Using the actual distribution of loan values and probabilities, we can see from Table 11A–3 that there is a 6.77 percent probability that the loan value will fall below $102.02, implying an approximate 5 percent actual VAR of over $107.09 − $102.02 = $5.07 million, and that there is a 1.47 percent probability that the loan value will fall below $98.10, imply-

ing an approximate 1 percent actual VAR of over $107.09 − $98.10 = $8.99. These actual VARs could be made less approximate by using linear interpolation to get the exact 5 percent and 1 percent VAR measures. For example, since the 1.47 percentile equals 98.10 and the 0.3 percentile equals 83.64, then, using linear interpolation, the 1.00 percentile equals $92.29. This suggests an actual 1 percent VAR of $107.09 − $92.29 = $14.80.

CAPITAL REQUIREMENTS

It is interesting to compare these VAR figures with the capital reserves against loans currently required by OSFI. While these requirements are explained in more detail in Chapter 20, they basically amount to a requirement that a bank hold a 7 percent ratio of the book value of the loan as a capital reserve against unexpected losses. In our example of a $100 million face (book) value BBB loan, the capital requirement would be $7 million. This contrasts to the two market-based VAR measures developed above. Using the 1 percent VAR based on the normal distribution, a capital requirement of $6.97 million would be required (i.e., less than OSFI's requirement), while using the 1 percent VAR based on the iterated value from the actual distribution, a $14.80 million capital requirement would be required (which is much greater than OSFI's capital requirement).

It should be noted that under the CreditMetrics approach, every loan is likely to have a different VAR and thus a different implied capital requirement.[5] This contrasts to the current BIS regulations, where all private sector loans of different ratings (AAA through CCC) and different maturities are subject to the same capital requirements.

[5] Although, as we discuss in Chapter 20, the 7 percent ratio and 100 percent risk weight for all commercial and corporate loans will be revised and fully implemented in 2007. Under the foundations and advanced approaches of Basel II (proposed), each loan will have an individual capital requirement.

Appendix 11B[1]   Credit Risk+

Credit Risk+ is a model developed by Credit Suisse Financial Products (CSFP).[2] Unlike CreditMetrics, which seeks to develop a full VAR framework, Credit Risk+ attempts to estimate the expected loss of loans and the distribution of those losses with a focus on calculating the FI's required capital reserves to meet losses above a certain level.

The key ideas come from the insurance literature (especially fire insurance), in which the losses incurred by an insurer reflect two things: (1) the probability of a house burning down (what an insurer calls the frequency of the event) and (2) the value of the house lost if it burns down (what the insurer calls severity of the loss). We can apply the same idea to loans, in which the loss distribution on a portfolio of loans reflects the combination (or product) of the frequency of loan defaults and their severity. This framework is shown in Figure 11B–1.

Unlike CreditMetrics, which assumes that there is a fixed probability of a loan defaulting in the next period (defined by its historic transition probability), it is assumed in its simplest form that (1) the probability of any individual loan defaulting in the portfolio of loans is random and (2) the correlation between the defaults on any pair of loans is zero (i.e., individual loan default probabilities are independent). This framework is therefore most appropriate for analyzing the default risk on large portfolios of small loans (e.g., small business loans, mortgages, and consumer loans) rather than portfolios that contain a few large loans. The model's assumptions about the probability (frequency) of default are shown in Figure 11B–2.

FIGURE 11B–1   Credit Risk+ Model of the Determinants of Loan Losses

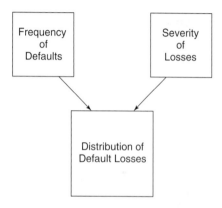

When the probability of default on individual loans is small and this probability is independent across loans in the portfolio, the frequency distribution of default rates can be modeled by a Poisson distribution. Below we look at an example.

Assume that:

1. The FI makes 100 loans of $100,000 each.
2. Historically, 3 percent (3 of 100) of loans have defaulted on average.
3. On default, the severity of loss on each of these loans is the same, at 20 cents per $1 (or $20,000 per $100,000 loan).

THE FREQUENCY DISTRIBUTION OF DEFAULT RATES

From the Poisson distribution, we can easily generate the probability of different numbers of defaults (in a 100-loan portfolio) occurring:

[1] This Appendix, which contains more technical topics, may be included in or dropped from the chapter reading depending on the rigour of the course.

[2] See Credit Suisse Financial Products, "Credit Risk+; Credit Risk Management Framework," October 1997, New York/London; and Saunders and Allen, *Credit Risk Measurement*, Chapter 7.

FIGURE 11B–2

Frequency of
Default on a
Loan Assumed
by Credit Risk+

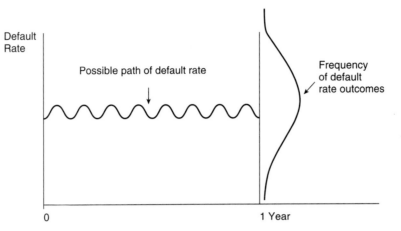

FIGURE 11B–3

Frequency
Distribution of
Default Rates
from Example

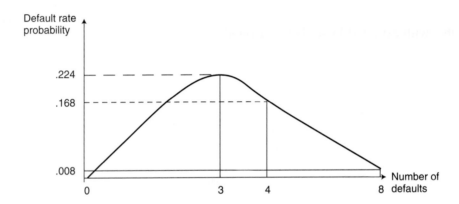

$$\text{Probability of } n \text{ defaults} = \frac{e^{-m}m^n}{n!}$$

Where e is exponential (2.71828), m is the historic average number of defaults (3 of 100, or 3 percent) for loans of this type, and $n!$ is n factorial, where n is the number of loans for which we are trying to determine the probability of default.

For example, the probability of 3 of 100 loans defaulting over the next year is:

$$\frac{(2.71828)^{-3} \times 3^3}{1 \times 2 \times 3} = .224$$

That is, there is a 22.4 percent probability of 3 loans defaulting. We can also determine the probability of 4 of the 100 loans defaulting:

$$\frac{(2.71828)^{-3} \times 3^4}{1 \times 2 \times 3 \times 4} = .168$$

or 16.8 percent. The frequency distribution of default rates is shown in Figure 11B–3.

We can multiply these default numbers by loss severity to get the distribution of dollar *losses* on the loan:

Dollar loss of 3 loans defaulting = 3 × 20c× $100,000
= $60,000

Dollar loss of 4 loans defaulting = 4 × 20c× $100,000
= $80,000

The distribution of dollar losses is shown in Figure 11B–4.

As under CreditMetrics, we may ask what the 1 percent worst-case loss scenario (i.e., the 99th worst year's loss out of 100 years) is. From the Poisson distribution, the probability of having 8 losses per 100 loans is approximately 1 percent; thus, there is a 1 percent chance of losing $160,000.[3] In the framework of Credit Risk+ the FI would hold a

---

[3] In actual practice, the probability of eight losses is 0.8 percent.

FIGURE 11B–4
Frequency
Distribution
of Losses on
Loan Portfolio
from Example

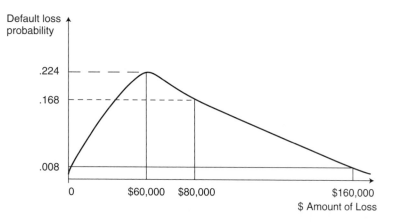

capital reserve to meet the difference between the unexpected (1 percent) loss rate and the average or expected loss rate (the losses associated with three defaults), with expected losses being covered by loan loss provisions and pricing. In our example the capital reserve would be $160,000 − $60,000 = $100,000, or approximately 1 percent of the value of the portfolio. One reason capital reserves are low in this case is that the severity of loss is assumed to be low and equal in each case (i.e., only 20 percent). If, for example, each of the loans in the portfolio lost 80 cents on default, the required capital reserve would rise to 4 percent of the loan portfolio's value. More-

over, in general, the severity of the losses themselves has a distribution. For example, if loan 1 defaults, the FI might lose 20 cents in $1, while if loan 2 defaults, it may lose 30 cents in $1, and so on. Allowing for a distribution in the severity of losses as well as in the number of defaults can easily be built into the Credit Risk+ framework, as can allowing the mean default rate itself to be variable (see the CSFP technical document for more details).[4]

---

[4] If the (variable) mean default rate is incorporated into the model, this allows the FI to analyze unexpected loan losses in recessions versus expansions. In general, allowing the mean default rate to vary over time increases unexpected losses and required capital reserves.

Appendix 11C Credit Analysis

This section discusses credit analysis for real estate lending, consumer and small-business lending, mid-market commercial and industrial lending, and large commercial and industrial lending. It also provides insights into the credit risk evaluation process from the perspective of a credit officer (or an FI manager) evaluating a loan application.

Real Estate Lending

Because of the importance of residential mortgages to banks, savings institutions, credit unions, and insurance companies, residential mortgage loan applications are among the most standardized of all credit applications. In this appendix, we look at the evaluation process that FIs (such as commercial banks, savings institutions, and finance companies) use to determine whether a real estate loan application should be approved.

Two considerations dominate an FI's decision to approve a mortgage loan application or not: (1) the applicant's ability and willingness to make timely interest and principal repayments and (2) the value of the borrower's collateral.

Ability and willingness of the borrower to repay debt outstanding is usually established by application of qualitative and quantitative models. The character of the applicant is also extremely important. Stability of residence, occupation, family status (e.g., married, single), previous history of savings, and credit (or bill payment) history are frequently used in assessing character. The loan officer also must establish whether the applicant has sufficient income. In particular, the loan amortization (i.e., principal payments) should be reasonable when compared with the applicant's income and age. The loan officer also should consider the applicant's monthly expenditures. Family responsibilities and marital stability are also important. Monthly financial obligations relating to auto, personal, and credit card loans should be ascertained, and an applicant's personal balance sheet and income statement should be constructed.

Two ratios are very useful in determining a customer's ability to maintain mortgage payments: the **GDS (gross debt service)** and the **TDS (total debt service) ratios.** Gross debt service ratio is the customer's total annual accommodation expenses (mortgage, lease, condominium, management fees, real estate taxes, etc.) divided by annual gross income. Total debt service ratio is the customer's total annual accommodation expenses plus all other debt service payments divided by annual gross income. These can be represented as follows:

$$GDS = \frac{\text{Annual mortgage payments} + \text{Property taxes}}{\text{Annual gross income}}$$

$$TDS = \frac{\text{Annual total debt payments}}{\text{Annual gross income}}$$

As a general rule, for an FI to consider an applicant, the GDS and TDS ratios must be less than an acceptable threshold. The threshold is commonly 25 to 30 percent for the GDS and 35 to 40 percent for the TDS ratios.[1]

FIs often combine the various factors affecting the ability and willingness to make loan repayments into a single credit score. A **credit-scoring system** (illustrated below) is a quantitative model that uses observed characteristics of the applicant to calculate a "score" representing the applicant's probability of default (versus repayment). Credit-scoring systems are developed by using borrower characteristics (e.g., income, age, loan payment history) for some past period. The credit-scoring model weights each characteristic to identify a boundary number (score) or range such that if past loan customers had an overall credit score (derived from the weighted characteristics) greater than the boundary number (score) they did not default on the loan, while if they had a credit score less than the boundary number they defaulted on the loan. The boundary number or range is derived by statistical analysis, such

---

EXAMPLE 11C–1

Calculation of the GDS and TDS Ratios

Consider two customers who have applied for a mortgage from an FI with a GDS threshold of 25 percent and a TDS threshold of 40 percent.

Customer	Gross Annual Income	Monthly Mortgage Payments	Annual Property Taxes	Monthly Other Debt Payments
1	$150,000	$3,000	$3,500	$2,000
2	60,000	500	1,500	200

The GDS and TDS ratios for the mortgage applicants are as follows:

Customer	GDS	TDS
1	$\frac{3,000(12) + 3,500}{150,000} = 26.33\%$	$\frac{3,000(12) + 3,500 + 2,000(12)}{150,000} = 42.33\%$
2	$\frac{500(12) + 1,500}{60,000} = 12.50\%$	$\frac{500(12) + 1,500 + 200(12)}{60,000} = 16.50\%$

Despite a higher level of gross income, Customer 1 does not meet the GDS or TDS thresholds because of relatively high mortgage, tax, and other debt payments. Customer 2, while earning less, has fewer required payments and meets both the FI's GDS and TDS thresholds.

---

[1] Other FIs may impose different thresholds. The numerator of the GDS is often increased to include home heating and property taxes. When the GDS ratio is used for consumer credit, rent is substituted for mortgage payments.

as logit or discriminant analysis.[2] Assuming new loan customers act like past customers, the credit-scoring system can then be used to calculate a credit score for new loan applicants and assign them to a high or low default risk group. The applicant's total score must be above the boundary score or range to be considered acceptable for a loan.

The theory behind credit scoring is that by selecting and combining different economic and financial characteristics, an FI manager may be able to separate good from bad loan customers based on the characteristics of borrowers who have defaulted in the past. One advantage of credit-scoring systems is that a loan applicant's credit quality is expressed as a single numerical value, rather than as a judg-mental assessment of several separate factors. This is beneficial for FIs that must evaluate small loan applicants quickly, at low cost, and consistently and who would otherwise have to employ many more credit analysts (each of whom might well apply inconsistent standards across different loan applicants as well as adding to the FI's labour costs).

If the FI uses a scoring system, the loan officer can give an immediate answer yes, maybe, or no—and the reasons for that answer. A maybe occurs in borderline cases or when the loan officer is uncertain of the classification of certain input information. A credit-scoring system allows an FI to reduce the ambiguity and turnaround time and increase the transparency of the credit approval process.

EXAMPLE 11C–2

Credit Scoring of a Real Estate Loan

An FI uses the following credit-scoring model to evaluate real estate loan applications:

Characteristic	Characteristic Values and Weights				
Annual gross income	<$10,000	$10,000–$25,000	$25,000–$50,000	$50,000–$100,000	>$100,000
Score	0	15	35	50	75
TDS	>50%	35%–50%	15%–35%	5%–15%	<5%
Score	0	10	20	35	50
Relations with FI	None	Chequing account	Savings account	Both	
Score	0	30	30	60	
Major credit cards	None	1 or more			
Score	0	20			
Age	<25	25–60	>60		
Score	5	30	35		
Residence	Rent	Own with mortgage	Own outright		
Score	5	20	50		
Length of residence	<1 year	1–5 years	>5 years		
Score	0	20	45		
Job stability	<1 year	1–5 years	>5 years		
Score	0	25	50		
Credit history	No record	Missed a payment in last 5 years	Met all payments		
Score	0	−15	50		

---

[2] For example, those credit-scoring systems based on a statistical technique called discriminant analysis are also referred to as discriminant analysis models. Discriminant analysis places borrowers into two groups (defaulting and nondefaulting) and, by seeking to maximize the difference in the variance of the characteristics (e.g., income) between these groups while minimizing the variance within each group, seeks to derive appropriate weights for the characteristics that discriminate between the defaulting and nondefaulting groups. This is the discriminant function that results from discriminant analysis.

The loan is automatically rejected if the applicant's *total* score is less than 120 (i.e., applicants with a score of 120 or less have, in the past, mainly defaulted on their loan); the loan is automatically approved if the total score is greater than 190 (i.e., applicants with a score of 190 or more have, in the past, mainly paid their loan in complete accordance with the loan agreement). A score between 120 and 190 is reviewed by a loan committee for a final decision.

A loan customer listing the following information on the loan application receives the following points:

Characteristic	Value	Score
Annual gross income	$67,000	50
TDS	12%	35
Relations with FI	None	0
Major credit cards	4	20
Age	37	30
Residence	Own/mortgage	20
Length of residence	2½ years	20
Job stability	2½ years	25
Credit history	Met all payments	50
Total store		250

The real estate loan for this customer would be automatically approved.

Verification of the borrower's financial statements is essential. If the answer is yes to a loan application, the loan officer states that the FI is prepared to grant the loan subject to a verification of his or her creditworthiness and obtains the applicant's permission to make all necessary inquiries. The collateral provided by the mortgage is normally considered only after the loan officer has established that the applicant can service the loan. If collateral secures a loan, the FI must make sure that its claim, should the borrower default, is free and clear from other claims. This process is referred to as **perfecting** a security interest in the **collateral.** Even if collateral secures the loan, no FI should become involved in a loan that is likely to go into default. In such a case, the FI would at best seize the property in a **foreclosure** (where the FI takes possession of the mortgaged property in satisfaction of the defaulting borrower's indebtedness, forgoing claim to any deficiency) or **power of sale** (where the FI takes the proceeds of the forced sale of a mortgaged property in satisfaction of the indebtedness and returns to the mortgagor the excess over the indebtedness or claims any shortfall as an unsecured creditor).

Before an FI accepts a mortgage, it must satisfy itself regarding the property involved in the loan by doing the following:

- Confirming the title and legal description of the property.
- Obtaining a surveyor's certificate confirming that the house is within the property boundaries.
- Checking with the tax office to confirm that no property taxes are unpaid.
- Requesting a land title search to determine that there are no other claims against the property.
- Obtaining an independent appraisal to confirm that the purchase price is in line with the market value.

Consumer (Individual) and Small-Business Lending

The techniques used for mortgage loan credit analysis are very similar to those applied to individual and small-business loans. Individual consumer loans are scored like mortgages, often without the borrower ever meeting the loan officer. Unlike mortgage loans for which the focus is on a property, however, nonmortgage consumer loans focus on the individual's ability to repay. Thus, credit-scoring models for such loans would put more weight on personal characteristics such as annual gross income, the TDS score, and so on.

Small-business loans are more complicated because the FI is frequently asked to assume the credit risk of an individual whose business cash flows require considerable analysis, often with incomplete accounting information available to the credit officer. The payoff for this analysis is also small, by definition, because loan principal amounts are usually small. A $50,000 loan with a 3 percent interest spread over the cost of funds provides only $1,500 of gross revenues before loan loss provisions, monitoring costs, and allocation of overheads. This low profitability has caused many FIs to build small-business scoring models similar to, but more sophisticated than, those used for mortgages and consumer credit. These models often combine computer-based financial analysis of borrower financial statements with behavioural analysis of the owner of the small business.

Mid-Market Commercial and Industrial Lending

In recent years, mid-market commercial and industrial lending has offered some of the most profitable opportunities for credit-granting FIs. Although definitions of mid-market corporates vary, they typically have sales revenues from $5 million to $100 million a year, have a recognizable corporate structure (unlike many small businesses), but do not have ready access to deep and liquid capital markets (as do large corporations).

Credit analysis of a mid-market corporate customer differs from that of a small business because, while still assessing the character of the firm's management, its main focus is on the business itself. The credit process begins with an account officer gathering information by meeting existing customers, checking referrals, and meeting with new business prospects. Having gathered information about the credit applicant, an account officer decides whether it is worthwhile to pursue the new business, given the applicant's needs, the FI's credit policies, the current economy, and the competitive lending environment. If it is, the account officer structures and prices the credit agreement with reference to the FI's credit granting policy. This includes several areas of analysis, including the five Cs of credit, cash flow analysis, ratio analysis, and financial statement comparisons (described below). At any time in this process, conditions could change or new information could be revealed, significantly changing the borrower's situation and forcing the account officer to begin the process again.

Once the applicant and an account officer tentatively agree on a loan, the account officer must obtain internal approval from the FI's credit risk management team. Generally, even for the smallest mid-market credit, at least two officers must approve a new loan customer. Larger credit requests must be presented formally (either in hard copy or through a computer network) to a credit approval officer and/or committee before they can be signed. This means that, during the negotiations, the account officer must be very well acquainted with the FI's overall credit philosophy and current strategy.

Five C's of Credit

To analyze the loan applicant's credit risk, the account officer must understand the customer's character, capacity, collateral, conditions, and capital (sometimes referred to as the *five Cs of credit*). Character refers to the probability that the loan applicant will try to honour the loan obligations. Capacity is a subjective judgment regarding the applicant's ability to pay the FI according to the terms of the loan. Collateral is represented by assets that the loan applicant offers as security backing the loan. Conditions refer to any general economic trends or special developments in certain geographic regions or sectors of the economy that might affect the applicant's ability to meet the loan obligations. Capital is measured by the general financial condition of the applicant as indicated by an analysis of the applicant's financial statements and his/her leverage. Some important questions that provide information on the five Cs follow.

Production (measures of capacity and conditions)
- On what production inputs does the applicant depend?
- To what extent does this cause supply risk?
- How do input price risks affect the applicant?
- How do costs of production compare with those of the competition?
- How does the quality of goods and services produced compare with those of the competition?

Management (measures of character and conditions)
- Is management trustworthy?
- Is management skilled at production? Marketing? Finance? Building an effective organization?
- To what extent does the company depend on one or a few key players?

- Is there a successful plan?
- Are credible and sensible accounting, budgeting, and control systems in place?

Marketing (measures of conditions)

- How are the changing needs of the applicant's customers likely to affect the applicant?
- How creditworthy are the applicant's customers?
- At what stage of their life cycles are the applicant's products and services?
- What are the market share and share growth of the applicant's products and services?
- What is the applicant's marketing policy?
- Who are the applicant's competitors? What policies are they pursuing? Why are they able to remain in business?
- How is the applicant meeting changing market needs?

Capital (measures of capital and collateral)

- How much equity is currently funding the firm's assets?
- How much access does the firm have to equity and debt markets?
- Will the company back the loan with the firm's assets?

Cash Flow Analysis

FIs require corporate loan applicants to provide cash flow information, which provides the FI with relevant information about the applicant's cash receipts and disbursements that are compared with the principal and interest payments on the loan.

Cash receipts include any transaction that results in an increase in cash assets (i.e., receipt of income, decrease in a noncash asset, increase in a liability, and increase in an equity account). *Cash disbursements* include any transaction that results in a decrease in cash assets (i.e., cash expenses, increase in a noncash asset, decrease in a liability, and decrease in equity).[3] The cash flow statement (or cash-based income statement) reconciles changes in the cash account over some period according to three cash flow activities: operating, investing, and financing activities. Operating activities include net income, depreciation, and changes in current assets and current liabilities other than cash and short-term debt. Investing activities include investments in or sales of fixed assets. Financing activities include cash raised by issuing short-term debt, long-term debt, or stock. Also, since dividends paid or cash used to buy back outstanding stock or bonds reduces the applicant's cash, such transactions are included as financing activities.

When evaluating the cash flow statement, FIs want to see that the loan applicant can pay back the loan with cash flows produced from the applicant's operations. FIs do not want the loan applicant to pay back the loan by selling fixed assets or issuing additional debt. Thus, the cash flows from the operating section of the cash flow statement are most critical to the FI in evaluating the loan applicant.

Importantly, cash flows generated from operations, as in the preceding example, are the source of cash used to repay the loan to the FI, and thus they play a key role in the credit decision process.

EXAMPLE 11C–3

Computation of Cash Flow Statement

Consider the financial statement for the loan applicant presented in Table 11C.1. The cash flow statement reconciles the change in the firm's cash assets account from 2006 to 2007 as equal to −$61 (see the first row of panel A). Construction of the cash flow statement begins with all cash flow items associated with the operating activities of the applicant. Panel A of Table 11C.1 shows that the cash flows from operations total −$78. Next, cash flows from investment activities (i.e., fixed-asset investments and other nonoperating investments of the firm) are calculated in Table 11C.2, Panel B, as −$168. Finally, cash flows from financing activities are shown in Panel C as $185. The sum of these cash flow activities, reported in Panel D, −$61, equals the change in the cash account from 2006 to 2007 (Table 11C.2, Panel A, first row). Given that the loan should be repaid from cash flows from operations, which are negative, i.e., −$78, this loan applicant will likely be rejected.

---

[3] For example, if a firm issues new bonds (increasing liabilities), it will have a(n) (increased) cash flow from the purchasers of the newly issued bonds. Similarly, a sale of new equity (such as common stock) will create a positive cash inflow to the firm from purchasers of the equity.

TABLE 11C–1   Financial Statements Used to Construct a Cash Flow Statement (in thousands of dollars)

Panel A: Balance Sheets

Assets	2006	2007	Change from 2006 to 2007	Liabilities/Equity	2006	2007	Change from 2006 to 2007
Cash	$ 133	$ 72	$ (61)	Notes payable	$ 657	$ 967	$ 310
Accounts receivable	1,399	1,846	447	Accounts payable	908	1,282	374
Inventory	1,255	1,779	524	Accruals	320	427	107
Gross fixed assets	876	1,033	157	Long-term debt	375	300	(75)
Less: depreciation	(277)	(350)	(73)	Common stock	700	700	0
Net fixed assets	599	683	84	Retained earnings	465	754	298
Temporary investments	39	50	11	Total	$3,425	$4,430	$1,005
Total assets	$3,425	$4,430	$1,005				

Panel B: Income Statement

	2007
Net sales	$12,430
Cost of goods sold	(8,255)
Gross profit	4,175
Cash operating expenses	(3,418)
Depreciation	(73)
Operating profit	684
Interest expense	(157)
Taxes	(188)
Net income	339
Dividends	(50)
Change in retained earnings	$289

Ratio Analysis

In addition to cash flow information, an applicant requesting specific levels of credit substantiates these business needs by presenting historical audited financial statements and projections of future needs. Historical financial statement analysis can be useful in determining whether cash flow and profit projections are plausible on the basis of the history of the applicant and in highlighting the applicant's risks.

Calculation of financial ratios is useful when performing financial statement analysis on a midmarket corporate applicant. Although stand-alone accounting ratios are used for determining the size of the credit facility, the analyst may find relative ratios more informative when determining how the applicant's business is changing over time. Ratios are particularly informative when they differ either from an industry average (or FI-determined standard of what is appropriate) or from the applicant's own past history. An optimal value is seldom given for any ratio because no two companies are identical. A ratio that differs from an industry average or an FI-determined standard, however, normally raises a "flag" and causes the account officer to investigate further. For example, a ratio that shifts radically from accounting period to accounting period may reveal a company weakness.

Hundreds of ratios could be calculated from any set of accounting statements. The following are a few that most credit analysts find useful.

Liquidity Ratios.

$$\text{Current ratio} = \frac{\text{Current assets}}{\text{Current liabilities}}$$

Quick ratio (acid-test ratio) =

$$\frac{\text{Cash} + \text{Cash equivalents} + \text{Receivables}}{\text{Current liabilities}}$$

TABLE 11C–2 Cash Flow Statement (in thousands of dollars)

		Cash Flow Impact
Panel A: Cash Flow from Operating Activities		
Net sales	$12,430	↑
Change in accounts receivable	(447)	↓
Cash receipts from sales	11,983	
Cost of goods sold	(8,255)	↓
Change in inventory	(524)	↓
Change in accounts payable	374	↑
Cash margin	3,578	
Cash operating expenses	(3,418)	↓
Change in accruals	107	↑
Cash before interest and taxes	267	
Interest expense	(157)	↓
Taxes	(188)	↓
Cash flows from operations	(78)	
Panel B: Cash Flow from Investing Activities		
Change in gross fixed assets	(157)	↓
Change in temporary investments	(11)	↓
Cash flows from investing activities	(168)	
Panel C: Cash Flows from Financing Activities		
Retirement of long-term debt	(75)	↓
Change in notes payable	310	↑
Change in common stock	0	—
Dividends paid	(50)	↓
Cash flow from financing activities	185	
Panel D: Net Increase (Decrease) in Cash		
	(61)*	

*This is equal to the change in cash for 2006–2007 reported in Panel A of Table 11C.1.

Liquidity provides the defensive cash and near-cash resources for firms to meet claims for payment. Liquidity ratios express the variability of liquid resources relative to potential claims. High levels of liquidity effectively guard against liquidity crises but at the cost of lower returns on investment. Note that a company with a very predictable cash flow can maintain low levels of liquidity without much liquidity risk. Account officers frequently request detailed cash flows from an applicant that specify exactly when cash inflows and outflows are anticipated.

Asset Management Ratios.

$$\text{Number of days sales in receivables} = \frac{\text{Accounts receivable} \times 365}{\text{Credit sales}}$$

$$\text{Number of days in inventory} = \frac{\text{Inventory} \times 365}{\text{Cost of goods sold}}$$

$$\text{Sales to working capital} = \frac{\text{Sales}}{\text{Working capital}}$$

$$\text{Sales to fixed assets} = \frac{\text{Sales}}{\text{Fixed assets}}$$

$$\text{Sales to total assets} \atop \text{(asset turnover)} = \frac{\text{Sales}}{\text{Total assets}}$$

The asset management ratios give the account officer clues to how well the applicant uses its assets relative to its past performance and the performance of the industry. For example, ratio analysis may reveal that the number of days that finished goods are in inventory is increasing. This suggests that finished goods inventories, relative to the sales they support, are not being used as well as in the past. If this increase is the result of a deliberate policy to increase inventories to offer customers a wider choice and if it results in higher future sales volumes or increased margins that more than compensate for increased capital tied up in inventory, the increased relative size of finished goods inventories is good for the applicant and, thus, the FI. An FI should be concerned, on the other hand, if increased finished goods inventories are the result of declining sales but steady purchases of supplies and production. Inventory aging schedules give more information than single ratios and should be requested by the account officer concerned about deteriorating ratios.

What a loan applicant often describes in words differs substantially from what the ratio analysis reveals. For example, a company that claims to be a high-volume producer but has low sales-to-assets ratios relative to the industry bears further investigation. In discussing the analysis with the applicant, the account officer not only gains a better appreciation of the applicant's strategy and needs but also may help the applicant better understand the company relative to financial and industry norms.

Debt and Solvency Ratios.

Debt-asset ratio =

$$\frac{\text{Short-term liabilities} + \text{Long-term liabilities}}{\text{Total assets}}$$

Fixed-charge coverage ratio =

$$\frac{\text{Earnings available to meet fixed charges}}{\text{Fixed charges}}$$

$$\text{Cash-flow-to-debt ratio} = \frac{\text{EBIT} + \text{Depreciation}}{\text{Debt}}$$

where **EBIT** represents earnings before interest and taxes.

Debt and solvency ratios give the account manager an idea of the extent to which the applicant finances its assets with debt versus equity. Specifically, the lower the debt-asset ratio, the less debt and more equity the applicant uses to finance its assets (i.e., the bigger the applicant's equity cushion). Similarly, the higher the fixed-charge coverage ratio and the cash-flow-to-debt, the more equity and less debt the applicant uses to finance its assets.

Adequate levels of equity capital are as critical to the health of a credit applicant as they are to the health of FIs. The account officer analyzing a credit application or renewal wishes to know whether a sufficient equity cushion exists to absorb fluctuations in the loan applicant's earnings and asset values and sufficient cash flow exists to make debt service payments. Clearly, the larger the fluctuations or variability of cash flows, the larger is the need for an equity cushion. Note that from a secured creditor's point of view (e.g., a bank lender), the unsecured creditors and subordinate lenders (such as subordinate bond holders) form part of the quasi-equity cushion in liquidation. The secured creditor must make sure, however, that it enjoys true seniority in cash payment so that the firm's assets are not liquidated in paying down the claims of the subordinate (junior) creditors and equity holders.

Whether a debt burden is too large can be analyzed with the help of a fixed-charge coverage ratio. This ratio measures the dollars available to meet fixed-charge obligations (earnings available to meet fixed charges). A value of 1 for this ratio means that $1 of earnings is available to meet each dollar of fixed-charge obligations. A value of less (greater) than 1 means that the applicant has less (more) than $1 of earnings available to pay each dollar of fixed-charge obligations. This ratio can be tailored to the applicant's situation, depending on what really constitutes fixed charges that must be paid. One version of it follows: (EBIT + Lease payments)/(Interest + Lease payments + Sinking fund/$(1 - T)$), where T is the marginal tax rate.[4] Here, it is assumed that sinking fund payments must be made.[5] They are adjusted by the division of $(1 - T)$ into a before-tax cash outflow so they can be added to other before-tax cash outflows. The variability of cash flows (the cash

---

[4] Another version adds to the denominator investments for replacing equipment that is needed for the applicant to remain in business.

[5] *Sinking funds* are required periodic payments into a fund that is used to retire the principal amounts on bonds outstanding.

flow ratio) provides a clue as to how much higher than 1 a fixed-charge coverage ratio should be.

The cash-flow-to-debt ratio is a variant of the fixed-charge coverage ratio. It measures the cash flow available for debt service in proportion to the debt principal being serviced and can be compared to the interest rate on the debt. If this ratio is equal to the interest rate on the debt, the applicant's cash flows are just sufficient to pay the required interest on the debt principal. The more the ratio exceeds the interest rate on the debt, the larger is the debt-service cushion.

Profitability Ratios.

$$\text{Gross margin} = \frac{\text{Gross profit}}{\text{Sales}}$$

$$\text{Operating profit margin} = \frac{\text{Operating profit}}{\text{Sales}}$$

$$\text{Income to sales} = \frac{\text{EBIT}}{\text{Sales}}$$

$$\text{Return on assets} = \frac{\text{EAT}}{\text{Average total assets}}$$

$$\text{Return on equity} = \frac{\text{EAT}}{\text{Total equity}}$$

$$\text{Dividend payout} = \frac{\text{Dividends}}{\text{EAT}}$$

where **EAT** represents earnings after taxes, or net income.

For all but the dividend payout ratio, the higher the value of the ratio, the higher the profitability of the firm. The dividend payout ratio measures how much of the profit is retained in the firm versus paid out to the stockholders as dividends. The lower the dividend payout ratio, the more profits (percentage wise) are retained in the firm. A profitable firm that retains its earnings increases its level of equity capital as well as its creditworthiness. The analyst should be concerned about large swings in profitability as well as profit trends.[6]

---

[6] *Market value ratios* such as the growth rate in the share price, price-earnings ratio, and dividend yield are also valuable indicators if they are available. For a mid-market corporation, however, they are probably unavailable since the debt and equity claims of most mid-market corporations are not publicly traded. The account officer may find it informative to substitute a similar listed firm (a comparability test).

Cautions with Ratio Analysis.

While ratio analysis provides useful information about a loan applicant's financial condition, it also has limitations that require care and judgment in its use. For example, many firms operate in more than one industry. For these companies, it is difficult to construct a meaningful set of industry averages. Further, different accounting practices can distort industry comparisons. For example, the loan applicant may be using straight-line depreciation for its fixed assets, while industry competitors are using an accelerated cost recovery method (ACRS), which causes depreciation to accrue quickly. ACRS methods will cause fixed asset values to be written down quickly and leave their book value lower than straight-line depreciation. This can distort the analysis of fixed asset-based ratios. In addition, it is sometimes difficult to generalize whether a particular value for a ratio is good or bad. For example, a high current ratio can be a sign of a highly liquid firm or one that holds excessive cash. FI loan officers need to be aware of the problems with ratio analysis in analyzing the loan applicant's financial statements and making a loan decision. Finally, concerns about how earnings are reported in recent high-profile cases such as Enron and WorldCom have accentuated the weakness of FI's relying totally on ratio analysis in making credit decisions.

Common Size Analysis and Growth Rates

In addition to the ratios listed above, an analyst can compute sets of ratios by dividing all income statement amounts by total sales revenue and all balance sheet amounts by total assets. These calculations yield common-size financial statements that can be used to identify changes in corporate performance. Year-to-year growth rates also give useful ratios for identifying trends. Common-size financial statements may provide quantitative clues as to the direction that the firm is moving and that the analysis should take.

Having reviewed the financial and other conditions of the applicant, the FI can include loan covenants as a part of the loan agreement. Loan covenants reduce the risk of the loan to the lender. They can include a variety of conditions such as maintenance of various ratios at or within stated ranges, key-person insurance policies on employees critical to the success of the project funded by the loan, and so on.

Following Approval

The credit process does not end when the applicant signs the loan agreement. As is the case for mortgage loans, before allowing a drawdown (the actual release of the funds to the borrower) of a mid-market credit, the account officer must make sure that **conditions precedent** have been cleared. Conditions precedent are those conditions specified in the credit agreement or term sheet for a credit that must be fulfilled before drawdowns are permitted. These include various title searches, perfecting of collateral, and the like. Following drawdown, the credit must be monitored throughout the loan's life to ensure that the borrower is living up to its commitments and to detect any deterioration in the borrower's creditworthiness so as to protect the FI's interest in the loan being repaid in full with the promised interest return.

Typically, the borrower's credit needs will change from time to time. A growing company has an expanding need for credit. A company moving into the international arena needs foreign exchange. A contractor may have periodic guarantee requests. Even if the credit agreements being offered do not change, a corporation's credit needs are usually reviewed on an annual basis to ensure that they comply with the terms of the original credit agreement. At that time, credit limits for individual customers will be set, including limits on other bank services such as forward exchange contracts or Banker's Acceptances (BAs) which give rise to credit risk for the FI. As well, the annual review allows account managers to maintain closer contact with customers so that they can respond to ongoing financial service requirements—both credit and noncredit—so that the relationship will develop into a permanent, mutually beneficial one (the customer relationship effect that FIs call relationship banking).

Appendix 16A   Mechanisms for Dealing with Sovereign Risk Exposure

Note: In the following discussion, all dollar figures refer to U.S. dollars, the currency of most LDC loans. The exports of many LDCs are commodities such as coffee, cocoa, oil, nickel, copper, etc., that are priced in U.S. dollars, providing a source of hard currency for interest and principal repayments.

In the text of the chapter, we identified methods and models FI managers can use to measure sovereign risk exposure before making credit decisions. In this Appendix, we consider the benefits and costs of using four alternative mechanisms to deal with problem sovereign credits once they have arisen. The four mechanisms are:

1. Debt-for-equity swaps.
2. Multiyear restructuring of loans (MYRAs).
3. Sale of LDC loans on the secondary market.
4. Bond-for-loan swaps (Brady bonds).

While restructuring keeps the loans in the portfolio, the other three mechanisms change the fundamental nature of the FI's claim itself or remove it from the balance sheet.

In this Appendix we look at the mechanics of loan restructuring and debt-for-equity swaps. Because we have already described LDC loan sales and bond-for-loan swaps (e.g., Brady bonds), we only summarize their benefits and costs here. Understanding each of these mechanisms, especially their benefits and costs, is important, since an FI can choose among the four in dealing with a problem sovereign loan or credit.

DEBT-FOR-EQUITY SWAPS

The market for LDC loan sales has a close link to debt-for-equity swap programs arranged by certain LDCs, such as Chile and Mexico, with outside investors that wish to make equity investments in debtor countries.[1] Indeed, while banks are the major sellers of LDC loans, important buyers are parties that wish to engage in long-term equity or real investments in those debtor countries.

For example, the 1985 Mexican debt-for-equity swap program allowed Mexican dollar loans to be swapped for Mexican equity in certain priority investment areas. These were the motor, tourism, and chemical industries. For example, American Express was an FI that exploited the opportunities of the Mexican debt-for-equity swap program by building seven hotels in Mexico. The estimated annual amount of debt-for-equity swaps is currently around $10 billion.[2]

To demonstrate the costs and benefits of a debt-for-equity swap for the FI and other parties participating in the transaction, we present a hypothetical example. Suppose that in November 2003, CIBC had $100 million loans outstanding to Chile and could have sold those loans on the secondary market for a bid price of $91 million, or $91 per $100. The advantages to CIBC from selling loans are the removal of these loans from its books and the freeing up of funds for other investments. However, CIBC has to accept a loss of $9 million on the loan. Given that the rest of the bank is profitable, the bank can offset this loss against other profits. Further, if the corporate tax rate is 34 percent, then CIBC's after-tax loss will be $9(1 − .34) million = $5.94 million.[3]

If CIBC sold this loan to Merrill Lynch for $91 million, Merrill Lynch, as a market maker, could reoffer the loan to an outside buyer at a slightly higher price—say, $93 million (or $93 per $100 of face value). Suppose IBM wants to build a computer factory in Chile and buys the $100 million face value loan from Merrill Lynch for $93 million to finance its investments in Chile. Thus, Merrill Lynch earns a profit of $93 million − $91 million = $2 million, and IBM knows that Chile has a debt-for-equity swap program. This means that at a given exchange rate, the Chilean government will allow IBM to convert the $100 million dollar loan it has purchased into local currency, or pesos. However, the Chilean government will be willing to do this only if it receives something in return.

---

[1] For more details, see R. Grosse, "The Debt/Equity Swap in Latin America—In Whose Interest?" *Journal of International Financial Management and Accounting* 4 (Spring 1992), pp. 13–39.

[2] Countries that have recently employed debt-for-equity swap programs include Argentina, Brazil, Chile, Costa Rica, Ecuador, Jamaica, Mexico, Uruguay, and Venezuela.

[3] CIBC reduced its exposure to LDC debt in 1989 through loan sales.

FIGURE 16A–1
Debt-for-Equity
Swaps and
Loan Sales

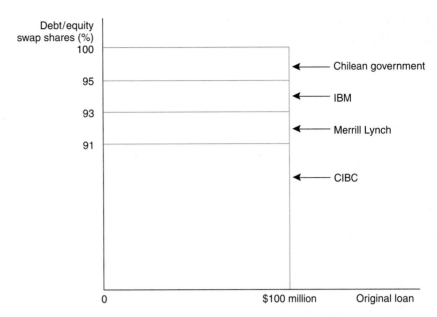

Thus, it may be willing to convert the dollars into pesos only at a 5 percent discount from the true free market dollar/peso exchange rate. If the free market exchange rate was 380 Chilean pesos to the U.S. dollar, the Chilean government will convert the dollars only at 361 pesos to the U.S. dollar. Thus IBM must bear a 5 percent discount on the face value of the purchased loan; that is, when converting the $100 million loan at the Chilean Central Bank, IBM receives $95 million equivalent in pesos.[4] Remember that IBM had originally bought the loan for only $93 million on the secondary market. Thus, its net savings from this debt-for-equity conversion program is $2 million.[5] However, note that the $95 million is in pesos that must be invested in Chilean equity, such as real estate for factories. In general, debt-for-equity swap investors face long periods before they can repatriate dividends (12 years in the Mexican case) and often large withholding taxes (55 percent in the Mexican case). Moreover, they face the risk of future expropriation or nationalization of those assets as well as peso currency risk. Thus, the $2 million spread reflects IBM's expectations about such risks.

Finally, what does the Chilean government get out of this debt-for-equity swap program? It has retired relatively expensive hard currency dollar debt with local currency pesos at a discount. Implicitly, it has retired a $100 million face value debt at a cost of $95 million in pesos; the difference reflects the debt-for-equity swap official exchange rate (361 pesos/$1) and the true exchange rate (380 pesos/$1). The cost to Chile is printing $95 million more in pesos. This may lead to a higher domestic inflation rate, as well as increased foreign ownership and control of Chilean real assets as a result of IBM's equity purchases.

We illustrate the division of the original $100 million face value loan among the four parties as a result of the loan sale and debt-for-equity swap in Figure 16A–1. CIBC gets 91 percent of the original face value of the loan; Merrill Lynch, 2 percent; IBM, 2 percent; and Chile, 5 percent. That is, the three parties have the 9 percent discount from face value accepted by CIBC: the investment bank, the corporation involved in the debt-for-equity swap, and the sponsoring country's government.

One puzzle from the preceding example is why CIBC does not sidestep both the investment bank and IBM and engage in a local currency debt-for-equity swap itself. That is, why doesn't CIBC directly swap its $100 million loan to Chile for the $95 million equivalent of local equity? The problem is that Canadian banks are restricted in their ability to buy real equity or engage in commerce. If a bank could buy and hold Chilean real assets, this might lower its potential losses from restructuring its

---

[4] In practice, debt-for-equity swaps convert into pesos at an official rate. This official rate is often less attractive than the rate quoted in official or unofficial parallel markets for private transactions.

[5] That is, in general, the swap is cheaper than direct local borrowing if this is an available alternative.

LDC loan portfolio. Nevertheless, note that although a loan sale directly removes a problem loan from the balance sheet, a debt-for-equity swap replaces that problem loan with a risky long-term peso-denominated equity position on its balance sheet. Thus, the improvement of the liquidity of the balance sheet through such a transaction is far from certain.

MULTIYEAR RESTRUCTURING AGREEMENTS (MYRAS)

If a country is unable to keep its payments on a loan current and an FI chooses to maintain the loan on its balance sheet rather than selling it or swapping it for equity or debt, the loan and its contractual terms would be rescheduled under a multiyear restructuring agreement (MYRA). A good example of a MYRA was the January 1998 agreement reached between South Korea and its major creditors to restructure $24 billion of short-term dollar loans that had been made by banks and corporations (and that were coming due in March 1998). Many of these loans had interest rates as high as 20 percent and maturities of 90 days or less.

As with the loan sale, the debt-for-equity swap, and the debt-for-debt swap, the crucial question for an FI is the amount it is willing to concede or give up to the borrower in the sovereign loan rescheduling process. The benefits and costs of this policy depend on a number of factors that are usually built into any MYRA, including the following:

1. The *fee* charged by the FI to the borrower for the costs of restructuring the loan. This fee may be as high as 1 percent of the face value of the loan if a large lending syndicate is involved in the negotiations.

2. The *interest rate* charged on the new loan. This is generally lower than the rate on the original loan to ease the repayment cash flow problems of the borrower. In the South Korean case, if the loan was rescheduled for one year, the new interest was LIBOR plus 2.25 percent; if it was rescheduled for two years, the new loan interest rate was LIBOR plus 2.5 percent; and if it was rescheduled for three years, the new interest rate was LIBOR plus 2.75 percent.

3. A *grace period* may be involved before interest and/or principal payments begin on the new loan to give the borrower time to accumulate

hard currency reserves to meet its future debt interest and principal obligations. In the South Korean case, no grace period was set.

4. The *maturity* of the loan is lengthened, normally to extend the interest and principal payments over a longer period. In the South Korean case the restructured loan maturities were set at between one and three years.

5. *Option and guarantee features* are often built into the MYRA to allow the lender (and sometimes the borrower) to choose the currency for repayment of interest and principal,[6] and/or to protect the lenders against default in the future. In the case of the South Korean loans, the government had to guarantee repayment of the $24 billion.

The magnitude and interaction of these factors determine the degree of the MYRA's concessionality (the net cost) to an FI. In general, the net cost or degree of concessionality can be defined as:

Concessionality

$$= \left(\begin{array}{c} \text{Present value of} \\ \text{original loan} \end{array} \right) - \left(\begin{array}{c} \text{Present value of} \\ \text{restructured loan} \end{array} \right)$$

$$= PV_0 - PV_R$$

The lower the present value of the restructured loan relative to the original loan, the greater are the *concessions* the FI has made to the borrower, that is, the greater the cost of loan restructuring.

LOAN SALES

The third mechanism for dealing with problem sovereign loans—LDC loan sales—was discussed earlier in this chapter. Here we summarize the main benefits and costs of the sales to the FI. The first major benefit is the removal of these loans from the balance sheet and, as a result, the freeing up of resources for other investments. Second, being able to sell these loans at a discount or loss signifies that the rest of the FI's balance sheet is sufficiently strong to bear the cost. In fact, a number of studies have found that announcements of FIs taking allowances against LDC loans—prior to their charge-off and sale—have a positive effect on bank stock prices.[7] Third, the FI shares part of the

---

[6] For example, the lender may choose to be repaid in dollars or in yen. Such option features add value to the cash flow stream for either the borrower or the lender, depending on who can exercise the currency option.

[7] See, for example, Grammatikos and Saunders, "Additions to Bank Loan Loss Reserves." *Journal of Monetary Economics* 25 (1990), pp. 289–304.

loan sale loss with the government because such losses provide a tax write-off for the lender.

The major cost is one of the loss itself—the tax-adjusted difference between the face value of the loan and its market value at the time of the sale.

BOND-FOR-LOAN SWAPS (BRADY BONDS)

The fourth mechanism is a bond-for-loan swap. The primary benefit of bond-for-loan swaps is that they transform an LDC loan into a highly marketable and liquid instrument—a bond. For example, FIs trade and clear Brady bonds (the most common of these types of swaps) in a fashion similar to most Eurobonds with relatively low transaction costs, small bid-ask spreads, and an efficient clearing and settlement system. In addition, because of full or partial collateral backing, these bonds are normally senior in status to any remaining LDC loans or sovereign bonds of that country. The major cost occurs when the bond is swapped for the loan because the bond usually has a longer stated maturity. Also, the swap of loan face value for debt face value is often less than dollar for dollar. Moreover, posting U.S. dollar debt as collateral can be very expensive for an LDC country with minimal hard currency exchange reserves.

Appendix 20A Internal Ratings-Based Approach to Measuring Credit Risk-Adjusted Assets

The main body of this chapter described the Standardized Approach to measuring credit risk-adjusted asset values for DTIs under Basel II. Rather than using the Standardized Approach, banks with a sufficient number of internal credit risk rating grades for loans and whose borrowers are largely unrated by the major credit rating agencies may (with regulatory approval) adopt one of two Internal Ratings-Based (IRB) approaches to calculating credit risk-adjusted assets for capital requirements: the *Foundations Approach* and the *Advanced Approach*.[1] The IRB results in an individualized capital requirement for each asset depending on five key variables. That is, in general, for asset *i*:

$$\text{Capital requirement}_i = f(PD_i, LGD_i, R_i, EAD_i, M_i)$$

where

PD_i = One-year probability of default of the *i*th borrower

LGD_i = Loss given default of the *i*th borrower

R_i = Correlation of the *i*th borrower with the rest of the portfolio

EAD_i = Amount (in dollars) of exposure at default

M_i = Maturity of the loan

Under the Foundations Approach to corporate, bank, and sovereign exposures, a bank internally estimates the one-year probability of default (*PD*) associated with a borrower class, while relying on supervisory rules for the estimation of other risk components. With regulatory approval, a bank may use the Advanced Approach, in which banks use internal estimates of three additional risk components: loss given default (*LGD*), exposure at default (*EAD*), and maturity (*M*). For both models, R is set by the regulator.

Under both approaches of IRB capital requirement calculations, benchmark risk weights (BRWs) are calculated for different loans. Under the Foundations Approach, the bank calculates the expected (mean) probability of default (*PD*) for each of its rating classes based on historical experience to generate the BRW. Then, given an *LGD* for the loan (assumed by the BIS to be 50 percent for unsecured loans, 45 percent for loans secured by physical non-real estate collateral, and 40 percent if secured by receivables), an effective maturity (M), and correlation (R) of between 10 and 20 percent, it calculates an individualized BRW and RW (risk weight) for each of its corporate loans. The BRW for each loan under the Foundations Approach is calculated using a formula that calibrates the default risk at the 99.9 percent level using the following formula:

$$\begin{aligned} BRW = 12.5 \times LGD \times M \times N[(1 - R)^{-0.5} \\ \times G(PD) + (R/(1 - R))^{0.5} \times G(0.999)] \end{aligned} \quad \textbf{(A1)}$$

where

$$M = 1 + 0.047 \times ((1 - PD)/PD^{0.44}) \quad \textbf{(A2)}$$

$$\begin{aligned} R = 0.10 \times [(1 - \exp^{-50PD})/(1 - \exp^{-50})] + 0.20 \\ \times [1 - (1 - \exp^{-50PD})/(1 - \exp^{-50})] \end{aligned} \quad \textbf{(A3)}$$

and the risk weight (RW) for a loan is:

$$RW = (LGD/50) \times BRW \quad \textbf{(A4)}$$

Note that in the Foundations Approach model, if the loan is not secured, LGD equals 50 percent (so that the ratio LGD/50 = 1). If, however, the loan is secured by collateral such as non-real estate collateral or receivables, the LGD/50 ratio is less than 1 (e.g., (45/50) or (40/50)), thus reducing the overall risk weight on the loan. The term "exp" in equation A3 stands for the natural exponential function; N(x) is the cumulative distribution function for a standard normal cumulative distribution function (i.e., the probability that a normal random variable with mean zero and variance of one is less than or equal to x), and G(z) is the inverse standard normal cumulative distribution function for a standard normal random variable (i.e., the value x such that N(x) = z).[2] Equation A2 denotes the

[1] For a more detailed analysis of these two approaches, see Basel Committee on Banking Supervision, "The New Basel Capital Accord," January 2001; "Potential Modifications to the Committee's Proposals," November 2001; and "International Convergence of Capital Measurement and Capital Standards," June 2004; www.bis.org. See also E. Altman, S. T. Bharath, and A. Saunders, "Credit Ratings and the BIS Reform Agenda," *Journal of Banking and Finance*, 2002, pp. 909–21.

maturity factor M given by the regulator. The correlation coefficient R is computed in equation A3. The correlation ranges from 0.20 for the lowest PD value to 0.10 for the highest PD value.

The LGD shows the severity of loss as a percent of original loan value, and RW shows the overall risk weight or the capital requirement on the loan.[3] Note that the 8 percent capital requirement on all loans under Basel I translates into a (one-year) probability of default (PD) of 1 percent. Thus, under Basel I, loans with PDs less than 1 percent generally "charged" too much capital and loans with PDs greater than 1 percent "charged" too little capital. Table 20A–1 shows the impact of the probability of default (PD) on capital requirements

under the IRB Foundations Approach assuming LGD equals 50 percent.

Under the Advanced Approach, the bank inputs (using its own data) the values of four variables: PD_i, EAD_i, M_i, and LGD_i for each borrower. The fifth variable is set by the regulators using the formula in equation A3.

TABLE 20A–1 Capital Requirements under IRB Foundations Approach

Probability of Default (PD)	Capital Requirement
0.03%	1.4%
0.10	2.7
0.25	4.3
0.50	5.9
0.75	7.1
1.00 (Basel I)	8.0
1.25	8.7
1.50	9.3
2.00	10.3
2.50	11.1
3.00	11.9
4.00	13.4
5.00	14.8
10.00	21.0
20.00	30.0

---

[2] According to the BIS, the functions N and G are generally available in spreadsheet and statistical packages. For both functions, the mean should be set equal to zero and the standard deviation should be set equal to 1. See BIS Consultative Document, "New Basel Capital Accord," January 2001, p. 36, footnote 28.

[3] For example, a PD of 1 percent translates to a capital requirement of 8 percent and to a risk weight of 100 percent [(100%/8%) × 8% = 100%]. Similarly, a PD of 20 percent translates to a capital requirement of 30 percent and to a risk weight of 375 percent [(100%/8%) × 30%].

Appendix 25A   Pricing an Interest Rate Swap

In this appendix, we discuss fair pricing of a swap at the time the parties enter into the swap agreement. As with much of financial theory, there are important no-arbitrage conditions that should hold in setting rates in a fixed-floating rate swap agreement. The most important no-arbitrage condition is that the expected present value of the cash flow payments made by the fixed-rate payer, the buyer, should equal the expected present value of the cash flow payments made by the floating-rate payer, the seller:

$$\text{Expected fixed-payment } PV$$
$$= \text{Expected floating-payment } PV$$

If this no-arbitrage condition does not hold, one party usually has to compensate the other with an up-front payment equal to the difference between the two expected present values of the cash flows.

For a U.S. dollar swap the fixed-rate payment of the swap is usually priced off the newly issued or *on-the-run* yield curve of U.S. Treasury notes and bonds. Thus, if four-year Treasuries are currently yielding 10 percent, a quote of 10.25 percent (bid) and 10.35 percent (offer) would mean that the commercial or investment bank acting as a swap dealer is willing to buy or become the fixed-rate payer in a swap agreement at a contractual swap rate of 10.25 percent. It is also willing to take the other side of the swap (become the fixed-rate receiver) if the swap fixed rate is set higher at 10.35 percent. The 10-basis-point spread is the dealer's spread or the return for intermediating the swap. As discussed earlier, in intermediating, the FI has to cover the credit risk assumed in the swap transaction and cover its costs of search and intermediation as well. In the next subsection of this appendix, we develop a detailed example of how a swap might be priced.

PRICING A SWAP: AN EXAMPLE

We develop an example of swap pricing under simplified assumptions by applying the no-arbitrage condition and pricing swaps off the Treasury yield curve. This provides an understanding of why expected cash flows from the swap agreement can differ from actual or realized cash flows. It also explains why, when yield curves slope upward, the fixed-rate payer (swap buyer) faces an inherent credit risk in any swap contract.

Assume that in a four-year swap agreement, the fixed-rate payer makes fixed-rate payments at the end of each year. Also assume that although these payments are made at the end of each year, interest rates are determined at the beginning of each year.[1] That is,

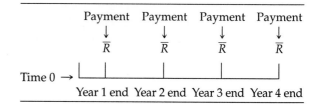

Since this is a four-year swap agreement, the fixed-rate payer knows in advance the annual interest rate to pay each year:

$$\overline{R}_1 = \overline{R}_2 = \overline{R}_3 = \overline{R}_4 = Fixed$$

Let R be priced off the current *Treasury bond par yield curve* for four-year, on-the-run Treasury note issues. The assumed current par yield curve is represented in Figure 25A–1. Suppose that newly issued four-year Treasury bonds are currently yielding 10 percent and that the fixed-rate payments on the swap are set at 10 percent for each of the four years

$$R_i = 10\% \qquad i = 1, \dots, 4$$

Here we ignore the usual markup in the swap market over Treasuries for simplicity. For the no-arbitrage condition to hold, the present value of these fixed payments made must equal the expected stream of variable one-year payments received from the floating-rate payer. If we assume that the expectations theory of interest rates holds, we can extract the expected one-year rates (payments) from the Treasury yield curve. Specifically, we wish to determine

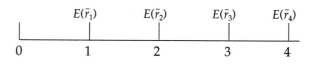

---

[1] This is not always the case. Further, in practice many swaps are now priced off the LIBOR yield curve (reflecting some credit risk premium over Treasuries).

FIGURE 25A–1
T-bond Par Yield
Curve

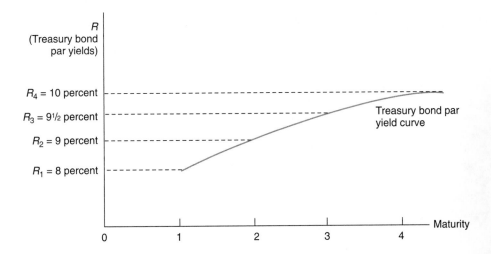

where $E(\bar{r}_i)$ are the expected one-year (forward) interest payments to be made at the end of years 1, 2, 3, and 4, respectively.

Extracting these expected one-year forward rates is a little awkward. We begin by extracting the spot or zero-coupon discount bond yield curve from the coupon par yield curve on Treasury bonds; then we derive expected one-year forward rates from this zero-coupon yield curve. The reason we need to extract the zero-coupon discount yield curve is that this yield curve reflects the time value of money for single payments (bonds) at 1 year's, 2 years', 3 years', and 4 years' time. Unfortunately, the yield to maturity on a coupon bond is a complex weighted average of the time value of money discount yields on zero-coupon bonds. Specifically, a yield to maturity on a coupon bond is the internal rate of return on that bond or the single interest rate (yield) that equates the promised cash flows on the bond to its price. Such a yield is not the same as the time value of money. For example, assuming annual coupon payments, the 10 percent yield to maturity on the four-year T-bond is a complex average of the yields to maturity on a one-year, two-year, three-year, and four-year zero-coupon discount bond.

To see this, consider the cash flows on the four-year coupon par value Treasury bond

$$100 = P_4 = \frac{10}{(1 + R_4)} + \frac{10}{(1 + R_4)^2}$$
$$+ \frac{10}{(1 + R_4)^3} + \frac{110}{(1 + R_4)^4}$$

and the yield to maturity on this par bond, $R_4 = 10$ percent. Thus,

$$P_4 = \frac{10}{(1.1)} + \frac{10}{(1.1)^2} + \frac{10}{(1.1)^3} + \frac{110}{(1.1)^4} = 100$$

Conceptually, this coupon bond could be broken down and sold as four separate zero-coupon bonds with one year, two years, three years, and four years to maturity. This is similar to how the U.S. Treasury currently creates zero-coupon bonds through its *Treasury Strips* program.[2] That is,

$$P_4 = \underbrace{\frac{10}{(1 + R_4)} + \frac{10}{(1 + R_4)^2} + \frac{10}{(1 + R_4)^3} + \frac{110}{(1 + R_4)^4}}_{\text{Coupon bond value}}$$
$$= \underbrace{\frac{10}{(1 + d_1)} + \frac{10}{(1 + d_2)^2} + \frac{10}{(1 + d_3)^3} + \frac{110}{(1 + d_4)^4}}_{\text{Sum of separate zero-coupon bond values}}$$

The first relationship is the value of the coupon bond as a whole, while the second is the value of four stripped coupon and principal discount bonds of 10, 10, 10, and 110, each sold separately to different investors. The time value of money for the single payments in each of the four years, or required discount yields, is d_1, d_2, d_3, and d_4. Further, this equation confirms that the yield to maturity on the four-year coupon bond, when sold as a whole bond (R_4), is a complex average of the discount rates on four different

---

[2] Apart from semiannual rather than annual coupon stripping, the other major difference in practice is that the final coupon payment of 10 is separated and sold independently from the 100 face value, even though both are paid at the same time and have the same time value of money.

zero-coupon bonds—d_1, d_2, d_3, and d_4—where the d_i are discount yields on single-payment bonds of i year to maturity, $i = 1, 2, 3,$ and 4

$$P_1^D = \frac{10}{(1 + d_1)}$$

$$P_2^D = \frac{10}{(1 + d_2)^2}$$

$$P_3^D = \frac{10}{(1 + d_3)^3}$$

$$P_4^D = \frac{10}{(1 + d_4)^4}$$

$$\text{and } P_4 = \sum_{i=1}^{4} P_i^D$$

P_i^D represent the market values of the four different stripped or zero-coupon bonds. The no-arbitrage condition requires that the values of the four zero-coupon bonds sum to the price of the four-year Treasury coupon bond (P_4) when sold as a whole.

To derive the expected one-year forward rates implied by the yield curve, we need to calculate the discount yields themselves: d_1, d_2, d_3, and d_4.

Solving the Discount Yield Curve

To calculate the discount yields, we use a process of forward iteration. From Figure 25A–1, which shows the T-bond yield curve, we note that one-year par value coupon Treasury bonds are currently yielding 8 percent

$$P_1 = \frac{108}{(1 + R_1)} = \frac{108}{1.08} = 100$$
$$R_1 = 8\%$$

Because the one-year coupon bond has exactly one year left to maturity, and thus only one final payment of interest (8) and principal (100), its valuation is exactly the same as a one-year zero-coupon bond with one payment at the end of the year. Thus, by definition, under no arbitrage,

$$R_1 = d_1 = 8\%$$

Once we have solved for d_1, we can go on to solve for d_2 by forward iteration. Specifically, from the par coupon yield curve we can see that two-year coupon-bearing bonds are yielding 9 percent

$$P_2 = \frac{9}{(1 + R_2)} + \frac{109}{(1 + R_2)^2}$$

$$= \frac{9}{(1.09)} + \frac{109}{(1.09)^2} = 100$$
$$R_1 = 9\%$$

The no-arbitrage condition between coupon bonds and zero-coupon bonds implies that

$$P_2 = \frac{9}{(1.09)} + \frac{109}{(1.09)^2}$$

$$= \frac{9}{(1 + d_1)} + \frac{109}{(1 + d_2)^2} = 100$$

Since we have solved for $d_1 = 8$ percent, we can directly solve for d_2

$$100 = \frac{9}{(1.08)} + \frac{109}{(1 + d_2)^2}$$

$$d_2 = 9.045\%$$

Similarly, we know from the current par T-bond yield curve that three-year coupon-bearing bonds are yielding $9\frac{1}{2}$ percent. The no arbitrage requires

$$P_3 = \frac{9\frac{1}{2}}{(1 + R_3)} + \frac{9\frac{1}{2}}{(1 + R_3)^2} + \frac{109\frac{1}{2}}{(1 + R_3)^3}$$

$$= \frac{9\frac{1}{2}}{(1 + d_1)} + \frac{9\frac{1}{2}}{(1 + d_2)^2} + \frac{109\frac{1}{2}}{(1 + d_3)^3} = 100$$

$$R_3 = 9\frac{1}{2}\%$$

To solve for d_3, the yield on a three-year zero-coupon bond, we have

$$100 = \frac{9\frac{1}{2}}{(1.08)} + \frac{9\frac{1}{2}}{(1.09045)^2} + \frac{109\frac{1}{2}}{(1 + d_3)^3}$$

Thus, since d_1 and d_2 have already been determined, $d_3 = 9.58$ percent.

Finally, to solve for the discount rate on a four-year zero-coupon bond (d_4), we know that

$$P_4 = 100 = \frac{10}{(1 + R_4)} + \frac{10}{(1 + R_4)^2}$$

$$+ \frac{10}{(1 + R_4)^3} + \frac{110}{(1 + R_4)^4}$$

$$= \frac{10}{(1 + d_1)} + \frac{10}{(1 + d_2)^2}$$

$$+ \frac{10}{(1 + d_3)^3} + \frac{110}{(1 + d_4)^4}$$

$$R_4 = 10\%$$

FIGURE 25A–2
Discount Yield
Curve versus Par
Yield Curve

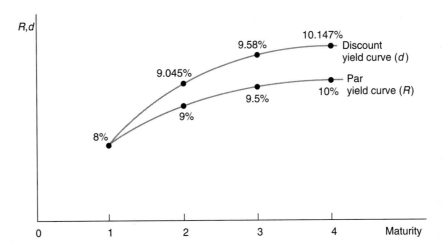

To solve for d_4, we have

$$100 = \frac{10}{(1.08)} + \frac{10}{(1.09045)^2}$$
$$+ \frac{10}{(1.0958)^3} + \frac{110}{(1 + d_4)^4}$$

As a result, since d_1, d_2, and d_3 were solved, $d_4 = 10.147$ percent.

In Figure 25A–2 we plot the derived zero-coupon discount bond yield curve alongside the coupon par yield curve. As you can see, the derived zero-coupon yield curve slopes upward faster than does the coupon bond yield curve. This result is a mathematical relationship and comes from the no-arbitrage derivation of the zero-coupon curve from the T-bond par yield curve. There is an intuitive explanation for this result as well. Remember that R_4 (= 10 percent, the yield to maturity or internal rate of return on a four-year coupon bond) can conceptually be viewed as a complex weighted average of the discount rates on four successive one-year zero-coupon bonds (d_1, d_2, d_3, and d_4). Since R_4 at 10 percent is higher than d_1 = 8 percent, d_2 = 9.045 percent, and d_3 = 9.58 percent, then d_4 (10.147 percent) must be above R_4 (10 percent) if R_4 is to be a weighted average of the individual zero-coupon discount rates. This same reasoning explains why $R_3 < d_3$ and $R_2 < d_2$.

Note, however, that if the coupon yield curve was flat, then $R_i = d_i$ for every maturity. If the coupon yield curve were downward sloping, the discount or zero-coupon yield curve would lie below the coupon yield curve (for the converse reason used to explain why it must be above when the coupon yield curve is rising). We can now solve

for the expected one-year floating rates implied by the zero-coupon yield curve.

We are assuming that floating interest rate payments are made at the end of each year and are based on the one-year interest rates that are set at the beginning of each year. We can use the zero-coupon bond yield curve to derive the expected one-year forward rates that reflect the expected floating swap payments at the end of each year.

Solving for the Implied Forward Rates/ Floating Payments on a Swap Agreement

End of Year 1 Payment

The expected end of year 1 payment $E(\tilde{r}_1)$ must be equal to the current one-year rate set for one-year discount bonds at time 0 since floating rates paid at the end of a period are assumed to depend on rates set or expected at the beginning of that period. That is, the expected first-year floating payment equals the current one-year discount rate

$$E(\tilde{r}_1) = d_1 = 8 \text{ percent}$$

End of Year 2 Payment

To determine the end of year 2 payment, we need to solve the expected one-year interest rate or forward rate in year 2. This is the rate that reflects expected payments at the end of year 2. We know that no arbitrage requires[3]

$$(1 + d_2)^2 = (1 + d_1)(1 + E(\tilde{r}_1))$$

That is, the yield from holding a two-year zero-coupon bond to maturity must equal the expected

---

[3] Under the pure expectations theory of interest rates.

FIGURE 25A–3
Fixed and Expected
Floating Swap
Payments

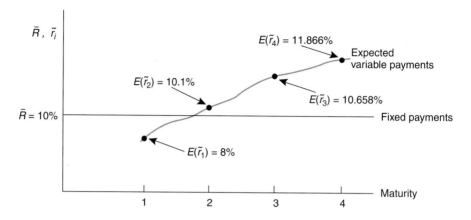

yield from holding the current one-year, zero-coupon bond to maturity times the expected yield from investing in a new one-year, zero-coupon bond in year 2. Rearranging this equation, we have

$$(1 + E(\tilde{r}_2)) = \frac{(1 + d_2)^2}{(1 + d_1)}$$

Since we have already solved for $d_2 = 9.045$ percent and $d_1 = 8$ percent, we can solve for $E(\tilde{r}_2)$

$$1 + E(\tilde{r}_2) = \frac{(1.09045)^2}{(1.08)}$$

$$E(\tilde{r}_2) = 10.1\%$$

End of Year 3 Payment

In a similar fashion

$$(1 + E(\tilde{r}_3)) = \frac{(1 + d_3)^3}{(1 + d_2)^2}$$

Substituting in the d_2 and d_3 values from the zero-coupon bond yield curve

$$1 + E(\tilde{r}_3) = \frac{(1.0958)^3}{(1.09045)^2}$$

$$E(\tilde{r}_3) = 10.658\%$$

End of Year 4 Payment

Using the same procedure

$$1 + E(\tilde{r}_4) = \frac{(1 + d_4)^4}{(1 + d_3)^3} = \frac{(1.10147)^4}{(1.0958)^3}$$

$$E(\tilde{r}_4) = 11.866\%$$

These four expected one-year payments by the floating-rate payer are plotted against the fixed-rate payments by the buyer of the swap in Figure 25A–3. Although expecting to pay a net payment $[\bar{R} - E(\tilde{r}_2)]$ of 2 percent to the floating-rate payer in the first year, the fixed-rate payer expects to receive net

payments of 0.1 percent, 0.658 percent, and 1.866 percent from the floating-rate seller in years 2, 3, and 4. This has important credit risk implications. It implies that when the yield curve is upward sloping, the fixed-rate payer can expect not only to pay more than the floating-rate payer in the early years of a swap agreement but also to receive higher cash flows from the seller or floating-rate payer in the later years of the swap agreement. Thus, the fixed-rate payer faces the risk that if expected rates are actually realized, the floating-rate payer may have an incentive to default toward the end of the swap agreement as a net payer. In this case the swap buyer might have to replace the swap at less favorable market conditions in the future.[4]

Finally, note that in this appendix we have been comparing expected cash flows in the swap agreement under no-arbitrage conditions. If the term structure shifts after the swap has been entered into, realized one-year rates (and payments) will not equal expected rates for the floating-rate payer. In our example, if the term structure shifts,

$$r_2 \neq E(\tilde{r}_2)$$
$$r_3 \neq E(\tilde{r}_3)$$
$$r_4 \neq E(\tilde{r}_4)$$

where r_2, r_3, and r_4 are realized or actual one-year rates on new one-year discount bonds issued in years 2, 3, and 4, respectively. Of course, the floating-rate payer has to make payments on actual or realized rates rather than expected rates, as we discussed in the first section of this chapter.

---

[4] This example is based on the discussion in C. W. Smith, C. W. Smithson, and L. M. Wakeman, "The Market for Interest Rate Swaps," *Financial Management* 17 (1988), pp. 34–44.

Index